D0328069

Oxford Essential

Spanish Dictionary

Oxford Essential Spanish Dictionary

SPANISH-ENGLISH

ENGLISH-SPANISH

ESPAÑOL-INGLÉS

INGLÉS-ESPAÑOL

OXFORD
UNIVERSITY PRESS

OXFORD
UNIVERSITY PRESS

Great Clarendon Street, Oxford OX2 6DP

Oxford University Press is a department of the University of Oxford.
It furthers the University's objective of excellence in research, scholarship,
and education by publishing worldwide in

Oxford New York

Auckland Cape Town Dar es Salaam Hong Kong Karachi
Kuala Lumpur Madrid Melbourne Mexico City Nairobi
New Delhi Shanghai Taipei Toronto

With offices in

Argentina Austria Brazil Chile Czech Republic France Greece
Guatemala Hungary Italy Japan Poland Portugal Singapore
South Korea Switzerland Thailand Turkey Ukraine Vietnam

Oxford is a registered trade mark of Oxford University Press
in the UK and in certain other countries

© Oxford University Press 2009

Database right Oxford University Press (maker)

Previously published as the *Oxford Spanish Mini Dictionary*, 2008

First edition 2009

British Library Cataloguing in Publication Data

Data available

ISBN 978-0-19-957644-9

6

Typeset by Interactive Sciences Ltd, Gloucester
Printed in Great Britain by Clays Ltd, St Ives plc

4643770599114886

Contents/Índice

Contributors/Colaboradores

Christine Lea
Carol Styles Carvajal
Michael Britton
Jane Horwood
Idoia Noble
Neil and Roswitha Morris
Susan Wilkin
Nicholas Rollin
Joanna Rubery
Pablo Pérez D'Ors
Oriana Orellana Jordán

Introduction

The *Oxford Essential Spanish Dictionary* is designed as an effective and practical reference tool for the student, adult learner, traveler, and business professional.

The wordlist has been revised and updated to reflect recent additions to both languages.

Another valuable feature of the dictionary is the special status given to more complex grammatical words which provide the basic structure of both languages. Boxed entries in the text for these *function words* provide extended treatment, including notes to warn of possible pitfalls.

The dictionary has an easy-to-use, streamlined layout. Bullets separate each new part of speech within an entry. Nuances of sense or usage are pinpointed by indicators or by typical collocates with which the word frequently occurs. Extra help is given in the form of symbols to mark the register of words and phrases. An exclamation mark ▣ indicates colloquial language, and a cross ▣ indicates slang.

Each English headword is followed by its phonetic transcription between slashes. The symbols used are those of the International Phonetic Alphabet. Pronunciation is also shown for derivatives and compounds where it is not easily deduced from that of a headword. The rules for the pronunciation of Spanish are given on pages xii–xiii.

The swung dash (∼) is used to represent a headword or that part of a headword preceding the vertical bar (|).

In both English and Spanish only irregular plurals are given. Normally Spanish nouns and adjectives ending in an unstressed vowel form the plural by adding s (e.g. *libro, libros*). Nouns and adjectives ending in a stressed vowel or a consonant add es (e.g. *rubí, rubíes, pared, paredes*). An accent on the final syllable is not required when es is added (e.g. *nación, naciones*). Final z becomes *ces* (e.g. *vez, veces*).

Spanish nouns and adjectives ending in o form the feminine by changing the final o to a (e.g. *hermano, hermana*). Most Spanish nouns and adjectives ending in anything other than final o do not have a separate feminine form, with the exception of those denoting nationality etc.; these add a to the masculine singular form (e.g. *español, española*). An accent on the penultimate syllable is then not required (e.g. *inglés, inglesa*). Adjectives ending in *án, ón,* or *or* behave like those denoting nationality, with the following exceptions: *inferior, mayor, mejor, menor, peor, superior,* where the feminine has the same form as the masculine. Spanish verb tables will be found at the end of the book.

The Spanish alphabet

In Spanish ñ is considered a separate letter and in the Spanish–English section, therefore, is alphabetized after *ny*.

Introducción

El *Oxford Essential Spanish Dictionary* ha sido concebid a fin de proporcionar una herramienta de referencia práctica y eficaz al estudiante, joven y adulto, al viajero y a la persona de negocios.

Se ha revisado la lista de palabras con el objeto de incorporar nuevos términos en ambos idiomas.

Otro valioso aspecto del diccionario es la importancia especial que se da a palabras con una función más compleja dentro de la gramática y que proveen la estructura básica de ambos idiomas. Estos *vocablos clave* están contenidos en recuadros dentro del texto, donde se les da un tratamiento amplio y se incluyen notas para advertir sobre posibles escollos.

El diccionario tiene una presentación clara y es fácil de usar. Símbolos distintivos separan las diferentes categorías gramaticales dentro de cada entrada. Los matices de sentido y de uso se muestran con precisión mediante indicadores o por colocaciones típicas con las que la palabra se usa frecuentemente. Se encuentra ayuda adicional en los signos que indican el registro idiomático de las palabras y frases. Un signo de exclamación 🅸 señala el uso coloquial y una cruz 🆇 el uso argot.

Cada palabra cabeza de artículo en inglés va seguida de su transcripción fonética entre barras oblicuas. Los símbolos que se usan son los del Alfabeto Fonético Internacional. También aparece la pronunciación de derivados y nombres compuestos cuando no es posible deducirla de la palabra cabeza de artículo. Las reglas sobre pronunciación inglesa se encuentran en la página xiv.

La tilde (~) se emplea para sustituir la palabra cabeza de artículo o aquella parte de tal palabra que precede a la barra vertical (|).

Tanto en inglés como en español se dan los plurales solamente si son irregulares. Para formar el plural regular en inglés se añade la letra s al sustantivo singular, pero se añade es cuando se trata de una palabra que termina en *ch*, *sh*, *s*, *ss*, *us*, *x*, *o*, *z* (p.ej. *sash*, *sashes*). En el caso de una palabra que termine en *y* precedida por una consonante, la *y* se transforma en *ies* (p.ej. *baby*, *babies*). Para formar el tiempo pasado y el participio pasado se añade *ed* al infinitivo de los verbos regulares ingleses (p.ej. *last*, *lasted*). En el caso de los verbos ingleses que terminan en e muda se añade sólo la *d* (p.ej. *move*, *moved*). En el caso de los verbos ingleses que terminan en *y*, se debe cambiar la *y* por *ied* (p.ej. *carry*, *carried*). Los verbos irregulares se encuentran en el diccionario por orden alfabético remitidos al infinitivo, y también en la lista que aparece en las últimas páginas del diccionario.

Pronunciation of Spanish

Vowels

a between pronunciation of *a* in English *cat* and *arm*

e like *e* in English *bed*

i like *ee* in English *see* but a little shorter

o like *o* in English *hot* but a little longer

u like *oo* in English *too*

y when a vowel is as Spanish **i**

Consonants

b (1) in initial position or after a nasal consonant is like English *b*

    (2) in other positions is between English *b* and English *v*

c (1) before **e** or **i** is like *th* in English *thin*. In Latin American Spanish is like English *s*.

    (2) in other positions is like *c* in English *cat*

ch like *ch* in English *chip*

d (1) in initial position, after nasal consonants and after **l** is like English *d*

    (2) in other positions is like *th* in English *this*

f like English *f*

g (1) before **e** or **i** is like *ch* in Scottish *loch*

    (2) in initial position is like *g* in English *get*

    (3) in other positions is like (2) but a little softer

....

....

j   like *ch* in Scottish *loch*

k   like English *k*

l   like English *l* but see also **ll**

ll   like *lli* in English *million*

m   like English *m*

n   like English *n*

ñ   like *ni* in English *opinion*

p   like English *p*

q   like English *k*

r   rolled or trilled

s   like *s* in English *sit*

t   like English *t*

v   (1) in initial position or after a nasal consonant is like
         English *b*
         (2) in other positions is between English b and English *v*

w   like Spanish **b** or **v**

x   like English *x*

y   like English *y*

z   like *th* in English *thin*

Pronunciación inglesa

Símbolos fonéticos

Vocales y diptongos

iː	see	ɔː	saw	eɪ	page	ɔɪ	join
ɪ	sit	ʊ	put	əʊ	home	ɪə	near
e	ten	uː	too	aɪ	five	eə	hair
æ	hat	ʌ	cup	aɪə	fire	ʊə	poor
ɑː	arm	ɜː	fur	aʊ	now		
ɒ	got	ə	ago	aʊə	flour		

Consonantes

p	pen	tʃ	chin	s	so	n	no
b	bad	dʒ	June	z	zoo	ŋ	sing
t	tea	f	fall	ʃ	she	l	leg
d	dip	v	voice	ʒ	measure	r	red
k	cat	θ	thin	h	how	j	yes
g	got	ð	then	m	man	w	wet

El símbolo ' precede a la sílaba sobre la cual recae el acento tónico.

a *preposición*

> Note that **a** followed by **el** becomes **al**, e.g. **vamos al cine**

····➤ (*dirección*) to. **fui a México** I went to Mexico. **muévete a la derecha** move to the right

····➤ (*posición*) **se sentaron a la mesa** they sat at the table. **al lado del banco** next to the bank. **a orillas del río** on the banks of the river

····➤ (*distancia*) **queda a 5 km** it's 5 km away. **a pocos metros de aquí** a few meters from here

····➤ (*fecha*) **hoy estamos a 5** today is the 5th. **¿a cuánto estamos?**, (*LAm*) **¿a cómo estamos?** what's the date?

····➤ (*hora, momento*) at. **a las 2** at 2 o'clock. **a fin de mes** at the end of the month. **a los 21 años** at the age of 21; (*después de*) after 21 years

····➤ (*precio*) **¿a cómo están las peras?** how much are the pears? **están a 3 euros el kilo** they're 3 euros a kilo. **salen a 15 euros cada uno** they work out at 15 euros each

····➤ (*medio, modo*) **fuimos a pie** we went on foot. **hecho a mano** hand made. **pollo al horno** (*LAm*) roast chicken

····➤ (*cuando precede al objeto directo de persona*) *no se traduce*. **conocí a Juan** I met Juan. **quieren mucho a sus hijos** they love their children very much

····➤ (*con objeto indirecto*) to. **se lo di a Juan** I gave it to Juan. **le vendí el coche a mi amigo** I sold my friend the car, I sold the car to my friend. **se lo compré a mi madre** I bought it from my mother; (*para*) I bought it for my mother

> ➡ Cuando la preposición **a** se emplea precedida de ciertos verbos como **empezar, faltar, ir, llegar** etc., ver bajo el respectivo verbo

ábaco *m* abacus

abadejo *m* pollack

abadía *f* abbey

abajo *adv* (*down*) below; (*dirección*) down(wards); (*en casa*) downstairs. ● *int* down with. ~ **de** (*LAm*) under(neath). **calle** ~ down the street. **el** ~ **firmante** the undersigned. **escaleras** ~ down the stairs. **la parte de** ~ the bottom (part). **más** ~ further down

abalanzarse 🔟 *vpr* rush (**hacia** towards)

abanderado *m* standard-bearer; (*Mex, en fútbol*) linesman

abandon|ado *adj* abandoned; (*descuidado*) neglected, (*persona*) untidy. ~**ar** *vt* leave (*un lugar*); abandon (*persona, cosa*). ● *vi* give up. ~**arse** *vpr* give in; (*descuidarse*) let o.s. go. ~**o** *m* abandonment; (*estado*) neglect

abani|car 🔽 *vt* fan. ~**co** *m* fan

abaratar *vt* reduce

abarcar 🔽 *vt* put one's arms around, embrace; (*comprender*) embrace

abarrotar *vt* overfill, pack full

abarrotes *mpl* (*LAm*) groceries; (*tienda*) grocer's shop

abast|ecer 🔟 *vt* supply. ~**ecimiento** *m* supply; (*acción*) supplying. ~**o** *m* supply. **no dar** ~**o** be unable to cope (**con** with)

abati|do *adj* depressed. ~**miento** *m* depression

abdicar 🔽 *vt* give up. ● *vi* abdicate

abdom|en *m* abdomen. ~**inal** *adj* abdominal

abec|é *m* 🔳 alphabet, ABC. ~**edario** *m* alphabet

abedul *m* birch (tree)

abej|a *f* bee. ~**orro** *m* bumble-bee

a

aberración f aberration

abertura f opening

abeto m fir (tree)

abierto pp véase **ABRIR**. • adj open

abism|al adj abysmal; (profundo) deep. **~ar** vt throw into an abyss; (fig, abatir) humble. **~arse** vpr be absorbed (en in), be lost (en in). **~o** m abyss; (fig, diferencia) world of difference

ablandar vt soften. **~se** vpr soften

abnega|ción f self-sacrifice. **~do** adj self-sacrificing

abochornar vt embarrass. **~se** vpr feel embarrassed

abofetear vt slap

aboga|cía f law. **~do** m lawyer, solicitor; (ante tribunal superior) barrister (Brit), attorney (Amer).

abolengo m ancestry

aboli|ción f abolition. **~cionismo** m abolitionism. **~cionista** m & f abolitionist. **~r** 24 vt abolish

abolla|dura f dent. **~r** vt dent

abolsado adj baggy

abomba|do adj convex; (LAm, atontado) dopey. **~r** vt make convex. **~rse** vpr (LAm, descomponerse) go bad

abominable adj abominable

abona|ble adj payable. **~do** adj paid. • m subscriber. **~r** vt pay; (en agricultura) fertilize. **~rse** vpr subscribe.

abono m payment; (estiércol) fertilizer; (a un periódico) subscription

aborda|ble adj reasonable; (persona) approachable. **~je** m boarding. **~r** vt tackle (un asunto); approach (una persona); (Naut) come alongside; (Mex, Aviac) board

aborigen adj & m native

aborrec|er 11 vt loathe. **~ible** adj loathsome. **~ido** adj loathed. **~imiento** m loathing

abort|ar vi have a miscarriage. **~ivo** adj abortive. **~o** m miscarriage; (voluntario) abortion. **hacerse un ~o** have an abortion

abotonar vt button (up). **~se** vpr button (up)

abovedado adj vaulted

abrasa|dor adj burning. **~r** vt burn. **~rse** vpr burn

abraz|ar vt 10 embrace. **~arse** vpr embrace. **~o** m hug. **un fuerte ~o de** (en una carta) with best wishes from

abre|botellas m invar bottle-opener. **~cartas** m invar paper-knife. **~latas** m invar tin opener (Brit), can opener

abrevia|ción f abbreviation; (texto abreviado) abridged text. **~do** adj brief; (texto) abridged. **~r** vt abbreviate; abridge (texto); cut short (viaje etc). • vi be brief. **~tura** f abbreviation

abrig|ado adj (lugar) sheltered; (persona) well wrapped up. **~ador** adj (Mex, ropa) warm. **~ar** 12 vt shelter; cherish (esperanza); harbour (duda, sospecha). **~arse** vpr (take) shelter; (con ropa) wrap up. **~o** m (over)coat; (lugar) shelter

abril m April. **~eño** adj April

abrillantar vt polish

abrir (pp abierto) vt/i open. **~se** vpr open; (extenderse) open out; (el tiempo) clear

abrochar vt do up; (con botones) button up

abruma|dor adj overwhelming. **~r** vt overwhelm

abrupto adj steep; (áspero) harsh

abrutado adj brutish

absentismo m absenteeism

absolución f (Relig) absolution; (Jurid) acquittal

absolut|amente adv absolutely, completely. **~o** adj absolute. **en ~o** (not) at all. **~orio** adj of acquittal

absolver 2 (pp absuelto) vt (Relig) absolve; (Jurid) acquit

absor|bente adj absorbent; (fig, interesante) absorbing. **~ber** vt absorb. **~ción** f absorption. **~to** adj absorbed

abstemio adj teetotal. • m teetotaller

absten|ción f abstention. **~erse** 40 vpr abstain, refrain (de from)

abstinencia f abstinence

abstra|cción f abstraction. **~cto** adj abstract. **~er** 41 vt abstract. **~erse**

vpr be lost in thought. **~ido** *adj* absent-minded

absuelto *adj* (*Relig*) absolved; (*Jurid*) acquitted

absurdo *adj* absurd. ● *m* absurd thing

abuche|ar *vt* boo. **~o** *m* booing

abuel|a *f* grandmother. **~o** *m* grandfather. **~os** *mpl* grandparents

ab|ulia *f* apathy. **~úlico** *adj* apathetic

abulta|do *adj* bulky. **~r** *vt* (*fig, exagerar*) exaggerate. ● *vi* be bulky

abunda|ncia *f* abundance. **nadar en la ~ncia** be rolling in money. **~nte** *adj* abundant, plentiful. **~r** *vi* be plentiful

aburguesarse *vpr* become middle-class

aburri|do *adj* (*con estar*) bored; (*con ser*) boring. **~dor** *adj* (*LAm*) boring. **~miento** *m* boredom; (*cosa pesada*) bore. **~r** *vt* bore. **~rse** *vpr* get bored

abus|ar *vi* take advantage. **~ar de la bebida** drink too much. **~ivo** *adj* excessive. **~o** *m* abuse

acá *adv* here. **~ y allá** here and there. **de ~ para allá** to and fro. **de ayer ~** since yesterday. **más ~** nearer

acaba|do *adj* finished; (*perfecto*) perfect. ● *m* finish. **~r** *vt/i* finish. **~rse** *vpr* finish; (*agotarse*) run out; (*morirse*) die. **~r con** put an end to. **~r de** (+ *infinitivo*) have just (+ *pp*). **~de llegar** he has just arrived. **~r por** (+ *infinitivo*) end up (+ *gerundio*). **¡se acabó!** that's it!

acabóse *m*. **ser el ~** be the end, be the limit

acad|emia *f* academy. **~émico** *adj* academic

acallar *vt* silence

acalora|do *adj* heated; (*persona*) hot. **~rse** *vpr* get hot; (*fig, excitarse*) get excited

acampar *vi* camp

acantilado *m* cliff

acapara|r *vt* hoard; (*monopolizar*) monopolize. **~miento** *m* hoarding; (*monopolio*) monopolizing

acariciar *vt* caress; (*animal*) stroke; (*idea*) nurture

ácaro *m* mite

acarre|ar *vt* transport; (*desgracias etc*) cause. **~o** *m* transport

acartona|do *adj* (*piel*) wizened. **~rse** *vpr* (*ponerse rígido*) go stiff; (*piel*) become wizened

acaso *adv* maybe, perhaps. ● *m* chance. **~ llueva mañana** perhaps it will rain tomorrow. **por si ~** (just) in case

acata|miento *m* compliance (**de** with). **~r** *vt* comply with

acatarrarse *vpr* catch a cold, get a cold

acaudalado *adj* well off

acceder *vi* agree; (*tener acceso*) have access

acces|ible *adj* accessible; (*persona*) approachable. **~o** *m* access, entry; (*Med, ataque*) attack

accesorio *adj & m* accessory

accident|ado *adj* (*terreno*) uneven; (*agitado*) troubled; (*persona*) injured. **~al** *adj* accidental. **~arse** *vpr* have an accident. **~e** *m* accident

acci|ón *f* (*incl Jurid*) action; (*hecho*) deed; (*Com*) share. **~onar** *vt* work. ● *vi* gesticulate. **~onista** *m & f* shareholder

acebo *m* holly (tree)

acech|ar *vt* lie in wait for. **~o** *m* spying. **al ~o** on the look-out

aceit|ar *vt* oil; (*Culin*) add oil to. **~e** *m* oil. **~e de oliva** olive oil. **~te de ricino** castor oil. **~era** *f* cruet; (*para engrasar*) oilcan. **~ero** *adj* oil. **~oso** *adj* oily

aceitun|a *f* olive. **~ado** *adj* olive. **~o** *m* olive tree

acelera|dor *m* accelerator. **~r** *vt* accelerate; (*fig*) speed up, quicken

acelga *f* chard

acent|o *m* accent; (*énfasis*) stress. **~uación** *f* accentuation. **~uar** [21] *vt* stress; (*fig*) emphasize. **~uarse** *vpr* become noticeable

acepción *f* meaning, sense

acepta|ble *adj* acceptable. **~ción** *f* acceptance; (*éxito*) success. **~r** *vt* accept

acequia *f* irrigation channel

acera *f* pavement (*Brit*), sidewalk (*Amer*)

acerca de *prep* about

a

acerca|miento m approach; (fig) reconciliation. **~r 7** vt bring near **~rse** vpr approach

acero m steel. **~ inoxidable** stainless steel

acérrimo adj (fig) staunch

acert|ado adj right, correct; (apropiado) appropriate. **~ar 1** vt (adivinar) get right, guess. ● vi get right; (en el blanco) hit. **~ar a** happen to. **~ar con** hit on. **~ijo** m riddle

achacar 7 vt attribute

achacoso adj sickly

achaque m ailment

achatar vt flatten

achicar 7 vt make smaller; (fig, fam, empequeñecer) belittle; (Naut) bale out. **~rse** vpr become smaller; (humillarse) be intimidated

achicharra|r vt burn; (fig) pester. **~rse** vpr burn

achichincle m & f (Mex) hanger-on

achicopalado adj (Mex) depressed

achicoria f chicory

achiote m (LAm) annatto

achispa|do adj tipsy. **~rse** vpr get tipsy

achulado adj cocky

acicala|do adj dressed up. **~r** vt dress up. **~rse** vpr get dressed up

acicate m spur

acidez f acidity; (Med) heartburn

ácido adj sour. ● m acid

acierto m success; (idea) good idea; (habilidad) skill

aclama|ción f acclaim; (aplausos) applause. **~r** vt acclaim; (aplaudir) applaud

aclara|ción f explanation. **~r** vt lighten (colores); (explicar) clarify; (enjuagar) rinse. ● vi (el tiempo) brighten up. **~rse** vpr become clear. **~torio** adj explanatory

aclimata|ción f acclimatization, acclimation (Amer). **~r** vt acclimatize, acclimate (Amer). **~rse** vpr become acclimatized, become acclimated (Amer)

acné m acne

acobardar vt intimidate. **~se** vpr lose one's nerve

acocil m (Mex) freshwater shrimp

acog|edor adj welcoming; (ambiente) friendly. **~er 14** vt welcome; (proteger) shelter; (recibir) receive. **~erse** vpr take refuge. **~ida** f welcome; (refugio) refuge

acolcha|do adj quilted. **~r** vt quilt, pad

acomedido adj (Mex) obliging

acomet|er vt attack; (emprender) undertake. **~ida** f attack

acomod|ado adj well off. **~ador** m usher. **~adora** f usherette. **~ar** vt arrange; (adaptar) adjust. ● vi be suitable. **~arse** vpr settle down; (adaptarse) conform

acompaña|miento m accompaniment. **~nte** m & f companion; (Mus) accompanist. **~r** vt go with; (hacer compañía) keep company; (adjuntar) enclose

acondicionar vt fit out; (preparar) prepare

aconseja|ble adj advisable. **~do** adj advised. **~r** vt advise. **~rse** vpr. **~rse con** consult

acontec|er 11 vi happen. **~imiento** m event

acopla|miento m coupling; (Elec) connection. **~r** vt fit; (Elec) connect; (Rail) couple

acorazado adj armour-plated. ● m battleship

acord|ar 2 vt agree (upon); (decidir) decide; (recordar) remind. **~arse** vpr remember. **~e** adj in agreement; (Mus) harmonious. ● m chord

acorde|ón m accordion. **~onista** m & f accordionist

acordona|do adj (lugar) cordoned off; (zapatos) lace-up. **~r** vt lace (up); (rodear) cordon off

acorralar vt round up (animales); corner (personas)

acortar vt shorten; cut short (permanencia). **~se** vpr get shorter

acos|ar vt hound; (fig) pester. **~o** m pursuit; (fig) pestering

acostar 2 vt put to bed; (Naut) bring alongside. ● vi (Naut) reach land. **~se** vpr go to bed; (echarse) lie down. **~se con** (fig) sleep with

acostumbra|do adj (habitual) usual. **~do a** used to. **~r** vt get used. **me**

ha ~**do a levantarme por la noche** he's got me used to getting up at night. ● *vi.* ~**r** be accustomed to. **acostumbro a comer a la una** I usually have lunch at one o'clock. ~**rse** *vpr* become accustomed, get used

acota|ción *f* (*nota*) margin note (*en el teatro*) stage direction; (*cota*) elevation mark. ~**miento** *m* (*Mex*) hard shoulder

acrecentar ❶ *vt* increase. ~**se** *vpr* increase

acredita|do *adj* reputable; (*Pol*) accredited. ~**r** *vt* prove; accredit (diplomático); (*garantizar*) guarantee; (*autorizar*) authorize. ~**rse** *vpr* make one's name

acreedor *adj* worthy (**de** of). ● *m* creditor

acribillar *vt* (*a balazos*) riddle (**a** with); (*a picotazos*) cover (**a** with); (*fig, a preguntas etc*) bombard (**a** with)

acr|obacia *f* acrobatics. ~**obacias aéreas** aerobatics. ~**óbata** *m & f* acrobat. ~**obático** *adj* acrobatic

acta *f* minutes; (*certificado*) certificate

actitud *f* posture, position; (*fig*) attitude, position

activ|ar *vt* activate; (*acelerar*) speed up. ~**idad** *f* activity. ~**o** *adj* active. ● *m* assets

acto *m* act; (*ceremonia*) ceremony. **en el** ~ Immediately

act|or *m* actor. ~**riz** *f* actress

actuación *f* action; (*conducta*) behaviour; (*Theat*) performance

actual *adj* present; (*asunto*) topical. ~**idad** *f* present; (*de asunto*) topicality. **en la** ~**idad** (*en este momento*) currently; (*hoy en día*) nowadays. ~**idades** *fpl* current affairs. ~**ización** *f* modernization. ~**izar** ❿ *vt* modernize. ~**mente** *adv* now, at the present time

actuar ㉑ *vi* act. ~ **de** act as

acuarel|a *f* watercolour. ~**ista** *m & f* watercolourist

acuario *m* aquarium. **A**~ Aquarius

acuartelar *vt* quarter, billet; (*mantener en cuartel*) confine to barracks

acuático *adj* aquatic

acuchillar *vt* slash; stab (persona)

acuci|ante *adj* urgent. ~**ar** *vt* urge on; (*dar prisa a*) hasten. ~**oso** *adj* keen

acudir *vi.* ~ **a** go to; (*asistir*) attend; turn up for (a una cita); (*en auxilio*) go to help

acueducto *m* aqueduct

acuerdo *m* agreement. ● *vb véase* **ACORDAR**. **¡de** ~**!** OK! **de** ~ **con** in accordance with. **estar de** ~ agree. **ponerse de** ~ agree

acuesto *vb véase* **ACOSTAR**

acumula|dor *m* accumulator. ~**r** *vt* accumulate. ~**rse** *vpr* accumulate

acunar *vt* rock

acuñar *vt* mint, coin

acupuntura *f* acupuncture

acurrucarse ❼ *vpr* curl up

acusa|do *adj* accused; (*destacado*) marked. ● *m* accused. ~**r** *vt* accuse; (*mostrar*) show; (*denunciar*) denounce; acknowledge (recibo)

acuse *m.* ~ **de recibo** acknowledgement of receipt

acus|ica *m & f* ① telltale. ~**ón** *m* ① telltale

acústic|a *f* acoustics. ~**o** *adj* acoustic

adapta|ble *adj* adaptable. ~**ción** *f* adaptation. ~**dor** *m* adapter. ~**r** *vt* adapt; (*ajustar*) fit. ~**rse** *vpr* adapt o.s.

adecua|do *adj* suitable. ~**r** *vt* adapt, make suitable

adelant|ado *adj* advanced; (niño) precocious; (reloj) fast. **por** ~**ado** in advance. ~**amiento** *m* advance(ment); (*Auto*) overtaking. ~**ar** *vt* advance, move forward; (*acelerar*) speed up; put forward (reloj); (*Auto*) overtake. ● *vi* advance, go forward; (reloj) gain, be fast. ~**arse** *vpr* advance, move forward; (reloj) gain; (*Auto*) overtake. ~**e** *adv* forward. ● *int* come in!; (¡siga!) carry on! **más** ~**e** (*lugar*) further on; (*tiempo*) later on. ~**o** *m* advance; (*progreso*) progress

adelgaza|miento *m* slimming. ~**r** ❿ *vt* make thin; lose (kilos). ● *vi* lose weight; (*adrede*) slim. ~**rse** *vpr* lose weight; (*adrede*) slim

ademán *m* gesture. **en** ~ **de** as if to. **ademanes** *mpl* (*modales*) manners.

a

además *adv* besides; (*también*) also; (*lo que es más*) what's more. ~ **de** besides

adentr|arse *vpr.* ~**arse en** penetrate into; study thoroughly (*tema* etc.). ~**o** *adv* in(side). ~ **de** (*LAm*) in(side). **mar** ~**o** out at sea. **tierra** ~**o** inland

adepto *m* supporter

aderez|ar 🔟 *vt* flavour (*bebidas*); (*condimentar*) season; dress (*ensalada*). ~**o** *m* flavouring; (*con condimentos*) seasoning; (*para ensalada*) dressing

adeud|ar *vt* owe. ~**o** *m* debit

adhe|rir 4 *vt/i* stick. ~**rirse** *vpr* stick; (*fig*) follow. ~**sión** *f* adhesion; (*fig*) support. ~**sivo** *adj & m* adhesive

adici|ón *f* addition. ~**onal** *adj* additional. ~**onar** *vt* add

adicto *adj* addicted. ● *m* addict; (*seguidor*) follower

adiestra|do *adj* trained. ~**miento** *m* training. ~**r** *vt* train. ~**rse** *vpr* practise

adinerado *adj* wealthy

adiós *int* goodbye!; (*al cruzarse con alguien*) hello!

adit|amento *m* addition; (*accesorio*) accessory. ~**ivo** *m* additive

adivin|anza *f* riddle. ~**ar** *vt* foretell; (*acertar*) guess. ~**o** *m* fortune-teller

adjetivo *adj* adjectival. ● *m* adjective

adjudica|ción *f* award. ~**r** 7 *vt* award. ~**rse** *vpr* appropriate. ~**tario** *m* winner of an award

adjunt|ar *vt* enclose. ~**o** *adj* enclosed; (*auxiliar*) assistant. ● *m* assistant

administra|ción *f* administration; (*gestión*) management. ~**dor** *m* administrator; (*gerente*) manager. ~**dora** *f* administrator; manageress. ~**r** *vt* administer. ~**tivo** *adj* administrative

admira|ble *adj* admirable. ~**ción** *f* admiration. ~**dor** *m* admirer. ~**r** *vt* admire; (*sorprender*) amaze. ~**rse** *vpr* be amazed

admi|sibilidad *f* admissibility. ~**sible** *adj* acceptable. ~**sión** *f* admission; (*aceptación*) acceptance. ~**tir** *vt* admit; (*aceptar*) accept

adobar *vt* (*Culin*) pickle; (*condimentar*) marinade

adobe *m* sun-dried brick

adobo *m* pickle; (*condimento*) marinade

adoctrinar *vt* indoctrinate

adolecer 🔟 *vi.* ~ **de** suffer from

adolescen|cia *f* adolescence. ~**te** *adj* adolescent. ● *m & f* teenager, adolescent

adonde *adv* where

adónde *adv* where?

adop|ción *f* adoption. ~**tar** *vt* adopt. ~**tivo** *adj* adoptive; (*hijo*) adopted; (*patria*) of adoption

adoqu|ín *m* paving stone; (*imbécil*) idiot. ~**inado** *m* paving. ~**inar** *vt* pave

adora|ción *f* adoration. ~**r** *vt* adore

adormec|er 🔟 *vt* send to sleep; (*fig, calmar*) calm, soothe. ~**erse** *vpr* fall asleep; (*un miembro*) go to sleep. ~**ido** *adj* sleepy; (*un miembro*) numb

adormilarse *vpr* doze

adorn|ar *vt* adorn (**con, de** with). ~**o** *m* decoration

adosar *vt* lean (**a** against); (*Mex, adjuntar*) to enclose

adqui|rir 4 *vt* acquire; (*comprar*) purchase. ~**sición** *f* acquisition; (*compra*) purchase. ~**sitivo** *adj* purchasing

adrede *adv* on purpose

adrenalina *f* adrenalin

aduan|a *f* customs. ~**ero** *adj* customs. ● *m* customs officer

aducir 47 *vt* allege

adueñarse *vpr* take possession

adul|ación *f* flattery. ~**ador** *adj* flattering. ● *m* flatterer. ~**ar** *vt* flatter

ad|ulterar *vt* adulterate. ~**ulterio** *m* adultery

adulto *adj & m* adult, grown-up

advenedizo *adj & m* upstart

advenimiento *m* advent, arrival; (*subida al trono*) accession

adverbio *m* adverb

advers|ario *m* adversary. ~**idad** *f* adversity. ~**o** *adj* adverse, unfavourable

advert|encia *f* warning. ~**ir** 4 *vt* warn; (*notar*) notice

adviento *m* Advent

adyacente *adj* adjacent

aéreo *adj* air; *(foto)* aerial; *(ferrocarril)* overhead

aeróbico *adj* aerobic

aerodeslizador *m* hovercraft

aero|ligero *m* microlight. ~**lito** *m* meteorite. ~**moza** *f (LAm)* flight attendant. ~**puerto** *m* airport. ~**sol** *m* aerosol

afab|ilidad *f* affability. ~**le** *adj* affable

afamado *adj* famous

af|án *m* hard work; *(deseo)* desire. ~**anador** *m (Mex)* cleaner. ~**anar** *vt* 🇽 pinch 🇽. ~**anarse** *vpr* strive (en, por to)

afear *vt* disfigure, make ugly; *(censurar)* censure

afecta|ción *f* affectation. ~**do** *adj* affected. ~**r** *vt* affect

afect|ivo *adj* sensitive. ~**o** *m (cariño)* affection. ● *a.* ~**o a** attached to. ~**uoso** *adj* affectionate. **con un** ~**uoso saludo** *(en cartas)* with kind regards. **suyo** ~**ísimo** *(en cartas)* yours sincerely

afeita|do *m* shave. ~**dora** *f* electric razor. ~**r** *vt* shave. ~**rse** *vpr* shave, have a shave

afeminado *adj* effeminate. ● *m* effeminate person

aferrar *vt* grasp. ~**se** *vpr* to cling (a to)

afianza|miento *m (refuerzo)* strengthening; *(garantía)* guarantee. ~**rse** 🔟 *vpr* become established

afiche *m (LAm)* poster

aficI|ón *f* liking; *(conjunto de aficionados)* fans. **por** ~**ón** as a hobby. ~**onado** *adj* keen (a on), fond (a of). ● *m* fan. ~**onar** *vt* make fond. ~**onarse** *vpr* take a liking to

afila|do *adj* sharp. ~**dor** *m* knifegrinder. ~**r** *vt* sharpen

afilia|ción *f* affiliation. ~**do** *adj* affiliated. ~**rse** *vpr* become a member (a of)

afín *adj* similar; *(contiguo)* adjacent; *(personas)* related

afina|ción *f (Auto, Mus)* tuning. ~**do** *adj (Mus)* in tune. ~**dor** *m* tuner. ~**r** *vt (afilar)* sharpen; *(Auto, Mus)* tune. ~**rse** *vpr* become thinner

afincarse 🔟 *vpr* settle

afinidad *f* affinity; *(parentesco)* relationship by marriage

afirma|ción *f* affirmation. ~**r** *vt* make firm; *(asentir)* affirm. ~**rse** *vpr* steady o.s. ~**tivo** *adj* affirmative

aflicción *f* affliction

afligi|do *adj* distressed. ~**r** 🔟 *vt* distress. ~**rse** *vpr* distress o.s.

aflojar *vt* loosen; *(relajar)* ease. ● *vi* let up. ~**se** *vpr* loosen

aflu|encia *f* flow. ~**ente** *adj* flowing. ● *m* tributary. ~**ir** 🔟 *vi* flow (a into)

afónico *adj* hoarse

aforismo *m* aphorism

aforo *m* capacity

afortunado *adj* fortunate, lucky

afrancesado *adj* Frenchified

afrenta *f* insult; *(vergüenza)* disgrace

África *f* Africa. ~ **del Sur** South Africa

africano *adj & m* African

afrodisiaco *adj & m* aphrodisiac

afrontar *vt* bring face to face; *(enfrentar)* face, confront

afuera *adv* out(side) **¡~!** out of the way! ~ **de** *(LAm)* outside. ~**s** *fpl* outskirts

agachar *vt* lower. ~**se** *vpr* bend over

agalla *f (de los peces)* gill. ~**s** *fpl (fig)* guts

agarradera *f (LAm)* handle

agarr|ado *adj (fig, fam)* mean. ~**ar** *vt* grasp; *(esp LAm)* take; *(LAm, pillar)* catch. ~**arse** *vpr* hold on; *(fam, reñirse)* have a fight. ~**ón** *m* tug; *(LAm, riña)* row

agarrotar *vt* tie tightly; *(el frío)* stiffen; garotte *(un reo)*. ~**se** *vpr* go stiff; *(Auto)* seize up

agasaj|ado *m* quest of honour. ~**ar** *vt* look after well. ~**o** *m* good treatment

agazaparse *vpr* crouch

agencia *f* agency. ~ **de viajes** travel agency. ~ **inmobiliaria** estate agency *(Brit)*, real estate agency *(Amer)*. ~**rse** *vpr* find (out) for o.s.

agenda *f* diary *(Brit)*, appointment book *(Amer)*; *(programa)* agenda

agente *m* agent; *(de policía)* policeman. ●*f* agent; *(de policía)* policewoman. ~ **de aduanas** customs of-

a

ficer. ∼ **de bolsa** stockbroker

ágil *adj* agile

agili|dad *f* agility. ∼**zación** *f* speeding up. ∼**zar** *vt* speed up

agita|ción *f* waving; (*de un líquido*) stirring; (*intranquilidad*) agitation. ∼**do** *adj* (el mar) rough; (*fig*) agitated. ∼**dor** *m* (*Pol*) agitator

agitar *vt* wave; shake (botellas etc); stir (líquidos); (*fig*) stir up. ∼**se** *vpr* wave; (el mar) get rough; (*fig*) get excited

aglomera|ción *f* agglomeration; (*de tráfico*) traffic jam. ∼**r** *vt* amass. ∼**se** *vpr* form a crowd

agnóstico *adj & m* agnostic

agobi|ante *adj* (trabajo) exhausting; (calor) oppressive. ∼**ar** *vt* weigh down; (*fig, abrumar*) overwhelm. ∼**o** *m* weight; (*cansancio*) exhaustion; (*opresión*) oppression

agolparse *vpr* crowd together

agon|ía *f* death throes; (*fig*) agony. ∼**izante** *adj* dying; (luz) failing. ∼**izar** 10 *vi* be dying

agosto *m* August. **hacer su** ∼ feather one's nest

agota|do *adj* exhausted; (*todo vendido*) sold out; (libro) out of print. ∼**dor** *adj* exhausting. ∼**miento** *m* exhaustion. ∼**r** *vt* exhaust. ∼**se** *vpr* be exhausted; (existencias) sell out; (libro) go out of print

agracia|do *adj* attractive; (*que tiene suerte*) lucky. ∼**r** *vt* make attractive

agradec|er 11 *vt* thank (persona); be grateful for (cosa). ∼**ido** *adj* grateful. ¡**muy** ∼**ido!** thanks a lot! ∼**imiento** *m* gratitude

agrado *m* pleasure; (*amabilidad*) friendliness

agrandar *vt* enlarge; (*fig*) exaggerate. ∼**se** *vpr* get bigger

agrario *adj* agrarian, land; (política) agricultural

agrava|nte *adj* aggravating. ● *f* additional problem. ∼**r** *vt* aggravate; (*aumentar el peso*) make heavier. ∼**rse** *vpr* get worse

agravi|ar *vt* offend; (*perjudicar*) wrong. ∼**o** *m* offence

agredir 24 *vt* attack. ∼ **de palabra** insult

agrega|do *m* aggregate; (*diplomático*) attaché. ∼**r** 12 *vt* add; appoint (persona). ∼**rse** *vpr* to join

agres|ión *f* aggression; (*ataque*) attack. ∼**ividad** *f* aggressiveness. ∼**ivo** *adj* aggressive. ∼**or** *m* aggressor

agreste *adj* country; (terreno) rough

agriar *regular, o raramente* 20 *vt* sour. ∼**se** *vpr* turn sour; (*fig*) become embittered

agr|ícola *adj* agricultural. ∼**icultor** *m* farmer. ∼**icultura** *f* agriculture, farming

agridulce *adj* bitter-sweet; (*Culin*) sweet-and-sour

agrietar *vt* crack. ∼**se** *vpr* crack; (piel) chap

agrio *adj* sour. ∼**s** *mpl* citrus fruits

agro|nomía *f* agronomy. ∼**pecuario** *adj* farming

agrupa|ción *f* group; (acción) grouping. ∼**r** *vt* group. ∼**rse** *vpr* form a group

agruras *fpl* (*Mex*) heartburn

agua *f* water; (*lluvia*) rain; (*marea*) tide; (*vertiente del tejado*) slope. ∼ **abajo** downstream. ∼ **arriba** upstream. ∼ **bendita** holy water. ∼ **corriente** running water. ∼ **de colonia** eau de cologne. ∼ **dulce** fresh water. ∼ **mineral con gas** fizzy mineral water. ∼ **mineral sin gas** still mineral water. ∼ **potable** drinking water. ∼ **salada** salt water. **hacer** ∼ (*Naut*) leak. **se me hizo** ∼ **la boca** (*LAm*) my mouth watered

aguacate *m* avocado pear; (*árbol*) avocado pear tree

aguacero *m* downpour, heavy shower

aguado *adj* watery; (*Mex, aburrido*) boring

agua|fiestas *m & f invar* spoilsport, wet blanket. ∼**mala** *f* (*Mex*), ∼**mar** *m* jellyfish. ∼**marina** *f* aquamarine

aguant|ar *vt* put up with, bear; (*sostener*) support. ● *vi* hold out. ∼**arse** *vpr* restrain o.s. ∼**e** *m* patience; (*resistencia*) endurance

aguar ⓯ *vt* water down

aguardar *vt* wait for. ● *vi* wait

agua|rdiente *m* (cheap) brandy. **~rrás** *m* turpentine, turps Ⓔ

agud|eza *f* sharpness; (*fig, perspicacia*) insight; (*fig, ingenio*) wit. **~izar** ⓾ *vt* sharpen. **~izarse** *vpr* (*enfermedad*) get worse. **~o** *adj* sharp; (*ángulo, enfermedad*) acute; (*voz*) high-pitched

agüero *m* omen. **ser de mal ~** be a bad omen

aguijón *m* sting; (*vara*) goad

águila *f* eagle; (*persona perspicaz*) astute person; (*Mex, de moneda*) heads. **¿~ o sol?** heads or tails?

aguileño *adj* aquiline

aguinaldo *m* Christmas box; (*LAm, paga*) Christmas bonus

aguja *f* needle; (*del reloj*) hand; (*de torre*) steeple. **~s** *fpl* (*Rail*) points

aguje|ear *vt* make holes in. **~o** *m* hole

agujetas *fpl* stiffness; (*Mex, de zapatos*) shoe laces. **tener ~** be stiff

aguzado *adj* sharp

ah *int* ah!, oh!

ahí *adv* there. **~ nomás** (*LAm*) just there. **de ~ que** that is why. **por ~** that way; (*aproximadamente*) thereabouts

ahija|da *f* god-daughter, godchild. **~do** *m* godson, godchild. **~dos** *mpl* godchildren

ahínco *m* enthusiasm; (*empeño*) insistence

ahog|ado *adj* (*en el agua*) drowned; (*asfixiado*) suffocated. **~ar** ⓬ *vt* (*en el agua*) drown; (*asfixiar*) suffocate; put out (*fuego*). **~arse** *vpr* (*en el agua*) drown; (*asfixiarse*) suffocate. **~o** *m* breathlessness; (*fig, angustia*) distress

ahondar *vt* deepen. ● *vi* go deep. **~ en** (*fig*) examine in depth. **~se** *vpr* get deeper

ahora *adv* now; (*hace muy poco*) just now; (*dentro de poco*) very soon. **~ bien** however. **~ mismo** right now. **de ~ en adelante** from now on, in future. **por ~** for the time being

ahorcar ⓻ *vt* hang. **~se** *vpr* hang o.s.

ahorita *adv* (*esp LAm fam*) now. **~ mismo** right now

ahorr|ador *adj* thrifty. **~ar** *vt* save. **~arse** *vpr* save o.s. **~o** *m* saving. **~os** *mpl* savings

ahuecar ⓻ *vt* hollow; fluff up (colchón); deepen (la voz)

ahuizote *m* (*Mex*) scourge

ahuma|do *adj* (*Culin*) smoked; (*de colores*) smoky. **~r** *vt* (*Culin*) smoke; (*llenar de humo*) fill with smoke. ● *vi* smoke. **~rse** *vpr* become smoky; (*comida*) acquire a smoky taste

ahuyentar *vt* drive away; banish (pensamientos etc)

aimará *adj & m* Aymara. ● *m & f* Aymara indian

airado *adj* annoyed

aire *m* air; (*viento*) breeze; (*corriente*) draught; (*aspecto*) appearance; (*Mus*) tune, air. **~ acondicionado** airconditioning. **al ~ libre** outdoors. **darse ~s** give o.s. airs. **~ar** *vt* air; (*ventilar*) ventilate; (*fig, publicar*) make public. **~arse** *vpr.* **salir para ~arse** go out for some fresh air

airoso *adj* graceful; (*exitoso*) successful

aisla|do *adj* isolated; (*Elec*) insulated. **~dor** *adj* (*Elec*) insulating. **~nte** *adj* insulating. **~r** ㉓ *vt* isolate; (*Elec*) insulate

ajar *vt* crumple; (*estropear*) spoil

ajedre|cista *m & f* chess-player. **~z** *m* chess

ajeno *adj* (*de otro*) someone else's; (*de otros*) other people's; (*extraño*) alien

ajetre|ado *adj* hectic, busy. **~o** *m* bustle

ají *m* (*LAm*) chilli; (*salsa*) chilli sauce

aj|illo *m* garlic. **al ~illo** cooked with garlic. **~o** *m* garlic. **~onjolí** *m* sesame

ajuar *m* furnishings; (*de novia*) trousseau; (*de bebé*) layette

ajust|ado *adj* right; (*vestido*) tight. **~ar** *vt* fit; (*adaptar*) adapt; (*acordar*) agree; settle (una cuenta); (*apretar*) tighten. ● *vi* fit. **~arse** *vpr* fit; (*adaptarse*) adapt o.s.; (*acordarse*) come to an agreement. **~e** *m* fitting; (*adaptación*) adjustment; (*acuerdo*) agreement; (*de una cuenta*) settlement

al = a + el

ala f wing; (de sombrero) brim. ● m & f (deportes) winger

alaba|nza f praise. ~**r** vt praise

alacena f cupboard (Brit), closet (Amer)

alacrán m scorpion

alambr|ada f wire fence. ~**ado** m (LAm) wire fence. ~**e** m wire. ~**e de púas** barbed wire

alameda f avenue; (plantío de álamos) poplar grove

álamo m poplar. ~ **temblón** aspen

alarde m show. **hacer** ~ **de** boast of

alarga|do adj long. ~**dor** m extension. ~**r** 12 vt lengthen; stretch out (mano etc); (dar) give, pass. ~**rse** vpr get longer

alarido m shriek

alarm|a f alarm. ~**ante** adj alarming. ~**ar** vt alarm, frighten. ~**arse** vpr be alarmed. ~**ista** m & f alarmist

alba f dawn

albacea m & f executor

albahaca f basil

albanés adj & m Albanian

Albania f Albania

albañil m builder; (que coloca ladrillos) bricklayer

albarán m delivery note

albaricoque m apricot. ~**ro** m apricot tree

albedrío m will. **libre** ~ free will

alberca f tank, reservoir; (Mex, piscina) swimming pool

alberg|ar 12 vt (alojar) put up; (vivienda) house; (dar refugio) shelter. ~**arse** vpr stay; (refugiarse) shelter. ~**ue** m accommodation; (refugio) shelter. ~**ue de juventud** youth hostel

albino adj & m albino

albóndiga f meatball, rissole

albornoz m bathrobe

alborot|ado adj excited; (aturdido) hasty. ~**ador** adj rowdy. ● m troublemaker. ~**ar** vt disturb, upset. ● vi make a racket. ~**arse** vpr get excited; (el mar) get rough. ~**o** m row, uproar

álbum m (pl ~**es** o ~**s**) album

alcachofa f artichoke

alcald|e m mayor. ~**esa** f mayoress. ~**ía** f mayoralty; (oficina) mayor's office

alcance m reach; (de arma, telescopio etc) range; (déficit) deficit

alcancía f money-box; (LAm, de niño) piggy bank

alcantarilla f sewer; (boca) drain

alcanzar 10 vt (llegar a) catch up; (coger) reach; catch (un autobús); (bala etc) strike, hit. ● vi reach; (ser suficiente) be enough. ~ **a** manage

alcaparra f caper

alcázar m fortress

alcoba f bedroom

alcoh|ol m alcohol. ~**ol desnaturalizado** methylated spirits, meths. ~**ólico** adj & m alcoholic. ~**olímetro** m Breathalyser . ~**olismo** m alcoholism

alcornoque m cork-oak; (persona torpe) idiot

aldaba f door-knocker

aldea f village. ~**no** adj village. ● m villager

alea|ción f alloy. ~**r** vt alloy

aleatorio adj uncertain

aleccionar vt instruct

aledaños mpl outskirts

alega|ción f allegation; (LAm, disputa) argument. ~**r** 12 vt claim; (Jurid) plead. ● vi (LAm) argue. ~**ta** f (Mex) argument. ~**to** m plea

alegoría f allegory

alegr|ar vt make happy; (avivar) brighten up. ~**arse** vpr be happy; (emborracharse) get merry. ~**e** adj happy; (achispado) merry, tight. ~**ía** f happiness

aleja|do adj distant. ~**miento** m removal; (entre personas) estrangement; (distancia) distance. ~**r** vt remove; (ahuyentar) get rid of; (fig, apartar) separate. ~**rse** vpr move away

alemán adj & m German

Alemania f Germany. ~ **Occidental** (historia) West Germany. ~ **Oriental** (historia) East Germany

alenta|dor adj encouraging. ~**r** 1 vt encourage. ● vi breathe

alerce m larch

al|ergia f allergy. ~**érgico** adj allergic

alero m (del tejado) eaves

alerta adj alert. ¡~! look out! **estar** ~ be alert; (en guardia) be on the alert. ~**r** vt alert

aleta f wing; (de pez) fin

aletarga|do adj lethargic. ~**r** 12 vt make lethargic. ~**rse** vpr become lethargic

alet|azo m (de un ave) flap of the wings; (de un pez) flick of the fin. ~**ear** vi flap its wings, flutter

alevosía f treachery

alfab|ético adj alphabetical. ~**etizar** 10 vt alphabetize; teach to read and write. ~**eto** m alphabet. ~**eto Morse** Morse code

alfalfa f alfalfa

alfar|ería m pottery. ~**ero** m potter

alféizar m (window)sill

alférez m second lieutenant

alfil m (en ajedrez) bishop

alfile|r m pln. ~**tero** m pincushion; (estuche) pin-case

alfombr|a f (grande) carpet; (pequeña) rug, mat. ~**ado** adj (LAm) carpeted. ~**ar** vt carpet. ~**illa** f rug, mat; (Med) type of measles

alforja f saddle-bag

algarabía f hubbub

algas fpl seaweed

álgebra f algebra

álgido adj (fig) decisive

algo pron something; (en frases interrogativas, condicionales) anything. ● adv rather. ¿~ **más?** anything else? ¿**quieres tomar** ~? would you like a drink?; (de comer) would you like something to eat?

algod|ón m cotton. ~**ón de azúcar** candy floss (Brit), cotton candy (Amer). ~**ón hidrófilo** cotton wool. ~**onero** adj cotton. ● m cotton plant

alguacil m bailiff

alguien pron someone, somebody; (en frases interrogativas, condicionales) anyone, anybody

algún véase **ALGUNO**

alguno adj (delante de nombres masculinos en singular **algún**) some; (en frases interrogativas, condicionales) any; (pospuesto al nombre en frases negativas) at all. **no tiene idea alguna** he hasn't any idea at all. **alguna que otra vez** from time to time. **algunas veces**, **alguna vez** sometimes. ● pron one; (en plural) some; (alguien) someone

alhaja f piece of jewellery; (fig) treasure. ~**s** fpl jewellery

alharaca f fuss

alhelí m wallflower

alia|do adj allied. ● m ally. ~**nza** f alliance; (anillo) wedding ring. ~**r** 20 vt combine. ~**rse** vpr be combined; (formar una alianza) form an alliance

alias adv & m alias

alicaído adj (fig, débil) weak; (fig, abatido) depressed

alicates mpl pliers

aliciente m incentive; (de un lugar) attraction

alienado adj mentally ill

aliento m breath; (ánimo) courage

aligerar vt make lighter; (aliviar) alleviate, ease; (apresurar) quicken

alijo m (de contrabando) consignment

alimaña f pest. ~**s** fpl vermin

aliment|ación f diet; (acción) feeding. ~**ar** vt feed; (nutrir) nourish. ● vi be nourishing. ~**arse** vpr feed (con, de on). ~**icio** adj nourishing. **productos** mpl ~**icios** foodstuffs. ~**o** m food. ~**os** mpl (Jurid) alimony

alinea|ción f alignment; (en deportes) line-up. ~**r** vt align, line up

aliñ|ar vt (Culin) season; dress (ensalada). ~**o** m seasoning; (para ensalada) dressing

alioli m garlic mayonnaise

alisar vt smooth

alistar vt put on a list; (Mil) enlist. ~**se** vpr enrol; (Mil) enlist; (LAm, prepararse) get ready

alivi|ar vt lighten; relieve (dolor, etc); (arg, hurtar) steal, pinch ⏻. ~**arse** vpr (dolor) diminish; (persona) get better. ~**o** m relief

aljibe m tank

allá adv (over) there. ¡~ **él!** that's his business! ~ **fuera** out there. ~ **por 1970** back in 1970. **el más** ~ the beyond. **más** ~ further on. **más** ~ **de** beyond. **por** ~ that way

allana|miento m. ~**miento (de morada)** breaking and entering: (LAm, por la autoridad) raid. ~**r** vt level; remove (obstáculos); (fig) iron out (dificultades etc); break into (una casa); (LAm, por la autoridad) raid

allega|do adj close. ● m close friend; (pariente) close relative. ~**r 12** vt collect

allí adv there; (tiempo) then. ~ **fuera** out there. **por** ~ that way

alma f soul; (habitante) inhabitant

almac|én m warehouse; (LAm, tienda) grocer's shop; (de un arma) magazine. ~**enes** mpl department store. ~**enaje** m storage; (derechos) storage charges. ~**enar** vt store; stock up with (provisiones)

almanaque m almanac

almeja f clam

almendr|a f almond. ~**ado** adj almond-shaped. ~**o** m almond tree

alm|íbar m syrup. ~**ibarar** vt cover in syrup

almid|ón m starch. ~**onado** adj starched; (fig, estirado) starchy

almirante m admiral

almizcle m musk. ~**ra** f muskrat

almohad|a f pillow. **consultar con la** ~**a** sleep on it. ~**illa** f small cushion. ~**ón** m large pillow, bolster

almorranas fpl haemorrhoids, piles

alm|orzar 2 & 10 vt (a mediodía) have for lunch; (desayunar) have for breakfast. ● vi (a mediodía) have lunch; (desayunar) have breakfast. ~**uerzo** m (a mediodía) lunch; (desayuno) breakfast

alocado adj scatter-brained

aloja|miento m accommodation. ~**r** vt put up. ~**rse** vpr stay

alondra f lark

alpaca f alpaca

alpargata f canvas shoe, espadrille

alpin|ismo m mountaineering, climbing. ~**ista** m & f mountaineer, climber. ~**o** adj Alpine

alpiste m birdseed

alquil|ar vt (tomar en alquiler) hire (vehículo), rent (piso, casa); (dar en alquiler) hire (out) (vehículo), rent (out) (piso, casa). **se alquila** to let (Brit), for

rent (Amer.) ~**er** m (acción — de alquilar un piso etc) renting; (— de alquilar un vehículo) hiring; (precio — por el que se alquila un piso etc) rent; (— por el que se alquila un vehículo) hire charge. **de** ~**er** for hire

alquimi|a f alchemy. ~**sta** m alchemist

alquitrán m tar

alrededor adv around. ~ **de** around; (con números) about. ~**es** mpl surroundings; (de una ciudad) outskirts

alta f discharge

altaner|ía f (arrogancia) arrogance. ~**o** adj arrogant, haughty

altar m altar

altavoz m loudspeaker

altera|ble adj changeable. ~**ción** f change, alteration. ~**r** vt change, alter; (perturbar) disturb; (enfadar) anger, irritate. ~**rse** vpr change, alter; (agitarse) get upset; (enfadarse) get angry; (comida) go off

altercado m argument

altern|ar vt/i alternate. ~**arse** vpr take turns. ~**ativa** f alternative. ~**ativo** adj alternating. ~**o** adj alternate; (Elec) alternating

Alteza f (título) Highness

altibajos mpl (de terreno) unevenness; (fig) ups and downs

altiplanicie f, **altiplano** m high plateau

altisonante adj pompous

altitud f altitude

altiv|ez f arrogance. ~**o** adj arrogant

alto adj high; (persona, edificio) tall; (voz) loud; (fig, elevado) lofty; (Mus) (nota) high(-pitched); (Mus) (voz, instrumento) alto; (horas) early. ● adv high; (de sonidos) loud(ly). ● m height; (de un edificio) top floor; (viola) viola; (voz) alto; (parada) stop. ● int halt!, stop! **en lo** ~ **de** on the top of. **tiene 3 metros de** ~ it is 3 metres high

altoparlante m (esp LAm) loudspeaker

altruis|mo m altruism. ~**ta** adj altruistic. ● m & f altruist

altura f height; (Aviac, Geog) altitude; (de agua) depth; (fig, cielo) sky. **a estas** ~**s** at this stage. **tiene 3 me-**

tros de ~ it is 3 metres high

alubia f (haricot) bean

alucinación f hallucination

alud m avalanche

aludi|do adj in question. **darse por
~do** take it personally. **no darse por
~do** turn a deaf ear. **~r** vi mention

alumbra|do adj lit. ● m lighting.
~miento m lighting; (parto) child-
birth. **~r** vt light

aluminio m aluminium (Brit), aluminum (Amer)

alumno m pupil; (Univ) student

aluniza|je m landing on the moon.
~r 🔟 vi land on the moon

alusi|ón f allusion. **~vo** adj allusive

alza f rise. **~da** f (de caballo) height;
(Jurid) appeal. **~do** adj raised; (Mex,
soberbio) vain; (precio) fixed.
~miento m (Pol) uprising. **~r** 🔟 vt
raise, lift (up); raise (precios). **~rse**
vpr (Pol) rise up

ama f lady of the house. **~ de casa**
housewife. **~ de cría** wet-nurse. **~
de llaves** housekeeper

amab|ilidad f kindness. **~le** adj kind;
(simpático) nice

amaestra|do adj trained. **~r** vt train

amag|ar 🔢 vt (mostrar intención de)
make as if to; (Mex, amenazar)
threaten. ● vi threaten; (algo bueno)
be in the offing. **~o** m threat; (señal)
sign; (Med) symptom

amainar vi let up

amalgama f amalgam. **~r** vt amalgamate

amamantar vt/i breast-feed; (animal)
to suckle

amanecer m dawn. ● vi dawn; (persona) wake up. **al ~** at dawn, at day-
break. **~se** vpr (Mex) stay up all night

amanera|do adj affected. **~rse** vpr
become affected

amansar vt tame; break in (un caballo); soothe (dolor etc). **~se** vpr calm
down

amante adj fond. ● m & f lover

amapola f poppy

amar vt love

amara|je m landing on water; (de as-
tronave) splash-down. **~r** vi land on
water; (astronave) splash down

amarg|ado adj embittered. **~ar** 🔢 vt
make bitter; embitter (persona).
~arse vpr become bitter. **~o** adj bitter. **~ura** f bitterness

amariconado adj 🔟 effeminate

amarill|ento adj yellowish; (tez) sal-
low. **~o** adj & m yellow

amarra|s fpl. **soltar las ~s** cast off.
~do adj (LAm) mean. **~r** vt moor;
(esp LAm, atar) tie. **~rse** vpr LAm
tie up

amas|ar vt knead; (acumular) to
amass. **~ijo** m dough; (acción)
kneading; (fig, fam, mezcla) hotchpotch

amate m (Mex) fig tree

amateur adj & m & f amateur

amazona f Amazon; (jinete) horse-
woman

ámbar m amber

ambici|ón f ambition. **~onar** vt as-
pire to. **~onar ser** have an ambition
to be. **~oso** adj ambitious. ● m ambitious person

ambidextro adj ambidextrous. ● m
ambidextrous person

ambient|ar vt give an atmosphere to.
~arse vpr adapt o.s. **~e** m atmosphere; (entorno) environment

ambig|üedad f ambiguity. **~uo** adj
ambiguous

ámbito m sphere; (alcance) scope

ambos adj & pron both

ambulancia f ambulance

ambulante adj travelling

ambulatorio m out-patients' department

amedrentar vt frighten, scare. **~se**
vpr be frightened

amén m amen. ● int amen! **en un
decir ~** in an instant

amenaza f threat. **~r** 🔟 vt threaten

amen|idad f pleasantness. **~izar** 🔟
vt brighten up. **~o** adj pleasant

América f America. **~ Central** Central
America. **~ del Norte** North America. **~ del Sur** South America. **~ Latina** Latin America

american|a f jacket. **~ismo** m Ameri-
canism. **~o** adj American

amerita|do adj (LAm) meritorious. **~r**
vt (LAm) deserve

amerizaje m véase **AMARAJE**

ametralla|dora f machine-gun. **~r** vt machine-gun

amianto m asbestos

amig|a f friend; (novia) girl-friend; (amante) lover. **~able** adj friendly. **~ablemente** adv amicably

am|ígdala f tonsil. **~igdalitis** f tonsillitis

amigo adj friendly. ● m friend; (novio) boyfriend; (amante) lover. **ser ~ de** be fond of. **ser muy ~s** be close friends

amilanar vt daunt. **~se** vpr be daunted

aminorar vt lessen; reduce (velocidad)

amist|ad f friendship. **~ades** fpl friends. **~oso** adj friendly

amn|esia f amnesia. **~ésico** adj amnesiac

amnist|ía f amnesty. **~iar** 20 vt grant an amnesty to

amo m master; (dueño) owner

amodorrarse vpr feel sleepy

amoldar vt mould; (adaptar) adapt; (acomodar) fit. **~se** vpr adapt

amonestar vt rebuke, reprimand; (anunciar la boda) publish the banns

amoniaco, amoníaco m ammonia

amontonar vt pile up; (fig, acumular) accumulate. **~se** vpr pile up; (gente) crowd together

amor m love. **~es** mpl (relaciones amorosas) love affairs. **~ propio** pride. **con mil ~es, de mil ~es** with (the greatest of) pleasure. **hacer el ~** make love. **por (el) ~ de Dios** for God's sake

amoratado adj purple; (de frío) blue

amordazar 10 vt gag; (fig) silence

amorfo adj amorphous, shapeless

amor|ío m affair. **~oso** adj loving; (cartas) love; (LAm, encantador) cute

amortajar vt shroud

amortigua|dor adj deadening. ● m (Auto) shock absorber. **~r** 15 vt deaden (ruido); dim (luz); cushion (golpe); tone down (color)

amortiza|ble adj redeemable. **~ción** f (de una deuda) repayment; (de bono etc) redemption. **~r** 10 vt repay (una deuda)

amotinar vt incite to riot. **~se** vpr rebel; (Mil) mutiny

ampar|ar vt help; (proteger) protect. **~arse** vpr seek protection; (de la lluvia) shelter. **~o** m protection; (de la lluvia) shelter. **al ~o de** under the protection of

amperio m ampere, amp 1

amplia|ción f extension; (photo) enlargement. **~r** 20 vt enlarge, extend; (photo) enlarge

amplifica|ción f amplification. **~dor** m amplifier. **~r** 7 amplify

ampli|o adj wide; (espacioso) spacious; (ropa) loose-fitting. **~tud** f extent; (espaciosidad) spaciousness; (espacio) space

ampolla f (Med) blister; (de medicamento) ampoule, phial

ampuloso adj pompous

amputar vt amputate; (fig) delete

amueblar vt furnish

amuleto m charm, amulet

amuralla|do adj walled. **~r** vt build a wall around

anacr|ónico adj anachronistic. **~onismo** m anachronism

anales mpl annals

analfabet|ismo m illiteracy. **~o** adj & m illiterate

analgésico adj analgesic. ● m painkiller

an|álisis m invar analysis. **~álisis de sangre** blood test. **~alista** m & f analyst. **~alítico** adj analytical. **~alizar** 10 vt analyze

an|alogía f analogy. **~álogo** adj analogous

anaranjado adj orangey

an|arquía f anarchy. **~árquico** adj anarchic. **~arquismo** m anarchism. **~arquista** adj anarchistic. ● m & f anarchist

anat|omía f anatomy. **~ómico** adj anatomical

anca f haunch; (parte superior) rump; (fam, nalgas) bottom. **en ~s** (LAm) on the crupper

ancestro m ancestor

ancho adj wide; (ropa) loose-fitting; (fig) relieved; (demasiado grande) too big; (ufano) smug. ● m width; (Rail)

gauge. ~ **de banda** bandwidth.
tiene 3 metros de ~ it is 3 metres
wide
anchoa f anchovy
anchura f width; (*medida*) measurement
ancian|o adj elderly, old. ● *m* elderly
man, old man. ~**a** f elderly woman,
old woman. **los** ~**os** old people
ancla f anchor. **echar** ~**s** drop anchor.
levar ~**s** weigh anchor. ~**r** vi anchor
andad|eras fpl (*Mex*) baby-walker. ~**or**
m baby-walker
Andalucía f Andalusia
andaluz adj & m Andalusian
andamio m platform. ~**s** mpl scaffolding
and|anzas fpl adventures. ~**ar** 🔳 vi
(*recorrer*) cover, go. ● vi walk; (*máquina*) go, work; (*estar*) be; (*moverse*)
move. ~**ar a caballo** (*LAm*) ride a
horse. ~**ar en bicicleta** (*LAm*) ride a
bicycle. **¡anda!** go on!, come on! ~**ar
por** be about. ~**arse** vpr (*LAm, en imperativo*) **¡andate!** go away! ● m walk.
~**ariego** adj fond of walking
andén m platform
Andes mpl. **los** ~ the Andes
andin|o adj Andean. ~**ismo** m (*LAm*)
mountaineering, climbing. ~**ista** m &
f (*LAm*) mountaineer, climber
andrajo m rag. ~**so** adj ragged
anduve vb véase **ANDAR**
anécdota f anecdote
anecdótico adj anecdotal
anegar 🔳 vt flood. ~**se** vpr be
flooded, flood
anejo adj véase **ANEXO**
an|emia f anaemia. ~**émico** adj anaemic
anest|esia f anaesthesia; (*droga*) anaesthetic. ~**esiar** vt anaesthetize.
~**ésico** adj & m anaesthetic. ~**esista**
m & f anaesthetist
anex|ar vt annex. ~**o** adj attached. ●
m annexe
anfibio adj amphibious. ● m amphibian
anfiteatro m amphitheatre; (*en un
teatro*) upper circle
anfitri|ón m host. ~**ona** f hostess
ángel m angel; (*encanto*) charm

angelical adj, **angélico** adj angelic
angina f. ~ **de pecho** angina
(pectoris). **tener** ~**s** have tonsillitis
anglicano adj & m Anglican
angl|icismo m Anglicism. ~**ófilo** adj &
m Anglophile. ~**ohispánico** adj
Anglo-Spanish. ~**osajón** adj & m
Anglo-Saxon
angosto adj narrow
angu|ila f eel. ~**la** f elver, baby eel
ángulo m angle; (*rincón, esquina*) corner; (*curva*) bend
angusti|a f anguish. ~**ar** vt distress;
(*inquietar*) worry. ~**arse** vpr get distressed; (*inquietarse*) get worried.
~**oso** adj anguished; (*que causa angustia*) distressing
anhel|ar vt (+ *nombre*) long for; (+ *verbo*)
long to. ~**o** m (*fig*) yearning
anidar vi nest
anill|a f ring. ~**o** m ring. ~**o de boda**
wedding ring
ánima f soul
anima|ción f (*de personas*) life; (*de
cosas*) liveliness; (*bullicio*) bustle; (*en el
cine*) animation. ~**do** adj lively; (*sitio
etc*) busy. ~**dor** m host. ~**dora** f
hostess; (*de un equipo*) cheerleader
animadversión f ill will
animal adj animal; (*fig, fam, torpe*)
stupid. ● m animal; (*fig, fam, idiota*)
idiot; (*fig, fam, bruto*) brute
animar vt give life to; (*dar ánimo*) encourage; (*dar vivacidad*) liven up. ~**se**
vpr (*decidirse*) decide; (*ponerse alegre*)
cheer up. **¿te animas a ir al cine?** do
you feel like going to the cinema?
ánimo m soul; (*mente*) mind; (*valor*)
courage; (*intención*) intention. **¡**~**!**
come on!, cheer up! **dar** ~**s** encourage
animos|idad f animosity. ~**o** adj
brave; (*resuelto*) determined
aniquilar vt annihilate; (*acabar con*)
ruin
anís m aniseed; (*licor*) anisette
aniversario m anniversary
anoche adv last night, yesterday evening
anochecer 🔳 vi get dark. **anochecí
en Madrid** I was in Madrid at dusk.
● m nightfall, dusk. **al** ~ at nightfall

a

anodino *adj* bland

an|omalía *f* anomaly. **~ómalo** *adj* anomalous

an|onimato *m* anonymity. **~ónimo** *adj* anonymous; (sociedad) limited. ● *m* (carta) anonymous letter

anormal *adj* abnormal. ● *m & f* 🚹 idiot. **~idad** *f* abnormality

anota|ción *f* (nota) note; (acción de poner notas) annotation. **~r** *vt* (poner nota) annotate; (apuntar) make a note of; (LAm) score (un gol)

anquilosa|miento *m* (fig) paralysis. **~rse** *vpr* become paralyzed

ansi|a *f* anxiety, worry; (anhelo) yearning. **~ar** 20 *vt* long for. **~edad** *f* anxiety. **~oso** *adj* anxious; (deseoso) eager

antag|ónico *adj* antagonistic. **~onismo** *m* antagonism. **~onista** *m & f* antagonist

antaño *adv* in days gone by

antártico *adj & m* Antarctic

ante *prep* in front of, before; (frente a) in the face of; (en vista de) in view of. ● *m* elk; (piel) suede. **~anoche** *adv* the night before last. **~ayer** *adv* the day before yesterday. **~brazo** *m* forearm

antece|dente *adj* previous. ● *m* antecedent. **~dentes** *mpl* history, background. **~dentes penales** criminal record. **~der** *vt* precede. **~sor** *m* predecessor; (antepasado) ancestor

antelación *f* (advance) notice. **con ~** in advance

antemano *adv*. **de ~** beforehand

antena *f* antenna; (radio, TV) aerial

antenoche *adv* (LAm) the night before last

anteoj|eras *fpl* blinkers. **~o** *m* telescope. **~os** *mpl* binoculars; (LAm, gafas) glasses, spectacles. **~os de sol** sunglasses

ante|pasados *mpl* forebears, ancestors. **~poner** 34 *vt* put in front (a of); (fig) put before, prefer. **~proyecto** *m* preliminary sketch; (fig) blueprint

anterior *adj* previous; (delantero) front. **~idad** *f*. **con ~idad** previously. **con ~idad a** prior to

antes *adv* before; (antiguamente) in the past; (mejor) rather; (primero) first. **~ de** before. **~ de ayer** the day before yesterday. **~ de que** + subjuntivo before. **~ de que llegue** before he arrives. **cuanto ~, lo ~ posible** as soon as possible

anti|aéreo *adj* anti-aircraft. **~biótico** *adj & m* antibiotic. **~ciclón** *m* anticyclone

anticip|ación *f*. **con ~ación** in advance. **con media hora de ~ación** half an hour early. **~ado** *adj* advance. **por ~ado** in advance. **~ar** *vt* bring forward; advance (dinero). **~arse** *vpr* be early. **~o** *m* (dinero) advance; (fig) foretaste

anti|conceptivo *adj & m* contraceptive. **~ de emergencia** morning-after pill. **~congelante** *m* antifreeze

anticua|do *adj* old-fashioned. **~rio** *m* antique dealer

anticuerpo *m* antibody

antídoto *m* antidote

anti|estético *adj* ugly. **~faz** *m* mask

antig|ualla *f* old relic. **~uamente** *adv* formerly; (hace mucho tiempo) long ago. **~üedad** *f* antiquity; (objeto) antique; (en un empleo) length of service. **~uo** *adj* old; (ruinas) ancient; (mueble) antique

Antillas *fpl*. **las ~** the West Indies

antílope *m* antelope

antinatural *adj* unnatural

antip|atía *f* dislike; (cualidad de antipático) unpleasantness. **~ático** *adj* unpleasant, unfriendly

anti|semita *m & f* anti-Semite. **~séptico** *adj & m* antiseptic. **~social** *adj* antisocial

antítesis *f invar* antithesis

antoj|adizo *adj* capricious. **~arse** *vpr* fancy. **se le ~a un caramelo** he fancies a sweet. **~itos** *mpl* (Mex) snacks bought at street stands. **~o** *m* whim; (de embarazada) craving

antología *f* anthology

antorcha *f* torch

ántrax *m* anthrax

antro *m* (fig) dump, hole. **~ de perversión** den of iniquity

antrop|ología f anthropology. **~ólogo** m anthropologist

anua|l adj annual. **~lidad** f annuity. **~lmente** adv yearly. **~rio** m yearbook

anudar vt tie, knot. **~se** vpr tie

anula|ción f annulment, cancellation. **~r** vt annul, cancel. ● adj (dedo) ring. ● m ring finger

anunci|ante m & f advertiser. **~ar** vt announce; advertise (producto comercial); (presagiar) be a sign of. **~o** m announcement; (para vender algo) advertisement, advert ⬛; (cartel) poster

anzuelo m (fish)hook; (fig) bait. **tragar el ~** swallow the bait

añadi|dura f addition. **por ~dura** in addition. **~r** vt add

añejo adj (vino) mature

añicos mpl. **hacer(se) ~** smash to pieces

año m year. **~ bisiesto** leap year. **~ nuevo** new year. **al ~** per year, a year. **¿cuántos ~s tiene?** how old is he? **tiene 5 ~s** he's 5 (years old). **el ~ pasado** last year. **el ~ que viene** next year. **entrado en ~s** elderly. **los ~s 60** the sixties

añora|nza f nostalgia. **~r** vt miss

apabulla|nte adj overwhelming. **~r** vt overwhelm

apacible adj gentle; (clima) mild

apacigua|r ⬛ vt pacify; (calmar) calm; relieve (dolor etc). **~rse** vpr calm down

apadrinar vt sponsor; be godfather to (a un niño)

apag|ado adj extinguished; (color) dull; (aparato eléctrico, luz) off; (persona) lifeless; (sonido) muffled. **~ar** ⬛ vt put out (fuego, incendio); turn off, switch off (aparato eléctrico, luz); quench (sed); muffle (sonido). **~arse** vpr (fuego, luz) go out; (sonido) die away. **~ón** m blackout

apalabrar vt make a verbal agreement; (contratar) engage

apalear vt winnow (grano); beat (alfombra, frutos, persona)

apantallar vt (Mex) impress

apañar vt (arreglar) fix; (remendar) mend; (agarrar) grasp, take hold of. **~se** vpr get along, manage

apapachar vt (Mex) cuddle

aparador m sideboard; (Mex, de tienda) shop window

aparato m apparatus; (máquina) machine; (doméstico) appliance; (teléfono) telephone; (radio, TV) set; (ostentación) show, pomp. **~so** adj showy, ostentatious; (caída) spectacular

aparca|miento m car park (Brit), parking lot (Amer). **~r** ⬛ vt/i park

aparear vt mate (animales). **~se** vpr mate

aparecer ⬛ vi appear. **~se** vpr appear

aparej|ado adj. **llevar ~ado, traer ~ado** mean, entail. **~o** m (avíos) equipment; (de caballo) tack; (de pesca) tackle

aparent|ar vt (afectar) feign; (parecer) look. ● vi show off. **~a 20 años** she looks like she's 20. **~e** adj apparent

apari|ción f appearance; (visión) apparition. **~encia** f appearance; (fig) show. **guardar las ~encias** keep up appearances

apartado adj separated; (aislado) isolated. ● m (de un texto) section. **~ (de correos)** post-office box, PO box

apartamento m apartment, flat (Brit)

apart|ar vt separate; (alejar) move away; (quitar) remove; (guardar) set aside. **~arse** vpr leave; (quitarse de en medio) get out of the way; (aislarse) cut o.s. off. **~e** adv apart; (por separado) separately; (además) besides. ● m aside; (párrafo) new paragraph. **~e de** apart from. **dejar ~e** leave aside. **eso ~e** apart from that

apasiona|do adj passionate; (entusiasta) enthusiastic; (falto de objetividad) biased. ● m. **~do de** lover. **~miento** m passion. **~r** vt excite. **~rse** vpr be mad (por about); (ser parcial) become biased

ap|atía f apathy. **~ático** adj apathetic

apea|dero m (Rail) halt. **~rse** vpr get off

apechugar ⬛ vi. ⬛ **~ con** put up with

apedrear vt stone

apeg|ado adj attached (**a** to). **~o** m
⚊ attachment. **tener ~o a** be
fond of

apela|ción f appeal. **~r** vi appeal; (*re-
currir*) resort (**a** to). ● vt (*apodar*) call.
~tivo m (nick)name

apellid|ar vt call. **~arse** vpr be called.
¿cómo te apellidas? what's your surname? **~o** m surname

apelmazarse vpr (*lana*) get matted

apenar vt sadden; (*LAm, avergonzar*)
embarrass. **~se** vpr be sad; (*LAm,
avergonzarse*) be embarrassed

apenas adv hardly, scarcely; (*Mex, sólo*)
only. ● conj (*esp LAm, en cuanto*) as
soon as. **~ si** ⚊ hardly

ap|éndice m appendix. **~endicitis** f
appendicitis

apergaminado adj (*piel*) wrinkled

aperitivo m (*bebida*) aperitif; (*comida*)
appetizer

aperos mpl implements; (*de labranza*)
agricultural equipment; (*LAm, de un
caballo*) tack

apertura f opening

apesadumbrar vt upset. **~se** vpr
sadden

apestar vt infect. ● vi stink (**a** of)

apet|ecer ⚊ vi. **¿te ~ece una copa?**
do you fancy a drink? do you feel like
a drink?. **no me ~ece** I don't feel
like it. **~ecible** adj attractive. **~ito** m
appetite; (*fig*) desire. **~itoso** adj appetizing

apiadarse vpr feel sorry (**de** for)

ápice m (*nada, en frases negativas*) anything. **no ceder un ~** not give an
inch

apilar vt pile up

apiñar vt pack in. **~se** vpr (*personas*)
crowd together; (*cosas*) be packed
tight

apio m celery

aplacar ⚊ vt placate; soothe (*dolor*)

aplanar vt level. **~ calles** (*LAm fam*)
loaf around

aplasta|nte adj overwhelming. **~r** vt
crush. **~rse** vpr flatten o.s.

aplau|dir vt clap, applaud; (*fig*) ap-
plaud. **~so** m applause; (*fig*) praise

aplaza|miento m postponement. **~r**
⚊ vt postpone; defer (*pago*)

aplica|ble adj applicable. **~ción** f ap-
plication. **~do** adj (*persona*) diligent.
~r ⚊ vt apply. ● vi (*LAm, a un puesto*)
apply (for). **~rse** vpr apply o.s.

aplom|ado adj composed. **~o** m com-
posure

apocado adj timid

apocar ⚊ vt belittle (*persona*). **~se**
vpr feel small

apodar vt nickname

apodera|do m representative. **~rse**
vpr seize

apodo m nickname

apogeo m (*fig*) height

apolilla|do adj moth-eaten. **~rse** vpr
get moth-eaten

apolítico adj non-political

apología f defence

apoltronarse vpr settle o.s. down

apoplejía f stroke

aporrear vt hit, thump; beat up (*persona*)

aport|ación f contribution. **~ar** vt
contribute. **~e** m (*LAm*) contribution

aposta adv on purpose

apostar¹ ⚊ vt/i bet

apostar² vt station. **~se** vpr station
o.s.

apóstol m apostle

apóstrofo m apostrophe

apoy|ar vt lean (**en** against); (*descan-
sar*) rest; (*asentar*) base; (*reforzar*)
support. **~arse** vpr lean, rest. **~o** m
support

apreci|able adj appreciable; (*digno de
estima*) worthy. **~ación** f appreci-
ation; (*valoración*) appraisal. **~ar** vt
value; (*estimar*) appreciate. **~o** m appraisal; (*fig*) esteem

apremi|ante adj urgent, pressing.
~ar vt urge; (*obligar*) compel; (*dar
prisa a*) hurry up. ● vi be urgent. **~o**
m urgency; (*obligación*) obligation

aprender vt/i learn. **~se** vpr learn

aprendiz m apprentice. **~aje** m learning; (*período*) apprenticeship

aprensi|ón f apprehension; (*miedo*)
fear. **~vo** adj apprehensive, fearful

apresar vt seize; (*capturar*) capture

aprestar vt prepare. **~se** vpr prepare

apresura|do adj in a hurry; (*hecho con prisa*) hurried. **~r** vt hurry. **~rse** vpr hurry up

apret|ado adj tight; (*difícil*) difficult; (*tacaño*) stingy, mean. **~ar ▇** vt tighten; press (*botón*); squeeze (*persona*); (*comprimir*) press down. ● vi be too tight. **~arse** vpr crowd together. **~ón** m squeeze. **~ón de manos** handshake

aprieto m difficulty. **verse en un ~** be in a tight spot

aprisa adv quickly

aprisionar vt trap

aproba|ción f approval. **~r ▇** vt approve (of); pass (*examen*). ● vi pass

apropia|ción f appropriation. **~do** adj appropriate. **~rse** vpr. **~rse de** appropriate, take

aprovecha|ble adj usable. **~do** adj (*aplicado*) diligent; (*ingenioso*) resourceful; (*oportunista*) opportunist. **bien ~do** well spent. **~miento** m advantage; (*uso*) use. **~r** vt take advantage of; (*utilizar*) make use of. ● vi make the most of it. **¡que aproveche!** enjoy your meal! **~rse** vpr. **~rse de** take advantage of

aprovisionar vt provision (**con, de** with). **~se** vpr stock up

aproxima|ción f approximation; (*proximidad*) closeness; (*en la lotería*) consolation prize. **~damente** adv roughly, approximately. **~do** adj approximate, rough. **~r** vt bring near; (*fig*) bring together (*personas*). **~rse** vpr come closer, approach

apt|itud f suitability; (*capacidad*) ability. **~o** adj (*capaz*) capable; (*adecuado*) suitable

apuesta f bet

apuesto m handsome. ● vb véase APOSTAR ¹

apuntalar vt shore up

apunt|ar vt aim (*arma*); (*señalar*) point at; (*anotar*) make a note of, note down; (*inscribir*) enrol; (*en el teatro*) prompt. ● vi (*con un arma*) to aim (**a** at). **~arse** vpr put one's name down; score (*triunfo, tanto* etc). **~e** m note; (*bosquejo*) sketch. **tomar ~s** take notes

apuñalar vt stab

apur|ado adj difficult; (*sin dinero*) hard up; (*LAm, con prisa*) in a hurry. **~ar** vt (*acabar*) finish; drain (*vaso* etc); (*causar vergüenza*) embarrass; (*LAm, apresurar*) hurry. **~arse** vpr worry; (*LAm, apresurarse*) hurry up. **~o** m tight spot, difficult situation; (*vergüenza*) embarrassment; (*estrechez*) hardship, want; (*LAm, prisa*) hurry

aquejar vt afflict

aquel adj (*f* **aquella**, *mpl* **aquellos**, *fpl* **aquellas**) that; (*en plural*) those

aquél pron (*f* **aquélla**, *mpl* **aquéllos**, *fpl* **aquéllas**) that one; (*en plural*) those

aquello pron that; (*asunto*) that business

aquí adv here. **de ~** from here. **de ~ a 15 días** in a fortnight's time. **~ mismo** right here. **de ~ para allá** to and fro. **de ~ que** that is why. **hasta ~** until now. **por ~** around here

aquietar vt calm (down)

árabe adj & m & f Arab; (*lengua*) Arabic

Arabia f Arabia. **~ Saudita, ~ Saudí** Saudi Arabia

arado m plough. **~r** m ploughman

arancel m tariff; (*impuesto*) duty. **~ario** adj tariff

arándano m blueberry

arandela f washer

araña f spider; (*lámpara*) chandelier. **~r** vt scratch

arar vt plough

arbitra|je m arbitration; (*en deportes*) refereeing. **~r** vt/i arbitrate; (*en fútbol* etc) referee; (*en tenis* etc) umpire

arbitr|ariedad f arbitrariness. **~ario** adj arbitrary. **~io** m (free) will

árbitro m arbitrator; (*en fútbol* etc) referee; (*en tenis* etc) umpire

árbol m tree; (*eje*) axle; (*palo*) mast. **~ genealógico** family tree. **~ de Navidad** Christmas tree

arbol|ado m trees. **~eda** f wood

arbusto m bush

arca f (*caja*) chest. **~ de Noé** Noah's ark

arcada f arcade; (*de un puente*) arch; (*náuseas*) retching

arcaico adj archaic

arce m maple (tree)

arcén m (de autopista) hard shoulder; (de carretera) verge

archipiélago m archipelago

archiv|ador m filing cabinet. **~ar** vt file (away). **~o** m file; (de documentos históricos) archives. **~o adjunto** (email) attachment

arcilla f clay

arco m arch; (Elec, Mat) arc; (Mus, arma) bow; (LAm, en fútbol) goal. **~ iris** rainbow

arder vi burn; (LAm, escocer) sting; (fig, de ira) seethe. **estar que arde** be very tense

ardid m trick, scheme

ardiente adj burning

ardilla f squirrel

ardor m heat; (fig) ardour; (LAm, escozor) smarting. **~ de estómago** heartburn

arduo adj arduous

área f area

arena f sand; (en deportes) arena; (en los toros) (bull)ring. **~ movediza** quicksand

arenoso adj sandy

arenque m herring. **~ ahumado** kipper

arete m (LAm) earring

Argel m Algiers. **~ia** f Algeria

Argentina f Argentina

argentino adj Argentinian, Argentine. ● m Argentinian

argolla f ring. **~ de matrimonio** (LAm) wedding ring

arg|ot m slang. **~ótico** adj slang

argucia f cunning argument

argüir 19 vt (probar) prove, show; (argumentar) argue. ● vi argue

argument|ación f argument. **~ar** vt/i argue. **~o** m argument; (de libro, película etc) story, plot

aria f aria

aridez f aridity, dryness

árido adj dry. **~s** mpl dry goods

Aries m Aries

arisco adj unfriendly

arist|ocracia f aristocracy. **~ócrata** m & f aristocrat. **~ocrático** adj aristocratic

aritmética f arithmetic

arma f arm, weapon; (sección) section. **~ de fuego** firearm. **~s de destrucción masiva** weapons of mass destruction. **~da** f navy; (flota) fleet. **~do** adj armed (de with). **~dura** f armour; (de gafas etc) frame; (Tec) framework. **~mentismo** m build up of arms. **~mento** m arms, armaments; (acción de armar) armament. **~r** vt arm (de with); (montar) put together. **~r un lío** kick up a fuss

armario m cupboard; (para ropa) wardrobe (Brit), closet (Amer)

armatoste m huge great thing

armazón m & f frame(work)

armiño m ermine

armisticio m armistice

armonía f harmony

armónica f harmonica, mouth organ

armoni|oso adj harmonious. **~zar** 10 vt harmonize. ● vi harmonize; (personas) get on well (con with); (colores) go well (con with)

arn|és m armour. **~eses** mpl harness

aro m ring, hoop

arom|a m aroma; (de flores) scent; (de vino) bouquet. **~ático** adj aromatic

arpa f harp

arpía f harpy; (fig) hag

arpillera f sackcloth, sacking

arpón m harpoon

arquear vt arch, bend. **~se** vpr arch, bend

arque|ología f archaeology. **~ológico** adj archaeological. **~ólogo** m archaeologist

arquero m archer; (LAm, en fútbol) goalkeeper

arquitect|o m architect. **~ónico** adj architectural. **~ura** f architecture

arrabal m suburb; (barrio pobre) poor area. **~es** mpl outskirts. **~ero** adj suburban; (de modales groseros) common

arraiga|do adj deeply rooted. **~r** 12 vi take root. **~rse** vpr take root; (fig) settle

arran|car 7 vt pull up (planta); pull out (diente); (arrebatar) snatch; (Auto) start. ● vi start. **~carse** vpr pull out. **~que** m sudden start; (Auto) start; (fig) outburst

arras *fpl* security; (*en boda*) coins

arrasar *vt* level, smooth; raze to the ground (*edificio etc*); (*llenar*) fill to the brim. ● *vi* (*en deportes*) sweep to victory; (*en política*) win a landslide victory

arrastr|ar *vt* pull; (*por el suelo*) drag (along); give rise to (*consecuencias*). ● *vi* trail on the ground. **~arse** *vpr* crawl; (*humillarse*) grovel. **~e** *m* dragging; (*transporte*) haulage. **estar para el ~e** 🆔 be done in

arre *int* gee up! **~ar** *vt* urge on

arrebat|ado *adj* (*irreflexivo*) impetuous. **~ar** *vt* snatch (away); (*fig*) win (over); captivate (*corazón etc*). **~arse** *vpr* get carried away. **~o** *m* (*de cólera etc*) fit; (*éxtasis*) ecstasy

arrech|ar *vt* (*LAm fam, enfurecer*) to infuriate. **~arse** *vpr* get furious. **~o** *adj* furious

arrecife *m* reef

arregl|ado *adj* neat; (*bien vestido*) well-dressed; (*LAm, amañado*) fixed. **~ar** *vt* arrange; (*poner en orden*) tidy up; sort out (*asunto, problema etc*); (*reparar*) mend. **~arse** *vpr* (*solucionarse*) get sorted out; (*prepararse*) get ready; (*apañarse*) manage, make do; (*ponerse de acuerdo*) come to an agreement. **~árselas** manage, get by. **~o** *m* (*incl Mus*) arrangement; (*acción de reparar*) repair; (*acuerdo*) agreement; (*solución*) solution. **con ~o a** according to

arrellanarse *vpr* settle o.s. (**en** into)

arremangar 🆔 *vt* roll up (*mangas*); tuck up (*falda*). **~se** *vpr* roll up one's sleeves

arremeter *vi* charge (**contra** at); (*atacar*) attack

arremolinarse *vpr* mill about; (*el agua*) to swirl

arrenda|dor *m* landlord. **~dora** *f* landlady. **~miento** *m* renting; (*contrato*) lease; (*precio*) rent. **~r** 🆔 *vt* (*dar casa en alquiler*) let; (*dar cosa en alquiler*) hire out; (*tomar en alquiler*) rent. **~tario** *m* tenant

arreos *mpl* tack

arrepenti|miento *m* repentance, regret. **~rse** 🆔 *vpr* (*retractarse*) to change one's mind; (*lamentarse*) be

sorry. **~rse de** regret; repent of (*pecados*)

arrest|ar *vt* arrest, detain; (*encarcelar*) imprison. **~o** *m* arrest; (*encarcelamiento*) imprisonment

arriar 🆔 *vt* lower (*bandera, vela*)

arriba *adv* up; (*dirección*) up(wards); (*en casa*) upstairs. ● *int* up with; (*¡levántate!*) up you get!; (*¡ánimo!*) come on! **¡~ España!** long live Spain! **~ de** (*LAm*) on top of. **~ mencionado** aforementioned. **calle ~** up the street. **de ~ abajo** from top to bottom. **de 10 euros para ~** over 10 euros. **escaleras ~** upstairs. **la parte de ~** the top part. **los de ~** those at the top. **más ~** higher up

arrib|ar *vi* (*barco*) reach port; (*esp LAm, llegar*) arrive. **~ista** *m & f* social climber. **~o** *m* (*esp LAm*) arrival

arriero *m* muleteer

arriesga|do *adj* risky; (*person*) daring. **~r** 🆔 *vt* risk; (*aventurar*) venture. **~rse** *vpr* take a risk

arrim|ar *vt* bring close(r). **~arse** *vpr* come closer, approach

arrincona|do *adj* forgotten; (*acorralado*) cornered. **~r** *vt* put in a corner; (*perseguir*) corner (*arrumbar*) put aside. **~rse** *vpr* become a recluse

arroba *f* (*Internet*) at (@); measure of weight

arrocero *adj* rice

arrodillarse *vpr* kneel (down)

arrogan|cia *f* arrogance; (*orgullo*) pride. **~te** *adj* arrogant; (*orgulloso*) proud

arroj|ar *vt* throw; (*emitir*) give off, throw out; (*producir*) produce. ● *vi* (*esp LAm, vomitar*) throw up. **~arse** *vpr* throw o.s. **~o** *m* courage

arrollar *vt* roll (up); (*atropellar*) run over; (*vencer*) crush

arropar *vt* wrap up; (*en la cama*) tuck up. **~se** *vpr* wrap (o.s.) up

arroy|o *m* stream; (*de una calle*) gutter. **~uelo** *m* small stream

arroz *m* rice. **~ con leche** rice pudding. **~al** *m* rice field

arruga *f* (*en la piel*) wrinkle, line; (*en tela*) crease. **~r** 🆔 *vt* wrinkle; crumple (*papel*); crease (*tela*). **~rse** *vpr* (la piel) become wrinkled; (tela) crease, get creased

arruinar *vt* ruin; (*destruir*) destroy. **~se** *vpr* (persona) be ruined

arrullar *vt* lull to sleep. ● *vi* (palomas) coo

arrumbar *vt* put aside

arsenal *m* (*astillero*) shipyard; (*de armas*) arsenal; (*fig*) mine

arsénico *m* arsenic

arte *m* (*f en plural*) art; (*habilidad*) skill; (*astucia*) cunning. **bellas ~s** fine arts. **con ~** skilfully. **malas ~s** trickery. **por amor al ~** for the fun of it

artefacto *m* device

arteria *f* artery; (*fig, calle*) main road

artesan|al *adj* craft. **~ía** *f* handicrafts. **objeto** *m* **de ~ía** traditional craft object. **~o** *m* artisan, craftsman

ártico *adj* Arctic. **Á~** *m*. **el Á~** the Arctic

articula|ción *f* joint; (*pronunciación*) articulation. **~do** *adj* articulated; (lenguaje) articulate. **~r** *vt* articulate

artículo *m* article. **~s** *mpl* (*géneros*) goods. **~ de exportación** export product. **~ de fondo** editorial, leader

artífice *m* & *f* artist; (*creador*) architect

artifici|al *adj* artificial. **~o** *m* (*habilidad*) skill; (*dispositivo*) device; (*engaño*) trick

artiller|ía *f* artillery. **~o** *m* artilleryman, gunner

artilugio *m* gadget

artimaña *f* trick

art|ista *m* & *f* artist. **~ístico** *adj* artistic

artritis *f* arthritis

arveja *f* (*LAm*) pea

arzobispo *m* archbishop

as *m* ace

asa *f* handle

asado *adj* roast(ed) ● *m* roast (meat), joint; (*LAm, reunión*) barbecue. **~o a la parrilla** grilled meat; (*LAm*) barbecued meat

asalariado *adj* salaried. ● *m* employee

asalt|ante *m* attacker; (*de un banco*) robber. **~ar** *vt* storm (fortaleza); attack (persona); raid (banco etc); (*fig*) (duda) assail; (*fig*) (idea etc) cross one's mind. **~o** *m* attack; (*robo*) rob-

bery; (*en boxeo*) round

asamblea *f* assembly; (*reunión*) meeting

asar *vt* roast. **~se** *vpr* be very hot. **~ a la parrilla** grill; (*LAm*) barbecue. **~ al horno** (*sin grasa*) bake; (*con grasa*) roast

asbesto *m* asbestos

ascend|encia *f* descent; (*LAm, influencia*) influence. **~ente** *adj* ascending. **~er** **1** *vt* promote. ● *vi* go up, ascend; (cuenta etc) come to, amount to; (*ser ascendido*) be promoted. **~iente** *m* & *f* ancestor; (*influencia*) influence

ascens|ión *f* ascent; (*de grado*) promotion. **día** *m* **de la A~ión** Ascension Day. **~o** *m* ascent; (*de grado*) promotion

ascensor *m* lift (*Brit*), elevator (*Amer*). **~ista** *m* & *f* lift attendant (*Brit*), elevator operator (*Amer*)

asco *m* disgust. **dar ~** be disgusting; (*fig, causar enfado*) be infuriating. **estar hecho un ~** be disgusting. **me da ~** it makes me feel sick. **¡qué ~!** how disgusting! **ser un ~** be disgusting

ascua *f* ember. **estar en ~s** be on tenterhooks

asea|do *adj* clean; (*arreglado*) neat. **~r** *vt* (*lavar*) wash; (*limpiar*) clean; (*arreglar*) tidy up

asedi|ar *vt* besiege; (*fig*) pester. **~o** *m* siege

asegura|do *adj* & *m* insured. **~dor** *m* insurer. **~r** *vt* secure, make safe; (*decir*) assure; (*concertar un seguro*) insure; (*preservar*) safeguard.**~rse** *vpr* make sure

asemejarse *vpr* be alike

asenta|do *adj* situated; (*arraigado*) established. **~r** **1** *vt* place; (*asegurar*) settle; (*anotar*) note down; (*Mex, afirmar*) state. **~rse** *vpr* settle; (*estar situado*) be situated; (*esp LAm, sentar cabeza*) settle down

asentir **4** *vi* agree (a to). **~ con la cabeza** nod

aseo *m* cleanliness. **~s** *mpl* toilets

asequible *adj* obtainable; (*precio*) reasonable; (*persona*) approachable

asesin|ar *vt* murder; (*Pol*) assassinate. **~ato** *m* murder; (*Pol*) assassination. **~o** *m* murderer; (*Pol*) assassin

asesor *m* adviser, consultant. **~ar** *vt* advise. **~arse** *vpr*. **~arse con** consult. **~ía** *f* consultancy; (*oficina*) consultant's office

asfalt|ado *adj* asphalt. **~ar** *vt* asphalt. **~o** *m* asphalt

asfixia *f* suffocation. **~nte** *adj* suffocating. **~r** *vt* suffocate. **~rse** *vpr* suffocate

así *adv* (*de esta manera*) like this, like that. ● *adj* such. **~ ~** so-so. **~ como** just as. **~ como ~**, (*LAm*) **~ nomás** just like that. **~ ... como** both ... and. **~ pues** so. **~ que** so; (*en cuanto*) as soon as. **~ sea** so be it. **~ y todo** even so. **aun ~** even so. **¿no es ~?** isn't that right? **si es ~** if that is the case. **y ~ (sucesivamente)** and so on

Asia *f* Asia

asiático *adj & m* Asian

asidero *m* handle; (*fig, pretexto*) excuse

asidu|amente *adv* regularly. **~o** *adj & m* regular

asiento *m* seat; (*en contabilidad*) entry. **~ delantero** front seat. **~ trasero** back seat

asignar *vt* assign; allot (*porción, tiempo etc*)

asignatura *f* subject. **~ pendiente** (*en enseñanza*) failed subject; (*fig*) matter still to be resolved

asil|ado *m* inmate; (*Pol*) refugee. **~o** *m* asylum; (*fig*) shelter; (*de ancianos etc*) home. **pedir ~o político** ask for political asylum

asimétrico *adj* asymmetrical

asimila|ción *f* assimilation. **~r** *vt* assimilate

asimismo *adv* also; (*igualmente*) in the same way, likewise

asir **45** *vt* grasp

asist|encia *f* attendance; (*gente*) people (present); (*en un teatro etc*) audience; (*ayuda*) assistance. **~encia médica** medical care. **~enta** *f* (*mujer de la limpieza*) charwoman. **~ente** *m & f* assistant. **~ente social** social worker. **~ido** *adj* assisted. **~ir** *vt* assist, help. ● *vi*. **~ir a** attend, be present at

asm|a *f* asthma. **~ático** *adj & m* asthmatic

asno *m* donkey; (*fig*) ass

asocia|ción *f* association; (*Com*) partnership. **~do** *adj* associated; (*socio*) associate. ● *m* associate. **~r** *vt* associate; (*Com*) take into partnership. **~rse** *vpr* associate; (*Com*) become a partner

asolar **1** *vt* devastate

asomar *vt* show. ● *vi* appear, show. **~se** *vpr* (*persona*) lean out (**a, por** of); (*cosa*) appear

asombr|ar *vt* (*pasmar*) amaze; (*sorprender*) surprise. **~arse** *vpr* be amazed; (*sorprenderse*) be surprised. **~o** *m* amazement, surprise. **~oso** *adj* amazing, astonishing

asomo *m* sign. **ni por ~** by no means

aspa *f* cross, X-shape; (*de molino*) (windmill) sail. **en ~** X-shaped

aspaviento *m* show, fuss. **~s** *mpl* gestures. **hacer ~s** make a big fuss

aspecto *m* look, appearance; (*fig*) aspect

aspereza *f* roughness; (*de sabor etc*) sourness

áspero *adj* rough; (*sabor etc*) bitter

aspersión *f* sprinkling

aspiración *f* breath; (*deseo*) ambition

aspirador *m*, **aspiradora** *f* vacuum cleaner

aspira|nte *m & f* candidate. **~r** *vt* breathe in; (*máquina*) suck up. ● *vi* breathe in; (*máquina*) suck. **~r a** aspire to

aspirina *f* aspirin

asquear *vt* sicken. ● *vi* be sickening. **~se** *vpr* be disgusted

asqueroso *adj* disgusting

asta *f* spear; (*de la bandera*) flagpole; (*cuerno*) horn. **a media ~** at half-mast. **~bandera** *f* (*Mex*) flagpole

asterisco *m* asterisk

astilla *f* splinter. **~s** *fpl* firewood

astillero *m* shipyard

astringente *adj & m* astringent

astr|o *m* star. **~ología** *f* astrology. **~ólogo** *m* astrologer. **~onauta** *m & f*

a

astronaut. **~onave** f spaceship.
~onomía f astronomy. **~ónomo** m
astronomer

astu|cia f cleverness; (*ardid*) cunning
trick. **~to** adj astute; (*taimado*) cunning

asumir vt assume

asunción f assumption. **la A~** the Assumption

asunto m (*cuestión*) matter; (*de una novela*) plot; (*negocio*) business. **~s**
mpl **exteriores** foreign affairs. **el ~ es
que** the fact is that

asusta|dizo adj easily frightened. **~r**
vt frighten. **~rse** vpr be frightened

ataca|nte m & f attacker. **~r 7** vt attack

atad|o adj tied. ● m bundle. **~ura** f tie

ataj|ar vi take a short cut; (*Mex, en tenis*) pick up the balls. ● vt (*LAm, agarrar*) catch. **~o** m short cut

atañer 22 vt concern

ataque m attack; (*Med*) fit, attack. **~
al corazón** heart attack. **~ de nervios** fit of hysterics

atar vt tie. **~se** vpr tie up

atarantar vt (*LAm*) fluster. **~se** vpr
(*LAm*) get flustered

atardecer 11 vi get dark. ● m dusk. **al
~** at dusk

atareado adj busy

atasc|ar 7 vt block; (*fig*) hinder.
~arse vpr get stuck; (*tubo etc*)
block. **~o** m blockage; (*Auto*) traffic
jam

ataúd m coffin

atav|iar 20 vt dress up. **~iarse** vpr
dress up, get dressed up. **~ío** m
dress, attire

atemorizar 10 vt frighten. **~se** vpr be
frightened

atención f attention; (*cortesía*) courtesy, kindness; (*interés*) interest. **¡~!**
look out!. **llamar la ~** attract attention, catch the eye; **prestar ~** pay
attention

atender 1 vt attend to; (*cuidar*) look
after. ● vi pay attention

atenerse 40 vpr abide (**a** by)

atentado m (*ataque*) attack; (*afrenta*)
affront (**contra** to). **~ contra la vida
de uno** attempt on s.o.'s life

atentamente adv attentively; (*con cortesía*) politely; (*con amabilidad*)
kindly. **lo saluda ~** (*en cartas*) yours
faithfully

atentar vi. **~ contra** threaten. **~
contra la vida de uno** make an attempt on s.o.'s life

atento adj attentive; (*cortés*) polite;
(*amable*) kind

atenua|nte adj extenuating. ● f extenuating circumstance. **~r 21** vt attenuate; (*hacer menor*) diminish,
lessen

ateo adj atheistic. ● m atheist

aterciopelado adj velvety

aterra|dor adj terrifying. **~r** vt terrify

aterriza|je m landing. **~je forzoso**
emergency landing. **~r 10** vt land

aterrorizar 10 vt terrify

atesorar vt hoard; amass (*fortuna*)

atesta|do adj packed, full up. ● m
sworn statement. **~r** vt fill up, pack;
(*Jurid*) testify

atestiguar 15 vt testify to; (*fig*) prove

atiborrar vt fill, stuff. **~se** vpr stuff
o.s.

ático m attic

atina|do adj right; (*juicioso*) wise, sensible. **~r** vt/i hit upon; (*acertar*) guess
right

atizar 10 vt poke; (*fig*) stir up

atlántico adj Atlantic. **el (océano) A~**
the Atlantic (Ocean)

atlas m atlas

atl|eta m & f athlete. **~ético** adj athletic. **~etismo** m athletics

atmósfera f atmosphere

atole m (*LAm*) boiled maize drink

atolladero m bog; (*fig*) tight corner

atolondra|do adj scatter-brained;
(*aturdido*) stunned. **~r** vt fluster;
(*pasmar*) stun. **~rse** vpr get flustered

at|ómico adj atomic. **~omizador** m
spray, atomizer

átomo m atom

atónito m amazed

atonta|do adj stunned; (*tonto*) stupid.
~r vt stun. **~rse** vpr get confused

atorar vt (*esp LAm*) to block; (*Mex, sujetar*) secure. **~se** vpr (*esp LAm, atragantarse*) choke; (*atascarse*) get blocked;

(puerta) get jammed

atormentar vt torture. ~**se** vpr worry, torment o.s.

atornillar vt screw on

atosigar 🔢 vt pester

atraca|dor m mugger; (de banco) bank robber. ~**r** 🔢 vt dock; (arrimar) bring alongside; hold up (banco); mug (persona). ● vi (barco) dock

atracci|ón f attraction. ~**ones** fpl entertainment, amusements

atrac|o m hold-up, robbery. ~**ón** m. darse un ~ón stuff o.s. (de with)

atractivo adj attractive. ● m attraction; (encanto) charm

atraer 🔢 vt attract

atragantarse vpr choke (con on). la historia se me atraganta I can't stand history

atrancar 🔢 vt bolt (puerta). ~**se** vpr get stuck

atrapar vt catch; (encerrar) trap

atrás adv back; (tiempo) previously, before. años ~ years ago. ~ de (LAm) behind. dar un paso ~ step backwards. hacia ~, para ~ backwards

atras|ado adj behind; (reloj) slow; (con deudas) in arrears; (país) backward. llegar ~ado (esp LAm) arrive late. ~**r** vt put back (reloj); (demorar) delay, postpone. ● vi (reloj) be slow. ~**arse** vpr be late; (reloj) be slow; (quedarse atrás) fall behind. ~**o** m delay; (de un reloj) slowness; (de un país) backwardness. ~**os** mpl (Com) arrears

atravesa|do adj lying across. ~**r** 🔢 vt cross; (traspasar) go through (poner transversalmente) lay across. ~**rse** vpr lie across; (en la garganta) get stuck, stick

atrayente adj attractive

atrev|erse vpr dare. ~**erse con** tackle. ~**ido** adj daring; (insolente) insolent. ~**imiento** m daring; (descaro) insolence

atribu|ción f attribution. ~**ciones** fpl authority. ~**ir** 🔢 vt attribute; confer (función). ~**irse** vpr claim

atribulado adj afflicted

atributo m attribute

atril m lectern; (Mus) music stand

atrocidad f atrocity. ¡qué ~! how awful!

atrofiarse vpr atrophy

atropell|ado adj hasty. ~**ar** vt knock down; (por encima) run over; (empujar) push aside; (fig) outrage, insult. ~**arse** vpr rush. ~**o** m (Auto) accident; (fig) outrage

atroz adj appalling; (fig) atrocious

atuendo m dress, attire

atún m tuna (fish)

aturdi|do adj bewildered; (por golpe) stunned. ~**r** vt bewilder; (golpe) stun; (ruido) deafen

auda|cia f boldness, audacity. ~**z** adj bold

audi|ble adj audible. ~**ción** f hearing; (prueba) audition. ~**encia** f audience; (tribunal) court; (sesión) hearing

auditor m auditor. ~**io** m audience; (sala) auditorium

auge m peak; (Com) boom

augur|ar vt predict; (cosas) augur. ~**io** m prediction. con nuestros mejores ~**los** para with our best wishes for. mal ~ bad omen

aula f class-room; (Univ) lecture room

aull|ar 🔢 vi howl. ~**ido** m howl

aument|ar vt increase; magnify (imagen). ● vi increase. ~**o** m increase; (de sueldo) rise

aun adv even. ~ así even so. ~ cuando although. más ~ even more. ni ~ not even

aún adv still, yet. ~ no ha llegado it still hasn't arrived, it hasn't arrived yet

aunar 🔢 vt join. ~**se** vpr join together

aunque conj although, (even) though

aúpa int up! de ~ wonderful

aureola f halo

auricular m (de teléfono) receiver. ~**es** mpl headphones

aurora f dawn

ausen|cia f absence. en ~**cia de** in the absence of. ~**tarse** vpr leave. ~**te** adj absent. ● m & f absentee; (Jurid) missing person. ~**tismo** m (LAm) absenteeism

auspici|ador m sponsor. ~**ar** vt sponsor. ~**o** m sponsorship; (signo) omen. bajo los ~**s** de sponsored by

a **auster|idad** *f* austerity. **~o** *adj* austere

austral *adj* southern

Australia *m* Australia

australiano *adj & m* Australian

Austria *f* Austria

austriaco, **austríaco** *adj & m* Austrian

aut|enticar **7** authenticate. **~entici-dad** *f* authenticity. **~éntico** *adj* authentic

auto *m* (*Jurid*) decision; (*orden*) order; (*Auto, fam*) car. **~s** *mpl* proceedings

auto|abastecimiento *m* self-sufficiency. **~biografia** *f* autobiography

autobús *m* bus. **en ~** by bus

autocar *m* (long-distance) bus, coach (*Brit*)

autocontrol *m* self-control

autóctono *adj* indigenous

auto|determinación *f* self-determination. **~didacta** *adj* self-taught. ● *m & f* self-taught person. **~escuela** *f* driving school. **~financiamiento** *m* self-financing

autógrafo *m* autograph

autómata *m* robot

autom|ático *adj* automatic. ● *m* press-stud. **~atización** *f* automation

automotor *m* diesel train

autom|óvil *adj* motor. ● *m* car. **~ovilismo** *m* motoring. **~ovilista** *m & f* driver, motorist

aut|onomía *f* autonomy. **~onómico** *adj*, **~ónomo** *adj* autonomous

autopista *f* motorway (*Brit*), freeway (*Amer*)

autopsia *f* autopsy

autor *m* author. **~a** *f* author(ess)

autori|dad *f* authority. **~tario** *adj* authoritarian

autoriza|ción *f* authorization. **~do** *adj* authorized, official; (*opinión etc*) authoritative. **~r** **10** *vt* authorize

auto|rretrato *m* self-portrait. **~servicio** *m* self-service restaurant. **~stop** *m* hitch-hiking. **hacer ~stop** hitch-hike

autosuficiente *adj* self-sufficient

autovía *f* dual carriageway

auxili|ar *adj* auxiliary; (*profesor*) assistant. ● *m & f* assistant. ● *vt* help. **~o** *m* help. **¡~o!** help! **en ~o de** in aid of. **pedir ~o** shout for help. **primeros ~os** first aid

Av. *abrev* (**Avenida**) Ave

aval *m* guarantee

avalancha *f* avalanche

avalar *vt* guarantee

aval|uar *vt* **21** (*LAm*) value. **~úo** *m* valuation

avance *m* advance; (*en el cine*) trailer. **avances** *mpl* (*Mex*) trailer

avanzar **10** *vt* move forward. **~ la pantalla** scroll up. ● *vi* advance

avar|icia *f* avarice. **~icioso** *adj*, **~iento** *adj* greedy; (*tacaño*) miserly. **~o** *adj* miserly. ● *m* miser

avasallar *vt* dominate

Avda. *abrev* (**Avenida**) Ave

ave *f* bird. **~ de paso** (*incl fig*) bird of passage. **~ de rapiña** bird of prey

---

> **AVE - Alta Velocidad Espa-ñola** A high-speed train service linking Madrid, Seville and Huelva via Cadiz, established in 1992 in time for the international exhibition, Expo 92 in Seville. Lines under construction include: Madrid-Barcelona, with an extension to France, and Barcelona-Valencia. An Ave service linking Madrid and Galicia is planned. *i*

---

avecinarse *vpr* approach

avejentar *vt* age

avellan|a *f* hazelnut. **~o** *m* hazel (tree)

avemaría *f* Hail Mary

avena *f* oats

avenida *f* (*calle*) avenue

avenir **53** *vt* reconcile. **~se** *vpr* come to an agreement; (*entenderse*) get on well (**con**) with

aventaja|do *adj* outstanding. **~r** *vt* be ahead of; (*superar*) surpass

avent|ar **1** *vt* fan; winnow (*grano etc*); (*Mex, lanzar*) throw; (*Mex, empujar*) push. **~arse** *vpr* (*Mex*) throw o.s.; (*atreverse*) dare. **~ón** *m* (*Mex*) ride, lift (*Brit*)

aventur|a f adventure. ~**a amorosa** love affair. ~**ado** adj risky. ~**ero** adj adventurous. ● m adventurer

avergonzar ⑩ & ⑯ vt shame; (abochornar) embarrass. ~**se** vpr be ashamed; (abochornarse) be embarrassed

aver|ía f (Auto) breakdown; (en máquina) failure. ~**iado** adj broken down. ~**iarse** ⑳ vpr break down

averigua|ción f inquiry; (Mex, disputa) argument. ~**r** ⑮ vt find out. ● vi (Mex) argue

aversión f aversion (**a, hacia, por** to)

avestruz m ostrich

avia|ción f aviation; (Mil) air force. ~**dor** m (piloto) pilot

av|ícola adj poultry. ~**icultura** f poultry farming

avidez f eagerness, greed

ávido adj eager, greedy

avinagra|do adj sour. ~**rse** vpr go sour; (fig) become embittered

avi|ón m aeroplane (Brit), airplane (Amer); (Mex, juego) hopscotch. ~**onazo** m (Mex) plane crash

avis|ar vt warn; (informar) notify, inform; call (médico etc). ~**o** m warning; (comunicación) notice; (LAm, anuncio, cartel) advertisement; (en televisión) commercial. **estar sobre** ~**o** be on the alert. **sin previo** ~**o** without prior warning

avisp|a f wasp. ~**ado** adj sharp. ~**ero** m wasps' nest; (fig) mess. ~**ón** m hornet

avistar vt catch sight of

avivar vt stoke up (fuego); brighten up (color); arouse (interés, pasión); intensify (dolor). ~**se** vpr revive; (animarse) cheer up; (LAm, despabilarse) wise up

axila f armpit, axilla

axioma m axiom

ay int (de dolor) ouch!; (de susto) oh!; (de pena) oh dear! **¡~ de ti!** poor you!

aya f governess, child's nurse

ayer adv yesterday. ● m past. **antes de** ~ the day before yesterday. ~ **por la mañana**, (LAm) ~ **en la mañana** yesterday morning

ayuda f help, aid. ~ **de cámara** valet. ~**nta** f, ~**nte** m assistant; (Mil) adjutant. ~**r** vt help

ayun|ar vi fast. ~**as** fpl. **estar en** ~**as** have had nothing to eat or drink; (fig, fam) be in the dark. ~**o** m fasting

ayuntamiento m town council, city council; (edificio) town hall

azabache m jet

azad|a f hoe. ~**ón** m (large) hoe

azafata f air hostess

azafate m (LAm) tray

azafrán m saffron

azahar m orange blossom; (del limonero) lemon blossom

azar m chance; (desgracia) misfortune. **al** ~ at random. **por** ~ by chance. ~**es** mpl ups and downs

azaros|amente adv hazardously. ~**o** adj hazardous, risky; (vida) eventful

azorar vt embarrass. ~**rse** vpr be embarrassed

Azores fpl. **las** ~ the Azores

azotador m (Mex) caterpillar

azot|ar vt whip, beat; (Mex, puerta) slam. ~**e** m whip; (golpe) smack; (fig, calamidad) calamity

azotea f flat roof

azteca adj & m & f Aztec

---

i

Aztecas A Náhuatl-speaking people who in the fourteenth century established a brilliant and tyrannical civilization in central and southern Mexico. Its capital was Tenochtitlán, built on reclaimed marshland, and which became Mexico City. The Aztec empire collapsed in 1521 after defeat by the Spaniards led by Hernán Cortés.

---

az|úcar m & f sugar. ~**ucarado** adj sweet, sugary. ~**ucarar** vt sweeten. ~**ucarero** m sugar bowl

azucena f (white) lily

azufre m sulphur

azul adj & m blue. ~**ado** adj bluish. ~ **marino** navy blue

azulejo m tile

azuzar ⑩ vt urge on, incite

Año Nuevo See
▷**Nochevieja**

Bb

bab|a f spittle. **~ear** vi drool, slobber; (niño) dribble. **caérsele la ~a a uno** be delighted. **~eo** m drooling; (de un niño) dribbling. **~ero** m bib

babor m port. **a ~** to port, on the port side

babosa f slug

babosada f (Mex) drivel

babos|ear vt slobber over; (niño) dribble over. ● vi (Mex) day dream. **~o** adj slimy; (LAm, tonto) silly

babucha f slipper

baca f luggage rack

bacalao m cod

bache m pothole; (fig) bad patch

bachillerato m school-leaving examination

bacteria f bacterium

bagaje m. **~ cultural** cultural knowledge; (de un pueblo) cultural heritage

bahía f bay

bail|able adj dance. **~aor** m Flamenco dancer. **~ar** vt/i dance. **ir a ~ar** go dancing. **~arín** m dancer. **~arina** f dancer; (de ballet) ballerina. **~e** m dance; (actividad) dancing. **~e de etiqueta** ball

baja f drop, fall; (Mil) casualty. **~ por maternidad** maternity leave. **darse de ~** take sick leave. **~da** f slope; (acto de bajar) descent; (camino) way down. **~r** vt lower; (llevar abajo) get down; go down (escalera); bow (la cabeza). ● vi go down; (temperatura, precio) fall. **~rse** vpr pull down (pantalones). **~r(se) de** get out of (coche); get off (autobús, caballo, tren, bicicleta)

bajeza f vile deed

bajío m shallows; (de arena) sandbank; (LAm, terreno bajo) low-lying area

bajo adj low; (de estatura) short, small; (cabeza, ojos) lowered; (humilde) humble, low; (vil) vile, low; (voz) low; (Mus) deep. ● m lowland; (Mus) bass. ● adv quietly; (volar) low. ● prep under. **~ cero** below zero. **~ la lluvia** in the rain. **los ~s** (LAm) ground floor (Brit), first floor (Amer); **los ~s fondos** the underworld

bajón m sharp drop; (de salud) sudden decline

bala f bullet; (de algodón etc) bale. (LAm, en atletismo) shot. **como una ~** like a shot. **lanzamiento de ~** (LAm) shot put

balada f ballad

balan|ce m balance; (documento) balance sheet; (resultado) outcome. **~cear** vt balance. **~cearse** vpr swing. **~ceo** m swinging. **~cín** m rocking chair; (de niños) seesaw. **~za** f scales; (Com) balance

balar vi bleat

balazo m (disparo) shot; (herida) bullet wound

balboa f (unidad monetaria panameña) balboa

balbuc|ear vt/i stammer; (niño) babble. **~eo** m stammering; (de niño) babbling. **~ir** 24 vt/i stammer; (niño) babble

balcón m balcony

balda f shelf

balde m bucket. **de ~** free (of charge). **en ~** in vain

baldío adj (terreno) waste

baldosa f (floor) tile; (losa) flagstone

bale|ar adj Balearic. ●**las (Islas) B~ares** the Balearics, the Balearic Islands. ●vt (LAm) to shoot. **~o** m (LAm, tiroteo) shooting

balero m (Mex) cup and ball toy; (rodamiento) bearing

balido m bleat; (varios sonidos) bleating

balística f ballistics

baliza f (Naut) buoy; (Aviac) beacon

ballena f whale

ballet /ba'le/ (pl **~s**) m ballet

balneario m spa; (con playa) seaside resort

balompié m soccer, football (Brit)

ball|ón m ball. **~oncesto** m basketball. **~onmano** m handball. **~onvolea** m volleyball

balotaje m (LAm) voting

balsa f (de agua) pool; (plataforma flotante) raft

bálsamo m balsam; (fig) balm

> **balseros** The name given to illegal immigrants who try to enter a country in small boats or on rafts. It applies particularly to Cubans who try to enter the US by sailing to Florida and to immigrants attempting to enter Spain by crossing the Straits of Gibraltar.

baluarte m (incl fig) bastion

bambalina f drop curtain. **entre ~s** behind the scenes

bambole|ar vi sway. **~arse** vpr sway; (mesa etc) wobble; (barco) rock. **~o** m swaying; (de mesa etc) wobbling; (de barco) rocking

bambú m (pl ~es) bamboo

banal adj banal. **~idad** f banality

banan|a f (esp LAm) banana. **~ero** adj banana. **~o** m (LAm) banana tree

banc|a f banking; (conjunto de bancos) banks; (en juegos) bank; (LAm, asiento) bench. **~ario** adj bank, banking. **~arrota** f bankruptcy. **hacer ~arrota, ir a la ~arrota** go bankrupt. **~o** m (asiento) bench; (Com) bank; (bajío) sandbank; (de peces) shoal

banda f (incl Mus, Radio) band; (Mex, para el pelo) hair band; (raya ancha) stripe; (cinta ancha) sash; (grupo) gang, group. **~ acha** broadband. **~ sonora** sound-track. **~da** f (de pájaros) flock; (de peces) shoal

bandeja f tray

bandejón m (Mex) central reservation (Brit), median strip (Amer)

bander|a f flag. **~illa** f banderilla. **~ear** vt stick the banderillas in. **~ero** m banderillero. **~ín** m pennant, small flag

bandido m bandit

bando m edict, proclamation; (facción) camp, side. **~s** mpl banns. **pasarse al otro ~** go over to the other side

bandolero m bandit

bandoneón m large accordion

banjo m banjo

banquero m banker

banquete m banquet; (de boda) wedding reception

banquillo m bench; (Jurid) dock; (taburete) footstool

bañ|ador m (de mujer) swimming costume; (de hombre) swimming trunks. **~ar** vt bath (niño); (Culin, recubrir) coat. **~arse** vpr go swimming, have a swim; (en casa) have a bath. **~era** f bath (tub). **~ista** m & f bather. **~o** m bath; (en piscina, mar etc) swim; (cuarto) bathroom; (LAm, wáter) toilet; (bañera) bath(tub); (capa) coat(ing)

baqueano (LAm), **baquiano** m guide

bar m bar

baraja f pack of cards. **~r** vt shuffle; juggle (cifras etc); consider (posibilidades); (Mex, explicar) explain

baranda, barandilla f rail; (de escalera) banisters

barat|a f (Mex) sale. **~ija** f trinket. **~illo** m junk shop; (géneros) cheap goods. **~o** adj cheap. ● adv cheap(ly)

barba f chin; (pelo) beard

barbacoa f barbecue; (carne) barbecued meat

barbari|dad f atrocity; (fam, mucho) awful lot 🔝. **¡qué ~dad!** how awful. **~e** f barbarity; (fig) ignorance. **~smo** m barbarism

bárbaro adj barbaric, cruel, (brutal) uncouth; (fam, estupendo) terrific 🔝 ● m barbarian. **¡qué ~!** how marvellous!

barbear vt (Mex, lisonjear) suck up to

barbecho m. **en ~** fallow

barber|ía f barber's (shop). **~o** m barber; (Mex, adulador) creep

barbilla f chin

barbitúrico m barbiturate

barbudo adj bearded

barca f (small) boat. **~ de pasaje** ferry. **~za** f barge

barcelonés adj of Barcelona, from Barcelona. ● m native of Barcelona

barco m boat; (navío) ship. **~ cisterna** tanker. **~ de vapor** steamer. **~ de vela** sailing boat. **ir en ~** go by boat

barda f (Mex) wall; (de madera) fence

barítono adj & m baritone

barman m (pl ∼s) barman

barniz m varnish; (para loza etc) glaze; (fig) veneer. ∼ar 🔟 vt varnish; glaze (loza etc)

barómetro m barometer

bar|ón m baron. ∼onesa f baroness

barquero m boatman

barquillo m wafer; (Mex, de helado) ice-cream cone

barra f bar; (pan) loaf of French bread; (palanca) lever; (de arena) sandbank; (LAm, de hinchas) supporters. ∼ de labios lipstick

barrabasada f mischief, prank

barraca f hut; (vivienda pobre) shack, shanty

barranco m ravine, gully; (despeñadero) cliff, precipice

barrer vt sweep; thrash (rival)

barrera f barrier. ∼ del sonido sound barrier

barriada f district; (LAm, barrio marginal) slum

barrial m (LAm) quagmire

barrida f sweep; (LAm, redada) police raid

barrig|a f belly. ∼ón adj, ∼udo adj pot-bellied

barril m barrel

barrio m district, area. ∼s bajos poor quarter, poor area. el otro ∼ (fig, fam) the other world. ∼bajero adj vulgar, common

barro m mud; (arcilla) clay; (arcilla cocida) earthenware

barroco adj Baroque. ● m Baroque style

barrote m bar

bartola f. tirarse a la ∼ take it easy

bártulos mpl things. liar los ∼ pack one's bags

barullo m racket; (confusión) confusion. a ∼ galore

basar vt base. ∼se vpr. ∼se en be based on

báscula f scales

base f base; (fig) basis, foundation. a ∼ de thanks to; (mediante) by means of; (en una receta) mainly consisting

of. ∼ de datos database. **partiendo de la ∼ de, tomando como ∼** on the basis of

básico adj basic

basílica f basilica

básquetbol, basquetbol m (LAm) basketball

---

bastante

● adjetivo/pronombre

····▶ (suficiente) enough. ¿hay ∼s sillas? are there enough chairs? ya tengo ∼ I have enough already

····▶ (mucho) quite a lot. vino ∼ gente quite a lot of people came. tiene ∼s amigos he has quite a lot of friends ¿te gusta?-sí, ∼ do you like it? — yes, quite a lot

● adverbio

····▶ (suficientemente) enough. no has estudiado ∼ you haven't studied enough. no es lo ∼ inteligente he's not clever enough (como para to)

····▶ bastante + adjetivo/adverbio (modificando la intensidad) quite, fairly. parece ∼ simpático he looks quite friendly. es ∼ fácil de hacer it's quite easy to do. canta ∼ bien he sings quite well

····▶ bastante con verbo (considerablemente) quite a lot. el lugar ha cambiado ∼ the place has changed quite a lot

---

bastar vi be enough. ¡basta! that's enough! **basta con decir que** suffice it to say that. **basta y sobra** that's more than enough

bastardilla f italics

bastardo adj & m bastard

bastidor m frame; (Auto) chassis. ∼es mpl (en el teatro) wings. **entre ∼es** behind the scenes

basto adj coarse. ∼s mpl (naipes) clubs

bast|ón m walking stick; (de esquí) ski pole. ∼onazo m blow with a stick; (de mando) staff of office

basur|a f rubbish, garbage (Amer); (en la calle) litter. ∼al m (LAm, lugar) rubbish dump. ∼ero m dustman (Brit), garbage collector (*Amer*); (*sitio*) rubbish dump; (*Mex*, *recipiente*) dustbin (*Brit*), garbage can (*Amer*)

bata *f* dressing-gown; (*de médico etc*) white coat; (*esp LAm*, *de baño*) bathrobe

batahola *f* (*LAm*) pandemonium

batall|a *f* battle. ~a campal pitched battle. de ~a everyday. ~ador *adj* fighting. ● *m* fighter. ~ar *vi* battle, fight. ~ón *m* battalion.

batata *f* sweet potato

bate *m* bat. ~ador *m* batter; (*cricket*) batsman. ~ar *vi* bat

batería *f* battery; (*Mus*) drums. ● *m & f* drummer. ~ de cocina kitchen utensils, pots and pans

baterista *m & f* drummer

batido *adj* beaten; (*nata*) whipped. ● *m* batter; (*bebida*) milk shake. ~ra *f* (*food*) mixer

batir *vt* beat; break (*récord*); whip (*nata*). ~ palmas clap. ~se *vpr* fight

batuta *f* baton. llevar la ~ be in command, be the boss

baúl *m* trunk

bauti|smal *adj* baptismal. ~smo *m* baptism, christening. ~zar **10** *vt* baptize, christen. ~zo *m* christening

baya *f* berry

bayeta *f* cloth

bayoneta *f* bayonet

baza *f* (*naipes*) trick; (*fig*) advantage. meter ~ interfere

bazar *m* bazaar

bazofia *f* revolting food; (*fig*) rubbish

beato *adj* blessed; (*piadoso*) devout; (*pey*) overpious

bebé *m* baby

beb|edero *m* drinking trough; (*sitio*) watering place. ~edizo *m* potion; (*veneno*) poison. ~edor *m* heavy drinker. ~er *vt/i* drink. ~ida *f* drink. ~ido *adj* drunk

beca *f* grant, scholarship. ~do *m* (*LAm*) scholarship holder, scholar. ~r **7** *vt* give a scholarship to. ~rio *m* scholarship holder, scholar

beige /beis, beʒ/ *adj & m* beige

béisbol *m*, (*Mex*) **beisbol** *m* baseball

belén *m* crib, nativity scene

belga *adj & m & f* Belgian

Bélgica *f* Belgium

bélico *adj*, **belicoso** *adj* warlike

bell|eza *f* beauty. ~o *adj* beautiful. ~as artes *fpl* fine arts

bellota *f* acorn

bemol *m* flat. tener (muchos) ~es be difficult

bend|ecir **46** (*pero imperativo* bendice, *futuro, condicional y pp regulares*) *vt* bless. ~ición *f* blessing. ~ito *adj* blessed; (*que tiene suerte*) lucky; (*feliz*) happy

benefactor *m* benefactor

benefic|encia *f* charity. de ~encia charitable. ~iar *vt* benefit. ~iarse *vpr* benefit. ~iario *m* beneficiary; (*de un cheque etc*) payee. ~io *m* benefit, (*ventaja*) advantage; (*ganancia*) profit, gain. ~ioso *adj* beneficial

benéfico *adj* beneficial; (*de beneficencia*) charitable

ben|evolencia *f* benevolence. ~évolo *adj* benevolent

bengala *f* flare. luz *f* de ~ flare

benigno *adj* kind; (*moderado*) gentle, mild; (*tumor*) benign

berberecho *m* cockle

berenjena *f* aubergine (*Brit*), eggplant (*Amer*)

berr|ear *vi* (*animales*) bellow; (*niño*) bawl. ~ido *m* bellow; (*de niño*) bawling

berrinche *m* temper; (*de un niño*) tantrum

berro *m* watercress

besamel(a) *f* white sauce

bes|ar *vt* kiss. ~arse *vpr* kiss (each other). ~o *m* kiss

bestia *f* beast; (*bruto*) brute; (*idiota*) idiot. ~ de carga beast of burden. ~l *adj* bestial, animal; (*fig*, *fam*) terrific. ~lidad *f* (*acción brutal*) horrid thing; (*insensatez*) stupidity

besugo *m* red bream

besuquear *vt* cover with kisses

betabel *f* (*Mex*) beetroot

betún *m* (*para el calzado*) shoe polish

biberón *m* feeding-bottle

Biblia *f* Bible

bibliografía *f* bibliography

biblioteca *f* library; (*mueble*) bookcase. ~ de consulta reference library. **~río** *m* librarian

bicarbonato *m* bicarbonate

bicho *m* insect, bug; (*animal*) small animal, creature. **~ raro** odd sort

bici *f* 1 bike. **~cleta** *f* bicycle. **ir en ~cleta** cycle. **~moto** (*LAm*) moped

bidé, bidet /bi'ðeɪ/ *m* bidet

bidón *m* drum, can

bien *adv* well; (*muy*) very, quite; (*correctamente*) right; (*de buena gana*) willingly. ● *m* good; (*efectos*) property. **¡~!** fine!, OK!, good! **~... (o) ~** either... or. **¡está ~!** fine!, alright!; (*basta*) that is enough!. **más ~** rather. **¡muy ~!** good! **no ~** as soon as. **¡qué ~!** marvellous!, great! 1. **si ~** although

bienal *adj* biennial

bien|aventurado *adj* fortunate. **~estar** *m* well-being. **~hablado** *adj* well-spoken. **~hechor** *m* benefactor. **~intencionado** *adj* well-meaning

bienio *m* two year-period

bienvenid|a *f* welcome. **dar la ~a a uno** welcome s.o. **~o** *adj* welcome. **¡~o!** welcome!

bifurca|ción *f* junction. **~rse** 7 *vpr* fork; (*rail*) branch off

b|igamia *f* bigamy. **~ígamo** *adj* bigamous. ● *m* bigamist

bigot|e *m* moustache. **~ón** *adj* (*Mex*), **~udo** *adj* with a big moustache

bikini *m* bikini

bilingüe *adj* bilingual

billar *m* billiards

billete *m* ticket; (*de banco*) (bank) note (*Brit*), bill (*Amer*). **~ de ida y vuelta** return ticket (*Brit*), round-trip ticket (*Amer*). **~ sencillo** single ticket (*Brit*), one-way ticket (*Amer*). **~ra** *f*, **~ro** *m* wallet, billfold (*Amer*)

billón *m* billion (*Brit*), trillion (*Amer*)

bi|mensual *adj* fortnightly, twice-monthly. **~mestral** *adj* two-monthly. **~mestre** two-month period. **~motor** *adj* twin-engined. ● *m* twin-engined plane

binoculares *mpl* binoculars

biocarburante *m* biofuel

bi|ografía *f* biography. **~ográfico** *adj* biographical

bi|ología *f* biology. **~ológico** *adj* biological. **~ólogo** *m* biologist

biombo *m* folding screen

biopsia *f* biopsy

bioterrorismo *m* bioterrorism

biplaza *m* two-seater

biquini *m* bikini

birlar *vt* 1 steal, pinch 1

bis *m* encore. **¡~!** encore! **vivo en el 3 ~** I live at 3A

bisabuel|a *f* great-grandmother. **~o** *m* great-grandfather. **~os** *mpl* great-grandparents

bisagra *f* hinge

bisiesto *adj*. **año** *m* **~** leap year

bisniet|a *f* great-granddaughter. **~o** *m* great-grandson. **~os** *mpl* great-grandchildren

bisonte *m* bison

bisoño *adj* inexperienced

bisté, bistec *m* steak

bisturí *m* scalpel

bisutería *f* costume jewellery

bitácora *f* binnacle

bizco *adj* cross-eyed

bizcocho *m* sponge (cake)

bizquear *vi* squint

blanc|a *f* white woman; (*Mus*) minim. **~o** *adj* white; (*tez*) fair. ● *m* white; (*persona*) white man; (*espacio*) blank; (*objetivo*) target. **dar en el ~o** hit the mark. **dejar en ~o** leave blank. **pasar la noche en ~o** have a sleepless night. **~ura** *f* whiteness

blandir 24 *vt* brandish

bland|o *adj* soft; (*carácter*) weak; (*cobarde*) cowardly; (*carne*) tender. **~ura** *f* softness; (*de la carne*) tenderness

blanque|ar *vt* whiten; whitewash (paredes); bleach (tela); launder (dinero). ● *vi* turn white. **~o** *m* whitening; (*de dinero*) laundering

blasón *m* coat of arms

bledo *m*. **me importa un ~** I couldn't care less

blinda|je *m* armour (plating). **~r** *vt* armour(-plate)

bloc *m* (*pl* **~s**) pad

bloque *m* block; (*Pol*) bloc. **en ~** en bloc. **~ar** *vt* block; (*Mil*) blockade;

(*Com*) freeze. **~o** *m* blockade; (*Com*) freezing

blusa *f* blouse

bob|ada *f* silly thing. **decir ~adas** talk nonsense. **~ería** *f* silly thing

bobina *f* reel; (*Elec*) coil

bobo *adj* silly, stupid. ● *m* idiot, fool

boca *f* mouth; (*fig, entrada*) entrance; (*de buzón*) slot; (*de cañón*) muzzle. **~ abajo** face down. **~ arriba** face up

bocacalle *f* junction. **la primera ~ a la derecha** the first turning on the right

bocad|illo *m* (filled) roll; (*fam, comida ligera*) snack. **~o** *m* mouthful; (*mordisco*) bite; (*de caballo*) bit

boca||jarro. a ~jarro point-blank. **~manga** *f* cuff

bocanada *f* puff; (*de vino etc*) mouthful; (*ráfaga*) gust

bocata *f* sandwich

bocatería *f* sandwich bar

bocaza *m & f invar* big-mouth

boceto *m* sketch; (*de proyecto*) outline

bochinche *m* row; (*alboroto*) racket. **~ro** *adj* (*LAm*) rowdy

bochorno *m* sultry weather; (*fig, vergüenza*) embarrassment. **¡qué ~!** how embarrassing!. **~so** *adj* oppressive; (*fig*) embarrassing

bocina *f* horn; (*LAm, auricular*) receiver. **tocar la ~** sound one's horn. **~zo** *m* toot

boda *f* wedding

bodeg|a *f* cellar; (*de vino*) wine cellar; (*LAm, almacén*) warehouse; (*de un barco*) hold. **~ón** *m* cheap restaurant; (*pintura*) still life

bodoque *m & f* (*fam, tonto*) thickhead; (*Mex, niño*) kid

bofes *mpl* lights. **echar los ~** slog away

bofet|ada *f* slap; (*fig*) blow. **~ón** *m* punch

boga *f* (*moda*) fashion. **estar en ~** be in fashion, be in vogue. **~r 12** *vt* row. **~vante** *m* (*crustáceo*) lobster

Bogotá *f* Bogotá

bogotano *adj* from Bogotá. ● *m* native of Bogotá

bohemio *adj & m* Bohemian

bohío *m* (*LAm*) hut

boicot *m* (*pl ~s*) boycott. **~ear** *vt* boycott. **~eo** *m* boycott. **hacer un ~** boycott

boina *f* beret

bola *f* ball; (*canica*) marble; (*mentira*) fib; (*Mex, reunión desordenada*) rowdy party; (*Mex, montón*). **una ~ de** a bunch of; (*Mex, revolución*) revolution; (*Mex, brillo*) shine

boleadoras (*LAm*) *fpl* bolas

bolear *vt* (*Mex*) polish, shine

bolera *f* bowling alley

bolero *m* (*baile, chaquetilla*) bolero; (*fig, fam, mentiroso*) liar; (*Mex, limpiabotas*) bootblack

bole|ta *f* (*LAm, de rifa*) ticket; (*Mex, de notas*) (school) report; (*Mex, electoral*) ballot paper. **~taje** *m* (*Mex*) tickets. **~tería** *f* (*LAm*) ticket office; (*de teatro, cine*) box office. **~tero** *m* (*LAm*) ticket-seller

boletín *m* bulletin; (*publicación periódica*) journal; (*de notas*) report

boleto *m* (*esp LAm*) ticket; (*Mex, de avión*) (air) ticket. **~ de ida y vuelta**, (*Mex*) **~ redondo** return ticket (*Brit*), round-trip ticket (*Amer*). **~ sencillo** single ticket (*Brit*), one-way ticket (*Amer*)

boli *m* 1 Biro (*P*), ball-point pen

boliche *m* (*juego*) bowls; (*bolera*) bowling alley

bolígrafo *m* Biro (*P*), ball-point pen

bolillo *m* bobbin; (*Mex, pan*) (bread) roll

bolívar *m* (*unidad monetaria venezolana*) bolívar

Bolivia *f* Bolivia

boliviano *adj* Bolivian. ● *m* Bolivian; (*unidad monetaria de Bolivia*) boliviano

boll|ería *f* baker's shop. **~o** *m* roll; (*con azúcar*) bun

bolo *m* skittle; (*Mex, en bautizo*) coins. **~s** *mpl* (*juego*) bowling

bols|a *f* bag; (*Mex, bolsillo*) pocket; (*Mex, de mujer*) handbag; (*Com*) stock exchange; (*cavidad*) cavity. **~a de agua caliente** hot-water bottle. **~illo** *m* pocket. **de ~illo** pocket. **~o** *m* (*de mujer*) handbag. **~o de mano**, **~o de viaje** (overnight) bag

bomba *f* bomb; (*máquina*) pump; (*noticia*) bombshell. ~ **de aceite** (*Auto*) oil pump. ~ **de agua** (*Auto*) water pump. **pasarlo** ~ have a marvellous time

bombachos *mpl* baggy trousers, baggy pants (*Amer*)

bombarde|ar *vt* bombard; (*desde avión*) bomb. ~**o** *m* bombardment; (*desde avión*) bombing. ~**ro** *m* (*avión*) bomber

bombazo *m* explosion

bombear *vt* pump

bombero *m* fireman. **cuerpo** *m* **de** ~**s** fire brigade (*Brit*), fire department (*Amer*)

bombilla *f* (light) bulb; (*LAm, para mate*) pipe for drinking maté

bombín *m* pump; (*fam, sombrero*) bowler (hat) (*Brit*), derby (*Amer*)

bombo *m* (*tambor*) bass drum. **a** ~ **y platillos** with a lot of fuss

bomb|ón *m* chocolate; (*Mex, malvavisco*) marshmallow. ~**ona** *f* gas cylinder

bonachón *adj* easygoing; (*bueno*) good-natured

bonaerense *adj* from Buenos Aires. ● *m* native of Buenos Aires

bondad *f* goodness; (*amabilidad*) kindness; (*del clima*) mildness. **tenga la** ~ **de** would you be kind enough to. ~**oso** *adj* kind

boniato *m* sweet potato

bonito *adj* nice; (*mono*) pretty. ¡**muy** ~!, ¡**qué** ~! that's nice!, very nice!. ● *m* bonito

bono *m* voucher; (*título*) bond. ~ **del Tesoro** government bond

boñiga *f* dung

boqueada *f* gasp. **dar la última** ~ be dying

boquerón *m* anchovy

boquete *m* hole; (*brecha*) breach

boquiabierto *adj* open-mouthed; (*fig*) amazed, dumbfounded. **quedarse** ~ be amazed

boquilla *f* mouthpiece; (*para cigarillos*) cigarette-holder; (*filtro de cigarillo*) tip

borbotón *m*. **hablar a borbotones** gabble. **salir a borbotones** gush out

borda|do *adj* embroidered. ● *m* embroidery. ~**r** *vt* embroider

borde *m* edge; (*de carretera*) side; (*de plato etc*) rim; (*de un vestido*) hem. **al** ~**e de** on the edge of; (*fig*) on the brink of. ● *adj* (*Esp fam*) stroppy. ~**ear** *vt* go round; (*fig*) border on. ~**illo** *m* kerb (*Brit*), curb (*esp Amer*)

bordo. a ~ on board

borla *f* tassel

borrach|era *f* drunkenness. **pegarse una** ~**era** get drunk. ~**ín** *m* drunk; (*habitual*) drunkard. ~**o** *adj* drunk. ● *m* drunkard. **estar** ~**o** be drunk. **ser** ~**o** be a drunkard

borrador *m* rough draft; (*de contrato*) draft; (*para la pizarra*) (black)board rubber; (*goma*) eraser

borrar *vt* rub out; (*tachar*) cross out; delete (*información*)

borrasc|a *f* depression; (*tormenta*) storm. ~**oso** *adj* stormy

borrego *m* year-old lamb; (*Mex, noticia falsa*) canard

borrico *m* donkey; (*fig, fam*) ass

borrón *m* smudge; (*de tinta*) inkblot. ~ **y cuenta nueva** let's forget about it!

borroso *adj* blurred; (*fig*) vague

bos|coso *adj* wooded. ~**que** *m* wood, forest

bosquej|ar *vt* sketch; outline (plan). ~**o** *m* sketch; (*de plan*) outline

bosta *f* dung

bostez|ar 🔟 *vi* yawn. ~**o** *m* yawn

bota *f* boot; (*recipiente*) wineskin

botana *f* (*Mex*) snack, appetizer

botánic|a *f* botany. ~**o** *adj* botanical. ● *m* botanist

botar *vt* launch; bounce (pelota); (*esp LAm, tirar*) throw away. ● *vi* bounce

botarate *m* irresponsible person; (*esp LAm, derrochador*) spendthrift

bote *m* boat; (*de una pelota*) bounce; (*lata*) tin, can; (*vasija*) jar. ~ **de la basura** (*Mex*) rubbish bin (*Brit*), trash can (*Amer*). ~ **salvavidas** lifeboat. **de** ~ **en** ~ packed

botella *f* bottle

botica *f* chemist's (shop) (*Brit*), drugstore (*Amer*). ~**rio** *m* chemist (*Brit*), druggist (*Amer*)

botijo m earthenware jug

botín m half boot; (de guerra) booty; (de ladrones) haul

botiquín m medicine chest; (de primeros auxilios) first aid kit

bot|ón m button; (yema) bud; (LAm, insignia) badge. **~ones** m invar bellboy (Brit), bellhop (Amer)

bóveda f vault

boxe|ador m boxer. **~ar** vi box. **~o** m boxing

boya f buoy; (corcho) float. **~nte** adj buoyant

bozal m (de perro etc) muzzle; (de caballo) halter

bracear vi wave one's arms, (nadar) swim, crawl

bracero m seasonal farm labourer

braga(s) f(pl) panties, knickers (Brit)

bragueta f flies

bram|ar vi bellow. **~ido** m bellowing

branquia f gill

bras|a f ember. **a la ~a** grilled. **~ero** m brazier

brasier m (Mex) bra

Brasil m. **(el)** ~ Brazil

brasile|ño adj & m Brazilian. **~ro** adj & m (LAm) Brazilian

bravío adj wild

brav|o adj fierce; (valeroso) brave; (mal) rough. **¡~!** int well done! bravo! **~ura** f ferocity; (valor) bravery

braz|a f fathom. **nadar a ~a** swim breast-stroke. **~ada** f (en natación) stroke. **~alete** m bracelet; (brazal) arm-band. **~o** m arm; (de caballo) foreleg; (rama) branch. **~o derecho** right-hand man. **del ~o** arm in arm

brea f tar, pitch

brebaje m potion; (pej) concoction

brecha f opening; (Mil) breach; (Med) gash. **~ generacional** generation gap. **estar en la ~** be in the thick of it

brega f struggle. **andar a la ~** work hard

breva f early fig

breve adj short. **en ~** soon, shortly. **en ~s momentos** soon. **~dad** f shortness

brib|ón m rogue, rascal. **~onada** f dirty trick

brida f bridle

brigad|a f squad; (Mil) brigade. **~ier** m brigadier (Brit), brigadier-general (Amer)

brill|ante adj bright; (lustroso) shiny; (persona) brilliant. ● m diamond. **~ar** vi shine; (centellear) sparkle. **~o** m shine; (brillantez) brilliance; (centelleo) sparkle. **sacar ~o** polish. **~oso** adj (LAm) shiny

brinc|ar 7 vi jump up and down. **~o** m jump. **dar un ~o, pegar un ~o** jump

brind|ar vt offer. ● vi. **~ar por** toast, drink a toast to. **~is** m toast

br|ío m energy; (decisión) determination. **~ioso** adj spirited; (garboso) elegant

brisa f breeze

británico adj British. ● m Briton, British person

brocha f paintbrush; (para afeitarse) shaving-brush

broche m clasp, fastener; (joya) brooch; (Mex, para el pelo) hairslide (Brit), barrete (Amer)

brocheta f skewer; (plato) kebab

brócoli m broccoli

brom|a f joke. **~a pesada** practical joke. **en ~a** in fun. **ni de ~a** no way. **~ear** vi joke. **~ista** adj fond of joking. ● m & f joker

bronca f row; (reprensión) telling-off; (LAm, rabia) foul mood. **dar ~ a uno** bug s.o.

bronce m bronze; (LAm) brass. **~ado** adj bronze; (por el sol) tanned. **~ar** vt tan (piel). **~arse** vpr get a suntan

bronquitis f bronchitis

brot|ar vi (plantas) sprout; (Med) break out; (líquido) gush forth; (lágrimas) well up. **~e** m shoot; (Med) outbreak

bruces: de ~ face down(wards). **caer de ~** fall flat on one's face

bruj|a f witch. **~ería** f witchcraft. **~o** m wizard, magician. ● adj (Mex) broke

brújula f compass

brum|a f mist; (fig) confusion. **~oso** adj misty, foggy

brusco adj (repentino) sudden; (persona) brusque

Bruselas f Brussels

brusquedad f roughness; (de movimiento) abruptness

brut|al adj brutal. ~**alidad** f brutality; (estupidez) stupidity. ~**o** adj ignorant; (tosco) rough; (peso, sueldo) gross

bucal adj oral; (lesión) mouth

buce|ar vi dive; (nadar) swim under water. ~**o** m diving; (natación) underwater swimming

bucle m ringlet

budín m pudding

budis|mo m Buddhism. ~**ta** m & f Buddhist

buen véase BUENO

buenaventura f good luck; (adivinación) fortune

bueno adj (delante de nombre masculino en singular **buen**) good; (agradable) nice; (tiempo) fine. • int well!; (de acuerdo) OK!, very well! **¡buena la has hecho!** you've gone and done it now! **¡buenas noches!** good night! **¡buenas tardes!** (antes del atardecer) good afternoon!; (después del atardecer) good evening! **¡~s días!** good morning! **estar de buenas** be in a good mood. **por las buenas** willingly. **¡qué bueno!** (LAm) great!

Buenos Aires m Buenos Aires

buey m ox

búfalo m buffalo

bufanda f scarf

bufar vi snort

bufete m (mesa) writing-desk; (despacho) lawyer's office

buf|o adj comic. ~**ón** adj comical. • m buffoon; (Historia) jester

buhardilla f attic; (ventana) dormer window

búho m owl

buhonero m pedlar

buitre m vulture

bujía f (Auto) spark plug

bulbo m bulb

bulevar m avenue, boulevard

Bulgaria f Bulgaria

búlgaro adj & m Bulgarian

bull|a f noise. ~**icio** m hubbub; (movimiento) bustle. ~**icioso** adj bustling; (ruidoso) noisy

bullir [22] vi boil; (burbujear) bubble; (fig) bustle

bulto m (volumen) bulk; (forma) shape; (paquete) package; (maleta etc) piece of luggage; (protuberancia) lump

buñuelo m fritter

BUP abrev (**Bachillerato Unificado Polivalente**) secondary school education

buque m ship, boat

burbuj|a f bubble. ~**ear** vi bubble; (vino) sparkle

burdel m brothel

burdo adj rough, coarse; (excusa) clumsy

burgu|és adj middle-class, bourgeois. • m middle-class person. ~**esía** f middle class, bourgeoisie

burla f taunt; (broma) joke; (engaño) trick. ~**r** vt evade. ~**rse** vpr. ~**rse de** mock, make fun of

burlesco adj (en literatura) burlesque

burlón adj mocking

bur|ocracia f bureaucracy; (Mex, funcionariado) civil service. ~**ócrata** m & f bureaucrat; (Mex, funcionario) civil servant. ~**ocrático** adj bureaucratic; (Mex) (empleado) government

burro adj stupid; (obstinado) pigheaded. • m donkey; (fig) ass

bursátil adj stock-exchange

bus m bus

busca f search. **a la ~ de** in search of. • m beeper

buscador m search engine

buscapleitos m & f invar (LAm) troublemaker

buscar [7] vt look for. • vi look. **buscársela** ask for it; **ir a ~ a uno** fetch s.o.

búsqueda f search

busto m bust

butaca f armchair; (en el teatro etc) seat

buzo m diver

buzón m postbox (Brit), mailbox (Amer)

Cc

C/ *abrev* (**Calle**) St, Rd

cabal *adj* exact; (*completo*) complete. **no estar en sus ~es** not be in one's right mind

cabalga|dura *f* mount, horse. **~r** 12 *vt* ride. ● *vi* ride, go riding. **~ta** *f* ride; (*desfile*) procession

caballa *f* mackerel

caballerango *m* (*Mex*) groom

caballeresco *adj* gentlemanly. **literatura** *f* **caballeresca** books of chivalry

caballer|ía *f* mount, horse. **~iza** *f* stable. **~izo** *m* groom

caballero *m* gentleman; (*de orden de caballería*) knight; (*tratamiento*) sir. **~so** *adj* gentlemanly

caballete *m* (*del tejado*) ridge; (*para mesa*) trestle; (*de pintor*) easel

caballito *m* pony. **~ del diablo** dragonfly. **~ de mar** sea-horse. **~s** *mpl* (*carrusel*) merry-go-round

caballo *m* horse; (*del ajedrez*) knight; (*de la baraja española*) queen. **~ de fuerza** horsepower. **a ~** on horseback

cabaña *f* hut

cabaret /kaba're/ *m* (*pl* **~s**) night-club

cabecear *vi* nod off; (*en fútbol*) head the ball; (*caballo*) toss its head

cabecera *f* (*de la cama*) headboard; (*de la mesa*) head; (*en un impreso*) heading

cabecilla *m* ringleader

cabello *m* hair. **~s** *mpl* hair

caber 28 *vi* fit (**en** into). **no cabe duda** there's no doubt

cabestr|illo *m* sling. **~o** *m* halter

cabeza *f* head; (*fig, inteligencia*) intelligence. **andar de ~** have a lot to do. **~da** *f* nod. **dar una ~da** nod off. **~zo** *m* butt; (*en fútbol*) header

cabida *f* capacity; (*extensión*) area; (*espacio*) room. **dar ~ a** have room for, accommodate

cabina *f* (*de pasajeros*) cabin; (*de pilotos*) cockpit; (*electoral*) booth; (*de ca-*

mión) cab. **~ telefónica** telephone box (*Brit*), telephone booth (*Amer*)

cabizbajo *adj* crestfallen

cable *m* cable

cabo *m* end; (*trozo*) bit; (*Mil*) corporal; (*mango*) handle; (*en geografía*) cape; (*Naut*) rope. **al ~ de** after. **de ~ a rabo** from beginning to end. **llevar a ~** carry out

cabr|a *f* goat. **~iola** *f* jump, skip. **~itilla** *f* kid. **~ito** *m* kid

cábula *m* (*Mex*) crook

cacahuate, (*Mex*) **cacahuete** *m* peanut

cacalote *m* (*Mex*) crow

cacao *m* (*planta y semillas*) cacao; (*polvo*) cocoa; (*fig*) confusion

cacarear *vt* boast about. ● *vi* (*gallo*) crow; (*gallina*) cluck

cacería *f* hunt. **ir de ~** go hunting

cacerola *f* saucepan, casserole

cacharro *m* (*earthenware*) pot; (*coche estropeado*) wreck; (*cosa inútil*) piece of junk; (*chisme*) thing. **~s** *mpl* pots and pans

cachear *vt* frisk

cachemir *m*, **cachemira** *f* cashmere

cacheo *m* frisking

cachetada *f* (*LAm*) slap

cache|te *m* slap; (*esp LAm, mejilla*) cheek. **~tear** *vt* (*LAm*) slap. **~tón** *adj* (*LAm*) chubby-cheeked

cachimba *f* pipe

cachiporra *f* club, truncheon

cachivache *m* piece of junk. **~s** *mpl* junk

cacho *m* bit, piece; (*LAm, cuerno*) horn

cachondeo *m* 1 joking, joke

cachorro *m* (*perrito*) puppy; (*de león, tigre*) cub

cachucha *f* (*Mex*) cup

caciqu|e *m* cacique, chief; (*Pol*) local political boss; (*hombre poderoso*) tyrant. **~il** *adj* despotic. **~ismo** *m* despotism

caco *m* thief

cacofonía *f* cacophony

cacto *m*, **cactus** *m invar* cactus

cada *adj invar* each, every. **~ uno** each one, everyone. **uno de ~ cinco** one in five. **~ vez más** more and more

cadáver *m* corpse

cadena f chain; (TV) channel. ~ **de fabricación** production line. ~ **de montañas** mountain range. ~ **perpetua** life imprisonment

cadera f hip

cadete m cadet

caduc|ar 7 vi expire. ~**idad** f. **fecha** f **de** ~**idad** sell-by date. ~**o** adj outdated

cae|r 29 vi fall. **dejar** ~**r** drop. **este vestido no me** ~ **bien** this dress doesn't suit me. **hacer** ~**r** knock over. **Juan me** ~ **bien** I like Juan. **su cumpleaños cayó en martes** his birthday fell on a Tuesday. ~**rse** vpr fall (over). **se le cayó** he dropped it

café m coffee; (cafetería) café; (Mex, marrón) brown. ● adj. **color** ~ coffee-coloured. ~ **con leche** white coffee. ~ **cortado** coffee with a little milk. ~ **negro** (LAm) expresso. ~ **solo** black coffee

cafe|ína f caffeine. ~**tal** m coffee plantation. ~**tera** f coffee-pot. ~**tería** f café. ~**tero** adj coffee

caíd|a f fall; (disminución) drop; (pendiente) slope. ~**o** adj fallen

---

cafetería In Spain, a place to have a coffee or other drinks, pastries and cakes. *Cafeterías* are frequently combined with *bares* and are very similar. However, *cafeterías* are usually smarter, and serve a wider variety of dishes. *i*

---

caigo vb véase **CAER**

caimán m cayman, alligator

caj|a f box; (de botellas) case; (ataúd) coffin; (en tienda) cash desk; (en supermercado) check-out; (en banco) cashier's desk. ~**a de ahorros** savings bank. ~**a de cambios** gearbox. ~**a de caudales**, ~**a fuerte** safe. ~**a negra** black box. ~**a registradora** till. ~**ero** m cashier. ~**ero automático** cash dispenser. ~**etilla** f packet. ~**ita** f small box. ~**ón** m (de mueble) drawer; (caja grande) crate; (LAm, ataúd) coffin; (Mex, en estacionamiento) parking space. **ser de** ~**ón** be obvious. ~**uela** f (Mex) boot (Brit), trunk (Amer)

cal m lime

cala f cove

calaba|cín m, **|cita** f (Mex) courgette (Brit), zucchini (Amer). ~**za** f pumpkin; (fig, fam, idiota) idiot. **dar** ~**zas a uno** give s.o. the brush-off

calabozo m prison; (celda) cell

calado adj soaked. **estar** ~ **hasta los huesos** be soaked to the skin. ● m (Naut) draught

calamar m squid

calambre m cramp

calami|dad f calamity, disaster. ~**toso** adj calamitous

calaña f sort

calar vt soak; (penetrar) pierce; (fig, penetrar) see through; rumble (persona); sample (fruta). ~**se** vpr get soaked; (zapatos) leak; (Auto) stall

calavera f skull; (Mex, Auto) tail light

calcar 7 vt trace; (fig) copy

calcet|a f. **hacer** ~ knit. ~**ín** m sock

calcetín m sock

calcinar vt burn

calcio m calcium

calcomanía f transfer

calcula|dor adj calculating. ~**dora** f calculator. ~**r** vt calculate; (suponer) reckon, think; (imaginar) imagine

cálculo m calculation; (Med) stone

caldear vt heat, warm. ~**se** vpr get hot

caldera f boiler

calderilla f small change

caldo m stock; (sopa) clear soup, broth

calefacción f heating. ~ **central** central heating

caleidoscopio m kaleidoscope

calendario m calendar; (programa) schedule

calent|ador m heater. ~**amiento** m warming; (en deportes) warm-up. ~**ar** 1 vt heat; (templar) warm. ~**arse** vpr get hot; (templarse) warm up; (LAm, enojarse) get mad. ~**ura** f fever, (high) temperature. ~**uriento** adj feverish

calibr|ar vt calibrate; (fig) weigh up. ~**e** m calibre; (diámetro) diameter; (fig) importance

calidad f quality; (condición) capacity. **en ~ de** as

calidez f (LAm) warmth

cálido adj warm

caliente adj hot; (habitación, ropa) warm; (LAm, enojado) angry

califica|ción f qualification; (evaluación) assessment; (nota) mark. **~do** adj (esp LAm) qualified; (mano de obra) skilled. **~r 🔽** vt qualify; (evaluar) assess; mark (examen etc). **~r de** describe as, label

cáliz m chalice; (en botánica) calyx

caliz|a f limestone. **~o** adj lime

calla|do adj quiet. **~r** vt silence; keep (secreto); hush up (asunto). ● vi be quiet, keep quiet, shut up 🅳. **~rse** vpr be quiet, keep quiet, shut up 🅳 **¡cállate!** be quiet!, shut up! 🅳

calle f street, road; (en deportes, autopista) lane. **~ de dirección única** one-way street. **~ mayor** high street, main street. **de ~** everyday. **~ja** f narrow street. **~jear** vi hang out in the streets. **~jero** adj street. ● m street plan. **~jón** m alley. **~ón sin salida** dead end. **~juela** f back street, side street

call|ista m & f chiropodist. **~o** m corn, callus. **~os** mpl tripe. **~osidad** f callus

calm|a f calm. **¡~a!** calm down!. **en ~a** calm, **perder la ~a** lose one's composure. **~ante** m tranquilizer; (para el dolor) painkiller. **~ar** vt calm; (aliviar) soothe. ● vi (viento) abate. **~arse** vpr calm down; (viento) abate. **~o** adj calm, **~oso** adj calm; (fam, flemático) slow

calor m heat; (afecto) warmth. **hace ~** it's hot. **tener ~** be hot. **~ía** f calorie. **~ífero** adj heat-producing. **~ífico** adj calorific

calumni|a f calumny; (oral) slander; (escrita) libel. **~ar** vt slander; (por escrito) libel. **~oso** adj slanderous; (cosa escrita) libellous

caluroso adj warm; (clima) hot

calv|a f bald head; (parte sin pelo) bald patch. **~icie** f baldness. **~o** adj bald

calza f wedge

calzada f road; (en autopista) carriageway

calza|do adj wearing shoes. ● m footwear, shoe. **~dor** m shoehorn. **~r 🔟** vt put shoes on; (llevar) wear. **¿qué número calza Vd?** what size shoe do you take? ● vi wear shoes. **~rse** vpr put on

calz|ón m shorts. **~ones** mpl shorts; (LAm, ropa interior) panties. **~oncillos** mpl underpants

cama f bed. **~ de matrimonio** double bed. **~ individual** single bed. **guardar ~** stay in bed

camada f litter

camafeo m cameo

camaleón m chameleon

cámara f (aposento) chamber; (fotográfica) camera. **~ fotográfica** camera. **a ~ lenta** in slow motion

camarad|a m & f colleague; (de colegio) schoolfriend; (Pol) comrade. **~ería** f camaraderie

camarer|a f chambermaid; (de restaurante etc) waitress. **~o** m waiter

camarógrafo m cameraman

camarón m shrimp

camarote m cabin

cambi|able adj changeable; (Com etc) exchangeable. **~ante** adj variable; (persona) moody. **~ar** vt change; (trocar) exchange. ● vi change. **~ar de idea** change one's mind. **~arse** vpr change. **~o** m change; (Com) exchange rate; (moneda menuda) (small) change; (Auto) gear. **~o climático** climate change. **en ~o** on the other hand

camello m camel

camellón m (Mex) traffic island

camerino m dressing room

camilla f stretcher

camin|ante m traveller. **~ar** vt/i walk. **~ata** f long walk. **~o** m road; (sendero) path, track; (dirección, ruta) way. **~o de** towards, on the way to. **abrir ~o** make way. **a medio ~o, a la mitad del ~o** half-way. **de ~o** on the way

cami|ón m truck, lorry; (Mex, autobús) bus. **~onero** m lorry-driver; (Mex, de autobús) bus driver. **~oneta** f van; (LAm, coche familiar) estate car

Camino de Santiago A pilgrimage route since the Middle Ages across north-western Spain to Santiago de Compostela in Galicia. The city was founded at a place where a shepherd is said to have discovered the tomb of St James the Apostle, and its cathedral reputedly houses the saint's relics.

camis|a f shirt. ~a de fuerza straitjacket. ~ería f shirtmaker's. ~eta f T-shirt; (ropa interior) vest. ~ón m nightdress

camorra f ① row. buscar ~ look for a fight

camote m (LAm) sweet potato

campamento m camp. de ~ adj camping

campan|a f bell. ~ada f stroke. ~ario m bell tower, belfry. ~illa f bell

campaña f campaign

campe|ón adj & m champion. ~onato m championship

campes|ino adj country. ● m peasant. ~tre adj country

camping /'kampin/ m (pl ~s) camping; (lugar) campsite. hacer ~ go camping

camp|iña f countryside. ~o m country; (agricultura, fig) field; (de fútbol) pitch; (de golf) course. ~osanto m cemetery

camufla|je m camouflage. ~r vt camouflage

cana f grey hair, white hair. peinar ~s be getting old

Canadá m. el ~ Canada

canadiense adj & m & f Canadian

canal m (incl TV) channel; (artificial) canal; (del tejado) gutter. ~ de la Mancha English Channel. ~ de Panamá Panama Canal. ~ón m (horizontal) gutter; (vertical) drain-pipe

canalla f rabble. ● m (fig, fam) swine. ~da f dirty trick

canapé m sofa, couch; (Culin) canapé

Canarias fpl. las (islas) ~ the Canary Islands, the Canaries

canario adj of the Canary Islands. ● m native of the Canary Islands; (pájaro) canary

canast|a f (large) basket. ~illa f small basket; (para un bebé) layette. ~illo m small basket. ~o m (large) basket

cancela|ción f cancellation. ~r vt cancel; write off (deuda)

cáncer m cancer. C~ Cancer

cancha f court; (LAm, de fútbol, rugby) pitch, ground

canciller m chancellor; (LAm, ministro) Minister of Foreign Affairs

canci|ón f song. ~ón de cuna lullaby. ~onero m song-book

candado m padlock

candel|a f candle. ~abro m candelabra. ~ero m candlestick

candente adj (rojo) red-hot; (fig) burning

candidato m candidate

candidez f innocence; (ingenuidad) naivety

cándido adj naive

candil m oil lamp. ~ejas fpl footlights

candor m innocence; (ingenuidad) naivety

canela f cinnamon

cangrejo m crab. ~ de río crayfish

canguro m kangaroo. ● m & f (persona) baby-sitter

caníbal adj & m & f cannibal

canica f marble

canijo adj weak; (Mex, terco) stubborn; (Mex, intenso) incredible

canilla f (LAm) shinbone

canino adj canine. ● m canine (tooth)

canje m exchange. ~ar vt exchange

cano adj grey. de pelo ~ grey-haired

canoa f canoe

can|ónigo m canon. ~onizar ⑩ vt canonize

canoso adj grey-haired

cansa|do adj tired; (que cansa) tiring. ~dor (LAm) tiring. ~ncio m tiredness. ~r vt tire; (aburrir) bore. ● vi be tiring; (aburrir) get boring. ~rse vpr get tired

canta|nte adj singing. ● m & f singer. ~or m Flamenco singer. ~r vt/i sing. ~rlas claras speak frankly. ● m singing; (*poema*) poem

cántaro *m* pitcher. **llover a ~s** pour down

cante *m* folk song. **~ flamenco**, **~ jondo** Flamenco singing

cantera *f* quarry

cantidad *f* quantity; (*número*) number; (*de dinero*) sum. **una ~ de** lots of

cantimplora *f* water-bottle

cantina *f* canteen; (*Rail*) buffet; (*LAm, bar*) bar

cant|inela *f* song. **~o** *m* singing; (*canción*) chant; (*borde*) edge; (*de un cuchillo*) blunt edge. **~o rodado** boulder; (*guijarro*) pebble. **de ~o** on edge

canturre|ar *vt/i* hum. **~o** *m* humming

canuto *m* tube

caña *f* (*planta*) reed; (*del trigo*) stalk; (*del bambú*) cane; (*de pescar*) rod; (*de la bota*) leg; (*vaso*) glass. **~ de azúcar** sugar-cane. **~da** *f* ravine; (*camino*) track; (*LAm, arroyo*) stream

cáñamo *m* hemp. **~ Indio** cannabis

cañ|ería *f* pipe; (*tubería*) piping. **~o** *m* pipe, tube; (*de fuente*) jet. **~ón** *m* (*de pluma*) quill; (*de artillería*) cannon; (*de arma de fuego*) barrel; (*desfiladero*) canyon. **~onera** *f* gunboat

caoba *f* mahogany

ca|os *m* chaos. **~ótico** *adj* chaotic

capa *f* layer; (*de pintura*) coat; (*Culin*) coating; (*prenda*) cloak; (*más corta*) cape; (*en geología*) stratum

capaci|dad *f* capacity; (*fig*) ability. **~tar** *vt* qualify, enable; (*instruir*) train

caparazón *m* shell

capataz *m* foreman

capaz *adj* capable, able

capcioso *adj* sly, insidious

capellán *m* chaplain

caperuza *f* hood; (*de bolígrafo*) cap

capilla *f* chapel

capital *adj* capital, very important. ● *m* (*dinero*) capital. ● *f* (*ciudad*) capital. **~ de provincia** county town. **~ino** *adj* (*LAm*) of/from the capital. **~ismo** *m* capitalism. **~ista** *adj* & *m* & *f* capitalist. **~izar** 10 *vt* capitalize

capit|án *m* captain; (*de pesquero*) skipper. **~anear** *vt* lead, command; skip-

per (*pesquero*); captain (*un equipo*)

capitel *m* (*de columna*) capital

capitulaci|ón *f* surrender. **~ones** *fpl* marriage contract

capítulo *m* chapter; (*de serie*) episode

capó *m* bonnet (*Brit*), hood (*Amer*)

capón *m* (*pollo*) capon

caporal *m* (*Mex*) foreman

capot|a *f* (*de mujer*) bonnet; (*Auto*) folding top; (*de cochecito*) hood. **~e** *m* cape; (*Mex, de coche*) bonnet (*Brit*), hood (*Amer*)

capricho *m* whim. **~so** *adj* capricious, whimsical

Capricornio *m* Capricorn

cápsula *f* capsule

captar *vt* harness (*agua*); grasp (*sentido*); capture (*atención*); win (*confianza*); (*radio*) pick up

captura *f* capture. **~r** *vt* capture

capucha *f* hood

capullo *m* bud; (*de insecto*) cocoon

caqui *m* khaki

cara *f* face; (*de una moneda*) heads; (*de un objeto*) side; (*aspecto*) look, appearance; (*descaro*) cheek. **~ a** a facing. **~ a ~** face to face. **~ dura** *véase* **CARADURA**. **~ o cruz** heads or tails. **dar la ~ a** face up to. **hacer ~** a face. **tener mala ~** look ill. **volver la ~** look the other way

carabela *f* caravel

carabina *f* carbine; (*fig, fam, señora*) chaperone

caracol *m* snail; (*de mar*) winkle; (*LAm, concha*) conch; (*de pelo*) curl. **¡~es!** Good Heavens!. **~a** *f* conch

carácter *m* (*pl* caracteres) character; (*índole*) nature. **con ~ de** as

característic|a *f* characteristic. **~o** *adj* characteristic, typical

caracteriza|do *adj* characterized; (*prestigioso*) distinguished. **~r** 10 *vt* characterize

caradura *f* cheek, nerve. ● *m* & *f* cheeky person

caramba *int* good heavens!

carambola *f* (*en billar*) cannon; (*Mex, choque múltiple*) pile-up. **de ~** by pure chance

caramelo *m* sweet (*Brit*), candy (*Amer*); (*azúcar fundido*) caramel

caraqueño adj from Caracas

carátula f (de disco) sleeve (Brit), jacket (Amer); (de video) case; (de libro) cover; (Mex, del reloj) face

caravana f caravan; (de vehículos) convoy; (Auto) long line, traffic jam; (remolque) caravan (Brit), trailer (Amer); (Mex, reverencia) bow

caray int ⓘ good heavens!

carb|ón m coal; (para dibujar) charcoal. ∼ de leña charcoal. ∼oncillo m charcoal. ∼onero adj coal. • m coal-merchant. ∼onizar ⓾ vt (fig) burn (to a cinder). ∼ono m carbon

carbura|dor m carburettor. ∼nte m fuel

carcajada f guffaw. reírse a ∼s roar with laughter. soltar una ∼ burst out laughing

cárcel f prison, jail

carcelero m jailer

carcom|er vt eat away; (fig) undermine. ∼erse vpr be eaten away; (fig) waste away

cardenal m cardinal; (contusión) bruise

cardiaco, cardíaco adj cardiac, heart

cardinal adj cardinal

cardo m thistle

carear vt bring face to face (personas); compare (cosas)

care|cer ⓲ vi. ∼cer de lack. ∼cer de sentido not to make sense. ∼ncia f lack. ∼nte adj lacking

care|ro adj pricey. ∼stía f (elevado) high cost

careta f mask

carey m tortoiseshell

carga f load; (fig) burden; (acción) loading; (de barco, avión) cargo; (de tren) freight; (de arma) charge; (Elec, ataque) charge; (obligación) obligation. llevar la ∼ de algo be responsible for sth. ∼da f (Mex, Pol) supporters. ∼do adj loaded; (fig) burdened; (atmósfera) heavy; (café) strong; (pila) charged. ∼mento m load; (acción) loading; (de un barco) cargo. ∼r ⓬ vt load; (fig) burden; (Elec, atacar) charge; fill (pluma etc). • vi load. ∼r con carry. ∼rse vpr (pila) charge. ∼rse de to load s.o. down with

cargo m (puesto) post; (acusación) charge. a ∼ de in the charge of. hacerse ∼ de take responsibility for. tener a su ∼ be in charge of

carguero m (Naut) cargo ship

caria|do adj decayed. ∼rse vpr decay

caribeño adj Caribbean

caricatura f caricature

caricia f caress; (a animal) stroke

caridad f charity. ¡por ∼! for goodness sake!

caries f invar tooth decay; (lesión) cavity

cariño m affection; (caricia) caress. ∼ mío my darling. con mucho ∼ (en carta) with love from. tener ∼ a be fond of. tomar ∼ a become fond of. ∼so adj affectionate

carisma m charisma

caritativo adj charitable

cariz m look

carmesí adj & m crimson

carmín m (de labios) lipstick; (color) red

carnal adj carnal. primo ∼ first cousin

carnaval m carnival. ∼esco adj carnival

carne f meat; (Anat, de frutos, pescado) flesh. ∼ de cerdo pork. ∼ de cordero lamb. ∼ de gallina goose pimples. ∼ molida (LAm), ∼ picada mince (Brit), ground beef (Amer). ∼ de ternera veal. ∼ de vaca beef. me pone la ∼ de gallina it gives me the creeps. ser de ∼ y hueso be only human

carné, carnet m card. ∼ de conducir driving licence (Brit), driver's license (Amer) ∼ de identidad identity card. ∼ de manejar (LAm) driving license (Brit), driver's license (Amer). ∼ de socio membership card

carnero m ram

carnicer|ía f butcher's (shop); (fig) massacre. ∼o adj carnivorous. • m butcher

carnívoro adj carnivorous. • m carnivore

carnoso adj fleshy; (pollo) meaty

caro adj expensive. • adv dear, dearly. costar ∼ a uno cost s.o. dear.

carpa f carp; (LAm, tienda) tent

carpeta f folder, file. **~zo** m. **dar ~zo a** shelve

carpinter|ía f carpentry. **~o** m carpinter, joiner

carraspe|ar vi clear one's throat. **~ra** f. **tener ~ra** have a frog in one's throat

carrera f run; (prisa) rush; (concurso) race; (estudios) degree course; (profesión) career; (de taxi) journey

carreta f cart. **~da** f cartload

carrete m reel; (película) film

carretear vi (LAm) taxi

carretera f road. **~ de circunvalación** bypass, ring road. **~ nacional** A road (Brit), highway (Amer)

carretilla f wheelbarrow

carril m lane; (Rail) rail

carrito m (en supermercado, para equipaje) trolley (Brit), cart (Amer)

carro m cart; (LAm, coche) car; (Mex, vagón) coach. **~ de combate** tank. **~cería** f (Auto) bodywork

carroña f carrion

carroza f coach, carriage; (en desfile de fiesta) float

carruaje m carriage

carrusel m merry-go-round

cart|a f letter; (lista de platos) menu; (lista de vinos) list; (mapa) map; (naipe) card. **~a blanca** free hand. **~a de crédito** letter of credit. **~a verde** green card. **~earse** vpr correspond

cartel m poster; (letrero) sign. **~era** f hoarding; (en periódico) listings; (LAm en escuela, oficina) notice board (Brit), bulletin board (Amer). **de ~** celebrated

carter|a f wallet; (de colegial) satchel; (para documentos) briefcase; (LAm, de mujer) handbag (Brit), purse (Amer). **~ista** m & f pickpocket

cartero m postman, mailman (Amer)

cartílago m cartilage

cartilla f first reading book. **~ de ahorros** savings book. **leerle la ~ a uno** tell s.o. off

cartón m cardboard

cartucho m cartridge

cartulina f card

casa f house; (hogar) home; (empresa) firm. **~ de huéspedes** boarding-house. **~ de socorro** first aid post. **ir a ~** go home. **salir de ~** go out

casaca f jacket

casado adj married. **los recién ~s** the newly-weds

casa|mentero m matchmaker. **~miento** m marriage; (ceremonia) wedding. **~r** vt marry. **~rse** vpr get married

cascabel m small bell; (de serpiente) rattle

cascada f waterfall

casca|nueces m invar nutcrackers. **~r 7** vt crack (nuez, huevo); (pegar) beat. **~rse** vpr crack

cáscara f (de huevo, nuez) shell; (de naranja) peel; (de plátano) skin

cascarrabias adj invar grumpy

casco m helmet; (de cerámica etc) piece, fragment; (cabeza) scalp; (de barco) hull; (envase) empty bottle; (de caballo) hoof; (de una ciudad) part, area

cascote m piece of rubble. **~s** mpl rubble

caserío m country house; (poblado) hamlet

casero adj home-made; (doméstico) domestic; (amante del hogar) home-loving; (reunión) family. ●m owner; (vigilante) caretaker

caseta f hut; (puesto) stand. **~ de baño** bathing hut

casete m & f cassette

casi adv almost, nearly; (en frases negativas) hardly. **~ ~** very nearly. **~ nada** hardly any. **¡~ nada!** is that all? **~ nunca** hardly ever

casill|a f hut; (en ajedrez etc) square; (en formulario) box; (compartimento) pigeonhole. **~ electrónica** e-mail address. **~ero** m pigeonholes; (compartimento) pigeonhole

casino m casino; (club social) club

caso m case. **el ~ es que** the fact is that. **en ~ de** in the event of. **en cualquier ~** in any case, whatever happens. **en ese ~** in that case. **en todo ~** in any case. **en último ~** as a last resort. **hacer ~ de** take notice of. **poner por ~** suppose

caspa f dandruff

casquivana f flirt

cassette m & f cassette

casta f (de animal) breed; (de persona) descent; (grupo social) caste

castaña f chestnut

castañetear vi (dientes) chatter

castaño adj chestnut; (ojos) brown. ● m chestnut (tree)

castañuela f castanet

castellano adj Castilian. ● m (persona) Castilian; (lengua) Castilian, Spanish. ~**parlante** adj Castilian-speaking, Spanish-speaking. ¿**habla Vd** ~? do you speak Spanish?

> **castellano** In Spain the term *castellano*, rather than *español*, refers to the Spanish language as opposed to Catalan, Basque etc. The choice of word has political overtones; *castellano* has separatist connotations and *español* is considered neutral. In Latin America *castellano* is another term for Spanish.

castidad f chastity

castig|ar 12 vt punish; (en deportes) penalize. ~**o** m punishment; (en deportes) penalty

castillo m castle

cast|izo adj traditional; (puro) pure. ~**o** adj chaste

castor m beaver

castrar vt castrate

castrense m military

casual adj chance, accidental. ~**idad** f chance, coincidence. **dar la** ~**idad** happen. **de** ~**idad, por** ~**idad** by chance. ¡**qué** ~**idad!** what a coincidence!. ~**mente** adv by chance; (precisamente) actually

cataclismo m cataclysm

catador m taster

catalán adj & m Catalan

catalizador m catalyst

cat|alogar 12 vt catalogue; (fig) classify. ~**álogo** m catalogue

Cataluña f Catalonia

catamarán m catamaran

catapulta f catapult

catar vt taste, try

catarata f waterfall, falls; (Med) cataract

catarro m cold

cat|ástrofe m catastrophe. ~**astrófico** adj catastrophic

catecismo m catechism

cátedra f (en universidad) professorship, chair; (en colegio) post of head of department

catedral f cathedral

catedrático m professor; (de colegio) teacher, head of department

categ|oría f category; (clase) class. **de** ~**oría** important. **de primera** ~**oría** first-class. ~**órico** adj categorical

cat|olicismo m catholicism. ~**ólico** adj (Roman) Catholic ● m (Roman) Catholic

catorce adj & m fourteen

cauce m river bed; (fig, artificial) channel

caucho m rubber

caudal m (de río) volume of flow; (riqueza) wealth. ~**oso** adj (río) large

caudillo m leader

causa f cause; (motivo) reason; (Jurid) trial. **a** ~ **de, por** ~ **de** because of. ~**r** vt cause

cautel|a f caution. ~**oso** adj cautious, wary

cauterizar 10 vt cauterize

cautiv|ar vt capture; (fig, fascinar) captivate. ~**erio** m, ~**idad** f captivity. ~**o** adj & m captive

cauto adj cautious

cavar vt/i dig

caverna f cave, cavern

caviar m caviare

cavidad f cavity

caza f hunting; (con fusil) shooting; (animales) game. ● m fighter. **andar a (la)** ~ **de** be in search of. ~ **mayor** game hunting. **dar** ~ chase, go after. **ir de** ~ go hunting/shooting. ~**dor** m hunter. ~**dora** f jacket. ~**r** 10 vt hunt; (con fusil) shoot; (fig) track down; (obtener) catch, get

caz|o m saucepan; (cucharón) ladle. ~**oleta** f (small) saucepan. ~**uela** f casserole

cebada *f* barley

ceb|ar *vt* fatten (up); bait (anzuelo); prime (arma de fuego). ~**o** *m* bait; (*de arma de fuego*) charge

ceboll|a *f* onion. ~**eta** *f* spring onion (*Brit*), scallion (*Amer*). ~**ino** *m* chive

cebra *f* zebra

cece|ar *vi* lisp. ~**o** *m* lisp

cedazo *m* sieve

ceder *vt* give up; (*transferir*) transfer. ● *vi* give in; (*disminuir*) ease off; (*romperse*) give way, collapse. **ceda el paso** give way (*Brit*), yield (*Amer*)

cedro *m* cedar

cédula *f* bond. ~ **de identidad** identity card

CE(E) *abrev* (**Comunidad (Económica) Europea**) E(E)C

ceg|ador *adj* blinding. ~**ar** **1** & **12** *vt* blind; (*tapar*) block up. ~**arse** *vpr* be blinded (**de** by). ~**uera** *f* blindness

ceja *f* eyebrow

cejar *vi* give way

celada *f* ambush; (*fig*) trap

cela|dor *m* (*de cárcel*) prison warder; (*de museo etc*) security guard. ~**r** *vt* watch

celda *f* cell

celebra|ción *f* celebration. ~**r** *vt* celebrate; (*alabar*) praise. ~**rse** *vpr* take place

célebre *adj* famous

celebridad *f* fame; (*persona*) celebrity

celest|e *adj* heavenly; (*vestido*) pale blue. **azul** ~**e** sky-blue. ~**ial** *adj* heavenly

celibato *m* celibacy

célibe *adj* celibate

celo *m* zeal; (*de las hembras*) heat; (*de los machos*) rut; (*cinta adhesiva*) Sellotape (P) (*Brit*), Scotch (P) tape (*Amer*). ~**s** *mpl* jealousy. **dar** ~**s** make jealous. **tener** ~**s** be jealous

celofán *m* cellophane

celoso *adj* conscientious; (*que tiene celos*) jealous

celta *adj* & *m* (*lengua*) Celtic. ● *m* & *f* Celt

célula *f* cell

celular *adj* cellular. ● *m* (*LAm*) mobile, cellphone

celulosa *f* cellulose

cementerio *m* cemetery

cemento *m* cement; (*hormigón*) concrete; (*LAm, cola*) glue

cena *f* dinner; (*comida ligera*) supper

cenag|al *m* marsh, bog; (*fig*) tight spot. ~**oso** *adj* boggy

cenar *vt* have for dinner; (*en cena ligera*) have for supper. ● *vi* have dinner; (*tomar cena ligera*) have supper

cenicero *m* ashtray

ceniza *f* ash

censo *m* census. ~ **electoral** electoral roll

censura *f* censure; (*de prensa etc*) censorship. ~**r** *vt* censure; censor (*prensa etc*)

centavo *adj* & *m* hundredth; (*moneda*) centavo

centell|a *f* flash; (*chispa*) spark. ~**ar**, ~**ear** *vi* sparkle

centena *f* hundred. ~**r** *m* hundred. **a** ~**res** by the hundred. ~**rio** *adj* centenarian. ● *m* centenary; (*persona*) centenarian

centeno *m* rye

centésim|a *f* hundredth. ~**o** *adj* hundredth

cent|igrado *adj* centigrade, Celsius. ● *m* centigrade. ~**igramo** *m* centigram. ~**ilitro** *m* centilitre. ~**ímetro** *m* centimetre

céntimo *adj* hundredth. ● *m* cent

centinela *f* sentry

centolla *f*, **centollo** *m* spider crab

central *adj* central. ● *f* head office. ~ **de correos** general post office. ~ **eléctrica** power station. ~ **nuclear** nuclear power station. ~ **telefónica** telephone exchange. ~**ita** *f* switchboard

centraliza|ción *f* centralization. ~**r** **10** *vt* centralize

centrar *vt* centre

céntrico *adj* central

centrífugo *adj* centrifugal

centro *m* centre. ~ **comercial** shopping centre (*Brit*), shopping mall (*Amer*). ~ **de llamadas** call centre

Centroamérica *f* Central America

centroamericano *adj* & *m* Central American

ceñi|do adj tight. ~**r** 5 & 22 vt take
(corona); (vestido) cling to. ~**rse** vpr
limit o.s. (**a** to)

ceñ|o m frown. **fruncir el ~o** frown.
~**udo** adj frowning

cepill|ar vt brush; (en carpintería)
plane. ~**o** m brush; (en carpintería)
plane. ~**o de dientes** toothbrush

cera f wax

cerámic|a f ceramics; (materia) pot-
tery; (objeto) piece of pottery. ~**o** adj
ceramic

cerca f fence; (de piedra) wall.● adv
near, close. ~ **de** prep close to, close
up, closely

cercan|ía f nearness, proximity. ~**ías**
fpl vicinity. **tren** m **de ~ías** local train.
~**o** adj near, close.

cercar 7 vt fence in, enclose; (gente)
surround; (asediar) besiege

cerciorar vt convince. ~**se** vpr make
sure

cerco m (asedio) siege; (círculo) ring;
(LAm, valla) fence; (LAm, seto) hedge

cerdo m pig; (carne) pork

cereal m cereal

cerebr|al adj cerebral. ~**o** m brain;
(persona) brains

ceremoni|a f ceremony. ~**al** adj cere-
monial. ~**oso** adj ceremonious

cerez|a f cherry. ~**o** m cherry tree

cerill|a f match. ~**o** m (Mex) match

cern|er 1 vt sieve. ~**erse** vpr hover.
~**idor** m sieve

cero m nought, zero; (fútbol) nil (Brit),
zero (Amer); (tenis) love; (persona)
nonentity

cerquillo m (LAm, flequillo) fringe
(Brit), bangs (Amer)

cerra|do adj shut, closed; (espacio)
shut in, enclosed; (cielo) overcast;
(curva) sharp. ~**dura** f lock; (acción
de cerrar) shutting, closing. ~**jero** m
locksmith. ~**r** 1 vt shut, close; (con
llave) lock; (cercar) enclose; turn off
(grifo); block up (agujero etc). ● vi
shut, close. ~**rse** vpr shut, close; (herida) heal. ~**r con llave** lock

cerro m hill

cerrojo m bolt. **echar el ~** bolt

certamen m competition, contest

certero adj accurate

certeza, **certidumbre** f certainty

certifica|do adj (carta etc) registered.
● m certificate. ~**r** 7 vt certify

certitud f certainty

cervatillo, **cervato** m fawn

cerve|cería f beerhouse, bar; (fábrica)
brewery. ~**za** f beer. ~**za de barril**
draught beer. ~**za rubia** lager

cesa|ción f cessation, suspension.
~**nte** adj redundant. ~**r** vt stop. ● vi
stop, cease; (dejar un empleo) resign.
sin ~r incessantly

cesárea f caesarian (section)

cese m cessation; (de un empleo) dismissal. ~ **del fuego** (LAm) ceasefire

césped m grass, lawn

cest|a f basket. ~**o** m basket. ~**o de
los papeles** waste-paper basket

chabacano adj common; (chiste etc)
vulgar. ● m (Mex, albaricoque) apricot

chabola f shack. ~**s** fpl shanty town

cháchara f 1 chatter; (Mex, objetos sin
valor) junk

chacharear vt (Mex) sell. ● vi 1 chatter

chacra f (LAm) farm

chal m shawl

chalado adj 1 crazy

chalé m house (with a garden), villa

chaleco m waistcoat, vest (Amer). ~
salvavidas life-jacket

chalet m (pl ~**s**) house (with a garden), villa

chalote m shallot

chamac|a f (esp Mex) girl. ~**o** m (esp
Mex) boy

chamarra f sheepskin jacket; (Mex,
chaqueta corta) jacket

chamb|a f (Mex, trabajo) work. **por
~a** by fluke. ~**ear** vi (Mex, fam) work

champán m, **champaña** m & f champagne

champiñón m mushroom

champú m (pl ~**es** o ~**s**) shampoo

chamuscar 7 vt scorch

chance m (esp LAm) chance

chancho m (LAm) pig

chanchullo m 1 swindle, fiddle 1

chanclo m clog; (de caucho) rubber
overshoe

chándal m (pl ~**s**) tracksuit

chantaje m blackmail. **~ar** vt blackmail

chanza f joke

chapa f plate, sheet; (*de madera*) plywood; (*de botella*) metal top; (*carrocería*) bodywork; (*LAm cerradura*) lock. **~do** adj plated. **~do a la antigua** old-fashioned. **~do en oro** gold-plated

chaparro adj (*LAm*) short, squat

chaparrón m downpour

chapopote m (*Mex*) tar

chapotear vi splash

chapucero adj (*persona*) slapdash; (*trabajo*) shoddy

chapulín m (*Mex*) locust; (*saltamontes*) grasshopper

chapurrar, chapurrear vt have a smattering of, speak a little

chapuza f botched job; (*trabajo ocasional*) odd job

chaquet|a f jacket. **cambiar de ~a** change sides. **~ón** m three-quarter length coat

charc|a f pond, pool. **~o** m puddle, pool

charcutería f delicatessen

charla f chat; (*conferencia*) talk. **~dor** adj talkative. **~r** vi ⬛ chat. **~tán** adj talkative. ● m chatterbox; (*vendedor*) cunning hawker; (*curandero*) charlatan

charol m varnish; (*cuero*) patent leather. **~a** f (*Mex*) tray

charr|a f (*Mex*) horsewoman, cowgirl. **~o** m (*Mex*) horseman, cowboy

chascar ⬛ vt crack (*látigo*); click (lengua); snap (*dedos*). ● vi (*madera*) creak. **~ con la lengua** click one's tongue

chasco m disappointment

chasis m (*Auto*) chassis

chasqu|ear vt crack (*látigo*); click (lengua); snap (*dedos*). ● vi (*madera*) creak. **~ con la lengua** click one's tongue. **~ido** m crack; (*de la lengua*) click; (*de los dedos*) snap

chatarra f scrap iron; (*fig*) scrap

chato adj (*nariz*) snub; (*objetos*) flat. ● m wine glass

chav|a f (*Mex*) girl, lass. **~al** m ⬛ boy, lad. **~o** m (*Mex*) boy, lad.

checa|da f (*Mex*) check; (*Mex, Med*) checkup. **~r** ⬛ vt (*Mex*) check; (*vigilar*) check up on. **~r tarjeta** clock in

checo adj & m Czech. **~slovaco** adj & m (*History*) Czechoslovak

chelín m shilling

chelo m cello

cheque m cheque. **~ de viaje** traveller's cheque. **~ar** vt check; (*LAm*) check in (equipaje). **~o** m check; (*Med*) checkup. **~ra** f cheque-book

chévere adj (*LAm*) great

chica f girl; (*criada*) maid, servant

chicano adj & m Chicano, Mexican-American

Chicano Chicanos are Mexican Americans, descendants of Mexican immigrants living in US. For long looked down by Americans of European descent, Chicanos have found a new pride in their origins and culture. There are numerous Chicano radio stations and many universities and colleges now offer courses in Chicano studies.

chícharo m (*Mex*) pea

chicharra f cicada; (*timbre*) buzzer

chichón m bump

chicle m chewing-gum

chico adj ⬛ small; (*esp LAm, de edad*) young. ● m boy. **~s** mpl children

chicoria f chicory

chifla|do adj ⬛ crazy, daft. **~r** vt whistle at, boo. ● vi (*LAm*) whistle; (⬛, *gustar mucho*) **me chifla el chocolate** I'm mad about chocolate. **~rse** vpr be mad (**por** about)

chilango adj (*Mex*) from Mexico City

chile m chilli

Chile m Chile

chileno adj & m Chilean

chill|ar vi scream, shriek; (*ratón*) squeak; (*cerdo*) squeal. **~ido** m scream, screech. **~ón** adj noisy; (colores) loud; (sonido) shrill

chimenea f chimney; (*hogar*) fireplace

chimpancé m chimpanzee

china f Chinese (woman)

China f China

chinche m drawing-pin (Brit), thumbtack (Amer); (insecto) bedbug; (fig) nuisance. ~**eta** f drawing-pin (Brit), thumbtack (Amer)

chinela f slipper

chino adj Chinese; (Mex rizado) curly. ● m Chinese (man); (Mex, de pelo rizado) curly-haired person

chipriota adj & m & f Cypriot

chiquero m pen; (LAm, pocilga) pigsty (Brit), pigpen (Amer)

chiquillo adj childish. ● m child, kid 🔢

chirimoya f custard apple

chiripa f fluke

chirri|ar 🔢 vi creak; (frenos) screech; (pájaro) chirp. ~**do** m creaking; (de frenos) screech; (de pájaros) chirping

chis int sh!, hush!; (fam, para llamar a uno) hey!, psst!

chism|e m gadget, thingumajig 🔢; (chismorreo) piece of gossip. ~**es** mpl things, bits and pieces. ~**orreo** m gossip. ~**oso** adj gossipy.● m gossip

chisp|a f spark; (pizca) drop; (gracia) wit; (fig) sparkle. **estar que echa** ~**a(s)** be furious. ~**eante** adj sparkling. ~**ear** vi spark; (lloviznar) drizzle; (fig) sparkle. ~**orrotear** vt throw out sparks; (fuego) crackle; (aceite) spit

chistar vi. **ni chistó** he didn't say a word. **sin** ~ without saying a word

chiste m joke, funny story. **tener** ~ be funny

chistera f top hat

chistoso adj funny

chiva|rse vpr tip-off; (niño) tell. ~**tazo** m tip-off. ~**to** m informer; (niño) telltale

chivo m kid; (LAm, macho cabrío) billy goat

choca|nte adj shocking; (Mex desagradable) unpleasant. ~**r** 🔢 vt clink (vasos); (LAm) crash (vehículo). **¡chócala!** give me five! ● vi collide, hit. ~**r con**, ~**r contra** crash into

choch|ear vi be gaga. ~**o** adj gaga; (fig) soft

choclo m (LAm) corn on the cob

chocolate m chocolate. **tableta** f **de** ~ bar of chocolate

chófer, (LAm) **chofer** m chauffeur; (conductor) driver

cholo adj & m (LAm) half-breed

chopo m poplar

choque m collision; (fig) clash; (eléctrico) shock; (Auto, Rail etc) crash, accident; (sacudida) jolt

chorizo m chorizo

chorro m jet, stream; (caudal pequeño) trickle; (fig) stream. **a** ~ (avión) jet. **a** ~**s** (fig) in abundance

chovinista adj chauvinistic. ● m & f chauvinist

choza f hut

chubas|co m shower. ~**quero** m raincoat, anorak

chuchería f trinket

chueco adj (LAm) crooked

chufa f tiger nut

chuleta f chop

chulo adj cocky; (bonito) lovely (Brit), neat (Amer); (Mex, atractivo) cute. ● m tough guy; (proxeneta) pimp

chup|ada f suck; (al helado) lick; (al cigarro) puff. ~**ado** adj skinny; (fam, fácil) very easy. ~**ar** vt suck; puff at (cigarro etc); (absorber) absorb. ~**ete** m dummy (Brit), pacifier (Amer). ~**ón** m sucker; (LAm) dummy (Brit), pacifier (Amer); (Mex, del biberón) teat

churrasco m barbecued steak

churro m fritter; 🔢 mess

chut|ar vi shoot. ~**e** m shot

cianuro m cyanide

cibernética f cybernetics

cicatriz f scar. ~**ar** 🔢 vt/i heal. ~**arse** vpr heal

cíclico adj cyclic(al)

ciclis|mo m cycling. ~**ta** adj cycle. ● m & f cyclist

ciclo m cycle; (de películas, conciertos) season; (de conferencias) series

ciclomotor m moped

ciclón m cyclone

ciego adj blind. ● m blind man, blind person. **a ciegas** in the dark

cielo m sky; (Relig) heaven; (persona) darling. **¡**~**s!** good heavens!, goodness me!

ciempiés m invar centipede

cien *adj* a hundred. ~ **por** ~ one hundred per cent

ciénaga *f* bog, swamp

ciencia *f* science; (*fig*) knowledge. ~**s** *fpl* (*Univ etc*) science. ~**s empresariales** business studies. **a** ~ **cierta** for certain

cieno *m* mud

científico *adj* scientific. ● *m* scientist

ciento *adj & m* a hundred, one hundred. ~**s de** hundreds of. **por** ~ per cent

cierre *m* fastener; (*acción de cerrar*) shutting, closing; (*LAm, cremallera*) zip, zipper (*Amer*)

cierto *adj* certain; (*verdad*) true. **estar en lo** ~ be right. **lo** ~ **es que** the fact is that. **no es** ~ that's not true. **¿no es** ~**?** isn't that right? **por** ~ by the way. **si bien es** ~ **que** although

ciervo *m* deer

cifra *f* figure, number; (*cantidad*) sum. **en** ~ coded, in code. ~**do** *adj* coded. ~**r** *vt* code; place (*esperanzas*)

cigala *f* crayfish

cigarra *f* cicada

cigarr|illera *f* cigarette box; (*de bolsillo*) cigarette case. ~**illo** *m* cigarette. ~**o** *m* (*cigarrillo*) cigarette; (*puro*) cigar

cigüeña *f* stork

cilantro *m* coriander

cil|índrico *adj* cylindrical. ~**indro** *m* cylinder

cima *f* top; (*fig*) summit

cimbr|ear *vt* shake. ~**earse** *vpr* sway. ~**onada** *f*, ~**onazo** *m* (*LAm*) jolt; (*de explosión*) blast

cimentar 🔟 *vt* lay the foundations of; (*fig, reforzar*) strengthen

cimientos *mpl* foundations

cinc *m* zinc

cincel *m* chisel. ~**ar** *vt* chisel

cinco *adj & m* five; (*en fechas*) fifth

cincuent|a *adj & m* fifty; (*quincuagésimo*) fiftieth. ~**ón** *adj* in his fifties

cine *m* cinema; (*local*) cinema (*Brit*), movie theater (*Amer*). ~**asta** *m & f* film maker (*Brit*), movie maker (*Amer*). ~**matográfico** *adj* film (*Brit*), movie (*Amer*)

cínico *adj* cynical. ● *m* cynic

cinismo *m* cynicism

cinta *f* ribbon; (*película*) film (*Brit*), movie (*Amer*); (*para grabar, en carreras*) tape. ~ **aislante** insulating tape. ~ **métrica** tape measure. ~ **virgen** blank tape

cintur|a *f* waist. ~**ón** *m* belt. ~**ón de seguridad** safety belt. ~**ón salvavidas** lifebelt

ciprés *m* cypress (tree)

circo *m* circus

circuito *m* circuit; (*viaje*) tour. ~ **cerrado** closed circuit. **corto** ~ short circuit

circula|ción *f* circulation; (*vehículos*) traffic. ~**r** *adj* circular. ● *vi* circulate; (*líquidos*) flow; (*conducir*) drive; (*caminar*) walk; (*autobús*) run

círculo *m* circle. ~ **vicioso** vicious circle. **en** ~ in a circle

circunci|dar *vt* circumcise. ~**sión** *f* circumcision

circunferencia *f* circumference

circunflejo *m* circumflex

circunscri|bir (*pp* **circunscrito**) *vt* confine. ~**birse** *vpr* confine o.s. (**a** to). ~**pción** *f* (*distrito*) district. ~**pción electoral** constituency

circunspecto *adj* circumspect

circunstancia *f* circumstance

circunv|alar *vt* bypass. ~**olar** *vt* 🔟 circle

cirio *m* candle

ciruela *f* plum. ~ **pasa** prune

ciru|gía *f* surgery. ~**jano** *m* surgeon

cisne *m* swan

cisterna *f* tank, cistern

cita *f* appointment; (*entre chico y chica*) date; (*referencia*) quotation. ~ **a ciegas** blind date. ~ **flash** speed dating. ~**ción** *f* quotation; (*Jurid*) summons. ~**do** *adj* aforementioned. ~**r** *vt* make an appointment with; (*mencionar*) quote; (*Jurid*) summons. ~**rse** *vpr* arrange to meet

cítara *f* zither

ciudad *f* town; (*grande*) city. ~ **balneario** (*LAm*) coastal resort. ~ **perdida** (*Mex*) shanty town. ~ **universitaria** university campus. ~**anía** *f* citizenship; (*habitantes*) citizens.

∼ano adj civic. ● m citizen, inhabitant

cívico adj civic

civil adj civil. ● m & f civil guard; (persona no militar) civilian

civiliza|ción f civilization. **∼r** 🔟 vt civilize. **∼rse** vpr become civilized

civismo m community spirit

clam|ar vi cry out, clamour. **∼or** m clamour; (protesta) outcry. **∼oroso** adj noisy; (éxito) resounding

clandestino adj clandestine, secret; (periódico) underground

clara f (de huevo) egg white

claraboya f skylight

clarear vi dawn; (aclarar) brighten up

clarete m rosé

claridad f clarity; (luz) light

clarifica|ción f clarification. **∼r** 🔳 vt clarify

clar|ín m bugle. **∼inete** m clarinet. **∼inetista** m & f clarinettist

clarividen|cia f clairvoyance; (fig) far-sightedness. **∼te** adj clairvoyant; (fig) far-sighted

claro adj clear; (luminoso) bright; (colores) light; (líquido) thin. ● m (en bosque etc) clearing; (espacio) gap. ● adv clearly. ● int of course! **¡∼ que sí!** yes, of course! **¡∼ que no!** of course not!

clase f class; (tipo) kind, sort; (aula) classroom. **∼ media** middle class. **∼ obrera** working class. **∼ social** social class. **dar ∼s** teach

clásico adj classical; (típico) classic. ● m classic

clasifica|ción f classification; (deportes) league. **∼r** 🔳 vt classify

claustro m cloister; (Univ) staff

claustrof|obia f claustrophobia. **∼óbico** adj claustrophobic

cláusula f clause

clausura f closure

clava|do adj fixed; (con clavo) nailed. **es ∼do a su padre** he's the spitting image of his father. ● m (LAm) dive. **∼r** vt knock in (clavo); stick in (cuchillo); (fijar) fix; (juntar) nail together

clave f key; (Mus) clef; (instrumento) harpsichord. **∼cín** m harpsichord

clavel m carnation

clavícula f collarbone, clavicle

clav|ija f peg; (Elec) plug. **∼o** m nail; (Culin) clove

claxon /'klakson/ m (pl ∼s) horn

clemencia f clemency, mercy

clementina f tangerine

cleptómano m kleptomaniac

clerical adj clerical

clérigo m priest

clero m clergy

clic m: **hacer ∼ en** to click on

cliché m cliché; (Foto) negative

cliente m customer; (de médico) patient; (de abogado) client. **∼la** f clientele, customers; (de médico) patients

clim|a m climate; (ambiente) atmosphere. **∼ático** adj climatic. **∼atizado** adj air-conditioned

clínic|a f clinic. **∼o** adj clinical

cloaca f drain, sewer

clon m clone

cloro m chlorine

club m (pl ∼s o ∼es) club

coacci|ón f coercion. **∼onar** vt coerce

coagular vt coagulate; clot (sangre); curdle (leche). **∼se** vpr coagulate; (sangre) clot; (leche) curdle

coalición f coalition

coarta|da f alibi. **∼r** vt hinder; restrict (libertad etc)

cobard|e adj cowardly. ● m coward. **∼ía** f cowardice

cobert|izo m shed. **∼ura** f covering; (en radio, TV) coverage

cobij|a f (Mex, manta) blanket. **∼as** fpl (LAm, ropa de cama) bedclothes. **∼ar** vt shelter. **∼arse** vpr (take) shelter. **∼o** m shelter

cobra f cobra

cobra|dor m collector; (de autobús) conductor. **∼r** vt collect; (ganar) earn; charge (precio); cash (cheque); (recuperar) recover. ● vi be paid

cobr|e m copper. **∼izo** adj coppery

cobro m collection; (de cheque) cashing; (pago) payment. **presentar al ∼** cash

coca|ína f cocaine. **∼lero** adj (of) coca farming. ● n coca farmer

cocción f cooking; (Tec) firing

coc|er ❷ & ❾ *vt/i* cook; (*hervir*) boil; (*Tec*) fire. **~ido** *m* stew

coche *m* car, automobile (*Amer*); (*de tren*) coach, carriage; (*de bebé*) pram (*Brit*), baby carriage (*Amer*). **~-cama** sleeper. **~ fúnebre** hearse. **~ restaurante** dining-car. **~s de choque** dodgems. **~ra** *f* garage; (*de autobuses*) depot

cochin|ada *f* dirty thing. **~o** *adj* dirty, filthy. ● *m* pig

cociente *m* quotient. **~ intelectual** intelligence quotient, IQ

cocin|a *f* kitchen; (*arte*) cookery, cuisine; (*aparato*) cooker. **~a de gas** gas cooker. **~a eléctrica** electric cooker. **~ar** *vt/i* cook. **~ero** *m* cook

coco *m* coconut; (*árbol*) coconut palm; (*cabeza*) head; (*que mete miedo*) bogeyman. **comerse el ~** think hard

cocoa *f* (*LAm*) cocoa

cocodrilo *m* crocodile

cocotero *m* coconut palm

cóctel *m* (*pl* **~s** o **~es**) cocktail

cod|azo *m* nudge (with one's elbow). **~ear** *vt/i* elbow, nudge. **~earse** *vpr* rub shoulders (**con** with)

codici|a *f* greed. **~ado** *adj* coveted, sought after. **~ar** *vt* covet. **~oso** *adj* greedy

código *m* code. **~ de la circulación** Highway Code

codo *m* elbow; (*dobladura*) bend. **~ a ~** side by side. **hablar (hasta) por los ~s** talk too much

codorniz *m* quail

coeficiente *m* coefficient. **~ Intelectual** intelligence quotient, IQ

coerción *f* constraint

coetáneo *adj* & *m* contemporary

coexist|encia *f* coexistence. **~ir** *vi* coexist

cofradía *f* brotherhood

cofre *m* chest; (*Mex*, *capó*) bonnet (*Brit*), hood (*Amer*)

coger ⓮ *vt* (*esp Esp*) take; catch (tren, autobús, pelota, catarro); (*agarrar*) take hold of; (*del suelo*) pick up; pick (frutos etc); (*LAm*, *vulgar*) to screw. **~se** *vpr* trap, catch; (*agarrarse*) hold on

cogollo *m* (*de lechuga etc*) heart; (*brote*) bud

cogote *m* nape; (*LAm*, *cuello*) neck

cohech|ar *vt* bribe. **~o** *m* bribery

cohe|rente *adj* coherent. **~sión** *f* cohesion

cohete *m* rocket

cohibi|do *adj* shy; (*inhibido*) awkward; (*incómodo*) awkward. **~r** *vt* inhibit; (*incomodar*) make s.o. feel embarrassed. **~rse** *vpr* feel inhibited

coima *f* (*LAm*) bribe

coincid|encia *f* coincidence. **dar la ~encia** happen. **~ir** *vt* coincide

coje|ar *vt* limp; (*mueble*) wobble. **~ra** *f* lameness

coj|ín *m* cushion. **~inete** *m* small cushion

cojo *adj* lame; (*mueble*) wobbly. ● *m* lame person

col *f* cabbage. **~es de Bruselas** Brussel sprouts

cola *f* tail; (*fila*) queue; (*para pegar*) glue. **a la ~** at the end. **hacer ~** queue (up) (*Brit*), line up (*Amer*)

colabora|ción *f* collaboration. **~dor** *m* collaborator. **~r** *vi* collaborate

colada *f* washing. **hacer la ~** do the washing

colador *m* strainer

colapso *m* collapse; (*fig*) standstill

colar ❷ *vt* strain; pass (moneda falsa etc). ● *vi* (*líquido*) seep through; (*fig*) be believed. **~se** *vpr* slip; (*en una cola*) jump the queue; (*en fiesta*) gatecrash

colch|a *f* bedspread. **~ón** *m* mattress. **~oneta** *f* air bed; (*en gimnasio*) mat

colear *vi* wag its tail; (*asunto*) not be resolved. **vivito y coleando** alive and kicking

colecci|ón *f* collection. **~onar** *vt* collect. **~onista** *m* & *f* collector

colecta *f* collection

colectivo *adj* collective

colega *m* & *f* colleague

colegi|al *m* schoolboy. **~ala** *f* schoolgirl. **~o** *m* school; (*de ciertas profesiones*) college. **~o mayor** hall of residence

cólera *m* cholera. ● *f* anger, fury. **montar en ~** fly into a rage

colérico *adj* furious, irate

colesterol *m* cholesterol

coleta *f* pigtail

colga|nte *adj* hanging. ● *m* pendant. ~**r** 🄴 & 🄸🄴 *vt* hang; hang out (ropa lavada); hang up (abrigo etc); put down (teléfono). ●*vi* hang; (teléfono) hang up. ~**rse** *vpr* hang o.s. **dejar a uno** ~**do** let s.o. down

colibrí *m* hummingbird

cólico *m* colic

coliflor *f* cauliflower

colilla *f* cigarette end

colina *f* hill

colinda|nte *adj* adjoining. ~**r** *vt* border (con on)

colisión *f* collision, crash; (fig) clash

collar *m* necklace; (de perro) collar

colmar *vt* fill to the brim; try (paciencia); (fig) fulfill. ~ **a uno de atenciones** lavish attention on s.o.

colmena *f* beehive, hive

colmillo *m* eye tooth, canine (tooth); (de elefante) tusk; (de carnívoro) fang

colmo *m* height. **ser el** ~ be the limit, be the last straw

coloca|ción *f* positioning; (empleo) job, position. ~**r** 🄷 *vt* put, place; (buscar empleo) find work for. ~**rse** *vpr* find a job

Colombia *f* Colombia

colombiano *adj* & *m* Colombian

colon *m* colon

colón *m* (unidad monetaria de Costa Rica y El Salvador) colon

colon|ia *f* colony; (comunidad) community; (agua de colonia) cologne; (Mex, barrio) residential suburb. ~**ia de verano** holiday camp. ~**iaje** *m* (LAm) colonial period. ~**ial** *adj* colonial. ~**ialista** *m* & *f* colonialist. ~**ización** *f* colonization. ~**izar** 🄸🄾 colonize. ~**o** *m* colonist, settler; (labrador) tenant farmer

coloqui|al *adj* colloquial. ~**o** *m* conversation; (congreso) conference

color *m* colour. **de** ~ colour. **en** ~(**es**) (fotos, película) colour. ~**ado** *adj* (rojo) red. ~**ante** *m* colouring. ~**ear** *vt/i* colour. ~**ete** *m* blusher. ~**ido** *m* colour

colosal *adj* colossal; (fig, fam, magnífico) terrific

columna *f* column; (en anatomía) spine. ~ **vertebral** spinal column; (fig) backbone

columpi|ar *vt* swing. ~**arse** *vpr* swing. ~**o** *m* swing

coma *f* comma; (Mat) point. ● *m* (Med) coma

comadre *f* (madrina) godmother; (amiga) friend. ~**ar** *vi* gossip

comadreja *f* weasel

comadrona *f* midwife

comal *m* (Mex) griddle

comand|ancia *f* command. ~**ante** *m* & *f* commander. ~**o** *m* command; (Mil, soldado) commando; (de terroristas) cell

comarca *f* area, region

comba *f* bend; (juguete) skipping-rope; (de viga) sag. **saltar a la** ~ skip. ~**rse** *vpr* bend; (viga) sag

combat|e *m* combat; (pelea) fight. ~**iente** *m* fighter. ~**ir** *vt/i* fight

combina|ción *f* combination; (enlace) connection; (prenda) slip. ~**r** *vt* combine; put together (colores)

combustible *m* fuel

comedia *f* comedy; (cualquier obra de teatro) play; (LAm, telenovela) soap (opera)

comedi|do *adj* restrained; (LAm, atento) obliging. ~**rse** 🄵 *vpr* show restraint

comedor *m* dining-room; (restaurante) restaurant

comensal *m* fellow diner

comentar *vt* comment on; discuss (tema); (mencionar) mention. ~**io** *m* commentary; (observación) comment. ~**ios** *mpl* gossip. ~**ista** *m* & *f* commentator

comenzar 🄱 & 🄸🄾 *vt/i* begin, start

comer *vt* eat; (a mediodía) have for lunch; (esp LAm, cenar) have for dinner; (corroer) eat away; (en ajedrez) take. ● *vi* eat; (a mediodía) have lunch; (esp LAm, cenar) have dinner. **dar de** ~ a feed. ~**se** *vpr* eat (up)

comerci|al *adj* commercial; (ruta) trade; (nombre, trato) business. ●*m* (LAm) commercial, ad. ~**ante** *m* trader; (*de tienda*) shopkeeper. **~ar** *vi* trade (**con** with, **en** in); (*con otra persona*) do business. **~o** *m* commerce; (*actividad*) trade; (*tienda*) shop; (*negocios*) business. **~o justo** fair trade

comestible *adj* edible. **~s** *mpl* food. **tienda de ~s** grocer's (shop) (*Brit*), grocery (*Amer*)

cometa *m* comet. ● *f* kite

comet|er *vt* commit; make (falta). **~ido** *m* task

comezón *m* itch

comicios *mpl* elections

cómico *adj* comic; (*gracioso*) funny. ● *m* comic actor; (*humorista*) comedian

comida *f* food; (*a mediodía*) lunch; (*esp LAm, cena*) dinner; (*acto*) meal

comidilla *f.* **ser la ~ del pueblo** be the talk of the town

comienzo *m* beginning, start

comillas *fpl* inverted commas

comil|ón *adj* greedy. **~ona** *f* feast

comino *m* cumin. **(no) me importa un ~** I couldn't care less

comisar|ía *f* police station. **~io** *m* commissioner; (*deportes*) steward

comisión *f* assignment; (*organismo*) commission, committee; (*Com*) commission

comisura *f* corner. **~ de los labios** corner of the mouth

comité *m* committee

como *prep* as; (*comparación*) like. ● *adv* about. ● *conj* as. **~ quieras** as you like. **~ si** as if

---
cómo adverbio

····▸ how. **¿~ se llega?** how do you get there? **¿~ es de alto?** how tall is it? **sé ~ pasó** I know how it happened

! Cuando **cómo** va seguido del verbo **llamar** se traduce por *what*, p. ej. **¿~ te llamas?** *what's your name?*

····▸ **cómo** + *ser* (*sugiriendo descripción*) **¿~ es su marido?** what's her husband like?; (*físicamente*) what does her husband look like? **no sé ~ es la comida** I don't
---

know what the food's like

····▸ (*por qué*) why. **¿~ no actuaron antes?** why didn't they act sooner?

····▸ (*pidiendo que se repita*) sorry?, pardon? **¿~? no te escuché** sorry? I didn't hear you

····▸ (*en exclamaciones*) **¡~ llueve!** it's really pouring! **¡~! ¿que no lo sabes?** what! you mean you don't know? **¡~ no!** of course!

cómoda *f* chest of drawers

comodidad *f* comfort. **a su ~** at your convenience

cómodo *adj* comfortable; (*conveniente*) convenient

comoquiera *conj.* **~ que sea** however it may be

compacto *adj* compact; (*denso*) dense; (líneas etc) close

compadecer 11 *vt* feel sorry for. **~se** *vpr.* **~se de** feel sorry for

compadre *m* godfather; (*amigo*) friend

compañ|ero *m* companion; (*de trabajo*) colleague; (*de clase*) classmate; (*pareja*) partner. **~ía** *f* company. **en ~ía de** with

compara|ble *adj* comparable. **~ción** *f* comparison. **~r** *vt* compare. **~tivo** *adj & m* comparative

comparecer 11 *vi* appear

comparsa *f* group. ● *m & f* (*en el teatro*) extra

compartim(i)ento *m* compartment

compartir *vt* share

compás *m* (*instrumento*) (pair of) compasses; (*ritmo*) rhythm; (*división*) bar (*Brit*), measure (*Amer*); (*Naut*) compass. **a ~** in time

compasi|ón *f* compassion, pity. **tener ~ón de** feel sorry for. **~vo** *adj* compassionate

compatib|ilidad *f* compatibility. **~le** *adj* compatible

compatriota *m & f* compatriot

compendio *m* summary

compensa|ción *f* compensation. **~ción por despido** redundancy payment. **~r** *vt* compensate

competen|cia f competition; (*capacidad*) competence; (*poder*) authority; (*incumbencia*) jurisdiction. **~te** *adj* competent

competi|ción f competition. **~dor** m competitor. **~r 5** vi compete

compinche m accomplice; (*fam, amigo*) friend, mate 🞂

complac|er 32 vt please. **~erse** vpr be pleased. **~iente** *adj* obliging; (*marido*) complaisant

complej|idad f complexity. **~o** *adj* & m complex

complement|ario *adj* complementary. **~o** m complement; (*Gram*) object, complement

complet|ar vt complete. **~o** *adj* complete; (*lleno*) full; (*exhaustivo*) comprehensive

complexión f build

complica|ción f complication; (*esp AmL, implicación*) involvement. **~r 7** vt complicate; involve (persona). **~rse** vpr become complicated; (*implicarse*) get involved

cómplice m & f accomplice

complot m (*pl* **~s**) plot

compon|ente *adj* component. ● m component; (*miembro*) member. **~er 34** vt make up; (*Mus, Literatura etc*) write, compose; (*esp LAm, reparar*) mend; (*LAm*) set (hueso); settle (estómago). **~erse** vpr be made up; (*arreglarse*) get better. **~érselas** manage

comporta|miento m behaviour. **~rse** vpr behave. **~rse mal** misbehave

composi|ción f composition. **~tor** m composer

compostura f composure; (*LAm, arreglo*) repair

compota f stewed fruit

compra f purchase. **~ a plazos** hire purchase. **hacer la(s) ~(s)** do the shopping. **ir de ~s** go shopping. **~dor** m buyer. **~r** vt buy. **~venta** f buying and selling; (*Jurid*) sale and purchase contract. **negocio** m **de ~venta** second-hand shop

compren|der vt understand; (*incluir*) include. **~sión** f understanding. **~sivo** *adj* understanding

compresa f compress; (*de mujer*) sanitary towel

compr|esión f compression. **~imido** *adj* compressed. ● m pill, tablet. **~imir** vt compress

comproba|nte m proof; (*recibo*) receipt. **~r** vt check; (*demostrar*) prove

comprom|eter vt compromise; (*arriesgar*) jeopardize. **~eterse** vpr compromise o.s.; (*obligarse*) agree to; (*novios*) get engaged. **~etido** *adj* (*situación*) awkward, delicate; (*autor*) politically committed. **~iso** m obligation; (*apuro*) predicament; (*cita*) appointment; (*acuerdo*) agreement. **sin ~iso** without obligation

compuesto *adj* compound; (*persona*) smart. ● m compound

computa|ción f (*esp LAm*) computing. **curso** m **de ~ción** computer course. **~dor** m, **computadora** f computer. **~r** vt calculate. **~rizar, computerizar 10** vt computerize

cómputo m calculation

comulgar 12 vi take Communion

común *adj* common; (*compartido*) joint. **en ~** in common. **por lo ~** generally. ● m **el ~ de** most

comunal *adj* communal

comunica|ción f communication. **~do** m communiqué. **~do de prensa** press release. **~r 7** vt communicate; (*informar*) inform; (*LAm, por teléfono*) put through. **está ~ndo** (*teléfono*) it's engaged. **~rse** vpr communicate; (*ponerse en contacto*) get in touch. **~tivo** *adj* communicative

comunidad f community. **~ de vecinos** residents' association. **C~ (Económica) Europea** European (Economic) Community. **en ~** together

---

Comunidad Autónoma In 1978 Spain was divided into *comunidades autónomas* or *autonomías*, which have far greater powers than the old *regiones*. The *comunidades autónomas* are: Andalusia, Aragon, Asturias, Balearic Islands, the Basque Country, Canary Islands, Cantabria, Castilla y León, Castilla-La Mancha, Catalonia,

Extremadura, Galicia, Madrid, Murcia, Navarre, La Rioja, Valencia and the North African enclaves of Ceuta and Melilla.

comunión f communion; (*Relig*) (Holy) Communion

comunis|mo m communism. **~ta** adj & m & f communist

con prep with; (+ *infinitivo*) by. **~ decir la verdad** by telling the truth. **~ que** so. **~ tal que** as long as

concebir 5 vt/i conceive

conceder vt concede, grant; award (*premio*); (*admitir*) admit

concej|al m councillor. **~ero** m (*LAm*) councillor. **~o** m council

concentra|ción f concentration; (*Pol*) rally. **~r** vt concentrate; assemble (*personas*). **~rse** vpr concentrate

concep|ción f conception. **~to** m concept; (*opinión*) opinion. **bajo ningún ~to** in no way

concerniente adj. **en lo ~ a** with regard to

concertar 1 vt arrange; agree (upon) (*plan*)

concesión f concession

concha f shell; (*carey*) tortoiseshell

conciencia f conscience; (*conocimiento*) awareness. **~ limpia** clear conscience. **~ sucia** guilty conscience. **a ~ de que** fully aware that. **en ~** honestly. **tener ~ de** be aware of. **tomar ~ de** become aware of. **~r** vt make aware. **~rse** vpr become aware

concientizar 10 vt (*esp LAm*) make aware. **~se** vpr become aware

concienzudo adj conscientious

concierto m concert; (*acuerdo*) agreement; (*Mus, composición*) concerto

concilia|ción f reconciliation. **~r** vt reconcile. **~r el sueño** get to sleep. **~rse** vpr gain

concilio m council

conciso m concise

conclu|ir 17 vt finish; (*deducir*) conclude. ● vi finish, end. **~sión** f conclusion. **~yente** adj conclusive

concord|ancia f agreement. **~ar** 2 vt reconcile. ● vi agree. **~e** adj in

agreement. **~ia** f harmony

concret|amente adv specifically, to be exact. **~ar** vt make specific. **~arse** vpr become definite; (*limitarse*) confine o.s. **~o** adj concrete; (*determinado*) specific, particular. **en ~o** definite; (*concretamente*) to be exact; (*en resumen*) in short. ● m (*LAm*, *hormigón*) concrete

concurr|encia f concurrence; (*reunión*) audience. **~ido** adj crowded, busy. **~ir** vi meet; ; (*coincidir*) agree. **~ a** (*asistir a*) attend

concurs|ante m & f competitor, contestant. **~ar** vi compete, take part. **~o** m competition; (*ayuda*) help

cond|ado m county. **~e** m earl, count

condena f sentence. **~ción** f condemnation. **~do** m convicted person. **~r** vt condemn; (*Jurid*) convict

condensa|ción f condensation. **~r** vt condense

condesa f countess

condescende|ncia f condescension; (*tolerancia*) indulgence. **~r** 1 vi agree; (*dignarse*) condescend

condici|ón f condition. **a ~ón de (que)** on condition that. **~onal** adj conditional. **~onar** vt condition

condiment|ar vt season. **~o** m seasoning

condolencia f condolence

condominio m joint ownership; (*LAm*, *edificio*) block of flats (*Brit*), condominium (*esp Amer*)

condón m condom

condonar vt (*perdonar*) reprieve; cancel (*deuda*)

conducir 47 vt drive (*vehículo*); carry (*electricidad, gas, agua*). ● vi drive; (*fig, llevar*) lead. **¿a qué conduce?** what's the point? **~se** vpr behave

conducta f behaviour

conducto m pipe, tube; (*en anatomía*) duct. **por ~ de** through. **~r** m driver; (*jefe*) leader; (*Elec*) conductor

conduzco vb véase **CONDUCIR**

conectar vt/i connect

conejo m rabbit

conexión f connection

confabularse vpr plot

confecci|ón f (de trajes) tailoring; (de vestidos) dressmaking. **~ones** fpl clothing, clothes. **de ~ón** ready-to-wear. **~onar** vt make

confederación f confederation

conferencia f conference; (al teléfono) long-distance call; (Univ) lecture. **~ en la cima, ~ (en la) cumbre** summit conference. **~nte** m & f lecturer

conferir ❹ vt confer; award (premio)

confes|ar ❶ vt/i confess. **~arse** vpr confess. **~ión** f confession. **~ionario** m confessional. **~or** m confessor

confeti m confetti

confia|do adj trusting; (seguro de sí mismo) confident. **~nza** f trust; (en sí mismo) confidence; (intimidad) familiarity. **~r** ⑳ vt entrust. ● vi. **~r en** trust

confiden|cia f confidence, secret. **~cial** adj confidential. **~te** m confidant. ● f confidante

configur|ación f configuration. **~ar** vt to configure

conf|ín m border. **~ines** mpl outermost parts. **~inar** vt confine; (desterrar) banish

confirma|ción f confirmation. **~r** vt confirm

confiscar ❼ vt confiscate

confit|ería f sweet-shop (Brit), candy store (Amer). **~ura** f jam

conflict|ivo adj difficult; (época) troubled; (polémico) controversial. **~o** m conflict

confluencia f confluence

conform|ación f conformation, shape. **~ar** vt (acomodar) adjust. ● vi agree. **~arse** vpr conform. **~e** adj in agreement;(contento) happy, satisfied; (según) according (con to). **~e a** in accordance with, according to. ● conj as. ● int OK!. **~idad** f agreement; (tolerancia) resignation. **~ista** m & f conformist

conforta|ble adj comfortable. **~nte** adj comforting. **~r** vt comfort

confronta|ción f confrontation. **~r** vt confront

confu|ndir vt (equivocar) mistake, confuse; (mezclar) mix up, confuse; (turbar) embarrass. **~ndirse** vpr become confused; (equivocarse) make a

mistake. **~sión** f confusion; (vergüenza) embarrassment. **~so** adj confused; (borroso) blurred

congela|do adj frozen. **~dor** m freezer. **~r** vt freeze

congeniar vi get on

congesti|ón f congestion. **~onado** adj congested. **~onarse** vpr become congested

congoja f distress; (pena) grief

congraciarse vpr ingratiate o.s.

congratular vt congratulate

congrega|ción f gathering; (Relig) congregation. **~rse** ⑫ vpr gather, assemble

congres|ista m & f delegate, member of a congress. **~o** m congress, conference. **C~o** Parliament. **C~o de los Diputados** Chamber of Deputies

cónico adj conical

conífer|a f conifer. **~o** adj coniferous

conjetura f conjecture, guess. **~r** vt conjecture, guess

conjuga|ción f conjugation. **~r** ⑫ vt conjugate

conjunción f conjunction

conjunto adj joint. ● m collection; (Mus) band; (ropa) suit, outfit. **en ~** altogether

conjurar vt exorcise; avert (peligro). ● vi plot, conspire

conllevar vt to entail

conmemora|ción f commemoration. **~r** vt commemorate

conmigo pron with me

conmo|ción f shock; (tumulto) upheaval. **~ cerebral** concussion. **~cionar** vt shock. **~ver** ❷ vt shake; (emocionar) move

conmuta|dor m switch; (LAm, de teléfonos) switchboard. **~r** vt exchange

connota|ción f connotation. **~do** adj (LAm, destacado) distinguished. **~r** vt connote

cono m cone

conoc|edor adj & m expert. **~er** ⓫ vt know; (por primera vez) meet; (reconocer) recognize, know. **se conoce que** apparently. **dar a ~er** make known. **~erse** vpr know o.s.; (dos personas) know each other; (notarse) be obvious. **~ido** adj well-known. ● m acquaintance. **~imiento** m knowledge; (*sentido*) consciousness. **sin ~imiento** unconscious. **tener ~imiento de** know about

conozco vb véase **CONOCER**

conque conj so

conquista f conquest. **~dor** adj conquering. ● m conqueror; (*de América*) conquistador. **~r** vt conquer, win

consabido adj usual, habitual

> **Conquistadores** The collective term for the succession of explorers, soldiers and adventurers who, from the sixteenth century onward led the settlement and exploitation of Spain's Latin American colonies.

consagra|ción f consecration. **~r** vt consecrate; (*fig*) devote. **~rse** vpr devote o.s.

consanguíneo m blood relation

consciente adj conscious

consecuen|cia f consequence; (*coherencia*) consistency. **a ~cia de** as a result of. **~te** adj consistent

consecutivo adj consecutive

conseguir 5 & 13 vt get, obtain; (*lograr*) manage; achieve (*objetivo*)

consej|ero m adviser; (*miembro de consejo*) member. **~o** m piece of advice; (*Pol*) council. **~o de ministros** cabinet

consenso m assent, consent

consenti|do adj (*niño*) spoilt. **~miento** m consent. **~r** 4 vt allow; spoil (*niño*). ● vi consent

conserje m porter, caretaker. **~ría** f porter's office

conserva f (*mermelada*) preserve; (*en lata*) tinned food. **en ~** tinned (*Brit*), canned. **~ción** f conservation; (*de alimentos*) preservation

conservador adj & m (*Pol*) conservative

conservar vt keep; preserve (*alimentos*). **~se** vpr keep; (*costumbre*) survive

conservatorio m conservatory

considera|ble adj considerable. **~ción** f consideration; (*respeto*) respect. **de ~ción** serious. **de mi**

~ción (*LAm, en cartas*) Dear Sir. **~do** adj considerate; (*respetado*) respected. **~r** vt consider; (*respetar*) respect

consigna f order; (*para equipaje*) left luggage office (*Brit*), baggage room (*Amer*); (*eslogan*) slogan

consigo pron (*él*) with him; (*ella*) with her; (*Ud, Uds*) with you; (*uno mismo*) with o.s.

consiguiente adj consequent. **por ~** consequently

consist|encia f consistency. **~ente** adj consisting (*en* of); (*firme*) solid; (*LAm, congruente*) consistent. **~ir** vi. **~ en** consist of; (*radicar en*) be due to

consola|ción f consolation. **~r** 2 vt console, comfort. **~rse** vpr console o.s.

consolidar vt consolidate. **~se** vpr consolidate

consomé m clear soup, consommé

consonante adj consonant. ● f consonant

consorcio m consortium

conspira|ción f conspiracy. **~dor** m conspirator. **~r** vi conspire

consta|ncia f constancy; (*prueba*) proof; (*LAm, documento*) written evidence. **~nte** adj constant. **~r** vi be clear; (*figurar*) appear, figure; (*componerse*) consist. **hacer ~r** state; (*por escrito*) put on record. **me ~ que** I'm sure that. **que conste que** believe me

constatar vt check; (*confirmar*) confirm

constipa|do m cold. ● adj. **estar ~do** have a cold; (*LAm, estreñido*) be constipated. **~rse** vpr catch a cold

constitu|ción f constitution; (*establecimiento*) setting up. **~cional** adj constitutional. **~ir** 17 vt constitute; (*formar*) form; (*crear*) set up, establish. **~irse** vpr set o.s. up (*en* as). **~tivo** adj, **~yente** adj constituent

constru|cción f construction. **~ctor** m builder. **~ir** 17 vt construct; build (*edificio*)

consuelo m consolation

consuetudinario adj customary

cónsul m & f consul

consulado m consulate

consult|a f consultation. **horas** fpl de **~a** surgery hours. **obra** f de **~a** reference book. **~ar** vt consult. **~orio** m surgery

consumar vt complete; commit (crimen); carry out (robo); consummate (matrimonio)

consum|ición f consumption; (bebida) drink; (comida) food. **~ición mínima** minimum charge. **~ido** adj (persona) skinny, wasted. **~idor** m consumer. **~ir** vt consume. **~irse** vpr (persona) waste away; (vela, cigarillo) burn down; (líquido) dry up. **~ismo** m consumerism. **~o** m consumption; (LAm, en restaurante etc) (bebida) drink; (comida) food. **~o mínimo** minimum charge

contab|ilidad f book-keeping; (profesión) accountancy. **~le** m & f accountant

contacto m contact. **ponerse en ~ con** get in touch with

conta|do adj. **al ~** cash. **~s** adj pl few. **tiene los días ~s** his days are numbered. **~dor** m meter; (LAm, persona) accountant

contagi|ar vt infect (persona); pass on (enfermedad); (fig) contaminate. **~o** m infection; (directo) contagion. **~oso** adj infectious; (por contacto directo) contagious

contamina|ción f contamination, pollution. **~r** vt contaminate, pollute

contante adj. **dinero** m **~** cash

contar 2 vt count; tell (relato). **se cuenta que** it's said that. ● vi count. **~ con** rely on, count on. **~se** vpr be included (entre among)

contempla|ción f contemplation. **sin ~ciones** unceremoniously. **~r** vt look at; (fig) contemplate

contemporáneo adj & m contemporary

conten|er 40 vt contain; hold (respiración). **~erse** vpr contain o.s. **~ido** adj contained. ● m contents

content|ar vt please. **~arse** vpr. **~arse con** be satisfied with, be pleased with. **~o** adj (alegre) happy; (satisfecho) pleased

contesta|ción f answer. **~dor** m. **~ automático** answering machine. **~r** vt/i answer; (replicar) answer back

contexto m context

contienda f conflict; (lucha) contest

contigo pron with you

contiguo adj adjacent

continen|tal adj continental. **~te** m continent

continu|ación f continuation. **a ~ación** immediately after. **~ar** 21 vt continue, resume. ● vi continue. **~idad** f continuity. **~o** adj continuous; (frecuente) continual. **corriente** f **~a** direct current

contorno m outline; (de árbol) girth; (de caderas) measurement. **~s** mpl surrounding area

contorsión f contortion

contra prep against. **en ~** against. ● m cons. ● f snag. **llevar la ~** contradict

contraata|car 7 vt/i counter-attack. **~que** m counter-attack

contrabaj|ista m & f double-bass player. **~o** m double-bass; (persona) double-bass player

contraband|ista m & f smuggler. **~o** m contraband

contracción f contraction

contrad|ecir 46 vt contradict. **~icción** f contradiction. **~ictorio** adj contradictory

contraer 41 vt contract. **~ matrimonio** marry. **~se** vpr contract

contralto m counter tenor. ● f contralto

contra|mano. a ~ in the wrong direction. **~partida** f compensation. **~pelo. a ~** the wrong way

contrapes|ar vt counterweight. **~o** m counterweight

contraproducente adj counterproductive

contrari|a f. **llevar la ~a** contradict. **~ado** adj upset; (enojado) annoyed. **~ar** 20 vt upset; (enojar) annoy. **~edad** f setback; (disgusto) annoyance. **~o** adj contrary (a to); (dirección) opposite. **al ~o** on the contrary. **al ~o de** contrary to. **de lo ~o** otherwise. **por el ~o** on the contrary. **ser** ～**o a** be opposed to, be against

contrarrestar vt counteract

contrasentido m contradiction

contraseña f (palabra) password; (en cine) stub

contrast|ar vt check, verify. ● vi contrast. ～**e** m contrast; (en oro, plata) hallmark

contratar vt contract (servicio); hire, take on (empleados); sign up (jugador)

contratiempo m setback; (accidente) mishap

contrat|ista m & f contractor. ～**o** m contract

contraven|ción f contravention. ～**ir** 53 vt contravene

contraventana f shutter

contribu|ción f contribution; (tributo) tax. ～**ir** 17 vt/i contribute. ～**yente** m & f contributor; (que paga impuestos) taxpayer

contrincante m rival, opponent

control m control; (vigilancia) check; (lugar) checkpoint. ～**ar** vt control; (vigilar) check. ～**arse** vpr control s.o.

controversia f controversy

contundente adj (arma) blunt; (argumento) convincing

contusión f bruise

convalec|encia f convalescence. ～**er** 11 vi convalesce. ～**iento** adj & m & f convalescent

convalidar vt recognize (título)

convenc|er 9 vt convince. ～**imiento** m conviction

convenci|ón f convention. ～**onal** adj conventional

conveni|encia f convenience; (aptitud) suitability. ～**ente** adj suitable; (aconsejable) advisable; (provechoso) useful. ～**o** m agreement. ～**r** 53 vt agree. ● vi agree (**en** on); (ser conveniente) be convenient for, suit; (ser aconsejable) be advisable

convento m (de monjes) monastery; (de monjas) convent

conversa|ción f conversation. ～**ciones** fpl talks. ～**r** vi converse, talk

conver|sión f conversion. ～**so** adj converted. ● m convert. ～**tible** adj

convertible. ● m (LAm) convertible. ～**tir** 4 vt convert. ～**tirse** vpr. ～**tirse en** turn into; (Relig) convert

convic|ción f conviction. ～**to** adj convicted

convida|do m guest. ～**r** vt invite

convincente adj convincing

conviv|encia f coexistence; (de parejas) life together. ～**ir** vi live together; (coexistir) coexist

convocar 7 vt call (huelga, elecciones); convene (reunión); summon (personas)

convulsión f convulsion

conyugal adj marital, conjugal; (vida) married

cónyuge m spouse. ～**s** mpl married couple

coñac m (pl ～s) brandy

coopera|ción f cooperation. ～**r** vi cooperate. ～**nte** m & f voluntary aid worker. ～**tiva** f cooperative. ～**tivo** adj cooperative

coordinar vt coordinate

copa f glass; (deportes, fig) cup; (de árbol) top. ～**s** fpl (naipes) hearts. **tomar una** ～ have a drink

copia f copy. ～ **en limpio** fair copy. **sacar una** ～ make a copy. ～**r** vt copy

copioso adj copious; (lluvia, nevada etc) heavy

copla f verse; (canción) folksong

copo m flake. ～ **de nieve** snowflake. ～**s de maíz** cornflakes

coquet|a f flirt; (mueble) dressing-table. ～**ear** vi flirt. ～**o** adj flirtatious

coraje m courage; (rabia) anger

coral adj choral. ● m coral; (Mus) chorale

coraza f cuirass; (Naut) armour-plating; (de tortuga) shell

coraz|ón m heart; (persona) darling. **sin** ～**ón** heartless. **tener buen** ～**ón** be good-hearted. ～**onada** f hunch; (impulso) impulse

corbata f tie, necktie (esp Amer). ～ **de lazo** bow tie

corche|a f quaver. ～**te** m fastener, hook and eye; (gancho) hook; (paréntesis) square bracket

corcho _m_ cork. **~lata** _f_ (Mex) (crown) cap

corcova _f_ hump

cordel _m_ cord, string

cordero _m_ lamb

cordial _adj_ cordial, friendly. ● _m_ tonic. **~idad** _f_ cordiality, warmth

cordillera _f_ mountain range

córdoba _m_ (_unidad monetaria de Nicaragua_) córdoba

cordón _m_ string; (_de zapatos_) lace; (_cable_) cord; (_fig_) cordon. **~ umbilical** umbilical cord

coreografía _f_ choreography

corista _f_ (_bailarina_) chorus girl

cornet|a _f_ bugle; (_Mex, de coche_) horn. **~ín** _m_ cornet

coro _m_ (_Mus_) choir; (_en teatro_) chorus

corona _f_ crown; (_de flores_) wreath, garland. **~ción** _f_ coronation. **~r** _vt_ crown

coronel _m_ colonel

coronilla _f_ crown. **estar hasta la ~** be fed up

corpora|ción _f_ corporation. **~l** _adj_ (_castigo_) corporal; (_trabajo_) physical

corpulento _adj_ stout

corral _m_ farmyard. **aves** _fpl_ **de ~** poultry

correa _f_ strap; (_de perro_) lead; (_cinturón_) belt

correc|ción _f_ correction; (_cortesía_) good manners. **~to** _adj_ correct; (_cortés_) polite

corrector ortográfico _m_ spell checker

corre|dizo _adj_ running. **nudo** _m_ **~dizo** slip knot. **puerta** _f_ **~diza** sliding door. **~dor** _m_ runner; (_pasillo_) corridor; (_agente_) agent, broker. **~dor de coches** racing driver

corregir 5 & 14 _vt_ correct

correlación _f_ correlation

correo _m_ post, mail; (_persona_) courier; (_LAm, oficina_) post office. **~s** _mpl_ post office. **~ electrónico** e-mail. **echar al ~** post

correr _vt_ run; (_mover_) move; draw (cortinas). ● _vi_ run; (_agua, electricidad etc_) flow; (_tiempo_) pass. **~se** _vpr_ (_apartarse_) move along; (colores) run

correspond|encia _f_ correspondence. **~er** _vi_ correspond; (_ser adecuado_) be fitting; (_contestar_) reply; (_pertenecer_) belong; (_incumbir_) fall to. **~erse** _vpr_ (_amarse_) love one another. **~iente** _adj_ corresponding

corresponsal _m_ correspondent

corrid|a _f_ run. **~a de toros** bullfight. **de ~a** from memory. **~o** _adj_ (_continuo_) continuous

corriente _adj_ (agua) running; (monedas, publicación, cuenta, año) current; (_ordinario_) ordinary. ● _f_ current; (_de aire_) draught; (_fig_) tendency. ● _m_ current month. **al ~** (_al día_) up-to-date; (_enterado_) aware

corr|illo _m_ small group. **~o** _m_ circle

corroborar _vt_ corroborate

corroer 24 & 37 _vt_ corrode; (_en geología_) erode; (_fig_) eat away

corromper _vt_ corrupt, rot (materia). **~se** _vpr_ become corrupted; (materia) rot; (alimentos) go bad

corrosi|ón _f_ corrosion. **~vo** _adj_ corrosive

corrupción _f_ corruption; (_de materia etc_) rot

corsé _m_ corset

corta|do _adj_ cut; (carretera) closed; (leche) curdled; (_avergonzado_) embarrassed; (_confuso_) confused. ● _m_ coffee with a little milk. **~dura** _f_ cut. **~nte** _adj_ sharp; (viento) biting; (frío) bitter. **~r** _vt_ cut; (_recortar_) cut out; (_aislar, separar, interrumpir_) cut off. ● _vi_ cut; (novios) break up. **~rse** _vpr_ cut o.s.; (leche etc) curdle; (_fig_) be embarrassed. **~rse el pelo** have one's hair cut. **~rse las uñas** cut one's nails. **~uñas** _m invar_ nail-clippers

corte _m_ cut; (_de tela_) length. **~ de luz** power cut. **~ y confección** dressmaking. ● _f_ court; (_LAm, tribunal_) Court of Appeal. **hacer la ~** court. **las C~s** the Spanish parliament. **la C~ Suprema** the Supreme Court

cortej|ar _vt_ court. **~o** _m_ (_de rey etc_) entourage. **~o fúnebre** cortège, funeral procession

cortés _adj_ polite

cortesía _f_ courtesy

corteza _f_ bark; (_de queso_) rind; (_de pan_) crust

cortijo *m* farm; (*casa*) farmhouse

cortina *f* curtain

corto *adj* short; (*apocado*) shy. ~ **de** short of. ~ **de alcances** dim, thick. ~ **de vista** short-sighted. **a la corta o a la larga** sooner or later. **quedarse** ~ fall short; (*subestimar*) underestimate. ~**circuito** *m* short circuit.

Coruña *f*. **La** ~ Corunna

cosa *f* thing; (*asunto*) business; (*idea*) idea. **como si tal** ~ just like that; (*como si no hubiera pasado nada*) as if nothing had happened. **decirle a uno cuatro** ~**s** tell s.o. a thing or two

cosecha *f* harvest; (*de vino*) vintage. ~**r** *vt* harvest

coser *vt* sew; sew on (*botón*); stitch (*herida*). ● *vi* sew. ~**se** *vpr* stick to s.o.

cosmético *adj* & *m* cosmetic

cósmico *adj* cosmic

cosmo|polita *adj* & *m* & *f* cosmopolitan. ~**s** *m* cosmos

cosquillas *fpl*. **dar** ~ tickle. **hacer** ~ tickle. **tener** ~ be ticklish

costa *f* coast. **a** ~ **de** at the expense of. **a toda** ~ at any cost

costado *m* side

costal *m* sack

costar ⊇ *vt* cost. ● *vi* cost; (*resultar difícil*) to be hard. ~ **caro** be expensive. **cueste lo que cueste** at any cost

costarricense *adj* & *m*, **costarriqueño** *adj* & *m* Costa Rican

cost|as *fpl* (*Jurid*) costs. ~**e** *m* cost. ~**ear** *vt* pay for; (*Naut*) sail along the coast

costero *adj* coastal

costilla *f* rib; (*chuleta*) chop

costo *m* cost. ~**so** *adj* expensive

costumbre *f* custom; (*de persona*) habit. **de** ~ usual; (*como adv*) usually

costur|a *f* sewing; (*línea*) seam; (*confección*) dressmaking. ~**era** *f* dressmaker. ~**ero** *m* sewing box

cotejar *vt* compare

cotidiano *adj* daily

cotille|ar *vt* gossip. ~**o** *m* gossip

cotiza|ción *f* quotation, price. ~**r** 🔟 *vt* (*en la bolsa*) quote. ● *vi* pay contri-

butions. ~**rse** *vpr* fetch; (*en la bolsa*) stand at; (*fig*) be valued

coto *m* enclosure; (*de caza*) preserve. ~ **de caza** game preserve

cotorr|a *f* parrot; (*fig*) chatterbox. ~**ear** *vi* chatter

coyuntura *f* joint

coz *f* kick

cráneo *m* skull

cráter *m* crater

crea|ción *f* creation. ~**dor** *adj* creative. ● *m* creator. ~**r** *vt* create

crec|er 🔢 *vi* grow; (*aumentar*) increase; (*río*) rise. ~**ida** *f* (*de río*) flood. ~**ido** *adj* (*persona*) grown-up; (*número*) large, considerable; (*plantas*) fully-grown. ~**iente** *adj* growing; (*luna*) crescent. ~**imiento** *m* growth

credencial *f* document. ● *adj*. **cartas** *fpl* ~**es** credentials

credibilidad *f* credibility

crédito *m* credit; (*préstamo*) loan. **digno de** ~ reliable

credo *m* creed

crédulo *adj* credulous

cre|encia *f* belief. ~**er** 🔢 *vt/i* believe; (*pensar*) think. ~**o que no** I don't think so, I think not. ~**o que sí** I think so. **no** ~**o** I don't think so. **¡ya lo** ~**o!** I should think so!. ~**erse** *vpr* consider o.s. **no me lo** ~**o** I don't believe it. ~**íble** *adj* credible

crema *f* cream; (*Culin*) custard; (*LAm, de la leche*) cream. ~ **batida** (*LAm*) whipped cream. ~ **bronceadora** suntan cream

cremallera *f* zip (*Brit*), zipper (*Amer*)

crematorio *m* crematorium

crepitar *vi* crackle

crepúsculo *m* twilight

crespo *adj* frizzy; (*LAm, rizado*) curly. ● *m* (*LAm*) curl

cresta *f* crest; (*de gallo*) comb

creyente *m* believer

cría *f* breeding; (*animal*) baby animal. **las** ~**s** the young

cria|da *f* maid, servant. ~**dero** *m* (*de pollos etc*) farm; (*de ostras*) bed; (*de plantas*) nursery. ● *m* servant. ~**dor** *m* breeder. ~**nza** *f* breeding. ~**r** 🔢 *vt* suckle; grow (*plantas*); breed (*animales*); (*educar*) bring up (*Brit*), raise (*esp*

Amer). ~**rse** *vpr* grow up

criatura *f* creature; *(niño)* baby

crim|en *m* (serious) crime; *(asesinato)* murder; *(fig)* crime. ~**inal** *adj & m & f* criminal

crin *f* mane

crío *m* child

criollo *adj* Creole; *(LAm, música, comida)* traditional. ● *m* Creole; *(LAm, nativo)* Peruvian, Chilean etc

crisantemo *m* chrysanthemum

crisis *f invar* crisis

crispar *vt* twitch; *(fam, irritar)* annoy. ~**le los nervios a uno** get on s.o.'s nerves

cristal *m* crystal; *(Esp, vidrio)* glass; *(Esp, de una ventana)* pane of glass. **limpiar los** ~**es** *(Esp)* clean the windows. ~**ino** *adj* crystalline; *(fig)* crystal-clear. ~**izar** 🔟 crystallize. ~**izarse** *vpr* crystallize

cristian|dad *f* Christendom. ~**ismo** *m* Christianity. ~**o** *adj* Christian. **ser** ~**o** be a Christian. ● *m* Christian

cristo *m* crucifix

Cristo *m* Christ

criterio *m* criterion; *(discernimiento)* judgement; *(opinión)* opinion

cr|ítica *f* criticism; *(reseña)* review. ~**iticar** 🔼 *vt* criticize. ~**ítico** *adj* critical. ● *m* critic

croar *vi* croak

crom|ado *adj* chromium-plated. ~**o** *m* chromium, chrome

crónic|a *f* chronicle; *(de radio, TV)* report; *(de periódico)* feature. ~ **deportiva** sport section. ~**o** *adj* chronic

cronista *m & f* reporter

crono|grama *m* schedule, timetable. ~**logía** *f* chronology

cron|ometrar *vt* time. ~**ómetro** *m* *(en deportes)* stop-watch

croqueta *f* croquette

cruce *m* crossing; *(de calles, carreteras)* crossroads; *(de peatones)* (pedestrian) crossing

crucial *adj* crucial

crucifi|car 🔼 *vt* crucify. ~**jo** *m* crucifix

crucigrama *m* crossword (puzzle)

crudo *adj* raw; *(fig)* harsh. ● *m* crude (oil)

cruel *adj* cruel. ~**dad** *f* cruelty

cruji|do *m* (de seda, de hojas secas) rustle; *(de muebles)* creak. ~**r** *vi* (seda, hojas secas) rustle; (muebles) creak

cruz *f* cross; *(de moneda)* tails. ~ **gamada** swastika. **la C**~ **Roja** the Red Cross

cruza|da *f* crusade. ~**r** 🔟 *vt* cross; exchange (palabras). ~**rse** *vpr* cross; *(pasar en la calle)* pass each other. ~**rse con** pass

cuaderno *m* exercise book; *(para apuntes)* notebook

cuadra *f* (caballeriza) stable; *(LAm, distancia)* block

cuadrado *adj & m* square

cuadragésimo *adj* fortieth

cuadr|ar *vt* square. ● *vi* suit; *(cuentas)* tally. ~**arse** *vpr* (Mil) stand to attention; *(fig)* dig one's heels in. ~**ilátero** *m* quadrilateral; *(Boxeo)* ring

cuadrilla *f* group; *(pandilla)* gang

cuadro *m* square; *(pintura)* painting; *(Teatro)* scene; *(de números)* table; *(de mando etc)* panel; *(conjunto del personal)* staff. ~ **de distribución** switchboard. **a** ~**s, de** ~**s** check. **¡qué** ~**!, ¡vaya un** ~**!** what a sight!

cuadrúpedo *m* quadruped

cuádruple *adj & m* quadruple

cuajar *vt* congeal (sangre); curdle (leche); *(llenar)* fill up. ● *vi* (nieve) settle; *(fig, fam)* work out. **cuajado de** full of. ~**se** *vpr* coagulate; (sangre) clot; (leche) curdle

cual *pron.* **el** ~**, la** ~ etc *(animales y cosas)* that, which; *(personas, sujeto)* who, that; *(personas, objeto)* whom. ● *adj (LAm, qué)* what. ~ **si** as if. **cada** ~ everyone. **lo** ~ which. **por lo** ~ because of which. **sea** ~ **sea** whatever

cuál *pron* which; *(LAm, qué)* what

cualidad *f* quality

cualquiera *adj (delante de nombres* **cualquier,** *pl* **cualesquiera)** any. ● *pron (pl* **cualesquiera)** anyone, anybody; *(cosas)* whatever, whichever. **un** ~ a nobody. **una** ~ a slut

cuando *adv* when. ● *conj* when; (*si*) if. ~ **más** at the most. ~ **menos** at the least. **aun** ~ even if. **de** ~ **en** ~ from time to time

cuándo *adv & conj* when. ¿**de** ~ **acá?**, ¿**desde** ~? since when? ¡~ **no!** (*LAm*) as usual, typical!

cuant|ía *f* quantity; (*extensión*) extent. ~**ioso** *adj* abundant. ~**o** *adj* as much ... as, as many ... as. ● *pron* as much as, as many as. ● *adv* as much as. ~**o antes** as soon as possible. ~**o más, mejor** the more the merrier. **en** ~**o** as soon as. **en** ~**o a** as for. **por** ~**o** since. **unos** ~**os** a few, some

cuánto *adj* (*interrogativo*) how much?; (*interrogativo en plural*) how many?; (*exclamativo*) what a lot of! ● *pron* how much?; (*en plural*) how many? ● *adv* how much. ¿~ **mides?** how tall are you? ¿~ **tiempo?** how long? ¡~ **tiempo sin verte!** it's been a long time! ¿**a** ~**s estamos?** what's the date today? **un Sr. no sé** ~**s** Mr So-and-So

cuáquero *m* Quaker

cuarent|a *adj & m* forty; (*cuadragésimo*) fortieth. ~**ena** *f* (*Med*) quarantine. ~**ón** *adj* about forty

cuaresma *f* Lent

cuarta *f* (*palmo*) span

cuartel *m* (*Mil*) barracks, ~ **general** headquarters

cuarteto *m* quartet

cuarto *adj* fourth. ● *m* quarter; (*habitación*) room. ~ **de baño** bathroom. ~ **de estar** living room. ~ **de hora** quarter of an hour. **estar sin un** ~ be broke. **y** ~ (a) quarter past

cuarzo *m* quartz

cuate *m* (*Mex*) twin; (*amigo*) friend; (🔲, *tipo*) guy

cuatro *adj & m* four. ~**cientos** *adj & m* four hundred

Cuba *f* Cuba

cuba|libre *m* rum and Coke (P). ~**no** *adj & m* Cuban

cúbico *adj* cubic

cubículo *m* cubicle

cubiert|a *f* cover; (*neumático*) tyre; (*Naut*) deck. ~**o** *adj* covered; (*cielo*) overcast. ● *m* place setting, piece of cutlery; (*en restaurante*) cover charge. **a** ~**o** under cover

cubilete *m* bowl; (*molde*) mould; (*para los dados*) cup

cubis|mo *m* cubism. ~**ta** *adj & m & f* cubist

cubo *m* bucket; (*Mat*) cube

cubrecama *m* bedspread

cubrir (*pp* **cubierto**) *vt* cover; fill (vacante). ~**se** *vpr* cover o.s.; (*ponerse el sombrero*) put on one's hat; (*el cielo*) cloud over, become overcast

cucaracha *f* cockroach

cuchar|a *f* spoon. ~**ada** *f* spoonful. ~**adita** *f* teaspoonful. ~**illa**, ~**ita** *f* teaspoon. ~**ón** *m* ladle

cuchichear *vi* whisper

cuchill|a *f* large knife; (*de carnicero*) cleaver; (*hoja de afeitar*) razor blade. ~**ada** *f* stab; (*herida*) knife wound. ~**o** *m* knife

cuchitril *m* (*fig*) hovel

cuclillas: **en** ~ *adv* squatting

cuco *adj* shrewd; (*mono*) pretty, nice. ● *m* cuckoo

cucurucho *m* cornet

cuello *m* neck; (*de camisa*) collar. **cortar(le) el** ~ **a uno** cut s.o.'s throat

cuenc|a *f* (*del ojo*) (eye) socket; (*de río*) basin. ~**o** *m* hollow; (*vasija*) bowl

cuenta *f* count; (*acción de contar*) counting; (*cálculo*) calculation; (*factura*) bill; (*en banco, relato*) account; (*de collar*) bead. ~ **corriente** current account, checking account (*Amer*). **dar** ~ **de** give an account of. **darse** ~ **de** realize. **en resumidas** ~**s** in short. **por mi propia** ~ on my own account. **tener en** ~ bear in mind

cuentakilómetros *m invar* milometer

cuent|ista *m & f* story-writer; (*de mentiras*) fibber. ~**o** *m* story; (*mentira*) fib, tall story. ~ **de hadas** fairy tale. ● *vb véase* **CONTAR**

cuerda *f* rope; (*más fina*) string; (*Mus*) string. ~ **floja** tightrope. **dar** ~ **a** wind up (un reloj)

cuerdo *adj* (*persona*) sane; (*acción*) sensible

cuerno *m* horn

cuero m leather; (*piel*) skin; (*del grifo*) washer. ~ **cabelludo** scalp. **en ~s (vivos)** stark naked

cuerpo m body

cuervo m crow

cuesta f slope, hill. ~ **abajo** downhill. ~ **arriba** uphill. **a ~s** on one's back

cuestión f matter; (*problema*) problem; (*cosa*) thing

cueva f cave

cuida|do m care; (*preocupación*) worry. **i~do!** watch out!. **tener ~do** be careful. **~doso** adj careful. **~r** vt look after. ● vi. **~r de** look after. **~rse** vpr look after o.s. **~rse de** be careful to

culata f (*de revólver, fusil*) butt. **~zo** m recoil

culebr|a f snake. **~ón** m soap opera

culinario adj culinary

culminar vi culminate

culo m 🔲 bottom; (*LAm vulg*) arse (*Brit vulg*), ass (*Amer vulg*)

culpa f fault. **echar la ~** blame. **por ~ de** because of. **tener la ~** be to blame (de for). **~bilidad** f guilt. **~ble** adj guilty. ● m & f culprit. **~r** vt blame (de for)

cultiv|ar vt farm; grow (plantas); (*fig*) cultivate. **~o** m farming; (*de plantas*) growing

cult|o adj (persona) educated. ● m cult; (*homenaje*) worship. **~ura** f culture. **~ural** adj cultural

culturismo m body-building

cumbre f summit

cumpleaños m invar birthday

cumplido adj perfect; (*cortés*) polite. ● m compliment. **de ~** courtesy. **por ~** out of a sense of duty. **~r** adj reliable

cumpli|miento m fulfilment; (*de ley*) observance; (*de orden*) carrying out. **~r** vt carry out; observe (ley); serve (condena); reach (años); keep (promesa). **hoy cumple 3 años** he's 3 (years old) today. ● vi do one's duty. **por ~r** as a mere formality. **~rse** vpr expire; (*realizarse*) be fulfilled

cuna f cradle; (*fig, nacimiento*) birthplace

cundir vi spread; (*rendir*) go a long way

cuneta f ditch

cuña f wedge

cuñad|a f sister-in-law. **~o** m brother-in-law

cuño m stamp. **de nuevo ~** new

cuota f quota; (*de sociedad etc*) membership, fee; (*LAm, plazo*) instalment; (*Mex, peaje*) toll

cupe vb véase **CABER**

cupo m cuota; (*LAm, capacidad*) room; (*Mex, plaza*) place

cupón m coupon

cúpula f dome

cura f cure; (*tratamiento*) treatment. ● m priest. **~ción** f healing. **~ndero** m faith-healer. **~r** vt (*incl Culin*) cure; dress (herida); (*tratar*) treat; (*fig*) remedy; tan (pieles). **~rse** vpr get better

curios|ear vi pry; (*mirar*) browse. **~idad** f curiosity. **~o** adj curious; (*raro*) odd, unusual ● m onlooker; (*fisgón*) busybody

curita f (*LAm*) (sticking) plaster

curriculum (vitae) m curriculum vitae, CV

cursar vt issue; (*estudiar*) study

cursi adj pretentious, showy

cursillo m short course

cursiva f italics

curso m course; (*Univ etc*) year. **en ~** under way; (año etc) current

cursor m cursor

curtir vt tan; (*fig*) harden. **~se** vpr become tanned; (*fig*) become hardened

curv|a f curve; (*de carretera*) bend. **~ar** vt bend; bow (estante). **~arse** vpr bend; (estante) bow; (madera) warp. **~ilíneo** adj curvilinear; (mujer) curvaceous. **~o** adj curved

cúspide f top; (*fig*) pinnacle

custodi|a f safe-keeping; (*Jurid*) custody. **~ar** vt guard; (*guardar*) look after. **~o** m guardian

cutáneo adj skin

cutis m skin, complexion

cuyo pron (*de persona*) whose, of whom; (*de cosa*) whose, of which. **en ~ caso** in which case

Dd

dactilógrafo m typist

dado m dice. ● adj given. ~ **que** since, given that

daltónico adj colour-blind

dama f lady. ~ **de honor** bridesmaid. ~**s** fpl draughts (Brit), checkers (Amer)

damasco m damask; (LAm, fruta) apricot

danés adj Danish. ● m Dane; (idioma) Danish

danza f dance; (acción) dancing. ~**r** 🔟 vt/i dance

dañ|ar vt damage. ~**se** vpr get damaged. ~**ino** adj harmful. ~**o** m damage; (a una persona) harm. ~**os y perjuicios** damages. **hacer** ~**o a** harm, hurt. **hacerse** ~**o** hurt o.s.

dar 🆖 vt give; bear (frutos); give out (calor); strike (la hora). ● vi give. **da igual** it doesn't matter. **¡dale!** go on! **da lo mismo** it doesn't matter. ~ **a** (ventana) look on to; (edificio) face. ~ **a luz** give birth. ~ **con** meet (persona); find (cosa). **¿qué más da?** it doesn't matter! ~**se** vpr have (baño). **dárselas de** make o.s. out to be. ~**se por** consider o.s.

dardo m dart

datar vi. ~ **de** date from

dátil m date

dato m piece of information. ~**s** mpl data, information. ~**s personales** personal details

---

de preposición

Note that **de** before **el** becomes **del**, e.g. **es del norte**

····▶ (contenido, material) of. **un vaso de agua** a glass of water. **es de madera** it's made of wood (pertenencia) **el coche de Juan** Juan's car. **es de ella** it's hers. **es de María** it's María's. **las llaves del coche** the car keys (procedencia, origen, época) from. **soy de** Madrid I'm from Madrid. **una llamada de Lima** a call from Lima. **es del siglo V** it's from the 5th century (causa, modo) **se murió de cáncer** he died of cancer. **temblar de miedo** to tremble with fear. **de dos en dos** two by two

····▶ (parte del día, hora) **de noche** at night. **de madrugada** early in the morning. **las diez de la mañana** ten (o'clock) in the morning. **de 9 a 12** from 9 to 12

····▶ (en oraciones pasivas) by. **rodeado de agua** surrounded by water. **va seguido de coma** it's followed by a comma. **es de Mozart** it's by Mozart

····▶ (al especificar) **el cajón de arriba** the top drawer. **la clase de inglés** the English lesson. **la chica de verde** the girl in green. **el de debajo** the one underneath

····▶ (en calidad de) as. **trabaja de oficinista** he works as a clerk. **vino de chaperón** he came as a chaperon

····▶ (en comparaciones) than. **pesa más de un kilo** it weighs more than a kilo

····▶ (con superlativo) **el más alto del mundo** the tallest in the world. **el mejor de todos** the best of all

····▶ (sentido condicional) if. **de haberlo sabido** if I had known. **de continuar así** if this goes on

➡️ Cuando la preposición **de** se emplea como parte de expresiones como **de prisa, de acuerdo** etc., y de nombres compuestos como **hombre de negocios, saco de dormir** etc., ver bajo el respectivo nombre

---

deambular vi roam (por about)

debajo adv underneath. ~ **de** under(neath). **el de** ~ the one underneath. **por** ~ underneath. **por** ~ **de** below

debat|e m debate. ~**ir** vt debate

deber vt owe. ● verbo auxiliar have to, must; (en condicional) should. **debo marcharme** I must go, I have to go. ● m duty. **~es** mpl homework. **~se** vpr. **~se a** be due to

debido adj due; (correcto) proper. **~ a** due to. **como es ~** as is proper

débil adj weak; (sonido) faint; (luz) dim

debili|dad f weakness. **~tar** vt weaken. **~tarse** vpr weaken, get weak

débito m debit. **~ bancario** (LAm) direct debit

debut m debut

debutar vi make one's debut

década f decade

deca|dencia f decline. **~dente** adj decadent. **~er 29** vi decline; (debilitarse) weaken. **~ido** adj in low spirits. **~imiento** m decline, weakening

decano m dean; (miembro más antiguo) senior member

decapitar vt behead

decena f ten. **una ~ de** about ten

decencia f decency

decenio m decade

decente adj decent; (decoroso) respectable; (limpio) clean, tidy

decepci|ón f disappointment. **~onar** vt disappoint

decidi|do adj decided; (persona) determined, resolute. **~r** vt decide; settle (cuestión etc). ● vi decide. **~rse** vpr make up one's mind

decimal adj & m decimal

décimo adj & m tenth. ● m (de lotería) tenth part of a lottery ticket

decir 46 vt say; (contar) tell. ● m saying. **~ que no** say no. **~ que sí** say yes. **dicho de otro modo** in other words. **dicho y hecho** no sooner said than done. **¿dígame?** can I help you? **¡dígame!** (al teléfono) hello! **digamos** let's say. **es ~** that is to say. **mejor dicho** rather. **¡no me digas!** you don't say!, really! **por así ~, por ~lo así** so to speak, as it were. **querer ~** mean. **se dice que** it is said that, they say that

decisi|ón f decision. **~vo** adj decisive

declara|ción f declaration; (a autoridad, prensa) statement. **~ción de**

renta income tax return. **~r** vt/i declare. **~rse** vpr declare o.s.; (epidemia etc) break out

declinar vt turn down; (Gram) decline

declive m slope; (fig) decline. **en ~** sloping

decola|je m (LAm) take-off. **~r** vi (LAm) take off

decolorarse vpr become discoloured, fade

decora|ción f decoration. **~do** m (en el teatro) set. **~r** vt decorate. **~tivo** adj decorative

decoro m decorum. **~so** adj decent, respectable

decrépito adj decrepit

decret|ar vt decree. **~o** m decree

dedal m thimble

dedica|ción f dedication. **~r 7** vt dedicate; devote (tiempo). **~rse** vpr. **~rse a** devote o.s. to. **¿a qué se dedica?** what does he do? **~toria** f dedication

dedo m finger; (del pie) toe. **~ anular** ring finger. **~ corazón** middle finger. **~ gordo** thumb; (del pie) big toe. **~ índice** index finger. **~ meñique** little finger. **~ pulgar** thumb

deduc|ción f deduction. **~ir 47** vt deduce; (descontar) deduct

defect|o m fault, defect. **~uoso** adj defective

defen|der 1 vt defend. **~sa** f defence. **~derse** vpr defend o.s. **~sivo** adj defensive. **~sor** m defender. **abogado m ~sor** defence counsel

defeño m (Mex) person from the Federal District

deficien|cia f deficiency. **~cia mental** mental handicap. **~te** adj poor, deficient. ● m & f **~te mental** mentally handicapped person

déficit m invar deficit

defini|ción f definition. **~do** adj defined. **~r** vt define. **~tivo** adj definitive. **en ~tiva** all in all

deform|ación f deformation; (de imagen etc) distortion. **~ar** vt deform; distort (imagen, metal). **~arse** vpr go out of shape. **~e** adj deformed

defraudar vt defraud; (decepcionar) disappoint

defunción f death

degenera|ción f degeneration; (cualidad) degeneracy. ~**do** adj degenerate. ~**r** vi degenerate

degollar 16 vt cut s.o.'s throat

degradar vt degrade; (Mil) demote. ~**se** vpr demean o.s..

degusta|ción f tasting. ~**r** vt taste

dehesa f pasture

deja|dez f slovenliness; (pereza) laziness. ~**do** adj slovenly; (descuidado) slack, negligent. ~**r** vt leave; (abandonar) abandon; give up (estudios); (prestar) lend; (permitir) let. ~**r a un lado** leave aside. ~**r de** stop

dejo m aftertaste, (tonillo) slight accent; (toque) touch

del = de + el

delantal m apron

delante adv in front. ~ **de** in front of. **de** ~ front. ~**ra** f front; (de teatro etc) front row; (ventaja) lead; (de equipo) forward line. **llevar la** ~**ra** be in the lead. ~**ro** adj front. ● m forward

delat|ar vt denounce. ~**or** m informer

delega|ción f delegation; (oficina) regional office; (Mex, comisaría) police station. ~**do** m delegate; (Com) agent, representative. ~**r** 12 vt delegate

deleit|ar vt delight. ~**e** m delight

deletrear vt spell (out)

delfín m dolphin

delgad|ez f thinness. ~**o** adj thin; (esbelto) slim. ~**ucho** adj skinny

delibera|ción f deliberation. ~**do** adj deliberate. ~**r** vi deliberate (**sobre** on)

delicad|eza f gentleness; (fragilidad) frailty; (tacto) tact. **falta de** ~**eza** tactlessness. **tener la** ~ **de** have the courtesy to. ~**o** adj delicate; (refinado) refined; (sensible) sensitive

delici|a f delight. ~**oso** adj delightful; (sabor etc) delicious

delimitar vt delimit

delincuen|cia f delinquency. ~**te** m & f criminal, delinquent

delinquir 8 vi commit a criminal offence

delir|ante adj delirious. ~**ar** vi be delirious; (fig) talk nonsense. ~**io** m delirium; (fig) frenzy

delito m crime, offence

demacrado adj haggard

demagogo m demagogue

demanda f demand; (Jurid) lawsuit. ~**do** m defendant. ~**nte** m & f (Jurid) plaintiff. ~**r** vt (Jurid) sue; (LAm, requerir) require

demarcación f demarcation

demás adj rest of the, other. ● pron rest, others. **lo** ~ the rest. **por** ~ extremely. **por lo** ~ otherwise

demas|ía f. **en** ~**ía** in excess. ~**iado** adj too much; (en plural) too many. ● adv too much; (con adjetivo) too

demen|cia f madness. ~**te** adj demented, mad

dem|ocracia f democracy. ~**ócrata** m & f democrat. ~**ocrático** adj democratic

demol|er 2 vt demolish. ~**ición** f demolition

demonio m devil, demon. **¡**~**s!** hell! **¿cómo** ~**s?** how the hell? **¡qué** ~**s!** what the hell!

demora f delay. ~**r** vt delay. ● vi stay on. ~**rse** vpr be too long; (LAm, cierto tiempo) **se** ~ **una hora en llegar** it takes him an hour to get there

demostra|ción f demonstration, show. ~**r** 2 vt demonstrate; (mostrar) show; (probar) prove. ~**tivo** adj demonstrative

dengue m dengue fever

denigrar vt denigrate

denominado adj named; (supuesto) so-called

dens|idad f density. ~**o** adj dense, thick

denta|dura f teeth. ~**dura postiza** dentures, false teeth. ~**l** adj dental

dent|era f. **darle** ~**era a uno** set s.o.'s teeth on edge. ~**ífrico** m toothpaste. ~**ista** m & f dentist

dentro adv inside; (de un edificio) indoors. ~ **de** in. ~ **de poco** soon. **por** ~ inside

denuncia f report; (acusación) accusation. ~**r** vt report; (periódico etc) denounce

d

departamento *m* department; (*LAm*, *apartamento*) flat (*Brit*), apartment (*Amer*)

depend|encia *f* dependence; (*sección*) section; (*oficina*) office. **~encias** *fpl* buildings. **~er** *vi* depend (**de** on). **~ienta** *f* shop assistant. **~iente** *adj* dependent (**de** on). ● *m* shop assistant

depila|r *vt* depilate. **~torio** *adj* depilatory

deplora|ble *adj* deplorable. **~r** *vt* deplore, regret

deponer 34 *vt* remove from office; depose (*rey*); lay down (*armas*). ● *vi* give evidence

deporta|ción *f* deportation. **~r** *vt* deport

deport|e *m* sport. **hacer ~e** take part in sports. **~ista** *m* sportsman. ● *f* sportswoman. **~ivo** *adj* sports. ● *m* sports car

dep|ositante *m & f* depositor. **~ositar** *vt* deposit; (*poner*) put, place. **~ósito** *m* deposit; (*almacén*) warehouse; (*Mil*) depot; (*de líquidos*) tank

depravado *adj* depraved

deprecia|ción *f* depreciation. **~r** *vt* depreciate. **~rse** *vpr* depreciate

depr|esión *f* depression. **~imido** *adj* depressed. **~imir** *vt* depress. **~imirse** *vpr* get depressed

depura|ción *f* purification. **~do** *adj* refined. **~r** *vt* purify; (*Pol*) purge; refine (*estilo*)

derech|a *f* (*mano*) right hand; (*lado*) right. **a la ~a** on the right; (*hacia el lado derecho*) to the right. **~ista** *adj* right-wing. ● *m & f* right-winger. **~o** *adj* right; (*vertical*) upright; (*recto*) straight. ● *adv* straight. **todo ~o** straight on. ● *m* right; (*Jurid*) law; (*lado*) right side. **~os** *mpl* dues. **~os de autor** royalties

deriva *f* drift. **a la ~** drifting, adrift

deriva|do *adj* derived. ● *m* derivative, by-product. **~r** *vt* divert. ● *vi*. **~r de** derive from, be derived from. **~rse** *vpr*. **~rse de** be derived from

derram|amiento *m* spilling. **~amiento de sangre** bloodshed. **~ar** *vt* spill; shed (*lágrimas*). **~arse** *vpr* spill. **~e** *m* spilling; (*pérdida*) leakage; (*Med*) discharge; (*Med, de sangre*) haemorrhage

derretir 5 *vt* melt

derribar *vt* knock down; bring down, overthrow (*gobierno etc*)

derrocar 7 *vt* bring down, overthrow (*gobierno etc*)

derroch|ar *vt* squander. **~e** *m* waste

derrot|a *f* defeat. **~ar** *vt* defeat. **~ado** *adj* defeated. **~ero** *m* course

derrumba|r *vt* knock down **~rse** *vpr* collapse; (*persona*) go to pieces

desabotonar *vt* unbutton, undo. **~se** *vpr* come undone; (*persona*) undo

desabrido *adj* tasteless; (*persona*) surly; (*LAm*) dull

desabrochar *vt* undo. **~se** *vpr* come undone; (*persona*) undo

desacato *m* defiance; (*Jurid*) contempt of court

desac|ertado *adj* ill-advised; (*erróneo*) wrong. **~ierto** *m* mistake

desacreditar *vt* discredit

desactivar *vt* defuse

desacuerdo *m* disagreement

desafiar 20 *vt* challenge; (*afrontar*) defy

desafina|do *adj* out of tune. **~r** *vi* be out of tune. **~rse** *vpr* go out of tune

desafío *m* challenge; (*a la muerte*) defiance; (*combate*) duel

desafortunad|amente *adv* unfortunately. **~o** *adj* unfortunate

desagrada|ble *adj* unpleasant. **~r** *vt* displease. ● *vi* be unpleasant. **me ~ el sabor** I don't like the taste

desagradecido *adj* ungrateful

desagrado *m* displeasure. **con ~** unwillingly

desagüe *m* drain; (*acción*) drainage. **tubo** *m* **de ~** drain-pipe

desahog|ado *adj* roomy; (*acomodado*) comfortable. **~ar** 12 *vt* vent. **~arse** *vpr* let off steam. **~o** *m* comfort; (*alivio*) relief

desahuci|ar *vt* declare terminally ill (*enfermo*); evict (*inquilino*). **~o** *m* eviction

desair|ar *vt* snub. **~e** *m* snub

desajuste *m* maladjustment; (*desequilibrio*) imbalance

desala|dora f desalination plant. **~r** vt to desalinate

desal|entador adj disheartening. **~entar** **1** vt discourage. **~iento** m discouragement

desaliñado adj slovenly

desalmado adj heartless

desalojar vt (ocupantes) evacuate; (policía) to clear; (LAm) evict (inquilino)

desampar|ado adj helpless; (lugar) unprotected. **~ar** vt abandon. **~o** m helplessness; (abandono) lack of protection

desangrar vt bleed. **~se** vpr bleed

desanima|do adj down-hearted. **~r** vt discourage. **~rse** vpr lose heart

desapar|ecer **11** vi disappear; (efecto) wear off. **~ecido** adj missing. ● m missing person. **~ición** f disappearance

desapego m indifference

desapercibido adj. pasar **~** go unnoticed

desaprobar **2** vt disapprove of

desarm|able adj collapsible; (estante) easy to dismantle. **~ar** vt disarm; (desmontar) dismantle; take apart; (LAm) take down (carpa). **~e** m disarmament

desarraig|ado adj rootless. **~ar** **12** vt uproot. **~o** m uprooting

desarregl|ar vt mess up; (alterar) disrupt. **~o** m disorder

desarroll|ar vt develop. **~arse** vpr (incl Foto) develop; (suceso) take place. **~o** m development

desaseado adj dirty; (desordenado) untidy

desasosiego m anxiety; (intranquilidad) restlessness

desastr|ado adj scruffy. **~e** m disaster. **~oso** adj disastrous

desatar vt untie; (fig, soltar) unleash. **~se** vpr come undone; to undo (zapatos)

desatascar **7** vt unblock

desaten|der **1** vt not pay attention to; neglect (deber etc). **~to** adj inattentive; (descortés) discourteous

desatin|ado adj silly. **~o** m silliness; (error) mistake

desatornillar vt unscrew

desautorizar **10** vt declare unauthorized; discredit (persona); (desmentir) deny

desavenencia f disagreement

desayun|ar vt have for breakfast. ● vi have breakfast. **~o** m breakfast

desazón m (fig) unease

desbandarse vpr (Mil) disband; (dispersarse) disperse

desbarajust|ar vt mess up. **~e** m mess

desbaratar vt spoil; (Mex) mess up (papeles)

desbloquear vt clear; release (mecanismo); unfreeze (cuenta)

desbocado adj (caballo) runaway; (escote) wide

desbordarse vpr overflow; (río) burst its banks

descabellado adj crazy

descafeinado adj decaffeinated. ● m decaffeinated coffee

descalabro m disaster

descalificar **7** vt disqualify; (desacreditar) discredit

descalz|ar **10** vt take off (zapatos). **~o** adj barefoot

descampado m open ground. **al ~** (LAm) in the open air

descans|ado adj rested; (trabajo) easy. **~ar** vt/i rest. **~illo** m landing. **~o** m rest; (del trabajo) break; (LAm, rellano) landing, (en deportes) half-time; (en el teatro etc) interval

descapotable adj convertible

descarado adj cheeky; (sin vergüenza) shameless

descarg|a f unloading; (Mil, Elec) discharge. **~ar** **12** vt unload; (Mil, Elec) discharge; (Informática) download. **~o** m (recibo) receipt; (Jurid) evidence

descaro m cheek, nerve

descarriarse **20** vpr go the wrong way; (res) stray; (fig) go astray

descarrila|miento m derailment. **~r** vi be derailed. **~rse** vpr (LAm) be derailed

descartar vt rule out

descascararse vpr (pintura) peel; (taza) chip

descen|dencia *f* descent; (*personas*) descendants. **~der** **1** *vt* go down (escalera etc). ● *vi* go down; (*temperatura*) fall, drop; (*provenir*) be descended (**de** from). **~diente** *m & f* descendent. **~so** *m* descent; (*de temperatura, fiebre etc*) fall, drop

descifrar *vt* decipher; decode (clave)

descolgar **2** & **12** *vt* take down; pick up (el teléfono). **~se** *vpr* lower o.s.

descolor|ar *vt* discolour, fade. **~ido** *adj* discoloured, faded; (persona) pale

descomp|oner **34** *vt* break down; decompose (materia); upset (estómago); (*esp LAm, estropear*) break; (*esp LAm, desarreglar*) mess up. **~onerse** *vpr* decompose; (*esp LAm, estropearse*) break down; (persona) feel sick. **~ostura** *f* (*esp LAm, de máquina*) breakdown; (*esp LAm, náuseas*) sickness; (*esp LAm, diarrea*) diarrhoea; (*LAm, falla*) fault. **~uesto** *adj* decomposed; (*encolerizado*) angry; (*esp LAm, estropeado*) broken. **estar ~uesto** (*del estómago*) have diarrhoea

descomunal *adj* enormous

desconc|ertante *adj* disconcerting. **~ertar** **1** *vt* disconcert; (*dejar perplejo*) puzzle. **~ertarse** *vpr* be put out, be disconcerted

desconectar *vt* disconnect

desconfia|do *adj* distrustful. **~nza** *f* distrust, suspicion. **~r** **20** *vi*. **~r de** mistrust; (*no creer*) doubt

descongelar *vt* defrost; (*Com*) unfreeze

desconoc|er **11** *vt* not know, not recognize. **~ido** *adj* unknown; (*cambiado*) unrecognizable. ● *m* stranger. **~imiento** *m* ignorance

desconsidera|ción *f* lack of consideration. **~do** *adj* inconsiderate

descons|olado *adj* distressed. **~uelo** *m* distress; (*tristeza*) sadness

desconta|do *adj*. **dar por ~do (que)** take for granted (that). **~r** **2** *vt* discount; deduct (impuestos etc)

descontento *adj* unhappy (**con** with), dissatisfied (**con** with). ● *m* discontent

descorazonar *vt* discourage. **~se** *vpr* lose heart

descorchar *vt* uncork

descorrer *vt* draw (cortina). **~ el cerrojo** unbolt the door

descort|és *adj* rude, discourteous. **~esía** *f* rudeness

descos|er *vt* unpick. **~erse** *vpr* come undone. **~ido** *adj* unstitched

descrédito *m* disrepute. **ir en ~ de** damage the reputation of

descremado *adj* skimmed

descri|bir (*pp* **descrito**) *vt* describe. **~pción** *f* description

descuartizar **10** *vt* cut up

descubierto *adj* discovered; (*no cubierto*) uncovered; (*vehículo*) open-top; (piscina) open-air; (cielo) clear; (cabeza) bare. ● *m* overdraft. **poner al ~** expose

descubri|miento *m* discovery. **~r** (*pp* **descubierto**) *vt* discover; (*destapar*) uncover; (*revelar*) reveal; unveil (estatua). **~rse** *vpr* (*quitarse el sombrero*) take off one's hat

descuento *m* discount; (*del sueldo*) deduction; (*en deportes*) injury time

descuid|ado *adj* careless; (aspecto etc) untidy; (*desprevenido*) unprepared. **~ar** *vt* neglect. ● *vi* not worry. **¡~a!** don't worry!. **~arse** *vpr* be careless **~o** *m* carelessness; (*negligencia*) negligence

desde *prep* (*lugar etc*) from; (*tiempo*) since, from. **~ ahora** from now on. **~ hace un mes** for a month. **~ luego** of course. **~ Madrid hasta Barcelona** from Madrid to Barcelona. **~ niño** since childhood

desdecirse **46** *vpr*. **~ de** take back (palabras etc); go back on (promesa)

desd|én *m* scorn. **~eñable** *adj* insignificant. **nada ~eñable** significant. **~eñar** *vt* scorn

desdicha *f* misfortune. **por ~** unfortunately. **~do** *adj* unfortunate

desdoblar *vt* (*desplegar*) unfold

desear *vt* want; wish (suerte etc). **le deseo un buen viaje** I hope you have a good journey. **¿qué desea Vd?** can I help you?

desech|able *adj* disposable. **~ar** *vt* throw out; (*rechazar*) reject. **~o** *m* waste

desembalar *vt* unpack

desembarcar 7 vt unload. • vi disembark

desemboca|dura f (de río) mouth; (de calle) opening. ~**r 7** vi. ~**r en** (río) flow into; (calle) lead to

desembolso m payment

desembragar 12 vi declutch

desempaquetar vt unwrap

desempat|ar vi break a tie. ~**e** m tiebreaker

desempeñ|ar vt redeem; play (papel); hold (cargo); perform, carry out (deber etc). ~**arse** vpr (LAm) perform. ~**arse bien** manage well. ~**o** m redemption; (de un deber, una función) discharge; (LAm, actuación) performance

desemple|ado adj unemployed. • m unemployed person. **los** ~**ados** the unemployed. ~**o** m unemployment

desencadenar vt unchain (preso); unleash (perro); (causar) trigger. ~**se** vpr be triggered off; (guerra etc) break out

desencajar vt dislocate; (desconectar) disconnect. ~**se** vpr become dislocated

desenchufar vt unplug

desenfad|ado adj uninhibited; (desenvuelto) self-assured. ~**o** m lack of inhibition; (desenvoltura) self-assurance

desenfocado adj out of focus

desenfren|ado adj unrestrained. ~**o** m licentiousness

desenganchar vt unhook; uncouple (vagón)

desengañ|ar vt disillusion. ~**arse** vpr become disillusioned; (darse cuenta) realize. ~**o** m disillusionment, disappointment

desenlace m outcome

desenmascarar vt unmask

desenredar vt untangle. ~**se** vpr untangle

desenro|llar vt unroll, unwind. ~**scar 7** vt unscrew

desentend|erse 1 vpr want nothing to do with. ~**ido** m. **hacerse el** ~**ido** (fingir no oír) pretend not to hear; (fingir ignorancia) pretend not to know

desenterrar 1 vt exhume; (fig) unearth

desentonar vi be out of tune; (colores) clash

desenvoltura f ease; (falta de timidez) confidence

desenvolver 2 (pp **desenvuelto**) vt unwrap; expound (idea etc). ~**se** vpr perform; (manejarse) manage

deseo m wish, desire. ~**so** adj eager. **estar** ~**so de** be eager to

desequilibr|ado adj unbalanced. ~**io** m imbalance

des|ertar vt desert; (Pol) defect. ~**értico** adj desert-like. ~**ertor** m deserter; (Pol) defector

desespera|ción f despair. ~**do** adj desperate. ~**nte** adj infuriating. ~**r** vt drive to despair. ~**rse** vpr despair

desestimar vt (rechazar) reject

desfachat|ado adj brazen, shameless. ~**ez** f nerve, cheek

desfallec|er 11 vt weaken. • vi become weak; (desmayarse) faint. ~**imiento** m weakness; (desmayo) faint

desfasado adj out of phase; (idea) outdated; (persona) out of touch

desfavorable adj unfavourable

desfil|adero m narrow mountain pass; (cañón) narrow gorge. ~**ar** vi march (past). ~**e** m procession, parade. ~**e de modelos** fashion show

desgana f, (LAm) **desgano** m (falta de apetito) lack of appetite; (Med) weakness, faintness; (fig) unwillingness

desgarr|ador adj heart-rending. ~**ar** vt tear; (fig) break (corazón). ~**o** m tear, rip

desgast|ar vt wear away; wear out (ropa). ~**arse** vpr wear away; (ropa) be worn out; (persona) wear o.s. out. ~**e** m wear

desgracia f misfortune; (accidente) accident; **por** ~ unfortunately. **¡qué** ~**!** what a shame!. ~**do** adj unlucky; (pobre) poor. • m unfortunate person, poor devil 🅸

desgranar vt shell (habas etc)

desgreñado adj ruffled, dishevelled

deshabitado adj uninhabited; (edificio) unoccupied

d

deshacer **31** vt undo; strip (cama); unpack (maleta); (*desmontar*) take to pieces; break (trato); (*derretir*) melt; (*disolver*) dissolve. ~**se** vpr come undone; (*disolverse*) dissolve; (*derretirse*) melt. ~**se de algo** get rid of sth. ~**se en lágrimas** dissolve into tears. ~**se por hacer algo** go out of one's way to do sth

desheredar vt disinherit

deshidratarse vpr become dehydrated

deshielo m thaw

deshilachado adj frayed

deshincha|do adj (neumático) flat. ~**r** vt deflate; (*Med*) reduce the swelling in. ~**rse** vpr go down

deshollinador m chimney sweep

deshon|esto adj dishonest; (*obsceno*) indecent. ~**ra** f disgrace. ~**rar** vt dishonour

deshora f. **a** ~ out of hours. **comer a** ~**s** eat between meals

deshuesar vt bone (carne); stone (fruta)

desidia f slackness; (*pereza*) laziness

desierto adj deserted. ● m desert

designar vt designate; (*fijar*) fix

desigual adj unequal; (terreno) uneven; (*distinto*) different. ~**dad** f inequality

desilusi|ón f disappointment; (*pérdida de ilusiones*) disillusionment. ~**onar** vt disappoint; (*quitar las ilusiones*) disillusion. ~**onarse** vpr be disappointed; (*perder las ilusiones*) become disillusioned

desinfecta|nte m disinfectant. ~**r** vt disinfect

desinflar vt deflate. ~**se** vpr go down

desinhibido adj uninhibited

desintegrar vt disintegrate. ~**se** vpr disintegrate

desinter|és m lack of interest; (*generosidad*) unselfishness. ~**esado** adj uninterested; (*liberal*) unselfish

desistir vi. ~ **de** give up

desleal adj disloyal. ~**tad** f disloyalty

desligar **12** vt untie; (*separar*) separate; (*fig, librar*) free. ~**se** vpr break away; (*de un compromiso*) free o.s. (**de** from)

desliza|dor m (*Mex*) hang glider. ~**r** **10** vt slide, slip. ~**se** vpr slide, slip; (patinador) glide; (tiempo) slip by, pass; (*fluir*) flow

deslucido adj tarnished; (*gastado*) worn out; (*fig*) undistinguished

deslumbrar vt dazzle

desmadr|arse vpr get out of control. ~**e** m excess

desmán m outrage

desmanchar vt (*LAm*) remove the stains from

desmantelar vt dismantle; (*despojar*) strip

desmaquillador m make-up remover

desmay|ado adj unconscious. ~**arse** vpr faint. ~**o** m faint

desmedido adj excessive

desmemoriado adj forgetful

desmenti|do m denial. ~**r** **4** vt deny; (*contradecir*) contradict

desmenuzar **10** vt crumble; shred (carne etc)

desmerecer **11** vi. **no** ~ **de** compare favourably with

desmesurado adj excessive; (*enorme*) enormous

desmonta|ble adj collapsible; (armario) easy to dismantle; (*separable*) removable. ~**r** vt (*quitar*) remove; (*desarmar*) dismantle, take apart. ● vi dismount

desmoralizar **10** vt demoralize

desmoronarse vpr crumble; (edificio) collapse

desnatado adj skimmed

desnivel m unevenness; (*fig*) difference, inequality

desnud|ar vt strip; undress, strip (persona). ~**arse** vpr undress. ~**ez** f nudity. ~**o** adj naked; (*fig*) bare. ● m nude

desnutri|ción f malnutrition. ~**do** adj undernourished

desobed|ecer **11** vt disobey. ~**iencia** f disobedience

desocupa|do adj (asiento etc) vacant, free; (*sin trabajo*) unemployed; (*ocioso*) idle. ~**r** vt vacate; (*vaciar*) empty; (*desalojar*) clear

desodorante m deodorant

desolado *adj* desolate; (persona) sorry, sad

desorbitante *adj* excessive

desorden *m* disorder, untidiness; (*confusión*) confusion. **~ado** *adj* untidy. **~ar** *vt* disarrange, make a mess of

desorganizar 🔟 *vt* disorganize; (*trastornar*) disturb

desorienta|do *adj* confused. **~r** *vt* disorientate. **~rse** *vpr* lose one's bearings

despabila|do *adj* wide awake; (*listo*) quick. **~r** *vt* (*despertar*) wake up; (*avivar*) wise up. **~rse** *vpr* wake up; (*avivarse*) wise up

despach|ar *vt* finish; (*tratar con*) deal with, (*atender*) serve, (*vender*) sell; (*enviar*) send; (*despedir*) fire. **~o** *m* dispatch; (*oficina*) office; (*venta*) sale; (*de localidades*) box office

despacio *adv* slowly

despampanante *adj* stunning

desparpajo *m* confidence; (*descaro*) impudence

desparramar *vt* scatter; spill (líquidos)

despavorido *adj* terrified

despecho *m* spite. **a ~ de** in spite of. **por ~** out of spite

despectivo *adj* contemptuous; (*sentido etc*) pejorative

despedazar 🔟 *vt* tear to pieces

despedi|da *f* goodbye, farewell. **~da de soltero** stag-party. **~r** 🔼 *vt* say goodbye to, see off; dismiss (empleado); evict (inquilino); (*arrojar*) throw; give off (olor etc). **~rse** *vpr* say goodbye (**de** to)

despeg|ar 🔢 *vt* unstick. ● *vi* (avión) take off. **~ue** *m* take-off

despeinar *vt* ruffle the hair of

despeja|do *adj* clear; (persona) wide awake. **~r** *vt* clear; (*aclarar*) clarify. ● *vi* clear. **~rse** *vpr* (*aclararse*) become clear; (tiempo) clear up

despellejar *vt* skin

despenalizar *vt* decriminalize

despensa *f* pantry, larder

despeñadero *m* cliff

desperdici|ar *vt* waste. **~o** *m* waste. **~os** *mpl* rubbish

desperta|dor *m* alarm clock. **~r** 🔟 *vt* wake (up); (*fig*) awaken. **~rse** *vpr* wake up

despiadado *adj* merciless

despido *m* dismissal

despierto *adj* awake; (*listo*) bright

despilfarr|ar *vt* waste. **~o** *m* squandering

despintarse *vpr* (Mex) run

despista|do *adj* (con estar) confused; (con ser) absent-minded. **~r** *vt* throw off the scent; (*fig*) mislead. **~rse** *vpr* (*fig*) get confused

despiste *m* mistake; (*confusión*) muddle

desplaza|miento *m* displacement; (de opinión etc) swing, shift. **~r** 🔟 *vt* displace. **~rse** *vpr* travel

desplegar 🔢 & 🔢 *vt* open out; spread (alas); (*fig*) show

desplomarse *vpr* collapse

despoblado *m* deserted area

despoj|ar *vt* deprive (persona); strip (cosa). **~os** *mpl* remains; (de res) offal; (de ave) giblets

despreci|able *adj* despicable; (cantidad) negligible. **~ar** *vt* despise; (*rechazar*) scorn. **~o** *m* contempt; (*desaire*) snub

desprender *vt* remove; give off (olor). **~se** *vpr* fall off; (*fig*) part with; (*deducirse*) follow

despreocupa|do *adj* unconcerned; (*descuidado*) careless. **~rse** *vpr* not worry

desprestigiar *vt* discredit

desprevenido *adj* unprepared. **pillar a uno ~** catch s.o. unawares

desproporcionado *adj* disproportionate

desprovisto *adj*. **~ de** lacking in, without

después *adv* after, afterwards; (*más tarde*) later; (*a continuación*) then. **~ de** after. **~ de comer** after eating. **~ de todo** after all. **~ (de) que** after. **poco ~** soon after

desquit|arse *vpr* get even (de with). **~e** *m* revenge

destaca|do *adj* outstanding. **~r** 🔽 *vt* emphasize. ● *vi* stand out. **~rse** *vpr* stand out. **~rse en** excel at

destajo *m.* trabajar a ∼ do piece-work

destap|ar *vt* uncover; open (botella). ∼**arse** *vpr* reveal one's true self. ∼**e** *m* (*fig*) permissiveness

destartalado *adj* (coche) clapped-out; (casa) ramshackle

destello *m* sparkle; (de estrella) twinkle; (*fig*) glimmer

destemplado *adj* discordant; (nervios) frayed

desteñir 5 & 22 *vt* fade. ● *vi* fade; (color) run. ∼**se** *vpr* fade; (color) run

desterra|do *m* exile. ∼**r** 1 *vt* banish

destetar *vt* wean

destiempo *m.* a ∼ at the wrong moment; (*Mus*) out of time

destierro *m* exile

destil|ar *vt* distil. ∼**ería** *f* distillery

destin|ar *vt* destine; (nombrar) post. ∼**atario** *m* addressee. ∼**o** *m* (uso) use, function; (lugar) destination; (suerte) destiny. **con** ∼**o a** (going) to

destituir 17 *vt* dismiss

destornilla|dor *m* screwdriver. ∼**r** *vt* unscrew

destreza *f* skill

destroz|ar 10 *vt* destroy; (*fig*) shatter. ∼**os** *mpl* destruction, damage

destru|cción *f* destruction. ∼**ir** 17 *vt* destroy

desus|ado *adj* old-fashioned; (insólito) unusual. ∼**o** *m* disuse. **caer en** ∼**o** fall into disuse

desvalido *adj* needy, destitute

desvalijar *vt* rob; ransack (casa)

desvalorizar 10 *vt* devalue

desván *m* loft

desvanec|er 11 *vt* make disappear; (borrar) blur; (*fig*) dispel. ∼**erse** *vpr* disappear; (desmayarse) faint. ∼**imiento** *m* (*Med*) faint

desvariar 20 *vi* be delirious; (*fig*) talk nonsense

desvel|ar *vt* keep awake. ∼**arse** *vpr* stay awake, have a sleepless night. ∼**o** *m* sleeplessness

desvencijado *adj* (mueble) rickety

desventaja *f* disadvantage

desventura *f* misfortune. ∼**do** *adj* unfortunate

desverg|onzado *adj* impudent, cheeky. ∼**üenza** *f* impudence, cheek

desvestirse 5 *vpr* undress

desv|iación *f* deviation; (*Auto*) diversion. ∼**iar** 20 *vt* divert; deflect (pelota). ∼**iarse** *vpr* (carretera) branch off; (del camino) make a detour; (del tema) stray. ∼**ío** *m* diversion

desvivirse *vpr.* ∼**se por** be completely devoted to; (esforzarse) go out of one's way to

detall|ar *vt* relate in detail. ∼**e** *m* detail; (*fig*) gesture. **al** ∼**e** retail. **entrar en** ∼**es** go into detail. **¡qué** ∼**e!** how thoughtful! ∼**ista** *m & f* retailer

detect|ar *vt* detect. ∼**ive** *m* detective

deten|ción *f* stopping; (*Jurid*) arrest; (en la cárcel) detention. ∼**er** 40 *vt* stop; (*Jurid*) arrest; (encarcelar) detain; (retrasar) delay. ∼**erse** *vpr* stop; (entretenerse) spend a lot of time. ∼**idamente** *adv* at length. ∼**ido** *adj* (*Jurid*) under arrest. ● *m* prisoner

detergente *adj & m* detergent

deterior|ar *vt* damage, spoil. ∼**arse** *vpr* deteriorate. ∼**o** *m* deterioration

determina|ción *f* determination; (decisión) decison. ∼**nte** *adj* decisive. ∼**r** *vt* determine; (decidir) decide

detestar *vt* detest

detrás *adv* behind; (en la parte posterior) on the back. ∼ **de** behind. **por** ∼ at the back; (por la espalda) from behind

detrimento *m* detriment. **en** ∼ **de** to the detriment of

deud|a *f* debt. ∼**or** *m* debtor

devalua|ción *f* devaluation. ∼**r** 21 *vt* devalue. ∼**se** *vpr* depreciate

devastador *adj* devastating

devoción *f* devotion

devol|ución *f* return; (*Com*) repayment, refund. ∼**ver** 5 (*pp* devuelto) *vt* return; (*Com*) repay, refund. ● *vi* be sick

devorar *vt* devour

devoto *adj* devout; (amigo etc) devoted. ● *m* admirer

di *vb véase* **DAR**, **DECIR**

día *m* day. ∼ **de fiesta** (public) holiday. ∼ **del santo** saint's day. ∼ **feriado** (*LAm*), ∼ **festivo** (public) holiday. **al**

~ up to date. **al ~ siguiente** (on) the following day. **¡buenos ~s!** good morning! **de ~** by day. **el ~ de hoy** today. **el ~ de mañana** tomorrow. **un ~ sí y otro no** every other day. **vivir al ~** live from hand to mouth

> **Día de la raza** In Latin America, the anniversary of Columbus's discovery of America, October 12. In Spain it is known as *Día de la Hispanidad*. It is a celebration of the cultural ties shared by Spanish-speaking countries.

diab|etes *f* diabetes. **~ético** *adj* diabetic

diab|lo *m* devil. **~lura** *f* mischief. **~ólico** *adj* diabolical

diadema *f* diadem

diáfano *adj* diaphanous; (cielo) clear

diafragma *m* diaphragm

diagn|osis *f* diagnosis. **~osticar** 🔢 *vt* diagnose. **~óstico** *m* diagnosis

diagonal *adj & f* diagonal

diagrama *m* diagram

dialecto *m* dialect

di|alogar 🔢 *vi* talk. **~álogo** *m* dialogue; (Pol) talks

diamante *m* diamond

diámetro *m* diameter

diana *f* reveille; (blanco) bull's-eye

diapositiva *f* slide, transparency

diario *adj* daily. ● *m* newspaper; (libro) diary. **a ~o** daily. **de ~o** everyday, ordinary

diarrea *f* diarrhoea

dibuj|ante *m* draughtsman. ● *f* draughtswoman. **~ar** *vt* draw. **~o** *m* drawing. **~os animados** cartoons

diccionario *m* dictionary

dich|a *f* happiness. **por ~a** fortunately. **~o** *adj* said; (tal) such. ● *m* saying. **~o y hecho** no sooner said than done. **mejor ~o** rather. **propiamente ~o** strictly speaking. **~oso** *adj* happy; (afortunado) fortunate

diciembre *m* December

dicta|do *m* dictation. **~dor** *m* dictator. **~dura** *f* dictatorship. **~men** *m* opinion; (informe) report. **~r** *vt* dic-

tate; pronounce (sentencia etc); (LAm) give (clase)

didáctico *adj* didactic

dieci|nueve *adj & m* nineteen. **~ocho** *adj & m* eighteen. **~séis** *adj & m* sixteen. **~siete** *adj & m* seventeen

diente *m* tooth; (de tenedor) prong; (de ajo) clove. **~ de león** dandelion. **hablar entre ~s** mumble

diestro *adj* right-handed; (hábil) skillful

dieta *f* diet

diez *adj & m* ten

diezmar *vt* decimate

difamación *f* (con palabras) slander; (por escrito) libel

diferen|cia *f* difference; (desacuerdo) disagreement. **~ciar** *vt* differentiate between. **~ciarse** *vpr* differ. **~te** *adj* different; (diversos) various

diferido *adj* (TV etc) **en ~** recorded

dif|ícil *adj* difficult; (poco probable) unlikely. **~icultad** *f* difficulty. **~icultar** *vt* make difficult

difteria *f* diphtheria

difundir *vt* spread; (TV etc) broadcast

difunto *adj* late, deceased. ● *m* deceased

difusión *f* spreading

dige|rir 🔢 *vt* digest. **~stión** *f* digestion. **~stivo** *adj* digestive

digital *adj* digital; (de los dedos) finger

dign|arse *vpr* deign to. **~atario** *m* dignitary. **~idad** *f* dignity. **~o** *adj* honourable; (decoroso) decent; (merecedor) worthy (de of). **~ de elogio** praiseworthy

digo *vb* véase **DECIR**

dije *vb* véase **DECIR**

dilatar *vt* expand; (Med) dilate; (prolongar) prolong. **~se** *vpr* expand; (Med) dilate; (extenderse) extend; (Mex, demorarse) be late

dilema *m* dilemma

diligen|cia *f* diligence; (gestión) job; (carruaje) stagecoach. **~te** *adj* diligent

dilucidar *vt* clarify; solve (misterio)

diluir 🔢 *vt* dilute

diluvio *m* flood

dimensión *f* dimension; (tamaño) size

diminut|ivo *adj & m* diminutive. **~o** *adj* minute

dimitir *vt/i* resign

Dinamarca *f* Denmark

dinamarqués *adj* Danish. ● *m* Dane

dinámic|a *f* dynamics. ~**o** *adj* dynamic

dinamita *f* dynamite

dínamo *m* dynamo

dinastía *f* dynasty

diner|al *m* fortune. ~**o** *m* money. ~**o** efectivo cash. ~**o suelto** change

dinosaurio *m* dinosaur

dios *m* god. ~**a** *f* goddess. ¡**D**~ mío! good heavens! ¡**gracias a D**~! thank God!

diplom|a *m* diploma. ~**acia** *f* diplomacy. ~**ado** *adj* qualified. ~**arse** *vpr* (*LAm*) graduate. ~**ático** *adj* diplomatic. ● *m* diplomat

diptongo *m* diphthong

diputa|ción *f* delegation. ~**ción provincial** county council. ~**do** *m* deputy; (*Pol, en España*) member of the Cortes; (*Pol, en Inglaterra*) Member of Parliament; (*Pol, en Estados Unidos*) congressman

dique *m* dike

direc|ción *f* direction; (*señas*) address; (*los que dirigen*) management; (*Pol*) leadership; (*Auto*) steering. ~**ción prohibida** no entry. ~**ción única** one-way. ~**ta** *f* (*Auto*) top gear. ~**tiva** *f* board; (*Pol*) executive committee. ~**tivas** *fpl* guidelines. ~**to** *adj* direct; (*línea*) straight; (*tren*) through. **en** ~**to** (*TV etc*) live. ~**tor** *m* director; (*Mus*) conductor; (*de escuela*) headmaster; (*de periódico*) editor; (*gerente*) manager. ~**tora** *f* (*de escuela etc*) headmistress. ~**torio** *m* board of directors; (*LAm, de teléfonos*) telephone directory

dirig|ente *adj* ruling. ● *m & f* leader; (*de empresa*) manager. ~**ir** 14 *vt* direct; (*Mus*) conduct; run (empresa etc); address (carta etc). ~**irse** *vpr* make one's way; (*hablar*) address

disciplina *f* discipline. ~**r** *vt* discipline. ~**rio** *adj* disciplinary

discípulo *m* disciple; (*alumno*) pupil

disco *m* disc; (*Mus*) record; (*deportes*) discus; (*de teléfono*) dial; (*de tráfico*) sign; (*Rail*) signal. ~ **duro** hard disk.

~ **flexible** floppy disk

disconforme *adj* not in agreement

discord|e *adj* discordant. ~**ia** *f* discord

discoteca *f* discothèque, disco 🔢; (*colección de discos*) record collection

discreción *f* discretion

discrepa|ncia *f* discrepancy; (*desacuerdo*) disagreement. ~**r** *vi* differ

discreto *adj* discreet; (*moderado*) moderate

discrimina|ción *f* discrimination. ~**r** *vt* (*distinguir*) discriminate between; (*tratar injustamente*) discriminate against

disculpa *f* apology; (*excusa*) excuse. **pedir** ~**s** apologize. ~**r** *vt* excuse, forgive. ~**rse** *vpr* apologize

discurs|ar *vi* speak (**sobre** about). ~**o** *m* speech

discusión *f* discussion; (*riña*) argument

discuti|ble *adj* debatable. ~**r** *vt* discuss; (*contradecir*) contradict. ● *vi* argue (**por** about)

disecar 7 *vt* stuff; (*cortar*) dissect

diseminar *vt* disseminate, spread

disentir 4 *vi* disagree (**de** with, **en** on)

diseñ|ador *m* designer. ~**ar** *vt* design. ~**o** *m* design; (*fig*) sketch

disertación *f* dissertation

disfraz *m* fancy dress; (*para engañar*) disguise. ~**ar** 10 *vt* dress up; (*para engañar*) disguise. ~**arse** *vpr*. ~**arse de** dress up as; (*para engañar*) disguise o.s. as.

disfrutar *vt* enjoy. ● *vi* enjoy o.s. ~ **de** enjoy

disgust|ar *vt* displease; (*molestar*) annoy. ~**arse** *vpr* get annoyed, get upset; (*dos personas*) fall out. ~**o** *m* annoyance; (*problema*) trouble; (*riña*) quarrel; (*dolor*) sorrow, grief

disidente *adj & m & f* dissident

disimular *vt* conceal. ● *vi* pretend

disipar *vt* dissipate; (*derrochar*) squander

dislocarse 7 *vpr* dislocate

disminu|ción *f* decrease. ~**ir** 17 *vi* diminish

disolver 🔢 (*pp* **disuelto**) *vt* dissolve. **~se** *vpr* dissolve

dispar *adj* different

disparar *vt* fire; (*Mex, pagar*) buy. ● *vi* shoot (**contra** at)

disparate *m* silly thing; (*error*) mistake. **decir ~s** talk nonsense. **¡qué ~!** how ridiculous!

disparidad *f* disparity

disparo *m* (*acción*) firing; (*tiro*) shot

dispensar *vt* give; (*eximir*) exempt. ● *vi*. **¡Vd dispense!** forgive me

dispers|ar *vt* scatter, disperse. **~arse** *vpr* scatter, disperse. **~ión** *f* dispersion. **~o** *adj* scattered

dispon|er 🔢 *vt* arrange; (*Jurid*) order. ● *vi*. **~er de** have; (*vender etc*) dispose of. **~erse** *vpr* prepare (**a** to). **~ibilidad** *f* availability. **~ible** *adj* available

disposición *f* arrangement; (*aptitud*) talent; (*disponibilidad*) disposal; (*Jurid*) order, decree. **~ de ánimo** frame of mind. **a la ~ de** at the disposal of. **a su ~** at your service

dispositivo *m* device

dispuesto *adj* ready; (*persona*) disposed (**a** to); (*servicial*) helpful

disputa *f* dispute; (*pelea*) argument

disquete *m* diskette, floppy disk

dista|ncia *f* distance, **a ~ncia** from a distance. **guardar las ~ncias** keep one's distance. **~nciar** *vt* space out; distance (*amigos*). **~nciarse** *vpr* (*dos personas*) fall out. **~nte** *adj* distant. **~r** *vi* be away; (*fig*) be far. **~ 5 kilómetros** it's 5 kilometres away

distin|ción *f* distinction; (*honor*) award. **~guido** *adj* distinguished. **~guir** 🔢 *vt/i* distinguish. **~guirse** *vpr* distinguish o.s.; (*diferenciarse*) differ. **~tivo** *adj* distinctive. ● *m* badge. **~to** *adj* different, distinct

distra|cción *f* amusement; (*descuido*) absent-mindedness, inattention. **~er** 🔢 *vt* distract; (*divertir*) amuse. **~erse** *vpr* amuse o.s.; (*descuidarse*) not pay attention. **~ido** *adj* (*desatento*) absent-minded

distribu|ción *f* distribution. **~idor** *m* distributor. **~ir** 🔢 *vt* distribute

distrito *m* district

disturbio *m* disturbance

disuadir *vt* deter, dissuade

diurno *adj* daytime

divagar 🔢 *vi* digress; (*hablar sin sentido*) ramble

diván *m* settee, sofa

diversi|dad *f* diversity. **~ficar** 🔢 *vt* diversify

diversión *f* amusement, entertainment; (*pasatiempo*) pastime

diverso *adj* different

diverti|do *adj* amusing; (*que tiene gracia*) funny. **~r** 🔢 *vt* amuse, entertain. **~rse** *vpr* enjoy o.s.

dividir *vt* divide; (*repartir*) share out

divino *adj* divine

divisa *f* emblem. **~s** *fpl* currency

divisar *vt* make out

división *f* division

divorci|ado *adj* divorced. ● *m* divorcee. **~ar** *vt* divorce. **~arse** *vpr* get divorced. **~o** *m* divorce

divulgar 🔢 *vt* spread; divulge (*secreto*)

dizque *adv* (*LAm*) apparently; (*supuestamente*) supposedly

do *m* C; (*solfa*) doh

DNI - Documento Nacional de Identidad See
▷**DOCUMENTO DE IDENTIDAD**

dobl|adillo *m* hem; (*de pantalón*) turn-up (*Brit*), cuff (*Amer*). **~ar** *vt* double; (*plegar*) fold; (*torcer*) bend; turn (*esquina*); dub (*película*). ● *vi* turn; (*campana*) toll. **~arse** *vpr* double; (*curvarse*) bend. **~e** *adj* double. ● *m* double. **el ~e** twice as much (**de, que** as). **~egar** 🔢 *vt* (*fig*) force to give in. **~egarse** *vpr* give in

doce *adj & m* twelve. **~na** *f* dozen

docente *adj* teaching. ● *m & f* teacher

dócil *adj* obedient

doctor *m* doctor. **~ado** *m* doctorate

doctrina *f* doctrine

document|ación *f* documentation, papers. **~al** *adj & m* documentary. **~o** *m* document. **D~o Nacional de Identidad** identity card

documento de identidad *i*
An identity card that all residents over a certain age in Spain and Latin America must carry at all times. Holders must quote their identity card number on most official forms. The card is also known as *carné de identidad*, and in Spain as the *DNI* (*Documento Nacional de Identidad*).

dólar *m* dollar

dolarizar *vt* dollarize

dol|er 2 *vi* hurt, ache; (*fig*) grieve. **me duele la cabeza** I have a headache. **le duele el estómago** he has a stomach-ache. **~or** *m* pain; (*sordo*) ache; (*fig*) sorrow. **~or de cabeza** headache. **~or de muelas** toothache. **~oroso** *adj* painful

domar *vt* tame; break in (*caballo*)

dom|esticar 7 *vt* domesticate. **~éstico** *adj* domestic

domicili|ar *vt*. **~ar los pagos** pay by direct debit. **~o** *m* address. **~o particular** home address. **reparto a ~** home delivery service

domina|nte *adj* dominant; (*persona*) domineering. **~r** *vt* dominate; (*contener*) control; (*conocer*) have a good command of. ● *vi* dominate. **~rse** *vpr* control o.s.

domingo *m* Sunday

dominio *m* authority; (*territorio*) domain; (*fig*) command

dominó *m* (*pl* **~s**) dominoes; (*ficha*) domino

don *m* talent, gift; (*en un sobre*) Mr. **~ Pedro** Pedro

donación *f* donation

donaire *m* grace, charm

dona|nte *m& f* (*de sangre*) donor. **~r** *vt* donate

doncella *f* maiden; (*criada*) maid

donde *adv* where

dónde *adv* where?; (*LAm, cómo*) how; **¿hasta ~?** how far? **¿por ~?** whereabouts? (*por qué camino?*) which way? **¿a ~ vas?** where are you going? **¿de ~ eres?** where are you from?

dondequiera *adv*. **~ que** wherever. **por ~** everywhere

doña *f* (*en un sobre*) Mrs. **~ María** María

dora|do *adj* golden; (*cubierto de oro*) gilt. **~r** *vt* gilt; (*Culin*) brown

dormi|do *adj* asleep. **quedarse ~do** fall asleep; (*no despertar*) oversleep. **~r** 6 *vt* send to sleep. ● *vi* sleep. **~rse** *vpr* fall asleep. **~r la siesta** have an afternoon nap, have a siesta. **~tar** *vi* doze. **~torio** *m* bedroom

dors|al *adj* back. ● *m* (*en deportes*) number. **~o** *m* back. **nadar de ~** (*Mex*) do (the) backstroke

dos *adj & m* two. **de ~ en ~** in twos, in pairs. **los ~, las ~** both (of them). **~cientos** *adj & m* two hundred

dosi|ficar 7 *vt* dose; (*fig*) measure out. **~s** *f invar* dose

dot|ado *adj* gifted. **~ar** *vt* give a dowry; (*proveer*) provide (**de** with). **~e** *m* dowry

doy *vb véase* **DAR**

dragar 12 *vt* dredge

drama *m* drama; (*obra de teatro*) play. **~turgo** *m* playwright

drástico *adj* drastic

droga *f* drug. **~dicto** *m* drug addict. **~do** *m* drug addict. **~r** 12 *vt* drug. **~rse** *vpr* take drugs

droguería *f* hardware store

ducha *f* shower. **~rse** *vpr* have a shower

dud|a *f* doubt. **poner en ~a** question. **sin ~a (alguna)** without a doubt. **~ar** *vt/i* doubt. **~oso** *adj* doubtful; (*sospechoso*) dubious

duelo *m* duel; (*luto*) mourning

duende *m* imp

dueñ|a *f* owner, proprietress; (*de una pensión*) landlady. **~o** *m* owner, proprietor; (*de una pensión*) landlord

duermo *vb véase* **DORMIR**

dul|ce *adj* sweet; (*agua*) fresh; (*suave*) soft, gentle. ● *m* (*LAm*) sweet. **~zura** *f* sweetness; (*fig*) gentleness

duna *f* dune

dúo *m* duet, duo

duplica|do *adj* duplicated. **por ~** in duplicate. ● *m* duplicate. **~r** 7 *vt* duplicate. **~rse** *vpr* double

duque *m* duke. **~sa** *f* duchess

dura|ción f duration, length. **~dero** adj lasting. **~nte** prep during; (medida de tiempo) for. **~ todo el año** all year round. **~r** vi last

durazno m (LAm, fruta) peach

dureza f hardness; (Culin) toughness; (fig) harshness

duro adj hard; (Culin) tough; (fig) harsh. ● adv (esp LAm) hard

DVD m (**Disco Versátil Digital**) DVD. **~teca** f DVD library

....

Ee

....

e conj and

Ébola m ebola

ebrio adj drunk

ebullición f boiling

eccema m eczema

echar vt throw; post (carta); give off (olor); pour (líquido); (expulsar) expel; (de recinto) throw out; fire (empleado); (poner) put on; get (gasolina); put out (raíces); show (película). **~ a start. ~ a perder** spoil. **~ de menos** miss. **~se atrás** (fig) back down. **echárselas de** feign. **~se** vpr throw o.s.; (tumbarse) lie down

eclesiástico adj ecclesiastical

eclipse m eclipse

eco m echo. **hacerse ~ de** echo

ecolog|ía f ecology. **~ista** m & f ecologist

economato m cooperative store

econ|omía f economy; (ciencia) economics. **~ómico** adj economic; (no caro) inexpensive. **~omista** m & f economist. **~omizar** 🔟 vt/i economize

ecoturismo m ecotourism

ecuación f equation

ecuador m equator. **el E~** the Equator. **E~** (país) Ecuador

ecuánime adj level-headed; (imparcial) impartial

ecuatoriano adj & m Ecuadorian

ecuestre adj equestrian

edad f age. **~ avanzada** old age. **E~ de Piedra** Stone Age. **E~ Media** Middle Ages. **¿qué ~ tiene?** how old is he?

edición f edition; (publicación) publication

edicto m edict

edific|ación f building. **~ante** adj edifying. **~ar** 🔟 vt build; (fig) edify. **~io** m building; (fig) structure

edit|ar vt edit; (publicar) publish. **~or** adj publishing. ● m editor; (que publica) publisher. **~orial** adj editorial. ● m leading article. ● f publishing house

edredón m duvet

educa|ción f upbringing, (modales) (good) manners; (enseñanza) education. **falta de ~ción** rudeness, bad manners. **~do** adj polite. **bien ~do** polite. **mal ~do** rude. **~r** 🔟 vt bring up; (enseñar) educate. **~tivo** adj educational

edulcorante m sweetener

EE.UU. abrev (**Estados Unidos**) USA

efect|ivamente adv really; (por supuesto) indeed. **~ivo** adj effective; (auténtico) real. ● m cash. **~o** m effect; (impresión) impression. **en ~o** really; (como respuesta) indeed. **~os** mpl belongings; (Com) goods. **~uar** 🔟 vt carry out; make (viaje, compras etc)

efervescente adj effervescent; (bebidas) fizzy

efica|cia f effectiveness; (de persona) efficiency. **~z** adj effective; (persona) efficient

eficien|cia f efficiency. **~te** adj efficient

efímero adj ephemeral

efusi|vidad f effusiveness. **~vo** adj effusive; (persona) demonstrative

egipcio adj & m Egyptian

Egipto m Egypt

ego|ísmo m selfishness, egotism. **~ista** adj selfish

egresar vi (LAm) graduate; (de colegio) leave school, graduate (Amer)

eje m axis; (Tec) axle

ejecu|ción f execution; (Mus) performance. **~tar** vt carry out; (Mus) perform; (*matar*) execute. ~**tivo** *m* executive

ejempl|ar *adj* exemplary; (*ideal*) model. ● *m* specimen; (*libro*) copy; (*revista*) issue, number. ~**ificar** **7** *vt* exemplify. ~**o** *m* example. **dar (el)** ~**o** set an example. **por** ~**o** for example

ejerc|er **9** *vt* exercise; practise (profesión); exert (influencia). ● *vi* practise. ~**icio** *m* exercise; (*de profesión*) practice. **hacer** ~**icios** take exercise. ~**itar** *vt* exercise

ejército *m* army

ejido *m* (*Mex*) cooperative

ejote *m* (*Mex*) green bean

---

el *artículo definido masculino* (*pl* **los**)

The masculine article **el** is also used before feminine nouns which begin with stressed **a** or **ha**, e.g. **el ala derecha**, **el hada madrina**. Also, **de** followed by **el** becomes **del** and **el** preceded by **a** becomes **al**

····➤ the. **el tren de las seis** the six o'clock train. **el vecino de al lado** the next-door neighbour. **cerca del hospital** near the hospital

····➤ *No se traduce en los siguientes casos:* (*con nombre abstracto, genérico*) **el tiempo vuela** time flies. **odio el queso** I hate cheese. **el hilo es muy durable** linen is very durable

····➤ (*con colores, días de la semana*) **el rojo está de moda** red is in fashion. **el lunes es fiesta** Monday is a holiday

····➤ (*con algunas instituciones*) **termino el colegio mañana** I finish school tomorrow. **lo ingresaron en el hospital** he was admitted to hospital

····➤ (*con nombres propios*) **el Sr. Díaz** Mr Díaz. **el doctor Lara** Doctor Lara

····➤ (*antes de infinitivo*) **es muy cuidadosa en el vestir** she takes great care in the way she dresses. **me di cuenta al verlo** I realized when I saw him

····➤ (*con partes del cuerpo, artículos personales*) *se traduce por un posesivo.* **apretó el puño** he clenched his fist. **tienes el zapato desatado** your shoe is undone

····➤ **el + de. es el de Pedro** it's Pedro's. **el del sombrero** the one with the hat

····➤ **el + que** (*persona*) **el que me atendió** the one who served me. (*cosa*) **el que se rompió** the one that broke.

····➤ **el + que** + *subjuntivo* (*quienquiera*) whoever. **el que gane la lotería** whoever wins the lottery. (*cualquiera*) whichever. **compra el que sea más barato** buy whichever is cheaper

él *pron* (*persona*) he; (*persona con prep*) him; (*cosa*) it. **es de** ~ it's his

elabora|ción *f* elaboration; (*fabricación*) manufacture. ~**r** *vt* elaborate; manufacture (producto); (*producir*) produce

el|asticidad *f* elasticity. ~**ástico** *adj & m* elastic

elec|ción *f* choice; (*de político etc*) election. ~**ciones** *fpl* (*Pol*) election. ~**tor** *m* voter. ~**torado** *m* electorate. ~**toral** *adj* electoral; (*campaña*) election

electrici|dad *f* electricity. ~**sta** *m & f* electrician

eléctrico *adj* electric; (*aparato*) electrical

electri|ficar **7** *vt* electrify. ~**zar** **10** *vt* electrify

electrocutar *vt* electrocute. ~**se** *vpr* be electrocuted

electrodoméstico *adj* electrical appliance

electrónic|a *f* electronics. ~**o** *adj* electronic

elefante *m* elephant

elegan|cia *f* elegance. ~**te** *adj* elegant

elegía *f* elegy

elegi|ble *adj* eligible. ~**do** *adj* chosen. ~**r** **5** & **14** *vt* choose; (*por votación*) elect

element|al *adj* elementary; (*esencial*) fundamental. ~**o** *m* element; (*per-*

sona) person, bloke (*Brit, fam*). ∼**os**
mpl (*nociones*) basic principles

elenco *m* (*en el teatro*) cast

eleva|ción *f* elevation; (*de precios*)
rise, increase; (*acción*) raising. ∼**dor**
m (*Mex*) lift (*Brit*), elevator (*Amer*). ∼**r**
vt raise; (*promover*) promote

elimina|ción *f* elimination. ∼**r** *vt*
eliminate; (*Informática*) delete.
∼**toria** *f* preliminary heat

élite /e'lit, e'lite/ *f* elite

ella *pron* (*persona*) she; (*persona con
prep*) her; (*cosa*) it. **es de** ∼**s** it's
theirs. ∼**s** *pron* pl they; (*con prep*)
them. **es de** ∼ it's hers

ello *pron* it

ellos *pron* pl they; (*con prep*) them. **es
de** ∼ it's theirs

elocuen|cia *f* eloquence. ∼**te** *adj* eloquent

elogi|ar *vt* praise. ∼**o** *m* praise

elote *m* (*Mex*) corncob; (*Culin*) corn on
the cob

eludir *vt* avoid, elude

emanar *vi* emanate (*de* from); (*originarse*) originate (*de* from, in)

emancipa|ción *f* emancipation. ∼**r** *vt*
emancipate. ∼**rse** *vpr* become emancipated

embadurnar *vt* smear

embajad|a *f* embassy. ∼**or** *m* ambassador

embalar *vt* pack

embaldosar *vt* tile

embalsamar *vt* embalm

embalse *m* reservoir

embaraz|ada *adj* pregnant. ● *f* pregnant woman. ∼**ar** 🔟 *vt* get pregnant.
∼**o** *m* pregnancy; (*apuro*) embarrassment; (*estorbo*) hindrance. ∼**oso** *adj*
awkward, embarrassing

embar|cación *f* vessel. ∼**cadero** *m*
jetty, pier. ∼**car** 🔢 *vt* load (*mercancías* etc). ∼**carse** *vpr* board. ∼**carse
en** (*fig*) embark upon

embargo *m* embargo; (*Jurid*) seizure.
sin ∼ however

embarque *m* loading; (*de pasajeros*)
boarding

embaucar 🔢 *vt* trick

embelesar *vt* captivate

embellecer 🔟 *vt* make beautiful

embesti|da *f* charge. ∼**r** 🔢 *vt/i*
charge

emblema *m* emblem

embolsarse *vpr* pocket

embonar *vt* (*Mex*) fit

emborrachar *vt* get drunk. ∼**se** *vpr*
get drunk

emboscada *f* ambush

embotar *vt* dull

embotella|miento *m* (*de vehículos*)
traffic jam. ∼**r** *vt* bottle

embrague *m* clutch

embriag|arse 🔢 *vpr* get drunk.
∼**uez** *f* drunkenness

embrión *m* embryo

embroll|ar *vt* mix up; involve (*persona*). ∼**arse** *vpr* get into a muddle;
(*en un asunto*) get involved. ∼**o** *m*
tangle; (*fig*) muddle

embruj|ado *adj* bewitched; (*casa*)
haunted. ∼**ar** *vt* bewitch. ∼**o** *m* spell

embrutecer 🔟 *vt* brutalize

embudo *m* funnel

embuste *m* lie. ∼**ro** *adj* deceitful. ● *m*
liar

embuti|do *m* (*Culin*) sausage. ∼**r** *vt*
stuff

emergencia *f* emergency

emerger 🔢 *vi* appear, emerge

emigra|ción *f* emigration. ∼**nte** *adj* &
m & f emigrant. ∼**r** *vi* emigrate

eminen|cia *f* eminence. ∼**te** *adj* eminent

emisario *m* emissary

emi|sión *f* emission; (*de dinero*) issue;
(*TV etc*) broadcast. ∼**sor** *adj* issuing;
(*TV etc*) broadcasting. ∼**sora** *f* radio
station. ∼**tir** *vt* emit, give out; (*TV
etc*) broadcast; cast (*voto*); (*poner en
circulación*) issue

emoci|ón *f* emotion; (*excitación*) excitement. **¡qué** ∼**ón!** how exciting!.
∼**onado** *adj* moved. ∼**onante** *adj* exciting; (*conmovedor*) moving. ∼**onar**
vt move. ∼**onarse** *vpr* get excited;
(*conmoverse*) be moved

emotivo *adj* emotional; (*conmovedor*)
moving

empacar 🔢 *vt* (*LAm*) pack

empacho *m* indigestion

empadronar vt register. **~se** vpr register

empalagoso adj sickly; (persona) cloying

empalizada f fence

empalm|ar vt connect, join. • vi meet. **~e** m junction; (de trenes) connection

empan|ada f (savoury) pie; (LAm, individual) pasty. **~adilla** f pasty

empantanarse vpr become swamped; (coche) get bogged down

empañar vt steam up; (fig) tarnish. **~se** vpr steam up

empapar vt soak. **~se** vpr get soaked

empapela|do m wallpaper. **~r** vt wallpaper

empaquetar vt package

emparedado m sandwich

emparentado adj related

empast|ar vt fill (muela). **~e** m filling

empat|ar vi draw. **~e** m draw

empedernido adj confirmed; (bebedor) inveterate

empedrar 🔢 vt pave

empeine m instep

empeñ|ado adj in debt; (decidido) determined (en to). **~ar** vt pawn; pledge (palabra). **~arse** vpr get into debt; (estar decidido a) be determined (en to). **~o** m pledge; (resolución) determination. **casa** f **de ~s** pawnshop. **~oso** adj (LAm) hardworking

empeorar vt make worse. • vi get worse. **~se** vpr get worse

empequeñecer 🔢 vt become smaller; (fig) belittle

empera|dor m emperor. **~triz** f empress

empezar 🔢 & 🔢 vt/i start, begin. **para ~** to begin with

empina|do adj (cuesta) steep. **~r** vt raise. **~rse** vpr (persona) stand on tiptoe

empírico adj empirical

emplasto m plaster

emplaza|miento m (Jurid) summons; (lugar) site. **~r** 🔢 vt summon; (situar) site

emple|ada f employee; (doméstica) maid. **~ado** m employee. **~ar** vt use; employ (persona); spend (tiempo). **~arse** vpr get a job. **~o** m use; (trabajo) employment; (puesto) job

empobrecer 🔢 vt impoverish. **~se** vpr become poor

empoll|ar vt incubate (huevos); (arg, estudiar) cram 🔢. • vi (ave) sit; (estudiante) 🔢 cram. **~ón** m 🔢 swot (Brit, fam), grind (Amer, fam)

empolvarse vpr powder

empotra|do adj built-in, fitted. **~r** vt fit

emprende|dor adj enterprising. **~r** vt undertake; set out on (viaje). **~rla con uno** pick a fight with s.o.

empresa f undertaking; (Com) company, firm. **~ puntocom** dot-com company. **~rio** m businessman; (patrón) employer; (de teatro etc) impresario

empuj|ar vt push. **~e** m (fig) drive. **~ón** m push, shove

empuña|dura f handle

emular vt emulate

en prep in; (sobre) on; (dentro) inside, in; (medio de transporte) by. **~ casa** at home. **~ coche** by car. **~ 10 días** in 10 days. **de pueblo ~ pueblo** from town to town

enagua f petticoat

enajena|ción f alienation. **~ción mental** insanity. **~r** vt alienate; (volver loco) derange

enamora|do adj in love. • m lover. **~r** vt win the love of. **~rse** vpr fall in love (**de** with)

enano adj & m dwarf

enardecer 🔢 vt inflame. **~se** vpr get excited (**por** about)

encabeza|do m (Mex) headline. **~miento** m heading; (de periódico) headline. **~r** 🔢 vt head; lead (revolución etc)

encabritarse vpr rear up

encadenar vt chain; (fig) tie down

encaj|ar vt fit; fit together (varias piezas). • vi fit; (cuadrar) tally. **~arse** vpr put on. **~e** m lace; (Com) reserve

encaminar vt direct. **~se** vpr make one's way

encandilar vt dazzle; (estimular) stimulate

encant|ado *adj* enchanted; (persona) delighted. **¡~ado!** pleased to meet you! **~ador** *adj* charming. **~amiento** *m* spell. **~ar** *vt* bewitch; (*fig*) charm, delight. **me ~a la leche** I love milk. **~o** *m* spell; (*fig*) delight

encapricharse *vpr*. **~ con** take a fancy to

encarar *vt* face; (*LAm*) stand up to (persona). **~se** *vpr*. **~se con** stand up to

encarcelar *vt* imprison

encarecer 🔟 *vt* put up the price of. **~se** *vpr* become more expensive

encarg|ado *adj* in charge. ● *m* manager, person in charge. **~ar** 🔢 *vt* entrust; (*pedir*) order. **~arse** *vpr* take charge (**de** of). **~o** *m* job; (*Com*) order; (*recado*) errand. **hecho de ~o** made to measure

encariñarse *vpr*. **~ con** take to, become fond of

encarna|ción *f* incarnation. **~do** *adj* incarnate; (*rojo*) red; (*uña*) ingrowing. ● *m* red

encarnizado *adj* bitter

encarpetar *vt* file; (*LAm*, *dar carpetazo*) shelve

encarrilar *vt* put back on the rails; (*fig*) direct, put on the right track

encasillar *vt* classify; (*fig*) pigeonhole

encauzar 🔟 *vt* channel

enceguecer *vt* 🔟 (*LAm*) blind

encend|edor *m* lighter. **~er** 🔟 *vt* light; switch on, turn on (aparato eléctrico); start (motor); (*fig*) arouse. **~erse** *vpr* light; (aparato eléctrico) come on; (*excitarse*) get excited; (*ruborizarse*) blush. **~ido** *adj* lit; (aparato eléctrico) on; (*rojo*) bright red. ● *m* (*Auto*) ignition

encera|do *adj* waxed. ● *m* (*pizarra*) blackboard. **~r** *vt* wax

encerr|ar 🔟 *vt* shut in; (*con llave*) lock up; (*fig*, *contener*) contain. **~ona** *f* trap

enchilar *vt* (*Mex*) add chili to

enchinar *vt* (*Mex*) perm

enchuf|ado *adj* switched on. **~ar** *vt* plug in; fit together (tubos etc). **~e** *m* socket; (*clavija*) plug; (*de tubos etc*) joint; (*fam*, *influencia*) contact. **tener**
~e have friends in the right places

encía *f* gum

enciclopedia *f* encyclopaedia

encierro *m* confinement; (*cárcel*) prison

encim|a *adv* on top; (*arriba*) above. **~ de** on, on top of; (*sobre*) over; (*además de*) besides, as well as. **por ~** on top; (*adj la ligera*) superficially. **por ~ de todo** above all. **~ar** *vt* (*Mex*) stack up. **~era** *f* worktop

encina *f* holm oak

encinta *adj* pregnant

enclenque *adj* weak; (*enfermizo*) sickly

encoger 🔢 *vt* shrink; (*contraer*) contract. **~se** *vpr* shrink. **~erse de hombros** shrug one's shoulders

encolar *vt* glue; (*pegar*) stick

encolerizar 🔟 *vt* make angry. **~se** *vpr* get furious

encomendar 🔢 *vt* entrust

encomi|ar *vt* praise. **~o** *m* praise. **~oso** *adj* (*LAm*) complimentary

encono *m* bitterness, ill will

encontra|do *adj* contrary, conflicting. **~r** 🔢 *vt* find; (*tropezar con*) meet. **~rse** *vpr* meet; (*hallarse*) be. **no ~rse** feel uncomfortable

encorvar *vt* hunch. **~se** *vpr* stoop

encrespa|do *adj* (pelo) curly; (mar) rough. **~r** *vt* curl (pelo); make rough (mar)

encrucijada *f* crossroads

encuaderna|ción *f* binding. **~dor** *m* bookbinder. **~r** *vt* bind

encub|ierto *adj* hidden. **~rir** (*pp* **encubierto**) *vt* hide, conceal; cover up (delito); shelter (delincuente)

encuentro *m* meeting; (*en deportes*) match; (*Mil*) encounter

encuesta *f* survey; (*investigación*) inquiry

encumbrado *adj* eminent; (*alto*) high

encurtidos *mpl* pickles

endeble *adj* weak

endemoniado *adj* possessed; (*muy malo*) wretched

enderezar 🔟 *vt* straighten out; (*poner vertical*) put upright; (*fig*, *arreglar*) put right, sort out; (*dirigir*) direct. **~se** *vpr* straighten out

endeudarse *vpr* get into debt

endiablado *adj* possessed; (*malo*) terrible; (*difícil*) difficult

endosar *vt* endorse (cheque)

endulzar [10] *vt* sweeten; (*fig*) soften

endurecer [11] *vt* harden. **~se** *vpr* harden

enemi|go *adj* enemy. ● *m* enemy. **~stad** *f* enmity. **~star** *vt* make an enemy of. **~starse** *vpr* fall out (**con** with)

en|ergía *f* energy. **~érgico** *adj* (*persona*) lively; (*decisión*) forceful

energúmeno *m* madman

enero *m* January

enésimo *adj* nth, umpteenth [1]

enfad|ado *adj* angry; (*molesto*) annoyed. **~ar** *vt* make cross, anger; (*molestar*) annoy. **~arse** *vpr* get angry; (*molestarse*) get annoyed. **~o** *m* anger; (*molestia*) annoyance

énfasis *m invar* emphasis, stress. **poner ~** stress, emphasize

enfático *adj* emphatic

enferm|ar *vi* fall ill. **~arse** *vpr* (*LAm*) fall ill. **~edad** *f* illness. **~era** *f* nurse. **~ería** *f* sick bay; (*carrera*) nursing. **~ero** *m* (male) nurse **~izo** *adj* sickly. **~o** *adj* ill. ● *m* patient

enflaquecer [11] *vt* make thin. ● *vi* lose weight

enfo|car [7] *vt* shine on; focus (lente); (*fig*) approach. **~que** *m* focus; (*fig*) approach

enfrentar *vt* face, confront; (*poner frente a frente*) bring face to face. **~se** *vpr*. **~se con** confront; (*en deportes*) meet

enfrente *adv* opposite. **~ de** opposite. **de ~** opposite

enfria|miento *m* cooling; (*catarro*) cold. **~r** [20] *vt* cool (down); (*fig*) cool down. **~rse** *vpr* go cold; (*fig*) cool off

enfurecer [11] *vt* infuriate. **~se** *vpr* get furious

engalanar *vt* adorn. **~se** *vpr* dress up

enganchar *vt* hook; hang up (ropa). **~se** *vpr* get caught; (*Mil*) enlist

engañ|ar *vt* deceive, trick; (*ser infiel*) be unfaithful. **~arse** *vpr* be wrong, be mistaken; (*no admitir la verdad*) deceive o.s. **~o** *m* deceit, trickery; (*error*) mistake. **~oso** *adj* deceptive; (*persona*) deceitful

engarzar [10] *vt* string (cuentas); set (joyas)

engatusar *vt* [1] coax

engendr|ar *vt* father; (*fig*) breed. **~o** *m* (*monstruo*) monster; (*fig*) brainchild

englobar *vt* include

engomar *vt* glue

engordar *vt* fatten, gain (kilo). ● *vi* get fatter, put on weight

engorro *m* nuisance

engranaje *m* (*Auto*) gear

engrandecer [11] *vt* (*enaltecer*) exalt, raise

engrasar *vt* grease; (*con aceite*) oil; (*ensuciar*) get grease on

engreído *adj* arrogant

engullir [22] *vt* gulp down

enhebrar *vt* thread

enhorabuena *f* congratulations. **dar la ~** congratulate

enigm|a *m* enigma. **~ático** *adj* enigmatic

enjabonar *vt* soap. **~se** *vpr* to soap o.s.

enjambre *m* swarm

enjaular *vt* put in a cage

enjuag|ar [12] *vt* rinse. **~ue** *m* rinsing; (*para la boca*) mouthwash

enjugar [12] *vt* wipe (away)

enjuiciar *vt* pass judgement on

enjuto *adj* (*persona*) skinny

enlace *m* connection; (*matrimonial*) wedding

enlatar *vt* tin, can

enlazar [10] *vt* link; tie together (cintas); (*Mex*, *casar*) marry

enlodar *vt*, **enlodazar** [10] *vt* cover in mud

enloquecer [11] *vt* drive mad. ● *vi* go mad. **~se** *vpr* go mad

enlosar *vt* (*con losas*) pave; (*con baldosas*) tile

enmarañar *vt* tangle (up), entangle; (*confundir*) confuse. **~se** *vpr* get into a tangle; (*confundirse*) get confused

enmarcar [7] *vt* frame

enm|endar *vt* correct. **~endarse** *vpr* mend one's way. **~ienda** *f* correction; (*de ley etc*) amendment

enmohecerse ⓫ *vpr* (*con óxido*) go rusty; (*con hongos*) go mouldy

enmudecer ⓫ *vi* be dumbstruck; (*callar*) fall silent

ennegrecer ⓫ *vt* blacken

ennoblecer ⓫ *vt* ennoble; (*fig*) add style to

enoj|adizo *adj* irritable. **~ado** *adj* angry; (*molesto*) annoyed. **~ar** *vt* anger; (*molestar*) annoy. **~arse** *vpr* get angry; (*molestarse*) get annoyed. **~o** *m* anger; (*molestia*) annoyance. **~oso** *adj* annoying

enorgullecerse ⓫ *vpr* be proud

enorm|e *adj* huge, enormous. **~emente** *adv* enormously. **~idad** *f* immensity; (*de crimen*) enormity

enraizado *adj* deeply rooted

enrarecido *adj* rarefied

enred|adera *f* creeper. **~ar** *vt* tangle (up), entangle; (*confundir*) confuse; (*involucrar*) involve. **~arse** *vpr* get tangled; (*confundirse*) get confused; (*persona*) get involved (**con** with). **~o** *m* tangle; (*fig*) muddle, mess

enrejado *m* bars

enriquecer ⓫ *vt* make rich; (*fig*) enrich. **~se** *vpr* get rich

enrojecerse ⓫ *vpr* (*persona*) go red, blush

enrolar *vt* enlist

enrollar *vt* roll (up), wind (hilo etc)

enroscar ⓬ *vt* coil; (*atornillar*) screw in

ensalad|a *f* salad. **armar una ~a** make a mess. **~era** *f* salad bowl. **~illa** *f* Russian salad

ensalzar ⓾ *vt* praise; (*enaltecer*) exalt

ensambla|dura *f*, **ensamblaje** *m* (*acción*) assembling; (*efecto*) joint. **~r** *vt* join

ensanch|ar *vt* widen; (*agrandar*) enlarge. **~arse** *vpr* get wider. **~e** *m* widening

ensangrentar ⓵ *vt* stain with blood

ensañarse *vpr*. **~ con** treat cruelly

ensartar *vt* string (cuentas etc)

ensay|ar *vt* test; rehearse (obra de teatro etc). **~o** *m* test, trial; (*composición literaria*) essay

enseguida *adv* at once, immediately

ensenada *f* inlet, cove

enseña|nza *f* education; (*acción de enseñar*) teaching. **~nza media** secondary education. **~r** *vt* teach; (*mostrar*) show

enseres *mpl* equipment

ensillar *vt* saddle

ensimismarse *vpr* be lost in thought

ensombrecer ⓫ *vt* darken

ensordecer ⓫ *vt* deafen. • *vi* go deaf

ensuciar *vt* dirty. **~se** *vpr* get dirty

ensueño *m* dream

entablar *vt* (*empezar*) start

entablillar *vt* put in a splint

entallar *vt* tailor (un vestido). • *vi* fit

entarimado *m* parquet; (*plataforma*) platform

ente *m* entity, being; (*fam, persona rara*) weirdo; (*Com*) firm, company

entend|er ⓵ *vt* understand; (*opinar*) believe, think. • *vi* understand. **~er de** know about. **a mi ~er** in my opinion. **dar a ~er** hint. **darse a ~er** (*LAm*) make o.s. understood. **~erse** *vpr* make o.s. understood; (*comprenderse*) be understood. **~erse con** get on with. **~ido** *adj* understood; (*enterado*) well-informed. **no darse por ~ido** pretend not to understand. • *interj* agreed!, OK! ⓵. **~imiento** *m* understanding

entera|do *adj* well-informed; (*que sabe*) aware. **darse por ~do** take the hint. **~r** *vt* inform (**de** of). **~rse** *vpr*. **~rse de** find out about, hear of. **¡entérate!** listen! **¿te ~s?** do you understand?

entereza *f* (*carácter*) strength of character

enternecer ⓫ *vt* (*fig*) move, touch. **~se** *vpr* be moved, be touched

entero *adj* entire, whole. **por ~** entirely, completely

enterra|dor *m* gravedigger. **~r** ⓵ *vt* bury

entibiar *vt* (*enfriar*) cool; (*calentar*) warm (up). **~se** *vpr* (*enfriarse*) cool down; (*fig*) cool; (*calentarse*) get warm

entidad *f* entity; (*organización*) organization; (*Com*) company; (*importancia*) significance

entierro *m* burial; (*ceremonia*) funeral

entona|ción *f* intonation. **~r** *vt* intone; sing (nota). ● *vi* (*Mus*) be in tune; (colores) match. **~rse** *vpr* (*emborracharse*) get tipsy

entonces *adv* then. **en aquel ~** at that time, then

entorn|ado *adj* (puerta) ajar; (ventana) slightly open. **~o** *m* environment; (*en literatura*) setting

e

entorpecer 11 *vt* dull; slow down (tráfico); (*dificultar*) hinder

entra|da *f* entrance; (*incorporación*) admission, entry; (*para cine etc*) ticket; (*de datos, Tec*) input; (*de una comida*) starter. **de ~da** right away. **~do** *adj*. **~do en años** elderly. **ya ~da la noche** late at night. **~nte** *adj* next, coming

entraña *f* (*fig*) heart. **~s** *fpl* entrails; (*fig*) heart. **~ble** *adj* (cariño) deep; (amigo) close. **~r** *vt* involve

entrar *vt* (*traer*) bring in; (*llevar*) take in. ● *vi* go in, enter; (*venir*) come in, enter; (*empezar*) start, begin; (*incorporarse*) join. **~ en**, (*LAm*) **~ a** go into

entre *prep* (*dos personas o cosas*) between; (*más de dos*) among(st)

entre|abierto *adj* half-open. **~abrir** (*pp* **entreabierto**) *vt* half open. **~acto** *m* interval. **~cejo** *m* forehead. **fruncir el ~cejo** frown. **~cerrar** 1 *vt* (*LAm*) half close. **~cortado** *adj* (voz) faltering; (respiración) laboured. **~cruzar** 10 *vt* intertwine

entrega *f* handing over; (*de mercancías etc*) delivery; (*de novela etc*) instalment; (*dedicación*) commitment. **~r** 12 *vt* deliver; (*dar*) give; hand in (deberes); hand over (poder). **~rse** *vpr* surrender, give o.s. up; (*dedicarse*) devote o.s. (**a** to)

entre|lazar 10 *vt* intertwine. **~més** *m* hors-d'oeuvre; (*en el teatro*) short comedy. **~mezclar** *vt* intermingle

entrena|dor *m* trainer. **~miento** *m* training. **~r** *vt* train. **~rse** *vpr* train

entre|pierna *f* crotch; *medida* inside leg measurement. **~piso** *m* (*LAm*) mezzanine. **~sacar** 7 *vt* pick out; (*peluquería*) thin out **~suelo** *m* mezzanine; (*de cine*) dress circle **~tanto** *adv* meanwhile, in the meantime **~tejer** *vt* weave; (*entrelazar*) interweave

entreten|ción *f* (*LAm*) entertainment. **~er** 40 *vt* entertain, amuse; (*detener*) delay, keep. **~erse** *vpr* amuse o.s.; (*tardar*) delay, linger. **~ido** *adj* (*con ser*) entertaining; (*con estar*) busy. **~imiento** *m* entertainment

entrever 43 *vt* make out, glimpse

entrevista *f* interview; (*reunión*) meeting. **~rse** *vpr* have an interview

entristecer 11 *vt* sadden, make sad. **~se** *vpr* grow sad

entromet|erse *vpr* interfere. **~ido** *adj* interfering

entumec|erse 11 *vpr* go numb. **~ido** *adj* numb

enturbiar *vt* cloud

entusi|asmar *vt* fill with enthusiasm; (*gustar mucho*) delight. **~asmarse** *vpr*. **~asmarse con** get enthusiastic about. **~asmo** *m* enthusiasm. **~asta** *adj* enthusiastic. ● *m & f* enthusiast

enumerar *vt* enumerate

envalentonar *vt* encourage. **~se** *vpr* become bolder

envas|ado *m* packaging; (*en latas*) canning; (*en botellas*) bottling. **~ar** *vt* package; (*en latas*) tin, can; (*en botellas*) bottle. **~e** *m* packing; (*lata*) tin, can; (*botella*) bottle

envejec|er 11 *vt* make (look) older. ● *vi* age, grow old. **~erse** *vpr* age, grow old

envenenar *vt* poison

envergadura *f* importance

envia|do *m* envoy; (*de la prensa*) correspondent. **~r** 20 *vt* send

enviciarse *vpr* become addicted (**con** to)

envidi|a *f* envy; (*celos*) jealousy. **~ar** *vt* envy, be envious of. **~oso** *adj* envious; (*celoso*) jealous. **tener ~a a** envy

envío *m* sending, dispatch; (*de mercancías*) consignment; (*de dinero*) remittance. **~ contra reembolso** cash on delivery. **gastos** *mpl* **de ~** postage and packing (costs)

enviudar *vi* be widowed

env|oltura *f* wrapping. **~olver** 2 (*pp* **envuelto**) *vt* wrap; (*cubrir*) cover; (*ro-*

dear) surround; (*fig*, *enredar*) involve. **~uelto** *adj* wrapped (up)

enyesar *vt* plaster; (*Med*) put in plaster

épica *f* epic

épico *adj* epic

epid|emia *f* epidemic. **~émico** *adj* epidemic

epil|epsia *f* epilepsy. **~éptico** *adj* epileptic

epílogo *m* epilogue

episodio *m* episode

epístola *f* epistle

epitafio *m* epitaph

época *f* age; (*período*) period. **hacer ~** make history, be epoch-making

equidad *f* equity

equilibr|ado *adj* (well-)balanced. **~ar** *vt* balance. **~io** *m* balance; (*de balanza*) equilibrium. **~ista** *m* & *f* tightrope walker

equinoccio *m* equinox

equipaje *m* luggage (*esp Brit*), baggage (*esp Amer*)

equipar *vt* equip; (*de ropa*) fit out

equiparar *vt* make equal; (*comparar*) compare

equipo *m* equipment; (*de personas*) team

equitación *f* riding

equivale|nte *adj* equivalent. **~r** 42 *vi* be equivalent; (*significar*) mean

equivoca|ción *f* mistake, error. **~do** *adj* wrong. **~rse** *vpr* make a mistake; (*estar en error*) be wrong, be mistaken. **~rse de** be wrong about. **~rse de número** dial the wrong number. **si no me equivoco** if I'm not mistaken

equívoco *adj* equivocal; (*sospechoso*) suspicious ● *m* misunderstanding; (*error*) mistake

era *f* era. ● *vb véase* SER

erario *m* treasury

erección *f* erection

eres *vb véase* SER

erguir 48 *vt* raise. **~se** *vpr* raise

erigir 14 *vt* erect. **~se** *vpr*. **~se en** set o.s. up as; (*llegar a ser*) become

eriza|do *adj* prickly. **~rse** 10 *vpr* stand on end; (*LAm*) (*persona*) get goose pimples

erizo *m* hedgehog; (*de mar*) sea urchin. **~ de mar** sea urchin

ermita *f* hermitage. **~ño** *m* hermit

erosi|ón *f* erosion. **~onar** *vt* erode

er|ótico *adj* erotic. **~otismo** *m* eroticism

err|ar 1 (*la* **i** *inicial pasa a ser* **y**) *vt* miss. ● *vi* wander; (*equivocarse*) make a mistake, be wrong. **~ata** *f* misprint. **~óneo** *adj* erroneous, wrong. **~or** *m* error, mistake. **estar en un ~or** be wrong, be mistaken

eruct|ar *vi* belch. **~o** *m* belch

erudi|ción *f* learning, erudition. **~to** *adj* learned; (*palabra*) erudite

erupción *f* eruption; (*Med*) rash

es *vb véase* SER

esa *adj véase* ESE

ésa *pron véase* ÉSE

esbelto *adj* slender, slim

esboz|ar 10 *vt* sketch, outline. **~o** *m* sketch, outline

escabeche *m* brine. **en ~** pickled

escabroso *adj* (*terreno*) rough; (*asunto*) difficult; (*atrevido*) crude

escabullirse 22 *vpr* slip away

escafandra *f* diving-suit

escala *f* scale; (*escalera de mano*) ladder; (*Aviac*) stopover. **hacer ~ en** stop at. **vuelo sin ~s** non-stop flight. **~da** *f* climbing; (*Pol*) escalation. **~r** *vt* climb; break into (*una casa*). ● *vi* climb, go climbing

escaldar *vt* scald

escalera *f* staircase, stairs; (*de mano*) ladder. **~ de caracol** spiral staircase. **~ de incendios** fire escape. **~ de tijera** step-ladder. **~ mecánica** escalator

escalfa|do *adj* poached. **~r** *vt* poach

escalinata *f* flight of steps

escalofrío *m* shiver. **tener ~s** be shivering

escalón *m* step, stair; (*de escala*) rung

escalope *m* escalope

escam|a *f* scale; (*de jabón, de la piel*) flake. **~oso** *adj* scaly; (*piel*) flaky

escamotear *vt* make disappear; (*robar*) steal, pinch

escampar *vi* stop raining

esc|andalizar 10 *vt* scandalize, shock. **~andalizarse** *vpr* be shocked. **~án-**

e

dalo *m* scandal; (*alboroto*) commotion, racket. **armar un** ~ make a scene. ~**andaloso** *adj* scandalous; (*alborotador*) noisy

escandinavo *adj & m* Scandinavian

escaño *m* bench; (*Pol*) seat

escapa|da *f* escape; (*visita*) flying visit. ~**r** *vi* escape. **dejar** ~**r** let out ~**rse** *vpr* escape; (*líquido, gas*) leak

escaparate *m* (shop) window

escap|atoria *f* (*fig*) way out. ~**e** *m* (*de gas, de líquido*) leak; (*fuga*) escape; (*Auto*) exhaust

escarabajo *m* beetle

escaramuza *f* skirmish

escarbar *vt* scratch; pick (dientes, herida); (*fig, escudriñar*) pry (**en** into). ~**se** *vpr* pick

escarcha *f* frost. ~**do** *adj* (fruta) crystallized

escarlat|a *adj invar* scarlet. ~**ina** *f* scarlet fever

escarm|entar 1 *vt* teach a lesson to. ● *vi* learn one's lesson. ~**iento** *m* punishment; (*lección*) lesson

escarola *f* endive

escarpado *adj* steep

escas|ear *vi* be scarce. ~**ez** *f* scarcity, shortage; (*pobreza*) poverty. ~**o** *adj* scarce; (*poco*) little; (*muy justo*) barely. ~**o de** short of

escatimar *vt* be sparing with

escayola *f* plaster

esc|ena *f* scene; (*escenario*) stage. ~**enario** *m* stage; (*fig*) scene. ~**énico** *adj* stage. ~**enografía** *f* set design

esc|epticismo *m* scepticism. ~**éptico** *adj* sceptical. ● *m* sceptic

esclarecer 11 *vt* (*fig*) throw light on, clarify

esclav|itud *f* slavery. ~**izar 10** *vt* enslave. ~**o** *m* slave

esclusa *f* lock; (*de presa*) floodgate

escoba *f* broom

escocer 2 & 9 *vi* sting

escocés *adj* Scottish. ● *m* Scot

Escocia *f* Scotland

escog|er 14 *vt* choose. ~**ido** *adj* chosen; (*mercancía*) choice; (*clientela*) select

escolar *adj* school. ● *m* schoolboy. ● *f* schoolgirl

escolta *f* escort

escombros *mpl* rubble

escond|er *vt* hide. ~**erse** *vpr* hide. ~**idas** *fpl* (*LAm, juego*) hide-and-seek. **a** ~**idas** secretly. ~**ite** *m* hiding place; (*juego*) hide-and-seek. ~**rijo** *m* hiding place

escopeta *f* shotgun

escoria *f* slag; (*fig*) dregs

escorpión *m* scorpion

Escorpión *m* Scorpio

escot|ado *adj* low-cut. ~**e** *m* low neckline. **pagar a** ~**e** share the expenses

escozor *m* stinging

escri|bano *m* clerk. ~**bir** (*pp* **escrito**) *vt/i* write. ~**bir a máquina** type. **¿cómo se escribe...?** how do you spell...? ~**birse** *vpr* write to each other. ~**to** *adj* written. **por** ~**to** in writing. ● *m* document. ~**tor** *m* writer. ~**torio** *m* desk; (*oficina*) office; (*LAm, en una casa*) study. ~**tura** *f* (hand)writing; (*Jurid*) deed

escr|úpulo *m* scruple. ~**upuloso** *adj* scrupulous

escrut|ar *vt* scrutinize; count (votos). ~**inio** *m* count

escuadr|a *f* (*instrumento*) square; (*Mil*) squad; (*Naut*) fleet. ~**ón** *m* squadron

escuálido *adj* skinny

escuchar *vt* listen to; (*esp LAm, oír*) hear. ● *vi* listen

escudo *m* shield. ~ **de armas** coat of arms

escudriñar *vt* examine

escuela *f* school. ~ **normal** teachers' training college

escueto *adj* simple

escuincle *m* (*Mex fam*) kid **1**

escul|pir *vt* sculpture. ~**tor** *m* sculptor. ~**tora** *f* sculptress. ~**tura** *f* sculpture

escupir *vt/i* spit

escurr|eplatos *m invar* plate rack. ~**idizo** *adj* slippery. ~**ir** *vt* drain; wring out (ropa). ● *vi* drain; (ropa) drip. ~**irse** *vpr* slip

ese *adj* (*f* **esa**) that; (*mpl* **esos**, *fpl* **esas**) those

ése *pron* (*f* **ésa**) that one: (*mpl* **ésos**, *fpl* **ésas**) those; (*primero de dos*) the former

esencia *f* essence. **∼l** *adj* essential. **lo ∼l** the main thing

esf|era *f* sphere; (*de reloj*) face. **∼érico** *adj* spherical

esf|orzarse ② & ⑩ *vpr* make an effort. **∼uerzo** *m* effort

esfumarse *vpr* fade away; (*persona*) vanish

esgrim|a *f* fencing. **∼ir** *vt* brandish; (*fig*) use

esguince *m* sprain

eslabón *m* link

eslavo *adj* Slavic, Slavonic

eslogan *m* slogan

esmalt|ar *vt* enamel. **∼e** *m* enamel. **∼e de uñas** nail polish

esmerado *adj* careful; (persona) painstaking

esmeralda *f* emerald

esmer|arse *vpr* take care (**en** over).

esmero *m* care

esmoquin (*pl* **esmóquines**) *m* dinner jacket, tuxedo (*Amer*)

esnob *adj invar* snobbish. ● *m & f* (*pl* **∼s**) snob. **∼ismo** *m* snobbery

esnórkel *m* snorkel

eso *pron* that. **¡∼ es!** that's it! **∼ mismo** exactly. **a ∼ de** about **en ∼** at that moment. **¿no es ∼?** isn't that right? **por ∼** that's why. **y ∼ que** even though

esos *adj pl véase* **ESE**

ésos *pron pl véase* **ÉSE**

espabila|do *adj* bright; (*despierto*) awake. **∼r** *vt* (*avivar*) brighten up; (*despertar*) wake up. **∼rse** *vpr* wake up; (*avivarse*) wise up; (*apresurarse*) hurry up

espaci|al *adj* space. **∼ar** *vt* space out. **∼o** *m* space. **∼oso** *adj* spacious

espada *f* sword. **∼s** *fpl* (*en naipes*) spades

espaguetis *mpl* spaghetti

espald|a *f* back. **a ∼as de uno** behind s.o.'s back. **volver la(s) ∼a(s) a uno** give s.o. the cold shoulder. **∼ mojada** wetback. **∼illa** *f* shoulder-blade

espant|ajo *m*, **∼apájaros** *m invar* scarecrow. **∼ar** *vt* frighten; (*ahuyen-*

tar) frighten away. **∼arse** *vpr* be frightened; (*ahuyentarse*) be frightened away. **∼o** *m* terror; (*horror*) horror. **¡qué ∼o!** how awful! **∼oso** *adj* horrific; (*terrible*) terrible

España *f* Spain

español *adj* Spanish. ● *m* (*persona*) Spaniard; (*lengua*) Spanish. **los ∼es** the Spanish

esparadrapo *m* (sticking) plaster

esparcir ⑨ *vt* scatter; (*difundir*) spread. **∼rse** *vpr* be scattered; (*difundirse*) spread; (*divertirse*) enjoy o.s.

espárrago *m* asparagus

espasm|o *m* spasm. **∼ódico** *adj* spasmodic

espátula *f* spatula; (*en pintura*) palette knife

especia *f* spice

especial *adj* special. **en ∼** especially. **∼idad** *f* speciality (*Brit*), specialty (*Amer*). **∼ista** *adj & m & f* specialist. **∼ización** *f* specialization. **∼izarse** ⑩ *vpr* specialize. **∼mente** *adv* especially

especie *f* kind, sort; (*en biología*) species. **en ∼** in kind

especifica|ción *f* specification. **∼r** ⑦ *vt* specify

específico *adj* specific

espect|áculo *m* sight; (*de circo etc*) show. **∼acular** *adj* spectacular. **∼ador** *m & f* spectator

espectro *m* spectre; (*en física*) spectrum

especula|dor *m* speculator. **∼r** *vi* speculate

espej|ismo *m* mirage. **∼o** *m* mirror. **∼o retrovisor** (*Auto*) rear-view mirror

espeluznante *adj* horrifying

espera *f* wait. **a la ∼** waiting (**de** for). **∼nza** *f* hope. **∼r** *vt* hope; (*aguardar*) wait for; expect (vista, carta, bebé). **espero que no** I hope not. **espero que sí** I hope so. ● *vi* (*aguardar*) wait. **∼rse** *vpr* hang on; (*prever*) expect

esperma *f* sperm

esperpento *m* fright

espes|ar *vt/i* thicken. **∼arse** *vpr* thicken. **∼o** *adj* thick. **∼or** *m* thickness

espetón *m* spit

esp|ía f spy. **~iar** 20 vt spy on. ● vi spy

espiga f (de trigo etc) ear

espina f thorn; (de pez) bone; (en anatomía) spine. **~ dorsal** spine

espinaca f spinach

espinazo m spine

espinilla f shin; (Med) blackhead; (LAm, grano) spot

espino m hawthorn. **~so** adj thorny; (fig) difficult

espionaje m espionage

espiral adj & f spiral

esp|iritista m & f spiritualist. **~íritu** m spirit; (mente) mind. **~iritual** adj spiritual

espl|éndido adj splendid; (persona) generous. **~endor** m splendour

espolear vt spur (on)

espolvorear vt sprinkle

esponj|a f sponge. **~oso** adj spongy

espont|aneidad f spontaneity. **~áneo** adj spontaneous

esporádico adj sporadic

espos|a f wife. **~as** fpl handcuffs. **~ar** vt handcuff. **~o** m husband

espuela f spur; (fig) incentive

espum|a f foam; (en bebidas) froth; (de jabón) lather; (de las olas) surf. **echar ~a** foam, froth. **~oso** adj (vino) sparkling

esqueleto m skeleton; (estructura) framework

esquema m outline

esqu|í m (pl **~ís**, **~íes**) ski; (deporte) skiing. **~iar** 20 vi ski

esquilar vt shear

esquimal adj & m Eskimo

esquina f corner

esquiv|ar vt avoid; dodge (golpe). **~o** adj elusive

esquizofrénico adj & m schizophrenic

esta adj véase ESTE

ésta pron véase ÉSTE

estab|ilidad f stability. **~le** adj stable

establec|er 11 vt establish. **~erse** vpr settle; (Com) set up. **~imiento** m establishment

establo m cattleshed

estaca f stake

estación f station; (del año) season. **~ de invierno** winter (sports) resort. **~ de servicio** service station

estaciona|miento m parking; (LAm, lugar) car park (Brit), parking lot (Amer). **~r** vt station; (Auto) park. **~rio** adj stationary

estadía f (LAm) stay

estadio m stadium; (fase) stage

estadista m statesman. ● f stateswoman

estadístic|a f statistics; (cifra) statistic. **~o** adj statistical

estado m state; (Med) condition. **~ civil** marital status. **~ de ánimo** frame of mind. **~ de cuenta** bank statement. **~ mayor** (Mil) staff. **en buen ~** in good condition

Estados Unidos mpl United States

estadounidense adj American, United States. ● m & f American

estafa f swindle. **~r** vt swindle

estafeta f (oficina de correos) (sub-)post office

estala|ctita f stalactite. **~gmita** f stalagmite

estall|ar vi explode; (olas) break; (guerra etc) break out; (fig) burst. **~ar en llanto** burst into tears. **~ar de risa** burst out laughing. **~ido** m explosion; (de guerra etc) outbreak

estamp|a f print; (aspecto) appearance. **~ado** adj printed. ● m printing; (motivo) pattern; (tela) cotton print. **~ar** vt stamp; (imprimir) print

estampido m bang

estampilla f (LAm, de correos) (postage) stamp

estanca|do adj stagnant. **~r** 7 vt stem. **~rse** vpr stagnate

estancia f stay; (cuarto) large room

estanco adj watertight. ● m tobacconist's (shop)

---

estanco In Spain, an establishment selling tobacco, stamps, bus and metro passes and other products whose sale is restricted. Cigarettes etc are sold in bars and cafés but at higher prices. *Estancos* also sell stationery and sometimes papers.

i

estandarte *m* standard, banner

estanque *m* pond; (*depósito de agua*) (water) tank

estanquero *m* tobacconist

estante *m* shelf. **~ría** *f* shelves; (*para libros*) bookcase

estaño *m* tin

---

estar 27

● *verbo intransitivo*

••••▶ to be ¿**cómo estás?** how are you?. **estoy enfermo** I'm ill. **está muy cerca** it's very near. ¿**está Pedro?** is Pedro in? ¿**cómo está el tiempo?** what's the weather like? **ya estamos en invierno** it's winter already

••••▶ (*quedarse*) to stay. **sólo ~é una semana** I'll only be staying for a week. **estoy en un hotel** I'm staying in a hotel

••••▶ (*con fecha*) ¿**a cuánto estamos?** what's the date today? **estamos a 8 de mayo** it's the 8th of May.

••••▶ (*en locuciones*) ¿**estamos?** all right? ¡**ahí está!** that's it! **~ por** (*apoyar a*) to support; (*LAm, encontrarse a punto de*) to be about to; (*quedar por*) **eso está por verse** that remains to be seen. **son cuentas que están por pagar** they're bills still to be paid

● *verbo auxiliar*

••••▶ (*con gerundio*) **estaba estudiando** I was studying

••••▶ (*con participio*) **está condenado a muerte** he's been sentenced to death. **está mal traducido** it's wrongly translated. **estarse** *verbo pronominal* to stay. **no se está quieto** he won't stay still

➡️ Cuando el verbo **estar** forma parte de expresiones como **estar de acuerdo**, **estar a la vista**, **estar constipado**, etc., ver bajo el respectivo nombre o adjetivo

---

estatal *adj* state

estático *adj* static

estatua *f* statue

estatura *f* height

estatuto *m* statute; (*norma*) rule

este *adj* (*región*) eastern; (*viento, lado*) east. ● *m* east. ● *adj* (*f* **esta**) this; (*mpl* **estos**, *fpl* **estas**) these. ● *int* (*LAm*) well, er

éste *pron* (*f* **ésta**) this one; (*mpl* **éstos**, *fpl* **éstas**) these; (*segundo de dos*) the latter

estela *f* wake; (*de avión*) trail; (*lápida*) carved stone

estera *f* mat; (*tejido*) matting

est|éreo *adj* stereo. **~ereofónico** *adj* stereo, stereophonic

estereotipo *m* stereotype

estéril *adj* sterile; (*terreno*) barren

esterilla *f* mat

esterlina *adj*. **libra** *f* **~** pound sterling

estético *adj* aesthetic

estiércol *m* dung; (*abono*) manure

estigma *m* stigma. **~s** *mpl* (*Relig*) stigmata

estil|arse *vpr* be used. **~o** *m* style; (*en natación*) stroke. **~ mariposa** butterfly. **~ pecho** (*LAm*) breaststroke. **por el ~o** of that sort

estilográfica *f* fountain pen

estima *f* esteem. **~do** *adj* (*amigo, colega*) valued. **~do señor** (*en cartas*) Dear Sir. **~r** *vt* esteem; have great respect for (*persona*); (*valorar*) value; (*juzgar*) consider

est|imulante *adj* stimulating. ● *m* stimulant. **~imular** *vt* stimulate; (*incitar*) incite. **~ímulo** *m* stimulus

estir|ado *adj* stretched; (*persona*) haughty. **~ar** *vt* stretch; (*fig*) stretch out. **~ón** *m* pull, tug; (*crecimiento*) sudden growth

estirpe *m* stock

esto *pron neutro* this; (*este asunto*) this business. **en ~** at this point. **en ~ de** in this business of. **por ~** therefore

estofa|do *adj* stewed. ● *m* stew. **~r** *vt* stew

estómago *m* stomach. **dolor** *m* **de ~** stomach ache

estorb|ar *vt* obstruct; (*molestar*) bother. ● *vi* be in the way. **~o** *m* hindrance; (*molestia*) nuisance

estornud|ar vi sneeze. **~o** m sneeze

estos adj mpl véase **ESTE**

éstos pron mpl véase **ÉSTE**

estoy vb véase **ESTAR**

estrabismo m squint

estrado m stage; (Mus) bandstand

estrafalario adj eccentric; (ropa) outlandish

estrago m devastation. **hacer ~os** devastate

estragón m tarragon

estrambótico adj eccentric; (ropa) outlandish

estrangula|dor m strangler; (Auto) choke. **~r** vt strangle

estratagema f stratagem

estrat|ega m & f strategist. **~egia** f strategy. **~égico** adj strategic

estrato m stratum

estrech|ar vt make narrower; take in (vestido); embrace (persona). **~ar la mano a uno** shake hands with s.o. **~arse** vpr become narrower; (abrazarse) embrace. **~ez** f narrowness. **~eces** fpl financial difficulties. **~o** adj narrow; (vestido etc) tight; (fig, íntimo) close. ● **~o de miras** narrow-minded. ● m strait(s)

estrella f star. **~ de mar** starfish. **~ado** adj starry

estrellar vt smash; crash (coche). **~se** vpr crash (**contra** into)

estremec|er 11 vt shake. **~erse** vpr shake; (de emoción etc) tremble (**de** with). **~imiento** m shaking

estren|ar vt wear for the first time (vestido etc); show for the first time (película). **~arse** vpr make one's début. **~o** m (de película) première; (de obra de teatro) first night; (de persona) debut

estreñi|do adj constipated. **~miento** m constipation

estrés m stress

estría f groove; (de la piel) stretch mark

estribillo m (incl Mus) refrain

estribo m stirrup; (de coche) step. **perder los ~s** lose one's temper

estribor m starboard

estricto adj strict

estridente adj strident, raucous

estrofa f stanza, verse

estropajo m scourer

estropear vt damage; (plan) spoil; ruin (ropa). **~se** vpr be damaged; (averiarse) break down; (ropa) get ruined; (fruta etc) go bad; (fracasar) fail

estructura f structure. **~l** adj structural

estruendo m roar; (de mucha gente) uproar

estrujar vt squeeze; wring (out) (ropa); (fig) drain

estuario m estuary

estuche m case

estudi|ante m & f student. **~antil** adj student. **~ar** vt study. **~o** m study; (de artista) studio. **~oso** adj studious

estufa f heater; (Mex, cocina) cooker

estupefac|iente m narcotic. **~to** adj astonished

estupendo adj marvellous; (persona) fantastic; **¡~!** that's great!

est|upidez f stupidity; (acto) stupid thing. **~úpido** adj stupid

estupor m amazement

estuve vb véase **ESTAR**

etapa f stage. **por ~s** in stages

etéreo adj ethereal

etern|idad f eternity. **~o** adj eternal

étic|a f ethics. **~o** adj ethical

etimología f etymology

etiqueta f ticket, tag; (ceremonial) etiquette. **de ~** formal

étnico adj ethnic

eucalipto m eucalyptus

eufemismo m euphemism

euforia f euphoria

euro m euro. **~escéptico** adj & m Eurosceptic

Europa f Europe

euro|peo adj & m European. **~zona** f eurozone

eutanasia f euthanasia

evacua|ción f evacuation. **~r** 21 vt evacuate

evadir vt avoid; evade (impuestos). **~se** vpr escape

evalua|ción f evaluation. **~r** 21 vt assess; evaluate (datos)

evangeli|o m gospel. **~sta** m & f evangelist; (*Mex, escribiente*) scribe

evapora|ción f evaporation. **~rse** vpr evaporate; (*fig*) disappear

evasi|ón f evasion; (*fuga*) escape. **~vo** adj evasive

evento m event; (*caso*) case

eventual adj possible. **~idad** f eventuality

eviden|cia f evidence. **poner en ~cia a uno** show s.o. up. **~ciar** vt show. **~ciarse** vpr be obvious. **~te** adj obvious. **~temente** adv obviously

evitar vt avoid; (*ahorrar*) spare; (*prevenir*) prevent

evocar 7 vt evoke

evoluci|ón f evolution. **~onar** vi evolve; (*Mil*) manoeuvre

ex prefijo ex-, former

exacerbar vt exacerbate

exact|amente adv exactly. **~itud** f exactness. **~o** adj exact; (*preciso*) accurate; (*puntual*) punctual. **¡~!** exactly!

exagera|ción f exaggeration. **~do** adj exaggerated. **~r** vt/i exaggerate

exalta|do adj exalted; (*excitado*) (over-)excited; (*fanático*) hot-headed. **~r** vt exalt. **~rse** vpr get excited

exam|en m exam, examination. **~inar** vt examine. **~inarse** vpr take an exam

exasperar vt exasperate. **~se** vpr get exasperated

excarcela|ción f release (from prison). **~r** vt release

excava|ción f excavation. **~dora** f digger. **~r** vt excavate

excede|ncia f leave of absence. **~nte** adj & m surplus. **~r** vi exceed. **~rse** vpr go too far

excelen|cia f excellence; (*tratamiento*) Excellency. **~te** adj excellent

exc|entricidad f eccentricity. **~éntrico** adj & m eccentric

excepci|ón f exception. **~onal** adj exceptional. **a ~ón de, con ~ón de** except (for)

except|o prep except (for). **~uar** 21 vt except

exces|ivo adj excessive. **~o** m excess. **~o de equipaje** excess luggage (*esp*

Brit), excess baggage (*esp Amer*)

excita|ción f excitement. **~r** vt excite; (*incitar*) incite. **~rse** vpr get excited

exclama|ción f exclamation. **~r** vi exclaim

exclu|ir 17 vt exclude. **~sión** f exclusion. **~siva** f sole right; (*reportaje*) exclusive (story). **~sivo** adj exclusive

excomu|lgar 12 vt excommunicate. **~nión** f excommunication

excremento m excrement

excursi|ón f excursion, outing. **~onista** m & f day-tripper

excusa f excuse; (*disculpa*) apology. **presentar sus ~s** apologize. **~r** vt excuse

exento adj exempt; (*libre*) free

exhalar vt exhale, breath out; give off (olor etc)

exhaust|ivo adj exhaustive. **~o** adj exhausted

exhibi|ción f exhibition; (*demostración*) display. **~cionista** m & f exhibitionist. **~r** vt exhibit **~rse** vpr show o.s.; (*hacerse notar*) draw attention to o.s.

exhumar vt exhume; (*fig*) dig up

exig|encia f demand. **~ente** adj demanding. **~ir** 14 vt demand

exiguo adj meagre

exil|(i)ado adj exiled. ● m exile. **~(i)arse** vpr go into exile. **~io** m exile

exim|ente m reason for exemption; (*Jurid*) grounds for acquittal. **~ir** vt exempt

existencia f existence. **~s** fpl stock. **~lismo** m existentialism

exist|ente adj existing. **~ir** vi exist

éxito m success. **no tener ~** fail. **tener ~** be successful

exitoso adj successful

éxodo m exodus

exonerar vt exonerate

exorbitante adj exorbitant

exorci|smo m exorcism. **~zar** 10 vt exorcise

exótico adj exotic

expan|dir vt expand; (*fig*) spread. **~dirse** vpr expand. **~sión** f expansion. **~sivo** adj expansive

expatria|do *adj & m* expatriate. **~rse** *vpr* emigrate; (*exiliarse*) go into exile

expectativa *f* prospect; (*esperanza*) expectation. **estar a la ~** be waiting

expedi|ción *f* expedition; (*de documento*) issue; (*de mercancías*) dispatch. **~ente** *m* record, file; (*Jurid*) proceedings. **~r** 5 *vt* issue; (*enviar*) dispatch, send. **~to** *adj* clear; (*LAm, fácil*) easy

expeler *vt* expel

expend|edor *m* dealer. **~edor automático** vending machine. **~io** *m* (*LAm*) shop; (*venta*) sale

expensas *fpl* (*Jurid*) costs. **a ~ de** at the expense of. **a mis ~** at my expense

experiencia *f* experience

experiment|al *adj* experimental. **~ar** *vt* test, experiment with; (*sentir*) experience. **~o** *m* experiment

experto *adj & m* expert

expiar 20 *vt* atone for

expirar *vi* expire

explanada *f* levelled area; (*paseo*) esplanade

explayarse *vpr* speak at length; (*desahogarse*) unburden o.s. (**con** to)

explica|ción *f* explanation. **~r** 7 *vt* explain. **~rse** *vpr* understand; (*hacerse comprender*) explain o.s. **no me lo explico** I can't understand it

explícito *adj* explicit

explora|ción *f* exploration. **~dor** *m* explorer; (*muchacho*) boy scout. **~r** *vt* explore

explosi|ón *f* explosion; (*fig*) outburst. **~onar** *vt* blow up. **~vo** *adj & m* explosive

explota|ción *f* working; (*abuso*) exploitation. **~r** *vt* work (mina); farm (tierra); (*abusar*) exploit. ● *vi* explode

expone|nte *m* exponent. **~r** 34 *vt* expose; display (mercancías); present (tema); set out (hechos); exhibit (cuadros etc); (*arriesgar*) risk. ● *vi* exhibit. **~rse** *vpr*. **~se a que** run the risk of

exporta|ción *f* export. **~dor** *m* exporter. **~r** *vt* export

exposición *f* exposure; (*de cuadros etc*) exhibition; (*de hechos*) exposition

expres|ar *vt* express. **~arse** *vpr* express o.s. **~ión** *f* expression. **~ivo** *adj* expressive; (*cariñoso*) affectionate

expreso *adj* express. ● *m* express; (*café*) expresso

exprimi|dor *m* squeezer. **~r** *vt* squeeze

expropiar *vt* expropriate

expuesto *adj* on display; (*lugar etc*) exposed; (*peligroso*) dangerous. **estar ~ a** be exposed to

expuls|ar *vt* expel; throw out (persona); send off (jugador). **~ión** *f* expulsion

exquisito *adj* exquisite; (*de sabor*) delicious

éxtasis *m invar* ecstasy

extend|er 1 *vt* spread (out); (*ampliar*) extend; issue (documento). **~erse** *vpr* spread; (*paisaje etc*) extend, stretch. **~ido** *adj* spread out; (*generalizado*) widespread; (*brazos*) outstretched

extens|amente *adv* widely; (*detalladamente*) in full. **~ión** *f* extension; (*área*) expanse; (*largo*) length. **~o** *adj* extensive

extenuar 21 *vt* exhaust

exterior *adj* external, exterior; (*del extranjero*) foreign; (*aspecto etc*) outward. ● *m* outside, exterior; (*países extranjeros*) abroad

extermin|ación *f* extermination. **~ar** *vt* exterminate. **~io** *m* extermination

externo *adj* external; (*signo etc*) outward. ● *m* day pupil

extin|ción *f* extinction. **~guidor** *m* (*LAm*) fire extinguisher. **~guir** 13 *vt* extinguish. **~guirse** *vpr* die out; (*fuego*) go out. **~to** *adj* (*raza etc*) extinct. **~tor** *m* fire extinguisher

extirpar *vt* eradicate; remove (tumor)

extorsión *f* extortion

extra *adj invar* extra; (*de buena calidad*) good-quality; (*huevos*) large. **paga** *f* **~** bonus

extracto *m* extract

extradición *f* extradition

extraer 41 *vt* extract

extranjer|ía *f* (*Esp*) **la ley de ~** immigration law. **~o** *adj* foreign. ●*m* foreigner; (*países*) foreign countries.

del ~ from abroad. **en el** ~, **por el** ~ abroad

extrañ|ar vt surprise; (encontrar extraño) find strange; (LAm, echar de menos) miss. **~arse** vpr be surprised (**de** at). **~eza** f strangeness; (asombro) surprise. **~o** adj strange. ● m stranger

extraoficial adj unofficial

extraordinario adj extraordinary

extrarradio m outlying districts

extraterrestre adj extraterrestrial. ● m alien

extravagan|cia f oddness, eccentricity. **~te** adj odd, eccentric

extrav|iado adj lost. **~iar** 20 vt lose. **~iarse** vpr get lost, (objetos) go missing. **~io** m loss

extremar vt take extra (precauciones); tighten up (vigilancia). **~se** vpr make every effort

extremeño adj from Extremadura

extrem|idad f end. **~idades** fpl extremities. **~ista** adj & m & f extremist. **~o** adj extreme. ● m end; (colmo) extreme. **en** ~o extremely. **en último** ~o as a last resort

extrovertido adj & m extrovert

exuberan|cia f exuberance. **~te** adj exuberant

eyacular vt/i ejaculate

· · · · · · · · · · · · · · · · · · ·

Ff

· · · · · · · · · · · · · · · · · · ·

fa m F; (solfa) fah

fabada f bean and pork stew

fábrica f factory. **marca** f **de** ~ trade mark

fabrica|ción f manufacture. **~ción en serie** mass production. **~nte** m & f manufacturer. **~r** 7 vt manufacture

fábula f fable; (mentira) fabrication

fabuloso adj fabulous

facci|ón f faction. **~ones** fpl (de la cara) features

faceta f facet

facha f (fam, aspecto) look. **~da** f façade

fácil adj easy; (probable) likely

facili|dad f ease; (disposición) aptitude. **~dades** fpl facilities. **~tar** vt facilitate; (proporcionar) provide

factible adj feasible

factor m factor

factura f bill, invoice. **~r** vt (hacer la factura) invoice; (al embarcar) check in

faculta|d f faculty; (capacidad) ability; (poder) power. **~tivo** adj optional

faena f job. **~s domésticas** housework

faisán m pheasant

faja f (de tierra) strip; (corsé) corset; (Mil etc) sash

fajo m bundle; (de billetes) wad

falda f skirt; (de montaña) side

falla f fault; (defecto) flaw. ~ **humana** (LAm) human error. **~r** vi fail. **me falló** he let me down. **sin** ~**r** without fail. ● vt (errar) miss

fallec|er 11 vi die. **~ido** m deceased

fallido adj vain; (fracasado) unsuccessful

fallo m (defecto) fault; (error) mistake. ~ **humano** human error; (en certamen) decision; (Jurid) ruling

falluca f (Mex) smuggled goods

fals|ear vt falsify, distort. **~ificación** f forgery. **~ificador** m forger. **~ificar** 7 vt forge. **~o** adj false; (falsificado) forged; (joya) fake

falt|a f lack; (ausencia) absence; (escasez) shortage; (defecto) fault, defect; (culpa) fault; (error) mistake; (en fútbol etc) foul; (en tenis) fault. **a** ~**a de** for lack of. **echar en** ~**a** miss. **hacer** ~**a** be necessary. **me hace** ~**a** I need. **sacar** ~**as** find fault. ~**o** adj lacking (**de** in)

---

faltar   verbo intransitivo

❗ cuando el verbo **faltar** va precedido del complemento indirecto **le** (o **les**, **nos** etc) el sujeto en español pasa a ser el objeto en inglés p.ej: **les falta experiencia** they lack experience

····▸ (no estar) to be missing **¿quién falta?** who's missing? **falta una de las chicas** one of the girls is missing. **al abrigo le faltan 3 botones** the coat has three buttons missing. ~ **a algo** (*no asistir*) to be absent from sth; (*no acudir*) to miss sth

····➤ (*no haber suficiente*) **va a ~ leche** there won't be enough milk. **nos faltó tiempo** we didn't have enough time

····➤ (*no tener*) **le falta cariño** he lacks affection

····➤ (*hacer falta*) **le falta sal** it needs more salt. **¡es lo que nos faltaba!** that's all we needed!

····➤ (*quedar*) **¿te falta mucho?** are you going to be much longer? **falta poco para Navidad** it's not long until Christmas. **aún falta mucho** (*distancia*) there's a long way to go yet **¡no faltaba más!** of course!

fama *f* fame; (*reputación*) reputation

famélico *adj* starving

familia *f* family; (*hijos*) children. ~ **numerosa** large family. ~**r** *adj* familiar; (*de la familia*) family; (*sin ceremonia*) informal; (*lenguaje*) colloquial. ● *m & f* relative. ~**ridad** *f* familiarity. ~**rizarse** 🔟 *vpr* become familiar (**con** with)

famoso *adj* famous

fanático *adj* fanatical. ● *m* fanatic

fanfarr|ón *adj* boastful. ● *m* braggart. ~**onear** *vi* show off

fango *m* mud. ~**so** *adj* muddy

fantasía *f* fantasy. **de** ~ fancy; (*joya*) imitation

fantasma *m* ghost

fantástico *adj* fantastic

fardo *m* bundle

faringe *f* pharynx

farmac|éutico *m* chemist (*Brit*), pharmacist, druggist (*Amer*). ~**ia** *f* (*ciencia*) pharmacy; (*tienda*) chemist's (shop) (*Brit*), pharmacy

faro *m* lighthouse; (*Aviac*) beacon; (*Auto*) headlight

farol *m* lantern; (*de la calle*) street lamp. ~**a** *f* street lamp

farr|a *f* partying. ~**ear** *vi* (*LAm*) go out partying

farsa *f* farce. ~**nte** *m & f* fraud

fascículo *m* instalment

fascinar *vt* fascinate

fascis|mo *m* fascism

fase *f* phase

fastidi|ar *vt* annoy; (*estropear*) spoil. ~**arse** *vpr* (*máquina*) break down; hurt (pierna); (*LAm, molestarse*) get annoyed. **¡para que te ~es!** so there!. ~**o** *m* nuisance; (*aburrimiento*) boredom. ~**oso** *adj* annoying

fatal *adj* fateful; (*mortal*) fatal; (*fam, pésimo*) terrible. ~**idad** *f* fate; (*desgracia*) misfortune

fatig|a *f* fatigue. ~**ar** 🔢 *vt* tire. ~**arse** *vpr* get tired. ~**oso** *adj* tiring

fauna *f* fauna

favor *m* favour. **a** ~ **de, en** ~ **de** in favour of. **haga el** ~ **de** would you be so kind as to, please. **por** ~ please

favorec|er 🔢 *vt* favour; (vestido, peinado etc) suit. ~**ido** *adj* favoured

favorito *adj & m* favourite

fax *m* fax

faxear *vt* fax

faz *f* face

fe *f* faith. **dar** ~ **de** certify. **de buena** ~ in good faith

febrero *m* February

febril *adj* feverish

fecha *f* date. **a estas** ~**s** now; (*todavía*) still. **hasta la** ~ so far. **poner la** ~ date. ~**r** *vt* date

fecund|ación *f* fertilization. ~**ación artificial** artificial insemination. ~**ar** *vt* fertilize. ~**o** *adj* fertile; (*fig*) prolific

federa|ción *f* federation. ~**l** *adj* federal

felici|dad *f* happiness. ~**dades** *fpl* best wishes; (*congratulaciones*) congratulations. ~**tación** *f* letter of congratulation. **¡~taciones!** (*LAm*) congratulations! ~**tar** *vt* congratulate

feligrés *m* parishioner

feliz *adj* happy; (*afortunado*) lucky. **¡Felices Pascuas!** Happy Christmas! **¡F~ Año Nuevo!** Happy New Year!

felpudo *m* doormat

fem|enil *adj* (*Mex*) women's. ~**enino** *adj* feminine; (*equipo*) women's; (*en*

biología) female. ● *m* feminine.
~**inista** *adj & m & f* feminist.
fen|omenal *adj* phenomenal.
~**ómeno** *m* phenomenon; *(monstruo)*
freak
feo *adj* ugly; *(desagradable)* nasty. ● *adv*
(LAm) (mal) bad
feria *f* fair; *(verbena)* carnival; *(Mex,*
cambio) small change. ~**do** *m* *(LAm)*
public holiday
ferment|ar *vt/i* ferment. ~**o** *m* fer-
ment
fero|cidad *f* ferocity. ~**z** *adj* fierce
férreo *adj* iron; *(disciplina)* strict
ferreter|ía *f* hardware store, iron-
monger's *(Brit)*. ~**o** *m* hardware
dealer, ironmonger *(Brit)*
ferro|carril *m* railway *(Brit)*, railroad
(Amer). ~**viario** *adj* rail. ● *m* railway-
man *(Brit)*, railroader *(Amer)*
fértil *adj* fertile
fertili|dad *f* fertility. ~**zante** *m* fertil-
izer. ~**zar** 🔟 *vt* fertilize
ferv|iente *adj* fervent. ~**or** *m* fervour
festej|ar *vt* celebrate; entertain (per-
sona). ~**o** *m* celebration
festiv|al *m* festival. ~**idad** *f* festivity.
~**o** *adj* festive. ● *m* public holiday
fétido *adj* stinking
feto *m* foetus
fiable *adj* reliable
fiado *m* al ~. on credit. ~**r** *m* *(Jurid)*
guarantor
fiambre *m* cold meat. ~**ría** *f* *(LAm)*
delicatessen
fianza *f* *(dinero)* deposit; *(objeto)*
surety. **bajo** ~. on bail
fiar 🔟 *vt* *(vender)* sell on credit; *(con-*
fiar) confide. ● *vi* give credit. ~**se** *vpr*.
~**se de** trust
fibra *f* fibre. ~ **de vidrio** fibreglass
ficción *f* fiction
fich|a *f* token; *(tarjeta)* index card; *(en*
juegos) counter. ~**ar** *vt* open a file
on. **estar** ~**ado** have a (police) record. ~**ero** *m* card index; *(en infor-*
mática) file
fidedigno *adj* reliable
fidelidad *f* faithfulness
fideos *mpl* noodles
fiebre *f* fever. ~ **aftosa** foot-and-
mouth disease. ~ **del heno** hay

fever. ~ **porcina** swine fever. **tener**
~ have a temperature
fiel *adj* faithful; *(memoria, relato etc)*
reliable. ● *m* believer
fieltro *m* felt
fier|a *f* wild animal. ~**o** *adj* fierce
fierro *m* *(LAm)* metal bar; *(hierro)* iron
fiesta *f* party; *(día festivo)* holiday. ~**s**
fpl celebrations

---

fiestas A *fiesta* in Spain can
be a day of local celebrations, a larger event for a town or
city, or a national holiday to com-
memorate a saint's day or a histor-
ical event. Famous Spanish *fiestas*
include The *fallas* in Valencia, the
Sanfermines in Pamplona, and the
Feria de Sevilla. In Latin America *fiestas patrias* are a period of one or
more days when each country cele-
brates its independence. There are
usually military parades, firework
displays, and cultural events typical
of the country.

---

figura *f* figure; *(forma)* shape. ~**r** *vi*
appear; *(destacar)* show off. ~**rse** *vpr*
imagine. **¡figúrate!** just imagine!
fij|ación *f* fixing; *(obsesión)* fixation.
~**ar** *vt* fix; establish *(residencia)*.
~**arse** *vpr* *(poner atención)* pay attention; *(precatarse)* notice. **¡fíjate!** just
imagine! ~**o** *adj* fixed; *(firme)* stable;
(permanente) permanent. ● *adv*. **mirar**
~**o** stare
fila *f* line; *(de soldados etc)* file; *(en el*
teatro, cine etc) row; *(cola)* queue. **po-**
nerse en ~ line up
filántropo *m* philanthropist
filat|elia *f* stamp collecting, philately.
~**élico** *adj* philatelic. ● *m* stamp collector, philatelist
filete *m* fillet
filial *adj* filial. ● *f* subsidiary
Filipinas *fpl.* **las (islas)** ~ the Philip-
pines
filipino *adj* Philippine, Filipino
filmar *vt* film; shoot *(película)*
filo *m* edge; *(de hoja)* cutting edge. **al**
~ **de las doce** at exactly twelve
o'clock. **sacar** ~ **a** sharpen
filología *f* philology

filón *m* vein; (*fig*) gold-mine

fil|osofía *f* philosophy. **∼ósofo** *m* philosopher

filtr|ar *vt* filter. **∼arse** *vpr* filter; (dinero) disappear; (noticia) leak. **∼o** *m* filter; (*bebida*) philtre. **∼ solar** sunscreen

fin *m* end; (*objetivo*) aim. **∼ de semana** weekend. **a ∼ de** in order to. **a ∼ de cuentas** at the end of the day. **a ∼ de que** in order that. **a ∼es de** at the end of. **al ∼** finally. **al ∼ y al cabo** after all. **dar ∼ a** end. **en ∼** in short. **por ∼** finally. **sin ∼** endless

final *adj* final. ● *m* end. ● *f* final. **∼idad** *f* aim. **∼ista** *m & f* finalist. **∼izar** 🔟 *vt* finish. ● *vi* end

financi|ación *f* financing; (*fondos*) funds; (*facilidades*) credit facilities. **∼ar** *vt* finance. **∼ero** *adj* financial. ● *m* financier

finca *f* property; (*tierras*) estate; (*rural*) farm; (*de recreo*) country house

fingir 🔢 *vt* feign; (*simular*) simulate. ● *vi* pretend. **∼se** *vpr* pretend to be

finlandés *adj* Finnish. ● *m* (*persona*) Finn; (*lengua*) Finnish

Finlandia *f* Finland

fino *adj* fine; (*delgado*) thin; (*oído*) acute; (*de modales*) refined; (*sutil*) subtle

firma *f* signature; (*acto*) signing; (*empresa*) firm

firmar *vt/i* sign

firme *adj* firm; (*estable*) stable, steady; (*color*) fast. ● *m* (*pavimento*) (road) surface. ● *adv* hard. **∼za** *f* firmness

fisc|al *adj* fiscal, tax. ● *m & f* public prosecutor. **∼o** *m* treasury

fisg|ar 🔢 *vi* snoop (around). **∼ón** *adj* nosy. ● *m* snooper

físic|a *f* physics. **∼o** *adj* physical. ● *m* physique; (*persona*) physicist

fisonomista *m & f.* **ser buen ∼** be good at remembering faces

fistol *m* (*Mex*) tiepin

flaco *adj* thin, skinny; (*débil*) weak

flagelo *m* scourge

flagrante *adj* flagrant. **en ∼** redhanded

flama *f* (*Mex*) flame

flamante *adj* splendid; (*nuevo*) brand-new

flamear *vi* flame; (bandera etc) flap

flamenco *adj* flamenco; (*de Flandes*) Flemish. ● *m* (*ave*) flamingo; (*música etc*) flamenco; (*idioma*) Flemish

---

flamenco Flamenco is performed in three forms: guitar, singing and dancing. Originally a gypsy art form, it also has Arabic and North African influences. Modern flamenco blends traditional forms with rock, jazz and salsa. In its pure form the music and lyrics are improvised, but tourists are more likely to see rehearsed performances.   *i*

---

flan *m* crème caramel

flaqueza *f* thinness; (*debilidad*) weakness

flauta *f* flute

flecha *f* arrow. **∼zo** *m* love at first sight

fleco *m* fringe; (*Mex, en el pelo*) fringe (*Brit*), bangs (*Amer*)

flem|a *f* phlegm. **∼ático** *adj* phlegmatic

flequillo *m* fringe (*Brit*), bangs (*Amer*)

fletar *vt* charter; (*LAm, transportar*) transport

flexible *adj* flexible

flirte|ar *vi* flirt. **∼o** *m* flirting

floj|ear *vi* flag; (*holgazanear*) laze around. **∼o** *adj* loose; (*poco fuerte*) weak; (*perezoso*) lazy

flor *f* flower. **la ∼ y nata** the cream. **∼a** *f* flora. **∼ecer** 🔟 *vi* flower, bloom; (*fig*) flourish. **∼eciente** *adj* (*fig*) flourishing. **∼ero** *m* flower vase. **∼ista** *m & f* florist

flot|a *f* fleet. **∼ador** *m* float; (*de niño*) rubber band. **∼ar** *vi* float. **∼e. a ∼e** afloat

fluctua|ción *f* fluctuation. **∼r** 🔢 *vi* fluctuate

flu|idez *f* fluidity; (*fig*) fluency. **∼ido** *adj* fluid; (*fig*) fluent. ● *m* fluid. **∼ir** 🔢 *vi* flow

fluoruro *m* fluoride

fluvial *adj* river

fobia f phobia

foca f seal

foco m focus; (lámpara) floodlight; (LAm, de coche) (head)light; (Mex, bombilla) light bulb

fogón m cooker; (LAm, fogata) bonfire

folio m sheet

folklórico adj folk

follaje m foliage

follet|ín m newspaper serial. ~o m pamphlet

follón m ⚊ mess; (alboroto) row; (problema) trouble

fomentar vt promote; boost (ahorro); stir up (odio)

fonda f (pensión) boarding-house; (LAm, restaurant) cheap restaurant

fondo m bottom; (de calle, pasillo) end; (de sala etc) back; (de escenario, pintura etc) background. ~ de reptiles slush fund. ~s mpl funds, money. a ~ thoroughly

fonétic|a f phonetics. ~o adj phonetic

fontanero m plumber

footing /'futin/ m jogging

forastero m stranger

forcejear vi struggle

forense adj forensic. ● m & f forensic scientist

forjar vt forge. ~se vpr forge; build up (ilusiones)

forma f form; (contorno) shape; (modo) way; (Mex, formulario) form. ~s fpl conventions. de todas ~s anyway. estar en ~ be in good form. ~ción f formation; (educación) training. ~l adj formal; (de fiar) reliable; (serio) serious. ~lidad f formality; (fiabilidad) reliability; (seriedad) seriousness. ~r vt form; (componer) make up; (enseñar) train. ~rse vpr form; (desarrollarse) develop; (educarse) to be educated. ~to m format

formidable adj formidable; (muy grande) enormous

fórmula f formula; (sistema) way. ~ de cortesía polite expression

formular vt formulate; make (queja etc). ~io m form

fornido adj well-built

forr|ar vt (en el interior) line; (en el exterior) cover. ~o m lining; (cubierta) cover

fortale|cer ⓫ vt strengthen. ~za f strength; (Mil) fortress; (fuerza moral) fortitude

fortuito adj fortuitous; (encuentro) chance

fortuna f fortune; (suerte) luck

forz|ar ② & ⓾ vt force; strain (vista). ~osamente adv necessarily. ~oso adj necessary

fosa f ditch; (tumba) grave. ~s nasales nostrils

fósforo m phosphorus; (cerilla) match

fósil adj & m fossil

foso m ditch; (en castillo) moat; (de teatro) pit

foto f photo. sacar ~s take photos

fotocopia f photocopy. ~dora f photocopier. ~r vt photocopy

fotogénico adj photogenic

fot|ografía f photography; (Foto) photograph. ~ografiar ⓴ vt photograph. ~ógrafo m photographer

foul /faʊl/ m (pl ~s) (LAm) foul

frac m (pl ~s o fraques) tails

fracas|ar vi fail. ~o m failure

fracción f fraction; (Pol) faction

fractura f fracture. ~r vt fracture. ~rse vpr fracture

fragan|cia f fragrance. ~te adj fragrant

frágil adj fragile

fragmento m fragment; (de canción etc) extract

fragua f forge. ~r ⓯ vt forge; (fig) concoct. ● vi set

fraile m friar; (monje) monk

frambuesa f raspberry

franc|és adj French. ● m (persona) Frenchman; (lengua) French. ~esa f Frenchwoman

Francia f France

franco adj frank; (evidente) marked; (Com) free. ● m (moneda) franc

francotirador m sniper

franela f flannel

franja f border; (banda) stripe; (de terreno) strip

franque|ar vt clear; (atravesar) cross; pay the postage on (carta). **~o** m postage

franqueza f frankness

frasco m bottle; (de mermelada etc) jar

frase f phrase; (oración) sentence. **~ hecha** set phrase

fratern|al adj fraternal. **~idad** f fraternity

fraud|e m fraud. **~ulento** adj fraudulent

fray m brother, friar

frecuen|cia f frequency. **con ~cia** frequently. **~tar** vt frequent. **~te** adj frequent

frega|dero m sink. **~r** ⓵ & ⓰ vt scrub; wash (los platos); mop (el suelo); (LAm, fam, molestar) annoy

freír ⓾ (pp frito) vt fry; **~se** vpr fry; (persona) roast

frenar vt brake; (fig) check

frenético adj frenzied; (furioso) furious

freno m (de caballería) bit; (Auto) brake; (fig) check

frente m front. **~ a** opposite. **~ a ~** face to face. **al ~** at the head; (hacia delante) forward. **chocar de ~** crash head on. **de ~ a** (LAm) facing. **hacer ~ a** face (cosa); stand up to (persona). ● f forehead. **arrugar la ~** frown

fresa f strawberry

fresc|o adj (frío) cool; (reciente) fresh; (descarado) cheeky. ● m fresh air; (frescor) coolness; (mural) fresco; (persona) impudent person. **al ~o** in the open air. **hacer ~o** be cool. **tomar el ~o** get some fresh air. **~or** m coolness. **~ura** f freshness; (frío) coolness; (descaro) cheek

frialdad f coldness; (fig) indifference

fricci|ón f rubbing; (fig, Tec) friction; (masaje) massage. **~onar** vt rub

frigidez f frigidity

frígido adj frigid

frigorífico m fridge, refrigerator

frijol m (LAm) bean. **~es refritos** (Mex) fried purée of beans

frío adj & m cold. **tomar ~** catch cold. **hacer ~** be cold. **tener ~** be cold

frito adj fried; (⒤, harto) fed up. **me tiene ~** I'm sick of him

fr|ivolidad f frivolity. **~ívolo** adj frivolous

fronter|a f border, frontier. **~izo** adj border; (país) bordering

frontón m pelota court; (pared) fronton

frotar vt rub; strike (cerilla)

fructífero adj fruitful

fruncir ⓽ vt gather (tela). **~ el ceño** frown

frustra|ción f frustration. **~r** vt frustrate. **~rse** vpr (fracasar) fail. **quedar ~do** be disappointed

frut|a f fruit. **~al** adj fruit. **~ería** f fruit shop. **~ero** m fruit seller; (recipiente) fruit bowl. **~icultura** f fruit-growing. **~o** m fruit

fucsia f fuchsia. ● m fuchsia

fuego m fire. **~s artificiales** fireworks. **a ~ lento** on a low heat. **tener ~** have a light

fuente f fountain; (manantial) spring; (plato) serving dish; (fig) source

fuera adv out; (al exterior) outside; (en otra parte) away; (en el extranjero) abroad. **~ de** outside; (excepto) except for, besides. **por ~** on the outside. ● vb véase **IR** y **SER**

fuerte adj strong; (color) bright; (sonido) loud; (dolor) severe; (duro) hard; (grande) large; (lluvia, nevada) heavy. ● m fort; (fig) strong point. ● adv hard; (con hablar etc) loudly; (llover) heavily; (mucho) a lot

fuerza f strength; (poder) power; (en física) force; (Mil) forces. **~ de voluntad** will-power. **a ~ de** by (dint of). **a la ~** by necessity. **por ~** by force; (por necesidad) by necessity. **tener ~s para** have the strength to

fuese vb véase **IR** y **SER**

fug|a f flight, escape; (de gas etc) leak; (Mus) fugue. **~arse** ⓰ vpr flee, escape. **~az** adj fleeting. **~itivo** adj & m fugitive

fui vb véase **IR**, **SER**

fulano m so-and-so. **~, mengano y zutano** every Tom, Dick and Harry

fulminar vt (fig, con mirada) look daggers at

fuma|dor adj smoking. ● m smoker. **~r** vt/i smoke. **~r en pipa** smoke a pipe. **~rse** *vpr* smoke. **~rada** *f* puff of smoke

funci|ón *f* function; (*de un cargo etc*) duty; (*de teatro*) show, performance. **~onal** *adj* functional. **~onar** *vi* work, function. **no ~ona** out of order. **~onario** *m* civil servant

funda *f* cover. **~ de almohada** pillow-case

funda|ción *f* foundation. **~mental** *adj* fundamental. **~mentar** *vt* base (**en** on). **~mento** *m* foundation. **~r** *vt* found; (*fig*) base. **~rse** *vpr* be based

fundi|ción *f* melting; (*de metales*) smelting; (*taller*) foundry. **~r** *vt* melt; smelt (*metales*); cast (*objeto*); blend (*colores*); (*fusionar*) merge; (*Elec*) blow; (*LAm*) seize up (*motor*). **~rse** *vpr* melt; (*unirse*) merge

fúnebre *adj* funeral; (*sombrío*) gloomy

funeral *adj* funeral. ● *m* funeral. **~es** *mpl* funeral

funicular *adj & m* funicular

furg|ón *m* van. **~oneta** *f* van

fur|ia *f* fury; (*violencia*) violence. **~ibundo** *adj* furious. **~ioso** *adj* furious. **~or** *m* fury

furtivo *adj* furtive. **cazador ~** poacher

furúnculo *m* boil

fusible *m* fuse

fusil *m* rifle. **~ar** *vt* shoot

fusión *f* melting; (*unión*) fusion; (*Com*) merger

fútbol *m*, (*Mex*) **futbol** *m* football

futbolista *m & f* footballer

futur|ista *adj* futuristic. ● *m & f* futurist. **~o** *adj & m* future

· ·

Gg

· ·

gabardina *f* raincoat

gabinete *m* (*Pol*) cabinet; (*en museo etc*) room; (*de dentista, médico etc*) consulting room

gaceta *f* gazette

gafa *f* hook. **~s** *fpl* glasses, spectacles. **~s de sol** sunglasses

gaf|ar *vt* 🔲 bring bad luck to. **~e** *m* jinx

gaita *f* bagpipes

gajo *m* segment

gala *f* gala. **~s** *fpl* finery, best clothes. **estar de ~** be dressed up. **hacer ~ de** show off

galán *m* (*en el teatro*) (romantic) hero; (*enamorado*) lover

galante *adj* gallant. **~ar** *vt* court. **~ría** *f* gallantry

galápago *m* turtle

galardón *m* award

galaxia *f* galaxy

galera *f* galley

galer|ía *f* gallery. **~ía comercial** (shopping) arcade. **~ón** *m* (*Mex*) hall

Gales *m* Wales. **país de ~** Wales

gal|és *adj* Welsh. ● *m* Welshman; (*lengua*) Welsh. **~esa** *f* Welshwoman

galgo *m* greyhound

Galicia *f* Galicia

galimatías *m invar* gibberish

gallard|ía *f* elegance. **~o** *adj* elegant

gallego *adj & m* Galician

galleta *f* biscuit (*Brit*), cookie (*Amer*)

gall|ina *f* hen, chicken; (*fig, fam*) coward. **~o** *m* cock

galón *m* gallon; (*cinta*) braid; (*Mil*) stripe

galop|ar *vi* gallop. **~e** *m* gallop

gama *f* scale; (*fig*) range

gamba *f* prawn (*Brit*), shrimp (*Amer*)

gamberro *m* hooligan

gamuza *f* (*piel*) chamois leather; (*de otro animal*) suede

gana *f* wish, desire; (*apetito*) appetite. **de buena ~** willingly. **de mala ~** reluctantly. **no me da la ~** I don't feel like it. **tener ~s de** (+ *infinitivo*) feel like (+ *gerundio*)

ganad|ería *f* cattle raising; (*ganado*) livestock. **~o** *m* livestock. **~o lanar** sheep. **~o porcino** pigs. **~o vacuno** cattle

gana|dor *adj* winning. ● *m* winner. **~ncia** *f* gain; (*Com*) profit. **~r** *vt* earn; (*en concurso, juego etc*) win; (*alcanzar*) reach. ● *vi* (*vencer*) win; (*mejorar*) improve. **~rle a uno** beat s.o. **~rse la vida** earn a living. **salir ~ndo** come out better off

ganch|illo m crochet. **hacer ~illo** crochet. **~o** m hook; (LAm, colgador) hanger. **tener ~o** be very attractive

ganga f bargain

ganso m goose

garabat|ear vt/i scribble. **~o** m scribble

garaje m garage

garant|e m & f guarantor. **~ía** f guarantee. **~izar** 🔟 vt guarantee

garapiña f (Mex) pineapple squash. **~do** adj. **almendras** fpl **~das** sugared almonds

garbanzo m chick-pea

garbo m poise; (de escrito) style. **~so** adj elegant

garganta f throat; (valle) gorge

gárgaras fpl. **hacer ~** gargle

garita f hut; (de centinela) sentry box

garra f (de animal) claw; (de ave) talon

garrafa f carafe

garrafal adj huge

garrapata f tick

garrapat|ear vi scribble. **~o** m scribble

garrote m club, cudgel; (tormento) garrotte

gar|úa f (LAm) drizzle. **~uar** vi 🔟 (LAm) drizzle

garza f heron

gas m gas. **con ~** fizzy. **sin ~** still

gasa f gauze

gaseosa f fizzy drink

gas|óleo m diesel. **~olina** f petrol (Brit), gasoline (Amer), gas (Amer). **~olinera** f petrol station (Brit), gas station (Amer)

gast|ado adj spent; (vestido etc) worn out. **~ador** m spendthrift. **~ar** vt spend; (consumir) use; (malgastar) waste; (desgastar) wear out; wear (vestido etc); crack (broma). **~arse** vpr wear out. **~o** m expense; (acción de gastar) spending

gastronomía f gastronomy

gat|a f cat. **a ~as** on all fours. **~ear** vi crawl

gatillo m trigger

gat|ito m kitten. **~o** m cat. **dar ~o por liebre** take s.o. in

gaucho m Gaucho

gaucho A peasant of the pampas of Argentina, Uruguay and Brazil. Modern gauchos work as foremen on farms and ranches and take part in rodeos. Traditionally, a gaucho's outfit was characterized by its baggy trousers, leather chaps, and chiripá, a waist-high garment. They also used boleadoras for catching cattle.

gaveta f drawer

gaviota f seagull

gazpacho m gazpacho

gelatina f gelatine; (jalea) jelly

gema f gem

gemelo m twin. **~s** mpl (anteojos) binoculars; (de camisa) cuff-links

gemido m groan

Géminis m Gemini

gemir 🔟 vi moan; (animal) whine, howl

gen m, **gene** m gene

geneal|ogía f genealogy. **~ógico** adj genealogical. **árbol** m **~ógico** family tree

generaci|ón f generation. **~onal** adj generation

general adj general. **en ~** in general. **por lo ~** generally. ● m general. **~izar** 🔟 vt/i generalize. **~mente** adv generally

generar vt generate

género m type, sort; (en biología) genus; (Gram) gender; (en literatura etc) genre; (producto) product; (tela) material. **~s de punto** knitwear. **~ humano** mankind

generos|idad f generosity. **~o** adj generous

genétic|a f genetics. **~o** adj genetic

geni|al adj brilliant; (divertido) funny. **~o** m temper; (carácter) nature; (talento, persona) genius

genital adj genital. **~es** mpl genitals

genoma m genome

gente f people; (nación) nation; (fam, familia) family, folks; (Mex, persona) person. ● adj (LAm) respectable; (amable) kind

gentil adj charming. **~eza** f kindness. **tener la ~eza de** be kind enough to

gentío m crowd
genuflexión f genuflection
genuino adj genuine
ge|ografía f geography. ~ográfico adj geographical.
ge|ología f geology. ~ólogo m geologist
geom|etría f geometry. ~étrico adj geometrical
geranio m geranium
geren|cia f management. ~ciar vt (LAm) manage. ~te m & f manager
germen m germ
germinar vi germinate
gestación f gestation
gesticula|ción f gesticulation. ~r vi gesticulate
gesti|ón f step; (administración) management. ~onar vt take steps to arrange; (dirigir) manage
gesto m expression; (ademán) gesture; (mueca) grimace
gibraltareño adj & m Gibraltarian
gigante adj gigantic. ● m giant. ~sco adj gigantic
gimn|asia f gymnastics. ~asio m gymnasium, gym 🔲. ~asta m & f gymnast. ~ástic adj gymnastic
gimotear vi whine
ginebra f gin
ginec|ólogo m gynaecologist
gira f tour. ~r vt spin; draw (cheque); transfer (dinero). ● vi rotate, go round; (en camino) turn
girasol m sunflower
gir|atorio adj revolving. ~o m turn; (Com) draft; (locución) expression. ~o postal money order
gitano adj & m gypsy
glacia|l adj icy. ~r m glacier
glándula f gland
glasear vt glaze; (Culin) ice
glob|al adj global; (fig) overall. ~alización f globalization. ~o m globe; (juguete) balloon
glóbulo m globule
gloria f glory; (placer) delight. ~rse vpr boast (de about)
glorieta f square; (Auto) roundabout (Brit), (traffic) circle (Amer)
glorificar 🔢 vt glorify

glorioso adj glorious
glotón adj gluttonous. ● m glutton
gnomo /'nomo/ m gnome
gob|ernación f government. Ministerio m de la G~ernación Home Office (Brit), Department of the Interior (Amer). ~ernador adj governing. ● m governor. ~ernante adj governing. ● m & f leader. ~ernar 🔟 vt govern. ~ierno m government
goce m enjoyment
gol m goal
golf m golf
golfo m gulf; (niño) urchin; (holgazán) layabout
golondrina f swallow
golos|ina f titbit; (dulce) sweet. ~o adj fond of sweets
golpe m blow; (puñetazo) punch; (choque) bump; (de emoción) shock; (arg, atraco) job 🔲; (en golf, en tenis, de remo) stroke. ~ de estado coup d'etat. ~ de fortuna stroke of luck. ~ de vista glance. ~ militar military coup. de ~ suddenly. de un ~ in one go. ~ar vt hit; (dar varios golpes) beat; (con mucho ruido) bang; (con el puño) punch. ● vi knock
goma f rubber; (para pegar) glue; (banda) rubber band; (de borrar) eraser. ~ de mascar chewing gum. ~ espuma foam rubber
googlear ® vt/i 🔲 to google
gord|a f (Mex) small thick tortilla. ~o adj (persona) (con ser) fat; (con estar) have put on weight; (carne) fatty; (grueso) thick; (grande) large, big. ● m first prize. ~ura f fatness; (grasa) fat
gorila f gorilla
gorje|ar vi chirp. ~o m chirping
gorra f cap. ~ de baño (LAm) bathing cap
gorrión m sparrow
gorro m cap; (de niño) bonnet. ~ de baño bathing cap
got|a f drop; (Med) gout. ni ~a nothing. ~ear vi drip. ~era f leak
gozar 🔟 vt enjoy. ● vi. ~ de enjoy
gozne m hinge
gozo m pleasure; (alegría) joy. ~so adj delighted

g

graba|ción *f* recording. **~do** *m* engraving, print; (*en libro*) illustration. **~dora** *f* tape-recorder. **~r** *vt* engrave; record (*discos etc*)

graci|a *f* grace; (*favor*) favour; (*humor*) wit. **~as** *fpl* thanks. **¡~as!** thank you!, thanks! **dar las ~as** thank. **hacer ~a** amuse; (*gustar*) please. **¡muchas ~as!** thank you very much! **tener ~a** be funny. **~oso** *adj* funny. ● *m* fool, comic character

grad|a *f* step. **~as** *fpl* stand(s). **~ación** *f* gradation. **~o** *m* degree; (*en enseñanza*) year (*Brit*), grade (*Amer*). **de buen ~o** willingly

gradua|ción *f* graduation; (*de alcohol*) proof. **~do** *m* graduate. **~l** *adj* gradual. **~r** 21 *vt* graduate; (*regular*) adjust. **~rse** *vpr* graduate

gráfic|a *f* graph. **~o** *adj* graphic. ● *m* graph

gram|ática *f* grammar. **~atical** *adj* grammatical

gramo *m* gram, gramme (*Brit*)

gran *adj véase* **GRANDE**

grana *f* (*color*) deep red

granada *f* pomegranate; (*Mil*) grenade

granate *m* (*color*) maroon

Gran Bretaña *f* Great Britain

grande *adj* (*delante de nombre en singular* **gran**) big, large; (*alto*) tall; (*fig*) great; (*LAm, de edad*) grown up. **~za** *f* greatness

grandioso *adj* magnificent

granel *m*. **a ~** in bulk; (*suelto*) loose; (*fig*) in abundance

granero *m* barn

granito *m* granite; (*grano*) small grain

graniz|ado *m* iced drink. **~ar** 10 *vi* hail. **~o** *m* hail

granj|a *f* farm. **~ero** *m* farmer

grano *m* grain; (*semilla*) seed; (*de café*) bean; (*Med*) spot. **~s** *mpl* cereals

granuja *m & f* rogue

grapa *f* staple. **~r** *vt* staple

gras|a *f* grease; (*Culin*) fat. **~iento** *adj* greasy

gratifica|ción *f* (*de sueldo*) bonus (*recompensa*) reward. **~r** 7 *vt* reward

grat|is *adv* free. **~itud** *f* gratitude. **~o** *adj* pleasant **~uito** *adj* free; (*fig*) uncalled for

grava|men *m* tax; (*carga*) burden; (*sobre inmueble*) encumbrance. **~r** *vt* tax; (*cargar*) burden

grave *adj* serious; (*voz*) deep; (*sonido*) low; (*acento*) grave. **~dad** *f* gravity

gravilla *f* gravel

gravitar *vi* gravitate; (*apoyarse*) rest (**sobre** on); (*peligro*) hang (**sobre** over)

gravoso *adj* costly

graznar *vi* (*cuervo*) caw; (*pato*) quack; honk (*ganso*)

Grecia *f* Greece

gremio *m* union

greña *f* mop of hair

gresca *f* rumpus; (*riña*) quarrel

griego *adj & m* Greek

grieta *f* crack

grifo *m* tap, faucet (*Amer*)

grilletes *mpl* shackles

grillo *m* cricket. **~s** *mpl* shackles

gringo *m* (*LAm*) foreigner; (*norteamericano*) Yankee 🇹

gripe *f* flu

gris *adj* grey. ● *m* grey; (*fam, policía*) policeman

grit|ar *vi* shout. **~ería** *f*, **~erío** *m* uproar. **~o** *m* shout; (*de dolor, sorpresa*) cry; (*chillido*) scream. **dar ~s** shout

grosella *f* redcurrant. **~ negra** blackcurrant

groser|ía *f* rudeness; (*ordinariez*) coarseness; (*comentario etc*) coarse remark; (*palabra*) swearword. **~o** *adj* coarse; (*descortés*) rude

grosor *m* thickness

grotesco *adj* grotesque

grúa *f* crane

grueso *adj* thick; (*persona*) fat, stout. ● *m* thickness; (*fig*) main body

grumo *m* lump

gruñi|do *m* grunt; (*de perro*) growl. **~r** 22 *vi* grunt; (*perro*) growl

grupa *f* hindquarters

grupo *m* group

gruta *f* grotto

guacamole *m* guacamole

guadaña *f* scythe

guaje *m* (*Mex*) gourd

guajolote *m* (*Mex*) turkey

guante m glove

guapo adj good-looking; (chica) pretty; (elegante) smart

guarda m & f guard; (de parque etc) keeper. **~barros** m invar mudguard. **~bosque** m gamekeeper. **~costas** m invar coastguard vessel. **~espaldas** m invar bodyguard. **~meta** m goalkeeper. **~r** vt keep; (proteger) protect; (en un lugar) put away; (reservar) save, keep. **~rse** vpr. **~rse de** (+ infinitivo) avoid (+ gerundio). **~rropa** m wardrobe; (en local público) cloakroom. **~vallas** m invar (LAm) goalkeeper

guardería f nursery

guardia f guard; (policía) policewoman; (de médico) shift. **G~** **Civil** Civil Guard. **~ municipal** police. **estar de ~** be on duty. **estar en ~** be on one's guard. **montar la ~** mount guard. **●** m policeman. **~ jurado** m & f security guard. **~ de tráfico** m traffic policeman. **●** f traffic policewoman

guardián m guardian; (de parque etc) keeper; (de edificio) security guard

guar|ecer 11 vt (albergar) give shelter to. **~ecerse** vpr take shelter. **~ida** f den, lair; (de personas) hideout

guarn|ecer 11 vt (adornar) adorn; (Culin) garnish. **~ición** f adornment; (de caballo) harness; (Culin) garnish; (Mil) garrison; (de piedra preciosa) setting

guas|a f joke. **~ón** adj humorous. **●** m joker

Guatemala f Guatemala

guatemalteco adj & m Guatemalan

guateque m party, bash

guayab|a f guava; (dulce) guava jelly. **~era** f lightweight jacket

gubernatura f (Mex) government

güero adj (Mex) fair

guerr|a f war; (método) warfare. **dar ~a** annoy. **~ero** adj warlike; (belicoso) fighting. **●** m warrior. **~illa** f band of guerrillas. **~illero** m guerrilla

guía m & f guide. **●** f guidebook; (de teléfonos) directory

guiar 20 vt guide; (llevar) lead; (Auto) drive. **~se** vpr be guided (**por** by)

guijarro m pebble

guillotina f guillotine

guind|a f morello cherry. **~illa** f chilli

guiñapo m rag; (fig, persona) wreck

guiñ|ar vt/i wink. **~o** m wink. **hacer ~os** wink

gui|ón m hyphen, dash; (de película etc) script. **~onista** m & f scriptwriter

guirnalda f garland

guisado m stew

guisante m pea. **~ de olor** sweet pea

guis|ar vt/i cook. **~o** m stew

guitarr|a f guitar. **~ista** m & f guitarist

gula f gluttony

gusano m worm; (larva de mosca) maggot

---

gustar

● verbo intransitivo

! Cuando el verbo **gustar** va precedido del complemento indirecto **le** (o **les, nos** etc), el sujeto en español pasa a ser el objeto en inglés. **me gusta mucho la música** I like music very much. **le gustan los helados** he likes ice cream. **a Juan no le gusta** Juan doesn't like it (or her etc)

····▸ gustar + infinitivo. **les gusta ver televisión** they like watching television

····▸ gustar que + subjuntivo. **me ~ía que vinieras** I'd like you to come. **no le gusta que lo corrijan** he doesn't like being corrected. **¿te ~ía que te lo comprara?** would you like me to buy it for you?

····▸ gustar de algo to like sth. **gustan de las fiestas** they like parties

····▸ (tener acogida) to go down well. **ese tipo de cosas que siempre gusta** those sort of things always go down well. **el libro no gustó** the book didn't go down well

····▸ (en frases de cortesía) to wish. **como guste** as you wish. **cuando gustes** whenever you wish

g

● *verbo transitivo*

····▶ (*LAm, querer*) **¿gusta un café?** would you like a coffee? **¿gustan pasar?** would you like to come in? **gustarse** *verbo pronominal* to like each other

gusto *m* taste; (*placer*) pleasure. **a ~ comfortable. a mi ~** to my liking. **buen ~** good taste. **con mucho ~** with pleasure. **dar ~** please. **mucho ~** pleased to meet you. **~so** *adj* tasty; (*de buen grado*) willingly

gutural *adj* guttural

g

h

. . . .

Hh

. . . .

ha *vb véase* **HABER**

haba *f* broad bean

Habana *f* **La ~** Havana

habano *m* (*puro*) Havana

haber *verbo auxiliar* **30** have. ● *v impersonal* (*presente s & pl* **hay**, *imperfecto s & pl* **había**, *pretérito s & pl* **hubo**). **hay una carta para ti** there's a letter for you. **hay 5 bancos en la plaza** there are 5 banks in the square. **hay que hacerlo** it must be done, you have to do it. **he aquí** here is, here are. **no hay de qué** don't mention it, not at all. **¿qué hay?** (*¿qué pasa?*) what's the matter?; (*¿qué tal?*) how are you?

habichuela *f* bean

hábil *adj* skilful; (*listo*) clever; (*día*) working; (*Jurid*) competent

habili|dad *f* skill; (*astucia*) cleverness; (*Jurid*) competence. **~tar** *vt* qualify

habita|ción *f* room; (*dormitorio*) bedroom; (*en biología*) habitat. **~ción de matrimonio**, **~ción doble** double room. **~ción individual**, **~ción sencilla** single room. **~do** *adj* inhabited. **~nte** *m* inhabitant. **~r** *vt* live in. ● *vi* live

hábito *m* habit

habitua|l *adj* usual, habitual; (*cliente*) regular. **~r** **21** *vt* accustom. **~rse** *vpr*. **~rse a** get used to

habla *f* speech; (*idioma*) language; (*dialecto*) dialect. **al ~** (*al teléfono*) speaking. **ponerse al ~ con** get in touch with. **~dor** *adj* talkative. ● *m* chatterbox. **~duría** *f* rumour. **~durías** *fpl* gossip. **~nte** *adj* speaking. ● *m & f* speaker. **~r** *vt* speak. ● *vi* speak, talk (**con** to); (*Mex, por teléfono*) call. **¡ni ~r!** out of the question! **se ~ español** Spanish spoken

hacend|ado *m* landowner; (*LAm*) farmer. **~oso** *adj* hard-working

hacer **31**

● *verbo transitivo*

····▶ to do. **¿qué haces?** what are you doing? **~ los deberes** to do one's homework. **no sé qué ~** I don't know what to do. **hazme un favor** can you do me a favour?

····▶ (*fabricar, preparar, producir*) to make. **me hizo un vestido** she made me a dress. **~ un café** to make a (cup of) coffee. **no hagas tanto ruido** don't make so much noise

····▶ (*construir*) to build (casa, puente)

····▶ **hacer que uno haga algo** to make s.o. do sth. **haz que se vaya** make him leave. **hizo que se equivocara** he made her go wrong

····▶ **hacer hacer algo** to have sth done. **hizo arreglar el techo** he had the roof repaired

➡ Cuando el verbo **hacer** se emplea en expresiones como **hacer una pregunta**, **hacer trampa** etc., ver bajo el respectivo nombre

● *verbo intransitivo*

····▶ (*actuar, obrar*) to do. **hiciste bien en llamar** you did the right thing to call **¿cómo haces para parecer tan joven?** what do you do to look so young?

····▶ (*fingir, simular*) **hacer como que** to pretend. **hizo como que no me conocía** he pretended not to know me. **haz como que**

estás dormido pretend you're asleep

····▸ **hacer de** (*en teatro*) to play the part of; (*ejercer la función de*) to act as

····▸ (*LAm, sentar*) **tanta sal hace mal** so much salt is not good for you. **dormir le hizo bien** the sleep did him good. **el pepino me hace mal** cucumber doesn't agree with me *verbo impersonal*

····▸ (*hablando del tiempo atmosférico*) to be. **hace sol** it's sunny. **hace 3 grados** it's 3 degrees

····▸ (*con expresiones temporales*) **hace una hora que espero** I've been waiting for an hour. **llegó hace 3 días** he arrived 3 days ago. **hace mucho tiempo** a long time ago. **hasta hace poco** until recently

● **hacerse** *verbo pronominal*

····▸ (*para sí*) to make o.s. (falda, café)

····▸ (*hacer que otro haga*) **se hizo la permanente** she had her hair permed. **me hice una piscina** I had a pool built

····▸ (*convertirse en*) to become. **se hicieron amigos** they became friends

····▸ (*acostumbrarse*) ~**se a algo** to get used to sth

····▸ (*fingirse*) to pretend. ~**se el enfermo** to pretend to be ill

····▸ (*moverse*) to move. **hazte para atrás** move back

····▸ **hacerse de** (*LAm*) to make (amigo, dinero)

hacha *f* axe; (*antorcha*) torch

hacia *prep* towards; (*cerca de*) near; (*con tiempo*) at about. ~ **abajo** downwards. ~ **arriba** upwards. ~ **atrás** backwards. ~ **las dos** (at) about two o'clock

hacienda *f* country estate; (*en LAm*) ranch; **la ~ pública** the Treasury. **Ministerio** *m* **de H~** Ministry of Finance; (*en Gran Bretaña*) Exchequer; (*en Estados Unidos*) Treasury

hada *f* fairy. **el ~ madrina** the fairy godmother

hago *vb véase* **HACER**

Haití *m* Haiti

halag|ar 12 *vt* flatter. ~**üeño** *adj* flattering; (*esperanzador*) promising

halcón *m* falcon

halla|r *vt* find; (*descubrir*) discover. ~**rse** *vpr* be. ~**zgo** *m* discovery

hamaca *f* hammock; (*asiento*) deckchair

hambr|e *f* hunger; (*de muchos*) famine. **tener ~e** be hungry. ~**iento** *adj* starving

hamburguesa *f* hamburger

harag|án *adj* lazy, idle. ● *m* layabout. ~**anear** *vi* laze around

harap|iento *adj* in rags. ~**o** *m* rag

harina *f* flour

hart|ar *vt* (*fastidiar*) annoy. **me estás** ~**ando** you're annoying me. ~**arse** *vpr* (*llenarse*) gorge o.s. (**de** on); (*cansarse*) get fed up (**de** with). ~**o** *adj* full; (*cansado*) tired; (*fastidiado*) fed up (**de** with). ● *adv* (*LAm*) (*muy*) very; (*mucho*) a lot

hasta *prep* as far as; (*en el tiempo*) until, till; (*Mex*) not until. ● *adv* even. **¡~ la vista!** goodbye!, see you! 🔟 **¡~ luego!** see you later! **¡~ mañana!** see you tomorrow! **¡~ pronto!** see you soon!

hast|iar 20 *vt* (*cansar*) weary, tire; (*aburrir*) bore. ● **~iarse** *vpr* got fed up (**de** with). ~**ío** *m* weariness; (*aburrimiento*) boredom

haya *f* beech (tree). ● *vb véase* **HABER**

hazaña *f* exploit

hazmerreír *m* laughing stock

he *vb véase* **HABER**

hebilla *f* buckle

hebra *f* thread; (*fibra*) fibre

hebreo *adj & m* Hebrew

hechi|cera *f* witch. ~**cería** *f* witchcraft. ~**cero** *m* wizard. ~**zar** 10 *vt* cast a spell on; (*fig*) captivate. ~**zo** *m* spell; (*fig*) charm

hech|o *pp de* hacer. ● *adj* (*manufacturado*) made; (*terminado*) done; (*vestidos etc*) ready-made; (*Culin*) done. ● *m* fact; (*acto*) deed; (*cuestión*) matter; (*suceso*) event. **de ~o** in fact. ~**ura** *f*

h

making; (*forma*) form; (*del cuerpo*) build; (*calidad de fabricación*) workmanship

hed|er ▮ *vi* stink. **~iondez** *f* stench. **~iondo** *adj* stinking, smelly. **~or** *m* stench

hela|da *f* frost. **~dera** *f* (*LAm*) fridge, refrigerator. **~dería** *f* ice-cream shop. **~do** *adj* freezing; (*congelado*) frozen; (*LAm, bebida*) chilled. ● *m* ice-cream. **~r** ▮ *vt/i* freeze. **anoche heló** there was a frost last night. **~rse** *vpr* freeze

helecho *m* fern

hélice *f* propeller

helicóptero *m* helicopter

hembra *f* female; (*mujer*) woman

hemorr|agia *f* haemorrhage. **~oides** *fpl* haemorrhoids

hendidura *f* crack, split; (*en geología*) fissure

heno *m* hay

heráldica *f* heraldry

hered|ar *vt/i* inherit. **~era** *f* heiress. **~ero** *m* heir. **~itario** *adj* hereditary

herej|e *m* heretic. **~ia** *f* heresy

herencia *f* inheritance; (*fig*) heritage

heri|da *f* injury; (*con arma*) wound. **~do** *adj* injured; (*con arma*) wounded; (*fig*) hurt. ● *m* injured person. **~r** ▮ *vt* injure; (*con arma*) wound; (*fig*) hurt. **~rse** *vpr* hurt o.s.

herman|a *f* sister. **~a política** sister-in-law. **~astra** *f* stepsister. **~astro** *m* stepbrother. **~o** *m* brother. **~o político** brother-in-law. **~os** *mpl* brothers; (*chicos y chicas*) brothers and sisters. **~os gemelos** twins

hermético *adj* hermetic; (*fig*) watertight

hermos|o *adj* beautiful; (*espléndido*) splendid. **~ura** *f* beauty

héroe *m* hero

hero|ico *adj* heroic. **~ína** *f* heroine; (*droga*) heroin. **~ísmo** *m* heroism

herr|adura *f* horseshoe. **~amienta** *f* tool. **~ero** *m* blacksmith

herv|idero *m* (*fig*) hotbed; (*multitud*) throng. **~ir** ▮ *vt/i* boil. **~or** *m* (*fig*) ardour. **romper el ~** come to the boil

hiberna|ción *f* hibernation. **~r** *vi* hibernate

híbrido *adj & m* hybrid

hice *vb* véase **HACER**

hidalgo *m* nobleman

hidrata|nte *adj* moisturizing. **~r** *vt* hydrate; (*crema etc*) moisturize

hidráulico *adj* hydraulic

hidr|oavión *m* seaplane. **~oeléctrico** *adj* hydroelectric. **~ofobia** *f* rabies. **~ófobo** *adj* rabid. **~ógeno** *m* hydrogen

hiedra *f* ivy

hielo *m* ice

hiena *f* hyena

hierba *f* grass; (*Culin, Med*) herb **mala ~** weed. **~buena** *f* mint.

hierro *m* iron

hígado *m* liver

higi|ene *f* hygiene. **~énico** *adj* hygienic

hig|o *m* fig. **~uera** *f* fig tree

hij|a *f* daughter. **~astra** *f* stepdaughter. **~astro** *m* stepson. **~o** *m* son. **~os** *mpl* sons; (*chicos y chicas*) children

hilar *vt* spin. **~ delgado** split hairs

hilera *f* row; (*Mil*) file

hilo *m* thread; (*Elec*) wire; (*de líquido*) trickle; (*lino*) linen

hilv|án *m* tacking. **~anar** *vt* tack; (*fig*) put together

himno *m* hymn. **~ nacional** anthem

hincapié *m*. **hacer ~ en** stress, insist on

hincar ▮ *vt* drive (estaca) (**en** into). **~se** *vpr*. **~se de rodillas** kneel down

hincha *f* ▮ grudge. ● *m & f* (*fam, aficionado*) fan

hincha|do *adj* inflated; (*Med*) swollen. **~r** *vt* inflate, blow up. **~rse** *vpr* swell up; (*fig, fam, comer mucho*) gorge o.s. **~zón** *f* swelling

hinojo *m* fennel

hiper|mercado *m* hypermarket. **~sensible** *adj* hypersensitive. **~tensión** *f* high blood pressure

hípic|a *f* horse racing. **~o** *adj* horse

hipn|osis *f* hypnosis. **~otismo** *m* hypnotism. **~otizar** ▮ *vt* hypnotize

hipo *m* hiccup. **tener ~** have hiccups

hipo|alérgeno *adj* hypoallergenic. **~condríaco** *adj & m* hypochondriac

hip|ocresía *f* hypocrisy. **~ócrita** *adj* hypocritical. ● *m & f* hypocrite

hipódromo *m* racecourse

hipopótamo *m* hippopotamus

hipoteca *f* mortgage. **~r 7** *vt* mortgage

hip|ótesis *f invar* hypothesis. **~otético** *adj* hypothetical

hiriente *adj* offensive, wounding

hirsuto *adj* (barba) bristly; (pelo) wiry

hispánico *adj* Hispanic

Hispanidad - Día de la See ▷**DÍA DE LA RAZA**   *i*

Hispanoamérica *f* Spanish America

hispano|americano *adj* Spanish American. **~hablante** *adj* Spanish-speaking

hist|eria *f* hysteria. **~érico** *adj* hysterical

hist|oria *f* history; (relato) story; (excusa) tale, excuse. **pasar a la ~oria** go down in history. **~oriador** *m* historian. **~órico** *adj* historical. **~orieta** *f* tale; (con dibujos) strip cartoon

hito *m* milestone

hizo *vb véase* **HACER**

hocico *m* snout

hockey /'(x)oki/ *m* hockey. **~ sobre hielo** ice hockey

hogar *m* home; (chimenea) hearth. **~eño** *adj* domestic; (persona) home-loving

hoguera *f* bonfire

hoja *f* leaf; (de papel, metal etc) sheet; (de cuchillo, espada etc) blade. **~ de afeitar** razor blade. **~lata** *f* tin

hojaldre *m* puff pastry

hojear *vt* leaf through

hola *int* hello!

Holanda *f* Holland

holand|és *adj* Dutch. ● *m* Dutchman; (lengua) Dutch. **~esa** *f* Dutchwoman. **los ~eses** the Dutch

holg|ado *adj* loose; (fig) comfortable. **~ar 2 & 12** *vi.* **huelga decir que** needless to say. **~azán** *adj* lazy. ● *m* idler. **~ura** *f* looseness; (fig) comfort

hollín *m* soot

hombre *m* man; (especie humana) man(kind). ● *int* Good Heavens!; (de duda) well. **~ de negocios** businessman. **~ rana** frogman

hombr|era *f* shoulder pad. **~o** *m* shoulder

homenaje *m* homage, tribute. **rendir ~ a** pay tribute to

home|ópata *m* homoeopath. **~opatía** *f* homoeopathy. **~opático** *adj* homoeopathic

homicid|a *adj* murderous. ● *m & f* murderer. **~io** *m* murder

homosexual *adj & m & f* homosexual. **~idad** *f* homosexuality

hond|o *adj* deep. **~onada** *f* hollow

Honduras *f* Honduras

hondureño *adj & m* Honduran

honest|idad *f* honesty. **~o** *adj* honest

hongo *m* fungus; (LAm, Culin) mushroom; (venenoso) toadstool

hon|or *m* honour. **~orable** *adj* honourable. **~orario** *adj* honorary. **~orarios** *mpl* fees. **~ra** *f* honour; (buena fama) good name. **~radez** *f* honesty. **~rado** *adj* honest. **~rar** *vt* honour

hora *f* hour; (momento puntual) time; (cita) appointment. **~ pico, ~ punta** rush hour. **~s** *fpl* **de trabajo** working hours. **~s** *fpl* **extraordinarias** overtime. **~s** *fpl* **libres** free time. **a estas ~s** now. **¿a qué ~?** (at) what time? **a última ~** at the last moment. **de última ~** last-minute. **en buena ~** at the right time. **media ~** half an hour. **pedir ~** to make an appointment. **¿qué ~ es?** what time is it?

horario *adj* hourly. ● *m* timetable. **~ de trabajo** working hours

horca *f* gallows

horcajadas *fpl.* **a ~** astride

horchata *f* tiger-nut milk

horizont|al *adj & f* horizontal. **~e** *m* horizon

horma *f* mould; (para fabricar calzado) last; (para conservar su forma) shoe-tree. **de ~ ancha** broad-fitting

hormiga *f* ant

hormigón *m* concrete

hormigue|ar *vi* tingle; (bullir) swarm. **me ~a la mano** I've got pins and needles in my hand. **~o** *m* tingling; (fig) anxiety

h

hormiguero *m* anthill; (*de gente*) swarm

hormona *f* hormone

horn|ada *f* batch. **~illa** *f* (*LAm*) burner. **~illo** *m* burner; (*cocina portátil*) portable electric cooker. **~o** *m* oven; (*para cerámica etc*) kiln; (*Tec*) furnace

horóscopo *m* horoscope

horquilla *f* pitchfork; (*para el pelo*) hairpin

horr|endo *adj* awful. **~ible** *adj* horrible. **~ipilante** *adj* terrifying. **~or** *m* horror; (*atrocidad*) atrocity. **¡qué ~or!** how awful!. **~orizar** 10 *vt* horrify. **~orizarse** *vpr* be horrified. **~oroso** *adj* horrifying

hort|aliza *f* vegetable. **~elano** *m* market gardener

hosco *adj* surly

hospeda|je *m* accommodation. **~r** *vt* put up. **~rse** *vpr* stay

hospital *m* hospital. **~ario** *adj* hospitable. **~idad** *f* hospitality

hostal *m* boarding-house

hostería *f* inn

hostia *f* (*Relig*) host

hostigar 12 *vt* whip; (*fig, molestar*) pester

hostil *adj* hostile. **~idad** *f* hostility

hotel *m* hotel. **~ero** *adj* hotel. ● *m* hotelier

hoy *adv* today. **~ (en) día** nowadays. **~ por ~** at the present time. **de ~ en adelante** from now on

hoy|o *m* hole. **~uelo** *m* dimple

hoz *f* sickle

hube *vb véase* **HABER**

hucha *f* money box

hueco *adj* hollow; (*palabras*) empty; (*voz*) resonant; (*persona*) superficial. ● *m* hollow; (*espacio*) space; (*vacío*) gap

huelg|a *f* strike. **~a de brazos caídos** sit-down strike. **~a de hambre** hunger strike. **declararse en ~a** come out on strike. **~uista** *m & f* striker

huella *f* footprint; (*de animal etc*) track. **~ de carbono** carbon footprint. **~ digital** fingerprint

huelo *vb véase* **OLER**

huérfano *adj* orphaned. ● *m* orphan. **~ de** without

huert|a *f* market garden (*Brit*), truck farm (*Amer*); (*terreno de regadío*) irrigated plain. **~o** *m* vegetable garden; (*de árboles frutales*) orchard

hueso *m* bone; (*de fruta*) stone

huésped *m* guest; (*que paga*) lodger

huesudo *adj* bony

huev|a *f* roe. **~o** *m* egg. **~o duro** hard-boiled egg. **~o escalfado** poached egg. **~o estrellado**, **~o frito** fried egg. **~o pasado por agua** boiled egg. **~os revueltos** scrambled eggs. **~o tibio** (*Mex*) boiled egg

hui|da *f* flight, escape. **~dizo** *adj* (*tímido*) shy; (*esquivo*) elusive

huipil *m* (*Mex*) traditional embroidered smock

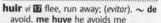

huipil A traditional garment worn by Indian and mestizo women in Mexico and Central America. *Huipiles* are generally made of richly embroidered cotton. They are very wide and low-cut, and are either waist- or thigh-length.

huir *vi* 17 flee, run away; (*evitar*). **~ de** avoid. **me huye** he avoids me

huitlacoche *m* (*Mex*) edible black fungus

hule *m* oilcloth; (*Mex, goma*) rubber

human|idad *f* mankind; (*fig*) humanity. **~itario** *adj* humanitarian. **~o** *adj* human; (*benévolo*) humane

humareda *f* cloud of smoke

humed|ad *f* dampness; (*en meteorología*) humidity; (*gotitas de agua*) moisture. **~ecer** 11 *vt* moisten. **~ecerse** *vpr* become moist

húmedo *adj* damp; (*clima*) humid; (*labios*) moist; (*mojado*) wet

humi|ldad *f* humility. **~lde** *adj* humble. **~llación** *f* humiliation. **~llar** *vt* humiliate. **~llarse** *vpr* lower o.s.

humo *m* smoke; (*vapor*) steam; (*gas nocivo*) fumes. **~s** *mpl* airs

humor *m* mood, temper; (*gracia*) humour. **estar de mal ~** be in a bad mood. **~ista** *m & f* humorist. **~ístico** *adj* humorous

hundi|miento m sinking. **~r** vt sink; destroy (persona). **~rse** vpr sink; (edificio) collapse

húngaro adj & m Hungarian

Hungría f Hungary

huracán m hurricane

huraño adj unsociable

hurgar 12 vi rummage (**en** through). **~se** vpr. **~se la nariz** pick one's nose

hurra int hurray!

hurtadillas fpl. **a ~** stealthily

hurt|ar vt steal. **~o** m theft; (cosa robada) stolen object

husmear vt sniff out; (fig) pry into

huyo vb véase **HUIR**

....

I i

....

iba véase **IR**

ibérico adj Iberian

iberoamericano adj & m Latin American

iceberg /iθˈber/ m (pl **~s**) iceberg

ictericia f jaundice

ida f outward journey; (partida) departure. **de ~ y vuelta** (billete) return (Brit), round-trip (Amer); (viaje) round

idea f idea; (opinión) opinion, **cambiar de ~** change one's mind. **no tener la más remota ~, no tener la menor ~** not have the slightest idea, not have a clue 1

ideal adj & m ideal. **~ista** m & f idealist. **~izar** 10 vt idealize

Idear vt think up, conceive; (inventar) invent

ídem pron & adv the same

idéntico adj identical

identi|dad f identity. **~ficación** f identification. **~ficar** 7 vt identify. **~ficarse** vpr identify o.s. **~ficarse con** identify with

ideol|ogía f ideology. **~ógico** adj ideological

idílico adj idyllic

idilio m idyll

idiom|a m language. **~ático** adj idiomatic

idiosincrasia f idiosyncrasy

idiot|a adj idiotic. ● m & f idiot. **~ez** f stupidity

idolatrar vt worship; (fig) idolize

ídolo m idol

idóneo adj suitable (**para** for)

iglesia f church

iglú m igloo

ignora|ncia f ignorance. **~nte** adj ignorant. ● m ignoramus. **~r** vt not know, be unaware of; (no hacer caso de) ignore

igual adj equal; (mismo) the same; (similar) like; (llano) even; (liso) smooth. ● adv the same. ● m equal. **~ que** (the same) as. **al ~ que** the same as. **da ~, es ~** it doesn't matter. **sin ~** unequalled

igual|ar vt make equal; equal (éxito, récord); (allanar) level. **~arse** vpr be equal. **~dad** f equality. **~mente** adv equally; (también) also, likewise; (respuesta de cortesía) the same to you

ilegal adj illegal

ilegible adj illegible

ilegítimo adj illegitimate

ileso adj unhurt

ilícito adj illicit

ilimitado adj unlimited

ilógico adj illogical

ilumina|ción f illumination; (alumbrado) lighting. **~r** vt light (up). **~rse** vpr light up

ilusi|ón f illusion; (sueño) dream; (alegría) joy. **hacerse ~ones** build up one's hopes. **me hace ~ón** I'm thrilled; I'm looking forward to (algo en el futuro). **~onado** adj excited. **~onar** vt give false hope. **~onarse** vpr have false hopes

ilusionis|mo m conjuring. **~ta** m & f conjurer

iluso adj naive. ● m dreamer. **~rio** adj illusory

ilustra|ción f learning; (dibujo) illustration. **~do** adj learned; (con dibujos) illustrated. **~r** vt explain; (instruir) instruct; (añadir dibujos etc) illustrate. **~rse** vpr acquire knowledge. **~tivo** adj illustrative

h

i

ilustre *adj* illustrious

imagen *f* image; (*TV etc*) picture

imagina|ble *adj* imaginable. ~**ción** *f* imagination. ~**r** *vt* imagine. ~**rse** *vpr* imagine. ~**rio** *m* imaginary. ~**tivo** *adj* imaginative

imán *m* magnet

imbécil *adj* stupid. ● *m & f* idiot

imborrable *adj* indelible; (*recuerdo* etc) unforgettable

imita|ción *f* imitation. ~**r** *vt* imitate

impacien|cia *f* impatience. ~**tarse** *vpr* lose one's patience. ~**te** *adj* impatient

impacto *m* impact; (*huella*) mark. ~ **de bala** bullet hole

impar *adj* odd

imparcial *adj* impartial. ~**idad** *f* impartiality

impartir *vt* impart, give

impasible *adj* impassive

impávido *adj* fearless; (*impasible*) impassive

impecable *adj* impeccable

impedi|do *adj* disabled. ~**mento** *m* impediment. ~**r** **5** *vt* prevent; (*obstruir*) hinder

impenetrable *adj* impenetrable

impensa|ble *adj* unthinkable. ~**do** *adj* unexpected

impera|r *vi* prevail. ~**tivo** *adj* imperative; (*necesidad*) urgent

imperceptible *adj* imperceptible

imperdible *m* safety pin

imperdonable *adj* unforgivable

imperfec|ción *f* imperfection. ~**to** *adj* imperfect

imperi|al *adj* imperial. ~**alismo** *m* imperialism. ~**o** *m* empire; (*poder*) rule. ~**oso** *adj* imperious

impermeable *adj* waterproof. ● *m* raincoat

impersonal *adj* impersonal

impertinen|cia *f* impertinence. ~**te** *adj* impertinent

imperturbable *adj* imperturbable

ímpetu *m* impetus; (*impulso*) impulse; (*violencia*) force

impetuos|idad *f* impetuosity. ~**o** *adj* impetuous

implacable *adj* implacable

implantar *vt* introduce

implementación *f* implementation

implica|ción *f* implication. ~**r** **7** *vt* implicate; (*significar*) imply

implícito *adj* implicit

implorar *vt* implore

impon|ente *adj* imposing; **🔲** terrific. ~**er** **34** *vt* impose; (*requerir*) demand; deposit (*dinero*). ~**erse** *vpr* (*hacerse obedecer*) assert o.s.; (*hacerse respetar*) command respect; (*prevalecer*) prevail. ~**ible** *adj* taxable

importa|ción *f* importation; (*artículo*) import. ~**ciones** *fpl* imports. ~**dor** *adj* importing. ● *m* importer

importa|ncia *f* importance. ~**nte** *adj* important; (*en cantidad*) considerable. ~**r** *vt* import; (*ascender a*) amount to. ● *vi* be important, matter. ¿le ~**ría...?** would you mind...? **no** ~ it doesn't matter

importe *m* price; (*total*) amount

importun|ar *vt* bother. ~**o** *adj* troublesome; (*inoportuno*) inopportune

imposib|ilidad *f* impossibility. ~**le** *adj* impossible. **hacer lo** ~**le para** do all one can to

imposición *f* imposition; (*impuesto*) tax

impostor *m* impostor

impoten|cia *f* impotence. ~**te** *adj* impotent

impracticable *adj* impracticable; (*intransitable*) unpassable

imprecis|ión *f* vagueness; (*error*) inaccuracy. ~**o** *adj* imprecise

impregnar *vt* impregnate; (*empapar*) soak

imprenta *f* printing; (*taller*) printing house, printer's

imprescindible *adj* indispensable, essential

impresi|ón *f* impression; (*acción de imprimir*) printing; (*tirada*) edition; (*huella*) imprint. ~**onable** *adj* impressionable. ~**onante** *adj* impressive; (*espantoso*) frightening. ~**onar** *vt* impress; (*negativamente*) shock; (*conmover*) move; (*Foto*) expose. ~**onarse** *vpr* be impressed; (*negativamente*) be shocked; (*conmover*) be moved

impresionis|mo *m* impressionism. **~ta** *adj & m & f* impressionist

impreso *adj* printed. ● *m* form. **~s** *mpl* printed matter. **~ra** *f* printer

imprevis|ible *adj* unforeseeable. **~to** *adj* unforeseen

imprimir (*pp* **impreso**) *vt* print (libro etc)

improbab|ilidad *f* improbability. **~le** *adj* unlikely, improbable

improcedente *adj* inadmissible; (conducta) improper; (despido) unfair

improductivo *adj* unproductive

improperio *m* insult. **~s** *mpl* abuse

impropio *adj* improper

improvis|ación *f* improvisation. **~ado** *adj* improvised. **~ar** *vt* improvise. **~o** *adj.* **de ~o** unexpectedly

impruden|cia *f* imprudence. **~te** *adj* imprudent

imp|udicia *f* indecency; (*desvergüenza*) shamelessness. **~údico** *adj* indecent; (*desvergonzado*) shameless. **~udor** *m* indecency; (*desvergüenza*) shamelessness

impuesto *adj* imposed. ● *m* tax. **~ a la renta** income tax. **~ sobre el valor agregado** (*LAm*), **~ sobre el valor añadido** VAT, value added tax

impuls|ar *vt* propel; drive (persona); boost (producción etc). **~ividad** *f* impulsiveness. **~ivo** *adj* impulsive. **~o** *m* impulse

impun|e *adj* unpunished. **~idad** *f* impunity

impur|eza *f* impurity. **~o** *adj* impure

imputa|ción *f* charge. **~r** *vt* attribute; (*acusar*) charge

inaccesible *adj* inaccessible

inaceptable *adj* unacceptable

inactiv|idad *f* inactivity. **~o** *adj* inactive

inadaptado *adj* maladjusted

inadecuado *adj* inadequate; (*inapropiado*) unsuitable

inadmisible *adj* inadmissible; (*inaceptable*) unacceptable

inadvertido *adj* distracted. **pasar ~** go unnoticed

inagotable *adj* inexhaustible

inaguantable *adj* unbearable

inaltera|ble *adj* impassive; (color) fast; (convicción) unalterable. **~do** *adj* unchanged

inapreciable *adj* invaluable; (*imperceptible*) imperceptible

inapropiado *adj* inappropriate

inasequible *adj* out of reach

inaudito *adj* unprecedented

inaugura|ción *f* inauguration. **~l** *adj* inaugural. **~r** *vt* inaugurate

inca *adj & m & f* Inca. **~ico** *adj* Inca

> **Incas** Founded in the twelfth
> century, the Andean empire
> of the Quechua-speaking Incas
> grew and extended from southern
> Colombia to Argentina and central
> Chile. Its capital was Cuzco. The
> Incas built an extensive road net-
> work and impressive buildings, in-
> cluding Machu Picchu. The empire
> collapsed in 1533 after defeat by
> the Spaniards led by Francisco Pi-
> zarro.

incalculable *adj* incalculable

incandescente *adj* incandescent

incansable *adj* tireless

incapa|cidad *f* incapacity; (*física*) disability. **~citado** *adj* disabled. **~citar** *vt* incapacitate. **~z** *adj* incapable

incauto *adj* unwary; (*fácil de engañar*) gullible

incendi|ar *vt* set fire to. **~arse** *vpr* catch fire. **~ario** *adj* incendiary. ● *m* arsonist. **~o** *m* fire

incentivo *m* incentive

incertidumbre *f* uncertainty

incesante *adj* incessant

incest|o *m* incest. **~uoso** *adj* incestuous

inciden|cia *f* incidence; (*efecto*) impact; (*incidente*) incident. **~tal** *adj* incidental. **~te** *m* incident

incidir *vi* fall (**en** into); (*influir*) influence

incienso *m* incense

incierto *adj* uncertain

incinera|dor *m* incinerator. **~r** *vt* incinerate; cremate (cadáver)

incipiente *adj* incipient

incisi|ón *f* incision. **~vo** *adj* incisive. ●
m incisor

incitar *vt* incite

inclemen|cia *f* harshness. **~te** *adj*
harsh

inclina|ción *f* slope; (*de la cabeza*)
nod; (*fig*) inclination. **~r** *vt* tilt; (*inducir*) incline. **~rse** *vpr* lean; (*en saludo*)
bow; (*tender*) be inclined (**a** to)

inclu|ido *adj* included; (*precio*) inclusive. **~ir** **17** *vt* include; (*en cartas*) enclose. **~sión** *f* inclusion. **~sive** *adv*
inclusive. **hasta el lunes ~sive** up to
and including Monday. **~so** *adv* even

incógnito *adj* unknown. **de ~** incognito

incoheren|cia *f* incoherence. **~te** *adj*
incoherent

incoloro *adj* colourless

incomestible *adj*, **incomible** *adj* uneatable, inedible

incomodar *vt* inconvenience; (*causar
vergüenza*) make feel uncomfortable.
~se *vpr* feel uncomfortable; (*enojarse*) get angry

incómodo *adj* uncomfortable; (*inconveniente*) inconvenient

incomparable *adj* incomparable

incompatib|ilidad *f* incompatibility.
~le *adj* incompatible

incompeten|cia *f* incompetence.
~te *adj* & *m* & *f* incompetent

incompleto *adj* incomplete

incompren|dido *adj* misunderstood.
~sible *adj* incomprehensible. **~sión** *f*
incomprehension

incomunicado *adj* cut off; (*preso*) in
solitary confinement

inconcebible *adj* inconceivable

inconcluso *adj* unfinished

incondicional *adj* unconditional

inconfundible *adj* unmistakable

incongruente *adj* incoherent; (*contradictorio*) inconsistent

inconmensurable *adj* immeasurable

inconscien|cia *f* unconsciousness;
(*irreflexión*) recklessness. **~te** *adj* unconscious; (*irreflexivo*) reckless

inconsecuente *adj* inconsistent

inconsistente *adj* flimsy

inconsolable *adj* unconsolable

inconstan|cia *f* lack of perseverance.
~te *adj* changeable; (*persona*) lacking
in perseverance; (*voluble*) fickle

incontable *adj* countless

incontenible *adj* irrepressible

incontinen|cia *f* incontinence. **~te**
adj incontinent

inconvenien|cia *f* inconvenience.
~te *adj* inconvenient; (*inapropiado*)
inappropriate; (*incorrecto*) improper.
● *m* problem; (*desventaja*) drawback

incorpora|ción *f* incorporation. **~r** *vt*
incorporate; (*Culin*) add. **~rse** *vpr* sit
up; join (sociedad, regimiento etc)

incorrecto *adj* incorrect; (*descortés*)
discourteous

incorregible *adj* incorrigible

incorruptible *adj* incorruptible

incrédulo *adj* sceptical; (mirada,
gesto) incredulous

increíble *adj* incredible

increment|ar *vt* increase. **~o** *m* increase

incriminar *vt* incriminate

incrustar *vt* encrust

incuba|ción *f* incubation. **~dora** *f* incubator. **~r** *vt* incubate; (*fig*) hatch

incuestionable *adj* unquestionable

inculcar **7** *vt* inculcate

inculpar *vt* accuse

inculto *adj* uneducated

incumplimiento *m* non-fulfilment;
(*de un contrato*) breach

incurable *adj* incurable

incurrir *vi.* **~ en** incur (gasto); fall
into (error); commit (crimen)

incursión *f* raid

indagar **12** *vt* investigate

indebido *adj* unjust; (*uso*) improper

indecen|cia *f* indecency. **~te** *adj* indecent

indecible *adj* indescribable

indecis|ión *f* indecision. **~o** *adj* (*con
ser*) indecisive; (*con estar*) undecided

indefenso *adj* defenceless

indefini|ble *adj* indefinable. **~do** *adj*
indefinite; (*impreciso*) undefined

indemnizar **10** *vt* compensate

independ|encia *f* independence.
~iente *adj* independent. **~izarse** **10**
vpr become independent

indes|cifrable *adj* indecipherable.
~**criptible** *adj* indescribable

indeseable *adj* undesirable

indestructible *adj* indestructible

indetermina|ble *adj* indeterminable.
~**do** *adj* indeterminate; (*tiempo*) indefinite

India *f*. **la ~** India

indica|ción *f* indication; (*señal*) signal.
~**ciones** *fpl* directions. ~**dor** *m* indicator; (*Tec*) gauge. ~**r** 7 *vt* show, indicate; (*apuntar*) point at; (*hacer saber*) point out; (*aconsejar*) advise.
~**tivo** *adj* indicative. ● *m* indicative;
(*al teléfono*) dialling code

índice *m* index; (*dedo*) index finger;
(*catálogo*) catalogue; (*indicación*) indication; (*aguja*) pointer

indicio *m* indication, sign; (*vestigio*)
trace

indiferen|cia *f* indifference. ~**te** *adj*
indifferent. **me es** ~**te** it's all the
same to me

indígena *adj* indigenous. ● *m & f* native

indigen|cia *f* poverty. ~**te** *adj* needy

indigest|ión *f* indigestion. ~**o** *adj* indigestible

indign|ación *f* indignation. ~**ado** *adj*
indignant. ~**ar** *vt* make indignant.
~**arse** *vpr* become indignant. ~**o** *adj*
unworthy; (*despreciable*) contemptible

indio *adj & m* Indian

indirect|a *f* hint. ~**o** *adj* indirect

indisciplinado *adj* undisciplined

indiscre|ción *f* indiscretion. ~**to** *adj*
indiscreet

indiscutible *adj* unquestionable

indisoluble *adj* indissoluble

indispensable *adj* indispensable

indisp|oner 34 *vt* (*enemistar*) set
against. ~**onerse** *vpr* fall out; (*ponerse enfermo*) fall ill. ~**osición** *f* indisposition. ~**uesto** *adj* indisposed

individu|al *adj* individual; (*cama*) single. ● *m* (*en tenis etc*) singles. ~**alidad** *f* individuality. ~**alista** *m & f* individualist. ~**alizar** 10 *vt* individualize.
~**o** *m* individual

indocumentado *m* person without
identity papers; (*inmigrante*) illegal immigrant

índole *f* nature; (*clase*) type

indolen|cia *f* indolence. ~**te** *adj* indolent

indoloro *adj* painless

indomable *adj* untameable

inducir 47 *vt* induce. ~ **a error** be
misleading

indudable *adj* undoubted

indulgen|cia *f* indulgence. ~**te** *adj* indulgent

indult|ar *vt* pardon. ~**o** *m* pardon

industria *f* industry. ~**l** *adj* industrial.
● *m & f* industrialist. ~**lización** *f* industrialization. ~**lizar** 10 *vt* industrialize

inédito *adj* unpublished; (*fig*) unknown

inefable *adj* indescribable

ineficaz *adj* ineffective; (*sistema etc*)
inefficient

ineficiente *adj* inefficient

ineludible *adj* inescapable, unavoidable

inept|itud *f* ineptitude. ~**o** *adj* inept

inequívoco *adj* unequivocal

inercia *f* inertia

inerte *adj* inert; (*sin vida*) lifeless

inesperado *adj* unexpected

inestable *adj* unstable

inestimable *adj* inestimable

inevitable *adj* inevitable

inexistente *adj* non-existent

inexorable *adj* inexorable

inexper|iencia *f* inexperience. ~**to**
adj inexperienced

inexplicable *adj* inexplicable

infalible *adj* infallible

infam|ar *vt* defame. ~**atorio** *adj* defamatory. ~**e** *adj* infamous; (*fig, fam,
muy malo*) awful. ~**ia** *f* infamy

infancia *f* infancy

infant|a *f* infanta, princess. ~**e** *m* infante, prince. ~**ería** *f* infantry. ~**il** *adj*
children's; (*población*) child; (*actitud
etc*) childish, infantile

infarto *m* heart attack

infec|ción *f* infection. ~**cioso** *adj* infectious. ~**tar** *vt* infect. ~**tarse** *vpr*
become infected. ~**to** *adj* infected;
1 disgusting

infeli|cidad *f* unhappiness. ~**z** *adj* unhappy

i

inferior *adj* inferior. ● *m & f* inferior. ~**idad** *f* inferiority

infernal *adj* infernal, hellish

infestar *vt* infest; (*fig*) inundate

infi|delidad *f* unfaithfulness. ~**el** *adj* unfaithful

infierno *m* hell

infiltra|ción *f* infiltration. ~**rse** *vpr* infiltrate

ínfimo *adj* lowest; (calidad) very poor

infini|dad *f* infinity. ~**tivo** *m* infinitive. ~**to** *adj* infinite. ● *m*. **el** ~**to** the infinite; (en matemáticas) infinity. ~**dad de** countless

inflación *f* inflation

inflama|ble *adj* (in)flammable. ~**ción** *f* inflammation. ~**r** *vt* set on fire; (fig, Med) inflame. ~**rse** *vpr* catch fire; (Med) become inflamed

inflar *vt* inflate; blow up (globo); (fig, exagerar) exaggerate

inflexi|ble *adj* inflexible. ~**ón** *f* inflexion

influ|encia *f* influence (**en** on). ~**ir** ⒄ *vt* influence. ● *vi*. ~ **en** influence. ~**jo** *m* influence. ~**yente** *adj* influential

informa|ción *f* information; (noticias) news; (en aeropuerto etc) information desk; (de teléfonos) directory enquiries. ~**dor** *m* informant

informal *adj* informal; (persona) unreliable

inform|ante *m & f* informant. ~**ar** *vt/i* inform. ~**arse** *vpr* find out. ~**ática** *f* information technology, computing. ~**ativo** *adj* informative; (programa) news. ~**atizar** ⒑ *vt* computerize

informe *adj* shapeless. ● *m* report. ~**s** *fpl* references, information

infracción *f* infringement. ~ **de tráfico** traffic offence

infraestructura *f* infrastructure

infranqueable *adj* impassable; (fig) insuperable

infrarrojo *adj* infrared

infringir ⒁ *vt* infringe

infructuoso *adj* fruitless

ínfulas *fpl*. **darse** ~ give o.s. airs. **tener** ~ **de** fancy o.s. as

infundado *adj* unfounded

infu|ndir *vt* instil. ~**sión** *f* infusion

ingeni|ar *vt* invent. ~**árselas para** find a way to

ingenier|ía *f* engineering. ~**o** *m* engineer

ingenio *m* ingenuity; (agudeza) wit; (LAm, de azúcar) refinery. ~**so** *adj* ingenious

ingenu|idad *f* naivety. ~**o** *adj* naive

Inglaterra *f* England

ingl|és *adj* English. ● *m* Englishman; (lengua) English. ~**esa** *f* Englishwoman. **los** ~**eses** the English

ingrat|itud *f* ingratitude. ~**o** *adj* ungrateful; (desagradable) thankless

ingrediente *m* ingredient

ingres|ar *vt* deposit. ● *vi*. ~**ar en** come in, enter; join (sociedad). ~**o** *m* entrance; (de dinero) deposit; (en sociedad, hospital) admission. ~**os** *mpl* income

inh|ábil *adj* unskilful; (no apto) unfit. ~**abilidad** *f* unskilfulness; (para cargo) ineligibility

inhabitable *adj* uninhabitable

inhala|dor *m* inhaler. ~**r** *vt* inhale

inherente *adj* inherent

inhibi|ción *f* inhibition. ~**r** *vt* inhibit

inhóspito *adj* inhospitable

inhumano *adj* inhuman

inici|ación *f* beginning. ~**al** *adj & f* initial. ~**ar** *vt* initiate; (comenzar) begin, start. ~**ativa** *f* initiative. ~**o** *m* beginning

inigualado *adj* unequalled

ininterrumpido *adj* uninterrupted

injert|ar *vt* graft. ~**to** *m* graft

injuri|a *f* insult. ~**ar** *vt* insult. ~**oso** *adj* insulting

injust|icia *f* injustice. ~**o** *adj* unjust, unfair

inmaculado *adj* immaculate

inmaduro *adj* unripe; (persona) immature

inmediaciones *fpl*. **las** ~ the vicinity, the surrounding area

inmediat|amente *adv* immediately. ~**o** *adj* immediate; (contiguo) next. **de** ~**o** immediately

inmejorable *adj* excellent

inmemorable *adj* immemorial

inmens|idad *f* immensity. ~**o** *adj* immense

inmersión f immersion
inmigra|ción f immigration. **~nte** adj & m & f immigrant. **~r** vt immigrate
inminen|cia f imminence. **~te** adj imminent
inmiscuirse 🔟 vpr interfere
inmobiliario adj property
inmolar vt sacrifice
inmoral adj immoral. **~idad** f immorality
inmortal adj immortal. **~izar** 🔟 vt immortalize
inmóvil adj immobile
inmovilizador m immobilizer
inmueble adj. **bienes ~s** property
inmund|icia f filth. **~o** adj filthy
inmun|e adj immune. **~idad** f immunity. **~ización** f immunization. **~izar** 🔟 vt immunize
inmuta|ble adj unchangeable. **~rse** vpr be perturbed. **sin ~rse** unperturbed
innato adj innate
innecesario adj unnecessary
innegable adj undeniable
innova|ción f innovation. **~r** vi innovate. ● vt make innovations in
innumerable adj innumerable
inocen|cia f innocence. **~tada** f practical joke. **~te** adj innocent. **~tón** adj naïve
inocuo adj innocuous
inodoro adj odourless. ● m toilet
inofensivo adj inoffensive
inolvidable adj unforgettable
inoperable adj inoperable
inoportuno adj untimely; (comentario) ill-timed
inoxidable adj stainless
inquiet|ar vt worry. **~arse** vpr get worried. **~o** adj worried; (agitado) restless. **~ud** f anxiety
inquilino m tenant
inquirir 🔟 vt enquire into, investigate
insaciable adj insatiable
insalubre adj unhealthy
insatisfecho adj unsatisfied; (descontento) dissatisfied
inscri|bir (pp **inscrito**) vt (en registro) register; (en curso) enrol; (grabar) in-scribe. **~birse** vpr register. **~pción** f inscription; (registro) registration
insect|icida m insecticide. **~o** m insect
insegur|idad f insecurity. **~o** adj insecure; (ciudad) unsafe, dangerous
insemina|ción f insemination. **~r** vt inseminate
insensato adj foolish
insensible adj insensitive
inseparable adj inseparable
insertar vt insert
insidi|a f malice. **~oso** adj insidious
insigne adj famous
insignia f badge; (bandera) flag
insignificante adj insignificant
insinu|ación f insinuation. **~ante** adj insinuating. **~ar** 🔟 vt imply; insinuate (algo ofensivo). **~arse** vpr. **~ársele a** make a pass at
insípido adj insipid
insist|encia f insistence. **~ente** adj insistent. **~ir** vi insist; (hacer hincapié) stress
insolación f sunstroke
insolen|cia f rudeness, insolence. **~te** adj rude, insolent
insólito adj unusual
insolven|cia f insolvency. **~te** adj & m & f insolvent
insomn|e adj sleepless. ● m & f insomniac. **~io** m insomnia
insondable adj unfathomable
insoportable adj unbearable
insospechado adj unexpected
insostenible adj untenable
inspec|ción f inspection. **~cionar** vt inspect. **~tor** m inspector
inspira|ción f inspiration. **~r** vt inspire. **~rse** vpr be inspired
instala|ción f installation. **~r** vt install. **~rse** vpr settle
instancia f request. **en última ~** as a last resort
instant|ánea f snapshot. **~áneo** adj instantaneous; (café etc) instant. **~e** m instant. **a cada ~e** constantly. **al ~e** immediately
instaura|ción f establishment. **~r** vt establish

instiga|ción f instigation. **~dor** m instigator. **~r** 12 vt instigate; (*incitar*) incite

instint|ivo adj instinctive. **~o** m instinct

institu|ción f institution. **~cional** adj institutional. **~ir** 17 vt establish. **~to** m institute; (*en enseñanza*) (secondary) school. **~triz** f governess

instru|cción f education; (*Mil*) training. **~cciones** fpl instruction. **~ctivo** adj instructive; (*película etc*) educational. **~ctor** m instructor. **~ir** 17 vt instruct, teach; (*Mil*) train

instrument|ación f instrumentation. **~al** adj instrumental. **~o** m instrument; (*herramienta*) tool

insubordina|ción f insubordination. **~r** vt stir up. **~rse** vpr rebel

insuficien|cia f insufficiency; (*inadecuación*) inadequacy. **~te** adj insufficient

insufrible adj insufferable

insular adj insular

insulina f insulin

insulso adj tasteless; (*fig*) insipid

insult|ar vt insult. **~o** m insult

insuperable adj insuperable; (*inmejorable*) unbeatable

insurgente adj insurgent

insurrec|ción f insurrection. **~to** adj insurgent

intachable adj irreproachable

intacto adj intact

intangible adj intangible

integra|ción f integration. **~l** adj integral; (*completo*) complete; (*incorporado*) built-in; (*pan*) wholemeal (*Brit*), wholewheat (*Amer*). **~r** vt make up

integridad f integrity; (*entereza*) wholeness

íntegro adj complete; (*fig*) upright

intelect|o m intellect. **~ual** adj & m & f intellectual

inteligen|cia f intelligence. **~te** adj intelligent

inteligible adj intelligible

intemperie f. **a la ~** in the open

intempestivo adj untimely

intenci|ón f intention. **con doble ~ón** implying sth else. **~onado** adj

deliberate. **bien ~onado** wellmeaning. **mal ~onado** malicious. **~onal** adj intentional

intens|idad f intensity. **~ificar** 7 vt intensify. **~ivo** adj intensive. **~o** adj intense

intent|ar vt try. **~o** m attempt; (*Mex, propósito*) intention

inter|calar vt insert. **~cambio** m exchange. **~ceder** vt intercede

interceptar vt intercept

interdicto m ban

inter|és m interest; (*egoísmo*) selfinterest. **~esado** adj interested; (*parcial*) biassed; (*egoísta*) selfish. **~esante** adj interesting. **~esar** vt interest; (*afectar*) concern. ● vi be of interest. **~esarse** vpr take an interest (**por** in)

interfaz m & f interface

interfer|encia f interference. **~ir** 4 vi interfere

interfono m intercom

interino adj temporary; (*persona*) acting. ● m stand-in

interior adj interior; (*comercio etc*) domestic. ● m inside. **Ministerio del I~** Interior Ministry

interjección f interjection

inter|locutor m speaker. **~mediario** adj & m intermediary. **~medio** adj intermediate. ● m interval

interminable adj interminable

intermitente adj intermittent. ● m indicator

internacional adj international

intern|ado m (*Escol*) boarding-school. **~ar** vt (*en manicomio*) commit; (*en hospital*) admit. **~arse** vpr penetrate

internauta m & f netsurfer

Internet m Internet

interno adj internal; (*en enseñanza*) boarding. ● m boarder

interponer 34 vt interpose. **~se** vpr intervene

int|erpretación f interpretation. **~erpretar** vt interpret; (*Mús etc*) play. **~érprete** m interpreter; (*Mus*) performer

interroga|ción f interrogation; (*signo*) question mark. **~r** 12 vt question. **~tivo** adj interrogative

interru|mpir vt interrupt; cut off (suministro); cut short (viaje etc); block (tráfico). **~pción** f interruption. **~ptor** m switch

inter|sección f intersection. **~urbano** adj inter-city; (llamada) long-distance

intervalo m interval; (espacio) space. **a ~s** at intervals

interven|ir 53 vt control; (Med) operate on. ● vi intervene; (participar) take part. **~tor** m inspector; (Com) auditor

intestino m intestine

intim|ar vi become friendly. **~idad** f intimacy

intimidar vt intimidate

íntimo adj intimate; (amigo) close. ● m close friend

intolera|ble adj intolerable. **~nte** adj intolerant

intoxicar 7 vt poison

intranquilo adj worried

intransigente adj intransigent

intransitable adj impassable

intransitivo adj intransitive

intratable adj impossible

intrépido adj intrepid

intriga f intrigue. **~nte** adj intriguing. **~r** 12 vt intrigue

intrincado adj intricate

intrínseco adj intrinsic

introduc|ción f introduction. **~ir** 47 vt introduce; (meter) insert. **~irse** vpr get into

intromisión f interference

introvertido adj introverted. ● m introvert

intruso m intruder

intui|ción f intuition. **~r** 17 vt sense. **~tivo** adj intuitive

inunda|ción f flooding. **~r** vt flood

inusitado adj unusual

in|útil adj useless; (vano) futile. **~utilidad** f uselessness

invadir vt invade

inv|alidez f invalidity; (Med) disability. **~álido** adj & m invalid

invariable adj invariable

invas|ión f invasion. **~or** adj invading. ● m invader

invencible adj invincible

inven|ción f invention. **~tar** vt invent

inventario m inventory

invent|iva f inventiveness. **~ivo** adj inventive. **~or** m inventor

invernadero m greenhouse

invernal adj winter

inverosímil adj implausible

inver|sión f inversion; (Com) investment. **~sionista** m & f investor

inverso adj inverse; (contrario) opposite. **a la inversa** the other way round. **a la inversa de** contrary to

inversor m investor

invertir 4 vt reverse; (Com) invest; put in (tiempo)

investidura f investiture

investiga|ción f investigation; (Univ) research. **~dor** m investigator; (Univ) researcher. **~r** 12 vt investigate; (Univ) research

investir 5 vt invest

invicto adj unbeaten

invierno m winter

inviolable adj inviolate

invisible adj invisible

invita|ción f invitation. **~do** m guest. **~r** vt invite. **te invito a una copa** I'll buy you a drink

invocar 7 vt invoke

involuntario adj involuntary

invulnerable adj invulnerable

inyec|ción f injection. **~tar** vt inject

---

ir 49

● verbo intransitivo

····▸ to go. **fui a verla** I went to see her. **ir a pie** to go on foot. **ir en coche** to go by car. **vamos a casa** let's go home. **fue (a) por el pan** he went to get some bread

! Cuando la acción del verbo **ir** significa trasladarse hacia o con el interlocutor la traducción es *to come*, p.ej: **¡ya voy!** *I'm coming!* **yo voy contigo** *I'll come with you*

····▸ (estar) to be. **iba con su**

novio she was with her boyfriend. **¿cómo te va?** how are you?

····▸ (*sentar*) to suit. **ese color no le va** that colour doesn't suit her. **no me va ni me viene** I don't mind at all

····▸ (*Méx, apoyar*) **irle a** to support. **le va al equipo local** he supports the local team

····▸ (*en exclamaciones*) **¡vamos!** come on! **¡vaya!** what a surprise!; (*contrariedad*) oh, dear! **¡vaya noche!** what a night! **¡qué va!** nonsense!

➡ Cuando el verbo intransitivo se emplea con expresiones como **ir de paseo, ir de compras, ir tirando** etc., ver bajo el respectivo nombre, verbo etc.

● *verbo auxiliar*

····▸ **ir a** + *infinitivo* (*para expresar futuro, propósito*) to be going to + *infinitive*; (*al prevenir*) **no te vayas a caer** be careful you don't fall. **no vaya a ser que llueva** in case it rains; (*en sugerencias*) **vamos a dormir** let's go to sleep. **vamos a ver** let's see

····▸ **ir** + *gerundio*. **ve arreglándote** start getting ready. **el tiempo va mejorando** the weather is gradually getting better.

● **irse** *verbo pronominal*

····▸ to go. **se ha ido a casa** he's gone home

····▸ (*marcharse*) to leave. **se fue sin despedirse** he left without saying goodbye. **se fue de casa** she left home

ira *f* anger. **~cundo** *adj* irascible

Irak *m* Iraq

Irán *m* Iran

iraní *adj & m & f* Iranian

iraquí *adj & m & f* Iraqi

iris *m* (*del ojo*) iris

Irlanda *f* Ireland

irland|és *adj* Irish. ● *m* Irishman; (*lengua*) Irish. **~esa** *f* Irishwoman. **los ~eses** the Irish

ir|onía *f* irony. **~ónico** *adj* ironic

irracional *adj* irrational

irradiar *vt* radiate

irreal *adj* unreal. **~idad** *f* unreality

irrealizable *adj* unattainable

irreconciliable *adj* irreconcilable

irreconocible *adj* unrecognizable

irrecuperable *adj* irretrievable

irreflexión *f* impetuosity

irregular *adj* irregular. **~idad** *f* irregularity

irreparable *adj* irreparable

irreprimible *adj* irrepressible

irreprochable *adj* irreproachable

irresistible *adj* irresistible

irrespetuoso *adj* disrespectful

irresponsable *adj* irresponsible

irriga|ción *f* irrigation. **~r** 🔢 *vt* irrigate

irrisorio *adj* derisory

irrita|ble *adj* irritable. **~ción** *f* irritation. **~r** *vt* irritate. **~rse** *vpr* get annoyed

irrumpir *vi* burst (**en** in)

isla *f* island. **las I~s Británicas** the British Isles

islámico *adj* Islamic

islandés *adj* Icelandic. ● *m* Icelander; (*lengua*) Icelandic

Islandia *f* Iceland

isleño *adj* island. ● *m* islander

Israel *m* Israel

israelí *adj & m* Israeli

Italia *f* Italy

italiano *adj & m* Italian

itinerario *adj* itinerary

IVA *abrev* (**impuesto sobre el valor agregado** (*LAm*), **impuesto sobre el valor añadido**) VAT

izar 🔟 *vt* hoist

izquierd|a *f*. **la ~a** the left hand; (*Pol*) left. **a la ~a** on the left; (*con movimiento*) to the left. **de ~a** left-wing. **~ista** *m & f* leftist. **~o** *adj* left

Jj

ja int ha!

jabalí m (pl ~es) wild boar

jabalina f javelin

jab|ón m soap. **~onar** vt soap. **~onoso** adj soapy

jaca f pony

jacinto m hyacinth

jactarse vpr boast

jadea|nte adj panting. **~r** vi pant

jaguar m jaguar

jaiba f (LAm) crab

jalar vt (LAm) pull

jalea f jelly

jaleo m row, uproar. **armar un ~** kick up a fuss

jalón m (LAm, tirón) pull; (Mex fam, trago) drink; (Mex, tramo) stretch

jamás adv never. **nunca ~** never ever

jamelgo m nag

jamón m ham. **~ de York** boiled ham. **~ serrano** cured ham

Japón m. **el ~** Japan

japonés adj & m Japanese

jaque m check. **~ mate** checkmate

jaqueca f migraine

jarabe m syrup

jardín m garden. **~ de la infancia**, (Mex) **~ de niños** kindergarten, nursery school

jardiner|ía f gardening. **~o** m gardener

jarr|a f jug. **en ~as** with hands on hips. **~o** m jug. **caer como un ~o de agua fría** come as a shock. **~ón** m vase

jaula f cage

jauría f pack of hounds

jazmín m jasmine

jef|a f boss. **~atura** f leadership; (sede) headquarters. **~e** m boss; (Pol etc) leader. **~e de camareros** head waiter. **~e de estación** stationmaster. **~e de ventas** sales manager

jengibre m ginger

jer|arquía f hierarchy. **~árquico** adj hierarchical

jerez m sherry. **al ~** with sherry

jerez Sherry is produced in an area around Jerez de la Frontera near Cádiz. Sherries are drunk worldwide as an aperitif, and in Spain as an accompaniment to tapas. The main types are: the pale *fino* and *manzanilla* and the darker *oloroso* and *amontillado*. It is from *Jerez* that sherry takes its English name.

jerga f coarse cloth; (argot) jargon

jerigonza f jargon; (galimatías) gibberish

jeringa f syringe; (LAm fam, molestia) nuisance. **~r** 12 vt (fig, fam, molestar) annoy

jeroglífico m hieroglyph(ic)

jersey m (pl ~s) jersey

Jesucristo m Jesus Christ. **antes de ~** BC, before Christ

jesuita adj & m Jesuit

Jesús m Jesus. • int good heavens!; (al estornudar) bless you!

jícara f (Mex) gourd

jilguero m goldfinch

jinete m & f rider

jipijapa m panama hat

jirafa f giraffe

jirón m shred, tatter

jitomate m (Mex) tomato

jorna|da f working day; (viaje) journey; (etapa) stage. **~l** m day's wage. **~lero** m day labourer

joroba f hump. **~do** adj hunchbacked. • m hunchback. **~r** vt 1 annoy

jota f letter J; (danza) jota, popular dance. **ni ~** nothing

joven (pl jóvenes) adj young. • m young man. • f young woman

jovial adj jovial

joy|a f jewel. **~as** fpl jewellery. **~ería** f jeweller's (shop). **~ero** m jeweller; (estuche) jewellery box

juanete m bunion

jubil|ación f retirement. **~ado** adj retired. **~ar** vt pension off. **~arse** vpr retire. **~eo** m jubilee

j

júbilo *m* joy

judaísmo *m* Judaism

judía *f* Jewish woman; (*alubia*) bean. **~ blanca** haricot bean. **~ escarlata** runner bean. **~ verde** French bean

judicial *adj* judicial

judío *adj* Jewish. ● *m* Jewish man

judo *m* judo

juego *m* play; (*de mesa, niños*) game; (*de azar*) gambling; (*conjunto*) set. **estar en ~** be at stake. **estar fuera de ~** be offside. **hacer ~** match. **~s** *mpl* **malabares** juggling. **J~s** *mpl* **Olímpicos** Olympic Games. ● *vb* véase **JUGAR**

juerga *f* spree

jueves *m invar* Thursday

juez *m* judge. **~ de instrucción** examining magistrate. **~ de línea** linesman

juga|dor *m* player; (*habitual, por dinero*) gambler. **~r 🇧** *vt* play. ● *vi* play; (*apostar fuerte*) gamble. **~rse** *vpr* risk. **~r al fútbol**, (*LAm*) **~r fútbol** play football

juglar *m* minstrel

jugo *m* juice; (*de carne*) gravy; (*fig*) substance. **~so** *adj* juicy; (*fig*) substantial

juguet|e *m* toy. **~ear** *vi* play. **~ón** *adj* playful

juicio *m* judgement; (*opinión*) opinion; (*razón*) reason. **a mi ~** in my opinion. **~so** *adj* wise

juliana *f* vegetable soup

julio *m* July

junco *m* rush, reed

jungla *f* jungle

junio *m* June

junt|a *f* meeting; (*consejo*) board, committee; (*Pol*) junta; (*Tec*) joint. **~ar** *vt* join; (*reunir*) collect. **~arse** *vpr* join; (*gente*) meet. **~o** *adj* joined; (*en plural*) together. **~o a** next to. **~ura** *f* joint

jura|do *adj* sworn. ● *m* jury; (*miembro de jurado*) juror. **~mento** *m* oath. **prestar ~mento** take an oath. **~r** *vt/i* swear. **~r en falso** commit perjury. **jurárselas a uno** have it in for s.o.

jurel *m* (type of) mackerel

jurídico *adj* legal

juris|dicción *f* jurisdiction. **~prudencia** *f* jurisprudence

justamente *adj* exactly; (*con justicia*) fairly

justicia *f* justice

justifica|ción *f* justification. **~r 🇷** *vt* justify

justo *adj* fair, just; (*exacto*) exact; (*ropa*) tight. ● *adv* just. **~ a tiempo** just in time

juven|il *adj* youthful. **~tud** *f* youth; (*gente joven*) young people

juzga|do *m* (*tribunal*) court. **~r 🇷** *vt* judge. **a ~r por** judging by

. . . .

Kk

. . . .

kilo *m*, **kilogramo** *m* kilo, kilogram

kil|ometraje *m* distance in kilometres, mileage. **~ométrico** *adj* 🇮 endless. **~ómetro** *m* kilometre. **~ómetro cuadrado** square kilometre

kilovatio *m* kilowatt

kiosco *m* kiosk

. . . .

Ll

. . . .

la artículo definido femenino (*pl* **las**)
⟶ the. **la flor azul** the blue flower. **la casa de al lado** the house next door. **cerca de la iglesia** near the church *No se traduce en los siguientes casos:*
⟶ (*con nombre abstracto, genérico*) **la paciencia es una virtud** patience is a virtue. **odio la leche** I hate milk. **la madera es muy versátil** wood is very versatile
⟶ (*con algunas instituciones*) **termino la universidad mañana** I finish university tomorrow. **no va nunca a la iglesia** he never

goes to church. **está en la cárcel** he's in jail

····▶ (con nombres propios) **la Sra. Díaz** Mrs Díaz. **la doctora Lara** doctor Lara

····▶ (con partes del cuerpo, artículos personales) se traduce por un posesivo. **apretó la mano** he clenched his fist. **tienes la camisa desabrochada** your shirt is undone

····▶ **la + de. es la de Ana** it's Ana's. **la del sombrero** the one with the hat

····▶ **la + que** (persona) **la que me atendió** the one who served me. (cosa) **la que se rompió** the one that broke

····▶ **la + que + subjuntivo** (quienquiera) whoever. **la que gane pasará a la final** whoever wins will go to the final. (cualquiera) whichever. **compra la que sea más barata** buy whichever is cheaper

laberinto m labyrinth, maze

labia f gift of the gab

labio m lip

labor f work. ~**es de aguja** needlework. ~**es de ganchillo** crochet. ~**es de punto** knitting. ~**es domésticas** housework. ~**able** adj working. ~**ar** vi work

laboratorio m laboratory

laborioso adj laborious

laborista adj Labour. ● m & f member of the Labour Party

labra|do adj worked; (madera) carved; (metal) wrought; (tierra) ploughed. ~**dor** m farmer; (obrero) farm labourer. ~**nza** f farming. ~**r** vt work; carve (madera); cut (piedra); till (la tierra). ~**rse** vpr. ~**rse un porvenir** carve out a future for o.s.

labriego m peasant

laca f lacquer

lacayo m lackey

lacio adj straight; (flojo) limp

lacón m shoulder of pork

lacónico adj laconic

lacr|ar vt seal. ~**e** m sealing wax

lactante adj (niño) still on milk

lácteo adj milky. **productos** mpl ~**s** dairy products

ladear vt tilt. ~**se** vpr lean

ladera f slope

ladino adj astute

lado m side. **al** ~ near. **al** ~ **de** next to, beside. **de** ~ sideways. **en todos** ~**s** everywhere. **los de al** ~ the next door neighbours. **por otro** ~ on the other hand. **por todos** ~**s** everywhere. **por un** ~ on the one hand

ladr|ar vi bark. ~**ido** m bark

ladrillo m brick

ladrón m thief, robber; (de casas) burglar

lagart|ija f (small) lizard. ~**o** m lizard

lago m lake

lágrima f tear

lagrimoso adj tearful

laguna f small lake; (fig, omisión) gap

laico adj lay

lament|able adj deplorable; (que da pena) pitiful; (pérdida) sad. ~**ar** vt be sorry about. ~**arse** vpr lament; (quejarse) complain. ~**o** m moan

lamer vt lick

lámina f sheet; (ilustración) plate; (estampa) picture card

lamina|do adj laminated. ~**r** vt laminate

lámpara f lamp. ~ **de pie** standard lamp

lamparón m stain

lampiño adj beardless; (cuerpo) hairless

lana f wool. **de** ~ wool(len)

lanceta f lancet

lancha f boat. ~ **motora** motor boat. ~ **salvavidas** lifeboat

langost|a f (de mar) lobster; (insecto) locust. ~**ino** m king prawn

languide|cer 🔢 vi languish. ~**z** f languor

lánguido adj languid; (decaído) listless

lanilla f nap; (tela fina) flannel

lanudo adj woolly; (perro) shaggy

lanza f lance, spear

lanza|llamas m invar flame-thrower. ~**miento** m throw; (acción de lanzar) throwing; (de proyectil, de producto) launch. **~miento de peso,** (*LAm*) **~miento de bala** shot put. **~r** [10] *vt* throw; (*de un avión*) drop; launch (proyectil, producto). **~rse** *vpr* throw o.s.

lapicero *m* (propelling) pencil

lápida *f* tombstone; (*placa conmemorativa*) memorial tablet

lapidar *vt* stone

lápiz *m* pencil. **~ de labios** lipstick. **a ~ in** pencil

lapso *m* lapse

laptop *m* laptop

larg|a *f.* **a la ~a** in the long run. **dar ~as** put off. **~ar** [12] *vt* (*Naut*) let out; (*fam, dar*) give; [LAm] deal (bofetada etc). **~arse** *vpr* [LAm] beat it [LAm]. **~o** *adj* long. ● *m* length. **¡~o!** go away! **a lo ~o** lengthwise. **a lo ~o de** along. **tener 100 metros de ~o** be 100 metres long

laring|e *f* larynx. **~itis** *f* laryngitis

larva *f* larva

las *artículo definido fpl* the. *véase tb* **LA**. ● *pron* them. **~ de** those, the ones. **~ de Vd** your ones, yours. **~ que** whoever, the ones

láser *m* laser

lástima *f* pity; (*queja*) complaint. **da ~ verlo así** it's sad to see him like that. **ella me da ~** I feel sorry for her. **¡qué ~!** what a pity!

lastim|ado *adj* hurt. **~ar** *vt* hurt. **~arse** *vpr* hurt o.s. **~ero** *adj* doleful. **~oso** *adj* pitiful

lastre *m* ballast; (*fig*) burden

lata *f* tinplate; (*envase*) tin (*esp Brit*), can; (*fam, molestia*) nuisance. **dar la ~** be a nuisance. **¡qué ~!** what a nuisance!

latente *adj* latent

lateral *adj* side, lateral

latido *m* beating; (*cada golpe*) beat

latifundio *m* large estate

latigazo *m* (*golpe*) lash; (*chasquido*) crack

látigo *m* whip

latín *m* Latin. **saber ~** [LAm] know what's what [LAm]

latino *adj* Latin. **L~américa** *f* Latin America. **~americano** *adj* & *m* Latin American

latir *vi* beat; (*herida*) throb

latitud *f* latitude

latón *m* brass

latoso *adj* annoying; (*pesado*) boring

laúd *m* lute

laureado *adj* honoured; (*premiado*) prize-winning

laurel *m* laurel; (*Culin*) bay

lava *f* lava

lava|ble *adj* washable. **~bo** *m* washbasin; (*retrete*) toilet. **~dero** *m* sink. **~do** *m* washing. **~do de cerebro** brainwashing. **~do en seco** drycleaning. **~dora** *f* washing machine. **~ndería** *f* laundry. **~ndería automática** launderette, laundromat (*esp Amer*). **~platos** *m* & *f invar* dishwasher. ● *m* (*Mex, fregadero*) sink. **~r** *vt* wash. **~r en seco** dry-clean. **~rse** *vpr* have a wash. **~rse las manos** (*incl fig*) wash one's hands. **~tiva** *f* enema. **~vajillas** *m invar* dishwasher; (*detergente*) washing-up liquid (*Brit*), dishwashing liquid (*Amer*)

laxante *adj* & *m* laxative

lazada *f* bow

lazarillo *m* guide for a blind person

lazo *m* knot; (*lazada*) bow; (*fig, vínculo*) tie; (*con nudo corredizo*) lasso; (*Mex, cuerda*) rope

le *pron* (*acusativo, él*) him; (*acusativo, Vd*) you; (*dativo, él*) (to) him; (*dativo, ella*) (to) her; (*dativo, cosa*) (to) it; (*dativo, Vd*) (to) you

leal *adj* loyal; (*fiel*) faithful. **~tad** *f* loyalty; (*fidelidad*) faithfulness

lección *f* lesson

leche *f* milk; (*golpe*) bash. **~ condensada** condensed milk. **~ desnatada** skimmed milk. **~ en polvo** powdered milk. **~ sin desnatar** whole milk. **tener mala ~** be spiteful. **~ra** *f* (*vasija*) milk jug. **~ría** *f* dairy. **~ro** *adj* milk, dairy. ● *m* milkman

lecho *m* (*en literatura*) bed. **~ de río** river bed

lechoso *adj* milky

lechuga *f* lettuce

lechuza *f* owl

lect|or *m* reader; (*Univ*) language assistant. **~ura** *f* reading

leer [18] *vt/i* read

legación f legation

legado m legacy; (*enviado*) legate

legajo m bundle, file

legal adj legal. **~idad** f legality. **~izar** 🔟 vt legalize; (*certificar*) authenticate. **~mente** adv legally

legar 🔢 vt bequeath

legible adj legible

legi|ón f legion. **~onario** m legionary. **~onella** f legionnaire's disease

legisla|ción f legislation. **~dor** m legislator. **~r** vi legislate. **~tura** f term (of office); (*año parlamentario*) session; (*LAm, cuerpo*) legislature

leg|itimidad f legitimacy. **~ítimo** adj legitimate; (*verdadero*) real

lego adj lay; (*ignorante*) ignorant. ● m layman

legua f league

legumbre f vegetable

lejan|ía f distance. **~o** adj distant

lejía f bleach

lejos adv far. **~ de** far from. **a lo ~** in the distance. **desde ~** from a distance, from afar

lema m motto

lencería f linen; (*de mujer*) lingerie

lengua f tongue; (*idioma*) language. **irse de la ~** talk too much. **morderse la ~** hold one's tongue

---

lenguas cooficiales The regional languages of Spain, *catalán*, *euskera* and *gallego*, which now have equal status with Castilian in the regions where they are spoken. Banned under Franco, they continued to be spoken privately. They are now widely used in public life, education, the media, cinema and literature.

---

lenguado m sole

lenguaje m language

lengüeta f (*de zapato*) tongue. **~da** f, **~zo** m lick

lente f lens. **~s** mpl glasses. **~s de contacto** contact lenses

lentej|a f lentil. **~uela** f sequin

lentilla f contact lens

lent|itud f slowness. **~o** adj slow

leñ|a f firewood. **~ador** m woodcutter. **~o** m log

Leo m Leo

le|ón m lion. **~ona** f lioness

leopardo m leopard

leotardo m thick tights

lepr|a f leprosy. **~oso** m leper

lerdo adj dim; (*torpe*) clumsy

les pron (*acusativo*) them; (*acusativo, Vds*) you; (*dativo*) (to) them; (*dativo, Vds*) (to) you

lesbiana f lesbian

lesi|ón f wound. **~onado** adj injured. **~onar** vt injure; (*dañar*) damage

letal adj lethal

let|árgico adj lethargic. **~argo** m lethargy

letr|a f letter; (*escritura*) handwriting; (*de una canción*) words, lyrics. **~a de cambio** bill of exchange. **~a de imprenta** print. **~ado** adj learned. **~ero** m notice; (*cartel*) poster

letrina f latrine

leucemia f leukaemia

levadura f yeast. **~ en polvo** baking powder

levanta|miento m lifting; (*sublevación*) uprising. **~r** vt raise, lift; (*construir*) build; (*recoger*) pick up. **~rse** vpr get up; (*ponerse de pie*) stand up; (*erguirse, sublevarse*) rise up

levante m east; (*viento*) east wind

levar vt. **~ anclas** weigh anchor

leve adj light; (*sospecha* etc) slight; (*enfermedad*) mild; (*de poca importancia*) trivial. **~dad** f lightness; (*fig*) slightness

léxico m vocabulary

lexicografía f lexicography

ley f law; (*parlamentaria*) act

leyenda f legend

liar 🔟 vt tie; (*envolver*) wrap up; roll (*cigarrillo*); (*fig, confundir*) confuse; (*fig, enredar*) involve. **~se** vpr get involved

libanés adj & m Lebanese

libelo m (*escrito*) libellous article; (*Jurid*) petition

libélula f dragonfly

libera|ción f liberation. **~dor** adj liberating. ● m liberator

liberal _adj_ & _m_ & _f_ liberal. **~idad** _f_ liberality

liber|ar _vt_ free. **~tad** _f_ freedom. **~tad de cultos** freedom of worship. **~tad de imprenta** freedom of the press. **~tad provisional** bail. **en ~tad** free. **~tador** _m_ liberator. **~tar** _vt_ free

libertino _m_ libertine

libido _f_ libido

libio _adj_ & _m_ Libyan

libra _f_ pound. **~ esterlina** pound sterling

Libra _m_ Libra

libra|dor _m_ (_Com_) drawer. **~r** _vt_ free; (_de un peligro_) save. **~rse** _vpr_ free o.s. **~rse de** get rid of

libre _adj_ free. **estilo ~** (_en natación_) freestyle. **~ de impuestos** tax-free

librea _f_ livery

libr|ería _f_ bookshop (_Brit_), bookstore (_Amer_); (_mueble_) bookcase. **~ero** _m_ bookseller; (_Mex, mueble_) bookcase. **~eta** _f_ notebook. **~o** _m_ book. **~o de bolsillo** paperback. **~o de ejercicios** exercise book. **~o de reclamaciones** complaints book

licencia _f_ permission; (_documento_) licence. **~do** _m_ graduate; (_Mex, abogado_) lawyer. **~ para manejar** (_Mex_) driving licence. **~r** _vt_ (_Mil_) discharge; (_echar_) dismiss. **~tura** _f_ degree

licencioso _adj_ licentious

licitar _vt_ bid for

lícito _adj_ legal; (_permisible_) permissible

licor _m_ liquor; (_dulce_) liqueur

licua|dora _f_ blender. **~r** 21 liquefy; (_Culin_) blend

lid _f_ fight. **en buena ~** by fair means. **~es** _fpl_ matters

líder _m_ leader

liderato _m_, **liderazgo** _m_ leadership

lidia _f_ bullfighting; (_lucha_) fight. **~r** _vt/i_ fight

liebre _f_ hare

lienzo _m_ linen; (_del pintor_) canvas; (_muro, pared_) wall

liga _f_ garter; (_alianza_) league; (_LAm, gomita_) rubber band. **~dura** _f_ bond; (_Mus_) slur; (_Med_) ligature. **~mento** _m_ ligament. **~r** 12 _vt_ bind; (_atar_) tie; (_Mus_) slur. ● _vi_ mix. **~r con** (_fig_) pick

up. **~rse** _vpr_ (_fig_) commit o.s.

liger|eza _f_ lightness; (_agilidad_) agility; (_rapidez_) swiftness; (_de carácter_) fickleness. **~o** _adj_ light; (_rápido_) quick; (_ágil_) agile; (_superficial_) superficial; (_de poca importancia_) slight. ● _adv_ quickly. **a la ~a** lightly, superficially

liguero _m_ suspender belt

lija _f_ dogfish; (_papel de lija_) sandpaper. **~r** _vt_ sand

lila _f_ lilac. ● _m_ (_color_) lilac

lima _f_ file; (_fruta_) lime. **~duras** _fpl_ filings. **~r** _vt_ file (down)

limita|ción _f_ limitation. **~do** _adj_ limited. **~r** _vt_ limit. **~r con** border on. **~tivo** _adj_ limiting

límite _m_ limit. **~ de velocidad** speed limit

limítrofe _adj_ bordering

lim|ón _m_ lemon; (_Mex_) lime. **~onada** _f_ lemonade

limosn|a _f_ alms. **pedir ~a** beg. **~ear** _vi_ beg

limpia|botas _m invar_ bootblack. **~parabrisas** _m invar_ windscreen wiper (_Brit_), windshield wiper (_Amer_). **~pipas** _m invar_ pipe-cleaner. **~r** _vt_ clean; (_enjugar_) wipe. **~vidrios** _m invar_ (_LAm_) window cleaner

limpi|eza _f_ cleanliness; (_acción de limpiar_) cleaning. **~eza en seco** dry-cleaning. **~o** _adj_ clean; (_cielo_) clear; (_fig, honrado_) honest; (_neto_) net. **pasar a ~o**, (_LAm_) **pasar en ~o** make a fair copy. ● _adv_ fairly. **jugar ~o** play fair

linaje _m_ lineage; (_fig, clase_) kind

lince _m_ lynx

linchar _vt_ lynch

lind|ar _vi_ border (**con** on). **~e** _f_ boundary. **~ero** _m_ border

lindo _adj_ pretty, lovely. **de lo ~** 1 a lot

línea _f_ line. **en ~** online. **en ~s generales** broadly speaking. **guardar la ~** watch one's figure

lingote _m_ ingot

lingü|ista _m_ & _f_ linguist. **~ística** _f_ linguistics. **~ístico** _adj_ linguistic

lino _m_ flax; (_tela_) linen

linterna f lantern; (*de bolsillo*) torch, flashlight (*Amer*)

lío m bundle; (*jaleo*) fuss; (*embrollo*) muddle; (*amorío*) affair

liquida|ción f liquidation; (*venta especial*) sale. ∼**r** vt liquify; (*Com*) liquidate; settle (*cuenta*)

líquido adj liquid; (*Com*) net. ● m liquid; (*Com*) cash

lira f lyre; (*moneda italiana*) lira

líric|a f lyric poetry. ∼**o** adj lyric(al)

lirio m iris

lirón m dormouse; (*fig*) sleepyhead. **dormir como un** ∼ sleep like a log

lisiado adj crippled

liso adj smooth; (*pelo*) straight; (*tierra*) flat; (*sencillo*) plain

lisonj|a f flattery. ∼**eador** adj flattering. ● m flatterer. ∼**ear** vt flatter. ∼**ero** adj flattering

lista f stripe; (*enumeración*) list. ∼ **de correos** poste restante. **a** ∼**s** striped. **pasar** ∼ take the register. ∼**do** adj striped

listo adj clever; (*preparado*) ready

listón m strip; (*en saltos*) bar; (*Mex, cinta*) ribbon

litera f (*en barco, tren*) berth; (*en habitación*) bunk bed

literal adj literal

litera|rio adj literary ∼**tura** f literature

litig|ar 12 vi dispute; (*Jurid*) litigate. ∼**lo** m dispute; (*Jurid*) litigation

litografía f (*arte*) lithography; (*cuadro*) lithograph

litoral adj coastal. ● m coast

litro m litre

lituano adj & m Lithuanian

liturgia f liturgy

liviano adj fickle; (*LAm, de poco peso*) light

lívido adj livid

llaga f wound; (*úlcera*) ulcer

llama f flame; (*animal*) llama

llamada f call

llama|do adj called. ● m (*LAm*) call. ∼**miento** m call. ∼**r** vt call; (*por teléfono*) phone. ● vi call; (*golpear en la puerta*) knock; (*tocar el timbre*) ring. ∼**r por teléfono** phone, telephone.

∼**rse** vpr be called. **¿cómo te** ∼**s?** what's your name?

llamarada f sudden blaze; (*fig, de pasión etc*) outburst

llamativo adj flashy; (*color*) loud; (*persona*) striking

llamear vi blaze

llano adj flat, level; (*persona*) natural; (*sencillo*) plain. ● m plain

llanta f (*Auto*) (wheel) rim; (*LAm, neumático*) tyre

llanto m crying

llanura f plain

llave f key; (*para tuercas*) spanner; (*LAm, del baño etc*) tap (*Brit*), faucet (*Amer*); (*Elec*) switch ∼ **inglesa** monkey wrench. **cerrar con** ∼ lock. **echar la** ∼ lock up. ∼**ro** m key-ring

llega|da f arrival. ∼**r** 12 vi arrive, come; (*alcanzar*) reach; (*bastar*) be enough. ∼**r a** (*conseguir*) manage to. ∼**r a saber** find out. ∼**r a ser** become. ∼**r hasta** go as far as

llen|ar vt fill (up); (*rellenar*) fill in; (*cubrir*) cover (**de** with). ∼**o** adj full. ● m (*en el teatro etc*) full house. **de** ∼ entirely

lleva|dero adj tolerable. ∼**r** vt carry; (*inducir, conducir*) lead; (*acompañar*) take; wear (*ropa*). **¿cuánto tiempo** ∼**s aquí?** how long have you been here? **llevo 3 años estudiando inglés** I've been studying English for 3 years. ∼**rse** vpr take away; win (*premio etc*); (*comprar*) take. ∼**rse bien** get on well together

llor|ar vi cry; (*ojos*) water. ∼**iquear** vi whine. ∼**iqueo** m whining. ∼**o** m crying. ∼**ón** adj whining. ● m crybaby. ∼**oso** adj tearful

llov|er 2 vi rain. ∼**izna** f drizzle. ∼**iznar** vi drizzle

llueve vb véase **LLOVER**

lluvi|a f rain; (*fig*) shower. ∼**oso** adj rainy; (*clima*) wet

lo artículo definido neutro. ∼ **importante** what is important, the important thing. ● pron (*él*) him; (*cosa*) it. ∼ **que** what, that which

loa f praise. ∼**ble** adj praiseworthy. ∼**r** vt praise

lobo m wolf

lóbrego *adj* gloomy

lóbulo *m* lobe

local *adj* local. ● *m* premises. ~**idad** *f* locality; (*de un espectáculo*) seat; (*entrada*) ticket. ~**izador** *m* pager; (*de reserva*) booking reference. ~**izar** 🔟 *vt* find, locate

loción *f* lotion

loco *adj* mad, crazy. ● *m* lunatic. ~ **de alegría** mad with joy. **estar** ~ **por** be crazy about. **volverse** ~ go mad

locomo|ción *f* locomotion. ~**tora** *f* locomotive

locuaz *adj* talkative

locución *f* expression

locura *f* madness; (*acto*) crazy thing. **con** ~ madly

locutor *m* broadcaster

lod|azal *m* quagmire. ~**o** *m* mud

lógic|a *f* logic. ~**o** *adj* logical

logr|ar *vt* get; win (premio). ~ **hacer** manage to do. ~**o** *m* achievement; (*de premio*) winning; (*éxito*) success

loma *f* small hill

lombriz *f* worm

lomo *m* back; (*de libro*) spine. ~ **de cerdo** loin of pork

lona *f* canvas

loncha *f* slice; (*de tocino*) rasher

londinense *adj* from London. ● *m* Londoner

Londres *m* London

loneta *f* thin canvas

longaniza *f* sausage

longev|idad *f* longevity. ~**o** *adj* long-lived

longitud *f* length; (*en geografía*) longitude

lonja *f* slice; (*de tocino*) rasher; (*Com*) market

loro *m* parrot

los *artículo definido mpl* the. *véase tb* **EL**. ● *pron* them. ~ **de Antonio** Antonio's. ~ **que** whoever, the ones

losa *f* (*baldosa*) flagstone. ~ **sepulcral** tombstone

lote *m* share; (*de productos*) batch; (*terreno*) plot (*Brit*), lot (*Amer*)

lotería *f* lottery

loto *m* lotus

loza *f* crockery; (*fina*) china

lozano *adj* fresh; (*vegetación*) lush; (*persona*) healthy-looking

lubina *f* sea bass

lubrica|nte *adj* lubricating. ● *m* lubricant. ~**r** 🔽 *vt* lubricate

lucero *m* bright star. ~ **del alba** morning star

lucha *f* fight; (*fig*) struggle. ~**dor** *m* fighter. ~**r** *vi* fight; (*fig*) struggle

lucid|ez *f* lucidity. ~**o** *adj* splendid

lúcido *adj* lucid

luciérnaga *f* glow-worm

lucimiento *m* brilliance

lucio *m* pike

lucir 🔢 *vt* (*fig*) show off. ● *vi* shine; (*joya*) sparkle; (*LAm, mostrarse*) look. ~**se** *vpr* (*fig*) shine, excel; (*presumir*) show off

lucr|ativo *adj* lucrative. ~**o** *m* gain

luego *adv* then; (*más tarde*) later (on); (*Mex, pronto*) soon. ● *conj* therefore. ~ **que** as soon as. **desde** ~ of course

lugar *m* place; (*espacio libre*) room. ~ **común** cliché. **dar** ~ **a** give rise to. **en** ~ **de** instead of. **en primer** ~ first. **hacer** ~ make room. **tener** ~ take place. ~**eño** *adj* local, village

lugarteniente *m* deputy

lúgubre *adj* gloomy

lujo *m* luxury. ~**so** *adj* luxurious. **de** ~ luxury

lumbago *m* lumbago

lumbre *f* fire; (*luz*) light

luminoso *adj* luminous; (*fig*) bright; (*letrero*) illuminated

luna *f* moon; (*espejo*) mirror. ~ **de miel** honeymoon. **claro de** ~ moonlight. **estar en la** ~ be miles away. ~**r** *adj* lunar. ● *m* mole; (*en tela*) spot

lunes *m invar* Monday

lupa *f* magnifying glass

lustr|abotas *m invar* (*LAm*) bootblack. ~**ar** *vt* shine, polish. ~**e** *m* shine; (*fig, esplendor*) splendour. **dar** ~**e a**, **sacar** ~**e a** polish. ~**oso** *adj* shining

luto *m* mourning. **estar de** ~ be in mourning

luz *f* light; (*electricidad*) electricity. **luces altas** (*LAm*) headlights on full beam. **luces bajas** (*LAm*), **luces cor-**

tas dipped headlights. **luces antinie-bla** fog light. **luces largas** headlights on full beam. **a la ~ de** in the light of. **a todas luces** obviously. **dar a ~** give birth. **hacer la ~ sobre** shed light on. **sacar a la ~** bring to light

Mm

macabro *adj* macabre

macaco *m* macaque (monkey)

macanudo *adj* ① great ①

macarrones *mpl* macaroni

macerar *vt* macerate (fruta); marinade (carne etc)

maceta *f* mallet; (*tiesto*) flowerpot

machacar ⑦ *vt* crush. ● *vi* go on (**sobre** about)

machamartillo. a ~ *adj* ardent; (*como adv*) firmly

machet|azo *m* blow with a machete; (*herida*) wound from a machete. **~e** *m* machete

mach|ista *m* male chauvinist. **~o** *adj* male; (*varonil*) macho

machu|car ⑦ *vt* bruise; (*aplastar*) crush. **~cón** *m* (*LAm*) bruise

macizo *adj* solid. ● *m* mass; (*de plantas*) bed

madeja *f* skein

madera *m* (*vino*) Madeira. ● *f* wood; (*naturaleza*) nature. **~ble** *adj* yielding timber. **~men** *m* woodwork

madero *m* log; (*de construcción*) timber

madona *f* Madonna

madr|astra *f* stepmother. **~e** *f* mother. **~eperla** *f* mother-of-pearl. **~eselva** *f* honeysuckle

madrigal *m* madrigal

madriguera *f* den; (*de conejo*) burrow

madrileño *adj* of Madrid. ● *m* person from Madrid

madrina *f* godmother; (*en una boda*) matron of honour

madrug|ada *f* dawn. **de ~ada** at dawn. **~ador** *adj* who gets up early.

● *m* early riser. **~ar** ⑫ *vi* get up early

madur|ación *f* maturing; (*de fruta*) ripening. **~ar** *vt/i* mature; (*fruta*) ripen. **~ez** *f* maturity; (*de fruta*) ripeness. **~o** *adj* mature; (*fruta*) ripe

maestr|ía *f* skill; (*Univ*) master's degree. **~o** *m* master; (*de escuela*) schoolteacher

mafia *f* mafia

magdalena *f* fairy cake (*Brit*), cup cake (*Amer*)

magia *f* magic

mágico *adj* magic; (*maravilloso*) magical

magist|erio *m* teaching (profession); (*conjunto de maestros*) teachers. **~rado** *m* magistrate; (*juez*) judge. **~ral** *adj* teaching; (*bien hecho*) masterly. **~ratura** *f* magistracy

magn|animidad *f* magnanimity. **~ánimo** *adj* magnanimous. **~ate** *m* magnate, tycoon

magnavoz *m* (*Mex*) megaphone

magnético *adj* magnetic

magneti|smo *m* magnetism. **~zar** ⑩ *vt* magnetize

magn|ificar *vt* extol; (*LAm*) magnify (*objeto*). **~ificencia** *f* magnificence. **~ífico** *adj* magnificent. **~itud** *f* magnitude

magnolia *f* magnolia

mago *m* magician; (*en cuentos*) wizard

magro *adj* lean; (*tierra*) poor

magulla|dura *f* bruise. **~r** *vt* bruise. **~rse** *vpr* bruise

mahometano *adj* Islamic

maíz *m* maize, corn (*Amer*)

majada *f* sheepfold; (*estiércol*) manure; (*LAm*) flock of sheep

majader|ía *f* silly thing. **~o** *m* idiot. ● *adj* stupid

majest|ad *f* majesty. **~uoso** *adj* majestic

majo *adj* nice

mal *adv* badly; (*poco*) poorly; (*difícilmente*) hardly; (*equivocadamente*) wrongly; (*desagradablemente*) bad. ● *adj*. **estar ~** be ill; (*anímicamente*) be in a bad way; (*incorrecto*) be wrong. **estar ~ de** (*escaso de*) be short of. *véase tb* **MALO**. ● *m* evil; (*daño*) harm;

(*enfermedad*) illness. ~ **que bien** somehow (or other). **de ~ en peor** from bad to worse. **hacer ~ en** be wrong to. **¡menos ~!** thank goodness!

malabaris|mo *m* juggling. ~**ta** *m & f* juggler

mala|consejado *adj* ill-advised. ~**costumbrado** *adj* spoilt. ~**crianza** (*LAm*) rudeness. ~**gradecido** *adj* ungrateful

malagueño *adj* of Málaga. ● *m* person from Málaga

malaria *f* malaria

Malasia *f* Malaysia

malavenido *adj* incompatible

malaventura *adj* unfortunate

malayo *adj* Malay(an)

malbaratar *vt* sell off cheap; (*malgastar*) squander

malcarado *adj* nasty looking

malcriado *adj* (niño) spoilt

maldad *f* evil; (*acción*) wicked thing

maldecir 46 (*pero imperativo* **maldice**, *futuro y condicional regulares, pp* **maldecido** *o* **maldito**) *vt* curse. ● *vi* curse; speak ill (**de** of)

maldi|ciente *adj* backbiting; (*que blasfema*) foul-mouthed. ~**ción** *f* curse. ~**to** *adj* damned. **¡~to sea!** damn (it)!

maleab|ilidad *f* malleability. ~**le** *adj* malleable

malea|nte *m* criminal. ~**r** *vt* damage; (*pervertir*) corrupt. ~**rse** *vpr* be spoilt; (*pervertirse*) be corrupted

malecón *m* breakwater; (*embarcadero*) jetty; (*Rail*) embankment; (*LAm, paseo marítimo*) seafront

maledicencia *f* slander

mal|eficio *m* curse. ~**éfico** *adj* evil

malestar *m* discomfort; (*fig*) uneasiness

malet|a *f* (suit)case. **hacer la ~a** pack (one's case). ~**ero** *m* porter; (*Auto*) boot, trunk (*Amer*). ~**ín** *m* small case; (*para documentos*) briefcase

mal|evolencia *f* malevolence. ~**évolo** *adj* malevolent

maleza *f* weeds; (*matorral*) undergrowth

mal|gastar *vt* waste. ~**hablado** *adj* foul-mouthed. ~**hechor** *m* criminal. ~**humorado** *adj* bad-tempered

malici|a *f* malice; (*picardía*) mischief. ~**arse** *vpr* suspect. ~**oso** *adj* malicious; (*pícaro*) mischievous

maligno *adj* malignant; (*persona*) evil

malintencionado *adj* malicious

malla *f* mesh; (*de armadura*) mail; (*de gimnasia*) leotard

Mallorca *f* Majorca

mallorquín *adj & m* Majorcan

malmirado *adj* (*con estar*) frowned upon

malo *adj* (*delante de nombre masculino en singular* **mal**) bad; (*enfermo*) ill. ~ **de** difficult to. **estar de malas** (*malhumorado*) be in a bad mood; (*LAm, con mala suerte*) be out of luck. **lo ~ es que** the trouble is that. **por las malas** by force

malogr|ar *vt* waste; (*estropear*) spoil. ~**arse** *vpr* fall through

maloliente *adj* smelly

malpensado *adj* nasty, malicious

malsano *adj* unhealthy

malsonante *adj* ill-sounding; (*grosero*) offensive

malt|a *f* malt. ~**eada** *f* (*LAm*) milk shake. ~**ear** *vt* malt

maltr|atar *vt* ill-treat; (*pegar*) batter; mistreat (juguete etc). ~**echo** *adj* battered

malucho *adj* ▣ under the weather

malva *f* mallow. (**color de**) ~ *adj invar* mauve

malvado *adj* wicked

malvavisco *m* marshmallow

malversa|ción *f* embezzlement. ~**dor** *adj* embezzling. ● *m* embezzler. ~**r** *vt* embezzle

Malvinas *fpl.* **las (islas)** ~ the Falklands, the Falkland Islands

mama *f* mammary gland; (*de mujer*) breast

mamá *f* mum; (*usado por niños*) mummy

mama|da *f* sucking. ~**r** *vt* suck; (*fig*) grow up with. ● *vi* (bebé) feed; (animal) suckle. **dar de ~** breastfeed

mamario *adj* mammary

mamarracho m clown; (cosa ridícula) (ridiculous) sight; (cosa mal hecha) botch; (cosa fea) mess. **ir hecho un ~** look a sight

mameluco m (LAm) overalls; (de niño) rompers

mamífero adj mammalian. ● m mammal

mamila f (Mex) feeding bottle

mamotreto m (libro) hefty volume; (armatoste) huge thing

mampara f screen

mampostería f masonry

mamut m mammoth

manada f herd; (de lobos) pack; (de leones) pride. **en ~** in crowds

mana|ntial m spring; (fig) source. **~r** vi flow; (fig) abound. ● vt drip with

manaza f big hand

mancha f stain; (en la piel) blotch. **~do** adj stained; (sucio) dirty; (animal) spotted. **~r** vt stain; (ensuciar) dirty. **~rse** vpr get stained; (ensuciarse) get dirty

manchego adj of la Mancha. ● m person from la Mancha

manchón m large stain

mancilla f blemish. **~r** vt stain

manco adj (de una mano) one-handed; (de las dos manos) handless; (de un brazo) one-armed; (de los dos brazos) armless

mancomun|adamente adv jointly. **~ar** vt unite; (Jurid) make jointly liable. **~arse** vpr unite. **~idad** f union

manda f (Mex) religious offering

manda|dero m messenger. **~do** m (LAm) shopping; (diligencia) errand. **hacer los ~dos** (LAm) do the shopping. **~miento** m order; (Relig) commandment. **~r** vt order; (enviar) send; (gobernar) rule. ● vi be in command. **¿mande?** (Mex) pardon?

mandarin|a f (naranja) mandarin (orange). **~o** m mandarin tree

mandat|ario m attorney; (Pol) head of state. **~o** m mandate; (Pol) term of office

mandíbula f jaw

mando m command. **~ a distancia** remote control. **al ~ de** in charge of. **altos ~s** mpl high-ranking officers

mandolina f mandolin

mandón adj bossy

manducar 7 vt 1 stuff oneself with

manecilla f hand

manej|able adj manageable. **~ar** vt use; handle (asunto etc); (fig) manage; (LAm, conducir) drive. **~arse** vpr get by. **~o** m handling. **~os** mpl scheming

manera f way. **~s** fpl manners. **de alguna ~** somehow. **de ~ que** so (that). **de ninguna ~** by no means. **de otra ~** otherwise. **de todas ~s** anyway

manga f sleeve; (tubo de goma) hose; (red) net; (para colar) filter; (LAm, de langostas) swarm

mango m handle; (fruta) mango. **~near** vt boss about. ● vi (entrometerse) interfere

manguera f hose(pipe)

manguito m muff

maní m (pl ~es) (LAm) peanut

manía f mania; (antipatía) dislike. **tener la ~ de** have an obsession with

maniaco adj, **maníaco** adj maniac(al). ● m maniac

maniatar vt tie s.o.'s hands

maniático adj maniac(al); (obsesivo) obsessive; (loco) crazy; (delicado) finicky

manicomio m lunatic asylum

manicura f manicure; (mujer) manicurist

manido adj stale

manifesta|ción f manifestation, sign; (Pol) demonstration. **~nte** m demonstrator. **~r** 1 vt show; (Pol) state. **~rse** vpr show; (Pol) demonstrate

manifiesto adj clear; (error) obvious; (verdad) manifest. ● m manifesto

manilargo adj light-fingered

manilla f (de cajón etc) handle; (de reloj) hand. **~r** m handlebar(s)

maniobra f manoeuvre. **~r** vt operate; (Rail) shunt. ● vt/i manoeuvre. **~s** fpl (Mil) manoeuvres

manipula|ción f manipulation. **~r** vt manipulate

maniquí m dummy. ● m & f model

mani|rroto adj & m spendthrift. ∼**ta** f, (LAm) ∼**to** m little hand

manivela f crank

manjar m delicacy

mano f hand; (de animales) front foot; (de perros, gatos) front paw. ∼ **de obra** work force. ¡∼**s arriba!** hands up! **a** ∼ by hand; (próximo) handy. **a** ∼ **derecha** on the right. **de segunda** ∼ second hand. **echar una** ∼ lend a hand. **tener buena** ∼ **para** be good at. ● m (LAm, fam) mate (Brit), buddy (Amer)

manojo m bunch

manose|ar vt handle. ∼**o** m handling

manotada f, **manotazo** m slap

manote|ar vi gesticulate. ∼**o** m gesticulation

mansalva: **a** ∼ adv without risk

mansarda f attic

mansión f mansion. ∼ **señorial** stately home

manso adj gentle; (animal) tame

manta f blanket

mantec|a f fat. ∼**oso** adj greasy

mantel m tablecloth; (del altar) altar cloth. ∼**ería** f table linen

manten|er 40 vt support; (conservar) keep; (sostener) maintain. ∼**erse** vpr support o.s.; (permanecer) remain. ∼**se de/con** live off. ∼**imiento** m maintenance

mantequ|era f butter churn. ∼**illa** f butter

mant|illa f mantilla. ∼**o** m cloak. ∼**ón** m shawl

manual adj & m manual

manubrio m crank; (LAm, de bicicleta) handlebars

manufactura f manufacture. ∼**r** vt manufacture, make

manuscrito adj handwritten. ● m manuscript

manutención f maintenance

manzana f apple; (de edificios) block. ∼**r** m (apple) orchard. ∼ **de Adán** (LAm) Adam's apple

manzan|illa f camomile tea. ● m manzanilla, pale dry sherry. ∼**o** m apple tree

maña f skill. ∼**s** fpl cunning

mañan|a f morning. ∼**a por la** ∼**a** tomorrow morning. **pasado** ∼**a** the day after tomorrow. **en la** ∼**a** (LAm), **por la** ∼**a** in the morning. ● m future. ● adv tomorrow. ∼**ero** adj who gets up early. ● m early riser

mañoso adj clever; (astuto) crafty; (LAm, caprichoso) difficult

mapa m map

mapache m racoon

maqueta f scale model

maquiladora f (Mex) cross-border assembly plant

maquilla|je m make-up. ∼**r** vt make up. ∼**rse** vpr make up

máquina f machine; (Rail) engine. ∼ **de afeitar** shaver. ∼ **de escribir** typewriter. ∼ **fotográfica** camera

maquin|ación f machination. ∼**al** adj mechanical. ∼**aria** f machinery. ∼**ista** m & f operator; (Rail) engine driver

mar m & f sea. **alta** ∼ high seas. **la** ∼ **de** ⓘ lots of

maraña f thicket; (enredo) tangle; (embrollo) muddle

maratón m & f marathon

maravill|a f wonder. **a las mil** ∼**as**, **de** ∼**as** marvellously. **contar/decir** ∼**as de** speak wonderfully of. **hacer** ∼**as** work wonders. ∼**ar** vt astonish. ∼**arse** vpr be astonished (de at). ∼**oso** adj marvellous, wonderful

marca f mark; (de coches etc) make; (de alimentos, cosméticos) brand; (Deportes) record. ∼ **de fábrica** trade mark. **de** ∼ brand name; (fig) excellent. **de** ∼ **mayor** ⓘ absolute. ∼**do** adj marked. ∼**dor** m marker; (Deportes) scoreboard. ∼**r** 7 vt mark; (señalar) show; score (un gol); dial (número de teléfono). ● vi score

marcha f (incl Mus) march; (Auto) gear; (desarrollo) course; (partida) departure. **a toda** ∼ at full speed. **dar/hacer** ∼ **atrás** put into reverse. **poner en** ∼ start; (fig) set in motion

marchante m (f **marchanta**) art dealer; (Mex, en mercado) stall holder

marchar vi go; (funcionar) work, go; (Mil) march. ∼**se** vpr leave

marchit|ar vt wither. ∼**arse** vpr wither. ∼**o** adj withered

marcial *adj* martial

marciano *adj & m* Martian

marco *m* frame; (*moneda alemana*) mark; (*deportes*) goal-posts

marea *f* tide. **~do** *adj* sick; (*en el mar*) seasick; (*aturdido*) dizzy; (*borracho*) drunk. **~r** *vt* make feel sick; (*aturdir*) make feel dizzy; (*confundir*) confuse. **~rse** *vpr* feel sick; (*en un barco*) get seasick; (*estar aturdido*) feel dizzy; (*irse la cabeza*) feel faint; (*emborracharse*) get slightly drunk; (*confundirse*) get confused

marejada *f* swell; (*fig*) wave

mareo *m* sickness; (*en el mar*) seasickness; (*aturdimiento*) dizziness; (*confusión*) muddle

marfil *m* ivory

margarina *f* margarine

margarita *f* daisy; (*cóctel*) margarita

marg|en *m* margin; (*de un camino*) side. ● *f* (*de un río*) bank. **~inado** *adj* excluded. ● *m* outcast. **al ~en** (*fig*) outside. **~inal** *adj* marginal. **~inar** *vt* (*excluir*) exclude; (*fijar márgenes*) set margins

mariachi *m* (*Mex*) (*música popular de Jalisco*) Mariachi music; (*conjunto*) Mariachi band; (*músico*) Mariachi musician

---

> **mariachi** The word can mean the traditional Mexican musical ensemble, the musicians and the lively mestizo music they play. *Mariachis* wearing costumes based on those worn by *charros* can be seen in the Plaza Garibaldi, in Mexico City, where they are hired for parties, or to sing *mañanitas* or serenades.

---

maric|a *m* 🛈 sissy 🛈. **~ón** *m* 🛈 homosexual, queer 🛈; (*LAm, cobarde*) wimp

marido *m* husband

mariguana *f*, **marihuana** *f* marijuana

marimacho *f* mannish woman

marimba *f* (type of) drum (*LAm, especie de xilofón*) marimba

marin|a *f* navy; (*barcos*) fleet; (*cuadro*) seascape. **~a de guerra** navy. **~a mercante** merchant navy. **~ería** *f*

seamanship; (*marineros*) sailors. **~ero** *adj* marine; (*barco*) seaworthy. ● *m* sailor. **a la ~era** in tomato and garlic sauce. **~o** *adj* marine

marioneta *f* puppet. **~s** *fpl* puppet show

maripos|a *f* butterfly. **~a nocturna** moth. **~ear** *vi* be fickle; (*galantear*) flirt. **~ón** *m* flirt

mariquita *f* ladybird (*Brit*), ladybug (*Amer*). ● *m* 🛈 sissy 🛈

mariscador *m* shell-fisher

mariscal *m* marshal

maris|car *vt* fish for shellfish. **~co** *m* seafood, shellfish. **~quero** *m* (*pescador de mariscos*) seafood fisherman; (*vendedor de mariscos*) seafood seller

marital *adj* marital; (*vida*) married

marítimo *adj* maritime; (*ciudad etc*) coastal, seaside

marmita *f* cooking pot

mármol *m* marble

marmota *f* marmot

maroma *f* rope; (*Mex, voltereta*) somersault

marqu|és *m* marquess. **~esa** *f* marchioness. **~esina** *f* glass canopy; (*en estadio*) roof

marran|a *f* sow. **~ada** *f* filthy thing; (*cochinada*) dirty trick. **~o** *adj* filthy. ● *m* hog

marrón *adj & m* brown

marroqu|í *adj & m & f* Moroccan. ● *m* (*leather*) morocco. **~inería** *f* leather goods

Marruecos *m* Morocco

marsopa *f* porpoise

marsupial *adj & m* marsupial

marta *f* marten

martajar *vt* (*Mex*) crush (*maíz*)

Marte *m* Mars

martes *m invar* Tuesday. **~ de carnaval** Shrove Tuesday

martill|ar *vt* hammer. **~azo** *m* blow with a hammer. **~ear** *vt* hammer. **~eo** *m* hammering. **~o** *m* hammer

martín *m* **pescador** kingfisher

martinete *m* (*del piano*) hammer; (*ave*) heron

martingala *f* (*ardid*) trick

mártir *m & f* martyr

m

martir|io *m* martyrdom; (*fig*) torment. **~izar** 🔟 *vt* martyr; (*fig*) torment, torture

marxis|mo *m* Marxism. **~ta** *adj & m &* *f* Marxist

marzo *m* March

más *adv & adj* (*comparativo*) more; (*superlativo*) most. **~ caro** dearer. **~ doloroso** more painful. **el ~ caro** the dearest; (*de dos*) the dearer. **el ~ curioso** the most curious; (*de dos*) the more curious. ● *prep* plus. ● *m* plus (sign). **~ bien** rather. **~ de** (*cantidad indeterminada*) more than. **~ o menos** more or less. **~ que** more than. **~ y ~** more and more. **a lo ~** at (the) most. **dos ~ dos** two plus two. **de ~** too many. **es ~** moreover. **nadie ~** nobody else. **no ~** no more

masa *f* mass; (*Culin*) dough. **en ~** en masse

masacre *f* massacre

masaj|e *m* massage. **~ear** *vt* massage. **~ista** *m* masseur. ● *f* masseuse

mascada *f* (*Mex*) scarf

mascar 🔟 *vt* chew

máscara *f* mask

mascar|ada *f* masquerade. **~illa** *f* mask. **~ón** *m* (*Naut*) figurehead

mascota *f* mascot

masculin|idad *f* masculinity. **~o** *adj* masculine; (*sexo*) male. ● *m* masculine

mascullar 🔟 *vt* mumble

masilla *f* putty

masivo *adj* massive, large-scale

mas|ón *m* Freemason. **~onería** *f* Freemasonry. **~ónico** *adj* Masonic

masoquis|mo *m* masochism. **~ta** *adj* masochistic. ● *m & f* masochist

mastica|ción *f* chewing. **~r** 🔟 *vt* chew

mástil *m* (*Naut*) mast; (*de bandera*) flagpole; (*de guitarra, violín*) neck

mastín *m* mastiff

mastodonte *m* mastodon; (*fig*) giant

masturba|ción *f* masturbation. **~rse** *vpr* masturbate

mata *f* (*arbusto*) bush; (*LAm, planta*) plant

matad|ero *m* slaughterhouse. **~or** *adj* killing. ● *m* (*torero*) matador

matamoscas *m invar* fly swatter

mata|nza *f* killing. **~r** *vt* kill (personas); slaughter (reses). **~rife** *m* butcher. **~rse** *vpr* kill o.s.; (*en un accidente*) be killed; (*Mex, para un examen*) cram. **~rse trabajando** work like mad

mata|polillas *m invar* moth killer. **~rratas** *m invar* rat poison

matasanos *m invar* quack

matasellos *m invar* postmark

mate *adj* matt. ● *m* (*ajedrez*) (check-)mate (*LAm, bebida*) maté

matemátic|as *fpl* mathematics, maths (*Brit*), math (*Amer*). **~o** *adj* mathematical. ● *m* mathematician

materia *f* matter; (*material*) material; (*LAm, asignatura*) subject. **~ prima** raw material. **en ~ de** on the question of

material *adj & m* material. **~idad** *f* material nature. **~ismo** *m* materialism. **~ista** *adj* materialistic. ● *m & f* materialist; (*Mex, constructor*) building contractor. **~izar** 🔟 *vt* materialize. **~izarse** *vpr* materialize. **~mente** *adv* materially; (*absolutamente*) absolutely

matern|al *adj* maternal; (*amor*) motherly. **~idad** *f* motherhood; (*hospital*) maternity hospital; (*sala*) maternity ward. **~o** *adj* motherly; (*lengua*) mother

matin|al *adj* morning. **~ée** *m* matinée

matiz *m* shade; (*fig*) nuance. **~ación** *f* combination of colours. **~ar** 🔟 *vt* blend (colores); (*introducir variedad*) vary; (*teñir*) tinge (**de** with)

mat|ón *m* bully; (*de barrio*) thug. **~onismo** *m* bullying; (*de barrio*) thuggery

matorral *m* scrub; (*conjunto de matas*) thicket

matraca *f* rattle. **dar ~** pester

matraz *m* flask

matriarca *f* matriarch. **~do** *m* matriarchy. **~l** *adj* matriarchal

matr|ícula *f* (*lista*) register, list; (*inscripción*) registration; (*Auto*) registration number; (*placa*) licence plate. **~icular** *vt* register. **~icularse** *vpr* enrol, register

matrimoni|al *adj* matrimonial. **~o** *m* marriage; (*pareja*) married couple

matriz *f* matrix; (*molde*) mould; (*útero*) womb, uterus

matrona *f* matron; (*partera*) midwife

matutino *adj* morning

maull|ar *vi* miaow. **~ido** *m* miaow

mausoleo *m* mausoleum

maxilar *adj* maxillary. ● *m* jaw(bone)

máxim|a *f* maxim. **~e** *adv* especially. **~o** *adj* maximum; (*punto*) highest. ● *m* maximum

maya *f* daisy. ● *adj* Mayan. ● *m & f* (*persona*) Maya

mayo *m* May

mayonesa *f* mayonnaise

mayor *adj* (*más grande, comparativo*) bigger; (*más grande, superlativo*) biggest; (*de edad, comparativo*) older; (*de edad, superlativo*) oldest; (*adulto*) grown-up; (*principal*) main, major; (*Mus*) major. ● *m & f* (*adulto*) adult. **al por ~** wholesale. **~al** *m* foreman. **~azgo** *m* entailed estate

mayordomo *m* butler

mayor|ía *f* majority. **~ista** *m & f* wholesaler. **~itario** *adj* majority; (*socio*) principal. **~mente** *adv* especially

mayúscul|a *f* capital (letter). **~o** *adj* capital; (*fig, grande*) big

mazacote *m* hard mass

mazapán *m* marzipan

mazmorra *f* dungeon

mazo *m* mallet; (*manojo*) bunch; (*LAm, de naipes*) pack (*Brit*), deck (*Amer*)

mazorca *f* cob. **~ de maíz** corncob

me *pron* (*acusativo*) me; (*dativo*) (to) me; (*reflexivo*) (to) myself

mecánic|a *f* mechanics. **~o** *adj* mechanical. ● *m* mechanic

mecani|smo *m* mechanism. **~zación** *f* mechanization. **~zar** 🔟 *vt* mechanize

mecanograf|ía *f* typing. **~iado** *adj* typed, typewritten. **~iar** 🔟 *vt* type

mecanógrafo *m* typist

mecate *m* (*Mex*) string; (*más grueso*) rope

mecedora *f* rocking chair

mecenas *m & f invar* patron

mecer 🔟 *vt* rock; swing (*columpio*). **~se** *vpr* rock; (*en un columpio*) swing

mecha *f* (*de vela*) wick; (*de explosivo*) fuse. **~s** *fpl* highlights

mechar *vt* stuff, lard

mechero *m* (cigarette) lighter

mechón *m* (*de pelo*) lock

medall|a *f* medal. **~ón** *m* medallion; (*relicario*) locket

media *f* stocking; (*promedio*) average. **a ~s** half each

mediación *f* mediation

mediado *adj* half full; (*a mitad de*) halfway through. **~s** *mpl*. **a ~s de marzo** in mid-March

mediador *m* mediator

medialuna *f* (*pl* **mediaslunas**) croissant

median|amente *adv* fairly. **~a** *f* (*Auto*) central reservation (*Brit*), median strip (*Amer*). **~era** *f* party wall. **~ero** *adj* (*muro*) party. **~o** *adj* medium; (*mediocre*) average, mediocre

medianoche *f* (*pl* **mediasnoches**) midnight; (*Culin*) type of roll

mediante *prep* through, by means of

mediar *vi* mediate; (*llegar a la mitad*) be halfway through; (*interceder*) intercede (*por* for)

medic|ación *f* medication. **~amento** *m* medicine. **~ina** *f* medicine. **~inal** *adj* medicinal

medición *f* measurement

médico *adj* medical. ● *m* doctor. **~ de cabecera** GP, general practitioner

medid|a *f* measurement; (*unidad*) measure; (*disposición*) measure, step; (*prudencia*) moderation. **a la ~a** made to measure. **a ~a que** as. **en cierta ~a** to a certain extent. **~or** *m* (*LAm*) meter

medieval *adj* medieval. **~ista** *m & f* medievalist

medio *adj* half (a); (*mediano*) average. **dos horas y media** two and a half hours. **~ litro** half a litre. **las dos y media** half past two. ● *m* middle; (*Math*) half; (*manera*) means; (*en deportes*) half(-back). **en ~** in the middle (**de** of). **por ~ de** through. **~ ambiente** *m* environment

medioambiental *adj* environmental

m

mediocr|e adj mediocre. **~idad** f mediocrity

mediodía m midday, noon; (sur) south

medioevo m Middle Ages

Medio Oriente m Middle East

medir 🖬 vt measure; weigh up (palabras etc). ● vi measure, be. ¿**cuánto mide de alto?** how tall is it? **~se** vpr (moderarse) measure o.s.; (Mex, probarse) try on

medita|bundo adj thoughtful. **~ción** f meditation. **~r** vt think about. ● vi meditate

mediterráneo adj Mediterranean

Mediterráneo m Mediterranean

médium m & f medium

médula f marrow

medusa f jellyfish

megáfono m megaphone

megalómano m megalomaniac

mejicano adj & m Mexican

Méjico m Mexico

mejilla f cheek

mejillón m mussel

mejor adj & adv (comparativo) better; (superlativo) best. **~ dicho** rather. **a lo ~** perhaps. **tanto ~** so much the better. **~a** f improvement. **~able** adj improvable. **~amiento** m improvement

mejorana f marjoram

mejorar vt improve, better. ● vi get better. **~se** vpr get better

mejunje m mixture

melanc|olía f melancholy. **~ólico** adj melancholic

melaza f molasses

melen|a f long hair; (de león) mane. **~udo** adj long-haired

melindr|es mpl affectation. **hacer ~es con la comida** be picky about food. **~oso** adj affected

mellizo adj & m twin

melocot|ón m peach. **~onero** m peach tree

mel|odía f melody. **~ódico** adj melodic. **~odioso** adj melodious

melodram|a m melodrama. **~ático** adj melodramatic

melómano m music lover

melón m melon

meloso adj sickly-sweet; (canción) slushy

membran|a f membrane. **~oso** adj membranous

membrete m letterhead

membrill|ero m quince tree. **~o** m quince

memo adj stupid. ● m idiot

memorable adj memorable

memorando m, **memorándum** m notebook; (nota) memorandum, memo

memori|a f memory; (informe) report; (tesis) thesis. **~as** fpl (autobiografía) memoirs. **de ~a** by heart; (citar) from memory. **~al** m memorial. **~ón** m good memory. **~zación** f memorizing. **~zar** 🔟 vt memorize

menaje m household goods. **~ de cocina** kitchenware

menci|ón f mention. **~onado** adj aforementioned. **~onar** vt mention

mendi|cidad f begging. **~gar** 🔃 vt beg for. ● vi beg. **~go** m beggar

mendrugo m piece of stale bread

mene|ar vt wag (rabo); shake (cabeza); wiggle (caderas). **~arse** vpr move; (con inquietud) fidget; (balancearse) swing. **~o** m movement; (sacudida) shake

menester m occupation. **ser ~** be necessary. **~oso** adj needy

menestra f vegetable stew

mengano m so-and-so

mengua f decrease; (falta) lack. **~do** adj diminished. **~nte** adj (luna) waning; (marea) ebb. **~r** 🖬 vt/i decrease, diminish

meningitis f meningitis

menjurje m mixture

menopausia f menopause

menor adj (más pequeño, comparativo) smaller; (más pequeño, superlativo) smallest; (más joven, comparativo) younger; (más joven, superlativo) youngest; (Mus) minor. ● m & f (menor de edad) minor. **al por ~** retail

menos adj (comparativo) less; (comparativo, con plural) fewer; (superlativo) least; (superlativo, con plural) fewest.

● adv (*comparativo*) less; (*superlativo*) least.● prep except. **al** ~ at least. **a** ~ **que** unless. **las dos** ~ **diez** ten to two. **ni mucho** ~ far from it. **por lo** ~ at least. ~**cabar** vt lessen; (*fig, estropear*) damage. ~**cabo** m lessening. ~**preciable** adj contemptible. ~**preciar** vt despise. ~**precio** m contempt

mensaje m message. ~**ro** m messenger

menso adj (*LAm, fam*) stupid

menstru|ación f menstruation. ~**al** adj menstrual. ~**ar** 21 vi menstruate

mensual adj monthly. ~**idad** f monthly pay; (*cuota*) monthly payment

mensurable adj measurable

menta f mint

mental adj mental. ~**idad** f mentality. ~**mente** adv mentally

mentar 1 vt mention, name

mente f mind

mentecato adj stupid. ● m idiot

mentir 4 vi lie. ~**a** f lie. ~**ijillas** fpl. **de** ~**ijillas** for a joke. ~**oso** adj lying. ● m liar

mentís m invar denial

mentor m mentor

menú m menu

menud|ear vi happen frequently; (*Mex, Com*) sell retail. ~**encia** f trifle. ~**encias** fpl (*LAm*) giblets. ~**eo** m (*Mex*) retail trade. ~**illos** mpl giblets. ~**o** adj small; (*lluvia*) fine. **a** ~**o** often. ~**os** mpl giblets

meñlque adj (*dedo*) little. ● m little finger

meollo m (*médula*) marrow; (*de tema etc*) heart

merca|chifle m hawker; (*fig*) profiteer. ~**der** m merchant. ~**dería** f (*LAm*) merchandise. ~**do** m market. **M~do Común** Common Market. ~**do negro** black market

mercan|cía(s) f(pl) goods, merchandise. ~**te** adj merchant. ● m merchant ship. ~**til** adj mercantile, commercial. ~**tilismo** m mercantilism

merced f favour. **su/vuestra** ~ your honour

mercenario adj & m mercenary

mercer|ía f haberdashery (*Brit*), notions (*Amer*).

mercurial adj mercurial

mercurio m mercury

merec|edor adj worthy (**de** of). ~**er** 11 vt deserve. ~**erse** vpr deserve. ~**idamente** adv deservedly. ~**ido** adj well deserved. ~**imiento** m (*mérito*) merit

merend|ar 1 vt have as an afternoon snack. ● vi have an afternoon snack. ~**ero** m snack bar; (*lugar*) picnic area

merengue m meringue

meridi|ano adj midday; (*fig*) dazzling. ● m meridian. ~**onal** adj southern. ● m southerner

merlenda f afternoon snack

merino adj merino

mérito m merit; (*valor*) worth

meritorio adj praiseworthy. ● m unpaid trainee

merluza f hake

merma f decrease. ~**r** vt/i decrease, reduce

mermelada f jam

mero adj mere; (*Mex, verdadero*) real. ● adv (*Mex, precisamente*) exactly; (*Mex, casi*) nearly. ● m grouper

merode|ador m prowler. ~**ar** vi prowl

mes m month

mesa f table; (*para escribir o estudiar*) desk. **poner la** ~ lay the table

mesarse vpr tear at one's hair

meser|a f (*LAm*) waitress. ~**o** m (*LAm*) waiter

meseta f plateau; (*descansillo*) landing

Mesías m Messiah

mesilla f, **mesita** f small table. ~ **de noche** bedside table

mesón m inn

mesoner|a f landlady. ~**o** m landlord

mestiz|aje m crossbreeding. ~**o** adj (*persona*) half-caste; (*animal*) crossbred. ● m (*persona*) half-caste; (*animal*) cross-breed

mesura f moderation. ~**do** adj moderate

meta f goal; (*de una carrera*) finish

metabolismo m metabolism

m

metafísic|a *f* metaphysics. **~o** *adj* metaphysical

met|áfora *f* metaphor. **~afórico** *adj* metaphorical

met|al *m* metal; (*de la voz*) timbre. **~ales** *mpl* (*instrumentos de latón*) brass. **~álico** *adj* (*objeto*) metal; (sonido) metallic

metal|urgia *f* metallurgy. **~úrgico** *adj* metallurgical

metamorfosis *f invar* metamorphosis

metedura de pata *f* blunder

mete|órico *adj* meteoric. **~orito** *m* meteorite. **~oro** *m* meteor. **~orología** *f* meteorology. **~orológico** *adj* meteorological. **~orólogo** *m* meteorologist

meter *vt* put; score (un gol); (*enredar*) involve; (*causar*) make. **~se** *vpr* get involved (**en** in); (*entrometerse*) meddle. **~se con uno** pick a quarrel with s.o.

meticulos|idad *f* meticulousness. **~o** *adj* meticulous

metida de pata *f* (*LAm*) blunder

metido *m* reprimand. ● *adj.* **~ en años** getting on. **estar ~ en algo** be involved in sth. **estar muy ~ con uno** be well in with s.o.

metódico *adj* methodical

metodis|mo *m* Methodism. **~ta** *adj & m & f* Methodist

método *m* method

metodología *f* methodology

metraje *m* length. **de largo ~** (*película*) feature

metrall|a *f* shrapnel. **~eta** *f* submachine gun

métric|a *f* metrics. **~o** *adj* metric; (verso) metrical

metro *m* metre; (*tren*) underground (*Brit*), subway (*Amer*). **~ cuadrado** square metre

metrónomo *m* metronome

metr|ópoli *f* metropolis. **~opolitano** *adj* metropolitan. ● *m* metropolitan; (*tren*) underground (*Brit*), subway (*Amer*)

mexicano *adj & m* Mexican

México *m* Mexico. **~ D. F.** Mexico City

mezcal *m* (*Mex*) mescal

mezc|la *f* (*acción*) mixing; (*substancia*) mixture; (*argamasa*) mortar. **~lador** *m* mixer. **~lar** *vt* mix; shuffle (los naipes). **~larse** *vpr* mix; (*intervenir*) interfere. **~olanza** *f* mixture

mezquin|dad *f* meanness. **~o** *adj* mean; (*escaso*) meagre. ● *m* mean person

mezquita *f* mosque

mi *adj* my. ● *m* (*Mus*) E; (*solfa*) mi

mí *pron* me

miau *m* miaow

mica *f* (*silicato*) mica

mico *m* (long-tailed) monkey

micro|bio *m* microbe. **~biología** *f* microbiology. **~cosmos** *m invar* microcosm. **~film(e)** *m* microfilm

micrófono *m* microphone

microonda *f* microwave. **~s** *m invar* microwave oven

microordenador *m* microcomputer

micros|cópico *adj* microscopic. **~copio** *m* microscope. **~urco** *m* long-playing record

miedo *m* fear (a for). **dar ~** frighten. **morirse de ~** be scared to death. **tener ~** be frightened. **~so** *adj* fearful

miel *f* honey

miembro *m* limb; (*persona*) member

mientras *conj* while. ● *adv* meanwhile. **~ que** whereas. **~ tanto** in the meantime

miércoles *m invar* Wednesday. **~ de ceniza** Ash Wednesday

mierda *f* (⊠) shit

mies *f* ripe, grain

miga *f* crumb; (*fig, meollo*) essence. **~jas** *fpl* crumbs; (*sobras*) scraps. **~r** 🔟 *vt* crumble

migra|ción *f* migration. **~torio** *adj* migratory

mijo *m* millet

mil *adj & m* a/one thousand. **~es de** thousands of. **~ novecientos noventa y nueve** nineteen ninety-nine. **~ euros** a thousand euros

milagro *m* miracle. **~so** *adj* miraculous

milen|ario *adj* millenial. **~io** *m* millennium

milésimo *adj & m* thousandth

mili *f* 🔲 military service. ~**cia** *f* soldiering; (*gente armada*) militia

mili|gramo *m* milligram. ~**litro** *m* millilitre

milímetro *m* millimetre

militante *adj & m & f* activist

militar *adj* military. ● *m* soldier. ~**ismo** *m* militarism. ~**ista** *adj* militaristic. ● *m & f* militarist. ~**izar** 🔟 *vt* militarize

milla *f* mile

millar *m* thousand. **a** ~**es** by the thousand

mill|ón *m* million. **un** ~**ón de libros** a million books. ~**onada** *f* fortune. ~**onario** *m* millionaire. ~**onésimo** *adj & m* millionth

milonga *f* popular dance and music from the River Plate region

milpa *f* (*Mex*) maize field, cornfield (*Amer*)

milpies *m invar* woodlouse

mimar *vt* spoil

mimbre *m & f* wicker. ~**arse** *vpr* sway. ~**ra** *f* osier. ~**ral** *m* osier-bed

mimetismo *m* mimicry

mímic|a *f* mime. ~**o** *adj* mimic

mimo *m* mime; (*adj un niño*) spoiling; (*caricia*) cuddle

mimosa *f* mimosa

mina *f* mine. ~**r** *vt* mine; (*fig*) undermine

minarete *m* minaret

mineral *m* mineral; (*mena*) ore. ~**ogía** *f* mineralogy. ~**ogista** *m & f* mineralogist

miner|ía *f* mining. ~**o** *adj* mining. ● *m* miner

miniatura *f* miniature

minifundio *m* smallholding

minimizar 🔟 *vt* minimize

mínim|o *adj & m* minimum. **como** ~ at least. ~**um** *m* minimum

minino *m* 🔲 cat, puss 🔲

minist|erial *adj* ministerial; (*reunión*) cabinet. ~**erio** *m* ministry. ~**ro** *m* minister

minor|ía *f* minority. ~**idad** *f* minority. ~**ista** *m & f* retailer

minuci|a *f* trifle. ~**osidad** *f* thoroughness. ~**oso** *adj* thorough; (*detallado*) detailed

minúscul|a *f* lower case letter. ~**o** *adj* tiny

minuta *f* draft copy; (*de abogado*) bill

minut|ero *m* minute hand. ~**o** *m* minute

mío *adj & pron* mine. **un amigo** ~ a friend of mine

miop|e *adj* short-sighted. ● *m & f* short-sighted person. ~**ia** *f* short-sightedness

mira *f* sight; (*fig, intención*) aim. **a la** ~ on the lookout. **con** ~**s a** with a view to. ~**da** *f* look. **echar una** ~**da a** a glance at. ~**do** *adj* careful with money; (*comedido*) considerate. **bien** ~**do** highly regarded. **no estar bien** ~**do** be frowned upon. ~**dor** *m* viewpoint. ~**miento** *m* consideration. ~**r** *vt* look at; (*observar*) watch; (*considerar*) consider. ~**r fijamente** a stare at. ● *vi* look (edificio etc). ~ **hacia** face. ~**rse** *vpr* (personas) look at each other

mirilla *f* peephole

miriñaque *m* crinoline

mirlo *m* blackbird

mirón *adj* nosey. ● *m* nosey-parker; (*espectador*) onlooker

mirto *m* myrtle

misa *f* mass. ~**l** *m* missal

misántropo *m* misanthropist

miscelánea *f* miscellany; (*Mex, tienda*) corner shop (*Brit*), small general store (*Amer*)

miser|able *adj* very poor; (*lastimoso*) miserable; (*tacaño*) mean. ~**ia** *f* extreme poverty; (*suciedad*) squalor

misericordi|a *f* pity; (*piedad*) mercy. ~**oso** *adj* merciful

mísero *adj* miserable; (*tacaño*) mean; (*malvado*) wicked

misil *m* missile

misi|ón *f* mission. ~**onero** *m* missionary

misiva *f* missive

mism|ísimo *adj* very same. ~**o** *adj* same; (*después de pronombre personal*) myself, yourself, himself, herself, itself, ourselves, yourselves, them-

m

selves; (enfático) very. ● *adv.* **ahora** ∼ right now. **aquí** ∼ right here. **lo** ∼ the same

misterio *m* mystery. ∼**so** *adj* mysterious

místic|a *f* mysticism. ∼**o** *adj* mystical. ● *m* mystic

mistifica|ción *f* mystification. ∼**r** **7** *vt* mystify

mitad *f* half; (*centro*) middle. **cortar algo por la** ∼ cut sth in half

mitigar **12** *vt* mitigate; quench (sed); relieve (dolor etc)

mitin *m*, **mitín** *m* meeting

mito *m* myth. ∼**logía** *f* mythology. ∼**lógico** *adj* mythological

mitón *m* mitten

mitote *m* (*Mex*) Aztec dance

mixt|o *adj* mixed. **educación mixta** coeducation

mobbing *m* harassment

mobiliario *m* furniture

moce|dad *f* youth. ∼**río** *m* young people. ∼**tón** *m* strapping lad. ∼**tona** *f* strapping girl

mochales *adj invar.* **estar** ∼ be round the bend

mochila *f* rucksack

mocho *adj* blunt. ● *m* butt end

mochuelo *m* little owl

moción *f* motion

moco *m* mucus. **limpiarse los** ∼**s** blow one's nose

moda *f* fashion. **estar de** ∼ be in fashion. ∼**l** *adj* modal. ∼**les** *mpl* manners. ∼**lidad** *f* kind

model|ado *m* modelling. ∼**ador** *m* modeller. ∼**ar** *vt* model; (*fig, configurar*) form. ∼**o** *m* & *f* model

módem *m* modem

modera|ción *f* moderation. ∼**do** *adj* moderate. ∼**r** *vt* moderate; reduce (velocidad). ∼**rse** *vpr* control oneself

modern|idad *f* modernity. ∼**ismo** *m* modernism. ∼**ista** *m* & *f* modernist. ∼**izar** **10** *vt* modernize. ∼**o** *adj* modern; (*a la moda*) fashionable

modest|ia *f* modesty. ∼**o** *adj* modest

módico *adj* moderate

modifica|ción *f* modification. ∼**r** **7** *vt* modify

modismo *m* idiom

modist|a *f* dressmaker. ∼**o** *m* designer

modo *m* manner, way; (*Gram*) mood; (*Mus*) mode. ∼ **de ser** character. **de** ∼ **que** so that. **de ningún** ∼ certainly not. **de todos** ∼**s** anyhow. **ni** ∼ (*LAm*) no way

modorra *f* drowsiness

modula|ción *f* modulation. ∼**dor** *m* modulator. ∼**r** *vt* modulate

módulo *m* module

mofa *f* mockery. ∼**rse** *vpr.* ∼**rse de** make fun of

mofeta *f* skunk

moflet|e *m* chubby cheek. ∼**udo** *adj* with chubby cheeks

mohín *m* grimace. **hacer un** ∼ pull a face

moho *m* mould; (*óxido*) rust. ∼**so** *adj* mouldy; (*metales*) rusty

moisés *m* Moses basket

mojado *adj* wet

mojar *vt* wet; (*empapar*) soak; (*humedecer*) moisten, dampen

mojigat|ería *f* prudishness. ∼**o** *m* prude. ● *adj* prudish

mojón *m* boundary post; (*señal*) signpost

molar *m* molar

mold|e *m* mould; (*aguja*) knitting needle. ∼**ear** *vt* mould, shape; (*fig*) form. ∼**ura** *f* moulding

mole *f* mass, bulk. ● *m* (*Mex, salsa*) chili sauce with chocolate and sesame

mol|écula *f* molecule. ∼**ecular** *adj* molecular

mole|dor *adj* grinding. ● *m* grinder. ∼**r** **2** grind

molest|ar *vt* annoy; (*incomodar*) bother. **¿le** ∼**a que fume?** do you mind if I smoke? ● *vi* be a nuisance. **no** ∼**ar** do not disturb. ∼**arse** *vpr* bother; (*ofenderse*) take offence. ∼**ia** *f* bother, nuisance; (*inconveniente*) inconvenience; (*incomodidad*) discomfort. ∼**o** *adj* annoying; (*inconveniente*) inconvenient; (*ofendido*) offended

molicie *f* softness; (*excesiva comodidad*) easy life

molido *adj* ground; (*fig, muy cansado*) worn out

molienda f grinding

molin|ero m miller. **~ete** m toy windmill. **~illo** m mill; (*juguete*) toy windmill. **~o** m mill. **~ de agua** watermill. **~o de viento** windmill

molleja f gizzard

mollera f (*de la cabeza*) crown; (*fig, sesera*) brains

molusco m mollusc

moment|áneamente adv momentarily. **~áneo** adj (*breve*) momentary; (*pasajero*) temporary. **~o** m moment; (*ocasión*) time. **al ~o** at once. **de ~o** for the moment

momi|a f mummy. **~ficar 7** vt mummify. **~ficarse** vpr become mummified

monacal adj monastic

monada f beautiful thing; (*niño bonito*) cute kid; (*acción tonta*) silliness

monaguillo m altar boy

mon|arca m & f monarch. **~arquía** f monarchy. **~árquico** adj monarchical

monasterio m monastery

mond|a f peeling; (*piel*) peel. **~adientes** m invar toothpick. **~adura** f peeling; (*piel*) peel. **~ar** vt peel (*fruta etc*). **~o** adj (*sin pelo*) bald

mondongo m innards

moned|a f coin; (*de un país*) currency. **~ero** m purse (*Brit*), change purse (*Amer*)

monetario adj monetary

mongolismo m Down's syndrome

monigote m weak character; (*muñeco*) rag doll; (*dibujo*) doodle

monitor m monitor

monj|a f nun. **~e** m monk. **~il** adj nun's; (*como de monja*) like a nun

mono m monkey; (*sobretodo*) overalls. ● adj pretty

monocromo adj & m monochrome

monóculo m monocle

mon|ogamia f monogamy. **~ógamo** adj monogamous

monogra|fía f monograph. **~ma** m monogram

mon|ologar 12 vi soliloquize. **~ólogo** m monologue

monoplano m monoplane

monopoli|o m monopoly. **~zar 10** vt monopolize

monos|ilábico adj monosyllabic. **~ílabo** m monosyllable

monoteís|mo m monotheism. **~ta** adj monotheistic. ● m & f monotheist

mon|otonía f monotony. **~ótono** adj monotonous

monseñor m monsignor

monstruo m monster. **~sidad** f monstrosity; (*atrocidad*) atrocity. **~so** adj monstrous

monta f mounting; (*valor*) total value

montacargas m invar service lift (*Brit*), service elevator (*Amer*)

monta|dor m fitter. **~je** m assembly; (*Cine*) montage; (*teatro*) staging, production

montañ|a f mountain. **~a rusa** roller coaster. **~ero** adj mountaineer. **~és** adj mountain. ● m highlander. **~ismo** m mountaineering. **~oso** adj mountainous

montaplatos m invar dumb waiter

montar vt ride; (*subirse a*) get on; (*ensamblar*) assemble; cock (arma); set up (una casa, un negocio). ● vi ride; (*subirse*) mount. **~ a caballo** ride a horse

monte m (*montaña*) mountain; (*terreno inculto*) scrub; (*bosque*) woodland. **~ de piedad** pawnshop

montepío m charitable fund for dependents

montés adj wild

montevideano adj & m Montevidean

montículo m hillock

montón m heap, pile. **a montones** in abundance. **un ~ de** loads of

montura f mount; (*silla*) saddle

monument|al adj monumental; (*fig, muy grande*) enormous. **~o** m monument

monzón m & f monsoon

moñ|a f ribbon. **~o** m bun; (*LAm, lazo*) bow

moque|o m runny nose. **~ro** m 1 handkerchief

moqueta f fitted carpet

moquillo m distemper

mora f mulberry; (*de zarzamora*) blackberry; (*Jurid*) default

morada f dwelling

morado *adj* purple

morador *m* inhabitant

moral *m* mulberry tree. ● *f* morals. ● *adj* moral. ~**eja** *f* moral. ~**idad** *f* morality. ~**ista** *m* & *f* moralist. ~**izador** *adj* moralizing. ● *m* moralist. ~**izar** 🔟 *vt* moralize

morar *vi* live

moratoria *f* moratorium

mórbido *adj* soft; (*malsano*) morbid

morbo *m* illness. ~**sidad** *f* morbidity. ~**so** *adj* unhealthy

morcilla *f* black pudding

morda|cidad *f* sharpness. ~**z** *adj* scathing

mordaza *f* gag

morde|dura *f* bite. ~**r** 🔁 *vt* bite; (*Mex*, *exigir soborno a*) extract a bribe from. ● *vi* bite. ~**rse** *vpr* bite o.s. ~**rse las uñas** bite one's nails

mordi|da *f* (*Mex*) bribe. ~**sco** *m* bite. ~**squear** *vt* nibble (at)

moreno *adj* (*con ser*) dark; (*de pelo obscuro*) dark-haired; (*de raza negra*) dark-skinned; (*con estar*) brown, tanned

morera *f* white mulberry tree

moretón *m* bruise

morfema *m* morpheme

morfin|a *f* morphine. ~**ómano** *m* morphine addict

morfol|ogía *f* morphology. ~**ógico** *adj* morphological

moribundo *adj* dying

morir 🔢 (*pp* **muerto**) *vi* die; (*fig, extinguirse*) die away; (*fig, terminar*) end. ~ **ahogado** drown. ~**se** *vpr* die. ~**se de hambre** starve to death; (*fig*) be starving. **se muere por una flauta** she's dying to have a flute

morisco *adj* Moorish. ● *m* Moor

morm|ón *m* Mormon. ~**ónico** *adj* Mormon. ~**onismo** *m* Mormonism

moro *adj* Moorish. ● *m* Moor

morral *m* (*mochila*) rucksack; (*de cazador*) gamebag; (*para caballos*) nosebag

morrillo *m* nape of the neck

morriña *f* homesickness

morro *m* snout

morrocotudo *adj* (🔳, *tremendo*) terrible; (*estupendo*) terrific 🔳

morsa *f* walrus

mortaja *f* shroud

mortal *adj* & *m* & *f* mortal. ~**idad** *f* mortality. ~**mente** *adv* mortally

mortandad *f* loss of life; (*Mil*) carnage

mortecino *adj* failing; (*color*) pale

mortero *m* mortar

mortífero *adj* deadly

mortifica|ción *f* mortification. ~**r** 🔢 *vt* (*atormentar*) torment. ~**rse** *vpr* distress o.s.

mortuorio *adj* death

mosaico *m* mosaic; (*Mex*, *baldosa*) floor tile

mosca *f* fly. ~**rda** *f* blowfly. ~**rdón** *m* botfly; (*de cuerpo azul*) bluebottle

moscatel *adj* muscatel

moscón *m* botfly; (*mosca de cuerpo azul*) bluebottle

moscovita *adj* & *m* & *f* Muscovite

mosque|arse *vpr* get cross. ~**o** *m* resentment

mosquete *m* musket. ~**ro** *m* musketeer

mosquit|ero *m* mosquito net. ~**o** *m* mosquito

mostacho *m* moustache

mostaza *f* mustard

mosto *m* must, grape juice

mostrador *m* counter

mostrar 🔁 *vt* show. ~**se** *vpr* (show oneself to) be. **se mostró muy amable** he was very kind

mota *f* spot, speck

mote *m* nickname

motea|do *adj* speckled. ~**r** *vt* speckle

motejar *vt* call

motel *m* motel

motete *m* motet

motín *m* riot; (*de tropas, tripulación*) mutiny

motiv|ación *f* motivation. ~**ar** *vt* motivate. ~**o** *m* reason. **con ~o de** because of

motocicl|eta *f* motor cycle, motor bike 🔳. ~**ista** *m* & *f* motorcyclist

motoneta *f* (*LAm*) (motor) scooter

motor *adj* motor. ● *m* motor, engine. ~ **de arranque** starter motor. ~**a** *f*

motor boat. **~ismo** m motorcycling.
~ista m & f motorist; (de una moto)
motorcyclist. **~izar** 🔟 vt motorize

motriz adj motor

move|dizo adj movable; (poco firme)
unstable; (persona) fickle. **~r** ② vt
move; shake (la cabeza); (provocar)
cause. **~rse** vpr move; (darse prisa)
hurry up

movi|ble adj movable. **~do** adj
moved; (Foto) blurred

móvil adj mobile; (Esp, teléfono) mobile
phone, cellphone. • m motive

movili|dad f mobility. **~zación** f mo-
bilization. **~zar** 🔟 vt mobilize

movimiento m movement, motion;
(agitación) bustle

moza f young girl. **~lbete** m lad

mozárabe adj Mozarabic. • m & f
Mozarab

moz|o m young boy. **~uela** f young
girl. **~uelo** m young boy/lad

mucam|a f (LAm) servant. **~o** m (LAm)
servant

muchach|a f girl; (sirvienta) servant,
maid. **~o** m boy, lad

muchedumbre f crowd

mucho adj a lot of; (en negativas, preguntas) much, a lot of. **~s** a lot of;
(en negativas, preguntas) many, a lot
of. • pron a lot; (personas) many
(people). **como ~** at the most. **ni ~**
menos by no means. **por ~ que**
however much. • adv a lot, very
much; (tiempo) long, a long time

mucos|idad f mucus. **~o** adj mucous

muda f change of clothing; (de animales) shedding. **~ble** adj changeable;
(personas) fickle. **~nza** f move, removal (Brit). **~r** vt change; shed
(piel). **~rse** vpr (de ropa) change
one's clothes; (de casa) move (house)

mudéjar adj & m & f Mudejar

mud|ez f dumbness. **~o** adj dumb;
(callado) silent

mueble adj movable. • m piece of furniture. **~s** mpl furniture

mueca f grimace, face. **hacer una ~**
pull a face

muela f back tooth, molar; (piedra de
afilar) grindstone; (piedra de molino)

millstone. **~ del juicio** wisdom tooth

muelle adj soft. • m spring; (Naut)
wharf; (malecón) jetty

muérdago m mistletoe

muero vb véase **MORIR**

muert|e f death; (homicidio) murder.
~o adj dead. • m dead person

muesca f nick; (ranura) slot

muestra f sample; (prueba) proof;
(modelo) model; (señal) sign. **~rio** m
collection of samples

muestro vb véase **MOSTRAR**

muevo vb véase **MOVER**

mugl|do m moo. **~r** 🔢 vi moo

mugr|e m dirt. **~iento** adj dirty, filthy

mugrón m sucker

mujer f woman; (esposa) wife. • int my
dear! **~iego** adj fond of the women.
• m womanizer. **~zuela** f prostitute

mula f mule. **~da** f drove of mules

mulato adj of mixed race (black and
white). • m person of mixed race

mulero m muleteer

muleta f crutch; (toreo) stick with a
red flag

mulli|do adj soft. **~r** 🔢 vt soften

mulo m mule

multa f fine. **~r** vt fine

multi|color adj multicoloured. **~co-**
pista m duplicator. **~cultural** adj
multicultural. **~forme** adj multiform.
~lateral adj multilateral. **~lingüe** adj
multilingual. **~millonario** m multi-
millionaire

múltiple adj multiple

multiplic|ación f multiplication. **~ar**
🔢 vt multiply. **~arse** vpr multiply.
~idad f multiplicity

múltiplo m multiple

multitud f multitude, crowd. **~inario**
adj mass; (concierto) with mass audience

mund|ano adj wordly; (de la sociedad
elegante) society. **~ial** adj world-wide.
la segunda guerra ~ial the Second
World War. **~illo** m world, circles.
~o m world. **todo el ~o** everybody

munición f ammunition; (provisiones)
supplies

m

municip|al *adj* municipal. **~alidad** *f* municipality. **~io** *m* municipality; (*ayuntamiento*) town council

muñe|ca *f* (*en anatomía*) wrist; (*juguete*) doll; (*maniquí*) dummy. **~co** *m* doll. **~quera** *f* wristband

muñón *m* stump

mura|l *adj* mural, wall. ● *m* mural. **~lla** *f* (city) wall. **~r** *vt* wall

murciélago *m* bat

murga *f* street band

murmullo *m* (*incl fig*) murmur

murmura|ción *f* gossip. **~dor** *adj* gossiping. ● *m* gossip. **~r** *vi* murmur; (*criticar*) gossip

muro *m* wall

murria *f* depression

mus *m* card game

musa *f* muse

musaraña *f* shrew

muscula|r *adj* muscular. **~tura** *f* muscles

músculo *m* muscle

musculoso *adj* muscular

muselina *f* muslin

museo *m* museum. **~ de arte** art gallery

musgo *m* moss. **~so** *adj* mossy

música *f* music

musical *adj & m* musical

músico *adj* musical. ● *m* musician

music|ología *f* musicology. **~ólogo** *m* musicologist

muslo *m* thigh

mustio *adj* (*plantas*) withered; (*cosas*) faded; (*personas*) gloomy; (*Mex, hipócrita*) two-faced

musulmán *adj & m* Muslim

muta|bilidad *f* mutability. **~ción** *f* mutation

mutila|ción *f* mutilation. **~do** *adj* crippled. ● *m* cripple. **~r** *vt* mutilate; maim (*persona*)

mutis *m* (*en el teatro*) exit. **~mo** *m* silence

mutu|alidad *f* mutuality; (*asociación*) friendly society. **~amente** *adv* mutually. **~o** *adj* mutual

muy *adv* very; (*demasiado*) too

Nn

nabo *m* turnip

nácar *m* mother-of-pearl

nac|er 11 *vi* be born; (*pollito*) hatch out; (*planta*) sprout. **~ido** *adj* born. **recien ~ido** newborn. **~iente** *adj* (*sol*) rising. **~imiento** *m* birth; (*de río*) source; (*belén*) crib. **lugar** *m* **de ~imiento** place of birth

naci|ón *f* nation. **~onal** *adj* national. **~onalidad** *f* nationality. **~onalismo** *m* nationalism. **~onalista** *m & f* nationalist. **~onalizar** 10 *vt* nationalize. **~onalizarse** *vpr* become naturalized

nada *pron* nothing, not anything. ● *adv* not at all. **¡~ de eso!** nothing of the sort! **antes que ~** first of all. **¡de ~!** (*después de gracias*) don't mention it! **para ~** (not) at all. **por ~ del mundo** not for anything in the world

nada|dor *m* swimmer. **~r** *vi* swim. **~r de espalda(s)** do (the) backstroke

nadería *f* trifle

nadie *pron* no one, nobody

nado *m* (*Mex*) swimming. ● *adv* **a ~** swimming

naipe *m* (playing) card. **juegos** *mpl* **de ~s** card games

nalga *f* buttock. **~s** *fpl* bottom. **~da** *f* (*Mex*) smack on the bottom

nana *f* lullaby

naranj|a *f* orange. **~ada** *f* orangeade. **~al** *m* orange grove. **~ero** *m* orange tree

narcótico *adj & m* narcotic

nariz *f* nose. **¡narices!** rubbish!

narra|ción *f* narration. **~dor** *m* narrator. **~r** *vt* tell. **~tivo** *adj* narrative

nasal *adj* nasal

nata *f* cream

natación *f* swimming

natal *adj* native; (*pueblo etc*) home. **~idad** *f* birth rate

natillas *fpl* custard

nativo *adj & m* native

nato *adj* born

natural *adj* natural. ● *m* native. **~eza** *f* nature. **~eza muerta** still life. **~idad** *f* naturalness. **~ista** *m* & *f* naturalist. **~izar** 🔟 *vt* naturalize. **~izarse** *vpr* become naturalized. **~mente** *adv* naturally. ● *int* of course!

naufrag|ar 🔢 *vi* (barco) sink; (persona) be shipwrecked; (*fig*) fail. **~io** *m* shipwreck

náufrago *adj* shipwrecked. ● *m* shipwrecked person

náuseas *fpl* nausea. **dar ~s a uno** make s.o. feel sick. **sentir ~s** feel sick

náutico *adj* nautical

navaja *f* penknife; (*de afeitar*) razor. **~zo** *m* slash

naval *adj* naval

nave *f* ship; (*de iglesia*) nave. **~ espacial** spaceship. **quemar las ~s** burn one's boats

navega|ble *adj* navigable; (barco) seaworthy. **~ción** *f* navigation; (*tráfico*) shipping. **~dor** *m* (*Informática*) browser. **~nte** *m* & *f* navigator. **~r** 🔢 *vi* sail; (*Informática*) browse

Navid|ad *f* Christmas. **~eño** *adj* Christmas. **en ~ades** at Christmas. **¡feliz ~ad!** Happy Christmas! **por ~ad** at Christmas

nazi *adj* & *m* & *f* Nazi. **~smo** *m* Nazism

neblina *f* mist

nebuloso *adj* misty; (*fig*) vague

necedad *f* foolishness. **decir ~es** talk nonsense. **hacer una ~** do sth stupid

necesari|amente *adv* necessarily. **~o** *adj* necessary

necesi|dad *f* need; (*cosa esencial*) necessity; (*pobreza*) poverty. **~dades** *fpl* hardships. **no hay ~dad** there's no need. **por ~dad** (out) of necessity. **~tado** *adj* in need (**de** of). **~tar** *vt* need. ● *vi*. **~tar de** need

necio *adj* silly. ● *m* idiot

néctar *m* nectar

nectarina *f* nectarine

nefasto *adj* unfortunate; (*consecuencia*) disastrous; (*influencia*) harmful

nega|ción *f* denial; (*Gram*) negative. **~do** *adj* useless. **~r** 🔢 & 🔢 *vt* deny; (*rehusar*) refuse. **~rse** *vpr* refuse (**a** to). **~tiva** *f* (*acción*) denial; (*acción de*

rehusar) refusal. **~tivo** *adj* & *m* negative

negligen|cia *f* negligence. **~te** *adj* negligent

negoci|able *adj* negotiable. **~ación** *f* negotiation. **~ante** *m* & *f* dealer. **~ar** *vt/i* negotiate. **~ar en** trade in. **~o** *m* business; (*Com, trato*) deal. **~os** *mpl* business. **hombre** *m* **de ~os** businessman

negr|a *f* black woman; (*Mus*) crotchet. **~o** *adj* black; (ojos) dark. ● *m* (*color*) black; (*persona*) black man. **~ura** *f* blackness. **~uzco** *adj* blackish

nen|a *f* little girl. **~o** *m* little boy

nenúfar *m* water lily

neocelandés *adj* from New Zealand. ● *m* New Zealander

neón *m* neon

nepotismo *m* nepotism

nervio *m* nerve; (*tendón*) sinew; (*en botánica*) vein. **~sidad** *f*, **~sismo** *m* nervousness; (*impaciencia*) impatience. **~so** *adj* nervous; (*de temperamento*) highly-strung. **ponerse ~so** get nervous

neto *adj* clear; (verdad) simple; (*Com*) net

neumático *adj* pneumatic. ● *m* tyre

neumonía *f* pneumonia

neur|algia *f* neuralgia. **~ología** *f* neurology. **~ólogo** *m* neurologist. **~osis** *f* neurosis. **~ótico** *adj* neurotic

neutr|al *adj* neutral. **~alidad** *f* neutrality. **~alizar** 🔟 *vt* neutralize. **~o** *adj* neutral; (*Gram*) neuter

neva|da *f* snowfall. **~r** 🔢 *vi* snow. **~sca** *f* blizzard

nevera *f* refrigerator, fridge (*Brit*)

nevisca *f* light snowfall

nexo *m* link

ni *conj*. **~...~** neither... nor. **~ aunque** not even if. **~ siquiera** not even. **sin...~** ... without ... or...

Nicaragua *f* Nicaragua

nicaragüense *adj* & *m* & *f* Nicaraguan

nicho *m* niche

nicotina *f* nicotine

nido *m* nest; (*de ladrones*) den

niebla *f* fog. **hay ~** it's foggy. **un día de ~** a foggy day

niet|a f granddaughter. **~o** m grandson. **~os** mpl grandchildren

nieve f snow; (Mex, helado) sorbet

niki m polo shirt

nimi|edad f triviality. **~o** adj insignificant

ninfa f nymph

ningún véase NINGUNO

ninguno adj (delante de nombre masculino en singular **ningún**) no; (con otro negativo) any. **de ninguna manera, de ningún modo** by no means. **en ninguna parte** nowhere. **sin ningún amigo** without any friends. ● pron (de dos) neither; (de más de dos) none; (nadie) no-one, nobody

niñ|a f (little) girl. **~era** f nanny. **~ería** f childish thing. **~ez** f childhood. **~o** adj childish. ● m (little) boy **de ~o** as a child. **desde ~o** from childhood

níquel m nickel

níspero m medlar

nitidez f clarity; (de foto, imagen) sharpness

nítido adj clear; (foto, imagen) sharp

nitrógeno m nitrogen

nivel m level; (fig) standard. **~ de vida** standard of living. **~ar** vt level. **~arse** vpr become level

no adv not; (como respuesta) no. ¿**~**? isn't it? **¡a que ~!** I bet you don't! **¡cómo ~!** of course! **Felipe ~ tiene hijos** Felipe has no children. **¡que ~!** certainly not!

nob|iliario adj noble. **~le** adj & m & f noble. **~leza** f nobility

noche f night. **~ vieja** New Year's Eve. **de ~** at night. **hacerse de ~** get dark. **hacer ~** spend the night. **media ~** midnight. **en la ~** (LAm), **por la ~** at night

---

Nochevieja In Spain and other Spanish-speaking countries, where it is known as Año Nuevo, it is customary to see the New Year in by eating twelve grapes for good luck, one on each chime of the clock at midnight.

Nochebuena f Christmas Eve

noción f notion. **nociones** fpl rudiments

nocivo adj harmful

nocturno adj nocturnal; (clase) evening; (tren etc) night. ● m nocturne

nodriza f wet nurse

nogal m walnut tree; (madera) walnut

nómada adj nomadic. ● m & f nomad

nombr|ado adj famous; (susodicho) aforementioned. **~amiento** m appointment. **~ar** vt appoint; (citar) mention. **~e** m name; (Gram) noun; (fama) renown. **~e de pila** Christian name. **en ~e de** in the name of. **no tener ~e** be unspeakable. **poner de ~e** call

nomeolvides m invar forget-me-not

nómina f payroll

nomina|l adj nominal. **~tivo** adj & m nominative. **~tivo a** (cheque etc) made out to

non adj odd. ● m odd number. **pares y ~es** odds and evens

nono adj ninth

nordeste adj (región) north-eastern; (viento) north-easterly. ● m northeast

nórdico adj Nordic. ● m Northern European

noria f water-wheel; (en una feria) big wheel (Brit), Ferris wheel (Amer)

norma f rule

normal adj normal. ● f teachers' training college. **~idad** f normality (Brit), normalcy (Amer). **~izar** [10] vt normalize. **~mente** adv normally, usually

noroeste adj (región) north-western; (viento) north-westerly. ● m northwest

norte adj (región) northern; (viento, lado) north. ● m north; (fig, meta) aim

Norteamérica f (North) America

norteamericano adj & m (North) American

norteño adj northern. ● m northerner

Noruega f Norway

noruego adj & m Norwegian

nos pron (acusativo) us; (dativo) (to) us; (reflexivo) (to) ourselves; (recíproco) (to) each other

nosotros pron we; (con prep) us

nost|algia f nostalgia; (de casa, de patria) homesickness. **~álgico** adj nostalgic

nota f note; (de examen etc) mark. **de ~** famous. **de mala ~** notorious. **digno de ~** notable. **~ble** adj notable. **~ción** f notation. **~r** vt notice. **es de ~r** it should be noted. **hacerse ~r** stand out

notario m notary

notici|a f (piece of) news. **~as** fpl news. **atrasado de ~as** behind with the news. **tener ~as de** hear from. **~ario**, (LAm) **~ero** m news

notifica|ción f notification. **~r** ⑦ vt notify

notori|edad f notoriety. **~o** adj well-known; (evidente) obvious; (notable) marked

novato adj inexperienced. ● m novice

novecientos adj & m nine hundred

noved|ad f newness; (cosa nueva) innovation; (cambio) change; (moda) latest fashion. **llegar sin ~ad** arrive safely. **~oso** adj novel

novel|a f novel. **~ista** m & f novelist

noveno adj ninth

noventa adj & m ninety; (nonagésimo) ninetieth

novia f girlfriend; (prometida) fiancée; (en boda) bride. **~r** vi (LAm) go out together. **~zgo** m engagement

novicio m novice

noviembre m November

novill|a f heifer. **~o** m bullock. **hacer ~os** play truant

novio m boyfriend; (prometido) fiancé; (en boda) bridegroom. **los ~s** the bride and groom

nub|arrón m large dark cloud. **~e** f cloud; (de insectos etc) swarm. **~lado** adj cloudy, overcast. ● m cloud. **~lar** vt cloud. **~larse** vpr become cloudy; (vista) cloud over. **~oso** adj cloudy

nuca f back of the neck

nuclear adj nuclear

núcleo m nucleus

nudillo m knuckle

nudis|mo m nudism. **~ta** m & f nudist

nudo m knot; (de asunto etc) crux. **tener un ~ en la garganta** have a

lump in one's throat. **~so** adj knotty

nuera f daughter-in-law

nuestro adj our. ● pron ours. **~ amigo** our friend. **un coche ~** a car of ours

nueva f (piece of) news. **~s** fpl news. **~mente** adv again

Nueva Zelanda f, (LAm) **Nueva Zelandia** f New Zealand

nueve adj & m nine

nuevo adj new. **de ~** again. **estar ~** be as good as new

nuez f walnut. **~ de Adán** Adam's apple. **~ moscada** nutmeg

nul|idad f nullity; (fam, persona) dead loss ①. **~o** adj useless; (Jurid) null and void

num|eración f numbering. **~eral** adj & m numeral. **~erar** vt number. **~érico** adj numerical

número m number; (arábigo, romano) numeral; (de zapatos etc) size; (billete de lotería) lottery ticket; (de publicación) issue. **sin ~** countless

numeroso adj numerous

nunca adv never. **~ (ja)más** never again. **casi ~** hardly ever. **como ~** like never before. **más que ~** more than ever

nupcial adj nuptial. **banquete ~** wedding breakfast

nutria f otter

nutri|ción f nutrition. **~do** adj nourished, fed; (fig) large; (aplausos) loud; (fuego) heavy. **~r** vt nourish, feed; (fig) feed. **~tivo** adj nutritious. **valor** m **~tivo** nutritional value

nylon m nylon

Ññ

ñapa f (LAm) extra goods given free

ñato adj (LAm) snub-nosed

ñoñ|ería f, **~ez** f insipidity. **~o** adj insipid; (tímido) bashful; (quisquilloso) prudish

Oo

o *conj* or. **~ bien** rather. **~... ~** either ... or

oasis *m invar* oasis

obed|ecer ⓫ *vt/i* obey. **~iencia** *f* obedience. **~iente** *adj* obedient

obes|idad *f* obesity. **~o** *adj* obese

obispo *m* bishop

obje|ción *f* objection. **~tar** *vt/i* object

objetivo *adj* objective. ● *m* objective; (*foto etc*) lens

objeto *m* object. **~r** *m* objector. **~ de conciencia** conscientious objector

oblicuo *adj* oblique

obliga|ción *f* obligation; (*Com*) bond. **~do** *adj* obliged; (*forzoso*) obligatory; **~r** ⓬ *vt* force, oblige. **~rse** *vpr*. **~rse a** undertake to. **~torio** *adj* obligatory

oboe *m* oboe. ● *m & f* (*músico*) oboist

obra *f* work; (*acción*) deed; (*de teatro*) play; (*construcción*) building work. **~ maestra** masterpiece. **en ~s** under construction. **por ~ de** thanks to. **~r** *vt* do

obrero *adj* labour; (*clase*) working. ● *m* workman; (*de fábrica, construcción*) worker

obscen|idad *f* obscenity. **~o** *adj* obscene

obscu... *véase* **oscu...**

obsequi|ar *vt* lavish attention on. **~ar con** give, present with. **~o** *m* gift, present; (*agasajo*) attention. **~oso** *adj* obliging

observa|ción *f* observation. **hacer una ~ción** make a remark. **~dor** *m* observer. **~ncia** *f* observance. **~r** *vt* observe; (*notar*) notice. **~torio** *m* observatory

obses|ión *f* obsession. **~ionar** *vt* obsess. **~ivo** *adj* obsessive. **~o** *adj* obsessed

obst|aculizar ⓾ *vt* hinder; hold up (*tráfico*). **~áculo** *m* obstacle

obstante: **no ~** *adv* however, nevertheless; (*como prep*) in spite of

obstar *vi*. **eso no obsta para que vaya** that should not prevent him from going

obstina|do *adj* obstinate. **~rse** *vpr*. **~rse en** (+ *infinitivo*) insist on (+ *gerundio*)

obstru|cción *f* obstruction. **~ir** ⓱ *vt* obstruct

obtener ⓵ *vt* get, obtain

obtura|dor *m* (*Foto*) shutter. **~r** *vt* plug; fill (*muela etc*)

obvio *adj* obvious

oca *f* goose

ocasi|ón *f* occasion; (*oportunidad*) opportunity. **aprovechar la ~ón** take the opportunity. **con ~ón de** on the occasion of. **de ~ón** bargain; (*usado*) second-hand. **en ~ones** sometimes. **perder una ~ón** miss a chance. **~onal** *adj* chance. **~onar** *vt* cause

ocaso *m* sunset; (*fig*) decline

occident|al *adj* western. ● *m & f* westerner. **~e** *m* west

océano *m* ocean

ochenta *adj & m* eighty

ocho *adj & m* eight. **~cientos** *adj & m* eight hundred

ocio *m* idleness; (*tiempo libre*) leisure time. **~sidad** *f* idleness. **~so** *adj* idle; (*inútil*) pointless

oct|agonal *adj* octagonal. **~ágono** *m* octagon

octano *m* octane

octav|a *f* octave. **~o** *adj & m* eighth

octogenario *adj & m* octogenarian

octubre *m* October

ocular *adj* eye

oculista *m & f* ophthalmologist, ophthalmic optician

ocult|ar *vt* hide. **~arse** *vpr* hide. **~o** *adj* hidden; (*secreto*) secret

ocupa|ción *f* occupation. **~do** *adj* occupied; (*persona*) busy. **estar ~do** (*asiento*) be taken; (*línea telefónica*) be engaged (*Brit*), be busy (*Amer*). **~nte** *m & f* occupant. **~r** *vt* occupy, take up (*espacio*). **~rse** *vpr* look after

ocurr|encia *f* occurrence, event; (*idea*) idea; (*que tiene gracia*) witty remark. **~ir** *vi* happen. **¿qué ~e?** what's the matter? **~irse** *vpr* occur. **se me ~e**

que it occurs to me that

oda f ode

odi|ar vt hate. ~**o** m hatred. ~**oso** adj hateful; (persona) horrible

oeste adj (región) western; (viento, lado) west. ● m west

ofen|der vt offend; (insultar) insult. ~**derse** vpr take offence. ~**sa** f offence. ~**siva** f offensive. ~**sivo** adj offensive

oferta f offer; (en subasta) bid. ~**s de empleo** situations vacant. **en** ~ on (special) offer

oficial adj official. ● m skilled worker; (Mil) officer

oficin|a f office. ~**a de colocación** employment office. ~**a de turismo** tourist office. **horas** fpl **de** ~**a** business hours. ~**ista** m & f office worker

oficio m trade. ~**so** adj (no oficial) unofficial

ofrec|er 🟦 vt offer; give (fiesta, banquete etc); (prometer) promise. ~**erse** vpr (persona) volunteer. ~**imiento** m offer

ofrenda f offering. ~**r** vt offer

ofuscar 🟦 vt blind; (confundir) confuse. ~**se** vpr get worked up

oí|ble adj audible. ~**do** m ear; (sentido) hearing. **al** ~**do** in one's ear. **de** ~**das** by hearsay. **conocer de** ~**das** have heard of. **de** ~**do** by ear. **duro de** ~**do** hard of hearing

oigo vb véase **OÍR**

oír 🟦 vt hear. **¡oiga!** listen!; (al teléfono) hello!

ojal m buttonhole

ojalá int I hope so! ● conj if only

ojea|da f glance. **dar una** ~**da a**, **echar una** ~**da a** have a quick glance at. ~**r** vt have a look at

ojeras fpl rings under one's eyes

ojeriza f ill will. **tener** ~ **a** have a grudge against

ojo m eye; (de cerradura) keyhole; (de un puente) span. **¡**~**!** careful!

ola f wave

olé int bravo!

olea|da f wave. ~**je** m swell

óleo m oil; (cuadro) oil painting

oleoducto m oil pipeline

oler 🟦 (las formas que empiecen por **ue** se escriben **hue**) vt smell. ● vi smell (**a** of). **me huele mal** (fig) it sounds fishy to me

olfat|ear vt sniff; scent (rastro). ~**o** m (sense of) smell; (fig) intuition

olimpiada f, **olimpíada** f Olympic games, Olympics

olímpico adj Olympic; (fig, fam) total

oliv|a f olive. ~**ar** m olive grove. ~**o** m olive tree

olla f pot, casserole. ~ **a/de presión**, ~ **exprés** pressure cooker

olmo m elm (tree)

olor m smell. ~**oso** adj sweet-smelling

olvid|adizo adj forgetful. ~**ar** vt forget. ~**arse** vpr forget. ~**arse de** forget. **se me** ~**ó** I forgot. ~**o** m oblivion; (acto) omission

ombligo m navel

omi|sión f omission. ~**tir** vt omit

ómnibus adj omnibus

omnipotente adj omnipotent

omóplato m shoulder blade

once adj & m eleven

ond|a f wave. ~**a corta** short wave. ~**a larga** long wave. **longitud** f **de** ~**a** wavelength. ~**ear** vi wave; (agua) ripple. ~**ulación** f undulation; (del pelo) wave. ~**ular** vi wave

onomásti|co adj (índice) of names. ● m (LAm) saint's day

> **onomástica**
See ▷**SANTO**   *i*

ONU abrev (**Organización de las Naciones Unidas**) UN

OPA f take-over bid

opac|ar 🟦 (LAm) make opaque; (deslucir) mar; (anular) overshadow. ~**o** adj opaque; (fig) dull

opci|ón f option. ~**onal** adj optional

open-jaw m open jaws ticket

ópera f opera

opera|ción f operation; (Com) transaction; ~ **retorno** (Esp) return to work (after the holidays). ~**dor** m operator; (TV) cameraman; (Mex, obrero) machinist. ~**r** vt operate on; work (milagro etc); (*Mex*) operate (máquina). ● *vi* operate; (*Com*) deal. **~rio** *m* machinist. **~rse** *vpr* take place; (*Med*) have an operation. **~torio** *adj* operative

opereta *f* operetta

opin|ar *vi* express one's opinion. ● *vt* think. **~ que** think that. ¿**qué opinas?** what do you think? **~ión** *f* opinion. **la ~ión pública** public opinion

opio *m* opium

opone|nte *adj* opposing. ● *m & f* opponent. **~r** *vt* oppose; offer (resistencia); raise (objeción). **~rse** *vpr* be opposed; (dos personas) oppose each other

oporto *m* port (wine)

oportun|idad *f* opportunity; (cualidad de oportuno) timeliness; (*LAm*, ocasión) occasion. **~ista** *m & f* opportunist. **~o** *adj* opportune; (apropiado) suitable

oposi|ción *f* opposition. **~ciones** *fpl* public examination. **~tor** *m* candidate; (*Pol*) opponent

opres|ión *f* oppression; (ahogo) difficulty in breathing. **~ivo** *adj* oppressive. **~or** *m* oppressor

oprimir *vt* squeeze; press (botón etc); (ropa) be too tight for; (fig) oppress

optar *vi* choose. **~ por** opt for

óptic|a *f* optics; (tienda) optician's (shop). **~o** *adj* optic(al). ● *m* optician

optimis|mo *m* optimism. **~ta** *adj* optimistic. ● *m & f* optimist

óptimo *adj* ideal; (condiciones) perfect

opuesto *adj* opposite; (opiniones) conflicting

opulen|cia *f* opulence. **~to** *adj* opulent

oración *f* prayer; (*Gram*) sentence

ora|dor *m* speaker. **~l** *adj* oral

órale *int* (*Mex*) come on!; (de acuerdo) OK!

orar *vi* pray (**por** for)

órbita *f* orbit

orden *f* order. **~ del día** agenda. **órdenes** *fpl* **sagradas** Holy Orders. **a sus órdenes** (esp *Mex*) can I help you? **~ de arresto** arrest warrant. **en ~** in

order. **por ~** in turn. **~ado** *adj* tidy

ordenador *m* computer

ordena|nza *f* ordinance. ● *m* (*Mil*) orderly. **~r** *vt* put in order; (mandar) order; (*Relig*) ordain; (*LAm*, en restaurante) order

ordeñar *vt* milk

ordinario *adj* ordinary; (grosero) common; (de mala calidad) poor-quality

orear *vt* air

orégano *m* oregano

oreja *f* ear

orfanato *m* orphanage

orfebre *m* goldsmith, silversmith

orfeón *m* choral society

orgánico *adj* organic

organillo *m* barrel-organ

organismo *m* organism

organista *m & f* organist

organiza|ción *f* organization. **~dor** *m* organizer. **~r** 🔟 *vt* organize. **~rse** *vpr* get organized

órgano *m* organ

orgasmo *m* orgasm

orgía *f* orgy

orgullo *m* pride. **~so** *adj* proud

orientación *f* orientation; (guía) guidance; (*Archit*) aspect

oriental *adj & m & f* oriental

orientar *vt* position; advise (persona). **~se** *vpr* point; (persona) find one's bearings

oriente *m* east

orificio *m* hole

orig|en *m* origin. **dar ~en a** give rise to. **~inal** *adj* original; (excéntrico) odd. **~inalidad** *f* originality. **~inar** *vt* give rise to. **~inario** *adj* original; (nativo) native. **ser ~inario de** come from. **~inarse** *vpr* originate; (incendio) start

orilla *f* (del mar) shore; (de río) bank; (borde) edge. **a ~s del mar** by the sea

orina *f* urine. **~l** *m* chamber-pot. **~r** *vi* urinate

oriundo *adj* native. **ser ~ de** (persona) come from; (especie etc) native to

ornamental *adj* ornamental

ornitología *f* ornithology

oro *m* gold. ~s *mpl* Spanish card suit. ~ **de ley** 9 carat gold. **hacerse de** ~ make a fortune. **prometer el** ~ **y el moro** promise the moon

orquesta *f* orchestra. ~**l** *adj* orchestral. ~**r** *vt* orchestrate

orquídea *f* orchid

ortiga *f* nettle

ortodoxo *adj* orthodox

ortografía *f* spelling

ortopédico *adj* orthopaedic

oruga *f* caterpillar

orzuelo *m* sty

os *pron* (*acusativo*) you; (*dativo*) (to) you; (*reflexivo*) (to) yourselves; (*recíproco*) (to) each other

osad|ía *f* boldness. ~**o** *adj* bold

oscila|ción *f* swinging; (*de precios*) fluctuation; (*Tec*) oscillation. ~**r** *vi* swing; (*precio*) fluctuate; (*Tec*) oscillate

oscur|ecer 🔢 *vi* get dark. ● *vt* darken; (*fig*) obscure. ~**ecerse** *vpr* grow dark; (*nublarse*) cloud over. ~**idad** *f* darkness; (*fig*) obscurity. ~**o** *adj* dark; (*fig*) obscure. **a** ~**as** in the dark

óseo *adj* bone

oso *m* bear. ~ **de felpa**, ~ **de peluche** teddy bear

ostensible *adj* obvious

ostent|ación *f* ostentation. ~**ar** *vt* show off; (*mostrar*) show. ~**oso** *adj* ostentatious

osteópata *m & f* osteopath

ostión *m* (*esp Mex*) oyster

ostra *f* oyster

ostracismo *m* ostracism

Otan *abrev* (**Organización del Tratado del Atlántico Norte**) NATO, North Atlantic Treaty Organization

otitis *f* inflammation of the ear

otoño *m* autumn (*Brit*), fall (*Amer*)

otorga|miento *m* granting. ~**r** 🔢 *vt* give; grant (*préstamo*); (*Jurid*) draw up (*testamento*)

otorrinolaringólogo *m* ear, nose and throat specialist

---

otro, otra

● *adjetivo*

····▸ another; (*con artículo, posesivo*) other. **come** ~ **pedazo** have another piece. **el** ~ **día** the other day. **mi** ~ **coche** my other car. **otra cosa** something else. **otra persona** somebody else. **otra vez** again

····▸ (*en plural*) other; (*con numeral*) another. **en otras ocasiones** on other occasions. ~**s 3 vasos** another 3 glasses

····▸ (*siguiente*) next. **al** ~ **día** the next day. **me bajo en la otra estación** I get off at the next station

● *pronombre*

····▸ (*cosa*) another one. **lo cambié por** ~ I changed it for another one

····▸ (*persona*) someone else. **invitó a** ~ she invited someone else

····▸ (*en plural*) (some) others. **tengo** ~**s en casa** I have (some) others at home. ~**s piensan lo contrario** others think the opposite

····▸ (*con artículo*) **el** ~ the other one. **los** ~**s** the others. **uno detrás del** ~ one after the other. **los** ~**s no vinieron** the others didn't come. **esta semana no, la otra** not this week, next week. **de un día para el** ~ from one day to the next

➡ Para usos complementarios ver **uno, tanto**

---

ovación *f* ovation

oval *adj*, **ovalado** *adj* oval

óvalo *m* oval

ovario *m* ovary

oveja *f* sheep; (*hembra*) ewe

overol *m* (*LAm*) overalls

ovillo *m* ball. **hacerse un** ~ curl up

OVNI *abrev* (**objeto volante no identificado**) UFO

ovulación *f* ovulation

oxida|ción *f* rusting. ~**r** *vi* rust. ~**rse** *vpr* go rusty

óxido *m* rust; (*en química*) oxide
oxígeno *m* oxygen
oye *vb véase* **oír**
oyente *adj* listening. ● *m & f* listener; (*Univ*) occasional student
ozono *m* ozone

Pp

pabellón *m* pavilion; (*en jardín*) summerhouse; (*en hospital*) block; (*de instrumento*) bell; (*bandera*) flag
pacer **11** *vi* graze
pachucho *adj* (*fruta*) overripe; (*persona*) poorly
pacien|cia *f* patience. **perder la** ~**cia** lose patience. ~**te** *adj & m & f* patient
pacificar **7** *vt* pacify. ~**se** *vpr* calm down
pacífico *adj* peaceful. **el** (**Océano**) **P**~ the Pacific (Ocean)
pacifis|mo *m* pacifism. ~**ta** *adj & m & f* pacifist
pact|ar *vi* agree, make a pact. ~**o** *m* pact, agreement
padec|er **11** *vt/i* suffer (**de** from); (*soportar*) bear. ~**er del corazón** have heart trouble. ~**imiento** *m* suffering
padrastro *m* stepfather
padre *adj* **1** terrible; (*Mex, estupendo*) great. ● *m* father. ~**s** *mpl* parents
padrino *m* godfather; (*en boda*) man who gives away the bride
padrón *m* register. ~ **electoral** (*LAm*) electoral roll
paella *f* paella
paga *f* payment; (*sueldo*) pay. ~**dero** *adj* payable
pagano *adj & m* pagan
pagar **12** *vt* pay; pay for (*compras*). ● *vi* pay. ~**é** *m* IOU
página *f* page
pago *m* payment
país *m* country; (*ciudadanos*) nation. ~ **natal** native land. **el P**~ **Vasco** the Basque Country. **los P**~**es Bajos** the Low Countries

paisaje *m* landscape, scenery
paisano *m* compatriot
paja *f* straw; (*en texto*) padding
pájaro *m* bird. ~ **carpintero** woodpecker
paje *m* page
pala *f* shovel; (*para cavar*) spade; (*para basura*) dustpan; (*de pimpón*) bat
palabr|a *f* word; (*habla*) speech. **pedir la** ~**a** ask to speak. **tomar la** ~**a** take the floor. ~**ota** *f* swear-word. **decir** ~**otas** swear
palacio *m* palace
paladar *m* palate
palanca *f* lever; (*fig*) influence. ~ **de cambio** (**de velocidades**) gear lever (*Brit*), gear shift (*Amer*)
palangana *f* washbasin (*Brit*), washbowl (*Amer*)
palco *m* (*en el teatro*) box
palestino *adj & m* Palestinian
paleta *f* (*de pintor*) palette; (*de albañil*) trowel
paleto *m* yokel
paliativo *adj & m* palliative
palide|cer **11** *vi* turn pale. ~**z** *f* paleness
pálido *adj* pale. **ponerse** ~ turn pale
palillo *m* (*de dientes*) toothpick; (*para comer*) chopstick
paliza *f* beating
palma *f* (*de la mano*) palm; (*árbol*) palm (tree); (*de dátiles*) date palm. **dar** ~**s** clap. ~**da** *f* pat; (*LAm*) slap. ~**das** *fpl* applause
palmera *f* palm tree
palmo *m* span; (*fig*) few inches. ~ **a** ~ inch by inch
palmote|ar *vi* clap. ~**o** *m* clapping, applause
palo *m* stick; (*de valla*) post; (*de golf*) club; (*golpe*) blow; (*de naipes*) suit; (*mástil*) mast
paloma *f* pigeon; (*blanca, símbolo*) dove
palomitas *fpl* popcorn
palpar *vt* feel
palpita|ción *f* palpitation. ~**nte** *adj* throbbing. ~**r** *vi* beat; (*latir con fuerza*) pound; (*vena, sien*) throb
palta *f* (*LAm*) avocado (pear)

paludismo m malaria
pamela f (woman's) broad-brimmed dress hat
pamp|a f pampas. ~**ero** adj of the pampas
pan m bread; (barra) loaf. ~ **integral** wholewheat bread, wholemeal bread (Brit). ~ **tostado** toast. ~ **rallado** breadcrumbs. **ganarse el** ~ earn one's living
pana f corduroy
panader|ía f bakery; (tienda) baker's (shop). ~**o** m baker
panal m honeycomb
panameño adj & m Panamanian
pancarta f banner, placard
panda m panda
pander|eta f (small) tambourine ~**o** m tambourine
pandilla f gang
panecillo m (bread) roll
panel m panel
panfleto m pamphlet
pánico m panic. **tener** ~ be terrified (a of)
panor|ama m panorama. ~**ámico** adj panoramic
panque m (Mex) sponge cake
pantaletas fpl (Mex) panties, knickers (Brit)
pantalla f screen; (de lámpara) (lamp-)shade
pantalón m, **pantalones** mpl trousers. ~ **a la cadera** bumsters
pantano m marsh; (embalse) reservoir. ~**so** adj marshy
pantera f panther
panti m, (Mex) **pantimedias** fpl tights (Brit), pantyhose (Amer)
pantomima f pantomime
pantorrilla f calf
pantufla f slipper
panz|a f belly. ~**udo** adj pot-bellied
pañal m nappy (Brit), diaper (Amer)
paño m material; (de lana) woollen cloth; (trapo) cloth. ~ **de cocina** dishcloth; (para secar) tea towel. ~ **higiénico** sanitary towel. **en** ~**s menores** in one's underclothes
pañuelo m handkerchief; (de cabeza) scarf

papa m pope. ●f (LAm) potato. ~**s fritas** (LAm) chips (Brit), French fries (Amer); (de paquete) crisps (Brit), chips (Amer)
papá m dad(dy). ~**s** mpl parents. **P~ Noel** Father Christmas
papada f (de persona) double chin
papagayo m parrot
papalote m (Mex) kite
papanatas m invar simpleton
paparrucha f (tontería) silly thing
papaya f papaya, pawpaw
papel m paper; (en el teatro etc) role. ~ **carbón** carbon paper. ~ **de calcar** tracing paper. ~ **de envolver** wrapping paper. ~ **de plata** silver paper. ~ **higiénico** toilet paper. ~ **pintado** wallpaper. ~ **secante** blotting paper. ~**eo** m paperwork. ~**era** f wastepaper basket. ~**ería** f stationer's (shop). ~**eta** f (para votar) (ballot) paper
paperas fpl mumps
paquete m packet; (bulto) parcel; (LAm, de papas fritas) bag; (Mex, problema) headache. ~ **postal** parcel
Paquistán m Pakistan
paquistaní adj & m Pakistani
par adj (número) even. ●m couple; (dos cosas iguales) pair. **a** ~**es** two by two. **de** ~ **en** ~ wide open. ~**es y nones** odds and evens. **sin** ~ without equal. ●f par. **a la** ~ (Com) at par. **a la** ~ **que** at the same time

para preposición
····▸ for. **es** ~ **ti** it's for you. ~ **siempre** for ever. **¿**~ **qué?** what for? ~ **mi cumpleaños** for my birthday
····▸ (con infinitivo) to. **es muy tarde** ~ **llamar** it's too late to call. **salió** ~ **divertirse** he went out to have fun. **lo hago** ~ **ahorrar** I do it (in order) to save money
····▸ (dirección) **iba** ~ **la oficina** he was going to the office. **empújalo** ~ **atrás** push it back. **¿vas** ~ **casa?** are you going home?
····▸ (tiempo) by. **debe estar listo** ~ **el 5** it must be ready by the

p

5th. ~ **entonces** by then
····> (LAm, hora) to. **son 5** ~ **la una** it's 5 to one
····> ~ **que** so (that). **grité** ~ **que me oyera** I shouted so (that) he could hear me.

Note that **para que** is always followed by a verb in the subjunctive

parabienes mpl congratulations
parábola f (narración) parable
parabólica f satellite dish
para|brisas m invar windscreen (Brit), windshield (Amer). **~caídas** m invar parachute. **~caidista** m & f parachutist; (Mil) paratrooper. **~choques** m invar bumper (Brit), fender (Amer) (Rail) buffer
parad|a f (acción) stop; (lugar) bus stop; (de taxis) rank; (Mil) parade. **~ero** m whereabouts; (LAm, lugar) bus stop. **~o** adj stationary; (desempleado) unemployed. **estar** ~ (LAm, de pie) be standing
paradoja f paradox
parador m state-owned hotel

parador (nacional de turismo) A national chain of hotels in Spain. They are often converted castles, palaces and monasteries. They provide a high standard of accommodation but are relatively inexpensive and often act as showcases for local craftsmanship and cooking.

parafina f paraffin
paraguas m invar umbrella
Paraguay m Paraguay
paraguayo adj & m Paraguayan
paraíso m paradise; (en el teatro) gallery
parallel|a f parallel (line). **~as** fpl parallel bars. **~o** adj & m parallel
par|álisis f invar paralysis. **~alítico** adj paralytic. **~alizar** 🔟 vt paralyse
parámetro m parameter
paramilitar adj paramilitary
páramo m bleak upland
parangón m comparison.

paraninfo m main hall
paranoi|a f paranoia. **~co** adj paranoiac
parar vt/i stop. **sin** ~ continuously. **~se** vpr stop; (LAm, ponerse de pie) stand
pararrayos m invar lightning conductor
parásito adj parasitic. ● m parasite
parcela f plot. **~r** vt divide into plots
parche m patch
parcial adj partial. **a tiempo** ~ part-time. **~idad** f prejudice
parco adj laconic; (sobrio) frugal
parear vt put into pairs
parec|er m opinion. **al** ~**er** apparently. **a mi** ~**er** in my opinion. ● vi 🇪🇸 seem; (asemejarse) look like; (tener aspecto de) look. **me** ~**e** I think. ~**e fácil** it looks easy. **¿qué te** ~**e?** what do you think? **según** ~**e** apparently. ~**erse** vpr look like. ~**ido** adj similar. **bien** ~**ido** good-looking. ● m similarity
pared f wall. ~ **por medio** next door. ~**ón** m (de fusilamiento) wall. **llevar al** ~**ón** shoot
parej|a f pair; (hombre y mujer) couple; (compañero) partner. ~**a de hecho** legalised partnership of unmarried couple. ~**o** adj the same; (LAm, sin desniveles) even; (LAm, liso) smooth; (Mex, equitativo) equal. ● adv (LAm) evenly
parente|la f relations. ~**sco** m relationship
paréntesis m invar parenthesis, bracket (Brit); (intervalo) break. **entre** ~ in brackets (Brit), in parenthesis; (fig) by the way
paria m & f outcast
paridad f equality; (Com) parity
pariente m & f relation, relative
parir vt give birth to. ● vi give birth
parisiense adj & m & f, **parisino** adj & m Parisian
parking /'parkin/ m car park (Brit), parking lot (Amer)
parlament|ar vi talk. ~**ario** adj parliamentary. ● m member of parliament (Brit), congressman (Amer). ~**o** m parliament

parlanchín *adj* talkative. ● *m* chatterbox

parlante *m* (*LAm*) loudspeaker

paro *m* stoppage; (*desempleo*) unemployment; (*subsidio*) unemployment benefit; (*LAm, huelga*) strike. ~ **cardíaco** cardiac arrest

parodia *f* parody

parpadear *vi* blink; (luz) flicker

párpado *m* eyelid

parque *m* park. ~ **de atracciones** funfair. ~ **eólico** wind farm. ~ **infantil** playground. ~ **zoológico** zoo, zoological gardens

parquímetro *m* parking meter

parra *f* grapevine

párrafo *m* paragraph

parrilla *f* grill; (*LAm, Auto*) luggage rack. **a la** ~ grilled. ~**da** *f* grill

párroco *m* parish priest

parroquia *f* parish; (*iglesia*) parish church. ~**no** *m* parishioner

parte *m* (*informe*) report. **dar** ~ report. **de mi** ~ for me ● *f* part; (*porción*) share; (*Jurid*) party; (*Mex*, *repuesto*) spare (part). **de** ~ **de** from. **¿de** ~ **de quién?** (*al teléfono*) who's speaking? **en cualquier** ~ anywhere. **en gran** ~ largely. **en** ~ partly. **en todas** ~**s** everywhere. **la mayor** ~ the majority. **la** ~ **superior** the top. **ninguna** ~ nowhere. **por otra** ~ on the other hand. **por todas** ~**s** everywhere

partera *f* midwife

partición *f* division; (*Pol*) partition

participa|ción *f* participation; (*noticia*) announcement; (*de lotería*) share. ~**nte** *adj* participating. ● *m & f* participant. ~**r** *vt* announce. ● *vi* take part

participio *m* participle

particular *adj* particular; (clase) private. **nada de** ~ nothing special. ● *m* private individual.

partida *f* departure; (*en registro*) entry; (*documento*) certificate; (*de mercancías*) consignment; (*juego*) game; (*de gente*) group

partidario *adj & m* partisan. ~ **de** in favour of

parti|do *m* (*Pol*) party; (*encuentro*) match, game; (*LAm, de ajedrez*) game. ~**r** *vt* cut; (*romper*) break; crack (nueces). ● *vi* leave. **a** ~**r de** from. ~ **de** start from. ~**rse** *vpr* (*romperse*) break; (*dividirse*) split

partitura *f* (*Mus*) score

parto *m* labour. **estar de** ~ be in labour

parvulario *m* kindergarten, nursery school (*Brit*)

pasa *f* raisin. ~ **de Corinto** currant

pasa|da *f* passing; (*de puntos*) row. **de** ~**da** in passing. ~**dero** *adj* passable. ~**dizo** *m* passage. ~**do** *adj* past; (día, mes etc) last; (*anticuado*) old-fashioned; (comida) bad, off. ~**do mañana** the day after tomorrow. ~**dos tres días** after three days. ~**dor** *m* bolt; (*de pelo*) hair-slide

pasaje *m* passage; (*pasajeros*) passengers; (*LAm, de avión etc*) ticket. ~**ro** *adj* passing. ● *m* passenger

pasamano(s) *m* handrail; (*barandilla de escalera*) banister(s)

pasamontañas *m invar* balaclava

pasaporte *m* passport

pasar *vt* pass; (*atravesar*) go through; (*filtrar*) strain; spend (tiempo); show (película); (*tolerar*) tolerate; give (mensaje, enfermedad). ● *vi* pass; (*suceder*) happen; (ir) go; (*venir*) come; (tiempo) go by. ~ **de** have no interest in. ~**lo bien** have a good time. ~ **frío** be cold. ~ **la aspiradora** vacuum. ~ **por alto** leave out. **lo que pasa es que** the fact is that. **pase lo que pase** whatever happens. **¡pase Vd!** come in!, go in! **¡que lo pases bien!** have a good time! **¿qué pasa?** what's the matter?, what's happening? ~**se** *vpr* pass; (dolor) go away; (flores) wither; (comida) go bad; spend (tiempo); (*excederse*) go too far

pasarela *f* footbridge; (*Naut*) gangway

pasatiempo *m* hobby, pastime

Pascua *f* (*fiesta de los hebreos*) Passover; (*de Resurrección*) Easter; (*Navidad*) Christmas. ~**s** *fpl* Christmas

pase *m* pass

pase|ante *m & f* passer-by. ~**ar** *vt* walk (perro); (*exhibir*) show off. ● *vi* walk.

ir a ∼ar, salir a ∼ar walk. ∼arse vpr walk. ∼o m walk; (en coche etc) ride; (calle) avenue. ∼o marítimo promenade. dar un ∼o, ir de ∼ go for a walk. ¡vete a ∼o! 🆒 get lost! 🆒

pasillo m corridor; (de cine, avión) aisle

pasión f passion

pasivo adj passive

pasm|ar vt astonish. ∼arse vpr be astonished

paso m step; (acción de pasar) passing; (camino) way; (entre montañas) pass; (estrecho) strait(s). ∼ a nivel level crossing (Brit), grade crossing (Amer). ∼ de cebra zebra crossing. ∼ de peatones pedestrian crossing. ∼ elevado flyover (Brit), overpass (Amer). a cada ∼ at every turn. a dos ∼s very near. de ∼ in passing. de ∼ por just passing through. oír ∼s hear footsteps. prohibido el ∼ no entry

pasota m & f drop-out

pasta f paste; (masa) dough; (sl, dinero) dough 🆒. ∼s fpl pasta; (pasteles) pastries. ∼ de dientes, ∼ dentífrica toothpaste

pastel m cake; (empanada) pie; (lápiz) pastel. ∼ería f cake shop

pasteurizado adj pasteurized

pastilla f pastille; (de jabón) bar; (de chocolate) piece

pasto m pasture; (hierba) grass; (LAm, césped) lawn. ∼r m shepherd; (Relig) minister. ∼ra f shepherdess

pata f leg; (pie de perro, gato) paw; (de ave) foot. ∼s arriba upside down. a cuatro ∼s on all fours. meter la ∼ put one's foot in it. tener mala ∼ have bad luck. ∼da f kick. ∼lear vi stamp one's feet; (niño) kick

patata f potato. ∼s fritas chips (Brit), French fries (Amer); (de bolsa) (potato) crisps (Brit), (potato) chips (Amer)

patente adj obvious. ● f licence

patern|al adj paternal; (cariño etc) fatherly. ∼idad f paternity. ∼o adj paternal; (cariño etc) fatherly

patético adj moving

patillas fpl sideburns

patín m skate; (con ruedas) roller skate. patines en línea Rollerblades (P)

patina|dor m skater. ∼je m skating. ∼r vi skate; (resbalar) slide; (coche) skid

patio m patio. ∼ de butacas stalls (Brit), orchestra (Amer)

pato m duck

patológico adj pathological

patoso adj clumsy

patraña f hoax

patria f homeland

patriarca m patriarch

patrimonio m patrimony; (fig) heritage

patri|ota adj patriotic. ● m & f patriot. ∼otismo m patriotism

patrocin|ar vt sponsor. ∼io m sponsorship

patrón m (jefe) boss; (de pensión etc) landlord; (en costura) pattern

patrulla f patrol; (fig, cuadrilla) group. ∼r vt/i patrol

pausa f pause. ∼do adj slow

pauta f guideline

paviment|ar vt pave. ∼o m pavement

pavo m turkey. ∼ real peacock

pavor m terror

payas|ada f buffoonery. ∼o m clown

paz f peace

peaje m toll

peatón m pedestrian

peca f freckle

peca|do m sin; (defecto) fault. ∼dor m sinner. ∼minoso adj sinful. ∼r 🔢 vi sin

pech|o m chest; (de mujer) breast; (fig, corazón) heart. dar el ∼o a un niño breast-feed a child. tomar a ∼o take to heart. ∼uga f breast

pecoso adj freckled

peculiar adj peculiar, particular. ∼idad f peculiarity

pedal m pedal. ∼ear vi pedal

pedante adj pedantic

pedazo m piece, bit. a ∼s in pieces. hacer(se) ∼s smash

pediatra m & f paediatrician

pedicuro m chiropodist

pedi|do m order; (LAm, solicitud) request. ∼r 🔢 vt ask for; (Com, en restaurante) order. ● vi ask. ∼r prestado borrow

pega|dizo adj catchy. **~joso** adj sticky

pega|mento m glue. **~r** 12 vt stick (on); (coser) sew on; give (enfermedad etc); (juntar) join; (golpear) hit; (dar) give. **~r fuego a** set fire to ● vi stick. **~rse** vpr stick; (pelearse) hit each other. **~tina** f sticker

pein|ado m hairstyle. **~ar** vt comb. **~arse** vpr comb one's hair. **~e** m comb. **~eta** f ornamental comb

p.ej. abrev (por ejemplo) e.g.

pelado adj (fruta) peeled; (cabeza) bald; (terreno) bare

pela|je m (de animal) fur; (fig, aspecto) appearance. **~mbre** m (de animal) fur; (de persona) thick hair

pelar vt peel; shell (habas); skin (tomates); pluck (ave)

peldaño m step; (de escalera de mano) rung

pelea f fight; (discusión) quarrel. **~r** vi fight; (discutir) quarrel. **~rse** vpr fight; (discutir) quarrel

peletería f fur shop

peliagudo adj difficult, tricky

pelícano m pelican

película f film (esp Brit), movie (esp Amer). **~ de dibujos animados** cartoon (film)

peligro m danger; (riesgo) hazard, risk. **poner en ~** endanger. **~so** adj dangerous

pelirrojo adj red-haired

pellejo m skin

pellizc|ar 7 vt pinch. **~o** m pinch

pelma m & f, **pelmazo** m bore, nuisance

pelo m hair. **no tener ~s en la lengua** be outspoken. **tomar el ~ a uno** pull s.o.'s leg

pelota f ball. **~ vasca** pelota. **hacer la ~ a uno** suck up to s.o.

pelotera f squabble

peluca f wig

peludo adj hairy

peluquer|ía f hairdresser's. **~o** m hairdresser

pelusa f down

pena f sadness; (lástima) pity; (LAm, vergüenza) embarrassment; (Jund) sentence. **~ de muerte** death pen-

alty. **a duras ~s** with difficulty. **da ~ que** it's a pity that. **me da ~** it makes me sad. **merecer la ~** be worthwhile. **pasar ~s** suffer hardship. **¡qué ~!** what a pity! **valer la ~** be worthwhile

penal adj penal; (derecho) criminal. ● m prison; (LAm, penalty) penalty. **~idad** f suffering; (Jurid) penalty. **~ty** m penalty

pendiente adj hanging; (cuenta) outstanding; (asunto etc) pending. ● m earring. ● f slope

péndulo m pendulum

pene m penis

penetra|nte adj penetrating; (sonido) piercing; (viento) bitter. **~r** vt penetrate; (fig) pierce. ● vi. **~r en** penetrate; (entrar) go into

penicilina f penicillin

pen|ínsula f peninsula. **~insular** adj peninsular

penique m penny

penitencia f penitence; (castigo) penance

penoso adj painful; (difícil) difficult; (LAm, tímido) shy; (l Am, embarazoso) embarrassing

pensa|do adj. **bien ~do** all things considered. **menos ~do** least expected. **~dor** m thinker. **~miento** m thought. **~r** 1 vt think; (considerar) consider. **cuando menos se piensa** when least expected. **¡ni ~rlo!** no way! **pienso que sí** I think so. ● vi think. **~r en** think about. **~tivo** adj thoughtful

pensi|ón f pension; (casa de huéspedes) guest-house. **~ón completa** full board. **~onista** m & f pensioner; (huésped) lodger

penúltimo adj & m penultimate, last but one

penumbra f half-light

penuria f shortage. **pasar ~s** suffer hardship

peñ|a f rock; (de amigos) group; (LAm, club) folk club. **~ón** m rock. **el P~ón de Gibraltar** The Rock (of Gibraltar)

peón m labourer; (en ajedrez) pawn; (en damas) piece

peonza f (spinning) top

p

peor adj (comparativo) worse; (superlativo) worst. ● adv worse. **de mal en** ~ from bad to worse. **lo** ~ the worst thing. **tanto** ~ so much the worse

pepin|illo m gherkin. ~**o** m cucumber. **(no) me importa un** ~**o** I couldn't care less

pepita f pip; (de oro) nugget

pequeñ|ez f smallness; (minucia) trifle. ~**o** adj small, little; (de edad) young; (menor) younger. ● m little one. **es el** ~**o** he's the youngest

pera f (fruta) pear. ~**l** m pear (tree)

percance m mishap

percatarse vpr. ~ **de** notice

perc|epción f perception. ~**ibir** vt perceive; earn (dinero)

percha f hanger; (de aves) perch

percusión f percussion

perde|dor adj losing. ● m loser. ~**r** ① vt lose; (malgastar) waste; miss (tren etc). ● vi lose. ~**rse** vpr get lost; (desaparecer) disappear; (desperdiciarse) be wasted; (estropearse) be spoilt. **echar(se) a** ~**r** spoil

pérdida f loss; (de líquido) leak; (de tiempo) waste

perdido adj lost

perdiz f partridge

perd|ón m pardon, forgiveness. **pedir** ~**ón** apologize. ● int sorry! ~**onar** vt excuse, forgive; (Jurid) pardon. **¡**~**one (Vd)!** sorry!

perdura|ble adj lasting. ~**r** vi last

perece|dero adj perishable. ~**r** ⑪ vi perish

peregrin|ación f pilgrimage. ~**o** adj strange. ● m pilgrim

perejil m parsley

perengano m so-and-so

perenne adj everlasting; (planta) perennial

perez|a f laziness. ~**oso** adj lazy

perfec|ción f perfection. **a la** ~**ción** perfectly, to perfection. ~**cionar** vt perfect; (mejorar) improve. ~**cionista** m & f perfectionist. ~**to** adj perfect; (completo) complete

perfil m profile; (contorno) outline. ~**ado** adj well-shaped

perfora|ción f perforation. ~**dora** f punch. ~**r** vt pierce, perforate; punch (papel, tarjeta etc)

perfum|ar vt perfume. ~**arse** vpr put perfume on. ~**e** m perfume, scent. ~**eria** f perfumery

pericia f skill

perif|eria f (de ciudad) outskirts. ~**érico** adj (barrio) outlying. ● m (Mex, carretera) ring road

perilla f (barba) goatee

perímetro m perimeter

periódico adj periodic(al). ● m newspaper

periodis|mo m journalism. ~**ta** m & f journalist

período m, **periodo** m period

periquito m budgerigar

periscopio m periscope

perito adj & m expert

perju|dicar ⑦ vt damage; (desfavorecer) not suit. ~**dicial** adj damaging. ~**icio** m damage. **en** ~**icio de** to the detriment of

perla f pearl. **de** ~**s** adv very well

permane|cer ⑪ vi remain. ~**ncia** f permanence; (estancia) stay. ~**nte** adj permanent. ● f perm. ● m (Mex) perm

permi|sivo adj permissive. ~**so** m permission; (documento) licence; (Mil etc) leave. ~**so de conducir** driving licence (Brit), driver's license (Amer). **con** ~**so** excuse me. ~**tir** vt allow, permit. **¿me** ~**te?** may I? ~**tirse** vpr allow s.o.

pernicioso adj pernicious; (persona) wicked

perno m bolt

pero conj but. ● m fault; (objeción) objection

perogrullada f platitude

perpendicular adj & f perpendicular

perpetrar vt perpetrate

perpetu|ar ㉑ vt perpetuate. ~**o** adj perpetual

perplejo adj perplexed

perr|a f (animal) bitch; (moneda) coin, penny (Brit), cent (Amer); (rabieta) tantrum. **estar sin una** ~**a** be broke. ~**era** f dog pound; (vehículo) dog catcher's van. ~**o** adj awful. ● m dog. ~**o galgo** greyhound. **de** ~**os** awful

persa *adj & m & f* Persian

perse|cución *f* pursuit; (*política etc*) persecution. ~**guir** 5 & 13 *vt* pursue; (*por ideología etc*) persecute

persevera|nte *adj* persevering. ~**r** *vi* persevere

persiana *f* blind; (*LAm, contraventana*) shutter

persignarse *vpr* cross o.s.

persist|ente *adj* persistent. ~**ir** *vi* persist

person|a *f* person. ~**as** *fpl* people. ~**aje** *m* (*persona importante*) important figure; (*de obra literaria*) character. ~**al** *adj* personal. ● *m* staff. ~**alidad** *f* personality. ~**arse** *vpr* appear in person. ~**ificar** 7 *vt* personify

perspectiva *f* perspective

perspica|cia *f* shrewdness; (*de vista*) keen eyesight. ~**z** *adj* shrewd; (vista) keen

persua|dir *vt* persuade. ~**sión** *f* persuasion. ~**sivo** *adj* persuasive

pertenecer 11 *vi* belong

pértiga *f* pole. **salto** *m* **con** ~ pole vault

pertinente *adj* relevant

perturba|ción *f* disturbance. ~**ción del orden público** breach of the peace. ~**r** *vt* disturb; disrupt (orden)

Perú *m*. **el** ~ Peru

peruano *adj & m* Peruvian

perver|so *adj* evil. ● *m* evil person. ~**tir** 4 *vt* pervert

pesa *f* weight. ~**dez** *f* weight; (*de cabeza etc*) heaviness; (*lentitud*) sluggishness; (*cualidad de fastidioso*) tediousness; (*cosa fastidiosa*) bore, nuisance

pesadilla *f* nightmare

pesado *adj* heavy; (*sueño*) deep; (*viaje*) tiring; (*duro*) hard; (*aburrido*) boring, tedious

pésame *m* sympathy, condolences

pesar *vt* weigh. ● *vi* be heavy. ● *m* sorrow; (*remordimiento*) regret. **a** ~ **de (que)** in spite of. **pese a (que)** in spite of

pesca *f* fishing; (*peces*) fish; (*pescado*) catch. **ir de** ~ go fishing. ~**da** *f* hake. ~**dería** *f* fish shop. ~**dilla** *f* whiting. ~**do** *m* fish. ~**dor** *adj* fishing. ● *m* fisherman. ~**r** 7 *vt* catch. ● *vi* fish

pescuezo *m* neck

pesebre *m* manger

pesero *m* (*Mex*) minibus

peseta *f* peseta

pesimista *adj* pessimistic. ● *m & f* pessimist

pésimo *adj* very bad, awful

peso *m* weight; (*moneda*) peso. ~ **bruto** gross weight. ~ **neto** net weight. **al** ~ by weight. **de** ~ influential

pesquero *adj* fishing

pestañ|a *f* eyelash. ~**ear** *vi* blink

pest|e *f* plague; (*hedor*) stench. ~**icida** *m* pesticide

pestillo *m* bolt; (*de cerradura*) latch

petaca *f* cigarette case; (*Mex, maleta*) suitcase

pétalo *m* petal

petardo *m* firecracker

petición *f* request; (*escrito*) petition

petirrojo *m* robin

petrificar 7 *vt* petrify

petr|óleo *m* oil. ~**olero** *adj* oil. ● *m* oil tanker

petulante *adj* smug

peyorativo *adj* pejorative

pez *f* fish; (*substancia negruzca*) pitch. ~ **espada** swordfish

pezón *m* nipple

pezuña *f* hoof

piadoso *adj* compassionate; (*devoto*) devout

pian|ista *m & f* pianist. ~**o** *m* piano. ~**o de cola** grand piano

piar 20 *vi* chirp

picad|a *f*. **caer en** ~**a** (*LAm*) nosedive. ~**o** *adj* perforated; (*carne*) minced (*Brit*), ground (*Amer*); (*ofendido*) offended; (*mar*) choppy; (*diente*) bad. ● *m*. **caer en** ~**o** nosedive. ~**ura** *f* bite, sting; (*de polilla*) moth hole

picaflor *m* (*LAm*) hummingbird

picante *adj* hot; (*chiste etc*) risqué

picaporte *m* door-handle; (*aldaba*) knocker

picar 7 *vt* (*ave*) peck; (*insecto, pez*) bite; (*abeja, avispa*) sting; (*comer poco*) pick at; mince (*Brit*), grind

p

picardía | **pista**

(*Amer*) (*carne*); chop (up) (cebolla etc); (*Mex, pinchar*) prick. ● *vi* itch; (*ave*) peck; (*insecto, pez*) bite; (*sol*) scorch; (*comida*) be hot

picardía *f* craftiness; (*travesura*) naughty thing

pícaro *adj* crafty; (*niño*) mischievous. ● *m* rogue

picazón *f* itch

pichón *m* pigeon; (*Mex, novato*) beginner

pico *m* beak; (*punta*) corner; (*herramienta*) pickaxe; (*cima*) peak. **y ~** (*con tiempo*) a little after; (*con cantidad*) a little more than. **~tear** *vt* peck; (*fam, comer*) pick at

picudo *adj* pointed

pido *vb véase* **PEDIR**

pie *m* foot; (*Bot, de vaso*) stem. **~ cuadrado** square foot. **a cuatro ~s** on all fours. **al ~ de la letra** literally. **a ~ on foot. a ~(s) juntillas** (*fig*) firmly. **buscarle tres ~s al gato** split hairs. **de ~** standing (up). **de ~s a cabeza** from head to toe. **en ~** standing (up). **ponerse de ~** stand up

piedad *f* pity; (*Relig*) piety

piedra *f* stone; (*de mechero*) flint

piel *f* skin; (*cuero*) leather

pienso *vb véase* **PENSAR**

pierdo *vb véase* **PERDER**

pierna *f* leg

pieza *f* piece; (*parte*) part; (*obra teatral*) play; (*moneda*) coin; (*habitación*) room. **~ de recambio** spare part

pijama *m* pyjamas

pila *f* (*montón*) pile; (*recipiente*) basin; (*eléctrica*) battery. **~ bautismal** font. **~r** *m* pillar

píldora *f* pill

pilla|je *m* pillage. **~r** *vt* catch

pillo *adj* wicked. ● *m* rogue

pilot|ar *vt* pilot. **~o** *m* pilot

pim|entero *m* (*vasija*) pepperpot. **~entón** *m* paprika; (*LAm, fruto*) pepper. **~ienta** *f* pepper. **grano** *m* **de ~ienta** peppercorn. **~iento** *m* pepper

pináculo *m* pinnacle

pinar *m* pine forest

pincel *m* paintbrush. **~ada** *f* brushstroke. **la última ~ada** (*fig*) the finishing touch

pinch|ar *vt* pierce, prick; puncture (*neumático*); (*fig, incitar*) push; (*Med, fam*) give an injection to. **~azo** *m* prick; (*en neumático*) puncture. **~itos** *mpl* kebab(s); (*tapas*) savoury snacks. **~o** *m* point

ping-pong *m* table tennis, pingpong

pingüino *m* penguin

pino *m* pine (tree)

pint|a *f* spot; (*fig, aspecto*) appearance. **tener ~a de** look like. **~ada** *f* graffiti. **~ar** *vt* paint. **no ~a nada** (*fig*) it doesn't count. **~arse** *vpr* put on make-up. **~or** *m* painter. **~oresco** *adj* picturesque. **~ura** *f* painting; (*material*) paint

pinza *f* (clothes-)peg (*Brit*), clothespin (*Amer*); (*de cangrejo etc*) claw. **~s** *fpl* tweezers

piñ|a *f* pine cone; (*fruta*) pineapple. **~ón** *m* (*semilla*) pine nut

pío *adj* pious. ● *m* chirp. **no decir ni ~** not say a word

piojo *m* louse

pionero *m* pioneer

pipa *f* pipe; (*semilla*) seed; (*de girasol*) sunflower seed

pique *m* resentment; (*rivalidad*) rivalry. **irse a ~** sink

piquete *m* picket; (*Mex, herida*) prick; (*Mex, de insecto*) sting

piragua *f* canoe

pirámide *f* pyramid

pirata *adj invar* pirate. ● *m & f* pirate

Pirineos *mpl*. **los ~** the Pyrenees

piropo *m* flattering comment

pirueta *f* pirouette

pirulí *m* lollipop

pisa|da *f* footstep; (*huella*) footprint. **~papeles** *m invar* paperweight. **~r** *vt* tread on. ● *vi* tread

piscina *f* swimming pool

Piscis *m* Pisces

piso *m* floor; (*vivienda*) flat (*Brit*), apartment (*Amer*); (*de autobús*) deck

pisotear *vt* trample (on)

pista *f* track; (*fig, indicio*) clue. **~ de aterrizaje** runway. **~ de baile** dance floor. ~ **de carreras** racing track. ~ **de hielo** ice-rink. ~ **de tenis** tennis court

pistol|a f pistol. ~**era** f holster. ~**ero** m gunman

pistón m piston

pit|ar, (LAm) ~**ear** vt whistle at; (conductor) hoot at; award (falta). ● vi blow a whistle; (Auto) sound one's horn. ~**ido** m whistle

pitill|era f cigarette case. ~**o** m cigarette

pito m whistle; (Auto) horn

pitón m python

pitorre|arse vpr. ~**arse de** make fun of. ~**o** m teasing

pitorro m spout

piyama m (LAm) pyjamas

pizarr|a f slate; (en aula) blackboard. ~**ón** m (LAm) blackboard

pizca f 🔟 tiny piece; (de sal) pinch. **ni** ~ not at all

placa f plate; (con inscripción) plaque; (distintivo) badge. ~ **de matrícula** number plate

place|ntero adj pleasant. ~**r** 🟥 vi. **haz lo que te plazca** do as you please. **me** ~ **hacerlo** I'm pleased to do it. ● m pleasure

plácido adj placid

plaga f (also fig) plague. ~**do** adj. ~**do de** filled with

plagio m plagiarism

plan m plan. **en** ~ **de** as

plana f page. **en primera** ~ on the front page

plancha f iron; (lámina) sheet. **a la** ~ grilled. **tirarse una** ~ put one's foot in it. ~**do** m ironing. ~**r** vt iron. ● vi do the ironing

planeador m glider

planear vt plan. ● vi glide

planeta m planet

planicie f plain

planifica|ción f planning. ~**r** 🟥 vt plan

planilla f (LAm) payroll; (personal) staff

plano adj flat. ● m plane; (de edificio) plan; (de ciudad) street plan. **primer** ~ foreground; (Foto) close-up

planta f (del pie) sole; (en botánica, fábrica) plant; (plano) ground plan; (piso) floor. ~ **baja** ground floor (Brit), first floor (Amer)

planta|ción f plantation. ~**r** vt plant; deal (golpe). ~**r en la calle** throw out. ~**rse** vpr stand; (fig) stand firm

plantear vt (exponer) expound; (causar) create; raise (cuestión)

plantilla f insole; (nómina) payroll; (personal) personnel

plaqué m plating. **de** ~ plated

plástico adj & m plastic

plata f silver; (fig, fam, dinero) money. ~ **de ley** hallmarked silver

plataforma f platform

platano m plane (tree); (fruta) banana. **platanero** m banana tree

platea f stalls (Brit), orchestra (Amer)

plateado adj silver-plated; (color de plata) silver

pl|ática f talk. ~**aticar** 🟥 vi (Mex) talk. ● vt (Mex) tell

platija f plaice

platillo m saucer; (Mus) cymbal. ~ **volador** (LAm), ~ **volante** flying saucer

platino m platinum. ~**s** mpl (Auto) points

plato m plate; (comida) dish; (parte de una comida) course

platónico adj platonic

playa f beach; (fig) seaside

plaza f square; (mercado) market (place); (sitio) place; (empleo) job. ~ **de toros** bullring

plazco vb véase **PLACER**

plazo m period; (pago) instalment; (fecha) date. **comprar a** ~**s** buy on hire purchase (Brit), buy on the installment plan (Amer)

plazuela f little square

pleamar f high tide

pleb|e f common people. ~**eyo** adj & m plebeian. ~**iscito** m plebiscite

plega|ble adj pliable; (silla) folding. ~**r** 🟦 & 🟥 vt fold. ~**rse** vpr bend; (fig) yield

pleito m (court) case; (fig) dispute

plenilunio m full moon

plen|itud f fullness; (fig) height. ~**o** adj full. **en** ~**o día** in broad daylight.

p

en ~o verano at the height of the summer

plieg|o *m* sheet. **~ue** *m* fold; (*en ropa*) pleat

plisar *vt* pleat

plom|ero *m* (*LAm*) plumber. **~o** *m* lead; (*Elec*) fuse. **con ~o** leaded. **sin ~o** unleaded

pluma *f* feather; (*para escribir*) pen. **~ atómica** (*Mex*) ballpoint pen. **~ estilográfica** fountain pen. **~je** *m* plumage

plum|ero *m* feather duster; (*para plumas, lápices etc*) pencil-case. **~ón** *m* down; (*edredón*) down-filled quilt

plural *adj & m* plural. **en ~** in the plural

pluri|empleo *m* having more than one job. **~partidismo** *m* multi-party system. **~étnico** *adj* multiethnic

plus *m* bonus

pluscuamperfecto *m* pluperfect

plusvalía *f* capital gain

pluvial *adj* rain

pobla|ción *f* population; (*ciudad*) city, town; (*pueblo*) village. **~do** *adj* populated. ● *m* village. **~r** **2** *vt* populate; (*habitar*) inhabit. **~rse** *vpr* get crowded

pobre *adj* poor. ● *m & f* poor person; (*fig*) poor thing. **¡~cito!** poor (little) thing! **¡~ de mí!** poor (old) me! **~za** *f* poverty

pocilga *f* pigsty

poción *f* potion

poco

● *adjetivo/pronombre*

····▸ **poco, poca** little, not much. **tiene poca paciencia** he has little patience. **¿cuánta leche queda? - poca** how much milk is there left? - not much

····▸ **pocos, pocas** few. **muy ~s días** very few days. **unos ~s dólares** a few dollars. **compré unos ~s** I bought a few. **aceptaron a muy ~s** very few (people) were accepted

····▸ **a ~ de llegar** soon after he arrived. **¡a ~!** (*Mex*) really? **dentro de ~** soon. **~ a ~**, (*LAm*) **de a ~** gradually, little by little.

hace ~ recently, not long ago. **por ~** nearly. **un ~** (*cantidad*) a little; (*tiempo*) a while. **un ~ de** a (little) bit of, a little, some

● *adverbio*

····▸ (*con verbo*) not much. **lee muy ~** he doesn't read very much

····▸ (*con adjetivo*) **un lugar ~ conocido** a little known place. **es ~ inteligente** he's not very intelligent

> **!** Cuando **poco** modifica a un adjetivo, muchas veces el inglés prefiere el uso del prefijo un-, p. ej. **poco amistoso** *unfriendly*. **poco agradecido** *ungrateful*

podar *vt* prune

poder **33** *verbo auxiliar* be able to. **no voy a ~ terminar** I won't be able to finish. **no pudo venir** he couldn't come. **¿puedo hacer algo?** can I do anything? **¿puedo pasar?** may I come in? **no ~ con** not be able to cope with; (*no aguantar*) not be able to stand. **no ~ más** be exhausted; (*estar harto de algo*) not be able to manage any more. **no ~ menos que** have no alternative but. **puede que** it is possible that. **puede ser** it is possible. **¿se puede ...?** may I...? ● *m* power. **en el ~** in power. **~es públicos** authorities. **~oso** *adj* powerful

podrido *adj* rotten

po|ema *m* poem. **~esía** *f* poetry; (*poema*) poem. **~eta** *m & f* poet. **~ético** *adj* poetic

polaco *adj* Polish. ● *m* Pole; (*lengua*) Polish

polar *adj* polar. **estrella ~** polestar

polea *f* pulley

pol|émica *f* controversy. **~emizar** **10** *vi* argue

polen *m* pollen

policía *f* police (force); (*persona*) policewoman. ● *m* policeman. **~co** *adj* police; (*novela etc*) detective

policromo *adj*, **polícromo** *adj* polychrome

polideportivo *m* sports centre

polietileno *m* polythene

poligamia *f* polygamy

polígono *m* polygon

polilla *f* moth

polio(mielitis) *f* polio(myelitis)

polític|a *f* politics; (*postura*) policy; (*mujer*) politician. **~ interior** domestic policy. **~o** *adj* political. **familia ~a** in-laws. ● *m* politician

póliza *f* (*de seguros*) policy

poll|o *m* chicken; (*gallo joven*) chick. **~uelo** *m* chick

polo *m* pole; (*helado*) ice lolly (*Brit*), Popsicle (P) (*Amer*); (*juego*) polo. **P~ norte** North Pole

Polonia *f* Poland

poltrona *f* armchair

polución *f* pollution

polv|areda *f* dust cloud; (*fig, escándalo*) uproar. **~era** *f* compact. **~o** *m* powder; (*suciedad*) dust. **~os** *mpl* powder. **en ~o** powdered. **estar hecho ~o** be exhausted. **quitar el ~o** dust

pólvora *f* gunpowder; (*fuegos artificiales*) fireworks

polvoriento *adj* dusty

pomada *f* ointment

pomelo *m* grapefruit

pómez *adj*. **piedra *f* ~** pumice stone

pomp|a *f* bubble; (*esplendor*) pomp. **~as fúnebres** funeral. **~oso** *adj* pompous; (*espléndido*) splendid

pómulo *m* cheekbone

ponchar *vt* (*Mex*) puncture

ponche *m* punch

poncho *m* poncho

ponderar *vt* (*alabar*) speak highly of

poner **34** *vt* put; put on (ropa, obra de teatro, TV etc); lay (la mesa, un huevo); set (examen, deberes); (*contribuir*) contribute; give (nombre); make (nervioso); pay (atención); show (película, interés); open (una tienda); equip (una casa). **~ con** (*al teléfono*) put through to. **~ por escrito** put into writing. **~ una multa** fine. **pongamos** let's suppose. ● *vi* lay. **~se** *vpr* put o.s.; (*volverse*) get; put on (ropa); (sol) set. **~se a** start to. **~se a mal con uno** fall out with s.o.

pongo *vb véase* **PONER**

poniente *m* west; (*viento*) west wind

pont|ificar **7** *vi* pontificate. **~ífice** *m* pontiff

popa *f* stern

popote *m* (*Mex*) (drinking) straw

popul|acho *m* masses. **~ar** *adj* popular; (*costumbre*) traditional; (*lenguaje*) colloquial. **~aridad** *f* popularity. **~arizar** **10** *vt* popularize.

póquer *m* poker

poquito *m*. **un ~** a little bit. ● *adv* a little

---

por *preposición*

····▸ for. **es ~ tu bien** it's for your own good. **lo compró por 5 dólares** he bought it for 5 dollars. **si no fuera por ti** if it weren't for you. **vino por una semana** he came for a week

⟹ Para expresiones como **por la mañana, por la noche** etc., ver bajo el respectivo nombre

····▸ (*causa*) because of. **se retrasó ~ la lluvia** he was late because of the rain. **no hay trenes ~ la huelga** there aren't any trains because of the strike

····▸ (*medio, agente*) by. **lo envié ~ correo** I sent it by post. **fue destruida ~ las bombas** it was destroyed by the bombs

····▸ (*a través de*) through. **entró ~ la ventana** he got in through the window. **me enteré ~ un amigo** I found out through a friend. **~ todo el país** throughout the country

····▸ (*a lo largo de*) along. **caminar ~ la playa** to walk along the beach. **cortar ~ la línea de puntos** cut along the dotted line

····▸ (*proporción*) per. **cobra 30 dólares ~ hora** he charges 30 dollars per hour. **uno ~ persona** one per person. **10 ~ ciento** 10 per cent

····▸ (*Mat*) times. **dos ~ dos (son) cuatro** two times two is four

····▸ (*modo*) in. **~ escrito** in

writing. **pagar** ~ **adelantado** to pay in advance

➡️ Para expresiones como **por dentro, por fuera** etc., ver bajo el respectivo adverbio

····▶ (en locuciones) ~ **más que** no matter how much. ¿~ **qué?** why? ~ **si** in case. ~ **supuesto** of course

porcelana f china
porcentaje m percentage
porcino adj pig
porción f portion; (de chocolate) piece
pordiosero m beggar
porfia|do adj stubborn. ~**r** 20 vi insist
pormenor m detail
pornogr|afia f pornography. ~**áfico** adj pornographic
poro m pore; (Mex, puerro) leek. ~**so** adj porous
porque conj because; (para que) so that
porqué m reason
porquería f filth; (basura) rubbish; (grosería) dirty trick
porra f club
porrón m wine jug (with a long spout)
portaaviones m invar aircraft carrier
portada f (de libro) title page; (de revista) cover
portadocumentos m invar (LAm) briefcase
portador m bearer
portaequipaje(s) m invar boot (Brit), trunk (Amer); (encima del coche) roof-rack
portal m hall; (puerta principal) main entrance. ~**es** mpl arcade
porta|ligas m invar suspender belt. ~**monedas** m invar purse
portarse vpr behave
portátil adj portable. ● m portable computer, laptop
portavoz m spokesman. ● f spokeswoman
portazo m bang. **dar un** ~ slam the door
porte m transport; (precio) carriage; (LAm, tamaño) size. ~**ador** m carrier

portento m marvel
porteño adj from Buenos Aires
porter|ía f porter's lodge; (en deportes) goal. ~**o** m caretaker, porter; (en deportes) goalkeeper. ~**o automático** entryphone
pórtico m portico
portorriqueño adj & m Puerto Rican
Portugal m Portugal
portugués adj & m Portuguese
porvenir m future
posada f inn. **dar** ~ give shelter
posar vt put. ● vi pose. ~**se** vpr (pájaro) perch; (avión) land
posdata f postscript
pose|edor m owner; (de récord, billete, etc) holder. ~**r** 18 vt own; hold (récord); have (conocimientos). ~**sión** f possession. ~**sionarse** vpr. ~**sionarse de** take possession of. ~**sivo** adj possessive
posgraduado adj & m postgraduate
posguerra f post-war years
posib|ilidad f possibility. ~**le** adj possible. **de ser** ~**le** if possible. **en lo** ~**le** as far as possible. **si es** ~**le** if possible
posición f position; (en sociedad) social standing
positivo adj positive
poso m sediment
posponer 34 vt put after; (diferir) postpone
posta f. **a** ~ on purpose
postal adj postal. ● f postcard
poste m pole; (de valla) post
póster m (pl ~s) poster
postergar 12 vt pass over; (diferir) postpone
posteri|dad f posterity. ~**or** adj back; (años) later; (capítulos) subsequent. ~**ormente** adv later
postigo m door; (contraventana) shutter
postizo adj false, artificial. ● m hairpiece
postrarse vpr prostrate o.s.
postre m dessert, pudding (Brit)
postular vt postulate; (LAm) nominate (candidato)
póstumo adj posthumous

p

postura f position, stance
potable adj drinkable; (agua) drinking
potaje m vegetable stew
potasio m potassium
pote m pot
poten|cia f power. ∼**cial** adj & m potential. ∼**te** adj powerful
potro m colt; (en gimnasia) horse
pozo m well; (hoyo seco) pit; (de mina) shaft; (fondo común) pool
práctica f practice. **en la** ∼ in practice
practica|nte m & f nurse. ∼**r** 🔢 vt practise; play (deportes); (ejecutar) carry out
práctico adj practical; (conveniente, útil) handy. ● m practitioner
prad|era f meadow; (terreno grande) prairie. ∼**o** m meadow
pragmático adj pragmatic
preámbulo m preamble
precario adj precarious; (medios) scarce
precaución f precaution; (cautela) caution. **con** ∼ cautiously
precaverse vpr take precautions
precede|ncia f precedence; (prioridad) priority. ∼**nte** adj preceding. ● m precedent. ∼**r** vt/i precede
precepto m precept. ∼**r** m tutor
precia|do adj valued; (don) valuable. ∼**rse** vpr. ∼**rse de** pride o.s. on
precio m price. ∼ **de venta al público** retail price. **al** ∼ **de** at the cost of. **no tener** ∼ be priceless. **¿qué** ∼ **tiene?** how much is it?
precios|idad f (cosa preciosa) beautiful thing. **¡es una** ∼**idad!** it's beautiful! ∼**o** adj precious; (bonito) beautiful
precipicio m precipice
precipita|ción f precipitation; (prisa) rush. ∼**damente** adv hastily. ∼**do** adj hasty. ∼**r** vt (apresurar) hasten; (arrojar) hurl. ∼**rse** vpr throw o.s.; (correr) rush; (actuar sin reflexionar) act rashly
precis|amente adv exactly. ∼**ar** vt require; (determinar) determine. ∼**ión** f precision. ∼**o** adj precise; (necesario) necessary. **si es** ∼**o** if necessary
preconcebido adj preconceived

precoz adj early; (niño) precocious
precursor m forerunner
predecesor m predecessor
predecir 46, (pero imperativo **predice**, futuro y condicional regulares) vt foretell
predestinado adj predestined
prédica f sermon
predicar 7 vt/i preach
predicción f prediction; (del tiempo) forecast
predilec|ción f predilection. ∼**to** adj favourite
predisponer 34 vt predispose
predomin|ante adj predominant. ∼**ar** vi predominate. ∼**io** m predominance
preeminente adj pre-eminent
prefabricado adj prefabricated
prefacio m preface
prefer|encia f preference; (Auto) right of way. **de** ∼**encia** preferably. ∼**ente** adj preferential. ∼**ible** adj preferable. ∼**ido** adj favourite. ∼**ir** 4 vt prefer
prefijo m prefix; (telefónico) dialling code
pregonar vt announce
pregunta f question. **hacer una** ∼ ask a question. ∼**r** vt/i ask (**por** about). ∼**rse** vpr wonder
prehistórico adj prehistoric
preju|icio m prejudice. ∼**zgar** 12 vt prejudge
preliminar adj & m preliminary
preludio m prelude
premarital adj, **prematrimonial** adj premarital
prematuro adj premature
premedita|ción f premeditation. ∼**r** vt premeditate
premi|ar vt give a prize to; (recompensar) reward. ∼**o** m prize; (recompensa) reward. ∼**o gordo** jackpot
premonición f premonition
prenatal adj antenatal
prenda f garment; (garantía) surety; (en juegos) forfeit. **en** ∼ **de** as a token of. ∼**r** vt captivate. ∼**rse** vpr fall in love (**de** with)
prende|dor m brooch. ∼**r** vt capture; (sujetar) fasten; light (cigarrillo); (LAm) turn on (gas, radio, etc). ● vi catch;

p

(*arraigar*) take root. ~**rse** *vpr* (*encenderse*) catch fire

prensa *f* press. ~**r** *vt* press

preñado *adj* pregnant; (*fig*) full

preocupa|ción *f* worry. ~**do** *adj* worried. ~**r** *vt* worry. ~**rse** *vpr* worry. ~**rse de** look after

prepara|ción *f* preparation. ~**do** *adj* prepared. • *m* preparation. ~**r** *vt* prepare. ~**rse** *vpr* get ready. ~**tivos** *mpl* preparations. ~**torio** *adj* preparatory

preposición *f* preposition

prepotente *adj* arrogant; (*actitud*) high-handed

prerrogativa *f* prerogative

presa *f* (*cosa*) prey; (*embalse*) dam

presagi|ar *vt* presage. ~**o** *m* omen

presb|iteriano *adj & m* Presbyterian. ~**ítero** *m* priest

prescindir *vi*. ~ **de** do without; (*deshacerse de*) dispense with

prescri|bir (*pp* prescrito) *vt* prescribe. ~**pción** *f* prescription

presencia *f* presence; (*aspecto*) appearance. **en** ~ **de** in the presence of. ~**r** *vt* be present at; (*ver*) witness

presenta|ble *adj* presentable. ~**ción** *f* presentation; (*de una persona a otra*) introduction. ~**dor** *m* presenter. ~**r** *vt* present; (*ofrecer*) offer; (*entregar*) hand in; (*hacer conocer*) introduce; show (película). ~**rse** *vpr* present o.s.; (*hacerse conocer*) introduce o.s.; (*aparecer*) turn up

presente *adj* present; (*actual*) this. • *m* present. **los** ~**s** those present. **tener** ~ remember

presenti|miento *m* premonition. ~**r** 4 *vt* have a feeling (**que** that)

preserva|r *vt* preserve. ~**tivo** *m* condom

presiden|cia *f* presidency; (*de asamblea*) chairmanship. ~**cial** *adj* presidential. ~**ta** *f* (woman) president. ~**te** *m* president; (*de asamblea*) chairman. ~**te del gobierno** prime minister

presidi|ario *m* convict. ~**o** *m* prison

presidir *vt* be president of; preside over (*tribunal*); chair (*reunión, comité*)

presi|ón *f* pressure. **a** ~**ón** under pressure. **hacer** ~**ón** press. ~**onar** *vt* press; (*fig*) put pressure on

preso *adj*. **estar** ~ be in prison. **llevarse** ~ **a uno** take s.o. away under arrest. • *m* prisoner

presta|do *adj* (*de uno*) lent; (*a uno*) borrowed. **pedir** ~**do** borrow. ~**mista** *m & f* moneylender

préstamo *m* loan; (*acción de pedir prestado*) borrowing; (*acción de prestar*) lending

prestar *vt* lend; give (ayuda etc); pay (atención). ~**se** *vpr*. ~**se a** be open to; (*ser apto*) be suitable (**para** for)

prestidigita|ción *f* conjuring. ~**dor** *m* conjurer

prestigio *m* prestige. ~**so** *adj* prestigious

presu|mido *adj* conceited. ~**mir** *vi* show off; boast (**de** about). ~**nción** *f* conceit; (*suposición*) presumption. ~**nto** *adj* alleged. ~**ntuoso** *adj* conceited

presup|oner 34 *vt* presuppose. ~**uesto** *m* budget; (*precio estimado*) estimate

preten|cioso *adj* pretentious. ~**der** *vt* try to; (*afirmar*) claim; (*solicitar*) apply for; (*cortejar*) court. ~**diente** *m* pretender; (*a una mujer*) suitor. ~**sión** *f* pretension; (*aspiración*) aspiration

pretérito *m* preterite, past

pretexto *m* pretext. **con el** ~ **de** on the pretext of

prevalecer 11 *vi* prevail (**sobre** over)

preven|ción *f* prevention; (*prejuicio*) prejudice. ~**ido** *adj* ready; (*precavido*) cautious. ~**ir** 53 *vt* prevent; (*advertir*) warn. ~**tiva** *f* (Mex) amber light. ~**tivo** *adj* preventive

prever 43 *vt* foresee; (*planear*) plan

previo *adj* previous

previs|ible *adj* predictable. ~**ión** *f* forecast; (*prudencia*) precaution

prima *f* (*pariente*) cousin; (*cantidad*) bonus

primario *adj* primary

primavera *f* spring. ~**l** *adj* spring

primer *adj véase* **PRIMERO**. ~**a** *f* (Auto) first (gear); (*en tren etc*) first class.

~**o** *adj* (*delante de nombre masculino en singular* **primer**) first; (*mejor*) best; (*principal*) leading. **la ~a fila** the front row. **lo ~o es** the most important thing is. **~a enseñanza** primary education. **a ~os de** at the beginning of. **de ~a** first-class. • *n* (the) first. • *adv* first

primitivo *adj* primitive

primo *m* cousin; 🔲 fool. **hacer el ~** be taken for a ride

primogénito *adj & m* first-born, eldest

primor *m* delicacy; (*cosa*) beautiful thing

primordial *adj* fundamental; (*interés*) paramount

princesa *f* princess

principal *adj* main. **lo ~ es que** the main thing is that

príncipe *m* prince

principi|ante *m & f* beginner. **~o** *m* beginning; (*moral, idea*) principle; (*origen*) origin. **al ~o** at first. **a ~o(s) de** at the beginning of. **desde el ~o** from the start. **en ~o** in principle. **~os** *mpl* (*nociones*) rudiments

prión *m* prion

prioridad *f* priority

prisa *f* hurry, haste. **darse ~** hurry (up). **de ~** quickly. **tener ~** be in a hurry

prisi|ón *f* prison; (*encarcelamiento*) imprisonment. **~onero** *m* prisoner

prismáticos *mpl* binoculars

priva|ción *f* deprivation. **~da** *f* (*Mex*) private road. **~do** *adj* (*particular*) private. **~r** *vt* deprive (**de** of). **~tivo** *adj* exclusive (**de** to)

privilegi|ado *adj* privileged; (*muy bueno*) exceptional. **~o** *m* privilege

pro *prep.* **en ~ de** for, in favour of. • *m* advantage. **los ~s y los contras** the pros and cons

proa *f* bow

probab|ilidad *f* probability. **~le** *adj* probable, likely. **~lemente** *adv* probably

proba|dor *m* fitting-room. **~r** 2 *vt* try; try on (*ropa*); (*demostrar*) prove. • *vi* try. **~rse** *vpr* try on

probeta *f* test-tube

problema *m* problem. **hacerse ~as** (*LAm*) worry

procaz *adj* indecent

proced|encia *f* origin. **~ente** *adj* (*razonable*) reasonable. **~ente de** (*coming*) from. **~er** *m* conduct. • *vi* proceed. **~er contra** start legal proceedings against. **~er de** come from. **~imiento** *m* procedure; (*sistema*) process; (*Jurid*) proceedings

proces|ador *m*. **~ de textos** word processor. **~al** *adj* procedural. **costas ~ales** legal costs. **~amiento** *m* processing; (*Jurid*) prosecution. **~amiento de textos** word-processing.. **~ar** *vt* process; (*Jurid*) prosecute

procesión *f* procession

proceso *m* process; (*Jurid*) trial; (*transcurso*) course

proclamar *vt* proclaim

procrea|ción *f* procreation. **~r** *vt* procreate

procura|dor *m* attorney, solicitor; (*asistente*) clerk (*Brit*), paralegal (*Amer*). **~r** *vt* try; (*obtener*) obtain

prodigar 12 *vt* lavish

prodigio *m* prodigy; (*maravilla*) wonder; (*milagro*) miracle. **~so** *adj* prodigious

pródigo *adj* prodigal

produc|ción *f* production. **~ir** 47 *vt* produce; (*causar*) cause. **~irse** *vpr* (*suceder*) happen. **~tivo** *adj* productive. **~to** *m* product. **~tos agrícolas** farm produce. **~tos alimenticios** foodstuffs. **~tos de belleza** cosmetics. **~tos de consumo** consumer goods. **~tor** *m* producer.

proeza *f* exploit

profana|ción *f* desecration. **~ar** *vt* desecrate. **~o** *adj* profane

profecía *f* prophecy

proferir 4 *vt* utter; hurl (*insultos etc*)

profes|ión *f* profession. **~ional** *adj* professional. **~or** *m* teacher; (*en universidad*) lecturer. **~orado** *m* teaching profession; (*conjunto de profesores*) staff

prof|eta *m* prophet. **~etizar** 10 *vt/i* prophesize

prófugo *adj & m* fugitive

p

profund|idad f depth. ~**o** adj deep; (fig) profound. **poco** ~**o** shallow

progenitor m ancestor

programa m programme; (de estudios) syllabus. ~ **concurso** quiz show. ~ **de entrevistas** chat show. ~**ción** f programming; (TV etc) programmes; (en periódico) TV guide. ~**r** vt programme. ~**dor** m computer programmer

progres|ar vi (make) progress. ~**ión** f progression. ~**ista** adj progressive. ~**ivo** adj progressive. ~**o** m progress. **hacer** ~**os** make progress

prohibi|ción f prohibition. ~**do** adj forbidden. **prohibido fumar** no smoking. ~**r** vt forbid. ~**tivo** adj prohibitive

prójimo m fellow man

prole f offspring

proletari|ado m proletariat. ~**o** adj & m proletarian

prol|iferación f proliferation. ~**iferar** vi proliferate. ~**ífico** adj prolific

prolijo adj long-winded

prólogo m prologue

prolongar 🔢 vt prolong; (alargar) lengthen. ~**se** vpr go on

promedio m average. **como** ~ on average

prome|sa f promise. ~**ter** vt promise. ● vi show promise. ~**terse** vpr (novios) get engaged. ~**tida** f fiancée. ~**tido** adj promised; (novios) engaged. ● m fiancé

prominente f prominence

promiscu|idad f promiscuity. ~**o** adj promiscuous

promo|ción f promotion. ~**tor** m promoter. ~**ver** 🔢 vt promote; (causar) cause

promulgar 🔢 vt promulgate

pronombre m pronoun

pron|osticar 🔢 vt predict; forecast (tiempo). ~**óstico** m prediction; (del tiempo) forecast; (Med) prognosis

pront|itud f promptness. ~**o** adj quick. ● adv quickly; (dentro de poco) soon; (temprano) early. **de** ~**o** suddenly. **por lo** ~**o** for the time being. **tan** ~**o como** as soon as

pronuncia|ción f pronunciation. ~**miento** m revolt. ~**r** vt pronounce; deliver (discurso). ~**rse** vpr (declararse) declare o.s.; (sublevarse) rise up

propagación f propagation

propaganda f propaganda; (anuncios) advertising

propagar 🔢 vt/i propagate. ~**se** vpr spread

propasarse vpr go too far

propens|ión f inclination. ~**o** adj inclined

propici|ar vt favour; (provocar) bring about. ~**o** adj favourable

propie|dad f property. ~**tario** m owner

propina f tip

propio adj own; (característico) typical; (natural) natural; (apropiado) proper. **el** ~ **médico** the doctor himself

proponer 🔢 vt propose; put forward (persona). ~**se** vpr. ~**se hacer** intend to do

proporci|ón f proportion. ~**onado** adj proportioned. ~**onal** adj proportional. ~**onar** vt provide

proposición f proposition

propósito m intention. **a** ~ (adrede) on purpose; (de paso) by the way. **a** ~ **de** with regard to

propuesta f proposal

propuls|ar vt propel; (fig) promote. ~**ión** f propulsion. ~**ión a chorro** jet propulsion

prórroga f extension

prorrogar 🔢 vt extend

prosa f prose. ~**ico** adj prosaic

proscri|bir (pp proscrito) vt exile; (prohibir) ban. ~**to** adj banned. ● m exile; (bandido) outlaw

proseguir 🔢 & 🔢 vt/i continue

prospecto m prospectus; (de fármaco) directions for use

prosper|ar vi prosper; (persona) do well. ~**idad** f prosperity

próspero adj prosperous. **¡P~ Año Nuevo!** Happy New Year!

prostit|ución f prostitution. ~**uta** f prostitute

protagonista m & f protagonist

prote|cción f protection. ~**ctor** adj protective. ● m protector; (benefactor) patron. ~**ger** 🔢 vt protect. ~**gida** f protegée. ~**gido** adj protected. ● m protegé

proteína f protein

protesta f protest; (manifestación) demonstration; (Mex, promesa) promise; (Mex, juramento) oath

protestante adj & m & f Protestant

protestar vt/i protest

protocolo m protocol

provecho m benefit. ¡buen ~! enjoy your meal! **de** ~ useful. **en** ~ **de** to the benefit of. **sacar** ~ **de** benefit from

proveer 🔢 (pp proveído y provisto) vt supply, provide

provenir 🔢 vi come (de from)

proverbi|al adj proverbial. ~**o** m proverb

provincia f province. ~**l** adj, ~**no** adj provincial

provisional adj provisional

provisto adj provided (de with)

provoca|ción f provocation. ~**r** 🔢 vt provoke; (causar) cause. ~**tivo** adj provocative

proximidad f proximity

próximo adj next; (cerca) near

proyec|ción f projection. ~**tar** vt hurl; cast (luz); show (película). ~**til** m missile. ~**to** m plan. ~**to de ley** bill. **en** ~**to** planned. ~**tor** m projector

pruden|cia f prudence; (cuidado) caution. ~**te** adj prudent, sensible

prueba f proof; (examen) test; (de ropa) fitting. **a** ~ on trial. **a** ~ **de** proof against. **a** ~ **de agua** waterproof. **poner a** ~ test

pruebo vb véase **PROBAR**

psicoan|álisis f psychoanalysis. ~**alista** m & f psychoanalyst. ~**alizar** 🔟 vt psychoanalyse

psic|ología f psychology. ~**ológico** adj psychological. ~**ólogo** m psychologist. ~**ópata** m & f psychopath. ~**osis** f invar psychosis

psiqu|e f psyche. ~**iatra** m & f psychiatrist. ~**iátrico** adj psychiatric

psíquico adj psychic

ptas, pts abrev (**pesetas**) pesetas

púa f sharp point; (espina) thorn; (de erizo) quill; (de peine) tooth; (Mus) plectrum

pubertad f puberty

publica|ción f publication. ~**r** 🔢 vt publish

publici|dad f publicity; (Com) advertising. ~**tario** adj advertising

público adj public. ● m public; (de espectáculo etc) audience

puchero m cooking pot; (guisado) stew. **hacer** ~**s** (fig, fam) pout

pude vb véase **PODER**

pudor m modesty. ~**oso** adj modest

pudrir (pp podrido) vt rot; (fig, molestar) annoy. ~**se** vpr rot

puebl|ecito m small village. ~**erino** m country bumpkin. ~**o** m town; (aldea) village; (nación) nation, people

puedo vb véase **PODER**

puente m bridge; (fig, fam) long weekend. ~ **colgante** suspension bridge. ~ **levadizo** drawbridge. **hacer** ~ 🔟 have a long weekend

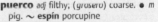

puente Puentes are very important in Spain and Latin America. Hacer Puente means that when a working day falls between two public holidays, it too is taken as a holiday

puerco adj filthy; (grosero) coarse. ● m pig. ~ **espín** porcupine

puerro m leek

puerta f door; (en deportes) goal; (de ciudad, en jardín) gate. ~ **principal** main entrance. **a** ~ **cerrada** behind closed doors

puerto m port; (fig, refugio) refuge; (entre montañas) pass. ~ **franco** free port

puertorriqueño adj & m Puerto Rican

pues adv (entonces) then; (bueno) well. ● conj since

puest|a f setting; (en juegos) bet. ~**a de sol** sunset. ~**a en escena** staging. ~**a en marcha** starting. ~**o** adj put; (vestido) dressed. ● m place;

(*empleo*) position, job; (*en mercado etc*) stall. ● *conj.* ~o que since

pugna *f* struggle. ~r *vi.* ~r por strive to

puja *f* struggle (**por** to); (*en subasta*) bid. ~r *vt* struggle; (*en subasta*) bid

pulcro *adj* neat

pulga *f* flea. **tener malas** ~s be bad-tempered

pulga|da *f* inch. ~r *m* thumb; (*del pie*) big toe

puli|do *adj* polished; (*modales*) refined. ~r *vt* polish; (*suavizar*) smooth

pulla *f* gibe

pulm|ón *m* lung. ~onar *adj* pulmonary. ~onía *f* pneumonia

pulpa *f* pulp

pulpería *f* (*LAm*) grocer's shop (*Brit*), grocery store (*Amer*)

púlpito *m* pulpit

pulpo *m* octopus

pulque *m* (*Mex*) pulque, alcoholic Mexican drink. ~ría *f* bar

pulsa|ción *f* pulsation. ~dor *m* button. ~r *vt* press; (*Mus*) pluck

pulsera *f* bracelet

pulso *m* pulse; (*firmeza*) steady hand. **echar un** ~ arm wrestle. **tomar el** ~ **a uno** take s.o.'s pulse

pulular *vi* teem with

puma *m* puma

puna *f* puna, high plateau

punitivo *adj* punitive

punta *f* point; (*extremo*) tip. **estar de** ~ be in a bad mood. **ponerse de** ~ **con uno** fall out with s.o. **sacar** ~ **a** sharpen

puntada *f* stitch

puntaje *m* (*LAm*) score

puntal *m* prop, support

puntapié *m* kick

puntear *vt* mark; (*Mus*) pluck; (*LAm, en deportes*) lead

puntería *f* aim; (*destreza*) markmanship

puntiagudo *adj* pointed; (*afilado*) sharp

puntilla *f* (*encaje*) lace. **en** ~s (*LAm*), **de** ~s on tiptoe

punto *m* point; (*señal, trazo*) dot; (*de examen*) mark; (*lugar*) spot, place; (*de taxis*) stand; (*momento*) moment; (*punto final*) full stop (*Brit*), period (*Amer*); (*puntada*) stitch. ~ **de vista** point of view. ~ **com** dot-com. ~ **final** full stop (*Brit*), period (*Amer*). ~ **muerto** (*Auto*) neutral (gear). ~ **y aparte** full stop, new paragraph (*Brit*), period, new paragraph (*Amer*). ~ **y coma** semicolon. **a** ~ on time; (*listo*) ready. **a** ~ **de** on the point of. **de** ~ knitted. **dos** ~s colon. **en** ~ exactly. **hacer** ~ knit. **hasta cierto** ~ to a certain extent

puntuación *f* punctuation; (*en deportes, acción*) scoring; (*en deportes, número de puntos*) score

puntual *adj* punctual; (*exacto*) accurate. ~idad *f* punctuality; (*exactitud*) accuracy

puntuar 21 *vt* punctuate; mark (*Brit*), grade (*Amer*) (*examen*). ● *vi* score (points)

punza|da *f* sharp pain; (*fig*) pang. ~nte *adj* sharp. ~r 10 *vt* prick

puñado *m* handful. **a** ~s by the handful

puñal *m* dagger. ~ada *f* stab

puñ|etazo *m* punch. ~o *m* fist; (*de ropa*) cuff; (*mango*) handle. **de su** ~o (**y letra**) in his own handwriting

pupa *f* (*fam, en los labios*) cold sore

pupila *f* pupil

pupitre *m* desk

puré *m* purée; (*sopa*) thick soup. ~ **de papas** (*LAm*), ~ **de patatas** mashed potatoes

pureza *f* purity

purga *f* purge. ~torio *m* purgatory

puri|ficación *f* purification. ~ificar 7 *vt* purify. ~sta *m & f* purist. ~tano *adj* puritanical. ● *m* puritan

puro *adj* pure; (*cielo*) clear. **de pura casualidad** by sheer chance. **de** ~ **tonto** out of sheer stupidity. ● *m* cigar

púrpura *f* purple

pus *m* pus

puse *vb véase* **PONER**

pusilánime *adj* fainthearted

puta *f* (*vulg*) whore

Qq

que *pron rel* (*personas, sujeto*) who; (*personas, complemento*) whom; (*cosas*) which, that. ● *conj* that. ¡~ **tengan Vds buen viaje!** have a good journey! ¡~ **venga!** let him come! ~ **venga o no venga** whether he comes or not. **creo** ~ **tiene razón** I think (that) he is right. **más** ~ more than. **lo** ~ what. **yo** ~ **tú** if I were you

qué *adj* (*con sustantivo*) what; (*con a o adv*) how. ● *pron* what. ¡~ **bonito!** how nice!. ¿**en** ~ **piensas?** what are you thinking about?

quebra|da *f* gorge; (*paso*) pass. ~**dizo** *adj* fragile. ~**do** *adj* broken; (*Com*) bankrupt. ● *m* (*Math*) fraction. ~**ntar** *vt* break; disturb (*paz*). ~**nto** *m* (*pérdida*) loss; (*daño*) damage. ~**r** **1** *vt* break. ● *vi* break; (*Com*) go bankrupt. ~**rse** *vpr* break

quechua *adj* Quechua. ● *m & f* Quechuan. ● *m* (*lengua*) Quechua

quedar *vi* stay, remain; (*estar*) be; (*haber todavía*) be left. ~ **bien** come off well. ~**se** *vpr* stay. ~ **con** arrange to meet. ~ **en** agree to. ~ **en nada** come to nothing. ~ **por** (+ *infinitivo*) remain to be (+ *pp*)

quehacer *m* work. ~**es domésticos** household chores

quej|a *f* complaint; (*de dolor*) moan. ~**arse** *vpr* complain (**de** about); (*gemir*) moan. ~**ido** *m* moan

quema|do *adj* burnt; (*LAm, bronceado*) tanned; (*fig*) annoyed. ~**dor** *m* burner. ~**dura** *f* burn. ~**r** *vt/i* burn. ~**rse** *vpr* burn o.s.; (*consumirse*) burn up; (*con el sol*) get sunburnt. ~**rropa** *adv.* **a** ~**rropa** point-blank

quena *f* Indian flute

quepo *vb véase* **CABER**

querella *f* (*riña*) quarrel, dispute; (*Jurid*) criminal action

quer|er **35** *vt* want; (*amar*) love; (*necesitar*) need. ~**er decir** mean. ● *m* love; (*amante*) lover. **como quiera**

que however. **cuando quiera que** whenever. **donde quiera** wherever. ¿**quieres darme ese libro?** would you pass me that book? ¿**quieres un helado?** would you like an ice-cream? **quisiera ir a la playa** I'd like to go to the beach. **sin** ~**er** without meaning to. ~**ido** *adj* dear; (*amado*) loved

querosén *m*, **queroseno** *m* kerosene

querubín *m* cherub

ques|adilla *f* (*Mex*) tortilla filled with cheese. ~**o** *m* cheese

quetzal *m* (*unidad monetaria ecuatoriana*) quetzal

quicio *m* frame. **sacar de** ~ **a uno** infuriate s.o.

quiebra *f* (*Com*) bankruptcy

quien *pron rel* (*sujeto*) who; (*complemento*) whom

quién *pron interrogativo* (*sujeto*) who; (*tras preposición*) ¿**con** ~? who with?, to whom?. ¿**de** ~ **son estos libros?** whose are these books?

quienquiera *pron* whoever

quiero *vb véase* **QUERER**

quiet|o *adj* still; (*inmóvil*) motionless; (*carácter etc*) calm. ~**ud** *f* stillness

quijada *f* jaw

quilate *m* carat

quilla *f* keel

quimera *f* (*fig*) illusion

químic|a *f* chemistry. ~**o** *adj* chemical. ● *m* chemist

quince *adj & m* fifteen. ~ **días** a fortnight. ~**na** *f* fortnight. ~**nal** *adj* fortnightly

quincuagésimo *adj* fiftieth

quiniela *f* pools coupon. ~**s** *fpl* (football) pools

quinientos *adj & m* five hundred

quinquenio *m* (period of) five years

quinta *f* (*casa*) villa

quintal *m* a hundred kilograms

quinteto *m* quintet

quinto *adj & m* fifth

quiosco *m* kiosk; (*en jardín*) summerhouse; (*en parque etc*) bandstand

quirúrgico *adj* surgical

quise *vb véase* **QUERER**

quisquill|a f trifle; (*camarón*) shrimp. ~**oso** adj irritable; (*exigente*) fussy

quita|esmalte m nail polish remover. ~**manchas** m invar stain remover. ~**nieves** m invar snow plough. ~**r** vt remove, take away; take off (*ropa*); (*robar*) steal. ~**ndo** (*fam, a excepción de*) apart from. ~**rse** vpr get rid of (*dolor*); take off (*ropa*). ~**rse de** (*no hacerlo más*) stop. ~**rse de en medio** get out of the way. ~**sol** m sunshade

quizá(s) adv perhaps

quórum m quorum

Rr

rábano m radish. ~ **picante** horseradish. **me importa un** ~ I couldn't care less

rabi|a f rabies; (*fig*) rage. ~**ar** vi (*de dolor*) be in great pain; (*estar enfadado*) be furious. **dar** ~**a** infuriate. ~**eta** f tantrum

rabino m rabbi

rabioso adj rabid; (*furioso*) furious

rabo m tail

racha f gust of wind; (*fig*) spate. **pasar por una mala** ~ go through a bad patch

racial adj racial

racimo m bunch

ración f share, ration; (*de comida*) portion

raciona|l adj rational. ~**lizar** 10 vt rationalize. ~**r** vt (*limitar*) ration; (*repartir*) ration out

racis|mo m racism. ~**ta** adj racist

radar m radar

radiación f radiation

radiactiv|idad f radioactivity. ~**o** adj radioactive

radiador m radiator

radiante adj radiant; (*brillante*) brilliant

radical adj & m & f radical

radicar 7 vi lie (*en* in). ~**se** vpr settle

radio m radius; (*de rueda*) spoke; (*LAm*) radio. ● f radio. ~**actividad** f radioactivity. ~**activo** adj radioactive.

~**difusión** f broadcasting. ~**emisora** f radio station. ~**escucha** m & f listener. ~**grafia** f radiography

radi|ólogo m radiologist. ~**oterapia** f radiotherapy

radioyente m & f listener

raer 36 vt scrape; (*quitar*) scrape off

ráfaga f (*de viento*) gust; (*de ametralladora*) burst

rafia f raffia

raído adj threadbare

raíz f root. **a** ~ **de** as a result of. **echar raíces** (*fig*) settle

raja f split; (*Culin*) slice. ~**r** vt split. ~**rse** vpr split; (*fig*) back out

rajatabla. a ~ rigorously

ralea f sort

ralla|dor m grater. ~**r** vt grate

ralo adj (*pelo*) thin

rama f branch. ~**je** m branches. ~**l** m branch

rambla f watercourse; (*avenida*) avenue

ramera f prostitute

ramifica|ción f ramification. ~**rse** 7 vpr branch out

ram|illete m bunch. ~**o** m branch; (*de flores*) bunch, bouquet

rampa f ramp, slope

rana f frog

ranch|era f (*Mex*) folk song. ~**ero** m cook; (*Mex, hacendado*) rancher. ~**o** m (*LAm, choza*) hut; (*LAm, casucha*) shanty; (*Mex, hacienda*) ranch

rancio adj rancid; (*vino*) old; (*fig*) ancient

rango m rank

ranúnculo m buttercup

ranura f groove; (*para moneda*) slot

rapar vt shave; crop (*pelo*)

rapaz adj rapacious; (*ave*) of prey

rape m monkfish

rapidez f speed

rápido adj fast, quick. ● adv quickly. ● m (*tren*) express. ~**s** mpl rapids

rapiña f robbery. **ave** f **de** ~ bird of prey

rapsodia f rhapsody

rapt|ar vt kidnap. ~**o** m kidnapping; (*de ira etc*) fit

raqueta f racquet

rar|eza f rarity; (cosa rara) oddity. ~o adj rare; (extraño) odd. **es** ~o **que** it is strange that. **¡qué** ~o! how strange!

ras. a ~ **de** level with

rasca|cielos m invar skyscraper. ~r **7** vt scratch; (raspar) scrape

rasgar **12** vt tear

rasgo m characteristic; (gesto) gesture; (de pincel) stroke. ~s mpl (facciones) features

rasguear vt strum

rasguñ|ar vt scratch. ~o m scratch

raso adj (cucharada etc) level; (vuelo etc) low. **al** ~ in the open air. ● m satin

raspa|dura f scratch; (acción) scratching. ~r vt scratch; (rozar) scrape

rastr|a. a ~**as** dragging. ~**ear** vt track. ~**ero** adj creeping. ~**illar** vt rake. ~**illo** m rake. ~**o** m track; (señal) sign. **ni** ~**o** not a trace

rata f rat

ratero m petty thief

ratifica|ción f ratification. ~r **7** vt ratify

rato m moment, short time. ~s **libres** spare time. **a** ~s at times. **a cada** ~ (LAm) always. **hace un** ~ a moment ago. **pasar un mal** ~ have a rough time

rat|ón m mouse. ~**onera** f mousetrap; (madriguera) mouse hole

raudal m torrent. **a** ~**les** in abundance

raya f line; (lista) stripe; (de pelo) parting. **a** ~s striped. **pasarse de la** ~ go too far. ~r vt scratch. ~r **en** border on

rayo m ray; (descarga eléctrica) lightning. ~ **de luna** moonbeam. ~ **láser** laser beam. ~s **X** X-rays

raza f race; (de animal) breed. **de** ~ (caballo) thoroughbred; (perro) pedigree

raz|ón f reason. **a** ~**ón de** at the rate of. **tener** ~**ón** be right. ~**onable** adj reasonable. ~**onar** vt reason out. ● vi reason

RDSI abrev (**Red Digital de Servicios Integrados**) ISDN

re m D; (solfa) re

reac|ción f reaction; (LAm, Pol) right wing. ~**ción en cadena** chain reaction. ~**cionario** adj & m reactionary. ~**tor** m reactor; (avión) jet

real adj real; (de rey etc) royal; (hecho) true. ● m real, old Spanish coin

realidad f reality; (verdad) truth. **en** ~ in fact. **hacerse** ~ come true

realis|mo m realism. ~**ta** adj realistic. ● m & f realist

realiza|ción f fulfilment. ~r **10** vt carry out; make (viaje); fulfil (ilusión); (vender) sell. ~**rse** vpr (sueño, predicción etc) come true; (persona) fulfil o.s.

realzar **10** vt (fig) enhance

reanimar vt revive. ~**se** vpr revive

reanudar vt resume; renew (amistad)

reavivar vt revive

rebaja f reduction. **en** ~s in the sale. ~**do** adj (precio) reduced. ~r vt lower; lose (peso)

rebanada f slice

rebaño m herd; (de ovejas) flock

rebasar vt exceed; (dejar atrás) leave behind; (Mex, Auto) overtake

rebatir vt refute

rebel|arse vpr rebel. ~**de** adj rebellious; (grupo) rebel. ● m rebel. ~**día** f rebelliousness. ~**ión** f rebellion

rebosa|nte adj brimming (**de** with). ~r vi overflow; (abundar) abound

rebot|ar vt bounce; (rechazar) repel. ● vi bounce; (bala) ricochet. ~**e** m bounce, rebound. **de** ~**e** on the rebound

reboz|ar **10** vt wrap up; (Culin) coat in batter. ~**o** m (LAm) shawl

rebusca|do adj affected; (complicado) over-elaborate. ~r **7** vt search through

rebuznar vi bray

recado m errand; (mensaje) message

reca|er **29** vi fall back; (Med) relapse; (fig) fall. ~**ida** f relapse

recalcar **7** vt stress

recalcitrante adj recalcitrant

recalentar **1** vt reheat; (demasiado) overheat

r

recámara f small room; (de arma de fuego) chamber; (Mex, dormitorio) bedroom

recambio m (Mec) spare (part); (de pluma etc) refill. **de ~** spare

recapitular vt sum up

recarg|ar 🔢 vt overload; (aumentar) increase; recharge (batería); top up (móvil). **~o** m increase

recat|ado adj modest. **~o** m prudence; (modestia) modesty. **sin ~o** openly

recauda|ción f (cantidad) takings. **~dor** m tax collector. **~r** vt collect

recel|ar vt suspect. ● vi be suspicious (de of). **~o** m distrust; (temor) fear. **~oso** adj suspicious

recepci|ón f reception. **~onista** m & f receptionist

receptáculo m receptacle

receptor m receiver

recesión f recession

receta f recipe; (Med) prescription

rechaz|ar 🔢 vt reject; defeat (moción); repel (ataque); (no aceptar) turn down. **~o** m rejection

rechifla f booing

rechinar vi squeak. **le rechinan los dientes** he grinds his teeth

rechoncho adj stout

recib|imiento m (acogida) welcome. **~ir** vt receive; (acoger) welcome ● vi entertain. **~irse** vpr graduate. **~o** m receipt. **acusar ~o** acknowledge receipt

reci|én adv recently; (LAm, hace poco) just. **~ casado** newly married. **~ nacido** newborn. **~ente** adj recent; (Culin) fresh

recinto m enclosure; (local) premises

recio adj strong; (voz) loud. ● adv hard; (en voz alta) loudly

recipiente m receptacle. ● m & f recipient

recíproco adj reciprocal; (sentimiento) mutual

recita|l m recital; (de poesías) reading. **~r** vt recite

reclama|ción f claim; (queja) complaint. **~r** vt claim. ● vi appeal

réclame m (LAm) advertisement

reclamo m (LAm) complaint

reclinar vi lean. **~se** vpr lean

reclus|ión f imprisonment. **~o** m prisoner

recluta m & f recruit. **~miento** m recruitment. **~r** vt recruit

recobrar vt recover. **~se** vpr recover

recodo m bend

recog|er 🔢 vt collect; pick up (cosa caída); (cosechar) harvest. **~erse** vpr withdraw; (ir a casa) go home; (acostarse) go to bed. **~ida** f collection; (cosecha) harvest

recomenda|ción f recommendation. **~r** 🔢 vt recommend; (encomendar) entrust

recomenzar 🔢 & 🔢 vt/i start again

recompensa f reward. **~r** vt reward

reconcilia|ción f reconciliation. **~r** vt reconcile. **~rse** vpr be reconciled

reconoc|er 🔢 vt recognize; (admitir) acknowledge; (examinar) examine. **~imiento** m recognition; (admisión) acknowledgement; (agradecimiento) gratitude; (examen) examination

reconozco vb véase **RECONOCER**

reconquista f reconquest. **~r** vt reconquer; (fig) win back

---

Reconquista The period in Spain's history during which the Christian kingdoms slowly recovered the territories occupied by the Moslem Moors of North Africa. The Moorish invasion began in 711 AD and was halted in 718. The expulsion of the last Moorish ruler of Granada in 1492 completed the *Reconquista*.

---

reconsiderar vt reconsider

reconstruir 🔢 vt reconstruct

récord /'rekor/ m (pl **~s**) record

recordar 🔢 vt remember; (hacer acordar) remind. ● vi remember. **que yo recuerde** as far as I remember. **si mal no recuerdo** if I remember rightly

recorr|er vt tour (país); go round (zona, museo); cover (distancia). **~ mundo** travel all around the world. **~ido** m journey; (trayecto) route

recort|ar vt cut (out). **~e** m cutting (out); (de periódico etc) cutting

175

recostar | refrigeración

recostar ② *vt* lean. **∼se** *vpr* lie down

recoveco *m* bend; (*rincón*) nook

recre|ación *f* recreation. **∼ar** *vt* recreate; (*divertir*) entertain. **∼arse** *vpr* amuse o.s. **∼ativo** *adj* recreational. **∼o** *m* recreation; (*en escuela*) break

recrudecer ⑪ *vi* intensify

recta *f* straight line. **∼ final** home stretch

rect|angular *adj* rectangular. **∼ángulo** *adj* rectangular; (*triángulo*) right-angled. ● *m* rectangle

rectifica|ción *f* rectification. **∼r** ⑦ *vt* rectify

rect|itud *f* straightness; (*fig*) honesty. **∼o** *adj* straight; (*fig, justo*) fair; (*fig, honrado*) honest. **todo ∼o** straight on. ● *m* rectum

rector *adj* governing. ● *m* rector

recubrir (*pp* **recubierto**) *vt* cover (*con, de* with)

recuerdo *m* memory; (*regalo*) souvenir. **∼s** *mpl* (*saludos*) regards. ● *vb* véase **RECORDAR**

recupera|ción *f* recovery. **∼r** *vt* recover. **∼r el tiempo perdido** make up for lost time. **∼rse** *vpr* recover

recur|rir *vi*. **∼rir a** resort to (*cosa*); turn to (*persona*). **∼so** *m* resort; (*medio*) resource; (*Jurid*) appeal. **∼sos** *mpl* resources

red *f* network, (*malla*) net; (*para equipaje*) luggage rack, (*Com*) chain; (*Elec, gas*) mains. **la R∼** the Net

redac|ción *f* writing; (*lenguaje*) wording; (*conjunto de redactores*) editorial staff; (*oficina*) editorial office; (*Escol, Univ*) essay. **∼tar** *vt* write. **∼tor** *m* writer; (*de periódico*) editor

redada *f* catch; (*de policía*) raid

redecilla *f* small net; (*para el pelo*) hairnet

redentor *adj* redeeming

redimir *vt* redeem

redoblar *vt* redouble; step up (*vigilancia*)

redomado *adj* utter

redond|a *f* (*de imprenta*) roman (type); (*Mus*) semibreve (*Brit*), whole note (*Amer*). **a la ∼a** around. **∼ear** *vt* round off. **∼el** *m* circle; (*de plaza de toros*) arena. **∼o** *adj* round; (*completo*)

complete; (*Mex, boleto*) return, round-trip (*Amer*). **en ∼o** round; (*categóricamente*) flatly

reduc|ción *f* reduction. **∼ido** *adj* reduced; (*limitado*) limited; (*pequeño*) small; (*precio*) low. **∼ir** ㊼ *vt* reduce. **∼irse** *vpr* be reduced; (*fig*) amount

reduje *vb* véase **REDUCIR**

redundan|cia *f* redundancy. **∼te** *adj* redundant

reduzco *vb* véase **REDUCIR**

reembols|ar *vt* reimburse. **∼o** *m* repayment. **contra ∼o** cash on delivery

reemplaz|ar ⑩ *vt* replace. **∼o** *m* replacement

refacci|ón *f* (*LAm*) refurbishment; (*Mex, Mec*) spare part. **∼onar** *vt* (*LAm*) refurbish. **∼onaria** *f* (*Mex*) repair shop

referencia *f* reference; (*información*) report. **con ∼ a** with reference to. **hacer ∼ a** refer to

referéndum *m* (*pl* **∼s**) referendum

referir ④ *vt* tell; (*remitir*) refer. **∼se** *vpr* refer. **por lo que se refiere a** as regards

refiero *vb* véase **REFERIR**

refilón. de ∼ obliquely

refin|amiento *m* refinement. **∼ar** *vt* refine. **∼eria** *f* refinery

reflector *m* reflector; (*proyector*) searchlight

reflej|ar *vt* reflect. **∼o** *adj* reflex. ● *m* reflection; (*Med*) reflex; (*en el pelo*) highlights

reflexi|ón *f* reflection. **sin ∼ón** without thinking. **∼onar** *vi* reflect. **∼vo** *adj* (*persona*) thoughtful; (*Gram*) reflexive

reforma *f* reform. **∼s** *fpl* (*reparaciones*) repairs. **∼r** *vt* reform. **∼rse** *vpr* reform

reforzar ② & ⑩ *vt* reinforce

refrac|ción *f* refraction. **∼tario** *adj* heat-resistant

refrán *m* saying

refregar ① & ⑫ *vt* scrub

refresc|ar ⑦ *vt* refresh; (*enfriar*) cool. ● *vi* get cooler. **∼arse** *vpr* refresh o.s. **∼o** *m* cold drink. **∼os** *mpl* refreshments

refrigera|ción *f* refrigeration; (*aire acondicionado*) air-conditioning; (*de* *motor)* cooling. **~r** *vt* refrigerate; air-condition *(lugar)*; cool *(motor)*. **~dor** *m* refrigerator

refuerzo *m* reinforcement

refugi|ado *m* refugee. **~arse** *vpr* take refuge. **~o** *m* refuge, shelter

refunfuñar *vi* grumble

refutar *vt* refute

regadera *f* watering-can; *(Mex, ducha)* shower

regala|do *adj* as a present, free; *(cómodo)* comfortable. **~r** *vt* give

regalo *m* present, gift

regañ|adientes. a ~adientes reluctantly. **~ar** *vt* scold. ● *vi* moan; *(dos personas)* quarrel. **~o** *m* *(represión)* scolding

regar 🔢 & 🔢 *vt* water

regata *f* boat race; *(serie)* regatta

regate|ar *vt* haggle over; *(economizar)* economize on. ● *vi* haggle; *(en deportes)* dribble. **~o** *m* haggling; *(en deportes)* dribbling

regazo *m* lap

regenerar *vt* regenerate

régimen *m* *(pl* **regímenes**) regime; *(Med)* diet; *(de lluvias)* pattern

regimiento *m* regiment

regi|ón *f* region. **~onal** *adj* regional

regir 🔢 & 🔢 *vt* govern. ● *vi* apply, be in force

registr|ado *adj* registered. **~ar** *vt* register; *(Mex)* check in *(equipaje)*; *(grabar)* record; *(examinar)* search. **~arse** *vpr* register; *(darse)* be reported. **~o** *m* *(acción de registrar)* registration; *(libro)* register; *(cosa anotada)* entry; *(inspección)* search. **~o civil** *(oficina)* registry office

regla *f* ruler; *(norma)* rule; *(menstruación)* period. **en ~** in order. **por ~ general** as a rule. **~mentación** *f* regulation. **~mentar** *vt* regulate. **~mentario** *adj* regulation; *(horario)* set. **~mento** *m* regulations

regocij|arse *vpr* be delighted. **~o** *m* delight

regode|arse *vpr* (+ *gerundio)* delight in (+ *gerund)*. **~o** *m* delight

regordete *adj* chubby

regres|ar *vi* return; *(LAm)* send back *(persona)*. **~arse** *vpr* *(LAm)* return.

~ivo *adj* backward. **~o** *m* return

regula|ble *adj* adjustable. **~dor** *m* control. **~r** *adj* regular; *(mediano)* average; *(no bueno)* so-so. ● *vt* regulate; adjust *(volumen* etc). **~ridad** *f* regularity. **con ~ridad** regularly

rehabilita|ción *f* rehabilitation; *(en empleo* etc) reinstatement. **~r** *vt* rehabilitate; *(en cargo)* reinstate

rehacer 🔢 *vt* redo; *(repetir)* repeat; rebuild *(vida)*. **~se** *vpr* recover

rehén *m* hostage

rehogar 🔢 *vt* sauté

rehuir 🔢 *vt* avoid

rehusar *vt/i* refuse

reimpr|esión *f* reprinting. **~imir** *(pp* **reimpreso)** *vt* reprint

reina *f* queen. **~do** *m* reign. **~nte** *adj* ruling; *(fig)* prevailing. **~r** *vi* reign; *(fig)* prevail

reincidir *vi* *(Jurid)* reoffend

reino *m* kingdom. **R~ Unido** United Kingdom

reintegr|ar *vt* reinstate *(persona)*; refund *(cantidad)*. **~arse** *vpr* return. **~o** *m* refund

reír 🔢 *vi* laugh. **~se** *vpr* laugh. **~se de** laugh at. **echarse a ~** burst out laughing

reivindica|ción *f* claim. **~r** 🔢 *vt* claim; *(rehabilitar)* restore

rej|a *f* grille; *(verja)* railing. **entre ~as** behind bars. **~illa** *f* grille, grating; *(red)* luggage rack

rejuvenecer 🔢 *vt/i* rejuvenate. **~se** *vpr* be rejuvenated

relaci|ón *f* connection; *(trato)* relation(ship); *(relato)* account; *(lista)* list. **con ~ón a, en ~ón a** in relation to. **~onado** *adj* related. **bien ~onado** well-connected. **~onar** *vt* relate **(con** to). **~onarse** *vpr* be connected; *(tratar)* mix **(con** with)

relaja|ción *f* relaxation; *(aflojamiento)* slackening. **~do** *adj* relaxed. **~r** *vt* relax; *(aflojar)* slacken. **~rse** *vpr* relax

relamerse *vpr* lick one's lips

relámpago *m* (flash of) lightning

relatar *vt* tell, relate

relativ|idad *f* relativity. **~o** *adj* relative

relato *m* tale; *(relación)* account

relegar 🔢 vt relegate. ~ **al olvido** consign to oblivion

relev|ante adj outstanding. ~**ar** vt relieve; (substituir) replace. ~**o** m relief. **carrera f de** ~**os** relay race

relieve m relief; (fig) importance. **de** ~ important. **poner de** ~ emphasize

religi|ón f religion. ~**osa** f nun. ~**oso** adj religious. ● m monk

relinch|ar vi neigh. ~**o** m neigh

reliquia f relic

rellano m landing

rellen|ar vt refill; (Culin) stuff; fill in (formulario). ~**o** adj full up; (Culin) stuffed. ● m filling; (Culin) stuffing

reloj m clock; (de bolsillo o pulsera) watch. ~ **de caja** grandfather clock. ~ **de pulsera** wrist-watch. ~ **de sol** sundial. ~ **despertador** alarm clock. ~**ería** f watchmaker's (shop). ~**ero** m watchmaker

reluci|ente adj shining. ~**r** 🔢 vi shine; (destellar) sparkle

relumbrar vi shine

remach|ar vt rivet. ~**e** m rivet

remangar 🔢 vt roll up

remar vi row

remat|ado adj (total) complete. ~**ar** vt finish off; (agotar) use up; (Com) sell off cheap; (LAm, subasta) auction; (en tenis) smash. ~**e** m end; (fig) finishing touch; (LAm, subastar) auction; (en tenis) smash. **de** ~**e** completely

remedar vt imitate

remedi|ar vt remedy; repair (daño); (fig, resolver) solve. **no lo pude** ~**ar** I couldn't help it. ~**o** m remedy; (fig) solution; (LAm, medicamento) medicine. **como último** ~**o** as a last resort. **no hay más** ~**o** there's no other way. **no tener más** ~**o** have no choice

remedo m poor imitation

rem|endar 🔢 vt repair. ~**iendo** m patch

remilg|ado adj fussy; (afectado) affected. ~**o** m fussiness; (afectación) affectation. ~**oso** adj (Mex) fussy

reminiscencia f reminiscence

remisión f remission; (envío) sending; (referencia) reference

remit|e m sender's name and address. ~**ente** m sender. ~**ir** vt send; (referir) refer ● vi diminish

remo m oar

remoj|ar vt soak; (fig, fam) celebrate. ~**o** m soaking. **poner a** ~**o** soak

remolacha f beetroot. ~ **azucarera** sugar beet

remolcar 🔢 vt tow

remolino m swirl; (de aire etc) whirl

remolque m towing; (cabo) tow-rope; (vehículo) trailer. **a** ~ on tow. **dar** ~ **a** tow

remontar vt overcome. ~ **el vuelo** soar up; (avión) gain height. ~**se** vpr soar up; (en el tiempo) go back to

remord|er 🔢 vi. **eso le remuerde** he feels guilty for it. **me remuerde la conciencia** I have a guilty conscience. ~**imiento** m remorse. **tener** ~**imientos** feel remorse

remoto adj remote; (época) distant

remover 🔢 vt stir (líquido); turn over (tierra); (quitar) remove; (fig, activar) revive

remunera|ción f remuneration. ~**r** vt remunerate

renac|er 🔢 vi be reborn; (fig) revive. ~**imiento** m rebirth. **R**~**imiento** Renaissance

renacuajo m tadpole; (fig) tiddler

rencilla f quarrel

rencor m bitterness. **guardar** ~ **a** have a grudge against. ~**oso** adj resentful

rendi|ción f surrender. ~**do** adj submissive; (agotado) exhausted

rendija f crack

rendi|miento m performance; (Com) yield. ~**r** 🔢 vt yield; (agotar) exhaust; pay (homenaje); present (informe). ● vi pay; (producir) produce. ~**rse** vpr surrender

renegar 🔢 & 🔢 vt deny. ● vi grumble. ~ **de** renounce (fe etc); disown (personas)

renglón m line; (Com) item. **a** ~ **seguido** straight away

reno m reindeer

renombr|ado adj renowned. ~**e** m renown

r

renova|ción *f* renewal; (*de edificio*) renovation; (*de mobiliario*) complete change. **~r** *vt* renew; renovate (edificio); change (mobiliario)

rent|a *f* income; (*Mex, alquiler*) rent. **~a vitalicia** (life) annuity. **~able** *adj* profitable. **~ar** *vt* yield; (*Mex, alquilar*) rent, hire. **~ista** *m* & *f* person of independent means

renuncia *f* renunciation; (*dimisión*) resignation. **~r** *vi*. **~r a** renounce, give up; (*dimitir*) resign

reñi|do *adj* hard-fought. **estar ~do con** be incompatible with (cosa); be on bad terms with (persona). **~r** ⑤ & ㉒ *vt* scold. ● *vi* quarrel

reo *m* & *f* (*Jurid*) accused; (*condenado*) convicted offender; (*pez*) sea trout

reojo. mirar de ~ look out of the corner of one's eye at

reorganizar ⑩ *vt* reorganize

repar|ación *f* repair; (*acción*) repairing (*fig, compensación*) reparation. **~ar** *vt* repair; (*fig*) make amends for; (*notar*) notice. ● *vi*. **~ar en** notice; (*hacer caso de*) pay attention to. **~o** *m* fault; (*objeción*) objection. **poner ~os** raise objections

repart|ir *vt* go over; check (cuenta); revise (texto); (*leer a la ligera*) glance through; (*coser*) mend. ● *vi* revise. **~o** *m* revision; (*de ropa*) mending. **dar un ~o** look through

repatria|ción *f* repatriation. **~r** *vt* repatriate

repele|nte *adj* repulsive. ● *m* insect repellent. **~r** *vt* repel

repent|e. de ~ suddenly. **~ino** *adj* sudden

repercu|sión *f* repercussion. **~tir** *vi* reverberate; (*fig*) have repercussions (**en** on)

repertorio *m* repertoire

repeti|ción *f* repetition; (*de programa*) repeat. **~damente** *adv* repeatedly. **~r** ⑤ *vt* repeat; have a second help-

ing of (plato); (*imitar*) copy. ● *vi* have a second helping of

repi|car ⑦ *vt* ring (campanas). **~que** *m* peal

repisa *f* shelf. **~ de chimenea** mantlepiece

repito *vb véase* REPETIR

replegarse ① & ⑫ *vpr* withdraw

repleto *adj* full up. **~ de gente** packed with people

réplica *adj* reply; (*copia*) replica

replicar ⑦ *vi* reply

repollo *m* cabbage

reponer ㉞ *vt* replace; revive (obra de teatro); (*contestar*) reply. **~se** *vpr* recover

report|aje *m* report; (*LAm, entrevista*) interview. **~ar** *vt* yield; (*LAm, denunciar*) report. **~e** *m* (*Mex, informe*) report; (*Mex, queja*) complaint. **~ero** *m* reporter

repos|ado *adj* quiet; (*sin prisa*) unhurried. **~ar** *vi* rest; (*líquido*) settle. **~o** *m* rest

repost|ar *vt* replenish. ● *vi* (*avión*) refuel; (*Auto*) fill up. **~ería** *f* pastrymaking

reprender *vt* reprimand

represalia *f* reprisal. **tomar ~s** retaliate

representa|ción *f* representation; (*en el teatro*) performance. **en ~ción de** representing. **~nte** *m* representative. **~r** *vt* represent; perform (obra de teatro); play (papel); (*aparentar*) look. **~rse** *vpr* imagine. **~tivo** *adj* representative

represi|ón *f* repression. **~vo** *adj* repressive

reprimenda *f* reprimand

reprimir *vt* supress. **~se** *vpr* control o.s.

reprobar ② *vt* condemn; (*LAm, Univ, etc*) fail

reproch|ar *vt* reproach. **~e** *m* reproach

reproduc|ción *f* reproduction. **~ir** ㊼ *vt* reproduce. **~tor** *adj* reproductive; (*animal*) breeding

reptil *m* reptile

rep|ública *f* republic. **~ublicano** *adj* & *m* republican

repudiar *vt* condemn; (*Jurid*) repudiate

repuesto *m* (*Mec*) spare (part). **de ~** spare

repugna|ncia *f* disgust. **~nte** *adj* repugnant; (olor) disgusting. **~r** *vt* disgust

repuls|a *f* rebuff. **~ión** *f* repulsion. **~ivo** *adj* repulsive

reputa|ción *f* reputation. **~do** *adj* reputable. **~r** *vt* consider

requeri|miento *m* request; (*necesidad*) requirement. **~r 4** *vt* require; summons (persona)

requesón *m* curd cheese

requete... *prefijo* (*fam*) extremely

requis|a *f* requisition; (*confiscación*) seizure; (*inspección*) inspection; (*Mil*) requisition. **~ar** *vt* requisition; (*confiscar*) seize; (*inspeccionar*) inspect. **~ito** *m* requirement

res *f* animal. **~ lanar** sheep. **~ vacuna** (*vaca*) cow; (*toro*) bull; (*buey*) ox. **carne de ~** (*Mex*) beef

resabido *adj* well-known; (persona) pedantic

resaca *f* undercurrent; (*después de beber*) hangover

resaltar *vi* stand out. **hacer ~** emphasize

resarcir 9 *vt* repay; (*compensar*) compensate. **~se** *vpr* make up for

resbal|adilla *f* (*Mex*) slide. **~adizo** *adj* slippery. **~ar** *vi* slip; (*Auto*) skid; (líquido) trickle. **~arse** *vpr* slip; (*Auto*) skid; (líquido) trickle. **~ón** *m* slip; (*de vehículo*) skid. **~oso** *adj* (*LAm*) slippery

rescat|ar *vt* rescue; (*fig*) recover. **~e** *m* ransom; (*recuperación*) recovery; (*salvamento*) rescue

rescoldo *m* embers

resecar 7 *vt* dry up. **~se** *vpr* dry up

resenti|do *adj* resentful. **~miento** *m* resentment. **~rse** *vpr* feel the effects; (*debilitarse*) be weakened; (*ofenderse*) take offence (**de** at)

reseña *f* summary; (*de persona*) description; (*en periódico*) report, review. **~r** *vt* describe; (*en periódico*) report on, review

reserva *f* reservation; (*provisión*) reserve(s). **de ~** in reserve. **~ción** *f*

(*LAm*) reservation. **~do** *adj* reserved. **~r** *vt* reserve; (*guardar*) keep, save. **~rse** *vpr* save o.s.

resfria|do *m* cold. **~rse** *vpr* catch a cold

resguard|ar *vt* protect. **~arse** *vpr* protect o.s.; (*fig*) take care. **~o** *m* protection; (*garantía*) guarantee; (*recibo*) receipt

resid|encia *f* residence; (*Univ*) hall of residence (*Brit*), dormitory (*Amer*); (*de ancianos etc*) home. **~encial** *adj* residential. **~ente** *adj & m & f* resident. **~ir** *vi* reside; (*fig*) lie (**en** in)

residu|al *adj* residual. **~o** *m* residue. **~os** *mpl* waste

resigna|ción *f* resignation. **~rse** *vpr* resign o.s. (**a** to)

resist|encia *f* resistence. **~ente** *adj* resistent. **~ir** *vt* resist; (*soportar*) bear. ● *vi* resist. **ya no resisto más** I can't take it any more

resol|ución *f* resolution; (*solución*) solution; (*decisión*) decision. **~ver 2** (*pp* **resuelto**) resolve; solve (problema etc). **~verse** *vpr* resolve itself; (*resultar bien*) work out; (*decidir*) decide

resona|ncia *f* resonance. **tener ~ncia** cause a stir. **~nte** *adj* resonant; (*fig*) resounding. **~r 2** *vi* resound

resorte *m* spring; (*Mex, elástico*) elastic. **tocar (todos los) ~s** (*fig*) pull strings

respald|ar *vt* back; (*escribir*) endorse. **~arse** *vpr* lean back. **~o** *m* backing; (*de asiento*) back

respect|ar *vi*. **en lo que ~a** a with regard to. **en lo que a mí ~a** as far as I'm concerned. **~ivo** *adj* respective. **~o** *m* respect. **al ~o** on this matter. (**con**) **~o a** with regard to

respet|able *adj* respectable. ● *m* audience. **~ar** *vt* respect. **~o** *m* respect. **faltar al ~o a** be disrespectful to. **~uoso** *adj* respectful

respir|ación *f* breathing; (*ventilación*) ventilation. **~ar** *vi* breathe; (*fig*) breathe a sigh of relief. **~o** *m* breathing; (*fig*) rest

respland|ecer 11 *vi* shine. **~eciente** *adj* shining. **~or** *m* brilliance; (*de llamas*) glow

r

responder *vi* answer; (*replicar*) answer back; (*reaccionar*) respond. ~ **de** be responsible for. ~ **por uno** vouch for s.o.

responsab|ilidad *f* responsibility. ~**le** *adj* responsible

respuesta *f* reply, answer

resquebrajar *vt* crack. ~**se** *vpr* crack

resquemor *m* (*fig*) uneasiness

resquicio *m* crack; (*fig*) possibility

resta *f* subtraction

restablecer 11 *vt* restore. ~**se** *vpr* recover

rest|ante *adj* remaining. **lo** ~**nte** the rest. ~**ar** *vt* take away; (*substraer*) subtract. ● *vi* be left

restaura|ción *f* restoration. ~**nte** *m* restaurant. ~**r** *vt* restore

restitu|ción *f* restitution. ~**ir** 17 *vt* return; (*restaurar*) restore

resto *m* rest, remainder; (*en matemática*) remainder. ~**s** *mpl* remains; (*de comida*) leftovers

restorán *m* restaurant

restregar 1 & 12 *vt* rub

restri|cción *f* restriction. ~**ngir** 14 *vt* restrict, limit

resucitar *vt* resuscitate; (*fig*) revive. ● *vi* return to life

resuello *m* breath; (*respiración*) heavy breathing

resuelto *adj* resolute

resulta|do *m* result (**en** in). ~**r** *vi* result; (*salir*) turn out; (*dar resultado*) work; (*ser*) be; (*costar*) come to

resum|en *m* summary. **en** ~**en** in short. ~**ir** *vt* summarize; (*recapitular*) sum up

resur|gir 14 *vi* reemerge; (*fig*) revive. ~**gimiento** *m* resurgence. ~**rección** *f* resurrection

retaguardia *f* (*Mil*) rearguard

retahíla *f* string

retar *vt* challenge

retardar *vt* slow down; (*demorar*) delay

retazo *m* remnant; (*fig*) piece, bit

reten|ción *f* retention. ~**er** 40 *vt* keep; (*en la memoria*) retain; (*no dar*) withhold

reticencia *f* insinuation; (*reserva*) reluctance

retina *f* retina

retir|ada *f* withdrawal. ~**ado** *adj* remote; (*vida*) secluded; (*jubilado*) retired. ~**ar** *vt* move away; (*quitar*) remove; withdraw (*dinero*); (*jubilar*) pension off. ~**arse** *vpr* draw back; (*Mil*) withdraw; (*jubilarse*) retire; (*acostarse*) go to bed. ~**o** *m* retirement; (*pensión*) pension; (*lugar apartado*) retreat; (*LAm, de apoyo, fondos*) withdrawal

reto *m* challenge

retocar 7 *vt* retouch

retoño *m* shoot; (*fig*) kid

retoque *m* (*acción*) retouching; (*efecto*) finishing touch

retorc|er 2 & 9 *vt* twist; wring (*ropa*). ~**erse** *vpr* get twisted up; (*de dolor*) writhe. ~**ijón** *m* (*LAm*) stomach cramp

retóric|a *f* rhetoric; (*grandilocuencia*) grandiloquence. ~**o** *m* rhetorical

retorn|ar *vt/i* return. ~**o** *m* return

retortijón *m* twist; (*de tripas*) stomach cramp

retractarse *vpr* retract. ~ **de lo dicho** withdraw what one said

retransmitir *vt* repeat; (*radio, TV*) broadcast. ~ **en directo** broadcast live

retras|ado *adj* (*con ser*) mentally handicapped; (*con estar*) behind; (*reloj*) slow; (*poco desarrollado*) backward; (*anticuado*) old-fashioned. ~**ar** *vt* delay; put back (*reloj*); (*retardar*) slow down; (*posponer*) postpone. ● *vi* (*reloj*) be slow. ~**arse** *vpr* be late; (*reloj*) be slow. ~**o** *m* delay; (*poco desarrollo*) backwardness; (*de reloj*) slowness. **traer** ~**o** be late. ~**os** *mpl* arrears

retrato *m* portrait; (*fig, descripción*) description. **ser el vivo** ~ **de** be the living image of

retrete *m* toilet

retribu|ción *f* payment; (*recompensa*) reward. ~**ir** 17 *vt* pay; (*recompensar*) reward; (*LAm*) return (favor)

retroce|der *vi* move back; (*fig*) back down. ~**so** *m* backward movement; (*de arma de fuego*) recoil; (*Med*) relapse

retrógrado *adj & m* (*Pol*) reactionary

r

retrospectivo adj retrospective

retrovisor m rear-view mirror

retumbar vt echo; (trueno etc) boom

reum|a m, **reúma** m rheumatism. **~ático** adj rheumatic. **~atismo** m rheumatism

reuni|ón f meeting; (entre amigos) reunion. **~r** 23 vt join together; (recoger) gather (together); raise (fondos). **~rse** vpr meet; (amigos etc) get together

revalidar vt confirm; (Mex, estudios) validate

revalorizar 10 vt, (LAm) **revaluar** 21 vt revalue; increase (pensiones). **~se** vpr appreciate

revancha f revenge; (en deportes) return match. **tomar la ~** get one's own back

revela|ción f revelation. **~do** m developing. **~dor** adj revealing. **~r** vt reveal; (Foto) develop

revent|ar 1 vi burst; (tener ganas) be dying to. **~arse** vpr burst. **~ón** m burst; (Auto) blow out; (Mex, fiesta) party

reveren|cia f reverence; (de hombre, niño) bow; (de mujer) curtsy. **~ciar** vt revere. **~do** adj (Relig) reverend. **~te** adj reverent

revers|ible adj reversible. **~o** m reverse; (de papel) back

revertir 4 vi revert (a to)

revés m wrong side; (de prenda) inside; (contratiempo) setback; (en deportes) backhand. **al ~** the other way round; (con lo de arriba abajo) upside down; (con lo de dentro fuera) inside out

revesti|miento m coating. **~r** 5 vt cover

revis|ar vt check; overhaul (mecanismo); service (coche etc); (LAm, equipaje) search. **~ión** f check(ing)); (Med) checkup; (de coche etc) service; (LAm, de equipaje) inspection. **~or** m inspector

revista f magazine; (inspección) inspection; (artículo) review; (espectáculo) revue. **pasar ~ a** inspect

revivir vi revive

revolcar 2 & 7 vt knock over. **~se** vpr roll around

revolotear vi flutter

revoltijo m, **revoltillo** m mess

revoltoso adj rebellious; (niño) naughty

revoluci|ón f revolution. **~onar** vt revolutionize. **~onario** adj & m revolutionary

revolver 2 (pp **revuelto**) vt mix; stir (líquido); (desordenar) mess up

revólver m revolver

revuelo m fluttering; (fig) stir

revuelt|a f revolt; (conmoción) disturbance. **~o** adj mixed up; (líquido) cloudy; (mar) rough; (tiempo) unsettled; (huevos) scrambled

rey m king. **los ~es** the king and queen. **los R~es Magos** the Three Wise Men

reyerta f brawl

rezagarse 12 vpr fall behind

rez|ar 10 vt say. ● vi pray; (decir) say. **~o** m praying; (oración) prayer

rezongar 12 vi grumble

ría f estuary

riachuelo m stream

riada f flood

ribera f bank

ribete m border; (fig) embellishment

rico adj rich; (Culin, fam) good, nice. ● m rich person

rid|ículo adj ridiculous. **~iculizar** 10 vt ridicule

riego m watering; (irrigación) irrigation

riel m rail

rienda f rein

riesgo m risk. **correr (el) ~ de** run the risk of

rifa f raffle. **~r** vt raffle

rifle m rifle

rig|idez f rigidity; (fig) inflexibility

rígido adj rigid; (fig) inflexible

rig|or m strictness; (exactitud) exactness; (de clima) severity. **de ~or** compulsory. **en ~or** strictly speaking. **~uroso** adj rigorous

rima f rhyme. **~r** vt/i rhyme

rimbombante adj resounding; (lenguaje) pompous; (fig, ostentoso) showy

rímel m mascara

rin m (Mex) rim

r

rincón m corner

rinoceronte m rhinoceros

riña f quarrel; (pelea) fight

riñón m kidney

río m river; (fig) stream. ~ abajo downstream. ~ arriba upstream. ● vb véase REÍR

riqueza f wealth; (fig) richness. ~s fpl riches

ris|a f laugh. desternillarse de ~a split one's sides laughing. la ~a laughter. ~otada f guffaw. ~ueño adj smiling; (fig) cheerful

rítmico adj rhythmic(al)

ritmo m rhythm; (fig) rate

rit|o m rite; (fig) ritual. ~ual adj & m ritual

rival adj & m & f rival. ~idad f rivalry. ~izar 🔟 vi rival

riz|ado adj curly. ~ar 🔟 vt curl; ripple (agua). ~o m curl; (en agua) ripple

róbalo m bass

robar vt steal (cosa); rob (banco); (raptar) kidnap

roble m oak (tree)

robo m theft; (de banco, museo) robbery; (en vivienda) burglary

robusto adj robust

roca f rock

roce m rubbing; (señal) mark; (fig, entre personas) regular contact; (Pol) friction. tener un ~ con uno have a brush with s.o.

rociar 🔟 vt spray

rocín m nag

rocío m dew

rodaballo m turbot

rodaja f slice. en ~s sliced

roda|je m (de película) shooting; (de coche) running in. ~r 🔟 vt shoot (película); run in (coche). ● vi roll; (coche) run; (hacer una película) shoot

rode|ar vt surround; (LAm) round up (ganado). ~arse vpr surround o.s. (de with). ~o m detour; (de ganado) round-up. andar con ~os beat about the bush. sin ~os plainly

rodill|a f knee. ponerse de ~as kneel down. ~era f knee-pad

rodillo m roller; (Culin) rolling-pin

roe|dor m rodent. ~r 🔟 vt gnaw

rogar 🔟 & 🔟 vt/i beg; (Relig) pray; se ruega a los Sres. pasajeros... passengers are requested.... se ruega no fumar please do not smoke

roj|izo adj reddish. ~o adj & m red. ponerse ~o blush

roll|izo adj plump; (bebé) chubby. ~o m roll; (de cuerda) coil; (Culin, rodillo) rolling-pin; (fig, fam, pesadez) bore

romance adj Romance. ● m (idilio) romance; (poema) ballad

roman|o adj & m Roman. a la ~a (Culin) (deep-)fried in batter

rom|anticismo m romanticism. ~ántico adj romantic

romería f pilgrimage; (LAm, multitud) mass

romero m rosemary

romo adj blunt; (nariz) snub

rompe|cabezas m invar puzzle; (de piezas) jigsaw (puzzle). ~olas m invar breakwater

romp|er (pp roto) vt break; tear (hoja, camisa etc); break off (relaciones etc). ● vi break; (novios) break up. ~er a burst out. ~erse vpr break

ron m rum

ronc|ar 🔟 vi snore. ~o adj hoarse

roncha f lump; (por alergia) rash

ronda f round; (patrulla) patrol; (serenata) serenade. ~r vt patrol. ● vi be on patrol; (merodear) hang around

ronqu|era f hoarseness. ~ido m snore

ronronear vi purr

roñ|a f (suciedad) grime. ~oso adj dirty; (oxidado) rusty; (tacaño) mean

rop|a f clothes, clothing. ~a blanca linen, underwear. ~a de cama bedclothes. ~a interior underwear. ~aje m robes; (excesivo) heavy clothing. ~ero m wardrobe

ros|a adj invar pink. ● f rose. ● m pink. ~áceo adj pinkish. ~ado adj pink; (mejillas) rosy. ● m (vino) rosé. ~al m rose-bush

rosario m rosary; (fig) series

ros|ca f (de tornillo) thread; (de pan) roll; (bollo) type of doughnut. ~co m roll. ~quilla f type of doughnut

rostro m face

rota|ción f rotation. **~r** vt/i rotate. **~rse** vpr take turns. **~tivo** adj rotary

roto adj broken

rótula f kneecap

rotulador m felt-tip pen

rótulo m sign; (etiqueta) label; (logotipo) logo

rotundo adj categorical

rotura f tear; (grieta) crack

rozadura f scratch

rozagante adj (LAm) healthy

rozar 🔟 vt rub against; (ligeramente) brush against; (rozpar) graze. **~se** vpr rub; (con otras personas) mix

Rte. abrev (**Remite(nte)**) sender

rubéola f German measles

rubí m ruby

rubicundo adj ruddy

rubio adj (pelo) fair; (persona) fair-haired; (tabaco) Virginia

rubor m blush; (Mex, cosmético) blusher. **~izarse** 🔟 vpr blush

rúbrica f (de firma) flourish; (firma) signature; (título) heading

rudeza f roughness

rudiment|ario adj rudimentary. **~os** mpl rudiments

rueca f distaff

rueda f wheel; (de mueble) castor; (de personas) ring; (Culin) slice. **~ de prensa** press conference

ruedo m edge; (redondel) bullring

ruego m request; (súplica) entreaty. ● vb véase **ROGAR**

rufián m pimp; (granuja) rogue

rugby m rugby

rugi|do m roar. **~r** 🔢 vi roar

ruibarbo m rhubarb

ruido m noise. **~so** adj noisy; (fig) sensational

ruin adj despicable; (tacaño) mean

ruin|a f ruin; (colapso) collapse. **~oso** adj ruinous

ruiseñor m nightingale

ruleta f roulette

rulo m curler

rumano adj & m Romanian

rumbo m direction; (fig) course; (fig, esplendidez) lavishness. **con ~** a in the direction of. **~so** adj lavish

rumia|nte adj & m ruminant. **~r** vt chew; (fig) brood over. ● vi ruminate

rumor m rumour; (ruido) murmur. **~earse** vpr **se ~ea que** rumour has it that. **~oso** adj murmuring

runrún m (de voces) murmur; (de motor) whirr

ruptura f breakup; (de relaciones etc) breaking off; (de contrato) breach

rural adj rural

ruso adj & m Russian

rústico adj rural; (de carácter) coarse. **en rústica** paperback

ruta f route; (fig) course

rutina f routine. **~rio** adj routine; (trabajo) monotonous

•••••••••••••••••••••••••••••••

Ss

•••••••••••••••••••••••••••••••

S.A. abrev (**Sociedad Anónima**) Ltd, plc, Inc (Amer)

sábado m Saturday

sábana f sheet

sabañón m chilblain

sabático adj sabbatical

sab|elotodo m & f invar know-all 🔲. **~er** 🔢 vt know; (ser capaz de) be able to, know how to; (enterarse de) find out. ● vi know. **~er a** taste of. **hacer ~er** let know. **¡qué sé yo!** how should I know? **que yo sepa** as far as I know. **¿~es nadar?** can you swim? **un no sé qué** a certain sth. **¡yo qué sé!** how should I know? **¡vete a ~er!** who knows? **~er** m knowledge. **~ido** adj well-known. **~iduría** f wisdom; (conocimientos) knowledge

sabi|endas. a ~ knowingly; (a propósito) on purpose. **~hondo** adj know-all. **~o** adj learned; (prudente) wise

sabor m taste, flavour; (fig) flavour. **~ear** vt taste; (fig) savour

sabot|aje m sabotage. **~eador** m saboteur. **~ear** vt sabotage

sabroso adj tasty; (chisme) juicy; (LAm, agradable) pleasant

sabueso *m* (*perro*) bloodhound; (*fig, detective*) detective

saca|corchos *m invar* corkscrew. **~puntas** *m invar* pencil-sharpener

sacar **7** *vt* take out; put out (*parte del cuerpo*); (*quitar*) remove; take (*foto*); win (*premio*); get (*billete, entrada*); withdraw (*dinero*); reach (*solución*); draw (*conclusión*); make (*copia*). **~ adelante** bring up (*niño*); carry on (*negocio*)

sacarina *f* saccharin

sacerdo|cio *m* priesthood. **~te** *m* priest

saciar *vt* satisfy; quench (*sed*)

saco *m* sack; (*LAm, chaqueta*) jacket. **~ de dormir** sleeping-bag

sacramento *m* sacrament

sacrific|ar **7** *vt* sacrifice; slaughter (*res*); put to sleep (*perro, gato*). **~arse** *vpr* sacrifice o.s. **~io** *m* sacrifice; (*de res*) slaughter

sacr|ilegio *m* sacrilege. **~ílego** *adj* sacrilegious

sacudi|da *f* shake; (*movimiento brusco*) jolt, jerk; (*fig*) shock. **~da eléctrica** electric shock. **~r** *vt* shake; (*golpear*) beat. **~rse** *vpr* shake off; (*fig*) get rid of

sádico *adj* sadistic. ● *m* sadist

sadismo *m* sadism

safari *m* safari

sagaz *adj* shrewd

Sagitario *m* Sagittarius

sagrado *adj* (*lugar*) holy, sacred; (*altar, escrituras*) holy; (*fig*) sacred

sal *f* salt. ● *vb véase* **SALIR**

sala *f* room; (*en casa*) living room; (*en hospital*) ward; (*para reuniones etc*) hall; (*en teatro*) house; (*Jurid*) courtroom. **~ de embarque** departure lounge. **~ de espera** waiting room. **~ de estar** living room. **~ de fiestas** nightclub

salado *adj* salty; (*agua del mar*) salt; (*no dulce*) savoury; (*fig*) witty

salario *m* wage

salchich|a *f* (*pork*) sausage. **~ón** *m* salami

sald|ar *vt* settle (*cuenta*); (*vender*) sell off. **~o** *m* balance. **~os** *mpl* sales. **venta de ~os** clearance sale

salero *m* salt-cellar

salgo *vb véase* **SALIR**

sali|da *f* departure; (*puerta*) exit, way out; (*de gas, de líquido*) leak; (*de astro*) rising; (*Com, venta*) sale; (*chiste*) witty remark; (*fig*) way out; **~da de emergencia** emergency exit. **~ente** *adj* (*Archit*) projecting; (*pómulo etc*) prominent. **~r** **52** *vi* leave; (*ir afuera*) go out; (*Informática*) exit; (*revista etc*) be published; (*resultar*) turn out; (*astro*) rise; (*aparecer*) appear. **~r adelante** get by. **~rse** *vpr* leave; (*recipiente, líquido etc*) leak. **~rse con la suya** get one's own way

saliva *f* saliva

salmo *m* psalm

salm|ón *m* salmon. **~onete** *m* red mullet

salón *m* living-room, lounge. **~ de actos** assembly hall. **~ de clases** classroom. **~ de fiestas** dancehall

salpica|dera *f* (*Mex*) mudguard. **~dero** *m* (*Auto*) dashboard. **~dura** *f* splash; (*acción*) splashing. **~r** **7** *vt* splash; (*fig*) sprinkle

sals|a *f* sauce; (*para carne asada*) gravy; (*Mus*) salsa. **~a verde** parsley sauce. **~era** *f* sauce-boat

salt|amontes *m invar* grasshopper. **~ar** *vt* jump (over); (*fig*) miss out. ● *vi* jump; (*romperse*) break; (*líquido*) spurt out; (*desprenderse*) come off; (*pelota*) bounce; (*estallar*) explode. **~eador** *m* highwayman. **~ear** *vt* (*Culin*) sauté

salt|o *m* jump; (*al agua*) dive. **~o de agua** waterfall. **~ mortal** somersault. **de un ~o** with one jump. **~ón** *adj* (*ojos*) bulging

salud *f* health. ● *int* cheers!; (*LAm, al estornudar*) bless you! **~able** *adj* healthy

salud|ar *vt* greet, say hello to; (*Mil*) salute. **lo ~a atentamente** (*en cartas*) yours faithfully. **~ con la mano** wave. **~o** *m* greeting; (*Mil*) salute. **~os** *mpl* best wishes

salva *f* salvo. **una ~ de aplausos** a burst of applause

salvación *f* salvation

salvado *m* bran

salvaguardia *f* safeguard

salvaje adj (planta, animal) wild; (primitivo) savage. ● m & f savage

salva|mento m rescue. ~r vt save, rescue; (atravesar); cross (recorrer); travel (fig) overcome. ~rse vpr save o.s. ~vidas m & f invar lifeguard. ● m lifebelt. **chaleco** m ~vidas life-jacket

salvo adj safe. ● adv & prep except (for). a ~ out of danger. **poner a** ~ put in a safe place. ~ **que** unless. ~**conducto** m safe-conduct.

San adj Saint, St. ~ **Miguel** St Michael

sana|r vt cure. ● vi recover; heal (herida). ~**torio** m sanatorium

sanci|ón f sanction. ~**onar** vt sanction

sandalia f sandal

sandía f watermelon

sándwich /'saŋgwitʃ/ m (pl ~s, ~es) sandwich

sangr|ante adj bleeding; (fig) flagrant. ~**ar** vt/i bleed. ~**e** f blood. a ~**e fría** in cold blood

sangría f (bebida) sangria

sangriento adj bloody

sangu|ijuela f leech. ~**ineo** adj blood

san|idad f health. ~**itario** adj sanitary. ● m (Mex) toilet. ~**o** adj healthy; (mente) sound. ~**o y salvo** safe and sound. **cortar por lo** ~**o** settle things once and for all

santiamén m, **en un** ~ in an instant

sant|idad f sanctity. ~**ificar** 7 vt sanctify. ~**iguarse** 12 vpr cross o.s. ~**o** adj holy; (delante de nombre) Saint, St. ● m saint; (día) saint's day, name day. ~**uario** m sanctuary. ~**urrón** adj sanctimonious

> **santo** Most first names in Spanish-speaking countries **ℹ**
> are those of saints. A person's santo (also known as onomástico in Latin America and onomástica in Spain) is the saint's day of the saint they are named after. As well as celebrating their calendar birthday many people also celebrate their santo.

saña f viciousness. **con** ~ viciously

sapo m toad

saque m (en tenis) service; (inicial en fútbol) kick-off. ~ **de banda** throw-in; (en rugby) line-out. ~ **de esquina** corner (kick)

saque|ar vt loot. ~**o** m looting

sarampión m measles

sarape m (Mex) colourful blanket

sarc|asmo m sarcasm. ~**ástico** adj sarcastic

sardina f sardine

sargento m sergeant

sarpullido m rash

sartén f or m frying-pan (Brit), fry-pan (Amer)

sastre m tailor. ~**ría** f tailoring; (tienda) tailor's (shop)

Sat|anás m Satan. ~**ánico** adj satanic

satélite m satellite

satinado adj shiny

sátira f satire

satírico adj satirical. ● m satirist

satisf|acción f satisfaction. ~**acer** 31 vt satisfy; (pagar) pay; (gustar) please; meet (gastos, requisitos). ~**acerse** vpr satisfy o.s.; (vengarse) take revenge. ~**actorio** adj satisfactory. ~**echo** adj satisfied. ~**echo de sí mismo** smug

satura|ción f saturation. ~**r** vt saturate

Saturno m Saturn

sauce m willow. ~ **llorón** weeping willow

sauna f, (LAm) **sauna** m sauna

saxofón m, **saxófono** m saxophone

sazona|do adj ripe; (Culin) seasoned. ~**r** vt ripen; (Culin) season

---

> **se** pronombre   **9**
>
> ● (en lugar de le, les) **se lo di** (a él) I gave it to him; (a ella) I gave it to her; (a usted, ustedes) I gave it to you; (a ellos, ellas) I gave it to them. **se lo compré** I bought it for him (or her etc). **se lo quité** I took it away from him (or her etc). **se lo dije** I told him (or her etc)
>
> ····▸ (reflexivo) **se secó** (él) he dried himself; (ella) she dried herself; (usted) you dried yourself. (sujeto no humano) it dried itself. **se secaron** (ellos, ellas) they dried themselves. (ustedes) you dried

yourselves. (con partes del cuerpo) **se lavó la cara** (él) he washed his face; (con efectos personales) **se limpian los zapatos** they clean their shoes

••••> (recíproco) each other, one another. **se ayudan mucho** they help each other a lot. **no se hablan** they don't speak to each other

••••> (cuando otro hace la acción) **va a operarse** she's going to have an operation. **se cortó el pelo** he had his hair cut

••••> (enfático) **se bebió el café** he drank his coffee. **se subió al tren** he got on the train

> **se** also forms part of certain pronominal verbs such as **equivocarse, arrepentirse, caerse** etc., which are treated under the respective entries

••••> (voz pasiva) **se construyeron muchas casas** many houses were built. **se vendió rápidamente** it was sold very quickly

••••> (impersonal) **antes se escuchaba más radio** people used to listen to the radio more in the past. **no se puede entrar** you can't get in. **se está bien aquí** it's very nice here

••••> (en instrucciones) **sírvase frío** serve cold

sé vb véase **SABER** y **SER**

sea vb véase **SER**

seca|dor m drier; (de pelo) hair-drier. **~nte** adj drying. ● m blotting-paper. **~r** 7 vt dry. **~rse** vpr dry; (río etc) dry up; (persona) dry o.s.

sección f section

seco adj dry; (frutos, flores) dried; (flaco) thin; (respuesta) curt. **a secas** just. **en ~** (bruscamente) suddenly. **lavar en ~** dry-clean

secretar|ía f secretariat; (Mex, ministerio) ministry. **~io** m secretary; (Mex, Pol) minister

secreto adj & m secret

secta f sect. **~rio** adj sectarian

sector m sector

secuela f consequence

secuencia f sequence

secuestr|ar vt confiscate; kidnap (persona); hijack (avión). **~o** m seizure; (de persona) kidnapping; (de avión) hijack(ing)

secundar vt second, help. **~io** adj secondary

sed f thirst. ● vb véase **SER. tener ~** be thirsty. **tener ~ de** (fig) be hungry for

seda f silk. **~ dental** dental floss

sedante adj & m sedative

sede f seat; (Relig) see; (de organismo) headquarters; (de congreso, juegos etc) venue

sedentario adj sedentary

sedici|ón f sedition. **~oso** adj seditious

sediento adj thirsty

seduc|ción f seduction. **~ir** 47 vt seduce; (atraer) attract. **~tor** adj seductive. ● m seducer

seglar adj secular. ● m layman

segrega|ción f segregation. **~r** 12 vt segregate

segui|da f. **en ~da** immediately. **~do** adj continuous; (en plural) consecutive. **~ de** followed by. ● adv straight; (LAm, a menudo) often. **todo ~do** straight ahead. **~dor** m follower; (en deportes) supporter. **~r** 5 & 13 vt follow. ● vi (continuar) continue; (por un camino) go on. **~r adelante** carry on

según prep according to. ● adv it depends; (a medida que) as

segund|a f (Auto) second gear; (en tren, avión etc) second class. **~o** adj & m second

segur|amente adv certainly; (muy probablemente) surely. **~idad** f security; (ausencia de peligro) safety; (certeza) certainty; (aplomo) confidence. **~idad en sí mismo** self-confidence. **~idad social** social security. **~o** adj safe; (cierto) certain, sure; (estable) secure; (de fiar) reliable. ● adv for certain. ● m insurance; (dispositivo de seguridad) safety device. **~o de sí mismo** self-confident. **~o contra terceros** third-party insurance

seis *adj & m* six. **~cientos** *adj & m* six hundred

seísmo *m* earthquake

selec|ción *f* selection. **~cionar** *vt* select, choose. **~tivo** *adj* selective. **~to** *adj* selected; (*fig*) choice

sell|ar *vt* stamp; (*cerrar*) seal. **~o** *m* stamp; (*precinto*) seal; (*fig, distintivo*) hallmark; (*LAm, en moneda*) reverse

selva *f* forest; (*jungla*) jungle

semáforo *m* (*Auto*) traffic lights; (*Rail*) signal; (*Naut*) semaphore

semana *f* week. **S~ Santa** Holy Week. **~l** *adj* weekly. **~rio** *adj & m* weekly

> **Semana Santa** The most famous Holy Week celebrations in the Spanish-speaking world are held in Sevilla between Palm Sunday and Easter Sunday. Lay brotherhoods, *cofradías*, process through the city in huge parades. During the processions they sing *saetas*, flamenco verses mourning Christ's passion.

semántic|a *f* semantics. **~o** *adj* semantic

semblante *m* face; (*fig*) look

sembrar 1 *vt* sow; (*fig*) scatter

semeja|nte *adj* similar; (*tal*) such. ● *m* fellow man. **~nza** *f* similarity. **a ~nza de** like, **~r** *vi*, **~r a** resemble

semen *m* semen. **~tal** *adj* stud. ● *m* stud animal

semestr|al *adj* half-yearly. **~e** *m* six months

semi|circular *adj* semicircular. **~círculo** *m* semicircle. **~final** *f* semifinal

semill|a *f* seed. **~ero** *m* seedbed; (*fig*) hotbed

seminario *m* (*Univ*) seminar; (*Relig*) seminary

sémola *f* semolina

senado *m* senate. **~r** *m* senator

sencill|ez *f* simplicity. **~o** *adj* simple; (*para viajar*) single ticket; (*disco*) single; (*LAm, dinero suelto*) change

senda *f*, **sendero** *m* path

sendos *adj pl* each

seno *m* bosom. **~ materno** womb

sensaci|ón *f* sensation; (*percepción, impresión*) feeling. **~onal** *adj* sensational

sensat|ez *f* good sense. **~o** *adj* sensible

sensi|bilidad *f* sensibility. **~ble** *adj* sensitive; (*notable*) notable; (*lamentable*) lamentable. **~tivo** *adj* (*órgano*) sense

sensual *adj* sensual. **~idad** *f* sensuality

senta|do *adj* sitting (down); **dar algo por ~do** take something for granted. **~dor** *adj* (*LAm*) flattering. **~r 1** *vt* sit; (*establecer*) establish. ● *vi* suit; (*de medidas*) fit; (*comida*) agree with. **~rse** *vpr* sit (down)

sentencia *f* (*Jurid*) sentence. **~r** *vt* sentence (**a** to)

sentido *adj* heartfelt; (*sensible*) sensitive. ● *m* sense; (*dirección*) direction; (*conocimiento*) consciousness. **~ común** common sense. **~ del humor** sense of humour. **~ único** one-way. **doble ~** double meaning. **no tener ~** not make sense. **perder el ~** faint. **sin ~** senseless

sentim|ental *adj* sentimental. **~iento** *m* feeling; (*sentido*) sense; (*pesar*) regret

sentir 4 *vt* feel; (*oír*) hear; (*lamentar*) be sorry for. **lo siento mucho** I'm really sorry. ● *m* (*opinión*) opinion. **~se** *vpr* feel; (*Mex, ofenderse*) be offended

seña *f* sign. **~s** *fpl* (*dirección*) address; (*descripción*) description. **dar ~s de** show signs of

señal *f* signal; (*letrero, aviso*) sign; (*telefónica*) tone; (*Com*) deposit. **dar ~es de** show signs of. **en ~ de** as a token of. **~ado** *adj* (*hora, día*) appointed. **~ar** *vt* signal; (*poner señales en*) mark; (*apuntar*) point out; (*manecilla, aguja*) point to; (*determinar*) fix. **~arse** *vpr* stand out

señor *m* man, gentleman; (*delante de nombre propio*) Mr; (*tratamiento directo*) sir. **~a** *f* lady, woman; (*delante de nombre propio*) Mrs; (*esposa*) wife; (*tratamiento directo*) madam. **el ~** Mr. **muy ~ mío** Dear Sir. **¡no ~!** certainly not!. **~ial** *adj* (*casa*) stately.

S

~**ita** f young lady; (delante de nombre propio) Miss; (tratamiento directo) miss. ~**ito** m young gentleman

señuelo m lure

sepa vb véase **SABER**

separa|ción f separation. ~**do** adj separate. **por** ~**do** separately. ~**r** vt separate; (de empleo) dismiss. ~**rse** vpr separate; (amigos) part. ~**tista** adj & m & f separatist

septentrional adj north(ern)

septiembre m September

séptimo adj seventh

sepulcro m sepulchre

sepult|ar vt bury. ~**ura** f burial; (tumba) grave. ~**urero** m gravedigger

sequ|edad f dryness. ~**ia** f drought

séquito m entourage; (fig) train

ser 39
● verbo intransitivo

····➤ to be. **es bajo** he's short. **es abogado** he's a lawyer. **ábreme, soy yo** open up, it's me. **¿cómo es?** (como persona) what's he like?; (físicamente) what does he look like? **era invierno** it was winter

····➤ **ser de** (indicando composición) to be made of. **es de hierro** it's made of iron. (provenir de) to be from. **es de México** he's from Mexico. (pertenecer a) to belong to. **el coche es de Juan** the car belongs to Juan, it's Juan's car

····➤ (sumar) **¿cuánto es todo?** how much is that altogether? **son 40 dólares** that's 40 dollars. **somos 10** there are 10 of us

····➤ (con la hora) **son las 3** it's 3 o'clock. ~**ía la una** it must have been one o'clock

····➤ (tener lugar) to be held. ~**á en la iglesia** it will be held in the church

····➤ (ocurrir) to happen **¿dónde fue el accidente?** where did the accident happen? **me contó cómo fue** he told me how it happened

····➤ (en locuciones) **a no** ~ **que**

unless. **como sea** no matter what. **cuando sea** whenever. **donde sea** wherever. **¡eso es!** that's it! **es que** the thing is. **lo que sea** anything. **no sea que, no vaya a** ~ **que** in case. **o sea** in other words. **sea ... sea ...** either ... or ... **sea como sea** at all costs

● nombre masculino being; (persona) person. **el** ~ **humano** the human being. **un** ~ **amargado** a bitter person. **los** ~**es queridos** the loved ones

seren|ar vt calm down. ~**arse** vpr calm down. ~**ata** f serenade. ~**idad** f serenity. ~**o** adj serene; (cielo) clear; (mar) calm

seri|al m serial. ~**e** f series. **fuera de** ~**e** (fig) out of this world. **producción** f **en** ~**e** mass production

seri|edad f seriousness. ~**o** adj serious; (confiable) reliable; **en** ~**o** seriously. **poco** ~**o** frivolous

sermón m sermon; (fig) lecture

serp|enteante adj winding. ~**entear** vi wind. ~**iente** f snake. ~**iente de cascabel** rattlesnake

serr|ar 1 vt saw. ~**in** m sawdust. ~**uchar** vt (LAm) saw. ~**ucho** m (hand)saw

servi|cial adj helpful. ~**cio** m service; (conjunto) set; (aseo) toilet; ~**cio a domicilio** delivery service. ~**dor** m servant. **su** ~**dor** (en cartas) yours faithfully. ~**dumbre** f servitude; (criados) servants, staff. ~**l** adj servile

servidor m server; (criado) servant

servilleta f napkin, serviette

servir 5 vt serve; (en restaurante) wait on. ● vi serve; (ser útil) be of use. ~**se** vpr help o.s.. ~**se de** use. **no** ~ **de nada** be useless. **para** ~**le** at your service. **sírvase sentarse** please sit down

sesent|a adj & m sixty. ~**ón** adj & m sixty-year-old

seseo m pronunciation of the Spanish c as an s

sesión f session; (en el cine, teatro) performance

seso *m* brain

seta *f* mushroom

sete|cientos *adj & m* seven hundred. ~**nta** *adj & m* seventy. ~**ntón** *adj & m* seventy-year-old

setiembre *m* September

seto *m* fence; (*de plantas*) hedge. ~ **vivo** hedge

seudónimo *m* pseudonym

sever|idad *f* severity; (*de profesor etc*) strictness. ~**o** *adj* severe; (*profesor etc*) strict

sevillan|as *fpl* popular dance from Seville. ~**o** *m* person from Seville

sexo *m* sex

sext|eto *m* sextet. ~**o** *adj* sixth

sexual *adj* sexual. ~**idad** *f* sexuality

si *m* (*Mus*) B; (*solfa*) te. ● *conj* if; (*dubitativo*) whether; ~ **no** otherwise. **por** ~ **(acaso)** in case

sí[1] *pron reflexivo* (*él*) himself; (*ella*) herself; (*de cosa*) itself; (*uno*) oneself; (*Vd*) yourself; (*ellos, ellas*) themselves; (*Vds*) yourselves; (*recíproco*) each other

sí[2] *adv* yes. ● *m* consent

sida *m* Aids

sidra *f* cider

siembra *f* sowing; (*época*) sowing time

siempre *adv* always; (*LAm, todavía*) still; (*Mex, por fin*) after all. ~ **que** if; (*cada vez*) whenever. **como** ~ as usual. **de** ~ (*acostumbrado*) usual. **lo de** ~ the usual thing. **para** ~ for ever

sien *f* temple

siento *vb véase* **SENTAR** *y* **SENTIR**

sierra *f* saw; (*cordillera*) mountain range

siesta *f* nap, siesta

siete *adj & m* seven

sífilis *f* syphilis

sifón *m* U-bend; (*de soda*) syphon

sigilo *m* stealth; (*fig*) secrecy

sigla *f* abbreviation

siglo *m* century; (*época*) age. **hace** ~**s que no escribe** he hasn't written for ages

significa|ción *f* significance. ~**do** *adj* (*conocido*) well-known. ● *m* meaning; (*importancia*) significance. ~**r** [7] *vt* mean; (*expresar*) express. ~**tivo** *adj* meaningful; (*importante*) significant

signo *m* sign. ~ **de admiración** exclamation mark. ~ **de interrogación** question mark

sigo *vb véase* **SEGUIR**

siguiente *adj* following, next. **lo** ~ the following

sílaba *f* syllable

silb|ar *vt/i* whistle. ~**ato** *m*, ~**ido** *m* whistle

silenci|ador *m* silencer. ~**ar** *vt* hush up. ~**o** *m* silence. ~**oso** *adj* silent

sill|a *f* chair; (*de montar*) saddle (*Relig*) see ~**a de ruedas** wheelchair. ~**in** *m* saddle. ~**ón** *m* armchair

silueta *f* silhouette; (*dibujo*) outline

silvestre *adj* wild

simb|ólico *adj* symbolic(al). ~**olismo** *m* symbolism. ~**olizar** [10] *vt* symbolize

símbolo *m* symbol

sim|etría *f* symmetry. ~**étrico** *adj* symmetric(al)

similar *adj* similar (**a** to)

simp|atía *f* friendliness; (*cariño*) affection. ~**ático** *adj* nice, likeable; (*ambiente*) pleasant. ~**atizante** *m & f* sympathizer. ~**atizar** [10] *vi* get on (well together)

simpl|e *adj* simple; (*mero*) mere. ~**eza** *f* simplicity; (*tontería*) stupid thing; (*insignificancia*) trifle. ~**icidad** *f* simplicity. ~**ificar** [7] *vt* simplify. ~**ista** *adj* simplistic. ~**ón** *m* simpleton

simula|ción *f* simulation. ~**r** *vt* simulate; (*fingir*) feign

simultáneo *adj* simultaneous

sin *prep* without. ~ **saber** without knowing. ~ **querer** accidentally

sinagoga *f* synagogue

sincer|idad *f* sincerity. ~**o** *adj* sincere

sincronizar [10] *vt* synchronize

sindica|l *adj* (*trade-*)union. ~**lista** *m & f* trade-unionist. ~**to** *m* trade union

síndrome *m* syndrome

sinfín *m* endless number (**de** of)

sinfonía *f* symphony

singular *adj* singular; (*excepcional*) exceptional. ~**izarse** *vpr* stand out

s

siniestro *adj* sinister. • *m* disaster; (*accidente*) accident

sinnúmero *m* endless number (**de** of)

sino *m* fate. • *conj* but

sinónimo *adj* synonymous. • *m* synonym (**de** for)

sintaxis *f* syntax

síntesis *f invar* synthesis; (*resumen*) summary

sint|ético *adj* synthetic. **~etizar** 🔟 *vt* synthesize; (*resumir*) summarize

síntoma *f* symptom

sintomático *adj* symptomatic

sinton|ía *f* tuning; (*Mus*) signature tune. **~izar** 🔟 *vt* (*con la radio*) tune (in) to

sinvergüenza *m & f* crook

siquiera *conj* even if. • *adv* at least. **ni ~** not even

sirena *f* siren; (*en cuentos*) mermaid

sirio *adj & m* Syrian

sirvient|a *f* maid. **~e** *m* servant

sirvo *vb véase* **SERVIR**

sísmico *adj* seismic

sismo *m* earthquake

sistem|a *m* system. **por ~a** as a rule. **~ático** *adj* systematic

sitiar *vt* besiege; (*fig*) surround

sitio *m* place; (*espacio*) space; (*Mil*) siege; (*Mex, parada de taxi*) taxi rank. **en cualquier ~** anywhere. **~ web** website

situa|ción *f* situation; (*estado, condición*) position. **~r** 🔢 *vt* place, put; locate (*edificio*). **~rse** *vpr* be successful, establish o.s.

slip /es'lip/ *m* (*pl* **~s**) underpants, briefs

smoking /es'mokin/ *m* (*pl* **~s**) dinner jacket (*Brit*), tuxedo (*Amer*)

sobaco *m* armpit

sobar *vt* handle; knead (*masa*)

soberan|ía *f* sovereignty. **~o** *adj* sovereign; (*fig*) supreme. • *m* sovereign

soberbi|a *f* pride; (*altanería*) arrogance. **~o** *adj* proud; (*altivo*) arrogant

soborn|ar *vt* bribe. **~o** *m* bribe

sobra *f* surplus. **de ~** more than enough. **~s** *fpl* leftovers. **~do** *adj* more than enough. **~nte** *adj* surplus.

~r *vi* be left over; (*estorbar*) be in the way

sobre *prep* on; (*encima de*) on top of; (*más o menos*) about; (*por encima de*) above; (*sin tocar*) over. **~ todo** above all, especially. • *m* envelope. **~cargar** 🔢 *vt* overload. **~coger** 🔢 *vt* startle; (*conmover*) move. **~cubierta** *f* dustcover. **~dosis** *f invar* overdose. **~entender** 🔟 *vt* understand, infer. **~girar** *vt* (*LAm*) overdraw. **~giro** *m* (*LAm*) overdraft. **~humano** *adj* superhuman. **~llevar** *vt* bear. **~mesa** *f*. **de ~mesa** after-dinner. **~natural** *adj* supernatural. **~nombre** *m* nickname. **~pasar** *vt* exceed. **~peso** *m* (*LAm*) excess baggage. **~poner** 🔢 *vt* superimpose. **~ponerse** *vpr* overcome. **~saliente** *adj* (*fig*) outstanding. • *m* excellent mark. **~salir** 🔢 *vi* stick out; (*fig*) stand out. **~saltar** *vt* startle. **~salto** *m* fright. **~sueldo** *m* bonus. **~todo** *m* overcoat. **~venir** 🔢 *vi* happen. **~viviente** *adj* surviving. • *m & f* survivor. **~vivir** *vi* survive. **~volar** *vt* fly over

sobriedad *f* moderation; (*de estilo*) simplicity

sobrin|a *f* niece. **~o** *m* nephew. **~os** (*varones*) nephews; (*varones y mujeres*) nieces and nephews

sobrio *adj* moderate, sober

socavar *vt* undermine

soci|able *adj* sociable. **~al** *adj* social. **~aldemócrata** *m & f* social democrat. **~alismo** *m* socialism. **~alista** *adj & m & f* socialist. **~edad** *f* society; (*Com*) company. **~edad anónima** limited company. **~o** *m* member; (*Com*) partner. **~ología** *f* sociology. **~ólogo** *m* sociologist

socorr|er *vt* help. **~o** *m* help

soda *f* (*bebida*) soda (water)

sodio *m* sodium

sofá *m* sofa, settee

sofistica|ción *f* sophistication. **~do** *adj* sophisticated

sofo|cante *adj* suffocating; (*fig*) stifling. **~car** 🟠 *vt* smother (*fuego*); (*fig*) stifle. **~carse** *vpr* get upset

soga *f* rope

soja *f* soya (bean)

sojuzgar 🔢 *vt* subdue

sol *m* sun; (*luz*) sunlight; (*Mus*) G; (*solfa*) soh. **al ~** in the sun. **día** *m* **de ~** sunny day. **hace ~, hay ~** it is sunny. **tomar el ~** sunbathe

solamente *adv* only

solapa *f* lapel; (*de bolsillo etc*) flap. **~do** *adj* sly

solar *adj* solar. ● *m* plot

solariego *adj* (*casa*) ancestral

soldado *m* soldier. **~ raso** private

solda|dor *m* welder; (*utensilio*) soldering iron. **~r** 🛈 *vt* weld, solder

soleado *adj* sunny

soledad *f* solitude; (*aislamiento*) loneliness

solemn|e *adj* solemn. **~idad** *f* solemnity

soler 🛈 *vi* be in the habit of. **suele despertarse a las 6** he usually wakes up at 6 o'clock

sol|icitante *m* applicant. **~ de asilo** asylum seeker. **~icitar** *vt* request, ask for; apply for (empleo). **~ícito** *adj* solicitous. **~icitud** *f* request; (*para un puesto*) application; (*formulario*) application form; (*preocupación*) concern

solidaridad *f* solidarity

solid|ez *f* solidity; (*de argumento etc*) soundness. **~ificarse** 🛈 *vpr* solidify

sólido *adj* solid; (*argumento etc*) sound. ● *m* solid

soliloquio *m* soliloquy

solista *m & f* soloist

solitario *adj* solitary; (*aislado*) lonely. ● *m* loner; (*juego, diamante*) solitaire

solloz|ar 🛈 *vi* sob. **~o** *m* sob

solo *adj* (*sin compañía*) alone; (*aislado*) lonely; (*sin ayuda*) by oneself; (*único*) only; (*Mus*) solo; (*café*) black. ● *m* solo; (*juego*) solitaire. **a solas** alone

sólo *adv* only. **~ que** except that. **no ~... sino también** not only... but also.... **tan ~** only

solomillo *m* sirloin

soltar 🛈 *vt* let go of; (*dejar ir*) release; (*dejar caer*) drop; (*dejar salir, decir*) let out; give (golpe etc). **~se** *vpr* come undone; (*librarse*) break loose

solter|a *f* single woman. **~o** *adj* single. ● *m* bachelor

soltura *f* looseness; (*fig*) ease, fluency

solu|ble *adj* soluble. **~ción** *f* solution. **~cionar** *vt* solve; settle (huelga, asunto)

solvente *adj & m* solvent

sombr|a *f* shadow; (*lugar sin sol*) shade. **a la ~a** in the shade. **~eado** *adj* shady

sombrero *m* hat. **~ hongo** bowler hat

sombrío *adj* sombre

somero *adj* superficial

someter *vt* subdue; subject (persona); (*presentar*) submit. **~se** *vpr* give in

somn|oliento *adj* sleepy. **~ífero** *m* sleeping-pill

somos *vb véase* **SER**

son *m* sound. ● *vb véase* **SER**

sonámbulo *m* sleepwalker. **ser ~** walk in one's sleep

sonar 🛈 *vt* blow; ring (timbre). ● *vi* sound; (*timbre, teléfono etc*) ring; (*despertador*) go off; (*Mus*) play; (*ser conocido*) be familiar. **~ a** sound like. **~se** *vpr* blow one's nose

sonde|ar *vt* sound out; explore (espacio); (*Naut*) sound. **~o** *m* poll; (*Naut*) sounding

soneto *m* sonnet

sonido *m* sound

sonoro *adj* sonorous; (*ruidoso*) loud

sonr|eír 🛈 *vi* smile. **~eírse** *vpr* smile. **~isa** *f* smile

sonroj|arse *vpr* blush. **~o** *m* blush

sonrosado *adj* rosy, pink

sonsacar 🛈 *vt* wheedle out

soñ|ado *adj* dream. **~ador** *m* dreamer. **~ar** 🛈 *vi* dream (**con** of). **¡ni ~arlo!** not likely!

sopa *f* soup

sopesar *vt* (*fig*) weigh up

sopl|ar *vt* blow; blow out (vela); blow off (polvo); (*Inflar*) blow up. ● *vi* blow. **~ete** *m* blowlamp. **~o** *m* puff

soport|al *m* porch. **~ales** *mpl* arcade. **~ar** *vt* support; (*fig*) bear, put up with. **~e** *m* support

soprano *f* soprano

sor *f* sister

sorb|er *vt* sip; (*con ruido*) slurp; (*absorber*) absorb. **~ por la nariz** sniff. **~ete** *m* sorbet, water-ice. **~o** *m* (*pe-*

s

queña cantidad) sip; (*trago grande*) gulp

sordera *f* deafness

sórdido *adj* squalid; (*asunto*) sordid

sordo *adj* deaf; (*ruido etc*) dull. ● *m* deaf person. **hacerse el** ~ turn a deaf ear. ~**mudo** *adj* deaf and dumb

soroche *m* (*LAm*) mountain sickness

sorpre|ndente *adj* surprising. ~**nder** *vt* surprise. ~**nderse** *vpr* be surprised. ~**sa** *f* surprise

sorte|ar *vt* draw lots for; (*fig*) avoid. ~**o** *m* draw. **por** ~**o** by drawing lots

sortija *f* ring; (*de pelo*) ringlet

sortilegio *m* sorcery; (*embrujo*) spell

sos|egar 1 & 12 *vt* calm. ~**iego** *m* calmness

soslayo. de ~ sideways

soso *adj* tasteless; (*fig*) dull

sospech|a *f* suspicion. ~**ar** *vt* suspect. ● *vi.* ~ **de** suspect. ~**oso** *adj* suspicious. ● *m* suspect

sost|én *m* support; (*prenda femenina*) bra **1**, brassière. ~**ener 40** *vt* support; bear (*peso*); (*sujetar*) hold; (*sustentar*) maintain; (*alimentar*) sustain. ~**enerse** *vpr* support o.s.; (*continuar*) remain. ~**enido** *adj* sustained; (*Mus*) sharp. ● *m* (*Mus*) sharp

sota *f* (*de naipes*) jack

sótano *m* basement

soviético *adj* (*Historia*) Soviet

soy *vb* véase **SER**

Sr. *abrev* (**Señor**) Mr. ~**a.** *abrev* (**Señora**) Mrs. ~**ta.** *abrev* (**Señorita**) Miss

su *adj* (*de él*) his; (*de ella*) her; (*de animal, objeto*) its; (*de uno*) one's; (*de Vd*) your; (*de ellos, de ellas*) their; (*de Vds*) your

suav|e *adj* smooth; (*fig*) gentle; (color, sonido) soft; (tabaco, sedante) mild. ~**idad** *f* smoothness, softness. ~**izante** *m* conditioner; (*para ropa*) softener. ~**izar 10** *vt* smooth, soften

subalimentado *adj* underfed

subarrendar 1 *vt* sublet

subasta *f* auction. ~**r** *vt* auction

sub|campeón *m* runner-up. ~**consciencia** *f* subconscious. ~**consciente** *adj & m* subconscious. ~**continente** *m* subcontinent. ~**desarrollado** *adj* under-developed. ~**director** *m* assistant manager

súbdito *m* subject

sub|dividir *vt* subdivide. ~**estimar** *vt* underestimate

subi|da *f* rise; (*a montaña*) ascent; (*pendiente*) slope. ~**do** *adj* (color) intense. ~**r** *vt* go up; climb (mountain); (*llevar*) take up; (*aumentar*) raise; turn up (radio, calefacción). ● *vi* go up. ~**r a** get into (coche); get on (autobús, avión, barco, tren); (*aumentar*) rise. ~ **a pie** walk up. ~**rse** *vpr* climb up. ~**rse a** get on (tren etc)

súbito *adj* sudden. **de** ~ suddenly

subjetivo *adj* subjective

subjuntivo *adj & m* subjunctive

subleva|ción *f* uprising. ~**rse** *vpr* rebel

sublim|ar *vt* sublimate. ~**e** *adj* sublime

submarino *adj* underwater. ● *m* submarine

subordinado *adj & m* subordinate

subrayar *vt* underline

subsanar *vt* rectify; overcome (dificultad); make up for (carencia)

subscri|bir *vt* (*pp* subscrito) sign. ~**birse** *vpr* subscribe (a to). ~**pción** *f* subscription

subsidi|ario *adj* subsidiary. ~**o** *m* subsidy. ~**o de desempleo,** ~ **de paro** unemployment benefit

subsiguiente *adj* subsequent

subsist|encia *f* subsistence. ~**ir** *vi* subsist; (*perdurar*) survive

substraer 41 *vt* take away

subterráneo *adj* underground

subtítulo *m* subtitle

suburb|ano *adj* suburban. ~**io** *m* suburb; (*barrio pobre*) depressed area

subvenci|ón *f* subsidy. ~**onar** *vt* subsidize

subver|sión *f* subversion. ~**sivo** *adj* subversive. ~**tir 4** *vt* subvert

succi|ón *f* suction. ~**onar** *vt* suck

suce|der *vi* happen; (*seguir*) ~ **a** follow. ● *vt* (*substituir*) succeed. **lo que** ~**de es que** the trouble is that. **¿qué** ~**de?** what's the matter? ~**sión** *f* succession. ~**sivo** *adj* successive; (*consecutivo*) consecutive. **en lo**

~**sivo** in future. ~**so** *m* event; (*inci-dente*) incident. ~**sor** *m* successor

suciedad *f* dirt; (*estado*) dirtiness

sucinto *adj* concise; (*prenda*) scanty

sucio *adj* dirty; (*conciencia*) guilty. **en ~** in rough

sucre *m* (*unidad monetaria del Ecuador*) sucre

suculento *adj* succulent

sucumbir *vi* succumb (**a** to)

sucursal *f* branch (office)

Sudáfrica *f* South Africa

sudafricano *adj & m* South African

Sudamérica *f* South America

sudamericano *adj & m* South American

sudar *vi* sweat

sud|este *m* south-east. ~**oeste** *m* south-west

sudor *m* sweat

Suecia *f* Sweden

sueco *adj* Swedish. ● *m* (*persona*) Swede; (*lengua*) Swedish. **hacerse el ~** pretend not to hear

suegr|a *f* mother-in-law. ~**o** *m* father-in-law. **mis ~os** my in-laws

suela *f* sole

sueldo *m* salary

suelo *m* ground; (*dentro de edificio*) floor; (*territorio*) soil; (*en la calle etc*) road surface. ● *vb véase* **SOLER**

suelto *adj* loose; (*cordones*) undone; (*sin pareja*) odd; (*lenguaje*) fluent. **con el pelo ~** with one's hair down. ● *m* change

sueño *m* sleep; (*lo soñado, ilusión*) dream. **tener ~** be sleepy

suerte *f* luck; (*destino*) fate; (*azar*) chance. **de otra ~** otherwise. **de ~ que** so. **echar ~s** draw lots. **por ~** fortunately. **tener ~** be lucky

suéter *m* sweater, jersey

suficien|cia *f* (*aptitud*) aptitude; (*presunción*) smugness. ~**te** *adj* enough, sufficient; (*presumido*) smug. ~**temente** *adv* sufficiently

sufijo *m* suffix

sufragio *m* (*voto*) vote

sufri|miento *m* suffering. ~**r** *vt* suffer; undergo (*cambio*); have (*accidente*). ● *vi* suffer

suge|rencia *f* suggestion. ~**rir** 🔳 *vt* suggest. ~**stión** *f* (*en psicología*) suggestion. **es pura ~stión** it's all in one's mind. ~**stionable** *adj* impressionable. ~**stionar** *vt* influence. ~**stivo** *adj* (*estimulante*) stimulating; (*atractivo*) sexy

suicid|a *adj* suicidal. ● *m & f* suicide victim; (*fig*) maniac. ~**arse** *vpr* commit suicide. ~**io** *m* suicide

Suiza *f* Switzerland

suizo *adj & m* Swiss

suje|ción *f* subjection. **con ~ a** in accordance with. ~**tador** *m* bra 🔳, brassière. ~**tapapeles** *m invar* paperclip. ~**tar** *vt* fasten; (*agarrar*) hold. ~**tarse** *vpr*. ~**se a** hold on to, (*someterse*) abide by. ~**to** *adj* fastened; (*susceptible*) subject (**a** to). ● *m* individual; (*Gram*) subject.

suma *f* sum; (*Math*) addition; (*combinación*) combination. **en ~** in short. ~**mente** *adv* extremely. ~**r** *vt* add (up); (*totalizar*) add up to. ● *vi* add up. ~**rse** *vpr*. ~**rse a** join in

sumario *adj* brief; (*Jurid*) summary. ● *m* table of contents; (*Jurid*) pre-trial proceedings

sumergi|ble *adj* submersible. ~**r** 🔳 *vt* submerge

suministr|ar *vt* supply. ~**o** *m* supply; (*acción*) supplying

sumir *vt* sink; (*fig*) plunge

sumis|ión *f* submission. ~**o** *adj* submissive

sumo *adj* great; (*supremo*) supreme. **a lo ~** at the most

suntuoso *adj* sumptuous

supe *vb véase* **SABER**

superar *vt* surpass; (*vencer*) overcome; beat (*marca*); (*dejar atrás*) get over. ~**se** *vpr* better o.s.

superchería *f* swindle

superfici|al *adj* superficial. ~**e** *f* surface; (*extensión*) area. **de ~e** surface

superfluo *adj* superfluous

superior *adj* superior; (*más alto*) higher; (*mejor*) better; (*piso*) upper. ● *m* superior. ~**idad** *f* superiority

superlativo *adj & m* superlative

supermercado *m* supermarket

superstici|ón *f* superstition. **~oso** *adj* superstitious

supervis|ar *vt* supervise. **~ión** *f* supervision. **~or** *m* supervisor

superviv|encia *f* survival. **~iente** *adj* surviving. ● *m & f* survivor

suplantar *vt* supplant

suplement|ario *adj* supplementary. **~o** *m* supplement

suplente *adj & m & f* substitute

súplica *f* entreaty; (*Jurid*) request

suplicar 7 *vt* beg

suplicio *m* torture

suplir *vt* make up for; (*reemplazar*) replace

supo|ner 34 *vt* suppose; (*significar*) mean; involve (gasto, trabajo). **~sición** *f* supposition

suprem|acía *f* supremacy. **~o** *adj* supreme

supr|esión *f* suppression; (*de impuesto*) abolition; (*de restricción*) lifting. **~imir** *vt* suppress; abolish (impuesto); lift (restricción); delete (párrafo)

supuesto *adj* supposed; (falso) false; (*denominado*) so-called. ● *m* assumption. **¡por ~!** of course!

sur *m* south; (*viento*) south wind

surc|ar 7 *vt* plough; cut through (agua). **~o** *m* furrow; (*de rueda*) rut

surfear *vi* (*Informática*) surf

surgir 14 *vi* spring up; (*elevarse*) loom up; (*aparecer*) appear; (dificultad, oportunidad) arise

surrealis|mo *m* surrealism. **~ta** *adj & m & f* surrealist

surti|do *adj* well-stocked; (*variado*) assorted. ● *m* assortment, selection. **~dor** *m* (*de gasolina*) petrol pump (*Brit*), gas pump (*Amer*). **~r** *vt* supply; have (efecto). **~rse** *vpr* provide o.s. (**de** with)

susceptib|ilidad *f* sensitivity. **~le** *adj* susceptible; (*sensible*) sensitive

suscitar *vt* provoke; arouse (curiosidad, interés)

suscr... *véase* **SUBSCR...**

susodicho *adj* aforementioned

suspen|der *vt* suspend; stop (tratamiento); call off (viaje); (*en examen*) fail; (*colgar*) hang (**de** from). **~se** *m*

suspense. **novela de ~se** thriller. **~sión** *f* suspension. **~so** *m* fail; (*LAm*, en libro, película) suspense. **en ~so** suspended

suspir|ar *vi* sigh. **~o** *m* sigh

sust... *véase* **SUBST...**

sustanci|a *f* substance. **~al** *adj* substantial. **~oso** *adj* substantial

sustantivo *m* noun

sustent|ación *f* support. **~ar** *vt* support; (*alimentar*) sustain; (*mantener*) maintain. **~o** *m* support; (*alimento*) sustenance

sustitu|ción *f* substitution; (*permanente*) replacement. **~ir** 17 *vt* substitute, replace. **~to** *m* substitute; (*permanente*) replacement

susto *m* fright

susurr|ar *vi* (*persona*) whisper; (agua) murmur; (hojas) rustle

sutil *adj* fine; (*fig*) subtle. **~eza** *f* subtlety

suyo *adj & pron* (*de él*) his; (*de ella*) hers; (*de animal*) its; (*de Vd*) yours; (*de ellos, de ellas*) theirs; (*de Vds*) yours. **un amigo ~** a friend of his, a friend of theirs, etc

·····························

Tt

·····························

tabac|alera *f* (state) tobacco monopoly. **~o** *m* tobacco; (*cigarrillos*) cigarettes

tabern|a *f* bar. **~ero** *m* barman; (*dueño*) landlord

tabique *m* partition wall; (*Mex, ladrillo*) brick

tabl|a *f* plank; (*del suelo*) floorboard; (*de vestido*) pleat; (*índice*) index; (*gráfico, en matemática etc*) table. **hacer ~as** (*en ajedrez*) draw. **~a de surf** surfboard. **~ado** *m* platform; (*en el teatro*) stage. **~ao** *m* place where flamenco shows are held. **~ero** *m* board. **~ero de mandos** dashboard

tableta *f* tablet; (*de chocolate*) bar

tabl|illa *f* splint; (*Mex, de chocolate*) bar. **~ón** *m* plank. **~ón de anuncios**

notice board (*esp Brit*), bulletin board (*Amer*)

tabú *m* (*pl* ~**es**, ~**s**) taboo

tabular *vt* tabulate

taburete *m* stool

tacaño *adj* mean

tacha *f* stain, blemish. **sin** ~ unblemished; (*conducta*) irreproachable. ~**r** *vt* (*con raya*) cross out; (*Jurid*) impeach. ~ **de** accuse of

tácito *adj* tacit

taciturno *adj* taciturn; (*triste*) glum

taco *m* plug; (*LAm, tacón*) heel; (*de billar*) cue; (*de billetes*) book; (*fig, fam, lío*) mess; (*palabrota*) swearword; (*Mex, Culin*) taco, filled tortilla

tacón *m* heel

táctic|a *f* tactics. ~**o** *adj* tactical

táctil *adj* tactile

tacto *m* touch; (*fig*) tact

tahúr *m* card-sharp

tailandés *adj & m* Thai

Tailandia *f* Thailand

taimado *adj* sly

taj|ada *f* slice. **sacar** ~**ada** profit. ~**ante** *adj* categorical; (*tono*) sharp. ~**ear** *vt* (*LAm*) slash. ~**o** *m* cut; (*en mina*) face

tal *adj* such. **de** ~ **manera** in such a way. **un** ~ someone called. ● *pron.* **como** ~ as such. **y** ~ and things like that. ● *adv.* **con** ~ **de que** as long as. ~ **como** the way. ~ **para cual** ① two of a kind. ~ **vez** maybe. ¿**qué** ~**?** how are you? ¿**qué** ~ **es ella?** what's she like?

taladr|ar *vt* drill. ~**o** *m* drill

talante *m* mood. **de buen** ~ (*estar*) in a good mood; (*ayudar*) willingly

talar *vt* fell

talco *m* talcum powder

talega *f*, **talego** *m* sack

talento *m* talent; (*fig*) talented person

talismán *m* talisman

talla *f* carving; (*de diamante etc*) cutting; (*estatura*) height; (*tamaño*) size. ~**do** *m* carving; (*de diamante etc*) cutting. ~**dor** *m* carver; (*cortador*) cutter; (*LAm, de naipes*) dealer. ~**r** *vt* carve; sculpt (*escultura*); cut (*diamante*); (*Mex, restregar*) scrub. ~**rse** *vpr* (*Mex*) rub o.s.

tallarín *m* noodle

talle *m* waist; (*figura*) figure

taller *m* workshop; (*de pintor etc*) studio; (*Auto*) garage

tallo *m* stem, stalk

tal|ón *m* heel; (*recibo*) counterfoil; (*cheque*) cheque. ~**onario** *m* receipt book; (*de cheques*) cheque book

tamal *m* (*LAm*) tamale

tamaño *adj* such a. ● *m* size. **de** ~ **natural** life-size

tambalearse *vpr* (*persona*) stagger; (*cosa*) wobble

también *adv* also, too

tambor *m* drum. ~ **del freno** brake drum. ~**ilear** *vi* drum

tamiz *m* sieve. ~**ar** ⑩ *vt* sieve

tampoco *adv* neither, nor, not either. **yo** ~ **fui** I didn't go either

tampón *m* tampon; (*para entintar*) ink-pad

tan *adv* so. ~**...** **como** as... as. ¿**qué** ~**...?** (*LAm*) how...?

tanda *f* group; (*de obreros*) shift

tang|ente *adj & f* tangent. ~**ible** *adj* tangible

tango *m* tango

tanque *m* tank

tante|ar *vt* estimate; sound up (*persona*); (*ensayar*) test; (*fig*) weigh up; (*LAm, palpar*) feel. ● *vi* (*LAm*) feel one's way. ~**o** *m* estimate; (*prueba*) test; (*en deportes*) score

tanto *adj* (*en singular*) so much; (*en plural*) so many; (*comparación en singular*) as much; (*comparación en plural*) as many. ● *pron* so much; (*en plural*) so many. ● *adv* so; (*con verbo*) so much. **hace** ~ **tiempo** it's been so long. ~**...** **como** both...and. ¿**qué** ~**...?** (*LAm*) how much...? ~ **como** as well as; (*cantidad*) as much. ~ **más... cuanto que** all the more ... because. ~ **si... como si** whether ... or. **a** ~**s de** sometime in. **en** ~, **entre** ~ meanwhile. **en** ~ **que** while. **entre** ~ meanwhile. **hasta que** until. **no es para** ~ it's not as bad as all that. **otro** ~ the same; (*el doble*) as much again. **por (lo)** ~ therefore. ● *m* certain amount; (*punto*) point; (*gol*) goal. **estar al** ~

de be up to date with

tañer 🔢 *vi* peal

tapa *f* lid; (*de botella*) top; (*de libro*) cover. **~s** *fpl* savoury snacks. **~dera** *f* cover, lid; (*fig*) cover. **~r** *vt* cover; (*abrigar*) wrap up; (*obturar*) plug. **~rrabo(s)** *m invar* loincloth

---

tapas In Spain these are small portions of food served in bars and cafés with a drink. There is a wide variety, including Spanish omelette, seafood, different kinds of cooked potatoes, cheese, ham, chorizo etc. The practice of going out for a drink and *tapas* is known as *tapeo*. *i*

---

tapete *m* (*de mesa*) table cover; (*Mex, alfombra*) rug

tapia *f* wall. **~r** *vt* enclose

tapi|cería *f* tapestry; (*de muebles*) upholstery. **~z** *m* tapestry. **~zar** 🔟 *vt* upholster (*muebles*)

tapón *m* stopper; (*Tec*) plug

taqu|igrafía *f* shorthand

taquill|a *f* ticket office; (*fig, dinero*) takings. **~ero** *adj* box-office

tara *f* (*peso*) tare; (*defecto*) defect

tarántula *f* tarantula

tararear *vt/i* hum

tarda|nza *f* delay. **~r** *vt* take. • *vi* (*retrasarse*) be late; (*emplear mucho tiempo*) take a long time. **a más ~r** at the latest. **sin ~r** without delay

tard|e *adv* late. • *f* (*antes del atardecer*) afternoon; (*después del atardecer*) evening. **en la ~e** (*LAm*), **por la ~e** in the afternoon. **~ío** *adj* late

tarea *f* task, job

tarifa *f* rate; (*en transporte*) fare; (*lista de precios*) tariff

tarima *f* dais

tarjeta *f* card. **~ de crédito** credit card. **~ de fidelidad** loyalty card. **~ postal** postcard. **T~ Sanitaria Europea** European Health Insurance Card. **t~ SIM** SIM card. **~ telefónica** telephone card

tarro *m* jar; (*Mex, taza*) mug

tarta *f* cake; (*con base de masa*) tart. **~ helada** ice-cream gateau

tartamud|ear *vi* stammer. **~o** *adj*. **es ~o** he stammers

tasa *f* valuation; (*impuesto*) tax; (*índice*) rate. **~r** *vt* value; (*limitar*) ration

tasca *f* bar

tatarabuel|a *f* great-great-grandmother. **~o** *m* great-great-grandfather. **~os** *mpl* great-great-grandparents

tatua|je *m* (*acción*) tattooing; (*dibujo*) tattoo. **~r** 🔢 *vt* tattoo

taurino *adj* bullfighting

Tauro *m* Taurus

tauromaquia *f* bullfighting

taxi *m* taxi. **~ista** *m & f* taxi-driver

taz|a *f* cup. **~ón** *m* bowl

te *pron* (*acusativo*) you; (*dativo*) (to) you; (*reflexivo*) (to) yourself

té *m* tea; (*LAm, reunión*) tea party

teatr|al *adj* theatre; (*exagerado*) theatrical. **~o** *m* theatre; (*literatura*) drama

tebeo *m* comic

tech|ado *m* roof. **~ar** *vt* roof. **~o** *m* (*interior*) ceiling; (*LAm, tejado*) roof. **~umbre** *f* roof

tecl|a *f* key. **~ado** *m* keyboard. **~ear** *vt* key in

técnica *f* technique

tecnicismo *m* technical nature; (*palabra*) technical term

técnico *adj* technical. • *m* technician; (*en deportes*) trainer

tecnol|ogía *f* technology. **~ógico** *adj* technological

tecolote *m* (*Mex*) owl

teja *f* tile. **~s de pizarra** slates. **~do** *m* roof. **a toca ~** cash

teje|dor *m* weaver. **~r** *vt* weave; (*hacer punto*) knit

tejemaneje *m* 🔢 intrigue. **~s** *mpl* scheming

tejido *m* material; (*Anat, fig*) tissue. **~s** *mpl* textiles

tejón *m* badger

tela *f* material, fabric; (*de araña*) web; (*en líquido*) skin

telar *m* loom. **~es** *mpl* textile mill

telaraña *f* spider's web, cobweb

tele *f* 🔢 TV, telly

tele|banca *f* telephone banking. **~comunicación** *f* telecommunication.

~diario m television news. **~diri-gido** adj remote-controlled; (misil) guided. **~férico** m cable-car

tel|efonear vt/i telephone. **~efónico** adj telephone. **~efonista** m & f telephonist.

teléfono m telephone. **~ celular** (LAm) mobile phone, cellular phone. **~ móvil** (Esp) mobile phone, cellular phone. **~ satélite** satphone

tel|egrafía f telegraphy. **~égrafo** m telegraph. **~egrama** m telegram

telenovela f television soap opera

teleobjetivo m telephoto lens

telep|atía f telepathy. **~ático** adj telepathic

telesc|ópico adj telescopic. **~opio** m telescope

telesilla m & f chair-lift

telespectador m viewer

telesquí m ski-lift

televi|dente m & f viewer. **~sar** vt televise. **~sión** f television. **~sor** m television (set)

télex m invar telex

telón m curtain

tema m subject; (Mus) theme

tembl|ar ■ vi shake; (de miedo) tremble; (de frío) shiver. **~or** m shaking; (de miedo) trembling; (de frío) shivering; **~or de tierra** earth tremor. **~oroso** adj trembling

tem|er vt be afraid (of). ● vi be afraid. **~erse** vpr be afraid. **~erario** adj reckless. **~eroso** adj frightened. **~ible** adj fearsome. **~or** m fear

témpano m floe

temperamento m temperament

temperatura f temperature

tempest|ad f storm. **~uoso** adj stormy

templ|ado adj (tibio) warm; (clima, tiempo) mild; (valiente) courageous. **~anza** f mildness. **~ar** vt temper; (calentar) warm up. **~e** m tempering; (coraje) courage; (humor) mood

templo m temple

tempora|da f season. **~l** adj temporary. ● m storm

tempran|ero adj (frutos) early. **ser ~ero** be an early riser. **~o** adj & adv early

tenacidad f tenacity

tenacillas fpl tongs

tenaz adj tenacious

tenaza f, **tenazas** fpl pliers; (de chimenea, Culin) tongs; (de cangrejo) pincer

tende|ncia f tendency. **~nte** adj. **~nte a** aimed at. **~r** ■ vt spread (out); hang out (ropa a secar); (colocar) lay. ● vi tend (a to). **~rse** vpr lie down

tender|ete m stall. **~o** m shopkeeper

tendido adj spread out; (ropa) hung out; (persona) lying down. ● m (en plaza de toros) front rows

tendón m tendon

tenebroso adj gloomy; (asunto) sinister

tenedor m fork; (poseedor) holder

---

tener **4U**

● verbo transitivo

! El presente del verbo **tener** admite dos traducciones: to have y to have got, este último de uso más extendido en el inglés británico.

····▶ to have. **¿tienen hijos?** do you have any children?, have you got any children? **no tenemos coche** we don't have a car, we haven't got a car. **tiene gripe** he has (the) flu, he's got (the) flu

····▶ to be. (dimensiones, edad) **tiene 1 metro de largo** it's 1 meter long. **tengo 20 años** I'm 20 (years old)

····▶ (sentir) **tener** + nombre to be + adjective. **~ celos** to be jealous. **~ frío** to be cold

····▶ (sujetar, sostener) to hold. **tenme la escalera** hold the ladder for me

····▶ (indicando estado) **tiene las manos sucias** his hands are dirty. **me tiene preocupada** I'm worried about him. **me tuvo esperando** he kept me waiting

····▶ (llevar puesto) to be wearing, to have on. **¡qué zapatos más elegantes tienes!** those are very smart shoes you're wearing! **tienes el suéter al revés** you have your sweater on inside out

····▸ (*considerar*) ~ **a uno por algo** to think s.o. is sth. **lo tenía por tímido** I thought he was shy

● *verbo auxiliar*

····▸ ~ **que hacer algo** to have to do sth. **tengo que irme** I have to go

····▸ **tener** + *participio pasado.* **tengo pensado comprarlo** I'm thinking of buying it. **tenía entendido otra cosa** I understood something else

····▸ (*LAm, con expresiones temporales*) **tienen 2 años de estar aquí** they've been here for 2 months. **tiene mucho tiempo sin verlo** she hasn't seen him for a long time

····▸ (*en locuciones*) **aquí tiene** here you are. **¿qué tienes?** what's the matter with you? **¿y eso qué tiene?** (*LAm*) and what's wrong with that?

● **tenerse** *verbo pronominal*

····▸ (*sostenerse*) **no podía ~se en pie** (*de cansancio*) he was dead on his feet; (*de borracho*) he could hardly stand

····▸ (*considerarse*) to consider o.s. **se tiene por afortunado** he considers himself lucky

tengo *vb véase* TENER

teniente *m* lieutenant

tenis *m* tennis. ~ **de mesa** table tennis. ~**ta** *m & f* tennis player

tenor *m* sense; (*Mus*) tenor. **a** ~ **de** according to

tens|ión *f* tension; (*arterial*) blood pressure; (*Elec*) voltage; (*estrés*) strain. ~**o** *adj* tense

tentación *f* temptation

tentáculo *m* tentacle

tenta|dor *adj* tempting. ~**r** **1** *vt* tempt; (*palpar*) feel

tentativa *f* attempt

tenue *adj* thin; (*luz, voz*) faint; (*color*) subdued

teñi|r **5** & **22** *vt* dye; (*fig*) tinge (**de** with). ~**rse** *vpr* dye one's hair

teología *f* theology

te|oría *f* theory. ~**órico** *adj* theoretical

tequila *f* tequila

terap|euta *m & f* therapist. ~**éutico** *adj* therapeutic. ~**ia** *f* therapy

terc|er *adj véase* TERCERO. ~**era** *f* (*Auto*) third (gear). ~**ero** *adj* (*delante de nombre masculino en singular* **tercer**) third. ● *m* third party. ~**io** *m* third

terciopelo *m* velvet

terco *adj* obstinate

tergiversar *vt* distort

termal *adj* thermal

térmico *adj* thermal

termina|ción *f* ending; (*conclusión*) conclusion. ~**l** *adj & m* terminal. ~**nte** *adj* categorical. ~**r** *vt* finish, end. ~**r por** end up. ~**rse** *vpr* come to an end

término *m* end; (*palabra*) term; (*plazo*) period. ~ **medio** average. **dar** ~ **a** finish off. **en primer** ~ first of all. **en último** ~ as a last resort. **estar en buenos** ~**s con** be on good terms with. **llevar a** ~ carry out

terminología *f* terminology

termita *f* termite

termo *m* Thermos (P) flask, flask

termómetro *m* thermometer

termo|nuclear *adj* thermonuclear. ~**stato** *m* thermostat

terner|a *f* (*carne*) veal. ~**o** *m* calf

ternura *f* tenderness

terquedad *f* stubbornness

terrado *m* flat roof

terraplén *m* embankment

terrateniente *m & f* landowner

terraza *f* terrace; (*balcón*) balcony; (*terrado*) flat roof

terremoto *m* earthquake

terre|no *adj* earthly. ● *m* land; (*solar*) plot (*fig*) field. ~**stre** *adj* land; (*Mil*) ground

terrible *adj* terrible. ~**mente** *adv* awfully

territori|al *adj* territorial. ~**o** *m* territory

terrón *m* (*de tierra*) clod; (*Culin*) lump

terror *m* terror. ~**ífico** *adj* terrifying. ~**ismo** *m* terrorism. ~**ista** *m & f* terrorist

terso *adj* smooth

tertulia *f* gathering

tesina *f* dissertation

tesón *m* tenacity

tesor|ería *f* treasury. **~ero** *m* treasurer. **~o** *m* treasure; (*tesorería*) treasury; (*libro*) thesaurus

testaferro *m* figurehead

testa|mento *m* will. **T~mento** (*Relig*) Testament. **~r** *vi* make a will

testarudo *adj* stubborn

testículo *m* testicle

testi|ficar 🔲 *vt/i* testify. **~go** *m* witness. **~go ocular**, **~go presencial** eyewitness. **ser ~go de** witness. **~monio** *m* testimony

teta *f* tit (*fam o vulg*); (*de biberón*) teat

tétanos *m* tetanus

tetera *f* (*para el té*) teapot

tetilla *f* nipple; (*de biberón*) teat

tétrico *adj* gloomy

textil *adj & m* textile

text|o *m* text. **~ual** *adj* textual; (*traducción*) literal; (*palabras*) exact

textura *f* texture

tez *f* complexion

ti *pron* you

tía *f* aunt; 🔲 woman

tiara *f* tiara

tibio *adj* lukewarm

tiburón *m* shark

tiempo *m* time; (*atmosférico*) weather; (*Mus*) tempo; (*Gram*) tense; (*en partido*) half. **a su ~** in due course. **a ~** in time. **¿cuánto ~?** how long? **hace buen ~** the weather is fine. **hace ~** some time ago. **mucho ~** a long time. **perder el ~** waste time

tienda *f* shop (*esp Brit*), store (*esp Amer*); (*de campaña*) tent. **~ de comestibles**, **~ de ultramarinos** grocer's (shop) (*Brit*), grocery store (*Amer*)

tiene *vb véase* TENER

tienta. **andar a ~s** feel one's way

tierno *adj* tender; (*joven*) young

tierra *f* land; (*planeta, Elec*) earth; (*suelo*) ground; (*en geología*) soil, earth; (*LAm, polvo*) dust. **por ~** overland, by land

tieso *adj* stiff; (*engreído*) conceited

tiesto *m* flowerpot

tifón *m* typhoon

tifus *m* typhus; (*fiebre tifoidea*) typhoid (fever)

tigre *m* tiger. **~sa** *f* tigress

tijera *f*, **tijeras** *fpl* scissors; (*de jardín*) shears

tijeretear *vt* snip

tila *f* (*infusión*) lime tea

tild|ar *vt*. **~ar de** (*fig*) brand as. **~e** *f* tilde

tilo *m* lime(-tree)

timar *vt* swindle

timbal *m* kettledrum; (*Culin*) timbale, meat pie. **~es** *mpl* (*Mus*) timpani

timbr|ar *vt* stamp. **~e** *m* (*sello*) fiscal stamp; (*Mex*) postage stamp; (*Elec*) bell; (*sonido*) timbre

timidez *f* shyness

tímido *adj* shy

timo *m* swindle

timón *m* rudder; (*rueda*) wheel; (*fig*) helm

tímpano *m* eardrum

tina *f* tub. **~co** *m* (*Mex*) water tank. **~ja** *f* large earthenware jar

tinglado *m* mess; (*asunto*) racket

tinieblas *fpl* darkness; (*fig*) confusion

tino *f* good sense; (*tacto*) tact

tint|a *f* ink. **de buena ~a** on good authority. **~e** *m* dyeing; (*color*) dye; (*fig*) tinge. **~ero** *m* ink-well

tintinear *vi* tinkle; (*vasos*) chink, clink

tinto *adj* (*vino*) red

tintorería *f* dry cleaner's

tintura *f* dyeing; (*color*) dye

tío *m* uncle; 🔲 man. **~s** *mpl* uncle and aunt

tiovivo *m* merry-go-round

típico *adj* typical

tipo *m* type; (*fam, persona*) person; (*figura de mujer*) figure; (*figura de hombre*) build; (*Com*) rate

tip|ografía *f* typography. **~ográfico** *adj* typographic(al)

tira *f* strip. **la ~ de** lots of

tirabuzón *m* corkscrew; (*de pelo*) ringlet

tirad|a *f* distance; (*serie*) series; (*de periódico etc*) print-run. **de una ~a** in one go. **~o** *adj* (*barato*) very cheap;

t

(*fam, fácil*) very easy. **~or** *m* (*asa*) handle

tiran|ía *f* tyranny. **~izar** 🔟 *vt* tyrannize. **~o** *adj* tyrannical. ● *m* tyrant

tirante *adj* tight; (*fig*) tense; (*relaciones*) strained. ● *m* strap. **~s** *mpl* braces (*esp Brit*), suspenders (*Amer*)

tirar *vt* throw; (*desechar*) throw away; (*derribar*) knock over; drop (*bomba*); fire (*cohete*); (*imprimir*) print. ● *vi* (*disparar*) shoot. **~ a** tend to (be); (*parecerse a*) resemble. **~ abajo** knock down. **~ de** pull. **a todo ~** at the most. **ir tirando** get by. **~se** *vpr* throw o.s.; (*tumbarse*) lie down

tirita *f* (sticking) plaster

tiritar *vi* shiver (**de** with)

tiro *m* throw; (*disparo*) shot. **~ libre** free kick. **a ~** within range. **errar el ~** miss. **pegarse un ~** shoot o.s.

tiroides *m* thyroid (gland)

tirón *m* tug. **de un ~** in one go

tirote|ar *vt* shoot at. **~o** *m* shooting

tisana *f* herb tea

tisú *m* (*pl* **~s**, **~es**) tissue

títere *m* puppet. **~s** *mpl* puppet show

titilar *vi* (*estrella*) twinkle

titiritero *m* puppeteer; (*acróbata*) acrobat

titube|ante *adj* faltering; (*fig*) hesitant. **~ar** *vi* falter. **~o** *m* hesitation

titula|do *adj* (*libro*) entitled; (*persona*) qualified. **~r** *m* headline; (*persona*) holder. ● *vt* call. **~rse** *vpr* be called; (*persona*) graduate

título *m* title; (*académico*) qualification; (*Univ*) degree. **a ~ de** as, by way of

tiza *f* chalk

tiz|nar *vt* dirty. **~ne** *m* soot

toall|a *f* towel. **~ero** *m* towel-rail

tobillo *m* ankle

tobogán *m* slide; (*para la nieve*) toboggan

tocadiscos *m invar* record-player

toca|do *adj* touched 🔟. ● *m* head-dress. **~dor** *m* dressing-table. **~nte** *adj*. **en lo ~nte a** with regard to. **~r** 🔟 *vt* touch; (*palpar*) feel; (*Mus*) play; ring (*timbre*); (*mencionar*) touch on; (*barco*) stop at. ● *vi* ring; (*corresponder a uno*). **te ~ a ti** it's your turn.

en lo que ~ a as for. **~rse** *vpr* touch; (*personas*); touch each other

tocayo *m* namesake

tocino *m* bacon

tocólogo *m* obstetrician

todavía *adv* still; (*con negativos*) yet. **~ no** not yet

---

todo , **toda**

● *adjetivo*

····▸ (*la totalidad*) all. **~ el vino** all the wine. **~s los edificios** all the buildings. **~ ese dinero** all that money. **~ el mundo** everyone. (*como adv*) **está toda sucia** it's all dirty

····▸ (*entero*) whole. **~ el día** the whole day, all day. **toda su familia** his whole family. **~ el tiempo** the whole time, all the time

····▸ (*cada, cualquiera*) every. **~ tipo de coche** every type of car. **~s los días** every day

····▸ (*enfático*) **a toda velocidad** at top speed. **es ~ un caballero** he's a real gentleman

····▸ (*en locuciones*) **ante ~** above all. **a ~ esto** meanwhile. **con ~** even so. **del ~** totally. **lo contrario** quite the opposite

> Para expresiones como **todo recto, todo seguido** etc., ver bajo el respectivo adjetivo

● *pronombre*

····▸ all; (*todas las cosas*) everything. **eso es ~** that's all. **lo perdieron ~** they lost everything. **quiere comprar ~** he wants to buy everything

····▸ **todos, todas** all; (*todo el mundo*) everyone. **los compró ~s** he bought them all, he bought all of them. **~s queríamos ir** we all wanted to go. **vinieron ~s** everyone came

● *nombre masculino* **el/un ~** the/a whole

---

toldo *m* awning

tolera|ncia *f* tolerance. **~nte** *adj* tolerant. **~r** *vt* tolerate

toma f taking; (de universidad etc) occupation; (Med) dose; (de agua) intake; (Elec) socket; (LAm, acequia) irrigation channel. ● int well!, fancy that! ~ **de corriente** power point. ~**dura** f. ~**dura de pelo** hoax. ~**r** vt take; catch (autobús, tren); occupy (universidad etc); (beber) drink, have; (comer) eat, have. ● vi take; (esp LAm, beber) drink; (LAm, dirigirse) go. ~**r a bien** take well. ~**r a mal** take badly. ~**r en serio** take seriously. ~**rla con uno** pick on s.o. ~**r por** take for. ~ **y daca** give and take. ¿**qué va a** ~**r?** what would you like? ~**rse** vpr take; (beber) drink, have; (comer) eat, have

tomate m tomato

tomillo m thyme

tomo m volume

ton: **sin** ~ **ni son** without rhyme or reason

tonad|a f tune; (canción) popular song; (LAm, acento) accent. ~**illa** f tune

tonel m barrel. ~**ada** f ton. ~**aje** m tonnage

tónic|a f trend; (bebida) tonic water. ~**o** adj tonic; (sílaba) stressed. ● m tonic

tonificar 7 vt invigorate

tono m tone; (Mus, modo) key; (color) shade

tont|ería f silliness; (cosa) silly thing; (dicho) silly remark. **dejarse de** ~**erías** stop fooling around. ~**o** adj silly. ● m fool, idiot; (payaso) clown. **hacer el** ~**o** act the fool. **hacerse el** ~**o** act dumb

topacio m topaz

topar vi. ~ **con** run into

tope adj maximum. ● m end; (de tren) buffer; (Mex, Auto) speed bump. **hasta los** ~**s** crammed full. **ir a** ~ go flat out

tópico adj trite. **de uso** ~ (Med) for external use only. ● m cliché

topo m mole

topogr|afía f topography. ~**áfico** adj topographical

toque m touch; (sonido) sound; (de campana) peal; (de reloj) stroke. ~ **de queda** curfew. **dar los últimos**

~**s** put the finishing touches. ~**tear** vt fiddle with

toquilla f shawl

tórax m invar thorax

torcer 2 & 9 vt twist; (doblar) bend; wring out (ropa). ● vi turn. ~**se** vpr twist

tordo adj dapple grey. ● m thrush

tore|ar vt fight; (evitar) dodge. ● vi fight (bulls). ~**o** m bullfighting. ~**ro** m bullfighter

torment|a f storm. ~**o** m torture. ~**oso** adj stormy

tornado m tornado

tornasolado adj irridescent

torneo m tournament

tornillo m screw

torniquete m (Med) tourniquet; (entrada) turnstile

torno m lathe; (de alfarero) wheel. **en** ~ **a** around

toro m bull. ~**s** mpl bullfighting. **ir a los** ~**s** go to a bullfight

---

(la fiesta de) los toros Bullfighting is popular in Spain and some Latin American countries. The season runs from March to October in Spain, from November to March in Latin America. The bullfighters who take part in a corrida gather in *cuadrillas*. The principal bullfighter or *matador* is assisted by *peones*.

---

toronja f (LAm) grapefruit

torpe adj clumsy; (estúpido) stupid

torpedo m torpedo

torpeza f clumsiness; (de inteligencia) slowness. **una** ~ a blunder

torre f tower; (en ajedrez) castle, rook; (Elec) pylon; (edificio) tower block (Brit), apartment block (Amer)

torren|cial adj torrential. ~**te** m torrent; (circulatorio) bloodstream; (fig) flood

tórrido adj torrid

torsión f twisting

torso m torso

torta f tart; (LAm, de verduras) pie; (golpe) slap, punch; (Mex, bocadillo) filled roll. **no entender ni** ~ not

t

understand a thing. ~**zo** *m* slap, punch. **pegarse un ~zo** have a bad accident

tortícolis *f* stiff neck

tortilla *f* omelette; (*Mex, de maíz*) tortilla. ~ **española** potato omelette. ~ **francesa** plain omelette

tórtola *f* turtle-dove

tortuoso *adj* winding; (*fig*) devious

tortura *f* torture. ~**r** *vt* torture

tos *f* cough. ~ **ferina** whooping cough

tosco *adj* crude; (persona) coarse

toser *vi* cough

tost|ada *f* piece of toast. ~**adas** *fpl* toast; (*Mex, de tortilla*) fried tortillas. ~**ado** *adj* (pan) toasted; (café) roasted; (persona, color) tanned. ~**ar** *vt* toast (pan); roast (café); tan (piel)

total *adj* total. ● *adv* after all. ~ **que** so, to cut a long story short. ● *m* total; (totalidad) whole. ~**idad** *f* whole. ~**itario** *adj* totalitarian. ~**izar** **10** *vt* total

tóxico *adj* toxic

toxi|cómano *m* drug addict. ~**na** *f* toxin

tozudo *adj* stubborn

traba *f* catch; (*fig, obstáculo*) obstacle. **poner ~s a** hinder

trabaj|ador *adj* hard-working. ● *m* worker. ~**ar** *vt* work; knead (masa). ● *vi* work (**de** as); (actor) act. ¿**en qué ~as?** what do you do? ~**o** *m* work. **costar ~o** be difficult. ~**oso** *adj* hard

trabalenguas *m invar* tonguetwister

traba|r *vt* (*sujetar*) fasten; (*unir*) join; (*entablar*) strike up. ~**rse** *vpr* get stuck. **trabársele la lengua** get tongue-tied

trácala *m* (*Mex*) cheat. ● *f* (*Mex*) trick

tracción *f* traction

tractor *m* tractor

tradici|ón *f* tradition. ~**onal** *adj* traditional

traduc|ción *f* translation. ~**ir** **47** *vt* translate (**a** into). ~**tor** *m* translator

traer **41** *vt* bring; (*llevar*) carry; (*causar*) cause. **traérselas** be difficult

trafica|nte *m & f* dealer. ~**r** **7** *vi* deal

tráfico *m* traffic; (*Com*) trade

traga|luz *m* skylight. ~**perras** *f invar* slot-machine. ~**r** **12** *vt* swallow; (*comer mucho*) devour; (*soportar*) put up with. **no lo trago** I can't stand him. ~**rse** *vpr* swallow; (*fig*) swallow up

tragedia *f* tragedy

trágico *adj* tragic. ● *m* tragedian

trag|o *m* swallow, gulp; (*pequeña porción*) sip; (*fig, disgusto*) blow; (*LAm, bebida alcohólica*) drink. **echar(se) un ~o** have a drink. ~**ón** *adj* greedy. ● *m* glutton.

trai|ción *f* treachery; (*Pol*) treason. ~**cionar** *vt* betray. ~**cionero** *adj* treacherous. ~**dor** *adj* treacherous. ● *m* traitor

traigo *vb véase* **TRAER**

traje *m* dress; (*de hombre*) suit. ~ **de baño** swimming-costume. ~ **de etiqueta**, ~ **de noche** evening dress. ● *vb véase* **TRAER**.

traj|ín *m* coming and going; (*ajetreo*) hustle and bustle. ~**inar** *vi* bustle about

trama *f* weft; (*fig, argumento*) plot. ~**r** *vt* weave; (*fig*) plot

tramitar *vt* negotiate

trámite *m* step. ~**s** *mpl* procedure

tramo *m* (*parte*) section; (*de escalera*) flight

tramp|a *f* trap; (*fig*) trick. **hacer ~a** cheat. ~**illa** *f* trapdoor

trampolín *m* trampoline; (*de piscina*) springboard; (*rígido*) diving board

tramposo *adj* cheating. ● *m* cheat

tranca *f* bar. ~**r** *vt* bar

trance *m* moment; (*hipnótico etc*) trance

tranco *m* stride

tranquil|idad *f* peace; (*de espíritu*) peace of mind. **con ~** calmly. ~**izar** **10** *vt* calm down; (*reconfortar*) reassure. ~**o** *adj* calm; (*lugar*) quiet; (*conciencia*) clear. **estáte ~o** don't worry

transa|cción *f* transaction; (*acuerdo*) settlement. ~**r** *vi* (*LAm*) compromise

transatlántico *adj* transatlantic. ● *m* (*ocean*) liner

transbord|ador m ferry. **~ar** vt transfer. **~o** m transfer. **hacer ~o** change (**en** at)

transcri|bir (pp **transcrito**) vt transcribe. **~pción** f transcription

transcur|rir vi pass. **~so** m course

transeúnte m & f passer-by

transfer|encia f transfer. **~ir 4** vt transfer

transforma|ción f transformation. **~dor** m transformer. **~r** vt transform

transfusión f transfusion

transgre|dir vt transgress. **~sión** f transgression

transición f transition

transigir 14 vi give in, compromise

transistor m transistor

transita|ble adj passable. **~r** vi go

transitivo adj transitive

tránsito m transit; (tráfico) traffic

transitorio adj transitory

transmi|sión f transmission; (radio, TV) broadcast **~sor** m transmitter. **~sora** f broadcasting station. **~tir** vt transmit; (radio, TV) broadcast; (fig) pass on

transparen|cia f transparency. **~tar** vt show. **~te** adj transparent

transpira|ción f perspiration. **~r** vi transpire; (sudar) sweat

transport|ar vt transport. **~e** m transport. **empresa** f **de ~es** removals company

transversal adj transverse. **una calle ~ a la Gran Vía** a street which crosses the Gran Vía

tranvía m tram

trapear vt (LAm) mop

trapecio m trapeze; (Math) trapezium

trapo m cloth. **~s** mpl rags; (**1**, ropa) clothes **a todo ~** out of control

tráquea f windpipe, trachea

traquete|ar vt bang, rattle; (persona) rush around. **~o** m banging, rattle

tras prep after; (detrás) behind

trascende|ncia f significance; (alcance) implication. **~ntal** adj transcendental; (importante) important. **~r 1** vi (saberse) become known; (extenderse) spread

trasero adj back, rear. ● m (de persona) bottom

trasfondo m background

traslad|ar vt move; transfer (empleado etc); (aplazar) postpone. **~o** m transfer; (copia) copy. (mudanza) removal. **dar ~o** notify

trasl|úcido adj translucent. **~ucirse 11** vpr be translucent; (dejarse ver) show through; (fig, revelarse) be revealed. **~uz** m. **al ~uz** against the light

trasmano. a ~ out of the way

trasnochar vt (acostarse tarde) go to bed late; (no acostarse) stay up all night; (no dormir) be unable to sleep

traspas|ar vt go through; (transferir) transfer; go beyond (límite). **se ~a** for sale. **~o** m transfer

traspié m trip; (fig) slip. **dar un ~** stumble; (fig) slip up

trasplant|ar vt transplant. **~e** m transplant

trastada f prank; (jugada) dirty trick

traste m fret. **dar al ~ con** ruin. **ir al ~** fall through. **~s** mpl (Mex) junk

trastero m storeroom

trasto m piece of junk. ● **~s** mpl junk

trastorn|ado adj mad. **~ar** vt upset; (volver loco) drive mad; (fig, fam, gustar mucho) delight. **~arse** vpr get upset; (volverse loco) go mad. **~o** m (incl Med) upset; (Pol) disturbance; (fig) confusion

trat|able adj friendly; (Med) treatable. **~ado** m treatise; (acuerdo) treaty **~amiento** m treatment; (título) title. **~ante** m & f dealer. **~ar** vt (incl Med) treat; deal with (asunto etc); (manejar) handle; (de tú, de Vd) address (**de** as). ● vi deal (with). **~ar con** have to do with; (Com) deal in. **~ar de** be about; (intentar) try. **¿de qué se ~a?** what's it about? **~o** m treatment; (acuerdo) agreement; (título) title; (relación) relationship. **¡~o hecho!** agreed! **~os** mpl dealings

traum|a m trauma. **~ático** adj traumatic

través: a ~ de through; (de lado a lado) crossways

travesaño m crossbeam; (de portería) crossbar

travesía f crossing; (calle) side-street

t

trav|esura f prank. **~ieso** adj (niño) mischievous, naughty

trayecto m (tramo) stretch; (ruta) route; (viaje) journey. **~ria** f trajectory; (fig) course

traz|a f (aspecto) appearance. **~as** fpl signs. **~ado** m plan. **~ar** 🔟 vt draw; (bosquejar) sketch. **~o** m stroke; (línea) line

trébol m clover. **~es** mpl (en naipes) clubs

trece adj & m thirteen

trecho m stretch; (distancia) distance; (tiempo) while. **a ~s** here and there. **de ~ en ~** at intervals

tregua f truce; (fig) respite

treinta adj & m thirty

tremendo adj terrible; (extraordinario) terrific

tren m train. **~ de aterrizaje** landing gear. **~ de vida** lifestyle

tren|cilla f braid. **~za** f braid; (de pelo) plait. **~zar** 🔟 vt plait

trepa|dor adj climbing. **~dora** f climber. **~r** vt/i climb. **~rse** vpr. **~rse a** climb (árbol); climb onto (silla etc)

tres adj & m three. **~cientos** adj & m three hundred. **~illo** m three-piece suite; (Mus) triplet

treta f trick

tri|angular adj triangular. **~ángulo** m triangle

trib|al adj tribal. **~u** f tribe

tribuna f platform; (de espectadores) stand. **~l** m court; (de examen etc) board; (fig) tribunal

tribut|ar vt pay. **~o** m tribute; (impuesto) tax

triciclo m tricycle

tricolor adj three-coloured

tricotar vt/i knit

tridimensional adj three-dimensional

trig|al m wheat field. **~o** m wheat

trigésimo adj thirtieth

trigueño adj olive-skinned; (pelo) dark blonde

trilla|do adj (fig, manoseado) trite; (fig, conocido) well-known. **~r** vt thresh

trilogía f trilogy

trimestr|al adj quarterly. **~e** m quarter; (en enseñanza) term

trin|ar vi warble. **estar que trina** be furious

trinchar vt carve

trinchera f ditch; (Mil) trench; (abrigo) trench coat

trineo m sledge

trinidad f trinity

trino m warble

trío m trio

tripa f intestine; (fig, vientre) tummy, belly. **~s** fpl (de máquina etc) parts, workings. **revolver las ~s** turn one's stomach

tripl|e adj triple. ● m. **el ~e (de)** three times as much (as). **~icado** adj. **por ~icado** in triplicate. **~icar** 🔟 vt treble

tripula|ción f crew. **~nte** m & f member of the crew. **~r** vt man

tris m. **estar en un ~** be on the point of

triste adj sad; (paisaje, tiempo etc) gloomy; (fig, insignificante) miserable. **~za** f sadness

triturar vt crush

triunf|al adj triumphal. **~ante** adj triumphant. **~ar** vi triumph (**de, sobre** over). **~o** m triumph

trivial adj trivial. **~idad** f triviality

trizas. hacer algo ~ smash sth to pieces. **hacerse ~** smash

trocear vt cut up, chop

trocha f narrow path; (LAm, rail) gauge

trofeo m trophy

tromba f whirlwind; (marina) waterspout. **~ de agua** heavy downpour

trombón m trombone

trombosis f invar thrombosis

trompa f horn; (de orquesta) French horn; (de elefante) trunk; (hocico) snout; (en anatomía) tube. **coger una ~** 🅘 get drunk. **~zo** m bump

trompet|a f trumpet; (músico) trumpet player; (Mil) trumpeter. **~illa** f ear-trumpet

trompo m (juguete) (spinning) top

tronar vt (Mex) shoot. ● vi thunder

tronchar vt bring down; (fig) cut short. **~se de risa** laugh a lot

tronco m trunk. **dormir como un ~** sleep like a log

trono *m* throne

trop|a *f* troops. **~el** *m* mob

tropez|ar **1** & **10** *vi* trip; (*fig*) slip up. **~ar con** run into. **~ón** *m* stumble; (*fig*) slip

tropical *adj* tropical

trópico *adj* tropical. ● *m* tropic

tropiezo *m* slip; (*desgracia*) hitch

trot|ar *vi* trot. **~e** *m* trot; (*fig*) toing and froing. **al ~e** at a trot; (*de prisa*) in a rush. **de mucho ~e** hard-wearing

trozo *m* piece, bit. **a ~s** in bits

trucha *f* trout

truco *m* trick. **coger el ~** get the knack

trueno *m* thunder; (*estampido*) bang

trueque *m* exchange; (*Com*) barter

trufa *f* truffle

truhán *m* rogue

truncar **7** *vt* truncate; (*fig*) cut short

tu *adj* your

tú *pron* you

tuba *f* tuba

tubérculo *m* tuber

tuberculosis *f* tuberculosis

tub|ería *f* pipes; (*oleoducto etc*) pipe-lIne. **~o** *m* tube. **~o de ensayo** test tube. **~o de escape** (*Auto*) exhaust (pipe) **~ular** *adj* tubular

tuerca *f* nut

tuerto *adj* one-eyed, blind in one eye. ● *m* one-eyed person

tuétano *m* marrow; (*fig*) heart. **hasta los ~s** completely

tufo *m* stench

tugurio *m* hovel

tul *m* tulle

tulipán *m* tulip

tulli|do *adj* paralysed. **~r** **22** *vt* cripple

tumba *f* grave, tomb

tumb|ar *vt* knock over, knock down (*estructura*); (*fig, fam, en examen*) fail. **~arse** *vpr* lie down. **~o** *m* jolt. **dar un ~o** tumble. **~ona** *f* sun lounger

tumor *m* tumour

tumulto *m* turmoil; (*Pol*) riot

tuna *f* prickly pear; (*de estudiantes*) student band

tunante *m* & *f* rogue

túnel *m* tunnel

túnica *f* tunic

tupé *m* toupee; (*fig*) nerve

tupido *adj* thick

turba *f* peat; (*muchedumbre*) mob

turbado *adj* upset

turbante *m* turban

turbar *vt* upset; (*molestar*) disturb. **~se** *vpr* be upset

turbina *f* turbine

turbi|o *adj* cloudy; (*vista*) blurred; (*asunto etc*) shady. **~ón** *m* squall

turbulen|cia *f* turbulence; (*disturbio*) disturbance. **~te** *adj* turbulent

turco *adj* Turkish. ● *m* Turk; (*lengua*) Turkish

tur|ismo *m* tourism; (*coche*) car. **hacer ~** travel around. **~ cultural** heritage tourism. **~ patrimonial** (*LAm*) heritage tourism. **~ista** *m* & *f* tourist. **~ístico** *adj* tourist

turn|arse *vpr* take turns (*para* to). **~o** *m* turn; (*de trabajo*) shift. **de ~** on duty

turquesa *f* turquoise

Turquía *f* Turkey

turrón *m* nougat

tutear *vt* address as *tú*. **~se** *vpr* be on familiar terms

tutela *f* (*Jurid*) guardianship; (*fig*) protection

tutor *m* guardian; (*en enseñanza*) form master

tuve *vb* *véase* **TENER**

tuyo *adj* & *pron* yours. **un amigo ~** a friend of yours

....

Uu

....

u *conj* or

ubic|ar *vt* (*LAm*) place; (*localizar*) find. **~arse** *vpr* (*LAm*) be situated; (*orientarse*) find one's way around

ubre *f* udder

Ud. *abrev* (**Usted**) you

UE *abrev* (**Unión Europea**) EU

uf *int* phew!; (*de repugnancia*) ugh!

ufan|arse *vpr* be proud (**con, de** of); (*jactarse*) boast (**con, de** about). **~o** *adj* proud

úlcera *f* ulcer

últimamente *adv* (*recientemente*) recently; (*finalmente*) finally

ultim|ar *vt* complete; (*LAm, matar*) kill. **~átum** *m* ultimatum

último *adj* last; (*más reciente*) latest; (*más lejano*) furthest; (*más alto*) top; (*más bajo*) bottom; (*definitivo*) final. ● *m* last one. **estar en las últimas** be on one's last legs; (*sin dinero*) be down to one's last penny. **por ~** finally. **vestido a la última** dressed in the latest fashion

ultra *adj* ultra, extreme

ultraj|ante *adj* offensive. **~e** *m* insult, outrage

ultramar *m*. **de ~** overseas; (*productos*) foreign. **~inos** *mpl* groceries. **tienda de ~s** grocer's (shop) (*Brit*), grocery store (*Amer*)

ultranza. **a ~** (*con decisión*) decisively; (*extremo*) out-and-out

ultravioleta *adj invar* ultraviolet

umbilical *adj* umbilical

umbral *m* threshold

---

un, **una** *artículo indefinido*

! The masculine article **un** is also used before feminine nouns which begin with stressed **a** or **ha**, e.g. **un alma piadosa, un hada madrina**

····➤ (*en sing*) a; (*antes de sonido vocálico*) an. **un perro** a dog. **una hora** an hour

····➤ **unos, unas** (*cantidad incierta*) some. **compré ~os libros** I bought some books. (*cantidad cierta*) **tiene ~os ojos preciosos** she has beautiful eyes. **tiene ~os hijos muy buenos** her children are very good. (*en aproximaciones*) about. **en ~as 3 horas** in about 3 hours

➡ For further information see **uno**

---

un|ánime *adj* unanimous. **~animidad** *f* unanimity

undécimo *adj* eleventh

ungüento *m* ointment

únic|amente *adv* only. **~o** *adj* only; (*fig, incomparable*) unique

unicornio *m* unicorn

unid|ad *f* unit; (*cualidad*) unity. **~ad de disco** disk drive. **~o** *adj* united

unifica|ción *f* unification. **~r 7** *vt* unite, unify

uniform|ar *vt* standardize. **~e** *adj & m* uniform. **~idad** *f* uniformity

unilateral *adj* unilateral

uni|ón *f* union; (*cualidad*) unity; (*Tec*) joint. **~r** *vt* join; mix (*líquidos*). **~rse** *vpr* join together; (*caminos*) converge; (*compañías*) merge

unísono *m* unison. **al ~** in unison

univers|al *adj* universal. **~idad** *f* university. **~itario** *adj* university. **~o** *m* universe

---

uno, **una**

● *adjetivo*

Note that **uno** becomes **un** before masculine nouns

····➤ one. **una peseta** one peseta. **un dólar** one dollar. **ni una persona** not one person, not a single person. **treinta y un años** thirty one years

● *pronombre*

····➤ one. **~ es mío** one (of them) is mine. **es la una** it's one o'clock. **se ayudan el ~ al otro** they help one another, they help each other. **lo que sienten el ~ por el otro** what they feel for each other

····➤ (*fam, alguien*) someone. **le pregunté a ~** I asked someone

····➤ **unos, unas** some. **no tenía vasos así es que le presté ~s** she didn't have any glasses so I lent her some. **a ~s les gusta, a otros no** some like it, others don't. **los ~s a los otros** one another, each other

····➤ (*impersonal*) you. **~ no sabe qué decir** you don't know what to say

untar *vt* grease; (*cubrir*) spread; (*fig, fam, sobornar*) bribe

uña *f* nail; (*de animal*) claw; (*casco*) hoof

uranio *m* uranium

Urano *m* Uranus

urban|idad *f* politeness. **~ismo** *m* town planning. **~ización** *f* development. **~izar** 🔟 *vt* develop. **~o** *adj* urban

urbe *f* big city

urdir *vt* (*fig*) plot

urg|encia *f* urgency; (*emergencia*) emergency. **~encias** A & E, (*Amer*) emergency room. **~ente** *adj* urgent; (*carta*) express. **~ir** 🔟 *vi* be urgent.

urinario *m* urinal

urna *f* urn; (*Pol*) ballot box

urraca *f* magpie

URSS *abrev* (*Historia*) USSR

Uruguay *m*. **el ~** Uruguay

uruguayo *adj & m* Uruguayan

us|ado *adj* (*con estar*) used; (*ropa etc*) worn; (*con ser*) secondhand. **~ar** *vt* use; (*llevar*) wear. **~arse** *vpr* (*LAm*) be in fashion. **~o** *m* use; (*costumbre*) custom. **al ~o de** in the style of

usted *pron* you. **~es** you

usual *adj* usual

usuario *adj* user

usur|a *f* usury. **~ero** *m* usurer

usurpar *vt* usurp

utensilio *m* utensil; (*herramienta*) tool

útero *m* womb, uterus

útil *adj* useful. **~es** *mpl* implements; (*equipo*) equipment

utili|dad *f* usefulness. **~dades** *fpl* (*LAm*) profits. **~zación** *f* use, utilization. **~zar** 🔟 *vt* use, utilize

utopía *f* Utopia

uva *f* grape. **~ pasa** raisin. **mala ~** bad mood

Vv

vaca *f* cow. **carne de ~,** beef

vacaciones *fpl* holiday(s), vacation(s) (*Amer*). **de ~** on holiday, on vacation (*Amer*)

vacante *adj* vacant. ● *f* vacancy

vaciar 🔟 *vt* empty; (*ahuecar*) hollow out; (*en molde*) cast

vacila|ción *f* hesitation. **~nte** *adj* unsteady; (*fig*) hesitant. **~r** *vi* hesitate (🔟, *bromear*) tease; (*LAm, divertirse*) have fun

vacío *adj* empty; (*frívolo*) frivolous. ● *m* empty space; (*estado*) emptiness; (*en física*) vacuum; (*fig*) void

vacuna *f* vaccine. **~ción** *f* vaccination. **~r** *vt* vaccinate

vacuno *adj* bovine

vad|ear *vt* ford. **~o** *m* ford

vaga|bundear *vi* wander. **~bundo** *adj* vagrant; (*perro*) stray. **niño ~** street urchin. ● *m* tramp, vagrant. **~ncia** *f* vagrancy; (*fig*) laziness. **~r** 🔟 *vi* wander (about)

vagina *f* vagina

vago *adj* vague; (*holgazán*) lazy. ● *m* layabout

vag|ón *m* coach, carriage; (*de mercancías*) wagon. **~ón restaurante** dining-car. **~oneta** *f* small freight wagon; (*Mex, para pasajeros*) van

vaho *m* breath; (*vapor*) steam. **~s** *mpl* inhalation

vain|a *f* sheath; (*de semillas*) pod. **~illa** *f* vanilla

vaiv|én *m* swinging; (*de tren etc*) rocking. **~enes** *mpl* (*fig, de suerte*) swings

vajilla *f* dishes, crockery

vale *m* voucher; (*pagaré*) IOU. **~dero** *adj* valid

valenciano *adj* from Valencia

valentía *f* bravery, courage

valer 🔟 *vt* be worth; (*costar*) cost; (*fig, significar*) mean. ● *vi* be worth; (*costar*) cost; (*servir*) be of use; (*ser valedero*) be valid; (*estar permitido*) be allowed. **~ la pena** be worthwhile,

u

v

be worth it. **¿cuánto vale?** how much is it? **no ~ para nada** be useless. **eso no me vale** (*Mex, fam*) I don't give a damn about that. **¡vale!** all right!, OK! ⊞

valeroso *adj* courageous

valgo *vb véase* **VALER**

valía *f* worth

validez *f* validity. **dar ~ a** validate

válido *adj* valid

valiente *adj* brave; (*en sentido irónico*) fine. ● *m* brave person

valija *f* suitcase. **~ diplomática** diplomatic bag

valioso *adj* valuable

valla *f* fence; (*en atletismo*) hurdle

valle *m* valley

val|or *m* value, worth; (*coraje*) courage. **objetos** *mpl* **de ~or** valuables. **sin ~or** worthless. **~ores** *mpl* securities. **~oración** *f* valuation. **~orar** *vt* value

vals *m invar* waltz

válvula *f* valve

vampiro *m* vampire

vanagloriarse *vpr* boast

vandalismo *m* vandalism

vándalo *m & f* vandal

vanguardia *f* vanguard. **de ~** (*en arte, música etc*) avant-garde

van|idad *f* vanity. **~idoso** *adj* vain. **~o** *adj* vain; (*inútil*) futile; (*palabras*) empty. **en ~** in vain

vapor *m* steam, vapour; (*Naut*) steamer. **al ~** (*Culin*) steamed. **~izador** *m* vaporizer. **~izar** 🔟 vaporize

vaquer|o *m* cowherd, cowboy. **~os** *mpl* jeans

vara *f* stick; (*de autoridad*) staff (*medida*) yard

varar *vi* run aground

varia|ble *adj & f* variable. **~ción** *f* variation. **~do** *adj* varied. **~nte** *f* variant; (*Auto*) by-pass. **~ntes** *fpl* hors d'oeuvres. **~r** 🔟 *vt* change; (*dar variedad a*) vary. ● *vi* vary; (*cambiar*) change

varicela *f* chickenpox

variedad *f* variety

varilla *f* stick; (*de metal*) rod

varios *adj* several

varita *f* wand

variz *f* (*pl* varices, (*LAm*) várices) varicose vein

var|ón *adj* male. ● *m* man; (*niño*) boy. **~onil** *adj* manly

vasco *adj & m* Basque

vaselina *f* Vaseline (P), petroleum jelly

vasija *f* vessel, pot

vaso *m* glass; (*en anatomía*) vessel

vástago *m* shoot; (*descendiente*) descendant

vasto *adj* vast

vaticin|ar *vt* forecast. **~io** *m* prediction, forecast

vatio *m* watt

vaya *vb véase* **IR**

Vd. *abrev* (**Usted**) you

vecin|al *adj* local. **~dad** *f* neighbourhood; (*vecinos*) residents; (*Mex, edificio*) tenement house. **~dario** *m* neighbourhood; (*vecinos*) residents. **~o** *adj* neighbouring. ● *m* neighbour; (*de barrio, edificio*) resident

ve|da *f* close season. **~do** *m* reserve. **~do de caza** game reserve. **~r** *vt* prohibit

vega *f* fertile plain

vegeta|ción *f* vegetation. **~l** *adj & m* plant, vegetable. **~r** *vi* grow; (*persona*) vegetate. **~riano** *adj & m* vegetarian

vehemente *adj* vehement

vehículo *m* vehicle

veinte *adj & m* twenty

veinti|cinco *adj & m* twenty-five. **~cuatro** *adj & m* twenty-four. **~dós** *adj & m* twenty-two. **~nueve** *adj & m* twenty-nine; **~ocho** *adj & m* twenty-eight. **~séis** *adj & m* twenty-six. **~siete** *adj & m* twenty-seven. **~trés** *adj & m* twenty-three. **~uno** *adj & m* (*delante de nombre masculino* **veintiún**) twenty-one

vejación *f* humiliation

vejar *vt* ill-treat

veje|storio *m* old crock; (*LAm, cosa*) old relic. **~z** *f* old age

vejiga *f* bladder

vela *f* (*Naut*) sail; (*de cera*) candle; (*vigilia*) vigil. **pasar la noche en ~** have a sleepless night

velada *f* evening

vela|do *adj* veiled; (*Foto*) exposed. ~r *vt* watch over; hold a wake over (*difunto*); (*encubrir*) veil; (*Foto*) expose. ● *vi* stay awake. ~r por look after. ~rse *vpr* (*Foto*) get exposed

velero *m* sailing-ship

veleta *f* weather vane

vell|o *m* hair; (*pelusa*) down. ~ón *m* fleece

velo *m* veil

veloc|idad *f* speed; (*Auto, Mec*) gear. a toda ~idad at full speed. ~ímetro *m* speedometer. ~ista *m & f* sprinter

velódromo *m* cycle-track

veloz *adj* fast, quick

vena *f* vein; (*en madera*) grain. estar de/en ~ be in the mood

venado *m* deer; (*Culin*) venison

vencedor *adj* winning. ● *m* winner

venc|er 9 *vt* defeat; (*superar*) overcome. ● *vi* win; (*pasaporte*) expire. ~erse *vpr* collapse; (*LAm, pasaporte*) expire. ~ido *adj* beaten; (*pasaporte*) expired; (*Com, atrasado*) in arrears. darse por ~ido give up. ~imiento *m* due date; (*de pasaporte*) expiry date

venda *f* bandage. ~je *m* dressing. ~r *vt* bandage

vendaval *m* gale

vende|dor *adj* selling. ● *m* seller; (*en tienda*) salesperson. ~dor ambulante pedlar. ~r *vt* sell. se ~ for sale. ~rse *vpr* (*persona*) sell out

vendimia *f* grape harvest

veneciano *adj* Venetian

veneno *m* poison; (*malevolencia*) venom. ~so *adj* poisonous

venera|ble *adj* venerable. ~ción *f* reverence. ~r *vt* revere

venéreo *adj* venereal

venezolano *adj & m* Venezuelan

Venezuela *f* Venezuela

venga|nza *f* revenge. ~r 12 *vt* avenge. ~rse *vpr* take revenge (de, por for) (en on). ~tivo *adj* vindictive

vengo *vb véase* VENIR

venia *f* (*permiso*) permission. ~l *adj* venial

veni|da *f* arrival; (*vuelta*) return. ~dero *adj* coming. ~r 53 *vi* come.

~r bien suit. la semana que viene next week. ¡venga! come on!

venta *f* sale; (*posada*) inn. en ~ for sale

ventaj|a *f* advantage. ~oso *adj* advantageous

ventan|a *f* (*inc informática*) window; (*de la nariz*) nostril. ~illa *f* window

ventarrón *m* 🅴 strong wind

ventila|ción *f* ventilation. ~dor *m* fan. ~r *vt* air

vent|isca *f* blizzard. ~olera *f* gust of wind. ~osa *f* sucker. ~osidad *f* wind, flatulence. ~oso *adj* windy

ventrílocuo *m* ventriloquist

ventur|a *f* happiness; (*suerte*) luck. a la ~a with no fixed plan. echar la buena ~a a uno tell s.o.'s fortune. por ~a fortunately; (*acaso*) perhaps. ~oso *adj* happy, lucky

Venus *m* Venus

ver 43 *vt* see; watch (*televisión*). ● *vi* see. a mi modo de ~ in my view. a ~ let's see. dejarse ~ show. no lo puedo ~ I can't stand him. no tener nada que ~ con have nothing to do with. vamos a ~ let's see. ya lo veo that's obvious. ya ~emos we'll see. ~se *vpr* see o.s.; (*encontrarse*) find o.s.; (*dos personas*) meet; (*LAm, parecer*) look

veran|eante *m & f* holidaymaker, vacationer (*Amer*). ~ear *vi* spend one's summer holiday. ~eo *m* ir de ~eo spend one's summer holiday. lugar *m* de ~eo summer resort. ~iego *adj* summer. ~o *m* summer

vera|s. de ~ really; (*verdadero*) real. ~z *adj* truthful

verbal *adj* verbal

verbena *f* (*fiesta*) fair; (*baile*) dance

verbo *m* verb. ~so *adj* verbose

verdad *f* truth. ¿~? isn't it?, aren't they?, won't it? etc. a decir ~ to tell the truth. de ~ really. ~eramente *adv* really. ~ero *adj* true; (*fig*) real

verd|e *adj* green; (fruta) unripe; (chiste) dirty. ● *m* green; (*hierba*) grass. ~or *m* greenness

verdugo *m* executioner; (*fig*) tyrant

verdu|lería *f* greengrocer's (shop). ~lero *m* greengrocer

V

vereda *f* path; (*LAm, acera*) pavement (*Brit*), sidewalk (*Amer*)

veredicto *m* verdict

verg|onzoso *adj* shameful; (*tímido*) shy. **~üenza** *f* shame; (*bochorno*) embarrassment. **¡es una ~üenza!** it's a disgrace! **me da ~üenza** I'm ashamed/embarrassed. **tener ~üenza** be ashamed/embarrassed

verídico *adj* true

verifica|ción *f* verification. **~r 7** *vt* check. **~rse** *vpr* take place; (*resultar verdad*) come true

verja *f* (*cerca*) railings; (*puerta*) iron gate

vermú *m*, **vermut** *m* vermouth

verosímil *adj* likely; (*relato*) credible

verruga *f* wart

versa|do *adj* versed. **~r** *vi*. **~ sobre** deal with

versátil *adj* versatile; (*fig*) fickle

versión *f* version; (*traducción*) translation

verso *m* verse; (*poema*) poem

vértebra *f* vertebra

verte|dero *m* dump; (*desagüe*) drain **~r 1** *vt* pour; (*derramar*) spill ● *vi* flow

vertical *adj & f* vertical

vértice *f* vertex

vertiente *f* slope

vertiginoso *adj* dizzy

vértigo *m* (*Med*) vertigo. **dar ~** make dizzy

vesícula *f* vesicle. **~ biliar** gall bladder

vespertino *adj* evening

vestíbulo *m* hall; (*de hotel, teatro*) foyer

vestido *m* dress

vestigio *m* trace. **~s** *mpl* remains

vest|imenta *f* clothes. **~ir 5** *vt* (*llevar*) wear; dress (*niño etc*) ● *vi* dress. **~ir de** wear. **~irse** *vpr* get dressed. **~irse de** wear; (*disfrazarse*) dress up as. **~uario** *m* wardrobe; (*en gimnasio etc*) changing room (*Brit*), locker room (*Amer*)

vetar *vt* veto

veterano *adj* veteran

veterinari|a *f* veterinary science. **~o** *adj* veterinary. ● *m* vet **1**, veterinary surgeon (*Brit*), veterinarian (*Amer*)

veto *m* veto

vez *f* time; (*turno*) turn. **a la ~** at the same time. **alguna ~** sometimes; (*en preguntas*) ever. **algunas veces** sometimes. **a su ~** in turn. **a veces** sometimes. **cada ~** each time. **cada ~ más** more and more. **de una ~** in one go. **de una ~ para siempre** once and for all. **de ~ en cuando** from time to time. **dos veces** twice. **en ~ de** instead of. **érase una ~, había una ~** once upon a time there was. **otra ~** again. **pocas veces, rara ~** seldom. **una ~ (que)** once

vía *f* road; (*Rail*) line; (*en anatomía*) tract; (*fig*) way. **~ férrea** railway (*Brit*), railroad (*Amer*). **~ rápida** fast lane. **estar en ~s de** be in the process of. ● *prep* via. **~ aérea** by air. **~ de comunicación** means of communication.

viab|ilidad *f* viability. **~le** *adj* viable

viaducto *m* viaduct

viaj|ante *m & f* commercial traveller. **~ar** *vi* travel. **~e** *m* journey; (*corto*) trip. **~e de novios** honeymoon. **¡buen ~e!** have a good journey!. **estar de ~** be away. **salir de ~** go on a trip. **~ero** *m* traveller; (*pasajero*) passenger

víbora *f* viper

vibra|ción *f* vibration. **~nte** *adj* vibrant. **~r** *vt/i* vibrate

vicario *m* vicar

viceversa *adv* vice versa

vici|ado *adj* (*texto*) corrupt; (*aire*) stale. **~ar** *vt* corrupt; (*estropear*) spoil. **~o** *m* vice; (*mala costumbre*) bad habit. **~oso** *adj* dissolute; (*círculo*) vicious

víctima *f* victim; (*de un accidente*) casualty

victori|a *f* victory. **~oso** *adj* victorious

vid *f* vine

vida *f* life; (*duración*) lifetime. **¡~ mía!** my darling! **de por ~** for life. **en mi ~** never (in my life). **estar con ~** be still alive

vídeo *m*, (*LAm*) **video** *m* video; (*cinta*) videotape; (*aparato*) video recorder

videojuego *m* video game

vidri|era f stained glass window; (puerta) glass door; (LAm, escaparate) shop window. **~ería** f glass works. **~ero** m glazier. **~o** m glass; (LAm, en ventana) window pane. **limpiar los ~os** clean the windows. **~oso** adj glassy

vieira f scallop

viejo adj old. • m old person

viene vb véase VENIR

viento m wind. **hacer ~** be windy

vientre m stomach; (cavidad) abdomen; (matriz) womb; (intestino) bowels; (de vasija etc) belly

viernes m invar Friday. **V~ Santo** Good Friday

viga f beam, (de metal) girder

vigen|cia f validity. **~te** adj valid; (ley) in force. **entrar en ~cia** come into force

vigésimo adj twentieth

vigía f watch-tower. • m & f (persona) lookout

vigil|ancia f vigilance. **~ante** adj vigilant. • m & f security guard; (nocturno) watchman. **~ar** vt keep an eye on. • vi be vigilant; (vigía) keep watch. **~ia** f vigil; (Relig) fasting

vigor m vigour; (vigencia) force. **entrar en ~** come into force. **~oso** adj vigorous

vil adj vile. **~eza** f vileness; (acción) vile deed

villa f (casa) villa; (Historia) town. **la V~** Madrid

villancico m (Christmas) carol

villano adj villanous; (Historia) peasant

vilo. en ~ in the air

vinagre m vinegar. **~ra** f vinegar bottle. **~ras** fpl cruet. **~ta** f vinaigrette

vincular vt bind

vínculo m tie, bond

vindicar 7 vt (rehabilitar) vindicate

vine vb véase VENIR

vinicult|or m wine-grower. **~ura** f wine growing

vino m wine. **~ de la casa** house wine. **~ de mesa** table wine. **~ tinto** red wine

viñ|a f vineyard. **~atero** m (LAm) wine-grower. **~edo** m vineyard

viola f viola

viola|ción f violation; (de una mujer) rape. **~r** vt violate; break (ley); rape (mujer)

violen|cia f violence; (fuerza) force. **~tarse** vpr get embarrassed. **~to** adj violent; (fig) awkward

violeta adj invar & f violet

viol|ín m violin. • m & f (músico) violinist. **~inista** m & f violinist. **~ón** m double bass. **~onc(h)elista** m & f cellist. **~onc(h)elo** m cello

vira|je m turn. **~r** vt turn. • vi turn; (fig) change direction. **~r bruscamente** swerve

virg|en adj. **ser ~en** be a virgin. • f virgin. **~inal** adj virginal. **~inidad** f virginity

Virgo m Virgo

viril adj virile. **~idad** f virility

virtu|al adj virtual. **~d** f virtue; (capacidad) power. **en ~ de** by virtue of. **~oso** adj virtuous. • m virtuoso

viruela f smallpox

virulento adj virulent

virus m invar virus

visa f (LAm) visa. **~ado** m visa. **~r** vt endorse

vísceras fpl entrails

viscoso adj viscous

visera f visor; (de gorra) peak

visib|ilidad f visibility. **~le** adj visible

visillo m (cortina) net curtain

visi|ón f vision; (vista) sight. **~onario** adj & m visionary

visita f visit; (visitante) visitor; (invitado) guest; (Internet) hit. **~nte** m & f visitor. **~r** vt visit

vislumbrar vt glimpse

viso m sheen; (aspecto) appearance

visón m mink

visor m viewfinder

víspera f day before, eve

vista f sight, vision; (aspecto, mirada) look; (panorama) view. **apartar la ~** look away. **a primera ~, a simple ~** at first sight. **con ~s a** with a view to. **en ~ de** in view of. **estar a la ~** be obvious. **hacer la ~ gorda** turn a blind eye. **perder la ~** lose one's sight. **tener a la ~** have in front of

V

one. **volver la** ~ **atrás** look back.
~**zo** m glance. **dar/echar un** ~**zo a**
glance at

visto adj seen; (poco original) common
(considerado) considered. ~ **que**
since. **bien** ~ acceptable. **está** ~
que it's obvious that. **mal** ~ unacceptable. **por lo** ~ apparently. ● vb
véase **VESTIR**. ~ **bueno** m approval.
~**so** adj colourful, bright

visual adj visual. **campo** ~ field of vision

vital adj vital. ~**icio** adj life; (cargo)
held for life. ~**idad** f vitality

vitamina f vitamin

viticult|or m wine-grower. ~**ura** f
wine growing

vitorear vt cheer

vítreo adj vitreous

vitrina f showcase; (en casa) glass
cabinet; (LAm, escaparate) shop window

viud|a f widow. ~**ez** f widowhood.
~**o** adj widowed. ● m widower

viva m cheer. ~**cidad** f liveliness.
~**mente** adv vividly. ~**z** adj lively

víveres mpl supplies

vivero m nursery; (de peces) hatchery;
(de moluscos) bed

viveza f vividness; (de inteligencia)
sharpness; (de carácter) liveliness

vívido adj vivid

vividor m pleasure seeker

vivienda f housing; (casa) house;
(piso) flat (Brit), apartment (esp Amer).
sin ~ homeless

viviente adj living

vivificar **7** vt (animar) enliven

vivir vt live through. ● vi live; (estar
vivo) be alive. **¡viva!** hurray! **¡viva el
rey!** long live the king! ● m life. ~ **de**
live on. **de mal** ~ dissolute

vivisección f vivisection

vivo adj alive; (viviente) living; (color)
bright; (listo) clever; (fig) lively. ● m
sharp operator

vocab|lo m word. ~**ulario** m vocabu-
lary

vocación f vocation

vocal adj vocal. ● f vowel. ● m & f member. ~**ista** m & f vocalist

voce|ar vt call (mercancías); (fig) pro-
claim; (Mex) page (persona). ● vi

shout. ~**río** m shouting. ~**ro** (LAm)
spokeperson

vociferar vi shout

vola|dor adj flying. ● m rocket.
~**ndas. en** ~**ndas** in the air. ~**nte**
adj flying. ● m (Auto) steering-wheel;
(nota) note; (rehilete) shuttlecock. ~**r**
2 vt blow up. ● vi fly; (fam, desaparecer) disappear

volátil adj volatile

volcán m volcano. ~**ico** adj volcanic

volcar **2** & **7** vt knock over; (vaciar)
empty out; turn over (molde). ● vi
overturn. ~**se** vpr fall over; (vehículo)
overturn; (fig) do one's utmost. ~**se**
en throw o.s. into

vóleibol m, (Mex) **volibol** m volleyball

voltaje m voltage

volte|ar vt turn over; (en el aire) toss;
ring (campanas); (LAm) turn over (colchón etc). ~**arse** vpr (LAm) turn
around; (carro) overturn. ~**reta** f
somersault

voltio m volt

voluble adj (fig) fickle

volum|en m volume. ~**inoso** adj volu-
minous

voluntad f will; (fuerza de voluntad)
willpower; (deseo) wish; (intención) intention. **buena** ~ goodwill. **mala** ~
ill will

voluntario adj voluntary. ● m volunteer

voluptuoso adj voluptuous

volver **2** (pp vuelto) vt turn; (de
arriba a abajo) turn over; (devolver)
restore. ● vi return; (fig) revert. ~ **a
hacer algo** do sth again. ~ **en sí**
come round. ~**se** vpr turn round; (hacerse) become

vomit|ar vt bring up. ● vi be sick,
vomit. ~**ivo** adj disgusting

vómito m vomit; (acción) vomiting

voraz adj voracious

vos pron (LAm) you. ~**otros** pron you;
(reflexivo) yourselves

vot|ación f voting; (voto) vote. ~**ante**
m & f voter. ~**ar** vt vote for. ● vi vote
(por for). ~**o** m vote; (Relig) vow

voy vb véase **IR**

voz f voice; (rumor) rumour; (palabra)
word. ~ **pública** public opinion. **a
media** ~ softly. **a una** ~ unani-

mously. **dar voces** shout. **en ~ alta** loudly

vuelco *m* upset. **el corazón me dio un ~** my heart missed a beat

vuelo *m* flight; (*acción*) flying; (*de ropa*) flare. **al ~** in flight; (*fig*) in passing

vuelta *f* turn; (*curva*) bend; (*paseo*) walk; (*revolución*) revolution; (*regreso*) return; (*dinero*) change. **a la ~** on one's return. **a la ~ de la esquina** round the corner. **dar la ~ al mundo** go round the world. **dar una ~** go for a walk. **estar de ~** be back

vuelvo *vb véase* **VOLVER**

vuestro *adj* your. ● *pron* yours. **un amigo ~** a friend of yours

vulg|ar *adj* vulgar; (persona) common. **~aridad** *f* vulgarity. **~arizar** 🔟 *vt* popularize. **~o** *m* common people

vulnerable *adj* vulnerable

wáter /'(g)water/ *m* toilet
Web *m* /'(g)web/. **el ~** the Web
whisky /'(g)wiski/ *m* whisky

y *conj* and
ya *adv* already; (*ahora*) now; (*con negativos*) any more; (*para afirmar*) yes, sure; (*en seguida*) immediately; (*pronto*) soon. **~ mismo** (*LAm*) right

away. ● *int* of course! **~ no** no longer. **~ que** since. **¡~, ~!** oh sure!

yacaré *m* (*LAm*) alligator

yac|er 🔟 *vi* lie. **~imiento** *m* deposit; (*de petróleo*) oilfield

yanqui *m & f* American, Yank(ee)

yate *m* yacht

yegua *f* mare

yelmo *m* helmet

yema *f* (*en botánica*) bud; (*de huevo*) yolk; (*golosina*) sweet. **~ del dedo** fingertip

yerba *f* (*LAm*) grass; (*Med*) herb

yergo *vb véase* **ERGUIR**

yermo *adj* uninhabited; (*no cultivable*) barren. ● *m* wasteland

yerno *m* son-in-law

yerro *m* mistake. ● *vb véase* **ERRAR**

yeso *m* plaster; (*mineral*) gypsum

yo *pron* I. **~ mismo** myself. **¿quién, ~?** who, me? **soy ~** it's me

yodo *m* iodine

yoga *m* yoga

yogur *m* yog(h)urt

yuca *f* yucca

yugo *m* yoke

Yugoslavia *f* Yugoslavia

yugoslavo *adj & m* Yugoslav

yunque *m* anvil

yunta *f* yoke

xenofobia *f* xenophobia
xilófono *m* xylophone

zafarrancho *m* (*confusión*) mess; (*riña*) quarrel

zafarse *vpr* escape; get out of (*obligación etc*); (*Mex, dislocarse*) dislocate

zafiro *m* sapphire

zaga *f* rear; (*en deportes*) defence. **a la ~** behind

zaguán *m* hall

zaherir 🔟 *vt* hurt

zahorí *m* dowser

zaino *adj* (*caballo*) chestnut; (*vaca*) black

zalamer|ía *f* flattery. **~o** *adj* flattering. ● *m* flatterer

zamarra *f* (*piel*) sheepskin; (*prenda*) sheepskin jacket

zamarrear *vt* shake

zamba *f* South American dance

zambulli|da *f* dive; (*baño*) dip. **~rse** *vpr* dive

zamparse *vpr* gobble up

zanahoria *f* carrot

zancad|a *f* stride. **~illa** *f* trip. **hacer una ~illa a uno** trip s.o. up

zanc|o *m* stilt. **~udo** *adj* long-legged; (ave) wading. ● *m* (*LAm*) mosquito

zanganear *vi* idle

zángano *m* drone. ●*m* & *f* (*persona*) idler

zangolotear *vt* shake. ● *vi* rattle; (persona) fidget

zanja *f* ditch; (*para tuberías etc*) trench. **~r** *vt* (*fig*) settle

zapat|ear *vi* tap with one's feet. **~ería** *f* shoe shop; (*arte*) shoemaking. **~ero** *m* shoemaker; (*el que remienda zapatos*) cobbler. **~illa** *f* slipper; (*de deportes*) trainer. **~illa de ballet** ballet shoe. **~o** *m* shoe

zarand|a *f* sieve. **~ear** *vt* (*sacudir*) shake

zarcillo *m* earring

zarpa *f* paw

zarpar *vi* set sail, weigh anchor

zarza *f* bramble. **~mora** *f* blackberry

zarzuela *f* Spanish operetta

---

zarzuela A musical drama consisting of alternating passages of dialogue, songs, choruses, and dancing that originated in Spain in the seventeenth century. Also popular in Latin America, its name derives from the Palacio de la Zarzuela, the Madrid palace where the Royal family now lives. **ⓘ**

---

zigzag *m* zigzag. **~uear** *vi* zigzag

zinc *m* zinc

zócalo *m* skirting-board; (*pedestal*) plinth; (*Mex, plaza*) main square

zodiaco *m*, **zodíaco** *m* zodiac

zona *f* zone; (*área*) area

zoo *m* zoo. **~logía** *f* zoology. **~lógico** *adj* zoological

zoólogo *m* zoologist

zopenco *adj* stupid. ● *m* idiot

zoquete *m* blockhead

zorr|a *f* vixen **~illo** *m* (*LAm*) skunk.. **~o** *m* fox

zorzal *m* thrush

zozobra *f* (*fig*) anxiety. **~r** *vi* founder

zueco *m* clog

zumb|ar *vt* 🔢 give (golpe etc). ● *vi* buzz. **~ido** *m* buzzing

zumo *m* juice

zurci|do *m* darning. **~r** 🔢 *vt* darn

zurdo *adj* left-handed; (mano) left

zurrar *vt* (*fig, fam, dar golpes*) beat (up)

zutano *m* so-and-so

a /ə/, *stressed form* /eɪ/

before vowel sound or silent 'h' **an**

indefinite article

····➤ un (*m*), una (*f*). **a problem** un problema. **an apple** una manzana. **have you got a pencil?** ¿tienes un lápiz?

❗ Feminine singular nouns beginning with stressed or accented *a* or *ha* take the article *un* instead of *una*, e.g. un *águila*, un *hada*

····➤ (*when talking about prices and quantities*) por. **30 miles an hour** 30 millas por hora. **twice a week** dos veces por semana, dos veces a la semana

❗ There are many cases in which **a** is not translated, such as when talking about people's professions, in exclamations, etc: **she's a lawyer** *es abogada*. **what a beautiful day!** *¡qué día más precioso!* **have you got a car?** *¿tienes coche?* **half a cup** *media taza*

A & E /eɪənd'iː/ *n* urgencias *fpl*

aback /ə'bæk/ *adv*. **be taken ~** quedar desconcertado

abandon /ə'bændən/ *vt* abandonar. ●*n* abandono *m*, desenfado *m*. **~ed** *a* abandonado

abashed /ə'bæʃt/ *adj* confuso

abate /ə'beɪt/ *vi* disminuir; (*storm etc*) calmarse

abattoir /'æbətwɑː(r)/ *n* matadero *m*

abbess /'æbɪs/ *n* abadesa *f*

abbey /'æbɪ/ *n* abadía *f*

abbot /'æbət/ *n* abad *m*

abbreviat|e /ə'briːvɪeɪt/ *vt* abreviar. **~ion** /-'eɪʃn/ *n* abreviatura *f*; (*act*) abreviación *f*

abdicat|e /'æbdɪkeɪt/ *vt/i* abdicar. **~ion** /-'eɪʃn/ *n* abdicación *f*

abdom|en /'æbdəmən/ *n* abdomen *m*. **~inal** /-'dɒmɪnl/ *adj* abdominal

abduct /æb'dʌkt/ *vt* secuestrar. **~ion** /-ʃn/ *n* secuestro *m*

abhor /əb'hɔː(r)/ *vt* (*pt* abhorred) aborrecer. **~rence** /-'hɒrəns/ *n* aborrecimiento *m*. **~rent** /-'hɒrənt/ *adj* aborrecible

abide /ə'baɪd/ *vt* (*pt* abided) soportar. ●*vi* (*old use*, *pt* abode) morar. □ **~ by** *vt* atenerse a; cumplir (*promise*)

ability /ə'bɪlətɪ/ *n* capacidad *f*; (*cleverness*) habilidad *f*

abject /'æbdʒekt/ *adj* (*wretched*) miserable

ablaze /ə'bleɪz/ *adj* en llamas

able /'eɪbl/ *adj* (**-er**, **-est**) capaz. **be ~** poder; (*know how to*) saber. **~-bodied** /-'bɒdɪd/ *adj* sano, no discapacitado

ably /'eɪblɪ/ *adv* hábilmente

abnormal /æb'nɔːml/ *adj* anormal. **~ity** /-'mælətɪ/ *n* anormalidad *f*

aboard /ə'bɔːd/ *adv* a bordo. ●*prep* a bordo de

abode /ə'bəʊd/ *see* ABIDE. ●*n* (*old use*) domicilio *m*

aboli|sh /ə'bɒlɪʃ/ *vt* abolir. **~tion** /æbə'lɪʃn/ *n* abolición *f*

abominable /ə'bɒmɪnəbl/ *adj* abominable

aborigin|al /æbə'rɪdʒənl/ *adj & n* aborigen (*m & f*), indígena (*m & f*). **~es** /-iːz/ *npl* aborígenes *mpl*

abort /ə'bɔːt/ *vt* hacer abortar. **~ion** /-ʃn/ *n* aborto *m* provocado; (*fig*) aborto *m*. **have an ~ion** hacerse un aborto. **~ive** *adj* fracasado

abound /ə'baʊnd/ *vi* abundar (**in** en)

about /ə'baʊt/ *adv* (*approximately*) alrededor de; (*here and there*) por todas partes; (*in existence*) por aquí. **~ here** por aquí. **be ~ to** estar a punto de. ●*prep* sobre; (*around*) alrededor de; (*somewhere in*) en. **talk ~** hablar de. **~-face**, **~-turn** *n* (*fig*) cambio *m* rotundo

a

above /ə'bʌv/ adv arriba. ● prep encima de; (more than) más de. ~ all sobre todo. ~ board adj legítimo. ● adv abiertamente. ~-mentioned adj susodicho

abrasi|on /ə'breɪʒn/ n abrasión f. ~ve /-sɪv/ adj abrasivo

abreast /ə'brest/ adv. march four ~ marchar en columna de cuatro en fondo. keep ~ of mantenerse al corriente de

abroad /ə'brɔːd/ adv (be) en el extranjero; (go) al extranjero; (far and wide) por todas partes

abrupt /ə'brʌpt/ adj brusco. ~ly adv (suddenly) repentinamente; (curtly) bruscamente

abscess /'æbsɪs/ n absceso m

abscond /əb'skɒnd/ vi fugarse

absen|ce /'æbsəns/ n ausencia f; (lack) falta f. ~t /'æbsənt/ adj ausente. ~t-minded /-'maɪndɪd/ adj distraído. ~t-mindedness n distracción f, despiste m. ~tee /-'tiː/ n ausente m & f. ~teeism n absentismo m, ausentismo m (LAm)

absolute /'æbsəluːt/ adj absoluto. ~ly adv absolutamente

absolve /əb'zɒlv/ vt (from sin) absolver; (from obligation) liberar

absor|b /əb'zɔːb/ vt absorber. ~bent /-bent/ adj absorbente. ~bent cotton n (Amer) algodón m hidrófilo. ~ption /əb'zɔːpʃən/ n absorción f

abstain /əb'steɪn/ vi abstenerse (from de)

abstemious /əb'stiːmɪəs/ adj abstemio

abstention /əb'stenʃn/ n abstención f

abstract /'æbstrækt/ adj abstracto. ● n (summary) resumen m; (painting) cuadro m abstracto. ● /əb'strækt/ vt extraer; (summarize) resumir. ~ion /-ʃn/ n abstracción f

absurd /əb'sɜːd/ adj absurdo. ~ity n absurdo m, disparate m

abundan|ce /ə'bʌndəns/ n abundancia f. ~t adj abundante

abus|e /ə'bjuːz/ vt (misuse) abusar de; (ill-treat) maltratar; (insult) insultar. ● /ə'bjuːs/ n abuso m; (insults) insultos mpl. ~ive /ə'bjuːsɪv/ adj injurioso

abysmal /ə'bɪzməl/ adj Ⅰ pésimo

abyss /ə'bɪs/ n abismo m

academic /ækə'demɪk/ adj académico; (pej) teórico. ● n universitario m, catedrático m

academy /ə'kædəmɪ/ n academia f.

accelerat|e /ək'seləreɪt/ vt acelerar. ● vi acelerar; (Auto) apretar el acelerador. ~ion /-'reɪʃn/ n aceleración f. ~or n acelerador m

accent /'æksənt/ n acento m

accept /ək'sept/ vt aceptar. ~able adj aceptable. ~ance n aceptación f; (approval) aprobación f

access /'ækses/ n acceso m. ~ible /ək'sesəbl/ adj accesible; (person) tratable

accession /æk'seʃn/ n (to power, throne etc) ascenso m; (thing added) adquisición f

accessory /ək'sesərɪ/ adj accesorio. ● n accesorio m, complemento m; (Jurid) cómplice m & f

accident /'æksɪdənt/ n accidente m; (chance) casualidad f. by ~ sin querer; (by chance) por casualidad. ~al /-'dentl/ adj accidental, fortuito. ~ally /-'dentəlɪ/ adv sin querer; (by chance) por casualidad. ~-prone adj propenso a los accidentes

acclaim /ə'kleɪm/ vt aclamar. ● n aclamación f

accolade /'ækəleɪd/ n (praise) encomio m

accommodat|e /ə'kɒmədeɪt/ vt (give hospitality to) alojar; (adapt) acomodar; (oblige) complacer. ~ing adj complaciente. ~ion /-'deɪʃn/ n, ~ions npl (Amer) alojamiento m

accompan|iment /ə'kʌmpənɪmənt/ n acompañamiento m. ~ist n acompañante m & f. ~y /ə'kʌmpənɪ/ vt acompañar

accomplice /ə'kʌmplɪs/ n cómplice m & f

accomplish /ə'kʌmplɪʃ/ vt (complete) acabar; (achieve) realizar; (carry out) llevar a cabo. ~ed adj consumado. ~ment n realización f; (ability) talento m; (thing achieved) triunfo m, logro m

accord /ə'kɔːd/ vi concordar. ● vt conceder. ● n acuerdo m; (harmony) armonía f. **of one's own** ~ espontáneamente. **~ance** n. **in ~ance with** de acuerdo con. **~ing** adv. **~ing to** según. **~ingly** adv en conformidad; (therefore) por consiguiente

accordion /ə'kɔːdɪən/ n acordeón m

accost /ə'kɒst/ vt abordar

account /ə'kaʊnt/ n cuenta f; (description) relato m. **~s** npl (in business) contabilidad f. **on** ~ **of** a causa de. **on no** ~ de ninguna manera. **on this** ~ por eso. **take into** ~ tener en cuenta. ● vt considerar. □ ~ **for** vt dar cuenta de, explicar

accountan|cy /ə'kaʊntənsɪ/ n contabilidad f. **~t** n contable m & f, contador m (LAm)

accumulat|e /ə'kjuːmjʊleɪt/ vt acumular. ● vi acumularse. **~ion** /-'leɪʃn/ n acumulación f

accura|cy /'ækjərəsɪ/ n exactitud f, precisión f. **~te** /-ət/ adj exacto, preciso

accus|ation /ækjuː'zeɪʃn/ n acusación f. **~e** /ə'kjuːz/ vt acusar

accustom /ə'kʌstəm/ vt acostumbrar. **~ed** adj. **be ~ed (to)** estar acostumbrado (a). **get ~ed (to)** acostumbrarse (a)

ace /eɪs/ n as m

ache /eɪk/ n dolor m. ● vi doler. **my leg ~s** me duele la pierna

achieve /ə'tʃiːv/ vt realizar; lograr (success). **~ment** n realización f; (feat) proeza f; (thing achieved) logro m

acid /'æsɪd/ adj & n ácido (m). **~ic** adj /ə'sɪdɪk/ adj ácido. ~ **rain** n lluvia f ácida

acknowledge /ək'nɒlɪdʒ/ vt reconocer. ~ **receipt of** acusar recibo de. **~ment** n reconocimiento m; (Com) acuse m de recibo

acne /'ækni/ n acné m

acorn /'eɪkɔːn/ n bellota f

acoustic /ə'kuːstɪk/ adj acústico. **~s** npl acústica f

acquaint /ə'kweɪnt/ vt. ~ **s.o. with** poner a uno al corriente de. **be ~ed with** conocer (person); saber (fact). **~ance** n conocimiento m; (person) conocido m

acquiesce /ækwɪ'es/ vi consentir (**in** en). **~nce** n aquiescencia f, consentimiento m

acqui|re /ə'kwaɪə(r)/ vt adquirir; aprender (language). **~re a taste for** tomar gusto a. **~sition** /ækwɪ'zɪʃn/ n adquisición f. **~sitive** /ə'kwɪzətɪv/ adj codicioso

acquit /ə'kwɪt/ vt (pt **acquitted**) absolver. **~tal** n absolución f

acre /'eɪkə(r)/ n acre m

acrid /'ækrɪd/ adj acre

acrimonious /ækrɪ'məʊnɪəs/ adj cáustico, mordaz

acrobat /'ækrəbæt/ n acróbata m & f. **~ic** /-'bætɪk/ adj acrobático. **~ics** npl acrobacia f

acronym /'ækrənɪm/ n acrónimo m, siglas fpl

across /ə'krɒs/ adv & prep (side to side) de un lado al otro; (on other side) al otro lado de; (crosswise) a través de. **it is 20 metres** ~ tiene 20 metros de ancho. **go** or **walk** ~ atravesar, cruzar

act /ækt/ n acto m; (action) acción f; (in variety show) número m; (decree) decreto m. ● vt hacer (part, role). ● vi actuar; (pretend) fingir. ~ **as** actuar de; (object) servir de. ~ **for** representar. **~ing** adj interino. ● n (of play) representación f; (by actor) interpretación f; (profession) profesión f de actor

action /'ækʃn/ n acción f; (Jurid) demanda f; (plot) argumento m. **out of** ~ (on sign) no funciona. **put out of** ~ inutilizar. **take** ~ tomar medidas ~ **replay** n repetición f de la jugada

activate /'æktɪveɪt/ vt activar

activ|e /'æktɪv/ adj activo; (energetic) lleno de energía; (volcano) en actividad. **~ist** n activista m & f. **~ity** /-'tɪvətɪ/ n actividad f

act|or /'æktə(r)/ n actor m. **~ress** /-trɪs/ n actriz f

actual /'æktʃʊəl/ adj verdadero. **~ly** adv en realidad, efectivamente; (even) incluso

acute /ə'kjuːt/ adj agudo. **~ly** adv agudamente

ad /æd/ n 🔢 anuncio m, aviso m (LAm)

AD /ˈeɪˈdiː/ abbr (= **Anno Domini**) d. de J.C.

Adam's apple /ˈædəmzˈæpl/ n nuez f (de Adán)

adapt /əˈdæpt/ vt adaptar. ● vi adaptarse. ~**ability** /əˈbɪləti/ n adaptabilidad f. ~**able** /-əbl/ adj adaptable. ~**ation** /ædæpˈteɪʃn/ n adaptación f; (of book etc) versión f. ~**or** /əˈdæptə(r)/ n (Elec, with several sockets) enchufe m múltiple; (Elec, for different sockets) adaptador m

add /æd/ vt añadir. ● vi sumar. □ ~ **up** vt sumar; (fig) tener sentido. ~ **up to** equivaler a

adder /ˈædə(r)/ n víbora f

addict /ˈædɪkt/ n adicto m; (fig) entusiasta m & f. ~**ed** /əˈdɪktɪd/ adj. ~**ed to** adicto a; (fig) fanático de. ~**ion** /əˈdɪkʃn/ n (Med) dependencia f; (fig) afición f. ~**ive** /əˈdɪktɪv/ adj que crea adicción; (fig) que crea hábito

addition /əˈdɪʃn/ n suma f. **in** ~ además. ~**al** adj suplementario

address /əˈdres/ n dirección f; (on form) domicilio m; (speech) discurso m. ● vt poner la dirección en; (speak to) dirigirse a. ~ **book** n libreta f de direcciones. ~**ee** /ædreˈsiː/ n destinatario m

adept /ˈædept/ adj & n experto (m)

adequa|cy /ˈædɪkwəsi/ n suficiencia f. ~**te** /-ət/ adj suficiente, adecuado. ~**tely** adv suficientemente, adecuadamente

adhere /ədˈhɪə(r)/ vi adherirse (**to** a); observar (rule). ~**nce** /-rəns/ n adhesión f; (to rules) observancia f

adhesi|on /ədˈhiːʒn/ n adherencia f. ~**ve** /-sɪv/ adj & n adhesivo (m)

adjacent /əˈdʒeɪsnt/ adj contiguo

adjective /ˈædʒɪktɪv/ n adjetivo m

adjourn /əˈdʒɜːn/ vt aplazar; suspender (meeting etc). ● vi suspenderse

adjust /əˈdʒʌst/ vt ajustar (machine); (arrange) arreglar. ● vi. ~ (**to**) adaptarse (a). ~**able** adj ajustable. ~**ment** n adaptación f; (Tec) ajuste m

administer /ədˈmɪnɪstə(r)/ vt administrar

administrat|ion /ədmɪnɪˈstreɪʃn/ n administración f. ~**ive** /əd-

ˈmɪnɪstrətɪv/ adj administrativo. ~**or** /ədˈmɪnɪstreɪtə(r)/ n administrador m

admirable /ˈædmərəbl/ adj admirable

admiral /ˈædmərəl/ n almirante m

admir|ation /ædməˈreɪʃn/ n admiración f. ~**e** /ədˈmaɪə(r)/ vt admirar. ~**er** /ədˈmaɪərə(r)/ n admirador m

admission /ədˈmɪʃn/ n admisión f; (entry) entrada f

admit /ədˈmɪt/ vt (pt **admitted**) dejar entrar; (acknowledge) admitir, reconocer. ~ **to** confesar. **be** ~**ted** (to hospital etc) ingresar. ~**tance** n entrada f. ~**tedly** adv es verdad que

admonish /ədˈmɒnɪʃ/ vt reprender; (advise) aconsejar

ado /əˈduː/ n alboroto m; (trouble) dificultad f. **without more** or **further** ~ en seguida, sin más

adolescen|ce /ædəˈlesns/ n adolescencia f. ~**t** adj & n adolescente (m & f)

adopt /əˈdɒpt/ vt adoptar. ~**ed** adj (child) adoptivo. ~**ion** /-ʃn/ n adopción f

ador|able /əˈdɔːrəbl/ adj adorable. ~**ation** /ædəˈreɪʃn/ n adoración f. ~**e** /əˈdɔː(r)/ vt adorar

adorn /əˈdɔːn/ vt adornar. ~**ment** n adorno m

adrift /əˈdrɪft/ adj & adv a la deriva

adult /ˈædʌlt/ adj & n adulto (m)

adulter|er /əˈdʌltərə(r)/ n adúltero m. ~**ess** /-ɪs/ n adúltera f. ~**y** n adulterio m

advance /ədˈvɑːns/ vt adelantar. ● vi adelantarse. ● n adelanto m. **in** ~ con anticipación, por adelantado. ~**d** adj avanzado; (studies) superior

advantage /ədˈvɑːntɪdʒ/ n ventaja f. **take** ~ **of** aprovecharse de; abusar de (person). ~**ous** /ædvənˈteɪdʒəs/ adj ventajoso

advent /ˈædvənt/ n venida f. **A**~ n adviento m

adventur|e /ədˈventʃə(r)/ n aventura f. ~**er** n aventurero m. ~**ous** adj (person) aventurero; (thing) arriesgado; (fig, bold) audaz

adverb /ˈædvɜːb/ n adverbio m

adversary /ˈædvəsəri/ n adversario m

advers|e /'ædvɜːs/ adj adverso, contrario, desfavorable. **~ity** /əd'vɜːsətɪ/ n infortunio m

advert /'ædvɜːt/ n 🔲 anuncio m, aviso m (LAm). **~ise** /'ædvətaɪz/ vt anunciar. ●vi hacer publicidad; (seek, sell) poner un anuncio. **~isement** /əd'vɜːtɪsmənt/ n anuncio m, aviso m (LAm). **~iser** /'ædvətaɪzə(r)/ n anunciante m & f

advice /əd'vaɪs/ n consejo m; (report) informe m

advis|able /əd'vaɪzəbl/ adj aconsejable. **~e** /əd'vaɪz/ vt aconsejar; (inform) avisar. **~e against** aconsejar en contra de. **~er** n consejero m; (consultant) asesor m. **~ory** adj consultivo

advocate /'ædvəkət/ n defensor m; (Jurid) abogado m. ● /'ædvəkeɪt/ vt recomendar

aerial /'eərɪəl/ adj aéreo. ●n antena f

aerobics /eə'rəʊbɪks/ npl aeróbica f

aerodrome /'eərədrəʊm/ n aeródromo m

aerodynamic /eərəʊdaɪ'næmɪk/ adj aerodinámico

aeroplane /'eərəpleɪn/ n avión m

aerosol /'eərəsɒl/ n aerosol m

aesthetic /iːs'θetɪk/ adj estético

afar /ə'fɑː(r)/ adv lejos

affable /'æfəbl/ adj afable

affair /ə'feə(r)/ n asunto m. (love) **~** aventura f, amorío m. **~s** npl (business) negocios mpl

affect /ə'fekt/ vt afectar; (pretend) fingir. **~ation** /æfek'teɪʃn/ n afectación f. **~ed** adj afectado, amanerado

affection /ə'fekʃn/ n cariño m. **~ate** /-ət/ adj cariñoso

affiliate /ə'fɪlɪeɪt/ vt afiliar

affirm /ə'fɜːm/ vt afirmar. **~ative** /-ətɪv/ adj afirmativo. ●n respuesta f afirmativa

afflict /ə'flɪkt/ vt afligir. **~ion** /-ʃn/ n aflicción f, pena f

affluen|ce /'æfluəns/ n riqueza f. **~t** adj rico.

afford /ə'fɔːd/ vt permitirse; (provide) dar. **he can't ~ a car** no le alcanza el dinero para comprar un coche

affront /ə'frʌnt/ n afrenta f, ofensa f. ●vt afrentar, ofender

afield /ə'fiːld/ adv. **far ~** muy lejos

afloat /ə'fləʊt/ adv a flote

afraid /ə'freɪd/ adj. **be ~** tener miedo (of a); (be sorry) sentir, lamentar

afresh /ə'freʃ/ adv de nuevo

Africa /'æfrɪkə/ n África f. **~n** adj & n africano (m). **~n-American** adj & n norteamericano (m) de origen africano

after /'ɑːftə(r)/ adv después; (behind) detrás. ● prep después de; (behind) detrás de. **it's twenty ~ four** (Amer) son las cuatro y veinte. **be ~** (seek) andar en busca de. ● conj después de que. ● adj posterior. **~-effect** n consecuencia f, efecto m secundario. **~math** /'ɑːftəmæθ/ n secuelas fpl. **~noon** /-'nuːn/ n tarde f. **~shave** n loción f para después de afeitarse. **~thought** n ocurrencia f tardía. **~wards** /-wədz/ adv después

again /ə'gen/ adv otra vez; (besides) además. **do ~** volver a hacer, hacer otra vez. **~ and ~** una y otra vez

against /ə'genst/ prep contra; (in opposition to) en contra de, contra

age /eɪdʒ/ n edad f. **at four years of ~** a los cuatro años. **under ~** menor de edad. **~s** npl 🔲 siglos mpl. ● vt/i (pres p ageing) envejecer. **~d** /'eɪdʒd/ adj de … años. **~d 10** de 10 años. **~d** /'eɪdʒɪd/ adj viejo, anciano

agency /'eɪdʒənsɪ/ n agencia f; (department) organismo m

agenda /ə'dʒendə/ n orden m del día

agent /'eɪdʒənt/ n agente m & f; (representative) representante m & f

aggravat|e /'ægrəveɪt/ vt agravar; (fam, irritate) irritar. **~ion** /-'veɪʃn/ n agravación f; (fam, irritation) irritación f

aggress|ion /ə'greʃn/ n agresión f. **~ive** adj agresivo. **~iveness** n agresividad f. **~or** n agresor m

aggrieved /ə'griːvd/ adj apenado, ofendido

aghast /ə'gɑːst/ adj horrorizado

agil|e /'ædʒaɪl/ adj ágil. **~ity** /ə'dʒɪlətɪ/ n agilidad f

aging /'eɪdʒɪŋ/ adj envejecido. ●n envejecimiento m

agitat|e /'ædʒɪteɪt/ vt agitar. ~**ed** adj nervioso. ~**ion** /-'teɪʃn/ n agitación f, excitación f. ~**or** n agitador m

ago /ə'gəʊ/ adv. **a long time** ~ hace mucho tiempo. **3 days** ~ hace 3 días

agon|ize /'ægənaɪz/ vi atormentarse. ~**izing** adj (pain) atroz; (experience) angustioso. ~**y** n dolor m (agudo); (mental) angustia f

agree /ə'gri:/ vt acordar. ● vi estar de acuerdo; (of figures) concordar; (get on) entenderse. □ ~ **on** vt acordar (date, details). □ ~ **with** vt (of food etc) sentarle bien a. ~**able** /ə'gri:əbl/ adj agradable. **be** ~**able** (willing) estar de acuerdo. ~**d** adj (time, place) convenido. ~**ment** /-mənt/ n acuerdo m. **in** ~**ment** de acuerdo

agricultur|al /ægrɪ'kʌltʃərəl/ adj agrícola. ~**e** /'ægrɪkʌltʃə(r)/ n agricultura f

aground /ə'graʊnd/ adv. **run** ~ (of ship) varar, encallar

ahead /ə'hed/ adv delante; (in time) antes de. **be** ~ ir delante

aid /eɪd/ vt ayudar. ● n ayuda f. **in** ~ **of** a beneficio de

AIDS /eɪdz/ n sida m

ailment /'eɪlmənt/ n enfermedad f

aim /eɪm/ vt apuntar; (fig) dirigir. ● vi apuntar; (fig) pretender. ● n puntería f; (fig) objetivo m. ~**less** adj, ~**lessly** adv sin objeto, sin rumbo

air /eə(r)/ n aire m. **be on the** ~ (Radio, TV) estar en el aire. **put on** ~**s** darse aires. ● vt airear. ~ **bag** n (Auto) bolsa f de aire. ~ **base** n base f aérea. ~**borne** adj en el aire; (Mil) aerotransportado. ~-**conditioned** adj climatizado, con aire acondicionado. ~ **conditioning** n aire m acondicionado. ~**craft** n (pl invar) avión m. ~**craft carrier** n portaaviones m. ~**field** n aeródromo m. **A**~ **Force** n fuerzas fpl aéreas. ~ **freshener** n ambientador m. ~**gun** n escopeta f de aire comprimido. ~ **hostess** n azafata f, aeromoza f (LAm). ~**line** n línea f aérea. ~ **mail** n correo m aéreo. ~**plane** n (Amer) avión m. ~**port** n aeropuerto m. ~**sick** adj mareado (en un avión). ~**tight** adj hermético. ~ **traffic controller** n controlador m

aéreo. ~**y** adj (-ier, -iest) aireado; (manner) desenfadado

aisle /aɪl/ n nave f lateral; (gangway) pasillo m

ajar /ə'dʒɑ:(r)/ adj entreabierto

alarm /ə'lɑ:m/ n alarma f. ● vt asustar. ~ **clock** n despertador m. ~**ist** n alarmista m & f

Albania /æl'beɪnɪə/ n Albania f. ~**n** adj & n albanés (m)

albatross /'ælbətrɒs/ n albatros m

album /'ælbəm/ n álbum m

alcohol /'ælkəhɒl/ n alcohol m. ~**ic** /-'hɒlɪk/ adj & n alcohólico (m)

alcove /'ælkəʊv/ n nicho m

ale /eɪl/ n cerveza f

alert /ə'lɜ:t/ adj vivo; (watchful) vigilante. ● n alerta f. **on the** ~ alerta. ● vt avisar

algebra /'ældʒɪbrə/ n álgebra f

Algeria /æl'dʒɪərɪə/ n Argelia f. ~**n** adj & n argelino (m)

alias /'eɪlɪəs/ n (pl -ases) alias m. ● adv alias

alibi /'ælɪbaɪ/ n (pl -is) coartada f

alien /'eɪlɪən/ n extranjero m. ● adj ajeno. ~**ate** /-eɪt/ vt enajenar. ~**ation** /-'neɪʃn/ n enajenación f

alienat|e /'eɪlɪəneɪt/ vt enajenar. ~**ion** /-'neɪʃn/ n enajenación f

alight /ə'laɪt/ adj ardiendo; (light) encendido

align /ə'laɪn/ vt alinear. ~**ment** n alineación f

alike /ə'laɪk/ adj parecido, semejante. **look** or **be** ~ parecerse. ● adv de la misma manera

alive /ə'laɪv/ adj vivo. ~ **with** lleno de

alkali /'ælkəlaɪ/ n (pl -is) álcali m. ~**ne** adj alcalino

all /ɔ:l/

● adjective todo, -da; (pl) todos, -das. ~ **day** todo el día. ~ **the windows** todas las ventanas. ~ **four of us went** fuimos los cuatro

● pronoun

····▸ (everything) todo. **that's** ~ eso es todo. **I did** ~ **I could to persuade her** hice todo lo que pude para convencerla

····➤ (*after pronoun*) todo, -da; (*pl*) todos, -das. **he helped us ~** nos ayudó a todos

····➤ **all of** todo, -da, (*pl*) todos, -das. **~ of the paintings** todos los cuadros. **~ of the milk** toda la leche

····➤ (*in phrases*) **all in all** en general. **not at all** (*in no way*) de ninguna manera; (*after thanks*) de nada, no hay de qué. **it's not at ~ bad** no está nada mal. **I don't like it at ~** no me gusta nada

● *adverb*

····➤ (*completely*) completamente. **she was ~ alone** estaba completamente sola. **I got ~ dirty** me ensucié todo/toda. **I don't know him ~ that well** no lo conozco tan bien

····➤ (*in scores*) **the score was one ~** iban empatados uno a uno

····➤ (*in phrases*) **to be all for sth** estar completamente a favor de algo. **to be all in** Ⓣ estar rendido

all-around /ɔːləˈraʊnd/ *adj* (*Amer*) completo

allay /əˈleɪ/ *vt* allviar (pain); aquietar (fears etc)

all clear /ɔːlˈklɪə(r)/ *n* fin *m* de (la) alarma; (*permission*) visto *m* bueno

alleg|ation /ælɪˈɡeɪʃn/ *n* alegato *m*. **~e** /əˈledʒ/ *vt* alegar. **~ed** *adj* presunto. **~edly** /-ɪdlɪ/ *adv* según se dice, supuestamente

allegiance /əˈliːdʒəns/ *n* lealtad *f*

allegory /ˈælɪɡərɪ/ *n* alegoría *f*

allerg|ic /əˈlɜːdʒɪk/ *adj* alérgico (**to** a). **~y** /ˈælədʒɪ/ *n* alergia *f*

alleviate /əˈliːvɪeɪt/ *vt* aliviar

alley /ˈælɪ/ (*pl* **-eys**) *n* callejuela *f*

alliance /əˈlaɪəns/ *n* alianza *f*

alligator /ˈælɪɡeɪtə(r)/ *n* caimán *m*

allocat|e /ˈæləkeɪt/ *vt* asignar; (*share out*) repartir. **~ion** /-ˈkeɪʃn/ *n* asignación *f*; (*distribution*) reparto *m*

allot /əˈlɒt/ *vt* (*pt* **allotted**) asignar. **~ment** *n* asignación *f*; (*land*) parcela *f*

allow /əˈlaʊ/ *vt* permitir; (*grant*) conceder; (*reckon on*) prever; (*agree*) admitir. □ **~ for** *vt* tener en cuenta. **~ance** /əˈlaʊəns/ *n* concesión *f*; (*pension*) pensión *f*; (*Com*) rebaja *f*. **make ~ances for** ser indulgente con (person); (*take into account*) tener en cuenta

alloy /ˈælɔɪ/ *n* aleación *f*

all ~ right *adj* & *adv* bien. ● *int* ¡vale!, ¡okey! (*esp LAm*), ¡órale! (*Mex*). **~-round** *adj* completo

allusion /əˈluːʒn/ *n* alusión *f*

ally /ˈælaɪ/ *n* aliado *m*. ● /əˈlaɪ/ *vt*. **~ o.s.** aliarse (**with** con)

almighty /ɔːlˈmaɪtɪ/ *adj* todopoderoso

almond /ˈɑːmənd/ *n* almendra *f*

almost /ˈɔːlməʊst/ *adv* casi

alone /əˈləʊn/ *adj* solo. ● *adv* sólo, solamente

along /əˈlɒŋ/ *prep* por, a lo largo de. ● *adv*. **~ with** junto con. **all ~** todo el tiempo. **come ~** venga. **~side** /-ˈsaɪd/ *adv* (*Naut*) al costado. ● *prep* al lado de

aloof /əˈluːf/ *adv* apartado. ● *adj* reservado

aloud /əˈlaʊd/ *adv* en voz alta

alphabet /ˈælfəbet/ *n* alfabeto *m*. **~ical** /-ˈbetɪkl/ *adj* alfabético

Alps /ælps/ *npl* **the ~** los Alpes

already /ɔːlˈredɪ/ *adv* ya

Alsatian /ælˈseɪʃn/ *n* pastor *m* alemán

also /ˈɔːlsəʊ/ *adv* también; (*moreover*) además

altar /ˈɔːltə(r)/ *n* altar *m*

alter /ˈɔːltə(r)/ *vt* cambiar. ● *vi* cambiarse. **~ation** /-ˈreɪʃn/ *n* modificación *f*; (*to garment*) arreglo *m*

alternate /ɔːlˈtɜːnət/ *adj* alterno; (*Amer*) see **ALTERNATIVE**. ● /ˈɔːltəneɪt/ *vt/i* alternar. **~ly** /ɔːlˈtɜːnətlɪ/ *adv* alternativamente

alternative /ɔːlˈtɜːnətɪv/ *adj* alternativo. ● *n* alternativa *f*. **~ly** *adv* en cambio, por otra parte

although /ɔːlˈðəʊ/ *conj* aunque

altitude /ˈæltɪtjuːd/ *n* altitud *f*

altogether /ɔːltəˈɡeðə(r)/ *adv* completamente; (*on the whole*) en total

a

aluminium /ælju'mınıəm/, **aluminum** /ə'lu:mınəm/ (*Amer*) *n* aluminio *m*

always /'ɔ:lweiz/ *adv* siempre

am /æm/ *see* BE

a.m. *abbr* (= **ante meridiem**) de la mañana

amalgamate /ə'mælgəmeɪt/ *vt* amalgamar. ● *vi* amalgamarse

amass /ə'mæs/ *vt* acumular

amateur /'æmətə(r)/ *adj & n* amateur (*m & f*). **~ish** *adj* (*pej*) torpe, chapucero

amaz|e /ə'meiz/ *vt* asombrar. **~ed** *adj* asombrado, estupefacto. **be ~ed at** quedarse asombrado de, asombrarse de. **~ement** *n* asombro *m*. **~ing** *adj* increíble

ambassador /æm'bæsədə(r)/ *n* embajador *m*

ambigu|ity /æmbɪ'gju:ətɪ/ *n* ambigüedad *f*. **~ous** /æm'bɪgjʊəs/ *adj* ambiguo

ambiti|on /æm'bɪʃn/ *n* ambición *f*. **~ous** /-ʃəs/ *adj* ambicioso

ambivalent /æm'bɪvələnt/ *adj* ambivalente

amble /'æmbl/ *vi* andar despacio, andar sin prisa

ambulance /'æmbjʊləns/ *n* ambulancia *f*

ambush /'æmbʊʃ/ *n* emboscada *f*. ● *vt* tender una emboscada a

amen /ɑ:'men/ *int* amén

amend /ə'mend/ *vt* enmendar. **~ment** *n* enmienda *f*. **~s** *npl*. **make ~s** reparar

amenities /ə'mi:nətɪz/ *npl* servicios *mpl*; (*of hotel, club*) instalaciones *fpl*

America /ə'merɪkə/ *n* (*continent*) América; (*North America*) Estados Unidos, Norteamérica *f*. **~n** *adj & n* americano (*m*); (*North American*) estadounidense (*m & f*), norteamericano (*m*). **~nism** *n* americanismo *m*

American dream El sueño americano se basa en la idea de que cualquier persona en los Estados Unidos puede prosperar mediante el trabajo duro. Para los inmigrantes y las minorías, el concepto abarca la libertad y la igualdad de derechos.

amiable /'eɪmɪəbl/ *adj* simpático

amicable /'æmɪkəbl/ *adj* amistoso

amid(st) /ə'mɪd(st)/ *prep* entre, en medio de

ammonia /ə'məʊnɪə/ *n* amoníaco *m*, amoniaco *m*

ammunition /æmjʊ'nɪʃn/ *n* municiones *fpl*

amnesty /'æmnəstɪ/ *n* amnistía *f*

amok /ə'mɒk/ *adv*. **run ~** volverse loco

among(st) /ə'mʌŋ(st)/ *prep* entre

amount /ə'maʊnt/ *n* cantidad *f*; (*total*) total *m*, suma *f*. □ **~ to** *vt* sumar; (*fig*) equivaler a, significar

amp(ere) /'æmp(eə(r))/ *n* amperio *m*

amphibi|an /æm'fɪbɪən/ *n* anfibio *m*. **~ous** /-əs/ *adj* anfibio

amphitheatre /'æmfɪθɪətə(r)/ *n* anfiteatro *m*

ampl|e /'æmpl/ *adj* (**-er, -est**) amplio; (*enough*) suficiente; (*plentiful*) abundante. **~y** *adv* ampliamente, bastante

amplif|ier /'æmplɪfaɪə(r)/ *n* amplificador *m*. **~y** /'æmplɪfaɪ/ *vt* amplificar

amputat|e /'æmpjʊteɪt/ *vt* amputar. **~ion** /-'teɪʃn/ *n* amputación *f*

amus|e /ə'mju:z/ *vt* divertir. **~ed** *adj* (*expression*) divertido. **keep s.o. ~ed** entretener a uno. **~ement** *n* diversión *f*. **~ing** *adj* divertido

an /ən, æn/ *see* A

anaemi|a /ə'ni:mɪə/ *n* anemia *f*. **~c** *adj* anémico

anaesthe|tic /ænɪs'θetɪk/ *n* anestésico *m*. **~tist** /ə'ni:sθɪtɪst/ *n* anestesista *m & f*

anagram /'ænəgræm/ *n* anagrama *m*

analogy /ə'nælədʒɪ/ *n* analogía *f*

analy|se /'ænəlaɪz/ *vt* analizar. **~sis** /ə'næləsɪs/ *n* (*pl* **-ses** /-si:z/) *n* análisis *m*. **~st** /'ænəlɪst/ *n* analista *m & f*. **~tic(al)** /ænə'lɪtɪk(əl)/ *adj* analítico

anarch|ist /'ænəkɪst/ *n* anarquista *m & f*. **~y** *n* anarquía *f*

anatom|ical /ænə'tɒmɪkl/ *adj* anatómico. **~y** /ə'nætəmɪ/ *n* anatomía *f*

ancest|or /'ænsestə(r)/ *n* antepasado *m*. **~ral** /-'sestrəl/ *adj* ancestral. **~ry**

/'ænsestrɪ/ n ascendencia f

anchor /'æŋkə(r)/ n ancla f. ● vt anclar; (fig) sujetar. ● vi anclar. ~**man** n (on TV) presentador m. ~**woman** n (on TV) presentadora f.

ancient /'eɪnʃənt/ adj antiguo, viejo

ancillary /æn'sɪlərɪ/ adj auxiliar

and /ənd, ænd/ conj y; (before i- and hi-) e. bread ~ butter pan m con mantequilla. go ~ see him ve a verlo. more ~ more cada vez más. try ~ come trata de venir

anecdot|al /ænɪk'dəʊtl/ adj anecdótico. ~**e** /'ænɪkdəʊt/ n anécdota f

anew /ə'nju:/ adv de nuevo

angel /'eɪndʒl/ n ángel m. ~**ic** /æn 'dʒelɪk/ adj angélico

anger /'æŋgə(r)/ n ira f. ● vt enfadar, (esp LAm) enojar

angle /'æŋgl/ n ángulo m; (fig) punto m de vista. ~**r** /'æŋglə(r)/ n pescador m

Anglican /'æŋglɪkən/ adj & n anglicano (m)

angr|ily /'æŋgrɪlɪ/ adv con enfado, (esp LAm) con enojo. ~**y** /'æŋgrɪ/ adj (-ier, -iest) enfadado, (esp LAm) enojado. get ~**y** enfadarse, enojarse (esp LAm)

anguish /'æŋgwɪʃ/ n angustia f

animal /'ænɪml/ adj & n animal (m)

animat|e /'ænɪmeɪt/ vt animar. ~**ion** /-'meɪʃn/ n animación f

animosity /ænɪ'mɒsətɪ/ n animosidad f

ankle /'æŋkl/ n tobillo m. ~ boot botín m. ~ sock calcetín m corto

annexe /'æneks/ n anexo m

annihilat|e /ə'naɪəleɪt/ vt aniquilar. ~**ion** /-'leɪʃn/ n aniquilación f

anniversary /ænɪ'vɜːsərɪ/ n aniversario m

announce /ə'naʊns/ vt anunciar, comunicar. ~**ment** n anuncio m; (official) comunicado m. ~**r** n (Radio, TV) locutor m

annoy /ə'nɔɪ/ vt molestar. ~**ance** n molestia m. ~**ed** adj enfadado, enojado (LAm). ~**ing** adj molesto

annual /'ænjʊəl/ adj anual. ● n anuario m. ~**ly** adv cada año

annul /ə'nʌl/ vt (pt annulled) anular. ~**ment** n anulación f

anonymous /ə'nɒnɪməs/ adj anónimo

anorak /'ænəræk/ n anorac m

another /ə'nʌðə(r)/ adj & pron otro. ~ 10 minutes 10 minutos más. in ~ way de otra manera. one ~ el uno al otro; (pl) unos a otros

answer /'ɑːnsə(r)/ n respuesta f; (solution) solución f. ● vt contestar; escuchar, oír (prayer). ~ the door abrir la puerta. ● vi contestar. □ ~ back vi contestar. □ ~ for vt ser responsable de. ~**able** adj responsable. ~**ing machine** n contestador m automático

ant /ænt/ n hormiga f

antagoni|sm /æn'tægənɪzəm/ n antagonismo m. ~**stic** /-'nɪstɪk/ adj antagónico, opuesto. ~**ze** /æn'tægənaɪz/ vt provocar la enemistad de

Antarctic /æn'tɑːktɪk/ adj antártico. ● n the ~ la región antártica

antelope /'æntɪləʊp/ n antílope m

antenatal /'æntɪneɪtl/ adj prenatal

antenna /æn'tenə/ (pl -nae /-niː/) (of insect etc) n antena f; (pl -nas) (of radio, TV) antena f

anthem /'ænθəm/ n himno m

anthology /æn'θɒlədʒɪ/ n antología f

anthrax /'ænθræks/ n ántrax m

anthropolog|ist /ænθrə'pɒlədʒɪst/ n antropólogo m. ~**y** n antropología f

anti- /ænti/ pref anti- **~ aircraft** /-'eəkrɑːft/ adj antiaéreo

antibiotic /æntɪbaɪ'ɒtɪk/ adj & n antibiótico (m)

anticipat|e /æn'tɪsɪpeɪt/ vt anticiparse a; (foresee) prever; (forestall) prevenir. ~**ion** /-'peɪʃn/ n (foresight) previsión f; (expectation) expectativa f

anti~climax /-'klaɪmæks/ n decepción f. ~**clockwise** /-'klɒkwaɪz/ adv & adj en sentido contrario al de las agujas del reloj

antidote /'æntɪdəʊt/ m antídoto m

antifreeze /'æntɪfriːz/ n anticongelante m

antiperspirant /æntɪ'pɜːspɪrənt/ n antitranspirante m

antiquated /'æntɪkweɪtɪd/ adj anticuado

a

antique /æn'ti:k/ adj antiguo. ●n antigüedad f. ~ **dealer** anticuario m. ~ **shop** tienda f de antigüedades

antiquity /æn'tɪkwətɪ/ n antigüedad f

anti ~**septic** /-'septɪk/ adj & n antiséptico (m). ~**social** /-'səʊʃl/ adj antisocial

antlers /'æntləz/ npl cornamenta f

anus /'eɪnəs/ n ano m

anvil /'ænvɪl/ n yunque m

anxi|ety /æŋ'zaɪətɪ/ n ansiedad f; (worry) inquietud f; (eagerness) anhelo m. ~**ous** /'æŋkʃəs/ adj inquieto; (eager) deseoso. ~**ously** adv con inquietud; (eagerly) con impaciencia

any /'enɪ/ adj algún; (negative) ningún m; (whatever) cualquier; (every) todo. **at** ~ **moment** en cualquier momento. **have you** ~ **wine?** ¿tienes vino? ●pron alguno; (negative) ninguno. **have we** ~? ¿tenemos algunos? **not** ~ ninguno. ●adv (a little) un poco, algo. **is it** ~ **better?** ¿está algo mejor?

anybody /'enɪbɒdɪ/ pron alguien; (after negative) nadie. ~ **can do it** cualquiera puede hacerlo

anyhow /'enɪhaʊ/ adv de todas formas; (in spite of all) a pesar de todo; (badly) de cualquier manera

anyone /'enɪwʌn/ pron see **ANYBODY**

anything /'enɪθɪŋ/ pron algo; (whatever) cualquier cosa; (after negative) nada. ~ **but** todo menos

anyway /'enɪweɪ/ adv de todas formas

anywhere /'enɪweə(r)/ adv en cualquier parte; (after negative) en ningún sitio. ~ **else** en cualquier otro lugar. ~ **you go** dondequiera que vayas

apart /ə'pɑːt/ adv aparte; (separated) separado. ~ **from** aparte de. **come** ~ romperse. **take** ~ desmontar

apartheid /ə'pɑːtheɪt/ n apartheid m

apartment /ə'pɑːtmənt/ n (Amer) apartamento m, piso m. ~ **building** n (Amer) edificio m de apartamentos, casa f de pisos

apath|etic /æpə'θetɪk/ adj apático. ~**y** /'æpəθɪ/ n apatía f

ape /eɪp/ n mono m. ●vt imitar

aperitif /ə'perətɪf/ n aperitivo m

aperture /'æpətʃʊə(r)/ n abertura f

apex /'eɪpeks/ n ápice m

aphrodisiac /æfrə'dɪzɪæk/ adj & n afrodisíaco (m), afrodisiaco (m)

apolog|etic /əpɒlə'dʒetɪk/ adj lleno de disculpas. **be** ~**etic** disculparse. ~**ize** /ə'pɒlədʒaɪz/ vi disculparse (**for** de). ~**y** /ə'pɒlədʒɪ/ n disculpa f

apostle /ə'pɒsl/ n apóstol m

apostrophe /ə'pɒstrəfɪ/ n apóstrofo m

appal /ə'pɔːl/ vt (pt appalled) horrorizar. ~**ling** adj espantoso

apparatus /æpə'reɪtəs/ n aparato m

apparel /ə'pærəl/ n (Amer) ropa f

apparent /ə'pærənt/ adj aparente; (clear) evidente. ~**ly** adv por lo visto

apparition /æpə'rɪʃn/ n aparición f

appeal /ə'piːl/ vi apelar; (attract) atraer. ●n llamamiento m; (attraction) atractivo m; (Jurid) apelación f. ~**ing** adj atrayente

appear /ə'pɪə(r)/ vi aparecer; (seem) parecer; (in court) comparecer. ~**ance** n aparición f; (aspect) aspecto m; (in court) comparecencia f

appease /ə'piːz/ vt aplacar; (pacify) apaciguar

append /ə'pend/ vt adjuntar

appendicitis /əpendɪ'saɪtɪs/ n apendicitis f

appendix /ə'pendɪks/ n (pl -ices /-ɪsiːz/) (of book) apéndice m. (pl -ixes) (organ) apéndice m

appetite /'æpɪtaɪt/ n apetito m

applau|d /ə'plɔːd/ vt/i aplaudir. ~**se** /ə'plɔːz/ n aplausos mpl. **round of** ~**se** aplauso m

apple /'æpl/ n manzana f. ~ **tree** n manzano m

appliance /ə'plaɪəns/ n aparato m. **electrical** ~ electrodoméstico m

applic|able /'æplɪkəbl/ adj aplicable; (relevant) pertinente. ~**ant** /'æplɪkənt/ n candidato m, solicitante m & f. ~**ation** /æplɪ'keɪʃn/ n aplicación f; (request) solicitud f. ~**ation form** formulario m (de solicitud)

appl|ied /ə'plaɪd/ adj aplicado. ~**y** /ə'plaɪ/ vt aplicar. ●vi aplicarse; (ask) presentar una solicitud. ~**y for** solicitar (job etc)

appoint /ə'pɔɪnt/ vt nombrar; (fix) señalar. ~**ment** n cita f

apprais|al /ə'preɪzl/ n evaluación f. **~e** /ə'preɪz/ vt evaluar

appreciable /ə'pri:ʃəbl/ adj (considerable) considerable

appreciat|e /ə'pri:ʃɪeɪt/ vt (value) apreciar; (understand) comprender; (be grateful for) agradecer. **~ion** /-'eɪʃn/ n aprecio m; (gratitude) agradecimiento m. **~ive** /ə'pri:ʃɪətɪv/ adj agradecido

apprehen|sion /æprɪ'henʃn/ n (fear) recelo f. **~sive** adj aprensivo

apprentice /ə'prentɪs/ n aprendiz m. • vt. be **~d** to s.o. estar de aprendiz con uno. **~ship** n aprendizaje m

approach /ə'prəʊtʃ/ vt acercarse a. • vi acercarse. • n acercamiento m; (to problem) enfoque m; (access) acceso m

appropriate /ə'prəʊprɪət/ adj apropiado. • /ə'prəʊprɪeɪt/ vt apropiarse de. **~ly** /-ətli/ adv apropiadamente

approv|al /ə'pru:vl/ n aprobación f. on **~al** a prueba. **~e** /ə'pru:v/ vt/i aprobar. **~ingly** adv con aprobación

approximat|e /ə'prɒksɪmət/ adj aproximado. • /ə'prɒksɪmeɪt/ vt aproximarse a. **~ely** /-ətlɪ/ adv aproximadamente. **~ion** /-'meɪʃn/ n aproximación f

apricot /'eɪprɪkɒt/ n albaricoque m, chabacano m (Mex)

April /'eɪprəl/ n abril m. **~ fool!** ¡inocentón!

apron /'eɪprən/ n delantal m

apt /æpt/ adj apropiado. be **~ to** tener tendencia a. **~itude** /'æptɪtju:d/ n aptitud f. **~ly** adv acertadamente

aquarium /ə'kweərɪəm/ n (pl -ums) acuario m

Aquarius /ə'kweərɪəs/ n Acuario m

aquatic /ə'kwætɪk/ adj acuático

aqueduct /'ækwɪdʌkt/ n acueducto m

Arab /'ærəb/ adj & n árabe (m & f). **~ian** /ə'reɪbɪən/ adj árabe. **~ic** /'ærəbɪk/ adj & n árabe (m). **~ic numerals** números mpl arábigos

arable /'ærəbl/ adj cultivable

arbitrary /'ɑ:bɪtrərɪ/ adj arbitrario

arbitrat|e /'ɑ:bɪtreɪt/ vi arbitrar. **~ion** /-'treɪʃn/ n arbitraje m. **~or** n árbitro m

arc /ɑ:k/ n arco m

arcade /ɑ:'keɪd/ n arcada f; (around square) soportales mpl; (shops) galería f

arch /ɑ:tʃ/ n arco m. • vt arquear. • vi arquearse

archaeolog|ical /ɑ:kɪə'lɒdʒɪkl/ adj arqueológico. **~ist** /u:kɪ'ɒlədʒɪst/ n arqueólogo m. **~y** /ɑ:kɪ'ɒlədʒɪ/ n arqueología f

archaic /ɑ:'keɪɪk/ adj arcaico

archbishop /ɑ:tʃ'bɪʃəp/ n arzobispo m

archer /'ɑ:tʃə(r)/ n arquero m. **~y** n tiro m con arco

architect /'ɑ:kɪtekt/ n arquitecto m. **~ure** /-tʃə(r)/ n arquitectura f. **~ural** /-'tektʃərəl/ adj arquitectónico

archives /'ɑ:kaɪvz/ npl archivo m

archway /'ɑ:tʃweɪ/ n arco m

Arctic /'ɑ:ktɪk/ adj ártico. • n. the **~** el Ártico

ard|ent /'ɑ:dənt/ adj fervoroso; (supporter, lover) apasionado. **~our** /'ɑ:də(r)/ n fervor m; (love) pasión f

arduous /'ɑ:djʊəs/ adj arduo

are /ɑ:(r)/ see BE

area /'eərɪə/ n (Math) superficie f; (of country) zona f; (of city) barrio m

arena /ə'ri:nə/ n arena f; (scene of activity) ruedo m

aren't /ɑ:nt/ = **are not**

Argentin|a /ɑ:dʒən'ti:nə/ n Argentina f. **~ian** /-'tɪnɪən/ adj & n argentino (m)

argu|able /'ɑ:gjʊəbl/ adj discutible. **~e** /'ɑ:gju:/ vi discutir; (reason) razonar. **~ment** /'ɑ:gjʊmənt/ n disputa f; (reasoning) argumento m. **~mentative** /ɑ:gjʊ'mentətɪv/ adj discutidor

arid /'ærɪd/ adj árido

Aries /'eərɪ:z/ n Aries m

arise /ə'raɪz/ vi (pt arose, pp arisen) surgir (from de)

aristocra|cy /ærɪ'stɒkrəsɪ/ n aristocracia f. **~t** /'ærɪstəkræt/ n aristócrata m & f. **~tic** /-'krætɪk/ adj aristocrático

arithmetic /ə'rɪθmətɪk/ n aritmética f

ark /ɑ:k/ n (Relig) arca f

arm /ɑ:m/ n brazo m; (of garment) manga f. **~s** npl armas fpl. • vt armar

armament /'ɑ:məmənt/ n armamento m

a

arm ∼band n brazalete m. **∼chair** n sillón m

armed /ɑːmd/ adj armado. **∼ robbery** n robo m a mano armada

armful /'ɑːmfʊl/ n brazada f

armour /'ɑːmə(r)/ n armadura f. **∼ed** /'ɑːməd/ adj blindado. **∼y** /'ɑːmərɪ/ n arsenal m

armpit /'ɑːmpɪt/ n sobaco m, axila f

army /'ɑːmɪ/ n ejército m

aroma /ə'rəʊmə/ n aroma m

arose /ə'rəʊz/ see **ARISE**

around /ə'raʊnd/ adv alrededor; (near) cerca. **all ∼** por todas partes. ● prep alrededor de; (with time) a eso de

arouse /ə'raʊz/ vt despertar

arrange /ə'reɪndʒ/ vt arreglar; (fix) fijar. **∼ment** n arreglo m; (agreement) acuerdo m. **∼ments** npl (plans) preparativos mpl

arrears /ə'rɪəz/ npl atrasos mpl. **in ∼** atrasado en el pago (with de)

arrest /ə'rest/ vt detener. ● n detención f. **under ∼** detenido

arriv|al /ə'raɪvl/ n llegada f. **new ∼al** recién llegado m. **∼e** /ə'raɪv/ vi llegar

arrogan|ce /'ærəgəns/ n arrogancia f. **∼t** adj arrogante. **∼tly** adv con arrogancia

arrow /'ærəʊ/ n flecha f

arse /ɑːs/ n (vulgar) culo m

arsenal /'ɑːsənl/ n arsenal m

arsenic /'ɑːsnɪk/ n arsénico m

arson /'ɑːsn/ n incendio m provocado. **∼ist** n incendiario m

art¹ /ɑːt/ n arte m. **A∼s** npl (Univ) Filosofía y Letras fpl. **fine ∼s** bellas artes fpl

art² /ɑːt/ (old use, with thou) see **ARE**

artery /'ɑːtərɪ/ n arteria f

art gallery n museo m de arte, pinacoteca f; (commercial) galería f de arte

arthritis /ɑː'θraɪtɪs/ n artritis f

article /'ɑːtɪkl/ n artículo m. **∼ of clothing** prenda f de vestir

articulat|e /ɑː'tɪkjʊlət/ adj (utterance) articulado; (person) que sabe expresarse. ● /ɑː'tɪkjʊleɪt/ vt/i articular. **∼ed lorry** n camión m articulado. **∼ion** /-'leɪʃn/ n articulación f

artificial /ɑːtɪ'fɪʃl/ adj artificial. **∼ respiration** respiración f artificial

artillery /ɑː'tɪlərɪ/ n artillería f

artist /'ɑːtɪst/ n artista m & f. **∼tic** /ɑː'tɪstɪk/ adj artístico. **∼ry** /'ɑːtɪstrɪ/ n arte m, habilidad f

as /æz, əz/ adv & conj como; (since) ya que; (while) mientras. **∼ big ∼** tan grande como. **∼ far ∼** (distance) hasta; (qualitative) en cuanto a. **∼ far ∼ I know** que yo sepa. **∼ if** como si. **∼ long ∼** mientras. **∼ much ∼** tanto como. **∼ soon ∼** tan pronto como. **∼ well** también

asbestos /æz'bestəs/ n amianto m, asbesto m

ascen|d /ə'send/ vt/i subir. **A∼sion** /ə'senʃn/ n. **the A∼sion** la Ascensión. **∼t** /ə'sent/ n subida f

ascertain /æsə'teɪn/ vt averiguar

ash /æʃ/ n ceniza f. ● n. **∼ (tree)** fresno m

ashamed /ə'ʃeɪmd/ adj avergonzado (of de). **be ∼ of s.o.** avergonzarse de uno

ashore /ə'ʃɔː(r)/ adv a tierra. **go ∼** desembarcar

ash ∼tray n cenicero m. **A∼ Wednesday** n Miércoles m de Ceniza

Asia /'eɪʃə/ n Asia f. **∼n** adj & n asiático (m). **∼tic** /-ɪ'ætɪk/ adj asiático

aside /ə'saɪd/ adv a un lado. ● n (in theatre) aparte m

ask /ɑːsk/ vt pedir; hacer (question); (invite) invitar. **∼ about** enterarse de. **∼ s.o. to do something** pedirle a uno que haga algo. □ **∼ after** vt preguntar por. □ **∼ for vt. ∼ for help** pedir ayuda. **∼ for trouble** buscarse problemas. □ **∼ in** vt. **∼ s.o. in** invitar a uno a pasar

askew /ə'skjuː/ adv & adj torcido

asleep /ə'sliːp/ adv & adj dormido. **fall ∼** dormirse

asparagus /ə'spærəgəs/ n espárrago m

aspect /'æspekt/ n aspecto m

asphalt /'æsfælt/ n asfalto m. ● vt asfaltar

aspir|ation /æspə'reɪʃn/ n aspiración f. **∼e** /əs'paɪə(r)/ vi aspirar

aspirin /'æsprɪn/ n aspirina f

ass /æs/ n asno m; (fig, fam) imbécil m; (Amer vulgar) culo m

assassin /ə'sæsɪn/ n asesino m. ~**ate** /-eɪt/ vt asesinar. ~**ation** /-'eɪʃn/ n asesinato m

assault /ə'sɔːlt/ n (Mil) ataque m; (Jurid) atentado m. ● vt asaltar

assembl|e /ə'sembl/ vt reunir; (Mec) montar. ● vi reunirse. ~**y** n reunión f; (Pol etc) asamblea f. ~**y line** n línea f de montaje

assent /ə'sent/ n asentimiento m. ● vi asentir

assert /ə'sɜːt/ vt afirmar; hacer valer (one's rights). ~**ion** /-ʃn/ n afirmación f. ~**ive** adj positivo, firme

assess /ə'ses/ vt evaluar; (determine) determinar; fijar (tax etc). ~**ment** n evaluación f

asset /'æset/ n (advantage) ventaja f. ~**s** npl (Com) bienes mpl

assign /ə'saɪn/ vt asignar; (appoint) nombrar. ~**ment** n asignación f; (mission) misión f; (task) función f; (for school) trabajo m

assimilate /ə'sɪmɪleɪt/ vt asimilar. ● vi asimilarse

assist /ə'sɪst/ vt/i ayudar. ~**ance** n ayuda f. ~**ant** n ayudante m & f; (shop) dependienta f, dependiente m. ● adj auxiliar, adjunto

associat|e /ə'səʊʃɪeɪt/ vt asociar. ● vi asociarse. ● /ə'səʊʃɪət/ adj asociado. ● n colega m & f; (Com) socio m. ~**ion** /-'eɪʃn/ n asociación f.

assort|ed /ə'sɔːtɪd/ adj surtido. ~**ment** n surtido m

assum|e /ə'sjuːm/ vt suponer; tomar (power, attitude); asumir (role, burden). ~**ption** /ə'sʌmpʃn/ n suposición f

assur|ance /ə'ʃʊərəns/ n seguridad f; (insurance) seguro m. ~**e** /ə'ʃʊə(r)/ vt asegurar. ~**ed** adj seguro

asterisk /'æstərɪsk/ n asterisco m

asthma /'æsmə/ n asma f. ~**tic** /-'mætɪk/ adj & n asmático (m)

astonish /ə'stɒnɪʃ/ vt asombrar. ~**ed** adj asombrado. ~**ing** adj asombroso. ~**ment** n asombro m

astound /ə'staʊnd/ vt asombrar. ~**ed** adj atónito. ~**ing** adj increíble

astray /ə'streɪ/ adv. go ~ extraviarse. lead ~ llevar por mal camino

astrology /ə'strɒlədʒɪ/ n astrología f

astronaut /'æstrənɔːt/ n astronauta m & f

astronom|er /ə'strɒnəmə(r)/ n astrónomo m. ~**ical** /æstrə'nɒmɪkl/ adj astronómico. ~**y** /ə'strɒnəmɪ/ n astronomía f

astute /ə'stjuːt/ adj astuto

asylum /ə'saɪləm/ n asilo m. **lunatic** ~ manicomio m. ~ **seeker** n solicitante m & f de asilo

at /æt/ preposition

····▸ (location) en. **she's at the office** está en la oficina. **at home** en casa. **call me at the office** llámame a la oficina

➡ For translations of phrases such as **at the top, at the front of, at the back of** see entries **top, front** etc

····▸ (at the house of) en casa de. **I'll be at Rachel's** estaré en casa de Rachel

····▸ (Comput: @) arroba f

····▸ (talking about time) **at 7 o'clock** a las siete. **at night** por la noche, de noche, en la noche (LAm). **at Christmas** en Navidad

····▸ (talking about age) a. **at six (years of age)** a los seis años

····▸ (with measurements, numbers etc) a. **at 60 miles an hour** a 60 millas por hora. **at a depth of** a una profundidad de. **three at a time** de tres en tres

➡ For translations of phrasal verbs with **at**, such as **look at**, see entries for those verbs

ate /et/ see EAT

atheis|m /'eɪθɪɪzəm/ n ateísmo m. ~**t** n ateo m

athlet|e /'æθliːt/ n atleta m & f. ~**ic** /-'letɪk/ adj atlético. ~**ics** npl atletismo *m*; (*Amer, Sport*) deportes *mpl*

Atlantic /ət'læntɪk/ *adj* atlántico. ● *n.* **the ~ (Ocean)** el (Océano) Atlántico

atlas /'ætləs/ *n* atlas *m*

ATM *abbr* (= **automated teller machine**) cajero *m* automático

atmospher|e /'ætməsfɪə(r)/ *n* atmósfera *f*; (*fig*) ambiente *m*. **~ic** /-'ferɪk/ *adj* atmosférico

atom /'ætəm/ *n* átomo *m*. **~ic** /ə'tɒmɪk/ *adj* atómico

atroci|ous /ə'trəʊʃəs/ *adj* atroz. **~ty** /ə'trɒsəti/ *n* atrocidad *f*

attach /ə'tætʃ/ *vt* sujetar; adjuntar (document etc). **be ~ed to** (*be fond of*) tener cariño a. **~ment** *n* (*affection*) cariño *m*; (*tool*) accesorio *m*; (*to email*) archivo *m* adjunto

attack /ə'tæk/ *n* ataque *m*. ● *vt/i* atacar. **~er** *n* agresor *m*

attain /ə'teɪn/ *vt* conseguir. **~able** *adj* alcanzable

attempt /ə'tempt/ *vt* intentar. ● *n* tentativa *f*; (*attack*) atentado *m*

attend /ə'tend/ *vt* asistir a; (*escort*) acompañar. ● *vi* prestar atención. □ **~ to** *vt* (*look after*) ocuparse de. **~ance** *n* asistencia *f*; (*people present*) concurrencia *f*

atten|tion /ə'tenʃn/ *n* atención *f*. **~tion!** (*Mil*) ¡firmes! **pay ~tion** prestar atención. **~tive** *adj* atento

attic /'ætɪk/ *n* desván *m*

attire /ə'taɪə(r)/ *n* atavío *m*

attitude /'ætɪtjuːd/ *n* postura *f*

attorney /ə'tɜːnɪ/ *n* (*pl* -**eys**) (*Amer*) abogado *m*

attract /ə'trækt/ *vt* atraer. **~ion** /-ʃn/ *n* atracción *f*; (*charm*) atractivo *m*. **~ive** *adj* atractivo; (*interesting*) atrayente

attribute /ə'trɪbjuːt/ *vt* atribuir. ● /'ætrɪbjuːt/ *n* atributo *m*

aubergine /'əʊbəʒiːn/ *n* berenjena *f*

auction /'ɔːkʃn/ *n* subasta *f*. ● *vt* subastar. **~eer** /-ə'nɪə(r)/ *n* subastador *m*

audaci|ous /ɔː'deɪʃəs/ *adj* audaz. **~ty** /ɔː'dæsəti/ *n* audacia *f*

audible /'ɔːdəbl/ *adj* audible

audience /'ɔːdɪəns/ *n* (*at play, film*) público *m*; (*TV*) audiencia *f*; (*interview*) audiencia *f*

audiovisual /ɔːdɪəʊ'vɪʒʊəl/ *adj* audiovisual

audit /'ɔːdɪt/ *n* revisión *f* de cuentas. ● *vt* revisar

audition /ɔː'dɪʃn/ *n* audición *f*. ● *vt* hacerle una audición a. ● *vi* dar una audición (**for** para)

auditor /'ɔːdɪtə(r)/ *n* interventor *m* de cuentas

auditorium /ɔːdɪ'tɔːrɪəm/ (*pl* -**riums** *or* -**ria** /-rɪə/) *n* sala *f*, auditorio *m*

augment /ɔːg'ment/ *vt* aumentar

augur /'ɔːgə(r)/ *vt* augurar. **it ~s well** es de buen agüero

August /'ɔːgəst/ *n* agosto *m*

aunt /ɑːnt/ *n* tía *f*

au pair /əʊ'peə(r)/ *n* chica *f* au pair

aura /'ɔːrə/ *n* aura *f*, halo *m*

auster|e /ɔː'stɪə(r)/ *adj* austero. **~ity** /ɔː'sterəti/ *n* austeridad *f*

Australia /ɒ'streɪlɪə/ *n* Australia *f*. **~n** *adj* & *n* australiano (*m*)

Austria /'ɒstrɪə/ *n* Austria *f*. **~n** *adj* & *n* austríaco (*m*)

authentic /ɔː'θentɪk/ *adj* auténtico. **~ate** /-keɪt/ *vt* autenticar. **~ity** /-ən'tɪsəti/ *n* autenticidad *f*

author /'ɔːθə(r)/ *n* autor *m*. **~ess** /-ɪs/ *n* autora *f*

authoritative /ɔː'θɒrɪtətɪv/ *adj* autorizado; (*manner*) autoritario

authority /ɔː'θɒrəti/ *n* autoridad *f*; (*permission*) autorización *f*

authoriz|ation /ɔːθəraɪ'zeɪʃn/ *n* autorización *f*. **~e** /'ɔːθəraɪz/ *vt* autorizar

autobiography /ɔːtəʊbaɪ'ɒgrəfɪ/ *n* autobiografía *f*

autograph /'ɔːtəgrɑːf/ *n* autógrafo *m*. ● *vt* firmar, autografiar

automat|e /'ɔːtəmeɪt/ *vt* automatizar. **~ic** /-'mætɪk/ *adj* automático. **~ion** /-'meɪʃn/ *n* automatización *f*. **~on** /ɔː'tɒmətən/ *n* (*pl* -**tons** *or* -**ta** /-tə/) autómata *m*

automobile /'ɔːtəməbiːl/ *n* (*Amer*) coche *m*, carro *m* (*LAm*), automóvil *m*

autonom|ous /ɔː'tɒnəməs/ *adj* autónomo. **~y** *n* autonomía *f*

autopsy /'ɔːtɒpsɪ/ *n* autopsia *f*

autumn /'ɔːtəm/ n otoño m. **~al** /ɔː'tʌmnəl/ adj otoñal

auxiliary /ɔːg'zɪlɪərɪ/ adj & n auxiliar (m & f)

avail /ə'veɪl/ n. **to no ~** inútil

availab|ility /əveɪlə'bɪlətɪ/ n disponibilidad f. **~le** /ə'veɪləbl/ adj disponible

avalanche /'ævəlɑːnʃ/ n avalancha f

avaric|e /'ævərɪs/ n avaricia f. **~ious** /-'rɪʃəs/ adj avaro

avenue /'ævənjuː/ n avenida f; (fig) vía f

average /'ævərɪdʒ/ n promedio m. **on ~** por término medio. ● adj medio

avers|e /ə'vɜːs/ adj. **be ~e to** ser reacio a. **~ion** /-ʃn/ n repugnancia f

avert /ə'vɜːt/ vt (turn away) apartar; (ward off) desviar

aviation /eɪvɪ'eɪʃn/ n aviación f

avid /'ævɪd/ adj ávido

avocado /ævə'kɑːdəʊ/ n (pl **-os**) aguacate m

avoid /ə'vɔɪd/ vt evitar. **~able** adj evitable. **~ance** n el evitar

await /ə'weɪt/ vt esperar

awake /ə'weɪk/ vt/i (pt awoke, pp awoken) despertar. ● adj despierto. **wide ~** completamente despierto; (fig) despabilado. **~n** /ə'weɪkən/ vt/i despertar. **~ning** n el despertar

award /ə'wɔːd/ vt otorgar, (Jurid) adjudicar. ● n premio m; (Jurid) adjudicación f; (scholarship) beca f

aware /ə'weə(r)/ adj. **be ~ of sth** ser consciente de algo, darse cuenta de algo. **~ness** n conciencia f

awash /ə'wɒʃ/ adj inundado

away /ə'weɪ/ adv (absent) fuera. **far ~** muy lejos. ● adj **~ match** partido m fuera de casa

awe /ɔː/ n temor m. **~-inspiring** adj impresionante. **~some** /-səm/ adj imponente

awful /'ɔːfʊl/ adj terrible, malísimo. **feel ~** sentirse muy mal

awkward /'ɔːkwəd/ adj difícil; (inconvenient) inoportuno; (clumsy) desmañado; (embarrassed) incómodo. **~ness** n dificultad f; (discomfort) molestia f; (clumsiness) torpeza f

awning /'ɔːnɪŋ/ n toldo m

awoke /ə'wəʊk/, **awoken** /ə'wəʊkən/ see **AWAKE**

axe /æks/ n hacha f. ● vt (pres p axing) cortar con hacha; (fig) recortar

axis /'æksɪs/ n (pl **axes** /-iːz/) eje m

axle /'æksl/ n eje m

a
b

Bb

BA /biː'eɪ/ abbr see **BACHELOR**

babble /'bæbl/ vi balbucir; (chatter) parlotear; (stream) murmullar.

baboon /bə'buːn/ n mandril m

baby /'beɪbɪ/ n niño m, bebé m. **~ buggy**, **~ carriage** n (Amer) cochecito m. **~ish** adj /'beɪbɪʃ/ infantil. **~-sit** vi cuidar a los niños, hacer de canguro. **~-sitter** n baby sitter m & f, canguro m & f

bachelor /'bætʃələ(r)/ n soltero m. **B~ of Arts (BA)** licenciado m en filosofía y letras. **B~ of Science (BSc)** licenciado m en ciencias

back /bæk/ n espalda f; (of car) parte f trasera; (of chair) respaldo m; (of cloth) revés m; (of house) parte f de atrás; (of animal, book) lomo m; (of hand, document) dorso m; (football) defensa m & f. **in the ~ of beyond** en el quinto infierno. ● adj trasero. **the ~ door** la puerta trasera. ● adv atrás; (returned) de vuelta. ● vt apoyar; (betting) apostar a; dar marcha atrás a (car). ● vi retroceder; (car) dar marcha atrás. □ **~ down** vi volverse atrás. □ **~ out** vi retirarse. □ **~ up** vt apoyar; (Comp) hacer una copia de seguridad de. **~ache** n dolor m de espalda. **~bone** n columna f vertebral; (fig) pilar m. **~date** /-'deɪt/ vt antedatar. **~er** n partidario m; (Com) financiador m. **~fire** /-'faɪə(r)/ vi (Auto) petardear; (fig) fallar. **his plan ~fired on him** le salió el tiro por la culata. **~ground** n fondo m; (environment) antecedentes mpl. **~hand** n (Sport) revés m. **~ing** n apoyo m. **~lash** n reacción f. **~log** n atrasos mpl. **~side**

/-'saɪd/ n ⚀ trasero m. ~**stage** /-'steɪdʒ/ adj de bastidores. ● adv entre bastidores. ~**stroke** n (tennis etc) revés m; (swimming) estilo m espalda, estilo m dorso (Mex). ~**-up** n apoyo m; (Comp) copia f de seguridad. ~**ward** /-wəd/ adj (step etc) hacia atrás; (retarded) retrasado; (undeveloped) atrasado. ● adv (Amer) see **BACKWARDS**. ~**wards** adv hacia atrás; (fall) de espaldas; (back to front) al revés. **go** ~**wards and forwards** ir de acá para allá. ~**water** n agua f estancada; (fig) lugar m apartado

bacon /'beɪkən/ n tocino m

bacteria /bæk'tɪərɪə/ npl bacterias fpl

bad /bæd/ adj (**worse, worst**) malo, (before masculine singular noun) mal; (serious) grave; (harmful) nocivo; (language) indecente. **feel** ~ sentirse mal

bade /beɪd/ see **BID**

badge /bædʒ/ n distintivo m, chapa f

badger /'bædʒə(r)/ n tejón m. ● vt acosar

bad ~**ly** adv mal. **want** ~**ly** desear muchísimo. ~**ly injured** gravemente herido. ~**ly off** mal de dinero. ~**-mannered** /-'mænəd/ adj mal educado

badminton /'bædmɪntən/ n bádminton m

bad-tempered /bæd'tempəd/ adj (always) de mal carácter; (temporarily) de mal humor

baffle /'bæfl/ vt desconcertar. ~**d** adj perplejo

bag /bæg/ n bolsa f; (handbag) bolso m. ● vt (pt **bagged**) ensacar; (take) coger (esp Spain), agarrar (LAm). ~**s** npl (luggage) equipaje m

baggage /'bægɪdʒ/ n equipaje m. ~ **room** n (Amer) consigna f

baggy /'bægɪ/ adj (clothes) holgado

bagpipes /'bægpaɪps/ npl gaita f

baguette /bæ'get/ n baguette f

bail[1] /beɪl/ n fianza f. ● vt poner en libertad bajo fianza. ~ **s.o. out** pagar la fianza a uno

bail[2] vt. ~ **out** (Naut) achicar

bait /beɪt/ n cebo m

bak|e /beɪk/ vt cocer al horno. ● vi cocerse. ~**er** n panadero m. ~**ery** n panadería f

balance /'bæləns/ n equilibrio m; (Com) balance m; (sum) saldo m; (scales) balanza f; (remainder) resto m. ● vt equilibrar (load); mantener en equilibrio (object); nivelar (budget). ● vi equilibrarse; (Com) cuadrar. ~**d** adj equilibrado

balcony /'bælkənɪ/ n balcón m

bald /bɔːld/ adj (-er, -est) calvo, pelón (Mex)

bale /beɪl/ n bala f, fardo m. ● vi. ~ **out** lanzarse en paracaídas

Balearic /bælɪ'ærɪk/ adj. the ~ **Islands** las Islas fpl Baleares

ball /bɔːl/ n bola f; (tennis etc) pelota f; (football etc) balón m, pelota f (esp LAm); (of yarn) ovillo m; (dance) baile m

ballad /'bæləd/ n balada f

ballast /'bæləst/ n lastre m

ball bearing n cojinete m de bolas

ballerina /bælə'riːnə/ f bailarina f

ballet /'bæleɪ/ n ballet m. ~ **dancer** n bailarín m de ballet, bailarina f de ballet

balloon /bə'luːn/ n globo m

ballot /'bælət/ n votación f. ~ **box** n urna f. ~ **paper** n papeleta f.

ball ~**point** n. ~**point (pen)** bolígrafo m, pluma f atómica (Mex). ~**room** n salón m de baile

bamboo /bæm'buː/ n bambú m

ban /bæn/ vt (pt **banned**) prohibir. ~ **s.o. from sth** prohibir algo a uno. ● n prohibición f

banal /bə'nɑːl/ adj banal. ~**ity** /bə'nælətɪ/ n banalidad f

banana /bə'nɑːnə/ n plátano m

band /bænd/ n (strip) banda f. ● n (Mus) orquesta f; (military, brass) banda f. □ ~ **together** vi juntarse

bandage /'bændɪdʒ/ n venda f. ● vt vendar

Band-Aid /'bændeɪd/ n (Amer, ®) tirita f, curita f (LAm)

B & B /'biːənbiː/ abbr (= **bed and breakfast**) cama f y desayuno; (place) pensión f

bandit /'bændɪt/ n bandido m

band ~**stand** n quiosco m de música. ~**wagon** n. **jump on the** ~**wagon** (fig) subirse al carro

bandy /'bændɪ/ adj (-ier, -iest) patizambo

bang /bæŋ/ n (noise) ruido m; (blow) golpe m; (of gun) estampido m; (of door) golpe m. ● vt (strike) golpear. ~ **the door** dar un portazo. ● adv exactamente. ● int ¡pum! ~**s** npl (Amer) flequillo m, cerquillo m (LAm), fleco m (Mex)

banger /'bæŋə(r)/ n petardo m; (🔲, Culin) salchicha f

bangle /'bæŋgl/ n brazalete m

banish /'bænɪʃ/ vt desterrar

banisters /'bænɪstəz/ npl pasamanos m

banjo /'bændʒəʊ/ n (pl -os) banjo m

bank /bæŋk/ n (Com) banco m; (of river) orilla f. ● vt depositar. ● vi (in flying) ladearse. □ ~ **on** vt contar con. □ ~ **with** vi tener una cuenta con. ~ **card** n tarjeta f bancaria; (Amer) tarjeta f de crédito (expedida por un banco). ~**er** n banquero m. ~ **holiday** n día m festivo, día m feriado (LAm). ~**ing** n (Com) banca f. ~**note** n billete m de banco

bankrupt /'bæŋkrʌpt/ adj & n quebrado (m). **go** ~ quebrar. ● vt hacer quebrar. ~**cy** /-rʌpsɪ/ n bancarrota f, quiebra f

bank statement n estado m de cuenta

banner /'bænə(r)/ n bandera f; (in demonstration) pancarta f

banquet /'bæŋkwɪt/ n banquete m

banter /'bæntə(r)/ n chanza f

bap /bæp/ n panecillo m blando

baptism /'bæptɪzəm/ n bautismo m; (act) bautizo m

Baptist /'bæptɪst/ n bautista m & f

baptize /bæp'taɪz/ vt bautizar

bar /bɑː(r)/ n barra f; (on window) reja f; (of chocolate) tableta f; (of soap) pastilla f; (pub) bar m; (Mus) compás m; (Jurid) abogacía f; (fig) obstáculo m. ● vt (pt **barred**) atrancar (door); (exclude) excluir; (prohibit) prohibir. ● prep excepto

barbar|ian /bɑː'beərɪən/ adj & n bárbaro (m). ~**ic** /bɑː'bærɪk/ adj bárbaro

barbecue /'bɑːbɪkjuː/ n barbacoa f. ● vt asar a la parrilla

barbed wire /bɑːbd 'waɪə(r)/ n alambre m de púas

barber /'bɑːbə(r)/ n peluquero m, barbero m

barbwire /'bɑːb'waɪə(r)/ n (Amer) see BARBED WIRE

bare /beə(r)/ adj (-er, -est) desnudo; (room) con pocos muebles; (mere) simple; (empty) vacío. ● vt desnudar; (uncover) descubrir. ~ **one's teeth** mostrar los dientes. ~**back** adv a pelo. ~**faced** adj descarado. ~**foot** adj descalzo. ~**headed** /-'hedɪd/ adj descubierto. ~**ly** adv apenas.

bargain /'bɑːgɪn/ n (agreement) pacto m; (good buy) ganga f. ● vi negociar; (haggle) regatear. □ ~ **for** vt esperar, contar con

barge /bɑːdʒ/ n barcaza f. ● vi. ~ **in** irrumpir

baritone /'bærɪtəʊn/ n barítono m

bark /bɑːk/ n (of dog) ladrido m; (of tree) corteza f. ● vi ladrar

barley /'bɑːlɪ/ n cebada f

bar ~**maid** n camarera f. ~**man** /-mən/ n camarero m, barman m

barmy /'bɑːmɪ/ adj 🔳 chiflado

barn /bɑːn/ n granero m

barometer /bə'rɒmɪtə(r)/ n barómetro m

baron /'bærən/ n barón m. ~**ess** /-ɪs/ n baronesa f

barracks /'bærəks/ npl cuartel m

barrage /'bærɑːʒ/ n (Mil) barrera f; (dam) presa f. **a** ~ **of questions** un aluvión de preguntas

barrel /'bærəl/ n barril m; (of gun) cañón m

barren /'bærən/ adj estéril

barrette /bə'ret/ n (Amer) pasador m

barricade /bærɪ'keɪd/ n barricada f. ● vt cerrar con barricadas

barrier /'bærɪə(r)/ n barrera f

barrister /'bærɪstə(r)/ n abogado m

bartender /'bɑːtendə(r)/ n (Amer) (male) camarero m, barman m; (female) camarera f

barter /'bɑːtə(r)/ n trueque m. ● vt trocar

base /beɪs/ n base f. ● vt basar. ~**ball** n béisbol m, beisbol m (Mex)

basement /'beɪsmənt/ n sótano m

bash /bæʃ/ vt golpear. ● n golpe m. **have a** ~ 🄴 probar

bashful /'bæʃfl/ adj tímido

basic /'beɪsɪk/ adj básico, fundamental. ~**ally** adv fundamentalmente

basin /'beɪsn/ n (for washing) palangana f; (for food) cuenco m; (of river) cuenca f

basis /'beɪsɪs/ n (pl **bases** /-siːz/) base f

bask /bɑːsk/ vi asolearse; (fig) gozar (in de)

basket /'bɑːskɪt/ n cesta f; (big) cesto m. ~**ball** n baloncesto m, básquetbol m (LAm)

bass¹ /beɪs/ adj bajo. ● n (Mus) bajo m

bass² /bæs/ n (fish) lubina f

bassoon /bə'suːn/ n fagot m

bastard /'bɑːstəd/ n bastardo m. **you** ~**!** (vulgar) ¡cabrón! (vulgar)

bat /bæt/ n (for baseball, cricket) bate m; (for table tennis) raqueta f; (mammal) murciélago m. **off one's own** ~ por sí solo. ● vt (pt **batted**) golpear. **without** ~**ting an eyelid** sin pestañear. ● vi batear

batch /bætʃ/ n (of people) grupo m; (of papers) pila f; (of goods) remesa f; (of bread) hornada f; (Comp) lote m

bated /'beɪtɪd/ adj. **with** ~ **breath** con aliento entrecortado

bath /bɑːθ/ n (pl -**s** /bɑːðz/) baño m; (tub) bañera f, tina f (LAm). ~**s** npl (swimming pool) piscina f, alberca f (Mex). **have a** ~, **take a** ~ (Amer) bañarse. ● vt bañar. ● vi bañarse

bathe /beɪð/ vt bañar. ● vi bañarse. ● n baño m. ~**r** n bañista m & f

bathing /'beɪðɪŋ/ n baños mpl. ~ **costume**, ~ **suit** n traje m de baño

bathroom /'bɑːθrʊm/ n cuarto m de baño; (Amer, toilet) servicio m, baño m (LAm)

batsman /'bætsmən/ n (pl -**men**) bateador m

battalion /bə'tæliən/ n batallón m

batter /'bætə(r)/ vt (beat) apalear; (cover with batter) rebozar. ● n batido

m para rebozar; (Amer, for cake) masa f. ~**ed** /'bætəd/ adj (car etc) estropeado; (wife etc) maltratado

battery /'bætərɪ/ n (Mil, Auto) batería f; (of torch, radio) pila f

battle /'bætl/ n batalla f; (fig) lucha f. ● vi luchar. ~**field** n campo m de batalla. ~**ship** n acorazado m

bawl /bɔːl/ vt/i gritar

bay /beɪ/ n (on coast) bahía f. **keep at** ~ mantener a raya

bayonet /'beɪənet/ n bayoneta f

bay window /beɪ 'wɪndəʊ/ n ventana f salediza

bazaar /bə'zɑː(r)/ n bazar m

BC abbr (= **before Christ**) a. de C., antes de Cristo

be /biː/

present **am, are, is**; past **was, were**; past participle **been**

● intransitive verb

! Spanish has two verbs meaning **be**, *ser* and *estar*. See those entries for further information about the differences between them.

····➤ (position, changed condition or state) estar. **where is the library?** ¿dónde está la biblioteca? **she's tired** está cansada. **how are you?** ¿cómo estás?

····➤ (identity, nature or permanent characteristics) ser. **she's tall** es alta. **he's Scottish** es escocés. **I'm a journalist** soy periodista. **he's very kind** es muy bondadoso

····➤ (feel) **to be** + adjective tener + sustantivo. **to be cold/hot** tener frío/calor. **he's hungry/thirsty** tiene hambre/sed

····➤ (age) **he's thirty** tiene treinta años

····➤ (weather) **it's cold/hot** hace frío/calor. **it was 40 degrees** hacía 40 grados

● auxiliary verb

····➤ (in tenses) estar. **I'm working** estoy trabajando. **they were singing** estaban cantando, cantaban

····▶ (*in tag questions*) **it's a beautiful house, isn't it?** es una casa preciosa, ¿verdad? *or* ¿no? *or* ¿no es cierto?

····▶ (*in short answers*) **are you disappointed? - yes, I am** ¿estás desilusionado? - sí (,lo estoy). **I'm surprised, aren't you?** estoy sorprendido, ¿tú no?

····▶ (*in passive sentences*) **it was built in 1834** fue construido en 1834, se construyó en 1834. **she was told that ...** le dijeron que..., se le dijo que ...

> ! Note that passive sentences in English are often translated using the pronoun *se* or using the third person plural.

beach /biːtʃ/ *n* playa *f*

beacon /'biːkən/ *n* faro *m*

bead /biːd/ *n* cuenta *f*; (*of glass*) abalorio *m*

beak /biːk/ *n* pico *m*

beaker /'biːkə(r)/ *n* taza *f* (*alta y sin asa*)

beam /biːm/ *n* (*of wood*) viga *f*; (*of light*) rayo *m*; (*Naut*) bao *m*. ● *vt* emitir. ● *vi* irradiar; (*smile*) sonreír

bean /biːn/ *n* alubia *f*, frijol *m* (*LAm*); (*broad bean*) haba *f*; (*of coffee*) grano *m*

bear /beə(r)/ *vt* (*pt* **bore**, *pp* **borne**) llevar; parir (niño); (*endure*) soportar. **~ right** torcer a la derecha. **~ in mind** tener en cuenta. □ **~ with** *vt* tener paciencia con. ● *n* oso *m*, **~able** *adj* soportable

beard /bɪəd/ *n* barba *f*. **~ed** *adj* barbudo

bearer /'beərə(r)/ *n* portador *m*; (*of passport*) titular *m & f*

bearing /'beərɪŋ/ *n* comportamiento *m*; (*relevance*) relación *f*; (*Mec*) cojinete *m*. **get one's ~s** orientarse. **lose one's ~s** desorientarse

beast /biːst/ *n* bestia *f*; (*person*) bruto *m*. **~ly** *adj* (**-ier, -iest**) bestial; Ⓣ horrible

beat /biːt/ *vt* (*pt* **beat**, *pp* **beaten**) (*hit*) pegar; (*Culin*) batir; (*defeat*) derrotar; (*better*) sobrepasar; batir (record); (*baffle*) dejar perplejo. **~ it** 🅧 largarse. ● *vi* (*heart*) latir. ● *n* latido *m*; (*Mus*) ritmo *m*; (*of policeman*) ronda *f*. □ **~ up** *vt* darle una paliza a; (*Culin*) batir. **~ up on** (*Amer, fam*) darle una paliza a. **~er** *n* batidor *m*. **~ing** *n* paliza *f*

beautician /bjuː'tɪʃn/ *n* esteticista *m & f*

beautiful /'bjuːtɪfl/ *adj* hermoso. **~ly** *adv* maravillosamente

beauty /'bjuːtɪ/ *n* belleza *f*. **~ salon**, **~ shop** (*Amer*) *n* salón *m* de belleza. **~ spot** *n* (*on face*) lunar *m*; (*site*) lugar *m* pintoresco

beaver /'biːvə(r)/ *n* castor *m*

became /bɪ'keɪm/ *see* **BECOME**

because /bɪ'kɒz/ *conj* porque. ● *adv*. **~ of** por, a causa de

beckon /'bekən/ *vt/i*. **~ (to)** hacer señas (a)

become /bɪ'kʌm/ *vi* (*pt* **became**, *pp* **become**) hacerse, llegar a ser, volverse, convertirse en. **what has ~ of her?** ¿qué es de ella?

bed /bed/ *n* cama *f*; (*layer*) estrato *m*; (*of sea, river*) fondo *m*; (*of flowers*) macizo *m*. **go to ~** acostarse. ● *vi* (*pt* **bedded**). **~ and breakfast (B & B)** cama y desayuno; (*place*) pensión *f*. **~bug** *n* chinche *f*. **~clothes** *npl*, **~ding** *n* ropa *f* de cama, cobijas *fpl* (*LAm*)

> **Bed and breakfast** Los bed & breakfast o B&B son casas privadas o pequeños hoteles que ofrecen alojamiento y desayuno a precios generalmente módicos.

bed ~room *n* dormitorio *m*, cuarto *m*, habitación *f*, recámara *f* (*Mex*). **~-sitter** /-'sɪtə(r)/ *n* habitación *f* con cama y uso de cocina y baño compartidos, estudio *m*. **~spread** *n* colcha *f*. **~time** *n* hora *f* de acostarse

bee /biː/ *n* abeja *f*; (*Amer, social gathering*) círculo *m*

beech /biːtʃ/ *n* haya *f*

beef /biːf/ *n* carne *f* de vaca, carne *f* de res (*Mex*). ● *vi* 🅧 quejarse. **~burger** *n* hamburguesa *f*. **~y** *adj* (**-ier, -iest**) musculoso

bee ~**hive** n colmena f. ~**line** n. **make a** ~**line for** ir en línea recta hacia

been /biːn/ see BE

beer /bɪə(r)/ n cerveza f

beet /biːt/ n (Amer) remolacha f, betabel f (Mex)

beetle /'biːtl/ n escarabajo m

beetroot /'biːtruːt/ n invar remolacha f, betabel f (Mex)

befall /bɪ'fɔːl/ vt (pt befell, pp befallen) ocurrirle a. ●vi ocurrir

before /bɪ'fɔː(r)/ prep (time) antes de; (place) delante de. ~ **leaving** antes de marcharse. ●adv (place) delante; (time) antes. **a week** ~ una semana antes. **the week** ~ la semana anterior. ●conj (time) antes de que. ~ **he leaves** antes de que se vaya. ~**hand** adv de antemano

befriend /bɪ'frend/ vt hacerse amigo de

beg /beg/ vt/i (pt begged) mendigar; (entreat) suplicar; (ask) pedir. ~ s.o.'s **pardon** pedir perdón a uno. **I** ~ **your pardon!** ¡perdone Vd! **I** ~ **your pardon?** ¿cómo?

began /bɪ'gæn/ see BEGIN

beggar /'begə(r)/ n mendigo m

begin /bɪ'gɪn/ vt/i (pt began, pp begun, pres p beginning) comenzar, empezar. ~**ner** n principiante m & f. ~**ning** n principio m

begrudge /bɪ'grʌdʒ/ vt envidiar; (give) dar de mala gana

begun /bɪ'gʌn/ see BEGIN

behalf /bɪ'hɑːf/ n. **on** ~ **of, in** ~ **of** (Amer) de parte de, en nombre de

behav|e /bɪ'heɪv/ vi comportarse, portarse. ~**e (o.s.)** portarse bien. ~**iour** /bɪ'heɪvjə(r)/ n comportamiento m

behead /bɪ'hed/ vt decapitar

behind /bɪ'haɪnd/ prep detrás de, atrás de (LAm). ●adv detrás; (late) atrasado. ●n 🔲 trasero m

beige /beɪʒ/ adj & n beige (m)

being /'biːɪŋ/ n ser m. **come into** ~ nacer

belated /bɪ'leɪtɪd/ adj tardío

belch /beltʃ/ vi eructar. □ ~ **out** vt arrojar (smoke)

belfry /'belfrɪ/ n campanario m

Belgi|an /'beldʒən/ adj & n belga (m & f). ~**um** /'beldʒəm/ n Bélgica f

belie|f /bɪ'liːf/ n (trust) fe f; (opinion) creencia f. ~**ve** /bɪ'liːv/ vt/i creer. ~**ve in** creer en. **make** ~**ve** fingir

belittle /bɪ'lɪtl/ vt menospreciar (achievements); denigrar (person)

bell /bel/ n campana f; (on door, bicycle) timbre m

belligerent /bɪ'lɪdʒərənt/ adj beligerante

bellow /'beləʊ/ vt gritar. ●vi bramar. ~**s** npl fuelle m

bell pepper n (Amer) pimiento m

belly /'belɪ/ n barriga f

belong /bɪ'lɒŋ/ vi pertenecer (to a); (club) ser socio (to de); (have as usual place) ir. ~**ings** /bɪ'lɒŋɪŋz/ npl pertenencias fpl. **personal** ~**ings** efectos mpl personales

beloved /bɪ'lʌvɪd/ adj querido

below /bɪ'ləʊ/ prep debajo de, abajo de (LAm); (fig) inferior a. ●adv abajo

belt /belt/ n cinturón m; (area) zona f. ●vt (fig) rodear; 🔲 darle una paliza a. ~**way** n (Amer) carretera f de circunvalación

bench /bentʃ/ n banco m

bend /bend/ n curva f. ●vt (pt & pp bent) doblar; torcer (arm, leg). ●vi doblarse; (road) torcerse. □ ~ **down** vi inclinarse □ ~ **over** vi agacharse

beneath /bɪ'niːθ/ prep debajo de; (fig) inferior a. ●adv abajo

beneficial /benɪ'fɪʃl/ adj provechoso

beneficiary /benɪ'fɪʃərɪ/ n beneficiario m

benefit /'benɪfɪt/ n provecho m, ventaja f; (allowance) prestación f; (for unemployed) subsidio m; (perk) beneficio m. ●vt (pt benefited, pres p benefiting) beneficiar. ●vi beneficiarse

benevolent /bə'nevələnt/ adj benévolo

benign /bɪ'naɪn/ adj benigno

bent /bent/ see BEND. ●n inclinación f. ●adj torcido; (🔲, corrupt) corrompido

bereave|d /bɪ'riːvd/ n. **the** ~**d** la familia del difunto. ~**ment** n pérdida f; (mourning) luto m

beret /'bereɪ/ n boina f

berry /'berɪ/ n baya f

berserk /bə'sɜːk/ adj. **go ~** volverse loco

berth /bɜːθ/ n litera f; (anchorage) amarradero m. **give a wide ~ to** evitar. ● vt/i atracar

beside /bɪ'saɪd/ prep al lado de. **be ~ o.s.** estar fuera de sí

besides /bɪ'saɪdz/ prep además de; (except) excepto. ● adv además

besiege /bɪ'siːdʒ/ vt sitiar, asediar; (fig) acosar

best /best/ adj (el) mejor. **the ~ thing is to...** lo mejor es... ● adv mejor. **like ~** preferir. ● n lo mejor. **at ~** a lo más. **do one's ~** hacer todo lo posible. **make the ~ of** contentarse con. **~ man** n padrino m (de boda)

bestow /bɪ'stəʊ/ vt conceder

bestseller /best'selə(r)/ n éxito m de librería, bestseller m

bet /bet/ n apuesta f. ● vt/i (pt **bet** or **betted**) apostar

betray /bɪ'treɪ/ vt traicionar. **~al** n traición f

better /'betə(r)/ adj & adv mejor. **~ off** en mejores condiciones; (richer) más rico. **get ~** mejorar. **all the ~** tanto mejor. **I'd ~ be off** me tengo que ir. **the ~ part of** la mayor parte de. ● vt mejorar; (beat) sobrepasar. **~ o.s.** superarse. ● n superior m. **get the ~ of** vencer a. **my ~s** mis superiores mpl

between /bɪ'twiːn/ prep entre. ● adv en medio

beverage /'bevərɪdʒ/ n bebida f

beware /bɪ'weə(r)/ vi tener cuidado. ● int ¡cuidado!

bewilder /bɪ'wɪldə(r)/ vt desconcertar. **~ment** n aturdimiento m

bewitch /bɪ'wɪtʃ/ vt hechizar; (delight) cautivar

beyond /bɪ'jɒnd/ prep más allá de; (fig) fuera de. **~ doubt** sin lugar a duda. ● adv más allá

bias /'baɪəs/ n tendencia f; (prejudice) prejuicio m. ● vt (pt **biased**) influir en. **~ed** adj parcial

bib /bɪb/ n babero m

Bible /'baɪbl/ n Biblia f

biblical /'bɪblɪkl/ adj bíblico

bibliography /bɪblɪ'ɒgrəfɪ/ n bibliografía f

biceps /'baɪseps/ n invar bíceps m

bicker /'bɪkə(r)/ vi altercar

bicycle /'baɪsɪkl/ n bicicleta f

bid /bɪd/ n (offer) oferta f; (attempt) tentativa f. ● vi hacer una oferta. ● vt (pt & pp **bid**, pres p **bidding**) ofrecer; (pt **bid**, pp **bidden**, pres p **bidding**) mandar; dar (welcome, good day etc). **~der** n postor m. **~ding** n (at auction) ofertas fpl; (order) mandato m

bide /baɪd/ vt. **~ one's time** esperar el momento oportuno

bifocals /baɪ'fəʊklz/ npl gafas fpl bifocales, anteojos mpl bifocales (LAm)

big /bɪg/ adj (**bigger**, **biggest**) grande, (before singular noun) gran. ● adv. **talk ~** fanfarronear

bigam|ist /'bɪgəmɪst/ n bígamo m. **~ous** /'bɪgəməs/ adj bígamo. **~y** n bigamia f

big-headed /-'hedɪd/ adj engreído

bigot /'bɪgət/ n fanático m. **~ed** adj fanático

bike /baɪk/ n 🆃 bici f 🆃

bikini /bɪ'kiːnɪ/ n (pl **-is**) bikini m

bile /baɪl/ n bilis f

bilingual /baɪ'lɪŋgwəl/ adj bilingüe

bill /bɪl/ n cuenta f; (invoice) factura f; (notice) cartel m; (Amer, banknote) billete m; (Pol) proyecto m de ley; (of bird) pico m

billet /'bɪlɪt/ n (Mil) alojamiento m. ● vt alojar

billfold /'bɪlfəʊld/ n (Amer) cartera f, billetera f

billiards /'bɪlɪədz/ n billar m

billion /'bɪlɪən/ n billón m; (Amer) mil millones mpl

bin /bɪn/ n recipiente m; (for rubbish) cubo m de basura, bote m de basura (Mex); (for waste paper) papelera f

bind /baɪnd/ vt (pt **bound**) atar; encuadernar (book); (Jurid) obligar. ● n 🆃 lata f. **~ing** n (of books) encuadernación f; (braid) ribete m

binge /bɪndʒ/ n 🆇, (of food) comilona f; (of drink) borrachera f. **go on a ~** ir de juerga

bingo /'bɪŋgəʊ/ n bingo m

binoculars /bɪ'nɒkjʊləz/ *npl* gemelos *mpl*

biofuel /'baɪəʊfjuːəl/ *n* biocarburante *m*

biograph|er /baɪ'ɒgrəfə(r)/ *n* biógrafo *m*. **~y** *n* biografía *f*

biolog|ical /baɪə'lɒdʒɪkl/ *adj* biológico. **~ist** /baɪ'ɒlədʒɪst/ *n* biólogo *m*. **~y** /baɪ'ɒlədʒɪ/ *n* biología *f*

bioterrorism /baɪəʊ'terərɪzm/ *n* bioterrorismo *m*

birch /bɜːtʃ/ *n* (*tree*) abedul *m*

bird /bɜːd/ *n* ave *f*; (*small*) pájaro *m*; (*sl, girl*) chica *f*

Biro /'baɪərəʊ/ *n* (*pl* **-os**) (®) bolígrafo *m*

birth /bɜːθ/ *n* nacimiento *m*. **give ~** dar a luz. **~ certificate** *n* partida *f* de nacimiento. **~ control** *n* control *m* de la natalidad. **~day** *n* cumpleaños *m*. **~mark** *n* marca *f* de nacimiento. **~place** *n* lugar *m* de nacimiento. **~rate** *n* natalidad *f*

biscuit /'bɪskɪt/ *n* galleta *f*

bisect /baɪ'sekt/ *vt* bisecar

bishop /'bɪʃəp/ *n* obispo *m*; (*Chess*) alfil *m*

bit /bɪt/ *see* **BITE**. ●*n* trozo *m*; (*quantity*) poco *m*; (*of horse*) bocado *m*; (*Mec*) broca *f*; (*Comp*) bit *m*

bitch /bɪtʃ/ *n* perra *f*; (*fam, woman*) bruja *f* 🔲

bit|e /baɪt/ *vt/i* (*pt* **bit**, *pp* **bitten**) morder; (*insect*) picar. **~e one's nails** morderse las uñas. ●*n* mordisco *m*; (*mouthful*) bocado *m*; (*of insect etc*) picadura *f*. **~ing** /'baɪtɪŋ/ *adj* mordaz

bitter /'bɪtə(r)/ *adj* amargo; (*of weather*) glacial. ●*n* cerveza *f* amarga. **~ly** *adv* amargamente. **it's ~ly cold** hace un frío glacial. **~ness** *n* amargor *m*; (*resentment*) amargura *f*

bizarre /bɪ'zɑː(r)/ *adj* extraño

black /blæk/ *adj* (**-er**, **-est**) negro. **~ and blue** amoratado. ●*n* negro *m*; (*coffee*) solo, negro (*LAm*). ●*vt* ennegrecer; limpiar (shoes). **~ out** *vi* desmayarse. **~ and white** *n* blanco y negro *m*. **~-and-white** *adj* en blanco y negro. **~berry** /-bərɪ/ *n* zarzamora *f*. **~bird** *n* mirlo *m*. **~board** *n* pizarra *f*. **~currant** /-'kʌrənt/ *n* grosella *f*

negra. **~en** *vt* ennegrecer. **~ eye** *n* ojo *m* morado. **~list** *vt* poner en la lista negra. **~mail** *n* chantaje *m*. ●*vt* chantajear. **~mailer** *n* chantajista *m* & *f*. **~out** *n* apagón *m*; (*Med*) desmayo *m*; (*of news*) censura *f*. **~smith** *n* herrero *m*

bladder /'blædə(r)/ *n* vejiga *f*

blade /bleɪd/ *n* (*of knife, sword*) hoja *f*. **~ of grass** brizna *f* de hierba

blame /bleɪm/ *vt* echar la culpa a. **be to ~** tener la culpa. ●*n* culpa *f*. **~less** *adj* inocente

bland /blænd/ *adj* (**-er**, **-est**) suave

blank /blæŋk/ *adj* (page, space) en blanco; (cassette) virgen; (cartridge) sin bala; (*fig*) vacío. ●*n* blanco *m*

blanket /'blæŋkɪt/ *n* manta *f*, cobija *f* (*LAm*), frazada (*LAm*); (*fig*) capa *f*. ●*vt* (*pt* **blanketed**) (*fig*) cubrir (**in, with** de)

blare /bleə(r)/ *vi* sonar muy fuerte. ●*n* estrépito *m*

blasphem|e /blæs'fiːm/ *vt/i* blasfemar. **~ous** /'blæsfəməs/ *adj* blasfemo. **~y** /'blæsfəmɪ/ *n* blasfemia *f*

blast /blɑːst/ *n* explosión *f*; (*gust*) ráfaga *f*; (*sound*) toque *m*. ●*vt* volar. **~ed** *adj* maldito. **~-off** *n* (*of missile*) despegue *m*

blatant /'bleɪtnt/ *adj* patente; (*shameless*) descarado

blaze /'bleɪz/ *n* llamarada *f*; (*of light*) resplandor *m*; (*fig*) arranque *m*. ●*vi* arder en llamas; (*fig*) brillar

blazer /'bleɪzə(r)/ *n* chaqueta *f*

bleach /bliːtʃ/ *n* lejía *f*, cloro *m* (*LAm*), blanqueador *m* (*LAm*). ●*vt* blanquear; decolorar (hair).

bleak /bliːk/ *adj* (**-er**, **-est**) desolado; (*fig*) sombrío

bleat /bliːt/ *n* balido *m*. ●*vi* balar

bleed /bliːd/ *vt/i* (*pt* **bled** /bled/) sangrar

bleep /bliːp/ *n* pitido *m*

blemish /'blemɪʃ/ *n* mancha *f*

blend /blend/ *n* mezcla *f*. ●*vt* mezclar. ●*vi* combinarse. **~er** *n* licuadora *f*

bless /bles/ *vt* bendecir. **~ you!** (*on sneezing*) ¡Jesús!, ¡salud! (*Mex*). **~ed** /'blesɪd/ *adj* bendito. **~ing** *n* bendición f; (*advantage*) ventaja f

blew /blu:/ *see* **BLOW**

blight /blaɪt/ n añublo m, tizón m; (*fig*) plaga f. ●vt añublar, atizonar; (*fig*) destrozar

blind /blaɪnd/ adj ciego. ~ **alley** callejón m sin salida. ●n persiana f; (*fig*) pretexto m. ●vt dejar ciego; (*dazzle*) deslumbrar. ~**fold** adj & adv con los ojos vendados. ●n venda f. ●vt vendar los ojos a. ~**ly** adv a ciegas. ~**ness** n ceguera f

blink /blɪŋk/ vi parpadear; (light) centellear. ~**ers** npl (on horse) anteojeras fpl

bliss /blɪs/ n felicidad f. ~**ful** adj feliz

blister /ˈblɪstə(r)/ n ampolla f

blizzard /ˈblɪzəd/ n ventisca f

bloated /ˈbləʊtɪd/ adj hinchado (**with** de)

blob /blɒb/ n (drip) gota f; (stain) mancha f

bloc /blɒk/ n (Pol) bloque m

block /blɒk/ n bloque m; (of wood) zoquete m; (of buildings) manzana f, cuadra f (LAm). **in** ~ **letters** en letra de imprenta. ~ **of flats** edificio m de apartamentos, casa f de pisos. ●vt bloquear. ~**ade** /blɒˈkeɪd/ n bloqueo m. ●vt bloquear. ~**age** /-ɪdʒ/ n obstrucción f. ~**head** n 🄸 zopenco m

bloke /bləʊk/ n 🄸 tipo m, tío m 🄸

blond /blɒnd/ adj & n rubio (m), güero (m) (Mex fam). ~**e** adj & n rubia (f), güera (f) (Mex fam)

blood /blʌd/ n sangre f. ~**bath** n masacre m. ~-**curdling** /-kɜːdlɪŋ/adj horripilante. ~**hound** n sabueso m. ~ **pressure** n tensión f arterial. **high** ~ **pressure** hipertensión f. ~**shed** n derramamiento m de sangre. ~**shot** adj sanguinolento; (eye) inyectado de sangre. ~**stream** n torrente m sanguíneo. ~**thirsty** adj sanguinario. ~**y** adj (-ier, -iest) sangriento; (stained) ensangrentado; 🅇 maldito

bloom /blu:m/ n flor f. ●vi florecer

blossom /ˈblɒsəm/ n flor f. ●vi florecer. ~ (**out**) **into** (fig) llegar a ser

blot /blɒt/ n borrón m. ●vt (pt blotted) manchar; (dry) secar. ▫~ **out** vt oscurecer

blotch /blɒtʃ/ n mancha f. ~**y** adj lleno de manchas

blotting-paper /ˈblɒtɪŋ/ n papel m secante

blouse /blaʊz/ n blusa f

blow /bləʊ/ vt (pt blew, pp blown) soplar; fundir (fuse); tocar (trumpet).●vi soplar; (fuse) fundirse; (sound) sonar. ●n golpe m. ▫~ **down** vt derribar. ▫~ **out** vi apagar (candle). ▫~ **over** vi pasar. ▫~ **up** vt inflar; (explode) volar; (Photo) ampliar. vi (explode) estallar; (burst) reventar. ~-**dry** vt secar con secador. ~**lamp** n soplete m. ~**out** n (of tyre) reventón m. ~ **torch** n soplete m

blue /blu:/ adj (-er, -est) azul; (joke) verde. ●n azul m. **out of the** ~ totalmente inesperado. ~**s** npl. **have the** ~**s** tener tristeza. ~**bell** n campanilla f. ~**berry** n arándano m. ~**bottle** n moscarda f. ~**print** n plano m; (fig, plan) programa m

bluff /blʌf/ n (poker) farol m, bluff m (LAm), blof m (Mex). ●vt engañar. ●vi tirarse un farol, hacer un bluf (LAm), blofear (Mex)

blunder /ˈblʌndə(r)/ vi cometer un error. ●n metedura f de pata

blunt /blʌnt/ adj desafilado; (person) directo, abrupto. ●vt desafilar. ~**ly** adv francamente

blur /blɜ:(r)/ n impresión f indistinta. ●vt (pt blurred) hacer borroso

blurb /blɜ:b/ n resumen m publicitario

blurt /blɜ:t/ vt. ▫~ **out** dejar escapar

blush /blʌʃ/ vi ruborizarse. ●n rubor m

boar /bɔ:(r)/ n verraco m. **wild** ~ jabalí m

board /bɔ:d/ n tabla f, tablero m; (for notices) tablón m de anuncios, tablero m de anuncios (LAm); (blackboard) pizarra f; (food) pensión f; (of company) junta f. ~ **and lodging** casa y comida. **full** ~ pensión f completa. **go by the** ~ ser abandonado. ●vt alojar; ~ **a ship** embarcarse. ●vi alojarse (**with** en casa de); (at school) ser interno. ~**er** n huésped m & f; (school) interno m. ~**ing card** n tarjeta f de embarque. ~**ing house** n casa f de huéspedes, pensión f. ~**ing**

pass n see ~ING CARD. ~ing school n internado m

boast /bəʊst/ vt enorgullecerse de. ● vi jactarse. ● n jactancia f. ~ful adj jactancioso

boat /bəʊt/ n barco m; (small) bote m, barca f

bob /bɒb/ vi (pt bobbed) menearse, subir y bajar. □ ~ up vi presentarse súbitamente

bobbin /'bɒbɪn/ n carrete m; (in sewing machine) canilla f, bobina f

bobby pin /'bɒbɪ/ n (Amer) horquilla f, pasador m (Mex). ~ sox /sɒks/ npl (Amer) calcetines mpl cortos

bobsleigh /'bɒbsleɪ/ n bob(sleigh) m

bode /bəʊd/ vi. ~ well/ill ser de buen/mal agüero

bodice /'bɒdɪs/ n corpiño m

bodily /'bɒdɪlɪ/ adj físico, corporal. ● adv físicamente

body /'bɒdɪ/ n cuerpo m; (dead) cadáver m. ~guard n guardaespaldas m. ~ part n pedazo m de cuerpo. ~work n carrocería f

bog /bɒg/ n ciénaga f. □ ~ down vt (pt bogged). get ~ged down empantanarse

boggle /'bɒgl/ vi sobresaltarse. the mind ~s uno se queda atónito

bogus /'bəʊgəs/ adj falso

boil /bɔɪl/ vt/i hervir. be ~ing hot estar ardiendo; (weather) hacer mucho calor. ● n furúnculo m. □ ~ away vi evaporarse. □ ~ down to vt reducirse a. □ ~ over vi rebosar. ~ed adj hervido; (egg) pasado por agua. ~er n caldera f. ~er suit n mono m, overol m (LAm)

boisterous /'bɔɪstərəs/ adj ruidoso, bullicioso

bold /bəʊld/ adj (-er, -est) audaz. ~ly adv con audacia, audazmente

Bolivia /bə'lɪvɪə/ n Bolivia f. ~n adj & n boliviano (m)

bolster /'bəʊlstə(r)/ □ ~ up vt sostener

bolt /bəʊlt/ n (on door) cerrojo m; (for nut) perno m; (lightning) rayo m; (leap) fuga f. ● vt echar el cerrojo a (door); engullir (food). ● vi fugarse. ● adv. ~ upright rígido

bomb /bɒm/ n bomba f. ● vt bombardear. ~ard /bɒm'bɑːd/ vt bombardear ~er /'bɒmə(r)/ n (plane) bombardero m; (terrorist) terrorista m & f. ~ing /'bɒmɪŋ/ n bombardeo m. ~shell n bomba f

bond /bɒnd/ n (agreement) obligación f; (link) lazo m; (Com) bono m. ● vi (stick) adherirse. ~age /-ɪdʒ/ n esclavitud f

bone /bəʊn/ n hueso m; (of fish) espina f. ● vt deshuesar; quitar las espinas a (fish). ~-dry adj completamente seco. ~ idle adj holgazán

bonfire /'bɒnfaɪə(r)/ n hoguera f, fogata f

bonnet /'bɒnɪt/ n gorra f; (Auto) capó m, capote m (Mex)

bonus /'bəʊnəs/ n (payment) bonificación f; (fig) ventaja f

bony /'bəʊnɪ/ adj (-ier, -iest) huesudo; (fish) lleno de espinas

boo /buː/ int ¡bu! ● vt/i abuchear

boob /buːb/ n (fam, mistake) metedura f de pata. ● vi Ⓣ meter la pata

book /bʊk/ n libro m; (of cheques etc) talonario m, chequera f; (notebook) libreta f; (exercise book) cuaderno m. ~s (mpl) (Com) cuentas fpl. ● vt (enter) registrar; (reserve) reservar. ● vi reservar. ~case n biblioteca f, librería f, librero m (Mex). ~ing n reserva f, reservación f (LAm). ~ing office n (in theatre) taquilla f, boletería f (LAm). ~keeping n contabilidad f. ~let /'bʊklɪt/ n folleto m. ~maker n corredor m de apuestas. ~mark n señal f. ~seller n librero m. ~shop, (Amer) ~store n librería f. ~worm n (fig) ratón m de biblioteca

boom /buːm/ vi retumbar; (fig) prosperar. ● n estampido m; (Com) boom m

boost /buːst/ vt estimular; reforzar (morale). ● n empuje m. ~er n (Med) revacunación f. ~er cable n (Amer) cable m de arranque

boot /buːt/ n bota f; (Auto) maletero m, cajuela f (Mex). □ ~ up vt (Comp) cargar

booth /buːð/ n cabina f; (at fair) puesto m

booze /buːz/ vi Ⓣ beber mucho. ● n Ⓣ alcohol m

border /'bɔːdə(r)/ n borde m; (frontier) frontera f; (in garden) arriate m. □ ~ **on** vt lindar con. ~**line** n línea f divisoria. ~**line case** n caso m dudoso

bor|e /bɔː(r)/ see **BEAR**. ● vt (annoy) aburrir; (Tec) taladrar. ● vi taladrar. ● n (person) pelmazo m; (thing) lata f. ~**ed** adj aburrido. **be** ~**ed** estar aburrido. **get** ~**ed** aburrirse. ~**edom** /'bɔːdəm/ n aburrimiento m. ~**ing** adj aburrido, pesado

born /bɔːn/ adj nato. **be** ~ nacer

borne /bɔːn/ see **BEAR**

borough /'bʌrə/ n municipio m

borrow /'bɒrəʊ/ vt pedir prestado

boss /bɒs/ n Ⓣ jefe m. ● vt. ~ **(about)** Ⓣ dar órdenes a, ~**y** adj mandón

botan|ical /bə'tænɪkl/ adj botánico. ~**ist** /'bɒtənɪst/ n botánico m. ~**y** /'bɒtənɪ/ n botánica f

both /bəʊθ/ adj & pron ambos (mpl), los dos (mpl). ● adv al mismo tiempo, a la vez. ~ **Ann and Brian came** tanto Ann como Bob vinieron.

bother /'bɒðə(r)/ vt (inconvenience) molestar; (worry) preocupar. ~ **it!** ¡caramba! ● vi molestarse. ~ **about** preocuparse de. ~ **doing** tomarse la molestia de hacer. ● n molestia f

bottle /'bɒtl/ n botella, mamila f (Mex); (for baby) biberón m. ● vt embotellar. □ ~ **up** vt (fig) reprimir. ~**neck** n (traffic jam) embotellamiento m. ~ **opener** n abrebotellas m, destapador m (LAm)

bottom /'bɒtəm/ n fondo m; (of hill) pie m; (buttocks) trasero m. ● adj de más abajo; (price) más bajo; (lip, edge) inferior. ~**less** adj sin fondo

bough /baʊ/ n rama f

bought /bɔːt/ see **BUY**

boulder /'bəʊldə(r)/ n canto m

bounce /baʊns/ vt hacer rebotar. ● vi rebotar; (person) saltar; Ⓣ (cheque) ser rechazado. ● n rebote m

bound /baʊnd/ see **BIND**. ● vi saltar. ● n (jump) salto m. ~**s** npl (limits) límites mpl. **out of** ~**s** zona f prohibida. ● adj. **be** ~ **for** dirigirse a. ~ **to** obligado a; (certain) seguro de

boundary /'baʊndərɪ/ n límite m

bouquet /bʊ'keɪ/ n ramo m; (of wine) buqué m, aroma m

bout /baʊt/ n período m; (Med) ataque m; (Sport) encuentro m

bow¹ /bəʊ/ n (weapon, Mus) arco m; (knot) lazo m, moño m (LAm)

bow² /baʊ/ n reverencia f; (Naut) proa f; ● vi inclinarse. ● vt inclinar

bowels /'baʊəlz/ npl intestinos mpl; (fig) entrañas fpl

bowl /bəʊl/ n (container) cuenco m; (for washing) palangana f; (ball) bola f. ● vt (cricket) arrojar. ● vi (cricket) arrojar la pelota. □ ~ **over** vt derribar

bowl ~**er** n (cricket) lanzador m. ~**er (hat)** sombrero m de hongo, bombín m. ~**ing** n bolos mpl. ~**ing alley** n bolera f

bow tie /bəʊ 'taɪ/ n corbata f de lazo, pajarita f

box /bɒks/ n caja f; (for jewels etc) estuche m; (in theatre) palco m. ● vt boxear contra. ~ **s.o.'s ears** dar una manotada a uno. ● vi boxear. ~**er** n boxeador m. ~**ing** n boxeo m. **B**~**ing Day** n el 26 de diciembre. ~ **office** n taquilla f, boletería f (LAm). ~ **room** n trastero m

boy /bɔɪ/ n chico m, muchacho m; (young) niño m

boy ~ **band** n grupo m pop de chicos. ~**friend** n novio m. ~**hood** n niñez f. ~**ish** adj de muchacho; (childish) infantil

boycott /'bɔɪkɒt/ vt boicotear. ● n boicoteo m

bra /brɑː/ n sostén m, sujetador m, brasier m (Mex)

brace /breɪs/ n abrazadera f. ● vt asegurar. ~ **o.s.** prepararse. ~**s** npl tirantes mpl; (Amer, dental) aparato(s) m(pl)

bracelet /'breɪslɪt/ n pulsera f

bracken /'brækən/ n helecho m

bracket /'brækɪt/ n soporte m; (group) categoría f; (parenthesis) paréntesis m. **square** ~**s** corchetes mpl. ● vt poner entre paréntesis; (join together) agrupar

brag /bræg/ vi (pt **bragged**) jactarse **(about** de)

braid /breɪd/ n galón m; (Amer, in hair) trenza f

brain /breɪn/ n cerebro m. ● vt romper la cabeza a. ~**child** n invento m. ~

drain n ① fuga f de cerebros.
~**storm** n ataque m de locura; (*Amer*, *brainwave*) idea f genial. ~**wash** vt lavar el cerebro. ~**wave** n idea f genial. ~**y** adj (**-ier, -iest**) inteligente

brake /breɪk/ n freno m. ● vt/i frenar. ~ **fluid** n líquido m de freno. ~ **lights** npl luces fpl de freno

bramble /ˈbræmbl/ n zarza f

bran /bræn/ n salvado m

branch /brɑːntʃ/ n rama f; (*of road*) bifurcación f; (*Com*) sucursal m; (*fig*) ramo m. □ ~ **off** vi bifurcarse. □ ~ **out** vi ramificarse

brand /brænd/ n marca f. ● vt marcar; (*label*) tildar de

brandish /ˈbrændɪʃ/ vt blandir

brand ~ **name** n marca f. ~-**new** /-ˈnjuː/ adj flamante

brandy /ˈbrændɪ/ n coñac m

brash /bræʃ/ adj descarado

brass /brɑːs/ n latón m. **get down to** ~ **tacks** (*fig*) ir al grano. ~ **band** n banda f de música

brassière /ˈbræsjeə(r)/ n see **BRA**

brat /bræt/ n (*pej*) mocoso m

bravado /brəˈvɑːdəʊ/ n bravata f

brave /breɪv/ adj (**-er, -est**) valiente. ● n (*North American Indian*) guerrero m indio. **the** ~ npl los valientes. ● vt afrontar. ~**ry** /-ərɪ/ n valentía f, valor m

brawl /brɔːl/ n alboroto m. ● vi pelearse

brazen /ˈbreɪzn/ adj descarado

Brazil /brəˈzɪl/ n Brasil m. ~**ian** /-jən/ adj & n brasileño (m)

breach /briːtʃ/ n infracción f, violación f; (*of contract*) incumplimiento m; (*gap*) brecha f. ~ **of the peace** alteración f del orden público. ● vt abrir una brecha en

bread /bred/ n pan m. **a loaf of** ~ un pan. ~**crumbs** npl migajas fpl; (*Culin*) pan m rallado, pan m molido (*Mex*)

breadth /bredθ/ n anchura f

breadwinner /ˈbredwɪnə(r)/ n sostén m de la familia

break /breɪk/ vt (*pt* **broke**, *pp* **broken**) romper; infringir, violar (law); batir (record); comunicar (news); interrumpir (journey). ● vi romperse; (news)

divulgarse. ● n ruptura f; (*interval*) intervalo m; (*fam, chance*) oportunidad f; (*in weather*) cambio m. □ ~ **away** vi escapar. □ ~ **down** vt derribar; analizar (figures). vi estropearse, descomponerse (*LAm*); (*Auto*) averiarse; (*cry*) deshacerse en lágrimas. □ ~ **in** vi (intruder) entrar (*para robar*). □ ~ **into** vt entrar en (*para robar*) (house etc); (*start doing*) ponerse a. □ ~ **off** vi interrumpirse. □ ~ **out** vi (war, disease) estallar; (*run away*) escaparse. □ ~ **up** vi romperse; (band, lovers) separarse; (schools) terminar. ~**able** adj frágil. ~**age** /-ɪdʒ/ n rotura f. ~**down** n (*Tec*) falla f; (*Med*) colapso m, crisis f nerviosa; (*of figures*) análisis f. ~**er** n (*wave*) ola f grande

breakfast /ˈbrekfəst/ n desayuno m. **have** ~ desayunar

break ~**through** n adelanto m. ~**water** n rompeolas m

breast /brest/ n pecho m; (*of chicken etc*) pechuga f. (estilo m) ~**stroke** n braza f, (estilo m) pecho m (*LAm*)

breath /breθ/ n aliento m, respiración f. **be out of** ~ estar sin aliento. **hold one's** ~ aguantar la respiración. **under one's** ~ a media voz

breath|e /briːð/ vt/i respirar. ~**er** n descanso m, pausa f. ~**ing** n respiración f

breathtaking /ˈbreθteɪkɪŋ/ adj impresionante

bred /bred/ see **BREED**

breed /briːd/ vt (*pt* **bred**) criar; (*fig*) engendrar. ● vi reproducirse. ● n raza f

breez|e /briːz/ n brisa f. ~**y** adj de mucho viento

brew /bruː/ vt hacer (beer); preparar (tea). ● vi hacer cerveza; (tea) reposar; (*fig*) prepararse. ● n infusión f. ~**er** n cervecero m. ~**ery** n cervecería f, fábrica f de cerveza

bribe /braɪb/ n soborno m. ● vt sobornar. ~**ry** /ˈbraɪbərɪ/ n soborno m

brick /brɪk/ n ladrillo m. ~**layer** n albañil m

bridal /ˈbraɪdl/ adj nupcial

bride /braɪd/ m novia f. ~**groom** n novio m. ~**smaid** /ˈbraɪdzmeɪd/ n dama f de honor

bridge /brɪdʒ/ n puente m; (*of nose*) caballete m; (*Cards*) bridge m. ● vt tender un puente sobre·. **~ a gap** llenar un vacío

bridle /'braɪdl/ n brida f. **~ path** n camino m de herradura

brief /bri:f/ adj (**-er, -est**) breve. ● n (Jurid) escrito m. ● vt dar instrucciones a. **~case** n maletín m, portafolio(s) m (LAm). **~ly** adv brevemente. **~s** npl (man's) calzoncillos mpl; (woman's) bragas fpl, calzones mpl (LAm), pantaletas fpl (Mex)

brigade /brɪ'geɪd/ n brigada f

bright /braɪt/ adj (**-er, -est**) brillante, claro; (clever) listo; (cheerful) alegre. **~en** vt aclarar; hacer más alegre (house etc). ● vi (weather) aclararse; (face) iluminarse

brillian|ce /'brɪljəns/ n brillantez f, brillo m. **~t** adj brillante

brim /brɪm/ n borde m; (of hat) ala f. □ **~ over** vi (pt **brimmed**) desbordarse

brine /braɪn/ n salmuera f

bring /brɪŋ/ vt (pt **brought**) traer; (lead) llevar. □ **~ about** vt causar. □ **~ back** vt devolver. □ **~ down** vt derribar. □ **~ off** vt lograr. □ **~ on** vt causar. □ **~ out** vt sacar; lanzar (product); publicar (book). □ **~ round/to** vt hacer volver en sí. □ **~ up** vt (Med) vomitar; educar (children); plantear (question)

brink /brɪŋk/ n borde m

brisk /brɪsk/ adj (**-er, -est**) enérgico, vivo

bristle /'brɪsl/ n cerda f. ● vi erizarse

Brit|ain /'brɪtən/ n Gran Bretaña f. **~ish** /'brɪtɪʃ/ adj británico. ● npl **the ~ish** los británicos. **~on** /'brɪtən/ n británico m

Brittany /'brɪtənɪ/ n Bretaña f

brittle /'brɪtl/ adj quebradizo

broach /brəʊtʃ/ vt abordar

broad /brɔ:d/ adj (**-er, -est**) ancho. **in ~ daylight** a plena luz del día. **~band** n banda f ancha. **~ bean** n haba f **~cast** n emisión f. ● vt (pt **broadcast**) emitir. ● vi hablar por la radio. **~caster** n locutor m. **~casting** n radio-difusión f. **~en** vt ensanchar. ● vi ensancharse. **~ly** adv en general. **~-minded** /-'maɪndɪd/ adj de miras amplias, tolerante

broccoli /'brɒkəlɪ/ n invar brécol m

brochure /'brəʊʃə(r)/ n folleto m

broil /brɔɪl/ vt (Amer) asar a la parrilla. **~er** n (Amer) parrilla f

broke /brəʊk/ see BREAK. ● adj Ⓘ sin blanca, en la ruina

broken /'brəʊkən/ see BREAK. ● adj roto

broker /'brəʊkə(r)/ n corredor m

brolly /'brɒlɪ/ n Ⓘ paraguas m

bronchitis /brɒŋ'kaɪtɪs/ n bronquitis f

bronze /brɒnz/ n bronce m. ● adj de bronce

brooch /brəʊtʃ/ n broche m

brood /bru:d/ n cría f; (humorous) prole m. ● vi empollar; (fig) meditar

brook /brʊk/ n arroyo m. ● vt soportar

broom /bru:m/ n escoba f. **~stick** n palo m de escoba

broth /brɒθ/ n caldo m

brothel /'brɒθl/ n burdel m

brother /'brʌðə(r)/ n hermano m. **~hood** n fraternidad f. **~-in-law** (pl **~s-in-law**) n cuñado m. **~ly** adj fraternal

brought /brɔ:t/ see BRING

brow /braʊ/ n frente f; (of hill) cima f. **~beat** vt (pt **-beaten**, pp **-beat**) intimidar

brown /braʊn/ adj (**-er, -est**) marrón, café (Mex); (hair) castaño; (skin) moreno; (tanned) bronceado. ● n marrón m, café m (Mex). ● vt poner moreno; (Culin) dorar. **~ bread** n pan m integral. **~ sugar** /braʊn 'ʃʊgə(r)/ n azúcar m moreno, azúcar f morena

browse /braʊz/ vi (in a shop) curiosear, (animal) pacer; (Comp) navegar. **~r** (Comp) browser m, navegador m

bruise /bru:z/ n magulladura f. ● vt magullar; machucar (fruit)

brunch /brʌntʃ/ n Ⓘ desayuno m tardío

brunette /bru:'net/ n morena f

brunt /brʌnt/ n. **bear o take the ~ of** sth sufrir algo

brush /brʌʃ/ n cepillo m; (large) escoba; (for decorating) brocha f; (artist's) pincel; (skirmish) escaramuza f. ● vt cepillar. □ **~ against** vt rozar. □ **~ aside** vt rechazar. □ **~ off** vt (rebuff) desairar. □ **~ up (on)** vt refrescar

brusque /bruːsk/ adj brusco. ~**ly** adv
bruscamente

Brussels /'brʌslz/ n Bruselas f. ~
sprout n col f de Bruselas

brutal /'bruːtl/ adj brutal. ~**ity**
/-'tælətɪ/ n brutalidad f. ~**ly** adv bru-
talmente

brute /bruːt/ n bestia f. ● **force**
fuerza f bruta

BSc abbr see **BACHELOR**

BSE abbr (**bovine spongiform en-
cephalopathy**) EBE f

bubbl|e /'bʌbl/ n burbuja f. ● vi burbu-
jear. □ ~ **over** vi desbordarse. ~**ly** adj
burbujeante

buck /bʌk/ adj macho. ● n (deer) ciervo
m; (Amer fam) dólar m. **pass the** ~
pasar la pelota

bucket /'bʌkɪt/ n balde m, cubo m, cu-
beta f (Mex)

buckle /'bʌkl/ n hebilla f. ● vt abrochar. ● vi torcerse

bud /bʌd/ n brote m. ● vi (pt **budded**)
brotar.

Buddhis|m /'bʊdɪzəm/ n budismo m.
~**t** adj & n budista (m & f)

budding /'bʌdɪŋ/ adj (fig) en ciernes

buddy /'bʌdɪ/ n 🇺🇸 amigo m, cuate m
(Mex)

budge /bʌdʒ/ vt mover. ● vi moverse

budgerigar /'bʌdʒərɪɡɑː(r)/ n periquito m

budget /'bʌdʒɪt/ n presupuesto m

buffalo /'bʌfələʊ/ n (pl **-oes** or **-o**) búfalo m

buffer /'bʌfə(r)/ n parachoques m

buffet[1] /'bʊfeɪ/ n (meal) buffet m; (in
train) bar m

buffet[2] /'bʌfɪt/ n golpe m

bug /bʌɡ/ n bicho m; 🇺🇸 (germ) microbio m; (fam, device) micrófono m
oculto. ● vt (pt **bugged**) 🇺🇸 ocultar un
micrófono en; (bother) molestar

buggy /'bʌɡɪ/ n. **baby** ~ sillita f de
paseo (plegable); (Amer) cochecito m

bugle /'bjuːɡl/ n corneta f

build /bɪld/ vt/i (pt **built**) construir. ● n
(of person) figura f, tipo m. □ ~ **up** vt/i
fortalecer; (increase) aumentar. ~**er** n
(contractor) contratista m & f; (labourer) albañil m. ~**ing** n edificio m;
(construction) construcción f. ~**up** n

aumento m; (of gas etc) acumulación f

built /bɪlt/ see **BUILD**. ~**-in** adj empo-
trado. ~**-up area** n zona f urbanizada

bulb /bʌlb/ n bulbo m; (Elec) bombilla
f, foco m (Mex)

Bulgaria /bʌl'ɡeərɪə/ n Bulgaria f. ~**n**
adj & n búlgaro (m)

bulg|e /bʌldʒ/ n protuberancia f. ● vi
pandearse. ~**ing** adj abultado; (eyes)
saltón

bulk /bʌlk/ n bulto m, volumen m. **in**
~ a granel; (loose) suelto. **the** ~ **of**
la mayor parte de. ~**y** adj voluminoso

bull /bʊl/ n toro m. ~**dog** n buldog m.
~**dozer** /-dəʊzə(r)/ n bulldozer m

bullet /'bʊlɪt/ n bala f

bulletin /'bʊlətɪn/ n anuncio m; (journal) boletín m. ~ **board** n (Amer) tablón m de anuncios, tablero m de
anuncios (LAm)

bulletproof /'bʊlɪtpruːf/ adj a prueba
de balas

bullfight /'bʊlfaɪt/ n corrida f (de
toros). ~**er** n torero m. ~**ing** n (deporte m de) los toros

bull ~**ring** n plaza f de toros.
~**'s-eye** n diana f. ~**shit** n (vulgar)
sandeces fpl 🇺🇸, gillipolleces fpl 🇪🇸

bully /'bʊlɪ/ n matón m. ● vt intimidar.
~**ing** n intimidación f

bum /bʌm/ n (fam, backside) trasero
m; (Amer fam, tramp) holgazán m

bumblebee /'bʌmblbiː/ n abejorro m

bump /bʌmp/ vt chocar contra. ● vi
dar sacudidas. ● n (blow) golpe m;
(jolt) sacudida f. □ ~ **into** vt chocar
contra; (meet) encontrar.

bumper /'bʌmpə(r)/ n parachoques m.
● adj récord. ~ **edition** n edición f especial

bun /bʌn/ n bollo m; (bread roll) panecillo m, bolillo m (Mex); (hair) moño m,
chongo m (Mex)

bunch /bʌntʃ/ n (of people) grupo m;
(of bananas, grapes) racimo m; (of
flowers) ramo m

bundle /'bʌndl/ n bulto m; (of papers)
legajo m. □ ~ **up** vt atar

bungalow /'bʌŋɡələʊ/ n casa f de un
solo piso

bungle /'bʌŋɡl/ vt echar a perder

bunk /bʌŋk/ n litera f

bunker /'bʌŋkə(r)/ n carbonera f; (Golf, Mil) búnker m

bunny /'bʌnɪ/ n conejito m

buoy /bɔɪ/ n boya f. □ ~ **up** vt hacer flotar; (fig) animar

buoyant /'bɔɪənt/ adj flotante; (fig) optimista

burden /'bɜːdn/ n carga f. ● vt cargar (with de)

bureau /'bjʊərəʊ/ n (pl -eaux /-əʊz/) agencia f; (desk) escritorio m; (Amer, chest of drawers) cómoda f

bureaucra|cy /bjʊə'rɒkrəsɪ/ n burocracia f. ~**t** /'bjʊərəkræt/ n burócrata m & f. ~**tic** /-'krætɪk/ adj burocrático

burger /'bɜːgə(r)/ n 🔲 hamburguesa f

burgl|ar /'bɜːglə(r)/ n ladrón m. ~ **ar alarm** n alarma f antirrobo. ~**ary** n robo m (en casa o edificio). ~**e** /'bɜːgl/ vt entrar a robar en. **we were** ~**ed** nos entraron a robar

burial /'berɪəl/ n entierro m

burly /'bɜːlɪ/ adj (-ier, -iest) corpulento

burn /bɜːn/ vt (pt burned or burnt) quemar. ● vi quemarse. ● n quemadura f. ~**er** n quemador m. □ ~ **down** vt incendiar. vi incendiarse

burnt /bɜːnt/ see BURN

burp /bɜːp/ n 🔲 eructo m. ● vi 🔲 cructar

burrow /'bʌrəʊ/ n madriguera f. ● vt excavar

burst /bɜːst/ vt (pt burst) reventar. ● vi reventarse. ~ **into tears** echarse a llorar. ~ **out laughing** echarse a reír. ● n (Mil) ráfaga f; (of activity) arrebato; (of applause) salva f

bury /'berɪ/ vt enterrar; (hide) ocultar

bus /bʌs/ n (pl buses) autobús m, camión m (Mex)

bush /bʊʃ/ n arbusto m; (land) monte m. ~**y** adj espeso

business /'bɪznɪs/ n negocio m; (Com) negocios mpl; (profession) ocupación f; (fig) asunto m. **mind one's own** ~ ocuparse de sus propios asuntos. ~**like** adj práctico, serio. ~**man** /-mən/ n hombre m de negocios. ~**woman** n mujer f de negocios

busker /'bʌskə(r)/ n músico m ambulante

bus stop n parada f de autobús, paradero m de autobús (LAm)

bust /bʌst/ n busto m; (chest) pecho m. ● vt (pt busted or bust) 🔲 romper. ● vi romperse. ● adj roto. **go** ~ 🔲 quebrar

bust-up /'bʌstʌp/ n 🔲 riña f

busy /'bɪzɪ/ adj (-ier, -iest) ocupado; (street) concurrido. **be** ~ (Amer) (phone) estar comunicando, estar ocupado (LAm). ● vt. ~ **o.s.** with ocuparse de. ~**body** n entrometido m

but /bʌt/ conj pero; (after negative) sino. ● prep menos. ~ **for** si no fuera por. **last** ~ **one** penúltimo

butcher /'bʊtʃə(r)/ n carnicero m. ● vt matar; (fig) hacer una carnicería con

butler /'bʌtlə(r)/ n mayordomo m

butt /bʌt/ n (of gun) culata f; (of cigarette) colilla f; (target) blanco m; (Amer fam, backside) trasero m. ● vi topar. □ ~ **in** vi interrumpir

butter /'bʌtə(r)/ n mantequilla f. ● vt untar con mantequilla. ~**cup** n ranúnculo m. ~**fingers** n manazas m, torpe m. ~**fly** n mariposa f; (swimming) estilo m mariposa

buttock /'bʌtək/ n nalga f

button /'bʌtn/ n botón m. ● vt abotonar. ● vi abotonarse. ~**hole** n ojal m. ● vt (fig) detener

buy /baɪ/ vt/i (pt bought) comprar. ● n compra f. ~**er** n comprador m

buzz /bʌz/ n zumbido m. ● vi zumbar. □ ~ **off** vi 🔲 largarse. ~**er** n timbre m

by /baɪ/ prep por; (near) cerca de; (before) antes de; (according to) según. ~ **and large** en conjunto, en general. ~ **car** en coche. ~ **oneself** por sí solo

bye /baɪ/, **bye-bye** /'baɪbaɪ/ int 🔲 ¡adiós!

by ~**-election** n elección f parcial. ~**-law** n reglamento m (local). ~**pass** n carretera f de circunvalación. ● vt eludir; (road) circunvalar. ~**product** n subproducto m. ~**stander** /-stændə(r)/ n espectador m

byte /baɪt/ n (Comp) byte m, octeto m

Cc

cab /kæb/ *n* taxi *m*; (*of lorry, train*) cabina *f*

cabaret /'kæbəreɪ/ *n* cabaret *m*

cabbage /'kæbɪdʒ/ *n* col *f*, repollo *m*

cabin /'kæbɪn/ *n* (*house*) cabaña *f*; (*in ship*) camarote *m*; (*in plane*) cabina *f*

cabinet /'kæbɪnɪt/ *n* (*cupboard*) armario *m*; (*for display*) vitrina *f*. **C~** (*Pol*) gabinete *m*

cable /'keɪbl/ *n* cable *m*. **~ car** *n* teleférico *m*. **~ TV** *n* televisión *f* por cable, cablevisión *f* (*LAm*)

cackle /'kækl/ *n* (*of hen*) cacareo *m*; (*laugh*) risotada *f*. ●*vi* cacarear; (*laugh*) reírse a carcajadas

cactus /'kæktəs/ *n* (*pl* **-ti** /-taɪ/ or **-tuses**) cacto *m*

caddie, caddy /'kædɪ/ *n* (*golf*) portador *m* de palos

cadet /kə'det/ *n* cadete *m*

cadge /kædʒ/ *vt/i* gorronear

café /'kæfeɪ/ *n* cafetería *f*

cafeteria /kæfɪ'tɪərɪə/ *n* restaurante *m* autoservicio

caffeine /'kæfiːn/ *n* cafeína *f*

cage /keɪdʒ/ *n* jaula *f*. ●*vt* enjaular

cake /keɪk/ *n* pastel *m*, tarta *f*; (*sponge*) bizcocho *m*. **~ of soap** pastilla *f* de jabón

calamity /kə'læmətɪ/ *n* calamidad *f*

calcium /'kælsɪəm/ *n* calcio *m*

calculat|e /'kælkjʊleɪt/ *vt/i* calcular. **~ion** /-'leɪʃn/ *n* cálculo *m*. **~or** *n* calculadora *f*

calculus /'kælkjʊləs/ *n* (*Math*) cálculo *m*

calendar /'kælɪndə(r)/ *n* calendario *m*

calf /kɑːf/ *n* (*pl* **calves**) (*animal*) ternero *m*; (*of leg*) pantorrilla *f*

calibre /'kælɪbə(r)/ *n* calibre *m*

call /kɔːl/ *vt/i* llamar. ●*n* llamada *f*; (*shout*) grito *m*; (*visit*) visita *f*. **be on ~** estar de guardia. **long-distance ~** llamada *f* de larga distancia, conferencia *f*. □ **~ back** *vt* hacer volver; (*on phone*) volver a llamar. *vi* volver; (*on phone*) volver a llamar. □ **~ for** *vt* pedir; (*fetch*) ir a buscar. □ **~ off** *vt* suspender. □ **~ on** *vt* pasar a visitar. □ **~ out** *vi* dar voces. □ **~ together** *vt* convocar. □ **~ up** *vt* (*Mil*) llamar al servicio militar; (*phone*) llamar. **~ box** *n* cabina *f* telefónica. **~ centre** *n* centro *m* de llamadas. **~er** *n* visita *f*; (*phone*) persona que llama *m*. **~ing** *n* vocación *f*

callous /'kæləs/ *adj* insensible, cruel

calm /kɑːm/ *adj* (**-er, -est**) tranquilo; (*sea*) en calma. ●*n* tranquilidad *f*, calma *f*. ●*vt* calmar. ●*vi* calmarse. **~ down** *vi* tranquilizarse. *vt* calmar. **~ly** *adv* con calma

calorie /'kælərɪ/ *n* caloría *f*

calves /kɑːvz/ *npl* see **CALF**

camcorder /'kæmkɔːdə(r)/ *n* videocámara *f*, camcórder *m*

came /keɪm/ see **COME**

camel /'kæml/ *n* camello *m*

camera /'kæmərə/ *n* cámara *f*, máquina *f* fotográfica **~man** /-mən/ *n* camarógrafo *m*, cámara *m*

camouflage /'kæməflɑːʒ/ *n* camuflaje *m*. ●*vt* camuflar

camp /kæmp/ *n* campamento *m*. ●*vi* acampar. **go ~ing** hacer camping

campaign /kæm'peɪn/ *n* campaña *f*. ●*vi* hacer campaña

camp ~bed *n* catre *m* de tijera. **~er** *n* campista *m & f*; (*vehicle*) cámper *m*. **~ground** *n* (*Amer*) see **~SITE**. **~ing** *n* camping *m*. **~site** *n* camping *m*

campus /'kæmpəs/ *n* (*pl* **-puses**) campus *m*, ciudad *f* universitaria

---

can¹ /kæn//kən/

negative **can't, cannot** (formal); past **could**

auxiliary verb

····▸ (*be able to*) poder. **I ~'t lift it** no lo puedo levantar. **she says she ~ come** dice que puede venir

····▸ (*be allowed to*) poder. **~ I smoke?** ¿puedo fumar?

····▸ (*know how to*) saber. **~ you swim?** ¿sabes nadar?

····▸ (*with verbs of perception*) *not translated*. **I ~'t see you** no te veo.

I ∼ **hear you better now** ahora te oigo mejor

····▸ (in requests) ∼ **I have a glass of water, please?** ¿me trae un vaso de agua, por favor?. ∼ I **have a kilo of cheese, please?** ¿me da un kilo de queso, por favor?

····▸ (in offers) ∼ **I help you?** ¿te ayudo?; (in shop) ¿lo/la atienden?

can² /kæn/ n lata f, bote m. ●vt (pt **canned**) enlatar. ∼**ned music** música f grabada

Canad|a /'kænədə/ n (el) Canadá m. ∼**ian** /kə'neɪdɪən/ adj & n canadiense (m & f)

canal /kə'næl/ n canal m

Canaries /kə'neərɪz/ npl = **CANARY ISLANDS**

canary /kə'neərɪ/ n canario m. **C∼ Islands** npl. **the C∼ Islands** las Islas Canarias

cancel /'kænsl/ vt (pt **cancelled**) cancelar; anular (command, cheque); (delete) tachar. ∼**lation** /-'leɪʃn/ n cancelación f

cancer /'kænsə(r)/ n cáncer m. **C∼** n (in astrology) Cáncer m. ∼**ous** adj canceroso

candid /'kændɪd/ adj franco

candidate /'kændɪdeɪt/ n candidato m

candle /'kændl/ n vela f. ∼**stick** n candelero m

candour /'kændə(r)/ n franqueza f

candy /'kændɪ/ n (Amer) caramelo m, dulce f (LAm). ∼**floss** /-flɒs/ n algodón m de azúcar

cane /keɪn/ n caña f; (for baskets) mimbre m; (stick) bastón m; (for punishment) palmeta f. ●vt castigar con palmeta

canister /'kænɪstə(r)/ n bote m

cannabis /'kænəbɪs/ n cáñamo m índico, hachís m, cannabis m

cannibal /'kænɪbl/ n caníbal m. ∼**ism** n canibalismo m

cannon /'kænən/ n invar cañón m. ∼**ball** n bala f de cañón

cannot /'kænət/ see **CAN¹**

canoe /kə'nuː/ n canoa f, piragua f. ●vi ir en canoa

canon /'kænən/ n canon m; (person) canónigo m. ∼**ize** vt canonizar

can opener n abrelatas m

canopy /'kænəpɪ/ n dosel m

can't /kɑːnt/ see **CAN¹**

cantankerous /kæn'tæŋkərəs/ adj mal humorado

canteen /kæn'tiːn/ n cantina f; (of cutlery) juego m de cubiertos

canter /'kæntə(r)/ n medio galope m. ●vi ir a medio galope

canvas /'kænvəs/ n lona f; (artist's) lienzo m

canvass /'kænvəs/ vi hacer campaña, solicitar votos. ∼**ing** n solicitación f (de votos)

canyon /'kænjən/ n cañón m

cap /kæp/ n gorra f; (lid) tapa f; (of cartridge) cápsula f; (of pen) capuchón m. ●vt (pt **capped**) tapar, poner cápsula a; (outdo) superar

capab|ility /keɪpə'bɪlətɪ/ n capacidad f. ∼**le** /'keɪpəbl/ adj capaz

capacity /kə'pæsɪtɪ/ n capacidad f; (function) calidad f

cape /keɪp/ n (cloak) capa f; (headland) cabo m

capital /'kæpɪtl/ adj capital. ∼ **letter** mayúscula f. ●n (town) capital f; (money) capital m. ∼**ism** n capitalismo m. ∼**ist** adj & n capitalista (m & f.) ∼**ize** vt capitalizar; escribir con mayúsculas (word). ●vi. ∼**ize on** aprovechar

capitulat|e /kə'pɪtʃuleɪt/ vi capitular. ∼**ion** /-'leɪʃn/ n capitulación f

Capitol El Capitolio o sede del Congreso (Congress) de EE.UU., en Washington DC. Situado en Capitol Hill, a menudo la prensa emplea este nombre para hacer referencia al Congreso de EE.UU.

Capricorn /'kæprɪkɔːn/ n Capricornio m

capsize /kæp'saɪz/ vt hacer volcar. ●vi volcarse

capsule /'kæpsjuːl/ n cápsula f

captain /'kæptɪn/ n capitán m; (of plane) comandante m & f. ●vt capitanear

caption /'kæpʃn/ n (*heading*) título m; (*of cartoon etc*) leyenda f

captivate /'kæptɪveɪt/ vt encantar

captiv|e /'kæptɪv/ adj & n cautivo (m). **~ity** /-'tɪvətɪ/ n cautiverio m, cautividad f

capture /'kæptʃə(r)/ vt capturar; atraer (*attention*); (*Mil*) tomar. ● n apresamiento m; (*Mil*) toma f

car /kɑː(r)/ n coche m, carro m (*LAm*); (*Amer, of train*) vagón m

caramel /'kærəmel/ n azúcar m quemado; (*sweet*) caramelo m, dulce m (*LAm*)

caravan /'kærəvæn/ n caravana f

carbohydrate /kɑːbəʊ'haɪdreɪt/ n hidrato m de carbono

carbon /'kɑːbən/ n carbono m; (*paper*) carbón m. **~ copy** n copia f al carbón. **~ dioxide** /daɪ'ɒksaɪd/ n anhídrido m carbónico. **~ footprint** n huella f de carbono. **~ monoxide** /mə'nɒksaɪd/ n monóxido de carbono

carburettor /kɑːbjʊ'retə(r)/ n carburador m

carcass /'kɑːkəs/ n cuerpo m de animal muerto; (*for meat*) res f muerta

card /kɑːd/ n tarjeta f; (*for games*) carta f; (*membership*) carnet m; (*records*) ficha f. **~board** n cartón m

cardigan /'kɑːdɪgən/ n chaqueta f de punto, rebeca f

cardinal /'kɑːdɪnəl/ adj cardinal. ● n cardenal m

care /keə(r)/ n cuidado m; (*worry*) preocupación f; (*protection*) cargo m. **~ of** a cuidado de, en casa de. **take ~** tener cuidado. **take ~ of** cuidar de (*person*); ocuparse de (*matter*). ● vi interesarse. **I don't ~** me da igual. □ **~ about** vt preocuparse por. □ **~ for** vt cuidar de; (*like*) querer

career /kə'rɪə(r)/ n carrera f. ● vi correr a toda velocidad

care: **~free** adj despreocupado. **~ful** adj cuidadoso; (*cautious*) prudente. **be ~ful** tener cuidado. **~fully** adv con cuidado. **~less** adj negligente; (*not worried*) indiferente. **~lessly** adv descuidadamente. **~lessness** n descuido m **~r** n persona que cuida de un discapacitado

caress /kə'res/ n caricia f. ● vt acariciar

caretaker /'keəteɪkə(r)/ n vigilante m; (*of flats etc*) portero m

car ferry n transbordador m de coches

cargo /'kɑːgəʊ/ n (*pl* **-oes**) carga f

Caribbean /kærɪ'biːən/ adj caribeño. **the ~ (Sea)** n el mar Caribe

caricature /'kærɪkətʃʊə(r)/ n caricatura f. ● vt caricaturizar

carnage /'kɑːnɪdʒ/ n carnicería f, matanza f

carnation /kɑː'neɪʃn/ n clavel m

carnival /'kɑːnɪvl/ n carnaval m

carol /'kærəl/ n villancico m

carousel /kærə'sel/ n tiovivo m, carrusel m (*LAm*); (*for baggage*) cinta f transportadora

carp /kɑːp/ n invar carpa f. □ **~ at** vi quejarse de

car park n aparcamiento m, estacionamiento m

carpent|er /'kɑːpɪntə(r)/ n carpintero m. **~ry** /-trɪ/ n carpintería f

carpet /'kɑːpɪt/ n alfombra f. **~ sweeper** n cepillo m mecánico

carriage /'kærɪdʒ/ n coche m; (*Mec*) carro m; (*transport*) transporte m; (*cost, bearing*) porte m; (*of train*) vagón m. **~way** n calzada f

carrier /'kærɪə(r)/ n transportista m & f; (*company*) empresa f de transportes; (*Med*) portador m. **~ bag** n bolsa f

carrot /'kærət/ n zanahoria f

carry /'kærɪ/ vt llevar; transportar (*goods*); (*involve*) llevar consigo, implicar. ● vi (*sounds*) llegar, oírse. □ **~ off** vt llevarse. □ **~ on** vi seguir, continuar. □ **~ out** vt realizar; cumplir (*promise, threat*). **~ cot** n cuna f portátil

carsick /'kɑːsɪk/ adj mareado (*por viajar en coche*)

cart /kɑːt/ n carro m; (*Amer, in supermarket, airport*) carrito m. ● vt acarrear; (*fam, carry*) llevar

carton /'kɑːtən/ n caja f de cartón

cartoon /kɑː'tuːn/ n caricatura f, chiste m; (*strip*) historieta f; (*film*) dibujos mpl animados

cartridge /'kɑːtrɪdʒ/ n cartucho m

carve /kɑːv/ vt tallar; trinchar (*meat*)

cascade /kæsˈkeɪd/ n cascada f. ● vi caer en cascadas

case /keɪs/ n caso m; (*Jurid*) proceso m; (*crate*) cajón m; (*box*) caja f; (*suitcase*) maleta f, petaca f (*Mex*). **in any ~** en todo caso. **in ~ he comes** por si viene. **in ~ of** en caso de

cash /kæʃ/ n dinero m efectivo. **pay (in) ~** pagar al contado. ● vt cobrar. **~ in (on)** aprovecharse de. **~ desk** n caja f. **~ dispenser** n cajero m automático

cashier /kæʃˈɪə(r)/ n cajero m

cashpoint /ˈkæʃpɔɪnt/ n cajero m automático

casino /kəˈsiːnəʊ/ n (pl **-os**) casino m

cask /kɑːsk/ n barril m

casket /ˈkɑːskɪt/ n cajita f; (*Amer*) ataúd m, cajón m (*LAm*)

casserole /ˈkæsərəʊl/ n cacerola f; (*stew*) guiso m, guisado m (*Mex*)

cassette /kəˈset/ n cassette m & f

cast /kɑːst/ vt (*pt* cast) arrojar; fundir (metal); emitir (vote). ● n lanzamiento m; (*in play*) reparto m; (*mould*) molde m

castanets /kæstəˈnets/ npl castañuelas fpl

castaway /ˈkɑːstəweɪ/ n náufrago m

caster /ˈkɑːstə(r)/ n ruedecita f. **~ sugar** n azúcar m extrafino

Castil|le /kæˈstiːl/ n Castilla f. **~lan** /kæˈstɪlɪən/ adj & n castellano (m)

cast ~ iron n hierro m fundido. **~-iron** adj (*fig*) sólido

castle /ˈkɑːsl/ n castillo m; (*Chess*) torre f

cast-offs /ˈkɑːstɒfs/ npl desechos mpl

castrat|e /kæˈstreɪt/ vt castrar. **~ion** /-ʃn/ n castración f

casual /ˈkæʒʊəl/ adj casual; (*meeting*) fortuito; (*work*) ocasional; (*attitude*) despreocupado; (*clothes*) informal, de sport. **~ly** adv de paso

casualt|y /ˈkæʒʊəltɪ/ n (*injured*) herido m; (*dead*) víctima f; (*in hospital*) urgencias fpl. **~ies** npl (*Mil*) bajas fpl

cat /kæt/ n gato m

Catalan /ˈkætəlæn/ adj & n catalán (m)

catalogue /ˈkætəlɒg/ n catálogo m. ● vt catalogar

Catalonia /kætəˈləʊnɪə/ n Cataluña f

catalyst /ˈkætəlɪst/ n catalizador m

catamaran /kætəməˈræn/ n catamarán m

catapult /ˈkætəpʌlt/ n catapulta f; (*child's*) tirachinas f, resortera f (*Mex*)

catarrh /kəˈtɑː(r)/ n catarro m

catastroph|e /kəˈtæstrəfɪ/ n catástrofe m. **~ic** /kætəˈstrɒfɪk/ adj catastrófico

catch /kætʃ/ vt (*pt* caught) coger (*esp* Spain), agarrar; tomar (train, bus); (*unawares*) sorprender, pillar; (*understand*) entender; contagiarse de (disease). **~ a cold** resfriarse. **~ sight of** avistar. ● vi (*get stuck*) engancharse; (*fire*) prenderse. ● n (*by goalkeeper*) parada f; (*of fish*) pesca f; (*on door*) pestillo m; (*on window*) cerradura f. **□~ on** vi 🅱 hacerse popular. **□~ up** vi poner al día. **~ up with** alcanzar; ponerse al corriente de (news etc). **~ing** adj contagioso. **~phrase** n eslogan m. **~y** adj pegadizo

categor|ical /kætɪˈgɒrɪkl/ adj categórico. **~y** /ˈkætɪgərɪ/ n categoría f

cater /ˈkeɪtə(r)/ vi encargarse del servicio de comida. **~ for** proveer a (needs). **~er** n proveedor m

caterpillar /ˈkætəpɪlə(r)/ n oruga f, azotador m (*Mex*)

cathedral /kəˈθiːdrəl/ n catedral f

catholic /ˈkæθəlɪk/ adj universal. **C~** adj & n católico (m). **C~ism** /kəˈθɒlɪsɪzəm/ n catolicismo m

cat ~nap n sueñecito m. **C~seyes** npl (®) catafaros mpl

cattle /ˈkætl/ npl ganado m

catwalk n pasarela f

Caucasian /kɔːˈkeɪʒən/ n. **a male ~** (*Amer*) un hombre de raza blanca

caught /kɔːt/ see **CATCH**

cauliflower /ˈkɒlɪflaʊə(r)/ n coliflor f

cause /kɔːz/ n causa f, motivo m. ● vt causar

cautio|n /ˈkɔːʃn/ n cautela f; (*warning*) advertencia f. ● vt advertir; (*Jurid*) amonestar. **~us** /-ʃəs/ adj cauteloso, prudente

cavalry /ˈkævəlrɪ/ n caballería f

cave /keɪv/ n cueva f. **□~ in** vi hundirse. **~man** n troglodita m

cavern /ˈkævən/ n caverna f

caviare /ˈkævɪɑː(r)/ n caviar m

cavity /ˈkævətɪ/ n cavidad f; (in tooth) caries f

CCTV abbr (**closed circuit television**) CCTV m

CD abbr (= **compact disc**) CD m. ∼ **player** (reproductor m de) compact-disc m. ∼**-ROM** n CD-ROM m

cease /siːs/ vt/i cesar. ∼**fire** n alto m el fuego

cedar /ˈsiːdə(r)/ n cedro m

ceiling /ˈsiːlɪŋ/ n techo m

celebrat|e /ˈselɪbreɪt/ vt celebrar. ● vi divertirse. ∼**ed** adj célebre. ∼**ion** /-ˈbreɪʃn/ n celebración f; (party) fiesta f

celebrity /sɪˈlebrətɪ/ n celebridad f

celery /ˈselərɪ/ n apio m

cell /sel/ n celda f; (in plants, electricity) célula f

cellar /ˈselə(r)/ n sótano m; (for wine) bodega f

cello /ˈtʃeləʊ/ n (pl **-os**) violonc(h)elo m, chelo m

Cellophane /ˈseləfeɪn/ n (®) celofán m (®)

cellphone /ˈselfəʊn/ n celular m (LAm), móvil m (Esp)

cellul|ar /ˈseljʊlə(r)/ adj celular. ∼ **phone** n teléfono celular m (LAm), teléfono móvil m (Esp). ∼**oid** n celuloide m

Celsius /ˈselsɪəs/ adj. **20 degrees** ∼ 20 grados centígrados or Celsio(s)

cement /sɪˈment/ n cemento m. ● vt cementar

cemetery /ˈsemətrɪ/ n cementerio m

cens|or /ˈsensə(r)/ n censor m. ● vt censurar. ∼**ship** n censura f. ∼**ure** /ˈsenʃə(r)/ vt censurar

census /ˈsensəs/ n censo m

cent /sent/ n ($) centavo m; (€) céntimo m

centenary /senˈtiːnərɪ/ n centenario m

centi|grade /ˈsentɪgreɪd/ adj centígrado. ∼**litre** n centilitro m. ∼**metre** n centímetro m. ∼**pede** /-piːd/ n ciempiés m

central /ˈsentrəl/ adj central; (of town) céntrico. ∼ **heating** n calefacción f central. ∼**ize** vt centralizar

centre /ˈsentə(r)/ n centro m. ● vt (pt **centred**) centrar. ● vi centrarse (**on** en)

century /ˈsentʃərɪ/ n siglo m

cereal /ˈsɪərɪəl/ n cereal m

ceremon|ial /serɪˈməʊnɪəl/ adj & n ceremonial (m). ∼**y** /ˈserɪmənɪ/ n ceremonia f

certain /ˈsɜːtn/ adj cierto. **for** ∼ seguro. **make** ∼ **of** asegurarse de. ∼**ly** adv desde luego

certificate /səˈtɪfɪkət/ n certificado m; (of birth, death etc) partida f

certify /ˈsɜːtɪfaɪ/ vt certificar

chafe /tʃeɪf/ vt rozar. ● vi rozarse

chaffinch /ˈtʃæfɪntʃ/ n pinzón m

chagrin /ˈʃægrɪn/ n disgusto m

chain /tʃeɪn/ n cadena f. ● vt encadenar. ∼ **reaction** n reacción f en cadena. ∼**-smoker** n fumador m que siempre tiene un cigarrillo encendido. ∼ **store** n tienda f de una cadena

chair /tʃeə(r)/ n silla f; (Univ) cátedra f. ● vt presidir. ∼**lift** n telesquí m, telesilla m (LAm). ∼**man** /-mən/ n presidente m

chalet /ˈʃæleɪ/ n chalé m

chalk /tʃɔːk/ n (in geology) creta f; (stick) tiza f, gis m (Mex)

challeng|e /ˈtʃælɪndʒ/ n desafío m; (fig) reto m. ● vt desafiar; (question) poner en duda. ∼**ing** adj estimulante

chamber /ˈtʃeɪmbə(r)/ n (old use) cámara f. ∼**maid** n camarera f. ∼ **pot** n orinal m

champagne /ʃæmˈpeɪn/ n champaña m, champán m

champion /ˈtʃæmpɪən/ n campeón m. ● vt defender. ∼**ship** n campeonato m

chance /tʃɑːns/ n casualidad f; (likelihood) posibilidad f; (opportunity) oportunidad f; (risk) riesgo m. **by** ∼ por casualidad. ● adj fortuito

chancellor /ˈtʃɑːnsələ(r)/ n canciller m; (Univ) rector m. **C**∼ **of the Exchequer** Ministro m de Hacienda

chandelier /ʃændəˈlɪə(r)/ n araña f (de luces)

chang|e /tʃeɪndʒ/ vt cambiar; (substitute) reemplazar. ∼ **one's mind** cambiar de idea. ● vi cambiarse. ● n cambio m; (coins) cambio m, sencillo m

(*LAm*), feria *f* (*Mex*); (*money returned*) cambio *m*, vuelta *f*, vuelto *m* (*LAm*). **~eable** *adj* cambiable; (*weather*) variable. **~ing room** *n* (*Sport*) vestuario *m*, vestidor *m* (*Mex*); (*in shop*) probador *m*

channel /'tʃænl/ *n* canal *m*; (*fig*) medio *m*. ● *vt* (*pt* **channelled**) acanalar; (*fig*) encauzar. **the (English) C~** el Canal de la Mancha. **C~ Islands** *npl*. **the C~ Islands** las islas Anglonormandas. **C~ Tunnel** *n*. **the C~ Tunnel** el Eurotúnel

chant /tʃɑːnt/ *n* canto *m*. ● *vt/i* cantar

chao|s /'keɪɒs/ *n* caos *m*. **~tic** /-'ɒtɪk/ *adj* caótico

chap /tʃæp/ *n* 🆃 tipo *m*, tío *m* 🆃. ● *vt* (*pt* **chapped**) agrietar. ● *vi* agrietarse

chapel /'tʃæpl/ *n* capilla *f*

chaperon /'ʃæpərəʊn/ *n* acompañante *f*

chapter /'tʃæptə(r)/ *n* capítulo *m*

char /tʃɑː(r)/ *vt* (*pt* **charred**) carbonizar

character /'kærəktə(r)/ *n* carácter *m*; (*in book, play*) personaje *m*. **in ~** característico. **~istic** /-'rɪstɪk/ *adj* típico. ● *n* característica *f*. **~ize** *vt* caracterizar

charade /ʃə'rɑːd/ *n* farsa *f*. **~s** *npl* (*game*) charada *f*

charcoal /'tʃɑːkəʊl/ *n* carbón *m* vegetal; (*for drawing*) carboncillo *m*

charge /tʃɑːdʒ/ *n* precio *m*; (*Elec, Mil*) carga *f*; (*Jurid*) acusación *f*; (*task, custody*) encargo *m*; (*responsibility*) responsabilidad *f*. **in ~ of** responsable de, encargado de. **the person in ~** la persona responsable. **take ~ of** encargarse de. ● *vt* pedir; (*Elec, Mil*) cargar; (*Jurid*) acusar. ● *vi* cargar; (*animal*) embestir (**at** contra)

charit|able /'tʃærɪtəbl/ *adj* caritativo. **~y** /'tʃærɪtɪ/ *n* caridad *f*; (*society*) institución *f* benéfica

charm /tʃɑːm/ *n* encanto *m*; (*spell*) hechizo *m*; (*on bracelet*) dije *m*, amuleto *m*. ● *vt* encantar. **~ing** *adj* encantador

chart /tʃɑːt/ *n* (*for navigation*) carta *f* de navegación; (*table*) tabla *f*

charter /'tʃɑːtə(r)/ *n* carta *f*. ● *vt* alquilar (bus, train); fletar (plane, ship). **~ flight** *n* vuelo *m* chárter

chase /tʃeɪs/ *vt* perseguir. ● *vi* correr (**after** tras). ● *n* persecución *f*. □ **~ away**, **~ off** *vt* ahuyentar

chassis /'ʃæsɪ/ *n* chasis *m*

chastise /tʃæs'taɪz/ *vt* castigar

chastity /'tʃæstətɪ/ *n* castidad *f*

chat /tʃæt/ *n* charla *f*, conversación *f* (*LAm*), plática *f* (*Mex*). ● *vi* (*pt* **chatted**) charlar, conversar (*LAm*), platicar (*Mex*)

chatter /'tʃætə(r)/ *n* charla *f*. ● *vi* charlar. **his teeth are ~ing** le castañetean los dientes. **~box** *n* parlanchín *m*

chauffeur /'ʃəʊfə(r)/ *n* chófer *m*

chauvinis|m /'ʃəʊvɪnɪzəm/ *n* patriotería *f*; (*male*) machismo *m*, **~t** *n* patriotero *m*; (*male*) machista *m*

cheap /tʃiːp/ *adj* (**-er**, **-est**) barato; (*poor quality*) de baja calidad; (*rate*) económico. **~(ly)** *adv* barato, a bajo precio

cheat /tʃiːt/ *vt* defraudar; (*deceive*) engañar. ● *vi* (*at cards*) hacer trampas. ● *n* trampa *f*; (*person*) tramposo *m*

check /tʃek/ *vt* comprobar; (*examine*) inspeccionar; (*curb*) frenar. ● *vi* comprobar. ● *n* comprobación *f*; (*of tickets*) control *m*; (*curb*) freno *m*; (*Chess*) jaque *m*; (*pattern*) cuadro *m*; (*Amer, bill*) cuenta *f*; (*Amer, cheque*) cheque *m*. □ **~ in** *vi* registrarse; (*at airport*) facturar el equipaje, chequear el equipaje (*LAm*), registrar el equipaje (*Mex*). □ **~ out** *vi* pagar la cuenta y marcharse. □ **~ up** *vi* confirmar. □ **~ up on** *vt* investigar. **~book** *n* (*Amer*) see **CHEQUEBOOK**. **~ered** /'tʃekəd/ *adj* (*Amer*) see **CHEQUERED**

checkers /'tʃekəz/ *n* (*Amer*) damas *fpl*

check ~mate *n* jaque *m* mate. ● *vt* dar mate a. **~out** *n* caja *f*. **~point** control *m*. **~up** *n* chequeo *m*, revisión

cheek /tʃiːk/ *n* mejilla *f*; (*fig*) descaro *m*. **~bone** *n* pómulo *m*. **~y** *adj* descarado

cheep /tʃiːp/ *vi* piar

cheer /tʃɪə(r)/ *n* alegría *f*; (*applause*) viva *m*. **~s!** ¡salud!. ● *vt* alegrar; (*applaud*) aplaudir. ● *vi* alegrarse; (*applaud*) aplaudir. **~ up!** ¡anímate! **~ful** *adj* alegre

cheerio /tʃɪərɪ'əʊ/ *int* 🔲 ¡adiós!, ¡hasta luego!

cheerless /'tʃɪəlɪs/ *adj* triste

cheese /tʃi:z/ *n* queso *m*

cheetah /'tʃi:tə/ *n* guepardo *m*

chef /ʃef/ *n* jefe *m* de cocina

chemical /'kemɪkl/ *adj* químico. ●*n* producto *m* químico

chemist /'kemɪst/ *n* farmacéutico *m*; (*scientist*) químico *m*. ~**ry** *n* química *f*. ~**'s (shop)** *n* farmacia *f*

cheque /tʃek/ *n* cheque *m*, talón *m*. ~**book** *n* chequera *f*, talonario *m*

cherish /'tʃerɪʃ/ *vt* cuidar; (*love*) querer; abrigar (hope)

cherry /'tʃerɪ/ *n* cereza *f*. ~ **tree** *n* cerezo *m*

chess /tʃes/ *n* ajedrez *m*. ~**board** *n* tablero *m* de ajedrez

chest /tʃest/ *n* pecho *m*; (box) cofre *m*, cajón *m*

chestnut /'tʃesnʌt/ *n* castaña *f*. ●*adj* castaño. ~ **tree** *n* castaño *m*

chest of drawers *n* cómoda *f*

chew /tʃu:/ *vt* masticar. ~**ing gum** *n* chicle *m*

chic /ʃi:k/ *adj* elegante

chick /tʃɪk/ *n* polluelo *m*. ~**en** /'tʃɪkɪn/ *n* pollo *m*. ●*adj* 🔲 cobarde. □ ~**en out** *vi* 🔲 acobardarse. ~**enpox** /'tʃɪkɪnpɒks/ *n* varicela *f*. ~**pea** *n* garbanzo *m*

chicory /'tʃɪkərɪ/ *n* (*in coffee*) achicoria *f*; (*in salad*) escarola *f*

chief /tʃi:f/ *n* jefe *m*. ●*adj* principal. ~**ly** *adv* principalmente

chilblain /'tʃɪlbleɪn/ *n* sabañón *m*

child /tʃaɪld/ *n* (*pl* **children** /'tʃɪldrən/) niño *m*; (*offspring*) hijo *m*. ~**birth** *n* parto *m*, niñez *f*. ~**ish** *adj* infantil. ~**less** *adj* sin hijos. ~**like** *adj* ingenuo, de niño

Chile /'tʃɪlɪ/ *n* Chile *m*. ~**an** *adj* & *n* chileno (*m*)

chill /tʃɪl/ *n* frío *m*; (*illness*) resfriado *m*. ●*adj* frío. ●*vt* enfriar; refrigerar (food)

chilli /'tʃɪlɪ/ *n* (*pl* **-ies**) chile *m*

chilly /'tʃɪlɪ/ *adj* frío

chime /tʃaɪm/ *n* carillón *m*. ●*vt* tocar (bells); dar (hours). ●*vi* repicar

chimney /'tʃɪmnɪ/ *n* (*pl* **-eys**) chimenea *f*. ~ **sweep** *n* deshollinador *m*

chimpanzee /tʃɪmpæn'zi:/ *n* chimpancé *m*

chin /tʃɪn/ *n* barbilla *f*

china /'tʃaɪnə/ *n* porcelana *f*

Chin|a /'tʃaɪnə/ *n* China *f*. ~**ese** /-'ni:z/ *adj* & *n* chino (*m*)

chink /tʃɪŋk/ *n* (*crack*) grieta *f*; (*sound*) tintín *m*. ●*vi* tintinear

chip /tʃɪp/ *n* pedacito *m*; (*splinter*) astilla *f*; (*Culin*) patata *f* frita, papa *f* frita (*LAm*); (*in gambling*) ficha *f*; (*Comp*) chip *m*. **have a ~ on one's shoulder** guardar rencor. ●*vt* (*pt* **chipped**) desportillar. □ ~ **in** *vi* 🔲 interrumpir; (*with money*) contribuir

chiropodist /kɪ'rɒpədɪst/ *n* callista *m* & *f*, pedicuro *m*

chirp /tʃɜ:p/ *n* pío *m*. ●*vi* piar. ~**y** *adj* alegre

chisel /'tʃɪzl/ *n* formón *m*. ●*vt* (*pt* **chiselled**) cincelar

chivalr|ous /'ʃɪvəlrəs/ *adj* caballeroso. ~**y** /-rɪ/ *n* caballerosidad *f*

chlorine /'klɔːriːn/ *n* cloro *m*

chock /tʃɒk/ *n* cuña *f*. ~**-a-block** *adj*, ~**-full** *adj* atestado

chocolate /'tʃɒklət/ *n* chocolate *m*; (*individual sweet*) bombón *m*, chocolate *m* (*LAm*)

choice /tʃɔɪs/ *n* elección *f*; (*preference*) preferencia *f*. ●*adj* escogido

choir /'kwaɪə(r)/ *n* coro *m*

choke /tʃəʊk/ *vt* sofocar. ●*vi* sofocarse. ●*n* (*Auto*) choke *m*, estárter *m*, ahogador *m* (*Mex*)

cholera /'kɒlərə/ *n* cólera *m*

cholesterol /kə'lestərɒl/ *n* colesterol *m*

choose /tʃuːz/ *vt/i* (*pt* **chose**, *pp* **chosen**) elegir, escoger. ~**y** *adj* 🔲 exigente

chop /tʃɒp/ *vt* (*pt* **chopped**) cortar. ●*n* (*Culin*) chuleta *f*. □ ~ **down** *vt* talar. □ ~ **off** *vt* cortar. ~**per** *n* hacha *f*; (*butcher's*) cuchilla *f*. ~**py** *adj* picado

chord /kɔːd/ *n* (*Mus*) acorde *m*

chore /tʃɔː(r)/ *n* tarea *f*, faena *f*. **household ~s** *npl* quehaceres *mpl* domésticos

chorus /'kɔːrəs/ *n* coro *m*; (*of song*) estribillo *m*

chose /tʃəʊz/, **chosen** /'tʃəʊzn/ *see* CHOOSE

Christ /kraɪst/ *n* Cristo *m*

christen /'krɪsn/ *vt* bautizar. ~**ing** *n* bautizo *m*

Christian /'krɪstjən/ *adj & n* cristiano (*m*). ~**ity** /krɪstɪ'ænətɪ/ *n* cristianismo *m*. ~ **name** *n* nombre *m* de pila

Christmas /'krɪsməs/ *n* Navidad *f*. Merry ~! ¡Feliz Navidad!, ¡Felices Pascuas! Father ~ Papá *m* Noel. ● *adj* de Navidad, navideño. ~ **card** *n* tarjeta *f* de Navidad. ~ **day** *n* día *m* de Navidad. ~ **Eve** *n* Nochebuena *f*. ~ **tree** *n* árbol *m* de Navidad

chrom|e /krəʊm/ *n* cromo *m*. ~**ium** /'krəʊmɪəm/ *n* cromo *m*

chromosome /'krəʊməsəʊm/ *n* cromosoma *m*

chronic /'krɒnɪk/ *adj* crónico; (*fam, bad*) terrible

chronicle /'krɒnɪkl/ *n* crónica *f*. ● *vt* historiar

chronological /krɒnə'lɒdʒɪkl/ *adj* cronológico

chubby /'tʃʌbɪ/ *adj* (-ier, -iest) regordete; (person) gordinflón 🆃

chuck /tʃʌk/ *vt* 🆄 tirar. ▫ ~ **out** *vt* tirar

chuckle /'tʃʌkl/ *n* risa *f* ahogada. ● *vi* reírse entre dientes

chug /tʃʌg/ *vi* (*pt* **chugged**) (*of motor*) traquetear

chum /tʃʌm/ *n* amigo *m*, compinche *m*, cuate *m* (*Mex*)

chunk /tʃʌŋk/ *n* trozo *m* grueso. ~**y** *adj* macizo

church /'tʃɜːtʃ/ *n* iglesia *f*. ~**yard** *n* cementerio *m*

churn /'tʃɜːn/ *n* (*for milk*) lechera *f*, cántara *f*; (*for making butter*) mantequera *f*. ● *vt* agitar. ▫ ~ **out** *vt* producir en profusión

chute /ʃuːt/ *n* tobogán *m*

cider /'saɪdə(r)/ *n* sidra *f*

cigar /sɪ'ɡɑː(r)/ *n* puro *m*

cigarette /sɪɡə'ret/ *n* cigarrillo *m*. ~ **end** *n* colilla *f*. ~ **holder** *n* boquilla *f*. ~ **lighter** *n* mechero *m*, encendedor *m*

cinecamera /'sɪnɪkæmərə/ *n* tomavistas *m*, filmadora *f* (*LAm*)

cinema /'sɪnəmə/ *n* cine *m*

cipher /'saɪfə(r)/ *n* (*Math, fig*) cero *m*; (*code*) clave *f*

circle /'sɜːkl/ *n* círculo *m*; (*in theatre*) anfiteatro *m*. ● *vt* girar alrededor de. ● *vi* dar vueltas

circuit /'sɜːkɪt/ *n* circuito *m*

circular /'sɜːkjʊlə(r)/ *adj & n* circular (*f*)

circulat|e /'sɜːkjʊleɪt/ *vt* hacer circular. ● *vi* circular. ~**ion** /-'leɪʃn/ *n* circulación *f*; (*number of copies*) tirada *f*

circumcise /'sɜːkəmsaɪz/ *vt* circuncidar

circumference /sə'kʌmfərəns/ *n* circunferencia *f*

circumstance /'sɜːkəmstəns/ *n* circunstancia *f*. ~**s** (*means*) *npl* situación *f* económica

circus /'sɜːkəs/ *n* circo *m*

cistern /'sɪstən/ *n* cisterna *f*

cite /saɪt/ *vt* citar

citizen /'sɪtɪzn/ *n* ciudadano *m*; (*inhabitant*) habitante *m & f*

citrus /'sɪtrəs/ *n*. ~ **fruits** cítricos *mpl*

city /'sɪtɪ/ *n* ciudad *f*; the C~ el centro *m* financiero de Londres

City - the Área ubicada dentro de los límites de la antigua ciudad de Londres. Actualmente es el centro financiero de la capital donde tienen sus sedes centrales muchas instituciones financieras. A menudo, cuando se habla de The City, se está refiriendo a ésas y no a la zona propiamente dicha.

civic /'sɪvɪk/ *adj* cívico

civil /'sɪvl/ *adj* civil; (*polite*) cortés

civilian /sɪ'vɪlɪən/ *adj & n* civil (*m & f*)

civiliz|ation /sɪvɪlaɪ'zeɪʃn/ *n* civilización *f*. ~**ed** /'sɪvɪlaɪzd/ *adj* civilizado

civil ~ partnership *n* matrimonio *m* de homosexuales. ~ **servant** *n* funcionario *m* (del Estado), burócrata *m & f* (*Mex*). ~ **service** *n* administración *f* pública. ~ **war** *n* guerra *f* civil

clad /klæd/ *see* CLOTHE

claim /kleɪm/ vt reclamar; (assert) pretender. ● n reclamación f; (right) derecho m; (Jurid) demanda f

clairvoyant /kleəˈvɔɪənt/ n clarividente m & f

clam /klæm/ n almeja f. ● vi (pt clammed). ~ **up** 🄸 ponerse muy poco comunicativo

clamber /ˈklæmbə(r)/ vi trepar a gatas

clammy /ˈklæmɪ/ adj (-ier, -iest) húmedo

clamour /ˈklæmə(r)/ n clamor m. ● vi. ~ **for** pedir a gritos

clamp /klæmp/ n abrazadera f; (Auto) cepo m. ● vt sujetar con abrazadera; poner cepo a (car). □ ~ **down on** vt reprimir

clan /klæn/ n clan m

clang /klæŋ/ n sonido m metálico

clap /klæp/ vt (pt clapped) aplaudir; batir (hands). ● vi aplaudir. ● n palmada f; (of thunder) trueno m

clarif|ication /klærɪfɪˈkeɪʃn/ n aclaración f. ~**y** /ˈklærɪfaɪ/ vt aclarar. ● vi aclararse

clarinet /klærɪˈnet/ n clarinete m

clarity /ˈklærətɪ/ n claridad f

clash /klæʃ/ n choque m; (noise) estruendo m; (contrast) contraste m; (fig) conflicto m. ● vt golpear. ● vi encontrarse; (colours) desentonar

clasp /klɑːsp/ n cierre m. ● vt agarrar; apretar (hand)

class /klɑːs/ n clase f. **evening** ~ clase nocturna. ● vt clasificar

classic /ˈklæsɪk/ adj & n clásico (m). ~**al** adj clásico. ~**s** npl estudios mpl clásicos

classif|ication /klæsɪfɪˈkeɪʃn/ n clasificación f. ~**y** /ˈklæsɪfaɪ/ vt clasificar

class ~**room** n aula f, clase f. ~**y** adj 🄸 elegante

clatter /ˈklætə(r)/ n ruido m; (of train) traqueteo m. ● vi hacer ruido

clause /klɔːz/ n cláusula f; (Gram) oración f

claustrophobia /klɔːstrəˈfəʊbɪə/ n claustrofobia f

claw /klɔː/ n garra f; (of cat) uña f; (of crab) pinza f. ● vt arañar

clay /kleɪ/ n arcilla f

clean /kliːn/ adj (-er, -est) limpio; (stroke) bien definido. ● adv completamente. ● vt limpiar. ● vi limpiar. □ ~ **up** vt hacer la limpieza. ~**er** n persona f que hace la limpieza. ~**liness** /ˈklenlɪnɪs/ n limpieza f

cleans|e /klenz/ vt limpiar. ~**er** n producto m de limpieza; (for skin) crema f de limpieza. ~**ing cream** n crema f de limpieza

clear /klɪə(r)/ adj (-er, -est) claro; (transparent) transparente; (without obstacles) libre; (profit) neto; (sky) despejado. **keep** ~ **of** evitar. ● adv claramente. ● vt despejar; liquidar (goods); (Jurid) absolver; (jump over) saltar por encima de; quitar, levantar (LAm) (table). □ ~ **off** vi 🄳, ~ **out** vi (🄸, go away) largarse. □ ~ **up** vt (tidy) ordenar; aclarar (mystery). vi (weather) despejarse. ~**ance** n (removal of obstructions) despeje m; (authorization) permiso m; (by security) acreditación f. ~**ing** n claro m. ~**ly** adv evidentemente. ~**way** n carretera f en la que no se permite parar

cleavage /ˈkliːvɪdʒ/ n escote m

clef /klef/ n (Mus) clave f

clench /klentʃ/ vt apretar

clergy /ˈklɜːdʒɪ/ n clero m. ~**man** /-mən/ n clérigo m

cleric /ˈklerɪk/ n clérigo m. ~**al** adj clerical; (of clerks) de oficina

clerk /klɑːk/ n empleado m; (Amer, salesclerk) vendedor m

clever /ˈklevə(r)/ adj (-er, -est) inteligente; (skilful) hábil. ~**ly** adv inteligentemente; (with skill) hábilmente. ~**ness** n inteligencia f

cliché /ˈkliːʃeɪ/ n lugar m común m, cliché m

click /klɪk/ n golpecito m. ● vi chascar; 🄸 llevarse bien. ~ **on sth** hacer clic en algo. ● vt chasquear

client /ˈklaɪənt/ n cliente m

cliff /klɪf/ n acantilado m

climat|e /ˈklaɪmət/ n clima m. ~**e change** n cambio m climático. ~**ic** /-ˈmætɪk/ adj climático

climax /ˈklaɪmæks/ n clímax m; (orgasm) orgasmo m

climb /klaɪm/ vt subir (stairs); trepar (tree); escalar (mountain). ● vi subir.

● *n* subida *f*. □ ~ **down** *vi* bajar; (*fig*) ceder. ~**er** *n* (*Sport*) alpinista *m & f*, andinista *m & f* (*LAm*); (*plant*) trepadora *f*

clinch /klɪntʃ/ *vt* cerrar (deal)

cling /klɪŋ/ *vi* (*pt* clung) agarrarse; (*stick*) pegarse

clinic /ˈklɪnɪk/ *n* centro *m* médico; (*private hospital*) clínica *f*. ~**al** *adj* clínico

clink /klɪŋk/ *n* tintineo *m*. ● *vt* hacer tintinear. ● *vi* tintinear

clip /klɪp/ *n* (*fastener*) clip *m*; (*for paper*) sujetapapeles *m*; (*for hair*) horquilla *f*. ● *vt* (*pt* clipped) (*cut*) cortar; (*join*) sujetar. ~**pers** /ˈklɪpəz/ *npl* (*for hair*) maquinilla *f* para cortar el pelo; (*for nails*) cortauñas *m*. ~**ping** *n* recorte *m*

cloak /kləʊk/ *n* capa *f*. ~**room** *n* guardarropa *m*; (*toilet*) lavabo *m*, baño *m* (*LAm*)

clock /klɒk/ *n* reloj *m*. ~**wise** *a/adv* en el sentido de las agujas del reloj. ~**work** *n* mecanismo *m* de relojería. like ~**work** con precisión

clog /klɒg/ *n* zueco *m*. ● *vt* (*pt* clogged) atascar

cloister /ˈklɔɪstə(r)/ *n* claustro *m*

clone /kləʊn/ *n* clon *m*

close[1] /kləʊs/ *adj* (-**er**, -**est**) cercano; (*together*) apretado; (*friend*) íntimo; (*weather*) bochornoso; (*link etc*) estrecho; (*game, battle*) reñido. **have a ~ shave** (*fig*) escaparse de milagro. ● *adv* cerca

close[2] /kləʊz/ *vt* cerrar. ● *vi* cerrarse; (*end*) terminar. ~ **down** *vt/i* cerrar. ● *n* fin *m*. ~**d** *adj* cerrado

closely /ˈkləʊslɪ/ *adv* estrechamente; (*at a short distance*) de cerca; (*with attention*) detenidamente; (*precisely*) rigurosamente

closet /ˈklɒzɪt/ *n* (*Amer*) armario *m*; (*for clothes*) armario *m*, closet *m* (*LAm*)

close-up /ˈkləʊsʌp/ *n* (*Cinema etc*) primer plano *m*

closure /ˈkləʊʒə(r)/ *n* cierre *m*

clot /klɒt/ *n* (*Med*) coágulo *m*; 🄴 tonto *m*. ● *vi* (*pt* clotted) cuajarse; (*blood*) coagularse

cloth /klɒθ/ *n* tela *f*; (*duster*) trapo *m*; (*tablecloth*) mantel *m*

cloth|e /kləʊð/ *vt* (*pt* clothed *or* clad) vestir. ~**es** /kləʊðz/ *npl* ropa. ~**espin**, ~**espeg** (*Amer*) *n* pinza *f* (para tender la ropa). ~**ing** *n* ropa *f*

cloud /klaʊd/ *n* nube *f*. ● ~ **over** *vi* nublarse. ~**y** *adj* (-**ier**, -**iest**) nublado; (*liquid*) turbio

clout /klaʊt/ *n* bofetada *f*. ● *vt* abofetear

clove /kləʊv/ *n* clavo *m*. ~ **of garlic** *n* diente *m* de ajo

clover /ˈkləʊvə(r)/ *n* trébol *m*

clown /klaʊn/ *n* payaso *m*. ● *vi* hacer el payaso

club /klʌb/ *n* club *m*; (*weapon*) porra *f*; (*golf club*) palo *m* de golf; (*at cards*) trébol *m*. ● *vt* (*pt* clubbed) aporrear. □ ~ **together** *vi* contribuir con dinero (**to** para)

cluck /klʌk/ *vi* cloquear

clue /kluː/ *n* pista *f*; (*in crosswords*) indicación *f*. **not to have a ~** no tener la menor idea

clump /klʌmp/ *n* grupo *m*. ● *vt* agrupar

clums|iness /ˈklʌmzɪnɪs/ *n* torpeza *f*. ~**y** /ˈklʌmzɪ/ *adj* (-**ier**, -**lest**) torpe

clung /klʌŋ/ *see* CLING

cluster /ˈklʌstə(r)/ *n* grupo *m*. ● *vi* agruparse

clutch /klʌtʃ/ *vt* agarrar. ● *n* (*Auto*) embrague *m*

clutter /ˈklʌtə(r)/ *n* desorden *m*. ● *vt*. ~ **(up)** abarrotar. ~**ed** /ˈklʌtəd/ *adj* abarrotado de cosas

coach /kəʊtʃ/ *n* autocar *m*, autobús *m*; (*of train*) vagón *m*; (*horse-drawn*) coche *m*; (*Sport*) entrenador *m*. ● *vt* (*Sport*) entrenar

coal /kəʊl/ *n* carbón *m*

coalition /kəʊəˈlɪʃn/ *n* coalición *f*

coarse /kɔːs/ *adj* (-**er**, -**est**) grueso; (*material*) basto; (*person, language*) ordinario

coast /kəʊst/ *n* costa *f*. ● *vi* (*with cycle*) deslizarse sin pedalear; (*with car*) ir en punto muerto. ~**al** *adj* costero. ~**guard** *n* guardacostas *m*. ~**line** *n* litoral *m*

coat /kəʊt/ *n* abrigo *m*; (*jacket*) chaqueta *f*; (*of animal*) pelo *m*; (*of paint*) mano f. ●vt cubrir, revestir. ~**hanger** n percha f, gancho m (LAm). ~**ing** n capa f. ~ **of arms** n escudo m de armas

coax /kəʊks/ vt engatusar

cobbler /ˈkɒblə(r)/ n zapatero m (remendón)

cobblestone /ˈkɒbəlstəʊn/ n adoquín m

cobweb /ˈkɒbweb/ n telaraña f

cocaine /kəˈkeɪn/ n cocaína f

cock /kɒk/ n (cockerel) gallo m; (male bird) macho m. ●vt amartillar (gun); aguzar (ears). ~**erel** /ˈkɒkərəl/ n gallo m. ~-**eyed** /-aɪd/ adj 🄸 torcido

cockney /ˈkɒkni/ adj & n (pl -eys) londinense (m & f) (del este de Londres)

cockpit /ˈkɒkpɪt/ n (in aircraft) cabina f del piloto

cockroach /ˈkɒkrəʊtʃ/ n cucaracha f

cocktail /ˈkɒkteɪl/ n cóctel m

cock-up /ˈkɒkʌp/ n 🄧 lío m

cocky /ˈkɒki/ adj (-ier, -iest) engreído

cocoa /ˈkəʊkəʊ/ n cacao m; (drink) chocolate m, cocoa f (LAm)

coconut /ˈkəʊkənʌt/ n coco m

cocoon /kəˈkuːn/ n capullo m

cod /kɒd/ n invar bacalao m

code /kəʊd/ n código m; (secret) clave f; in ~ en clave

coeducational /kəʊedʒʊˈkeɪʃənl/ adj mixto

coerc|e /kəʊˈɜːs/ vt coaccionar. ~**ion** /-ʃn/ n coacción f

coffee /ˈkɒfi/ n café m. ~ **bean** n grano m de café. ~ **maker** n cafetera f. ~**pot** n cafetera f

coffin /ˈkɒfɪn/ n ataúd m, cajón m (LAm)

cog /kɒg/ n diente m; (fig) pieza f

coherent /kəʊˈhɪərənt/ adj coherente

coil /kɔɪl/ vt enrollar. ●n rollo m; (one ring) vuelta f

coin /kɔɪn/ n moneda f. ●vt acuñar

coincide /kəʊɪnˈsaɪd/ vi coincidir. ~**nce** /kəʊˈɪnsɪdəns/ n casualidad f. ~**ntal** /kəʊɪnsɪˈdentl/ adj casual

coke /kəʊk/ n (coal) coque m. **C~** (®) Coca-Cola f (®)

colander /ˈkʌləndə(r)/ n colador m

cold /kəʊld/ adj (-er, -est) frío. be ~ (person) tener frío. it is ~ (weather) hace frío. ●n frío m; (Med) resfriado m. have a ~ estar resfriado. ~-**blooded** /-ˈblʌdɪd/ adj (animal) de sangre fría; (murder) a sangre fría. ~-**shoulder** /-ˈʃəʊldə(r)/ vt tratar con frialdad. ~ **sore** n herpes m labial. ~ **storage** n conservación f en frigorífico

coleslaw /ˈkəʊlslɔː/ n ensalada f de col

collaborat|e /kəˈlæbəreɪt/ vi colaborar. ~**ion** /-ˈreɪʃn/ n colaboración f. ~**or** n colaborador m

collaps|e /kəˈlæps/ vi derrumbarse; (Med) sufrir un colapso. ●n derrumbamiento m; (Med) colapso m. ~**ible** /-əbl/ adj plegable

collar /ˈkɒlə(r)/ n cuello m; (for animals) collar m. ●vt 🄸 hurtar. ~**bone** n clavícula f

colleague /ˈkɒliːg/ n colega m & f

collect /kəˈlekt/ vt reunir; (hobby) coleccionar, juntar (LAm); (pick up) recoger; cobrar (rent). ●vi (people) reunirse; (things) acumularse. ~**ion** /-ʃn/ n colección f; (in church) colecta f; (of post) recogida f. ~**or** n coleccionista m & f

college /ˈkɒlɪdʒ/ n colegio m; (of art, music etc) escuela f; (Amer) universidad f

colli|de /kəˈlaɪd/ vi chocar. ~**sion** /-ˈlɪʒn/ n choque m

colloquial /kəˈləʊkwɪəl/ adj coloquial

Colombia /kəˈlʌmbɪə/ n Colombia f. ~**n** adj & n colombiano (m)

colon /ˈkəʊlən/ n (Gram) dos puntos mpl; (Med) colon m

colonel /ˈkɜːnl/ n coronel m

colon|ial /kəˈləʊnɪəl/ adj colonial. ~**ize** /ˈkɒlənaɪz/ vt colonizar. ~**y** /ˈkɒləni/ n colonia f

colossal /kəˈlɒsl/ adj colosal

colour /ˈkʌlə(r)/ n color m. off ~ (fig) indispuesto. ●adj de color(es), en color(es) ●vt colorear; (dye) teñir. ~-**blind** adj daltónico. ~**ed** /ˈkʌləd/ adj de color. ~**ful** adj lleno de color; (fig) pintoresco. ~**ing** n color; (food *colouring*) colorante *m*. **~less** *adj* incoloro

column /'kɒləm/ *n* columna *f*. **~ist** *n* columnista *m & f*

coma /'kəʊmə/ *n* coma *m*

comb /kəʊm/ *n* peine *m*. ● *vt* (*search*) registrar. **~ one's hair** peinarse

combat /'kɒmbæt/ *n* combate *m*. ● *vt* (*pt* **combated**) combatir

combination /kɒmbɪ'neɪʃn/ *n* combinación *f*

combine /kəm'baɪn/ *vt* combinar. ● *vi* combinarse. ● /'kɒmbaɪn/ *n* asociación *f*. **~ harvester** *n* cosechadora *f*

combustion /kəm'bʌstʃən/ *n* combustión *f*

come /kʌm/ *vi* (*pt* **came**, *pp* **come**) venir; (*occur*) pasar. □ **~ across** *vt* encontrarse con (person); encontrar (object). □ **~ apart** *vi* deshacerse. □ **~ away** *vi* (*leave*) salir; (*become detached*) salirse. □ **~ back** *vi* volver. □ **~ by** *vt* obtener. □ **~ down** *vi* bajar. □ **~ in** *vi* entrar; (*arrive*) llegar. □ **~ into** *vt* entrar en; heredar (money). □ **~ off** *vi* desprenderse; (*succeed*) tener éxito. *vt*. **~ off it!** Ⓔ ¡no me vengas con eso! □ **~ on** *vi* (*start to work*) encenderse. **~ on, hurry up!** ¡vamos, date prisa! □ **~ out** *vi* salir. □ **~ round** *vi* (*after fainting*) volver en sí; (*be converted*) cambiar de idea; (*visit*) venir. □ **~ to** *vt* llegar a (decision etc). □ **~ up** *vi* subir; (*fig*) surgir. □ **~ up with** *vt* proponer (idea). **~back** *n* retorno *m*; (*retort*) réplica *f*

comedian /kə'miːdɪən/ *n* cómico *m*

comedy /'kɒmədɪ/ *n* comedia *f*

comet /'kɒmɪt/ *n* cometa *m*

comfort /'kʌmfət/ *n* comodidad *f*; (*consolation*) consuelo *m*. ● *vt* consolar. **~able** *adj* cómodo. **~er** *n* (*for baby*) chupete *m*, chupón *m* (LAm); (*Amer, for bed*) edredón *m*

comic /'kɒmɪk/ *adj* cómico. ● *n* cómico *m*; (*periodical*) revista *f* de historietas, tebeo *m*. **~al** *adj* cómico. **~ strip** *n* tira *f* cómica

coming /'kʌmɪŋ/ *n* llegada *f*. **~s and goings** idas *fpl* y venidas. ● *adj* próximo; (*week, month etc*) que viene

comma /'kɒmə/ *n* coma *f*

command /kə'mɑːnd/ *n* orden *f*; (*mastery*) dominio *m*. ● *vt* ordenar; imponer (respect)

commandeer /kɒmən'dɪə(r)/ *vt* requisar

command **~er** *n* comandante *m*. **~ing** *adj* imponente. **~ment** *n* mandamiento *m*

commando /kə'mɑːndəʊ/ *n* (*pl* **-os**) comando *m*

commemorat|e /kə'meməreɪt/ *vt* conmemorar. **~ion** /-'reɪʃn/ *n* conmemoración *f*. **~ive** /-ətɪv/ *adj* conmemorativo

commence /kə'mens/ *vt* dar comienzo a. ● *vi* iniciarse

commend /kə'mend/ *vt* alabar. **~able** *adj* loable. **~ation** /kɒmen'deɪʃn/ *n* elogio *m*

comment /'kɒment/ *n* observación *f*. ● *vi* hacer observaciones (**on** sobre)

commentary /'kɒməntrɪ/ *n* comentario *m*; (*Radio, TV*) reportaje *m*

commentat|e /'kɒmənteɪt/ *vi* narrar. **~or** *n* (*Radio, TV*) locutor *m*

commerc|e /'kɒmɜːs/ *n* comercio *m*. **~ial** /kə'mɜːʃl/ *adj* comercial. ● *n* anuncio *m*; aviso *m* (LAm). **~ialize** *vt* comercializar

commiserat|e /kə'mɪzəreɪt/ *vi* compadecerse (**with** de). **~ion** /-'reɪʃn/ *n* conmiseración *f*

commission /kə'mɪʃn/ *n* comisión *f*. **out of ~** fuera de servicio. ● *vt* encargar; (*Mil*) nombrar oficial

commissionaire /kəmɪʃə'neə(r)/ *n* portero *m*

commit /kə'mɪt/ *vt* (*pt* **committed**) cometer; (*entrust*) confiar. **~ o.s.** comprometerse. **~ment** *n* compromiso *m*

committee /kə'mɪtɪ/ *n* comité *m*

commodity /kə'mɒdətɪ/ *n* producto *m*, artículo *m*

common /'kɒmən/ *adj* (**-er**, **-est**) común; (*usual*) corriente; (*vulgar*) ordinario. ● *n*. **in ~** en común. **~er** *n* plebeyo *m*. **~ law** *n* derecho *m* consuetudinario. **~ly** *adv* comúnmente. **C~ Market** *n* Mercado *m* Común. **~place** *adj* banal. ● *n* banalidad *f*. **~ room** *n* sala *f* común, salón *m* común.

C~s *n.* the (House of) C~s la Cámara de los Comunes. **~ sense** *n* sentido *m* común. **C~wealth** *n.* the C~wealth la Mancomunidad *f* Británica

commotion /kə'məʊʃn/ *n* confusión *f*

Commonwealth *La Commonwealth* es una asociación de las antiguas colonias y territorios que conformaban el Imperio Británico. Cada dos años se celebra una reunión de sus jefes de gobierno. Entre los países miembros existen muchos vínculos culturales, educativos y deportivos. En EE.UU., es el término oficial para referirse a cuatro estados: Kentucky, Massachussets, Pensilvania y Virginia.

---

commune /'kɒmju:n/ *n* comuna *f*

communicat|e /kə'mju:nɪkeɪt/ *vt* comunicar. ● *vi* comunicarse. **~ion** /-'keɪʃn/ *n* comunicación *f*. **~ive** /-ətɪv/ *adj* comunicativo

communion /kə'mju:nɪən/ *n* comunión *f*

communis|m /'kɒmjʊnɪsəm/ *n* comunismo *m*. **~t** *n* comunista *m & f*

community /kə'mju:nətɪ/ *n* comunidad *f*. **~ centre** *n* centro *m* social

commute /kə'mju:t/ *vi* viajar diariamente (*entre el lugar de residencia y el trabajo*). ● *vt* (*Jurid*) conmutar. **~r** *n* viajero *m* diario

compact /kəm'pækt/ *adj* compacto. ● /'kɒmpækt/ *n* (*for powder*) polvera *f*. **~ disc**, **~ disk** /'kɒmpækt/ *n* disco *m* compacto, compact-disc *m*. **~ disc player** *n* (reproductor *m* de) compact-disc

companion /kəm'pænɪən/ *n* compañero *m*. **~ship** *n* compañía *f*

company /'kʌmpənɪ/ *n* compañía *f*; (*guests*) visita *f*; (*Com*) sociedad *f*

compar|able /'kɒmpərəbl/ *adj* comparable. **~ative** /kəm'pærətɪv/ *adj* comparativo; (*fig*) relativo. ● *n* (*Gram*) comparativo *m*. **~e** /kəm'peə(r)/ *vt* comparar. **~ison** /kəm'pærɪsn/ *n* comparación *f*

compartment /kəm'pɑ:tmənt/ *n* compartim(i)ento *m*

compass /'kʌmpəs/ *n* brújula *f*. **~es** *npl* compás *m*

compassion /kəm'pæʃn/ *n* compasión *f*. **~ate** /-ət/ *adj* compasivo

compatible /kəm'pætəbl/ *adj* compatible

compel /kəm'pel/ *vt* (*pt* **compelled**) obligar. **~ling** *adj* irresistible

compensat|e /'kɒmpənseɪt/ *vt* compensar; (*for loss*) indemnizar. ● *vi.* **~e for sth** compensar algo. **~ion** /-'seɪʃn/ *n* compensación *f*; (*financial*) indemnización *f*

compère /'kɒmpeə(r)/ *n* presentador *m*. ● *vt* presentar

compete /kəm'pi:t/ *vi* competir

competen|ce /'kɒmpətəns/ *n* competencia *f*. **~t** *adj* competente

competit|ion /kɒmpə'tɪʃn/ *n* (*contest*) concurso *m*; (*Sport*) competición *f*, competencia *f* (*LAm*); (*Com*) competencia *f*. **~ive** /kəm'petətɪv/ *adj* competidor; (*price*) competitivo. **~or** /kəm'petɪtə(r)/ *n* competidor *m*; (*in contest*) concursante *m & f*

compile /kəm'paɪl/ *vt* compilar

complacen|cy /kəm'pleɪsənsɪ/ *n* autosuficiencia *f*. **~t** *adj* satisfecho de sí mismo

complain /kəm'pleɪn/ *vi.* **~ (about)** quejarse (de). ● *vt.* **~ that** quejarse de que. **~t** *n* queja *f*; (*Med*) enfermedad *f*

complement /'kɒmplɪmənt/ *n* complemento *m*. ● *vt* complementar. **~ary** /-'mentrɪ/ *adj* complementario

complet|e /kəm'pli:t/ *adj* completo; (*finished*) acabado; (*downright*) total. ● *vt* acabar; llenar (a form). **~ely** *adv* completamente. **~ion** /-ʃn/ *n* finalización *f*

complex /'kɒmpleks/ *adj* complejo. ● *n* complejo *m*

complexion /kəm'plekʃn/ *n* tez *f*; (*fig*) aspecto *m*

complexity /kəm'pleksətɪ/ *n* complejidad *f*

complicat|e /'kɒmplɪkeɪt/ *vt* complicar. **~ed** *adj* complicado. **~ion** /-'keɪʃn/ *n* complicación *f*

compliment /'kɒmplɪmənt/ *n* cumplido *m*; (*amorous*) piropo *m*. ● *vt* felicitar. **~ary** /-'mentrɪ/ *adj* halagador; (*given free*) de regalo. **~s** *npl* saludos *mpl*

comply /kəm'plaɪ/ *vi.* **~ with** conformarse con

component /kəm'pəʊnənt/ *adj & n* componente (*m*)

compos|e /kəm'pəʊz/ *vt* componer. **be ~ed of** estar compuesto de. **~er** *n* compositor *m*. **~ition** /kɒmpə'zɪʃn/ *n* composición *f*

compost /'kɒmpɒst/ *n* abono *m*

composure /kəm'pəʊʒə(r)/ *n* serenidad *f*

compound /'kɒmpaʊnd/ *n* compuesto *m*; (*enclosure*) recinto *m*. ● *adj* compuesto; (*fracture*) complicado

comprehen|d /kɒmprɪ'hend/ *vt* comprender. **~sion** /kɒmprɪ'henʃn/ *n* comprensión *f*. **~sive** /kɒmprɪ'hensɪv/ *adj* extenso; (*insurance*) contra todo riesgo. **~sive (school)** *n* instituto *m* de enseñanza secundaria

compress /'kɒmpres/ *n* (*Med*) compresa *f*. ● /kəm'pres/ *vt* comprimir. **~ion** /-'preʃn/ *n* compresión *f*

comprise /kəm'praɪz/ *vt* comprender

compromis|e /'kɒmprəmaɪz/ *n* acuerdo *m*, compromiso *m*, arreglo *m*. ● *vt* comprometer. ● *vi* llegar a un acuerdo. **~ing** *adj* (*situation*) comprometido

compuls|ion /kəm'pʌlʃn/ *n* (*force*) coacción *f*; (*obsession*) compulsión *f*. **~ive** /kəm'pʌlsɪv/ *adj* compulsivo. **~ory** /kəm'pʌlsərɪ/ *adj* obligatorio

comput|e /kəm'pjuːt/ *vb* calcular. **comput|er** *n* ordenador *m*, computadora *f* (*LAm*). **~erize** *vt* computarizar, computerizar. **~er studies** *n*, **~ing** *n* informática *f*, computación *f*

comrade /'kɒmreɪd/ *n* camarada *m & f*

con /kɒn/ *vt* (*pt* **conned**) 🔢 estafar. ● *n* (*fraud*) estafa *f*; (*objection*) *see* **PRO**

concave /'kɒŋkeɪv/ *adj* cóncavo

conceal /kən'siːl/ *vt* ocultar

concede /kən'siːd/ *vt* conceder

conceit /kən'siːt/ *n* vanidad *f*. **~ed** *adj* engreído

conceiv|able /kən'siːvəbl/ *adj* concebible. **~e** /kən'siːv/ *vt/i* concebir

concentrat|e /'kɒnsəntreɪt/ *vt* concentrar. ● *vi* concentrarse (**on** en). **~ion** /-'treɪʃn/ *n* concentración *f*

concept /'kɒnsept/ *n* concepto *m*

conception /kən'sepʃn/ *n* concepción *f*

concern /kən'sɜːn/ *n* asunto *m*; (*worry*) preocupación *f*; (*Com*) empresa *f*. ● *vt* tener que ver con; (*deal with*) tratar de. **as far as I'm ~ed** en cuanto a mí. **be ~ed about** preocuparse por. **~ing** *prep* acerca de

concert /'kɒnsət/ *n* concierto *m*. **~ed** /kən'sɜːtɪd/ *adj* concertado

concertina /kɒnsə'tiːnə/ *n* concertina *f*

concerto /kən'tʃɜːtəʊ/ *n* (*pl* **-os** *or* **-ti** /-tɪ/) concierto *m*

concession /kən'seʃn/ *n* concesión *f*

concise /kən'saɪs/ *adj* conciso

conclu|de /kən'kluːd/ *vt/i* concluir. **~ding** *adj* final. **~sion** /-ʃn/ *n* conclusión *f*. **~sive** /-sɪv/ *adj* decisivo. **~sively** *adv* concluyentemente

concoct /kən'kɒkt/ *vt* confeccionar; (*fig*) inventar. **~ion** /-ʃn/ *n* mezcla *f*; (*drink*) brebaje *m*

concrete /'kɒŋkriːt/ *n* hormigón *m*, concreto *m* (*LAm*). ● *adj* concreto

concussion /kən'kʌʃn/ *n* conmoción *f* cerebral

condemn /kən'dem/ *vt* condenar. **~ation** /kɒndem'neɪʃn/ *n* condena *f*

condens|ation /kɒnden'seɪʃn/ *n* condensación *f*. **~e** /kən'dens/ *vt* condensar. ● *vi* condensarse

condescend /kɒndɪ'send/ *vi* dignarse (**to** a). **~ing** *adj* superior

condition /kən'dɪʃn/ *n* condición *f*. **on ~ that** a condición de que. ● *vt* condicionar. **~al** *adj* condicional. **~er** *n* (*for hair*) suavizante *m*, enjuague *m* (*LAm*)

condo /'kɒndəʊ/ *n* (*pl* **-os**) (*Amer fam*) *see* **CONDOMINIUM**

condolences /kən'dəʊlənsɪz/ *npl* pésame *m*

condom /'kɒndɒm/ *n* condón *m*

condominium /kɒndə'mɪnɪəm/ *n* (*Amer*) apartamento *m*, piso *m* (en régimen de propiedad horizontal)

condone /kən'dəʊn/ *vt* condonar

conduct /kən'dʌkt/ vt llevar a cabo (business, experiment); conducir (electricity); dirigir (orchestra). ● /'kɒndʌkt/ n conducta f. **~or** /kən'dʌktə(r)/ n director m; (of bus) cobrador m. **~ress** /kən'dʌktrɪs/ n cobradora f

cone /kəʊn/ n cono m; (for ice cream) cucurucho m, barquillo m (Mex)

confectionery /kən'fekʃənrɪ/ n productos mpl de confitería

confederation /kənfedə'reɪʃn/ n confederación f

conference /'kɒnfərəns/ n congreso m; **an international ~ on ...** un congreso internacional sobre ...

confess /kən'fes/ vt confesar. ● vi confesarse. **~ion** /-ʃn/ n confesión f

confetti /kən'fetɪ/ n confeti m

confide /kən'faɪd/ vt/i confiar

confiden|ce /'kɒnfɪdəns/ n confianza f; (self-confidence) confianza f en sí mismo; (secret) confidencia f. **~ce trick** n estafa f, timo m. **~t** /'kɒnfɪdənt/ adj seguro de sí mismo. **be ~t of** confiar en

confidential /kɒnfɪ'denʃl/ adj confidencial. **~ity** /-denʃɪ'ælətɪ/ n confidencialidad f

configur|ation /kənfɪgə'reɪʃn/ n configuración f. **~e** /kən'fɪgə(r)/ vt configurar

confine /kən'faɪn/ vt confinar; (limit) limitar. **~ment** n (imprisonment) prisión f

confirm /kən'fɜːm/ vt confirmar. **~ation** /kɒnfə'meɪʃn/ n confirmación f. **~ed** adj inveterado

confiscat|e /'kɒnfɪskeɪt/ vt confiscar. **~ion** /-'keɪʃn/ n confiscación f

conflict /'kɒnflɪkt/ n conflicto m. ● /kən'flɪkt/ vi chocar. **~ing** /kən'flɪktɪŋ/ adj contradictorio

conform /kən'fɔːm/ vi conformarse. **~ist** n conformista m & f

confound /kən'faʊnd/ vt confundir. **~ed** adj 🄴 maldito

confront /kən'frʌnt/ vt hacer frente a; (face) enfrentarse con. **~ation** /kɒnfrʌn'teɪʃn/ n confrontación f

confus|e /kən'fjuːz/ vt confundir. **~ed** adj confundido. **get ~ed** confundirse.

~ing adj confuso. **~ion** /-ʒn/ n confusión f

congeal /kən'dʒiːl/ vi coagularse

congest|ed /kən'dʒestɪd/ adj congestionado. **~ion** /-tʃən/ n congestión f

congratulat|e /kən'grætjʊleɪt/ vt felicitar. **~ions** /-'leɪʃnz/ npl enhorabuena f, felicitaciones fpl (LAm)

congregat|e /'kɒŋgrɪgeɪt/ vi congregarse. **~ion** /-'geɪʃn/ n asamblea f; (Relig) fieles mpl, feligreses mpl

congress /'kɒŋgres/ n congreso m. **C~** (Amer) el Congreso. **~man** /-mən/ n (Amer) miembro m del Congreso. **~woman** n (Amer) miembro f del Congreso.

ℹ️

Congress El Congreso es el organismo legislativo de EE.UU. Se reúne en el Capitolio (Capitol) y está compuesto por dos cámaras: El Senado y la Cámara de Representantes. Se renueva cada dos años y su función es elaborar leyes que deben ser aprobadas, primero, por las dos cámaras y posteriormente por el Presidente.

---

conifer /'kɒnɪfə(r)/ n conífera f

conjugat|e /'kɒndʒʊgeɪt/ vt conjugar. **~ion** /-'geɪʃn/ n conjugación f

conjunction /kən'dʒʌŋkʃn/ n conjunción f

conjur|e /'kʌndʒə(r)/ vi hacer juegos de manos. ● vt. ☐ **~e up** vt evocar. **~er, ~or** n prestidigitador m

conk /kɒŋk/ vi. **~ out** 🄴 fallar; (person) desmayarse

conker /'kɒŋkə(r)/ n 🄴 castaña f de Indias

conman /'kɒnmæn/ n (pl **-men**) 🄴 estafador m, timador m

connect /kə'nekt/ vt conectar; (associate) relacionar. ● vi (be fitted) estar conectado (to a). ☐ **~ with** vt (train) enlazar con. **~ed** adj unido; (related) relacionado. **be ~ed with** tener que ver con, estar emparentado con. **~ion** /-ʃn/ n conexión f; (Rail) enlace m; (fig) relación f. **in ~ion with** a propósito de, con respecto a

connive /kə'naɪv/ vi. **~e at** ser cómplice en

connoisseur /kɒnəˈsɜː(r)/ n experto m

connotation /kɒnəˈteɪʃn/ n connotación f

conquer /ˈkɒŋkə(r)/ vt conquistar; (fig) vencer. **~or** n conquistador m

conquest /ˈkɒŋkwest/ n conquista f

conscience /ˈkɒnʃəns/ n conciencia f

conscientious /kɒnʃɪˈenʃəs/ adj concienzudo

conscious /ˈkɒnʃəs/ adj consciente; (deliberate) intencional. **~ly** adv a sabiendas. **~ness** n consciencia f; (Med) conocimiento m

conscript /ˈkɒnskrɪpt/ n recluta m & f, conscripto m (LAm). ● /kənˈskrɪpt/ vt reclutar. **~ion** /kənˈnkrɪpʃn/ n reclutamiento m, conscripción f (LAm)

consecrate /ˈkɒnsɪkreɪt/ vt consagrar

consecutive /kənˈsekjʊtɪv/ adj sucesivo

consensus /kənˈsensəs/ n consenso m

consent /kənˈsent/ vi consentir. ● n consentimiento m

consequen|ce /ˈkɒnsɪkwəns/ n consecuencia f. **~t** adj consiguiente. **~tly** adv por consiguiente

conservation /kɒnsəˈveɪʃn/ n conservación f, preservación f. **~ist** n conservacionista m & f

conservative /kənˈsɜːvətɪv/ adj conservador; (modest) prudente, moderado. **C~** adj & n conservador (m)

conservatory /kənˈsɜːvətrɪ/ n invernadero m

conserve /kənˈsɜːv/ vt conservar

consider /kənˈsɪdə(r)/ vt considerar; (take into account) tomar en cuenta. **~able** adj considerable. **~ably** adv considerablemente

considerat|e /kənˈsɪdərət/ adj considerado. **~ion** /-ˈreɪʃn/ n consideración f. **take sth into ~ion** tomar algo en cuenta

considering /kənˈsɪdərɪŋ/ prep teniendo en cuenta. ● conj. **~ (that)** teniendo en cuenta que

consign /kənˈsaɪn/ vt consignar; (send) enviar. **~ment** n envío m

consist /kənˈsɪst/ vi. **~ of** consistir en. **~ency** n consistencia f; (fig) coherencia f. **~ent** adj coherente; (unchan-

ging) constante. **~ent with** compatible con. **~ently** adv constantemente

consolation /kɒnsəˈleɪʃn/ n consuelo m

console /kənˈsəʊl/ vt consolar. ● /ˈkɒnsəʊl/ n consola f

consolidate /kənˈsɒlɪdeɪt/ vt consolidar

consonant /ˈkɒnsənənt/ n consonante f

conspicuous /kənˈspɪkjʊəs/ adj (easily seen) visible; (showy) llamativo; (noteworthy) notable

conspir|acy /kənˈspɪrəsɪ/ n conspiración f. **~ator** /kənˈspɪrətə(r)/ n conspirador m. **~e** /kənˈspaɪə(r)/ vi conspirar

constable /ˈkʌnstəbl/ n agente m & f de policía

constant /ˈkɒnstənt/ adj constante. **~ly** adv constantemente

constellation /kɒnstəˈleɪʃn/ n constelación f

consternation /kɒnstəˈneɪʃn/ n consternación f

constipat|ed /ˈkɒnstɪpeɪtɪd/ adj estreñido. **~ion** /-ˈpeɪʃn/ n estreñimiento m

constituen|cy /kənˈstɪtjuənsɪ/ n distrito m electoral. **~t** n (Pol) elector m. ● adj constituyente, constitutivo

constitut|e /ˈkɒnstɪtjuːt/ vt constituir. **~ion** /-ˈtjuːʃn/ n constitución f **~ional** /-ˈtjuːʃənl/ adj constitucional. ● n paseo m

constrict /kənˈstrɪkt/ vt apretar. **~ion** /-ʃn/ n constricción f

construct /kənˈstrʌkt/ vt construir. **~ion** /-ʃn/ n construcción f. **~ive** adj constructivo

consul /ˈkɒnsl/ n cónsul m & f. **~ate** /ˈkɒnsjʊlət/ n consulado m

consult /kənˈsʌlt/ vt/i consultar. **~ancy** n asesoría. **~ant** n asesor m; (Med) especialista m & f; (Tec) consejero m técnico. **~ation** /kɒnsəlˈteɪʃn/ n consulta f

consume /kənˈsjuːm/ vt consumir. **~r** n consumidor m. ● adj de consumo

consummate /ˈkɒnsəmət/ adj consumado. ● /ˈkɒnsəmeɪt/ vt consumar

consumption /kənˈsʌmpʃn/ n consumo m

contact /ˈkɒntækt/ n contacto m. ● vt ponerse en contacto con. ~ **lens** n lentilla f, lente f de contacto (LAm)

contagious /kənˈteɪdʒəs/ adj contagioso

contain /kənˈteɪn/ vt contener. ~ **o.s.** contenerse. ~**er** n recipiente m; (Com) contenedor m

contaminat|e /kənˈtæmɪneɪt/ vt contaminar. ~**ion** /-ˈneɪʃn/ n contaminación f

contemplate /ˈkɒntəmpleɪt/ vt contemplar; (consider) considerar

contemporary /kənˈtempərərɪ/ adj & n contemporáneo (m)

contempt /kənˈtempt/ n desprecio m. ~**ible** adj despreciable. ~**uous** /-tjʊəs/ adj desdeñoso

contend /kənˈtend/ vt competir. ~**er** n aspirante m & f (**for** a)

content /ˈkɒntent/ adj satisfecho. ● /ˈkɒntent/ n contenido m. ● /kən ˈtent/ vt contentar. ~**ed** /kənˈtentɪd/ adj satisfecho. ~**ment** /kənˈtentmənt/ n satisfacción f. ~**s** /ˈkɒntents/ n contenido m; (of book) índice m de materias

contest /ˈkɒntest/ n (competition) concurso m; (Sport) competición f, competencia f (LAm). ● /kənˈtest/ vt disputar. ~**ant** /kənˈtestənt/ n concursante m & f

context /ˈkɒntekst/ n contexto m

continent /ˈkɒntɪnənt/ n continente m. **the C**~ Europa f. ~**al** /-ˈnentl/ adj continental. ~**al quilt** n edredón m

contingen|cy /kənˈtɪndʒənsɪ/ n contingencia f. ~**t** adj & n contingente (m)

continu|al /kənˈtɪnjʊəl/ adj continuo. ~**ally** adv continuamente. ~**ation** /-ˈeɪʃn/ n continuación f. ~**e** /kən ˈtɪnjuː/ vt/i continuar, seguir. ~**ed** adj continuo. ~**ity** /kɒntɪˈnjuːətɪ/ n continuidad f. ~**ous** /kənˈtɪnjʊəs/ adj continuo. ~**ously** adv continuamente

contort /kənˈtɔːt/ vt retorcer. ~**ion** /-ʃn/ n contorsión f. ~**ionist** /-ʃənɪst/ n contorsionista m & f

contour /ˈkɒntʊə(r)/ n contorno m

contraband /ˈkɒntrəbænd/ n contrabando m

contracepti|on /kɒntrəˈsepʃn/ n anticoncepción f. ~**ve** /-tɪv/ adj & n anticonceptivo (m)

contract /ˈkɒntrækt/ n contrato m. ● /kənˈtrækt/ vt contraer. ● vi contraerse. ~**ion** /kənˈtrækʃn/ n contracción f. ~**or** /kənˈtræktə(r)/ n contratista m & f

contradict /kɒntrəˈdɪkt/ vt contradecir. ~**ion** /-ʃn/ n contradicción f. ~**ory** adj contradictorio

contraption /kənˈtræpʃn/ n 🄸 artilugio m

contrary /ˈkɒntrərɪ/ adj contrario. **the** ~ lo contrario. **on the** ~ al contrario. ● adv. ~ **to** contrariamente a. ● /kənˈtreərɪ/ adj (obstinate) terco

contrast /ˈkɒntrɑːst/ n contraste m. ● /kənˈtrɑːst/ vt/i contrastar. ~**ing** adj contrastante

contravene /kɒntrəˈviːn/ vt contravenir

contribut|e /kənˈtrɪbjuːt/ vt contribuir con. ● vi contribuir. ~**e to** escribir para (newspaper). ~**ion** /kɒntrɪ ˈbjuːʃn/ n contribución f. ~**or** n contribuyente m & f; (to newspaper) colaborador m

contrite /ˈkɒntraɪt/ adj arrepentido, pesaroso

contriv|e /kənˈtraɪv/ vt idear. ~**e to** conseguir. ~**ed** adj artificioso

control /kənˈtrəʊl/ vt (pt **controlled**) controlar. ● n control m. ~**ler** n director m. ~**s** npl (Mec) mandos mpl

controvers|ial /kɒntrəˈvɜːʃl/ controvertido. ~**y** /ˈkɒntrəvɜːsɪ/ n controversia f

conundrum /kəˈnʌndrəm/ n adivinanza f

convalesce /kɒnvəˈles/ vi convalecer. ~**nce** n convalecencia f

convector /kənˈvektə(r)/ n estufa f de convección

convene /kənˈviːn/ vt convocar. ● vi reunirse

convenien|ce /kənˈviːnɪəns/ n conveniencia f, comodidad f. **all modern** ~**ces** todas las comodidades. **at your** ~**ce** según le convenga. ~**ces** npl servicios mpl, baños mpl (LAm). ~**t** adj conveniente; (place) bien situado; (time) oportuno. **be** ~**t** convenir.

~tly adv convenientemente

convent /'kɒnvənt/ n convento m

convention /kən'venʃn/ n convención f. **~al** adj convencional

converge /kən'vɜːdʒ/ vi converger

conversation /kɒnvə'seɪʃn/ n conversación f. **~al** adj familiar, coloquial.

converse /kən'vɜːs/ vi conversar. ● /'kɒnvɜːs/ adj inverso. ● n lo contrario. **~ly** adv a la inversa

conver|sion /kən'vɜːʃn/ n conversión f. **~t** /kən'vɜːt/ vt convertir. ● /'kɒnvɜːt/ n converso m. **~tible** /kən'vɜːtɪbl/ adj convertible. **~n** (Auto) descapotable m, convertible m (LAm)

convex /'kɒnveks/ adj convexo

convey /kən'veɪ/ vt transportar (goods, people); comunicar (idea, feeling). **~or belt** n cinta f transportadora, banda f transportadora (LAm)

convict /kən'vɪkt/ vt condenar. ● /'kɒnvɪkt/ n presidiario m. **~ion** /kən'vɪkʃn/ n condena f; (belief) creencia f

convinc|e /kən'vɪns/ vt convencer. **~ing** adj convincente

convoluted /'kɒnvəluːtɪd/ adj (argument) intrincado

convoy /'kɒnvɔɪ/ n convoy m

convuls|e /kən'vʌls/ vt convulsionar. **be ~ed with laughter** desternillarse de risa. **~ion** /-ʃn/ n convulsión f

coo /kuː/ vi arrullar

cook /kʊk/ vt hacer, preparar. ● vi cocinar; (food) hacerse. ● n cocinero m. □ **~ up** vt inventar. **~book** n libro m de cocina. **~er** n cocina f, estufa f (Mex). **~ery** n cocina f

cookie /'kʊkɪ/ n (Amer) galleta f

cool /kuːl/ adj (-er, -est) fresco; (calm) tranquilo; (unfriendly) frío. ● n fresco m; ✗ calma f. ● vt enfriar. ● vi enfriarse. □ **~ down** vi (person) calmarse. **~ly** adv tranquilamente

coop /kuːp/ n gallinero m. □ **~ up** vt encerrar

co-op /'kəʊɒp/ n cooperativa f

cooperat|e /kəʊ'ɒpəreɪt/ vi cooperar. **~ion** /-'reɪʃn/ n cooperación f. **~ive** /kəʊ'ɒpərətɪv/ adj cooperativo. ● n cooperativa f

co-opt /kəʊ'ɒpt/ vt cooptar

co-ordinat|e /kəʊ'ɔːdɪneɪt/ vt coordinar. ● /kəʊ'ɔːdɪnət/ n (Math) coordenada f. **~es** npl prendas fpl para combinar. **~ion** /kəʊɒdɪ'neɪʃn/ n coordinación f

cop /kɒp/ n 🅟 poli m & f 🅟, tira m & f (Mex, fam)

cope /kəʊp/ vi arreglárselas. **~ with** hacer frente a

copious /'kəʊpɪəs/ adj abundante

copper /'kɒpə(r)/ n cobre m; (coin) perra f; 🅟 poli m & f 🅟, tira m & f (Mex, fam). ● adj de cobre

copy /'kɒpɪ/ n copia f; (of book, newspaper) ejemplar m. ● vt copiar. **~right** n derechos mpl de reproducción

coral /'kɒrəl/ n coral m

cord /kɔːd/ n cuerda f; (fabric) pana f; (Amer, Elec) cordón m, cable m

cordial /'kɔːdɪəl/ adj cordial. ● n refresco m (concentrado)

cordon /'kɔːdn/ n cordón m. □ **~ off** vt acordonar

core /kɔː(r)/ n (of apple) corazón m; (of Earth) centro m; (of problem) meollo m

cork /kɔːk/ n corcho m. **~screw** n sacacorchos m

corn /kɔːn/ n (wheat) trigo m; (Amer) maíz m; (hard skin) callo m

corned beef /kɔːnd 'biːf/ n carne f de vaca en lata

corner /'kɔːnə(r)/ n ángulo m; (inside) rincón m; (outside) esquina f; (football) córner m. ● vt arrinconar; (Com) acaparar

cornet /'kɔːnɪt/ n (Mus) corneta f; (for ice cream) cucurucho m, barquillo m (Mex)

corn ~flakes npl copos mpl de maíz. **~flour** n maizena f (®)

Cornish /'kɔːnɪʃ/ adj de Cornualles

cornstarch /'kɔːnstɑːtʃ/ n (Amer) maizena f (®)

corny /'kɔːnɪ/ adj (fam, trite) gastado

coronation /kɒrə'neɪʃn/ n coronación f

coroner /'kɒrənə(r)/ n juez m de primera instancia

corporal /'kɔːpərəl/ n cabo m. ● adj corporal

corporate /'kɔːpərət/ adj corporativo

corporation /kɔːpə'reɪʃn/ n corporación f; (Amer) sociedad f anónima

corps /kɔː(r)/ n (pl **corps**/kɔːz/) cuerpo m

corpse /kɔːps/ n cadáver m

corpulent /'kɔːpjʊlənt/ adj corpulento

corral /kə'rɑːl/ n (Amer) corral m

correct /kə'rekt/ adj correcto; (time) exacto. ● vt corregir. ~**ion** /-ʃn/ n corrección f

correspond /kɒrɪ'spɒnd/ vi corresponder; (write) escribirse. ~**ence** n correspondencia f. ~**ent** n corresponsal m & f

corridor /'kɒrɪdɔː(r)/ n pasillo m

corro|de /kə'rəʊd/ vt corroer. ● vi corroerse. ~**sion** /-ʒn/ n corrosión f. ~**sive** /-sɪv/ adj corrosivo

corrugated /'kɒrəgeɪtɪd/ adj ondulado. ~ **iron** n chapa f de zinc

corrupt /kə'rʌpt/ adj corrompido. ● vt corromper. ~**ion** /-ʃn/ n corrupción f

corset /'kɔːsɪt/ n corsé m

cosmetic /kɒz'metɪk/ adj & n cosmético (m)

cosmic /'kɒzmɪk/ adj cósmico

cosmopolitan /kɒzmə'pɒlɪtən/ adj & n cosmopolita (m & f)

cosmos /'kɒzmɒs/ n cosmos m

cosset /'kɒsɪt/ vt (pt **cosseted**) mimar

cost /kɒst/ vt (pt **cost**) costar; (pt **costed**) calcular el coste de, calcular el costo de (LAm). ● n coste m, costo m (LAm). **at all** ~**s** cueste lo que cueste. **to one's** ~ a sus expensas. ~**s** npl (Jurid) costas fpl

Costa Rica /kɒstə'riːkə/ n Costa f Rica. ~**n** adj & n costarricense (m & f), costarriqueño (m & f)

cost ~**-effective** adj rentable. ~**ly** adj (**-ier**, **-iest**) costoso

costume /'kɒstjuːm/ n traje m; (for party, disguise) disfraz m

cosy /'kəʊzɪ/ adj (**-ier**, **-iest**) acogedor. ● n cubreteras m

cot /kɒt/ n cuna f

cottage /'kɒtɪdʒ/ n casita f. ~ **cheese** n requesón m. ~ **pie** n pastel m de carne cubierta con puré

cotton /'kɒtn/ n algodón m; (thread) hilo m; (Amer) see ~ **WOOL**. □ ~ **on** vi 🔢 comprender. ~ **bud** n bastoncillo m, cotonete m (Mex). ~ **candy** n (Amer) algodón m de azúcar. ~ **swab** n (Amer) see ~ **BUD**. ~ **wool** n algodón m hidrófilo

couch /kaʊtʃ/ n sofá m

cough /kɒf/ vi toser. ● n tos f. □ ~ **up** vt 🔢 pagar. ~ **mixture** n jarabe m para la tos

could /kʊd/ pt of **CAN¹**

couldn't /'kʊdnt/ = **could not**

council /'kaʊnsl/ n consejo m; (of town) ayuntamiento m. ~ **house** n vivienda f subvencionada. ~**lor** n concejal m

counsel /'kaʊnsl/ n consejo m; (pl invar) (Jurid) abogado m. ● vt (pt **counselled**) aconsejar. ~**ling** n terapia f de apoyo. ~**lor** n consejero m

count /kaʊnt/ n recuento m; (nobleman) conde m. ● vt/i contar. □ ~ **on** vt contar. ~**down** n cuenta f atrás

counter /'kaʊntə(r)/ n (in shop) mostrador m; (in bank, post office) ventanilla f; (token) ficha f. ● adv. ~ **to** en contra de. ● adj opuesto. ● vt oponerse a; parar (blow)

counter... /'kaʊntə(r)/ pref contra.... ~**act** /-'ækt/ vt contrarrestar. ~**-attack** n contraataque m. ● vt/i contraatacar. ~**balance** n contrapeso m. ● vt/i contrapesar. ~**clockwise** /-'klɒkwaɪz/ a/adv (Amer) en sentido contrario al de las agujas del reloj

counterfeit /'kaʊntəfɪt/ adj falsificado. ● n falsificación f. ● vt falsificar

counterfoil /'kaʊntəfɔɪl/ n matriz f, talón m (LAm)

counter-productive /kaʊntəprə'dʌktɪv/ adj contraproducente

countess /'kaʊntɪs/ n condesa f

countless /'kaʊntlɪs/ adj innumerable

country /'kʌntrɪ/ n (native land) país m; (countryside) campo m; (Mus) (música f) country m. ~**-and-western** /-en'westən/ (música f) country m. ~**man** /-mən/ n (of one's own country) compatriota m. ~**side** n campo m; (landscape) paisaje m

county /'kaʊntɪ/ n condado m

coup /kuː/ n golpe m

couple /'kʌpl/ n (of things) par m; (of people) pareja f; (married) matrimonio m. **a ~ of** un par de

coupon /'kuːpɒn/ n cupón m

courage /'kʌrɪdʒ/ n valor m. **~ous** /kə'reɪdʒəs/ adj valiente

courgette /kʊə'ʒet/ n calabacín m

courier /'kʊrɪə(r)/ n mensajero m; (for tourists) guía m & f

course /kɔːs/ n curso m; (behaviour) conducta f; (in navigation) rumbo m; (Culin) plato m; (for golf) campo m. **in due ~** a su debido tiempo. **in the ~ of** en el transcurso de, durante. **of ~** claro, por supuesto. **of ~ not** claro que no, por supuesto que no

court /kɔːt/ n corte f; (tennis) pista f; cancha f (LAm); (Jurid) tribunal m. ● vt cortejar; buscar (danger)

courteous /'kɜːtɪəs/ adj cortés

courtesy /'kɜːtəsɪ/ n cortesía f

courtier /'kɔːtɪə(r)/ n (old use) cortesano m

court: **~ martial** n (pl **~s martial**) consejo m de guerra. **-martial** vt (pt **~ martialled**) juzgar en consejo de guerra. **~ship** n cortejo m. **~yard** n patio m

cousin /'kʌzn/ n primo m. **first ~** primo carnal. **second ~** primo segundo

cove /kəʊv/ n ensenada f, cala f

Coventry /'kɒvntrɪ/ n. **send s.o. to ~** hacer el vacío a uno

cover /'kʌvə(r)/ vt cubrir. ● n cubierta f; (shelter) abrigo m; (lid) tapa f; (for furniture) funda f; (pretext) pretexto m; (of magazine) portada f. □ **~ up** vt cubrir; (fig) ocultar. **~age** n cobertura f. **~ charge** n precio m del cubierto. **~ing** n cubierta f. **~ing letter** n carta f adjunta

covet /'kʌvɪt/ vt codiciar

cow /kaʊ/ n vaca f

coward /'kaʊəd/ n cobarde m. **~ice** /'kaʊədɪs/ n cobardía f. **~ly** adj cobarde.

cowboy /'kaʊbɔɪ/ n vaquero m

cower /'kaʊə(r)/ vi encogerse, acobardarse

coxswain /'kɒksn/ n timonel m

coy /kɔɪ/ adj (-er, -est) (shy) tímido; (evasive) evasivo

crab /kræb/ n cangrejo m, jaiba f (LAm)

crack /kræk/ n grieta f; (noise) crujido m; (of whip) chasquido m; (drug) crack m. ● adj 🅄 de primera. ● vt agrietar; chasquear (whip, fingers); cascar (nut); gastar (joke); resolver (problem). ● vi agrietarse. **get ~ing** 🅄 darse prisa. □ **~ down on** vt 🅄 tomar medidas enérgicas contra

cracker /'krækə(r)/ n (Culin) cracker f, galleta f (salada); (Christmas cracker) sorpresa f (que estalla al abrirla)

crackle /'krækl/ vi crepitar. ● n crepitación f, crujido m

crackpot /'krækpɒt/ n 🅄 chiflado m

cradle /'kreɪdl/ n cuna f. ● vt acunar

craft /krɑːft/ n destreza f; (technique) arte f; (cunning) astucia f. ● n invar (boat) barco m

craftsman /'krɑːftsmən/ n (pl **-men**) artesano m. **~ship** n artesanía f

crafty /'krɑːftɪ/ adj (-ier, -iest) astuto

cram /kræm/ vt (pt **crammed**) rellenar. **~ with** llenar de. ● vi (for exams) memorizar, empollar 🅴, zambutir (Mex)

cramp /kræmp/ n calambre m

cramped /kræmpt/ adj apretado

crane /kreɪn/ n grúa f. ● vt estirar (neck)

crank /kræŋk/ n manivela f; (person) excéntrico m. **~y** adj excéntrico

cranny /'krænɪ/ n grieta f

crash /kræʃ/ n accidente m; (noise) estruendo m; (collision) choque m; (Com) quiebra f. ● vt estrellar. ● vi quebrar con estrépito; (have accident) tener un accidente; (car etc) estrellarse, chocar; (fail) fracasar. **~ course** n curso m intensivo. **~ helmet** n casco m protector. **~-land** vi hacer un aterrizaje forzoso

crass /kræs/ adj craso, burdo

crate /kreɪt/ n cajón m. ● vt embalar

crater /'kreɪtə(r)/ n cráter m

crav|e /kreɪv/ vt ansiar. **~ing** n ansia f

crawl /krɔːl/ vi (baby) gatear; (move slowly) avanzar lentamente; (drag o.s.)

arrastrarse. ~ to humillarse ante. ~ with hervir de. ●n (*swimming*) crol *m*. at a ~ a paso lento

crayon /'kreɪən/ n lápiz *m* de color; (*made of wax*) lápiz *m* de cera, crayola *f* (®), crayón *m* (*Mex*)

craz|e /kreɪz/ n manía *f*. ~**y** /'kreɪzɪ/ adj (-**ier**, -**iest**) loco. **be ~y about** estar loco por

creak /kriːk/ n crujido *m*; (*of hinge*) chirrido *m*. ●vi crujir; (hinge) chirriar

cream /kriːm/ n crema *f*; (*fresh*) nata *f*, crema *f* (*LAm*). ●adj (*colour*) color crema. ●vt (*beat*) batir. ~ **cheese** n queso *m* para untar, queso *m* crema (*LAm*). ~**y** adj cremoso

crease /kriːs/ n raya *f*, pliegue *m* (*Mex*); (*crumple*) arruga *f*. ●vt plegar; (*wrinkle*) arrugar. ●vi arrugarse

creat|e /kriːˈeɪt/ vt crear. ~**ion** /-ˈʃn/ n creación *f*. ~**ive** adj creativo. ~**or** n creador *m*

creature /'kriːtʃə(r)/ n criatura *f*

crèche /kreʃ/ n guardería *f* (infantil)

credib|ility /kredəˈbɪlətɪ/ n credibilidad *f*. ~**le** /'kredəbl/ adj creíble

credit /'kredɪt/ n crédito *m*; (*honour*) mérito *m*. **take the ~ for** atribuirse el mérito de. ●vt (*pt* **credited**) acreditar; (*believe*) creer. ~ **s.o. with** atribuir a uno. ~ **card** n tarjeta *f* de crédito. ~**or** n acreedor *m*

creed /kriːd/ n credo *m*

creek /kriːk/ n ensenada *f*. **up the ~** 🅰 en apuros

creep /kriːp/ vi (*pt* **crept**) arrastrarse; (*plant*) trepar. ●n 🅰 adulador. ~**s** /kriːps/ npl. **give s.o. the ~s** poner los pelos de punta a uno. ~**er** n enredadera *f*

cremat|e /krɪˈmeɪt/ vt incinerar. ~**ion** /-ˈʃn/ n cremación *f*. ~**orium** /kremə'tɔːrɪəm/ n (*pl* -**ia** /-ɪə/) crematorio *m*

crept /krept/ *see* **CREEP**

crescendo /krɪˈʃendəʊ/ n (*pl* -**os**) crescendo *m*

crescent /'kresnt/ n media luna *f*; (*street*) calle *f* en forma de media luna

crest /krest/ n cresta *f*; (*on coat of arms*) emblema *m*

crevice /'krevɪs/ n grieta *f*

crew /kruː/ n tripulación *f*; (*gang*) pandilla *f*. ~ **cut** n corte *m* al rape

crib /krɪb/ n (*Amer*) cuna *f*; (*Relig*) belén *m*. ●vt/i (*pt* **cribbed**) copiar

crick /krɪk/ n calambre *m*; (*in neck*) tortícolis *f*

cricket /'krɪkɪt/ n (*Sport*) críquet *m*; (*insect*) grillo *m*

crim|e /kraɪm/ n delito *m*; (*murder*) crimen *m*; (*acts*) delincuencia *f*. ~**inal** /'krɪmɪnl/ adj & n criminal (*m & f*)

crimson /'krɪmzn/ adj & n carmesí (*m*)

cringe /krɪndʒ/ vi encogerse; (*fig*) humillarse

crinkle /'krɪŋkl/ vt arrugar. ●vi arrugarse. ●n arruga *f*

cripple /'krɪpl/ n lisiado *m*. ●vt lisiar; (*fig*) paralizar

crisis /'kraɪsɪs/ n (*pl* **crises** /-siːz/) crisis *f*

crisp /krɪsp/ adj (-**er**, -**est**) (*Culin*) crujiente; (air) vigorizador. ~**s** npl patatas *fpl* fritas, papas *fpl* fritas (*LAm*) (*de bolsa*)

crisscross /'krɪskrɒs/ adj entrecruzado. ●vt entrecruzar. ●vi entrecruzarse

criterion /kraɪˈtɪərɪən/ n (*pl* -**ia** /-ɪə/) criterio *m*

critic /'krɪtɪk/ n crítico *m*. ~**al** adj crítico. ~**ally** adv críticamente; (*ill*) gravemente

critici|sm /'krɪtɪsɪzəm/ n crítica *f*. ~**ze** /'krɪtɪsaɪz/ vt/i criticar

croak /krəʊk/ n (*of person*) gruñido *m*; (*of frog*) canto *m*. ●vi gruñir; (frog) croar

Croat /'krəʊæt/ n croata *m & f*. ~**ia** /krəʊˈeɪʃə/ n Croacia *f*. ~**ian** adj croata

crochet /'krəʊʃeɪ/ n crochet *m*, ganchillo *m*. ●vt tejer a crochet or a ganchillo

crockery /'krɒkərɪ/ n loza *f*

crocodile /'krɒkədaɪl/ n cocodrilo *m*. ~ **tears** npl lágrimas *fpl* de cocodrilo

crocus /'krəʊkəs/ n (*pl* -**es**) azafrán *m* de primavera

crook /krʊk/ n 🅰 sinvergüenza *m & f*. ~**ed** /'krʊkɪd/ adj torcido, chueco

(*LAm*); (*winding*) tortuoso; (*dishonest*) deshonesto

crop /krɒp/ n cosecha f; (*haircut*) corte m de pelo muy corto. ● vt (*pt* **cropped**) cortar. □ ~ **up** vi surgir

croquet /ˈkrəʊkeɪ/ n croquet m

cross /krɒs/ n cruz f; (*of animals*) cruce m. ● vt cruzar; (*oppose*) contrariar. ~ **s.o.'s mind** ocurrírsele a uno. ● vi cruzar. ~ **o.s.** santiguarse. ● adj enfadado, enojado (*esp LAm*). □ ~ **out** vt tachar. ~**bar** n travesaño m. ~**-examine** /-ɪgˈzæmɪn/ vt interrogar. ~**-eyed** adj bizco. ~**fire** n fuego m cruzado. ~**ing** n (*by boat*) travesía f; (*on road*) cruce m peatonal. ~**ly** adv con enfado, con enojo (*esp LAm*). ~**-purposes** /-ˈpɜːpəsɪz/ npl. **talk at** ~**-purposes** hablar sin entenderse. ~**-reference** /-ˈrefrəns/ n remisión f. ~**roads** n invar cruce m. ~**-section** /-ˈsekʃn/ n sección f transversal; (*fig*) muestra f representativa. ~**walk** n (*Amer*) paso de peatones. ~**word** n ~**word (puzzle)** crucigrama m

crotch /krɒtʃ/ n entrepiernas fpl

crouch /kraʊtʃ/ vi agacharse

crow /krəʊ/ n cuervo m. **as the** ~ **flies** en línea recta. ● vi cacarear. ~**bar** n palanca f

crowd /kraʊd/ n muchedumbre f. ● vt amontonar; (*fill*) llenar. ● vi amontonarse; (*gather*) reunirse. ~**ed** adj atestado

crown /kraʊn/ n corona f; (*of hill*) cumbre f; (*of head*) coronilla f. ● vt coronar

crucial /ˈkruːʃl/ adj crucial

crucifix /ˈkruːsɪfɪks/ n crucifijo m. ~**ion** /-ˈfɪkʃn/ n crucifixión f

crucify /ˈkruːsɪfaɪ/ vt crucificar

crude /kruːd/ adj (**-er, -est**) (*raw*) crudo; (*rough*) tosco; (*vulgar*) ordinario

cruel /ˈkruːəl/ adj (**crueller, cruellest**) cruel. ~**ty** n crueldad f

cruet /ˈkruːɪt/ n vinagrera f

cruise /kruːz/ n crucero m. ● vi hacer un crucero; (*of car*) circular lentamente. ~**r** n crucero m

crumb /krʌm/ n miga f

crumble /ˈkrʌmbl/ vt desmenuzar. ● vi desmenuzarse; (*collapse*) derrumbarse

crummy /ˈkrʌmɪ/ adj (**-ier, -iest**) ⊠ miserable

crumpet /ˈkrʌmpɪt/ n bollo m blando

crumple /ˈkrʌmpl/ vt arrugar. ● vi arrugarse

crunch /krʌntʃ/ vt hacer crujir; (*bite*) masticar. ~**y** adj crujiente

crusade /kruːˈseɪd/ n cruzada f. ~**r** n cruzado m

crush /krʌʃ/ vt aplastar; arrugar (*clothes*). ● n (*crowd*) aglomeración f. **have a** ~ **on** 🄸 estar chiflado por

crust /krʌst/ n corteza f. ~**y** adj (*bread*) de corteza dura

crutch /krʌtʃ/ n muleta f; (*between legs*) entrepiernas fpl

crux /krʌks/ n (*pl* **cruxes**). **the** ~ (*of the matter*) el quid (de la cuestión)

cry /kraɪ/ n grito m. **be a far** ~ **from** (*fig*) distar mucho de. ● vi llorar; (*call out*) gritar. □ ~ **off** vi echarse atrás, rajarse. ~**baby** n llorón m

crypt /krɪpt/ n cripta f

cryptic /ˈkrɪptɪk/ adj enigmático

crystal /ˈkrɪstl/ n cristal m. ~**lize** vi cristalizarse

cub /kʌb/ n cachorro m. **C**~ (**Scout**) n lobato m

Cuba /ˈkjuːbə/ n Cuba f. ~**n** adj & n cubano (m)

cubbyhole /ˈkʌbɪhəʊl/ n cuchitril m

cub|e /kjuːb/ n cubo m. ~**ic** adj cúbico

cubicle /ˈkjuːbɪkl/ n cubículo m; (*changing room*) probador m

cuckoo /ˈkʊkuː/ n cuco m, cuclillo m

cucumber /ˈkjuːkʌmbə(r)/ n pepino m

cuddl|e /ˈkʌdl/ vt abrazar. ● vi abrazarse. ● n abrazo m. ~**y** adj adorable

cue /kjuː/ n (*Mus*) entrada f; (*in theatre*) pie m; (*in snooker*) taco m

cuff /kʌf/ n puño m; (*Amer, of trousers*) vuelta f, dobladillo m; (*blow*) bofetada f. **speak off the** ~ hablar de improviso. ● vt abofetear. ~**link** n gemelo m, mancuerna f (*Mex*)

cul-de-sac /ˈkʌldəsæk/ n callejón m sin salida

culinary /ˈkʌlɪnərɪ/ adj culinario

cull /kʌl/ vt sacrificar en forma selectiva (*animals*)

culminat|e /'kʌlmɪneɪt/ vi culminar. **~ion** /-'neɪʃn/ n culminación f

culprit /'kʌlprɪt/ n culpable m & f

cult /kʌlt/ n culto m

cultivat|e /'kʌltɪveɪt/ vt cultivar. **~ion** /-'veɪʃn/ n cultivo m

cultur|al /'kʌltʃərəl/ adj cultural. **~e** /'kʌltʃə(r)/ n cultura f; (Bot etc) cultivo m. **~ed** adj cultivado; (person) culto

cumbersome /'kʌmbəsəm/ adj incómodo; (heavy) pesado

cunning /'kʌnɪŋ/ adj astuto. **●**n astucia f

cup /kʌp/ n taza f; (trophy) copa f

cupboard /'kʌbəd/ n armario m

curator /kjʊə'reɪtə(r)/ n (of museum) conservador m

curb /kɜːb/ n freno m; (Amer) bordillo m (de la acera), borde m de la banqueta (Mex). **●**vt refrenar

curdle /'kɜːdl/ vt cuajar. **●**vi cuajarse; (go bad) cortarse

cure /kjʊə(r)/ vt curar. **●**n cura f

curfew /'kɜːfjuː/ n toque m de queda

curio|sity /kjʊərɪ'ɒsəti/ n curiosidad f. **~us** /'kjʊərɪəs/ adj curioso

curl /kɜːl/ vt rizar, enchinar (Mex). **~ o.s. up** acurrucarse. **●**vi (hair) rizarse, enchinarse (Mex); (paper) ondularse. **●**n rizo m, chino m (Mex). **~er** n rulo m, chino m (Mex). **~y** adj (-ier, -iest) rizado, chino (Mex)

currant /'kʌrənt/ n pasa f de Corinto

currency /'kʌrənsi/ n moneda f

current /'kʌrənt/ adj & n corriente (f); (existing) actual. **~ affairs** npl sucesos de actualidad. **~ly** adv actualmente

curriculum /kə'rɪkjʊləm/ n (pl **-la**) programa m de estudios. **~ vitae** n currículum m vitae

curry /'kʌri/ n curry m. **●**vt preparar al curry

curse /kɜːs/ n maldición f; (oath) palabrota f. **●**vt maldecir. **●**vi decir palabrotas

cursory /'kɜːsəri/ adj superficial

curt /kɜːt/ adj brusco

curtain /'kɜːtn/ n cortina f; (in theatre) telón m

curtsey, curtsy /'kɜːtsɪ/ n reverencia f. **●**vi hacer una reverencia

curve /kɜːv/ n curva f. **●**vi estar curvado; (road) torcerse

cushion /'kʊʃn/ n cojín m, almohadón m

cushy /'kʊʃɪ/ adj (-ier, -iest) 🄳 fácil

custard /'kʌstəd/ n natillas fpl

custody /'kʌstədɪ/ n custodia f; **be in ~** Jurid estar detenido

custom /'kʌstəm/ n costumbre f; (Com) clientela f. **~ary** /-əri/ adj acostumbrado. **~er** n cliente m. **~s** npl aduana f. **~s officer** n aduanero m

cut /kʌt/ vt/i (pt cut, pres p cutting) cortar; reducir (prices). **●**n corte m; (reduction) reducción f. □ **~ across** vt cortar camino por. □ **~ back, ~ down** vt reducir. □ **~ in** vi interrumpir. □ **~ off** vt cortar; (phone) desconectar; (fig) aislar. □ **~ out** vt recortar; (omit) suprimir. □ **~ through** vt cortar camino por. □ **~ up** vt cortar en pedazos

cute /kjuːt/ adj (-er, -est) 🄳 mono, amoroso (LAm); (Amer, attractive) guapo, buen mozo (LAm)

cutlery /'kʌtləri/ n cubiertos mpl

cutlet /'kʌtlɪt/ n chuleta f

cut ~-price, (Amer) **~-rate** adj a precio reducido. **●**n corte **~-throat** adj despiadado. **~ting** adj cortante; (remark) mordaz. **●**n (from newspaper) recorte m; (of plant) esqueje m

CV n (= **curriculum vitae**) currículum m (vitae)

cyberspace /'saɪbəspeɪs/ ciberespacio m

cycl|e /'saɪkl/ n ciclo m; (bicycle) bicicleta f. **●**vi ir en bicicleta. **~ing** n ciclismo m. **~ist** n ciclista m & f

cylind|er /'sɪlɪmdə(r)/ n cilindro m. **~er head** (Auto) n culata f. **~rical** /-'lɪndrɪkl/ adj cilíndrico

cymbal /'sɪmbl/ n címbalo m

cynic /'sɪnɪk/ n cínico m. **~al** adj cínico. **~ism** /-sɪzəm/ n cinismo m

Czech /tʃek/ adj & n checo (m). **~oslovakia** /-əslə'vækɪə/ n (History) Checoslovaquia f. **~ Republic** n. **the ~ Republic** n la República Checa

Dd

dab /dæb/ vt (pt **dabbed**) tocar ligeramente. ●n toque m suave. **a ~ of** un poquito de

dad /dæd/ n 🔲 papá m. **~dy** n papi m. **~dy-long-legs** n invar (cranefly) típula f; (Amer, harvestman) segador m, falangio m

daffodil /'dæfədɪl/ n narciso m

daft /dɑːft/ adj (**-er, -est**) 🔲 tonto

dagger /'dægə(r)/ n daga f, puñal m

daily /'deɪlɪ/ adj diario. ●adv diariamente, cada día

> **Dáil Éireann** Es el nombre de la cámara baja del Parlamento de la República de Irlanda. Se pronuncia /dɔɪl/ y consta de 166 representantes o diputados, comúnmente llamados TDs, que representan 41 circunscripciones. Se eligen por medio del sistema de representación proporcional. Según la Constitución debe haber un diputado por cada 20.000 a 30.000 personas.

dainty /'deɪntɪ/ adj (**-ier, -iest**) delicado

dairy /'deərɪ/ n vaquería f; (shop) lechería f

daisy /'deɪzɪ/ n margarita f

dam /dæm/ n presa f, represa f (LAm)

damage /'dæmɪdʒ/ n daño m; **~s** (npl, Jurid) daños mpl y perjuicios mpl. ●vt (fig) dañar, estropear. **~ing** adj perjudicial

dame /deɪm/ n (old use) dama f; (Amer, sl) chica f

damn /dæm/ vt condenar; (curse) maldecir. ●int 🔲 ¡caray! 🔲. ●adj maldito. ●n **I don't give a ~** (no) me importa un comino

damp /dæmp/ n humedad f. ●adj (**-er, -est**) húmedo. ●vt mojar. **~ness** n humedad f

dance /dɑːns/ vt/i bailar. ●n baile m. **~e hall** n salón m de baile. **~er** n

bailador m; (professional) bailarín m. **~ing** n baile m

dandelion /'dændɪlaɪən/ n diente m de león

dandruff /'dændrʌf/ n caspa f

dandy /'dændɪ/ n petimetre m

Dane /deɪn/ n danés m

danger /'deɪndʒə(r)/ n peligro m; (risk) riesgo m. **~ous** adj peligroso

dangle /'dæŋgl/ vt balancear. ●vi suspender, colgar

Danish /'deɪnɪʃ/ adj danés. ●m (language) danés m

dar|e /deə(r)/ vt desafiar. ●vi atreverse a. **I ~ say** probablemente. ●n desafío m. **~edevil** n atrevido m, **~ing** adj atrevido

dark /dɑːk/ adj (**-er, -est**) oscuro; (skin, hair) moreno. ●n oscuridad f; (nightfall) atardecer. **in the ~** a oscuras. **~en** vt oscurecer. ●vi oscurecerse. **~ness** n oscuridad f. **~room** n cámara f oscura

darling /'dɑːlɪŋ/ adj querido. ●n cariño m

darn /dɑːn/ vt zurcir

dart /dɑːt/ n dardo m. ●vi lanzarse; (run) precipitarse. **~board** n diana f. **~s** npl los dardos mpl

dash /dæʃ/ vi precipitarse. ●vt tirar; (break) romper; defraudar (hopes). ●n (small amount) poquito m; (punctuation mark) guión m. □ **~ off** vi marcharse apresuradamente. **~ out** vi salir corriendo. **~board** n tablero m de mandos

data /'deɪtə/ npl datos mpl. **~base** n base f de datos. **~ processing** n proceso m de datos

date /deɪt/ n fecha f; (appointment) cita f; (fruit) dátil m. **to ~** hasta la fecha. ●vt fechar. ●vi datar; datar (remains); (be old-fashioned) quedar anticuado. **~d** adj pasado de moda

daub /dɔːb/ vt embadurnar

daughter /'dɔːtə(r)/ n hija f. **~-in-law** n nuera f

dawdle /'dɔːdl/ vi andar despacio; (waste time) perder el tiempo

dawn /dɔːn/ n amanecer m. ●vi amanecer; (fig) nacer. **it ~ed on me that** caí en la cuenta de que

d

day /deɪ/ n día m; (*whole day*) jornada f; (*period*) época f. **~break** n amanecer m. **~ care center** n (*Amer*) guardería f infantil. **~dream** n ensueño m. ● vi soñar despierto. **~light** n luz f del día. **~time** n día m

daze /deɪz/ vt aturdir. ● n aturdimiento m. **in a ~** aturdido. **~d** adj aturdido

dazzle /'dæzl/ vt deslumbrar

dead /ded/ adj muerto; (*numb*) dormido. ● adv justo; (🆒, *completely*) completamente. **~ beat** rendido. **~ slow** muy lento. **stop ~** parar en seco. **~en** vt amortiguar (sound, blow); calmar (pain). **~ end** n callejón m sin salida. **~line** n fecha f tope, plazo m de entrega. **~lock** n punto m muerto. **~ly** adj (**-ier**, **-iest**) mortal

deaf /def/ adj (**-er**, **-est**) sordo. **~en** vt ensordecer. **~ness** n sordera f

deal /diːl/ n (*agreement*) acuerdo m; (*treatment*) trato m. **a good ~** bastante. **a great ~ (of)** muchísimo. ● vt (*pt* **dealt**) dar (a blow, cards). ● vi (*cards*) dar, repartir. □ **~ in** vt comerciar en. □ **~ out** vt repartir, distribuir. □ **~ with** vt tratar con (person); tratar de (subject); ocuparse de (problem). **~er** n comerciante m. **drug ~er** traficante m & f de drogas

dean /diːn/ n deán m; (*Univ*) decano m

dear /dɪə(r)/ adj (**-er**, **-est**) querido; (*expensive*) caro. ● n querido m. ● adv caro. ● int **oh ~!** ¡ay por Dios! **~ me!** ¡Dios mío! **~ly** adv (*pay*) caro; (*very much*) muchísimo

death /deθ/ n muerte f. **~ sentence** n pena f de muerte. **~ trap** n lugar m peligroso.

debat|able /dɪ'beɪtəbl/ adj discutible. **~e** /dɪ'beɪt/ n debate m. ● vt debatir, discutir

debauchery /dɪ'bɔːtʃərɪ/ vt libertinaje m

debit /'debɪt/ n débito m. ● vt debitar, cargar. **~ card** n tarjeta f de cobro automático

debris /'debriː/ n escombros mpl

debt /det/ n deuda f. **be in ~** tener deudas. **~or** n deudor m

debut /'debjuː/ n debut m

decade /'dekeɪd/ n década f

decaden|ce /'dekədəns/ n decadencia f. **~t** adj decadente

decay /dɪ'keɪ/ vi descomponerse; (tooth) cariarse. ● n descomposición f; (*of tooth*) caries f

deceased /dɪ'siːst/ adj difunto

deceit /dɪ'siːt/ n engaño m. **~ful** adj falso. **~fully** adv falsamente

deceive /dɪ'siːv/ vt engañar

December /dɪ'sembə(r)/ n diciembre m

decen|cy /'diːsənsɪ/ n decencia f. **~t** adj decente; (*fam*, good) bueno; (*fam*, kind) amable. **~tly** adv decentemente

decepti|on /dɪ'sepʃn/ n engaño m. **~ve** /-tɪv/ adj engañoso

decibel /'desɪbel/ n decibel(io) m

decide /dɪ'saɪd/ vt/i decidir. **~d** adj resuelto; (*unquestionable*) indudable

decimal /'desɪml/ adj & n decimal (m). **~ point** n coma f (decimal), punto m decimal

decipher /dɪ'saɪfə(r)/ vt descifrar

decis|ion /dɪ'sɪʒn/ n decisión f. **~ive** /dɪ'saɪsɪv/ adj decisivo; (*manner*) decidido

deck /dek/ n (*Naut*) cubierta f; (*Amer*, of cards) baraja f; (*of bus*) piso m. ● vt adornar. **~chair** n tumbona f, silla f de playa

declar|ation /deklə'reɪʃn/ n declaración f. **~e** /dɪ'kleə(r)/ vt declarar

decline /dɪ'klaɪn/ vt rehusar; (*Gram*) declinar. ● vi disminuir; (*deteriorate*) deteriorarse. ● n decadencia f; (*decrease*) disminución f

decode /diː'kəʊd/ vt descifrar

decompose /diːkəm'pəʊz/ vi descomponerse

décor /'deɪkɔː(r)/ n decoración f

decorat|e /'dekəreɪt/ vt adornar, decorar (*LAm*); empapelar y pintar (room). **~ion** /-'reɪʃn/ n (*act*) decoración f; (*ornament*) adorno m. **~ive** /-ətɪv/ adj decorativo. **~or** n pintor m decorador

decoy /'diːkɔɪ/ n señuelo m. ● /dɪ'kɔɪ/ vt atraer con señuelo

decrease /dɪ'kriːs/ vt/i disminuir. ● /'diːkriːs/ n disminución f

decree /dɪ'kriː/ n decreto m. ● vt decretar

decrepit /dɪˈkrepɪt/ adj decrépito

decriminalize /diːˈkrɪmɪnəlaɪz/ vt despenalizar

dedicat|e /ˈdedɪkeɪt/ vt dedicar. ~**ion** /-ˈkeɪʃn/ n dedicación f

deduce /dɪˈdjuːs/ vt deducir

deduct /dɪˈdʌkt/ vt deducir. ~**ion** /-ʃn/ n deducción f

deed /diːd/ n hecho m; (Jurid) escritura f

deem /diːm/ vt juzgar, considerar

deep /diːp/ adj (-er, -est) adv profundo. ● adv profundamente. **be ~ in thought** estar absorto en sus pensamientos. ~**en** vt hacer más profundo. ● vi hacerse más profundo. ~**freeze** n congelador m, freezer m (LAm). ~**ly** adv profundamente

deer /dɪə(r)/ n invar ciervo m

deface /dɪˈfeɪs/ vt desfigurar

default /dɪˈfɔːlt/ vi faltar. ● n opción por defecto. **by ~** en rebeldía

defeat /dɪˈfiːt/ vt vencer; (frustrate) frustrar. ● n derrota f. ~**ism** n derrotismo m. ~**ist** n derrotista a & (m & f)

defect /ˈdiːfekt/ n defecto m. ● /dɪˈfekt/ vi desertar. **~ to** pasar a. ~**ion** /dɪˈfekʃn/ n (Pol) defección f. ~**ive** /dɪˈfektɪv/ adj defectuoso

defence /dɪˈfens/ n defensa f. ~**less** adj indefenso

deten|d /dɪˈfend/ vt defender. ~**dant** n (Jurid) acusado m. ~**sive** /-sɪv/ adj defensivo. ● n defensiva f

defer /dɪˈfɜː(r)/ vt (pt deferred) aplazar. ~**ence** /ˈdefərəns/ n deferencia f. ~**ential** /defəˈrenʃl/ adj deferente

defian|ce /dɪˈfaɪəns/ n desafío m. **in ~ce of** a despecho de. ~**t** adj desafiante. ~**tly** adv con actitud desafiante

deficien|cy /dɪˈfɪʃənsɪ/ n falta f. ~**t** adj deficiente. **be ~t in** carecer de

deficit /ˈdefɪsɪt/ n déficit m

define /dɪˈfaɪn/ vt definir

definite /ˈdefɪnɪt/ adj (final) definitivo; (certain) seguro; (clear) claro; (firm) firme. ~**ly** adv seguramente; (definitively) definitivamente

definition /defɪˈnɪʃn/ n definición f

definitive /dɪˈfɪnətɪv/ adj definitivo

deflate /dɪˈfleɪt/ vt desinflar. ● vi desinflarse

deflect /dɪˈflekt/ vt desviar

deform /dɪˈfɔːm/ vt deformar. ~**ed** adj deforme. ~**ity** n deformidad f

defrost /diːˈfrɒst/ vt descongelar. ● vi descongelarse

deft /deft/ adj (-er, -est) hábil. ~**ly** adv hábilmente f

defuse /diːˈfjuːz/ vt desactivar (bomb); (fig) calmar

defy /dɪˈfaɪ/ vt desafiar

degenerate /dɪˈdʒenəreɪt/ vi degenerar. ● /dɪˈdʒenərət/ adj & n degenerado (m)

degrad|ation /degrəˈdeɪʃn/ n degradación f. ~**e** /dɪˈɡreɪd/ vt degradar

degree /dɪˈɡriː/ n grado m; (Univ) licenciatura f; (rank) rango m. **to a certain ~** hasta cierto punto

deign /deɪn/ vi. **~ to** dignarse

deity /ˈdiːɪtɪ/ n deidad f

deject|ed /dɪˈdʒektɪd/ adj desanimado. ~**ion** /-ʃn/ n abatimiento m

delay /dɪˈleɪ/ vt retrasar, demorar (LAm). ● vi tardar, demorar (LAm). ● n retraso m, demora f (LAm)

delegat|e /ˈdelɪɡeɪt/ vt/i delegar. ● /ˈdelɪɡət/ n delegado m. ~**ion** /-ˈɡeɪʃn/ n delegación f

delet|e /dɪˈliːt/ vt tachar. ~**ion** /-ʃn/ n supresión f

deliberat|e /dɪˈlɪbəreɪt/ vt/i deliberar. ● /dɪˈlɪbərət/ adj intencionado; (steps etc) pausado. ~**ely** adv a proposito. ~**ion** /-ˈreɪʃn/ n deliberación f

delica|cy /ˈdelɪkəsɪ/ n delicadeza f; (food) manjar m. ~**te** /ˈdelɪkət/ adj delicado

delicatessen /delɪkəˈtesn/ n charcutería f, salchichonería f (Mex)

delicious /dɪˈlɪʃəs/ adj delicioso

delight /dɪˈlaɪt/ n placer m. ● vt encantar. ● vi deleitarse. ~**ed** adj encantado. ~**ful** adj delicioso

deliri|ous /dɪˈlɪrɪəs/ adj delirante. ~**um** /-əm/ n delirio m

deliver /dɪˈlɪvə(r)/ vt entregar; (distribute) repartir; (aim) lanzar; (Med) **he ~ed the baby** la asistió en el parto. ~**ance** n liberación f. ~**y** n entrega f; (of post) reparto m; (Med) parto m

d

delta /'deltə/ n (of river) delta m

delude /dɪ'lu:d/ vt engañar. **~ o.s.** engañarse

deluge /'delju:dʒ/ n diluvio m

delusion /dɪ'lu:ʒn/ n ilusión f

deluxe /dɪ'lʌks/ adj de lujo

delve /delv/ vi hurgar. **~ into** (investigate) ahondar en

demand /dɪ'mɑ:nd/ vt exigir. ●n petición f, pedido m (LAm); (claim) exigencia f; (Com) demanda f. **in ~** muy popular, muy solicitado. **on ~** a solicitud. **~ing** adj exigente. **~s** npl exigencias fpl

demented /dɪ'mentɪd/ adj demente

demo /'deməʊ/ n (pl **-os**) 🅐 manifestación f

democra|cy /dɪ'mɒkrəsɪ/ n democracia f. **~t** /'deməkræt/ n demócrata m & f. **D~t** a & n (in US) demócrata (m & f). **~tic** /demə'krætɪk/ adj democrático

demoli|sh /dɪ'mɒlɪʃ/ vt derribar. **~tion** /demə'lɪʃn/ n demolición f

demon /'di:mən/ n demonio m

demonstrat|e /'demənstreɪt/ vt demostrar. ●vi manifestarse, hacer una manifestación. **~ion** /-'streɪʃn/ n demostración f; (Pol) manifestación f. **~or** /'demənstreɪtə(r)/n (Pol) manifestante m & f; (marketing) demostrador m

demoralize /dɪ'mɒrəlaɪz/ vt desmoralizar

demote /dɪ'məʊt/ vt bajar de categoría

demure /dɪ'mjʊə(r)/ adj recatado

den /den/ n (of animal) guarida f, madriguera f

denial /dɪ'naɪəl/ n denegación f; (statement) desmentimiento m

denim /'denɪm/ n tela f vaquera or de jeans, mezclilla (Mex) f. **~s** npl vaqueros mpl, jeans mpl, tejanos mpl, pantalones mpl de mezclilla (Mex)

Denmark /'denmɑ:k/ n Dinamarca f

denote /dɪ'nəʊt/ vt denotar

denounce /dɪ'naʊns/ vt denunciar

dens|e /dens/ adj (**-er, -est**) espeso; (person) torpe. **~ely** adv densamente. **~ity** n densidad f

dent /dent/ n abolladura f. ●vt abollar

dental /'dentl/ adj dental. **~ floss** /flɒs/ n hilo m or seda f dental. **~ surgeon** n dentista m & f

dentist /'dentɪst/ n dentista m & f. **~ry** n odontología f

dentures /'dentʃəz/ npl dentadura f postiza

deny /dɪ'naɪ/ vt negar; desmentir (rumour); denegar (request)

deodorant /dɪ'əʊdərənt/ adj & n desodorante (m)

depart /dɪ'pɑ:t/ vi partir, salir. **~ from** (deviate from) apartarse de

department /dɪ'pɑ:tment/ n departamento m; (Pol) ministerio m, secretaría f (Mex). **~ store** n grandes almacenes mpl, tienda f de departamentos (Mex)

departure /dɪ'pɑ:tʃə(r)/ n partida f; (of train etc) salida f

depend /dɪ'pend/ vi depender. **~ on** depender de. **~able** adj digno de confianza. **~ant** /dɪ'pendənt/ n familiar m & f dependiente. **~ence** n dependencia f. **~ent** adj dependiente. **be ~ent on** depender de

depict /dɪ'pɪkt/ vt representar; (in words) describir

deplete /dɪ'pli:t/ vt agotar

deplor|able /dɪ'plɔ:rəbl/ adj deplorable. **~e** /dɪ'plɔ:(r)/ vt deplorar

deploy /dɪ'plɔɪ/ vt desplegar

deport /dɪ'pɔ:t/ vt deportar. **~ation** /-'teɪʃn/ n deportación f

depose /dɪ'pəʊz/ vt deponer

deposit /dɪ'pɒzɪt/ vt (pt **deposited**) depositar. ●n depósito m

depot /'depəʊ/ n depósito m; (Amer) estación f de autobuses

deprav|ed /dɪ'preɪvd/ adj depravado. **~ity** /dɪ'prævətɪ/ n depravación f

depress /dɪ'pres/ vt deprimir; (press down) apretar. **~ed** adj deprimido. **~ing** adj deprimente. **~ion** /-ʃn/ n depresión f

depriv|ation /deprɪ'veɪʃn/ n privación f. **~e** /dɪ'praɪv/ vt. **~e of** privar de. **~d** adj carenciado

depth /depθ/ n profundidad f. **be out of one's ~** perder pie; (fig) meterse en honduras. **in ~** a fondo

deput|ize /ˈdepjʊtaɪz/ vi. ~**ize for** sustituir a. ~**y** /ˈdepjʊti/ n sustituto m. ~**y chairman** n vicepresidente m

derail /dɪˈreɪl/ vt hacer descarrilar. ~**ment** n descarrilamiento m

derelict /ˈderəlɪkt/ adj abandonado y en ruinas

deri|de /dɪˈraɪd/ vt mofarse de. ~**sion** /dɪˈrɪʒn/ n mofa f. ~**sive** /dɪˈraɪsɪv/ adj burlón. ~**sory** /dɪˈraɪsərɪ/ adj (offer etc) irrisorio

deriv|ation /derɪˈveɪʃn/ n derivación f. ~**ative** /dɪˈrɪvətɪv/ n derivado m. ~**e** /dɪˈraɪv/ vt/i derivar

derogatory /dɪˈrɒgətrɪ/ adj despectivo

descen|d /dɪˈsend/ vt/i descender, bajar. ~**dant** n descendiente m & f. ~**t** n descenso m, bajada f; (lineage) ascendencia f

descri|be /dɪsˈkraɪb/ vt describir. ~**ption** /-ˈkrɪpʃn/ n descripción f. ~**ptive** /-ˈkrɪptɪv/ adj descriptivo

desecrate /ˈdesɪkreɪt/ vt profanar

desert¹ /dɪˈzɜːt/ vt abandonar. ● vi (Mil) desertar. ~**er** /dɪˈzɜːtə(r)/ n desertor m

desert² /ˈdezət/ adj & n desierto (m)

deserts /dɪˈzɜːts/ npl lo merecido. **get one's just** ~ llevarse su merecido

deserv|e /dɪˈzɜːv/ vt merecer. ~**ing** adj (cause) meritorio

design /dɪˈzaɪn/ n diseño m; (plan) plan m. ~**s** (intentions) propósitos mpl. ● vt diseñar; (plan) planear

designate /ˈdezɪgneɪt/ vt designar

designer /dɪˈzaɪnə(r)/ n diseñador m; (fashion ~) diseñador m de modas. ● adj (clothes) de diseño exclusivo

desirable /dɪˈzaɪərəbl/ adj deseable

desire /dɪˈzaɪə(r)/ n deseo m. ● vt desear

desk /desk/ n escritorio m; (at school) pupitre m; (in hotel) recepción f; (Com) caja f. ~**top publishing** n autoedición f, edición f electrónica

desolat|e /ˈdesələt/ adj desolado; (uninhabited) deshabitado. ~**ion** /-ˈleɪʃn/ n desolación f

despair /dɪˈspeə(r)/ n desesperación f. **be in** ~ estar desesperado. ● vi. ~ **of** desesperarse de

despatch /dɪˈspætʃ/ vt, n see **DISPATCH**

desperat|e /ˈdespərət/ adj desesperado. ~**ely** adv desesperadamente. ~**ion** /-ˈreɪʃn/ n desesperación f

despicable /dɪˈspɪkəbl/ adj despreciable

despise /dɪˈspaɪz/ vt despreciar

despite /dɪˈspaɪt/ prep a pesar de

despondent /dɪˈspɒndənt/ adj abatido

despot /ˈdespɒt/ n déspota m

dessert /dɪˈzɜːt/ n postre m. ~**spoon** n cuchara f de postre

destination /destɪˈneɪʃn/ n destino m

destiny /ˈdestɪnɪ/ n destino m

destitute /ˈdestɪtjuːt/ adj indigente

destroy /dɪˈstrɔɪ/ vt destruir. ~**er** n destructor m

destructi|on /dɪˈstrʌkʃn/ n destrucción f. ~**ve** /-ɪv/ adj destructivo

desultory /ˈdesəltrɪ/ adj desganado

detach /dɪˈtætʃ/ vt separar. ~**able** adj separable. ~**ed** adj (aloof) distante; (house) no adosado. ~**ment** n desprendimiento m; (Mil) destacamento m; (aloofness) indiferencia f

detail /ˈdiːteɪl/ n detalle m. **explain sth in** ~ explicar algo detalladamente. ● vt detallar; (Mil) destacar. ~**ed** adj detallado

detain /dɪˈteɪn/ vt detener; (delay) retener. ~**ee** /diːteɪˈniː/ n detenido m

detect /dɪˈtekt/ vt percibir; (discover) descubrir. ~**ive** n (private) detective m; (in police) agente m & f. ~**or** n detector m

detention /dɪˈtenʃn/ n detención f

deter /dɪˈtɜː(r)/ vt (pt deterred) disuadir; (prevent) impedir

detergent /dɪˈtɜːdʒənt/ adj & n detergente (m)

deteriorat|e /dɪˈtɪərɪəreɪt/ vi deteriorarse. ~**ion** /-ˈreɪʃn/ n deterioro m

determin|ation /dɪtɜːmɪˈneɪʃn/ n determinación f. ~**e** /dɪˈtɜːmɪn/ vt determinar; (decide) decidir. ~**ed** adj determinado; (resolute) decidido

deterrent /dɪˈterənt/ n elemento m de disuasión

detest /dɪˈtest/ vt aborrecer. ~**able** adj odioso

detonat|e /ˈdetəneɪt/ vt hacer detonar. ● vi detonar. ~**ion** /-ˈneɪʃn/ n detonación f. ~**or** n detonador m

detour /'di:tʊə(r)/ n rodeo m; (Amer, of transport) desvío m, desviación f. ● vt (Amer) desviar

detract /dɪ'trækt/ vi. ~ **from** disminuir

detriment /'detrɪmənt/ n. to the ~ of en perjuicio de. ~**al** /-'mentl/ adj perjudicial

devalue /di:'vælju:/ vt desvalorizar

devastat|e /'devəsteɪt/ vt devastar. ~**ing** adj devastador; (fig) arrollador. ~**ion** /-'steɪʃn/ n devastación f

develop /dɪ'veləp/ vt desarrollar; contraer (illness); urbanizar (land). ● vi desarrollarse; (appear) surgir. ~**ing** adj (country) en vías de desarrollo. ~**ment** n desarrollo m. (new) ~**ment** novedad f

deviant /'di:vɪənt/ adj desviado

deviat|e /'di:vɪeɪt/ vi desviarse. ~**ion** /-'eɪʃn/ n desviación f

device /dɪ'vaɪs/ n dispositivo m; (scheme) estratagema f

devil /'devl/ n diablo m

devious /'di:vɪəs/ adj taimado

devise /dɪ'vaɪz/ vt idear

devoid /dɪ'vɔɪd/ adj. be ~ of carecer de

devolution /di:və'lu:ʃn/ n descentralización f; (of power) delegación f

devot|e /dɪ'vəʊt/ vt dedicar. ~**ed** adj (couple) unido; (service) leal. ~**ee** /devə'ti:/ n partidario m. ~**ion** /-ʃn/ n devoción f

devour /dɪ'vaʊə(r)/ vt devorar

devout /dɪ'vaʊt/ adj devoto

dew /dju:/ n rocío m

dexterity /dek'sterətɪ/ n destreza f

diabet|es /daɪə'bi:ti:z/ n diabetes f. ~**ic** /-'betɪk/ adj & n diabético (m)

diabolical /daɪə'bɒlɪkl/ adj diabólico

diagnos|e /'daɪəgnəʊz/ vt diagnosticar. ~**is** /-'nəʊsɪs/ n (pl -**oses**/-si:z/) diagnóstico m

diagonal /daɪ'ægənl/ adj & n diagonal (f)

diagram /'daɪəgræm/ n diagrama m

dial /'daɪəl/ n cuadrante m; (on clock, watch) esfera f; (on phone) disco m. ● vt (pt dialled) marcar, discar (LAm)

dialect /'daɪəlekt/ n dialecto m

dialling: ~ **code** n prefijo m, código m de la zona (LAm). ~ **tone** n tono m de marcar, tono m de discado (LAm)

dialogue /'daɪəlɒg/ n diálogo m

dial tone n (Amer) see DIALLING TONE

diameter /daɪ'æmɪtə(r)/ n diámetro m

diamond /'daɪəmənd/ n diamante m; (shape) rombo m. ~**s** npl (Cards) diamantes mpl

diaper /'daɪəpə(r)/ n (Amer) pañal m

diaphragm /'daɪəfræm/ n diafragma m

diarrhoea /daɪə'rɪə/ n diarrea f

diary /'daɪərɪ/ n diario m; (book) agenda f

dice /daɪs/ n invar dado m. ● vt (Culin) cortar en cubitos

dictat|e /dɪk'teɪt/ vt/i dictar. ~**ion** /dɪk'teɪʃn/ n dictado m. ~**or** n dictador m. ~**orship** n dictadura f

dictionary /'dɪkʃənərɪ/ n diccionario m

did /dɪd/ see DO

didn't /'dɪdnt/ = **did not**

die /daɪ/ vi (pres p dying) morir. be dying to morirse por. □ ~ **down** vi irse apagando. □ ~ **out** vi extinguirse

diesel /'di:zl/ n (fuel) gasóleo m. ~ **engine** n motor m diesel

diet /'daɪət/ n alimentación f; (restricted) régimen m. be on a ~ estar a régimen. ● vi estar a régimen

differ /'dɪfə(r)/ vi ser distinto; (disagree) no estar de acuerdo. ~**ence** /'dɪfrəns/ n diferencia f; (disagreement) desacuerdo m. ~**ent** /'dɪfrənt/ adj distinto, diferente. ~**ently** adv de otra manera

difficult /'dɪfɪkəlt/ adj difícil. ~**y** n dificultad f

diffus|e /dɪ'fju:s/ adj difuso. ● /dɪ'fju:z/ vt difundir. ● vi difundirse. ~**ion** /-ʒn/ n difusión f

dig /dɪg/ n (poke) empujón m; (poke with elbow) codazo m; (remark) indirecta f. ~**s** npl 🅸 alojamiento m ● vt (pt dug, pres p digging) cavar; (thrust) empujar. ● vi cavar. □ ~ **out** vt extraer. □ ~ **up** vt desenterrar

digest /'daɪdʒest/ n resumen m. ● /daɪ'dʒest/ vt digerir. ~**ion** /-'dʒestʃn/ n digestión f. **∼ive** /-'dʒestɪv/ adj digestivo

digger /'dɪgə(r)/ n (Mec) excavadora f

digit /'dɪdʒɪt/ n dígito m; (finger) dedo m. **∼al** /'dɪdʒɪtl/ adj digital

dignified /'dɪgnɪfaɪd/ adj solemne

dignitary /'dɪgnɪtərɪ/ n dignatario m

dignity /'dɪgnətɪ/ n dignidad f

digress /daɪ'gres/ vi divagar. **∼ from** apartarse de. **∼ion** /-ʃn/ n digresión f

dike /daɪk/ n dique m

dilapidated /dɪ'læpɪdeɪtɪd/ adj ruinoso

dilate /daɪ'leɪt/ vt dilatar. ● vi dilatarse

dilemma /daɪ'lemə/ n dilema m

diligent /'dɪlɪdʒənt/ adj diligente

dilute /daɪ'ljuːt/ vt diluir

dim /dɪm/ adj (**dimmer, dimmest**) (light) débil; (room) oscuro; (fam, stupid) torpe. ● vt (pt **dimmed**) atenuar. **∼ one's headlights** (Amer) poner las (luces) cortas or de cruce, poner las (luces) bajas (LAm). ● vi (light) irse atenuando

dime /daɪm/ n (Amer) moneda de diez centavos

dimension /daɪ'menʃn/ n dimensión f

diminish /dɪ'mɪnɪʃ/ vt/i disminuir

dimple /'dɪmpl/ n hoyuelo m

din /dɪn/ n jaleo m

dine /daɪn/ vi cenar. **∼r** n comensal m & f. (Amer, restaurant) cafetería f

dinghy /'dɪŋgɪ/ n bote m; (inflatable) bote m neumático

dingy /'dɪndʒɪ/ adj (**-ier, -iest**) miserable, sucio

dinner /'dɪnə(r)/ n cena f, comida f (LAm). **have ∼** cenar, comer (LAm). **∼ party** n cena f, comida f (LAm)

dinosaur /'daɪnəsɔː(r)/ n dinosaurio m

dint /dɪnt/ n. **by ∼ of** a fuerza de

dip /dɪp/ vt (pt **dipped**) meter; (in liquid) mojar. **∼ one's headlights** poner las (luces) cortas or de cruce, poner las (luces) bajas (LAm). ● vi bajar. ● n (slope) inclinación f; (in sea) baño m. □ **∼ into** vt hojear (book)

diphthong /'dɪfθɒŋ/ n diptongo m

diploma /dɪ'pləʊmə/ n diploma m

diploma|cy /dɪ'pləʊməsɪ/ n diplomacia f. **∼t** /'dɪpləmæt/ n diplomático m.
∼tic /-'mætɪk/ adj diplomático

dipstick /'dɪpstɪk/ n (Auto) varilla f del nivel de aceite

dire /daɪə(r)/ adj (**-er, -est**) terrible; (need, poverty) extremo

direct /dɪ'rekt/ adj directo. ● adv directamente. ● vt dirigir; (show the way) indicar. **∼ion** /-ʃn/ n dirección f.
∼ions npl instrucciones fpl. **∼ly** adv directamente; (at once) en seguida.
● conj [] en cuanto. **∼or** n director m; (of company) directivo m

directory /dɪ'rektərɪ/ n guía f; (Comp) directorio m

dirt /dɜːt/ n suciedad f. **∼y** adj (**-ier, -iest**) sucio. ● vt ensuciar

disab|ility /dɪsə'bɪlətɪ/ n invalidez f.
∼le /dɪs'eɪbl/ vt incapacitar. **∼led** adj minusválido

disadvantage /dɪsəd'vɑːntɪdʒ/ n desventaja f. **∼d** adj desfavorecido

disagree /dɪsə'griː/ vi no estar de acuerdo (with con). **∼ with** (food, climate) sentarle mal a. **∼able** adj desagradable. **∼ment** n desacuerdo m; (quarrel) riña f

disappear /dɪsə'pɪə(r)/ vi desaparecer.
∼ance n desaparición f

disappoint /dɪsə'pɔɪnt/ vt decepcionar. **∼ing** adj decepcionante. **∼ment** n decepción f

disapprov|al /dɪsə'pruːvl/ n desaprobación f. **∼e** /dɪsə'pruːv/ vi. **∼e of** desaprobar. **∼ing** adj de reproche

disarm /dɪs'ɑːm/ vt desarmar. ● vi desarmarse. **∼ament** n desarme m

disarray /dɪsə'reɪ/ n desorden m

disast|er /dɪ'zɑːstə(r)/ n desastre m.
∼rous /-strəs/ adj catastrófico

disband /dɪs'bænd/ vt disolver. ● vi disolverse

disbelief /dɪsbɪ'liːf/ n incredulidad f

disc /dɪsk/ n disco m

discard /dɪs'kɑːd/ vt descartar; abandonar (beliefs etc)

discern /dɪ'sɜːn/ vt percibir. **∼ing** adj exigente; (ear, eye) educado

discharge /dɪs'tʃɑːdʒ/ vt descargar; cumplir (duty); (Mil) licenciar.
● /'dɪstʃɑːdʒ/ n descarga f; (Med) secreción f; (Mil) licenciamiento m

disciple /dɪ'saɪpl/ n discípulo m

disciplin|ary /dɪsə'plɪnərɪ/ adj discipli-
nario. **~e** /'dɪsɪplɪn/ n disciplina f. ● vt
disciplinar; (punish) sancionar

disc jockey /'dɪskdʒɒkɪ/ n pinchadis-
cos m & f

disclaim /dɪs'kleɪm/ vt desconocer.
~er n (Jurid) descargo m de responsabilidad

disclos|e /dɪs'kləʊz/ vt revelar. **~ure**
/-ʒə(r)/ n revelación f

disco /'dɪskəʊ/ n (pl **-os**) 🔲 discoteca f

discolour /dɪs'kʌlə(r)/ vt decolorar.
● vi decolorarse

discomfort /dɪs'kʌmfət/ n malestar
m; (lack of comfort) incomodidad f

disconcert /dɪskən'sɜːt/ vt desconcertar

disconnect /dɪskə'nekt/ vt separar;
(Elec) desconectar

disconsolate /dɪs'kɒnsələt/ adj des-
consolado

discontent /dɪskən'tent/ n descontento m. **~ed** adj descontento

discontinue /dɪskən'tɪnjuː/ vt interrumpir

discord /'dɪskɔːd/ n discordia f; (Mus)
disonancia f. **~ant** /-'skɔːdənt/ adj dis-
corde; (Mus) disonante

discotheque /'dɪskətek/ n discoteca f

discount /'dɪskaʊnt/ n descuento m.
● /dɪs'kaʊnt/ vt hacer caso omiso de;
(Com) descontar

discourag|e /dɪs'kʌrɪdʒ/ vt desani-
mar; (dissuade) disuadir. **~ing** adj
desalentador

discourteous /dɪs'kɜːtɪəs/ adj descortés

discover /dɪs'kʌvə(r)/ vt descubrir.
~y n descubrimiento m

discredit /dɪs'kredɪt/ vt (pt **dis-
credited**) desacreditar. ● n descrédito m

discreet /dɪs'kriːt/ adj discreto. **~ly**
adv discretamente

discrepancy /dɪ'skrepənsɪ/ n discre-
pancia f

discretion /dɪ'skreʃn/ n discreción f

discriminat|e /dɪs'krɪmɪneɪt/ vt dis-
criminar. **~e between** distinguir
entre. **~ing** adj persplcaz. **~ion**
/-'neɪʃn/ n discernimiento m; (bias)
discriminación f

discus /'dɪskəs/ n disco m

discuss /dɪ'skʌs/ vt discutir. **~ion**
/-ʃn/ n discusión f

disdain /dɪs'deɪn/ n desdén m. **~ful**
adj desdeñoso

disease /dɪ'ziːz/ n enfermedad f

disembark /dɪsɪm'bɑːk/ vi desembarcar

disenchant|ed /dɪsɪn'tʃɑːntɪd/ adj
desilusionado. **~ment** n desen-
canto m

disentangle /dɪsɪn'tæŋgl/ vt desenredar

disfigure /dɪs'fɪgə(r)/ vt desfigurar

disgrace /dɪs'greɪs/ n vergüenza f. ● vt
deshonrar. **~ful** adj vergonzoso

disgruntled /dɪs'grʌntld/ adj descontento

disguise /dɪs'gaɪz/ vt disfrazar. ● n disfraz m. **in ~** disfrazado

disgust /dɪs'gʌst/ n repugnancia f,
asco m. ● vt dar asco a. **~ed** adj indignado; (stronger) asqueado. **~ing** adj
repugnante, asqueroso

dish /dɪʃ/ n plato m. **wash** or **do the
~es** fregar los platos, lavar los trastes (Mex). □ **~ up** vt/i servir. **~cloth** n
bayeta f

disheartening /dɪs'hɑːtnɪŋ/ adj desalentador

dishonest /dɪs'ɒnɪst/ adj deshonesto.
~y n falta f de honradez

dishonour /dɪs'ɒnə(r)/ n deshonra f

dish ~ soap n (Amer) lavavajillas m. **~
towel** n paño m de cocina.
~washer n lavaplatos m, lavavajillas
m. **~washing liquid** n (Amer) see
~ SOAP

disillusion /dɪsɪ'luːʒn/ vt desilusionar.
~ment n desilusión f

disinfect /dɪsɪn'fekt/ vt desinfectar.
~ant n desinfectante m

disintegrate /dɪs'ɪntɪgreɪt/ vt desintegrar. ● vi desintegrarse

disinterested /dɪs'ɪntrəstɪd/ adj desinteresado

disjointed /dɪs'dʒɔɪntɪd/ adj inconexo

disk /dɪsk/ n disco m. **~ drive** (Comp)
unidad f de discos. **~ette** /dɪs'ket/ n
disquete m

dislike /dɪs'laɪk/ n aversión f. ● vt. **I ~
dogs** no me gustan los perros

dislocate /'dɪsləkeɪt/ vt dislocar(se) (limb)

dislodge /dɪs'lɒdʒ/ vt sacar

disloyal /dɪs'lɔɪəl/ adj desleal. ~**ty** n deslealtad f

dismal /'dɪzməl/ adj triste; (bad) fatal

dismantle /dɪs'mæntl/ vt desmontar

dismay /dɪs'meɪ/ n consternación f. ● vt consternar

dismiss /dɪs'mɪs/ vt despedir; (reject) rechazar. ~**al** n despido m; (of idea) rechazo m

dismount /dɪs'maʊnt/ vi desmontar

disobe|dience /dɪsə'biːdɪəns/ n desobediencia f. ~**dient** adj desobediente. ~**y** /dɪsə'heɪ/ vt/i desobedecer

disorder /dɪs'ɔːdə(r)/ n desorden m; (ailment) afección f. ~**ly** adj desordenado

disorganized /dɪs'ɔːɡənaɪzd/ adj desorganizado

disorientate /dɪs'ɔːrɪənteɪt/ vt desorientar

disown /dɪs'əʊn/ vt repudiar

disparaging /dɪs'pærɪdʒɪŋ/ adj despreciativo

dispatch /dɪs'pætʃ/ vt despachar. ● n despacho m. ~**rider** n mensajero m

dispel /dɪs'pel/ vt (pt dispelled) disipar

dispens|able /dɪs'pensəbl/ adj prescindible. ~**e** vt distribuir; (Med) preparar. □ ~ **with** vt prescindir de

dispers|al /dɪ'spɜːsl/ n dispersión f. ~**e** /dɪ'spɜːs/ vt dispersar. ● vi dispersarse

dispirited /dɪs'pɪrɪtɪd/ adj desanimado

display /dɪs'pleɪ/ vt exponer (goods); demostrar (feelings). ● n exposición f; (of feelings) demostración f

displeas|e /dɪs'pliːz/ vt desagradar. be ~**ed with** estar disgustado con. ~**ure** /-'pleʒə(r)/ n desagrado m

dispos|able /dɪs'pəʊzəbl/ adj desechable. ~**al** n (of waste) eliminación f. at s.o.'s ~**al** a la disposición de uno. ~**e of** /dɪs'pəʊz/ vt deshacerse de

disproportionate /dɪsprə'pɔːʃənət/ adj desproporcionado

disprove /dɪs'pruːv/ vt desmentir (claim); refutar (theory)

dispute /dɪs'pjuːt/ vt discutir. ● n disputa f. in ~ disputado

disqualif|ication /dɪskwɒlɪfɪ'keɪʃn/ n descalificación f. ~**y** /dɪs'kwɒlɪfaɪ/ vt incapacitar; (Sport) descalificar

disregard /dɪsrɪ'ɡɑːd/ vt no hacer caso de. ● n indiferencia f (for a)

disreputable /dɪs'repjʊtəbl/ adj de mala fama

disrespect /dɪsrɪ'spekt/ n falta f de respeto

disrupt /dɪs'rʌpt/ vt interrumpir; trastornar (plans). ~**ion** /-ʃn/ n trastorno m. ~**ive** adj (influence) perjudicial, negativo

dissatis|faction /dɪsætɪs'fækʃn/ n descontento m. ~**fied** /dɪ'sætɪsfaɪd/ adj descontento

dissect /dɪ'sekt/ vt disecar

dissent /dɪ'sent/ vi disentir. ● n disentimiento m

dissertation /dɪsə'teɪʃn/ n (Univ) tesis f

dissident /'dɪsɪdənt/ adj & n disidente (m & f)

dissimilar /dɪ'sɪmɪlə(r)/ adj distinto

dissolute /'dɪsəluːt/ adj disoluto

dissolve /dɪ'zɒlv/ vt disolver. ● vi disolverse

dissuade /dɪ'sweɪd/ vt disuadir

distan|ce /'dɪstəns/ n distancia f. from a ~**ce** desde lejos. in the ~**ce** a lo lejos. ~**t** adj distante, lejano; (aloof) distante

distaste /dɪs'teɪst/ n desagrado m. ~**ful** adj desagradable

distil /dɪs'tɪl/ vt (pt distilled) destilar. ~**lery** /dɪs'tɪlərɪ/ n destilería f

distinct /dɪs'tɪŋkt/ adj distinto; (clear) claro; (marked) marcado. ~**ion** /-ʃn/ n distinción f; (in exam) sobresaliente m. ~**ive** adj distintivo

distinguish /dɪs'tɪŋɡwɪʃ/ vt/i distinguir. ~**ed** adj distinguido

distort /dɪs'tɔːt/ vt torcer. ~**ion** /-ʃn/ n deformación f

distract /dɪs'trækt/ vt distraer. ~**ed** adj distraído. ~**ion** /-ʃn/ n distracción f; (confusion) aturdimiento m

distraught /dɪs'trɔːt/ adj consternado, angustiado

d

distress /dɪsˈtres/ n angustia f. ● vt afligir. ～ed adj afligido. ～ing adj penoso

distribut|e /dɪˈstrɪbjuːt/ vt repartir, distribuir. ～ion /-ˈbjuːʃn/ n distribución f. ～or n distribuidor m; (Auto) distribuidor m (del encendido)

district /ˈdɪstrɪkt/ n zona f, región f; (of town) barrio m

distrust /dɪsˈtrʌst/ n desconfianza f. ● vt desconfiar de

disturb /dɪsˈtɜːb/ vt molestar; (perturb) inquietar; (move) desordenar; (interrupt) interrumpir. ～ance n disturbio m; (tumult) alboroto m. ～ed adj trastornado. ～ing adj inquietante

disused /dɪsˈjuːzd/ adj fuera de uso

ditch /dɪtʃ/ n zanja f; (for irrigation) acequia f. ● vt 🄴 abandonar

dither /ˈdɪðə(r)/ vi vacilar

ditto /ˈdɪtəʊ/ adv ídem

divan /dɪˈvæn/ n diván m

dive /daɪv/ vi tirarse (al agua), zambullirse; (rush) meterse (precipitadamente). ● n (into water) zambullida f; (Sport) salto m (de trampolín); (of plane) descenso m en picado, descenso m en picada (LAm); (🄴, place) antro m. ～r n saltador m; (underwater) buzo m

diverge /daɪˈvɜːdʒ/ vi divergir. ～nt adj divergente

divers|e /daɪˈvɜːs/ adj diverso. ～ify vt diversificar. ～ity n diversidad f

diver|sion /daɪˈvɜːʃn/ n desvío m; desviación f; (distraction) diversión f. ～t /daɪˈvɜːt/ vt desviar; (entertain) divertir

divide /dɪˈvaɪd/ vt dividir. ● vi dividirse. ～d highway n (Amer) autovía f, carretera f de doble pista

dividend /ˈdɪvɪdend/ n dividendo m

divine /dɪˈvaɪn/ adj divino

division /dɪˈvɪʒn/ n división f

divorce /dɪˈvɔːs/ n divorcio m. ● vt divorciarse de. **get ～d** divorciarse. ● vi divorciarse. ～e /dɪvɔːˈsiː/ n divorciado m

divulge /daɪˈvʌldʒ/ vt divulgar

DIY abbr see **DO-IT-YOURSELF**

dizz|iness /ˈdɪzɪnɪs/ n vértigo m. ～y adj (-ier, -iest) mareado. **be** or **feel ～y** marearse

DJ abbr see **DISC JOCKEY**

do /duː//dʊ, də/

3rd person singular present **does**; past **did**; past participle **done**

● transitive verb

····▸ hacer. **he does what he wants** hace lo que quiere. **to do one's homework** hacer los deberes. **to do the cooking** preparar la comida, cocinar. **well done!** ¡muy bien!

····▸ (clean) lavar (dishes). limpiar (windows)

····▸ (as job) **what does he do?** ¿en qué trabaja?

····▸ (swindle) estafar. **I've been done!** ¡me han estafado!

····▸ (achieve) **she's done it!** ¡lo ha logrado!

● intransitive verb

····▸ hacer. **do as you're told!** ¡haz lo que se te dice!

····▸ (fare) **how are you doing?** (with a task) ¿qué tal te va? **how do you do?**, (as greeting) mucho gusto, encantado

····▸ (perform) **she did well/badly** le fue bien/mal

····▸ (be suitable) **will this do?** ¿esto sirve?

····▸ (be enough) ser suficiente, bastar. **one box will do** con una caja basta, con una caja es suficiente

● auxiliary verb

····▸ (to form interrogative and negative) **do you speak Spanish?** ¿hablas español?. **I don't want to** no quiero. **don't shut the door** no cierres la puerta

····▸ (in tag questions) **you eat meat, don't you?** ¿comes carne, ¿verdad? or ¿no? **he lives in London, doesn't he?** vive en Londres, ¿no? or ¿verdad? or ¿no es cierto?

····▸ (in short answers) **do you like it? - yes, I do** ¿te gusta? - sí. **who wrote it? - I did** ¿quién lo escribió? - yo

····▸ (emphasizing) **do come in!**

¡pase Ud!. **you do exaggerate!** ¡cómo exageras! □ **do away with** vt abolir. □ **do in** vt (sl, kill) eliminar. □ **do up** vt abrochar (coat etc); arreglar (house). □ **do with** vt (need) (with can, could) necesitar; (expressing connection) **It has nothing to do with that** no tiene nada que ver con eso. □ **do without** vt prescindir de

docile /'dəʊsaɪl/ adj dócil

dock /dɒk/ n (Naut) dársena f; (wharf, quay) muelle m; (Jurid) banquillo m de los acusados. ~**s** npl (port) puerto m. ● vt cortar (tail); atracar (ship). ● vi (ship) atracar. ~**er** n estibador m. ~**yard** n astillero m

doctor /'dɒktə(r)/ n médico m, doctor m

doctrine /'dɒktrɪn/ n doctrina f

document /'dɒkjʊmənt/ n documento m. ~**ary** /-'mentrɪ/ adj & n documental (m)

dodg|e /dɒdʒ/ vt esquivar. ● vi esquivarse. ● n treta f. ~**ems** /'dɒdʒəmz/ npl autos mpl de choque. ~**y** adj (-ier, -iest) (awkward) difícil

doe /dəʊ/ n (rabbit) coneja f; (hare) liebre f hembra; (deer) cierva f

does /dʌz/ see **DO**

doesn't /'dʌznt/ = **does not**

dog /dɒg/ n perro m. ● vt (pt dogged) perseguir

dogged /'dɒgɪd/ adj obstinado

doghouse /'dɒghaʊs/ n (Amer) casa f del perro. **in the ~** 🄸 en desgracia

dogma /'dɒgmə/ n dogma m. ~**tic** /-'mætɪk/ adj dogmático

do|ings npl actividades fpl. ~**-it-yourself** /'duːɪtjɔː'self/ n bricolaje m

dole /dəʊl/ n 🄸 subsidio m de paro, subsidio m de desempleo. **on the ~** 🄸 parado, desempleado. □ ~ **out** vt distribuir

doleful /'dəʊlfl/ adj triste

doll /dɒl/ n muñeca f

dollar /'dɒlə(r)/ n dólar m

dollarization /dɒlərar'zeɪʃn/ n dolarización f

dollop /'dɒləp/ n 🄸 porción f

dolphin /'dɒlfɪn/ n delfín m

domain /dəʊ'meɪn/ n dominio m

dome /dəʊm/ n cúpula f

domestic /də'mestɪk/ adj doméstico; (trade, flights, etc) nacional. ~**ated** /də'mestɪkeɪtɪd/ adj (animal) domesticado. ~ **science** n economía f doméstica

domin|ance /'dɒmɪnəns/ n dominio m. ~**ant** adj dominante. ~**ate** /-eɪt/ vt/i dominar. ~**ation** /-'neɪʃn/ n dominación f. ~**eering** adj dominante

Dominican Republic /də'mɪnɪkən/ n República f Dominicana

dominion /də'mɪnjən/ n dominio m

domino /'dɒmɪnəʊ/ n (pl -oes) ficha f de dominó. ~**es** npl (game) dominó m

donat|e /dəʊ'neɪt/ vt donar. ~**ion** /-ʃn/ n donativo m, donación f

done /dʌn/ see **DO**

donkey /'dɒŋkɪ/ n burro m, asno m. ~**'s years** 🄸 siglos mpl

donor /'dəʊnə(r)/ n donante m & f

don't /dəʊnt/ = **do not**

doodle /'duːdl/ vi/t garrapatear

doom /duːm/ n destino m; (death) muerte f. ● vt. **be ~ed to** estar condenado a

door /dɔː(r)/ n puerta f. ~**bell** n timbre m. ~ **knob** n pomo m (de la puerta). ~**mat** n felpudo m. ~**step** n peldaño m. ~**way** n entrada f

dope /dəʊp/ n 🄸 droga f; (sl, idiot) imbécil m. ● vt 🄸 drogar

dormant /'dɔːmənt/ adj aletargado, (volcano) inactivo

dormice /'dɔːmaɪs/ see **DORMOUSE**

dormitory /'dɔːmɪtrɪ/ n dormitorio m

dormouse /'dɔːmaʊs/ n (pl -mice) lirón m

DOS /dɒs/ abbr (= **disc-operating system**) DOS m

dos|age /'dəʊsɪdʒ/ n dosis f. ~**e** /dəʊs/ n dosis f

dot /dɒt/ n punto m. **on the ~** en punto. ~**-com** n punto m com. ~**-com company** empresa f punto-com

dote /dəʊt/ vi. ~ **on** adorar

dotty /'dɒtɪ/ adj (-ier, -iest) 🄸 chiflado

double /'dʌbl/ adj doble. ● adv el doble. ● n doble m; (person) doble m & f. **at the ~** corriendo. ● vt doblar;

redoblar (efforts etc). ● vi doblarse. **~ bass** /beɪs/ n contrabajo m. **~ bed** n cama f de matrimonio, cama f de doa plazas (*LAm*). **~ chin** n papada f. **~ click** vt hacer doble clic en. **~-cross** /-ˈkrɒs/ vt traicionar. **~-decker** /-ˈdekə(r)/ n autobús m de dos pisos. **~ Dutch** n Ⓣ chino m. **~ glazing** /-ˈgleɪzɪŋ/ n doble ventana f. **~s** npl (*tennis*) dobles mpl

doubly /ˈdʌblɪ/ adv doblemente

doubt /daʊt/ n duda f. ● vt dudar; (*distrust*) dudar de. **~ful** adj dudoso. **~less** adv sin duda

dough /dəʊ/ n masa f; (*sl, money*) pasta f Ⓧ, lana f (*LAm fam*). **~nut** n donut m, dona f (*Mex*)

dove /dʌv/ n paloma f

down /daʊn/ adv abajo. **~ with** abajo. **come ~** bajar. **go ~** bajar; (sun) ponerse. ● prep abajo. ● adj Ⓣ deprimido. ● vt derribar; (*fam, drink*) beber. ● n (*feathers*) plumón m. **~ and out** adj en la miseria. **~cast** adj abatido. **~fall** n perdición f; (*of king, dictator*) caída f. **~hearted** /-ˈhɑːtɪd/ adj abatido. **~hill** /-ˈhɪl/ adv cuesta abajo. **~load** /-ˈləʊd/ vt (*Comp*) bajar. **~market** /-ˈmɑːkɪt/ adj (newspaper) popular; (store) barato. **~ payment** n depósito m. **~pour** n aguacero m. **~right** adj completo. ● adv completamente. **~s** npl colinas fpl. **~stairs** /-ˈsteəz/ adv abajo. ● /-ˈsteəz/ adj de abajo. **~stream** adv río abajo. **~-to-earth** /-tʊˈɜːθ/ adj práctico. **~town** /-ˈtaʊn/ n centro m (de la ciudad). ● adv. **go ~town** ir al centro. **~ under** adv en las antípodas; (*in Australia*) en Australia. **~ward** /-wəd/ adj & adv, **~wards** adv hacia abajo

dowry /ˈdaʊərɪ/ n dote f

Downing Street Es una calle en el barrio londinense de Westminster. El número 10 es la residencia oficial del Primer Ministro y el 11, la del *Chancellor of the Exchequer* (Ministro de Economía y Hacienda). Los periodistas suelen utilizar las expresiones *Downing Street* o *Number 10* para referirse al Primér Ministro y al Gobierno.

---

doze /dəʊz/ vi dormitar

dozen /ˈdʌzn/ n docena f. **a ~ eggs** una docena de huevos. **~s of** Ⓣ miles de, muchos

Dr /ˈdɒktə(r)/ abbr (**Doctor**)

drab /dræb/ adj monótono

draft /drɑːft/ n borrador m; (*Com*) letra f de cambio; (*Amer, Mil*) reclutamiento m; (*Amer, of air*) corriente f de aire. ● vt redactar el borrador de; (*Amer, conscript*) reclutar

drag /dræg/ vt (*pt* **dragged**) arrastrar. ● n Ⓣ lata f

dragon /ˈdrægən/ n dragón m. **~fly** n libélula f

drain /dreɪn/ vt vaciar (tank, glass); drenar (land); (*fig*) agotar. ● vi escurrirse. ● n (*pipe*) sumidero m, resumidero m (*LAm*); (*plughole*) desagüe m. **~board** (*Amer*), **~ing board** n escurridero m

drama /ˈdrɑːmə/ n drama m; (*art*) arte m teatral. **~tic** /drəˈmætɪk/ adj dramático. **~tist** /ˈdræmətɪst/ n dramaturgo m. **~tize** /ˈdræmətaɪz/ vt adaptar al teatro; (*fig*) dramatizar

drank /dræŋk/ see **DRINK**

drape /dreɪp/ vt cubrir; (*hang*) colgar. **~s** npl (*Amer*) cortinas fpl

drastic /ˈdræstɪk/ adj drástico

draught /drɑːft/ n corriente f de aire. **~ beer** n cerveza f de barril. **~s** npl (*game*) juego m de damas fpl. **~y** adj lleno de corrientes de aire

draw /drɔː/ vt (*pt* **drew**, *pp* **drawn**) tirar; (*attract*) atraer; dibujar (picture); trazar (line). **~ the line** trazar el límite. ● vi (*Art*) dibujar; (*Sport*) empatar; **~ near** acercarse. ● n (*Sport*) empate m; (*in lottery*) sorteo m. □ **~ in** vi (days) acortarse. □ **~ out** vt sacar (money). □ **~ up** vi pararse. vt redactar (document); acercar (chair). **~back** n desventaja f. **~bridge** n puente m levadizo

drawer /drɔː(r)/ n cajón m, gaveta f (*Mex*). **~s** npl calzones mpl

drawing /ˈdrɔːɪŋ/ n dibujo m. **~ pin** n tachuela f, chincheta f, chinche f. **~ room** n salón m

drawl /drɔːl/ n habla f lenta

drawn /drɔːn/ see **DRAW**

dread /dred/ n terror m. ● vt temer.
~**ful** adj terrible. ~**fully** adv terriblemente

dream /dri:m/ n sueño m. ● vt/i (pt
dreamed or **dreamt** /dremt/) soñar.
□ ~ **up** vt idear. adj ideal. ~**er** n soñador m

dreary /'drɪərɪ/ adj (-ier, -iest) triste;
(boring) monótono

dredge /dredʒ/ n draga f. ● vt dragar.
~**r** n draga f

dregs /dregz/ npl posos mpl, heces fpl;
(fig) hez f

drench /drentʃ/ vt empapar

dress /dres/ n vestido m; (clothing)
ropa f. ● vt vestir; (decorate) adornar;
(Med) vendar. ● vi vestirse. □ ~ **up** vi
ponerse elegante. □ ~ **up as** disfrazarse de. ~ **circle** n primer palco m

dressing /'dresɪŋ/ n (sauce) aliño m;
(bandage) vendaje m. ~**-down**
/-'daʊn/ n rapapolvo m, reprensión f.
~ **gown** n bata f. ~ **room** n vestidor
m; (in theatre) camarín m. ~ **table** n
tocador m

dress ~**maker** n modista m & f.
~**making** n costura f. ~ **rehearsal** n ensayo m general

drew /dru:/ see **DRAW**

dribble /'drɪbl/ vi (baby) babear; (in
football) driblar, driblear

drie|d /draɪd/ adj (food) seco; (milk)
en polvo. ~**r** /'draɪə(r)/ n secador m

drift /drɪft/ vi ir a la deriva; (snow)
amontonarse. ● n (movement) dirección f; (of snow) montón m

drill /drɪl/ n (tool) taladro m; (of dentist) torno m; (training) ejercicio m.
● vt taladrar, perforar; (train) entrenar.
● vi entrenarse

drink /drɪŋk/ vt/i (pt **drank**, pp **drunk**)
beber, tomar (LAm). ● n bebida f.
~**able** adj bebible; (water) potable.
~**er** n bebedor m. ~**ing water** n
agua f potable

drip /drɪp/ vi (pt **dripped**) gotear. ● n
gota f; (Med) goteo m intravenoso;
(fam, person) soso m. ~**-dry** /-'draɪ/
adj de lava y pon. ~**ping** adj. be
~**ping wet** estar chorreando

drive /draɪv/ vt (pt **drove**, pp **driven**)
conducir, manejar (LAm) (car etc). ~
s.o. **mad** volver loco a uno. ~ s.o. **to**

do sth llevar a uno a hacer algo. ● vi
conducir, manejar (LAm). ~ **at** querer
decir. ~ **in** (in car) entrar en coche.
● n paseo m; (road) calle f; (private
road) camino m de entrada; (fig) empuje m. ~**r** n conductor m, chofer m
(LAm). ~**r's license** n (Amer) see **DRIVING LICENSE**

drivel /'drɪvl/ n tonterías fpl

driving /'draɪvɪŋ/ n conducción f. ~
licence n permiso m de conducir, licencia f de conducción (LAm), licencia
f (de manejar) (Mex). ~ **test** n examen m de conducir, examen m de
manejar (LAm)

drizzle /'drɪzl/ n llovizna f. ● vi lloviznar

drone /drəʊn/ n zumbido m. ● vi zumbar

drool /dru:l/ vi babear

droop /dru:p/ vi inclinarse; (flowers)
marchitarse

drop /drɒp/ n gota f; (fall) caída f;
(decrease) descenso m. ● vt (pt
dropped) dejar caer; (lower) bajar.
● vi caer. □ ~ **in** vi pasar por casa
de. □ ~ **off** vi (sleep) dormirse. □ ~
out vi retirarse; (student) abandonar
los estudios. ~**out** n marginado m

drought /draʊt/ n sequía f

drove /drəʊv/ see **DRIVE**. ● n manada f

drown /draʊn/ vt ahogar. ● vi ahogarse

drowsy /'draʊzɪ/ adj soñoliento

drudgery /'drʌdʒərɪ/ n trabajo m pesado

drug /drʌg/ n droga f; (Med) medicamento m. ● vt (pt **drugged**) drogar. ~
addict n drogadicto m. ~**gist** n
(Amer) farmacéutico m. ~**store** n
(Amer) farmacia f (que vende otros
artículos también)

drum /drʌm/ n tambor m; (for oil)
bidón m. ● vi (pt **drummed**) tocar el
tambor. ● vt. ~ **sth into s.o.** hacerle
aprender algo a uno a fuerza de repetírselo. ~**mer** n tambor m; (in
group) batería f. ~**s** npl batería f.
~**stick** n baqueta f; (Culin) muslo m

drunk /drʌŋk/ see **DRINK**. ● adj borracho. **get** ~ emborracharse. ● n borracho m. ~**ard** /-əd/ n borracho m.
~**en** adj borracho

d

dry /draɪ/ adj (**drier, driest**) seco. ● vt secar. ● vi secarse. ◻ ~ **up** vi (stream) secarse; (funds) agotarse. ~**-clean** vt limpiar en seco. ~**-cleaner's** tintorería f. ~**er** n see **DRIER**

DTD abbrev **Document Type Definition** DTD m

dual /'dju:əl/ adj doble. ~ **carriageway** n autovía f, carretera f de doble pista

dub /dʌb/ vt (pt **dubbed**) doblar (film)

dubious /'dju:bɪəs/ adj dudoso; (person) sospechoso

duchess /'dʌtʃɪs/ n duquesa f

duck /dʌk/ n pato m. ● vt sumergir; bajar (head). ● vi agacharse. ~**ling** /'dʌklɪŋ/ n patito m

duct /dʌkt/ n conducto m

dud /dʌd/ adj inútil; (cheque) sin fondos

due /dju:/ adj debido; (expected) esperado. ~ **to** debido a. ● adv. ~ **north** derecho hacia el norte. ~**s** npl derechos mpl

duel /'dju:əl/ n duelo m

duet /dju:'et/ n dúo m

duffel, duffle /'dʌfl/: ~ **bag** n bolsa f de lona. ~ **coat** n trenca f

dug /dʌg/ see **DIG**

duke /dju:k/ n duque m

dull /dʌl/ adj (**-er, -est**) (weather) gris; (colour) apagado; (person, play, etc) pesado; (sound) sordo

dumb /dʌm/ adj (**-er, -est**) mudo; 🄳 estúpido. ◻ ~ **down** vt reducir el valor intelectual de. ~**found** /dʌm'faʊnd/ vt pasmar

dummy /'dʌmɪ/ n muñeco m; (of tailor) maniquí m; (for baby) chupete m. ● adj falso. ~ **run** prueba f

dump /dʌmp/ vt tirar, botar (LAm). ● n vertedero m; (Mil) depósito m; 🄳 lugar m desagradable. **be down in the** ~**s** estar deprimido

dumpling /'dʌmplɪŋ/ n bola f de masa hervida

Dumpster /'dʌmpstə(r)/ n (Amer, ®) contenedor m (para escombros)

dumpy /'dʌmpɪ/ adj (**-ier, -iest**) regordete

dunce /dʌns/ n burro m

dung /dʌŋ/ n (manure) estiércol m

dungarees /dʌŋgə'ri:z/ npl mono m, peto m

dungeon /'dʌndʒən/ n calabozo m

dunk /dʌŋk/ vt remojar

dupe /dju:p/ vt engañar. ● n inocentón m

duplicat|e /'dju:plɪkət/ adj & n duplicado (m). ● /'dju:plɪkeɪt/ vt duplicar; (on machine) reproducir. ~**ing machine, ~or** n multicopista f

durable /'djʊərəbl/ adj durable

duration /djʊ'reɪʃn/ n duración f

duress /djʊ'res/ n. **under** ~ bajo coacción

during /'djʊərɪŋ/ prep durante

dusk /dʌsk/ n anochecer m

dust /dʌst/ n polvo m. ● vt quitar el polvo a; (sprinkle) espolvorear (**with** con). ~**bin** n cubo m de la basura, bote m de la basura (Mex). ~ **cloth** (Amer), ~**er** n trapo m. ~**jacket** n sobrecubierta f. ~**man** /-mən/ n basurero m. ~**pan** n recogedor m. ~**y** adj (**-ier, -iest**) polvoriento

Dutch /dʌtʃ/ adj holandés. ● n (language) holandés m. **the** ~ (people) los holandeses. ~**man** /-mən/ m holandés m. ~**woman** n holandesa f

duty /'dju:tɪ/ n deber m; (tax) derechos mpl de aduana. **on** ~ de servicio. ~**-free** /-'fri:/ adj libre de impuestos

duvet /'dju:veɪ/ n edredón m

DVD abbr (= **digital video disc**) DVD m

dwarf /dwɔ:f/ n (pl **-s** or **dwarves**) enano m

dwell /dwel/ vi (pt **dwelt** or **dwelled**) morar. ◻ ~ **on** vt detenerse en. ~**ing** n morada f

dwindle /'dwɪndl/ vi disminuir

dye /daɪ/ vt (pres p **dyeing**) teñir. ● n tinte m

dying /'daɪɪŋ/ see **DIE**

dynamic /daɪ'næmɪk/ adj dinámico. ~**s** npl dinámica f

dynamite /'daɪnəmaɪt/ n dinamita f. ● vt dinamitar

dynamo /'daɪnəməʊ/ n (pl **-os**) dinamo f, dínamo f, dinamo m (LAm), dínamo m (LAm)

dynasty /'dɪnəstɪ/ n dinastía f

d

Ee

E *abbr* (= **East**) E

each /iːtʃ/ *adj* cada. ● *pron* cada uno. ~ **one** cada uno. ~ **other** uno a otro, el uno al otro. **they love** ~ **other** se aman

eager /'iːgə(r)/ *adj* impaciente; (*enthusiastic*) ávido. ~**ness** *n* impaciencia *f*; (*enthusiasm*) entusiasmo *m*

eagle /'iːgl/ *n* águila *f*

ear /ɪə(r)/ *n* oído *m*; (*outer*) oreja *f*; (*of corn*) espiga *f*. ~**ache** *n* dolor *m* de oído. ~**drum** *n* tímpano *m*

earl /ɜːl/ *n* conde *m*

early /'ɜːlɪ/ *adj* (**-ier, -iest**) temprano; (*before expected time*) prematuro. ● *adv* temprano; (*ahead of time*) con anticipación

earn /ɜːn/ *vt* ganar; (*deserve*) merecer

earnest /'ɜːnɪst/ *adj* serio. **in** ~ en serio

earnings /'ɜːnɪŋz/ *npl* ingresos *mpl*; (*Com*) ganancias *fpl*

ear ~**phone** *n* audífono *m*. ~**ring** *n* pendiente *m*, arete *m* (*LAm*). ~**shot** *n*. **within** ~**shot** al alcance del oído

earth /ɜːθ/ *n* tierra *f*. **the E**~ (*planet*) la Tierra. ● *vt* (*Elec*) conectar a tierra. ~**quake** *n* terremoto *m*

earwig /'ɪəwɪg/ *n* tijereta *f*

ease /iːz/ *n* facilidad *f*; (*comfort*) tranquilidad *f*. **at** ~ a gusto; (*Mil*) en posición de descanso. **ill at** ~ molesto. **with** ~ fácilmente. ● *vt* calmar; aliviar (*pain*). ● *vi* calmarse; (*lessen*) disminuir

easel /'iːzl/ *n* caballete *m*

easily /'iːzɪlɪ/ *adv* fácilmente

east /iːst/ *n* este *m*. ● *adj* este, oriental; (*wind*) del este. ● *adv* hacia el este.

Easter /'iːstə(r)/ *n* Semana *f* Santa; (*Relig*) Pascua *f* de Resurrección. ~ **egg** *n* huevo *m* de Pascua

east ~**erly** /-əlɪ/ *adj* (*wind*) del este. ~**ern** /-ən/ *adj* este, oriental. ~**ward** /-wəd/, ~**wards** *adv* hacia el este

easy /'iːzɪ/ *adj* (**-ier, -iest**) fácil. ● *adv*. **go** ~ **on sth** 🄸 no pasarse con algo. **take it** ~ tomarse las cosas con calma. ● *int* ¡despacio! ~ **chair** *n* sillón *m*. ~**going** /-'gəʊɪŋ/ *adj* acomodadizo

eat /iːt/ *vt/i* (*pt* **ate**, *pp* **eaten**) comer. □ ~ **into** *vt* corroer. ~**er** *n* comedor *m*

eaves /iːvz/ *npl* alero *m*. ~**drop** *vi* (*pt* -**dropped**). ~**drop (on)** escuchar a escondidas

ebb /eb/ *n* reflujo *m*. ● *vi* bajar; (*fig*) decaer

ebola /iː'bəʊlə/ *n* Ébola *m*

ebony /'ebənɪ/ *n* ébano *m*

EC /iː'siː/ *abbr* (= **European Community**) CE *f* (Comunidad *f* Europea)

eccentric /ɪk'sentrɪk/ *adj* & *n* excéntrico (*m*). ~**ity** /eksen'trɪsətɪ/ *n* excentricidad *f*

echo /'ekəʊ/ *n* (*pl* -**oes**) eco *m*. ● *vi* hacer eco

eclipse /ɪ'klɪps/ *n* eclipse *m*. ● *vt* eclipsar

ecolog|ical /iːkə'lɒdʒɪkl/ *adj* ecológico. ~**y** *n* ecología *f*

e-commerce /iː'kɒmɜːs/ *n* comercio *m* electrónico

econom|ic /iːkə'nɒmɪk/ *adj* económico; ~ **refugee** refugiado *m* económico. ~**ical** *adj* económico. ~**ics** /iːkə'nɒmɪks/ *n* economía. ~**ist** /ɪ'kɒnəmɪst/ *n* economista *m* & *f*. ~**ize** /ɪ'kɒnəmaɪz/ *vi* economizar. ~**ize on sth** economizar algo. ~**y** /ɪ'kɒnəmɪ/ *n* economía *f*

ecsta|sy /'ekstəsɪ/ *n* éxtasis *f*. ~**tic** /ɪk'stætɪk/ *adj* extático

Ecuador /'ekwədɔː(r)/ *n* Ecuador *m*. ~**ean** /ekwə'dɔːrɪən/ *adj* & *n* ecuatoriano (*m*)

edg|e /edʒ/ *n* borde *m*; (*of knife*) filo *m*; (*of town*) afueras *fpl*. **have the** ~**e on** 🄸 llevar la ventaja a. **on** ~**e** nervioso. ● *vt* ribetear. ● *vi* avanzar cautelosamente. ~**eways** *adv* de lado. ~**y** *adj* nervioso

edible /'edɪbl/ *adj* comestible

edit /'edɪt/ *vt* dirigir (*newspaper*); preparar una edición de (*text*); editar (*film*). ~**ion** /ɪ'dɪʃn/ *n* edición *f*. ~**or** *n* (*of newspaper*) director *m*; (*of text*) redactor *m*. ~**orial** /edɪ'tɔːrɪəl/ *adj* editorial. ●n artículo m de fondo

Edinburgh Festival Es el principal acontecimiento cultural británico que, desde 1947, se celebra en agosto, en la capital de Escocia. El festival atrae a un gran número de visitantes y un aspecto muy importante del mismo son los espectáculos que no forman parte del programa oficial, que se conocen como the Fringe.

educat|e /'edʒʊkeɪt/ vt educar. **~ed** adj culto. **~ion** /-'keɪʃn/ n educación f; (knowledge, culture) cultura f. **~ional** /-'keɪʃənl/ adj instructivo

EC /iː'siː/ abbr (= European Commission) CE f (Comisión f Europea)

eel /iːl/ n anguila f

eerie /'ɪərɪ/ adj (-ier, -iest) misterioso

effect /ɪ'fekt/ n efecto m. **in ~** efectivamente. **take ~** entrar en vigor. **~ive** adj eficaz; (striking) impresionante; (real) efectivo. **~ively** adv eficazmente. **~iveness** n eficacia f

effeminate /ɪ'femɪnət/ adj afeminado

efficien|cy /ɪ'fɪʃənsɪ/ n eficiencia f; (Mec) rendimiento m. **~t** adj eficiente. **~tly** adv eficientemente

effort /'efət/ n esfuerzo m. **~less** adj fácil

e.g. /iː'dʒiː/ abbr (= exempli gratia) p.ej., por ejemplo

egg /eg/ n huevo m. □ **~ on** vt ⊞ incitar. **~cup** n huevera f. **~plant** n (Amer) berenjena f. **~shell** n cáscara f de huevo

ego /'iːgəʊ/ n (pl -os) yo m. **~ism** n egoísmo m. **~ist** n egoísta m & f. **~centric** /iːgəʊ'sentrɪk/ adj egocéntrico. **~tism** n egotismo m. **~tist** n egotista m & f

eh /eɪ/ int ⊞ ¡eh!

eiderdown /'aɪdədaʊn/ n edredón m

eight /eɪt/ adj & n ocho (m). **~een** /eɪ'tiːn/ adj & n dieciocho (m). **~eenth** adj decimoctavo. ●n dieciochavo m. **~h** /eɪtθ/ adj & n octavo (m) **~ieth** /'eɪtɪəθ/ adj octogésimo. ●n ochentavo m. **~y** /'eɪtɪ/ adj & n ochenta (m)

either /'aɪðə(r)/ adj cualquiera de los dos; (negative) ninguno de los dos;

(each) cada. ●pron uno u otro; (with negative) ni uno ni otro. ●adv (negative) tampoco. ●conj o. **~ Tuesday or Wednesday** o el martes o el miércoles; (with negative) ni el martes ni el miércoles

eject /ɪ'dʒekt/ vt expulsar

eke /iːk/ vt. **~ out** hacer alcanzar (resources). **~ out a living** ganarse la vida a duras penas

elaborate /ɪ'læbərət/ adj complicado. ●/ɪ'læbəreɪt/ vt elaborar. ●/ɪ'læbəreɪt/ vi explicarse

elapse /ɪ'læps/ vi transcurrir

elastic /ɪ'læstɪk/ adj & n elástico (m). **~ band** n goma f (elástica), liga f (Mex)

elat|ed /ɪ'leɪtɪd/ adj regocijado. **~ion** /-ʃn/ n regocijo m

elbow /'elbəʊ/ n codo m. ●vt dar un codazo a

elder /'eldə(r)/ adj mayor. ●n mayor m & f; (tree) saúco m. **~ly** /'eldəlɪ/ adj mayor, anciano

eldest /'eldɪst/ adj & n mayor (m & f)

elect /ɪ'lekt/ vt elegir. **~ to do** decidir hacer. ●adj electo. **~ion** /-ʃn/ n elección f. **~or** n elector m. **~oral** adj electoral. **~orate** /-ət/ n electorado m

electric /ɪ'lektrɪk/ adj eléctrico. **~al** adj eléctrico. **~ blanket** n manta f eléctrica. **~ian** /ɪlek'trɪʃn/ n electricista m & f. **~ity** /ɪlek'trɪsətɪ/ n electricidad f

electrify /ɪ'lektrɪfaɪ/ vt electrificar; (fig) electrizar

electrocute /ɪ'lektrəkjuːt/ vt electrocutar

electrode /ɪ'lektrəʊd/ n electrodo m

electron /ɪ'lektrɒn/ n electrón m

electronic /ɪlek'trɒnɪk/ adj electrónico. **~ mail** n correo m electrónico. **~s** n electrónica f

elegan|ce /'elɪgəns/ n elegancia f. **~t** adj elegante. **~tly** adv elegantemente

element /'elɪmənt/ n elemento m. **~ary** /-'mentrɪ/ adj elemental. **~ary school** n (Amer) escuela f primaria

elephant /'elɪfənt/ n elefante m

elevat|e /'elɪveɪt/ vt elevar. **~ion** /-'veɪʃn/ n elevación f. **~or** n (Amer) ascensor m

eleven /ɪ'levn/ adj & n once (m). **~th** adj undécimo. ●n onceavo m

elf /elf/ n (pl **elves**) duende m

eligible /'elɪdʒəbl/ adj elegible. **be ~ for** tener derecho a

eliminat|e /ɪ'lɪmɪneɪt/ vt eliminar. **~ion** /-'neɪʃn/ n eliminación f

élite /er'liːt/ n elite f, élite f

ellip|se /ɪ'lɪps/ n elipse f. **~tical** adj elíptico

elm /elm/ n olmo m

elope /ɪ'ləʊp/ vi fugarse con el amante

eloquen|ce /'eləkwəns/ n elocuencia f. **~t** adj elocuente

El Salvador /el'sælvədɔː(r)/ n El Salvador

else /els/ adv. **somebody ~** otra persona. **everybody ~** todos los demás. **nobody ~** ningún otro, nadie más. **nothing ~** nada más. **or ~** o bien. **somewhere ~** en otra parte. **~where** adv en otra parte

elu|de /ɪ'luːd/ vt eludir. **~sive** /-sɪv/ adj esquivo

elves /elvz/ see **ELF**

emaciated /ɪ'meɪʃɪeɪtɪd/ adj consumido

email, e-mail /'iːmeɪl/ n correo m electrónico, correo-e m. ●vt mandar por correo electrónico, emailear. **~ address** n casilla f electrónica, dirección f de correo electrónico

emancipat|e /ɪ'mænsɪpeɪt/ vt emancipar. **~ion** /-'peɪʃn/ n emancipación f

embankment /ɪm'bæŋkmənt/ n terraplén m; (of river) dique m

embargo /ɪm'bɑːɡəʊ/ n (pl **-oes**) embargo m

embark /ɪm'bɑːk/ vi embarcarse. **~ on** (fig) emprender. **~ation** /embɑː'keɪʃn/ n embarque m

embarrass /ɪm'bærəs/ vt avergonzar. **~ed** adj avergonzado. **~ing** adj embarazoso. **~ment** n vergüenza f

embassy /'embəsɪ/ n embajada f

embellish /ɪm'belɪʃ/ vt adornar. **~ment** n adorno m

embers /'embəz/ npl ascuas fpl

embezzle /ɪm'bezl/ vt desfalcar. **~ment** n desfalco m

emblem /'embləm/ n emblema m

embrace /ɪm'breɪs/ vt abrazar; (fig) abarcar. ●vi abrazarse. ●n abrazo m

embroider /ɪm'brɔɪdə(r)/ vt bordar. **~y** n bordado m

embroil /ɪm'brɔɪl/ vt enredar

embryo /'embrɪəʊ/ n (pl **-os**) embrión m. **~nic** /-'brɒnɪk/ adj embrionario

emend /ɪ'mend/ vt enmendar

emerald /'emərəld/ n esmeralda f

emerge /ɪ'mɜːdʒ/ vi salir. **~nce** /-əns/ n aparición f

emergency /ɪ'mɜːdʒənsɪ/ n emergencia f; (Med) urgencia f. **in an ~** en caso de emergencia. **~ exit** n salida f de emergencia. **~ room** urgencias fpl

emigra|nt /'emɪɡrənt/ n emigrante m & f. **~te** /'emɪɡreɪt/ vi emigrar. **~tion** /-'ɡreɪʃn/ n emigración f

eminen|ce /'emɪnəns/ n eminencia f. **~t** adj eminente.

emi|ssion /ɪ'mɪʃn/ n emisión f. **~t** vt (pt emitted) emitir

emoti|on /ɪ'məʊʃn/ n emoción f. **~onal** adj emocional; (person) emotivo; (moving) conmovedor. **~ve** /ɪ'məʊtɪv/ adj emotivo

empathy /'empəθɪ/ n empatía f

emperor /'empərə(r)/ n emperador m

empha|sis /'emfəsɪs/ n (pl **~ses** /-siːz/) énfasis m. **~size** /'emfəsaɪz/ vt enfatizar. **~tic** /ɪm'fætɪk/ adj (gesture) enfático; (assertion) categórico

empire /'empaɪə(r)/ n imperio m

empirical /ɪm'pɪrɪkl/ adj empírico

employ /ɪm'plɔɪ/ vt emplear. **~ee** /emplɔɪ'iː/ n empleado m. **~er** n patrón m. **~ment** n empleo m. **~ment agency** n agencia f de trabajo

empower /ɪm'paʊə(r)/ vt autorizar (**to do** a hacer)

empress /'emprɪs/ n emperatriz f

empty /'emptɪ/ adj vacío; (promise) vano. **on an ~y stomach** con el estómago vacío. ●n Ⓔ envase m (vacío). ●vt vaciar. ●vi vaciarse

emulate /'emjʊleɪt/ vt emular

emulsion /ɪ'mʌlʃn/ n emulsión f

enable /ɪ'neɪbl/ vt. **~ s.o. to do sth** permitir a uno hacer algo

enact /ɪ'nækt/ vt (Jurid) decretar; (in theatre) representar

enamel /ɪ'næml/ n esmalte m. ● vt (pt **enamelled**) esmaltar

enchant /ɪn'tʃɑ:nt/ vt encantar. ~**ing** adj encantador. ~**ment** n encanto m

encircle /ɪn'sɜ:kl/ vt rodear

enclave /'enkleɪv/ n enclave m

enclos|e /ɪn'kləʊz/ vt cercar (land); (Com) adjuntar. ~**ed** adj (space) cerrado; (Com) adjunto. ~**ure** /ɪn'kləʊʒə(r)/ n cercamiento m

encode /ɪn'kəʊd/ vt codificar, cifrar

encore /'ɒŋkɔ:(r)/ int ¡otra! ● n bis m, repetición f

encounter /ɪn'kaʊntə(r)/ vt encontrar. ● n encuentro m

encourag|e /ɪn'kʌrɪdʒ/ vt animar; (stimulate) fomentar. ~**ement** n ánimo m. ~**ing** adj alentador

encroach /ɪn'krəʊtʃ/ vi. ~ **on** invadir (land); quitar (time)

encyclopaedi|a /ɪnsaɪklə'pi:dɪə/ n enciclopedia f. ~**c** adj enciclopédico

end /end/ n fin m; (furthest point) extremo m. **in the ~** por fin. **make ~s meet** poder llegar a fin de mes. **put an ~ to** poner fin a. **no ~ of** muchísimos. **on ~** de pie; (consecutive) seguido. ● vt/i terminar, acabar

endanger /ɪn'deɪndʒə(r)/ vt poner en peligro. ~**ed** adj (species) en peligro

endearing /ɪn'dɪərɪŋ/ adj simpático

endeavour /ɪn'devə(r)/ n esfuerzo m, intento m. ● vi. ~ **to** esforzarse por

ending /'endɪŋ/ n fin m

endless /'endlɪs/ adj interminable

endorse /ɪn'dɔ:s/ vt endosar; (fig) aprobar. ~**ment** n endoso m; (fig) aprobación f; (Auto) nota f de inhabilitación

endur|ance /ɪn'djʊərəns/ n resistencia f. ~**e** /ɪn'djʊə(r)/ vt aguantar. ~**ing** adj perdurable

enemy /'enəmɪ/ n & a enemigo (m)

energ|etic /enə'dʒetɪk/ adj enérgico. ~**y** /'enədʒɪ/ n energía f. ~**y-efficient** adj energéticamente eficiente

enforce /ɪn'fɔ:s/ vt hacer cumplir (law); hacer valer (claim). ~**d** adj forzado

engag|e /ɪn'geɪdʒ/ vt emplear (staff); captar (attention); (Mec) hacer engranar. ● vi (Mec) engranar. ~**e in** dedicarse a. ~**ed** adj prometido, comprometido (LAm); (busy) ocupado. **be ~ed** (of phone) estar comunicando, estar ocupado (LAm). **get ~ed** prometerse, comprometerse (LAm). ~**ement** n compromiso m

engine /'endʒɪn/ n motor m; (of train) locomotora f. ~ **driver** n maquinista m

engineer /endʒɪ'nɪə(r)/ n ingeniero m; (mechanic) mecánico m; (Amer, Rail) maquinista m. ● vt (contrive) fraguar. ~**ing** n ingeniería f

England /'ɪŋglənd/ n Inglaterra f

English /'ɪŋglɪʃ/ adj inglés. ● n (language) inglés m. ● npl. **the ~** los ingleses. ~**man** /-mən/ n inglés m. ~**woman** n inglesa f

engrav|e /ɪn'greɪv/ vt grabar. ~**ing** n grabado m

engrossed /ɪn'grəʊst/ adj absorto

engulf /ɪn'gʌlf/ vt envolver

enhance /ɪn'hɑ:ns/ vt realzar; aumentar (value)

enigma /ɪ'nɪgmə/ n enigma m. ~**tic** /enɪg'mætɪk/ adj enigmático

enjoy /ɪn'dʒɔɪ/ vt. **I ~ reading** me gusta la lectura. ~ **o.s.** divertirse. ~**able** adj agradable. ~**ment** n placer m

enlarge /ɪn'lɑ:dʒ/ vt agrandar; (Photo) ampliar. ● vi agrandarse. ~ **upon** extenderse sobre. ~**ment** n (Photo) ampliación f

enlighten /ɪn'laɪtn/ vt ilustrar. ~**ment** n. **the E~ment** el siglo de la luces

enlist /ɪn'lɪst/ vt alistar; conseguir (support). ● vi alistarse

enliven /ɪn'laɪvn/ vt animar

enorm|ity /ɪ'nɔ:mətɪ/ n enormidad f. ~**ous** /ɪ'nɔ:məs/ adj enorme. ~**ously** adv enormemente

enough /ɪ'nʌf/ adj & adv bastante. ● n bastante m, suficiente m. ● int ¡basta!

enquir|e /ɪn'kwaɪə(r)/ vt/i preguntar. ~**e about** informarse de. ~**y** n pregunta f; (investigation) investigación f

enrage /ɪn'reɪdʒ/ vt enfurecer

enrol /ɪn'rəʊl/ vt (pt **enrolled**) inscribir, matricular (student). ● vi inscribirse, matricularse

ensue /ɪn'sjuː/ vi seguir

ensure /ɪn'ʃʊə(r)/ vt asegurar

entail /ɪn'teɪl/ vt suponer; acarrear (expense)

entangle /ɪn'tæŋgl/ vt enredar. **~ment** n enredo m

enter /'entə(r)/ vt entrar en, entrar a (esp LAm); presentarse a (competition); inscribirse en (race); (write) escribir. ● vi entrar

enterpris|e /'entəpraɪz/ n empresa f; (fig) iniciativa f. **~ing** adj emprendedor

entertain /entə'teɪn/ vt entretener; recibir (guests); abrigar (ideas, hopes); (consider) considerar. **~ing** adj entretenido. **~ment** n entretenimiento m; (show) espectáculo m

enthral /ɪn'θrɔːl/ vt (pt **enthralled**) cautivar

enthuse /ɪn'θjuːz/ vi. **~ over** entusiasmarse por

enthusias|m /ɪn'θjuːzɪæzəm/ n entusiasmo m. **~t** n entusiasta m & f. **~tic** /-'æstɪk/ adj entusiasta. **~tically** adv con entusiasmo

entice /ɪn'taɪs/ vt atraer

entire /ɪn'taɪə(r)/ adj entero. **~ly** adv completamente. **~ty** /ɪn'taɪərəti/ n. **in its ~ty** en su totalidad

entitle /ɪn'taɪtl/ vt titular; (give a right) dar derecho a. **be ~d to** tener derecho a. **~ment** n derecho m

entity /'entəti/ n entidad f

entrails /'entreɪlz/ npl entrañas fpl

entrance /'entrəns/ n entrada f. ● /ɪn'trɑːns/ vt encantar

entrant /'entrənt/ n participante m & f; (in exam) candidato m

entreat /ɪn'triːt/ vt suplicar. **~y** n súplica f

entrenched /ɪn'trentʃt/ adj (position) afianzado

entrust /ɪn'trʌst/ vt confiar

entry /'entri/ n entrada f

entwine /ɪn'twaɪn/ vt entrelazar

enumerate /ɪ'njuːməreɪt/ vt enumerar

envelop /ɪn'veləp/ vt envolver

envelope /'envələʊp/ n sobre m

enviable /'envɪəbl/ adj envidiable

envious /'envɪəs/ adj envidioso

environment /ɪn'vaɪərənmənt/ n medio m ambiente. **~al** /-'mentl/ adj ambiental

envisage /ɪn'vɪzɪdʒ/ vt prever; (imagine) imaginar

envision /ɪn'vɪʒn/ vt (Amer) prever

envoy /'envɔɪ/ n enviado m

envy /'envi/ n envidia f. ● vt envidiar

enzyme /'enzaɪm/ n enzima f

ephemeral /ɪ'femərəl/ adj efímero

epic /'epɪk/ n épica f. ● adj épico

epidemic /epɪ'demɪk/ n epidemia f. ● adj epidémico

epilep|sy /'epɪlepsi/ n epilepsia f. **~tic** /-'leptɪk/ adj & n epiléptico (m)

epilogue /'epɪlɒg/ n epílogo m

episode /'epɪsəʊd/ n episodio m

epitaph /'epɪtɑːf/ n epitafio m

epitom|e /ɪ'pɪtəmi/ n personificación f, epítome m. **~ize** vt ser la personificación de

epoch /'iːpɒk/ n época f

equal /'iːkwəl/ adj & n igual (m & f). **~ to** (a task) a la altura de. ● vt (pt **equalled**) ser igual a; (Math) ser. **~ity** /ɪ'kwɒləti/ n igualdad f. **~ize** vt igualar. ● vi (Sport) empatar. **~izer** n (Sport) gol m del empate. **~ly** adv igualmente; (share) por igual

equation /ɪ'kweɪʒn/ n ecuación f

equator /ɪ'kweɪtə(r)/ n ecuador m. **~ial** /ekwə'tɔːrɪəl/ adj ecuatorial

equilibrium /iːkwɪ'lɪbrɪəm/ n equilibrio m

equinox /'iːkwɪnɒks/ n equinoccio m

equip /ɪ'kwɪp/ vt (pt **equipped**) equipar. **~ sth with** proveer algo de. **~ment** n equipo m

equivalen|ce /ɪ'kwɪvələns/ n equivalencia f. **~t** adj & n equivalente (m). **be ~t to** equivaler

equivocal /ɪ'kwɪvəkl/ adj equívoco

era /'ɪərə/ n era f

eradicate /ɪ'rædɪkeɪt/ vt erradicar, extirpar

erase /ɪ'reɪz/ vt borrar. **~r** n goma f (de borrar)

erect /ɪ'rekt/ adj erguido. ● vt levantar. ~**ion** /-ʃn/ n construcción f; (physiology) erección f

ero|de /ɪ'rəʊd/ vt erosionar. ~**sion** /-ʒn/ n erosión f

erotic /ɪ'rɒtɪk/ adj erótico

err /ɜ:(r)/ vi errar; (sin) pecar

errand /'erənd/ n recado m, mandado m (LAm)

erratic /ɪ'rætɪk/ adj desigual; (person) voluble

erroneous /ɪ'rəʊnɪəs/ adj erróneo

error /'erə(r)/ n error m

erudit|e /'eru:daɪt/ adj erudito. ~**ion** /-'dɪʃn/ n erudición f

erupt /ɪ'rʌpt/ vi entrar en erupción; (fig) estallar. ~**ion** /-ʃn/ n erupción f

escalat|e /'eskəleɪt/ vt intensificar. ● vi intensificarse. ~**ion** /-'leɪʃn/ n intensificación f. ~**or** n escalera f mecánica

escapade /eskə'peɪd/ n aventura f

escap|e /ɪ'skeɪp/ vi escaparse. ● vt evitar. ● n fuga f; (of gas, water) escape m. **have a narrow ~e** escapar por un pelo. ~**ism** /-ɪzəm/ n escapismo m

escort /'eskɔ:t/ n acompañante m; (Mil) escolta f. ● /ɪ'skɔ:t/ vt acompañar; (Mil) escoltar

Eskimo /'eskɪməʊ/ n (pl **-os** or invar) esquimal m & f

especial /ɪ'speʃl/ adj especial. ~**ly** adv especialmente

espionage /'espɪənɑ:ʒ/ n espionaje m

Esq. /ɪ'skwaɪə(r)/ abbr (= **Esquire**) (in address) **E. Ashton**, ~ Sr. Don E. Ashton

essay /'eseɪ/ n ensayo m; (at school) composición f

essence /'esns/ n esencia f. **in** ~ esencialmente

essential /ɪ'senʃl/ adj esencial. ● n elemento m esencial. ~**ly** adv esencialmente

establish /ɪ'stæblɪʃ/ vt establecer. ~**ment** n establecimiento m. **the E~ment** los que mandan

estate /ɪ'steɪt/ n finca f; (housing estate) complejo m habitacional, urbanización f, fraccionamiento m (Mex); (possessions) bienes mpl. ~ **agent** n agente m inmobiliario. ~ **car** n ran-

chera f, (coche m) familiar m, camioneta f (LAm)

esteem /ɪ'sti:m/ n estima f

estimat|e /'estɪmət/ n cálculo m; (Com) presupuesto m. ● /'estɪmeɪt/ vt calcular. ~**ion** /-'meɪʃn/ n estimación f; (opinion) opinión f

estranged /ɪs'treɪndʒd/ adj alejado

estuary /'estʃʊərɪ/ n estuario m

etc /et'setrə/ abbr (= **et cetera**) etc.

etching /'etʃɪŋ/ n aguafuerte m

etern|al /ɪ'tɜ:nl/ adj eterno. ~**ity** /-ətɪ/ n eternidad f

ether /'i:θə(r)/ n éter m

ethic /'eθɪk/ n ética f. ~**al** adj ético. ~**s** npl ética f

ethnic /'eθnɪk/ adj étnico

etiquette /'etɪket/ n etiqueta f

etymology /etɪ'mɒlədʒɪ/ n etimología f

EU /i:'ju:/ abbr (**European Union**) UE (Unión Europea)

euphemism /'ju:fəmɪzəm/ n eufemismo m

euphoria /ju:'fɔ:rɪə/ n euforia f

euro /'jʊərəʊ/ n euro m

Europe /'jʊərəp/ n Europa f. ~**an** /-'pɪən/ adj & n europeo (m). ~**an Health Insurance Card** n Tarjeta f Sanitaria Europea. ~**an Union** n Unión f Europea

euthanasia /ju:θə'neɪzɪə/ n eutanasia f

evacuat|e /ɪ'vækjʊeɪt/ vt evacuar; desocupar (building). ~**ion** /-'eɪʃn/ n evacuación f

evade /ɪ'veɪd/ vt evadir

evalua|te /ɪ'væljʊeɪt/ vt evaluar. ~**tion** /-'eɪʃn/ n evaluación f

evangelical /i:væn'dʒelɪkl/ adj evangélico

evaporat|e /ɪ'væpəreɪt/ vi evaporarse. ~**ion** /-'reɪʃn/ n evaporación f

evasi|on /ɪ'veɪʒn/ n evasión f. ~**ve** /ɪ'veɪsɪv/ adj evasivo

eve /i:v/ n víspera f

even /'i:vn/ adj (flat, smooth) plano; (colour) uniforme; (distribution) equitativo; (number) par. **get ~ with** desquitarse con. ● vt nivelar. □ ~ **up** vt equilibrar. ● adv aun, hasta, incluso.

~ **if** aunque. ~ **so** aun así. **not** ~ ni siquiera

evening /'iːvnɪŋ/ n tarde f; (*after dark*) noche f. ~ **class** n clase f nocturna

event /ɪ'vent/ n acontecimiento m; (*Sport*) prueba f. **in the** ~ **of** en caso dc. ~**ful** adj lleno de acontecimientos

eventual /ɪ'ventʃʊəl/ adj final, definitivo. ~**ity** /-'ælətɪ/ n eventualidad f. ~**ly** adv finalmente

ever /'evə(r)/ adv (*negative*) nunca, jamás; (*at all times*) siempre. **have you ~ been to Greece?** ¿has estado (alguna vez) en Grecia?, ~ **after** desde entonces. ~ **since** desde entonces. ~ **so** Ⓔ muy. **for** ~ para siempre. **hardly** ~ casi nunca. ~**green** adj de hoja perenne. ● n árbol m de hoja perenne. ~**lasting** adj eterno.

every /'evrɪ/ adj cada, todo. ~ **child** todos los niños. ~ **one** cada uno. ~ **other day** un día sí y otro no. ~**body** pron todos, todo el mundo. ~**day** adj de todos los días. ~**one** pron todos, todo el mundo. ~**thing** pron todo. ~**where** adv (*be*) en todas partes, (*go*) a todos lados

evict /ɪ'vɪkt/ vt desahuciar. ~**ion** /-ʃn/ n desahucio m

eviden|ce /'evɪdəns/ n evidencia f; (*proof*) pruebas fpl; (*Jurid*) testimonio m; **give ~ to** prestar declaración. ~**ce of** señales de. **in** ~**ce** visible. ~t adj evidente. ~**tly** adv evidentemente

evil /'iːvl/ adj malvado. ● n mal m

evo|cative /ɪ'vɒkətɪv/ adj evocador. ~**ke** /ɪ'vəʊk/ vt evocar

evolution /iːvə'luːʃn/ n evolución f

evolve /ɪ'vɒlv/ vt desarrollar. ● vi evolucionar

ewe /juː/ n oveja f

exact /ɪg'zækt/ adj exacto. ● vt exigir (**from** a). ~**ing** adj exigente. ~**ly** adv exactamente

exaggerat|e /ɪg'zædʒəreɪt/ vt exagerar. ~**ion** /-'reɪʃn/ n exageración f

exam /ɪg'zæm/ n examen m. ~**ination** /ɪgzæmɪ'neɪʃn/ n examen m. ~**ine** /ɪg 'zæmɪn/ vt examinar; interrogar (*witness*). ~**iner** n examinador m

example /ɪg'zɑːmpl/ n ejemplo m. **for** ~ por ejemplo. **make an** ~ **of s.o.** darle un castigo ejemplar a uno

exasperat|e /ɪg'zæspəreɪt/ vt exasperar. ~**ing** adj exasperante. ~**ion** /-'reɪʃn/ n exasperación f

excavat|e /'ekskəveɪt/ vt excavar. ~**ion** /-'veɪʃn/ n excavación f

exceed /ɪk'siːd/ vt exceder. ~**ingly** adv sumamente

excel /ɪk'sel/ vi (*pt* excelled) sobresalir. ● vt. ~ **o.s.** lucirse. ~**lence** /'eksələns/ n excelencia f. ~**lent** adj excelente

except /ɪk'sept/ prep menos, excepto. ~ **for** si no fuera por. ● vt exceptuar. ~**ing** prep con excepción de

exception /ɪk'sepʃən/ n excepción f. **take ~ to** ofenderse por. ~**al** adj excepcional. ~**ally** adv excepcionalmente

excerpt /'eksɜːpt/ n extracto m

excess /ɪk'ses/ n exceso m. ● /'ekses/ adj excedente. ~ **fare** suplemento m. ~ **luggage** exceso m de equipaje. ~**ive** adj excesivo

exchange /ɪk'stʃeɪndʒ/ vt cambiar. ● n intercambio m; (*of money*) cambio m. (**telephone**) ~ central f telefónica

excise /'eksaɪz/ n impuestos mpl interos. ● /ek'saɪz/ vt quitar

excit|able /ɪk'saɪtəbl/ adj excitable. ~**e** /ɪk'saɪt/ vt emocionar; (*stimulate*) excitar. ~**ed** adj entusiasmado. **get** ~**ed** entusiasmarse. ~**ement** n emoción f; (*enthusiasm*) entusiasmo m. ~**ing** adj emocionante

excla|im /ɪk'skleɪm/ vi/t exclamar. ~**mation** /eksklə'meɪʃn/ n exclamación f. ~**mation mark** n signo m de admiración f

exclu|de /ɪk'skluːd/ vt excluir. ~**sion** /-ʒən/ n exclusión f. ~**sive** /ɪk 'skluːsɪv/ adj exclusivo; (club) selecto. ~**sive of** excluyendo. ~**sively** adv exclusivamente

excruciating /ɪk'skruːʃɪeɪtɪŋ/ adj atroz, insoportable

excursion /ɪk'skɜːʃn/ n excursión f

excus|able /ɪk'skjuːzəbl/ adj perdonable. ~**e** /ɪk'skjuːz/ vt perdonar. ~**e from** dispensar de. ~**e me!** ¡perdón! ● /ɪk'skjuːs/ n excusa f

ex-directory /eksdɪˈrektərɪ/ *adj* que no figura en la guía telefónica, privado (*Mex*)

execut|e /ˈeksɪkjuːt/ *vt* ejecutar. **~ion** /eksɪˈkjuːʃn/ *n* ejecución f. **~ioner** *n* verdugo *m*

executive /ɪgˈzekjʊtɪv/ *adj & n* ejecutivo (*m*)

exempt /ɪgˈzempt/ *adj* exento (**from** de). ● *vt* dispensar. **~ion** /-ʃn/ *n* exención f

exercise /ˈeksəsaɪz/ *n* ejercicio *m*. ● *vt* ejercer. ● *vi* hacer ejercicio. **~ book** *n* cuaderno *m*

exert /ɪgˈzɜːt/ *vt* ejercer. **~ o.s.** hacer un gran esfuerzo. **~ion** /-ʃn/ *n* esfuerzo *m*

exhale /eksˈheɪl/ *vt/i* exhalar

exhaust /ɪgˈzɔːst/ *vt* agotar. ● *n* (*Auto*) tubo *m* de escape. **~ed** *adj* agotado. **~ion** /-stʃən/ *n* agotamiento *m*. **~ive** *adj* exhaustivo

exhibit /ɪgˈzɪbɪt/ *vt* exponer; (*fig*) mostrar. ● *n* objeto *m* expuesto; (*Jurid*) documento *m*. **~ion** /eksɪˈbɪʃn/ *n* exposición. **~ionist** *n* exhibicionista *m & f*. **~or** /ɪgˈzɪbɪtə(r)/ *n* expositor *m*

exhilarat|ing /ɪgˈzɪləreɪtɪŋ/ *adj* excitante. **~ion** /-ˈreɪʃn/ *n* regocijo *m*

exhort /ɪgˈzɔːt/ *vt* exhortar

exile /ˈeksaɪl/ *n* exilio *m*; (*person*) exiliado *m*. ● *vt* desterrar

exist /ɪgˈzɪst/ *vi* existir. **~ence** *n* existencia f. **in ~ence** existente

exit /ˈeksɪt/ *n* salida f

exorbitant /ɪgˈzɔːbɪtənt/ *adj* exorbitante

exorcis|e /ˈeksɔːsaɪz/ *vt* exorcizar. **~m** /-sɪzəm/ *n* exorcismo *m*. **~t** *n* exorcista *m & f*

exotic /ɪgˈzɒtɪk/ *adj* exótico

expand /ɪkˈspænd/ *vt* expandir; (*develop*) desarrollar. ● *vi* expandirse

expanse /ɪkˈspæns/ *n* extensión f

expansion /ɪkˈspænʃn/ *n* expansión f

expatriate /eksˈpætrɪət/ *adj & n* expatriado (*m*)

expect /ɪkˈspekt/ *vt* esperar; (*suppose*) suponer; (*demand*) contar con. **I ~ so** supongo que sí. **~ancy** *n* esperanza f. **life ~ancy** esperanza f de vida. **~ant** *adj* expectante. **~ant**

mother *n* futura madre f

expectation /ekspekˈteɪʃn/ *n* expectativa f

expedient /ɪkˈspiːdɪənt/ *adj* conveniente. ● *n* expediente *m*

expedition /ekspɪˈdɪʃn/ *n* expedición f

expel /ɪkˈspel/ *vt* (*pt* **expelled**) expulsar

expend /ɪkˈspend/ *vt* gastar. **~able** *adj* prescindible. **~iture** /-ɪtʃə(r)/ *n* gastos *mpl*

expens|e /ɪkˈspens/ *n* gasto *m*. **at s.o.'s ~e** a costa de uno. **~es** *npl* (*Com*) gastos *mpl*. **~ive** *adj* caro

experience /ɪkˈspɪərɪəns/ *n* experiencia. ● *vt* experimentar. **~d** *adj* con experiencia; (*driver*) experimentado

experiment /ɪkˈsperɪmənt/ *n* experimento *m*. ● *vi* experimentar. **~al** /-ˈmentl/ *adj* experimental

expert /ˈekspɜːt/ *adj & n* experto (*m*). **~ise** /ekspɜːˈtiːz/ *n* pericia f. **~ly** *adv* hábilmente

expir|e /ɪkˈspaɪə(r)/ *vi* (*passport, ticket*) caducar; (*contract*) vencer. **~y** *n* vencimiento *m*, caducidad f

expla|in /ɪkˈspleɪn/ *vt* explicar. **~nation** /ekspləˈneɪʃn/ *n* explicación f. **~natory** /ɪksˈplænətərɪ/ *adj* explicativo

explicit /ɪkˈsplɪsɪt/ *adj* explícito

explode /ɪkˈspləʊd/ *vt* hacer explotar. ● *vi* estallar

exploit /ˈeksplɔɪt/ *n* hazaña f. ● /ɪkˈsplɔɪt/ *vt* explotar. **~ation** /eksplɔɪˈteɪʃn/ *n* explotación f

explor|ation /ekspləˈreɪʃn/ *n* exploración f. **~atory** /ɪkˈsplɒrətrɪ/ *adj* exploratorio. **~e** /ɪkˈsplɔː(r)/ *vt* explorar. **~er** *n* explorador *m*

explosi|on /ɪkˈspləʊʒn/ *n* explosión f. **~ve** /-sɪv/ *adj & n* explosivo (*m*)

export /ɪkˈspɔːt/ *vt* exportar. ● /ˈekspɔːt/ *n* exportación f; (*item*) artículo *m* de exportación. **~er** /ɪksˈpɔːtə(r)/ *n* exportador *m*

expos|e /ɪkˈspəʊz/ *vt* exponer; (*reveal*) descubrir. **~ure** /-ʒə(r)/ *n* exposición f. **die of ~ure** morir de frío

express /ɪkˈspres/ *vt* expresar. ● *adj* expreso; (*letter*) urgente. ● *adv* (*by ex-*

press post) por correo urgente. ● _n_ (_train_) rápido _m_, expreso _m_. ~**ion** _n_ expresión _f_. ~**ive** _adj_ expresivo. ~**ly** _adv_ expresadamente. ~**way** _n_ (_Amer_) autopista _f_

expulsion /ɪk'spʌlʃn/ _n_ expulsión _f_

exquisite /'ekskwɪzɪt/ _adj_ exquisito

exten|d /ɪk'stend/ _vt_ extender; (_prolong_) prolongar; ampliar (_house_). ● _vi_ extenderse. ~**sion** /-ʃn/ _n_ extensión _f_; (_of road, time_) prolongación _f_; (_building_) anejo _m_. ~**sive** /-sɪv/ _adj_ extenso. ~**sively** _adv_ extensamente. ~**t** _n_ extensión _f_; (_fig_) alcance _m_. **to a certain** ~**t** hasta cierto punto

exterior /ɪk'stɪərɪə(r)/ _adj & n_ exterior (_m_)

exterminat|e /ɪk'stɜːmɪneɪt/ _vt_ exterminar. ~**ion** /-'neɪʃn/ _n_ exterminio _m_

external /ɪk'stɜːnl/ _adj_ externo

extinct /ɪk'stɪŋkt/ _adj_ extinto. ~**ion** /-ʃn/ _n_ extinción _f_

extinguish /ɪk'stɪŋgwɪʃ/ _vt_ extinguir. ~**er** _n_ extintor _m_, extinguidor _m_ (_LAm_)

extol /ɪk'stəʊl/ _vt_ (_pt_ **extolled**) alabar

extort /ɪk'stɔːt/ _vt_ sacar por la fuerza. ~**ion** /-ʃn/ _n_ exacción _f_. ~**ionate** /-ənət/ _adj_ exorbitante

extra /'ekstrə/ _adj_ de más. ● _adv_ extraordinariamente. ● _n_ suplemento _m_; (_Cinema_) extra _m & f_

extract /'ekstrækt/ _n_ extracto _m_. ● /ɪk'strækt/ _vt_ extraer. ~**ion** /ɪk'strækʃn/ _n_ extracción _f_

extradit|e /'ekstrədaɪt/ _vt_ extraditar. ~**ion** /-'dɪʃn/ _n_ extradición _f_

extra ~**ordinary** /ɪk'strɔːdnrɪ/ _adj_ extraordinario. ~**sensory** /ekstrə 'sensərɪ/ _adj_ extrasensorial

extravagan|ce /ɪk'strævəgəns/ _n_ prodigalidad _f_; (_of gestures, dress_) extravagancia _f_. ~**t** _adj_ pródigo; (_behaviour_) extravagante. ~**za** _n_ gran espectáculo _m_

extrem|e /ɪk'striːm/ _adj & n_ extremo (_m_). ~**ely** _adv_ extremadamente. ~**ist** _n_ extremista _m & f_

extricate /'ekstrɪkeɪt/ _vt_ desenredar, librar

extrovert /'ekstrəvɜːt/ _n_ extrovertido _m_

exuberan|ce /ɪg'zjuːbərəns/ _n_ exuberancia _f_. ~**t** _adj_ exuberante

exude /ɪg'zjuːd/ _vt_ rezumar

exult /ɪg'zʌlt/ _vi_ exultar. ~**ation** /egzʌl'teɪʃn/ _n_ exultación _f_

eye /aɪ/ _n_ ojo _m_. **keep an** ~ **on** no perder de vista. **see** ~ **to** ~ **with s.o.** estar de acuerdo con uno. ● _vt_ (_pt_ **eyed**, _pres p_ **eyeing**) mirar. ~**ball** _n_ globo _m_ ocular. ~**brow** _n_ ceja _f_. ~**drops** _npl_ colirio _m_. ~**lash** _n_ pestaña _f_. ~**lid** _n_ párpado _m_. ~**opener** _n_ 🄴 revelación _f_. ~**shadow** _n_ sombra _f_ de ojos. ~**sight** _n_ vista _f_. ~**sore** _n_ (_fig, fam_) monstruosidad _f_, adefesio _m_. ~**witness** _n_ testigo _m_ ocular

Ff

fable /'feɪbl/ _n_ fábula _f_

fabric /'fæbrɪk/ _n_ tejido _m_, tela _f_

fabricate /'fæbrɪkeɪt/ _vt_ inventar. ~**ation** /-'keɪʃn/ _n_ invención _f_

fabulous /'fæbjʊləs/ _adj_ fabuloso

facade /fə'sɑːd/ _n_ fachada _f_

face /feɪs/ _n_ cara _f_, rostro _m_; (_of watch_) esfera _f_, carátula _f_ (_Mex_); (_aspect_) aspecto _m_. ~ **down(wards)** boca abajo. ~ **up(wards)** boca arriba. **in the** ~ **of** frente a. **lose** ~ quedar mal. **pull** ~**s** hacer muecas. ● _vt_ mirar hacia; (_house_) dar a; (_confront_) enfrentarse con. ● _vi_ volverse. □ ~ **up to** _vt_ enfrentarse con. ~ **flannel** _n_ paño _m_ (para lavarse la cara). ~**less** _adj_ anónimo. ~ **lift** _n_ cirugía _f_ estética en la cara

facetious /fə'siːʃəs/ _adj_ burlón

facial /'feɪʃl/ _adj_ facial

facile /'fæsaɪl/ _adj_ superficial, simplista

facilitate /fə'sɪlɪteɪt/ _vt_ facilitar

facility /fə'sɪlɪtɪ/ _n_ facilidad _f_

fact /fækt/ _n_ hecho _m_. **as a matter of** ~, **in** ~ en realidad, de hecho

faction /'fækʃn/ _n_ facción _f_

factor /'fæktə(r)/ _n_ factor _m_

factory /'fæktərɪ/ _n_ fábrica _f_

factual /'fæktʃʋəl/ *adj* basado en hechos, factual

faculty /'fækəltɪ/ *n* facultad *f*

fad /fæd/ *n* manía *f*, capricho *m*

fade /feɪd/ *vi* (colour) desteñirse; (flowers) marchitarse; (light) apagarse; (memory, sound) desvanecerse

fag /fæg/ *n* (*fam*, *chore*) faena *f*; (*sl*, *cigarette*) cigarrillo *m*, pitillo *m*

Fahrenheit /'færənhaɪt/ *adj* Fahrenheit

fail /feɪl/ *vi* fracasar; (brakes) fallar; (*in an exam*) suspender, ser reprobado (*LAm*). **he ~ed to arrive** no llegó. ●*vt* suspender, ser reprobado en (*LAm*) (exam); suspender, reprobar (*LAm*) (candidate). ●*n*. **without ~** sin falta. **~ing** *n* defecto *m*. ●*prep*. **~ing that,** ... si eso no resulta.... **~ure** /'feɪljə(r)/ *n* fracaso *m*

faint /feɪnt/ *adj* (-er, -est) (*weak*) débil; (*indistinct*) indistinto. **feel ~** estar mareado. **the ~est idea** la más remota idea. ●*vi* desmayarse. ●*n* desmayo *m*. **~-hearted** /-'hɑːtɪd/ *adj* pusilánime, cobarde. **~ly** *adv* (*weakly*) débilmente; (*indistinctly*) indistintamente; (*slightly*) ligeramente

fair /feə(r)/ *adj* (-er, -est) (*just*) justo; (weather) bueno; (amount) razonable; (hair) rubio, güero (*Mex fam*); (skin) blanco. ●*adv* limpio. ●*n* feria *f*. **~-haired** /-'heəd/ *adj* rubio, güero (*Mex fam*). **~ly** *adv* (*justly*) justamente; (*rather*) bastante. **~ness** *n* justicia *f*. **in all ~ness** sinceramente. **~ play** *n* juego *m* limpio. **~ trade** *n* comercio *m* justo

fairy /'feərɪ/ *n* hada *f*. **~ story,** **~ tale** *n* cuento *m* de hadas

faith /feɪθ/ *n* (trust) confianza *f*; (*Relig*) fe *f*. **~ful** *adj* fiel. **~fully** *adv* fielmente. **yours ~fully** (*in letters*) (le saluda) atentamente

fake /feɪk/ *n* falsificación *f*; (*person*) farsante *m*. ●*adj* falso. ●*vt* falsificar

falcon /'fɔːlkən/ *n* halcón *m*

Falkland Islands /'fɔːlklənd/ *npl*. **the Falkland Islands, the Falklands** las (Islas) Malvinas

fall /fɔːl/ *vi* (*pt* fell, *pp* fallen) caer; (*decrease*) bajar. ●*n* caída *f*; (*Amer*, *autumn*) otoño *m*; (*in price*) bajada *f*. □ **~ apart** *vi* deshacerse. □ **~ back on** *vt* recurrir a. □ **~ down** *vi* (*fall*) caerse. □ **~ for** *vt* 🛈 enamorarse de (person); dejarse engañar por (trick). □ **~ in** *vi* (*Mil*) formar filas. □ **~ off** *vi* caerse; (*diminish*) disminuir. □ **~ out** *vi* (quarrel) reñir (**with** con); (*drop out*) caerse; (*Mil*) romper filas. □ **~ over** *vi* caerse. *vt* tropezar con. □ **~ through** *vi* no salir adelante

fallacy /'fæləsɪ/ *n* falacia *f*

fallible /'fælɪbl/ *adj* falible

fallout /'fɔːlaʋt/ *n* lluvia *f* radiactiva. **~ shelter** *n* refugio *m* antinuclear

fallow /'fæləʋ/ *adj* en barbecho

false /fɔːls/ *adj* falso. **~ alarm** *n* falsa alarma. **~hood** *n* mentira *f*. **~ly** *adv* falsamente. **~ teeth** *npl* dentadura *f* postiza

falsify /'fɔːlsɪfaɪ/ *vt* falsificar

falter /'fɔːltə(r)/ *vi* vacilar

fame /feɪm/ *n* fama *f*. **~d** *adj* famoso

familiar /fə'mɪlɪə(r)/ *adj* familiar. **the name sounds ~** el nombre me suena. **be ~ with** conocer. **~ity** /-'ærətɪ/ *n* familiaridad *f*. **~ize** *vt* familiarizar

family /'fæməlɪ/ *n* familia *f*. ●*adj* de (la) familia, familiar. **~ tree** *n* árbol *m* genealógico

famine /'fæmɪn/ *n* hambre *f*, hambruna *f*

famished /'fæmɪʃt/ *adj* hambriento

famous /'feɪməs/ *adj* famoso

fan /fæn/ *n* abanico *m*; (*Mec*) ventilador *m*; (*enthusiast*) aficionado *m*; (*of group, actor*) fan *m* & *f*; (*of sport, team*) hincha *m* & *f*. ●*vt* (*pt* fanned) abanicar; avivar (interest). □ **~ out** *vi* desparramarse en forma de abanico

fanatic /fə'nætɪk/ *n* fanático *m*. **~al** *adj* fanático. **~ism** /-sɪzəm/ *n* fanatismo *m*

fan belt *n* correa *f* de ventilador, banda *f* del ventilador (*Mex*)

fanciful /'fænsɪfl/ *adj* (*imaginative*) imaginativo; (*impractical*) extravagante

fancy /'fænsɪ/ *n* imaginación *f*; (*liking*) gusto *m*. **take a ~ to** tomar cariño a (person); aficionarse a (thing). ●*adj* de lujo. ●*vt* (*imagine*) imaginar; (*believe*) creer; (*fam*, *want*) apetecer a.

~ **dress** *n* disfraz *m*

fanfare /'fænfeə(r)/ *n* fanfarria *f*

fang /fæŋ/ *n* (*of animal*) colmillo *m*; (*of snake*) diente *m*

fantasize /'fæntəsaɪz/ *vi* fantasear

fantastic /fæn'tæstɪk/ *adj* fantástico

fantasy /'fæntəsɪ/ *n* fantasía *f*

far /fɑː(r)/ *adv* lejos; (*much*) mucho. **as ~ as** hasta. **as ~ as I know** que yo sepa. **by ~** con mucho. ● *adj* (**further, furthest** *or* **farther, farthest**) lejano. **~ away** lejano

farc|e /fɑːs/ *n* farsa *f*. **~ical** *adj* ridículo

fare /feə(r)/ *n* (*on bus*) precio *m* del billete, precio *m* del boleto (*LAm*); (*on train, plane*) precio *m* del billete, precio *m* del pasaje (*LAm*); (*food*) comida *f*

Far East /fɑːr'iːst/ *n* Extremo *or* Lejano Oriente *m*

farewell /feə'wel/ *int & n* adiós (*m*)

far-fetched /fɑː'fetʃt/ *adj* improbable

farm /fɑːm/ *n* granja *f*. ● *vt* cultivar. □ **~ out** *vt* encargar (a terceros). ● *vi* ser agricultor. **~er** *n* agricultor *m*, granjero *m*. **~house** *n* granja *f*. **~ing** *n* agricultura *f*. **~yard** *n* corral *m*

far ~-off *adj* lejano. **~-reaching** /fɑː'riːtʃɪŋ/ *adj* trascendental. **~-sighted** /fɑː'saɪtɪd/ *adj* con visión del futuro; (*Med, Amer*) hipermétrope

farther, farthest /'fɑːðə(r), 'fɑːðəst/ *see* **FAR**

fascinat|e /'fæsɪneɪt/ *vt* fascinar. **~ed** *adj* fascinado. **~ing** *adj* fascinante. **~ion** /-'neɪʃn/ *n* fascinación *f*

fascis|m /'fæʃɪzəm/ *n* fascismo *m*. **~t** *adj & n* fascista (*m & f*)

fashion /'fæʃn/ *n* (*manner*) manera *f*; (*vogue*) moda *f*. **be in/out of ~** estar de moda/estar pasado de moda. **~able** *adj* de moda

fast /fɑːst/ *adj* (**-er, -est**) rápido; (*clock*) adelantado; (*secure*) fijo; (*colours*) sólido. ● *adv* rápidamente; (*securely*) firmemente. **~ asleep** profundamente dormido. ● *vi* ayunar. ● *n* ayuno *m*

fasten /'fɑːsn/ *vt* sujetar; cerrar (*case*); abrochar (*belt etc*). ● *vi* (*case*) cerrar; (*belt etc*) cerrarse. **~er, ~ing** *n* (*on box, window*) cierre *m*; (*on door*) cerrojo *m*

fat /fæt/ *n* grasa *f*. ● *adj* (**fatter, fattest**) gordo; (*meat*) que tiene mucha grasa; (*thick*) grueso. **get ~** engordar

fatal /'feɪtl/ *adj* mortal; (*fateful*) fatídico. **~ity** /fə'tælətɪ/ muerto *m*. **~ly** *adv* mortalmente

fate /feɪt/ *n* destino *m*; (*one's lot*) suerte *f*. **~d** *adj* predestinado. **~ful** *adj* fatídico

father /'fɑːðə(r)/ *n* padre *m*. **~hood** *m* paternidad *f*. **~-in-law** *m* (*pl* **~s-in-law**) *m* suegro *m*. **~ly** *adj* paternal

fathom /'fæðəm/ *n* braza *f*. ● *vt*. **~ (out)** comprender

fatigue /fə'tiːg/ *n* fatiga *f*. ● *vt* fatigar

fat|ten *vt*. **~ten (up)** cebar (*animal*). **~tening** *adj* que engorda. **~ty** *adj* graso, grasoso (*LAm*). ● *n* 🄵 gordinflón *m*

fatuous /'fætjʊəs/ *adj* fatuo

faucet /'fɔːsɪt/ *n* (*Amer*) grifo *m*, llave *f* (*LAm*)

fault /fɔːlt/ *n* defecto *m*; (*blame*) culpa *f*; (*tennis*) falta *f*; (*in geology*) falla *f*. **at ~** culpable. ● *vt* encontrarle defectos a. **~less** *adj* impecable. **~y** *adj* defectuoso

favour /'feɪvə(r)/ *n* favor *m*. ● *vt* favorecer; (*support*) estar a favor de; (*prefer*) preferir. **~able** *adj* favorable. **~ably** *adv* favorablemente. **~ite** *adj & n* preferido (*m*). **~itism** *n* favoritismo *m*

fawn /fɔːn/ *n* cervato *m*. ● *adj* beige, beis. ● *vi*. **~ on** adular

fax /fæks/ *n* fax *m*. ● *vt* faxear

fear /fɪə(r)/ *n* miedo *m*. ● *vt* temer. **~ful** *adj* (*frightening*) espantoso; (*frightened*) temeroso. **~less** *adj* intrépido. **~some** /-səm/ *adj* espantoso

feasib|ility /fiːzə'bɪlətɪ/ *n* viabilidad *f*. **~le** /'fiːzəbl/ *adj* factible; (*likely*) posible

feast /fiːst/ *n* (*Relig*) fiesta *f*; (*meal*) banquete *m*

feat /fiːt/ *n* hazaña *f*

feather /'feðə(r)/ *n* pluma *f*. **~weight** *n* peso *m* pluma

feature /'fiːtʃə(r)/ *n* (*on face*) rasgo *m*; (*characteristic*) característica *f*; (*in newspaper*) artículo *m*; **~ (film)** película *f* principal, largometraje *m*. ● *vt* presentar; (*give prominence to*) destacar

February /'februəri/ *n* febrero *m*

fed /fed/ *see* FEED

feder|al /'fedərəl/ *adj* federal. **~ation** /fedə'reɪʃn/ *n* federación *f*

fed up *adj* 🔟 harto (**with** de)

fee /fiː/ *n* (*professional*) honorarios *mpl*; (*enrolment*) derechos *mpl*; (*club*) cuota *f*

feeble /'fiːbl/ *adj* (**-er, -est**) débil

feed /fiːd/ *vt* (*pt* **fed**) dar de comer a; (*supply*) alimentar. ● *vi* comer. ● *n* (*for animals*) pienso *m*; (*for babies*) comida *f*. **~back** *n* reacción *f*

feel /fiːl/ *vt* (*pt* **felt**) sentir; (*touch*) tocar; (*think*) considerar. **do you ~ it's a good idea?** ¿te parece buena idea? **~ as if** tener la impresión de que. **~ hot/hungry** tener calor/hambre. **~ like** (*fam, want*) tener ganas de. ● *n* sensación *f*. **get the ~ of sth** acostumbrarse a algo. **~er** *n* (*of insect*) antena *f*. **~ing** *n* sentimiento *m*; (*physical*) sensación *f*

feet /fiːt/ *see* FOOT

feign /feɪn/ *vt* fingir

feint /feɪnt/ *n* finta *f*

fell /fel/ *see* FALL. ● *vt* derribar; talar (tree)

fellow /'feləʊ/ *n* 🔟 tipo *m*; (*comrade*) compañero *m*; (*of society*) socio *m*. **~ countryman** *n* compatriota *m*. **~ passenger/traveller** *n* compañero *m* de viaje

felony /'feləni/ *n* delito *m* grave

felt /felt/ *n see* FEEL. ● *n* fieltro *m*

female /'fiːmeɪl/ *adj* hembra; (*voice, sex etc*) femenino. ● *n* mujer *f*; (*animal*) hembra *f*

femini|ne /'femənɪn/ *adj & n* femenino (*m*). **~nity** /-'nɪnəti/ *n* feminidad *f*. **~st** *adj* & *n* feminista *m & f*

fenc|e /fens/ *n* cerca *f*, cerco *m* (*LAm*). ● *vt*. **~e (in)** encerrar, cercar. ● *vi* (*Sport*) practicar la esgrima. **~er** *n* esgrimidor *m*. **~ing** *n* (*Sport*) esgrima *f*

fend /fend/ *vi*. **~ for o.s.** valerse por sí mismo. **~ off** *vt* defenderse de

fender /'fendə(r)/ *n* rejilla *f*; (*Amer, Auto*) guardabarros *m*, salpicadera *f* (*Mex*)

ferment /fə'ment/ *vt/i* fermentar. **~ation** /-'teɪʃn/ *n* fermentación *f*

fern /fɜːn/ *n* helecho *m*

feroci|ous /fə'rəʊʃəs/ *adj* feroz. **~ty** /fə'rɒsəti/ *n* ferocidad *f*

ferret /'ferɪt/ *n* hurón *m*. ● *vi* (*pt* **ferreted**) **~ about** husmear. ● *vt*. **~ out** descubrir

ferry /'feri/ *n* ferry *m*. ● *vt* transportar

fertil|e /'fɜːtaɪl/ *adj* fértil. **~ity** /-'tɪləti/ *n* fertilidad *f*. **~ize** /'fɜːtəlaɪz/ *vt* fecundar, abonar (soil). **~izer** *n* fertilizante *m*

ferv|ent /'fɜːvənt/ *adj* ferviente. **~our** /-və(r)/ *n* fervor *m*

fester /'festə(r)/ *vi* enconarse

festival /'festəvl/ *n* fiesta *f*; (*of arts*) festival *m*

festiv|e /'festɪv/ *adj* festivo. **the ~e season** *n* las Navidades. **~ity** /fe'stɪvəti/ *n* festividad *f*

fetch /fetʃ/ *vt* (*go for*) ir a buscar; (*bring*) traer; (*be sold for*) venderse en. **~ing** *adj* atractivo

fête /feɪt/ *n* fiesta *f*. ● *vt* festejar

fetish /'fetɪʃ/ *n* fetiche *m*

fetter /'fetə(r)/ *vt* encadenar

feud /fjuːd/ *n* contienda *f*

feudal /'fjuːdl/ *adj* feudal. **~ism** *n* feudalismo *m*

fever /'fiːvə(r)/ *n* fiebre *f*. **~ish** *adj* febril

few /fjuː/ *adj* pocos. **a ~ houses** algunas casas. ● *n* pocos *mpl*. **a ~** unos (pocos). **a good ~, quite a ~** 🔟 muchos. **~er** *adj & n* menos. **~est** *adj* el menor número de

fiancé /fɪ'ɒnseɪ/ *n* novio *m*. **~e** /fɪ'ɒnseɪ/ *n* novia *f*

fiasco /fɪ'æskəʊ/ *n* (*pl* **-os**) fiasco *m*

fib /fɪb/ *n* 🔟 mentirilla *f*. ● *vi* 🔟 mentir, decir mentirillas

fibre /'faɪbə(r)/ *n* fibra *f*. **~glass** *n* fibra *f* de vidrio

fickle /'fɪkl/ *adj* inconstante

ficti|on /'fɪkʃn/ *n* ficción *f*. (**works of**) **~** novelas *fpl*. **~onal** *adj* novelesco. **~tious** /fɪk'tɪʃəs/ *adj* ficticio

fiddle /'fɪdl/ *n* 🔟 violín *m*; (*fam, swindle*) trampa *f*. ● *vt* 🔟 falsificar. **~ with** juguetear con

fidget /'fɪdʒɪt/ vi (pt **fidgeted**) moverse, ponerse nervioso. ~ **with** juguetear con. ●n persona f inquieta. ~**y** adj inquieto

field /fi:ld/ n campo m. ~ **day** n. have a ~ **day** hacer su agosto. ~ **glasses** npl gemelos mpl. **F~ Marshal** n mariscal m de campo. ~ **trip** n viaje m de estudio. ~**work** n investigaciones fpl en el terreno

fiend /fi:nd/ n demonio m. ~**ish** adj diabólico

fierce /fɪəs/ adj (**-er, -est**) feroz; (attack) violento. ~**ly** adv (growl) con ferocidad; (fight) con fiereza

fiery /'faɪərɪ/ adj (**-ier, -iest**) ardiente; (temper) exaltado

fifteen /fɪf'ti:n/ adj & n quince (m). ~**th** adj decimoquinto. ●n quinceavo m

fifth /fɪfθ/ adj & n quinto (m)

fift|ieth /'fɪftɪəθ/ adj quincuagésimo. ●n cincuentavo m. ~**y** adj & n cincuenta (m). ~**y-~y** adv mitad y mitad, a medias. ●adj. a ~**y-~y** **chance** una posibilidad de cada dos

fig /fɪg/ n higo m

fight /faɪt/ vi (pt **fought**) luchar; (quarrel) disputar. ●vt luchar contra. ●n pelea m; (struggle) lucha f; (quarrel) disputa f; (Mil) combate m. □ ~ **back** vi defenderse. □ ~ **off** vt rechazar (attack); luchar contra (illness). ~**er** n luchador m; (aircraft) avión m de caza. ~. **Ing** n luchas fpl

figment /'fɪgmənt/ n. ~ **of the imagination** producto m de la imaginación

figurative /'fɪgjʊrətɪv/ adj figurado

figure /'fɪgə(r)/ n (number) cifra f; (person) figura f; (shape) forma f; (of woman) tipo m. ●vt imaginar; (Amer fam, reckon) calcular. ●vi figurar. **that** ~**s** (fam) es lógico. □ ~ **out** vt entender. ~**head** n testaferro m, mascarón m de proa. ~ **of speech** n figura f retórica

filch /fɪltʃ/ vt ① hurtar

file /faɪl/ n (tool, for nails) lima f; (folder) carpeta f; (set of papers) expediente m; (Comp) archivo m; (row) fila f. **in single** ~ en fila india. ●vt archivar (papers); limar (metal, nails).

~ **in** vi entrar en fila. ~ **past** vt desfilar ante

filing cabinet /'faɪlɪŋ/ n archivador m

fill /fɪl/ vt llenar. ●vi llenarse. ●n. **eat one's** ~ hartarse de comer. have had one's ~ **of** estar harto de □ ~ **in** vt rellenar (form, hole). □ ~ **out** vt rellenar (form). vi (get fatter) engordar. □ ~ **up** vt llenar. vi llenarse

fillet /'fɪlɪt/ n filete m. ●vt (pt **filleted**) cortar en filetes (meat); quitar la espina a (fish)

filling /'fɪlɪŋ/ n (in tooth) empaste m, tapadura f (Mex). ~ **station** n gasolinera f

film /fɪlm/ n película f ●vt filmar. ~ **star** n estrella f de cine

filter /'fɪltə(r)/ n filtro m. ●vt filtrar. ●vi filtrarse. ~**-tipped** adj con filtro

filth /fɪlθ/ n mugre f. ~**y** adj mugriento

fin /fɪn/ n aleta f

final /'faɪnl/ adj último; (conclusive) decisivo. ●n (Sport) final f. ~**s** npl (Schol) exámenes mpl de fin de curso

finale /fɪ'nɑ:lɪ/ n final m

final|ist n finalista m & f. ~**ize** vt ultimar. ~**ly** adv (lastly) finalmente, por fin

financ|e /'faɪnæns/ n finanzas fpl. ●vt financiar. ~**ial** /faɪ'nænʃl/ adj financiero; (difficulties) económico

find /faɪnd/ vt (pt **found**) encontrar. ~ **out** vt descubrir. ●vi (learn) enterarse. ~**ings** npl conclusiones fpl

fine /faɪn/ adj (**-er, -est**) (delicate) fino; (excellent) excelente. ●adv muy bien. ●n multa f. ●vt multar. ~ **arts** npl bellas artes fpl. ~**ly** adv (cut) en trozos pequeños; (adjust) con precisión

finger /'fɪŋgə(r)/ n dedo m. ●vt tocar. ~**nail** n uña f. ~**print** n huella f digital. ~**tip** n punta f del dedo

finish /'fɪnɪʃ/ vt/i terminar, acabar. ~ **doing** terminar de hacer. ●n fin m; (of race) llegada f

finite /'faɪnaɪt/ adj finito

Fin|land /'fɪnlənd/ n Finlandia f. ~**n** n finlandés m. ~**nish** adj & n finlandés (m)

fiord /fjɔ:d/ n fiordo m

fir /fɜ:(r)/ n abeto m

f

fire /faɪə(r)/ n fuego m; (*conflagration*) incendio m. ● vt disparar (gun); (*dismiss*) despedir; avivar (imagination). ● vi disparar. ~ **alarm** n alarma f contra incendios. ~**arm** n arma f de fuego. ~ **brigade**, ~ **department** (*Amer*) n cuerpo m de bomberos. ~ **engine** n coche m de bomberos, carro m de bomberos (*Mex*). ~**-escape** n escalera f de incendios. ~ **extinguisher** n extintor m, extinguidor m (*LAm*). ~**fighter** n bombero m. ~**man** /-mən/ n bombero m. ~**place** n chimenea f. ~**side** n hogar m. ~ **truck** n (*Amer*) see ~ ENGINE. ~**wood** n leña f. ~**work** n fuego m artificial

firm /fɜːm/ n empresa f. ● adj (-**er**, -**est**) firme. ~**ly** adv firmemente

first /fɜːst/ adj primero, (*before masculine singular noun*) primer. **at** ~ **hand** directamente. ● n primero m. ● adv primero; (*first time*) por primera vez. ~ **of all** primero. ~ **aid** n primeros auxilios mpl. ~ **aid kit** n botiquín m. ~ **class** /-'klɑːs/ adv (travel) en primera clase. ~**-class** adj de primera clase. ~ **floor** n primer piso m; (*Amer*) planta f baja. **F~ Lady** n (*Amer*) Primera Dama f. ~**ly** adv en primer lugar. ~ **name** n nombre m de pila. ~**-rate** /-'reɪt/ adj excelente

fish /fɪʃ/ n (*pl invar or* -**es**) pez m; (*as food*) pescado m. ● vi pescar. **go** ~**ing** ir de pesca. □ ~ **out** vt sacar. ~**erman** n pescador m. ~**ing** n pesca f. ~**ing pole** (*Amer*), ~**ing rod** n caña f de pesca. ~**monger** n pescadero m. ~ **shop** n pescadería f. ~**y** adj (smell) a pescado; (*fam, questionable*) sospechoso

fission /'fɪʃn/ n fisión f

fist /fɪst/ n puño m

fit /fɪt/ adj (**fitter**, **fittest**) (*healthy*) en forma; (*good enough*) adecuado; (*able*) capaz. ● n (*attack*) ataque; (*of clothes*) corte m. ● vt (*pt* **fitted**) (*adapt*) adaptar; (*be the right size for*) quedarle bien a; (*install*) colocar. ● vi encajar; (*in certain space*) caber; (clothes) quedarle bien a uno. □ ~ **in** vi caber. ~**ful** adj irregular. ~**ness** n salud f; (*Sport*) (buena) forma f física. ~**ting** adj apropiado. ● n (*of clothes*)

prueba f. ~**ting room** n probador m

five /faɪv/ adj & n cinco (m)

fix /fɪks/ vt fijar; (*mend, deal with*) arreglar. ● n. **in a** ~ en un aprieto. ~**ed** adj fijo. ~**ture** /'fɪkstʃə(r)/ n (*Sport*) partido m

fizz /fɪz/ vi burbujear. ● n efervescencia f. ~**le** /fɪzl/ vi. ~**le out** fracasar. ~**y** adj efervescente; (water) con gas

fjord /fjɔːd/ n fiordo m

flabbergasted /'flæbəgɑːstɪd/ adj estupefacto

flabby /'flæbɪ/ adj flojo

flag /flæg/ n bandera f. ● vi (*pt* **flagged**) (*weaken*) flaquear; (*conversation*) languidecer

flagon /'flægən/ n botella f grande, jarro m

flagpole /'flægpəʊl/ n asta f de bandera

flagrant /'fleɪgrənt/ adj flagrante

flair /fleə(r)/ n don m (**for** de)

flak|e /fleɪk/ n copo m; (*of paint, metal*) escama f. ● vi desconcharse. ~**y** adj escamoso

flamboyant /flæm'bɔɪənt/ adj (clothes) vistoso; (manner) extravagante

flame /fleɪm/ n llama f. **go up in** ~**s** incendiarse

flamingo /flə'mɪŋgəʊ/ n (*pl* -**o(e)s** flamenco m

flammable /'flæməbl/ adj inflamable

flan /flæn/ n tartaleta f

flank /flæŋk/ n (*of animal*) ijada f; (*of person*) costado m; (*Mil, Sport*) flanco m

flannel /'flænl/ n franela f; (*for face*) paño m (para lavarse la cara).

flap /flæp/ vi (*pt* **flapped**) ondear; (wings) aletear. ● vt batir (wings); agitar (arms). ● n (*cover*) tapa f; (*of pocket*) cartera f; (*of table*) ala f. **get into a** ~ 🔲 ponerse nervioso

flare /fleə(r)/ ● n llamarada f; (*Mil*) bengala f; (*in skirt*) vuelo m. □ ~ **up** vi llamear; (fighting) estallar; (person) encolerizarse

flash /flæʃ/ ● vi destellar. ● vt (*aim torch*) dirigir; (*flaunt*) hacer ostentación de. ~ **past** pasar como un rayo. ● n destello m; (*Photo*) flash m. ~**back** n escena f retrospectiva. ~**light** n

(*Amer, torch*) linterna *f*. ~**y** *adj* ostentoso

flask /flɑːsk/ *n* frasco *m*; (*vacuum flask*) termo *m*

flat /flæt/ *adj* (**flatter, flattest**) plano; (tyre) deslnflado; (*refusal*) categórico; (*fare, rate*) fijo; (*Mus*) bemol. ● *adv* (*Mus*) demasiado bajo. ~ **out** (*at top speed*) a toda velocidad. ● *n* (*rooms*) apartamento *m*, piso *m*; 🔲 pinchazo *m*; (*Mus*) (*Auto, esp Amer*) bemol *m*. ~**ly** *adv* categóricamente. ~**ten** *vt* allanar, aplanar

flatter /flætə(r)/ *vt* adular. ~**ing** *adj* (*person*) lisonjero; (*clothes*) favorecedor. ~**y** *n* adulación *f*

flaunt /flɔːnt/ *vt* hacer ostentación de

flavour /ˈfleɪvə(r)/ *n* sabor *m*. ● *vt* sazonar. ~**ing** *n* condimento *m*

flaw /flɔː/ *n* defecto *m*. ~**less** *adj* perfecto

flea /fliː/ *n* pulga *f*

fleck /flek/ *n* mancha *f*, pinta *f*

fled /fled/ *see* **FLEE**

flee /fliː/ *vi* (*pt* **fled**) huir. ● *vt* huir de

fleece /fliːs/ *n* vellón *m*. ● *vt* 🔲 desplumar

fleet /fliːt/ *n* flota *f*; (*of cars*) parque *m* móvil

fleeting /ˈfliːtɪŋ/ *adj* fugaz

Flemish /ˈflemɪʃ/ *adj & n* flamenco (*m*)

flesh /fleʃ/ *n* carne *f*. **in the** ~ en persona

flew /fluː/ *see* **FLY**

flex /fleks/ *vt* doblar; flexionar (*muscle*). ● *n* (*Elec*) cable *m*

flexib|ility /fleksəˈbɪlətɪ/ *n* flexibilidad *f*. ~**le** /ˈfleksəbl/ *adj* flexible

flexitime /ˈfleksɪtaɪm/, (*Amer*) **flextime** /ˈflekstaɪm/ *n* horario *m* flexible

flick /flɪk/ *n* golpecito *m*. ● *vt* dar un golpecito a. □ ~ **through** *vt* hojear

flicker /ˈflɪkə(r)/ *vi* parpadear. ● *n* parpadeo *m*; (*of hope*) resquicio *m*

flies /flaɪz/ *npl* (*on trousers*) bragueta *f*

flight /flaɪt/ *n* vuelo *m*; (*fleeing*) huida *f*, fuga *f*. ~ **of stairs** tramo *m* de escalera *f*. **take** (**to**) ~ darse a la fuga. ~ **attendant** *n* (*male*) sobrecargo *m*, aeromozo *m* (*LAm*); (*female*) azafata *f*,

aeromoza *f* (*LAm*). ~**deck** *n* cubierta *f* de vuelo

flimsy /ˈflɪmzɪ/ *adj* (**-ier, -iest**) flojo, débil, poco sólido

flinch /flɪntʃ/ *vi* retroceder (**from** ante)

fling /flɪŋ/ *vt* (*pt* **flung**) arrojar. ● *n* (*love affair*) aventura *f*; (*wild time*) juerga *f*

flint /flɪnt/ *n* pedernal *m*; (*for lighter*) piedra *f*

flip /flɪp/ *vt* (*pt* **flipped**) dar un golpecito a. ● *n* golpecito *m*. □ ~ **through** *vt* hojear.

flippant /ˈflɪpənt/ *adj* poco serio

flipper /ˈflɪpə(r)/ *n* aleta *f*

flirt /flɜːt/ *vi* coquetear. ● *n* (*woman*) coqueta *f*; (*man*) coqueto *m*

flit /flɪt/ *vi* (*pt* **flitted**) revolotear

float /fləʊt/ *vi* flotar. ● *vt* hacer flotar; introducir en Bolsa (*company*). ● *n* flotador *m*; (*cash*) caja *f* chica

flock /flɒk/ *n* (*of birds*) bandada *f*; (*of sheep*) rebaño *m*. ● *vi* congregarse

flog /flɒg/ *vt* (*pt* **flogged**) (*beat*) azotar; (*fam, sell*) vender

flood /flʌd/ *n* inundación *f*; (*fig*) avalancha *f*. ● *vt* inundar. ● *vi* (*building etc*) inundarse; (*river*) desbordar. ~**light** *n* foco *m*. ● *vt* (*pt* ~**lit**) iluminar (*con focos*)

floor /flɔː(r)/ *n* suelo *m*; (*storey*) piso *m*; (*for dancing*) pista *f*. ● *vt* derribar; (*baffle*) confundir

flop /flɒp/ *vi* (*pt* **flopped**) dejarse caer pesadamente; (*fam, fall*) fracasar. ● *n* 🔲 fracaso *m*. ~**py** *adj* flojo. ● *n* *see* ~**PY DISK**. ~**py disk** *n* disquete *m*, floppy (*disk*) *m*

floral /ˈflɔːrəl/ *adj* floral

florid /ˈflɒrɪd/ *adj* florido

florist /ˈflɒrɪst/ *n* florista *m & f*

flounder /ˈflaʊndə(r)/ *vi* (*in water*) luchar para mantenerse a flote; (*speaker*) quedar sin saber qué decir

flour /ˈflaʊə(r)/ *n* harina *f*

flourish /ˈflʌrɪʃ/ *vi* florecer; (*business*) prosperar. ● *vt* blandir. ● *n* ademán *m* elegante; (*in handwriting*) rasgo *m*. ~**ing** *adj* próspero

flout /flaʊt/ *vt* burlarse de

flow /fləʊ/ vi fluir; (blood) correr; (*hang loosely*) caer. • n flujo m; (*stream*) corriente f; (*of traffic, information*) circulación f. **~ chart** n organigrama m

flower /'flaʊə(r)/ n flor f. • vi florecer, florear (*Mex*). **~ bed** n macizo m de flores. **~y** adj florido

flown /fləʊn/ see FLY

flu /fluː/ n gripe f

fluctuat|e /'flʌktjʊeɪt/ vi fluctuar. **~ion** /-'eɪʃn/ n fluctuación f

flue /fluː/ n tiro m

fluen|cy /'fluːənsɪ/ n fluidez f. **~t** adj (*style*) fluido; (*speaker*) elocuente. **be ~t in a language** hablar un idioma con fluidez. **~tly** adv con fluidez

fluff /flʌf/ n pelusa f. **~y** adj (**-ier, -iest**) velloso

fluid /'fluːɪd/ adj & n fluido (m)

flung /flʌŋ/ see FLING

fluorescent /flʊə'resnt/ adj fluorescente

flush /flʌʃ/ vi ruborizarse. • vt. **~ the toilet** tirar de la cadena, jalarle a la cadena (*LAm*). • n (*blush*) rubor m

fluster /'flʌstə(r)/ vt poner nervioso

flute /fluːt/ n flauta f

flutter /'flʌtə(r)/ vi ondear; (*bird*) revolotear. • n (*of wings*) revoloteo m; (*fig*) agitación f

flux /flʌks/ n flujo m. **be in a state of ~** estar siempre cambiando

fly /flaɪ/ vi (*pt* flew, *pp* flown) volar; (*passenger*) ir en avión; (*flag*) flotar; (*rush*) correr. • vt pilotar, pilotear (*LAm*) (*aircraft*); transportar en avión (*passengers, goods*); izar (*flag*). • n mosca f; (*of trousers*) see FLIES. **~ing** adj volante. **~ing visit** visita f relámpago. • n (*activity*) aviación f. **~leaf** n guarda f. **~over** n paso m elevado

foal /fəʊl/ n potro m

foam /fəʊm/ n espuma f. • vi espumar. **~ rubber** n goma f espuma, hule m espuma (*Mex*)

fob /fɒb/ vt (*pt* fobbed). **~ sth off onto s.o.** (*palm off*) encajarle algo a uno

focal /'fəʊkl/ adj focal

focus /'fəʊkəs/ n (*pl* **-cuses** or **-ci** /-saɪ/) foco m; (*fig*) centro m. **in ~** enfocado. **out of ~** desenfocado. • vt (*pt* focused) enfocar (*fig*) concentrar. • vi enfocar; (*fig*) concentrarse (**on** en)

fodder /'fɒdə(r)/ n forraje m

foe /fəʊ/ n enemigo m

foetus /'fiːtəs/ n (*pl* **-tuses**) feto m

fog /fɒg/ n niebla f

fog|gy adj (**-ier, -iest**) nebuloso. **it is ~gy** hay niebla. **~horn** n sirena f de niebla

foible /'fɔɪbl/ n punto m débil

foil /fɔɪl/ vt (*thwart*) frustrar. • n papel m de plata

foist /fɔɪst/ vt encajar (**on** a)

fold /fəʊld/ vt doblar; cruzar (arms). • vi doblarse; (*fail*) fracasar. • n pliegue m. (*for sheep*) redil m. **~er** n carpeta f. **~ing** adj plegable

foliage /'fəʊlɪɪdʒ/ n follaje m

folk /fəʊk/ n gente f. • adj popular. **~lore** /-lɔː(r)/ n folklore m. **~ music** n música f folklórica; (*modern*) música f folk. **~s** npl (*one's relatives*) familia f

follow /'fɒləʊ/ vt/i seguir. □ **~ up** vt seguir. **~er** n seguidor m. **~ing** n partidarios mpl. • adj siguiente. • prep después de

folly /'fɒlɪ/ n locura f

fond /fɒnd/ adj (**-er, -est**) (*loving*) cariñoso; (*hope*) vivo. **be ~ of s.o.** tener(le) cariño a uno. **be ~ of sth** ser aficionado a algo

fondle /'fɒndl/ vt acariciar

fondness /'fɒndnɪs/ n cariño m; (*for things*) afición f

font /fɒnt/ n pila f bautismal

food /fuːd/ n comida f. **~ processor** n robot m de cocina

fool /fuːl/ n idiota m & f • vt engañar. □ **~ about** vi hacer payasadas. **~hardy** adj temerario. **~ish** adj tonto. **~ishly** adv tontamente. **~ishness** n tontería f. **~proof** adj infalible

foot /fʊt/ n (*pl* feet) pie m; (*measure*) pie m (= 30,48cm); (*of animal, furniture*) pata f. **get under s.o.'s feet** estorbar a uno. **on ~** a pie. **on/to one's feet** de pie. **put one's ~ in it** meter la pata. • vt pagar (bill). **~age** /-ɪdʒ/ n (*of film*) secuencia f. **~and-**

mouth disease n fiebre f aftosa. **~ball** n (ball) balón m; (game) fútbol m; (American ~ball) fútbol m americano. **~baller** n futbolista m & f. **~bridge** n puente m para peatones. **~hills** npl estribaciones fpl. **~hold** n punto m de apoyo. **~ing** n pie m. **on an equal ~ing** en igualdad de condiciones. **~lights** npl candilejas fpl. **~man** /-mən/ n lacayo m. **~note** n nota f (al pie de la página). **~path** n (in country) senda f; (in town) acera f, banqueta f (Mex). **~print** n huella f. **~step** n paso m. **~wear** n calzado m

for /fɔː(r)//fə(r)/
● preposition
····▸ (intended for) para. **it's ~ my mother** es para mi madre. **she works ~ a multinational** trabaja para una multinacional
····▸ (on behalf of) por. **I did it ~ you** lo hice por ti

➡️ See entries **para** and **por** for further information

····▸ (expressing purpose) para. **I use it ~ washing the car** lo uso para limpiar el coche. **what ~?** ¿para qué?. **to go out ~ a meal** salir a comer fuera
····▸ (in favour of) a favor de. **are you ~ or against the idea?** ¿estás a favor o en contra de la idea?
····▸ (indicating cost, in exchange for) por. **I bought it ~ 30 pounds** lo compré por 30 libras. **she left him ~ another man** lo dejó por otro. **thanks ~ everything** gracias por todo. **what's the Spanish ~ toad'?** ¿cómo se dice toad' en español?
····▸ (expressing duration) **he read ~ two hours** leyó durante dos horas. **how long are you going ~?** ¿por cuánto tiempo vas? **I've been waiting ~ three hours** hace tres horas que estoy esperando, llevo tres horas esperando
····▸ (in the direction of) para. **the train ~ Santiago** el tren para Santiago
● conjunction (because) porque, pues

(literary usage). **she left at once, ~ it was getting late** se fue en seguida, porque or pues se hacía tarde

forage /'fɒrɪdʒ/ vi forrajear. ● n forraje m

forbade /fə'bæd/ see **FORBID**

forbearance /fɔː'beərəns/ n paciencia f

forbid /fə'bɪd/ vt (pt **forbade**, pp **forbidden**) prohibir (s.o. to do a uno hacer). **~ s.o. sth** prohibir algo a uno. **~ding** adj imponente

force /fɔːs/ n fuerza f. **by ~** a la fuerza. **come into ~** entrar en vigor. **the ~s** las fuerzas fpl armadas. ● vt forzar; (compel) obligar (s.o. to do sth a uno a hacer algo). **~ on** imponer a. **~ open** forzar. **~d** adj forzado. **~-feed** vt alimentar a la fuerza. **~ful** adj enérgico

forceps /'fɔːseps/ n fórceps m

forcibl|e /'fɔːsəbl/ adj a la fuerza. **~y** adv a la fuerza

ford /fɔːd/ n vado m ● vt vadear

fore /fɔː(r)/ adj anterior. ● n. **come to the ~** hacerse evidente

forearm /'fɔːrɑːm/ n antebrazo m

foreboding /fɔː'bəʊdɪŋ/ n presentimiento m

forecast /'fɔːkɑːst/ vt (pt **forecast**) pronosticar (weather); prever (result). ● n pronóstico m. **weather ~** pronóstico m del tiempo

forecourt /'fɔːkɔːt/ n patio m delantero

forefinger /'fɔːfɪŋgə(r)/ n (dedo m) índice m

forefront /'fɔːfrʌnt/ n vanguardia f. **in the ~** a la vanguardia

forego /fɔː'gəʊ/ vt (pt **forewent**, pp **foregone**) see **FORGO**

foregone /'fɔːgɒn/ adj. **~ conclusion** resultado m previsto

foreground /'fɔːgraʊnd/ n. **in the ~** en primer plano

forehead /'fɒrɪd/ n frente f

foreign /'fɒrən/ adj extranjero; (trade) exterior; (travel) al extranjero, en el extranjero. **~er** n extranjero m

f

foreman /'fɔːmən/ (pl **-men** /-mən/) n capataz m

foremost /'fɔːməʊst/ adj primero. ● adv. first and ~ ante todo

forerunner /'fɔːrʌnə(r)/ n precursor m

foresee /fɔː'siː/ vt (pt **-saw**, pp **-seen**) prever. ~**able** adj previsible

foresight /'fɔːsaɪt/ n previsión f

forest /'fɒrɪst/ n bosque m

forestall /fɔː'stɔːl/ vt (prevent) prevenir; (preempt) anticiparse a

forestry /'fɒrɪstrɪ/ n silvicultura f

foretaste /'fɔːteɪst/ n anticipo m

foretell /fɔː'tel/ vt (pt **foretold**) predecir

forever /fə'revə(r)/ adv para siempre; (always) siempre

forewarn /fɔː'wɔːn/ vt advertir

forewent /fɔː'went/ see FOREGO

foreword /'fɔːwɜːd/ n prefacio m

forfeit /'fɔːfɪt/ n (penalty) pena f; (in game) prenda f. ● vt perder; perder el derecho a (property)

forgave /fə'geɪv/ see FORGIVE

forge /fɔːdʒ/ n fragua f. ● vt fraguar; (copy) falsificar. □ ~ **ahead** vi adelantarse rápidamente. ~**r** n falsificador m. ~**ry** n falsificación f

forget /fə'get/ vt (pt **forgot**, pp **forgotten**) olvidar, olvidarse de. ● vi olvidarse (**about** de). **I forgot** se me olvidó. ~**ful** adj olvidadizo

forgive /fə'gɪv/ vt (pt **forgave**, pp **forgiven**) perdonar. ~ **s.o. for sth** perdonar algo a uno. ~**ness** n perdón m

forgo /fɔː'gəʊ/ vt (pt **forwent**, pp **forgone**) renunciar a

fork /fɔːk/ n tenedor m; (for digging) horca f; (in road) bifurcación f. ● vi (road) bifurcarse. □ ~ **out** vt 🅸 desembolsar, aflojar 🅸. ~**lift truck** n carretilla f elevadora

forlorn /fə'lɔːn/ adj (hope, attempt) desesperado; (smile) triste

form /fɔːm/ n forma f; (document) formulario m; (Schol) clase f. ● vt formar. ● vi formarse

formal /'fɔːml/ adj formal; (person) formalista; (dress) de etiqueta. ~**ity** /-'mælɪtɪ/ n formalidad f. ~**ly** adv oficialmente

format /'fɔːmæt/ n formato m. ● vt (pt **formatted**) (Comp) formatear

formation /fɔː'meɪʃn/ n formación f

former /'fɔːmə(r)/ adj anterior; (first of two) primero. ● n. the ~ el primero m, la primera f, los primeros mpl, las primeras fpl. ~**ly** adv antes

formidable /'fɔːmɪdəbl/ adj formidable

formula /'fɔːmjʊlə/ n (pl **-ae** /-iː/ or **-as**) fórmula f. ~**te** /-leɪt/ vt formular

forsake /fə'seɪk/ vt (pt **forsook**, pp **forsaken**) abandonar

fort /fɔːt/ n fuerte m

forth /fɔːθ/ adv. **and so** ~ y así sucesivamente. ~**coming** /-'kʌmɪŋ/ adj próximo, venidero; (sociable) comunicativo. ~**right** adj directo. ~**with** /-'wɪθ/ adv inmediatamente

fortieth /'fɔːtɪɪθ/ adj cuadragésimo. ● n cuadragésima parte f

fortnight /'fɔːtnaɪt/ n quince días mpl, quincena f. ~**ly** adj bimensual. ● adv cada quince días

fortress /'fɔːtrɪs/ n fortaleza f

fortunate /'fɔːtʃənət/ adj afortunado. **be** ~ tener suerte. ~**ly** adv afortunadamente

fortune /'fɔːtʃuːn/ n fortuna f. ~**-teller** n adivino m

forty /'fɔːtɪ/ adj & n cuarenta (m). ~ **winks** un sueñecito

forum /'fɔːrəm/ n foro m

forward /'fɔːwəd/ adj (movement) hacia adelante; (advanced) precoz; (pert) impertinente. ● n (Sport) delantero m. ● adv adelante. **go** ~ avanzar. ● vt hacer seguir (letter); enviar (goods). ~**s** adv adelante

forwent /fɔː'went/ see FORGO

fossil /'fɒsl/ adj & n fósil (m)

foster /'fɒstə(r)/ vt (promote) fomentar; criar (child). ~ **child** n hijo m adoptivo

fought /fɔːt/ see FIGHT

foul /faʊl/ adj (-er, -est) (smell) nauseabundo; (weather) pésimo; (person) asqueroso; (dirty) sucio; (language) obsceno. ● n (Sport) falta f. ● vt contaminar; (entangle) enredar. ~ **play** n (Sport) jugada f sucia; (crime) delito m

found /faʊnd/ see FIND. ● vt fundar.

foundation /faʊnˈdeɪʃn/ n fundación f; (basis) fundamento. (cosmetic) base f (de maquillaje). **~s** npl (of building) cimientos mpl

founder /ˈfaʊndə(r)/ n fundador m. ● vi (ship) hundirse

fountain /ˈfaʊntɪn/ n fuente f. **~ pen** n pluma f (estilográfica) f, estilográfica f

four /fɔː(r)/ adj & n cuatro (m). **~fold** adj cuádruple. ● adv cuatro veces. **~some** /-səm/ n grupo m de cuatro personas **~teen** /ˈfɔːtiːn/ adj & n catorce (m). **~teenth** adj & n decimocuarto (m). **~th** /fɔːθ/ adj & n cuarto (m). **~-wheel drive** n tracción f integral

fowl /faʊl/ n ave f

fox /fɒks/ n zorro m, zorra f. ● vt 🔲 confundir

foyer /ˈfɔɪeɪ/ n (of theatre) foyer m; (of hotel) vestíbulo m

fraction /ˈfrækʃn/ n fracción f

fracture /ˈfræktʃə(r)/ n fractura f. ● vt fracturar. ● vi fracturarse

fragile /ˈfrædʒaɪl/ adj frágil

fragment /ˈfrægmənt/ n fragmento m. **~ary** /-ərɪ/ adj fragmentario

fragran|ce /ˈfreɪɡrəns/ n fragancia f. **~t** adj fragante

frail /freɪl/ adj (-er, -est) frágil

frame /freɪm/ n (of picture, door, window) marco m; (of spectacles) montura f; (fig, structure) estructura f. ● vt enmarcar (picture); formular (plan, question); (fam, incriminate unjustly) incriminar falsamente. **~work** n estructura f; (context) marco m

France /frɑːns/ n Francia f

frank /fræŋk/ adj franco. ● vt franquear. **~ly** adv francamente

frantic /ˈfræntɪk/ adj frenético. **~ with** loco de

fratern|al /frəˈtɜːnl/ adj fraternal. **~ity** /frəˈtɜːnɪtɪ/ n fraternidad f; (club) asociación f. **~ize** /ˈfrætənaɪz/ vi fraternizar

fraud /frɔːd/ n fraude m; (person) impostor m. **~ulent** /-jʊlənt/ adj fraudulento

fraught /frɔːt/ adj (tense) tenso. **~ with** cargado de

fray /freɪ/ n riña f

freak /friːk/ n fenómeno m; (monster) monstruo m. ● adj anormal. **~ish** adj anormal

freckle /ˈfrekl/ n peca f. **~d** adj pecoso

free /friː/ adj (freer /ˈfriːə(r)/, freest /ˈfriːɪst/) libre; (gratis) gratuito. **~ of charge** gratis. ● vt (pt freed) (set at liberty) poner en libertad; (relieve from) liberar (from/of de); (untangle) desenredar. **~dom** n libertad f. **~hold** n propiedad f absoluta. **~ kick** n tiro m libre. **~lance** adj & adv por cuenta propia. **~ly** adv libremente. **~mason** n masón m. **~-range** adj (eggs) de granja. **~ speech** n libertad f de expresión. **~style** n estilo m libre. **~way** n (Amer) autopista f

freez|e /friːz/ vt (pt froze, pp frozen) helar; congelar (food, wages). ● vi helarse; (become motionless) quedarse inmóvil. ● n (on wages, prices) congelación f. **~er** n congelador m. **~ing** adj glacial. ● n. **~ing (point)** punto m de congelación f. **below ~ing** bajo cero

freight /freɪt/ n (goods) mercancías fpl. **~er** n buque m de carga

French /frentʃ/ adj francés. ● n (language) francés m. ● npl. **the ~** (people) los franceses. **~ fries** npl patatas fpl fritas, papas fpl fritas (LAm). **~man** /-mən/ n francés m. **~ window** n puerta f ventana. **~woman** f francesa f

frenz|ied /ˈfrenzɪd/ adj frenético. **~y** n frenesí m

frequency /ˈfriːkwənsɪ/ n frecuencia f

frequent /frɪˈkwent/ vt frecuentar. ● /ˈfriːkwənt/ adj frecuente. **~ly** adv frecuentemente

fresh /freʃ/ adj (-er, -est) fresco; (different, additional) nuevo; (water) dulce. **~en** vi refrescar. ▫ **~en up** vi (person) refrescarse. **~er** n 🔲 see **~MAN. ~ly** adv recientemente. **~man** n /-mən/ estudiante m de primer año. **~ness** n frescura f

fret /fret/ vi (pt fretted) preocuparse. **~ful** adj (discontented) quejoso; (irritable) irritable

friction /'frɪkʃn/ n fricción f

Friday /'fraɪdeɪ/ n viernes m

fridge /frɪdʒ/ n 🔳 frigorífico m, nevera f, refrigerador m (LAm)

fried /fraɪd/ see **FRY**. ● adj frito

friend /frend/ n amigo m. ~**liness** n simpatía f. ~**ly** adj (-ier, -iest) simpático. ~**ship** n amistad f

fries /fraɪz/ npl see **FRENCH FRIES**

frieze /friːz/ n friso m

frigate /'frɪɡət/ n fragata f

fright /fraɪt/ n miedo m; (shock) susto m. ~**en** vt asustar. □ ~ **off** vt ahuyentar. ~**ened** adj asustado. **be** ~**ened** tener miedo (**of** de.) ~**ful** adj espantoso, horrible. ~**fully** adv terriblemente

frigid /'frɪdʒɪd/ adj frígido

frill /frɪl/ n volante m, olán m (Mex). ~**s** npl (fig) adornos mpl. **with no** ~**s** sencillo

fringe /frɪndʒ/ n (sewing) fleco m; (ornamental border) franja f; (of hair) flequillo m, cerquillo m (LAm), fleco m (Mex); (of area) periferia f; (of society) margen m

fritter /'frɪtə(r)/ vt. □ ~ **away** vt desperdiciar (time); malgastar (money)

frivol|ity /frɪ'vɒlətɪ/ n frivolidad f. ~**ous** /'frɪvələs/ adj frívolo

fro /frəʊ/ see **TO AND FRO**

frock /frɒk/ n vestido m

frog /frɒɡ/ n rana f. **have a** ~ **in one's throat** tener carraspera. ~**man** /-mən/ n hombre m rana. ~**spawn** n huevos mpl de rana

frolic /'frɒlɪk/ vi (pt frolicked) retozar

from /frɒm//frəm/ prep de; (indicating starting point) desde; (habit, conviction) por; ~ **then on** a partir de ahí

front /frʌnt/ n parte f delantera; (of building) fachada f; (of clothes) delantera f; (Mil, Pol) frente f; (of book) principio m; (fig, appearance) apariencia f; (seafront) paseo m marítimo, malecón m (LAm). **in** ~ **of** delante de. ● adj delantero; (first) primero. ~**al** adj frontal; (attack) de frente. ~ **door** n puerta f principal

frontier /'frʌntɪə(r)/ n frontera f

front page n (of newspaper) primera plana f

frost /frɒst/ n (freezing) helada f; (frozen dew) escarcha f. ~**bite** n congelación f. ~**bitten** adj congelado. ~**ed** adj (glass) esmerilado. ~**ing** n (Amer) glaseado m. ~**y** adj (weather) helado; (night) de helada; (fig) glacial

froth /frɒθ/ n espuma f. ● vi espumar. ~**y** adj espumoso

frown /fraʊn/ vi fruncir el entrecejo ● n ceño m. □ ~ **on** vt desaprobar.

froze /frəʊz/ see **FREEZE**. ~**n** /'frəʊzn/ see **FREEZE**. ● adj congelado; (region) helado

frugal /'fruːɡl/ adj frugal

fruit /fruːt/ n (in botany) fruto m; (as food) fruta f. ~**ful** /'fruːtfl/ adj fértil; (fig) fructífero. ~**ion** /fruː'ɪʃn/ n. **come to** ~**ion** realizarse. ~**less** adj infructuoso. ~ **salad** n macedonia f de frutas. ~**y** adj que sabe a fruta

frustrat|e /frʌ'streɪt/ vt frustrar. ~**ion** /-ʃn/ n frustración f. ~**ed** adj frustrado. ~**ing** adj frustrante

fry /fraɪ/ vt (pt fried) freír. ● vi freírse. ~**ing pan** n sartén f, sartén m (LAm)

fudge /fʌdʒ/ n dulce m de azúcar

fuel /'fjuːəl/ n combustible m

fugitive /'fjuːdʒɪtɪv/ adj & n fugitivo (m)

fulfil /fʊl'fɪl/ vt (pt fulfilled) cumplir (con) (promise, obligation); satisfacer (condition); hacer realidad (ambition). ~**ment** n (of promise, obligation) cumplimiento m; (of conditions) satisfacción f; (of hopes, plans) realización f

full /fʊl/ adj (-er, -est) lleno; (bus, hotel) completo; (account) detallado. **at** ~ **speed** a máxima velocidad. **be** ~ (**up**) (with food) no poder más. ● n. **in** ~ sin quitar nada. **to the** ~ completamente. **write in** ~ escribir con todas las letras. ~**back** n (Sport) defensa m & f. ~**-blown** /fʊl'bləʊn/ adj verdadero. ~**-fledged** /-'fledʒd/ adj (Amer) see **FULLY-FLEDGED**. ~ **moon** n luna f llena. ~**-scale** /-'skeɪl/ adj (drawing) de tamaño natural; (fig) amplio. ~ **stop** n punto m. ~**-time** adj (employment) de jornada completa. ● /-'taɪm/ adv a tiempo completo. ~**y** adv completamente. ~**-fledged** /-'fledʒd/ adj (chick) capaz de volar; (lawyer, nurse) hecho y derecho

fulsome /'fʊlsəm/ adj excesivo

fumble /'fʌmbl/ vi buscar (a tientas)

fume /fju:m/ vi despedir gases; (fig, be furious) estar furioso. ~s npl gases mpl

fumigate /'fju:mɪgeɪt/ vt fumigar

fun /fʌn/ n (amusement) diversión f; (merriment) alegría f. **for** ~ en broma. **have** ~ divertirse. **make** ~ **of** burlarse de

function /'fʌŋkʃn/ n (purpose, duty) función f; (reception) recepción f. ● vi funcionar. ~**al** adj funcional

fund /fʌnd/ n fondo m. ● vt financiar

fundamental /fʌndə'mentl/ adj fundamental. ~**ist** adj & n fundamentalista (m & f)

funeral /'fju:nərəl/ n entierro m, funerales mpl. ~ **director** n director m de pompas fúnebres

funfair /'fʌnfeə(r)/ n feria f; (permanent) parque m de atracciones, parque m de diversiones (LAm)

fungus /'fʌŋgəs/ n (pl -**gi** /-gaɪ/) hongo m

funnel /'fʌnl/ n (for pouring) embudo m; (of ship) chimenea f

funn|ily /'fʌnɪlɪ/ adv (oddly) curiosamente. ~**y** adj (-**ier, -iest**) divertido, gracioso; (odd) curioso, raro

fur /fɜː(r)/ n pelo m; (pelt) piel f

furious /'fjʊərɪəs/ adj furioso. ~**ly** adv furiosamente

furlough /'fɜːləʊ/ n (Amer) permiso m. **on** ~ de permiso

furnace /'fɜːnɪs/ n horno m

furnish /'fɜːnɪʃ/ vt amueblar, amoblar (LAm); (supply) proveer. ~**ings** npl muebles mpl, mobiliario m

furniture /'fɜːnɪtʃə(r)/ n muebles mpl, mobiliario m. **a piece of** ~ un mueble

furrow /'fʌrəʊ/ n surco m

furry /'fɜːrɪ/ adj peludo

furthe|r /'fɜːðə(r)/ adj más lejano; (additional) nuevo. ● adv más lejos; (more) además. ● vt fomentar. ~**rmore** adv además. ~**st** adj más lejano. ● adv más lejos

furtive /'fɜːtɪv/ adj furtivo

fury /'fjʊərɪ/ n furia f

fuse /fju:z/ vt (melt) fundir; (fig, unite) fusionar. ~ **the lights** fundir los plomos. ● vi fundirse; (fig) fusionarse. ● n fusible m, plomo m; (of bomb) mecha f. ~**box** n caja f de fusibles

fuselage /'fju:zəlɑːʒ/ n fuselaje m

fusion /'fju:ʒn/ n fusión f

fuss /fʌs/ n (commotion) jaleo m. **kick up a** ~ armar un lío, armar una bronca. **make a** ~ **of** tratar con mucha atención. ● vi preocuparse. ~**y** adj (-**ier, -iest**) (finicky) remilgado; (demanding) exigente

futil|e /'fju:taɪl/ adj inútil, vano. ~**ity** /fju:'tɪlətɪ/ n inutilidad f

futur|e /'fju:tʃə(r)/ adj futuro. ● n futuro m. **in** ~**e** de ahora en adelante. ~**istic** /fju:tʃə'rɪstɪk/ adj futurista

fuzz /fʌz/ n pelusa f. ~**y** adj (hair) crespo; (photograph) borroso

f

g

gab /gæb/ n. **have the gift of the** ~ tener un pico de oro

gabardine /gæbə'diːn/ n gabardina f

gabble /'gæbl/ vi hablar atropelladamente

gable /'geɪbl/ n aguilón m

gad /gæd/ vi (pt gadded). ~ **about** callejear

gadget /'gædʒɪt/ n chisme m

Gaelic /'geɪlɪk/ adj & n gaélico (m)

gaffe /gæf/ n plancha f, metedura f de pata, metida f de pata (LAm)

gag /gæg/ n mordaza f; (joke) chiste m. ● vt (pt gagged) amordazar. ● vi hacer arcadas

gaiety /'geɪətɪ/ n alegría f

gaily /'geɪlɪ/ adv alegremente

gain /geɪn/ vt ganar; (acquire) adquirir; (obtain) conseguir. ● vi (clock) adelantar. ● n ganancia f; (increase) aumento m

gait /geɪt/ n modo m de andar

gala /'gɑːlə/ n fiesta f. ~ **performance** (función f de) gala f

galaxy /'gæləksɪ/ n galaxia f

gale /geɪl/ n vendaval m

gall /gɔːl/ n bilis f; (fig) hiel f; (impudence) descaro m

gallant /'gælənt/ adj (brave) valiente; (chivalrous) galante. ~**ry** n valor m

gall bladder /'gɔːlblædə(r)/ n vesícula f biliar

gallery /'gælərɪ/ n galería f

galley /'gælɪ/ n (ship) galera f; (ship's kitchen) cocina f. ~ (**proof**) n galerada f

gallivant /'gælɪvænt/ vi 🅸 callejear

gallon /'gælən/ n galón m (imperial = 4,546l; Amer = 3,785l)

gallop /'gæləp/ n galope m. ● vi (pt **galloped**) galopar

gallows /'gæləʊz/ n horca f

galore /gə'lɔː(r)/ adj en abundancia

galvanize /'gælvənaɪz/ vt galvanizar

gambl|e /'gæmbl/ vi jugar. ~**e on** contar con. ● vt jugarse. ● n (venture) empresa f arriesgada; (bet) apuesta f; (risk) riesgo m. ~**er** n jugador m. ~**ing** n juego m

game /geɪm/ n juego m; (match) partido m; (animals, birds) caza f. ● adj valiente. ~ **for** listo para. ~**keeper** n guardabosque m. ~**s** n (in school) deportes mpl

gammon /'gæmən/ n jamón m fresco

gamut /'gæmət/ n gama f

gander /'gændə(r)/ n ganso m

gang /gæŋ/ n pandilla f; (of workmen) equipo m. ~**master** n contratista de mano de obra indocumentada. ☐ ~ **up** vi unirse (on contra)

gangling /'gæŋglɪŋ/ adj larguirucho

gangrene /'gæŋgriːn/ n gangrena f

gangster /'gæŋstə(r)/ n bandido m, gángster m & f

gangway /'gæŋweɪ/ n pasillo m; (of ship) pasarela f

gaol /dʒeɪl/ n cárcel f. ~**er** n carcelero m

gap /gæp/ n espacio m; (in fence, hedge) hueco m; (in time) intervalo m; (in knowledge) laguna f; (difference) diferencia f

gap year En Gran Bretaña, es el periodo, entre el final de los estudios secundarios y el ingreso a la universidad, que muchos estudiantes destinan a obtener experiencia laboral relacionada con sus futuras carreras. Otros emprenden actividades no relacionadas con los estudios y para algunos es la oportunidad para ahorrar dinero o viajar.

gap|e /geɪp/ vi quedarse boquiabierto; (be wide open) estar muy abierto. ~**ing** adj abierto; (person) boquiabierto

garage /'gærɑːʒ/ n garaje m, garage m (LAm), cochera f (Mex); (petrol station) gasolinera f; (for repairs, sales) taller m, garage m (LAm)

garbage /'gɑːbɪdʒ/ n basura f. ~ **can** n (Amer) cubo m de la basura, bote m de la basura (Mex). ~ **collector**, ~ **man** n (Amer) basurero m

garble /'gɑːbl/ vt tergiversar, embrollar

garden /'gɑːdn/ n (of flowers) jardín m; (of vegetables/fruit) huerto m. ● vi trabajar en el jardín. ~**er** /'gɑːdnə(r)/ n jardinero m. ~**ing** n jardinería f; (vegetable growing) horticultura f

gargle /'gɑːgl/ vi hacer gárgaras

gargoyle /'gɑːgɔɪl/ n gárgola f

garish /'geərɪʃ/ adj chillón

garland /'gɑːlənd/ n guirnalda f

garlic /'gɑːlɪk/ n ajo m

garment /'gɑːmənt/ n prenda f (de vestir)

garnish /'gɑːnɪʃ/ vt adornar, decorar. ● n adorno m

garret /'gærət/ n buhardilla f

garrison /'gærɪsn/ n guarnición f

garrulous /'gærələs/ adj hablador

garter /'gɑːtə(r)/ n liga f

gas /gæs/ n (pl **gases**) gas m; (anaesthetic) anestésico m; (Amer, petrol) gasolina f. ● vt (pt **gassed**) asfixiar con gas

gash /gæʃ/ n tajo m. ● vt hacer un tajo de

gasket /'gæskɪt/ n junta f

gas ~ mask n careta f antigás. ~ **meter** n contador m de gas

gasoline /'gæsəli:n/ n (Amer) gasolina f

gasp /gɑ:sp/ vi jadear; (with surprise) dar un grito ahogado. ●n exclamación f, grito m

gas ~ ring n hornillo m de gas. **~ station** n (Amer) gasolinera f

gastric /'gæstrɪk/ adj gástrico

gate /geɪt/ n puerta f; (of metal) verja f; (barrier) barrera f

gate ~crash vt colarse en. **~crasher** n intruso m (que ha entrado sin ser invitado). **~way** n puerta f

gather /'gæðə(r)/ vt reunir (people, things); (accumulate) acumular; (pick up) recoger; recoger (flowers); (fig, infer) deducir; (sewing) fruncir. **~ speed** acelerar. ●vi (people) reunirse; (things) acumularse. **~ing** n reunión f

gaudy /'gɔ:dɪ/ adj (-ier, -iest) chillón

gauge /geɪdʒ/ n (measurement) medida f; (Rail) entrevía f; (instrument) indicador m. ●vt medir; (fig) estimar

gaunt /gɔ:nt/ adj descarnado; (from illness) demacrado

gauntlet /'gɔ:ntlɪt/ n. run the ~ of aguantar el acoso de

gauze /gɔ:z/ n gasa f

gave /geɪv/ see GIVE

gawky /'gɔ:kɪ/ adj (-ier, -iest) torpe

gawp /gɔ:p/ vi. ~ at mirar como un tonto

gay /geɪ/ adj (-er, -est) (fam, homosexual) homosexual, gay Ⓐ; (dated, joyful) alegre

gaze /geɪz/ vi. ~ (at) mirar (fijamente). ●n mirada f (fija)

gazelle /gə'zel/ n (pl invar or -s) gacela f

GB abbr see GREAT BRITAIN

gear /gɪə(r)/ n equipo m; (Tec) engranaje m; (Auto) marcha f, cambio m. in ~ engranado. out of ~ desengranado. change ~, shift ~ (Amer) cambiar de marcha. ●vt adaptar. **~box** n (Auto) caja f de cambios

geese /gi:s/ see GOOSE

gel /dʒel/ n gel m

gelatine /'dʒeləti:n/ n gelatina f

gelignite /'dʒelɪgnaɪt/ n gelignita f

gem /dʒem/ n piedra f preciosa

Gemini /'dʒemɪnaɪ/ n Géminis mpl

gender /'dʒendə(r)/ n género m

gene /dʒi:n/ n gen m, gene m

genealogy /dʒi:nɪ'ælədʒɪ/ n genealogía f

general /'dʒenərəl/ adj general. ●n general m. in ~ en general. **~ election** n elecciones fpl generales. **~ization** /-'zeɪʃn/ n generalización f. **~ize** vt/i generalizar. **~ knowledge** n cultura f general. **~ly** adv generalmente. **~ practitioner** n médico m de cabecera

generat|e /'dʒenəreɪt/ vt generar. **~ion** /-'reɪʃn/ n generación f. **~ion gap** n brecha f generacional. **~or** n generador m

genero|sity /dʒenə'rɒsətɪ/ n generosidad f. **~us** /'dʒenərəs/ adj generoso; (plentiful) abundante

genetic /dʒɪ'netɪk/ adj genético. **~s** n genética f

Geneva /dʒɪ'ni:və/ n Ginebra f

genial /'dʒi:nɪəl/ adj simpático, afable

genital /'dʒenɪtl/ adj genital. **~s** npl genitales mpl

genitive /'dʒenɪtɪv/ adj & n genitivo (m)

genius /'dʒi:nɪəs/ n (pl -uses) genio m

genocide /'dʒenəsaɪd/ n genocidio m

genome /'dʒi:nəʊm/ n genoma m

genre /ʒɑ:ŋr/ n género m

gent /dʒent/ n Ⓔ señor m. **~s** n aseo m de caballeros

genteel /dʒen'ti:l/ adj distinguido

gentl|e /'dʒentl/ adj (-er, -est) (person) dulce; (murmur, breeze) suave; (hint) discreto. **~eman** n señor m; (well-bred) caballero m. **~eness** n amabilidad f

genuine /'dʒenjʊɪn/ adj verdadero; (person) sincero

geograph|er /dʒɪ'ɒgrəfə(r)/ n geógrafo m. **~ical** /dʒɪə'græfɪkl/ adj geográfico. **~y** /dʒɪ'ɒgrəfɪ/ n geografía f

geolog|ical /dʒɪə'lɒdʒɪkl/ adj geológico. **~ist** /dʒɪ'ɒlədʒɪst/ n geólogo m. **~y** /dʒɪ'ɒlədʒɪ/ n geología f

geometr|ic(al) /dʒɪə'metrɪk(l)/ adj geométrico. **~y** /dʒɪ'ɒmətrɪ/ n geometría f

geranium /dʒə'reɪnɪəm/ n geranio m

g

geriatric /dʒerɪˈætrɪk/ adj (patient) anciano; (ward) de geriatría. ~s n geriatría f

germ /dʒɜːm/ n microbio m, germen m

German /ˈdʒɜːmən/ adj & n alemán (m). ~ic /dʒɜːˈmænɪk/ adj germánico. ~ measles n rubéola f. ~y n Alemania f

germinate /ˈdʒɜːmɪneɪt/ vi germinar

gesticulate /dʒeˈstɪkjʊleɪt/ vi hacer ademanes, gesticular

gesture /ˈdʒestʃə(r)/ n gesto m, ademán m; (fig) gesto m. ● vi hacer gestos

g

get /get/

past **got**; past participle **got**, **gotten** (Amer); present participle **getting**

● transitive verb

····▸ (obtain) conseguir, obtener. **did you get the job?** ¿conseguiste el trabajo?

····▸ (buy) comprar. **I got it in the sales** lo compré en las rebajas

····▸ (achieve, win) sacar. **she got very good marks** sacó muy buenas notas

····▸ (receive) recibir. **I got a letter from Alex** recibí una carta de Alex

····▸ (fetch) ir a buscar. ~ **your coat** vete a buscar tu abrigo

····▸ (experience) llevarse. **I got a terrible shock** me llevé un shock espantoso

····▸ (fam, understand) entender. **I don't ~ what you mean** no entiendo lo que quieres decir

····▸ (ask or persuade) **to ~ s.o. to do sth** hacer que uno haga algo

Note that *hacer que* is followed by the subjunctive form of the verb

····▸ (cause to be done or happen) **I must ~ this watch fixed** tengo que llevar a arreglar este reloj. **they got the roof mended** hicieron arreglar el techo

● intransitive verb

····▸ (arrive, reach) llegar. **I got there late** llegué tarde. **how do you ~ to Paddington?** ¿cómo se llega a Paddington?

····▸ (become) **to ~ tired** cansarse. **she got very angry** se puso furiosa. **it's ~ting late** se está haciendo tarde

➡ For translations of expressions such as **get better**, **get old** see entries **better**, **old** etc. See also **got**

····▸ **to get to do sth** (manage to) llegar a. **did you get to see him?** ¿llegaste a verlo? □ **get along** vi (manage) arreglárselas; (progress) hacer progresos. □ **get along with** vt llevarse bien con. □ **get at** vt (reach) llegar a; (imply) querer decir. □ **get away** vi (escape) escaparse. □ **get back** vi volver. vt (recover) recobrar. □ **get by** vi (manage) arreglárselas; (pass) pasar. □ **get down** vi bajar. vt (make depressed) deprimir. □ **get in** vi entrar. □ **get into** vt entrar en; subir a (car) □ **get off** vt bajar(se) de (train etc). vi (from train etc) bajarse; (Jurid) salir absuelto. □ **get on** vi (progress) hacer progresos; (succeed) tener éxito. vt subirse a (train etc). □ **get on with** vt (be on good terms with) llevarse bien con; (continue) seguir con. □ **get out** vi salir. vt (take out) sacar. □ **get out of** vt (fig) librarse de. □ **get over** vt reponerse de (illness). □ **get round** vt soslayar (difficulty etc); engatusar (person). □ **get through** vi pasar; (on phone) comunicarse con. □ **get together** vi (meet up) reunirse. vt (assemble) reunir. □ **get up** vi levantarse; (climb) subir

geyser /ˈgiːzə(r)/ n géiser m

ghastly /ˈgɑːstlɪ/ adj (-ier, -iest) horrible

gherkin /ˈgɜːkɪn/ n pepinillo m

ghetto /ˈgetəʊ/ n (pl -os) gueto m

ghost /gəʊst/ n fantasma m. ~ly adj espectral

giant /ˈdʒaɪənt/ n gigante m. ● adj gigantesco

gibberish /'dʒɪbərɪʃ/ n jerigonza f

gibe /dʒaɪb/ n pulla f

giblets /'dʒɪblɪts/ npl menudillos mpl

gidd|iness /'gɪdɪnɪs/ n vértigo m. ~**y** adj (**-ier, -iest**) mareado. **be/feel** ~**y** estar/sentirse mareado

gift /gɪft/ n regalo m; (ability) don m. ~**ed** adj dotado de talento. ~**-wrap** vt envolver para regalo

gigantic /dʒaɪ'gæntɪk/ adj gigantesco

giggle /'gɪgl/ vi reírse tontamente. ● n risita f

gild /gɪld/ vt dorar

gills /gɪlz/ npl agallas fpl

gilt /gɪlt/ n dorado m. ● adj dorado

gimmick /'gɪmɪk/ n truco m

gin /dʒɪn/ n ginebra f

ginger /'dʒɪndʒə(r)/ n jengibre m. ● adj rojizo. **he has** ~ **hair** es pelirrojo. ~**bread** n pan m de jengibre

gipsy /'dʒɪpsɪ/ n gitano m

giraffe /dʒɪ'rɑːf/ n jirafa f

girder /'gɜːdə(r)/ n viga f

girdle /'gɜːdl/ n (belt) cinturón m; (corset) corsé m

girl /gɜːl/ n chica f, muchacha f; (child) niña f. ~**band** n grupo m pop de chicas. ~**friend** n amiga f; (of boy) novia f. ~**ish** adj de niña; (boy) afeminado. ~ **scout** n (Amer) exploradora f, guía f

giro /'dʒaɪrəʊ/ n (pl -os) giro m (bancario)

girth /gɜːθ/ n circunferencia f

gist /dʒɪst/ n lo esencial

give /gɪv/ vt (pt gave, pp given) dar; (deliver) entregar; regalar (present); prestar (aid, attention). ~ **o.s. to** darse a. ● vi dar; (yield) ceder; (stretch) dar de sí. ● n elasticidad f. □ ~ **away** vt regalar; revelar (secret). □ ~ **back** vt devolver. □ ~ **in** vi ceder. □ ~ **off** vt emitir. □ ~ **out** vt distribuir. (become used up) agotarse. □ ~ **up** vt renunciar a; (yield) ceder. ~ **up doing sth** dejar de hacer algo. ~ **o.s. up** entregarse (**to** a). vi rendirse. ~**n** /'gɪvn/ see **GIVE**. ● adj dado. ~**n name** n nombre m de pila

glacier /'glæsɪə(r)/ n glaciar m

glad /glæd/ adj contento. **be** ~ alegrarse (**about** de). ~**den** vt alegrar

gladly /'glædlɪ/ adv alegremente; (willingly) con mucho gusto

glamo|rous /'glæmərəs/ adj glamoroso. ~**ur** /'glæmə(r)/ n glamour m

glance /glɑːns/ n ojeada f. ● vi. ~ **at** dar un vistazo a

gland /glænd/ n glándula f

glar|e /gleə(r)/ vi (light) deslumbrar; (stare angrily) mirar airadamente. ● n resplandor m; (stare) mirada f airada. ~**ing** adj deslumbrante; (obvious) manifiesto

glass /glɑːs/ n (material) cristal m, vidrio m; (without stem or for wine) vaso m; (with stem) copa f; (for beer) caña f; (mirror) espejo m. ~**es** npl (spectacles) gafas fpl, lentes fpl (LAm), anteojos mpl (LAm). ~**y** adj vítreo

glaze /gleɪz/ vt poner cristal(es) or vidrio(s) a (windows, doors); vidriar (pottery). ● vi. ~ (**over**) (eyes) vidriarse. ● n barniz m; (for pottery) esmalte m

gleam /gliːm/ n destello m. ● vi destellar

glean /gliːn/ vt espigar; recoger (information)

glee /gliː/ n regocijo m

glib /glɪb/ adj de mucha labia; (reply) fácil

glid|e /glaɪd/ vi deslizarse; (plane) planear. ~**er** n planeador m. ~**ing** n planeo m

glimmer /'glɪmə(r)/ n destello m. ● vi destellar

glimpse /glɪmps/ n. **catch a** ~ **of** vislumbrar, ver brevemente. ● vt vislumbrar

glint /glɪnt/ n destello m. ● vi destellar

glisten /'glɪsn/ vi brillar

glitter /'glɪtə(r)/ vi brillar. ● n brillo m

gloat /gləʊt/ vi. ~ **on/over** regodearse sobre

glob|al /'gləʊbl/ adj (worldwide) mundial; (all-embracing) global. ~**alization** n globalización f. ~**al warming** n calentamiento m global. ~**e** /gləʊb/ n globo m

gloom /gluːm/ n oscuridad f; (sadness, fig) tristeza f. ~**y** adj (**-ier, -iest**) triste; (pessimistic) pesimista

glor|ify /ˈglɔːrɪfaɪ/ vt glorificar. **~ious** /ˈglɔːrɪəs/ adj espléndido; (deed, hero etc) glorioso. **~y** /ˈglɔːrɪ/ n gloria f

gloss /glɒs/ n lustre m. **~ (paint)** (pintura f al or de) esmalte m. □ **~ over** vt (make light of) minimizar; (cover up) encubrir

glossary /ˈglɒsərɪ/ n glosario m

glossy /ˈglɒsɪ/ adj brillante

glove /glʌv/ n guante m. **~ compartment** n (Auto) guantera f

glow /gləʊ/ vi brillar. ● n brillo m. **~ing** /ˈgləʊɪŋ/ adj incandescente; (account) entusiasta; (complexion) rojo

glucose /ˈgluːkəʊs/ n glucosa f

glue /gluː/ n cola f, goma f de pegar. ● vt (pres p gluing) pegar

glum /glʌm/ adj (glummer, glummest) triste

glutton /ˈglʌtn/ n glotón m

gnarled /nɑːld/ adj nudoso

gnash /næʃ/ vt. **~ one's teeth** rechinar los dientes

gnat /næt/ n jején m, mosquito m

gnaw /nɔː/ vt roer. ● vi. **~ at** roer

gnome /nəʊm/ n gnomo m

---

go /gəʊ/

3rd pers sing present **goes**; past **went**; past participle **gone**

● intransitive verb

····▶ ir. **I'm going to France** voy a Francia. **to go shopping** ir de compras. **to go swimming** ir a nadar

····▶ (leave) irse. **we're going on Friday** nos vamos el viernes

····▶ (work, function) (engine, clock) funcionar

····▶ (become) **to go deaf** quedarse sordo. **to go mad** volverse loco. **his face went red** se puso colorado

····▶ (stop) (headache, pain) irse (+ me/te/le). **the pain's gone** se me ha ido el dolor

····▶ (turn out, progress) ir. **everything's going very well** todo va muy bien. **how did the exam go?** ¿qué tal te fue en el examen?

····▶ (match, suit) combinar. **the jacket and the trousers go well together** la chaqueta y los pantalones combinan bien.

····▶ (cease to function) (bulb, fuse) fundirse. **the brakes have gone** los frenos no funcionan

● auxiliary verb **to be going to** + infinitive ir a + infinitivo. **it's going to rain** va a llover. **she's going to win!** ¡va a ganar!

● noun (pl **goes**)

····▶ (turn) turno m. **you have three goes** tienes tres turnos. **it's your go** te toca a ti

····▶ (attempt) **to have a go at doing sth** intentar hacer algo. **have another go** inténtalo de nuevo

····▶ (energy, drive) empuje m. **she has a lot of go** tiene mucho empuje

····▶ (in phrases) **I've been on the go all day** no he parado en todo el día. **to make a go of sth** sacar algo adelante □ **go across** vt/vi cruzar. □ **go after** vi perseguir. □ **go away** vi irse. □ **go back** vi volver. □ **go back on** vt faltar a (promise etc). □ **go by** vi pasar. □ **go down** vi bajar; (sun) ponerse. □ **go for** vt (fam, attack) atacar. □ **go in** vi entrar. □ **go in for** vt presentarse para (exam); participar en (competition). □ **go off** vi (leave) irse; (go bad) pasarse; (explode) estallar; (lights) apagarse. □ **go on** vi seguir; (happen) pasar; (be switched on) encenderse, prenderse (LAm). □ **go out** vi salir; (fire, light) apagarse. □ **go over** vt (check) revisar; (revise) repasar. □ **go through** vt pasar por; (search) registrar; (check) examinar. □ **go up** vi/vt subir. □ **go without** vt pasar sin

---

goad /gəʊd/ vt aguijonear

go-ahead /ˈgəʊəhed/ n luz f verde. ● adj dinámico

goal /gəʊl/ n (Sport) gol m; (objective) meta f. **~ie** /ˈgəʊlɪ/ n ▯, **~keeper** n portero m, arquero m (LAm). **~post** n poste *m* de la portería, poste *m* del arco (*LAm*)

goat /gəʊt/ *n* cabra *f*

gobble /'gɒbl/ *vt* engullir

goblin /'gɒblɪn/ *n* duende *m*

god /gɒd/ *n* dios *m*. **G~** *n* Dios *m*. **~child** *n* ahijado *m*. **~daughter** *n* ahijada *f*. **~dess** /'gɒdes/ *n* diosa *f*. **~father** *n* padrino *m*. **~forsaken** *adj* olvidado de Dios. **~mother** *n* madrina *f*. **~send** *n* beneficio *m* inesperado. **~son** *n* ahijado *m*

going /'gəʊɪŋ/ *n* camino *m*; (*racing*) (estado *m* del) terreno *m*. **it is slow/ hard ~** es lento/difícil. ● *adj* (*price*) actual; (*concern*) en funcionamiento

gold /gəʊld/ *n* oro *m*. ● *adj* de oro. **~en** *adj* de oro; (*in colour*) dorado; (*opportunity*) único. **~en wedding** *n* bodas *fpl* de oro. **~fish** *n invar* pez *m* de colores. **~mine** *n* mina *f* de oro; (*fig*) fuente *f* de gran riqueza. **~-plated** /-'pleɪtɪd/ *adj* chapado en oro. **~smith** *n* orfebre *m*

golf /gɒlf/ *n* golf *m*. **~ ball** *n* pelota *f* de golf. **~ club** *n* palo *m* de golf; (*place*) club *m* de golf. **~course** *n* campo *m* de golf. **~er** *n* jugador *m* de golf

gondola /'gɒndələ/ *n* góndola *f*

gone /gɒn/ *see* **GO**. ● *adj* pasado. **~ six o'clock** después de las seis

gong /gɒŋ/ *n* gong(o) *m*

good /gʊd/ *adj* (**better, best**) bueno, (*before masculine singular noun*) buen. **~ afternoon** buenas tardes. **~ evening** (*before dark*) buenas tardes; (*after dark*) buenas noches. **~ morning** buenos días, **~ night** buenas noches. **as ~ as** (*almost*) casi. **feel ~** sentirse bien. **have a ~ time** divertirse. ● *n* bien *m*. **for ~** para siempre. **it is no ~ shouting** es inútil gritar *etc*. **~bye** /-'baɪ/ *int* ¡adiós! ● *n* adiós *m*. **say ~bye to** despedirse de. **~-fornothing** /-fənʌθɪŋ/ *adj & n* inútil (*m*). **G~ Friday** *n* Viernes *m* Santo. **~-looking** /-'lʊkɪŋ/ *adj* guapo, buen mozo *m* (*LAm*), buena moza *f* (*LAm*). **~ness** *n* bondad *f*. **~ness!, ~ness gracious!, ~ness me!, my ~ness!** ¡Dios mío! **~s** *npl* mercancías *fpl*. **~will** /-'wɪl/ *n* buena voluntad *f*. **~y**

n (*Culin, fam*) golosina *f*; (*in film*) bueno *m*

gooey /'guːɪ/ *adj* (**gooier, gooiest**) 🄵 pegajoso; (*fig*) sentimental

goofy /'guːfɪ/ *adj* (*Amer*) necio

google (®) /'guːgl/ *vt, vi* 🄵 googlear 🄵

goose /guːs/ *n* (*pl* **geese**) oca *f*, ganso *m*. **~berry** /'gʊzbərɪ/ *n* uva *f* espina, grosella *f* espinosa. **~-flesh** *n*, **~-pimples** *npl* carne *f* de gallina

gore /gɔː(r)/ *n* sangre *f*. ● *vt* cornear

gorge /gɔːdʒ/ *n* (*of river*) garganta *f*. ● *vt*. **~ o.s.** hartarse (**on** de)

gorgeous /'gɔːdʒəs/ *adj* precioso; (*splendid*) magnífico

gorilla /gə'rɪlə/ *n* gorila *m*

gorse /gɔːs/ *n* aulaga *f*

gory /'gɔːrɪ/ *adj* (**-ier, -iest**) 🄵 sangriento

gosh /gɒʃ/ *int* ¡caramba!

go-slow /gəʊ'sləʊ/ *n* huelga *f* de celo, huelga *f* pasiva

gospel /'gɒspl/ *n* evangelio *m*

gossip /'gɒsɪp/ *n* (*chatter*) chismorreo *m*; (*person*) chismoso *m*. ● *vi* (*pt* **gossiped**) (*chatter*) chismorrear, (*repeat scandal*) contar chismes

got /gɒt/ *see* **GET**. **have ~** tener. **I've ~ to do it** tengo que hacerlo.

gotten /'gɒtn/ *see* **GET**

gouge /gaʊdʒ/ *vt* abrir (*hole*). □ **~ out** *vt* sacar

gourmet /'gʊəmeɪ/ *n* gastrónomo *m*

govern /'gʌvən/ *vt/i* gobernar. **~ess** *n* institutriz *f*. **~ment** *n* gobierno *m*. **~or** *n* gobernador *m*

gown /gaʊn/ *n* vestido *m*; (*of judge, teacher*) toga *f*

GP *abbr see* **GENERAL PRACTITIONER**

GPS *abbrev* **Global Positioning System** GPS *m*

grab /græb/ *vt* (*pt* **grabbed**) agarrar

grace /greɪs/ *n* gracia *f*. **~ful** *adj* elegante

gracious /'greɪʃəs/ *adj* (*kind*) amable; (*elegant*) elegante

grade /greɪd/ *n* clase *f*, categoría *f*; (*of goods*) clase *f*, calidad *f*; (*on scale*) grado *m*; (*school mark*) nota *f*; (*Amer, class*) curso *m*, año *m*

g

gradient /'greɪdɪənt/ n pendiente f,
gradiente f (LAm)

gradual /'grædʒʊəl/ adj gradual. ∼ly
adv gradualmente, poco a poco

graduat|e /'grædʒʊət/ n (Univ) licen-
ciado. ● /'grædʒʊeɪt/ vi licenciarse.
∼ion /-'eɪʃn/ n graduación f

graffiti /grə'fi:tɪ/ npl graffiti mpl, pinta-
das fpl

graft /grɑ:ft/ n (Med, Bot) injerto m;
(Amer fam, bribery) chanchullos mpl. ● vt
injertar

grain /greɪn/ n grano m

gram /græm/ n gramo m

gramma|r /'græmə(r)/ n gramática f.
∼tical /grə'mætɪkl/ adj gramatical

gramme /græm/ n gramo m

grand /grænd/ adj (-er, -est) magnífico; (fam, excellent) estupendo.
∼child n nieto m. ∼daughter n
nieta f. ∼eur /'grændʒə(r)/ n gran-
diosidad f. ∼father n abuelo m.
∼father clock n reloj m de caja.
∼iose /'grændɪəʊs/ adj grandioso.
∼mother n abuela f. ∼parents npl
abuelos mpl. ∼ piano n piano m de
cola. ∼son n nieto m. ∼stand
/'grænstænd/ n tribuna f

granite /'grænɪt/ n granito m

granny /'grænɪ/ n 🔲 abuela f

grant /grɑ:nt/ vt conceder; (give)
donar; (admit) admitir (that que).
take for ∼ed dar por sentado. ● n
concesión f; (Univ) beca f

granule /'grænu:l/ n gránulo m

grape /greɪp/ n uva f. ∼fruit n invar
pomelo m, toronja f (LAm)

graph /grɑ:f/ n gráfica f

graphic /'græfɪk/ adj gráfico. ∼s npl
diseño m gráfico; (Comp) gráficos mpl

grapple /'græpl/ vi. ∼ with forcejear
con; (mentally) lidiar con

grasp /grɑ:sp/ vt agarrar. ● n (hold)
agarro m; (fig) comprensión f. ∼ing
adj avaro

grass /grɑ:s/ n hierba f. ∼hopper n
saltamontes m. ∼ roots npl base f popular. ● adj de las bases. ∼y adj cubierto de hierba

grate /greɪt/ n rejilla f; (fireplace) chimenea f. ● vt rallar. ● vi rechinar; (be

irritating) ser crispante

grateful /'greɪtfl/ adj agradecido. ∼ly
adv con gratitud

grater /'greɪtə(r)/ n rallador m

gratif|ied /'grætɪfaɪd/ adj contento.
∼y /'grætɪfaɪ/ vt satisfacer; (please)
agradar a. ∼ying adj agradable

grating /'greɪtɪŋ/ n reja f

gratitude /'grætɪtju:d/ n gratitud f

gratuitous /grə'tju:ɪtəs/ adj gratuito

gratuity /grə'tju:ətɪ/ n (tip) propina f

grave /greɪv/ n sepultura f. ● adj (-er,
-est) (serious) grave

gravel /'grævl/ n grava f

gravely /'greɪvlɪ/ adv (seriously) seriamente; (solemnly) con gravedad

grave ∼**stone** n lápida f. ∼**yard** n
cementerio m

gravitate /'grævɪteɪt/ vi gravitar

gravity /'grævətɪ/ n gravedad f

gravy /'greɪvɪ/ n salsa f

gray /greɪ/ adj & n (Amer) see **GREY**

graze /greɪz/ vi (eat) pacer. ● vt (touch)
rozar; (scrape) raspar. ● n rasguño m

greas|e /gri:s/ n grasa f. ● vt engrasar.
∼eproof paper n papel m encerado
or de cera. ∼y adj (hands) grasiento;
(food) graso; (hair, skin) graso, gra-
soso (LAm)

great /greɪt/ adj (-er, -est) grande, (before singular noun) gran; (fam, very
good) estupendo. **G**∼ **Britain** n Gran
Bretaña f. ∼**-grandfather**
/-'grænfɑ:ðə(r)/ n bisabuelo m.
∼**-grandmother** /-'grænmʌðə(r)/ n
bisabuela f. ∼**ly** adv (very) muy;
(much) mucho

Greece /gri:s/ n Grecia f

greed /gri:d/ n avaricia f; (for food)
glotonería f. ∼y adj avaro; (for food)
glotón

Greek /gri:k/ adj & n griego (m)

green /gri:n/ adj (-er, -est) verde. ● n
verde m; (grass) césped m. ∼ **belt** n
zona f verde. ∼ **card** n (Amer) permiso m de residencia y trabajo. ∼**ery**
n verdor m. ∼**gage** /-geɪdʒ/ n claudia
f. ∼**grocer** n verdulero m. ∼**house** n
invernadero m. **the** ∼**house effect** el
efecto invernadero. ∼ **light** n luz f
verde. ∼**s** npl verduras fpl

Green Card En EE.UU., documento oficial que toda persona que no sea ciudadana norteamericana debe obtener para residir y trabajar en este país. En el Reino Unido, es el documento que se debe obtener de la compañía de seguros, cuando se lleva un automóvil al extranjero, a fin de que siga vigente la cobertura de la póliza.

greet /gri:t/ vt saludar; (receive) recibir. ∼**ing** n saludo m

gregarious /grɪˈɡeərɪəs/ adj gregario; (person) sociable

grenade /grɪˈneɪd/ n granada f

grew /gru:/ see **GROW**

grey /greɪ/ adj (-er, -est) gris. **have** ∼ **hair** ser canoso. ● n gris m. ∼**hound** n galgo m

grid /grɪd/ n reja f; (Elec, network) red f; (on map) cuadriculado m

grief /gri:f/ n dolor m. **come to** ∼ (person) acabar mal; (fail) fracasar

grievance /ˈgri:vns/ n queja f formal

grieve /gri:v/ vt apenar. ● vi afligirse. ∼ **for** llorar

grievous /ˈgri:vəs/ adj doloroso; (serious) grave. ∼ **bodily harm** (Jurid) lesiones fpl (corporales) graves

grill /grɪl/ n parrilla f. ● vt asar a la parrilla; (🄸, interrogate) interrogar

grille /grɪl/ n rejilla f

grim /grɪm/ adj (**grimmer**, **grimmest**) severo

grimace /ˈgrɪməs/ n mueca f ● vi hacer muecas

grim|e /graɪm/ n mugre f. ∼**y** adj mugriento

grin /grɪn/ vt (pt **grinned**) sonreír. ● n sonrisa f (abierta)

grind /graɪnd/ vt (pt **ground**) moler (coffee, corn etc); (pulverize) pulverizar; (sharpen) afilar; (Amer) picar, moler (meat)

grip /grɪp/ vt (pt **gripped**) agarrar; (interest) captar. ● n (hold) agarro m; (strength of hand) apretón m; (hairgrip) horquilla f, pasador m (Mex). **come to** ∼s **with** entender (subject)

grisly /ˈgrɪzlɪ/ adj (-ier, -iest) horrible

gristle /ˈgrɪsl/ n cartílago m

grit /grɪt/ n arenilla f; (fig) agallas fpl. ● vt (pt **gritted**) echar arena en (road). ∼ **one's teeth** (fig) acorazarse

groan /grəʊn/ vi gemir. ● n gemido m

grocer /ˈgrəʊsə(r)/ n tendero m, abarrotero m (Mex). ∼**ies** npl comestibles mpl. ∼**y** n tienda f de comestibles, tienda f de abarrotes (Mex)

groggy /ˈgrɒgɪ/ adj (weak) débil; (unsteady) inseguro; (ill) malucho

groin /grɔɪn/ n ingle f

groom /gru:m/ n mozo m de caballos; (bridegroom) novio m. ● vt almohazar (horses); (fig) preparar

groove /gru:v/ n ranura f; (in record) surco m

grope /grəʊp/ vi (find one's way) moverse a tientas. ∼ **for** buscar a tientas

gross /grəʊs/ adj (-er, -est) (coarse) grosero; (Com) bruto; (fat) grueso; (flagrant) flagrante. ● n invar gruesa f. ∼**ly** adv (very) enormemente

grotesque /grəʊˈtesk/ adj grotesco

ground /graʊnd/ see **GRIND**. ● n suelo m; (area) terreno m; (reason) razón f; (Amer, Elec) toma f de tierra. ● vt fundar (theory); retirar del servicio (aircraft). ∼**s** npl jardines mpl; (sediment) poso m. ∼ **beef** n (Amer) carne f picada, carne f molida. ∼ **cloth** n (Amer) see ∼**SHEET**. ∼ **floor** n planta f baja. ∼**ing** n base f, conocimientos mpl (in de). ∼**less** adj infundado. ∼**sheet** n suelo m impermeable (de una tienda de campaña). ∼**work** n trabajo m preparatorio

group /gru:p/ n grupo m. ● vt agrupar. ● vi agruparse

grouse /graʊs/ n invar (bird) urogallo m. ● vi 🄸 rezongar

grovel /ˈgrɒvl/ vi (pt **grovelled**) postrarse; (fig) arrastrarse

grow /grəʊ/ vi (pt **grew**, pp **grown**) crecer; (become) volverse, ponerse. ● vt cultivar. ∼ **a beard** dejarse (crecer) la barba. □ ∼ **up** vi hacerse mayor. ∼**ing** adj (quantity) cada vez mayor; (influence) creciente

growl /graʊl/ vi gruñir. ● n gruñido m

grown /grəʊn/ see **GROW**. ● adj adulto. ∼-**up** adj & n adulto (m)

growth /grəʊθ/ n crecimiento m; (increase) aumento m; (development) desarrollo m; (Med) bulto m, tumor m

grub /grʌb/ n (larva) larva f; (fam, food) comida f

grubby /ˈgrʌbɪ/ adj (-ier, -iest) mugriento

grudg|e /grʌdʒ/ vt see BEGRUDGE. ● n rencilla f. **bear/have a ~e against s.o.** guardarle rencor a uno. **~ingly** adv de mala gana

gruelling /ˈgruːəlɪŋ/ adj agotador

gruesome /ˈgruːsəm/ adj horrible

gruff /grʌf/ adj (-er, -est) (manners) brusco; (voice) ronco

grumble /ˈgrʌmbl/ vi rezongar

grumpy /ˈgrʌmpɪ/ adj (-ier, -iest) malhumorado

grunt /grʌnt/ vi gruñir. ● n gruñido m

guarant|ee /gærənˈtiː/ n garantía f. ● vt garantizar. **~or** n garante m & f

guard /gɑːd/ vt proteger; (watch) vigilar. ● n (vigilance, Mil group) guardia f; (person) guardia m; (on train) jefe m de tren. □ ~ **against** vt evitar; protegerse contra (risk). **~ed** adj cauteloso. **~ian** /-ɪən/ n guardián m; (of orphan) tutor m

Guatemala /gwɑːtəˈmɑːlə/ n Guatemala f. **~n** adj & n guatemalteco (m)

guer(r)illa /gəˈrɪlə/ n guerrillero m. **~ warfare** n guerrilla f

guess /ges/ vt adivinar; (Amer, suppose) suponer. ● n conjetura f. **~work** n conjeturas fpl

guest /gest/ n invitado m; (in hotel) huésped m. **~house** n casa f de huéspedes

guffaw /gʌˈfɔː/ n carcajada f. ● vi reírse a carcajadas

guidance /ˈgaɪdəns/ n (advice) consejos mpl; (information) información f

guide /gaɪd/ n (person) guía m & f; (book) guía f. **Girl G~** exploradora f, guía f. ● vt guiar. **~book** n guía f. **~dog** n perro m guía, perro m lazarillo. **~d missile** n proyectil m teledirigido. **~lines** npl pauta f

guild /gɪld/ n gremio m

guile /gaɪl/ n astucia f

guillotine /ˈgɪlətiːn/ n guillotina f

guilt /gɪlt/ n culpa f; (Jurid) culpabilidad f. **~y** adj culpable

guinea pig /ˈgɪnɪ/ n conejillo m de Indias, cobaya f

guitar /gɪˈtɑː(r)/ n guitarra f. **~ist** n guitarrista m & f

gulf /gʌlf/ n (part of sea) golfo m; (gap) abismo m

gull /gʌl/ n gaviota f

gullet /ˈgʌlɪt/ n garganta f, gaznate m 🔲

gullible /ˈgʌləbl/ adj crédulo

gully /ˈgʌlɪ/ n (ravine) barranco m

gulp /gʌlp/ vt. ~ **(down)** tragarse de prisa. ● vi tragar saliva. ● n trago m

gum /gʌm/ n (in mouth) encía f; (glue) goma f de pegar; (for chewing) chicle m. ● vt (pt gummed) engomar

gun /gʌn/ n (pistol) pistola f; (rifle) fusil m, escopeta f; (artillery piece) cañón m. ● vt (pt gunned). □ ~ **down** vt abatir a tiros. **~fire** n tiros mpl

gun~man /-mən/ n pistolero m, gatillero m (Mex). **~powder** n pólvora f. **~shot** n disparo m

gurgle /ˈgɜːgl/ vi (liquid) gorgotear; (baby) gorjear

gush /gʌʃ/ vi. ~ **(out)** salir a borbotones. ● n (of liquid) chorro m; (fig) torrente m

gusset /ˈgʌsɪt/ n entretela f

gust /gʌst/ n ráfaga f

gusto /ˈgʌstəʊ/ n entusiasmo m

gusty /ˈgʌstɪ/ adj borrascoso

gut /gʌt/ n intestino m. ● vt (pt gutted) destripar; (fire) destruir. **~s** npl tripas fpl; (fam, courage) agallas fpl

gutter /ˈgʌtə(r)/ n (on roof) canalón m, canaleta f; (in street) cuneta f; (fig, slum) arroyo m

guttural /ˈgʌtərəl/ adj gutural

guy /gaɪ/ n (fam, man) tipo m 🔲, tío m 🔲

guzzle /ˈgʌzl/ vt (drink) chupar 🔲; (eat) tragarse

gym /dʒɪm/ n 🔲 (gymnasium) gimnasio m; (gymnastics) gimnasia f

gymnasium /dʒɪmˈneɪzɪəm/ n gimnasio m

gymnast /ˈdʒɪmnæst/ n gimnasta m & f. **~ics** /dʒɪmˈnæstɪks/ npl gimnasia f

gymslip /'dʒɪmslɪp/ n túnica f (de gimnasia)

gynaecolog|ist /gaɪnɪ'kɒlədʒɪst/ n ginecólogo m. **~y** n ginecología f

gypsy /'dʒɪpsɪ/ n gitano m

gyrate /dʒaɪə'reɪt/ vi girar

⋯⋯⋯⋯⋯⋯⋯⋯⋯⋯

Hh

⋯⋯⋯⋯⋯⋯⋯⋯⋯⋯

haberdashery /'hæbədæʃərɪ/ n mercería f; (Amer, clothes) ropa f y accesorios mpl para caballeros

habit /'hæbɪt/ n costumbre f; (Relig, costume) hábito m. **be in the ~ of** (+ gerund) tener la costumbre de (+ infinitivo), soler (+ infinitivo). **get into the ~ of** (+ gerund) acostumbrarse a (+ infinitivo)

habitable /'hæbɪtəbl/ adj habitable

habitat /'hæbɪtæt/ n hábitat m

habitation /hæbɪ'teɪʃn/ n habitación f

habitual /hə'bɪtjʊəl/ adj habitual; (liar) inveterado. **~ly** adv de costumbre

hack /hæk/ n (old horse) jamelgo m; (writer) escritorzuelo m. ● vt cortar. **~er** n (Comp) pirata m informático

hackneyed /'hæknɪd/ adj manido

had /hæd/ see **HAVE**

haddock /'hædək/ n invar eglefino m

haemorrhage /'hemərɪdʒ/ n hemorragia f

haemorrhoids /'hemərɔɪdz/ npl hemorroides fpl

hag /hæg/ n bruja f

haggard /'hægəd/ adj demacrado

hail /heɪl/ n granizo m. ● vi granizar. ● vt (greet) saludar; llamar (taxi). □ **~ from** vt venir de. **~stone** n grano m de granizo

hair /heə(r)/ n pelo m. **~band** n cinta f, banda f (Mex). **~brush** n cepillo m (para el pelo). **~cut** n corte m de pelo. **have a ~cut** cortarse el pelo. **~do** n 𝕀 peinado m. **~dresser** n peluquero m. **~dresser's (shop)** n peluquería f. **~dryer** n secador m, secadora f (Mex). **~grip** n horquilla f, pasador m (Mex). **~pin** n horquilla f.

~pin bend n curva f cerrada. **~-raising** adj espeluznante. **~spray** n laca f, fijador m (para el pelo). **~style** n peinado m. **~y** adj (-ier, -iest) peludo

half /hɑːf/ n (pl halves) mitad f. ● adj medio. **~ a dozen** media docena f. **~ an hour** media hora f. ● adv medio, a medias. **~-hearted** /-'hɑːtɪd/ adj poco entusiasta. **~-mast** /-'mɑːst/ n. **at ~-mast** a media asta. **~ term** n vacaciones fpl de medio trimestre. **~-time** n (Sport) descanso m, medio tiempo m (LAm). **~way** adj medio. ● adv a medio camino

hall /hɔːl/ n (entrance) vestíbulo m; (for public events) sala f, salón m. **~ of residence** residencia f universitaria, colegio m mayor. **~mark** /-mɑːk/ n (on gold, silver) contraste m; (fig) sello m (distintivo)

hallo /hə'ləʊ/ int see **HELLO**

Hallowe'en /'hæləʊ'iːn/ n víspera f de Todos los Santos

hallucination /həluːsɪ'neɪʃn/ n alucinación f

halo /'heɪləʊ/ n (pl -oes) aureola f

halt /hɔːlt/ n. **come to a ~** pararse. ● vt parar. ● vi pararse

halve /hɑːv/ vt reducir a la mitad; (divide into halves) partir por la mitad

halves /hɑːvz/ see **HALF**

ham /hæm/ n jamón m

hamburger /'hæmbɜːgə(r)/ n hamburguesa f

hammer /'hæmə(r)/ n martillo m. ● vt martill(e)ar

hammock /'hæmək/ n hamaca f

hamper /'hæmpə(r)/ n cesta f. ● vt estorbar

hamster /'hæmstə(r)/ n hámster m

hand /hænd/ n mano f; (of clock, watch) manecilla f; (worker) obrero m. **by ~** a mano. **lend a ~** echar una mano. **on ~** a mano. **on the one ~... on the other ~** por un lado... por otro. **out of ~** fuera de control. **to ~** a mano. ● vt pasar. □ **~ down** vt pasar. □ **~ in** vt entregar. □ **~ over** vt entregar. □ **~ out** vt distribuir. **~bag** n bolso m, cartera f (LAm), bolsa f (Mex). **~brake** n (in car) freno m de mano. **~cuffs** npl esposas fpl.

g

h

~**ful** n puñado m; (fam, person) persona f difícil

handicap /'hændɪkæp/ n desventaja f; (Sport) hándicap m. ~**ped** adj minusválido

handicraft /'hændɪkrɑːft/ n artesanía f

handkerchief /'hæŋkətʃɪf/ n (pl -fs or -chieves /-'tʃiːvz/) pañuelo m

handle /'hændl/ n (of door) picaporte m; (of drawer) tirador m; (of implement) mango m; (of cup, bag, jug) asa f. ● vt manejar; (touch) tocar. ~**bars** npl manillar m, manubrio m (LAm).

hand ~**out** n folleto m; (of money, food) dádiva f. ~**shake** n apretón m de manos

handsome /'hænsəm/ adj (goodlooking) guapo, buen mozo, buena moza (LAm); (generous) generoso

handwriting /'hændraɪtɪŋ/ n letra f

handy /'hændɪ/ adj (-ier, -iest) (useful) práctico; (person) diestro; (near) a mano. **come in** ~ venir muy bien. ~**man** n hombre m habilidoso

hang /hæŋ/ vt (pt **hung**) colgar; (pt **hanged**) (capital punishment) ahorcar. ● vi colgar; (clothing) caer. ● n. **get the** ~ **of sth** coger el truco de algo. □ ~ **about**, □ ~ **around** vi holgazanear. □ ~ **on** vi (wait) esperar. □ ~ **out** vt tender (washing). □ ~ **up** vi (also telephone) colgar

hangar /'hæŋə(r)/ n hangar m

hang ~**er** n (for clothes) percha f. ~**-glider** n alta f delta, deslizador m (Mex). ~**over** (after drinking) resaca f. ~**-up** n 🔢 complejo m

hankie, hanky /'hæŋkɪ/ n 🔢 pañuelo m

haphazard /hæp'hæzəd/ adj fortuito. ~**ly** adv al azar

happen /'hæpən/ vi pasar, suceder, ocurrir. **if he** ~**s to come** si acaso viene. ~**ing** n acontecimiento m

happ|ily /'hæpɪlɪ/ adv alegremente; (fortunately) afortunadamente. ~**iness** n felicidad f. ~**y** adj (-ier, -iest) feliz; (satisfied) contento

harass /'hærəs/ vt acosar. ~**ment** n acoso m

harbour /'hɑːbə(r)/ n puerto m

hard /hɑːd/ adj (-er, -est) duro; (difficult) difícil. ● adv (work) mucho; (pull) con fuerza. ~ **done by** tratado injustamente. ~**-boiled egg** /-'bɔɪld/ n huevo m duro. ~ **disk** n disco m duro. ~**en** vt endurecer. ● vi endurecerse. ~**-headed** /-'hedɪd/ adj realista

hardly /'hɑːdlɪ/ adv apenas. ~ **ever** casi nunca

hard ~**ness** n dureza f. ~**ship** n apuro m. ~ **shoulder** n arcén m, acotamiento m (Mex). ~**ware** n /-weə(r)/ ferretería f; (Comp) hardware m. ~**ware store** n (Amer) ferretería f. ~**-working** /-'wɜːkɪŋ/ adj trabajador

hardy /'hɑːdɪ/ adj (-ier, -iest) fuerte; (plants) resistente

hare /heə(r)/ n liebre f

hark /hɑːk/ vi escuchar. □ ~ **back to** vt volver a

harm /hɑːm/ n daño m. **there is no** ~ **in asking** con preguntar no se pierde nada. ● vt hacer daño a (person); dañar (thing); perjudicar (interests). ~**ful** adj perjudicial. ~**less** adj inofensivo

harmonica /hɑː'mɒnɪkə/ n armónica f

harmon|ious /hɑː'məʊnɪəs/ adj armonioso. ~**y** /'hɑːmənɪ/ n armonía f

harness /'hɑːnɪs/ n arnés m. ● vt poner el arnés a (horse); (fig) aprovechar

harp /hɑːp/ n arpa f. ● vi. ~ **on (about)** machacar (con)

harpoon /hɑː'puːn/ n arpón m

harpsichord /'hɑːpsɪkɔːd/ n clavicémbalo m, clave m

harrowing /'hærəʊɪŋ/ adj desgarrador

harsh /hɑːʃ/ adj (-er, -est) duro, severo; (light) fuerte; (climate) riguroso. ~**ly** adv severamente. ~**ness** n severidad f

harvest /'hɑːvɪst/ n cosecha f. ● vt cosechar

has /hæz/ see **HAVE**

hassle /'hæsl/ n 🔢 lío m 🔢, rollo m 🔢. ● vt (harass) fastidiar

hast|e /heɪst/ n prisa f, apuro m (LAm). **make** ~**e** darse prisa. ~**ily** /'heɪstɪlɪ/ adv de prisa. ~**y** /'heɪstɪ/ adj (-ier, -iest) rápido; (rash) precipitado

h

hat /hæt/ n sombrero m

hatch /hætʃ/ n (for food) ventanilla f; (Naut) escotilla f. ● vt empollar (eggs); tramar (plot). ● vi salir del cascarón. **~back** n coche m con tres/cinco puertas; (door) puerta f trasera

hatchet /ˈhætʃɪt/ n hacha f

hat|e /heɪt/ n odio m. ● vt odiar. **~eful** adj odioso. **~red** /ˈheɪtrɪd/ n odio m

haughty /ˈhɔːtɪ/ adj (-ier, -iest) altivo

haul /hɔːl/ vt arrastrar; transportar (goods). ● n (catch) redada f; (stolen goods) botín m; (journey) recorrido m. **~age** /-ɪdʒ/ n transporte m. **~er** (Amer), **~ier** n transportista m & f

haunt /hɔːnt/ vt frecuentar; (ghost) rondar. ● n sitio m preferido. **~ed** adj (house) embrujado; (look) angustiado

---

have /hæv//həv, əv/

3rd person singular present **has**, past **had**

● transitive verb

····➤ tener. I **~ three sisters** tengo tres hermanas. **do you ~ a credit card?** ¿tiene una tarjeta de crédito?

····➤ (in requests) **can I ~ a kilo of apples, please?** ¿me da un kilo de manzanas, por favor?

····➤ (eat) comer. **I had a pizza** comí una pizza

····➤ (drink) tomar. **come and ~ a drink** ven a tomar una copa

····➤ (smoke) fumar (cigarette)

····➤ (hold, organize) hacer (party, meeting)

····➤ (get, receive) **I had a letter from Tony yesterday** recibí una carta de Tony ayer. **we've had no news of her** no hemos tenido noticias suyas

····➤ (illness) tener (flu, headache). **to ~ a cold** estar resfriado, tener catarro

····➤ **to have sth done: we had it painted** lo hicimos pintar. **I had my hair cut** me corté el pelo

····➤ **to have it in for s.o.** tenerle manía a uno

● auxiliary verb

····➤ haber. **I've seen her already**

ya la he visto, ya la vi (LAm)

····➤ **to have just done sth** acabar de hacer algo. **I've just seen her** acabo de verla

····➤ **to have to do sth** tener que hacer algo. **I ~ to** or **I've got to go to the bank** tengo que ir al banco

····➤ (in tag questions) **you've met her, ~n't you?** ya la conoces, ¿no? or ¿verdad? or ¿no es cierto?

····➤ (in short answers) **you've forgotten something - have I?** has olvidado algo - ¿sí?

---

haven /ˈheɪvn/ n puerto m; (refuge) refugio m

haversack /ˈhævəsæk/ n mochila f

havoc /ˈhævək/ n estragos mpl

hawk /hɔːk/ n halcón m

hawthorn /ˈhɔːθɔːn/ n espino m

hay /heɪ/ n heno m. **~ fever** n fiebre f del heno. **~stack** n almiar m. **~wire** adj. **go ~wire** (plans) desorganizarse; (machine) estropearse

hazard /ˈhæzəd/ n riesgo m. **~ous** adj arriesgado

haze /heɪz/ n neblina f

hazel /ˈheɪzl/ n avellano m. **~nut** n avellana f

hazy /ˈheɪzɪ/ adj (-ier, -iest) nebuloso

he /hiː/ pron él

head /hed/ n cabeza f; (of family, government) jefe m; (of organization) director m; (of beer) espuma f. **~s or tails** cara o cruz. ● adj principal. ● vt encabezar, cabecear (ball). □ **~ for** vt dirigirse a. **~ache** n dolor m de cabeza. **~er** n (football) cabezazo m. **~first** / ˈfɜːst/ adv de cabeza. **~ing** n título m, encabezamiento m. **~lamp** n faro m, foco m (LAm). **~land** /-lənd/ n promontorio m. **~line** n titular m. **the news ~lines** el resumen informativo. **~long** adv de cabeza; (precipitately) precipitadamente. **~master** n director m. **~mistress** n directora f. **~on** /-ˈɒn/ adj & adv de frente. **~phones** npl auriculares mpl, cascos mpl. **~quarters** /-ˈkwɔːtəz/ n (of business) oficina f central; (Mil) cuartel m general. **~strong** adj testarudo. **~teacher** /-ˈtiːtʃə(r)/ n director _m._ ~**y** _adj_ (**-ier, -iest**) (_scent_) embriagador

heal /hi:l/ _vt_ curar. ● _vi_ cicatrizarse

health /helθ/ _n_ salud _f._ ~**y** _adj_ sano

heap /hi:p/ _n_ montón _m._ ● _vt_ amontonar.

hear /hɪə(r)/ _vt/i_ (_pt_ **heard** /hɜ:d/) oír. ~**, ~!** ¡bravo! ~ **about** oír hablar de. ~ **from** recibir noticias de. ~**ing** _n_ oído _m._ (_Jurid_) vista _f._ ~**ing-aid** _n_ audífono _m._ ~**say** _n_ rumores _mpl_

hearse /hɜ:s/ _n_ coche _m_ fúnebre

heart / ha:t/ _n_ corazón _m._ **at** ~ en el fondo. **by** ~ de memoria. **lose** ~ descorazonarse. ~**ache** _n_ congoja _f._ ~ **attack** _n_ ataque _m_ al corazón, infarto _m._ ~**break** _n_ congoja _f._ ~**breaking** _adj_ desgarrador. ~**burn** _n_ ardor _m_ de estómago. ~**felt** _adj_ sincero

hearth /ha:θ/ _n_ hogar _m_

heart ~**ily** _adv_ de buena gana. ~**less** _adj_ cruel. ~**y** _adj_ (_welcome_) caluroso; (_meal_) abundante

heat /hi:t/ _n_ calor _m._ (_contest_) (prueba _f_) eliminatoria _f._ ● _vt_ calentar. ● _vi_ calentarse. ~**ed** _adj_ (_fig_) acalorado. ~**er** _n_ calentador _m_

heath /hi:θ/ _n_ brezal _m_, monte _m_

heathen /'hi:ðn/ _n & a_ pagano (_m_)

heather /'heðə(r)/ _n_ brezo _m_

heat ~**ing** _n_ calefacción _f._ ~**stroke** _n_ insolación _f._ ~**wave** _n_ ola _f_ de calor

heave /hi:v/ _vt_ (_lift_) levantar; exhalar (_sigh_); (_fam, throw_) tirar. ● _vi_ (_pull_) tirar, jalar (_LAm_); (🄵, _retch_) dar arcadas

heaven /'hevn/ _n_ cielo _m._ ~**ly** _adj_ celestial; (_astronomy_) celeste; (_fam, excellent_) divino

heav|ily /'hevɪlɪ/ _adv_ pesadamente; (_smoke, drink_) mucho. ~**y** _adj_ (**-ier, -iest**) pesado; (rain) fuerte; (traffic) denso. ~**yweight** _n_ peso _m_ pesado

heckle /'hekl/ _vt_ interrumpir

hectic /'hektɪk/ _adj_ febril

he'd /hi:d/ = **he had, he would**

hedge /hedʒ/ _n_ seto _m_ (vivo). ● _vi_ escaparse por la tangente. ~**hog** _n_ erizo _m_

heed /hi:d/ _vt_ hacer caso de. ● _n._ **take** ~ tener cuidado

heel /hi:l/ _n_ talón _m;_ (_of shoe_) tacón _m_

hefty /'heftɪ/ _adj_ (**-ier, -iest**) (_sturdy_) fuerte; (_heavy_) pesado

heifer /'hefə(r)/ _n_ novilla _f_

height /haɪt/ _n_ altura _f;_ (_of person_) estatura _f;_ (_of fame, glory_) cumbre _f._ ~**en** _vt_ elevar; (_fig_) aumentar

heir /eə(r)/ _n_ heredero _m._ ~**ess** _n_ heredera _f._ ~**loom** _n_ reliquia _f_ heredada

held /held/ _see_ **HOLD**

helicopter /'helɪkɒptə(r)/ _n_ helicóptero _m_

hell /hel/ _n_ infierno _m_

he'll /hi:l/ = **he will**

hello /hə'ləʊ/ _int_ ¡hola!; (_Telephone, caller_) ¡oiga!, ¡bueno! (_Mex_); (_Telephone, person answering_) ¡diga!, ¡bueno! (_Mex_). **say** ~ **to** saludar

helm /helm/ _n_ (_Naut_) timón _m_

helmet /'helmɪt/ _n_ casco _m_

help /help/ _vt/i_ ayudar. **he cannot** ~ **laughing** no puede menos de reír. ~ **o.s. to** servirse. **it cannot be** ~**ed** no hay más remedio. ● _n_ ayuda _f._ ● _int_ ¡socorro! ~**er** _n_ ayudante _m._ ~**ful** _adj_ útil; (person) amable. ~**ing** _n_ porción _f._ ~**less** _adj_ (_unable to manage_) incapaz; (_defenceless_) indefenso

hem /hem/ _n_ dobladillo _m_

hemisphere /'hemɪsfɪə(r)/ _n_ hemisferio _m_

hen /hen/ _n_ (_chicken_) gallina _f;_ (_female bird_) hembra _f_

hence /hens/ _adv_ de aquí. ~**forth** _adv_ de ahora en adelante

henpecked /'henpekt/ _adj_ dominado por su mujer

her /hɜ:(r)/ _pron_ (_direct object_) la; (_indirect object_) le; (_after prep_) ella. **I know** ~ la conozco. ● _adj_ su, sus _pl_

herb /hɜ:b/ _n_ hierba _f._ ~**al** _adj_ de hierbas

herd /hɜ:d/ _n_ (_of cattle, pigs_) manada _f;_ (_of goats_) rebaño _m._ ● _vt_ arrear. ~ **together** reunir

here /hɪə(r)/ _adv_ aquí, acá (_esp LAm_). ~**!** (_take this_) ¡tenga! ~**abouts** /-ə'baʊts/ _adv_ por aquí. ~**after** /-'a:ftə(r)/ _adv_ en el futuro. ~**by** /-'baɪ/ _adv_ por este medio

heredit|ary /hɪ'redɪtərɪ/ _adj_ hereditario

here|sy /'herəsɪ/ n herejía f. **∼tic** n hereje m & f

herewith /hɪə'wɪð/ adv adjunto

heritage /'herɪtɪdʒ/ n herencia f; (fig) patrimonio m. **∼ tourism** n turismo m cultural, turismo m patrimonial (LAm)

hermetically /hɜː'metɪklɪ/ adv. **∼ sealed** herméticamente cerrado

hermit /'hɜːmɪt/ n ermitaño m, eremita m

hernia /'hɜːnɪə/ n hernia f

hero /'hɪərəʊ/ n (pl **-oes**) héroe m. **∼ic** /hɪ'rəʊɪk/ adj heroico

heroin /'herəʊɪn/ n heroína f

hero ∼ine /'herəʊɪn/ n heroína f. **∼ism** /'herəʊɪzm/ n heroísmo m

heron /'herən/ n garza f (real)

herring /'herɪŋ/ n arenque m

hers /hɜːz/ poss pron (el) suyo m, (la) suya f, (los) suyos mpl, (las) suyas fpl

herself /hɜː'self/ pron ella misma; (reflexive) se; (after prep) sí misma

he's /hiːz/ = **he is, he has**

hesit|ant /'hezɪtənt/ adj vacilante. **∼ate** /-teɪt/ vi vacilar. **∼ation** /-'teɪʃn/ n vacilación f

heterosexual /hetərəʊ'seksjʊəl/ adj & n heterosexual (m & f)

het up /het'ʌp/ adj 🔲 nervioso

hew /hjuː/ vt (pp **hewed** or **hewn**) cortar; (cut into shape) tallar

hexagon /'heksəgən/ n hexágono m. **∼al** /-'ægənl/ adj hexagonal

hey /heɪ/ int ¡eh!; (expressing dismay, protest) ¡oye!

heyday /'heɪdeɪ/ n apogeo m

hi /haɪ/ int 🔲 ¡hola!

hibernat|e /'haɪbəneɪt/ vi hibernar. **∼ion** /-'neɪʃn/ n hibernación f

hiccough, hiccup /'hɪkʌp/ n hipo m. **have (the) ∼s** tener hipo. ● vi hipar

hide /haɪd/ vt (pt **hid**, pp **hidden**) esconder. ● vi esconderse. ● n piel f; (tanned) cuero m. **∼-and-seek** /'haɪdnsiːk/ n. **play ∼-and-seek** jugar al escondite, jugar a las escondidas (LAm)

hideous /'hɪdɪəs/ adj (dreadful) horrible; (ugly) feo

hideout /'haɪdaʊt/ n escondrijo m

hiding /'haɪdɪŋ/ n (🔲, thrashing) paliza f. **go into ∼** esconderse. **∼ place** n escondite m, escondrijo m

hierarchy /'haɪərɑːkɪ/ n jerarquía f

hieroglyphics /haɪərə'glɪfɪks/ n jeroglíficos mpl

hi-fi /'haɪfaɪ/ adj de alta fidelidad. ● n equipo m de alta fidelidad, hi-fi m

high /haɪ/ adj (**-er, -est**) alto; (ideals) elevado; (wind) fuerte; (fam, drugged) drogado, colocado 🔲; (voice) agudo; (meat) pasado. ● n alto nivel m. **a (new) ∼** un récord. ● adv alto. **∼er education** n enseñanza f superior. **∼-handed** /-'hændɪd/ adj prepotente. **∼ heels** npl zapatos mpl de tacón alto. **∼lands** /-ləndz/ npl tierras fpl altas. **∼-level** adj de alto nivel. **∼light** n punto m culminante. ● vt destacar; (Art) realzar. **∼ly** adv muy; (paid) muy bien. **∼ly strung** adj nervioso. **H∼ness** n (title) alteza f. **∼-rise** adj (building) alto. **∼ school** n (Amer) instituto m, colegio m secundario. **∼ street** n calle f principal. **∼-strung** adj (Amer) nervioso. **∼way** n carretera f

High School En EE.UU., el último ciclo del colegio secundario, generalmente para alumnos de edades comprendidas entre los 14 y los 18 años. En Gran Bretaña, algunos colegios secundarios también reciben el nombre de high schools.

hijack /'haɪdʒæk/ vt secuestrar. ● n secuestro m. **∼er** n secuestrador

hike /haɪk/ n caminata f. ● vi ir de caminata. **∼r** n excursionista m & f

hilarious /hɪ'leərɪəs/ adj muy divertido

hill /hɪl/ n colina f; (slope) cuesta f. **∼side** n ladera f. **∼y** adj accidentado

hilt /hɪlt/ n (of sword) puño m. **to the ∼** (fig) totalmente

him /hɪm/ pron (direct object) lo, le (only Spain); (indirect object) le; (after prep) él. **I know ∼** lo/le conozco. **∼self** pron él mismo; (reflexive) se; (after prep) sí mismo

hind|er /'hɪndə(r)/ vt estorbar. **~rance** /'hɪndrəns/ n obstáculo m

hindsight /'haɪnsaɪt/ n. **with ~** retrospectivamente

Hindu /'hɪndu:/ n & a hindú (m & f). **~ism** n hinduismo m

hinge /hɪndʒ/ n bisagra f

hint /hɪnt/ n indirecta f; (advice) consejo m. ● vi soltar una indirecta. **~ at** dar a entender

hip /hɪp/ n cadera f

hippie /'hɪpɪ/ n hippy m & f

hippopotamus /hɪpə'pɒtəməs/ n (pl -muses or **-mi** /-maɪ/) hipopótamo m

hire /haɪə(r)/ vt alquilar (thing); contratar (person). ● n alquiler m. **car ~** alquiler m de coches. **~ purchase** n compra f a plazos

his /hɪz/ adj su, sus pl. ● poss pron (el) suyo m, (la) suya f, (los) suyos mpl, (las) suyas fpl

Hispan|ic /hɪ'spænɪk/ adj hispánico. ● n (Amer) hispano m. **~ist** /'hɪspənɪst/ n hispanista m & f

hiss /hɪs/ n silbido. ● vt/i silbar

histor|ian /hɪ'stɔ:rɪən/ n historiador m. **~ic(al)** /hɪ'stɒrɪk(l)/ adj histórico. **~y** /'hɪstərɪ/ n historia f.

hit /hɪt/ vt (pt hit, pres p hitting) golpear (object); pegarle a (person); (collide with) chocar con; (affect) afectar. **~ it off with** hacer buenas migas con. □ **~ on** vt dar con. ● n (blow) golpe m; (success) éxito m. (Internet) visita f

hitch /hɪtʃ/ vt (fasten) enganchar. ● n (snag) problema m. **~ a lift**, **~ a ride** (Amer) see **~HIKE**. **~hike** vi hacer autostop, hacer dedo, ir de aventón (Mex). **~hiker** n autoestopista m & f

hither /'hɪðə(r)/ adv aquí, acá. **~ and thither** acá y allá. **~to** adv hasta ahora

hit-or-miss /hɪtɔ:'mɪs/ adj (approach) poco científico

hive /haɪv/ n colmena f

hoard /hɔ:d/ vt acumular. ● n provisión f; (of money) tesoro m

hoarding /'hɔ:dɪŋ/ n valla f publicitaria

hoarse /hɔ:s/ adj (-er, -est) ronco. **~ly** adv con voz ronca

hoax /həʊks/ n engaño m. ● vt engañar

hob /hɒb/ n (of cooker) hornillos mpl, hornillas fpl (LAm)

hobble /'hɒbl/ vi cojear, renguear (LAm)

hobby /'hɒbɪ/ n pasatiempo m. **~horse** n (toy) caballito m (de niño); (fixation) caballo m de batalla

hockey /'hɒkɪ/ n hockey m; (Amer) hockey m sobre hielo

hoe /həʊ/ n azada f. ● vt (pres p hoeing) azadonar

hog /hɒg/ n (Amer) cerdo m. ● vt (pt hogged) 🔲 acaparar

hoist /hɔɪst/ vt levantar; izar (flag). ● n montacargas m

hold /həʊld/ vt (pt held) tener; (grasp) coger (esp Spain), agarrar; (contain) contener; mantener (interest); (believe) creer. ● vi mantenerse. ● n (influence) influencia f; (Naut, Aviat) bodega f. **get ~ of** agarrar; (fig, acquire) adquirir. □ **~ back** vt (contain) contener. □ **~ on** vi (stand firm) resistir; (wait) esperar. □ **~ on to** vt (keep) guardar; (cling to) agarrarse a. □ **~ out** vt (offer) ofrecer. vi (resist) resistir. □ **~ up** vt (raise) levantar; (support) sostener; (delay) retrasar; (rob) atracar. **~all** n bolsa f (de viaje). **~er** n tenedor m; (of post) titular m; (wallet) funda f. **~up** n atraco m

hole /həʊl/ n agujero m; (in ground) hoyo m; (in road) bache m. ● vt agujerear

holiday /'hɒlɪdeɪ/ n vacaciones fpl; (public) fiesta f. **go on ~** ir de vacaciones. **~maker** n veraneante m & f

holiness /'həʊlɪnɪs/ n santidad f

Holland /'hɒlənd/ n Holanda f

hollow /'hɒləʊ/ adj & n hueco (m)

holly /'hɒlɪ/ n acebo m

holocaust /'hɒləkɔ:st/ n holocausto m

holster /'həʊlstə(r)/ n pistolera f

holy /'həʊlɪ/ adj (-ier, -iest) santo, sagrado. **H~ Ghost** n, **H~ Spirit** n Espíritu m Santo. **~ water** n agua f bendita

homage /'hɒmɪdʒ/ n homenaje m. **pay ~ to** rendir homenaje a

home /həʊm/ n casa f; (for old people) residencia f de ancianos; (native land)

h

patria f. ● adj (cooking) casero; (address) particular; (background) familiar; (Pol) interior; (match) de casa. ● adv. **(at)** ~ en casa. ~**land** n patria f. ~**land security** seguridad f nacional. ~**less** adj sin hogar. ~**ly** adj (-ier, -iest) casero; (Amer, ugly) feo. ~**-made** adj hecho en casa. ~ **page** n (Comp) página f frontal. ~**sick** adj. be ~**sick** echar de menos a su familia/su país, extrañar a su ciudad/su país (LAm). ~ **town** n ciudad f natal. ~**work** n deberes mpl

homicide /ˈhɒmɪsaɪd/ n homicidio m

homoeopathic /həʊmɪəʊˈpæθɪk/ adj homeopático

homogeneous /hɒməʊˈdʒiːnɪəs/ adj homogéneo

homosexual /həʊməʊˈseksjʊəl/ adj & n homosexual (m)

honest /ˈɒnɪst/ adj honrado; (frank) sincero. ~**ly** adv honradamente. ~**y** n honradez f

honey /ˈhʌnɪ/ n miel f. ~**comb** n panal m. ~**moon** n luna f de miel. ~**suckle** n madreselva f

honorary /ˈɒnərərɪ/ adj honorario

honour /ˈɒnə(r)/ n honor m. ● vt honrar; cumplir (con) (promise). ~**able** adj honorable

hood /hʊd/ n capucha f; (car roof) capota f; (Amer, car bonnet) capó m, capote m (Mex)

hoodwink /ˈhʊdwɪŋk/ vt engañar

hoof /huːf/ n (pl hoofs or hooves) (of horse) casco m, pezuña f (Mex); (of cow) pezuña f

hook /hʊk/ n gancho m; (on garment) corchete m; (for fishing) anzuelo m. let s.o. off the ~ dejar salir a uno del atolladero. off the ~ (telephone) descolgado. ● vt. ~**ed on** 🔲 adicto a. □ ~ **up** vt enganchar. ~**ed** adj (tool) en forma de gancho; (nose) aguileño

hookey /ˈhʊkɪ/ n. **play** ~ (Amer fam) faltar a clase, hacer novillos

hooligan /ˈhuːlɪgən/ n vándalo m, gamberro m

hoop /huːp/ n aro m

hooray /hʊˈreɪ/ int & n ¡viva! (m)

hoot /huːt/ n (of horn) bocinazo m; (of owl) ululato m. ● vi tocar la bocina; (owl) ulular

Hoover /ˈhuːvə(r)/ n (®) aspiradora f. ● vt pasar la aspiradora por, aspirar (LAm)

hooves /huːvz/ see HOOF

hop /hɒp/ vi (pt hopped) saltar a la pata coja; (frog, rabbit) brincar, saltar; (bird) dar saltitos. ● n salto m; (flight) etapa f. ~**(s)** (plant) lúpulo m

hope /həʊp/ n esperanza f. ● vt/i esperar. ~ **for** esperar. ~**ful** adj (optimistic) esperanzado; (promising) esperanzador. ~**fully** adv con optimismo; (it is hoped) se espera. ~**less** adj desesperado

horde /hɔːd/ n horda f

horizon /həˈraɪzn/ n horizonte m

horizontal /hɒrɪˈzɒntl/ adj horizontal. ~**ly** adv horizontalmente

hormone /ˈhɔːməʊn/ n hormona f

horn /hɔːn/ n cuerno m, asta f, cacho m (LAm); (of car) bocina f; (Mus) trompa f. ~**ed** adj con cuernos

hornet /ˈhɔːnɪt/ n avispón m

horoscope /ˈhɒrəskəʊp/ n horóscopo m

horrible /ˈhɒrəbl/ adj horrible

horrid /ˈhɒrɪd/ adj horrible

horrific /həˈrɪfɪk/ adj horroroso

horrify /ˈhɒrɪfaɪ/ vt horrorizar

horror /ˈhɒrə(r)/ n horror m

hors-d'oeuvre /ɔːˈdɜːvr/ n (pl -s /ˈdɜːvr/) entremés m, botana f (Mex)

horse /hɔːs/ n caballo m. ~**back** n, on ~**back** a caballo. ~**power** n (unit) caballo m (de fuerza). ~**racing** n carreras fpl de caballos. ~**shoe** n herradura f

horticultur|al /hɔːtɪˈkʌltʃərəl/ adj hortícola. ~**e** /ˈhɔːtɪkʌltʃə(r)/ n horticultura f

hose /həʊz/ n manguera f, manga f. ● vt. ~ **down** lavar (con manguera). ~**pipe** n manga f

hosiery /ˈhəʊzɪərɪ/ n calcetería f

hospice /ˈhɒspɪs/ n residencia f para enfermos desahuciados

hospitable /hɒˈspɪtəbl/ adj hospitalario

hospital /ˈhɒspɪtl/ n hospital m

hospitality /hɒspɪˈtælətɪ/ n hospitalidad f

host /həʊst/ n (*master of house*) anfitrión m; (*Radio, TV*) presentador m; (*multitude*) gran cantidad f; (*Relig*) hostia f

hostage /ˈhɒstɪdʒ/ n rehén m

hostel /ˈhɒstl/ n (*for students*) residencia f; (*for homeless people*) hogar m

hostess /ˈhəʊstɪs/ n anfitriona f

hostil|e /ˈhɒstaɪl/ adj hostil. ~**ity** /-ˈtɪlətɪ/ n hostilidad f

hot /hɒt/ adj (**hotter, hottest**) caliente; (weather, day) caluroso; (climate) cálido; (*Culin*) picante; (news) de última hora. **be/feel** ~ tener calor. **get** ~ calentarse. **it is** ~ hace calor. ~**bed** n (*fig*) semillero m

hotchpotch /ˈhɒtʃpɒtʃ/ n mezcolanza f

hot dog n perrito m caliente

hotel /həʊˈtel/ n hotel m. ~**ier** /-ɪeɪ/ n hotelero m

hot ~**house** n invernadero m. ~**plate** n placa f, hornilla f (*LAm*). ~**-water bottle** /-ˈwɔːtə(r)/ n bolsa f de agua caliente

hound /haʊnd/ n perro m de caza. ● vt perseguir

hour /aʊə(r)/ n hora f. ~**ly** adj (rate) por hora. ● adv (*every hour*) cada hora; (*by the hour*) por hora

house /haʊs/ n (pl -s /ˈhaʊzɪz/) casa f; (*Pol*) cámara f. ● /haʊz/ vt alojar; (*keep*) guardar. ~**hold** n casa f. ~**holder** n dueño m de una casa. ~**keeper** n ama f de llaves. ~**maid** n criada f, mucama f (*LAm*). ~**-proud** adj meticuloso. ~**warming** (party) n fiesta f de inauguración de una casa. ~**wife** n ama f de casa. ~**work** n tareas fpl domésticas

housing /ˈhaʊzɪŋ/ n alojamiento m. ~ **development** (*Amer*), ~ **estate** n complejo m habitacional, urbanización f

hovel /ˈhɒvl/ n casucha f

hover /ˈhɒvə(r)/ vi (bird, threat etc) cernerse; (*loiter*) rondar. ~**craft** n (pl invar or -**crafts**) aerodeslizador m

how /haʊ/ adv cómo. ~ **about a walk?** ¿qué te parece si damos un paseo? ~ **are you?** ¿cómo está Vd? ~ **do you do?** (*in introduction*) mucho gusto. ~ **long?** (*in time*)

¿cuánto tiempo? ~ **long is the room?** ¿cuánto mide de largo el cuarto? ~ **often?** ¿cuántas veces?

however /haʊˈevə(r)/ adv (*nevertheless*) no obstante, sin embargo; (*with verb*) de cualquier manera que (+ subjunctive); (*with adjective or adverb*) por... que (+ subjunctive). ~ **much it rains** por mucho que llueva

howl /haʊl/ n aullido. ● vi aullar

hp abbr see **HORSEPOWER**

HP abbr see **HIRE-PURCHASE**

hub /hʌb/ n (of wheel) cubo m; (*fig*) centro m

hubcap /ˈhʌbkæp/ n tapacubos m

huddle /ˈhʌdl/ vi apiñarse

hue /hjuː/ n (colour) color m

huff /hʌf/ n. **be in a** ~ estar enfurruñado

hug /hʌɡ/ vt (pt **hugged**) abrazar. ● n abrazo m

huge /hjuːdʒ/ adj enorme. ~**ly** adv enormemente

hulk /hʌlk/ n (of ship) barco m viejo

hull /hʌl/ n (of ship) casco m

hullo /həˈləʊ/ int see **HELLO**

hum /hʌm/ vt/i (pt **hummed**) (person) canturrear; (insect, engine) zumbar. ● n zumbido m

human /ˈhjuːmən/ adj & n humano (m). ~ **being** n ser m humano. ~**e** /hjuːˈmeɪn/ adj humano. ~**itarian** /hjuːmænɪˈteərɪən/ adj humanitario. ~**ity** /hjuːˈmænətɪ/ n humanidad f

humbl|e /ˈhʌmbl/ adj (-**er**, -**est**) humilde. ● vt humillar. ~**y** adv humildemente

humdrum /ˈhʌmdrʌm/ adj monótono

humid /ˈhjuːmɪd/ adj húmedo. ~**ity** /hjuːˈmɪdətɪ/ n humedad f

humiliat|e /hjuːˈmɪlɪeɪt/ vt humillar. ~**ion** /-ˈeɪʃn/ n humillación f

humility /hjuːˈmɪlətɪ/ n humildad f

humongous /hjuːˈmʌŋɡəs/ adj 🄸 de primera

humo|rist /ˈhjuːmərɪst/ n humorista m & f. ~**rous** /-rəs/ adj humorístico. ~**rously** adv con gracia. ~**ur** /ˈhjuːmə(r)/ n humor m. **sense of** ~ sentido m del humor

hump /hʌmp/ n (of person, camel) joroba f; (in ground) montículo m

hunch /hʌntʃ/ vt encorvar. ●n presentimiento m; (lump) joroba f. **~back** n jorobado m

hundred /'hʌndrəd/ adj ciento, (before noun) cien. **one ~ and ninety-eight** ciento noventa y ocho. **two ~** doscientos. **three ~ pages** trescientas páginas. **four ~** cuatrocientos. **five ~** quinientos. ●n ciento m. **~s of** centenares de. **~th** adj & n centésimo (m). **~weight** n 50,8kg; (Amer) 45,36kg

hung /hʌŋ/ see HANG

Hungar|ian /hʌŋ'geərɪən/ adj & n húngaro (m). **~y** /'hʌŋgərɪ/ n Hungría f

hung|er /'hʌŋgə(r)/ n hambre f. ●vi. **~er for** tener hambre de. **~rily** /'hʌŋgrəlɪ/ adv ávidamente. **~ry** adj (-ier, -iest) hambriento. **be ~ry** tener hambre

hunk /hʌŋk/ n (buen) pedazo m

hunt /hʌnt/ vt cazar. ●vi cazar. **~ for** buscar. ●n caza f. **~er** n cazador m. **~ing** n caza f. **go ~ing** ir de caza

hurl /hɜːl/ vt lanzar

hurrah /hʊ'rɑː/, **hurray** /hʊ'reɪ/ int & n ¡viva! (m)

hurricane /'hʌrɪkən/ n huracán m

hurr|ied /'hʌrɪd/ adj apresurado. **~iedly** adv apresuradamente. **~y** vi darse prisa, apurarse (LAm). ●vt meter prisa a, apurar (LAm). ●n prisa f. **be in a ~y** tener prisa, estar apurado (LAm)

hurt /hɜːt/ vt (pt hurt) hacer daño a, lastimar (LAm). **~ s.o.'s feelings** ofender a uno. ●vi doler. **my head ~s** me duele la cabeza. **~ful** adj hiriente

hurtle /'hɜːtl/ vt ir volando. ●vi. **~ along** mover rápidamente

husband /'hʌzbənd/ n marido m, esposo m

hush /hʌʃ/ vt acallar. ●n silencio m. □ **~ up** vt acallar (affair). **~-hush** adj 🇹 super secreto

husk /hʌsk/ n cáscara f

husky /'hʌskɪ/ adj (-ier, -iest) (hoarse) ronco

hustle /'hʌsl/ vt (jostle) empujar. ●vi (hurry) darse prisa, apurarse (LAm). ●n empuje m

hut /hʌt/ n cabaña f

hutch /hʌtʃ/ n conejera f

hybrid /'haɪbrɪd/ adj & n híbrido (m)

hydrangea /haɪ'dreɪndʒə/ n hortensia f

hydrant /'haɪdrənt/ n. **(fire) ~** n boca f de riego, boca f de incendios (LAm)

hydraulic /haɪ'drɔːlɪk/ adj hidráulico

hydroelectric /haɪdrəʊɪ'lektrɪk/ adj hidroeléctrico

hydrofoil /'haɪdrəfɔɪl/ n hidrodeslizador m

hydrogen /'haɪdrədʒən/ n hidrógeno m

hyena /haɪ'iːnə/ n hiena f

hygien|e /'haɪdʒiːn/ n higiene f. **~ic** /haɪ'dʒiːnɪk/ adj higiénico

hymn /hɪm/ n himno m

hyper... /'haɪpə(r)/ pref hiper...

hyphen /'haɪfn/ n guión m. **~ate** /-eɪt/ vt escribir con quión

hypno|sis /hɪp'nəʊsɪs/ n hipnosis f. **~tic** /-'nɒtɪk/ adj hipnótico. **~tism** /'hɪpnətɪzəm/ n hipnotismo m. **~tist** /'hɪpnətɪst/ n hipnotista m & f. **~tize** /'hɪpnətaɪz/ vt hipnotizar

hypochondriac /haɪpə'kɒndrɪæk/ n hipocondríaco m

hypocri|sy /hɪ'pɒkrəsɪ/ n hipocresía f. **~te** /'hɪpəkrɪt/ n hipócrita m & f. **~tical** /hɪpə'krɪtɪkl/ adj hipócrita

hypodermic /haɪpə'dɜːmɪk/ adj hipodérmico. ●n hipodérmica f

hypothe|sis /haɪ'pɒθəsɪs/ n (pl -theses /-siːz/) hipótesis f. **~tical** /-ə'θetɪkl/ adj hipotético

hysteri|a /hɪ'stɪərɪə/ n histerismo m. **~cal** /-'terɪkl/ adj histérico. **~cs** /hɪ'sterɪks/ npl histerismo m **have ~cs** ponerse histérico; (laugh) morir de risa

. . . .

I i

. . . .

I /aɪ/ pron yo

ice /aɪs/ n hielo m. ●vt helar; glasear (cake). ●vi. **~ (up)** helarse, congelarse. **~berg** /-bɜːg/ n iceberg m. **~ box** n (compartment) congelador; (Amer fam, refrigerator) frigorífico m, refrigerador m (LAm). **~cream** n helado m. **~ cube** n cubito m de hielo

Iceland /'aɪslənd/ n Islandia f

ice ~ lolly polo m, paleta f helada (LAm). **~ rink** n pista f de hielo. **~ skating** n patinaje m sobre hielo

icicle /'aɪsɪkl/ n carámbano m

icing /'aɪsɪŋ/ n glaseado m

icon /'aɪkɒn/ n icono m

icy /'aɪsɪ/ adj (-ier, -iest) helado; (fig) glacial

I'd /aɪd/ = I had, I would

idea /aɪ'dɪə/ n idea f

ideal /aɪ'dɪəl/ adj & n ideal (m). **~ism** n idealismo m. **~ist** n idealista m & f. **~istic** /-'lɪstɪk/ adj idealista. **~ize** vt idealizar. **~ly** adv idealmente

identical /aɪ'dentɪkl/ adj idéntico. **~ twins** npl gemelos mpl idénticos, gemelos mpl (LAm)

identif|ication /aɪdentɪfɪ'keɪʃn/ n identificación f. **~y** /aɪ'dentɪfaɪ/ vt identificar. ● vi. **~y with** identificarse con

identity /aɪ'dentɪtɪ/ n identidad f. **~ card** n carné m de identidad. **~ theft** n robo m de identidad

ideolog|ical /aɪdɪə'lɒdʒɪkl/ adj ideológico. **~y** /aɪdɪ'ɒlədʒɪ/ n ideología f

idiocy /'ɪdɪəsɪ/ n idiotez f

idiom /'ɪdɪəm/ n locución f. **~atic** /-'mætɪk/ adj idiomático

idiot /'ɪdɪət/ n idiota m & f. **~ic** /-'ɒtɪk/ adj idiota

idle /'aɪdl/ adj (-er, -est) ocioso; (lazy) holgazán; (out of work) desocupado; (machine) parado. ● vi (engine) andar al ralentí. **~ness** n ociosidad f; (laziness) holgazanería f

idol /'aɪdl/ n ídolo m. **~ize** vt idolatrar

idyllic /ɪ'dɪlɪk/ adj idílico

i.e. abbr (= id est) es decir

if /ɪf/ conj si

igloo /'ɪglu:/ n iglú m

ignit|e /ɪg'naɪt/ vt encender. ● vi encenderse. **~ion** /-'nɪʃn/ n ignición f; (Auto) encendido m. **~ion key** n llave f de contacto

ignoramus /ɪgnə'reɪməs/ n (pl-muses) ignorante

ignoran|ce /'ɪgnərəns/ n ignorancia f. **~t** adj ignorante

ignore /ɪg'nɔ:(r)/ vt no hacer caso de; hacer caso omiso de (warning)

ill /ɪl/ adj enfermo. ● adv mal. ● n mal m

I'll /aɪl/ = I will

ill ~-advised /-əd'vaɪzd/ adj imprudente. **~ at ease** /-ət'i:z/ adj incómodo. **~-bred** /-'bred/ adj mal educado

illegal /ɪ'li:gl/ adj ilegal

illegible /ɪ'ledʒəbl/ adj ilegible

illegitima|cy /ɪlɪ'dʒɪtɪməsɪ/ n ilegitimidad f. **~te** /-ət/ adj ilegítimo

illitera|cy /ɪ'lɪtərəsɪ/ n analfabetismo m. **~te** /-ət/ adj analfabeto

illness /'ɪlnɪs/ n enfermedad f

illogical /ɪ'lɒdʒɪkl/ adj ilógico

illuminat|e /ɪ'lu:mɪneɪt/ vt iluminar. **~ion** /-'neɪʃn/ n iluminación f

illus|ion /ɪ'lu:ʒn/ n ilusión f. **~sory** /-sɛrɪ/ adj ilusorio

illustrat|e /'ɪləstreɪt/ vt ilustrar. **~ion** /-'streɪʃn/ n ilustración f; (example) ejemplo m

illustrious /ɪ'lʌstrɪəs/ adj ilustre

ill will /ɪl'wɪl/ n mala voluntad f

I'm /aɪm/ = I am

image /'ɪmɪdʒ/ n imagen f. **~ry** n imágenes fpl

imagin|able /ɪ'mædʒɪnəbl/ adj imaginable. **~ary** adj imaginario. **~ation** /-'neɪʃn/ n imaginación f. **~ative** adj imaginativo. **~e** /ɪ'mædʒɪn/ vt imaginar(se)

imbalance /ɪm'bæləns/ n desequilibrio m

imbecile /'ɪmbəsi:l/ n imbécil m & f

imitat|e /'ɪmɪteɪt/ vt imitar. **~ion** /-'teɪʃn/ n imitación f. ● adj de imitación. **~or** n imitador m

immaculate /ɪ'mækjʊlət/ adj inmaculado

immatur|e /ɪmə'tjʊə(r)/ adj inmaduro. **~ity** n inmadurez f

immediate /ɪ'mi:dɪət/ adj inmediato. **~ly** adv inmediatamente. ● conj en cuanto (+ subjunctive)

immens|e /ɪ'mens/ adj inmenso. **~ely** adv inmensamente; (fam, very much) muchísimo

immers|e /ɪ'mɜ:s/ vt sumergir. **~ion** /-ʃn/ n inmersión f. **~ion heater** n calentador *m* de inmersión

immigra|nt /'ɪmɪgrənt/ *adj & n* inmigrante (*m & f*). **~tion** /-'greɪʃn/ *n* inmigración *f*

imminent /'ɪmɪnənt/ *adj* inminente

immobil|e /ɪ'məʊbaɪl/ *adj* inmóvil. **~ize** /-bɪlaɪz/ *vt* inmovilizar. **~izer** /-bɪlaɪzə(r)/ *n* inmovilizador *m*

immoderate /ɪ'mɒdərət/ *adj* inmoderado

immodest /ɪ'mɒdɪst/ *adj* inmodesto

immoral /ɪ'mɒrəl/ *adj* inmoral. **~ity** /ɪmə'rælətɪ/ *n* inmoralidad *f*

immortal /ɪ'mɔːtl/ *adj* inmortal. **~ity** /-'tælətɪ/ *n* inmortalidad *f*. **~ize** *vt* inmortalizar

immun|e /ɪ'mjuːn/ *adj* inmune (**to** *a*). **~ity** *n* inmunidad *f*. **~ization** /ɪmjʊnar'zeɪʃn/ *n* inmunización *f*. **~ize** /ɪmjʊnaɪz/ *vt* inmunizar

imp /ɪmp/ *n* diablillo *m*

impact /'ɪmpækt/ *n* impacto *m*

impair /ɪm'peə(r)/ *vt* perjudicar

impale /ɪm'peɪl/ *vt* atravesar (**on** *con*)

impart /ɪm'pɑːt/ *vt* comunicar (*news*); impartir (*knowledge*)

impartial /ɪm'pɑːʃl/ *adj* imparcial. **~ity** /-ɪ'ælətɪ/ *n* imparcialidad *f*

impassable /ɪm'pɑːsəbl/ *adj* (*road*) intransitable

impassive /ɪm'pæsɪv/ *adj* impasible

impatien|ce /ɪm'peɪʃəns/ *n* impaciencia *f*. **~t** *adj* impaciente. **get ~t** impacientarse. **~tly** *adv* con impaciencia

impeccable /ɪm'pekəbl/ *adj* impecable

impede /ɪm'piːd/ *vt* estorbar

impediment /ɪm'pedɪmənt/ obstáculo *m*. (**speech**) **~** *n* defecto *m* del habla

impending /ɪm'pendɪŋ/ *adj* inminente

impenetrable /ɪm'penɪtrəbl/ *adj* impenetrable

imperative /ɪm'perətɪv/ *adj* imprescindible. ●*n* (*Gram*) imperativo *m*

imperceptible /ɪmpə'septəbl/ *adj* imperceptible

imperfect /ɪm'pɜːfɪkt/ *adj* imperfecto. **~ion** /ɪmpə'fekʃn/ *n* imperfección *f*

imperial /ɪm'pɪərɪəl/ *adj* imperial. **~ism** *n* imperialismo *m*

impersonal /ɪm'pɜːsənl/ *adj* impersonal

impersonat|e /ɪm'pɜːsəneɪt/ *vt* hacerse pasar por; (*mimic*) imitar. **~ion** /-'neɪʃn/ *n* imitación *f*. **~or** *n* imitador *m*

impertinen|ce /ɪm'pɜːtməns/ *n* impertinencia *f*. **~t** *adj* impertinente

impervious /ɪm'pɜːvɪəs/ *adj*. **~ to** impermeable a

impetuous /ɪm'petjʊəs/ *adj* impetuoso

impetus /'ɪmpɪtəs/ *n* ímpetu *m*

implacable /ɪm'plækəbl/ *adj* implacable

implant /ɪm'plɑːnt/ *vt* implantar

implement /'ɪmplɪmənt/ *n* instrumento *m*, implemento *m* (*LAm*). ●/'ɪmplɪment/ *vt* implementar

implementation /ɪmplɪmen'teɪʃn/ *n* implementación *f*

implicat|e /'ɪmplɪkeɪt/ *vt* implicar. **~ion** /-'keɪʃn/ *n* implicación *f*

implicit /ɪm'plɪsɪt/ *adj* (*implied*) implícito; (*unquestioning*) absoluto

implore /ɪm'plɔː(r)/ *vt* implorar

imply /ɪm'plaɪ/ *vt* (*involve*) implicar; (*insinuate*) dar a entender, insinuar

impolite /ɪmpə'laɪt/ *adj* mal educado

import /ɪm'pɔːt/ *vt* importar. ●/'ɪmpɔːt/ *n* importación *f*; (*item*) artículo *m* de importación; (*meaning*) significación *f*

importan|ce /ɪm'pɔːtəns/ *n* importancia *f*. **~t** *adj* importante

importer /ɪm'pɔːtə(r)/ *n* importador *m*

impos|e /ɪm'pəʊz/ *vt* imponer. ●*vi*. **~e on** abusar de la amabilidad de. **~ing** *adj* imponente. **~ition** /ɪmpə'zɪʃn/ *n* imposición *f*; (*fig*) abuso *m*

impossib|ility /ɪmpɒsə'bɪlətɪ/ *n* imposibilidad *f*. **~le** /ɪm'pɒsəbl/ *adj* imposible

impostor /ɪm'pɒstə(r)/ *n* impostor *m*

impoten|ce /'ɪmpətəns/ *n* impotencia *f*. **~t** *adj* impotente

impound /ɪm'paʊnd/ *vt* confiscar

impoverished /ɪm'pɒvərɪʃt/ *adj* empobrecido

impractical /ɪm'præktɪkl/ *adj* poco práctico

impregnable /ɪm'preɡnəbl/ adj inexpugnable

impregnate /'ɪmpreɡneɪt/ vt impregnar (**with** con, de)

impress /ɪm'pres/ vt impresionar; (make good impression) causar una buena impresión a. ● vi impresionar

impression /ɪm'preʃn/ n impresión f. ~**able** adj impresionable. ~**ism** n impresionismo m

impressive /ɪm'presɪv/ adj impresionante

imprint /'ɪmprɪnt/ n impresión f. ● /ɪm'prɪnt/ vt imprimir

imprison /ɪm'prɪzn/ vt encarcelar. ~**ment** n encarcelamiento m

improbab|ility /ɪmprɒbə'bɪlətɪ/ n improbabilidad f. ~**le** /ɪm'prɒbəbl/ adj improbable

impromptu /ɪm'prɒmptjuː/ adj improvisado. ● adv de improviso

improper /ɪm'prɒpə(r)/ adj impropio; (incorrect) incorrecto

improve /ɪm'pruːv/ vt mejorar. ● vi mejorar. ~**ment** n mejora f

improvis|ation /ɪmprəvaɪ'zeɪʃn/ n improvisación f. ~**e** /'ɪmprəvaɪz/ vt/i improvisar

impuden|ce /'ɪmpjʊdəns/ n insolencia f. ~**t** adj insolente

impuls|e /'ɪmpʌls/ n impulso m. **on** ~**e** sin reflexionar. ~**ive** adj irreflexivo

impur|e /ɪm'pjʊə(r)/ adj impuro. ~**ity** n impureza f

in /ɪn/ prep en; (within) dentro de. ~ **a firm manner** de una manera terminante. ~ **an hour('s time)** dentro de una hora. ~ **doing** al hacer. ~ **so far as** en la medida en que. ~ **the evening** por la tarde. ~ **the rain** bajo la lluvia. ~ **the sun** al sol. **one** ~ **ten** uno de cada diez. **the best** ~ **the world** el mejor del mundo. ● adv (inside) dentro; (at home) en casa. **come** ~ entrar. ● n. **the** ~**s and outs of** los detalles de

inability /ɪnə'bɪlətɪ/ n incapacidad f

inaccessible /ɪnæk'sesəbl/ adj inaccesible

inaccura|cy /ɪn'ækjʊrəsɪ/ n inexactitud f. ~**te** /-ət/ adj inexacto

inactiv|e /ɪn'æktɪv/ adj inactivo. ~**ity** /-'tɪvətɪ/ n inactividad f

inadequa|cy /ɪn'ædɪkwəsɪ/ adj insuficiencia f. ~**te** /-ət/ adj insuficiente

inadvertently /ɪnəd'vɜːtəntlɪ/ adv sin querer

inadvisable /ɪnəd'vaɪzəbl/ adj desaconsejable

inane /ɪ'neɪm/ adj estúpido

inanimate /ɪn'ænɪmət/ adj inanimado

inappropriate /ɪnə'prəʊprɪət/ adj inoportuno

inarticulate /ɪnɑː'tɪkjʊlət/ adj incapaz de expresarse claramente

inattentive /ɪnə'tentɪv/ adj desatento

inaudible /ɪn'ɔːdəbl/ adj inaudible

inaugurate /ɪ'nɔːɡjʊreɪt/ vt inaugurar

inborn /'ɪnbɔːn/ adj innato

inbred /ɪn'bred/ adj (inborn) innato; (social group) endogámico

Inc /ɪŋk/ abbr (Amer) (= **Incorporated**) S.A., Sociedad Anónima

incalculable /ɪn'kælkjʊləbl/ adj incalculable

incapable /ɪn'keɪpəbl/ adj incapaz

incapacit|ate /ɪnkə'pæsɪteɪt/ vt incapacitar. ~**y** n incapacidad f

incarcerate /ɪn'kɑːsəreɪt/ vt encarcelar

incarnat|e /ɪn'kɑːnət/ adj encarnado. ~**ion** /-'neɪʃn/ n encarnación f

incendiary /ɪn'sendɪərɪ/ adj incendiario. ~ **bomb** bomba f incendiaria

incense /'ɪnsens/ n incienso m. ● /ɪn'sens/ vt enfurecer

incentive /ɪn'sentɪv/ n incentivo m

incessant /ɪn'sesnt/ adj incesante. ~**ly** adv sin cesar

incest /'ɪnsest/ n incesto m. ~**uous** /ɪn'sestjʊəs/ adj incestuoso

inch /ɪntʃ/ n pulgada f; (= 2,54cm). ● vi. ~ **forward** avanzar lentamente

incidence /'ɪnsɪdəns/ n frecuencia f

incident /'ɪnsɪdənt/ n incidente m

incidental /ɪnsɪ'dentl/ adj (effect) secundario; (minor) incidental. ~**ly** adv a propósito

incinerat|e /ɪn'sɪnəreɪt/ vt incinerar. ~**or** n incinerador m

incision /ɪn'sɪʒn/ n incisión f

incite /ɪnˈsaɪt/ vt incitar. ~**ment** n incitación f

inclination /ɪnklɪˈneɪʃn/ n inclinación f. **have no** ~ **to** no tener deseos de

incline /ɪnˈklaɪn/ vt inclinar. **be** ~**d to** tener tendencia a. ● vi inclinarse. ● /ˈɪnklaɪn/ n pendiente f

inclu|de /ɪnˈkluːd/ vt incluir. ~**ding** prep incluso. ~**sion** /-ʒn/ n inclusión f. ~**sive** /-sɪv/ adj inclusivo

incognito /ɪnkɒɡˈniːtəʊ/ adv de incógnito

incoherent /ɪnkəʊˈhɪərənt/ adj incoherente

incom|e /ˈɪnkʌm/ n ingresos mpl. ~**e tax** n impuesto m sobre la renta. ~**ing** adj (tide) ascendente

incomparable /ɪnˈkɒmpərəbl/ adj incomparable

incompatible /ɪnkəmˈpætəbl/ adj incompatible

incompeten|ce /ɪnˈkɒmpɪtəns/ n incompetencia f. ~**t** adj incompetente

incomplete /ɪnkəmˈpliːt/ adj incompleto

incomprehensible /ɪnkɒmprɪˈhensəbl/ adj incomprensible

inconceivable /ɪnkənˈsiːvəbl/ adj inconcebible

inconclusive /ɪnkənˈkluːsɪv/ adj no concluyente

incongruous /ɪnˈkɒŋɡrʊəs/ adj incongruente

inconsiderate /ɪnkənˈsɪdərət/ adj desconsiderado

inconsisten|cy /ɪnkənˈsɪstənsɪ/ n inconsecuencia f. ~**t** adj inconsecuente. **be** ~**t with** no concordar con

inconspicuous /ɪnkənˈspɪkjʊəs/ adj que no llama la atención. ~**ly** adv sin llamar la atención

incontinent /ɪnˈkɒntɪnənt/ adj incontinente

inconvenien|ce /ɪnkənˈviːnɪəns/ adj inconveniencia f; (drawback) inconveniente m. ~**t** adj inconveniente

incorporate /ɪnˈkɔːpəreɪt/ vt incorporar; (include) incluir; (Com) constituir (en sociedad)

incorrect /ɪnkəˈrekt/ adj incorrecto

increas|e /ˈɪnkriːs/ n aumento m (in de). ● /ɪnˈkriːs/ vt/i aumentar. ~**ing** /ɪnˈkriːsɪŋ/ adj creciente. ~**ingly** adv cada vez más

incredible /ɪnˈkredəbl/ adj increíble

incredulous /ɪnˈkredjʊləs/ adj incrédulo

incriminat|e /ɪnˈkrɪmɪneɪt/ vt incriminar. ~**ing** adj comprometedor

incubat|e /ˈɪŋkjʊbeɪt/ vt incubar. ~**ion** /-ˈbeɪʃn/ n incubación f. ~**or** n incubadora f

incur /ɪnˈkɜː(r)/ vt (pt **incurred**) incurrir en; contraer (debts)

incurable /ɪnˈkjʊərəbl/ adj (disease) incurable; (romantic) empedernido

indebted /ɪnˈdetɪd/ adj. **be** ~ **to s.o.** estar en deuda con uno

indecen|cy /ɪnˈdiːsnsɪ/ n indecencia f. ~**t** adj indecente

indecisi|on /ɪndɪˈsɪʒn/ n indecisión f. ~**ve** /-ˈsaɪsɪv/ adj indeciso

indeed /ɪnˈdiːd/ adv en efecto; (really?) ¿de veras?

indefinable /ɪndɪˈfaɪnəbl/ adj indefinible

indefinite /ɪnˈdefnət/ adj indefinido. ~**ly** adv indefinidamente

indelible /ɪnˈdelɪbl/ adj indeleble

indemni|fy /ɪnˈdemnɪfaɪ/ vt (insure) asegurar; (compensate) indemnizar. ~**ty** /-ətɪ/ n (insurance) indemnidad f; (payment) indemnización f

indent /ɪnˈdent/ vt sangrar (text). ~**ation** /-ˈteɪʃn/ n mella f

independen|ce /ɪndɪˈpendəns/ n independencia f. ~**t** adj independiente. ~**tly** adv independientemente

in-depth /ɪnˈdepθ/ adj a fondo

indescribable /ɪndɪˈskraɪbəbl/ adj indescriptible

indestructible /ɪndɪˈstrʌktəbl/ adj indestructible

indeterminate /ɪndɪˈtɜːmɪnət/ adj indeterminado

index /ˈɪndeks/ n (pl **indexes**) (in book) índice m; (pl **indexes** or **indices**) (Com, Math) índice m. ● vt poner índice a; (enter in index) poner en un índice. ~ **finger** n (dedo m) índice m. ~**-linked** /-ˈlɪŋkt/ adj indexado

India /ˈɪndɪə/ n la India. ~**n** adj & n indio (m)

indicat|e /ˈɪndɪkeɪt/ *vt* indicar. **∼ion** /-ˈkeɪʃn/ *n* indicación *f*. **∼ive** /ɪnˈdɪkətɪv/ *adj & n* indicativo (*m*). **∼or** /ˈɪndɪkeɪtə(r)/ *n* indicador *m*; (*Auto*) intermitente *m*

indices /ˈɪndɪsiːz/ *see* INDEX

indict /ɪnˈdaɪt/ *vt* acusar. **∼ment** *n* acusación *f*

indifferen|ce /ɪnˈdɪfrəns/ *n* indiferencia *f*. **∼t** *adj* indiferente; (*not good*) mediocre

indigesti|ble /ɪndɪˈdʒestəbl/ *adj* indigesto. **∼on** /-tʃən/ *n* indigestión *f*

indigna|nt /ɪnˈdɪgnənt/ *adj* indignado. **∼tion** /-ˈneɪʃn/ *n* indignación *f*

indirect /ɪndɪˈrekt/ *adj* indirecto. **∼ly** *adv* indirectamente

indiscre|et /ɪndɪˈskriːt/ *adj* indiscreto. **∼tion** /-ˈkreʃn/ *n* indiscreción *f*

indiscriminate /ɪndɪˈskrɪmɪnət/ *adj* indistinto. **∼ly** *adv* indistintamente

indispensable /ɪndɪˈspensəbl/ *adj* indispensable, imprescindible

indisposed /ɪndɪˈspəʊzd/ *adj* indispuesto

indisputable /ɪndɪˈspjuːtəbl/ *adj* indiscutible

indistinguishable /ɪndɪˈstɪŋgwɪʃəbl/ *adj* indistinguible (**from** de)

individual /ɪndɪˈvɪdjʊəl/ *adj* individual. ● *n* individuo *m*. **∼ly** *adv* individualmente

indoctrinat|e /ɪnˈdɒktrɪneɪt/ *vt* adoctrinar. **∼ion** /-ˈneɪʃn/ *n* adoctrinamiento *m*

indolen|ce /ˈɪndələns/ *n* indolencia *f*. **∼t** *adj* indolente

indomitable /ɪnˈdɒmɪtəbl/ *adj* indómito

indoor /ˈɪndɔː(r)/ *adj* interior; (clothes etc) de casa; (*covered*) cubierto. **∼s** *adv* dentro, adentro (*LAm*)

induc|e /ɪnˈdjuːs/ *vt* inducir. **∼ement** *n* incentivo *m*

indulge /ɪnˈdʌldʒ/ *vt* satisfacer (desires); complacer (person). ● *vi.* **∼ in** permitirse. **∼nce** /-əns/ *n* (*of desires*) satisfacción *f*; (*extravagance*) lujo *m*. **∼nt** *adj* indulgente

industrial /ɪnˈdʌstrɪəl/ *adj* industrial; (unrest) laboral. **∼ist** *n* industrial *m & f*. **∼ized** *adj* industrializado

industrious /ɪnˈdʌstrɪəs/ *adj* trabajador

industry /ˈɪndəstrɪ/ *n* industria *f*; (*zeal*) aplicación *f*

inebriated /ɪˈniːbrɪeɪtɪd/ *adj* beodo, ebrio

inedible /ɪnˈedɪbl/ *adj* incomible

ineffective /ɪnɪˈfektɪv/ *adj* ineficaz; (person) incompetente

ineffectual /ɪnɪˈfektjʊəl/ *adj* ineficaz

inefficien|cy /ɪnɪˈfɪʃnsɪ/ *n* ineficacia *f*; (*of person*) incompetencia *f*. **∼t** *adj* ineficaz; (person) incompetente

ineligible /ɪnˈelɪdʒəbl/ *adj* inelegible. **be ∼ for** no tener derecho a

inept /ɪˈnept/ *adj* inepto

inequality /ɪnɪˈkwɒlətɪ/ *n* desigualdad *f*

inert /ɪˈnɜːt/ *adj* inerte. **∼ia** /ɪˈnɜːʃə/ *n* inercia *f*

inescapable /ɪnɪˈskeɪpəbl/ *adj* ineludible

inevitabl|e /ɪnˈevɪtəbl/ *adj* inevitable. ● *n*. **the ∼e** lo inevitable. **∼y** *adv* inevitablemente

inexact /ɪnɪgˈzækt/ *adj* inexacto

inexcusable /ɪnɪkˈskjuːsəbl/ *adj* imperdonable

inexpensive /ɪnɪkˈspensɪv/ *adj* económico, barato

inexperience /ɪnɪkˈspɪərɪəns/ *n* falta *f* de experiencia. **∼d** *adj* inexperto

inexplicable /ɪnɪkˈsplɪkəbl/ *adj* inexplicable

infallib|ility /ɪnfæləˈbɪlətɪ/ *n* infalibilidad *f*. **∼le** /ɪnˈfæləbl/ *adj* infalible

infam|ous /ˈɪnfəməs/ *adj* infame. **∼y** *n* infamia *f*

infan|cy /ˈɪnfənsɪ/ *n* infancia *f*. **∼t** *n* niño *m*. **∼tile** /ˈɪnfəntaɪl/ *adj* infantil

infantry /ˈɪnfəntrɪ/ *n* infantería *f*

infatuat|ed /ɪnˈfætjʊeɪtɪd/ *adj*. **be ∼ed with** estar encaprichado con. **∼ion** /-ˈeɪʃn/ *n* encaprichamiento *m*

infect /ɪnˈfekt/ *vt* infectar; (*fig*) contagiar. **∼ s.o. with sth** contagiarle algo a uno. **∼ion** /-ʃn/ *n* infección *f*. **∼ious** /-ʃəs/ *adj* contagioso

infer /ɪnˈfɜː(r)/ *vt* (*pt* **inferred**) deducir

inferior /ɪnˈfɪərɪə(r)/ *adj & n* inferior (*m & f*). **∼ity** /-ˈɒrətɪ/ *n* inferioridad *f*

inferno /ɪnˈfɜːnəʊ/ n (pl -os) infierno m

infertil|e /ɪnˈfɜːtaɪl/ adj estéril. ~**ity** /-ˈtɪlətɪ/ n esterilidad f

infest /ɪnˈfest/ vt infestar

infidelity /ɪnfɪˈdelətɪ/ n infidelidad f

infiltrat|e /ˈɪnfɪltreɪt/ vt infiltrarse en. ● vi infiltrarse. ~**or** n infiltrado m

infinite /ˈɪnfɪnət/ adj infinito. ~**ly** adv infinitamente

infinitesimal /ɪnfɪnɪˈtesɪml/ adj infinitesimal

infinitive /ɪnˈfɪnətɪv/ n infinitivo m

infinity /ɪnˈfɪnətɪ/ n (infinite distance) infinito m; (infinite quantity) infinidad f

infirm /ɪnˈfɜːm/ adj enfermizo. ~**ity** n enfermedad f

inflam|e /ɪnˈfleɪm/ vt inflamar. ~**mable** /ɪnˈflæməbl/ adj inflamable. ~**mation** /-əˈmeɪʃn/ n inflamación f

inflat|e /ɪnˈfleɪt/ vt inflar. ~**ion** /-ʃn/ n inflación f. ~**ionary** adj inflacionario

inflection /ɪnˈflekʃn/ n inflexión f

inflexible /ɪnˈfleksəbl/ adj inflexible

inflict /ɪnˈflɪkt/ vt infligir (**on** a)

influen|ce /ˈɪnflʊəns/ n influencia f. **under the** ~**ce** (fam, drunk) borracho. ● vt influir (en). ~**tial** /-ˈenʃl/ adj influyente

influenza /ɪnflʊˈenzə/ n gripe f

influx /ˈɪnflʌks/ n afluencia f

inform /ɪnˈfɔːm/ vt informar. **keep** ~**ed** tener al corriente. ● vi. ~ **on** s.o. delatar a uno

informal /ɪnˈfɔːml/ adj informal; (language) familiar. ~**ity** /-ˈmælətɪ/ n falta f de ceremonia. ~**ly** adv (casually) de manera informal; (unofficially) informalmente

inform|ation /ɪnfəˈmeɪʃn/ n información f. ~**ation technology** n informática f. ~**ative** adj /ɪnˈfɔːmətɪv/ informativo. ~**er** /ɪbˈfɔːmə(r)/ n informante m

infrared /ɪnfrəˈred/ adj infrarrojo

infrequent /ɪnˈfriːkwənt/ adj poco frecuente. ~**ly** adv raramente

infringe /ɪnˈfrɪndʒ/ vt infringir. ~ **on** violar. ~**ment** n violación f

infuriat|e /ɪnˈfjʊərɪeɪt/ vt enfurecer. ~**ing** adj exasperante

ingen|ious /ɪnˈdʒiːnɪəs/ adj ingenioso. ~**uity** /ɪndʒɪˈnjuːətɪ/ n ingeniosidad f

ingot /ˈɪŋgət/ n lingote m

ingrained /ɪnˈgreɪnd/ adj (belief) arraigado

ingratiate /ɪnˈgreɪʃɪeɪt/ vt. ~ **o.s. with** congraciarse con

ingratitude /ɪnˈgrætɪtjuːd/ n ingratitud f

ingredient /ɪnˈgriːdɪənt/ n ingrediente m

ingrowing /ˈɪngrəʊɪŋ/, **ingrown** /ˈɪngrəʊn/ adj. ~ **nail** n uñero m, uña f encarnada

inhabit /ɪnˈhæbɪt/ vt habitar. ~**able** adj habitable. ~**ant** n habitante m

inhale /ɪnˈheɪl/ vt aspirar. ● vi (when smoking) aspirar el humo. ~**r** n inhalador m

inherent /ɪnˈhɪərənt/ adj inherente. ~**ly** adv intrínsecamente

inherit /ɪnˈherɪt/ vt heredar. ~**ance** /-əns/ n herencia f

inhibit /ɪnˈhɪbɪt/ vt inhibir. ~**ed** adj inhibido. ~**ion** /-ˈbɪʃn/ n inhibición f

inhospitable /ɪnhəˈspɪtəbl/ adj (place) inhóspito; (person) inhospitalario

inhuman /ɪnˈhjuːmən/ adj inhumano. ~**e** /ɪnhjuːˈmeɪn/ adj inhumano. ~**ity** /ɪnhjuːˈmænətɪ/ n inhumanidad f

initial /ɪˈnɪʃl/ n inicial f. ● vt (pt **initialled**) firmar con iniciales. ● adj inicial. ~**ly** adv al principio

initiat|e /ɪˈnɪʃɪeɪt/ vt iniciar; promover (scheme etc). ~**ion** /-ˈeɪʃn/ n iniciación f

initiative /ɪˈnɪʃətɪv/ n iniciativa f. **on one's own** ~ por iniciativa propia. **take the** ~ tomar la iniciativa

inject /ɪnˈdʒekt/ vt inyectar. ~**ion** /-ʃn/ n inyección f

injur|e /ˈɪndʒə(r)/ vt herir. ~**y** n herida f

injustice /ɪnˈdʒʌstɪs/ n injusticia f

ink /ɪŋk/ n tinta f. ~**well** n tintero m. ~**y** adj manchado de tinta

inland /ˈɪnlənd/ adj interior. ● /ɪn ˈlænd/ adv tierra adentro. **I~ Revenue** /ˈɪnlənd/ n Hacienda f

in-laws /ˈɪnlɔːz/ npl parientes mpl políticos

inlay /ɪnˈleɪ/ vt (pt **inlaid**) taracear, incrustar. • /ˈɪnleɪ/ n taracea f, incrustación f

inlet /ˈɪnlet/ n (in coastline) ensenada f; (of river, sea) brazo m

inmate /ˈɪnmeɪt/ n (of asylum) interno m; (of prison) preso m

inn /ɪn/ n posada f

innate /ɪˈneɪt/ adj innato

inner /ˈɪnə(r)/ adj interior; (fig) íntimo. ~**most** adj más íntimo. ~ **tube** n cámara f

innocen|ce /ˈɪnəsns/ n inocencia f. ~**t** adj & n inocente (m & f)

innocuous /ɪˈnɒkjuəs/ adj inocuo

innovat|e /ˈɪnəveɪt/ vi innovar. ~**ion** /-ˈveɪʃn/ n innovación f. ~**ive** /ˈɪnəvətɪv/ adj innovador. ~**or** n innovador m

innuendo /ɪnjuːˈendəʊ/ n (pl -oes) insinuación f

innumerable /ɪˈnjuːmərəbl/ adj innumerable

inoculat|e /ɪˈnɒkjʊleɪt/ vt inocular. ~**ion** /-ˈleɪʃn/ n inoculación f

inoffensive /ɪnəˈfensɪv/ adj inofensivo

inopportune /ɪnˈɒpətjuːn/ adj inoportuno

input /ˈɪnpʊt/ n aportación f, aporte m (LAm); (Comp) entrada f. • vt (pt **input**, pres p **inputting**) entrar (data)

inquest /ˈɪnkwest/ n investigación f judicial

inquir|e /ɪnˈkwaɪə(r)/ vt/i preguntar. ~**e about** informarse de. ~**y** n pregunta f; (investigation) investigación f

inquisition /ɪnkwɪˈzɪʃn/ n inquisición f

inquisitive /ɪnˈkwɪzətɪv/ adj inquisitivo

insan|e /ɪnˈseɪn/ adj loco. ~**ity** /ɪnˈsænəti/ n locura f

insatiable /ɪnˈseɪʃəbl/ adj insaciable

inscri|be /ɪnˈskraɪb/ vt inscribir (letters); grabar (design). ~**ption** /-ɪpʃn/ n inscripción f

inscrutable /ɪnˈskruːtəbl/ adj inescrutable

insect /ˈɪnsekt/ n insecto m. ~**icide** /ɪnˈsektɪsaɪd/ n insecticida f

insecur|e /ɪnsɪˈkjʊə(r)/ adj inseguro. ~**ity** n inseguridad f

insensitive /ɪnˈsensətɪv/ adj insensible

inseparable /ɪnˈsepərəbl/ adj inseparable

insert /ˈɪnsɜːt/ n materia f insertada. • /ɪnˈsɜːt/ vt insertar. ~**ion** /ɪnˈsɜːʃn/ n inserción f

inside /ɪnˈsaɪd/ n interior m. ~ **out** al revés; (thoroughly) a fondo. • adj interior. • adv dentro, adentro (LAm). • prep dentro de. ~**s** npl tripas fpl

insight /ˈɪnsaɪt/ n perspicacia f. **gain an** ~ **into** llegar a comprender bien

insignificant /ɪnsɪgˈnɪfɪkənt/ adj insignificante

insincer|e /ɪnsɪnˈsɪə(r)/ adj poco sincero. ~**ity** /-ˈserəti/ n falta f de sinceridad

insinuat|e /ɪnˈsɪnjʊeɪt/ vt insinuar. ~**ion** /-ˈeɪʃn/ n insinuación f

insipid /ɪnˈsɪpɪd/ adj insípido

insist /ɪnˈsɪst/ vt insistir (**that** en que). • vi insistir. ~ **on** insistir en. ~**ence** /-əns/ n insistencia f. ~**ent** adj insistente. ~**ently** adv con insistencia

insolen|ce /ˈɪnsələns/ n insolencia f. ~**t** adj insolente

insoluble /ɪnˈsɒljʊbl/ adj insoluble

insolvent /ɪnˈsɒlvənt/ adj insolvente

insomnia /ɪnˈsɒmnɪə/ n insomnio m. ~**c** /-ɪæk/ n insomne m & f

inspect /ɪnˈspekt/ vt (officially) inspeccionar; (look at closely) revisar, examinar . ~**ion** /-ʃn/ n inspección f. ~**or** n inspector m; (on train, bus) revisor m, inspector m (LAm)

inspir|ation /ɪnspəˈreɪʃn/ n inspiración f. ~**e** /ɪnˈspaɪə(r)/ vt inspirar. ~**ing** adj inspirador

instability /ɪnstəˈbɪləti/ n inestabilidad f

install /ɪnˈstɔːl/ vt instalar. ~**ation** /-əˈleɪʃn/ n instalación f

instalment /ɪnˈstɔːlmənt/ n (payment) plazo m; (of publication) entrega f; (of radio, TV serial) episodio m

instance /ˈɪnstəns/ n ejemplo m; (case) caso m. **for** ~ por ejemplo. **in the first** ~ en primer lugar

instant /ˈɪnstənt/ adj instantáneo. • n instante m. ~**aneous** /ɪnstənˈteɪmɪəs/ adj instantáneo

instead /ɪnˈsted/ adv en cambio. ~ of en vez de, en lugar de

instigat|e /ˈɪnstɪɡeɪt/ vt instigar. ~ion /-ˈɡeɪʃn/ n instigación f

instinct /ˈɪnstɪŋkt/ n instinto m. ~ive adj instintivo

institut|e /ˈɪnstɪtjuːt/ n instituto m. ● vt instituir; iniciar (enquiry etc). ~ion /-ˈtjuːʃn/ n institución f. ~ional adj institucional

instruct /ɪnˈstrʌkt/ vt instruir; (order) mandar. ~ s.o. in sth enseñar algo a uno. ~ion /-ʃn/ n instrucción f. ~ions npl (for use) modo m de empleo. ~ive adj instructivo. ~or n instructor m

instrument /ˈɪnstrəmənt/ n instrumento m. ~al /ɪnstrəˈmentl/ adj instrumental. **be ~al in** jugar un papel decisivo en

insubordinat|e /ɪnsəˈbɔːdɪnət/ adj insubordinado. ~ion /-ˈneɪʃn/ n insubordinación f

insufferable /ɪnˈsʌfərəbl/ adj (person) insufrible; (heat) insoportable

insufficient /ɪnsəˈfɪʃnt/ adj insuficiente

insular /ˈɪnsjʊlə(r)/ adj insular, (narrow-minded) estrecho de miras

insulat|e /ˈɪnsjʊleɪt/ vt aislar. ~ion /-ˈleɪʃn/ n aislamiento m

insulin /ˈɪnsjʊlɪn/ n insulina f

insult /ɪnˈsʌlt/ vt insultar. ● /ˈɪnsʌlt/ n insulto m. ~ing /ɪnˈsʌltɪŋ/ adj insultante

insur|ance /ɪnˈʃʊərəns/ n seguro m. ~e /ɪnˈʃʊə(r)/ vt (Com) asegurar; (Amer) see **ENSURE**

insurmountable /ɪnsəˈmaʊntəbl/ adj insuperable

intact /ɪnˈtækt/ adj intacto

integral /ˈɪntɪɡrəl/ adj integral

integrat|e /ˈɪntɪɡreɪt/ vt integrar. ● vi integrarse. ~ion /-ˈɡreɪʃn/ n integración f

integrity /ɪnˈteɡrəti/ n integridad f

intellect /ˈɪntəlekt/ n intelecto m. ~ual /ɪntəˈlektʃʊəl/ adj & n intelectual (m)

intelligen|ce /ɪnˈtelɪdʒəns/ n inteligencia f. ~t adj inteligente. ~tly adv inteligentemente

intelligible /ɪnˈtelɪdʒəbl/ adj inteligible

intend /ɪnˈtend/ vt. ~ to do pensar hacer

intens|e /ɪnˈtens/ adj intenso; (person) apasionado. ~ely adv intensamente; (very) sumamente. ~ify /-ɪfaɪ/ vt intensificar. ● vi intensificarse. ~ity /-ɪti/ n intensidad f

intensive /ɪnˈtensɪv/ adj intensivo. ~ **care** n cuidados mpl intensivos

intent /ɪnˈtent/ n propósito m. ● adj atento. ~ **on** absorto en. ~ **on doing** resuelto a hacer

intention /ɪnˈtenʃn/ n intención f. ~al adj intencional

intently /ɪnˈtentli/ adv atentamente

interact /ɪntərˈækt/ vi relacionarse. ~ion /-ʃn/ n interacción f

intercept /ɪntəˈsept/ vt interceptar. ~ion /-ʃn/ n interceptación f

interchange /ɪntəˈtʃeɪndʒ/ vt intercambiar. ● /ˈɪntətʃeɪndʒ/ n intercambio m; (road junction) cruce m. ~able /-ˈtʃeɪndʒəbl/ adj intercambiable

intercity /ɪntəˈsɪti/ adj rápido interurbano m

intercourse /ˈɪntəkɔːs/ n trato m; (sexual) acto m sexual

interest /ˈɪntrest/ n interés m. ● vt interesar. ~ed adj interesado. **be ~ed in** interesarse por. ~ing adj interesante

interface /ˈɪntəfeɪs/ interfaz m & f; (interaction) interrelación f

interfere /ɪntəˈfɪə(r)/ vi entrometerse. ~ **in** entrometerse en. ~ **with** afectar (a); interferir (radio). ~nce /-rəns/ n intromisión f; (Radio) interferencia f

interior /ɪnˈtɪərɪə(r)/ adj & n interior (m)

interjection /ɪntəˈdʒekʃn/ n interjección f

interlude /ˈɪntəluːd/ n intervalo m; (theatre, music) interludio m

intermediary /ɪntəˈmiːdɪərɪ/ adj & n intermediario (m)

interminable /ɪnˈtɜːmɪnəbl/ adj interminable

intermittent /ɪntəˈmɪtnt/ adj intermitente. ~ly adv con discontinuidad

intern /ɪnˈtɜːn/ vt internar. ● /ˈɪntɜːn/ n (Amer, doctor) interno m

internal /ɪnˈtɜːnl/ adj interno. ~**ly** adv internamente. **I~ Revenue Service** n (Amer) Hacienda f

international /ɪntəˈnæʃənl/ adj internacional

Internet /ˈɪntənet/ n. **the ~** el Internet

interpret /ɪnˈtɜːprɪt/ vt/i interpretar. ~**ation** /-ˈteɪʃn/ n interpretación f. ~**er** n intérprete m & f

interrogat|e /ɪnˈterəɡeɪt/ vt interrogar. ~**ion** /-ˈɡeɪʃn/ n interrogatorio m. ~**ive** /-ˈrɒɡətɪv/ adj interrogativo

interrupt /ɪntəˈrʌpt/ vt/i interrumpir. ~**ion** /-ʃn/ n interrupción f

intersect /ɪntəˈsekt/ vt cruzar. ● vi (roads) cruzarse; (geometry) intersecarse. ~**ion** /-ʃn/ n (roads) cruce m; (geometry) intersección f

intersperse /ɪntəˈspɜːs/ vt intercalar

interstate (highway) /ˈɪntəsteɪt/ n (Amer) carretera f interestal

intertwine /ɪntəˈtwaɪn/ vt entrelazar. ● vi entrelazarse

interval /ˈɪntəvl/ n intervalo m; (theatre) descanso m. **at ~s** a intervalos

interven|e /ɪntəˈviːn/ vi intervenir. ~**tion** /-ˈvenʃn/ n intervención f

interview /ˈɪntəvjuː/ n entrevista f. ● vt entrevistar. ~**ee** /-ˈiː/ n entrevistado m. ~**er** n entrevistador m

intestine /ɪnˈtestɪn/ n intestino m

intimacy /ˈɪntɪməsɪ/ n intimidad f

intimate /ˈɪntɪmət/ adj íntimo. ● /ˈɪntɪmeɪt/ vt (state) anunciar; (imply) dar a entender. ~**ly** /ˈɪntɪmətlɪ/ adv íntimamente

intimidat|e /ɪnˈtɪmɪdeɪt/ vt intimidar. ~**ion** /-ˈdeɪʃn/ n intimidación f

into/ˈɪntu://ˈɪntə/ prep en; (translate) a

intolerable /ɪnˈtɒlərəbl/ adj intolerable

intoleran|ce /ɪnˈtɒlərəns/ n intolerancia f. ~**t** adj intolerante

intoxicat|e /ɪnˈtɒksɪkeɪt/ vt embriagar; (Med) intoxicar. ~**ed** adj ebrio. ~**ing** adj (substance) estupefaciente. ~**ion** /-ˈkeɪʃn/ n embriaguez f; (Med) intoxicación f

intransitive /ɪnˈtrænsɪtɪv/ adj intransitivo

intravenous /ɪntrəˈviːnəs/ adj intravenoso

intrepid /ɪnˈtrepɪd/ adj intrépido

intrica|cy /ˈɪntrɪkəsɪ/ n complejidad f. ~**te** /-ət/ adj complejo

intrigu|e /ɪnˈtriːɡ/ vt/i intrigar. ● /ˈɪntriːɡ/ n intriga f. ~**ing** /ɪnˈtriːɡɪn/ adj intrigante

intrinsic /ɪnˈtrɪnsɪk/ adj intrínseco. ~**ally** adv intrínsecamente

introduc|e /ɪntrəˈdjuːs/ vt introducir; presentar (person). ~**tion** /ɪntrəˈdʌkʃn/ n introducción f; (to person) presentación f. ~**tory** /ɪntrəˈdʌktərɪ/ adj preliminar; (course) de introducción

introvert /ˈɪntrəvɜːt/ n introvertido m

intru|de /ɪnˈtruːd/ vi entrometerse; (disturb) importunar. ~**der** n intruso m. ~**sion** /-ʒn/ n intrusión f. ~**sive** /-sɪv/ adj impertinente

intuiti|on /ɪntjuːˈɪʃn/ n intuición f. ~**ve** /ɪnˈtjuːɪtɪv/ adj intuitivo

inundat|e /ˈɪnʌndeɪt/ vt inundar. ~**ion** /-ˈdeɪʃn/ n inundación f

invade /ɪnˈveɪd/ vt invadir. ~**r** n invasor m

invalid /ˈɪnvəlɪd/ n inválido m. ● /ɪnˈvælɪd/ adj inválido. ~**ate** /ɪnˈvælɪdeɪt/ vt invalidar

invaluable /ɪnˈvæljʊəbl/ adj inestimable, invalorable (LAm)

invariabl|e /ɪnˈveərɪəbl/ adj invariable. ~**y** adv invariablemente

invasion /ɪnˈveɪʒn/ n invasión f

invent /ɪnˈvent/ vt inventar. ~**ion** /-ˈvenʃn/ n invención f. ~**ive** adj inventivo. ~**or** n inventor m

inventory /ˈɪnvəntrɪ/ n inventario m

invertebrate /ɪnˈvɜːtɪbrət/ n invertebrado m

inverted commas /ɪnvɜːtɪd ˈkɒməz/npl comillas fpl

invest /ɪnˈvest/ vt invertir. ● vi. **~ in** invertir en

investigat|e /ɪnˈvestɪɡeɪt/ vt investigar. ~**ion** /-ˈɡeɪʃn/ n investigación f. **under ~ion** sometido a examen. ~**or** n investigador m

investment /ɪnˈvestmənt/ inversión *f*

investor /ɪnˈvestə(r)/ inversionista *m & f*

inveterate /ɪnˈvetərət/ *adj* inveterado

invidious /ɪnˈvɪdɪəs/ *adj* (*hateful*) odioso; (*unfair*) injusto

invigorating /ɪnˈvɪɡəreɪtɪŋ/ *adj* vigorizante; (*stimulating*) estimulante

invincible /ɪnˈvɪnsɪbl/ *adj* invencible

invisible /ɪnˈvɪzəbl/ *adj* invisible

invit|ation /ɪnvɪˈteɪʃn/ *n* invitación *f*. **~e** /ɪnˈvaɪt/ *vt* invitar; (*ask for*) pedir. ● /ˈɪnvaɪt/ *n* Ⓘ invitación *f*. **~ing** /ɪnˈvaɪtɪŋ/ *adj* atrayente

invoice /ˈɪnvɔɪs/ *n* factura *f*. ● *vt*. **~ s.o. (for sth)** pasarle a uno factura (por algo)

involuntary /ɪnˈvɒləntərɪ/ *adj* involuntario

involve /ɪnˈvɒlv/ *vt* (*entail*) suponer; (*implicate*) implicar. **~d in** envuelto en. **~d** *adj* (*complex*) complicado. **~ment** *n* participación *f*; (*relationship*) enredo *m*

inward /ˈɪnwəd/ *adj* interior. ● *adv* hacia adentro. **~s** *adv* hacia dentro

iodine /ˈaɪədiːn/ *n* yodo *m*

ion /ˈaɪən/ *n* ion *m*

iota /aɪˈəʊtə/ *n* (*amount*) pizca *f*

IOU /aɪəʊˈjuː/ *abbr* (= **I owe you**) pagaré *m*

IQ *abbr* (= **intelligence quotient**) CI *m*, cociente *m* intelectual

Iran /ɪˈrɑːn/ *n* Irán *m*. **~ian** /ɪˈreɪnɪən/ *adj & n* Iraní (*m*)

Iraq /ɪˈrɑːk/ *n* Irak *m*. **~i** *adj & n* iraquí (*m & f*)

irate /aɪˈreɪt/ *adj* colérico

Ireland /ˈaɪələnd/ *n* Irlanda *f*

iris /ˈaɪərɪs/ *n* (*of eye*) iris *m*; (*flower*) lirio *m*

Irish /ˈaɪərɪʃ/ *adj* irlandés. ● *n* (*language*) irlandés *m*. *npl*. **the ~** (*people*) los irlandeses. **~man** /-mən/ *n* irlandés *m*. **~woman** *n* irlandesa *f*

iron /ˈaɪən/ *n* hierro *m*; (*appliance*) plancha *f*. ● *adj* de hierro. ● *vt* planchar. □ **~ out** *vt* allanar

ironic /aɪˈrɒnɪk/ *adj* irónico. **~ally** *adv* irónicamente

ironing board /ˈaɪənɪŋ/ *n* tabla *f* de planchar, burro *m* de planchar (*Mex*)

iron ~monger /-mʌŋɡə(r)/ *n* ferretero *m*. **~monger's** *n* ferretería *f*

irony /ˈaɪərənɪ/ *n* ironía *f*

irrational /ɪˈræʃənl/ *adj* irracional

irrefutable /ɪrɪˈfjuːtəbl/ *adj* irrefutable

irregular /ɪˈreɡjʊlə(r)/ *adj* irregular. **~ity** /-ˈlærətɪ/ *n* irregularidad *f*

irrelevan|ce /ɪˈreləvəns/ *n* irrelevancia *f*. **~t** *adj* irrelevante

irreparable /ɪˈrepərəbl/ *adj* irreparable

irreplaceable /ɪrɪˈpleɪsəbl/ *adj* irreemplazable

irresistible /ɪrɪˈzɪstəbl/ *adj* irresistible

irrespective /ɪrɪˈspektɪv/ *adj*. **~ of** sin tomar en cuenta

irresponsible /ɪrɪˈspɒnsəbl/ *adj* irresponsable

irretrievable /ɪrɪˈtriːvəbl/ *adj* irrecuperable

irreverent /ɪˈrevərənt/ *adj* irreverente

irrevocable /ɪˈrevəkəbl/ *adj* irrevocable

irrigat|e /ˈɪrɪɡeɪt/ *vt* regar, irrigar. **~ion** /-ˈɡeɪʃn/ *n* riego *m*, irrigación *f*

irritable /ˈɪrɪtəbl/ *adj* irritable

irritat|e /ˈɪrɪteɪt/ *vt* irritar. **~ed** *adj* irritado. **~ing** *adj* irritante. **~ion** /-ˈteɪʃn/ *n* irritación *f*

IRS *abbr* (*Amer*) *see* **INTERNAL REVENUE SERVICE**

is /ɪz/ *see* **BE**

ISDN *abbr* (**Integrated Services Digital Network**) RDSI

Islam /ˈɪzlɑːm/ *n* el Islam. **~ic** /ɪzˈlæmɪk/ *adj* Islámico

island /ˈaɪlənd/ *n* isla *f*. **~er** *n* isleño *m*

isolat|e /ˈaɪsəleɪt/ *vt* aislar. **~ion** /-ˈleɪʃn/ *n* aislamiento *m*

Israel /ˈɪzreɪl/ *n* Israel *m*. **~i** /ɪzˈreɪlɪ/ *adj & n* israelí (*m*)

issue /ˈɪʃuː/ *n* tema *m*, asunto *m*; (*of magazine etc*) número *m*; (*of stamps, bank notes*) emisión *f*; (*of documents*) expedición *f*. **take ~ with** discrepar de. ● *vt* hacer público (*statement*); expedir (*documents*); emitir (*stamps etc*); prestar (*library book*)

it /ɪt/ *pronoun*

····▸ (*as subject*) generally not translated. **it's huge** es enorme. **where is it?** ¿dónde está?. **it's all lies** son todas mentiras

····▸ (*as direct object*) lo (*m*), la (*f*). **he read it to me** me lo/la leyó. **give it to me** dámelo/dámela

····▸ (*as indirect object*) le. **I gave it another coat of paint** le di otra mano de pintura

····▸ (*after a preposition*) generally not translated. **there's nothing behind it** no hay nada detrás

! Note, however, that in some cases *él* or *ella* must be used e.g. **he picked up the spoon and hit me with it** *agarró la cuchara y me golpeó con ella*

····▸ (*at door*) **who is it?** ¿quién es?. **it's me** soy yo; (*on telephone*) **who is it, please?** ¿quién habla, por favor?; (*before passing on to sb else*) ¿de parte de quién, por favor? **it's Carol** soy Carol (*Spain*), habla Carol

····▸ (*in impersonal constructions*) **it is well known that ...** bien se sabe que ... **it's five o'clock** son las cinco. **so it seems** así parece

····▸ **that's it** (*that's right*) eso es; (*that's enough, that's finished*) ya está

Italian /ɪˈtæljən/ *adj & n* italiano (*m*)
italics /ɪˈtælɪks/ *npl* (letra *f*) cursiva *f*
Italy /ˈɪtəlɪ/ *n* Italia *f*
itch /ɪtʃ/ *n* picazón *f*. ● *vi* picar. **I'm ∼ing to** estoy que me muero por. **my arm ∼es** me pica el brazo. **∼y** *adj* que pica. **I've got an ∼y nose** me pica la nariz
it'd /ɪtəd/ = **it had**, **it would**
item /ˈaɪtəm/ *n* artículo *m*; (*on agenda*) punto *m*. **news ∼** noticia *f*. **∼ize** *vt* detallar
itinerary /aɪˈtɪnərərɪ/ *n* itinerario *m*
it'll /ˈɪtl/ = **it will**
its /ɪts/ *adj* su, sus (*pl*). ● *pron* (el) suyo *m*, (la) suya *f*, (los) suyos *mpl*, (las) suyas *fpl*
it's /ɪts/ = **it is**, **it has**

itself /ɪtˈself/ *pron* él mismo, ella misma, ello mismo; (*reflexive*) se; (*after prep*) sí mismo, sí misma
I've /aɪv/ = **I have**
ivory /ˈaɪvərɪ/ *n* marfil *m*. **∼ tower** *n* torre *f* de marfil
ivy /ˈaɪvɪ/ *n* hiedra *f*

Ivy League - the El grupo de universidades más antiguas y respetadas de EE.UU. Situadas al noreste del país, son: Harvard, Yale, Columbia, Cornell, Dartmouth College, Brown, Princeton y Pensylvania. El término proviene de la hiedra que crece en los antiguos edificios de estos establecimientos.

Jj

jab /dʒæb/ *vt* (*pt* **jabbed**) pinchar; (*thrust*) hurgonear. ● *n* pinchazo *m*
jack /dʒæk/ *n* (*Mec*) gato *m*; (*socket*) enchufe *m* hembra; (*Cards*) sota *f*. ▫ **∼ up** *vt* alzar con gato
jackal /ˈdʒækl/ *n* chacal *m*
jackdaw /ˈdʒækdɔː/ *n* grajilla *f*
jacket /ˈdʒækɪt/ *n* chaqueta *f*; (*casual*) americana *f*, saco *m* (*LAm*); (*Amer, of book*) sobrecubierta *f*; (*of record*) funda *f*, carátula *f*
jack ∼ knife *vi* (*lorry*) plegarse. **∼pot** *n* premio *m* gordo. **hit the ∼pot** sacar el premio gordo
jade /dʒeɪd/ *n* (*stone*) jade *m*
jagged /ˈdʒægɪd/ *adj* (edge, cut) irregular; (rock) recortado
jaguar /ˈdʒægjʊə(r)/ *n* jaguar *m*
jail /dʒeɪl/ *n* cárcel *m*, prisión *f*. ● *vt* encarcelar. **∼er** *n* carcelero *m*. **∼house** *n* (*Amer*) cárcel *f*
jam /dʒæm/ *vt* (*pt* **jammed**) interferir con (radio); atestar (road). **∼ sth into sth** meter algo a la fuerza en algo. ● *vi* (brakes) bloquearse; (machine) trancarse. ● *n* mermelada *f*; (*fam, situation*) apuro *m*

jangle /'dʒæŋgl/ n sonido m metálico (y áspero). ● vi hacer ruido (metálico)

janitor /'dʒænɪtə(r)/ n portero m

January /'dʒænjʊərɪ/ n enero m

Japan /dʒə'pæn/ n (el) Japón m. **∼ese** /dʒæpə'niːz/ adj & n invar Japonés (m)

jar /dʒɑː(r)/ n tarro m, bote m. ● vi (pt **jarred**) (clash) desentonar. ● vt sacudir

jargon /'dʒɑːgən/ n jerga f

jaundice /'dʒɔːndɪs/ n ictericia f

jaunt /dʒɔːnt/ n excursión f

jaunty /'dʒɔːntɪ/ adj (**-ier, -iest**) garboso

jaw /dʒɔː/ n mandíbula f. **∼s** npl fauces fpl. **∼bone** n mandíbula f, maxilar m; (of animal) quijada f

jay /dʒeɪ/ n arrendajo m. **∼walk** vi cruzar la calle descuidadamente. **∼walker** n peatón m imprudente

jazz /dʒæz/ n jazz m. □ **∼ up** vt animar. **∼y** adj chillón

jealous /'dʒeləs/ adj celoso; (envious) envidioso. **∼y** n celos mpl

jeans /dʒiːnz/ npl vaqueros mpl, jeans mpl, tejanos mpl, pantalones mpl de mezclilla (Mex)

Jeep (P), **jeep** /dʒiːp/ n Jeep m (P)

jeer /dʒɪə(r)/ vi. **∼ at** mofarse de; (boo) abuchear. ● n burla f; (boo) abucheo m

Jell-O /'dʒeləʊ/ n (P) (Amer) gelatina f (con sabor a frutas)

jelly /'dʒelɪ/ n (clear jam) jalea f; (pudding) see **JELL-O**; (substance) gelatina f. **∼fish** n (pl invar or **-es**) medusa f

jeopardize /'dʒepədaɪz/ vt arriesgar

jerk /dʒɜːk/ n sacudida f; (sl, fool) idiota m & f. ● vt sacudir

jersey /'dʒɜːzɪ/ n (pl **-eys**) jersey m, suéter m, pulóver m

jest /dʒest/ n broma f. ● vi bromear

Jesus /'dʒiːzəs/ n Jesús m

jet /dʒet/ n (stream) chorro m; (plane) avión m (con motor a reacción); (mineral) azabache m. **∼-black** /-'blæk/ adj azabache negro a invar. **∼ lag** n jet lag m, desfase f horario. **have ∼ lag** estar desfasado. **∼-propelled** /-prə'peld/ adj (de propulsión) a reacción

jettison /'dʒetɪsn/ vt echar al mar; (fig, discard) deshacerse de

jetty /'dʒetɪ/ n muelle m

Jew /dʒuː/ n judío m

jewel /'dʒuːəl/ n joya f. **∼ler** n joyero m. **∼lery** n joyas fpl

Jewish /'dʒuːɪʃ/ adj judío

jiffy /'dʒɪfɪ/ n momentito m. **do sth in a ∼** hacer algo en un santiamén

jig /dʒɪg/ n (dance) giga f

jigsaw /'dʒɪgsɔː/ n. **∼ (puzzle)** rompecabezas m

jilt /dʒɪlt/ vt dejar plantado

jingle /'dʒɪŋgl/ vt hacer sonar. ● vi tintinear. ● n tintineo m; (advert) jingle m (publicitario)

job /dʒɒb/ n empleo m, trabajo m; (piece of work) trabajo m. **It Is a good ∼ that** menos mal que. **∼less** adj desempleado

jockey /'dʒɒkɪ/ n jockey m

jocular /'dʒɒkjʊlə(r)/ adj jocoso

jog /dʒɒg/ vt (pt **jogged**) empujar; refrescar (memory). **∼vi** hacer footing, hacer jogging. **∼er** n persona f que hace footing. **∼ging** n footing m, jogging m. **go ∼ging** salir a hacer footing or jogging

join /dʒɔɪn/ vt (link) unir; hacerse socio de (club); hacerse miembro de (political group); alistarse en (army); reunirse con (another person). ● n juntura. ● vi. **∼ together** (parts) unirse; (roads etc) empalmar; (rivers) confluir. □ **∼ in** vi participar (en). □ **∼ up** vi (Mil) alistarse. **∼er** n carpintero m

joint /dʒɔɪnt/ adj conjunto. ● n (join) unión f, junta f; (in limbs) articulación f. (Culin) trozo m de carne (para asar). **out of ∼** descoyuntado. **∼ account** n cuenta f conjunta. **∼ly** adv conjuntamente. **∼ owner** n copropietario m.

joist /dʒɔɪst/ n viga f

jok|e /dʒəʊk/ n (story) chiste m; (practical joke) broma f. ● vi bromear. **∼er** n bromista m & f; (Cards) comodín m. **∼y** adj jocoso

jolly /'dʒɒlɪ/ adj (**-ier, -iest**) alegre. ● adv 🄵 muy

jolt /dʒɒlt/ vt sacudir. ● vi (vehicle) dar una sacudida. ● n sacudida f

jostle /'dʒɒsl/ vt empujar. ● vi empujarse

j

jot /dʒɒt/ n pizca f. ● vt (pt **jotted**). □ ~ **down** vt apuntar (rápidamente). ~**ter** n bloc m

journal /'dʒɜːnl/ n (diary) diario m; (newspaper) periódico m; (magazine) revista f. ~**ism** n periodismo m. ~**ist** n periodista m & f

journey /'dʒɜːnɪ/ n viaje m. **go on a ~** hacer un viaje. ● vi viajar

jovial /'dʒəʊvɪəl/ adj jovial

joy /dʒɔɪ/ n alegría f. ~**ful** adj feliz. ~**ous** adj feliz. ~**rider** n joven m que roba un coche para dar una vuelta. ~**stick** n (in aircraft) palanca f de mando; (Comp) mando m, joystick m

jubila|nt /'dʒuːbɪlənt/ adj jubiloso. ~**tion** /-'leɪʃn/ n júbilo m

jubilee /'dʒuːbɪliː/ n aniversario m especial

Judaism /'dʒuːdeɪɪzəm/ n judaísmo m

judge /dʒʌdʒ/ n juez m. ● vt juzgar. ~**ment** n juicio m

judicia|l /dʒuː'dɪʃl/ adj judicial. ~**ry** /-ərɪ/ n judicatura f

judo /'dʒuːdəʊ/ n judo m

jug /dʒʌg/ n jarra f

juggernaut /'dʒʌgənɔːt/ n camión m grande

juggle /'dʒʌgl/ vi hacer malabarismos. ● vt hacer malabarismos con. ~**r** n malabarista m & f

juic|e /dʒuːs/ n jugo m, zumo m. ~**y** adj jugoso, zumoso; (story etc) Ⓣ picante

jukebox /'dʒuːkbɒks/ n máquina f de discos, rocola f (LAm)

July /dʒuː'laɪ/ n julio m

jumble /'dʒʌmbl/ vt. ~ **(up)** mezclar. ● n (muddle) revoltijo m. ~ **sale** n venta f de objetos usados m

jumbo /'dʒʌmbəʊ/ adj gigante. ~ **jet** n jumbo m

jump /dʒʌmp/ vt saltar. ~ **rope** (Amer) saltar a la comba, saltar a la cuerda. ~ **the gun** obrar prematuramente. ~ **the queue** colarse. ● vi saltar; (start) sobresaltarse; (prices) alzarse. ~ **at an opportunity** apresurarse a aprovechar una oportunidad. ● n salto m; (start) susto m; (increase) aumento m. ~**er** n jersey m, suéter m, pulóver m; (Amer, dress) pichi m, jumper m & f (LAm). ~**er cables** (Amer), ~ **leads**

npl cables mpl de arranque. ~ **rope** (Amer) comba f, cuerda f, reata f (Mex). ~**suit** n mono m. ~**y** adj nervioso

junction /'dʒʌŋkʃn/ n (of roads, rails) cruce m; (Elec) empalme m

June /dʒuːn/ n junio m

jungle /'dʒʌŋgl/ n selva f, jungla f

junior /'dʒuːnɪə(r)/ adj (in age) más joven (**to** que); (in rank) subalterno. ● n menor m

junk /dʒʌŋk/ n trastos mpl viejos; (worthless stuff) basura f. ● vt Ⓣ tirar. ~ **food** n comida f basura, alimento m chatarra (Mex). ~**ie** /'dʒʌŋkɪ/ n Ⓣ drogadicto m, yonqui m & f Ⓣ. ~ **mail** n propaganda f que se recibe por correo. ~ **shop** n tienda f de trastos viejos

junta /'dʒʌntə/ n junta f militar

Jupiter /'dʒuːpɪtə(r)/ n Júpiter m

jurisdiction /dʒʊərɪs'dɪkʃn/ n jurisdicción f

jur|or /'dʒʊərə(r)/ n (miembro m de un) jurado m. ~**y** n jurado m

just /dʒʌst/ adj (fair) justo. ● adv exactamente, justo; (barely) justo; (only) sólo, solamente. ~ **as tall** tan alto (as como). ~ **listen!** ¡escucha! he has ~ **arrived** acaba de llegar, recién llegó (LAm)

justice /'dʒʌstɪs/ n justicia f. **J~ of the Peace** juez m de paz

justif|iable /dʒʌstɪ'faɪəbl/ adj justificable. ~**iably** adv con razón. ~**ication** /dʒʌstɪfɪ'keɪʃn/ n justificación f. ~**y** /'dʒʌstɪfaɪ/ vt justificiar

jut /dʒʌt/ vi (pt **jutted**). ~ **(out)** sobresalir

juvenile /'dʒuːvənaɪl/ adj juvenil; (childish) infantil. ● n (Jurid) menor m & f

Kk

kaleidoscope /kə'laɪdəskəʊp/ n caleidoscopio m

kangaroo /kæŋgə'ruː/ n canguro m

karate /kə'rɑːtɪ/ n kárate m, karate m (LAm)

keel /kiːl/ n (of ship) quilla f. □ ~ **over** vi volcar(se)

keen /kiːn/ adj (-er, -est) (interest, feeling) vivo; (wind, mind, analysis) penetrante; (eyesight) agudo; (eager) entusiasta. **I'm ~ on golf** me encanta el golf. **he's ~ on Shostakovich** le gusta Shostakovich. **~ly** adv vivamente; (enthusiastically) con entusiasmo. **~ness** n intensidad f; (enthusiasm) entusiasmo m.

keep /kiːp/ vt (pt kept) guardar; cumplir (promise); tener (shop, animals); mantener (family); observar (rule); (celebrate) celebrar; (delay) detener; (prevent) impedir. ● vi (food) conservarse; (remain) quedarse; (continue) seguir. ~ **doing** seguir haciendo. ● n subsistencia f; (of castle) torreón m. **for ~s** 🄸 para siempre. □ ~ **back** vt retener. ● vi no acercarse. □ ~ **in** vt no dejar salir. □ ~ **off** vt mantenerse alejado de (land). '~ **off the grass**' 'prohibido pisar el césped'. □ ~ **on** vi seguir. ~ **on doing sth** seguir haciendo. □ ~ **out** vt no dejar entrar. □ ~ **up** vt mantener. □ ~ **up with** vt estar al día en

kennel /ˈkenl/ n casa f del perro; (Amer, for boarding) residencia f canina. **~s** n invar residencia f canina

kept /kept/ see KEEP

kerb /kɜːb/ n bordillo m (de la acera), borde m de la banqueta (Mex)

kerosene /ˈkerəsiːn/ n queroseno m

ketchup /ˈketʃʌp/ n salsa f de tomate

kettle /ˈketl/ n pava f, tetera f (para calentar agua)

key /kiː/ n llave f; (of computer, piano) tecla f; (Mus) tono m. **be off ~** no estar en el tono. ● adj clave. □ ~ **in** vt teclear. **~board** n teclado m. **~hole** n ojo m de la cerradura. **~ring** n llavero m

khaki /ˈkɑːkɪ/ adj caqui

kick /kɪk/ vt dar una patada a (person); patear (ball). ● vi dar patadas; (horse) cocear. ● n patada f; (of horse) coz f; (fam, thrill) placer m. □ ~ **out** vt 🄸 echar. □ ~ **up** vt armar (fuss etc). **~off** n (Sport) saque m inicial. ~ **start** vt arrancar (con el pedal de arranque) (engine)

kid /kɪd/ n (young goat) cabrito m; (fam, child) niño m, chaval m, escuincle m (Mex). ● vt (pt kidded) tomar el pelo a. ● vi bromear

kidnap /ˈkɪdnæp/ vt (pt kidnapped) secuestrar. **~per** n secuestrador m. **~ping** n secuestro m

kidney /ˈkɪdnɪ/ n riñón m

kill /kɪl/ vt matar; (fig) acabar con. ● n matanza f. □ ~ **off** vt matar. **~er** n asesino m. **~ing** n matanza f; (murder) asesinato m. **make a ~ing** (fig) hacer un gran negocio

kiln /kɪln/ n horno m

kilo /ˈkiːləʊ/ n (pl -os) kilo m. **~gram(me)** /ˈkɪləɡræm/ n kilogramo m. **~metre** /ˈkɪləmiːtə(r)/, /kɪˈlɒmɪtə(r)/ n kilómetro m. **~watt** /ˈkɪləwɒt/ n kilovatio m

kilt /kɪlt/ n falda f escocesa

kin /kɪn/ n familiares mpl

kind /kaɪnd/ n tipo m, clase f. ~ **of** (fam, somewhat) un poco. **in ~** en especie. **be two of a ~** ser tal para cual. ● adj amable

kindergarten /ˈkɪndəɡɑːtn/ n jardín m de infancia

kind-hearted /kaɪndˈhɑːtɪd/ adj bondadoso

kindle /ˈkɪndl/ vt encender

kind|ly adj (-ier, -iest) bondadoso. ● adv amablemente; (please) haga el favor de. **~ness** n bondad f; (act) favor m

king /kɪŋ/ n rey m. **~dom** n reino m. **~fisher** n martín m pescador. **~-size(d)** adj extragrande

kink /kɪŋk/ n (in rope) vuelta f, curva f; (in hair) onda f. **~y** adj 🄸 pervertido

kiosk /ˈkiːɒsk/ n quiosco m

kipper /ˈkɪpə(r)/ n arenque m ahumado

kiss /kɪs/ n beso m. ● vt besar. ● vi besarse

kit /kɪt/ n avíos mpl. **tool ~** caja f de herramientas. □ ~ **out** vt (pt kitted) equipar

kitchen /ˈkɪtʃɪn/ n cocina f

kite /kaɪt/ n cometa f, papalote m (Mex)

kitten /ˈkɪtn/ n gatito m

knack /næk/ n truco m

knapsack /ˈnæpsæk/ n mochila f

knead /niːd/ vt amasar

knee /niː/ n rodilla f. **~cap** n rótula f

kneel /niːl/ vi (pt **kneeled** or **knelt**). ~ **(down)** arrodillarse; (be on one's knees) estar arrodillado

knelt /nelt/ see KNEEL

knew /njuː/ see KNOW

knickers /'nɪkəz/ npl bragas fpl, calzones mpl (LAm), pantaletas fpl (Mex)

knife /naɪf/ n (pl **knives**) cuchillo m. ● vt acuchillar

knight /naɪt/ n caballero m; (Chess) caballo m. ● vt conceder el título de Sir a. **~hood** n título m de Sir

knit /nɪt/ vt (pt **knitted** or **knit**) hacer, tejer (LAm). ● vi tejer, hacer punto. ~ **one's brow** fruncir el ceño. **~ting** n tejido m, punto m. **~ting needle** n aguja f de hacer punto, aguja f de tejer

knives /naɪvz/ see KNIFE

knob /nɒb/ n botón m; (of door, drawer etc) tirador m. **~bly** adj nudoso

knock /nɒk/ vt golpear; (criticize) criticar. ● vi golpear; (at door) llamar, golpear (LAm). ● n golpe m. □ ~ **about** vt maltratar. □ ~ **down** vt derribar; atropellar (person). □ ~ **off** vt hacer caer. ● vi (fam, finish work) terminar, salir del trabajo. □ ~ **out** vt (by blow) dejar sin sentido; (eliminate) eliminar. □ ~ **over** vt tirar; atropellar (person). **~er** n aldaba f. **~-kneed** /-'niːd/ adj patizambo. **~out** n (Boxing) nocaut m

knot /nɒt/ n nudo m. ● vt (pt **knotted**) anudar

know /nəʊ/ vt (pt **knew**) saber; (be acquainted with) conocer. **let s.o. ~ sth** decirle algo a uno; (warn) avisarle algo a uno. ● vi saber. ~ **how to do sth** saber hacer algo. ~ **about** entender de (cars etc). ~ **of** saber de. ● n. **be in the** ~ estar enterado. **~-all** n n sabelotodo m & f. **~-how** n knowhow m, conocimientos mpl y experiencia. **~ingly** adv a sabiendas. **~-it-all** n (Amer) see **~-ALL**

knowledge /'nɒlɪdʒ/ n saber m; (awareness) conocimiento m; (learning) conocimientos mpl. **~able** adj informado

known /nəʊn/ see KNOW. ● adj conocido

knuckle /'nʌkl/ n nudillo m. □ ~ **under** vi someterse

Korea /kə'rɪə/ n Corea f. **~n** adj & n coreano (m)

kudos /'kjuːdɒs/ n prestigio m

Ll

lab /læb/ n 🅣 laboratorio m

label /'leɪbl/ n etiqueta f. ● vt (pt **labelled**) poner etiqueta a; (fig, describe as) tachar de

laboratory /lə'bɒrətərɪ/ n laboratorio m

laborious /lə'bɔːrɪəs/ adj penoso

labour /'leɪbə(r)/ n trabajo m; (workers) mano f de obra; (Med) parto m. **in ~** de parto. ● vi trabajar. ● vt insistir en. **L~** n el partido m laborista. ● adj laborista. **~er** n peón m

lace /leɪs/ n encaje m; (of shoe) cordón m, agujeta f (Mex). ● vt (fasten) atar

lacerate /'læsəreɪt/ vt lacerar

lack /læk/ n falta f. **for ~ of** por falta de. ● vt faltarle a uno. **he ~s confidence** le falta confianza en sí mismo. **~ing** adj. **be ~ing** faltar. **be ~ing in** no tener

lad /læd/ n muchacho m

ladder /'lædə(r)/ n escalera f (de mano); (in stocking) carrera f. ● vt hacerse una carrera en. ● vi hacérsele una carrera a

laden /'leɪdn/ adj cargado (**with** de)

ladle /'leɪdl/ n cucharón m

lady /'leɪdɪ/ n señora f. **young ~** señorita f. **~bird** n, **~bug** n (Amer) mariquita f, catarina f (Mex). **~-in-waiting** n dama f de honor. **~like** adj fino

lag /læg/ vi (pt **lagged**). ~ **(behind)** retrasarse. ● vt revestir (pipes). ● n (interval) intervalo m

lager /'lɑːɡə(r)/ n cerveza f (rubia)

lagging /'læɡɪŋ/ n revestimiento m

lagoon /lə'ɡuːn/ n laguna f

laid /leɪd/ see LAY

lain /leɪn/ see LIE¹

lair /leə(r)/ n guarida f

lake /leɪk/ n lago m

lamb /læm/ n cordero m

lame /leɪm/ adj (-er, -est) cojo, rengo (LAm); (excuse) pobre, malo

lament /lə'ment/ n lamento m. ● vt lamentar. ~**able** /'læməntəbl/ adj lamentable

lamp /læmp/ n lámpara f

lamp ~**post** n farol m. ~**shade** n pantalla f

lance /lɑːns/ n lanza f

land /lænd/ n tierra f; (country) país m; (plot) terreno m. ● vt desembarcar; (obtain) conseguir; dar (blow). ● vi (from ship) desembarcar; (aircraft) aterrizar. □ ~ **up** vi ir a parar. ~**ing** n desembarque m; (by aircraft) aterrizaje m; (top of stairs) descanso m. ~**lady** n casera f; (of inn) dueña f. ~**lord** n casero m, dueño m; (of inn) dueño m. ~**mark** n punto m destacado. ~**scape** /-skeɪp/ n paisaje m. ~**slide** n desprendimiento m de tierras; (Pol) victoria f arrolladora

lane /leɪn/ n (path, road) camino m, sendero m; (strip of road) carril m

language /'læŋgwɪdʒ/ n idioma m; (speech, style) lenguaje m

lank /læŋk/ adj (hair) lacio. ~**y** adj (-ier, -iest) larguirucho

lantern /'læntən/ n linterna f

lap /læp/ n (of body) rodillas fpl; (Sport) vuelta f. □ ~ **up** vt (pt lapped) beber a lengüetazos; (fig) aceptar con entusiasmo. ● vi (waves) chapotear

lapel /lə'pel/ n solapa f

lapse /læps/ vi (decline) degradarse; (expire) caducar; (time) transcurrir. ~ **into silence** callarse. ● n error m; (of time) intervalo m

laptop /'læptɒp/ n. ~ **(computer)** laptop m, portátil m

lard /lɑːd/ n manteca f de cerdo

larder /'lɑːdə(r)/ n despensa f

large /lɑːdʒ/ adj (-er, -est) grande, (before singular noun) gran. ● n. at ~ en libertad. ~**ly** adv en gran parte

lark /lɑːk/ n (bird) alondra f; (joke) broma f; (bit of fun) travesura f. □ ~ **about** vt hacer el tonto ⊞

larva /'lɑːvə/ n (pl -vae/-viː/) larva f

laser /'leɪzə(r)/ n láser m. ~ **beam** n rayo m láser. ~ **printer** n impresora f láser

lash /læʃ/ vt azotar. □ ~ **out** vi atacar. ~ **out against** vt atacar. ● n latigazo m; (eyelash) pestaña f; (whip) látigo m

lashings /'læʃɪŋz/ npl. ~ **of** (fam, cream etc) montones de

lass /læs/ n muchacha f

lasso /læ'suː/ n (pl -os) lazo m

last /lɑːst/ adj último; (week etc) pasado. ~ **Monday** el lunes pasado. ~ **night** anoche. ● adv por último; (most recently) la última vez. **he came** ~ llegó el último. ● n último m; (remainder) lo que queda. ~ **but one** penúltimo. **at (long)** ~ por fin. ● vi/t durar. □ ~ **out** vi sobrevivir. ~**ing** adj duradero. ~**ly** adv por último

latch /lætʃ/ n pestillo m

late /leɪt/ adj (-er, -est) (not on time) tarde; (recent) reciente; (former) antiguo, ex. **be** ~ llegar tarde. **in** ~ **July** a fines de julio. **the** ~ **Dr Phillips** el difunto Dr. Phillips. ● adv tarde. ~**ly** adv últimamente

latent /'leɪtnt/ adj latente

later /'leɪtə(r)/ adv más tarde

lateral /'lætərəl/ adj lateral

latest /'leɪtɪst/ adj último. ● n. **at the** ~ a más tardar

lathe /leɪð/ n torno m

lather /'lɑːðə(r)/ n espuma f

Latin /'lætɪn/ n (language) latín m. ● adj latino. ~ **America** n América f Latina, Latinoamérica f. ~ **American** adj & n latinoamericano f

latitude /'lætɪtjuːd/ n latitud m

latter /'lætə(r)/ adj último; (of two) segundo. ● n. **the** ~ éste m, ésta f, éstos mpl, éstas fpl

laugh /lɑːf/ vi reír(se). ~ **at** reírse de. ● n risa f. ~**able** adj ridículo. ~**ing stock** n hazmerreír m. ~**ter** n risas fpl

launch /lɔːntʃ/ vt lanzar; botar (new vessel). ● n lanzamiento m; (of new vessel) botadura; (boat) lancha f (a motor). ~**ing pad**, ~ **pad** n plataforma f de lanzamiento

laund|er /'lɔːndə(r)/ vt lavar (y planchar). ~**erette** /-et/, **L~romat** /'lɔːndrəmæt/ (Amer) (P) n lavandería f automática. **~ry** n (*place*) lavandería f; (*dirty clothes*) ropa f sucia; (*clean clothes*) ropa f limpia

lava /'lɑːvə/ n lava f

lavatory /'lævətərɪ/ n (cuarto m de) baño m. **public ~** servicios mpl, baños mpl (*LAm*)

lavish /'lævɪʃ/ adj (*lifestyle*) de derroche; (*meal*) espléndido; (*production*) fastuoso. • vt prodigar (**on** a)

law /lɔː/ n ley f; (*profession, subject of study*) derecho m. **~ and order** n orden m público. **~ court** n tribunal m

lawn /lɔːn/ n césped m, pasto m (*LAm*). **~mower** n cortacésped f, cortadora f de pasto (*LAm*)

lawsuit /'lɔːsuːt/ n juicio m

lawyer /'lɔːjə(r)/ n abogado m

lax /læks/ adj descuidado; (*morals etc*) laxo

laxative /'læksətɪv/ n laxante m

lay /leɪ/ see **LIE**. • vt (pt **laid**) poner (*also table, eggs*); tender (*trap*); formar (*plan*). **~ hands on** echar mano a. **~ hold of** agarrar. • adj (*non-clerical*) laico; (*opinion etc*) profano. □ **~ down** vt dejar a un lado; imponer (*condition*). □ **~ into** vt ⊠ dar una paliza a. □ **~ off** vt despedir (*worker*). vi ⊞ terminar. □ **~ on** vt (*provide*) proveer. □ **~ out** vt (*design*) disponer; (*display*) exponer; gastar (*money*). **~about** n holgazán. **~-by** n área f de reposo

layer /'leɪə(r)/ n capa f

layette /leɪ'et/ n canastilla f

layman /'leɪmən/ n (pl **-men**) lego m

layout /'leɪaʊt/ n disposición f

laz|e /leɪz/ vi holgazanear; (*relax*) descansar. **~iness** n pereza f. **~y** adj perezoso. **~ybones** n holgazán m

lead¹ /liːd/ vt (pt **led**) conducir; dirigir (*team*); llevar (*life*); encabezar (*parade, attack*). **I was led to believe that ...** me dieron a entender que .... • vi (*go first*) ir delante; (*in race*) aventajar. • n mando m; (*clue*) pista f; (*leash*) correa f; (*wire*) cable m. **be in the ~** llevar la delantera

lead² /led/ n plomo m; (*of pencil*) mina f. **~ed** adj (*fuel*) con plomo

lead /liːd/ **~er** n jefe m; (*Pol*) líder m & f; (*of gang*) cabecilla m. **~ership** n dirección f. **~ing** adj principal; (*in front*) delantero

leaf /liːf/ n (pl **leaves**) hoja f. □ **~ through** vi hojear **~let** /'liːflɪt/ n folleto m. **~y** adj frondoso

league /liːg/ n liga f. **be in ~ with** estar aliado con

leak /liːk/ n (*hole*) agujero m; (*of gas, liquid*) escape m; (*of information*) filtración f; (*in roof*) gotera f; (*in boat*) vía f de agua. • vi gotear; (*liquid*) salirse; (*boat*) hacer agua. • vt perder; filtrar (*information*). **~y** adj (*receptacle*) agujereado; (*roof*) que tiene goteras

lean /liːn/ (pt **leaned** or **leant** /lent/) vt apoyar. • vi inclinarse. □ **~ against** vt apoyarse en. □ **~ on** vt apoyarse en. □ **~ out** vt asomarse (**of** a). □ **~ over** vi inclinarse • adj (**-er**, **-est**) (*person*) delgado; (*animal*) flaco; (*meat*) magro. **~ing** adj inclinado. **~-to** n colgadizo m

leap /liːp/ vi (pt **leaped** or **leapt** /lept/) saltar. • n salto m. **~frog** n. play **~frog** saltar al potro, jugar a la pídola, brincar al burro (*Mex*). • vi (pt **-frogged**) saltar. **~ year** n año m bisiesto

learn /lɜːn/ vt/i (pt **learned** or **learnt**) aprender (**to do** a hacer). **~ed** /-ɪd/ adj culto. **~er** n principiante m & f; (*apprentice*) aprendiz m. **~ing** n saber m. **~ing curve** n curva f del aprendizaje

lease /liːs/ n arriendo m. • vt arrendar

leash /liːʃ/ n correa f

least /liːst/ adj (*smallest amount of*) mínimo; (*slightest*) menor; (*smallest*) más pequeño. • n. **the ~** lo menos. **at ~** por lo menos. **not in the ~** en absoluto. • adv menos

leather /'leðə(r)/ n piel f, cuero m

leave /liːv/ vt (pt **left**) dejar; (*depart from*) salir de. **~ alone** dejar de tocar (*thing*); dejar en paz (*person*). • vi marcharse; (*train*) salir. • n permiso m. □ **~ behind** vt dejar. □ **~ out** vt omitir. □ **~ over** vt. **be left over** quedar. **on ~** (*Mil*) de permiso

leaves /liːvz/ see **LEAF**

lecture /'lektʃə(r)/ n conferencia f; (Univ) clase f; (rebuke) sermón m. ● vi dar clase. ● vt (scold) sermonear. ~r n conferenciante m & f, conferencista m & f (LAm); (Univ) profesor m universitario

led /led/ see **LEAD**¹

ledge /ledʒ/ n cornisa f; (of window) alféizar m

leek /liːk/ n puerro m

leer /'lɪə(r)/ vi. ~ **at** mirar impúdicamente. ● n mirada impúdica f

left /left/ see **LEAVE**. adj izquierdo. ● adv a la izquierda. ● n izquierda f. ~**-handed** /-'hændɪd/ adj zurdo. ~**luggage** n consigna f. ~**overs** npl restos mpl. ~ **wing** /-'wɪŋ/ adj izquierdista

leg /leg/ n pierna f; (of animal, furniture) pata f; (of pork) pernil m; (of lamb) pierna f; (of journey) etapa f. **on its last** ~**s** en las últimas. **pull s.o.'s** ~ ⊞ tomarle el pelo a uno

legacy /'legəsɪ/ n herencia f

legal /'liːgl/ adj (permitted by law) lícito; (recognized by law) legítimo; (system etc) jurídico. ~**ity** /liː'gælətɪ/ n legalidad f. ~**ize** vt legalizar, ~**ly** adv legalmente

legend /'ledʒənd/ n leyenda f. ~**ary** adj legendario

legible /'ledʒəbl/ adj legible

legislat|e /'ledʒɪsleɪt/ vi legislar. ~**ion** /-'leɪʃn/ n legislación f

legitimate /lɪ'dʒɪtɪmət/ adj legítimo

leisure /'leʒə(r)/ n ocio m. **at your** ~ cuando le venga bien. ~**ly** adj lento, pausado

lemon /'lemən/ n limón m. ~**ade** /-'neɪd/ n (fizzy) gaseosa f (de limón); (still) limonada f

lend /lend/ vt (pt **lent**) prestar. ~**ing** n préstamo m

length /leŋθ/ n largo m; (of time) duración f; (of cloth) largo m. **at** ~ (at last) por fin. **at (great)** ~ detalladamente. ~**en** /'leŋθən/ vt alargar. ● vi alargarse. ~**ways** adv a lo largo. ~**y** adj largo

lenient /'liːnɪənt/ adj indulgente

lens /lenz/ n lente f; (of camera) objetivo m. **(contact)** ~**es** npl (optics) lentillas fpl, lentes mpl de contacto (LAm)

lent /lent/ see **LEND**

Lent /lent/ n cuaresma f

Leo /'liːəʊ/ n Leo m

leopard /'lepəd/ n leopardo m

leotard /'liːətɑːd/ n malla f

lesbian /'lezbɪən/ n lesbiana f. ● adj lesbiano

less /les/ adj & n & adv & prep menos. ~ **than** menos que; (with numbers) menos de. ~ **and** ~ cada vez menos. **none the** ~ sin embargo. ~**en** vt/i disminuir

lesson /'lesn/ n clase f

lest /lest/ conj no sea que (+ subjunctive)

let /let/ vt (pt **let**, pres p **letting**) dejar; (lease) alquilar. ~ **me do it** déjame hacerlo. ● modal verb. ~**'s go!** ¡vamos!, ¡vámonos! ~**'s see** (vamos) a ver. ~**'s talk/drink** hablemos/bebamos. □ ~ **down** vt bajar; (deflate) desinflar; (fig) defraudar. □ ~ **go** vt soltar. □ ~ **in** vt dejar entrar. □ ~ **off** vt disparar (gun); (cause to explode) hacer explotar; hacer estallar (firework); (excuse) perdonar. □ ~ **out** vt dejar salir. □ ~ **through** vt dejar pasar. □ ~ **up** vi disminuir. ~**down** n desilusión f

lethal /'liːθl/ adj (dose, wound) mortal; (weapon) mortífero

letharg|ic /lɪ'θɑːdʒɪk/ adj letárgico. ~**y** /'leθədʒɪ/ n letargo m

letter /'letə(r)/ n (of alphabet) letra f; (written message) carta f. ~ **bomb** n carta f bomba. ~**box** n buzón m. ~**ing** n letras fpl

lettuce /'letɪs/ n lechuga f

let-up /'letʌp/ n interrupción f

leukaemia /luː'kiːmɪə/ n leucemia f

level /'levl/ adj (flat, even) plano, parejo (LAm); (spoonful) raso. ~ **with** (at same height) al nivel de. ● n nivel m. ● vt (pt **levelled**) nivelar; (aim) apuntar. ~ **crossing** n paso m a nivel, crucero m (Mex)

lever /'liːvə(r)/ n palanca f. ● vt apalancar. ~ **open** abrir haciendo palanca. ~**age** /-ɪdʒ/ n apalancamiento m

levy /'levɪ/ vt imponer (tax). ● n impuesto m

lewd /luːd/ adj (-er, -est) lascivo

liab|ility /laɪə'bɪlətɪ/ n responsabilidad f; (fam, disadvantage) lastre m.

~**ilities** *npl* (*debts*) deudas *fpl*. ~**le** /ˈlaɪəbl/ *adj*. **be** ~**le to do** tener tendencia a hacer. ~**le for** responsable de. ~**le to** susceptible de; expuesto a (*fine*)

liais|e /lɪˈeɪz/ *vi* actuar de enlace (**with** con). ~**on** /-ɒn/ *n* enlace *m*

liar /ˈlaɪə(r)/ *n* mentiroso *m*

libel /ˈlaɪbl/ *n* difamación *f*. ● *vt* (*pt* **libelled**) difamar (por escrito)

liberal /ˈlɪbərəl/ *adj* liberal; (*generous*) generoso. **L**~ (*Pol*) del Partido Liberal. ● *n* liberal *m* & *f*. ~**ly** *adv* liberalmente; (*generously*) generosamente

liberat|e /ˈlɪbəreɪt/ *vt* liberar. ~**ion** /-ˈreɪʃn/ *n* liberación *f*

liberty /ˈlɪbətɪ/ *n* libertad *f*. **take liberties** tomarse libertades. **take the** ~ **of** tomarse la libertad de

Libra /ˈliːbrə/ *n* Libra *f*

librar|ian /laɪˈbreərɪən/ *n* bibliotecario *m*. ~**y** /ˈlaɪbrərɪ/ *n* biblioteca *f*

Library of Congress La biblioteca nacional de EEUU, situada en Washington DC. Fundada por el Congreso *Congress*, alberga más de ochenta millones de libros en 470 idiomas, y otros objetos.

---

lice /laɪs/ *see* **LOUSE**

licence /ˈlaɪsns/ *n* licencia *f*, permiso *m*

license /ˈlaɪsns/ *vt* autorizar. ● *n* (*Amer*) *see* **LICENCE**. ~ **number** *n* (*Amer*) (número *m* de) matrícula *f*. ~ **plate** *n* (*Amer*) matrícula *f*, placa *f* (*LAm*)

lick /lɪk/ *vt* lamer; (*sl, defeat*) dar una paliza a. ● *n* lametón *m*

licorice /ˈlɪkərɪs/ *n* (*Amer*) regaliz *m*

lid /lɪd/ *n* tapa *f*; (*eyelid*) párpado *m*

lie[1] /laɪ/ *vi* (*pt* **lay**, *pp* **lain**, *pres p* **lying**) echarse, tenderse; (*be in lying position*) estar tendido; (*be*) estar, encontrarse. ~ **low** quedarse escondido. □ ~ **down** *vi* echarse, tenderse

lie[2] /laɪ/ *n* mentira *f*. ● *vi* (*pt* **lied**, *pres p* **lying**) mentir

lie-in /laɪˈɪn/ *n*. **have a** ~ quedarse en la cama

lieutenant /lefˈtenənt/ *n* (*Mil*) teniente *m*

life /laɪf/ *n* (*pl* **lives**) vida *f*. ~ **belt** *n* salvavidas *m*. ~**boat** *n* lancha *f* de sal-

vamento; (*on ship*) bote *m* salvavidas. ~**buoy** *n* boya *f* salvavidas. ~ **coach** *n* coach *m* & *f* personal. ~**guard** *n* salvavidas *m* & *f*, socorrista *m* & *f*. ~ **jacket** *n* chaleco *m* salvavidas. ~**less** *adj* sin vida. ~**like** *adj* verosímil. ~**line** *n* cuerda *f* de salvamento; (*fig*) tabla *f* de salvación. ~**long** *adj* de toda la vida. ~ **preserver** *n* (*Amer, buoy*) *see* ~**BUOY**; (*jacket*) *see* ~ **JACKET**. ~ **ring** *n* (*Amer*) *see* ~ **BELT**. ~**saver** *n* (*person*) salvavidas *m* & *f*; (*fig*) salvación *f*. ~**-size(d)** *adj* (de) tamaño natural. ~**time** *n* vida *f*. ~ **vest** *n* (*Amer*) *see* ~ **JACKET**

lift /lɪft/ *vt* levantar. ● *vi* (*fog*) disiparse. ● *n* ascensor *m*. **give a** ~ **to s.o.** llevar a uno en su coche, dar aventón a uno (*Mex*). □ ~ **up** *vt* levantar. ~**-off** *n* despegue *m*

light /laɪt/ *n* luz *f*; (*lamp*) lámpara *f*, luz *f*; (*flame*) fuego *m*. **come to** ~ salir a la luz. **have you got a** ~? ¿tienes fuego? **the** ~**s** *npl* (*traffic signals*) el semáforo; (*on vehicle*) las luces. ● *adj* (**-er**, **-est**) (*in colour*) claro; (*not heavy*) ligero. ● *vt* (*pt* **lit** or **lighted**) encender, prender (*LAm*); (*illuminate*) iluminar. ● *vi* encenderse, prenderse (*LAm*). ~ **up** *vt* iluminar. ● *vi* iluminarse. ~ **bulb** *n* bombilla *f*, foco *m* (*Mex*). ~**en** *vt* (*make less heavy*) aligerar, alivianar (*LAm*); (*give light to*) iluminar; (*make brighter*) aclarar. ~**er** *n* (*for cigarettes*) mechero *m*, encendedor *m*. ~**-hearted** /-ˈhɑːtɪd/ *adj* alegre. ~**house** *n* faro *m*. ~**ly** *adv* ligeramente

lightning /ˈlaɪtnɪŋ/ *n*. **flash of** ~ relámpago *m*. ● *adj* relámpago

lightweight *adj* ligero, liviano (*LAm*)

like /laɪk/ *adj* parecido. ● *prep* como. ● *conj* 🄴 como. ● *vt*. **I** ~ **chocolate** me gusta el chocolate. **they** ~ **swimming** (a ellos) les gusta nadar. **would you** ~ **a coffee?** ¿quieres un café?. ~**able** *adj* simpático.

like|lihood /ˈlaɪklɪhʊd/ *n* probabilidad *f*. ~**ly** *adj* (**-ier**, **-iest**) probable. **he is** ~**ly to come** es probable que venga. ● *adv* probablemente. **not** ~**ly!** ¡ni hablar! ~**n** *vt* comparar (**to** con, a). ~**ness** *n* parecido *m*. **be a good** ~**ness** parecerse mucho. ~**wise** *adv* (*also*) también; (*the same way*) lo mismo

liking /ˈlaɪkɪŋ/ n (*for thing*) afición f; (*for person*) simpatía f

lilac /ˈlaɪlək/ adj lila. ●n lila f; (*color*) lila m

lily /ˈlɪlɪ/ n lirio m; (*white*) azucena f

limb /lɪm/ n miembro m. **out on a ~** aislado

lime /laɪm/ n (*white substance*) cal f; (*fruit*) lima f. **~light** n. **be in the ~light** ser el centro de atención

limerick /ˈlɪmərɪk/ n quintilla f humorística

limit /ˈlɪmɪt/ n límite m. ●vt limitar. **~ation** /-ˈteɪʃn/ n limitación f. **~ed** adj limitado. **~ed company** n sociedad f anónima

limousine /ˈlɪməziːn/ n limusina f

limp /lɪmp/ vi cojear, renguear (*LAm*). ●n cojera f, renguera f (*LAm*). **have a ~** cojear. ●adj (-er, -est) flojo

linden /ˈlɪndn/ n (*Amer*) tilo m

line /laɪn/ n línea f; (*track*) vía f; (*wrinkle*) arruga f; (*row*) fila f; (*of poem*) verso m; (*rope*) cuerda f; (*of goods*) surtido m; (*Amer, queue*) cola f. **stand in ~** (*Amer*) hacer cola. **get in ~** (*Amer*) ponerse en la cola.. **cut in ~** (*Amer*) colarse. **in ~ with** de acuerdo con. ●vt forrar (skirt, box); bordear (streets etc). □ **~ up** vi alinearse; (*in queue*) hacer cola. vt (*form into line*) poner en fila; (*align*) alinear. **~d** /laɪnd/ adj (paper) con renglones; (*with fabric*) forrado

linen /ˈlɪnɪn/ n (*sheets etc*) ropa f blanca; (*material*) lino m

liner /ˈlaɪnə(r)/ n (*ship*) transatlántico m

linger /ˈlɪŋɡə(r)/ vi tardar en marcharse. **~ (on)** (smells etc) persistir. □ **~ over** vt dilatarse en

lingerie /ˈlænʒərɪ/ n lencería f

linguist /ˈlɪŋɡwɪst/ n políglota m & f; lingüista m & f. **~ic** /lɪŋˈɡwɪstɪk/ adj lingüístico. **~ics** n lingüística f

lining /ˈlaɪnɪŋ/ n forro m

link /lɪŋk/ n (*of chain*) eslabón m; (*connection*) conexión f; (*bond*) vínculo m; (*transport, telecommunications*) conexión f, enlace m. ●vt conectar; relacio-

nar (facts, events). □ **~ up** vt/i conectar

lino /ˈlaɪnəʊ/ n (*pl* -os) linóleo m

lint /lɪnt/ n (*Med*) hilas fpl

lion /ˈlaɪən/ n león m. **~ess** /-nɪs/ n leona f

lip /lɪp/ n labio m; (*edge*) borde m. **~read** vi leer los labios. **~salve** n crema f para los labios. **~ service** n. **pay ~ service to** aprobar de boquilla, aprobar de los dientes para afuera (*Mex*). **~stick** n lápiz m de labios

liqueur /lɪˈkjʊə(r)/ n licor m

liquid /ˈlɪkwɪd/ adj & n líquido (m)

liquidate /ˈlɪkwɪdeɪt/ vt liquidar

liquidize /ˈlɪkwɪdaɪz/ vt licuar. **~r** n licuadora f

liquor /ˈlɪkə(r)/ n bebidas fpl alcohólicas

liquorice /ˈlɪkərɪs/ n regaliz m

liquor store n (*Amer*) tienda f de bebidas alcohólicas

lisp /lɪsp/ n ceceo m. **speak with a ~** cecear. ●vi cecear

list /lɪst/ n lista f. ●vt hacer una lista de; (*enter in a list*) inscribir. ●vi (*ship*) escorar

listen /ˈlɪsn/ vi escuchar. **~ in (to)** escuchar. **~ to** escuchar. **~er** n oyente m & f

listless /ˈlɪstlɪs/ adj apático

lit /lɪt/ see **LIGHT**

literacy /ˈlɪtərəsɪ/ n alfabetismo m

literal /ˈlɪtərəl/ adj literal. **~ly** adv literalmente

literary /ˈlɪtərərɪ/ adj literario

literate /ˈlɪtərət/ adj alfabetizado

literature /ˈlɪtərətʃə(r)/ n literatura f; (*fig*) folletos mpl

lithe /laɪð/ adj ágil

litre /ˈliːtə(r)/ n litro m

litter /ˈlɪtə(r)/ n basura f; (*of animals*) camada f. ●vt ensuciar; (*scatter*) esparcir. **~ed with** lleno de. **~ bin** n papelera f. **~bug**, **~ lout** n persona f que tira basura en lugares públicos

little /ˈlɪtl/ adj pequeño; (*not much*) poco. **a ~ water** un poco de agua. ●pron poco, poca. **a ~** un poco. ●adv poco. **~ by ~** poco a poco. **~ finger** n (dedo m) meñique m

l

live /lɪv/ vt/i vivir. □ ~ **down** vt lograr borrar. □ ~ **off** vt vivir a costa de (family, friends); (feed on) alimentarse de. □ ~ **on** vt (feed o.s. on) vivir de. vi (memory) seguir presente; (tradition) seguir existiendo. □ ~ **up** vt. ~ **it up** 🄸 darse la gran vida. □ ~ **up to** vt vivir de acuerdo con; cumplir (promise). ● /laɪv/ adj vivo; (wire) con corriente; (broadcast) en directo

livelihood /'laɪvlɪhʊd/ n sustento m

lively /'laɪvlɪ/ adj (-ier, -iest) vivo

liven up /'laɪvn/ vt animar. ● vi animar(se)

liver /'lɪvə(r)/ n hígado m

lives /laɪvz/ see **LIFE**

livestock /'laɪvstɒk/ n animales mpl (de cría); (cattle) ganado m

livid /'lɪvɪd/ adj lívido; (fam, angry) furioso

living /'lɪvɪŋ/ adj vivo. ● n vida f. **make a** ~ ganarse la vida. ~ **room** n salón m, sala f (de estar), living m (LAm)

lizard /'lɪzəd/ n lagartija f; (big) lagarto m

load /ləʊd/ n (also Elec) carga f; (quantity) cantidad f; (weight, strain) peso m. ~**s of** 🄸 montones de. ● vt cargar. ~**ed** adj cargado

loaf /ləʊf/ n (pl **loaves**) pan m; (stick of bread) barra f de pan. ● vi. ~ **(about)** holgazanear

loan /ləʊn/ n préstamo m. **on** ~ prestado. ● vt prestar

loath|e /ləʊð/ vt odiar. ~**ing** n odio m (of a). ~**esome** /-səm/ adj repugnante

lobby /'lɒbɪ/ n vestíbulo m; (Pol) grupo m de presión. ● vt ejercer presión sobre. ● vi. ~ **for sth** ejercer presión para obtener algo

lobe /ləʊb/ n lóbulo m

lobster /'lɒbstə(r)/ n langosta f, bogavante m

local /'ləʊkl/ adj local. ~ **(phone) call** llamada f urbana. ● n (fam, pub) bar m. **the** ~**s** los vecinos mpl. ~ **government** n administración f municipal. ~**ity** /-'kælətɪ/ n localidad f. ~**ization** n localización f. ~**ly** adv (live, work) en la zona

locat|e /ləʊ'keɪt/ vt (situate) situar, ubicar (LAm); (find) localizar, ubicar (LAm). ~**ion** /-ʃn/ n situación f, ubicación f (LAm). **to film on** ~**ion in Andalusia** rodar en Andalucía

lock /lɒk/ n (of door etc) cerradura f; (on canal) esclusa f; (of hair) mechón m. ● vt cerrar con llave. ● vi cerrarse con llave. □ ~ **in** vt encerrar. □ ~ **out** vt cerrar la puerta a. □ ~ **up** vt encerrar (person); cerrar con llave (building)

locker /'lɒkə(r)/ n armario m, locker m (LAm). ~ **room** n (Amer) vestuario m, vestidor m (Mex)

locket /'lɒkɪt/ n medallón m

lock ~**out** /'lɒkaʊt/ n cierre m patronal, paro m patronal (LAm). ~**smith** n cerrajero m

locomotive /ləʊkə'məʊtɪv/ n locomotora f

lodg|e /lɒdʒ/ n (of porter) portería f. ● vt alojar; presentar (complaint). ~**er** n huésped m. ~**ings** n alojamiento m; (room) habitación f alquilada

loft /lɒft/ n desván m, altillo m (LAm)

lofty /'lɒftɪ/ adj (-ier, -iest) elevado; (haughty) altanero

log /lɒg/ n (of wood) tronco m; (as fuel) leño m; (record) diario m. **sleep like a** ~ dormir como un tronco. ● vt (pt **logged**) registrar. □ ~ **in**, ~ **on** vi (Comp) entrar (al sistema). □ ~ **off**, ~ **out** vi (Comp) salir (del sistema)

logarithm /'lɒgərɪðəm/ n logaritmo m

loggerheads /'lɒgəhedz/ npl. **be at** ~ **with** estar a matar con

logic /'lɒdʒɪk/ adj lógica f. ~**al** adj lógico. ~**ally** adv lógicamente

logistics /lə'dʒɪstɪks/ n logística f. ● npl (practicalities) problemas mpl logísticos

logo /'ləʊgəʊ/ n (pl **-os**) logo m

loin /lɔɪn/ n (Culin) lomo m. ~**s** npl entrañas fpl

loiter /'lɔɪtə(r)/ vi perder el tiempo

loll /lɒl/ vi repantigarse

loll|ipop /'lɒlɪpɒp/ n pirulí m. ~**y** n polo m, paleta f (helada) (LAm)

London /'lʌndən/ n Londres m. ● adj londinense. ~**er** n londinense m & f

lone /ləʊn/ adj solitario. ~**ly** adj (-**ier**, -**iest**) solitario. **feel** ~**ly** sentirse muy solo. ~**r** n solitario m. ~**some** /-səm/ adj solitario

long /lɒŋ/ adj (-**er**, -**est**) largo. **a** ~ **time** mucho tiempo. **how** ~ **is it?** ¿cuánto tiene de largo? ● adv largo/ mucho tiempo. **as** ~ **as** (while) mientras; (provided that) con tal que (+ subjunctive). **before** ~ dentro de poco. **so** ~! ¡hasta luego! **so** ~ **as** (provided that) con tal que (+ subjunctive). □ ~ **for** vi anhelar. ~ **to do** estar deseando hacer. ~-**distance** /-ˈdɪstəns/ adj de larga distancia. ~-**distance phone call** llamada f de larga distancia, conferencia f. ~**er** adv. **no** ~**er** ya no. ~-**haul** /-ˈhɔːl/ adj de larga distancia. ~**ing** n anhelo m, ansia f

longitude /ˈlɒŋɡɪtjuːd/ n longitud f

long ~ **jump** n salto m de longitud. ~-**playing record** n elepé m. ~-**range** adj de largo alcance. ~-**sighted** /-ˈsaɪtɪd/ adj hipermétrope. ~-**term** adj a largo plazo. ~-**winded** /-ˈwɪndɪd/ adj prolijo

loo /luː/ n 🇬🇧 váter m, baño m (LAm)

look /lʊk/ vt mirar; representar (age). ● vi mirar; (seem) parecer; (search) buscar. ● n mirada f; (appearance) aspecto m. **good** ~**s** belleza f. □ ~ **after** vt cuidar (person); (he responsible for) encargarse (in) de. □ ~ **at** vt mirar; (consider) considerar. □ ~ **down on** vt despreciar. □ ~ **for** vt buscar. □ ~ **forward to** vt esperar con ansia. □ ~ **into** vt investigar. □ ~ **like** vt parecerse a. □ ~ **on** vi mirar. □ ~ **out** vi tener cuidado. □ ~ **out for** vt buscar; (watch) tener cuidado con. □ ~ **round** vi volver la cabeza. □ ~ **through** vt hojear. □ ~ **up** vt buscar (word); (visit) ir a ver. □ ~ **up to** vt admirar. ~-**alike** n 🇬🇧 doble m & f. ~**out** n (Mil, person) vigía m. **be on the** ~**out for** andar a la caza de. ~**s** npl belleza f

loom /luːm/ n telar m. ● vi aparecerse

looney, loony /ˈluːnɪ/ adj & n 🇬🇧 chiflado (m) 🇬🇧, loco (m)

loop /luːp/ n (shape) curva f; (in string) lazada f. ● vt hacer una lazada con. ~**hole** n (in rule) escapatoria f

loose /luːs/ adj (-**er**, -**est**) suelto; (garment, thread, hair) flojo; (inexact) vago; (not packed) suelto. **be at a** ~ **end** no tener nada que hacer. ~**ly** adv sueltamente; (roughly) aproximadamente. ~**n** vt aflojar

loot /luːt/ n botín m. ● vt/i saquear. ~**er** n saqueador m

lop /lɒp/ vt (pt **lopped**). ~ **off** cortar

lop-sided /-ˈsaɪdɪd/ adj ladeado

lord /lɔːd/ n señor m; (British title) lord m. (**good**) **L**~! ¡Dios mío! **the L**~ el Señor. **the (House of) L**~**s** la Cámara de los Lores

lorry /ˈlɒrɪ/ n camión m. ~ **driver** n camionero m

lose /luːz/ vt/i (pt **lost**) perder. ~**r** n perdedor m

loss /lɒs/ n pérdida f. **be at a** ~ estar perplejo. **be at a** ~ **for words** no encontrar palabras

lost /lɒst/ see LOSE. ● adj perdido. **get** ~ perderse. ~ **property** n, ~ **and found** (Amer) oficina f de objetos perdidos

lot /lɒt/ n (fate) suerte f; (at auction) lote m; (land) solar m. **a** ~ **(of)** muchos. **quite a** ~ **of** 🇬🇧 bastante. ~**s (of)** 🇬🇧 muchos. **they ate the** ~ se lo comieron todo

lotion /ˈləʊʃn/ n loción f

lottery /ˈlɒtərɪ/ n lotería f

loud /laʊd/ adj (-**er**, -**est**) fuerte; (noisy) ruidoso; (gaudy) chillón. **out** ~ en voz alta. ~**hailer** /-ˈheɪlə(r)/ n megáfono m. ~**ly** adv (speak) en voz alta; (shout) fuerte; (complain) a voz en grito. ~**speaker** /-ˈspiːkə(r)/ n altavoz m, altoparlante m (LAm)

lounge /laʊndʒ/ vi repantigarse. ● n salón m, sala f (de estar), living m (LAm)

lous|e /laʊs/ n (pl **lice**) piojo m. ~**y** /ˈlaʊzɪ/ adj (-**ier**, -**iest**) (sl, bad) malísimo

lout /laʊt/ n patán m

lov|able /ˈlʌvəbl/ adj adorable. ~**e** /lʌv/ n amor m; (tennis) cero m. **be in** ~**e (with)** estar enamorado (de). **fall in** ~**e (with)** enamorarse (de). ● vt querer, amar (person). **I** ~ **milk** me encanta la leche. ~**e affair** n aventura f, amorío m

lovely /'lʌvlɪ/ adj (-ier, -iest) (appearance) precioso, lindo (LAm); (person) encantador, amoroso (LAm)

lover /'lʌvə(r)/ n amante m & f

loving /'lʌvɪŋ/ adj cariñoso

low /ləʊ/ adj & adv (-er, -est) bajo. ● vi (cattle) mugir. ~er vt bajar. ~er o.s. envilecerse. ~-level adj a bajo nivel. ~ly adj (-ier, -iest) humilde

loyal /'lɔɪəl/ adj leal, fiel. ~ty n lealtad f. ~ty card tarjeta f de fidelidad

lozenge /'lɒzɪndʒ/ n (shape) rombo m; (tablet) pastilla f

LP abbr (= **long-playing record**) elepé m

Ltd /'lɪmɪtɪd/ abbr (= **Limited**) S.A., Sociedad Anónima

lubricate /'lu:brɪkeɪt/ vt lubricar

lucid /'lu:sɪd/ adj lúcido

luck /lʌk/ n suerte f. **good** ~! ¡(buena) suerte! ~ily adv por suerte. ~y adj (-ier, -iest) (person) con suerte. **be** ~y tener suerte. ~y **number** número m de la suerte

lucrative /'lu:krətɪv/ adj lucrativo

ludicrous /'lu:dɪkrəs/ adj ridículo

lug /lʌɡ/ vt (pt lugged) 🔢 arrastrar

luggage /'lʌɡɪdʒ/ n equipaje m. ~ **rack** n rejilla f

lukewarm /'lu:kwɔ:m/ adj tibio; (fig) poco entusiasta

lull /lʌl/ vt (soothe, send to sleep) adormecer; (calm) calmar. ● n periodo m de calma

lullaby /'lʌləbaɪ/ n canción f de cuna

lumber /'lʌmbə(r)/ n trastos mpl viejos; (wood) maderos mpl. ● vt. ~ **s.o. with sth** 🔢 endilgar algo a uno. ~**jack** n leñador m

luminous /'lu:mɪnəs/ adj luminoso

lump /'lʌmp/ n (swelling) bulto m; (as result of knock) chichón m; (in liquid) grumo m; (of sugar) terrón m. ● vt. ~ **together** agrupar. ~ **it** 🔢 aguantarse. ~ **sum** n suma f global. ~y adj (sauce) grumoso; (mattress, cushions) lleno de protuberancias

lunacy /'lu:nəsɪ/ n locura f

lunar /'lu:nə(r)/ adj lunar

lunatic /'lu:nətɪk/ n loco m

lunch /lʌntʃ/ n comida f, almuerzo m. **have** ~ comer, almorzar

luncheon /'lʌntʃən/ n comida f, almuerzo m. ~ **voucher** n vale m de comida

lung /lʌŋ/ n pulmón m

lunge /lʌndʒ/ n arremetida f. ● vi. ~ **at** arremeter contra

lurch /lɜ:tʃ/ vi tambalearse. ● n. **leave in the** ~ dejar plantado

lure /ljʊə(r)/ vt atraer

lurid /'ljʊərɪd/ adj (colour) chillón; (shocking) morboso

lurk /lɜ:k/ vi merodear; (in ambush) estar al acecho

luscious /'lʌʃəs/ adj delicioso

lush /lʌʃ/ adj exuberante

lust /lʌst/ n lujuria f; (craving) deseo m. ● vi. ~ **after** codiciar

lute /lu:t/ n laúd m

Luxembourg, Luxemburg /'lʌksəmbɜ:ɡ/ n Luxemburgo m

luxuriant /lʌɡ'zjʊərɪənt/ adj exuberante

luxur|ious /lʌɡ'zjʊərɪəs/ adj lujoso. ~y /'lʌkʃərɪ/ n lujo m. ● adj de lujo

lying /'laɪɪŋ/ see LIE¹, LIE². ● n mentiras fpl. ● adj mentiroso

lynch /lɪntʃ/ vt linchar

lyric /'lɪrɪk/ adj lírico. ~al adj lírico. ~s npl letra f

• •

Mm

• •

MA /em'eɪ/ abbr see MASTER

mac /mæk/ n 🔢 impermeable m

macabre /mə'kɑ:brə/ adj macabro

macaroni /mækə'rəʊnɪ/ n macarrones mpl

mace /meɪs/ n (staff) maza f; (spice) macis f. **M**~ (P) (Amer) gas m para defensa personal

machine /mə'ʃi:n/ n máquina f. ~ **gun** n ametralladora f. ~**ry** n maquinaria f; (working parts, fig) mecanismo m

mackintosh /'mækɪntɒʃ/ n impermeable m

macro /'mækrəʊ/ n (pl -os) (Comp) macro m

macrobiotic /mækrəʊbaɪˈɒtɪk/ *adj* macrobiótico

mad /mæd/ *adj* (**madder, maddest**) loco; (*fam, angry*) furioso. **be ~ about** estar loco por

madam /ˈmædəm/ *n* señora *f*

mad ~cap *adj* atolondrado. **~ cow disease** *f* enfermedad *f* de las vacas locas. **~den** *vt* (*make mad*) enloquecer; (*make angry*) enfurecer

made /meɪd/ *see* MAKE. **~-to-measure** hecho a (la) medida

mad ~house *n* manicomio *m*. **~ly** *adv* (*interested, in love etc*) locamente; (*frantically*) como un loco. **~man** /-mən/ *n* loco *m*. **~ness** *n* locura *f*

Madonna /məˈdɒnə/ *n*. **the ~** (*Relig*) la Virgen

maestro /ˈmaɪstrəʊ/ *n* (*pl* **maestri** /-striː/ *or* **-os**) maestro *m*

Mafia /ˈmæfɪə/ *n* mafia *f*

magazine /mægəˈziːn/ *n* revista *f*; (*of gun*) recámara *f*

magenta /məˈdʒentə/ *adj* magenta, morado

maggot /ˈmægət/ *n* gusano *m*

magic /ˈmædʒɪk/ *n* magia *f*. ● *adj* mágico. **~al** *adj* mágico. **~ian** /mə ˈdʒɪʃn/ *n* mago *m*

magistrate /ˈmædʒɪstreɪt/ *n* juez *m* que conoce de faltas y asuntos civiles de menor importancia

magnet /ˈmægnɪt/ *n* imán *m*. **~ic** /-ˈnetɪk/ *adj* magnético; (*fig*) lleno de magnetismo. **~ism** *n* magnetismo *m*. **~ize** *vt* imantar, magnetizar

magnif|ication /mægnɪfɪˈkeɪʃn/ *n* aumento *m*. **~y** /ˈmægnɪfaɪ/ *vt* aumentar. **~ying glass** *n* lupa *f*

magnificen|ce /mægˈnɪfɪsns/ *adj* magnificencia *f*. **~t** *adj* magnífico

magnitude /ˈmægnɪtjuːd/ *n* magnitud *f*

magpie /ˈmægpaɪ/ *n* urraca *f*

mahogany /məˈhɒgənɪ/ *n* caoba *f*

maid /meɪd/ *n* (*servant*) criada *f*, sirvienta *f*; (*girl, old use*) doncella *f*. **old ~** solterona *f*

maiden /ˈmeɪdn/ *n* doncella *f*. ● *adj* (*voyage*) inaugural. **~ name** *n* apellido *m* de soltera

mail /meɪl/ *n* correo *m*; (*armour*) (cota *f* de) malla *f*. ● *adj* correo. ● *vt* echar al correo (*letter*); (*send*) enviar por correo. **~box** *n* (*Amer*) buzón *m*. **~ing list** *n* lista *f* de direcciones. **~man** /-mən/ *n* (*Amer*) cartero *m*. **~ order** *n* venta *f* por correo

maim /meɪm/ *vt* mutilar

main /meɪn/ *n*. (**water/gas**) **~** cañería *f* principal. **in the ~** en su mayor parte. **the ~s** *npl* (*Elec*) la red *f* de suministro. ● *adj* principal. **~ course** *n* plato *m* principal, plato *m* fuerte. **~ frame** *n* (*Comp*) unidad *f* central. **~land** *n*. **the ~land** la masa territorial de un país excluyendo sus islas. ● *adj*. **~land China** (la) China continental. **~ly** *adv* principalmente. **~ road** *n* carretera *f* principal. **~stream** *adj* (*culture*) establecido. **~ street** *n* calle *f* principal

maint|ain /meɪnˈteɪn/ *vt* mantener. **~enance** /ˈmeɪntənəns/ *n* mantenimiento *m*

maisonette /meɪzəˈnet/ *n* (*small house*) casita *f*; (*part of house*) dúplex *m*

maize /meɪz/ *n* maíz *m*

majestic /məˈdʒestɪk/ *adj* majestuoso

majesty /ˈmædʒəstɪ/ *n* majestad *f*

major /ˈmeɪdʒə(r)/ *adj* (*important*) muy importante; (*Mus*) mayor. **a ~ road** una calle prioritaria. ● *n* comandante *m & f*, mayor *m & f* (*LAm*). ● *vi*. **~ in** (*Amer, Univ*) especializarse en

Majorca /məˈjɔːkə/ *n* Mallorca *f*

majority /məˈdʒɒrətɪ/ *n* mayoría *f*. ● *adj* mayoritario

make /meɪk/ *vt* (*pt* **made**) hacer; (*manufacture*) fabricar; ganar (*money*); tomar (*decision*); llegar a (*destination*). **~ s.o. do sth** obligar a uno a hacer algo. **be made of** estar hecho de. **I ~ it two o'clock** yo tengo las dos. **~ believe** fingir. **~ do** (*manage*) arreglarse. **~ do with** (*content o.s.*) contentarse con. **~ it** llegar; (*succeed*) tener éxito. ● *n* marca *f*. **~ for** *vt* dirigirse a. **~ good** *vt* compensar; (*repair*) reparar. □ **~ off** *vi* escaparse (**with** con). □ **~ out** *vt* distinguir; (*understand*) entender; (*write out*) hacer; (*assert*) dar a entender. *vi*

m

(*cope*) arreglárselas. □ ~ **up** vt (*constitute*) formar; (*prepare*) preparar; inventar (*story*); ~ **it up** (*become reconciled*) hacer las paces. ~ **up** (*one's face*) maquillarse. □ ~ **up for** vt compensar. ~-**believe** adj fingido, simulado. n ficción f. ~**over** n (*Amer*) maquillaje m. ~**r** n fabricante m & f. ~**shift** adj (*temporary*) provisional, provisorio (*LAm*); (*improvised*) improvisado. ~**up** n maquillaje m. **put on** ~**up** maquillarse.

making /'meɪkɪŋ/ n. **he has the ~s of** tiene madera de. **in the ~** en vías de formación

maladjusted /mælə'dʒʌstɪd/ adj inadaptado

malaria /mə'leərɪə/ n malaria f, paludismo m

Malaysia /mə'leɪzɪə/ n Malasia f. ~**n** adj & n malaisio (m)

male /meɪl/ adj macho; (*voice, attitude*) masculino. ● n macho m; (*man*) varón m

malevolent /mə'levələnt/ adj malévolo

malfunction /mæl'fʌŋkʃn/ vi fallar, funcionar mal

malic|e /'mælɪs/ n mala intención f, maldad f. **bear s.o.** ~**e** guardar rencor a uno. ~**ious** /mə'lɪʃəs/ adj malintencionado. ~**iously** adv con malevolencia

malignant /mə'lɪgnənt/ adj maligno

mallet /'mælɪt/ n mazo m

malnutrition /mælnjuː'trɪʃn/ n desnutrición f

malpractice /mæl'præktɪs/ n mala práctica f (en el ejercicio de una profesión)

malt /mɔːlt/ n malta f

Malt|a /'mɔːltə/ n Malta f. ~**ese** /-'tiːz/ adj & n maltés (m)

mammal /'mæml/ n mamífero m

mammoth /'mæməθ/ n mamut m. ● adj gigantesco

man /mæn/ n (pl **men** /men/) hombre m; (*Chess*) pieza f. ~ **in the street** hombre m de la calle. ● vt (pt **manned**) encargarse de (switchboard); tripular (ship); servir (guns)

manacles /'mænəklz/ n (*for wrists*) esposas fpl; (*for legs*) grillos mpl

manag|e /'mænɪdʒ/ vt dirigir; administrar (land, finances); (*handle*) manejar. ● vi (*Com*) dirigir; (*cope*) arreglárselas. ~**e to do** lograr hacer. ~**eable** adj (task) posible de alcanzar; (size) razonable. ~**ement** n dirección f. ~**er** n director m; (*of shop*) encargado m; (*of soccer team*) entrenador m, director m técnico (*LAm*). ~**eress** /-'res/ n encargada f. ~**erial** /-'dʒɪərɪəl/ adj directivo, gerencial (*LAm*). ~**ing director** n director m ejecutivo

mandate /'mændeɪt/ n mandato m

mandatory /'mændətərɪ/ adj obligatorio

mane /meɪn/ n (*of horse*) crin(es) f(pl); (*of lion*) melena f

mangle /'mæŋgl/ n rodillo m (escurridor). ● vt destrozar

man ~handle vt mover a pulso; (*treat roughly*) maltratar. ~**hole** n registro m. ~**hood** n madurez f; (*quality*) virilidad f. ~-**hour** n hora f hombre. ~-**hunt** n persecución f

mania /'meɪnɪə/ n manía f. ~**c** /-ɪæk/ n maníaco m

manicure /'mænɪkjʊə(r)/ n manicura f, manicure f (*LAm*)

manifest /'mænɪfest/ adj manifiesto. ● vt manifestar. ~**ation** /-'steɪʃn/ n manifestación f

manifesto /mænɪ'festəʊ/ n (pl -**os**) manifiesto m

manipulat|e /mə'nɪpjʊleɪt/ vt manipular. ~**ion** /-'leɪʃn/ n manipulación f. ~**ive** /-lətɪv/ adj manipulador

man ~kind n humanidad f. ~**ly** adj viril. ~-**made** adj artificial

manner /'mænə(r)/ n manera f; (*demeanour*) actitud f; (*kind*) clase f. ~**ed** adj amanerado. ~**s** npl modales mpl, educación f. **bad** ~**s** mala educación

manoeuvre /mə'nuːvə(r)/ n maniobra f. ● vt/i maniobrar

manor /'mænə(r)/ n. ~ **house** casa f solariega

manpower n mano f de obra

mansion /'mænʃn/ n mansión f

man ~-size(d) adj grande. ~**slaughter** n homicidio m sin premeditación

mantelpiece /'mæntlpiːs/ n repisa f de la chimenea

manual /'mænjʊəl/ adj manual. ●n (handbook) manual m

manufacture /mænjʊ'fæktʃə(r)/ vt fabricar. ●n fabricación f. ~r n fabricante m & f

manure /mə'njʊə(r)/ n estiércol m

manuscript /'mænjʊskrɪpt/ n manuscrito m

many /'menɪ/ adj & pron muchos, muchas. ~ **people** mucha gente. **a great/good** ~ muchísimos. **how** ~? ¿cuántos? **so** ~ tantos. **too** ~ demasiados

map /mæp/ n mapa m; (of streets etc) plano m

mar /mɑː(r)/ vt (pt marred) estropear

marathon /'mærəθən/ n maratón m & f

marble /'mɑːbl/ n mármol m; (for game) canica f

march /mɑːtʃ/ vi (Mil) marchar. ~ **off** vi irse. ●n marcha f

March /mɑːtʃ/ n marzo m

march-past /'mɑːtʃpɑːst/ n desfile m

mare /meə(r)/ n yegua f

margarine /mɑːdʒə'riːn/ n margarina f

margin /'mɑːdʒɪn/ n margen f. ~al adj marginal

marijuana /mærɪ'hwɑːnə/ n marihuana f

marina /mə'riːnə/ n puerto m deportivo

marine /mə'riːn/ adj marino. ●n (sailor) infante m de marina

marionette /mærɪə'net/ n marioneta f

marital status /mærɪtl 'steɪtəs/ n estado m civil

mark /mɑːk/ n marca f; (stain) mancha f; (Schol) nota f; (target) blanco m. ●vt (indicate) señalar, marcar; (stain) manchar; corregir (exam). ~ **time** marcar el paso. □ ~ **out** vt (select) señalar; (distinguish) distinguir. ~ed adj marcado. ~edly /-kɪdlɪ/ adv marcadamente. ~er n marcador m. ~er (pen) n rotulador m, marcador m (LAm)

market /'mɑːkɪt/ n mercado m. **on the** ~ en venta. ●vt comercializar. ~ **garden** n huerta f. ~ing n marketing m

marking /'mɑːkɪŋ/ n marcas fpl; (on animal, plant) mancha f

marksman /'mɑːksmən/ n (pl -men) tirador m. ~ship n puntería f

marmalade /'mɑːməleɪd/ n mermelada f (de cítricos)

maroon /mə'ruːn/ adj & n granate (m). ●vt abandonar (en una isla desierta)

marquee /mɑː'kiː/ n toldo m, entoldado m; (Amer, awning) marquesina f

marriage /'mærɪdʒ/ n matrimonio m; (ceremony) casamiento m

married /'mærɪd/ adj casado; (life) conyugal

marrow /'mærəʊ/ n (of bone) tuétano m; (vegetable) calabaza f verde alargada. ~ **squash** n (Amer) calabaza f verde alargada

marry /'mærɪ/ vt casarse con; (give or unite in marriage) casar. ●vi casarse. **get married** casarse (**to** con)

Mars /mɑːz/ n Marte m

marsh /mɑːʃ/ n pantano m

marshal /'mɑːʃl/ n (Mil) mariscal m; (Amer, police chief) jefe m de policía. ●vt (pt marshalled) reunir; poner en orden (thoughts)

marsh ~**mallow** /-'mæləʊ/ n malvavisco m, bombón m (LAm). ~y adj pantanoso

martial /'mɑːʃl/ adj marcial. ~ **arts** npl artes fpl marciales. ~ **law** n ley f marcial

martyr /'mɑːtə(r)/ n mártir m & f

marvel /'mɑːvl/ n maravilla f. ●vi (pt marvelled) maravillarse (**at** de). ~lous adj maravilloso

Marxis|m /'mɑːksɪzəm/ n marxismo m. ~t adj & n marxista (m & f)

marzipan /'mɑːzɪpæn/ n mazapán m

mascara /mæ'skɑːrə/ n rímel® m

mascot /'mæskɒt/ n mascota f

masculin|e /'mæskjʊlɪn/ adj & n masculino (m). ~ity /-'lɪnətɪ/ n masculinidad f

mash /mæʃ/ n (Brit ①, potatoes) puré m de patatas, puré m de papas (LAm). ●vt hacer puré de, moler (Mex). ~ed

potatoes *n* puré *m* de patatas, puré *m* de papas (*LAm*)

mask /mɑːsk/ *n* máscara *f*; (*Sport*) careta *f*. ● *vt* ocultar

masochis|m /'mæsəkɪzəm/ *n* masoquismo *m*. ~**t** *n* masoquista *m* & *f*. ~**tic** /-'kɪstɪk/ *adj* masoquista

mason /'meɪsn/ *n* (*stone* ~) mampostero *m*. **M~** (*freemason*) masón *m*. ~**ry** /'meɪsnrɪ/ *n* albañilería *f*

masquerade /mɑːskə'reɪd/ *n* mascarada *f*. ● *vi*. ~ **as** hacerse pasar por

mass /mæs/ *n* masa *f*; (*Relig*) misa *f*; (*large quantity*) montón *m*. **the** ~**es** las masas. ● *vi* concentrarse

massacre /'mæsəkə(r)/ *n* masacre *f*, matanza *f*. ● *vt* masacrar

mass|age /'mæsɑːʒ/ *n* masaje *m*. ● *vt* masajear. ~**eur** /mæ'sɜː(r)/ *n* masajista *m*. ~**euse** /mæ'sɜːz/ *n* masajista *f*

massive /'mæsɪv/ *adj* masivo; (*heavy*) macizo; (*huge*) enorme

mass ~ **media** *n* medios *mpl* de comunicación. ~**-produce** /-prə'djuːs/ *vt* fabricar en serie

mast /mɑːst/ *n* mástil *m*; (*for radio, TV*) antena *f* repetidora

master /'mɑːstə(r)/ *n* amo *m*; (*expert*) maestro *m*; (*in secondary school*) profesor *m*; (*of ship*) capitán *m*; (*master copy*) original *m*. ~'**s degree** master *m*, maestría *f*. **M~ of Arts (MA)** poseedor *m* de una maestría en folosofía y letras. **M~ of Science (MSc)** poseedor *m* de una maestría en ciencias. ● *vt* llegar a dominar. ~**key** *n* llave *f* maestra. ~**mind** *n* cerebro *m*. ● *vt* dirigir. ~**piece** *n* obra *f* maestra. ~**stroke** *n* golpe *m* de maestro. ~**y** *n* dominio *m*; (*skill*) maestría *f*

masturbat|e /'mæstəbeɪt/ *vi* masturbarse. ~**ion** /-'beɪʃn/ *n* masturbación *f*

mat /mæt/ *n* estera *f*; (*at door*) felpudo *m*. ● *adj* (*Amer*) see **MATT**

match /mætʃ/ *n* (*Sport*) partido *m*; (*for fire*) cerilla *f*, fósforo *m* (*LAm*), cerillo *m* (*Mex*); (*equal*) igual *m*. ● *vt* emparejar; (*equal*) igualar; (*clothes, colours*) hacer juego con. ● *vi* hacer juego. ~**box** *n* caja *f* de cerillas, caja *f* de fósforos (*LAm*), caja *f* de cerillos (*Mex*). ~**ing** *adj* que hace juego. ~**stick** *n*

cerilla *f*, fósforo *m* (*LAm*), cerillo *m* (*Mex*)

mate /meɪt/ *n* (*of person*) pareja *f*; (*of animals, male*) macho *m*; (*of animals, female*) hembra *f*; (*assistant*) ayudante *m*; (🆸, *friend*) amigo *m*, cuate *m* (*Mex*); (*Chess*) (jaque *m*) mate *m*. ● *vi* aparearse

material /mə'tɪərɪəl/ *n* material *m*; (*cloth*) tela *f*. ● *adj* material. ~**istic** /-'lɪstɪk/ *adj* materialista. ~**ize** *vi* materializarse. ~**s** *npl* materiales *mpl*

matern|al /mə'tɜːnl/ *adj* maternal. ~**ity** /-ətɪ/ *n* maternidad *f*. ● *adj* (*ward*) de obstetricia; (*clothes*) premamá, de embarazada

math /mæθ/ *n* (*Amer*) see **MATHS**

mathematic|ian /mæθəmə'tɪʃn/ *n* matemático *m*. ~**al** /-'mætɪkl/ *adj* matemático. ~**s** /-'mætɪks/ *n* matemática(s) *f(pl)*

maths /mæθs/ *n* matemática(s) *f(pl)*

matinée, matinee /'mætɪneɪ/ *n* (*Theatre*) función *f* de tarde; (*Cinema*) primera sesión *f* (de la tarde)

matrices /'meɪtrɪsiːz/ *see* **MATRIX**

matriculat|e /mə'trɪkjʊleɪt/ *vi* matricularse. ~**ion** /-'leɪʃn/ *n* matrícula *f*

matrimon|ial /mætrɪ'məʊnɪəl/ *adj* matrimonial. ~**y** /'mætrɪmənɪ/ *n* matrimonio *m*

matrix /'meɪtrɪks/ *n* (*pl* **matrices**) matriz *f*

matron /'meɪtrən/ *n* (*married, elderly*) matrona *f*; (*in school*) ama *f* de llaves; (*former use, in hospital*) enfermera *f* jefe

matt, matte (*Amer*) /mæt/ *adj* mate

matted /'mætɪd/ *adj* enmarañado y apelmazado

matter /'mætə(r)/ *n* (*substance*) materia *f*; (*affair*) asunto *m*; (*pus*) pus *m*. **as a** ~ **of fact** en realidad. **no** ~ no importa. **what is the** ~? ¿qué pasa? **to make** ~**s worse** para colmo (de males). ● *vi* importar. **it doesn't** ~ no importa. ~**-of-fact** /-əv'fækt/ *adj* (*person*) práctico

mattress /'mætrɪs/ *n* colchón *m*

matur|e /mə'tjʊə(r)/ *adj* maduro. ● *vi* madurar. ~**ity** *n* madurez *f*

maudlin /'mɔːdlɪn/ *adj* llorón

maul /mɔːl/ vt atacar (y herir)

mauve /məʊv/ adj & n malva (m)

maverick /'mævərɪk/ n inconformista m & f

maxim /'mæksɪm/ n máxima f

maxim|ize /'mæksɪmaɪz/ vt maximizar. **~um** /-əm/ adj & n máximo (m)

---

may /meɪ/,

past **might**

auxiliary verb

····▸ (*expressing possibility*) he ~ come puede que venga, es posible que venga. it ~ be true puede ser verdad. she ~ not have seen him es posible que or puede que no lo haya visto

····▸ (*asking for or giving permission*) ~ I smoke? ¿puedo fumar?, ¿se puede fumar? ~ I have your name and address, please? ¿quiere darme su nombre y dirección, por favor?

····▸ (*expressing a wish*) ~ he be happy que sea feliz

····▸ (*conceding*) he ~ not have much experience, but he's very hardworking no tendrá mucha experiencia, pero es muy trabajador. that's as ~ be puede ser

····▸ I ~ as well stay más vale quedarme

May /meɪ/ n mayo m

maybe /'meɪbɪ/ adv quizá(s), tal vez, a lo mejor

May Day n el primero de mayo

mayhem /'meɪhem/ n caos m

mayonnaise /meɪə'neɪz/ n mayonesa f, mahonesa f

mayor /meə(r)/ n alcalde m, alcaldesa f. **~ess** /-ɪs/ n alcaldesa f

maze /meɪz/ n laberinto m

me /miː/ pron me; (*after prep*) mí. he knows ~ me conoce. it's ~ soy yo

meadow /'medəʊ/ n prado m, pradera f

meagre /'miːgə(r)/ adj escaso

meal /miːl/ n comida f. **~time** n hora f de comer

mean /miːn/ vt (pt meant) (*intend*) tener la intención de, querer; (*signify*)

querer decir, significar. ~ to do tener la intención de hacer. ~ well tener buenas intenciones. be meant for estar destinado a. ●adj (-er, -est) (*miserly*) tacaño; (*unkind*) malo; (*Math*) medio. ●n media f; (*average*) promedio m

meander /mɪ'ændə(r)/ vi (river) serpentear

meaning /'miːnɪŋ/ n sentido m. **~ful** adj significativo. **~less** adj sin sentido

meanness /'miːnnɪs/ n (*miserliness*) tacañería f; (*unkindness*) maldad f

means /miːnz/ n medio m. by ~ of por medio de, mediante. by all ~ por supuesto. by no ~ de ninguna manera. ●npl (*wealth*) medios mpl, recursos mpl. ~ test n investigación f de ingresos

meant /ment/ see MEAN

meantime /'miːntaɪm/ adv mientras tanto, entretanto. ●n. in the ~ mientras tanto, entretanto

meanwhile /'miːnwaɪl/ adv mientras tanto, entretanto

measl|es /'miːzlz/ n sarampión m. **~y** /'miːzlɪ/ adj ☐ miserable

measure /'meʒə(r)/ n medida f; (*ruler*) regla f. ●vt/i medir. □~ up to vt estar a la altura de. **~ment** n medida f

meat /miːt/ n carne f. **~ball** n albóndiga f. **~y** adj (taste, smell) a carne; (soup, stew) con mucha carne

mechan|ic /mɪ'kænɪk/ n mecánico m. **~ical** adj mecánico. **~ics** n mecánica f. **~ism** /'mekənɪzəm/ n mecanismo m. **~ize** /'mekənaɪz/ vt mecanizar

medal /'medl/ n medalla f. **~list** /'medəlɪst/ n medallista m & f. be a gold **~list** ganar una medalla de oro

meddle /'medl/ vi meterse, entrometerse (in en). ~ with (*tinker*) toquetear

media /'miːdɪə/ see MEDIUM. ●npl. the ~ los medios de comunicación

mediat|e /'miːdɪeɪt/ vi mediar. **~ion** /-'eɪʃn/ n mediación f. **~or** n mediador m

medical /'medɪkl/ adj médico; (*student*) de medicina. ●n revisión m médica

m

medicat|ed /'medɪkeɪtɪd/ adj medicinal. ~**ion** /-'keɪʃn/ n medicación f
medicin|al /mɪ'dɪsɪnl/ adj medicinal. ~**e** /'medsɪn/ n medicina f
medieval /medɪ'iːvl/ adj medieval
mediocre /miːdɪ'əʊkə(r)/ adj mediocre
meditat|e /'medɪteɪt/ vi meditar. ~**ion** /-'teɪʃn/ n meditación f
Mediterranean /medɪtə'reɪnɪən/ adj mediterráneo. ●n. the ~ el Mediterráneo
medium /'miːdɪəm/ n (pl **media**) medio m. **happy** ~ término m medio. ●adj mediano. ~**-size(d)** /-saɪz(d)/ adj de tamaño mediano
medley /'medlɪ/ n (Mus) popurrí m; (mixture) mezcla f
meek /miːk/ adj (**-er, -est**) dócil
meet /miːt/ vt (pt **met**) encontrar; (bump into s.o.) encontrarse con; (fetch) ir a buscar; (get to know, be introduced to) conocer. ●vi encontrarse; (get to know) conocerse; (have meeting) reunirse. ~ **up** vi encontrarse (**with** con). □ ~ **with** vt ser recibido con; (Amer, meet) encontrarse con. ~**ing** n reunión f; (accidental between two people) encuentro m
megabyte /'megəbaɪt/ n (Comp) megabyte m, megaocteto m
megaphone /'megəfəʊn/ n megáfono m
melanchol|ic /melən'kɒlɪk/ adj melancólico. ~**y** /'melənkɒlɪ/ n melancolía f. ●adj melancólico
mellow /'meləʊ/ adj (**-er, -est**) (fruit) maduro m; (sound) dulce; (colour) tenue; (person) apacible
melodrama /'melədrɑːmə/ n melodrama m. ~**tic** /melədrə'mætɪk/ adj melodramático
melody /'melədɪ/ n melodía f
melon /'melən/ n melón m
melt /melt/ vt (make liquid) derretir; fundir (metals). ●vi (become liquid) derretirse; (metals) fundirse. □ ~ **down** vt fundir
member /'membə(r)/ n miembro m & f; (of club) socio m. ~ **of staff** empleado m. **M~ of Congress** n (Amer) miembro m & f del Congreso. **M~ of**

Parliament n diputado m. ~**ship** n calidad f de socio; (members) socios mpl, membresía f (LAm)
membrane /'membreɪn/ n membrana f
memento /mɪ'mentəʊ/ n (pl **-os** or **-oes**) recuerdo m
memo /'meməʊ/ n (pl **-os**) memorándum m, memo m
memoir /'memwɑː(r)/ n memoria f
memorable /'memərəbl/ adj memorable
memorandum /memə'rændəm/ n (pl **-ums** or **-da** /-də/) memorándum m
memorial /mɪ'mɔːrɪəl/ n monumento m. ●adj conmemorativo
memor|ize /'meməraɪz/ vt aprender de memoria. ~**y** /'memərɪ/ n (faculty) memoria f; (thing remembered) recuerdo m. **from** ~**y** de memoria. **in** ~**y of** a la memoria de
men /men/ see MAN
menac|e /'menəs/ n amenaza f; (fam, nuisance) peligro m público. ●vt amenazar. ~**ing** adj amenazador
mend /mend/ vt reparar; arreglar (garment). ~ **one's ways** enmendarse. ●n remiendo m. **be on the** ~ ir mejorando
menfolk /'menfəʊk/ n hombres mpl
menial /'miːnɪəl/ adj servil
meningitis /menɪn'dʒaɪtɪs/ n meningitis f
menopause /'menəpɔːz/ n menopausia f
menstruat|e /'menstrʊeɪt/ vi menstruar. ~**ion** /-'eɪʃn/ n menstruación f
mental /'mentl/ adj mental; (hospital) psiquiátrico. ~**ity** /-'tælətɪ/ n mentalidad f. ~**ly** adv mentalmente. **be** ~**ly ill** ser un enfermo mental
mention /'menʃn/ vt mencionar. **don't** ~ **it!** ¡no hay de qué! ●n mención f
mentor /'mentɔː(r)/ n mentor m
menu /'menjuː/ n menú m
meow /mɪ'aʊ/ n & vi see MEW
mercenary /'mɜːsɪnərɪ/ adj & n mercenario (m)
merchandise /'mɜːtʃəndaɪz/ n mercancías fpl, mercadería f (LAm)

merchant /ˈmɜːtʃənt/ n comerciante m. ● adj (ship, navy) mercante. ~ **bank** n banco m mercantil

merci|ful /ˈmɜːsɪfl/ adj misericordioso. ~**less** adj despiadado

mercury /ˈmɜːkjʊrɪ/ n mercurio m. M~ (planet) Mercurio m

mercy /ˈmɜːsɪ/ n compasión f. **at the** ~ **of** a merced de

mere /mɪə(r)/ adj simple. ~**ly** adv simplemente

merge /mɜːdʒ/ vt unir; fusionar (companies). ● vi unirse; (companies) fusionarse. ~**r** n fusión f

meridian /məˈrɪdɪən/ n meridiano m

meringue /məˈræŋ/ n merengue m

merit /ˈmerɪt/ n mérito m. ● vt (pt merited) merecer

mermaid /ˈmɜːmeɪd/ n sirena f

merr|ily /ˈmerəlɪ/ adv alegremente. ~**lment** /ˈmerɪmənt/ n alegría f. ~**y** /ˈmerɪ/ adj (-ier, -iest) alegre. **make** ~ divertirse. ~**y-go-round** n tiovivo m, carrusel m (LAm). ~**y-making** n jolgorio m

mesh /meʃ/ n malla f

mesmerize /ˈmezməraɪz/ vt hipnotizar; (fascinate) cautivar

mess /mes/ n desorden m; (dirt) suciedad f; (Mil) rancho m. **make a** ~ **of** estropear. □ ~ **up** vt desordenar; (dirty) ensuciar; estropear (plans). □ ~ **about** vi tontear. □ ~ **with** vt (tinker with) manosear

mess|age /ˈmesɪdʒ/ n mensaje m; (when phoning) recado m. ~**enger** /ˈmesɪndʒə(r)/ n mensajero m

Messiah /mɪˈsaɪə/ n Mesías m

Messrs /ˈmesəz/ npl. ~ **Smith** los señores Smith, los Sres. Smith

messy /ˈmesɪ/ adj (-ier, -iest) en desorden; (dirty) sucio

met /met/ see **MEET**

metabolism /mɪˈtæbəlɪzəm/ n metabolismo m

metal /ˈmetl/ n metal. ● adj de metal. ~**lic** /məˈtælɪk/ adj metálico

metaphor /ˈmetəfə(r)/ n metáfora f. ~**ical** /-ˈfɒrɪkl/ adj metafórico

mete /miːt/ vt. ~ **out** repartir; dar (punishment)

meteor /ˈmiːtɪə(r)/ n meteoro m. ~**ic** /-ˈɒrɪk/ adj meteórico. ~**ite** /ˈmiːtɪəraɪt/ n meteorito m

meteorolog|ical /miːtɪərəˈlɒdʒɪkl/ adj meteorológico. ~**ist** /-ˈrɒlədʒɪst/ n meteorólogo m. ~**y** /ˈrɒlədʒɪ/ n meteorología f

meter /ˈmiːtə(r)/ n contador m, medidor m (LAm); (Amer) see **METRE**

method /ˈmeθəd/ n método m. ~**ical** /mɪˈθɒdɪkl/ adj metódico. **M~ist** /ˈmeθədɪst/ adj & n metodista (m & f)

methylated /ˈmeθɪleɪtɪd/ adj. ~ **spirit(s)** n alcohol m desnaturalizado

meticulous /mɪˈtɪkjʊləs/ adj meticuloso

metre /ˈmiːtə(r)/ n metro m

metric /ˈmetrɪk/ adj métrico

metropoli|s /mɪˈtrɒpəlɪs/ n metrópoli(s) f

mettle /ˈmetl/ n. be on one's ~ (fig) estar dispuesto a dar lo mejor de sí

mew /mjuː/ n maullido m. ● vi maullar

Mexic|an /ˈmeksɪkən/ adj & n mejicano (m), mexicano (m). ~**o** /-kəʊ/ n Méjico m, México m

miaow /miːˈaʊ/ n & vi see **MEW**

mice /maɪs/ see **MOUSE**

mickey /ˈmɪkɪ/ n. take the ~ out of 🅸 tomar el pelo a

micro... /ˈmaɪkrəʊ/ pref micro...

microbe /ˈmaɪkrəʊb/ n microbio m

micro ~**chip** n pastilla f. ~**film** n microfilme m. ~**light** n aeroligero m. ~**phone** n micrófono m. ~**processor** /-ˈprəʊsesə(r)/ n microprocesador m. ~**scope** n microscopio m. ~**scopic** /-ˈskɒpɪk/ adj microscópico. ~**wave** n microonda f. ~**wave oven** n horno m de microondas

mid- /mɪd/ pref. **in** ~ **air** en pleno aire. **in** ~ **March** a mediados de marzo

midday /mɪdˈdeɪ/ n mediodía m

middl|e /ˈmɪdl/ adj de en medio. ● n medio m. **in the** ~**e of** en medio de. ~**e-aged** /-ˈeɪdʒd/ adj de mediana edad. **M~e Ages** npl Edad f Media. ~**e class** n clase f media. ~**e-class** adj de la clase media. **M~e East** n Oriente m Medio. ~**eman** n intermediario m. ~**e name** n segundo nombre m. ~**ing** adj regular

m

midge /mɪdʒ/ n mosquito m

midget /ˈmɪdʒɪt/ n enano m. ● adj minúsculo

Midlands /ˈmɪdləndz/ npl región f central de Inglaterra

midnight /ˈmɪdnaɪt/ n medianoche f

midriff /ˈmɪdrɪf/ n diafragma m

midst /mɪdst/ n. in our ~ entre nosotros. in the ~ of en medio de

midsummer /mɪdˈsʌmə(r)/ n pleno verano m; (solstice) solsticio m de verano

midway /mɪdˈweɪ/ adv a mitad de camino

Midwest /ˈmɪdˈwest/ región f central de los EE.UU.

midwife /ˈmɪdwaɪf/ n comadrona f, partera f

midwinter /mɪdˈwɪntə(r)/ n pleno invierno m

might /maɪt/ see MAY. ● n (strength) fuerza f; (power) poder m. ~y adj (strong) fuerte; (powerful) poderoso. ● adv 🔲 muy

migraine /ˈmiːɡreɪn/ n jaqueca f

migra|nt /ˈmaɪɡrənt/ adj migratorio. ● n (person) emigrante m & f. ~te /maɪˈɡreɪt/ vi emigrar. ~tion /-ˈɡreɪʃn/ n migración f

mild /maɪld/ adj (-er, -est) (person) afable; (climate) templado; (slight) ligero; (taste, manner) suave

mildew /ˈmɪldjuː/ n moho m; (on plants) mildeu m, mildiu m

mildly /ˈmaɪldlɪ/ adv (gently) suavemente; (slightly) ligeramente

mile /maɪl/ n milla f. ~s better 🔲 mucho mejor. ~s too big 🔲 demasiado grande. ~age /-ɪdʒ/ n (loosely) kilometraje m. ~ometer /maɪˈlɒmɪtə(r)/ n (loosely) cuentakilómetros m. ~stone n mojón m; (event, stage, fig) hito m

militant /ˈmɪlɪtənt/ adj & n militante (m & f)

military /ˈmɪlɪtərɪ/ adj militar

militia /mɪˈlɪʃə/ n milicia f

milk /mɪlk/ n leche f. ● adj (product) lácteo; (chocolate) con leche. ● vt ordeñar (cow). ~man /-mən/ n lechero m. ~ shake n batido m, (leche f)

malteada f (LAm), licuado m con leche (LAm) lechoso. **M~y Way** n Vía f Láctea

mill /mɪl/ n molino m; (for coffee, pepper) molinillo m; (factory) fábrica f de tejidos de algodón. ● vt moler. □ ~ **about, mill around** vi dar vueltas

millennium /mɪˈlenɪəm/ n (pl -ia /-ɪə/ or -iums) milenio m

miller /ˈmɪlə(r)/ n molinero m

milli... /ˈmɪlɪ/ pref mili... ~gram(me) n miligramo m. ~metre n milímetro m

milliner /ˈmɪlɪnə(r)/ n sombrerero m

million /ˈmɪlɪən/ n millón m. a ~ **pounds** un millón de libras. ~aire /-ˈeə(r)/ n millonario m

millstone /ˈmɪlstəʊn/ n muela f (de molino); (fig, burden) carga f

mime /maɪm/ n mímica f. ● vt imitar, hacer la mímica de. ● vi hacer la mímica

mimic /ˈmɪmɪk/ vt (pt mimicked) imitar. ● n imitador m. ~ry n imitación f

mince /mɪns/ vt picar, moler (LAm) (meat). **not to ~ matters/words** no andar(se) con rodeos. ● n carne f picada, carne f molida (LAm). ~ **pie** n pastelito m de Navidad (pastelito relleno de picadillo de frutos secos). ~r n máquina f de picar carne, máquina f de moler carne (LAm)

mind /maɪnd/ n mente f; (sanity) juicio m. **to my ~** a mi parecer. **be on one's mind** preocuparle a uno. **make up one's ~** decidirse.● vt (look after) cuidar (de); atender (shop). ~ **the steps!** ¡cuidado con las escaleras! **never ~ him** no le hagas caso. **I don't ~ the noise** no me molesta el ruido. **would you ~ closing the door?** ¿le importaría cerrar la puerta? ● vi. **never ~** no importa, no te preocupes. **I don't ~** (don't object) me da igual. **do you ~ if I smoke?** ¿le importa si fumo? ~**ful** adj atento (of a). ~**less** adj (activity) mecánico; (violence) ciego

mine¹ /maɪn/ poss pron (sing) mío, mía; (pl) míos, mías. **it is** ~ es mío. ~ **are blue** los míos/las mías son azules. **a friend of** ~ un amigo mío/una amiga mía

mine² /maɪn/ n mina f; (Mil) mina f.
● vt extraer. ~**field** n campo m de
minas. ~**r** n minero m

mineral /'mɪnərəl/ adj & n mineral (m).
~ **water** n agua f mineral

mingle /'mɪŋgl/ vi mezclarse

mini... /'mɪnɪ/ pref mini...

miniature /'mɪnɪtʃə(r)/ n miniatura f.
● adj en miniatura

mini ~**bus** n microbús m. ~**cab** n
taxi m (que se pide por teléfono)

minim|al /'mɪnɪml/ adj mínimo. ~**ize**
vt reducir al mínimo. ~**um** /-məm/
adj & n (pl -**ima** /-mə/) mínimo (m)

mining /'maɪnɪŋ/ n minería f. ● adj minero

miniskirt /'mɪnɪskɜːt/ n minifalda f

minist|er /'mɪnɪstə(r)/ n ministro m,
secretario m (Mex); (Relig) pastor m.
~**erial** /-'stɪərɪəl/ adj ministerial. ~**ry**
n ministerio m, secretaría f (Mex)

mink /mɪŋk/ n visón m

minor /'maɪnə(r)/ adj (also Mus) menor;
(injury) leve; (change) pequeño; (operation) de poca importancia. ● n
menor m & f de edad. ~**ity** /maɪ
'nɒrətɪ/ n minoría f. ● adj minoritario

minstrel /'mɪnstrəl/ n juglar m

mint /mɪnt/ n (plant) menta f; (sweet)
pastilla f de menta, (Finance) casa f de
la moneda. **in** ~ **condition** como
nuevo. ● vt acuñar

minus /'maɪnəs/ prep menos; (fam,
without) sin. ● n (sign) menos m. **five**
~ **three is two** cinco menos tres is
igual a dos. ~ **sign** n (signo m de)
menos m

minute¹ /'mɪnɪt/ n minuto m. **the** ~**s**
npl (of meeting) el acta f

minute² /maɪ'njuːt/ adj diminuto; (de-
tailed) minucioso

mirac|le /'mɪrəkl/ n milagro m.
~**ulous** /mɪ'rækjʊləs/ adj milagroso

mirage /'mɪrɑːʒ/ n espejismo m

mirror /'mɪrə(r)/ n espejo m; (driving
~) (espejo m) retrovisor m. ● vt reflejar

mirth /mɜːθ/ n regocijo m; (laughter)
risas fpl

misapprehension /mɪsæprɪ'henʃn/
n malentendido m

misbehav|e /mɪsbɪ'heɪv/ vi portarse
mal. ~**iour** n mala conducta

miscalculat|e /mɪs'kælkjʊleɪt/ vt/i
calcular mal. ~**ion** /-'leɪʃn/ n error m
de cálculo

miscarr|iage /'mɪskærɪdʒ/ n aborto m
espontáneo. ~**iage of justice** n injusticia f. ~**y** vi abortar

miscellaneous /mɪsə'leɪnɪəs/ adj he-
terogéneo

mischie|f /'mɪstʃɪf/ n (foolish conduct)
travesura f; (harm) daño m. **get into**
~**f** hacer travesuras. **make** ~**f** causar
daños. ~**vous** /'mɪstʃɪvəs/ adj travieso; (grin) pícaro

misconception /mɪskən'sepʃn/ n
equivocación f

misconduct /mɪs'kɒndʌkt/ n mala
conducta f

misdeed /mɪs'diːd/ n fechoría f

misdemeanour /mɪsdɪ'miːnə(r)/ n
delito m menor, falta f

miser /'maɪzə(r)/ n avaro m

miserable /'mɪzərəbl/ adj (sad) triste;
(in low spirits) abatido; (wretched,
poor) mísero; (weather) pésimo

miserly /'maɪzəlɪ/ adj avariento

misery /'mɪzərɪ/ n (unhappiness) tristeza f; (pain) sufrimiento m

misfire /mɪs'faɪə(r)/ vi fallar

misfit /'mɪsfɪt/ n inadaptado m

misfortune /mɪs'fɔːtʃuːn/ n desgracia f

misgiving /mɪs'gɪvɪŋ/ n recelo m

misguided /mɪs'gaɪdɪd/ adj equivocado

mishap /'mɪshæp/ n percance m

misinform /mɪsɪn'fɔːm/ vt informar
mal

misinterpret /mɪsɪn'tɜːprɪt/ vt interpretar mal

misjudge /mɪs'dʒʌdʒ/ vt juzgar mal;
(miscalculate) calcular mal

mislay /mɪs'leɪ/ vt (pt mislaid) extraviar, perder

mislead /mɪs'liːd/ vt (pt misled /mɪs
'led/) engañar. ~**ing** adj engañoso

mismanage /mɪs'mænɪdʒ/ vt administrar mal. ~**ment** n mala administración f

misplace /mɪs'pleɪs/ vt (lose) extraviar,
perder

m

misprint /'mɪsprɪnt/ n errata f

miss /mɪs/ vt (fail to hit) no dar en; (regret absence of) echar de menos, extrañar (LAm); perder (train, party); perder (chance). ~ **the point** no comprender. ●vi errar el tiro, fallar; (bullet) no dar en el blanco. ●n fallo m, falla f (LAm); (title) señorita f. □ ~ **out** vt saltarse (line). ~out **on sth** perderse algo

misshapen /mɪs'ʃeɪpən/ adj deforme

missile /'mɪsaɪl/ n (Mil) misil m

missing /'mɪsɪŋ/ adj (lost) perdido. **be** ~ faltar. **go** ~ desaparecer. ~ **person** desaparecido m

mission /'mɪʃn/ n misión f. ~**ary** /'mɪʃənərɪ/ n misionero m

mist /mɪst/ n neblina f; (at sea) bruma f. □ ~ **up** vi empañarse

mistake /mɪ'steɪk/ n error m. **make a** ~ cometer un error. **by** ~ por error. ●vt (pt **mistook**, pp **mistaken**) confundir. ~ **for** confundir con. ~**n** /-ən/ adj equivocado. **be** ~**n** equivocarse

mistletoe /'mɪsltəʊ/ n muérdago m

mistreat /mɪs'triːt/ vt maltratar

mistress /'mɪstrɪs/ n (of house) señora f; (lover) amante f

mistrust /mɪs'trʌst/ vt desconfiar de. ●n desconfianza f. ~**ful** adj desconfiado

misty /'mɪstɪ/ adj (-ier, -iest) neblinoso; (day) de neblina. **it's** ~ hay neblina

misunderstand /mɪsʌndə'stænd/ vt (pt **-stood**) entender mal. ~**ing** n malentendido m

misuse /mɪs'juːz/ vt emplear mal; malversar (funds). ●/mɪs'juːs/ n mal uso m; (unfair use) abuso m; (of funds) malversación f

mite /maɪt/ n (insect) ácaro m

mitten /'mɪtn/ n mitón m

mix /mɪks/ vt mezclar. ●vi mezclarse; (go together) combinar. ~ **with** tratarse con (people). ●n mezcla f. □ ~ **up** vt mezclar; (confuse) confundir. ~**ed** adj (school etc) mixto; (assorted) mezclado. **be** ~**ed up** estar confuso. ~**er** n (Culin) batidora f; (TV, machine) mezcladora f. ~**ture** /'mɪkstʃə(r)/ n mezcla f. ~**-up** n lío m

moan /məʊn/ n gemido m. ●vi gemir; (complain) quejarse (**about** de)

moat /məʊt/ n foso m

mob /mɒb/ n turba f. ●vt (pt **mobbed**) acosar

mobil|e /'məʊbaɪl/ adj móvil. ~**e home** n caravana f fija, trailer m (LAm). ~**e (phone)** n (teléfono m) móvil m, (teléfono m) celular m (LAm). ●n móvil m. ~**ize** /'məʊbɪlaɪz/ vt movilizar. ●vi movilizarse

mock /mɒk/ vt burlarse de. ●adj (anger) fingido; (exam) de práctica. ~**ery** /'mɒkərɪ/ n burla f. **make a** ~**ery of sth** ridiculizar algo

model /'mɒdl/ n (example) modelo m; (mock-up) maqueta f; (person) modelo m. ●adj (exemplary) modelo; (car etc) en miniatura. ●vt (pt **modelled**) modelar. ~ **s.o. on s.o.** tomar a uno como modelo

modem /'məʊdem/ n (Comp) módem m

moderat|e /'mɒdərət/ adj & n moderado (m). ●/'mɒdəreɪt/ vt moderar. ~**ely** /'mɒdərətlɪ/ adv (fairly) medianamente. ~**ion** /-'reɪʃn/ n moderación f. **in** ~**ion** con moderación

modern /'mɒdn/ adj moderno. ~**ize** vt modernizar

modest /'mɒdɪst/ adj modesto. ~**y** n modestia f

modif|ication /mɒdɪfɪ'keɪʃn/ n modificación f. ~**y** /-faɪ/ vt modificar

module /'mɒdjuːl/ n módulo m

moist /mɔɪst/ adj (-er, -est) húmedo. ~**en** /'mɔɪsn/ vt humedecer

moistur|e /'mɔɪstʃə(r)/ n humedad f. ~**ize** vt hidratar. ~**izer**, ~**izing cream** n crema f hidratante

mole /məʊl/ n (animal) topo m; (on skin) lunar m

molecule /'mɒlɪkjuːl/ n molécula f

molest /mə'lest/ vt abusar (sexualmente) de

mollify /'mɒlɪfaɪ/ vt aplacar

mollusc /'mɒləsk/ n molusco m

mollycoddle /'mɒlɪkɒdl/ vt mimar

molten /'məʊltən/ adj fundido; (lava) líquido

mom /mɒm/ n (Amer, 🔢) mamá f 🔢

moment /'məʊmənt/ n momento m.
at the ~ en este momento. **for the
~** de momento. **~ary**
/'məʊməntəri/ adj momentáneo

momentous /mə'mentəs/ adj trascendental

momentum /mə'mentəm/ n momento m; (speed) velocidad f

mommy /'mɒmɪ/ n (Amer, fam) mamá
m [T]

monarch /'mɒnək/ n monarca m. **~y**
n monarquía f

monastery /'mɒnəstəri/ n monasterio m

Monday /'mʌndeɪ/ n lunes m

money /'mʌnɪ/ n dinero m, plata f
(LAm). **~box** n hucha f, alcancia f
(LAm). **~ order** n giro m postal

mongrel /'mʌŋɡrəl/ n perro m mestizo, chucho m [T]

monitor /'mɒnɪtə(r)/ n (Tec) monitor
m. ● vt observar (elections); seguir
(progress); (electronically) monitorizar,
escuchar

monk /mʌŋk/ n monje m. **~fish** n
rape m

monkey /'mʌŋkɪ/ n mono m. **~-nut** n
cacahuete m, cacahuate m (Mex), maní
m (LAm). **~wrench** n llave f inglesa

mono /'mɒnəʊ/ n monofonía f

monologue /'mɒnəlɒɡ/ n monó-
logo m

monopol|ize /mə'nɒpəlaɪz/ vt mono-
polizar; acaparar (conversation). **~y** n
monopolio m

monoton|e /'mɒnətəʊn/ n tono m
monocorde. **~ous** /mə'nɒtənəs/ adj
monótono. **~y** n monotonía f

monsoon /mɒn'suːn/ n monzón m

monst|er /'mɒnstə(r)/ n monstruo m.
~rous /-strəs/ adj monstruoso

month /mʌnθ/ n mes m. **£200 a ~**
200 libras mensuales or al mes. **~ly**
adj mensual. **~ly payment** mensuali-
dad f, cuota f mensual (LAm). ● adv
mensualmente

monument /'mɒnjʊmənt/ n monumento m. **~al** /-'mentl/ adj monu-
mental

moo /muː/ n mugido m. ● vi mugir

mood /muːd/ n humor m. **be in a
good/bad ~** estar de buen/mal

humor. **~y** adj (-ier, -iest) temperamental; (bad-tempered) malhumorado

moon /muːn/ n luna f. **~light** n luz f
de la luna. **~lighting** n pluriempleo
m. **~lit** adj iluminado por la luna;
(night) de luna

moor /mʊə(r)/ n páramo m; (of heather) brezal m. ● vt amarrar. **~ing** n
(place) amarradero m. **~ings** npl
(ropes) amarras fpl

moose /muːs/ n invar alce m americano

mop /mɒp/ n fregona f, trapeador m
(LAm). **~ of hair** pelambrera f. ● vt (pt
mopped). **~ (up)** limpiar

mope /məʊp/ vi estar abatido

moped /'məʊped/ n ciclomotor m

moral /'mɒrəl/ adj moral. ● n (of tale)
moraleja f

morale /mə'rɑːl/ n moral f

moral|ity /mə'rælətɪ/ n moralidad f.
~ly adv moralmente. **~s** npl morali-
dad f

morbid /'mɔːbɪd/ adj morboso

more /mɔː(r)/ adj más. **two ~ bottles**
dos botellas más. ● pron más. **you ate
~ than me** comiste más que yo.
some ~ más. **~ than six** más de
seis. **the ~ he has, the ~ he wants**
cuánto más tiene, más quiere. ● adv
más. **~ and ~** cada vez más. **~ or
less** más o menos. **once ~** una vez
más. **she doesn't live here any ~** ya
no vive aquí. **~over** /mɔː'rəʊvə(r)/
adv además

morgue /mɔːɡ/ n depósito m de cadáveres, morgue f (LAm)

morning /'mɔːnɪŋ/ n mañana f; (early
hours) madrugada f. **at 11 o'clock in
the ~** a las once de la mañana. **in
the ~** por la mañana, en la mañana
(LAm). **tomorrow/yesterday ~**
mañana/ayer por la mañana or (LAm)
en la mañana. **(good) ~!** ¡buenos
días!

Morocc|an /mə'rɒkən/ adj & n marro-
quí (m & f). **~o** /-kəʊ/ n Marruecos m

moron /'mɔːrɒn/ n imbécil m & f

morose /mə'rəʊs/ adj taciturno

Morse /mɔːs/ n Morse m. **in ~ (code)**
n en (código) morse

morsel /'mɔːsl/ n bocado m

m

mortal /'mɔːtl/ adj & n mortal (m).
~**ity** /-'tælɪtɪ/ n mortalidad f

mortar /'mɔːtə(r)/ n (all senses) mortero m

mortgage /'mɔːgɪdʒ/ n hipoteca f. ● vt hipotecar

mortify /'mɔːtɪfaɪ/ vt darle mucha vergüenza a

mortuary /'mɔːtjʊərɪ/ n depósito m de cadáveres, morgue f (LAm)

mosaic /məʊ'zeɪk/ n mosaico m

mosque /mɒsk/ n mezquita f

mosquito /mɒs'kiːtəʊ/ n (pl -oes) mosquito m, zancudo m (LAm)

moss /mɒs/ n musgo m

most /məʊst/ adj la mayoría de, la mayor parte de. ~ **days** casi todos los días. ● pron la mayoría, la mayor parte. **at** ~ como máximo. **make the** ~ **of** aprovechar al máximo. ● adv más; (very) muy; (Amer, almost) casi. ~**ly** adv principalmente

MOT n. ~ (**test**) ITV f, inspección f técnica de vehículos

motel /məʊ'tel/ n motel m

moth /mɒθ/ n mariposa f de la luz, palomilla f; (in clothes) polilla f

mother /mʌðə(r)/ n madre f. ● vt mimar. ~**-in-law** n (pl ~s-in-law) suegra f. ~**land** n patria f. ~**ly** adj maternal. ~**-of-pearl** n nácar m, madreperla f. **M**~**'s Day** n el día m de la Madre. ~**-to-be** n futura madre f. ~ **tongue** n lengua f materna

motif /məʊ'tiːf/ n motivo m

motion /'məʊʃn/ n movimiento m; (proposal) moción f. **put** or **set in** ~ poner algo en marcha. ● vt/i. ~ (**to**) **s.o. to** hacerle señas a uno para que. ~**less** adj inmóvil

motiv|ate /'məʊtɪveɪt/ vt motivar. ~**ation** /-'veɪʃn/ n motivación f. ~**e** /'məʊtɪv/ n motivo m

motley /'mɒtlɪ/ adj variopinto

motor /'məʊtə(r)/ n motor m. ● adj motor; (fem) motora, motriz. ~ **bike** n Ⓘ motocicleta f, moto f Ⓘ. ~ **boat** n lancha f a motor. ~ **car** n automóvil m. ~ **cycle** n motocicleta f. ~**cyclist** n motociclista m & f. ~**ing** n automovilismo m. ~**ist** n automovilista m & f. ~**way** n autopista f

motto /'mɒtəʊ/ n (pl -oes) lema m

mould /məʊld/ n molde m; (fungus) moho m. ● vt moldear; formar (character). ~**ing** n (on wall etc) moldura f. ~**y** adj mohoso

moult /məʊlt/ vi mudar de pelo/piel/plumas

mound /maʊnd/ n montículo m; (pile, fig) montón m

mount /maʊnt/ vt montar (horse); engarzar (gem); preparar (attack). ● vi subir, crecer. ● n. montura f; (mountain) monte m. □ ~ **up** vi irse acumulando

mountain /'maʊntɪn/ n montaña f. ~**eer** /maʊntɪ'nɪə(r)/ n alpinista m & f. ~**eering** n alpinismo m. ~**ous** adj montañoso

mourn /mɔːn/ vt llorar. ● vi lamentarse. ~ **for s.o.** llorar a uno. ~**er** n doliente m & f. ~**ful** adj triste. ~**ing** n duelo m, luto m. **be in** ~**ing** estar de duelo

mouse /maʊs/ n (pl mice) ratón m. ~**trap** n ratonera f

mousse /muːs/ n (Culin) mousse f or m; (for hair) mousse f

moustache /mə'stɑːʃ/ n bigote m

mouth /maʊθ/ n boca f; (of cave) entrada f; (of river) desembocadura f. ~**ful** n bocado m. ~**organ** n armónica f. ~**wash** n enjuague m bucal

move /muːv/ vt mover; (relocate) trasladar; (with emotion) conmover; (propose) proponer. ~ **the television** cambiar de lugar la televisión. ~ **house** mudarse de casa. ● vi moverse; (be in motion) estar en movimiento; (take action) tomar medidas. ● n movimiento m; (in game) jugada f; (player's turn) turno m; (removal) mudanza f. □ ~ **away** vi alejarse. □ ~ **in** vi instalarse. ~ **in with s.o.** irse a vivir con uno. □ ~ **over** vi correrse. ~**ment** n movimiento m

movie /'muːvɪ/ n (Amer) película f. **the** ~**s** npl el cine. ~ **camera** n (Amer) tomavistas m, filmadora f (LAm)

moving /'muːvɪŋ/ adj en movimiento; (touching) conmovedor

mow /məʊ/ vt (pt mowed or mown /məʊn/) cortar (lawn); segar (hay). □ ~ **down** vt acribillar. ~**er** n (for *lawn*) cortacésped *m*

MP *abbr see* **MEMBER OF PARLIAMENT**

Mr /'mɪstə(r)/ *abbr* (*pl* **Messrs**) (= **Mister**) Sr. ~ **Coldbeck** Sr. Coldbeck

Mrs /'mɪsɪz/ *abbr* (*pl* **Mrs**) (= **Missis**) Sra. ~ **Andrews** Sra. Andrews

Ms /mɪz/ *abbr* (title of married or unmarried woman)

MSc *abbr see* **MASTER**

much /mʌtʃ/ *adj & pron* mucho, mucha. ● *adv* mucho; (*before pp*) muy. ~ **as** por mucho que. ~ **the same** más o menos lo mismo. **how** ~? ¿cuánto?. **so** ~ tanto. **too** ~ demasiado

muck /mʌk/ *n* estiércol *m*; (*fam, dirt*) mugre *f*. □ ~ **about** *vi* 🔲 tontear

mud /mʌd/ *n* barro *m*, lodo *m*

muddle /'mʌdl/ *vt* embrollar. ● *n* desorden *m*; (*mix-up*) lío *m*. □ ~ **through** *vi* salir del paso

muddy *adj* lodoso; (hands etc) cubierto de lodo. ~**guard** *n* guardabarros *m*, salpicadera *f* (*Mex*)

muffle /'mʌfl/ *vt* amortiguar (sound). ~**r** *n* (*scarf*) bufanda *f*; (*Amer, Auto*) silenciador *m*

mug /mʌg/ *n* taza *f* (alta y sin platillo), tarro *m* (*Mex*); (*for beer*) jarra *f*; (*fam, face*) cara *f*, jeta *f* 🔲; (*fam, fool*) idiota *m & f*. ● *vt* (*pt* **mugged**) asaltar. ~**ger** *n* asaltante *m & f*. ~**ging** *n* asalto *m*

muggy /'mʌgɪ/ *adj* bochornoso

mule /mjuːl/ *n* mula *f*

mull /mʌl/ (*Amer*), ~ **over** *vt* reflexionar sobre

multi|coloured /mʌltɪ'kʌləd/ *adj* multicolor. ~**national** /-'næʃənl/ *adj & n* multinacional (*f*)

multipl|e /'mʌltɪpl/ *adj* múltiple. ● *n* múltiplo *m*. ~**ication** /mʌltɪplɪ'keɪʃn/ *n* multiplicación *f*. ~**y** /'mʌltɪplaɪ/ *vt* multiplicar. ● *vi* (*Math*) multiplicar; (*increase*) multiplicarse

multitude /'mʌltɪtjuːd/ *n*. **a** ~ **of problems** múltiples problemas

mum /mʌm/ *n* 🔲 mamá *f* 🔲

mumble /'mʌmbl/ *vt* mascullar. ● *vi* hablar entre dientes

mummy /'mʌmɪ/ *n* (*fam, mother*) mamá *f* 🔲; (*archaeology*) momia *f*

mumps /mʌmps/ *n* paperas *fpl*

munch /mʌntʃ/ *vt/i* mascar

mundane /mʌn'deɪn/ *adj* mundano

municipal /mjuː'nɪsɪpl/ *adj* municipal

mural /'mjʊərəl/ *adj & n* mural (*f*)

murder /'mɜːdə(r)/ *n* asesinato *m*. ● *vt* asesinar. ~**er** *n* asesino *m*

murky /'mɜːkɪ/ *adj* (**-ier, -iest**) turbio

murmur /'mɜːmə(r)/ *n* murmullo *m*. ● *vt/i* murmurar

musc|le /'mʌsl/ *n* músculo *m*. ~**ular** /'mʌskjʊlə(r)/ *adj* muscular; (arm, body) musculoso

muse /mjuːz/ *vi* meditar (**on** sobre)

museum /mjuː'zɪəm/ *n* museo *m*

mush /mʌʃ/ *n* papilla *f*

mushroom /'mʌʃrʊm/ *n* champiñón *m*; (*in botany*) seta *f*. ● *vi* aparecer como hongos

mushy /'mʌʃɪ/ *adj* blando

music /'mjuːzɪk/ *n* música *f*. ~**al** *adj* musical. **be** ~ tener sentido musical. ● *n* musical *m*. ~**ian** /mjuː'zɪʃn/ *n* músico *m*

Muslim /'mʊzlɪm/ *adj & n* musulmán (*m*)

mussel /'mʌsl/ *n* mejillón *m*

must /mʌst/ *modal verb* deber, tener que; (*expressing supposition*) deber (de). **he** ~ **be old** debe (de) ser viejo. **I** ~ **have done** it debo (de) haberlo hecho. ● *n*. **be a** ~ ser imprescindible

mustache /'mʌstæʃ/ *n* (*Amer*) bigote *m*

mustard /'mʌstəd/ *n* mostaza *f*

muster /'mʌstə(r)/ *vt* reunir

musty /'mʌstɪ/ *adj* (**-ier, -iest**) que huele a humedad

mutation /mjuː'teɪʃn/ *n* mutación *f*

mute /mjuːt/ *adj* mudo

mutilate /'mjuːtɪleɪt/ *vt* mutilar

mutiny /'mjuːtɪnɪ/ *n* motín *m*. ● *vi* amotinarse

mutter /'mʌtə(r)/ *vt/i* murmurar

mutton /'mʌtn/ *n* carne *f* de ovino

mutual /'mjuːtʃʊəl/ *adj* mutuo; (*fam, common*) común

muzzle /'mʌzl/ *n* (*snout*) hocico *m*; (*device*) bozal *m*

m

my /maɪ/ *adj* (*sing*) mi; (*pl*) mis

myself /maɪˈself/ *pron* (*reflexive*) me; (*used for emphasis*) yo mismo *m*, yo misma *f*. **I cut ~** me corté. **I made it ~** lo hice yo mismo/misma. **I was by ~** estaba solo/sola

myster|ious /mɪˈstɪərɪəs/ *adj* misterioso. **~y** /ˈmɪstərɪ/ *n* misterio *m*

mystical /ˈmɪstɪkl/ *adj* místico

mystify /ˈmɪstɪfaɪ/ *vt* dejar perplejo

mystique /mɪˈstiːk/ *n* mística *f*

myth /mɪθ/ *n* mito *m*. **~ical** *adj* mítico. **~ology** /mɪˈθɒlədʒɪ/ *n* mitología *f*

Nn

N *abbr* (= **north**) N

nab /næb/ *vt* (*pt* **nabbed**) (*sl, arrest*) pescar; (*snatch*) agarrar

nag /næg/ *vt* (*pt* **nagged**) fastidiar; (*scold*) estarle encima a. ● *vi* criticar

nail /neɪl/ *n* clavo *m*; (*of finger, toe*) uña *f*. **~ polish** esmalte *m* para las uñas. ● *vt*. **~ (down)** clavar

naive /naɪˈiːv/ *adj* ingenuo

naked /ˈneɪkɪd/ *adj* desnudo. **to the ~ eye** a simple vista

name /neɪm/ *n* nombre *m*; (*of book, film*) título *m*; (*fig*) fama *f*. **my ~ is Chris** me llamo Chris. **good ~** buena reputación. ● *vt* ponerle nombre a; (*appoint*) nombrar. **a man ~d Jones** un hombre llamado Jones. **she was ~d after** *or* (*Amer*) **for her grandmother** le pusieron el nombre de su abuela. **~less** *adj* anónimo. **~ly** *adv* a saber. **~sake** *n* (*person*) tocayo *m*

nanny /ˈnænɪ/ *n* niñera *f*

nap /næp/ *n* (*sleep*) sueñecito *m*; (*after lunch*) siesta *f*. **have a ~** echarse un sueño

napkin /ˈnæpkɪn/ *n* servilleta *f*

nappy /ˈnæpɪ/ *n* pañal *m*

narcotic /nɑːˈkɒtɪk/ *adj & n* narcótico (*m*)

narrat|e /nəˈreɪt/ *vt* narrar. **~ive** /ˈnærətɪv/ *n* narración *f*. **~or** /nəˈreɪtə(r)/ *n* narrador *m*

narrow /ˈnærəʊ/ *adj* (**-er, -est**) estrecho, angosto (*LAm*). **have a ~ escape** salvarse de milagro. ● *vt* estrechar; (*limit*) limitar. ● *vi* estrecharse. **~ly** *adv* (*just*) por poco. **~-minded** /-ˈmaɪndɪd/ *adj* de miras estrechas

nasal /ˈneɪzl/ *adj* nasal; (voice) gangoso

nasty /ˈnɑːstɪ/ *adj* (**-ier, -iest**) desagradable; (*spiteful*) malo (**to** con); (taste, smell) asqueroso; (cut) feo

nation /ˈneɪʃn/ *n* nación *f*

national /ˈnæʃənl/ *adj* nacional. ● *n* ciudadano *m*. **~ anthem** *n* himno *m* nacional. **~ism** *n* nacionalismo *m*. **~ity** /næʃəˈnælɪtɪ/ *n* nacionalidad *f*. **~ize** *vt* nacionalizar. **~ly** *adv* a escala nacional

National Trust Fundación británica cuyo objetivo es la conservación de lugares de interés histórico o de belleza natural. Se financia mediante legados y subvenciones privadas. Es la mayor propietaria de tierras de Gran Bretaña. En Escocia, es independiente y recibe el nombre de *National Trust for Scotland*.

nationwide /ˈneɪʃnwaɪd/ *adj & adv* a escala nacional

native /ˈneɪtɪv/ *n* natural *m & f*. **be a ~ of** ser natural de. ● *adj* nativo; (country, town) natal; (language) materno; (plant, animal) autóctono. **N~ American** indio *m* americano

nativity /nəˈtɪvətɪ/ *n*. **the N~** la Natividad *f*

NATO /ˈneɪtəʊ/ *abbr* (= **North Atlantic Treaty Organization**) OTAN *f*

natter /ˈnætə(r)/ 🔲 *vi* charlar. ● *n* charla *f*

natural /ˈnætʃərəl/ *adj* natural. **~ history** *n* historia *f* natural. **~ist** *n* naturalista *m & f*. **~ized** *adj* (citizen) naturalizado. **~ly** *adv* (*of course*) naturalmente; (*by nature*) por naturaleza

nature /ˈneɪtʃə(r)/ *n* naturaleza *f*; (*of person*) carácter *m*; (*of things*) naturaleza *f*

naught /nɔːt/ *n* cero *m*

naughty /'nɔːtɪ/ adj (-ier, -iest) malo, travieso

nause|a /'nɔːzɪə/ n náuseas fpl. ~ous /-ɪəs/ adj nauseabundo

nautical /'nɔːtɪkl/ adj náutico. ~ mile n milla f marina

naval /'neɪvl/ adj naval; (officer) de marina

nave /neɪv/ n nave f

navel /'neɪvl/ n ombligo m

naviga|ble /'nævɪɡəbl/ adj navegable. ~te /'nævɪɡeɪt/ vt navegar por (sea etc); gobernar (ship). ● vi navegar. ~tion /-'ɡeɪʃn/ n navegación f. ~tor n oficial m & f de derrota

navy /'neɪvɪ/ n marina f de guerra. ~ (blue) a & n azul (m) marino

NE abbr (= **north-east**) NE

near /nɪə(r)/ adv cerca. draw ~ acercarse. ● prep. ~ (to) cerca de. go ~ (to) sth acercarse a algo. ● adj cercano. ~by adj cerca. ~ly adv casi. he ~ly died por poco se muere, casi se muere. not ~ly ni con mucho. ~sighted /-'saɪtɪd/ adj miope, corto de vista

neat /niːt/ adj (-er, -est) (person) pulcro; (room etc) bien arreglado; (ingenious) hábil; (whisky, gin) solo; ; (Amer fam, great) fantástico 🆘. ~ly adv pulcramente; (organized) cuidadosamente

necessar|ily /nɒsə'serɪlɪ/ adv necesariamente. ~y /'nesəserɪ/ adj necesario

necessit|ate /nə'sesɪteɪt/ vt exigir. ~y /nɪ'sesətɪ/ n necesidad f. the bare ~ies lo indispensable

neck /nek/ n (of person, bottle, dress) cuello m; (of animal) pescuezo m. ~ and ~ a la par, parejos (LAm). ~lace /'nekləs/ n collar m. ~line n escote m

nectar /'nektə(r)/ n néctar m

nectarine /'nektərɪn/ n nectarina f

née /neɪ/ adj de soltera

need /niːd/ n necesidad f (for de). ● vt necesitar; (demand) exigir. you ~ not speak no tienes que hablar

needle /'niːdl/ n aguja f. ● vt (fam, annoy) pinchar

needless /'niːdlɪs/ adj innecesario

needlework /'niːdlwɜːk/ n labores fpl de aguja; (embroidery) bordado m

needy /'niːdɪ/ adj (-ier, -iest) necesitado

negative /'neɡətɪv/ adj negativo. ● n (of photograph) negativo m; (no) negativa f

neglect /nɪ'ɡlekt/ vt descuidar (house); desatender (children); no cumplir con (duty). ● n negligencia f. (state of) ~ abandono m. ~ful adj negligente

neglig|ence /'neɡlɪdʒəns/ n negligencia f, descuido m. ~ent adj negligente. ~ible /'neɡlɪdʒəbl/ adj insignificante

negotia|ble /nɪ'ɡəʊʃəbl/ adj negociable. ~te /nɪ'ɡəʊʃɪeɪt/ vt/i negociar. ~tion /-'eɪʃn/ n negociación f. ~tor n negociador m

neigh /neɪ/ vi relinchar

neighbour /'neɪbə(r)/ n vecino m. ~hood n vecindad f, barrio m. in the ~hood of alrededor de. ~ing adj vecino

neither /'naɪðə(r)/ adj. ~ book ninguno de los libros. ● pron ninguno, -na. ● conj. neither...nor ni...ni. ~ do I yo tampoco

neon /'niːɒn/ n neón m. ● adj (lamp etc) de neón

nephew /'nevjuː/ n sobrino m

Neptune /'neptjuːn/ n Neptuno m

nerv|e /nɜːv/ n nervio m; (courage) valor m; (calm) sangre f fría; (fam, impudence) descaro m. ~es npl (before exams etc) nervios mpl. get on s.o.'s ~es ponerle los nervios de punta a uno. ~e-racking adj exasperante. ~ous /'nɜːvəs/ adj nervioso. be/feel ~ous estar nervioso. ~ousness n nerviosismo m. ~y /'nɜːvɪ/ adj nervioso; (Amer fam) descarado

nest /nest/ n nido m. ● vi anidar

nestle /'nesl/ vi acurrucarse

net /net/ n red f. the N~ (Comp) la Red. ● vt (pt netted) pescar (con red) (fish). ● adj neto. ~ball n especie de baloncesto

Netherlands /'neðələndz/ npl. the ~ los Países Bajos

netting /'netɪŋ/ n redes fpl. wire ~ tela f metálica

nettle /'netl/ n ortiga f

network /'netwɜ:k/ n red f; (TV) cadena f

neuro|sis /njʊə'rəʊsɪs/ n (pl -oses /-si:z/) neurosis f. **~tic** /-'rɒtɪk/ adj & n neurótico (m)

neuter /'nju:tə(r)/ adj & n neutro (m). ● vt castrar (animals)

neutral /'nju:trəl/ adj neutral; (colour) neutro; (Elec) neutro. **~ (gear)** (Auto) punto m muerto. **~ize** vt neutralizar

neutron /'nju:trɒn/ n neutrón m

never /nevə(r)/ adv nunca; (more emphatic) jamás; (fam, not) no. **~ again** nunca más. **he ~ smiles** no sonríe nunca, nunca sonríe. **I ~ saw him** ⊞ no lo vi. **~-ending** adj interminable. **~theless** /-ðə'les/ adv sin embargo, no obstante

new /nju:/ adj (-er, -est) nuevo. **~born** adj recién nacido. **~comer** n recién llegado m. **~fangled** /-'fæŋgld/ adj (pej) moderno. **~ly** adv recién. **~ly-weds** npl recién casados mpl

news /nju:z/ n. **a piece of ~** una noticia. **good/bad ~** buenas/malas noticias. **the ~** (TV, Radio) las noticias. **~agent** n vendedor m de periódicos. **~caster** n locutor m. **~dealer** n (Amer) see **~AGENT**. **~flash** n información f de última hora. **~letter** n boletín m, informativo m. **~paper** n periódico m, diario m. **~reader** n locutor m

newt /nju:t/ n tritón m

New Year /nju:'jɪə(r)/ n Año m Nuevo. **N~'s Day** n día m de Año Nuevo. **N~'s Eve** n noche f vieja, noche f de fin de Año

New Zealand /nju:'zi:lənd/ n Nueva Zeland(i)a f

next /nekst/ adj próximo; (week, month etc) que viene, próximo; (adjoining) vecino; (following) siguiente. ● adv luego, después. **~ to** al lado de. **when you see me ~** la próxima vez que me veas. **~ to nothing** casi nada. **~ door** al lado (**to** de). **~-door** adj de al lado. **~ of kin** n familiar(es) m(pl) más cercano(s)

nib /nɪb/ n plumilla f

nibble /'nɪbl/ vt/i mordisquear. ● n mordisco m

Nicaragua /nɪkə'ræɡjʊə/ n Nicaragua f. **~n** adj & n nicaragüense (m & f)

nice /naɪs/ adj (-er, -est) agradable; (likeable) simpático; (kind) amable; (weather, food) bueno. **we had a ~ time** lo pasamos bien. **~ly** adv (kindly) amablemente; (politely) con buenos modales

niche /nɪtʃ, ni:ʃ/ n nicho m

nick /nɪk/ n corte m pequeño. **in the ~ of time** justo a tiempo. ● vt (sl, steal) afanar ⊠

nickel /'nɪkl/ n (metal) níquel m; (Amer) moneda f de cinco centavos

nickname /'nɪkneɪm/ n apodo m. ● vt apodar

nicotine /'nɪkəti:n/ n nicotina f

niece /ni:s/ n sobrina f

niggling /'nɪɡlɪŋ/ adj (doubt) constante

night /naɪt/ n noche f; (evening) tarde f. **at ~** por la noche, de noche. **good ~** ¡buenas noches! ● adj nocturno, de noche. **~cap** n (drink) bebida f (tomada antes de acostarse). **~club** n club m nocturno. **~dress** n camisón m. **~fall** n anochecer m. **~gown**, **~ie** /'naɪtɪ/ ⊞ n camisón m. **~life** n vida f nocturna. **~ly** adj de todas las noches. **~mare** n pesadilla f. **~ school** n escuela f nocturna. **~-time** n noche f. **~watchman** n sereno m

nil /nɪl/ n nada f; (Sport) cero m

nimble /'nɪmbl/ adj (-er, -est) ágil

nine /naɪn/ adj & n nueve (m). **~teen** /naɪn'ti:n/ adj & n diecinueve (m). **~teenth** adj decimonoveno. ● n diecinueveavo m. **~tieth** /'naɪntɪəθ/ adj nonagésimo. ● n noventavo m. **~ty** adj & n noventa (m)

ninth /'naɪnθ/ adj & n noveno (m)

nip /nɪp/ vt (pt nipped) (pinch) pellizcar; (bite) mordisquear. ● vi (fam, rush) correr

nipple /'nɪpl/ n (of woman) pezón m; (of man) tetilla f; (of baby's bottle) tetina f, chupón m (Mex)

nippy /'nɪpɪ/ adj (-ier, -iest) (fam, chilly) fresquito

nitrogen /'naɪtrədʒən/ n nitrógeno m

no /nəʊ/ adj ninguno, (before masculine singular noun) ningún. **I have ~ money** no tengo dinero. **there's ~**

food left no queda nada de comida. **it has ~ windows** no tiene ventanas. **I'm ~ expert** no soy ningún experto. **~ smoking** prohibido fumar. **~ way!** [!] ¡ni hablar! ● *adv & int* no. ● *n* (*pl* **noes**) no *m*

noble /'nəʊbl/ *adj* (**-er, -est**) noble. **~man** /-mən/ *n* noble *m*

nobody /'nəʊbədɪ/ *pron* nadie. **there's ~ there** no hay nadie

nocturnal /nɒk'tɜːnl/ *adj* nocturno

nod /nɒd/ *vt* (*pt* **nodded**). **~ one's head** asentir con la cabeza. ● *vi* (*in agreement*) asentir con la cabeza; (*in greeting*) saludar con la cabeza. □ **~ off** *vi* dormirse

nois|e /nɔɪz/ *n* ruido *m*. **~ily** *adv* ruidosamente. **~y** *adj* (**ier, iest**) ruidoso. **it's too ~y here** hay demasiado ruido aquí

nomad /'nəʊmæd/ *n* nómada *m & f*. **~ic** /-'mædɪk/ *adj* nómada

no man's land *n* tierra *f* de nadie

nominat|e /'nɒmɪneɪt/ *vt* (*put forward*) proponer; postular (*LAm*); (*appoint*) nombrar. **~ion** /-'neɪʃn/ *n* nombramiento *m*; (*Amer, Pol*) proclamación *f*

non-... /nɒn/ *pref* no ...

nonchalant /'nɒnʃələnt/ *adj* despreocupado

non-committal /nɒnkə'mɪtl/ *adj* evasivo

nondescript /'nɒndɪskrɪpt/ *adj* anodino

none /nʌn/ *pron* ninguno, ninguna. **there were ~ left** no quedaba ninguno/ninguna. **~ of us** ninguno de nosotros. ● *adv* no, de ninguna manera. **he is ~ the happier** no está más contento

nonentity /nɒ'nentətɪ/ *n* persona *f* insignificante

non-existent /nɒnɪg'zɪstənt/ *adj* inexistente

nonplussed /nɒn'plʌst/ *adj* perplejo

nonsens|e /'nɒnsns/ *n* tonterías *fpl*, disparates *mpl*. **~ical** /-'sensɪkl/ *adj* disparatado

non-smoker /nɒn'sməʊkə(r)/ *n* no fumador *m*. **I'm a ~** no fumo

non-stop /nɒn'stɒp/ *adj* (train) directo; (flight) sin escalas. ● *adv* sin

parar; (by train) directamente; (by air) sin escalas

noodles /'nuːdlz/ *npl* fideos *mpl*

nook /nʊk/ *n* rincón *m*

noon /nuːn/ *n* mediodía *m*

no-one /'nəʊwʌn/ *pron* nadie

noose /nuːs/ *n* soga *f*

nor /nɔː(r)/ *conj* ni, tampoco. **neither blue ~ red** ni azul ni rojo. **he doesn't play the piano, ~ do I** no sabe tocar el piano, ni yo tampoco

norm /nɔːm/ *n* norma *f*

normal /'nɔːml/ *adj* normal. **~cy** (*Amer*) normalidad *f*. **~ity** /-'mælətɪ/ *n* normalidad *f*. **~ly** *adv* normalmente

north /nɔːθ/ *n* norte *m*. ● *adj* norte. ● *adv* hacia el norte. **N~ America** *n* América *f* del Norte, Norteamérica *f*. **N~ American** *adj & n* norteamericano (*m*). **~east** *n* nor(d)este *m*. ● *adj* nor(d)este. ● *adv* (go) hacia el nor(d)este. **it's ~east of Leeds** está al nor(d)este de Leeds. **~erly** /'nɔːðəlɪ/ *adj* (wind) del norte. **~ern** /'nɔːðən/ *adj* del norte. **~erner** *n* norteño *m*. **N~ern Ireland** *n* Irlanda *f* del Norte. **N~ Sea** *n* mar *m* del Norte. **~ward** /'nɔːθwəd/, **~wards** *adv* hacia el norte. **~west** *n* noroeste *m*. ● *adj* noroeste. ● *adv* hacia el noroeste

Norw|ay /'nɔːweɪ/ *n* Noruega *f*. **~egian** /-'wiːdʒən/ *adj & n* noruego (*m*)

nose /nəʊz/ *n* nariz *f*. **~bleed** *n* hemorragia *f* nasal. **~dive** *vi* descender en picado, descender en picada (*LAm*)

nostalgi|a /nɒ'stældʒə/ *n* nostalgia *f*. **~c** *adj* nostálgico

nostril /'nɒstrɪl/ *n* ventana *f* de la nariz *f*

nosy /'nəʊzɪ/ *adj* (**-ier, -iest**) [!] entrometido, metiche (*LAm*)

not /nɒt/

Cuando **not** va precedido del verbo auxiliar **do** or **have** o de un verbo modal como **should** etc, se suele emplear la forma contraída **don't, haven't, shouldn't** etc

adverb

····➤ no. **I don't know** no sé. **~ yet**

todavía no. ~ **me** yo no
····▸ (*replacing a clause*) **I suppose**
~ supongo que no. **of course** ~
por supuesto que no. **are you
going to help me or** ~? ¿me
vas a ayudar o no?
····▸ (*emphatic*) ni. ~ **a penny
more!** ¡ni un penique más!
····▸ (*in phrases*) **certainly** ~ de
ninguna manera . ~ **you again!**
¡tú otra vez!

notabl|e /ˈnəʊtəbl/ *adj* notable;
(*author*) distinguido. ~**y** /ˈnəʊtəblɪ/
adv notablemente; (*in particular*) particularmente

notch /nɒtʃ/ *n* muesca *f*. □ ~ **up** *vt*
apuntarse

note /nəʊt/ *n* (*incl Mus*) nota *f*; (*banknote*) billete *m*. **take** ~**s** tomar apuntes. ● *vt* (*notice*) observar; (*record*)
anotar. □ ~ **down** *vt* apuntar.
~**book** *n* cuaderno *m*. ~**d** *adj* célebre. ~**paper** *n* papel *m* de carta(s)

nothing /ˈnʌθɪŋ/ *pron* nada. **he eats** ~
no come nada. **for** ~ (*free*) gratis; (*in
vain*) en vano. ~ **else** nada más. ~
much happened no pasó gran cosa.
he does ~ **but complain** no hace
más que quejarse

notice /ˈnəʊtɪs/ *n* (*sign*) letrero *m*;
(*item of information*) anuncio *m*; (*noti-
fication*) aviso *m*; (*of termination of
employment*) preaviso *m*; ~ **(of dismissal)** despido *m*. **take** ~ **of** hacer
caso a (a person). ● *vt* notar. ● *vi* darse
cuenta. ~**able** *adj* perceptible. ~**ably**
adv perceptiblemente. ~**board** *n* tablón *m* de anuncios, tablero *m* de
anuncios (*LAm*)

notif|ication /nəʊtɪfɪˈkeɪʃn/ *n* notifi-
cación *f*. ~**y** /ˈnəʊtɪfaɪ/ *vt* informar;
(*in writing*) notificar. ~**y s.o. of sth**
comunicarle algo a uno

notion /ˈnəʊʃn/ *n* (*concept*) concepto
m; (*idea*) idea *f*

notorious /nəʊˈtɔːrɪəs/ *adj* notorio

notwithstanding /nɒtwɪθˈstændɪŋ/
prep a pesar de. ● *adv* no obstante

nougat /ˈnuːgɑː/ *n* turrón *m*

nought /nɔːt/ *n* cero *m*

noun /naʊn/ *n* sustantivo *m*, nombre *m*

nourish /ˈnʌrɪʃ/ *vt* alimentar. ~**ment**
n alimento *m*

novel /ˈnɒvl/ *n* novela *f*. ● *adj* original,
novedoso. ~**ist** *n* novelista *m & f*.
~**ty** *n* novedad *f*

November /nəʊˈvembə(r)/ *n* noviembre *m*

novice /ˈnɒvɪs/ *n* principiante *m & f*

now /naʊ/ *adv* ahora. ~ **and again,** ~
and then de vez en cuando. **right** ~
ahora mismo. **from** ~ **on** a partir de
ahora. ● *conj*. ~ **(that)** ahora que.
~**adays** /ˈnaʊədeɪz/ *adv* hoy (en) día

nowhere /ˈnəʊweə(r)/ *adv* por ninguna parte, por ningún lado; (*after
motion towards*) a ninguna parte, a
ningún lado

nozzle /ˈnɒzl/ *n* (*on hose*) boca *f*; (*on
fire extinguisher*) boquilla *f*

nuance /ˈnjuːɑːns/ *n* matiz *m*

nuclear /ˈnjuːklɪə(r)/ *adj* nuclear

nucleus /ˈnjuːklɪəs/ *n* (*pl* **-lei** /-lɪaɪ/)
núcleo *m*

nude /njuːd/ *adj & n* desnudo (*m*). **in
the** ~ desnudo

nudge /nʌdʒ/ *vt* codear (ligeramente).
● *n* golpe *m* (suave) con el codo

nudi|st /ˈnjuːdɪst/ *n* nudista *m & f*. ~**ty**
/ˈnjuːdətɪ/ *n* desnudez *f*

nuisance /ˈnjuːsns/ *n* (*thing, event*)
molestia *f*, fastidio *m*; (*person*) pesado *m*

null /nʌl/ *adj* nulo

numb /nʌm/ *adj* entumecido. **go** ~
entumecerse ● *vt* entumecer

number /ˈnʌmbə(r)/ *n* número *m*;
(*telephone number*) número *m* de teléfono. **a** ~ **of people** varias personas.
● *vt* numerar; (*count, include*) contar.
~**plate** *n* matrícula *f*, placa *f* (*LAm*)

numer|al /ˈnjuːmərəl/ *n* número *m*.
~**ical** /njuːˈmerɪkl/ *adj* numérico.
~**ous** /ˈnjuːmərəs/ *adj* numeroso

nun /nʌn/ *n* monja *f*

nurse /nɜːs/ *n* enfermero *m*, enfermera
f; (*nanny*) niñera *f*. ● *vt* cuidar; abrigar
(hope etc)

nursery /ˈnɜːsərɪ/ *n* (*for plants*) vivero
m; (*day* ~) guardería *f*. ~ **rhyme** *n*
canción *f* infantil. ~ **school** *n* jardín *m*
de infancia, jardín *m* infantil (*LAm*)

n

nursing home /'nɜːsɪŋ/ n (for older people) residencia f de ancianos (con mayor nivel de asistencia médica)

nut /nʌt/ n fruto m seco (nuez, almendra, avellana etc); (Tec) tuerca f. ~**case** n 🄸 chiflado m. ~**crackers** npl cascanueces m. ~**meg** /-meg/ n nuez f moscada

nutri|ent /'njuːtrɪənt/ n nutriente m. ~**tion** /njuː'trɪʃn/ n nutrición f. ~**tious** /njuː'trɪʃəs/ adj nutritivo

nuts /nʌts/ adj (fam, crazy) chiflado

nutshell /'nʌtʃel/ n cáscara f de nuez. **in a** ~ en pocas palabras

NW abbr (= **north-west**) NO

nylon /'naɪlɒn/ n nylon m

....

Oo

....

oaf /əʊf/ n zoquete m

oak /əʊk/ n roble m

OAP /əʊer'piː/ abbr (= **old-age pensioner**) n pensionista m & f, pensionado m

oar /ɔː(r)/ n remo m

oasis /əʊ'eɪsɪs/ n (pl oases /-siːz/) oasis m

oath /əʊθ/ n juramento m

oat|meal /'əʊtmiːl/ n harina f de avena; (Amer, flakes) avena f (en copos). ~**s** /əʊts/ npl avena f

obedien|ce /ə'biːdɪəns/ n obediencia f. ~**t** adj obediente. ~**tly** adv obedientemente

obes|e /əʊ'biːs/ adj obeso. ~**ity** n obesidad f

obey /əʊ'beɪ/ vt/i obedecer

obituary /ə'bɪtʃʊərɪ/ n nota f necrológica, obituario m

object /'ɒbdʒɪkt/ n objeto m; (aim) objetivo m. ● /əb'dʒekt/ vi oponerse (**to** a). ~**ion** /əb'dʒekʃn/ n objeción f. ~**ionable** adj censurable; (unpleasant) desagradable. ~**ive** /əb'dʒektɪv/ adj & n objetivo (m)

oblig|ation /ɒblɪ'geɪʃn/ n obligación f. **be under an** ~**ation to** estar obligado a. ~**atory** /ə'blɪgətrɪ/ adj obli-

gatorio. ~**e** /ə'blaɪdʒ/ vt obligar. **I'd be much** ~**ed if you could help me** le quedaría muy agradecido si pudiera ayudarme. ● vi hacer un favor. ~**ing** adj atento

oblique /ə'bliːk/ adj oblicuo

obliterate /ə'blɪtəreɪt/ vt arrasar; (erase) borrar

oblivio|n /ə'blɪvɪən/ n olvido m. ~**us** /-vɪəs/ adj (unaware) inconsciente (**to, of** de)

oblong /'ɒblɒŋ/ adj oblongo. ● n rectángulo m

obnoxious /əb'nɒkʃəs/ adj odioso

oboe /'əʊbəʊ/ n oboe m

obscen|e /əb'siːn/ adj obsceno. ~**ity** /əb'senətɪ/ n obscenidad f

obscur|e /əb'skjʊə(r)/ adj oscuro. ● vt ocultar; impedir ver claramente (issue). ~**ity** n oscuridad f

obsequious /əb'siːkwɪəs/ adj servil

observ|ant /əb'zɜːvənt/ adj observador. ~**ation** /ɒbzə'veɪʃn/ n observación f. ~**atory** /əb'zɜːvətrɪ/ n observatorio m. ~**e** /əb'zɜːv/ vt observar. ~**er** n observador m

obsess /əb'ses/ vt obsesionar. ~**ed** /əb'sest/ adj obsesionado. ~**ion** /-ʃn/ n obsesión f. ~**ive** adj obsesivo

obsolete /'ɒbsəliːt/ adj obsoleto

obstacle /'ɒbstəkl/ n obstáculo m

obstina|cy /'ɒbstɪnəsɪ/ n obstinación f. ~**te** /-ət/ adj obstinado. ~**tely** adv obstinadamente

obstruct /əb'strʌkt/ vt obstruir; bloquear (traffic). ~**ion** /-ʃn/ n obstrucción f

obtain /əb'teɪn/ vt conseguir, obtener. ~**able** adj asequible

obtrusive /əb'truːsɪv/ adj (presence) demasiado prominente; (noise) molesto

obtuse /əb'tjuːs/ adj obtuso

obvious /'ɒbvɪəs/ adj obvio. ~**ly** adv obviamente

occasion /ə'keɪʒn/ n ocasión f. ~**al** adj esporádico. ~**ally** adv de vez en cuando

occult /ɒ'kʌlt/ adj oculto

occup|ant /'ɒkjʊpənt/ n ocupante m & f. ~**ation** /ɒkjʊ'peɪʃn/ n ocupación f. ~**ier** /'ɒkjʊpaɪə(r)/ n ocupante m & f.

n

o

~y /'ɒkjʊpaɪ/ vt ocupar. **keep o.s. ~ied** entretenerse

occur /ə'kɜː(r)/ vi (pt **occurred**) tener lugar, ocurrir; (change) producirse; (exist) encontrarse. **it ~red to me that** se me ocurrió que. **~rence** /ə'kʌrəns/ n (incidence) incidencia f. **it is a rare ~rence** no es algo frecuente

ocean /'əʊʃn/ n océano m

o'clock /ə'klɒk/ adv. **it is 7 ~** son las siete. **it's one ~** es la una

octagon /'ɒktəgən/ n octágono m

octave /'ɒktɪv/ n octava f

October /ɒk'təʊbə(r)/ n octubre m

octopus /'ɒktəpəs/ n (pl **-puses**) pulpo m

odd /ɒd/ adj (**-er, -est**) extraño, raro; (number) impar; (one of pair) desparejado. **smoke the ~ cigarette** fumarse algún que otro cigarillo. **fifty-~** unos cincuenta, cincuenta y pico. **the ~ one out** la excepción. **~ity** n (thing) rareza f; (person) bicho m raro. **~ly** adv de una manera extraña. **~ly enough** por extraño que parezca. **~ment** n retazo m. **~s** npl probabilidades fpl; (in betting) apuesta f. **be at ~s** estar en desacuerdo. **~s and ends** mpl 🔢 cosas fpl sueltas

odious /'əʊdɪəs/ adj odioso

odometer /ɒ'dɒmətə(r)/ n (Amer) cuentakilómetros m

odour /'əʊdə(r)/ n olor m

---

of /ɒv//əv/ preposition

····▶ de. **a pound of cheese** una libra de queso. **it's made of wood** es de madera. **a girl of ten** una niña de diez años

····▶ (in dates) de. **the fifth of November** el cinco de noviembre

····▶ (Amer, when telling the time) **it's ten (minutes) of five** son las cinco menos diez, son diez para las cinco (LAm)

❗ **of** is not translated in cases such as the following: **a colleague of mine** un colega mío; **there were six of us** éramos seis; **that's very kind of you** es Ud muy amable

---

off /ɒf/ prep (from) de. **he picked it up ~ the floor** lo recogió del suelo; (distant from) **just ~ the coast of Texas** a poca distancia de la costa de Tejas. **2 ft ~ the ground** a dos pies del suelo; (absent from) **I've been ~ work for a week** hace una semana que no voy a trabajar. ● adv (removed) **the lid was ~** la tapa no estaba puesta; (distant) **some way ~** a cierta distancia; (leaving) **I'm ~** me voy; (switched off) (light, TV) apagado; (water) cortado; (cancelled) (match) cancelado; (not on duty) (day) libre. ● adj. **be ~** (meat) estar malo, estar pasado; (milk) estar cortado. **~-beat** adj poco convencional. **~ chance** n. **on the ~ chance** por si acaso

---

off-licence En el Reino Unido, es una tienda que tiene licencia para vender bebidas alcohólicas y se deben consumir fuera del local. Abren cuando los bares y **pubs** están cerrados y también suelen vender bebidas no alcohólicas, tabaco, golosinas etc. A menudo alquilan vasos y copas para fiestas, etc.

---

offen|ce /ə'fens/ n (breach of law) infracción f; (criminal ~ce) delito m; (cause of outrage) atentado m; (Amer, attack) ataque m. **take ~ce** ofenderse. **~d** vt ofender. **~der** n delincuente m & f. **~sive** /-sɪv/ adj ofensivo; (disgusting) desagradable

offer /'ɒfə(r)/ vt ofrecer. **~ to do sth** ofrecerse a hacer algo. ● n oferta f. **on ~** de oferta

offhand /ɒf'hænd/ adj (brusque) brusco. **say sth in an ~ way** decir algo a la ligera. ● adv de improviso

office /'ɒfɪs/ n oficina f; (post) cargo m. **doctor's ~** (Amer) consultorio m, consulta m. **~ block** n edificio m de oficinas **~r** n oficial m & f; (police ~r) policía m & f; (as form of address) agente

offici|al /ə'fɪʃl/ adj oficial. ● n funcionario m del Estado; (of party, union) dirigente m & f. **~ally** adv oficialmente. **~ous** /ə'fɪʃəs/ adj oficioso

offing /'ɒfɪŋ/ n. **in the ~** en perspectiva

off ~-licence n tienda f de vinos y licores. **~-putting** adj (disconcerting) desconcertante; (disagreeable) desagradable. **~set** vt (pt **-set**, pres p **-setting**) compensar. **~shore** adj (breeze) que sopla desde la tierra; (drilling) offshore; (well) submarino. ● adv a un lugar de mano de obra barata. **~side** /ɒf'saɪd/ adj (Sport) fuera de juego. **~spring** n invar prole f. **~-stage** /-'steɪdʒ/ adv fuera del escenario. **~-white** adj color hueso

often /'ɒfn/ adv a menudo, con frecuencia. **how ~?** ¿con qué frecuencia? **more ~** con más frecuencia

ogle /'əʊgl/ vt comerse con los ojos

ogre /'əʊgə(r)/ n ogro m

oh /əʊ/ int ¡ah!; (expressing dismay) ¡ay!

oil /ɔɪl/ n aceite m; (petroleum) petróleo m. ● vt lubricar. **~field** n yacimiento m petrolífero. **~ painting** n pintura f al óleo; (picture) óleo m. **~ rig** n plataforma f petrolífera. **~y** adj (substance) oleaginoso; (food) aceitoso

ointment /'ɔɪntmənt/ n ungüento m

OK /əʊ'keɪ/ int ¡vale!, ¡de acuerdo!, ¡bueno! (LAm). ● adj **~, thanks** bien, gracias. **the job's ~** el trabajo no está mal

old /əʊld/ adj (~er, ~est) viejo; (not modern) antiguo; (former) antiguo; **an ~ friend** un viejo amigo. **how ~ is she?** ¿cuántos años tiene? **she is ten years ~** tiene diez años. **his ~er sister** su hermana mayor. **~ age** n vejez f. **~-fashioned** /-'fæʃənd/ adj anticuado

olive /'ɒlɪv/ n aceituna f.

Olympic /ə'lɪmpɪk/ adj olímpico. **the ~s** npl, **the ~ Games** npl los Juegos Olímpicos

omelette /'ɒmlɪt/ n tortilla f francesa, omelette m (LAm)

omen /'əʊmen/ n agüero m

omi|ssion /ə'mɪʃn/ n omisión f. **~t** /əʊ'mɪt/ vt (pt **omitted**) omitir

on /ɒn/ prep en, sobre; (about) sobre. **~ foot** a pie. **~ Monday** el lunes. **~ seeing** al ver. **I heard it ~ the radio**

lo oí por la radio. ● adv (light etc) encendido, prendido (LAm); (machine) en marcha; (tap) abierto. **~ and ~** sin cesar. **and so ~** y así sucesivamente. **have a hat ~** llevar (puesto) un sombrero. **further ~** un poco más allá. **what's ~ at the Odeon?** ¿qué dan en el Odeon? **go ~** continuar. **later ~** más tarde

once /wʌns/ adv una vez; (formerly) antes. **at ~** inmediatamente. **~ upon a time there was...** érase una vez.... **~ and for all** de una vez por todas. ● conj una vez que

one /wʌn/ adj uno, (before masculine singular noun) un. **the ~ person I trusted** la única persona en la que confiaba. ● n uno m. **~ by ~** uno a uno.. ● pron uno (m), una (f). **the blue ~** el/la azul. **this ~** éste/ésta. **~ another** el uno al otro

onerous /'ɒnərəs/ adj (task) pesado

one ~self /-'self/ pron (reflexive) se; (after prep) sí (mismo); (emphatic use) uno mismo, una misma. **by ~self** solo. **~-way** adj (street) de sentido único; (ticket) de ida, sencillo

onion /'ʌnɪən/ n cebolla f

online /ɒn'laɪn/ adj en línea

onlooker /'ɒnlʊkə(r)/ n espectador m

only /'əʊnlɪ/ adj único. **she's an ~ child** es hija única. ● adv sólo, solamente. **~ just** (barely) apenas. **I've just arrived** acabo de llegar. ● conj pero, sólo que

onset /'ɒnset/ n comienzo m; (of disease) aparición f

onshore /'ɒnʃɔː(r)/ adj (breeze) que sopla desde el mar; (oil field) en tierra

onslaught /'ɒnslɔːt/ n ataque m

onus /'əʊnəs/ n responsabilidad f

onward(s) /'ɒnwəd(z)/ adj & adv hacia adelante

ooze /uːz/ vt/i rezumar

opaque /əʊ'peɪk/ adj opaco

open /'əʊpən/ adj abierto; (question) discutible. ● n. **in the ~** al aire libre. ● vt/i abrir. **~ing** n abertura f; (beginning) principio m. **~ly** adv abiertamente. **~-minded** /-'maɪndɪd/ adj de actitud abierta

o

Open University La universidad a distancia británica, fundada en 1969. La enseñanza se imparte fundamentalmente por correspondencia, mediante materiales impresos, material enviado por internet y programas de televisión emitidos por la BBC. También hay cursos de verano a los que los alumnos deben asistir. No se exigen calificaciones académicas para su ingreso.

opera /'ɒprə/ n ópera f

operate /'ɒpəreɪt/ vt manejar, operar (Mex) (machine). ● vi funcionar; (company) operar. ~ (on) (Med) operar (a)

operatic /ɒpə'rætɪk/ adj operístico

operation /ɒpə'reɪʃn/ n operación f; (Mec) funcionamiento m; (using of machine) manejo m. he had an ~ lo operaron. in ~ en vigor. ~al adj operacional

operative /'ɒpərətɪv/ adj. be ~ estar en vigor

operator n operador m

opinion /ə'pɪnɪən/ n opinión f. in my ~ en mi opinión, a mi parecer

opponent /ə'pəʊnənt/ n adversario m; (in sport) contrincante m & f

opportun|e /'ɒpətjuːn/ adj oportuno. ~ist /ɒpə'tjuːnɪst/ n oportunista m & f. ~ity /ɒpə'tjuːnəti/ n oportunidad f

oppos|e /ə'pəʊz/ vt oponerse a. be ~ed to oponerse a, estar en contra de. ~ing adj opuesto. ~ite /'ɒpəzɪt/ adj (contrary) opuesto; (facing) de enfrente. ● n. the ~ite lo contrario. quite the ~ite al contrario. ● adv enfrente. ● prep enfrente de. ~ite number n homólogo m. ~ition /ɒpə'zɪʃn/ n oposición f; (resistance) resistencia f

oppress /ə'pres/ vt oprimir. ~ion /-ʃn/ n opresión f. ~ive adj (cruel) opresivo; (heat) sofocante

opt /ɒpt/ vi. ~ to optar por. □ ~ out vi decidir no tomar parte

optic|al /'ɒptɪkl/ adj óptico. ~ian /ɒp'tɪʃn/ n óptico m

optimis|m /'ɒptɪmɪzəm/ n optimismo m. ~t n optimista m & f. ~tic /-'mɪstɪk/ adj optimista

option /'ɒpʃn/ n opción f. ~al adj facultativo

or /ɔː(r)/ conj o; (before o- and ho-) u; (after negative) ni. ~ else si no, o bien

oral /'ɔːrəl/ adj oral. ● n 🆃 examen m oral

orange /'ɒrɪndʒ/ n naranja f; (colour) naranja m. ● adj naranja. ~ade /-'eɪd/ n naranjada f

orbit /'ɔːbɪt/ n órbita f. ● vt orbitar

orchard /'ɔːtʃəd/ n huerto m

orchestra /'ɔːkɪstrə/ n orquesta f; (Amer, in theatre) platea f. ~l /-'kestrəl/ adj orquestal. ~te /-eɪt/ vt orquestar

orchid /'ɔːkɪd/ n orquídea f

ordain /ɔː'deɪn/ vt (Relig) ordenar; (decree) decretar

ordeal /ɔː'diːl/ n dura prueba f

order /'ɔːdə(r)/ n orden m; (Com) pedido m; (command) orden f. in ~ that para que. in ~ to para. ● vt (command) ordenar, mandar; (Com) pedir; (in restaurant) pedir, ordenar (LAm); encargar (book); llamar, ordenar (LAm) (taxi). ~ly adj ordenado. ● n camillero m

ordinary /'ɔːdɪnrɪ/ adj corriente; (average) medio; (mediocre) ordinario

ore /ɔː(r)/ n mena f

organ /'ɔːgən/ n órgano m

organ|ic /ɔː'gænɪk/ adj orgánico. ~ism /'ɔːgənɪzəm/ n organismo m. ~ist /'ɔːgənɪst/ n organista m & f. ~ization /ɔːgənaɪ'zeɪʃn/ n organización f. ~ize /'ɔːgənaɪz/ vt organizar. ~izer n organizador m

orgasm /'ɔːgæzəm/ n orgasmo m

orgy /'ɔːdʒɪ/ n orgía f

Orient /'ɔːrɪənt/ n Oriente m. ~al /-'entl/ adj oriental

orientat|e /'ɔːrɪənteɪt/ vt orientar. ~ion /-'teɪʃn/ n orientación f

origin /'ɒrɪdʒɪn/ n origen m. ~al /ə'rɪdʒənl/ adj original. ~ally adv originariamente. ~ate /ə'rɪdʒɪneɪt/ vi. ~ate from provenir de

ornament /'ɔːnəmənt/ n adorno m. ~al /-'mentl/ adj de adorno

ornate /ɔː'neɪt/ adj ornamentado; (style) recargado

ornithology /ɔ:nɪˈθɒlədʒɪ/ n ornitología f

orphan /ˈɔ:fn/ n huérfano m. ● vt. be ~ed quedar huérfano. ~age /-ɪdʒ/ n orfanato m

orthodox /ˈɔ:θədɒks/ adj ortodoxo

oscillate /ˈɒsɪleɪt/ vi oscilar

ostentatious /ɒstenˈteɪʃəs/ adj ostentoso

osteopath /ˈɒstɪəpæθ/ n osteópata m & f

ostracize /ˈɒstrəsaɪz/ vt hacerle vacío a

ostrich /ˈɒstrɪtʃ/ n avestruz m

other /ˈʌðə(r)/ adj & pron otro. ~ than aparte de. the ~ one el otro. ~wise adv de lo contrario, si no

otter /ˈɒtə(r)/ n nutria f

ouch /aʊtʃ/ int ¡ay!

ought /ɔ:t/ modal verb. I ~ to see it debería verlo. he ~ to have done it debería haberlo hecho

ounce /aʊns/ n onza f (= 28.35 gr.)

our /ˈaʊə(r)/ adj (sing) nuestro, nuestra, (pl) nuestros, nuestras. ~s /ˈaʊəz/ poss pron (sing) nuestro, nuestra; (pl) nuestros, nuestras. ~s is red el nuestro es rojo. a friend of ~s un amigo nuestro. ~selves /-ˈselvz/ pron (reflexive) nos; (used for emphasis and after prepositions) nosotros mismos, nosotras mismas. we behaved ~selves nos portamos bien. we did it ~selves lo hicimos nosotros mismos/ nosotras mismas

oust /aʊst/ vt desbancar; derrocar (government)

out /aʊt/ adv (outside) fuera, afuera (LAm). (not lighted, not on) apagado; (in blossom) en flor; (in error) equivocado. he's ~ (not at home) no está; be ~ to estar resuelto a. ~ of prep (from inside) de; (outside) fuera, afuera (LAm). five ~ of six cinco de cada seis. made ~ of hecho de. we're ~ of bread nos hemos quedado sin pan. ~break n (of war) estallido m; (of disease) brote m. ~burst n arrebato m. ~cast n paria m & f. ~come n resultado m. ~cry n protesta f. ~dated /-ˈdeɪtɪd/ adj anticuado. ~do /-ˈdu:/ vt (pt -did, pp -done) superar. ~door adj (clothes) de calle; (pool) descubierto. ~doors /-ˈdɔ:z/ adv al aire libre

outer /ˈaʊtə(r)/ adj exterior

out ~fit n equipo m; (clothes) conjunto m. ~going adj (minister etc) saliente; (sociable) abierto. ~goings npl gastos mpl. ~grow /-ˈgrəʊ/ vt (pt -grew, pp -grown) crecer más que (person). he's ~grown his new shoes le han quedado pequeños los zapatos nuevos. ~ing n excursión f

outlandish /aʊtˈlændɪʃ/ adj extravagante

out ~law n forajido m. ● vt proscribir. ~lay n gastos mpl. ~let n salida f; (Com) punto m de venta; (Amer, Elec) toma f de corriente. ~line n contorno m; (summary) resumen m; (plan of project) esquema m.● vt trazar; (summarize) esbozar. ~live /-ˈlɪv/ vt sobrevivir a. ~look n perspectiva fpl; (attitude) punto m de vista. ~lying adj alejado. ~number /-ˈnʌmbə(r)/ vt superar en número. ~-of-date adj (ideas) desfasado; (clothes) pasado de moda. ~patient n paciente m externo. ~post n avanzada f. ~put n producción f; (of machine, worker) rendimiento m. ~right adv completamente; (frankly) abiertamente; (kill) en el acto. ● adj completo; (refusal) rotundo. ~set n principio m. ~side adj & n exterior (m). at the ~ como máximo. ● /-ˈsaɪd/ adv fuera, afuera (LAm). ● prep fuera de. ~size adj de talla gigante. ~skirts npl afueras fpl. ~spoken /-ˈspəʊkn/ adj directo, franco. ~standing /-ˈstændɪŋ/ adj excepcional; (debt) pendiente. ~stretched /aʊtˈstretʃt/ adj extendido. ~strip /-ˈstrɪp/ vt (pt -stripped) (run faster than) tomarle la delantera a; (exceed) sobrepasar. ~ward /-wəd/ adj (appearance) exterior; (sign) externo; (journey) de ida. ~wardly adv por fuera, exteriormente. ~(s) adv hacia afuera. ~weigh /-ˈweɪ/ vt ser mayor que. ~wit /-ˈwɪt/ vt (pt -witted) burlar

oval /ˈəʊvl/ adj ovalado, oval. ● n óvalo m

Oval Office El Despacho Oval es el despacho oficial del Presidente de los Estados Unidos, ubicado en el ala oeste de la Casa Blanca. La forma oval fue determinada por George Washington, lo que le permitiría tener contacto visual con todos durante las reuniones. Originariamente, quería que todas las habitaciones de la Casa Blanca fueran ovales, pero pronto comprendió que este diseño era poco práctico.

ovary /'əʊvərɪ/ n ovario m

ovation /əʊ'veɪʃn/ n ovación f

oven /'ʌvn/ n horno m

over /'əʊvə(r)/ prep por encima de; (across) al otro lado de; (during) durante; (more than) más de. ~ **and above** por encima de. ● adv por encima; (ended) terminado; (more) más; (in excess) de sobra. ~ **again** otra vez. ~ **and** ~ una y otra vez. ~ **here** por aquí. ~ **there** por allí. **all** ~ (finished) acabado; (everywhere) por todas partes

over... /'əʊvə(r)/ pref excesivamente, demasiado

over ~**all** /-'ɔːl/ adj global; (length, cost) total. ● adv en conjunto. ● /'əʊvərɔːl/ n, ~**alls** npl mono m, overol m (LAm); (Amer, dungarees) peto m, overol m. ~**awe** /-'ɔː/ vt intimidar. ~**balance** /-'bæləns/ vi perder el equilibrio. ~**bearing** /-'beərɪŋ/ adj dominante. ~**board** adv (throw) por la borda. ~**cast** /-'kɑːst/ adj (day) nublado; (sky) cubierto. ~**charge** /-'tʃɑːdʒ/ vt cobrarle de más a. ~**coat** n abrigo m. ~**come** /-'kʌm/ vt (pt -came, pp -come) superar, vencer. ~**crowded** /-'kraʊdɪd/ adj abarrotado (de gente). ~**do** /-'duː/ vt (pt -did, pp -done) exagerar; (Culin) recocer. ~**dose** n sobredosis f. ~**draft** n descubierto m. ~**draw** /-'drɔː/ vt (pt -drew, pp -drawn) girar en descubierto. **be** ~**drawn** tener un descubierto. ~**due** /-'djuː/ adj. **the book is a month** ~**due** el plazo de devolución del libro venció hace un mes. ~**esti**

mate /-'estɪmeɪt/ vt sobreestimar. ~**flow** /-'fləʊ/ vi desbordarse. ● n /-fləʊ/ (excess) exceso m; (outlet) rebosadero m. ~**flow car park** n estacionamento m extra (LAm), aparcamiento m extra (Esp). ~**grown** /-'grəʊn/ adj demasiado grande; (garden) lleno de maleza. ~**haul** /-'hɔːl/ vt revisar. ● /-hɔːl/ n revisión f. ~**head** /-'hed/ adv por encima. ● /-hed/ adj de arriba. ~**heads** /-hedz/ npl, ~**head** n (Amer) gastos mpl indirectos. ~**hear** /-'hɪə(r)/ vt (pt -heard) oír por casualidad. ~**joyed** /-'dʒɔɪd/ adj encantado. ~**land** a/adv por tierra. ~**lap** /-'læp/ vi (pt -lapped) traslaparse. ~**leaf** /-'liːf/ adv al dorso. ~**load** /-'ləʊd/ vt sobrecargar. ~**look** /-'lʊk/ vt (room) dar a; (not notice) pasar por alto; (disregard) disculpar. ~**night** /-'naɪt/ adv durante la noche. **stay** ~**night** quedarse a pasar la noche. ● adj (journey) de noche; (stay) de una noche. ~**pass** n paso m elevado, paso m a desnivel (Mex). ~**pay** /-'peɪ/ vt (pt -paid) pagar demasiado. ~**power** /-'paʊə(r)/ vt dominar (opponent); (emotion) abrumar. ~**powering** /-'paʊərɪŋ/ adj (smell) muy fuerte; (desire) irresistible. ~**priced** /-'praɪst/ adj demasiado caro. ~**rated** /-'reɪtɪd/ adj sobrevalorado. ~**react** /-rɪ'ækt/ vi reaccionar en forma exagerada. ~**ride** /-'raɪd/ vt (pt -rode, pp -ridden) invalidar. ~**riding** /-'raɪdɪŋ/ adj dominante. ~**rule** /-'ruːl/ vt anular; rechazar (objection). ~**run** /-'rʌn/ vt (pt -ran, pp -run, pres p -running) invadir; exceder (limit). ~**seas** /-'siːz/ adj (trade) exterior; (investments) en el exterior; (visitor) extranjero. ● adv al extranjero. ~**see** /-'siː/ vt (pt -saw, pp -seen) supervisar. ~**seer** /-sɪə(r)/ n capataz m & f, supervisor m. ~**shadow** /-'ʃædəʊ/ vt eclipsar. ~**shoot** /-'ʃuːt/ vt (pt -shot) excederse. ~**sight** n descuido m. ~**sleep** /-'sliːp/ vi (pt -slept) quedarse dormido. ~**step** /-'step/ vt (pt -stepped) sobrepasar. ~**step the mark** pasarse de la raya

overt /'əʊvɜːt/ adj manifiesto

over: ~**take** /-'teɪk/ vt/i (pt -**took**, pp -**taken**) sobrepasar; (Auto) adelantar, rebasar (Mex). ~**throw** /-'θrəʊ/ vt (pt -**threw**, pp -**thrown**) derrocar. ~**time** n horas fpl extra

overture /'əʊvətjʊə(r)/ n obertura f

over: ~**turn** /-'tɜːn/ vt darle la vuelta a. ● vi volcar. ~**weight** /-'weɪt/ adj demasiado gordo. **be** ~**weight** pesar demasiado. ~**whelm** /-'welm/ vt aplastar; (with emotion) abrumar. ~**whelming** adj aplastante; (fig) abrumador. ~**work** /-'wɜːk/ vt hacer trabajar demasiado. ● vi trabajar demasiado. ● n agotamiento m

ow|e /əʊ/ vt deber. ~**ing to** debido a

owl /aʊl/ n búho m

own /əʊn/ adj propio. **my** ~ **house** mi propia casa. ● pron. **it's my** ~ es mío (propio)/mía (propia). **on one's** ~ solo. **get one's** ~ **back** 🄸 desquitarse. ● vt tener. ▫ ~ **up** vi. 🄸 confesarse culpable. ~**er** n propietario m, dueño m. ~**ership** n propiedad f

oxygen /'ɒksɪdʒən/ n oxígeno m

Oxbridge Término usado para referirse conjuntamente a las universidades más antiguas y de más prestigio en el Reino Unido; Oxford y Cambridge, especialmente cuando se quiere destacar el ambiente de privilegio con el que se las relaciona. Últimamente se han hecho grandes esfuerzos para atraer a estudiantes de todos los medios sociales. *i*

---

oyster /'ɔɪstə(r)/ n ostra f

Pp

p abbr (= **pence, penny**) penique(s) (m(pl))

p. (pl **pp.**) (= **page**) pág., p.

pace /peɪs/ n paso m. **keep** ~ **with** s.o. seguirle el ritmo a uno. ● vi. ~ **up and down** andar de un lado para otro. ~**maker** n (runner) liebre f;

(Med) marcapasos m

Pacific /pə'sɪfɪk/ n. **the** ~ **(Ocean)** el (Océano) Pacífico m

pacif|ist /'pæsɪfɪst/ n pacifista m & f. ~**y** /'pæsɪfaɪ/ vt apaciguar

pack /pæk/ n fardo m; (of cigarettes) paquete m, cajetilla f; (of cards) baraja f; (of hounds) jauría f; (of wolves) manada f. **a** ~ **of lies** una sarta de mentiras. ● vt empaquetar; hacer (suitcase); (press down) apisonar. ● vi hacer la maleta, empacar (LAm). ~**age** /-ɪdʒ/ n paquete m. ~**age holiday** n vacaciones fpl organizadas. ~**ed** /pækt/ adj lleno (de gente). ~**et** /'pækɪt/ n paquete m

pact /pækt/ n pacto m, acuerdo m

pad /pæd/ n (for writing) bloc m. **shoulder** ~**s** hombreras fpl. ● vt (pt **padded**) rellenar

paddle /'pædl/ n pala f. ● vi mojarse los pies; (in canoe) remar (con pala)

paddock /'pædək/ n prado m

padlock /'pædlɒk/ n candado m. ● vt cerrar con candado

paed|iatrician /piːdɪə'trɪʃn/ n pediatra m & f. ~**ophile** /'piːdəfaɪl/ n pedófilo m

pagan /'peɪgən/ adj & n pagano (m)

page /peɪdʒ/ n página f; (attendant) paje m; (in hotel) botones m. ● vt llamar por megafonía/por buscapersonas, vocear (LAm)

paid /peɪd/ see **PAY**. ● adj. **put** ~ **to** 🄸 acabar con

pail /peɪl/ n balde m, cubo m

pain /peɪn/ n dolor m. **I have a** ~ **in my back** me duele la espalda. m. **be in** ~ tener dolores. **be a** ~ **in the neck** 🄸 ser un pesado; (thing) ser una lata. ● vt doler. ~**ful** adj doloroso. **it's very** ~**ful** duele mucho. ~**killer** n analgésico m. ~**less** adj indoloro. ~**staking** /'peɪnzteɪkɪŋ/ adj concienzudo

paint /peɪnt/ n pintura f. ● vt/i pintar. ~**er** n pintor m. ~**ing** n (medium) pintura f; (picture) cuadro m

pair /peə(r)/ n par m; (of people) pareja f. **a** ~ **of trousers** unos pantalones. ▫ ~**off**, ~ **up** vi formar parejas

pajamas /pə'dʒɑːməz/ npl (Amer) pijama m

o

p

Pakistan /pɑːkɪˈstɑːn/ n Pakistán m. ~**i** adj & n paquistaní (m & f)

pal /pæl/ n 🔢 amigo m

palace /ˈpælɪs/ n palacio m

palat|able /ˈpælətəbl/ adj agradable. ~**e** /ˈpælət/ n paladar m

pale /peɪl/ adj (-er, -est) pálido. **go** ~, **turn** ~ palidecer. ~**ness** n palidez f

Palestin|e /ˈpælɪstaɪn/ n Palestina f. ~**ian** /-ˈstɪnɪən/ adj & n palestino (m)

palette /ˈpælɪt/ n paleta f

palm /pɑːm/ n palma f. ◻ ~ **off** vt encajar (**on a**). **P**~ **Sunday** n Domingo m de Ramos

palpable /ˈpælpəbl/ adj palpable

palpitat|e /ˈpælpɪteɪt/ vi palpitar. ~**ion** /-ˈteɪʃn/ n palpitación f

pamper /ˈpæmpə(r)/ vt mimar

pamphlet /ˈpæmflɪt/ n folleto m

pan /pæn/ n cacerola f; (for frying) sartén f

panacea /pænəˈsɪə/ n panacea f

Panama /ˈpænəmɑː/ n Panamá m. ~**nian** /-ˈmeɪnɪən/ adj & n panameño (m)

pancake /ˈpænkeɪk/ n crep(e) m, panqueque m (LAm)

panda /ˈpændə/ n panda m

pandemonium /pændɪˈməʊnɪəm/ n pandemonio m

pander /ˈpændə(r)/ vi. ~ **to s.o.** consentirle los caprichos a uno

pane /peɪn/ n vidrio m, cristal m

panel /ˈpænl/ n panel m; (group of people) jurado m. ~**ling** n paneles mpl

pang /pæŋ/ n punzada f

panic /ˈpænɪk/ n pánico m. ● vi (pt panicked) dejarse llevar por el pánico. ~**-stricken** adj aterrorizado

panoram|a /pænəˈrɑːmə/ n panorama m. ~**ic** /-ˈræmɪk/ adj panorámico

pansy /ˈpænzɪ/ n (flower) pensamiento m

pant /pænt/ vi jadear

panther /ˈpænθə(r)/ n pantera f

panties /ˈpæntɪz/ npl bragas fpl, calzones mpl (LAm), pantaletas fpl (Mex)

pantihose /ˈpæntɪhəʊz/ npl see **PANTY-HOSE**

pantomime /ˈpæntəmaɪm/ n pantomima f

pantry /ˈpæntrɪ/ n despensa f

pants /pænts/ npl (man's) calzoncillos mpl; (woman's) bragas fpl, calzones mpl (LAm), pantaletas fpl (Mex); (Amer, trousers) pantalones mpl

pantyhose /ˈpæntɪhəʊz/ npl (Amer) panty m, medias fpl, pantimedias fpl (Mex)

paper /ˈpeɪpə(r)/ n papel m; (newspaper) diario m, periódico m; (exam) examen m; (document) documento m. ● vt empapelar, tapizar (Mex). ~**back** n libro m en rústica. ~ **clip** n sujetapapeles m, clip m. ~**weight** n pisapapeles m. ~**work** n papeleo m, trabajo m administrativo

parable /ˈpærəbl/ n parábola f

parachut|e /ˈpærəʃuːt/ n paracaídas m. ● vi saltar en paracaídas. ~**ist** n paracaidista m & f

parade /pəˈreɪd/ n desfile m; (Mil) formación f. ● vi desfilar. ● vt hacer alarde de

paradise /ˈpærədaɪs/ n paraíso m

paraffin /ˈpærəfɪn/ n queroseno m

paragraph /ˈpærəɡrɑːf/ n párrafo m

Paraguay /ˈpærəɡwaɪ/ n Paraguay m. ~**an** adj & n paraguayo (m)

parallel /ˈpærəlel/ adj paralelo. ● n paralelo m; (line) paralela f

paraly|se /ˈpærəlaɪz/ vt paralizar. ~**sis** /pəˈræləsɪs/ n (pl -ses /-siːz/) parálisis f

parameter /pəˈræmɪtə(r)/ n parámetro m

paranoia /pærəˈnɔɪə/ n paranoia f

parapet /ˈpærəpɪt/ n parapeto m

paraphernalia /pærəfəˈneɪlɪə/ n trastos mpl

parasite /ˈpærəsaɪt/ n parásito m

paratrooper /ˈpærətruːpə(r)/ n paracaidista m (del ejército)

parcel /ˈpɑːsl/ n paquete m

parch /pɑːtʃ/ vt resecar. **be** ~**ed** 🔢 estar muerto de sed

parchment /ˈpɑːtʃmənt/ n pergamino m

pardon /ˈpɑːdn/ n perdón m; (Jurid) indulto m. **I beg your** ~ perdón. (**I beg your**) ~**?** ¿cómo?, ¿mande? (Mex). ● vt perdonar; (Jurid) indultar. ~ **me?** (Amer) ¿cómo?

parent /'peərənt/ n (*father*) padre *m*; (*mother*) madre *f*. **my ~s** mis padres. **~al** /pə'rentl/ adj de los padres

parenthesis /pə'renθəsɪs/ n (*pl* **-theses** /-siːz/) paréntesis *m*

parenthood /'peərənthʊd/ n el ser padre/madre

Paris /'pærɪs/ n París *m*

parish /'pærɪʃ/ n parroquia *f*; (*municipal*) distrito *m*. **~ioner** /pə'rɪʃənə(r)/ n feligrés *m*

park /pɑːk/ n parque *m*. **~-and-ride** estacionamiento *m* disuasorio (*LAm*), aparcamiento *m* disuasorio (*Esp*). ● *vt/i* aparcar, estacionar (*LAm*)

parking /'pɑːkɪŋ/ n: **~ lot** n (*Amer*) aparcamiento *m*, estacionamiento *m* (*LAm*). **~ meter** n parquímetro *m*

parkway /'pɑːkweɪ/ n (*Amer*) carretera *f* ajardinada

parliament /'pɑːləmənt/ n parlamento *m*. **~ary** /-'mentrɪ/ adj parlamentario

Parliament El Parlamento británico, el más alto organismo legislativo. Está formado por la Cámara de los Lores y la Cámara de los Comunes. La primera, consta de 703 miembros, en la mayoría nombrados, con un número de cargos hereditarios, lo que es objeto de reforma en la actualidad. La Cámara de los Comunes consta de 659 miembros elegidos por el pueblo. Ver ▷**Dáil Éireann**, ▷**Scottish Parliament**, ▷**Welsh Assembly**.

parlour /'pɑːlə(r)/ n salón *m*

parochial /pə'rəʊkɪəl/ adj (*fig*) provinciano

parody /'pærədɪ/ n parodia *f*. ● *vt* parodiar

parole /pə'rəʊl/ n libertad *f* condicional

parrot /'pærət/ n loro *m*, papagayo *m*

parsley /'pɑːslɪ/ n perejil *m*

parsnip /'pɑːsnɪp/ n pastinaca *f*

part /pɑːt/ n parte *f*; (*of machine*) pieza *f*; (*of serial*) episodio *m*; (*in play*) papel *m*; (*Amer, in hair*) raya *f*. **take ~ in** tomar parte en, participar en. **for the**

most ~ en su mayor parte. ● adv en parte. ● *vt* separar. ● *vi* separarse. □ **~ with** *vt* desprenderse de

partial /'pɑːʃl/ adj parcial. **be ~ to** tener debilidad por. **~ly** adv parcialmente

participa|nt /pɑː'tɪsɪpənt/ n participante *m & f*. **~te** /-peɪt/ *vi* participar. **~tion** /-'peɪʃn/ n participación *f*

particle /'pɑːtɪkl/ n partícula *f*

particular /pə'tɪkjʊlə(r)/ adj particular; (*precise*) meticuloso; (*fastidious*) quisquilloso. **in ~** en particular. ● *n* detalle *m*. **~ly** adv particularmente; (*specifically*) específicamente

parting /'pɑːtɪŋ/ n despedida *f*; (*in hair*) raya *f*. ● adj de despedida

partition /pɑː'tɪʃn/ n partición *f*; (*wall*) tabique *m*. ● *vt* dividir

partly /'pɑːtlɪ/ adv en parte

partner /'pɑːtnə(r)/ n socio *m*; (*Sport*) pareja *f*. **~ship** n asociación *f*; (*Com*) sociedad *f*

partridge /'pɑːtrɪdʒ/ n perdiz *f*

part-time /pɑːt'taɪm/ adj & adv a tiempo parcial, de medio tiempo (*LAm*)

party /'pɑːtɪ/ n reunión *f*, fiesta *f*; (*group*) grupo *m*; (*Pol*) partido *m*; (*Jurid*) parte *f*

pass /pɑːs/ *vt* (*hand, convey*) pasar; (*go past*) pasar por delante de; (*overtake*) adelantar, rebasar (*Mex*); (*approve*) aprobar (*exam, bill, law*); pronunciar (*judgement*). ● *vi* pasar; (*pain*) pasarse; (*Sport*) pasar la pelota. □ **~ away** *vi* fallecer. □ **~ down** *vt* transmitir. □ **~ out** *vi* desmayarse. □ **~ round** *vt* distribuir. □ **~ up** *vt* 🄣 dejar pasar. ● *n* (*permit*) pase *m*; (*ticket*) abono *m*; (*in mountains*) puerto *m*, desfiladero *m*; (*Sport*) pase *m*; (*in exam*) aprobado *m*. **make a ~ at** 🄣 intentar besar. **~able** adj pasable; (*road*) transitable

passage /'pæsɪdʒ/ n (*voyage*) travesía *f*; (*corridor*) pasillo *m*; (*alleyway*) pasaje *m*; (*in book*) pasaje *m*

passenger /'pæsɪndʒə(r)/ n pasajero *m*

passer-by /pɑːsə'baɪ/ n (*pl* **passers-by**) transeúnte *m & f*

passion /'pæʃn/ n pasión f. ~**ate** /-ət/ adj apasionado. ~**ately** adv apasionadamente

passive /'pæsɪv/ adj pasivo

Passover /'pɑːsəʊvə(r)/ n Pascua f de los hebreos

pass ~**port** n pasaporte m. ~**word** n contraseña f

past /pɑːst/ adj anterior; (life) pasado; (week, year) último. **in times** ~ en tiempos pasados. ●n pasado m. **in the** ~ (formerly) antes, antiguamente. ●prep por delante de; (beyond) más allá de. **it's twenty** ~ **four** son las cuatro y veinte. ●adv. **drive** ~ pasar en coche. **go** ~ pasar

paste /peɪst/ n pasta f; (glue) engrudo m; (wallpaper ~) pegamento m; (jewellery) estrás m

pastel /'pæstl/ adj & n pastel (m)

pasteurize /'pɑːstʃəraɪz/ vt pasteurizar

pastime /'pɑːstaɪm/ n pasatiempo m

pastry /'peɪstrɪ/ n masa f; (cake) pastelito m

pasture /'pɑːstʃə(r)/ n pasto(s) mpl

pasty /'pæstɪ/ n empanadilla f, empanada f (LAm)

pat /pæt/ vt (pt patted) darle palmaditas. ●n palmadita f; (of butter) porción f

patch /pætʃ/ n (on clothes) remiendo m, parche m; (over eye) parche m. **a bad** ~ una mala racha. ●vt remendar. □ ~ **up** vt hacerle un arreglo a

patent /'peɪtnt/ adj patente. ●n patente f. ●vt patentar. ~ **leather** n charol m. ~**ly** adv. **it's** ~**ly obvious that...** está clarísimo que...

patern|al /pə'tɜːnl/ adj paterno. ~**ity** /-ətɪ/ n paternidad f

path /pɑːθ/ n (pl -s/pɑːðz/) sendero m; (Sport) pista f; (of rocket) trayectoria f; (fig) camino m

pathetic /pə'θetɪk/ adj (pitiful) patético; (excuse) pobre. **don't be so** ~ no seas tan pusilánime

patien|ce /'peɪʃns/ n paciencia f. ~**t** adj & n paciente (m & f). **be** ~**t with s.o.** tener paciencia con uno. ~**tly** adv pacientemente

patio /'pætɪəʊ/ n (pl -os) patio m

patriot /'pætrɪət/ n patriota m & f. ~**ic** /-'ɒtrɪk/ adj patriótico. ~**ism** n patriotismo m

patrol /pə'trəʊl/ n patrulla f. ●vt/i patrullar

patron /'peɪtrən/ n (of the arts) mecenas m & f; (of charity) patrocinador m; (customer) cliente m & f. ~**age** /'pætrənɪdʒ/ n (sponsorship) patrocinio m; (of the arts) mecenazgo m. ~**ize** /'pætrənaɪz/ vt ser cliente de; (fig) tratar con condescendencia. ~**izing** adj condescendiente

pattern /'pætn/ n diseño m; (sample) muestra f; (in dressmaking) patrón m

paunch /pɔːntʃ/ n panza f

pause /pɔːz/ n pausa f. ●vi hacer una pausa

pave /peɪv/ vt pavimentar; (with flagstones) enlosar. ~**ment** n pavimento m; (at side of road) acera f, banqueta f (Mex)

paving stone /'peɪvɪŋstəʊn/ n losa f

paw /pɔː/ n pata f

pawn /pɔːn/ n (Chess) peón m; (fig) título m. ●vt empeñar. ~**broker** n prestamista m & f

pay /peɪ/ vt (pt paid) pagar; prestar (attention); hacer (compliment, visit). ~ **cash** pagar al contado. ●vi pagar; (be profitable) rendir. ●n paga f. **in the** ~ **of** al servicio de. □ ~ **back** vt devolver; pagar (loan). □ ~ **in** vt ingresar, depositar (LAm). □ ~ **off** vt cancelar, saldar (debt). vi valer la pena. □ ~ **up** vi pagar. ~**able** adj pagadero. ~**ment** n pago m. ~**roll** n nómina f

pea /piː/ n guisante m, arveja f (LAm), chícharo m (Mex)

peace /piːs/ n paz f. ~ **of mind** tranquilidad f. ~**ful** adj tranquilo. ~**maker** n conciliador m

peach /piːtʃ/ n melocotón m, durazno m (LAm)

peacock /'piːkɒk/ n pavo m real

peak /piːk/ n cumbre f; (of career) apogeo m; (maximum) máximo m. ~ **hours** npl horas fpl de mayor demanda (o consumo etc)

peal /piːl/ n repique m. ~**s of laughter** risotadas fpl

peanut /'piːnʌt/ n cacahuete m, maní m (LAm), cacahuate m (Mex)

pear /peə(r)/ n pera f. ~ **(tree)** peral m

pearl /pɜːl/ n perla f

peasant /'peznt/ n campesino m

peat /piːt/ n turba f

pebble /'pebl/ n guijarro m

peck /pek/ vt picotear. ● n picotazo m; (kiss) besito m

peculiar /pɪ'kjuːlɪə(r)/ adj raro; (special) especial. ~**ity** /-'ærətɪ/ n rareza f; (feature) particularidad f

pedal /'pedl/ n pedal m. ● vi pedalear

pedantic /pɪ'dæntɪk/ adj pedante

peddle /'pedl/ vt vender por las calles

pedestal /'pedɪstl/ n pedestal m

pedestrian /pɪ'destrɪən/ n peatón m. ~ **crossing** paso m de peatones. ● adj pedestre; (dull) prosaico

pedigree /'pedɪgriː/ linaje m; (of animal) pedigrí m. ● adj (animal) de raza

peek /piːk/ vi mirar a hurtadillas

peel /piːl/ n piel f, cáscara f. ● vt pelar (fruit, vegetables). ● vi pelarse

peep /piːp/ vi. ~ **at** echarle un vistazo a. ● n (look) vistazo m; (bird sound) pío m

peer /pɪə(r)/ vi mirar. ~ **at** escudriñar. ● n (equal) par m & f; (contemporary) coetáneo m; (lord) par m. ~**age** /-ɪdʒ/ n nobleza f

peg /peg/ n (in ground) estaca f; (on violin) clavija f; (for washing) pinza f; (hook) gancho m; (for tent) estaquilla f **off the** ~ de confección. ● vt (pt pegged) sujetar (con estacas, etc); fijar (precios)

pejorative /pɪ'dʒɒrətɪv/ adj peyorativo, despectivo

pelican /'pelɪkən/ n pelícano m

pellet /'pelɪt/ n bolita f; (for gun) perdigón m

pelt /pelt/ n pellejo m. ● vt. ~ **s.o. with sth** lanzarle algo a uno. ● vi. ~ **with rain**, ~ **down** llover a cántaros

pelvis /'pelvɪs/ n pelvis f

pen /pen/ (for writing) pluma f; (ballpoint) bolígrafo m; (sheep ~) redil m; (cattle ~) corral m

penal /'piːnl/ adj penal. ~**ize** vt sancionar. ~**ty** /'penltɪ/ n pena f; (fine) multa f; (in soccer) penalty m; (in US football) castigo m. ~**ty kick** n (in soccer) penalty m

penance /'penəns/ n penitencia f

pence /pens/ see PENNY

pencil /'pensl/ n lápiz m. ● vt (pt pencilled) escribir con lápiz. ~**-sharpener** n sacapuntas m

pendulum /'pendjʊləm/ n péndulo m

penetrat|e /'penɪtreɪt/ vt/i penetrar. ~**ing** adj penetrante. ~**ion** /-'treɪʃn/ n penetración f

penguin /'peŋgwɪn/ n pingüino m

penicillin /penɪ'sɪlɪn/ n penicilina f

peninsula /pə'nɪnsjʊlə/ n península f

penis /'piːnɪs/ n pene m

pen ~knife /'pennaɪf/ n (pl penknives) navaja f. ~**-name** n seudónimo m

penn|iless /'penɪlɪs/ adj sin un céntimo. ~**y** /'penɪ/ n (pl pennies or pence) penique m

pension /'penʃn/ n pensión f; (for retirement) pensión f de jubilación. ~**er** n jubilado m

pensive /'pensɪv/ adj pensativo

Pentecost /'pentɪkɒst/ n Pentecostés m

penthouse /'penthaʊs/ n penthouse m

pent-up /pent'ʌp/ adj reprimido; (confined) encerrado

penultimate /pen'ʌltɪmət/ adj penúltimo

people /'piːpl/ npl gente f; (citizens) pueblo m. ~ **say (that)** se dice que, dicen que. **English** ~ los ingleses. **young** ~ los jóvenes. **the** ~ (nation) el pueblo. ● vt poblar

pepper /'pepə(r)/ n pimienta f; (vegetable) pimiento m. ● vt (intersperse) salpicar (with de). ~**box** n (Amer) pimentero m. ~**corn** n grano m de pimienta. ~**mint** n menta f; (sweet) caramelo m de menta. ~**pot** n pimentero m

per /pɜː(r)/ prep por. ~ **annum** al año. ~ **cent** see PERCENT. ~ **head** por cabeza, por persona. **ten miles** ~ **hour** diez millas por hora

perceive /pə'siːv/ vt percibir; (notice) darse cuenta de

P

percent, **per cent** /pə'sent/ n (no pl) porcentaje m. ● adv por ciento. ~**age** /-ɪdʒ/ n porcentaje m

percepti|ble /pə'septəbl/ adj perceptible. ~**on** /-ʃn/ n percepción f. ~**ve** /-tɪv/ adj perspicaz

perch /pɜːtʃ/ n (of bird) percha f; (fish) perca f. ● vi (bird) posarse. ~ **on** (person) sentarse en el borde de

percolat|e /'pɜːkəleɪt/ vi filtrarse. ~**or** n cafetera f eléctrica

percussion /pə'kʌʃn/ n percusión f

perfect /'pɜːfɪkt/ adj perfecto; (place, day) ideal. ● /pə'fekt/ vt perfeccionar. ~**ion** /pə'fekʃn/ n perfección f. **to** ~**ion** a la perfección. ~**ly** /'pɜːfɪktlɪ/ adv perfectamente

perform /pə'fɔːm/ vt desempeñar (function, role); ejecutar (task); realizar (experiment); representar (play); (Mus) interpretar. ~ **an operation** (Med) operar. ● vi (actor) actuar; (musician) tocar; (produce results) (vehicle) responder; (company) rendir. ~**ance** /-əns/ n ejecución f; (of play) representación f; (of actor, musician) interpretación f; (of team) actuación f; (of car) rendimiento m. ~**er** n (actor) actor m; (entertainer) artista m & f

perfume /'pɜːfjuːm/ n perfume m

perhaps /pə'hæps/ adv quizá(s), tal vez, a lo mejor

peril /'perəl/ n peligro m. ~**ous** adj arriesgado, peligroso

perimeter /pə'rɪmɪtə(r)/ n perímetro m

period /'pɪərɪəd/ n período m; (in history) época f; (lesson) clase f; (Amer, Gram) punto m; (menstruation) período m, regla f. ● adj de (la) época. ~**ic** /-'ɒdɪk/ adj periódico. ~**ical** /pɪərɪ'ɒdɪkl/ n revista f. ~**ically** adv periódico

peripher|al /pə'rɪfərəl/ adj secundario; (Comp) periférico. ~**y** /pə'rɪfərɪ/ n periferia f

perish /'perɪʃ/ vi perecer; (rot) deteriorarse. ~**able** adj perecedero. ~**ing** adj Ⓣ glacial

perjur|e /'pɜːdʒə(r)/ vr. ~**e o.s.** perjurarse. ~**y** n perjurio m

perk /pɜːk/ n gaje m. □ ~ **up** vt reanimar. vi reanimarse

perm /pɜːm/ n permanente f. ● vt. **have one's hair** ~**ed** hacerse la permanente

permanen|ce /'pɜːmənəns/ n permanencia f. ~**t** adj permanente. ~**tly** adv permanentemente

permissible /pə'mɪsəbl/ adj permisible

permission /pə'mɪʃn/ n permiso m

permit /pə'mɪt/ vt (pt permitted) permitir. ● /'pɜːmɪt/ n permiso m

peroxide /pə'rɒksaɪd/ n peróxido m

perpendicular /pɜːpən'dɪkjʊlə(r)/ adj & n perpendicular (f)

perpetrat|e /'pɜːpɪtreɪt/ vt cometer. ~**or** n autor m

perpetua|l /pə'petʃʊəl/ adj perpetuo. ~**te** /pə'petʃʊeɪt/ vt perpetuar

perplex /pə'pleks/ vt dejar perplejo. ~**ed** adj perplejo

persecut|e /'pɜːsɪkjuːt/ vt perseguir. ~**ion** /-'kjuːʃn/ n persecución f

persever|ance /pɜːsɪ'vɪərəns/ n perseverancia f. ~**e** /pɜːsɪ'vɪə(r)/ vi perseverar, persistir

Persian /'pɜːʃn/ adj persa. **the** ~ **Gulf** n el golfo Pérsico

persist /pə'sɪst/ vi persistir. ~**ence** /-əns/ n persistencia f. ~**ent** adj persistente; (continual) continuo

person /'pɜːsn/ n persona f. **in** ~ en persona. ~**al** adj personal; (call) particular; (property) privado. ~**al assistant** n secretario m personal. ~**ality** /-'nælətɪ/ n personalidad f. ~**ally** adv personalmente. ~**nel** /pɜːsə'nel/ n personal m. **P**~ (department) sección f de personal

perspective /pə'spektɪv/ n perspectiva f

perspir|ation /pɜːspə'reɪʃn/ n transpiración f. ~**e** /pəs'paɪə(r)/ vi transpirar

persua|de /pə'sweɪd/ vt convencer, persuadir. ~**e s.o. to do sth** convencer a uno para que haga algo. ~**sion** n /-ʃn/ persuasión f. ~**sive** /-sɪv/ adj persuasivo

pertinent /'pɜːtɪnənt/ adj pertinente. ~**ly** adv pertinentemente

perturb /pə'tɜːb/ vt perturbar

Peru /pə'ruː/ n el Perú m

peruse /pə'ruːz/ vt leer cuidadosamente

Peruvian /pə'ruːviən/ adj & n peruano (m)

perver|se /pə'vɜːs/ adj retorcido; (stubborn) obstinado. ~**sion** n perversión f. ~**t** /pə'vɜːt/ vt pervertir. • /'pɜːvɜːt/ n pervertido m

pessimis|m /'pesɪmɪzəm/ n pesimismo m. ~**t** n pesimista m & f. ~**tic** /-'mɪstɪk/ adj pesimista

pest /pest/ n plaga f; (🔢, person, thing) peste f

pester /'pestə(r)/ vt importunar

pesticide /'pestɪsaɪd/ n pesticida f

pet /pet/ n animal m doméstico; (favourite) favorito m. • adj preferido. **my ~ hate** lo que más odio. • vt (pt **petted**) acariciar

petal /'petl/ n pétalo m

petition /pɪ'tɪʃn/ n petición f

pet name n apodo m

petrified /'petrɪfaɪd/ adj (terrified) muerto de miedo; (rock) petrificado

petrol /'petrəl/ n gasolina f. ~ **pump** n surtidor m. ~ **station** n gasolinera f. ~ **tank** n depósito m de gasolina ~**eum** /pɪ'trəʊliəm/ n petróleo m.

petticoat /'petɪkəʊt/ n enagua f; (slip) combinación f

petty /'peti/ adj (-ier, -iest) insignificante; (mean) mezquino. ~**y cash** n dinero m para gastos menores

petulant /'petjʊlənt/ adj irritable

pew /pjuː/ n banco m (de iglesia)

phantom /'fæntəm/ n fantasma m

pharma|ceutical /fɑːmə'sjuːtɪkl/ adj farmacéutico. ~**cist** /'fɑːməsɪst/ n farmacéutico m. ~**cy** /'fɑːməsi/ n farmacia f

phase /feɪz/ n etapa f. □ ~ **out** vt retirar progresivamente

PhD abbr (= **Doctor of Philosophy**) n doctorado m; (person) Dr., Dra.

pheasant /'feznt/ n faisán m

phenomen|al /fɪ'nɒmɪnl/ adj fenomenal. ~**on** /-mən/ n (pl -**ena** /-ɪnə/) fenómeno m

philistine /'fɪlɪstaɪn/ adj & n filisteo (m)

philosoph|er /fɪ'lɒsəfə(r)/ n filósofo m. ~**ical** /-ə'sɒfɪkl/ adj filosófico. ~**y** /fɪ'lɒsəfi/ n filosofía f

phlegm /flem/ n flema f. ~**atic** /fleg'mætɪk/ adj flemático

phobia /'fəʊbiə/ n fobia f

phone /fəʊn/ n 🔢 teléfono m. • vt/i llamar (por teléfono). ~ **back** (call again) volver a llamar; (return call) llamar (más tarde). ~ **book** n guía f telefónica, directorio m (LAm). ~ **booth**, ~ **box** n cabina f telefónica. ~ **call** n llamada f (telefónica). ~ **card** n tarjeta f telefónica. ~ **number** n número m de teléfono

phonetic /fə'netɪk/ adj fonético. ~**s** n fonética f

phoney /'fəʊni/ adj (-ier. -iest) 🔢 falso

phosph|ate /'fɒsfeɪt/ n fosfato m. ~**orus** /'fɒsfərəs/ n fósforo m

photo /'fəʊtəʊ/ n (pl -**os**) 🔢 foto f. **take a ~** sacar una foto. ~**copier** /-kɒpiə(r)/ n fotocopiadora f. ~**copy** n fotocopia f. • vt fotocopiar. ~**genic** /-'dʒenɪk/ adj fotogénico. ~**graph** /-grɑːf/ n fotografía f. • vt fotografiar. ~**grapher** /fə'tɒgrəfə(r)/ n fotógrafo m. ~**graphic** /-'græfɪk/ adj fotográfico. ~**graphy** /fə'tɒgrəfi/ n fotografía f

phrase /freɪz/ n frase f. • vt expresar. ~ **book** n manual m de conversación

physi|cal /'fɪzɪkl/ adj físico. ~**cian** /fɪ'zɪʃn/ n médico m. ~**cist** /'fɪzɪsɪst/ n físico m. ~**cs** /'fɪzɪks/ n física f. ~**ology** /fɪzɪ'ɒlədʒi/ n fisiología f. ~**otherapist** /fɪzɪəʊ'θerəpɪst/ n fisioterapeuta m & f. ~**otherapy** /fɪzɪəʊ'θerəpi/ n fisioterapia f. ~**que** /fɪ'ziːk/ n físico m

pian|ist /'pɪənɪst/ n pianista m & f. ~**o** /pɪ'ænəʊ/ n (pl -**os**) piano m

pick /pɪk/ (tool) pico m. • vt escoger; cortar (flowers); recoger (fruit, cotton); abrir con una ganzúa (lock). ~ **a quarrel** buscar camorra. ~ **holes in** criticar. □ ~ **on** vt meterse con. □ ~ **out** vt escoger; (identify) reconocer. □ ~ **up** vt recoger; (lift) levantar; (learn) aprender; adquirir (habit, etc); contagiarse de (illness). • vi mejorar; (sales) subir. ~**axe** n pico m

p

picket /'pɪkɪt/ n (*group*) piquete m. ∼ **line** n piquete m. ● vt formar un piquete frente a

pickle /'pɪkl/ n (*in vinegar*) encurtido m; (*Amer, gherkin*) pepinillo m; (*relish*) salsa f (*a base de encurtidos*). ● vt encurtir

pick ∼**pocket** n carterista m & f. ∼**-up** n (*truck*) camioneta f

picnic /'pɪknɪk/ n picnic m

picture /'pɪktʃə(r)/ n (*painting*) cuadro m; (*photo*) foto f; (*drawing*) dibujo m; (*illustration*) ilustración f; (*film*) película f; (*fig*) descripción f. ● vt imaginarse. ∼**sque** /-'resk/ adj pintoresco

pie /paɪ/ n empanada f; (*sweet*) pastel m, tarta f

piece /piːs/ n pedazo m, trozo m; (*part of machine*) pieza f; (*coin*) moneda f; (*in chess*) figura f. **a** ∼ **of advice** un consejo. **a** ∼ **of furniture** un mueble. **a** ∼ **of news** una noticia. **take to** ∼**s** desmontar. ▢ ∼ **together** vt juntar. ∼**meal** adj gradual; (*unsystematic*) poco sistemático. ● adv poco a poco

pier /pɪə(r)/ n muelle m; (*with amusements*) paseo con atracciones sobre un muelle

pierc|e /pɪəs/ vt perforar. ∼**ing** adj penetrante

piety /'paɪətɪ/ n piedad f

pig /pɪɡ/ n cerdo m, chancho m (*LAm*)

pigeon /'pɪdʒɪn/ n paloma f; (*Culin*) pichón m. ∼**-hole** n casillero m; (*fig*) casilla f

piggy /'pɪɡɪ/ n cerdito m. ∼**back** n. **give s.o. a** ∼**back** llevar a uno a cuestas. ∼ **bank** n hucha f

pig-headed /-'hedɪd/ adj terco

pigment /'pɪɡmənt/ n pigmento m

pig|sty /'pɪɡstaɪ/ n pocilga f. ∼**tail** n (*plait*) trenza f; (*bunch*) coleta f

pike /paɪk/ n invar (*fish*) lucio m

pilchard /'pɪltʃəd/ n sardina f

pile /paɪl/ n (*heap*) montón m; (*of fabric*) pelo m. ● vt amontonar. ∼ **it on** exagerar. ● vi amontonarse. ▢ ∼ **up** vt amontonar. ● vi amontonarse. ∼**s** /paɪlz/ npl (*Med*) almorranas fpl. ∼**-up** n choque m múltiple

pilgrim /'pɪlɡrɪm/ n peregrino. ∼**age** /-ɪdʒ/ n peregrinación f

pill /pɪl/ n pastilla f

pillar /'pɪlə(r)/ n columna f. ∼ **box** n buzón m

pillow /'pɪləʊ/ n almohada f. ∼**case** n funda f de almohada

pilot /'paɪlət/ n piloto m. ● vt pilotar. ∼ **light** n fuego m piloto

pimple /'pɪmpl/ n grano m, espinilla f (*LAm*)

pin /pɪn/ n alfiler m; (*Mec*) perno m. ∼**s and needles** hormigueo m. ● vt (*pt* **pinned**) prender con alfileres; (*fix*) sujetar

PIN /pɪn/ n (= **personal identification number**) NIP m

pinafore /'pɪnəfɔː(r)/ n delantal m. ∼ **dress** n pichi m, jumper m & f (*LAm*)

pincers /'pɪnsəz/ npl tenazas fpl

pinch /pɪntʃ/ vt pellizcar; (*fam, steal*) hurtar. ● vi (*shoe*) apretar. ● n pellizco m; (*small amount*) pizca f. **at a** ∼ si fuera necesario

pine /paɪn/ n pino m. ● vi. ∼ **for sth** suspirar por algo. ▢ ∼ **away** vi languidecer de añoranza. ∼**apple** /'paɪnæpl/ n piña f

ping-pong /'pɪŋpɒŋ/ n ping-pong m

pink /pɪŋk/ adj & n rosa (m), rosado (m)

pinnacle /'pɪnəkl/ n pináculo m

pin ∼**point** vt determinar con precisión f. ∼**stripe** n raya f fina

pint /paɪnt/ n pinta f (= 0.57 *litros*)

pioneer /paɪə'nɪə(r)/ n pionero m

pious /'paɪəs/ adj piadoso

pip /pɪp/ n (*seed*) pepita f; (*time signal*) señal f

pipe /paɪp/ n tubo m; (*Mus*) caramillo m; (*for smoking*) pipa f. ● vt llevar por tuberías. ∼**-dream** n ilusión f. ∼**line** n conducto m; (*for oil*) oleoducto m. **in the** ∼**line** en preparación f

piping /'paɪpɪŋ/ n tubería f. ● adv. ∼ **hot** muy caliente, hirviendo

pira|cy /'paɪərəsɪ/ n piratería f. ∼**te** /'paɪərət/ n pirata m

Pisces /'paɪsiːz/ n Piscis m

piss /pɪs/ vi 🗷 mear. ▢ ∼ **off** vi 🗷. ∼ **off!** ¡vete a la mierda! ∼**ed** /pɪst/ adj (🗷, *drunk*) como una cuba; (*Amer, fed up*) cabreado

pistol /'pɪstl/ n pistola f

piston /'pɪstən/ n pistón m

pit /pɪt/ n hoyo m; (mine) mina f; (Amer, in fruit) hueso m

pitch /pɪtʃ/ n (substance) brea f; (degree) grado m; (Mus) tono m; (Sport) campo m. ● vt (throw) lanzar; armar (tent). ● vi (ship) cabecear. **~-black** /-'blæk/ adj oscuro como boca de lobo. **~er** n jarra f

pitfall /'pɪtfɔːl/ n trampa f

pith /pɪθ/ n (of orange, lemon) médula f; (fig) meollo m

pitiful /'pɪtɪfl/ adj lastimoso

pittance /'pɪtns/ n miseria f

pity /'pɪti/ n lástima f, pena f; (compassion) piedad f. **it's a ~ you can't come** es una lástima que no puedas venir. ● vt tenerle lástima a

pivot /'pɪvət/ n pivote m. ● vi pivotar; (fig) depender (**on** de)

placard /'plækɑːd/ n pancarta f; (sign) letrero m

placate /plə'keɪt/ vt apaciguar

place /pleɪs/ n lugar m; (seat) asiento m; (in firm, team) puesto m; (fam, house) casa f. **feel out of ~** sentirse fuera de lugar. **take ~** tener lugar. ● vt poner, colocar; (identify) identificar. **be ~d** (in race) colocarse. **~-mat** n mantel m individual

placid /'plæsɪd/ adj plácido

plague /pleɪg/ n peste f; (fig) plaga f. ● vt atormentar

plaice /pleɪs/ n invar platija f

plain /pleɪn/ adj (-er, -est) (clear) claro; (simple) sencillo; (candid) franco; (ugly) feo. **in ~ clothes** de civil. ● adv totalmente. ● n llanura f. **~ly** adv claramente; (frankly) francamente; (simply) con sencillez

plaintiff /'pleɪntɪf/ n demandante m & f

plait /plæt/ vt trenzar. ● n trenza f

plan /plæn/ n plan m; (map) plano m; (of book, essay) esquema f. ● vt (pt planned) planear; planificar (strategies). **I'm ~ning to go to Greece** pienso ir a Grecia

plane /pleɪn/ n (tree) plátano m; (level) nivel m; (aircraft) avión m; (tool) cepillo m. ● vt cepillar

planet /'plænɪt/ n planeta m. **~ary** adj planetario

plank /plæŋk/ n tabla f

planning /'plænɪŋ/ n planificación f. **family ~** planificación familiar. **town ~** urbanismo m

plant /plɑːnt/ n planta f; (Mec) maquinaria f; (factory) fábrica f. ● vt plantar; (place in position) colocar. **~ation** /plæn'teɪʃn/ n plantación f

plaque /plæk/ n placa f

plasma /'plæzmə/ n plasma m

plaster /'plɑːstə(r)/ n yeso m; (on walls) revoque m; (sticking plaster) tirita f (®), curita f (®) (LAm); (for setting bones) yeso m, escayola f. ● vt revocar; rellenar con yeso (cracks)

plastic /'plæstɪk/ adj & n plástico (m)

Plasticine /'plæstɪsiːn/ n (®) plastilina f (®)

plastic surgery /plæstɪk'sɜːdʒərɪ/ n cirugía f estética

plate /pleɪt/ n plato m; (of metal) chapa f; (silverware) vajilla f de plata; (in book) lámina f. ● vt recubrir (**with** de)

platform /'plætfɔːm/ n plataforma f; (Rail) andén m

platinum /'plætɪnəm/ n platino m

platitude /'plætɪtjuːd/ n lugar m común

platonic /plə'tɒnɪk/ adj platónico

plausible /'plɔːzəbl/ adj verosímil; (person) convincente

play /pleɪ/ vt jugar a (game, cards); jugar a, jugar (LAm) (football, chess); tocar (instrument); (act role) representar el papel de. ● vi jugar. ● n juego m; (drama) obra f de teatro. **~ down** vt minimizar. **~ up** vi 1 (child) dar guerra; (car, TV) no funcionar bien. **~er** n jugador m; (Mus) músico m. **~ful** adj juguetón. **~ground** n parque m de juegos infantiles; (in school) patio m de recreo. **~group** n jardín m de la infancia. **~ing card** n naipe m. **~ing field** n campo m de deportes. **~pen** n corralito m. **~wright** /-raɪt/ n dramaturgo m

plc abbr (= **public limited company**) S.A.

plea /pliː/ n súplica f; (excuse) excusa f; (Jurid) defensa f

plead /pliːd/ vt (Jurid) alegar; (as excuse) pretextar. ● vi suplicar. **~ with**

suplicarle a. ~ **guilty** declararse culpable

pleasant /'pleznt/ adj agradable

pleas|e /pli:z/ int por favor. ● vt complacer; (satisfy) contentar. ● vi agradar; (wish) querer. ~**ed** adj (satisfied) satisfecho; (happy) contento. ~**ed with** satisfecho de. ~**ing** adj agradable; (news) grato. ~**ure** /'pleʒə(r)/ n placer m

pleat /pli:t/ n pliegue m

pledge /pledʒ/ n cantidad f prometida

plent|iful /'plentɪfl/ adj abundante. ~**y** /'plentɪ/ n abundancia f. ● pron. ~**y of** muchos, -chas; (of sth uncountable) mucho, -cha

pliable /'plaɪəbl/ adj flexible

pliers /'plaɪəz/ npl alicates mpl

plight /plaɪt/ n situación f difícil

plimsolls /'plɪmsəlz/ npl zapatillas fpl de lona

plod /plɒd/ vi (pt plodded) caminar con paso pesado

plot /plɒt/ n complot m; (of novel etc) argumento m; (piece of land) parcela f. ● vt (pt plotted) tramar; (mark out) trazar. ● vi conspirar

plough /plaʊ/ n arado m. ● vt/i arar. □ ~ **into** vt estrellarse contra. □ ~ **through** vt avanzar laboriosamente por

ploy /plɔɪ/ n treta f

pluck /plʌk/ vt arrancar; depilarse (eyebrows); desplumar (bird). ~ **up courage to** armarse de valor para. ● n valor m. ~**y** adj (-ier, -iest) valiente

plug /plʌg/ n (in bath) tapón m; (Elec) enchufe m; (spark ~) bujía f. ● vt (pt plugged) tapar; (fam, advertise) hacerle propaganda a. □ ~ **in** vt (Elec) enchufar. ~**hole** n desagüe m

plum /plʌm/ n ciruela f

plumage /'plu:mɪdʒ/ n plumaje m

plumb|er /'plʌmə(r)/ n fontanero m, plomero m (LAm). ~**ing** n instalación f sanitaria, instalación f de cañerías

plume /plu:m/ n pluma f

plump /plʌmp/ adj (-er, -est) rechoncho

plunge /plʌndʒ/ vt hundir (knife); (in water) sumergir; (into state, condition)

sumir. ● vi zambullirse; (fall) caer. ● n zambullida f

plural /'plʊərəl/ n plural m. ● adj en plural

plus /plʌs/ prep más. ● adj positivo. ● n signo m de más; (fig) ventaja f

plush /plʌʃ/ adj lujoso

Pluto /'plu:təʊ/ n Plutón m

plutonium /plu:'təʊnɪəm/ n plutonio m

ply /plaɪ/ vt manejar (tool); ejercer (trade). ~ **s.o. with drink** dar continuamente de beber a uno. ~**wood** n contrachapado m

p.m. abbr (= post meridiem) de la tarde

pneumatic drill /nju:'mætɪk/ adj martillo m neumático

pneumonia /nju:'məʊnjə/ n pulmonía f

poach /pəʊtʃ/ vt escalfar (egg); cocer (fish etc); (steal) cazar furtivamente. ~**er** n cazador m furtivo

PO box /pi:'əʊ/ n Apdo. postal

pocket /'pɒkɪt/ n bolsillo m; (of air, resistance) bolsa f. ● vt poner en el bolsillo. ~**book** n (notebook) libro m de bolsillo; (Amer, wallet) cartera f; (Amer, handbag) bolso m, cartera f (LAm), bolsa f (Mex). ~ **money** n dinero m de bolsillo, mesada f (LAm)

pod /pɒd/ n vaina f

poem /'pəʊɪm/ n poema f

poet /'pəʊɪt/ n poeta m. ~**ic** /-'etɪk/ adj poético. ~**ry** /'pəʊɪtrɪ/ n poesía f

poignant /'pɔɪnjənt/ adj conmovedor

point /pɔɪnt/ n (dot, on scale) punto m; (sharp end) punta f; (in time) momento m; (statement) observación; (on agenda, in discussion) punto m; (Elec) toma f de corriente. **to the ~** pertinente. **up to a ~** hasta cierto punto. **be on the ~ of** estar a punto de. **get to the ~** ir al grano. **there's no ~ (in) arguing** no sirve de nada discutir. ● vt (aim) apuntar; (show) indicar. ● vi señalar. ~ **at/to sth** señalar algo. □ ~ **out** vt señalar. ~**-blank** adj & adv a quemarropa. ~**ed** adj (chin, nose) puntiagudo; (fig) mordaz. ~**less** adj inútil

poise /pɔɪz/ n porte m; (composure) desenvoltura f

poison /ˈpɔɪzn/ n veneno m. ● vt envenenar. **~ous** adj venenoso; (chemical etc) tóxico

poke /pəʊk/ vt empujar; atizar (fire). ● vi hurgar; (pry) meterse. ● n golpe m. □ **~ about** vi fisgonear. **~r** /ˈpəʊkə(r)/ n atizador m; (Cards) póquer m

poky /ˈpəʊkɪ/ adj (-ier, -iest) diminuto

Poland /ˈpəʊlənd/ n Polonia f

polar /ˈpəʊlə(r)/ adj polar. **~ bear** n oso m blanco

pole /pəʊl/ n palo m; (fixed) poste m; (for flag) mástil m; (in geography) polo m

police /pəˈliːs/ n policía f. **~man** /-mən/ n policía m, agente m. **~ station** n comisaría f. **~woman** n policía f, agente f

policy /ˈpɒlɪsɪ/ n política f; (insurance) póliza f (de seguros)

polish /ˈpɒlɪʃ/ n (for shoes) betún m; (furniture ~) cera f para muebles; (floor ~) abrillantador m de suelos; (shine) brillo m; (fig) finura f. ● vt darle brillo a; limpiar (shoes); (refine) pulir. □ **~ off** vt despachar. **~ed** adj pulido

Polish /ˈpəʊlɪʃ/ adj & n polaco (m)

polite /pəˈlaɪt/ adj cortés. **~ly** adv cortésmente. **~ness** n cortesía f

politic|al /pəˈlɪtɪkl/ adj político. **~ian** /pɒlɪˈtɪʃn/ n político m. **~s** /ˈpɒlətɪks/ n política f

poll /pəʊl/ n elección f; (survey) encuesta f. ● vt obtener (votes)

pollack /ˈpɒlæk/ n abadejo m

pollen /ˈpɒlən/ n polen m

polling booth n cabina f de votar

pollut|e /pəˈluːt/ vt contaminar. **~ion** /-ʃn/ n contaminación f

polo /ˈpəʊləʊ/ n polo m. **~ neck** n cuello m vuelto

poly|styrene /pɒlɪˈstaɪriːn/ n poliestireno m. **~thene** /ˈpɒlɪθiːn/ n plástico, polietileno m

pomp /pɒmp/ n pompa f. **~ous** adj pomposa

pond /pɒnd/ n (natural) laguna f; (artificial) estanque m

ponder /ˈpɒndə(r)/ vt considerar. **~ous** adj pesado

pony /ˈpəʊnɪ/ n poni m. **~-tail** n cola f de caballo

poodle /ˈpuːdl/ n caniche m

pool /puːl/ n charca f; (artificial) estanque m; (puddle) charco m. (common fund) fondos mpl comunes; (snooker) billar m americano. **(swimming) ~** n piscina f, alberca f (Mex). **~s** npl quinielas fpl. ● vt aunar

poor /pʊə(r)/ adj (-er, -est) pobre; (quality, diet) malo. **be in ~ health** estar mal de salud. **~ly** adj 🔢 malito. ● adv mal

pop /pɒp/ n (Mus) música f pop; (Amer fam, father) papá m. ● vt (pt popped) hacer reventar; (put) poner. □ **~ in** vi (visit) pasar por. □ **~ out** vi saltar; (person) salir un rato. □ **~ up** vi surgir, aparecer

popcorn /ˈpɒpkɔːn/ n palomitas fpl

pope /pəʊp/ n papa m

poplar /ˈpɒplə(r)/ n álamo m (blanco)

poppy /ˈpɒpɪ/ n amapola f

popular /ˈpɒpjʊlə(r)/ adj popular. **~ity** /-ˈlærətɪ/ n popularidad f. **~ize** vt popularizar

populat|e /ˈpɒpjʊleɪt/ vt poblar. **~ion** /ˈleɪʃn/ n población f

pop-up /ˈpɒpʌp/ n ventana f emergente, pop-up m

porcelain /ˈpɔːsəlɪn/ n porcelana f

porch /pɔːtʃ/ n porche m

porcupine /ˈpɔːkjʊpaɪn/ n puerco m espín

pore /pɔː(r)/ n poro m

pork /pɔːk/ n carne f de cerdo m, carne f de puerco m (Mex)

porn /pɔːn/ n 🔢 pornografía f. **~ographic** /-əˈɡræfɪk/ adj pornográfico. **~ography** /pɔːˈnɒɡrəfɪ/ n pornografía f

porpoise /ˈpɔːpəs/ n marsopa f

porridge /ˈpɒrɪdʒ/ n avena f (cocida)

port /pɔːt/ n puerto m; (Naut) babor m; (Comp) puerto m; (Culin) oporto m

portable /ˈpɔːtəbl/ adj portátil

porter /ˈpɔːtə(r)/ n (for luggage) maletero m; (concierge) portero m

porthole /ˈpɔːthəʊl/ n portilla f

portion /ˈpɔːʃn/ n porción f; (part) parte f

portrait /ˈpɔːtrɪt/ n retrato m

p

portray /pɔːˈtreɪ/ vt representar. ∼**al** n representación f

Portug|al /ˈpɔːtjʊɡl/ n Portugal m. ∼**uese** /-ˈɡiːz/ adj & n portugués (m)

pose /pəʊz/ n pose f, postura f. ● vt representar (threat); plantear (problem, question). ● vi posar. ∼ **as** hacerse pasar por

posh /pɒʃ/ adj 🔲 elegante

position /pəˈzɪʃn/ n posición f; (job) puesto m; (situation) situación f. ● vt colocar

positive /ˈpɒzətɪv/ adj positivo; (real) auténtico; (certain) seguro. ● n (Photo) positiva f. ∼**ly** adv positivamente

possess /pəˈzes/ vt poseer. ∼**ion** /-ʃn/ n posesión f; (Jurid) bien m. ∼**ive** adj posesivo

possib|ility /pɒsəˈbɪlətɪ/ n posibilidad f. ∼**le** /ˈpɒsəbl/ adj posible. ∼**ly** adv posiblemente

post /pəʊst/ n (pole) poste m; (job) puesto m; (mail) correo m. ● vt echar al correo (letter); (send) enviar por correo. **keep s.o.** ∼**ed** mantener a uno al corriente

post... /pəʊst/ pref post, pos

post ∼**age** /-ɪdʒ/ /-ɪdʒ/ n franqueo m. ∼**al** adj postal. ∼**al order** n giro m postal. ∼**box** n buzón m. ∼**card** n (tarjeta f) postal f. ∼**code** n código m postal

poster /ˈpəʊstə(r)/ n cartel m, póster m

posterity /pɒsˈterətɪ/ n posteridad f

posthumous /ˈpɒstjʊməs/ adj póstumo

post ∼**man** /-mən/ n cartero m. ∼**mark** n matasellos m

post mortem /pəʊstˈmɔːtəm/ n autopsia f

post office n oficina f de correos, correos mpl, correo m (LAm)

postpone /pəʊstˈpəʊn/ vt aplazar, posponer. ∼**ment** n aplazamiento m

postscript /ˈpəʊstskrɪpt/ n posdata f

posture /ˈpɒstʃə(r)/ n postura f

posy /ˈpəʊzɪ/ n ramillete m

pot /pɒt/ n (for cooking) olla f; (for jam, honey) tarro m; (for flowers) tiesto m; (in pottery) vasija f. ∼**s and pans** cacharros mpl

potato /pəˈteɪtəʊ/ n (pl -**oes**) patata f, papa f (LAm)

potent /ˈpəʊtnt/ adj potente; (drink) fuerte

potential /pəʊˈtenʃl/ adj & n potencial (m). ∼**ly** adv potencialmente

pot ∼**hole** n cueva f subterránea; (in road) bache m. ∼**holing** n espeleología f

potion /ˈpəʊʃn/ n poción f

pot-shot n tiro m al azar

potter /ˈpɒtə(r)/ n alfarero m. ● vi hacer pequeños trabajos agradables. ∼**y** n (pots) cerámica f; (workshop, craft) alfarería f

potty /ˈpɒtɪ/ adj (-**ier**, -**iest**) 🔲 chiflado. ● n orinal m

pouch /paʊtʃ/ n bolsa f pequeña; (for correspondence) valija f

poultry /ˈpəʊltrɪ/ n aves fpl de corral

pounce /paʊns/ vi saltar. ∼ **on** abalanzarse sobre

pound /paʊnd/ n (weight) libra f (= 454g); (money) libra f (esterlina); (for cars) depósito m. ● vt (crush) machacar. ● vi aporrear; (heart) palpitar; (sound) retumbar

pour /pɔː(r)/ vt verter; echar (salt). ∼ (**out**) servir (drink). ● vi (blood) manar; (water) salir; (rain) llover a cántaros. □ ∼ **out** vi (people) salir en tropel. ∼**ing** adj. ∼**ing rain** lluvia f torrencial

pout /paʊt/ vi hacer pucheros

poverty /ˈpɒvətɪ/ n pobreza f

powder /ˈpaʊdə(r)/ n polvo m; (cosmetic) polvos mpl. ● vt empolvar. ∼ **one's face** ponerse polvos en la cara. ∼**y** adj como polvo

power /ˈpaʊə(r)/ n poder m; (energy) energía f; (electricity) electricidad f; (nation) potencia f. ● vt. ∼**ed by** impulsado por ∼ **cut** n apagón m. ∼**ed** adj con motor. ∼**ful** adj poderoso. ∼**less** adj impotente. ∼ **plant**, ∼**-station** n central f eléctrica

PR = **public relations**

practicable /ˈpræktɪkəbl/ adj practicable

practical /ˈpræktɪkl/ adj práctico. ∼ **joke** n broma f. ∼**ly** adv prácticamente

practi|ce /'præktɪs/ n práctica f; (custom) costumbre f; (exercise) ejercicio m; (Sport) entrenamiento m; (clients) clientela f. **he's out of ~ce** le falta práctica. **in ~ce** (in fact) en la práctica. **~se** /'præktɪs/ vt practicar; ensayar (act); ejercer (profession). ● vi practicar; (professional) ejercer. **~tioner** /-'tɪʃənə(r)/ n médico m

prairie /'preərɪ/ n pradera f

praise /preɪz/ vt (Relig) alabar; (compliment) elogiar. ● n (credit) elogios mpl. **~worthy** adj loable

pram /præm/ n cochecito m

prank /præŋk/ n travesura f

prawn /prɔːn/ n gamba f, camarón m (LAm)

pray /preɪ/ vi rezar (for por). **~er** /preə(r)/ n oración f

pre.. /priː/ pref pre...

preach /priːtʃ/ vt/i predicar. **~er** n predicador m; (Amer, minister) pastor m

pre-arrange /priːə'reɪndʒ/ vt concertar de antemano

precarious /prɪ'keərɪəs/ adj precario. **~ly** adv precariamente

precaution /prɪ'kɔːʃn/ n precaución f

precede /prɪ'siːd/ vt preceder. **~nce** /'presədəns/ n precedencia f. **~nt** /'presədənt/ n precedente m

preceding /prɪ'siːdɪŋ/ adj anterior

precept /'priːsept/ n precepto m

precinct /'priːsɪŋkt/ n recinto m; (Amer, police district) distrito m policial; (Amer, voting district) circunscripción f. **pedestrian ~** zona f peatonal. **~s** (of city) límites mpl

precious /'preʃəs/ adj precioso. ● adv Ⅱ muy

precipice /'presɪpɪs/ n precipicio m

precipitate /prɪ'sɪpɪteɪt/ vt precipitar. ● /prɪ'sɪpɪtət/ n precipitado m. ● /prɪ'sɪpɪtət/ adj precipitado

precis|e /prɪ'saɪs/ adj (accurate) exacto; (specific) preciso; (meticulous) minucioso. **~ely** adv con precisión. **~!** ¡exacto! **~ion** /-'sɪʒn/ n precisión f

preclude /prɪ'kluːd/ vt excluir

precocious /prɪ'kəʊʃəs/ adj precoz. **~ly** adv precozmente

preconce|ived /priːkən'siːvd/ adj preconcebido. **~ption** /-'sepʃn/ n preconcepción f

precursor /priː'kɜːsə(r)/ n precursor m

predator /'predətə(r)/ n depredador m. **~y** adj predador

predecessor /'priːdɪsesə(r)/ n predecesor m, antecesor m

predicament /prɪ'dɪkəmənt/ n aprieto m

predict /prɪ'dɪkt/ vt predecir. **~ion** /-ʃn/ n predicción f

preen /priːn/ vt arreglar. **~ o.s.** atildarse

prefab /'priːfæb/ n Ⅱ casa f prefabricada. **~ricated** /-'fæbrɪkeɪtɪd/ adj prefabricado

preface /'prefəs/ n prefacio m; (to event) prólogo m

prefect /'priːfekt/ n (Schol) monitor m; (official) prefecto m

prefer /prɪ'fɜː(r)/ vt (pt preferred) preferir. **~ sth to sth** preferir algo a algo. **~able** /'prefrəbl/ adj preferible. **~ence** /'prefrəns/ n preferencia f. **~ential** /-ə'renʃl/ adj preferente

pregnan|cy /'pregnənsɪ/ n embarazo m. **~t** adj embarazada

prehistoric /priːhɪ'stɒrɪk/ adj prehistórico

prejudge /priː'dʒʌdʒ/ vt prejuzgar

prejudice /'predʒʊdɪs/ n prejuicio m. ● vt predisponer; (harm) perjudicar. **~d** adj lleno de prejuicios

preliminary /prɪ'lɪmɪnərɪ/ adj preliminar

prelude /'preljuːd/ n preludio m

premature /'premətjʊə(r)/ adj prematuro

premeditated /priː'medɪteɪtɪd/ adj premeditado

premier /'premɪə(r)/ n (Pol) primer ministro m

première /'premɪeə(r)/ n estreno m

premise /'premɪs/ n premisa f. **~s** /'premɪsɪz/ npl local m. **on the ~s** en el local

premium /'priːmɪəm/ n (insurance ~) prima f de seguro. **be at a ~** escasear

premonition /priːməˈnɪʃn/ n premonición f, presentimiento m

preoccup|ation /priːɒkjʊˈpeɪʃn/ n (obsession) obsesión f; (concern) preocupación f. ~**ied** /-ˈɒkjʊpaɪd/ adj absorto; (worried) preocupado

preparat|ion /prepəˈreɪʃn/ n preparación f. ~**ions** npl preparativos mpl. ~**ory** /prɪˈpærətrɪ/ adj preparatorio

prepare /prɪˈpeə(r)/ vt preparar. ● vi prepararse. ● adj preparado (willing). **be ~d to** estar dispuesto a

preposition /prepəˈzɪʃn/ n preposición f

preposterous /prɪˈpɒstərəs/ adj absurdo

prerequisite /priːˈrekwɪzɪt/ n requisito m esencial

prerogative /prɪˈrɒɡətɪv/ n prerrogativa f

Presbyterian /prezbɪˈtɪərɪən/ adj & n presbiteriano (m)

prescri|be /prɪˈskraɪb/ vt prescribir; (Med) recetar. ~**ption** /-ˈɪpʃn/ n (Med) receta f

presence /ˈprezns/ n presencia f. ~ **of mind** presencia f de ánimo

present /ˈpreznt/ n (gift) regalo m; (current time) presente m. **at ~** actualmente. **for the ~** por ahora. ● adj presente. ● /prɪˈzent/ vt presentar; (give) obsequiar. ~ **s.o. with** obsequiar a uno con. ~**able** /prɪˈzentəbl/ adj presentable. ~**ation** /prezn'teɪʃn/ n presentación f; (ceremony) ceremonia f de entrega. ~**er** /prɪˈzentə(r)/ n presentador m. ~**ly** /ˈprezntlɪ/ adv dentro de poco

preserv|ation /prezəˈveɪʃn/ n conservación f. ~**ative** /prɪˈzɜːvətɪv/ n conservante m. ~**e** /prɪˈzɜːv/ vt conservar; (maintain) mantener; (Culin) hacer conserva de. ● n coto m; (jam) confitura f. **wildlife ~e** (Amer) reserva f de animales

preside /prɪˈzaɪd/ vi presidir. ~ **over** presidir

presiden|cy /ˈprezɪdənsɪ/ n presidencia f. ~**t** n presidente m. ~**tial** /-ˈdenʃl/ adj presidencial

press /pres/ vt apretar; prensar (grapes); (put pressure on) presionar; (iron) planchar. **be ~ed for time**

andar escaso de tiempo. ● vi apretar; (time) apremiar; (fig) urgir. ● n (Mec, newspapers) prensa f; (printing) imprenta f. □ ~ **on** vi seguir adelante (**with** con). ~ **conference** n rueda f de prensa. ~ **cutting** n recorte m de periódico. ~**ing** adj urgente. ~-**up** n flexión f, fondo m

pressur|e /ˈpreʃə(r)/ n presión f. ● vt presionar. ~**e-cooker** n olla f a presión. ~**ize** vt presionar

prestig|e /preˈstiːʒ/ n prestigio m. ~**ious** /-ˈstɪdʒəs/ adj prestigioso

presum|ably /prɪˈzjuːməblɪ/ adv. ~... supongo que..., me imagino que... ~**e** /prɪˈzjuːm/ vt suponer. ~**ptuous** /prɪˈzʌmptʃʊəs/ adj impertinente

presuppose /priːsəˈpəʊz/ vt presuponer

preten|ce /prɪˈtens/ n fingimiento m; (claim) pretensión f; (pretext) pretexto m. ~**d** /-ˈtend/ vt/i fingir. ~**sion** /-ˈtenʃən/ n pretensión f. ~**tious** /-ˈtenʃəs/ adj pretencioso

pretext /ˈpriːtekst/ n pretexto m

pretty /ˈprɪtɪ/ adj (-ier, -iest) adv bonito, lindo (esp LAm)

prevail /prɪˈveɪl/ vi predominar; (win) prevalecer. □ ~ **on** vt persuadir

prevalen|ce /ˈprevələns/ n (occurrence) preponderancia f; (predominance) predominio m. ~**t** adj extendido

prevent /prɪˈvent/ vt (hinder) impedir; (forestall) prevenir, evitar. ~**ion** /-ʃn/ n prevención f. ~**ive** adj preventivo

preview /ˈpriːvjuː/ n preestreno m; (trailer) avance m

previous /ˈpriːvɪəs/ adj anterior. ~ **to** antes de. ~**ly** adv antes

prey /preɪ/ n presa f. **bird of ~** ave f de rapiña

price /praɪs/ n precio m. ● vt fijar el precio de. ~**less** adj inestimable; (fam, amusing) muy divertido. ~**y** adj 🔲 carito

prick /prɪk/ vt/i pinchar. ● n pinchazo m

prickl|e /ˈprɪkl/ n (thorn) espina f; (of animal) púa f; (sensation) picor m. ~**y** adj espinoso; (animal) con púas; (touchy) quisquilloso

pride /praɪd/ n orgullo m. ● vr. ~ **o.s. on** enorgullecerse de

priest /priːst/ n sacerdote m. **~hood** n sacerdocio m

prim /prɪm/ adj (**primmer, primmest**) mojigato; (affected) remilgado

primar|ily /'praɪmərɪlɪ/ adv en primer lugar. **~y** /'praɪmərɪ/ adj (principal) primordial; (first, basic) primario. **~ school** n escuela f primaria

prime /praɪm/ vt cebar (gun); (prepare) preparar; aprestar (surface). ● adj principal; (first rate) excelente. **~ minister** n primer ministro m. ● n. **be in one's ~** estar en la flor de la vida. **~r** n (paint) imprimación f

primeval /praɪ'miːvl/ adj primigenio

primitive /'prɪmɪtɪv/ adj primitivo

primrose /'prɪmrəʊz/ n primavera f

prince /prɪns/ n príncipe m. **~ss** /prɪn'ses/ n princesa f

principal /'prɪnsəpl/ adj principal. ● n (of school) director m; (of university) rector m. **~ly** /'prɪnsɪpəlɪ/ adv principalmente

principle /'prɪnsəpl/ n principio m. **in ~** en principio. **on ~** por principio

print /prɪnt/ vt imprimir; (write in capitals) escribir con letras de molde. **~ed matter** impresos mpl. ● n (characters) letra f; (picture) grabado m; (Photo) copia f; (fabric) estampado m. **in ~** (published) publicado; (available) a la venta. **out of ~** agotado. **~er** /'prɪntə(r)/ n impresor m; (machine) impresora f. **~ing** n impresión f; (trade) imprenta f. **~out** n listado m

prion /'praɪɒn/ n prión m

prior /'praɪə(r)/ n prior m. ● adj previo. **~ to** antes de. **~ity** /praɪ'ɒrətɪ/ n prioridad f. **~y** n priorato m

prise /praɪz/ vt. **~ open** abrir haciendo palanca

prison /'prɪzn/ n cárcel m. **~er** n prisionero m; (in prison) preso m; (under arrest) detenido m. **~ officer** n funcionario m de prisiones

priva|cy /'prɪvəsɪ/ n privacidad f. **~te** /'praɪvɪt/ adj privado; (confidential) personal; (lessons, house) particular. **in ~te** en privado; (secretly) en secreto. ● n soldado m raso. **~te detective** n detective m & f privado. **~tely** adv en privado. **~tion** /praɪ-

'veɪʃn/ n privación f

privilege /'prɪvəlɪdʒ/ n privilegio m. **~d** adj privilegiado. **be ~d to** tener el privilegio de

prize /praɪz/ n premio m. ● adj (idiot etc) de remate. ● vt estimar

pro /prəʊ/ n. **~s and cons** los pros m y los contras

probab|ility /prɒbə'bɪlətɪ/ n probabilidad f. **~le** /'prɒbəbl/ adj probable. **~ly** adv probablemente

probation /prə'beɪʃn/ n período m de prueba; (Jurid) libertad f condicional

probe /prəʊb/ n sonda f; (fig) investigación f. ● vt sondar. ● vi. **~ into** investigar

problem /'prɒbləm/ n problema m. ● adj difícil. **~atic** /-'mætɪk/ adj problemático

procedure /prə'siːdʒə(r)/ n procedimiento m

proceed /prə'siːd/ vi proceder; (move forward) avanzar. **~ings** npl (report) actas fpl; (Jurid) proceso m. **~s** /'prəʊsiːdz/ npl. **the ~s** lo recaudado

process /'prəʊses/ n proceso m. **in the ~ of** en vías de. ● vt tratar; revelar (photo); tramitar (order). **~ion** /prə'seʃn/ n desfile m; (Relig) procesión f. **~or** n procesador m. **food ~** procesador m de alimentos

proclaim /prə'kleɪm/ vt proclamar. **~mation** /prɒklə'meɪʃn/ n proclamación f

procure /prə'kjʊə(r)/ vt obtener

prod /prɒd/ vt (pt prodded) (with sth sharp) pinchar; (with elbow) darle un codazo a. ● n (with sth sharp) pinchazo m; (with elbow) codazo m

produc|e /prə'djuːs/ vt producir; surtir (effect); sacar (gun); producir (film); poner en escena (play). ● /'prɒdjuːs/ n productos mpl. **~er** /prə'djuːsə(r)/ n (TV, Cinema) productor m; (in theatre) director m; (manufacturer) fabricante m & f. **~t** /'prɒdʌkt/ n producto m. **~tion** /prə'dʌkʃn/ n (manufacture) fabricación f; (output) producción f; (of play) producción f. **~tive** /prə'dʌktɪv/ adj productivo. **~tivity** /prɒdʌk'tɪvətɪ/ n productividad f

profess /prə'fes/ vt profesar; (pretend) pretender. **~ion** /-'feʃn/ n profesión f.

~**ional** *adj & n* profesional (*m & f*).
~**or** /-'fesə(r)/ *n* catedrático *m*; (*Amer*) profesor *m*

proficien|cy /prə'fɪʃənsɪ/ *n* competencia *f*. ~**t** *adj* competente

profile /'prəʊfaɪl/ *n* perfil *m*

profit /'prɒfɪt/ *n* (*Com*) ganancia *f*; (*fig*) provecho *m*. ● *vi*. ~ **from** sacar provecho de. ~**able** *adj* provechoso

profound /prə'faʊnd/ *adj* profundo. ~**ly** *adv* profundamente

profus|e /prə'fjuːs/ *adj* profuso. ~**ely** *adv* profusamente

prognosis /prɒg'nəʊsɪs/ *n* (*pl* -oses) pronóstico *m*

program /'prəʊgræm/ *n* (*Comp*) programa *m*; (*Amer, course*) curso *m*. ~**me** /'prəʊgræm/ *n* programa *m*. ● *vt* (*pt* -med) programar. ~**mer** *n* programador *m*

progress /'prəʊgres/ *n* progreso *m*; (*development*) desarrollo *m*. **make** ~ hacer progresos. **in** ~ en curso.
● /prə'gres/ *vi* hacer progresos; (*develop*) desarrollarse. ~**ion** /prə'greʃn/ *n* progresión *f*; (*advance*) evolución *f*. ~**ive** /prə'gresɪv/ *adj* progresivo; (*reforming*) progresista. ~**ively** *adv* progresivamente

prohibit /prə'hɪbɪt/ *vt* prohibir; (*prevent*) impedir. ~**ive** *adj* prohibitivo

project /prə'dʒekt/ *vt* proyectar. ● *vi* (*stick out*) sobresalir. ● /'prɒdʒekt/ *n* proyecto *m*; (*Schol*) trabajo *m*; (*Amer, housing* ~) complejo *m* de viviendas subvencionadas. ~**or** /prə'dʒektə(r)/ *n* proyector *m*

prolific /prə'lɪfɪk/ *adj* prolífico

prologue /'prəʊlɒg/ *n* prólogo *m*

prolong /prə'lɒŋ/ *vt* prolongar

prom /prɒm/ *n* (*Amer*) baile *m* del colegio. ~**enade** /prɒmə'nɑːd/ *n* paseo *m* marítimo. ● *vi* pasearse.

> *i*
> **Prom** En EE.UU. un *prom* es un baile que se celebra para los estudiantes que terminan el *High School*. En Londres *the Proms* son una serie de conciertos de música clásica, durante los cuales una gran parte del público permanece de pie. Tienen lugar en el *Albert Hall* en el verano, durante ocho

semanas. Oficialmente, son conocidos como los *Henry Wood Promenade Concerts*, en memoria de su fundador.

prominen|ce /'prɒmɪnəns/ *n* prominencia *f*; (*fig*) importancia *f*. ~**t** *adj* prominente; (*important*) importante; (*conspicuous*) destacado

promiscu|ity /prɒmɪ'skjuːətɪ/ *n* promiscuidad *f*. ~**ous** /prə'mɪskjʊəs/ *adj* promiscuo

promis|e /'prɒmɪs/ *n* promesa *f*. ● *vt/i* prometer. ~**ing** *adj* prometedor; (*future*) halagüeño

promot|e /prə'məʊt/ *vt* promover; promocionar (*product*); (*in rank*) ascender. ~**ion** /-'məʊʃn/ *n* promoción *f*; (*in rank*) ascenso *m*

prompt /prɒmpt/ *adj* rápido; (*punctual*) puntual. ● *adv* en punto. ● *n* (*Comp*) presto *m*. ● *vt* incitar; apuntar (*actor*). ~**ly** *adv* puntualmente

prone /prəʊn/ *adj* (*tendido*) boca abajo. **be** ~ **to** ser propenso a

pronoun /'prəʊnaʊn/ *n* pronombre *m*

pronounc|e /prə'naʊns/ *vt* pronunciar; (*declare*) declarar. ~**ement** *n* declaración *f*. ~**ed** *adj* pronunciado; (*noticeable*) marcado

pronunciation /prənʌnsɪ'eɪʃn/ *n* pronunciación *f*

proof /pruːf/ *n* prueba *f*, pruebas *fpl*; (*of alcohol*) graduación *f* normal.
● *adj*. ~ **against** a prueba de.
~**-reading** *n* corrección *f* de pruebas

propaganda /prɒpə'gændə/ *n* propaganda *f*

propagate /'prɒpəgeɪt/ *vt* propagar. ● *vi* propagarse

propel /prə'pel/ *vt* (*pt* propelled) propulsar. ~**ler** *n* hélice *f*

proper /'prɒpə(r)/ *adj* correcto; (*suitable*) apropiado; (*Gram*) propio; (*fam, real*) verdadero. ~**ly** *adv* correctamente; (*eat, work*) bien

property /'prɒpətɪ/ *n* propiedad *f*; (*things owned*) bienes *mpl*. ● *adj* inmobiliario

prophe|cy /'prɒfəsɪ/ *n* profecía *f*. ~**sy** /'prɒfɪsaɪ/ *vt/i* profetizar. ~**t** /'prɒfɪt/ *n* profeta *m*. ~**tic** /prə'fetɪk/ *adj* profético

proportion /prə'pɔ:ʃn/ n proporción f.
~**al** adj. ~**ate** /-ət/ adj proporcional

propos|al /prə'pəʊzl/ n propuesta f;
(of marriage) proposición f matrimonial. ~**e** /prə'pəʊz/ vt proponer. ● vi.
~**e to s.o.** hacerle una oferta de matrimonio a una. ~**ition** /propə'zıʃn/
n propuesta f; (offer) oferta f

proprietor /prə'praıətə(r)/ n propietario m

pro rata /'prəʊ'rɑːtə/ adv a prorrata

prose /prəʊz/ n prosa f

prosecut|e /'prɒsıkjuːt/ vt procesar
(for por); (carry on) proseguir. ~**ion**
/-'kjuːʃn/ n proceso m. **the ~** (side) la
acusación. ~**or** n fiscal m & f; (in private prosecutions) abogado m de la
acusación

prospect /'prɒspekt/ n (possibility)
posibilidad f (**of** de); (situation envisaged) perspectiva f. ~**s** (chances)
perspectivas fpl. ~**ive** /prə'spektıv/
adj posible; (future) futuro. ~**or** /prə
'spektə(r)/ n prospector m. ~**us** /prə
'spektəs/ n folleto m informativo

prosper /'prɒspə(r)/ vi prosperar.
~**ity** /-'sperətı/ n prosperidad f.
~**ous** adj próspero

prostitut|e /'prɒstıtjuːt/ n prostituta f.
~**ion** /-'tjuːʃn/ n prostitución f

prostrate /'prɒstreıt/ adj postrado

protagonist /prə'tægənıst/ n protagonista m & f

protect /prə'tekt/ vt proteger. ~**ion**
/-ʃn/ n protección f. ~**ive** adj protector. ~**or** n protector m

protein /'prəʊtiːn/ n proteína f

protest /'prəʊtest/ n protesta f. **in ~**
(**against**) en señal de protesta (contra). **under ~** bajo protesta. ● /prə
'test/ vt/i protestar

Protestant /'prɒtıstənt/ adj & n protestante (m & f)

protester /prə'testə(r)/ n manifestante m & f

protocol /'prəʊtəkɒl/ n protocolo m

protrud|e /prə'truːd/ vi sobresalir.
~**ing** adj (chin) prominente. ~**ing
eyes** ojos saltones

proud /praʊd/ adj orgulloso. ~**ly** adv
con orgullo; (arrogantly) orgullosamente

prove /pruːv/ vt probar; demostrar
(loyalty). ● vi resultar. ~**n** adj probado

proverb /'prɒvɜːb/ n refrán m, proverbio m

provide /prə'vaıd/ vt proporcionar;
dar (accommodation). ~ **s.o. with
sth** proveer a uno de algo. ● vi. ~ **for**
(allow for) prever; mantener (person).
~**d** conj. ~**d** (**that**) con tal de que,
siempre que

providen|ce /'prɒvıdəns/ n providencia f. ~**tial** /-'denʃl/ adj providencial

providing /prə'vaıdıŋ/ conj. ~ **that**
con tal de que, siempre que

provinc|e /'prɒvıns/ n provincia f; (fig)
competencia f. ~**ial** /prə'vınʃl/ adj
provincial

provision /prə'vıʒn/ n provisión f;
(supply) suministro m; (stipulation) disposición f. ~**s** npl provisiones fpl, víveres mpl. ~**al** adj provisional

provo|cation /prɒvə'keıʃn/ n provocación f. ~**cative** /-'vɒkətıv/ adj provocador. ~**ke** /prə'vəʊk/ vt provocar

prow /praʊ/ n proa f

prowess /'praʊıs/ n destreza f; (valour) valor m

prowl /praʊl/ vi merodear. ~**er** n merodeador m

proximity /prɒk'sımətı/ n proximidad f

prude /pruːd/ n mojigato m

pruden|ce /'pruːdəns/ n prudencia f.
~**t** adj prudente. ~**tly** adv prudentemente

prudish /'pruːdıʃ/ adj mojigato

prune /pruːn/ n ciruela f pasa. ● vt
podar

pry /praı/ vi curiosear. ~ **into sth** entrometerse en algo. vt (Amer) see
PRISE

PS n (postscript) P.D.

psalm /sɑːm/ n salmo m

psychiatr|ic /saıkı'ætrık/ adj psiquiátrico. ~**ist** /saı'kaıətrıst/ n psiquiatra
m & f. ~**y** /saı'kaıətrı/ n psiquiatría f

psychic /'saıkık/ adj para(p)sicológico

psycho|analysis /saıkəʊə'næləsıs/ n
(p)sicoanálisis m. ~**logical** /saıkə
'lɒdʒıkl/ adj (p)sicológico. ~**logist**
/saı'kɒlədʒıst/ n (p)sicólogo m.
~**logy** /saı'kɒlədʒı/ n (p)sicología f.

~**therapy** /-'θerəpɪ/ n (p)sicoterapia f
pub /pʌb/ n bar m

> **pub** En Gran Bretaña, esta-
> blecimiento donde se vende ⓘ
> cerveza y otras bebidas (alcohólicas
> y no alcohólicas) para consumir en
> el local. *Pub* es la forma abreviada
> de *public house*. Suelen ofrecer co-
> midas y una variedad de juegos, es-
> pecialmente dardos, billar etc. Re-
> cientemente, las horas en que
> pueden abrir dependen de la licen-
> cia, siendo lo normal de 11 - 23
> horas.

puberty /'pju:bətɪ/ n pubertad f
pubic /'pju:bɪk/ adj pubiano, púbico
public /'pʌblɪk/ adj público. ~**an** n ta-
bernero m. ~**ation** /-'keɪʃn/ n publicación f. ~ **holiday** n día m festivo,
día m feriado (LAm). ~ **house** n bar
m. ~**ity** /pʌb'lɪsətɪ/ n publicidad f.
~**ize** /'pʌblɪsaɪz/ vt hacer público.
~**ly** adv públicamente. ~ **school** n
colegio m privado; (Amer) instituto m,
escuela f pública

> **public school** En Inglaterra y
> Gales, un colegio privado ⓘ
> para alumnos de edades compren-
> didas entre los 13 y 18 años. La
> mayoría de estos colegios tiene ré-
> gimen de internado y a menudo
> son mixtos. En EE.UU. y Escocia, el
> término se utiliza para referirse a
> un colegio estatal.

publish /'pʌblɪʃ/ vt publicar. ~**er** n
editor m. ~**ing** n publicación f. ~**ing
house** editorial f
pudding /'pʊdɪŋ/ n postre m;
(steamed) budín m
puddle /'pʌdl/ n charco m
Puerto Ric|an /pwɜ:təʊ'ri:kən/ adj & n
portorriqueño (m), puertorriqueño
(m). ~**o** /-əʊ/ n Puerto Rico m
puff /pʌf/ n (of wind) ráfaga f; (of
smoke) nube f; (action) soplo m; (on
cigarette) chupada f, calada f. ● vt/i soplar. ~ **at** dar chupadas a (pipe). ~
out (swell up) inflar, hinchar. ~**ed** adj
(out of breath) sin aliento. ~ **paste**
(Amer), ~ **pastry** n hojaldre m. ~**y** adj
hinchado

pull /pʊl/ vt tirar de, jalar (LAm); desgarrarse (muscle). ~ **a face** hacer una
mueca. ~ **a fast one** hacer una mala
jugada. ● vi tirar, jalar (LAm). ~ **at**
tirar de, jalar (LAm). ● n tirón m, jalón
m (LAm); (pulling force) fuerza f; (influence) influencia f. □ ~ **away** vi (Auto)
alejarse. □ ~ **back** vi retirarse. □ ~
down vt echar abajo (building);
(lower) bajar. □ ~ **in** vi (Auto) parar.
□ ~ **off** vt (remove) quitar; (achieve)
conseguir. □ ~ **out** vt sacar; retirar
(team). vi (Auto) salirse. □ ~ **through**
vi recobrar la salud. □ ~ **up** vi (Auto)
parar. vt (uproot) arrancar; (reprimand)
regañar
pullover /'pʊləʊvə(r)/ n suéter m, pulóver m, jersey m
pulp /pʌlp/ n pulpa f; (for paper)
pasta f
pulpit /'pʊlpɪt/ n púlpito m
pulse /pʌls/ n (Med) pulso m; (Culin) legumbre f
pummel /'pʌml/ vt (pt pummelled)
aporrear
pump /pʌmp/ n bomba f; (for petrol)
surtidor m. ● vt sacar con una bomba.
□ ~ **up** vt inflar
pumpkin /'pʌmpkɪn/ n calabaza f
pun /pʌn/ n juego m de palabras
punch /pʌntʃ/ vt darle un puñetazo a;
(perforate) perforar; hacer (hole). ● n
puñetazo m; (vigour) fuerza f; (device)
perforadora f; (drink) ponche m. ~ **in**
vi (Amer) fichar (al entrar al trabajo). ~
out vi (Amer) fichar (al salir del trabajo)
punctual /'pʌŋktʃʊəl/ adj puntual.
~**ity** /-'ælətɪ/ n puntualidad f. ~**ly**
adv puntualmente
punctuat|e /'pʌŋktʃʊeɪt/ vt puntuar.
~**ion** /-'eɪʃn/ n puntuación f
puncture /'pʌŋktʃə(r)/ n (in tyre) pinchazo m. **have a** ~ pinchar. ● vt pinchar. ● vi pincharse
punish /'pʌnɪʃ/ vt castigar. ~**ment** n
castigo m
punk /pʌŋk/ n punk m & f, punki m & f;
(Music) punk m; (Amer, hoodlum) vándalo m
punt /pʌnt/ n (boat) batea f. ~**er** n
apostante m & f
puny /'pju:nɪ/ adj (-ier, -iest) enclen-
que

pup /pʌp/ n cachorro m

pupil /'pjuːpl/ n alumno m; (of eye) pupila f

puppet /'pʌpɪt/ n marioneta f, títere m; (glove ∼) títere m

puppy /'pʌpɪ/ n cachorro m

purchase /'pɜːtʃəs/ vt adquirir. ● n adquisición f. ∼r n comprador m

pur|e /'pjʊə(r)/ adj (-er, -est) puro. ∼ity n pureza f

purgatory /'pɜːgətrɪ/ n purgatorio m

purge /pɜːdʒ/ vt purgar. ● n purga f

purif|ication /pjʊərɪfɪ'keɪʃn/ n purificación f. ∼y /'pjʊərɪfaɪ/ vt purificar

purist /'pjʊərɪst/ n purista m & f

puritan /'pjʊərɪtən/ n puritano m. ∼ical /-'tænɪkl/ adj puritano

purple /'pɜːpl/ adj morado. ● n morado m, púrpura f

purport /pə'pɔːt/ vt. ∼ to be pretender ser

purpose /'pɜːpəs/ n propósito m; (determination) resolución f. on ∼ a propósito. **serve a** ∼ servir de algo. ∼ful adj (resolute) resuelto. ∼ly adv a propósito

purr /pɜː(r)/ vi ronronear

purse /pɜːs/ n monedero m; (Amer) bolso m, cartera f (LAm), bolsa f (Mex)

pursu|e /pə'sjuː/ vt perseguir, continuar con (course of action). ∼it /pə'sjuːt/ n persecución f; (pastime) actividad f

pus /pʌs/ n pus m

push /pʊʃ/ vt empujar; apretar (button). ● vi empujar. ● n empujón m; (effort) esfuerzo m. □ ∼ **back** vt hacer retroceder. □ ∼ **off** vi 🔲 largarse. ∼chair n sillita f de paseo, carreola f (Mex). ∼y adj (pej) ambicioso

pussy /pʊsɪ/ (pl -sies), **pussycat** /'pʊsɪkæt/ n 🔲 minino m

put /pʊt/ vt (pt put, pres p **putting**) poner; (with care, precision) colocar; (inside sth) meter; (express) decir. □ ∼ **across** vt comunicar. □ ∼ **away** vt guardar. □ ∼ **back** vt volver a poner; retrasar (clock). □ ∼ **by** vt guardar; ahorrar (money). □ ∼ **down** vt (on a surface) dejar; colgar (phone); (suppress) sofocar; (write) apuntar; (kill) sacrificar. □ ∼ **forward** vt presentar

(plan); proponer (candidate); adelantar (clocks); adelantar (meeting). □ ∼ **in** vt (instal) poner; presentar (claim). □ ∼ **in for** vt solicitar. □ ∼ **off** vt aplazar, posponer; (disconcert) desconcertar. □ ∼ **on** vt (wear) ponerse; poner (CD, music); encender (light). □ ∼ **out** vt (extinguish) apagar; (inconvenience) incomodar; extender (hand); (disconcert) desconcertar. □ ∼ **through** vt (phone) poner, pasar (to con). □ ∼ **up** vt levantar; aumentar (rent); subir (price); poner (sign); alojar (guest). □ ∼ **up with** vt aguantar, soportar

putrid /'pjuːtrɪd/ adj putrefacto

putt /pʌt/ n (golf) golpe m suave

puzzl|e /'pʌzl/ n misterio m; (game) rompecabezas m. ● vt dejar perplejo. ∼ed adj (expression) de desconcierto. **I'm** ∼ed **about it** me tiene perplejo. ∼ing adj incomprensible; (odd) curioso

pygmy /'pɪgmɪ/ n pigmeo m

pyjamas /pə'dʒɑːməz/ npl pijama m, piyama m or f (LAm)

pylon /'paɪlɒn/ n pilón m

pyramid /'pɪrəmɪd/ n pirámide f

python /'paɪθn/ n pitón m

Qq

quack /kwæk/ n (of duck) graznido m; (person) charlatán m. ∼ **doctor** n curandero m

quadrangle /'kwɒdræŋgl/ n cuadrilátero m

quadruped /'kwɒdrʊped/ n cuadrúpedo m

quadruple /'kwɒdrʊpl/ adj & n cuádruplo (m). ● vt cuadruplicar

quagmire /'kwægmaɪə(r)/ n lodazal m

quail /kweɪl/ n codorniz f

quaint /kweɪnt/ adj (-er, -est) pintoresco; (odd) curioso

quake /kweɪk/ vi temblar. ● n 🔲 terremoto m

qualif|ication /kwɒlɪfɪ'keɪʃn/ n título m; (requirement) requisito m; (ability) capacidad f; (Sport) clasificación f; (fig) reserva f. ~ied /'kwɒlɪfaɪd/ adj cualificado; (with degree, diploma) titulado; (competent) capacitado. ~y /'kwɒlɪfaɪ/ vt calificar; (limit) limitar. ● vi titularse; (Sport) clasificarse. ~y for sth (be entitled to) tener derecho a algo

qualit|ative /'kwɒlɪtətɪv/ adj cualitativo. ~y /'kwɒlɪtɪ/ n calidad f; (attribute) cualidad f

qualm /kwɑːm/ n reparo m

quandary /'kwɒndrɪ/ n dilema m

quanti|fy /'kwɒntɪfaɪ/ vt cuantificar. ~ty /-tɪ/ n cantidad f

quarantine /'kwɒrəntiːn/ n cuarentena f. ● vt poner en cuarentena

quarrel /'kwɒrəl/ n pelea f. ● vi (pt quarrelled) pelearse, discutir. ~some /-səm/ adj pendenciero

quarry /'kwɒrɪ/ n (excavation) cantera f; (prey) presa f

quart /kwɔːt/ n cuarto m de galón

quarter /'kwɔːtə(r)/ n cuarto m; (of year) trimestre m; (district) barrio m. a ~ of an hour un cuarto de hora. ● vt dividir en cuartos; (Mil) acuartelar. ~-final n cuarto m de final. ~ly adj trimestral. ● adv trimestralmente

quartz /kwɔːts/ n cuarzo m

quay /kiː/ n muelle m

queasy /'kwiːzɪ/ adj mareado

queen /kwiːn/ n reina f. ~ mother n reina f madre

queer /kwɪə(r)/ adj (-er, -est) extraño

quench /kwentʃ/ vt quitar (thirst); sofocar (desire)

query /'kwɪərɪ/ n pregunta f. ● vt preguntar; (doubt) poner en duda

quest /kwest/ n busca f

question /'kwestʃən/ n pregunta f; (for discussion) cuestión f. in ~ en cuestión. out of the ~ imposible. without ~ sin duda. ● vt hacer preguntas a; (police etc) interrogar; (doubt) poner en duda. ~able adj discutible. ~ mark n signo m de interrogación. ~naire /-'neə(r)/ n cuestionario m

queue /kjuː/ n cola f. ● vi (pres p queuing) hacer cola

quibble /'kwɪbl/ vi discutir; (split hairs) sutilizar

quick /kwɪk/ adj (-er, -est) rápido. be ~! ¡date prisa! ● adv rápido. ~en vt acelerar. ● vi acelerarse. ~ly adv rápido. ~sand n arena f movediza. ~-tempered /-'tempəd/ adj irascible

quid /kwɪd/ n invar Ⓘ libra f (esterlina)

quiet /'kwaɪət/ adj (-er, -est) tranquilo; (silent) callado; (discreet) discreto. ● n tranquilidad f. ● vt/i (Amer) see **QUIETEN**. ~en vt calmar. ● n calmarse. ~ly adv tranquilamente; (silently) silenciosamente; (discreetly) discretamente. ~ness n tranquilidad f

quilt /kwɪlt/ n edredón m. ~ed adj acolchado

quintet /kwɪn'tet/ n quinteto m

quirk /kwɜːk/ n peculiaridad f

quit /kwɪt/ vt (pt quitted) dejar. ~ doing (Amer, cease) dejar de hacer. ● vi (give in) abandonar; (stop) parar; (resign) dimitir

quite /kwaɪt/ adv bastante; (completely) totalmente; (really) verdaderamente. ~ (so!) ¡claro! ~ a few bastante

quits /kwɪts/ adj. be ~ estar en paz. call it ~ darlo por terminado

quiver /'kwɪvə(r)/ vi temblar

quiz /kwɪz/ n (pl quizzes) serie f de preguntas; (game) concurso m. ● vt (pt quizzed) interrogar. ~zical adj burlón

quota /'kwəʊtə/ n cuota f

quot|ation /kwəʊ'teɪʃn/ n cita f; (price) presupuesto m. ~ation marks npl comillas fpl. ~e /kwəʊt/ vt citar; (Com) cotizar. ● n Ⓘ cita f; (price) presupuesto m. in ~es npl entre comillas

· ·

Rr

· ·

rabbi /'ræbaɪ/ n rabino m

rabbit /'ræbɪt/ n conejo m

rabi|d /'ræbɪd/ adj feroz; (dog) rabioso. ~es /'reɪbiːz/ n rabia f

race /reɪs/ n (in sport) carrera f; (ethnic group) raza f. ● vt hacer correr (horse). ● vi (run) correr, ir corriendo; (rush) ir

de prisa. **~course** n hipódromo m.
~horse n caballo m de carreras. **~**
relations npl relaciones fpl raciales.
~track n hipódromo m

racial /'reɪʃl/ adj racial

racing /'reɪsɪŋ/ n carreras fpl. **~ car** n
coche m de carreras

racis|m /'reɪsɪzəm/ n racismo m. **~t**
adj & n racista (m & f)

rack¹ /ræk/ n (shelf) estante m; (for
luggage) rejilla f; (for plates) escurre-
platos m. ●vt. **~ one's brains** deva-
narse los sesos

rack² /ræk/ n. **go to ~ and ruin** quedarse en la ruina

racket /'rækɪt/ n (for sports) raqueta;
(din) alboroto m; (swindle) estafa f
~eer /-ə'tɪə(r)/ n estafador m

racy /'reɪsɪ/ adj (-ier, -iest) vivo

radar /'reɪdɑː(r)/ n radar m

radian|ce /'reɪdɪəns/ n resplandor m.
~t adj radiante

radiat|e /'reɪdɪeɪt/ vt irradiar. ●vi di-
vergir. **~ion** /-'eɪʃn/ n radiación f.
~or n radiador m

radical /'rædɪkl/ adj & n radical (m)

radio /'reɪdɪəʊ/ n (pl -os) radio f or m.
●vt transmitir por radio. **~active**
/reɪdɪəʊ'æktɪv/ adj radiactivo. **~ac-**
tivity /-'tɪvətɪ/ n radiactividad f

radish /'rædɪʃ/ n rábano m

radius /'reɪdɪəs/ n (pl -dii /-dɪaɪ/)
radio m

raffle /'ræfl/ n rifa f

raft /rɑːft/ n balsa f

rafter /'rɑːftə(r)/ n cabrio m

rag /ræg/ n andrajo m, (for wiping)
trapo m. **in ~s** (person) andrajoso

rage /reɪdʒ/ n rabia f; (fashion) moda
f. ●vi estar furioso; (storm) bramar

ragged /'rægɪd/ adj (person) andrajoso; (clothes) hecho jirones

raid /reɪd/ n (Mil) incursión f; (by police
etc) redada f; (by thieves) asalto m.
●vt (Mil) atacar; (police) hacer una redada en; (thieves) asaltar. **~er** n invasor m; (thief) ladrón m

rail /reɪl/ n barandilla f; (for train) riel
m; (rod) barra f. **by ~** por ferrocarril.
~ing n barandilla f; (fence) verja f.
~road n (Amer), **~way** n ferrocarril

m. **~way station** n estación f de ferrocarril

rain /reɪn/ n lluvia f. ●vi llover. **~bow**
/-bəʊ/ n arco m iris. **~coat** n impermeable m. **~fall** n precipitación f. **~y**
adj (-ier, -iest) lluvioso

raise /reɪz/ vt levantar; (breed) criar;
obtener (money etc); formular (question); plantear (problem); subir
(price). ●n (Amer) aumento m

raisin /'reɪzn/ n (uva f) pasa f

rake /reɪk/ n rastrillo m. ●vt rastrillar;
(search) buscar en. **□ ~ up** vt remover

rally /'rælɪ/ vt reunir; (revive) reanimar.
●n reunión f; (Auto) rally m

ram /ræm/ n carnero m. ●vt (pt
rammed) (thrust) meter por la
fuerza; (crash into) chocar con

RAM /ræm/ n (Comp) RAM f

rambl|e /'ræmbl/ n excursión f a pie.
●vi ir de paseo; (in speech) divagar.
□ ~e on vi divagar. **~er** n excursionista m & f. **~ing** adj (speech) divaga-
dor

ramp /ræmp/ n rampa f

rampage /ræm'peɪdʒ/ vi alborotarse.
●/'ræmpeɪdʒ/ n. **go on the ~** alborotarse

ramshackle /'ræmʃækl/ adj desvencijado

ran /ræn/ see RUN

ranch /rɑːntʃ/ n hacienda f

random /'rændəm/ adj hecho al azar;
(chance) fortuito. ●n. **at ~** al azar

rang /ræŋ/ see RING²

range /reɪndʒ/ n alcance m; (distance)
distancia f; (series) serie f; (of mountains) cordillera f; (extent) extensión f;
(Com) surtido m; (stove) cocina f económica. ●vi extenderse; (vary) variar.
~r n guardabosque m

rank /ræŋk/ n posición f, categoría f;
(row) fila f; (for taxis) parada f. **the ~**
and file la masa f. **~s** npl soldados
mpl rasos. ●adj (-er, -est) (smell) fétido; (fig) completo. ●vt clasificar. ●vi
clasificarse

ransack /'rænsæk/ vt registrar; (pil-
lage) saquear

ransom /'rænsəm/ n rescate m. **hold**
s.o. to ~ exigir rescate por uno. ●vt
rescatar; (redeem) redimir

r

rant /rænt/ vi despotricar

rap /ræp/ n golpe m seco. ● vt/i (pt **rapped**) golpear

rape /reɪp/ vt violar. ● n violación f

rapid /'ræpɪd/ adj rápido. ~s npl rápidos mpl

rapist /'reɪpɪst/ n violador m

rapture /'ræptʃə(r)/ n éxtasis m. ~ous /-rəs/ adj extático

rare /reə(r)/ adj (-er, -est) raro; (Culin) poco hecho. ~fied /'reərɪfaɪd/ adj enrarecido. ~ly adv raramente

raring /'reərɪŋ/ adj 🔲. ~ to impaciente por

rarity /'reərətɪ/ n rareza f

rascal /'rɑːskl/ n granuja m & f

rash /ræʃ/ adj (-er, -est) precipitado, imprudente. ● n erupción f

rasher /'ræʃə(r)/ n loncha f

rashly /'ræʃlɪ/ adv precipitadamente, imprudentemente

rasp /rɑːsp/ n (file) escofina f

raspberry /'rɑːzbrɪ/ n frambuesa f

rat /ræt/ n rata f

rate /reɪt/ n (ratio) proporción f; (speed) velocidad f; (price) precio m; (of interest) tipo m. **at any** ~ de todas formas. **at this** ~ así. ~s npl (taxes) impuestos mpl municipales. ● vt valorar; (consider) considerar; (Amer, deserve) merecer. ● vi ser considerado

rather /'rɑːðə(r)/ adv mejor dicho; (fairly) bastante; (a little) un poco. ● int claro. **I would** ~ **not** prefiero no

rating /'reɪtɪŋ/ n clasificación f; (sailor) marinero m; (number, TV) índice m

ratio /'reɪʃɪəʊ/ n (pl **-os**) proporción f

ration /'ræʃn/ n ración f. ~s npl (provisions) víveres mpl. ● vt racionar

rational /'ræʃənəl/ adj racional. ~ize vt racionalizar

rattle /'rætl/ vi traquetear. ● vt (shake) agitar; 🔲 desconcertar. ● n traqueteo m; (toy) sonajero m. □ ~ **off** vt (fig) decir de corrida

raucous /'rɔːkəs/ adj estridente

ravage /'rævɪdʒ/ vt estragar

rave /reɪv/ vi delirar; (in anger) despotricar. ~ **about sth** poner a algo por las nubes

raven /'reɪvn/ n cuervo m

ravenous /'rævənəs/ adj voraz; (person) hambriento. **be** ~ morirse de hambre

ravine /rə'viːn/ n barranco m

raving /'reɪvɪŋ/ adj. ~ **mad** loco de atar

ravishing /'rævɪʃɪŋ/ adj (enchanting) encantador

raw /rɔː/ adj (-er, -est) crudo; (sugar) sin refinar; (inexperienced) inexperto. ~ **deal** n tratamiento m injusto, injusticia f. ~ **materials** npl materias fpl primas

ray /reɪ/ n rayo m

raze /reɪz/ vt arrasar

razor /'reɪzə(r)/ n navaja f de afeitar; (electric) maquinilla f de afeitar

Rd /rəʊd/ abbr (= **Road**) C/, Calle f

re /riː/ prep con referencia a. ● pref re.

reach /riːtʃ/ vt alcanzar; (extend) extender; (arrive at) llegar a; (achieve) lograr; (hand over) pasar, dar. ● vi extenderse. ● n alcance m. **within** ~ **of** al alcance de; (close to) a corta distancia de. □ ~ **out** vi alargar la mano

react /rɪ'ækt/ vi reaccionar. ~**ion** /rɪ'ækʃn/ n reacción f. ~**ionary** adj & n reaccionario (m). ~**or** /rɪ'æktə(r)/ n reactor m

read /riːd/ vt (pt **read** /red/) leer; (study) estudiar; (interpret) interpretar. ● vi leer; (instrument) indicar. □ ~ **out** vt leer en voz alta. ~**able** adj (clear) legible. ~**er** n lector m

readily /'redɪlɪ/ adv (willingly) de buena gana; (easily) fácilmente

reading /'riːdɪŋ/ n lectura f

readjust /riːə'dʒʌst/ vt reajustar. ● vi readaptarse (**to** a)

ready /'redɪ/ adj (-ier, -iest) listo, preparado. **get** ~ prepararse. ~**-made** adj confeccionado

real /rɪəl/ adj verdadero. ● adv (Amer fam) verdaderamente. ~ **estate** n bienes mpl raíces, propiedad f inmobiliaria. ~ **estate agent** see **REALTOR**. ~**ism** n realismo m. ~**ist** n realista m & f. ~**istic** /-'lɪstɪk/ adj realista. ~**ity** /rɪ'ælətɪ/ n realidad f. ~**ization** /rɪəlaɪ'zeɪʃn/ n comprensión f. ~**ize** /'rɪəlaɪz/ vt darse cuenta de; (fulfil, Com) realizar. ~**ly** /'rɪəlɪ/ adv verdaderamente

realm /relm/ n reino m

realtor /'ri:əltə(r)/ n (*Amer*) agente m inmobiliario

reap /ri:p/ vt segar; (*fig*) cosechar

reappear /ri:ə'pɪə(r)/ vi reaparecer

rear /rɪə(r)/ n parte f de atrás. ● adj posterior, trasero. ● vt (*bring up, breed*) criar. ● vi ~ (**up**) (*horse*) encabritarse

rearguard /'rɪəgɑ:d/ n retaguardia f

rearrange /ri:ə'reɪndʒ/ vt arreglar de otra manera

reason /'ri:zn/ n razón f, motivo m. **within** ~ dentro de lo razonable. ● vi razonar. ~**able** adj razonable. ~**ing** n razonamiento m

reassur|ance /ri:ə'ʃʊərəns/ n promesa f tranquilizadora; (*guarantee*) garantía f. ~**e** /ri:ə'ʃʊə(r)/ vt tranquilizar

rebate /'ri:beɪt/ n (*discount*) rebaja f

rebel /'rebl/ n rebelde m & f. ● /rɪ'bel/ vi (*pt* **rebelled**) rebelarse. ~**lion** /rɪ'belɪən/ n rebelión f. ~**lious** adj rebelde

rebound /rɪ'baʊnd/ vi rebotar; (*fig*) recaer. ● /'ri:baʊnd/ n rebote m

rebuff /rɪ'bʌf/ vt rechazar. ● n desaire m

rebuild /ri:'bɪld/ vt (*pt* **rebuilt**) reconstruir

rebuke /rɪ'bju:k/ vt reprender. ● n reprimenda f

recall /rɪ'kɔ:l/ vt (*call s.o. back*) llamar; (*remember*) recordar. ● n /'ri:kɔ:l/ (*of goods, ambassador*) retirada f; (*memory*) memoria f

recap /'ri:kæp/ vt/i (*pt* **recapped**) ⊤ resumir

recapitulate /ri:kə'pɪtʃʊleɪt/ vt/i resumir

recapture /ri:'kæptʃə(r)/ vt recobrar; (*recall*) hacer revivir

recede /rɪ'si:d/ vi retroceder

receipt /rɪ'si:t/ n recibo m. ~**s** npl (*Com*) ingresos mpl

receive /rɪ'si:v/ vt recibir. ~**r** n (*of stolen goods*) perista m & f; (*part of phone*) auricular m

recent /'ri:snt/ adj reciente. ~**ly** adv recientemente

recept|ion /rɪ'sepʃn/ n recepción f; (*welcome*) acogida f. ~**ionist** n recepcionista m & f. ~**ive** /-tɪv/ adj receptivo

recess /rɪ'ses/ n hueco m; (*holiday*) vacaciones fpl. ~**ion** /rɪ'seʃn/ n recesión f

recharge /ri:'tʃɑ:dʒ/ vt cargar de nuevo, recargar

recipe /'resəpi/ n receta f. ~ **book** n libro m de cocina

recipient /rɪ'sɪpɪənt/ n recipiente m & f; (*of letter*) destinatario m

recit|al /rɪ'saɪtl/ n (*Mus*) recital m. ~**e** /rɪ'saɪt/ vt recitar; (*list*) enumerar

reckless /'reklɪs/ adj imprudente. ~**ly** adv imprudentemente

reckon /'rekən/ vt/i calcular; (*consider*) considerar; (*think*) pensar. □ ~ **on** vt (*rely*) contar con

reclaim /rɪ'kleɪm/ vt reclamar; recuperar (*land*)

reclin|e /rɪ'klaɪn/ vi recostarse. ~**ing** adj acostado; (*seat*) reclinable

recluse /rɪ'klu:s/ n ermitaño m

recogni|tion /rekəg'nɪʃn/ n reconocimiento m. **beyond** ~**tion** irreconocible. ~**ze** /'rekəgnaɪz/ vt reconocer

recoil /rɪ'kɔɪl/ vi retroceder. ● /'ri:kɔɪl/ n (*of gun*) culatazo m

recollect /rekə'lekt/ vt recordar. ~**ion** /-ʃn/ n recuerdo m

recommend /rekə'mend/ vt recomendar. ~**ation** /-'deɪʃn/ n recomendación f

reconcil|e /'rekənsaɪl/ vt reconciliar (*people*); conciliar (facts). ~**e o.s.** resignarse (**to** a). ~**iation** /-sɪlɪ'eɪʃn/ n reconciliación f

reconnaissance /rɪ'kɒnɪsns/ n reconocimiento m

reconnoitre /rekə'nɔɪtə(r)/ vt (*pres p* -**tring**) (*Mil*) reconocer

re ~**consider** /ri:kən'sɪdə(r)/ vt volver a considerar. ~**construct** /ri:kən'strʌkt/ vt reconstruir

record /rɪ'kɔ:d/ vt (*in register*) registrar; (*in diary*) apuntar; (*Mus*) grabar. ● /'rekɔ:d/ n (*document*) documento m; (*of events*) registro m; (*Mus*) disco m; (*Sport*) récord m. **off the** ~ en confianza. ~**er** /rɪ'kɔ:də(r)/ n registrador

r

m; (*Mus*) flauta *f* dulce. **~ing** /rɪˈkɔːdɪŋ/ *n* grabación *f*. **~-player** /ˈrekɔːd-/ *n* tocadiscos *m* invar

recount /rɪˈkaʊnt/ *vt* contar, relatar

re-count /ˈriːkaʊnt/ *vt* volver a contar; recontar (votes). ● /ˈriːkaʊnt/ *n* (*Pol*) recuento *m*

recover /rɪˈkʌvə(r)/ *vt* recuperar. ● *vi* reponerse. **~y** *n* recuperación *f*

recreation /rekrɪˈeɪʃn/ *n* recreo *m*. **~al** *adj* de recreo

recruit /rɪˈkruːt/ *n* recluta *m*. ● *vt* reclutar; contratar (staff). **~ment** *n* reclutamiento *m*

rectang|le /ˈrektæŋgl/ *n* rectángulo *m*. **~ular** /-ˈtæŋgjʊlə(r)/ *adj* rectangular

rectify /ˈrektɪfaɪ/ *vt* rectificar

rector /ˈrektə(r)/ *n* párroco *m*; (*of college*) rector *m*. **~y** *n* rectoría *f*

recuperat|e /rɪˈkuːpəreɪt/ *vt* recuperar. ● *vi* reponerse. **~ion** /-ˈreɪʃn/ *n* recuperación *f*

recur /rɪˈkɜː(r)/ *vi* (*pt* recurred) repetirse. **~rence** /rɪˈkʌrns/ *n* repetición *f*. **~rent** /rɪˈkʌrənt/ *adj* repetido

recycle /riːˈsaɪkl/ *vt* reciclar

red /red/ *adj* (redder, reddest) rojo. ● *n* rojo. **be in the ~** estar en números rojos. **~den** *vi* enrojecerse. **~dish** *adj* rojizo

redecorate /riːˈdekəreɪt/ *vt* pintar de nuevo

rede|em /rɪˈdiːm/ *vt* redimir. **~mption** /-ˈdempʃn/ *n* redención *f*

red ~-handed /-ˈhændɪd/ *adj*. **catch s.o. ~handed** agarrar a uno con las manos en la masa. **~ herring** *n* (*fig*) pista *f* falsa. **~-hot** *adj* al rojo vivo. **~ light** *n* luz *f* roja

redo /riːˈduː/ *vt* (*pt* redid, *pp* redone) rehacer

redouble /rɪˈdʌbl/ *vt* redoblar

red tape /redˈteɪp/ *n* (*fig*) papeleo *m*

reduc|e /rɪˈdjuːs/ *vt* reducir; aliviar (pain). ● *vi* (*Amer*, *slim*) adelgazar. **~tion** /rɪˈdʌkʃn/ *n* reducción *f*

redundan|cy /rɪˈdʌndənsɪ/ *n* superfluidad *f*; (*unemployment*) despido *m*. **~t** superfluo. **she was made ~t** la despidieron por reducción de plantilla

reed /riːd/ *n* caña *f*; (*Mus*) lengüeta *f*

reef /riːf/ *n* arrecife *m*

reek /riːk/ *n* mal olor *m*. ● *vi*. **~ (of)** apestar a

reel /riːl/ *n* carrete *m*. ● *vi* dar vueltas; (*stagger*) tambalearse. □ **~ off** *vt* (*fig*) enumerar

refectory /rɪˈfektərɪ/ *n* refectorio *m*

refer /rɪˈfɜː(r)/ *vt* (*pt* referred) remitir. ● *vi* referirse. **~ to** referirse a; (*consult*) consultar. **~ee** /refəˈriː/ *n* árbitro *m*; (*for job*) referencia *f*. ● *vi* (*pt* refereed) arbitrar. **~ence** /ˈrefrəns/ *n* referencia *f*. **~ence book** *n* libro *m* de consulta. **in ~ to, with ~ to** con referencia a; (*Com*) respecto a. **~endum** /refəˈrendəm/ *n* (*pl* -ums or -da) referéndum *m*

refill /riːˈfɪl/ *vt* volver a llenar. ● /ˈriːfɪl/ *n* recambio *m*

refine /rɪˈfaɪn/ *vt* refinar. **~d** *adj* refinado. **~ry** /-ərɪ/ *n* refinería *f*

reflect /rɪˈflekt/ *vt* reflejar. ● *vi* reflejarse; (*think*) reflexionar. □ **~ badly upon** perjudicar. **~ion** /-ʃn/ *n* reflexión *f*; (*image*) reflejo *m*. **~or** *n* reflector *m*

reflex /ˈriːfleks/ *adj & n* reflejo (*m*). **~ive** /rɪˈfleksɪv/ *adj* (*Gram*) reflexivo

reform /rɪˈfɔːm/ *vt* reformar. ● *vi* reformarse. ● *n* reforma *f*

refrain /rɪˈfreɪn/ *n* estribillo *m*. ● *vi* abstenerse (**from** de)

refresh /rɪˈfreʃ/ *vt* refrescar. **~ing** *adj* refrescante. **~ments** *npl* (*food and drink*) refrigerio *m*

refrigerat|e /rɪˈfrɪdʒəreɪt/ *vt* refrigerar. **~or** *n* frigorífico *m*, refrigerador *m* (*LAm*)

refuel /riːˈfjuːəl/ *vt/i* (*pt* refuelled) repostar

refuge /ˈrefjuːdʒ/ *n* refugio *m*. **take ~** refugiarse. **~e** /refjʊˈdʒiː/ *n* refugiado *m*

refund /rɪˈfʌnd/ *vt* reembolsar. ● /ˈriːfʌnd/ *n* reembolso *m*

refusal /rɪˈfjuːzl/ *n* negativa *f*

refuse /rɪˈfjuːz/ *vt* rehusar. ● *vi* negarse. ● /ˈrefjuːs/ *n* residuos *mpl*

refute /rɪˈfjuːt/ *vt* refutar

regain /rɪˈgeɪn/ *vt* recobrar

regal /ˈriːgl/ *adj* real

regard /rɪ'gɑːd/ vt considerar; (look at) contemplar. **as ~s** en lo que se refiere a. ● n (consideration) consideración f; (esteem) estima f. **~s** npl saludos mpl. **kind ~s** recuerdos. **~ing** prep en lo que se refiere a. **~less** adv a pesar de todo. **~less of** sin tener en cuenta

regatta /rɪ'gætə/ n regata f

regime /reɪ'ʒiːm/ n régimen m

regiment /'redʒɪmənt/ n regimiento m. **~al** /-'mentl/ adj del regimiento

region /'riːdʒən/ n región f. **in the ~ of** alrededor de. **~al** adj regional

register /'redʒɪstə(r)/ n registro m. ● vt registrar; matricular (vehicle); declarar (birth); certificar (letter); facturar (luggage). ● vi (enrol) inscribirse; (fig) producir impresión

registrar /redʒɪ'strɑː(r)/ n secretario m del registro civil; (Univ) secretario m general

registration /redʒɪ'streɪʃn/ n registro m; (in register) inscripción f. **~ number** n (Auto) (número de) matrícula f

registry /'redʒɪstrɪ/ n. **~ office** n registro m civil

regret /rɪ'gret/ n pesar m; (remorse) arrepentimiento m. ● vt (pt **regretted**) lamentar. **I ~ that** siento (que). **~table** adj lamentable

regula|r /'regjʊlə(r)/ adj regular; (usual) habitual. ● n 🆃 cliente m habitual. **~rity** /-'lærətɪ/ n regularidad f. **~rly** adv con regularidad. **~te** /'regjʊleɪt/ vt regular. **~tion** /-'leɪʃn/ n regulación f; (rule) regla f

rehears|al /rɪ'hɜːsl/ n ensayo m. **~e** /rɪ'hɜːs/ vt ensayar

reign /reɪn/ n reinado m. ● vi reinar

reindeer /'reɪndɪə(r)/ n invar reno m

reinforce /riːɪn'fɔːs/ vt reforzar. **~ment** n refuerzo m

reins /reɪnz/ npl riendas fpl

reiterate /riː'ɪtəreɪt/ vt reiterar

reject /rɪ'dʒekt/ vt rechazar. ● /'riːdʒekt/ n producto m defectuoso. **~ion** /rɪ'dʒekʃn/ n rechazo m; (after job application) respuesta f negativa

rejoice /rɪ'dʒɔɪs/ vi regocijarse

rejoin /rɪ'dʒɔɪn/ vt reunirse con

rejuvenate /rɪ'dʒuːvəneɪt/ vt rejuvenecer

relapse /rɪ'læps/ n recaída f. ● vi recaer; (into crime) reincidir

relat|e /rɪ'leɪt/ vt contar; (connect) relacionar. ● vi relacionarse (**to** con). **~ed** adj emparentado; (ideas etc) relacionado. **~ion** /rɪ'leɪʃn/ n relación f; (person) pariente m & f. **~ionship** n relación f; (blood tie) parentesco m; (affair) relaciones fpl. **~ive** /'relətɪv/ n pariente m & f. ● adj relativo. **~ively** adv relativamente

relax /rɪ'læks/ vt relajar. ● vi relajarse. **~ation** /-'seɪʃn/ n relajación f; (rest) descanso m; (recreation) recreo m. **~ing** adj relajante

relay /'riːleɪ/ n relevo m. **~ (race)** n carrera f de relevos. ● /rɪ'leɪ/ vt transmitir

release /rɪ'liːs/ vt soltar; poner en libertad (prisoner); estrenar (film); (Mec) soltar; publicar (news). ● n liberación f; (of film) estreno m; (record) disco m nuevo

relent /rɪ'lent/ vi ceder. **~less** adj implacable; (continuous) incesante

relevan|ce /'reləvəns/ n pertinencia f. **~t** adj pertinente

relia|bility /rɪlaɪə'bɪlətɪ/ n fiabilidad f. **~ble** /rɪ'laɪəbl/ adj (person) de confianza; (car) fiable. **~nce** /rɪ'laɪəns/ n dependencia f; (trust) confianza f. **~nt** /rɪ'laɪənt/ adj confiado

relic /'relɪk/ n reliquia f

relie|f /rɪ'liːf/ n alivio m; (assistance) socorro m. **be on ~f** (Amer) recibir prestaciones de la seguridad social. **~ve** /rɪ'liːv/ vt aliviar; (take over from) relevar. **~ved** adj aliviado. **feel ~ved** sentir un gran alivio

religio|n /rɪ'lɪdʒən/ n religión f. **~us** /rɪ'lɪdʒəs/ adj religioso

relinquish /rɪ'lɪŋkwɪʃ/ vt abandonar, renunciar

relish /'relɪʃ/ n gusto m; (Culin) salsa f. ● vt saborear

reluctan|ce /rɪ'lʌktəns/ n desgana f. **~t** adj mal dispuesto. **be ~t to** no tener ganas de. **~tly** adv de mala gana

rely /rɪ'laɪ/ vi. **~ on** contar con; (trust) fiarse de; (depend) depender

r

remain /rɪ'meɪn/ vi (be left) quedar; (stay) quedarse; (continue to be) seguir. **~der** n resto m. **~s** npl restos mpl; (left-overs) sobras fpl

remand /rɪ'mɑːnd/ vt. **~ in custody** mantener bajo custodia. ●n. **on ~** en prisión preventiva

remark /rɪ'mɑːk/ n observación f. ●vt observar. **~able** adj notable

remarry /riː'mærɪ/ vi volver a casarse

remedy /'remədɪ/ n remedio m. ●vt remediar

remember /rɪ'membə(r)/ vt acordarse de, recordar. ●vi acordarse

remind /rɪ'maɪnd/ vt recordar. **~er** n recordatorio m

reminisce /remɪ'nɪs/ vi rememorar los viejos tiempos. **~nces** /-ənsɪz/ npl recuerdos mpl. **~nt** /-'nɪsnt/ adj. **be ~nt of** recordar

remnant /'remnənt/ n resto m; (of cloth) retazo m; (trace) vestigio m

remorse /rɪ'mɔːs/ n remordimiento m. **~ful** adj arrepentido. **~less** adj implacable

remote /rɪ'məʊt/ adj remoto. **~ control** n mando m a distancia. **~ly** adv remotamente

remov|able /rɪ'muːvəbl/ adj (detachable) de quita y pon; (handle) desmontable. **~al** n eliminación f; (from house) mudanza f. **~e** /rɪ'muːv/ vt quitar; (dismiss) destituir; (get rid of) eliminar

render /'rendə(r)/ vt rendir (homage); prestar (help etc). **~ sth useless** hacer que algo resulte inútil

rendezvous /'rɒndɪvuː/ n (pl -vous /-vuːz/) cita f

renegade /'renɪɡeɪd/ n renegado

renew /rɪ'njuː/ vt renovar; (resume) reanudar. **~al** n renovación f

renounce /rɪ'naʊns/ vt renunciar a

renovat|e /'renəveɪt/ vt renovar. **~ion** /-'veɪʃn/ n renovación f

renown /rɪ'naʊn/ n renombre m. **~ed** adj de renombre

rent /rent/ n alquiler m. ●vt alquilar. **~al** n alquiler m. **car ~** (Amer) alquiler m de coche

renunciation /rɪnʌnsɪ'eɪʃn/ n renuncia f

reopen /riː'əʊpən/ vt volver a abrir. ●vi reabrirse

reorganize /riː'ɔːɡənaɪz/ vt reorganizar

rep /rep/ n (Com) representante m & f

repair /rɪ'peə(r)/ vt arreglar, reparar; arreglar (clothes, shoes). ●n reparación f; (patch) remiendo m. **in good ~** en buen estado. **it's beyond ~** ya no tiene arreglo

repatriat|e /riː'pætrɪeɪt/ vt repatriar

repay /riː'peɪ/ vt (pt **repaid**) reembolsar; pagar (debt); corresponder a (kindness). **~ment** n pago m

repeal /rɪ'piːl/ vt revocar. ●n revocación f

repeat /rɪ'piːt/ vt repetir. ●vi repetir(se). ●n repetición f. **~edly** adv repetidas veces

repel /rɪ'pel/ vt (pt **repelled**) repeler. **~lent** adj repelente

repent /rɪ'pent/ vi arrepentirse. **~ant** adj arrepentido

repercussion /riːpə'kʌʃn/ n repercusión f

repertoire /'repətwɑː(r)/ n repertorio m

repetit|ion /repɪ'tɪʃn/ n repetición f. **~ious** /-'tɪʃəs/ adj, **~ive** /rɪ'petətɪv/ adj repetitivo

replace /rɪ'pleɪs/ vt reponer; cambiar (battery); (take the place of) sustituir. **~ment** n sustitución f; (person) sustituto m

replay /'riːpleɪ/ n (Sport) repetición f del partido; (recording) repetición f inmediata

replenish /rɪ'plenɪʃ/ vt reponer

replica /'replɪkə/ n réplica f

reply /rɪ'plaɪ/ vt/i responder, contestar. **~ to sth** responder a algo, contestar algo. ●n respuesta f

report /rɪ'pɔːt/ vt (reporter) informar sobre; informar de (accident); (denounce) denunciar. ●vi informar; (present o.s.) presentarse. ●n informe m; (Schol) boletín m de notas; (rumour) rumor m; (in newspaper) reportaje m. **~ card** (Amer) n boletín m de calificaciones. **~edly** adv según se dice. **~er** n periodista m & f, reportero m

reprehensible /reprɪˈhensəbl/ adj reprensible

represent /reprɪˈzent/ vt representar. **~ation** /-ˈteɪʃn/ n representación f. **~ative** adj representativo. ● n representante m & f; (Amer, in government) diputado m

repress /rɪˈpres/ vt reprimir. **~ion** /-ʃn/ n represión f. **~ive** adj represivo

reprieve /rɪˈpriːv/ n indulto m; (fig) respiro m. ● vt indultar

reprimand /ˈreprɪmɑːnd/ vt reprender. ● n represión f

reprisal /rɪˈpraɪzl/ n represalia f

reproach /rɪˈprəʊtʃ/ vt reprochar. ● n reproche m. **~ful** adj de reproche

reproduc|e /riːprəˈdjuːs/ vt reproducir. ● vi reproducirse. **~tion** /-ˈdʌkʃn/ n reproducción f. **~tive** /-ˈdʌktɪv/ adj reproductor

reprove /rɪˈpruːv/ vt reprender

reptile /ˈreptaɪl/ n reptil m

republic /rɪˈpʌblɪk/ n república f. **~an** adj & n republicano (m). R**~** a & n (in US) republicano (m)

repugnan|ce /rɪˈpʌɡnəns/ n repugnancia f. **~t** adj repugnante

repuls|e /rɪˈpʌls/ vt rechazar, repulsar. **~ion** /-ʃn/ n repulsión f. **~ive** adj repulsivo

reput|able /ˈrepjʊtəbl/ adj acreditado, reputado. **~ation** /repjʊˈteɪʃn/ n reputación f

request /rɪˈkwest/ n petición f. ● vt pedir

require /rɪˈkwaɪə(r)/ vt requerir; (need) necesitar; (demand) exigir. **~d** adj necesario. **~ment** n requisito m

rescue /ˈreskjuː/ vt rescatar, salvar. ● n rescate m. **~r** n salvador m

research /rɪˈsɜːtʃ/ n investigación f. ● vt investigar. **~er** n investigador m

resembl|ance /rɪˈzembləns/ n parecido m. **~e** /rɪˈzembl/ vt parecerse a

resent /rɪˈzent/ vt guardarle rencor a (person). **she ~ed his success** le molestaba que él tuviera éxito. **~ful** adj resentido. **~ment** n resentimiento m

reserv|ation /rezəˈveɪʃn/ n reserva f; (booking) reserva f. **~e** /rɪˈzɜːv/ vt reservar. ● n reserva f; (in sports) suplente m & f. **~ed** adj reservado. **~oir** /ˈrezəvwɑː(r)/ n embalse m

reshuffle /riːˈʃʌfl/ n (Pol) reorganización f

residen|ce /ˈrezɪdəns/ n residencia f. **~t** adj & n residente (m & f). **~tial** /rezɪˈdenʃl/ adj residencial

residue /ˈrezɪdjuː/ n residuo m

resign /rɪˈzaɪn/ vt/i dimitir. **~ o.s. to** resignarse a. **~ation** /rezɪɡˈneɪʃn/ n resignación f; (from job) dimisión f. **~ed** adj resignado

resilien|ce /rɪˈzɪliəns/ n elasticidad f; (of person) resistencia f. **~t** adj elástico; (person) resistente

resin /ˈrezɪn/ n resina f

resist /rɪˈzɪst/ vt resistir. ● vi resistirse. **~ance** n resistencia f. **~ant** adj resistente

resolut|e /ˈrezəluːt/ adj resuelto. **~ion** /-ˈluːʃn/ n resolución f

resolve /rɪˈzɒlv/ vt resolver. **~ to do** resolver a hacer. ● n resolución f

resort /rɪˈzɔːt/ n recurso m; (place) lugar m turístico. **in the last ~** como último recurso. □ **~ to** vt recurrir a.

resource /rɪˈsɔːs/ n recurso m. **~ful** adj ingenioso

respect /rɪˈspekt/ n (esteem) respeto m; (aspect) respecto m. **with ~ to** con respecto a. ● vt respetar. **~able** adj respetable. **~ful** adj respetuoso. **~ive** adj respectivo. **~ively** adv respectivamente

respiration /respəˈreɪʃn/ n respiración f

respite /ˈrespaɪt/ n respiro m

respon|d /rɪˈspɒnd/ vi responder. **~se** /rɪˈspɒns/ n respuesta f; (reaction) reacción f

responsib|ility /rɪspɒnsəˈbɪləti/ n responsabilidad f. **~le** /rɪˈspɒnsəbl/ adj responsable; (job) de responsabilidad. **~ly** adv con formalidad

responsive /rɪˈspɒnsɪv/ adj que reacciona bien. **~ to** sensible a

rest /rest/ vt descansar; (lean) apoyar. ● vi descansar; (lean) apoyarse. ● n descanso m; (Mus) pausa f; (remainder) resto m, lo demás; (people) los demás, los otros mpl. **to have a ~** tomarse un descanso. □ **~ up** vi (Amer) descansar

r

restaurant /'restərɒnt/ n restaurante m

rest ~**ful** adj sosegado. ~**ive** adj impaciente. ~**less** adj inquieto

restor|ation /restə'reɪʃn/ n restablecimiento m; (of building, monarch) restauración f. ~**e** /rɪ'stɔ:(r)/ vt restablecer; restaurar (building); devolver (confidence, health)

restrain /rɪ'streɪn/ vt contener. ~ **o.s.** contenerse. ~**ed** adj (moderate) moderado; (in control of self) comedido; ~**t** n restricción f; (moderation) compostura f

restrict /rɪ'strɪkt/ vt restringir. ~**ion** /-ʃn/ n restricción f. ~**ive** adj restrictivo

rest room n (Amer) baño m, servicio m

result /rɪ'zʌlt/ n resultado m. **as a** ~ **of** como consecuencia de. ● vi. ~ **from** resultar de. ~ **in** dar como resultado

resume /rɪ'zju:m/ vt reanudar. ● vi reanudarse

résumé /'rezjʊmeɪ/ n resumen m; (Amer, CV) currículum m, historial m personal

resurrect /rezə'rekt/ vt resucitar. ~**ion** /-ʃn/ n resurrección f

resuscitat|e /rɪ'sʌsɪteɪt/ vt resucitar. ~**ion** /-'teɪʃn/ n resucitación f

retail /'ri:teɪl/ n venta f al por menor. ● adj & adv al por menor. ● vt vender al por menor. ● vi venderse al por menor. ~**er** n minorista m & f

retain /rɪ'teɪn/ vt retener; conservar (heat)

retaliat|e /rɪ'tælɪeɪt/ vi desquitarse; (Mil) tomar represalias. ~**ion** /-'eɪʃn/ n represalias fpl

retarded /rɪ'tɑ:dɪd/ adj retrasado

rethink /ri:'θɪŋk/ vt (pt rethought) reconsiderar

reticen|ce /'retɪsns/ n reticencia f. ~**t** adj reticente

retina /'retɪnə/ n retina f

retinue /'retɪnju:/ n séquito m

retir|e /rɪ'taɪə(r)/ vi (from work) jubilarse; (withdraw) retirarse; (go to bed) acostarse. ~**ed** adj jubilado. ~**ement** n jubilación f. ~**ing** adj retraído

retort /rɪ'tɔ:t/ vt/i replicar. ● n réplica f

retrace /ri:'treɪs/ vt. ~ **one's steps** volver sobre sus pasos

retract /rɪ'trækt/ vt retirar (statement). ● vi retractarse

retrain /ri:'treɪn/ vi hacer un curso de reciclaje

retreat /rɪ'tri:t/ vi retirarse. ● n retirada f; (place) refugio m

retrial /ri:'traɪəl/ n nuevo juicio m

retriev|al /rɪ'tri:vl/ n recuperación f. ~**e** /rɪ'tri:v/ vt recuperar. ~**er** n (dog) perro m cobrador

retro|grade /'retrəgreɪd/ adj retrógrado. ~**spect** /-spekt/ n. **in** ~ en retrospectiva. ~**spective** /-'spektɪv/ adj retrospectivo

return /rɪ'tɜ:n/ vi volver, regresar; (symptom) reaparecer. ● vt devolver; corresponder a (affection). ● n regreso m, vuelta f; (Com) rendimiento m; (to owner) devolución f. **in** ~ **for** a cambio de. **many happy** ~**s!** ¡feliz cumpleaños! ~ **ticket** n billete m or (LAm) boleto m de ida y vuelta, boleto m redondo (Mex). ~**s** npl (Com) ingresos mpl

reun|ion /ri:'ju:nɪən/ n reunión f. ~**ite** /ri:ju:'naɪt/ vt reunir

rev /rev/ n (Auto, fam) revolución f. ● vt/i. ~ (**up**) (pt **revved**) (Auto, fam) acelerar(se)

reveal /rɪ'vi:l/ vt revelar. ~**ing** adj revelador

revel /'revl/ vi (pt **revelled**) tener un jolgorio. ~ **in** deleitarse en. ~**ry** n jolgorio m

revelation /revə'leɪʃn/ n revelación f

revenge /rɪ'vendʒ/ n venganza f. **take** ~ vengarse. ● vt vengar

revenue /'revənju:/ n ingresos mpl

revere /rɪ'vɪə(r)/ vt venerar. ~**nce** /'revərəns/ n reverencia f.

Reverend /'revərənd/ adj reverendo

reverent /'revərənt/ adj reverente

reverie /'revərɪ/ n ensueño m

revers|al /rɪ'vɜ:sl/ n inversión f. ~**e** /rɪ'vɜ:s/ adj inverso. ● n contrario m; (back) revés m; (Auto) marcha f atrás. ● vt invertir; anular (decision); (Auto) dar marcha atrás a. ● vi (Auto) dar marcha atrás

revert /rɪ'vɜːt/ vi. ~ **to** volver a; (Jurid) revertir a

review /rɪ'vjuː/ n revisión f; (Mil) revista f; (of book, play, etc) crítica f. ● vt examinar (situation); reseñar (book, play, etc); (Amer, for exam) repasar

revis|e /rɪ'vaɪz/ vt revisar; (Schol) repasar. ~**ion** /rɪ'vɪʒn/ n revisión f; (Schol) repaso m

revive /rɪ'vaɪv/ vt resucitar (person)

revolt /rɪ'vəʊlt/ vi sublevarse. ● n revuelta f. ~**ing** adj asqueroso

revolution /revə'luːʃn/ n revolución f. ~**ary** adj & n revolucionario (m). ~**ize** vt revolucionar

revolv|e /rɪ'vɒlv/ vi girar. ~**er** n revólver m. ~**ing** /rɪ'vɒlvɪŋ/ adj giratorio

revue /rɪ'vjuː/ n revista f

revulsion /rɪ'vʌlʃn/ n asco m

reward /rɪ'wɔːd/ n recompensa f. ● vt recompensar. ~**ing** adj gratificante

rewrite /riː'raɪt/ vt (pt rewrote, pp rewritten) volver a escribir or redactar; (copy out) escribir otra vez

rhetoric /'retərɪk/ n retórica f. ~**al** /rɪ'tɒrɪkl/ adj retórico

rheumatism /'ruːmətɪzəm/ n reumatismo m

rhinoceros /raɪ'nɒsərəs/ n (pl -oses or invar) rinoceronte m

rhubarb /'ruːbɑːb/ n ruibarbo m

rhyme /raɪm/ n rima f; (poem) poesía f. ● vt/i rimar

rhythm /'rɪðəm/ n ritmo m. ~**ic(al)** /'rɪðmɪk(l)/ adj rítmico

rib /rɪb/ n costilla f

ribbon /'rɪbən/ n cinta f

rice /raɪs/ n arroz m. ~ **pudding** n arroz con leche

rich /rɪtʃ/ adj (-er, -est) rico. ● n ricos mpl. ~**es** npl riquezas fpl

ricochet /'rɪkəʃeɪ/ vi rebotar

rid /rɪd/ vt (pt rid, pres p ridding) librar (of de). **get** ~ **of** deshacerse de. ~**dance** /'rɪdns/ n. **good** ~**dance!** ¡adiós y buen viaje!

ridden /'rɪdn/ see **RIDE**

riddle /'rɪdl/ n acertijo m. ● vt acribillar. **be** ~**d with** estar lleno de

ride /raɪd/ vi (pt rode, pp ridden) (on horseback) montar a caballo; (go) ir (en bicicleta, a caballo etc). ● vt montar a (horse); ir en (bicycle); (Amer) ir en (bus, train); recorrer (distance). ● n (on horse) cabalgata f; (in car) paseo m en coche. **take s.o. for a** ~ 🔟 engañarle a uno. ~**r** n (on horse) jinete m; (cyclist) ciclista m & f

ridge /rɪdʒ/ n (of hills) cadena f; (hilltop) cresta f

ridicul|e /'rɪdɪkjuːl/ n burlas fpl. ● vt ridiculizar. ~**ous** /rɪ'dɪkjʊləs/ adj ridículo

rife /raɪf/ adj difundido

rifle /'raɪfl/ n fusil m

rift /rɪft/ n grieta f; (fig) ruptura f

rig /rɪg/ vt (pt rigged) (pej) amañar. ● n (at sea) plataforma f de perforación. □ ~ **up** vt improvisar

right /raɪt/ adj (answer) correcto; (morally) bueno; (not left) derecho; (suitable) adecuado. **be** ~ (person) tener razón; (clock) estar bien. **it is** ~ (just, moral) es justo. **put** ~ rectificar. **the** ~ **person for the job** la persona indicada para el puesto. ● n (entitlement) derecho m; (not left) derecha f; (not evil) bien m. ~ **of way** (Auto) prioridad f. **be in the** ~ tener razón. **on the** ~ a la derecha. ● vt enderezar; (fig) reparar. ● adv a la derecha; (directly) derecho; (completely) completamente. ~ **angle** n ángulo m recto. ~ **away** adv inmediatamente. ~**eous** /'raɪtʃəs/ adj recto; (cause) justo. ~**ful** /'raɪtfl/ adj legítimo. ~-**handed** /-'hændɪd/ adj diestro. ~-**hand man** n brazo m derecho. ~**ly** adv justamente. ~ **wing** adj (Pol) derechista

rigid /'rɪdʒɪd/ adj rígido

rig|orous /'rɪgərəs/ adj riguroso. ~**our** /'rɪgə(r)/ n rigor m

rim /rɪm/ n borde m; (of wheel) llanta f; (of glasses) montura f

rind /raɪnd/ n corteza f; (of fruit) cáscara f

ring[1] /rɪŋ/ n (circle) círculo m; (circle of metal etc) aro m; (on finger) anillo m; (on finger with stone) sortija f; (Boxing) cuadrilátero m; (bullring) ruedo m; (for circus) pista f. ● vt cercar

ring[2] /rɪŋ/ n (of bell) toque m; (tinkle) tintineo m; (telephone call) llamada f.

● vt (pt **rang**, pp **rung**) hacer sonar; (telephone) llamar por teléfono. ~ **the bell** tocar el timbre. ● vi sonar. ~ **back** vt/i volver a llamar. □ ~ **up** vt llamar por teléfono

ring: ~**leader** /'rɪŋli:də(r)/ n cabecilla m & f. ~ **road** n carretera f de circunvalación

rink /rɪŋk/ n pista f

rinse /rɪns/ vt enjuagar. ● n aclarado m; (of dishes) enjuague m; (for hair) tintura f (no permanente)

riot /'raɪət/ n disturbio m; (of colours) profusión f. **run** ~ desenfrenarse. ● vi causar disturbios

rip /rɪp/ vt (pt **ripped**) rasgar. ● vi rasgarse. ● n rasgón m. □ ~ **off** vt (pull off) arrancar; (⊠, cheat) robar

ripe /raɪp/ adj (-**er**, -**est**) maduro. ~**n** /'raɪpn/ vt/i madurar

rip-off /'rɪpɒf/ n ⊠ timo m

ripple /'rɪpl/ n (on water) onda f

ris|e /raɪz/ vi (pt **rose**, pp **risen**) subir; (sun) salir; (river) crecer; (prices) subir; (land) elevarse; (get up) levantarse. ● n subida f; (land) altura f; (increase) aumento m; (to power) ascenso m. **give** ~**e to** ocasionar. ~**er** n. **early** ~**er** n madrugador m. ~**ing** n. ● adj (sun) naciente; (number) creciente; (prices) en alza

risk /rɪsk/ n riesgo m. ● vt arriesgar. ~**y** adj (-**ier**, -**iest**) arriesgado

rite /raɪt/ n rito m

ritual /'rɪtʃʊəl/ adj & n ritual (m)

rival /'raɪvl/ adj & n rival (m). ~**ry** n rivalidad f

river /'rɪvə(r)/ n río m

rivet /'rɪvɪt/ n remache m. ~**ing** adj fascinante

road /rəʊd/ n (in town) calle f; (between towns) carretera f; (route, way) camino m. ~ **map** n mapa m de carreteras. ~**side** n borde m de la carretera. ~**works** npl obras fpl. ~**worthy** adj (vehicle) apto para circular

roam /rəʊm/ vi vagar

roar /rɔ:(r)/ n rugido m; (laughter) carcajada f. ● vt/i rugir. ~ **past** (vehicles) pasar con estruendo. ~ **with laugh-**ter reírse a carcajadas. ~**ing** adj (trade etc) activo

roast /rəʊst/ vt asar; tostar (coffee). ● adj & n asado (m). ~ **beef** n rosbif m

rob /rɒb/ vt (pt **robbed**) atracar, asaltar (bank); robarle a (person). ~ **of** (deprive of) privar de. ~**ber** n ladrón m; (of bank) atracador m. ~**bery** n robo m; (of bank) atraco m

robe /rəʊb/ n bata f; (Univ etc) toga f

robin /'rɒbɪn/ n petirrojo m

robot /'rəʊbɒt/ n robot m

robust /rəʊ'bʌst/ adj robusto

rock /rɒk/ n roca f; (crag, cliff) peñasco m. ● vt mecer; (shake) sacudir. ● vi mecerse; (shake) sacudirse. ● n (Mus) música f rock. ~**-bottom** /-'bɒtəm/ adj ⊞ bajísimo

rocket /'rɒkɪt/ n cohete m

rock ~**ing-chair** n mecedora f. ~**y** adj (-**ier**, -**iest**) rocoso; (fig, shaky) bamboleante

rod /rɒd/ n vara f; (for fishing) caña f; (metal) barra f

rode /rəʊd/ see RIDE

rodent /'rəʊdnt/ n roedor m

rogue /rəʊg/ n pícaro m

role /rəʊl/ n papel m

roll /rəʊl/ vt hacer rodar; (roll up) enrollar; allanar (lawn); aplanar (pastry). ● vi rodar; (ship) balancearse; (on floor) revolcarse. **be** ~**ing in money** ⊞ nadar en dinero ● n rollo m; (of ship) balanceo m; (of drum) redoble m; (of thunder) retumbo m; (bread) panecillo m, bolillo m (Mex). □ ~ **over** vi (turn over) dar una vuelta. □ ~ **up** vt enrollar; arremangar (sleeve). vi ⊞ llegar. ~**-call** n lista f

roller /'rəʊlə(r)/ n rodillo m; (wheel) rueda f; (for hair) rulo m. **R**~ **blades** npl (P) patines mpl en línea. ~**-coaster** n montaña f rusa. ~**-skate** n patín m de ruedas. ~**-skating** patinaje m (sobre ruedas)

rolling /'rəʊlɪŋ/ adj ondulado. ~**-pin** n rodillo m

ROM /rɒm/ n (= **read-only memory**) ROM f

Roman /'rəʊmən/ adj & n romano (m). ~ **Catholic** adj & n católico (m) (romano)

romance /rəʊˈmæns/ n novela f romántica; (love) amor m; (affair) aventura f

Romania /ruːˈmeɪnɪə/ n Rumania f, Rumanía f. **~n** adj & n rumano (m)

romantic /rəʊˈmæntɪk/ adj romántico

Rome /ˈrəʊm/ n Roma f

romp /rɒmp/ vi retozar

roof /ruːf/ n techo m, tejado m; (of mouth) paladar m. ● vt techar. **~rack** n baca f. **~top** n tejado m

rook /rʊk/ n grajo m; (in chess) torre f

room /ruːm/ n cuarto m, habitación f; (bedroom) dormitorio m; (space) espacio m; (large hall) sala f. **~y** adj espacioso

roost /ruːst/ vi posarse. **~er** n gallo m

root /ruːt/ n raíz f. **take ~** echar raíces; (idea) arraigarse. ● vi echar raíces. **~ about** vi hurgar. □ **~ for** vt [T] alentar. □ **~ out** vt extirpar

rope /rəʊp/ n cuerda f. **know the ~s** estar al corriente. ● vt atar; (Amer, lasso) enlazar. □ **~ in** vt agarrar

rose¹ /rəʊz/ n rosa f; (nozzle) roseta f

rose² /rəʊz/ see RISE

rosé /ˈrəʊzeɪ/ n (vino m) rosado m

rot /rɒt/ vt (pt rotted) pudrir. ● vi pudrirse. ● n putrefacción f

rota /ˈrəʊtə/ n lista f (de turnos)

rotary /ˈrəʊtərɪ/ adj rotatorio

rotatle /rəʊˈteɪt/ vt girar; (change round) alternar. ● vi girar; (change round) alternarse. **~ion** /-ʃn/ n rotación f

rote /rəʊt/ n. **by ~** de memoria

rotten /ˈrɒtn/ adj podrido; [T] pésimo [T]; (weather) horrible

rough /rʌf/ adj (-er, -est) áspero; (person) tosco; (bad) malo; (ground) accidentado; (violent) brutal; (approximate) aproximado; (diamond) bruto. ● adv duro. **~ copy**, **~ draft** borrador m. ● vt. **~ it** vivir sin comodidades. **~age** /ˈrʌfɪdʒ/ n fibra f. **~-and-ready** adj improvisado. **~ly** adv bruscamente; (more or less) aproximadamente

roulette /ruːˈlet/ n ruleta f

round /raʊnd/ adj (-er, -est) redondo. ● n círculo m; (of visits, drinks) ronda f; (of competition) vuelta f; (Boxing)

asalto m. ● prep alrededor de. ● adv alrededor. **~ about** (approximately) aproximadamente. **come ~ to**, **go ~ to** (a friend etc) pasar por casa de. ● vt doblar (corner). □ **~ off** vt terminar; redondear (number). □ **~ up** vt rodear (cattle); hacer una redada de (suspects). **~about** n tiovivo m, carrusel m (LAm); (for traffic) glorieta f, rotonda f. ● adj in directo. **~ trip** n viaje m de ida y vuelta. **~-up** n resumen m; (of suspects) redada f

rous|e /raʊz/ vt despertar. **~ing** adj enardecedor

route /ruːt/ n ruta f; (Naut, Aviat) rumbo m; (of bus) línea f

routine /ruːˈtiːn/ n rutina f. ● adj rutinario

row¹ /rəʊ/ n fila f. ● vi remar

row² /raʊ/ n (fam, noise) bulla f [T]; (quarrel) pelea f. ● vi [T] pelearse

rowboat /ˈrəʊbəʊt/ (Amer) n bote m de remos

rowdy /ˈraʊdɪ/ adj (-ier, -iest) n escandaloso, alborotador

rowing /ˈrəʊɪŋ/ n remo m. **~ boat** n bote m de remos

royal /ˈrɔɪəl/ adj real. **~ist** adj & n monárquico (m). **~ly** adv magníficamente. **~ty** n realeza f

rub /rʌb/ vt (pt rubbed) frotar. □ **~ out** vt borrar

rubber /ˈrʌbə(r)/ n goma f, caucho m, hule m (Mex); (eraser) goma f (de borrar). **~ band** n goma f (elástica). **~-stamp** vt (fig) autorizar. **~y** adj parecido al caucho

rubbish /ˈrʌbɪʃ/ n basura f; (junk) trastos mpl; (fig) tonterías fpl. **~ bin** n cubo m de la basura, bote m de la basura (Mex). **~y** adj sin valor

rubble /ˈrʌbl/ n escombros mpl

ruby /ˈruːbɪ/ n rubí m

rucksack /ˈrʌksæk/ n mochila f

rudder /ˈrʌdə(r)/ n timón m

rude /ruːd/ adj (-er, -est) grosero, mal educado; (improper) indecente; (brusque) brusco. **~ly** adv groseramente. **~ness** n mala educación f

rudimentary /ruːdɪˈmentrɪ/ adj rudimentario

ruffian /ˈrʌfɪən/ n rufián m

r

ruffle /'rʌfl/ vt despeinar (hair); arrugar (clothes)

rug /rʌg/ n alfombra f, tapete m (Mex); (blanket) manta f de viaje

rugged /'rʌgɪd/ adj (coast) escarpado; (landscape) escabroso

ruin /'ruːɪn/ n ruina f. ● vt arruinar; (spoil) estropear

rul|e /ruːl/ n regla f; (Pol) dominio m. **as a ~** por regla general. ● vt gobernar; (master) dominar; (Jurid) dictaminar. **~e out** vt descartar. **~ed paper** n papel m rayado. **~er** n (sovereign) soberano m; (leader) gobernante m & f; (measure) regla f. **~ing** adj (class) dirigente. ● n decisión f

rum /rʌm/ n ron m

rumble /'rʌmbl/ vi retumbar; (stomach) hacer ruidos

rummage /'rʌmɪdʒ/ vi hurgar

rumour /'ruːmə(r)/ n rumor m. ● vt. **it is ~ed that** se rumorea que

rump steak /rʌmpsteɪk/ n filete m de cadera

run /rʌn/ vi (pt ran, pp run, pres p running) correr; (water) correr; (function) funcionar; (melt) derretirse; (makeup) corrense; (colour) desteñir; (bus etc) circular; (in election) presentarse. ● vt correr (race); dirigir (business); correr (risk); (move, pass) pasar; tender (wire); preparar (bath). **~ a temperature** tener fiebre. ● n corrida f, carrera f; (outing) paseo m (en coche); (ski) pista f. **in the long ~** a la larga. **be on the ~** estar prófugo. □ **~ away** vi huir, escaparse. □ **~ down** vi bajar corriendo; (battery) descargarse. vt (Auto) atropellar; (belittle) denigrar. □ **~ in** vi entrar corriendo. □ **~ into** vt toparse con (friend); (hit) chocar con. □ **~ off** vt sacar (copies). □ **~ out** vi salir corriendo; (liquid) salirse; (fig) agotarse. □ **~ out of** vt quedarse sin. □ **~ over** vt (Auto) atropellar. □ **~ through** vt (review) ensayar; (rehearse) repasar. □ **~ up** vt ir acumulando (bill). vi subir corriendo. **~away** n fugitivo m. **~ down** adj (person) agotado

rung¹ /rʌŋ/ n (of ladder) peldaño m

rung² /rʌŋ/ see RING

run ~ner /'rʌnə(r)/ n corredor m; (on sledge) patín m. **~ner bean** n judía f escarlata. **~ner-up** n. be **~er-up** quedar en segundo lugar. **~ning** n. **be in the ~ning** tener posibilidades de ganar. ● adj (water) corriente; (commentary) en directo. **four times ~ning** cuatro veces seguidas. **~ny** /'rʌnɪ/ adj líquido; (nose) que moquea. **~way** n pista f de aterrizaje

rupture /'rʌptʃə(r)/ n ruptura f. ● vt romper

rural /'rʊərəl/ adj rural

ruse /ruːz/ n ardid m

rush /rʌʃ/ n (haste) prisa f; (crush) bullicio m; (plant) junco m. ● vi precipitarse. ● vt apresurar; (Mil) asaltar. **~-hour** n hora f punta, hora f pico (LAm)

Russia /'rʌʃə/ n Rusia f. **~n** adj & n ruso (m)

rust /rʌst/ n orín m. ● vt oxidar. ● vi oxidarse

rustle /'rʌsl/ vt hacer susurrar; (Amer) robar. ● vi susurrar □ **~ up** vt 🄸 preparar.

rust ~proof adj inoxidable. **~y** (-ier, -iest) oxidado

rut /rʌt/ n surco m. **be in a ~** estar anquilosado

ruthless /'ruːθlɪs/ adj despiadado

rye /raɪ/ n centeno m

Ss

S abbr (= **south**) S

sabot|age /'sæbətɑːʒ/ n sabotaje m. ● vt sabotear. **~eur** /-'tɜː(r)/ n saboteador m

saccharin /'sækərɪn/ n sacarina f

sachet /'sæʃeɪ/ n bolsita f

sack /sæk/ n saco m. **get the ~** 🄸 ser despedido. ● vt 🄸 despedir, echar

sacrament /'sækrəmənt/ n sacramento m

sacred /'seɪkrɪd/ adj sagrado

sacrifice /'sækrɪfaɪs/ n sacrificio m. ● vt sacrificar

sacrileg|e /'sækrılıdʒ/ n sacrilegio m. **~ious** /-'lıdʒəs/ adj sacrílego

sad /sæd/ adj (**sadder, saddest**) triste. **~den** vt entristecer

saddle /'sædl/ n silla f de montar. ● vt ensillar (horse). **~ s.o. with sth** (fig) endilgarle algo a uno

sadlst /'seɪdɪst/ n sádico m. **~tic** /sə'dɪstɪk/ adj sádico

sadly /'sædlɪ/ adv tristemente; (fig) desgraciadamente. **~ness** n tristeza f

safe /seɪf/ adj (-er, -est) seguro; (out of danger) salvo; (cautious) prudente. **~ and sound** sano y salvo. ● n caja f fuerte. **~ deposit** n caja f de seguridad. **~guard** n salvaguardia f. ● vt salvaguardar. **~ly** adv sin peligro; (in safe place) en lugar seguro. **~ty** n seguridad f. **~ty belt** n cinturón m de seguridad. **~ty pin** n imperdible m

sag /sæg/ vi (pt **sagged**) (ceiling) combarse; (bed) hundirse

saga /'sɑːgə/ n saga f

Sagittarius /sædʒɪ'teərɪəs/ n Sagitario m

said /sed/ see SAY

sail /seɪl/ n vela f; (trip) paseo m (en barco). **set ~** zarpar. ● vi navegar; (leave) partir; (Sport) practicar la vela; (fig) deslizarse. **go ~ing** salir a navegar. vt gobernar (boat). **~boat** n (Amer) barco m de vela. **~ing** n (Sport) vela f. **~ing boat** n, **~ing ship** n barco m de vela. **~or** n marinero m

saint /seɪnt//sənt/ n santo m. **~ly** adj santo

sake /seɪk/ n. **for the ~ of** por. **for God's ~** por el amor de Dios

salad /'sæləd/ n ensalada f. **~ bowl** n ensaladera f. **~ dressing** n aliño m

salary /'sælərɪ/ n sueldo m

sale /seɪl/ n venta f; (at reduced prices) liquidación f. **for ~** (sign) se vende. **be for ~** estar a la venta. **be on ~** (Amer, reduced) estar en liquidación. **~able** adj vendible. (for sale) estar a la venta. **~s clerk** n (Amer) dependiente m, dependienta f. **~sman** /-mən/ n vendedor m; (in shop) dependiente m. **~swoman** n vendedora f; (in shop) dependienta f

saliva /sə'laɪvə/ n saliva f

salmon /'sæmən/ n invar salmón m

saloon /sə'luːn/ n (on ship) salón m; (Amer, bar) bar m; (Auto) turismo m

salt /sɔːlt/ n sal f. ● vt salar. **~ cellar** n salero m. **~y** adj salado

salute /sə'luːt/ n saludo m. ● vt saludar. ● vi hacer un saludo

Salvadorean, Salvadorian /sælvə'dɔːrɪən/ adj & n salvadoreño (m)

salvage /'sælvɪdʒ/ vt salvar

salvation /sæl'veɪʃn/ n salvación f

same /seɪm/ adj igual (as que); (before noun) mismo (as que). **at the ~ time** al mismo tiempo. ● pron. **the ~** lo mismo. **all the ~** de todas formas. ● adv. **the ~** igual

sample /'sɑːmpl/ n muestra f. ● vt degustar (food)

sanct|ify /'sæŋktɪfaɪ/ vt santificar. **~ion** /'sæŋkʃn/ n sanción f. ● vt sancionar. **~uary** /'sæŋktʃʊərɪ/ n (Relig) santuario m; (for wildlife) reserva f; (refuge) asilo m

sand /sænd/ n arena f. ● vt pulir (floor). □ **~ down** vt lijar (wood)

sandal /'sændl/ n sandalia f

sand ~castle n castillo m de arena. **~paper** n papel m de lija. ● vt lijar. **~storm** n tormenta f de arena

sandwich /'sænwɪdʒ/ n bocadillo m, sandwich m. ● vt. **be ~ed between** (person) estar apretujado entre

sandy /'sændɪ/ adj arenoso

sane /seɪn/ adj (-er, -est) (person) cuerdo; (sensible) sensato

sang /sæŋ/ see SING

sanitary /'sænɪtrɪ/ adj higiénico; (system etc) sanitario. **~ towel, ~ napkin** n (Amer) compresa f (higiénica)

sanitation /sænɪ'teɪʃn/ n higiene f; (drainage) sistema m sanitario

sanlty /'sænɪtɪ/ n cordura f

sank /sæŋk/ see SINK

Santa (Claus) /'sæntə(klɔːz)/ n Papá m Noel

sap /sæp/ n (in plants) savia f. ● (pt **sapped**) minar

sapling /'sæplɪŋ/ n árbol m joven

sapphire /'sæfaɪə(r)/ n zafiro m

sarcas|m /'sɑːkæzəm/ n sarcasmo m. **~tic** /-'kæstɪk/ adj sarcástico

sardine /sɑː'diːn/ n sardina f

sash /sæʃ/ n (over shoulder) banda f; (round waist) fajín m.

sat /sæt/ see **SIT**

SAT abbr (Amer) (**Scholastic Aptitude Test**); (Brit) (**Standard Assessment Task**)

satchel /'sætʃl/ n cartera f

satellite /'sætəlaɪt/ n & a satélite (m). ~ **TV** n televisión f por satélite

satin /'sætɪn/ n raso m. ● adj de raso

satir|e /'sætaɪə(r)/ n sátira f. ~**ical** /sə'tɪrɪkl/ adj satírico. ~**ize** /'sætəraɪz/ vt satirizar

satis|faction /sætɪs'fækʃn/ n satisfacción f. ~**factorily** /-'fæktərɪlɪ/ adv satisfactoriamente. ~**factory** /-'fæktərɪ/ adj satisfactorio. ~**fy** /'sætɪsfaɪ/ vt satisfacer; (convince) convencer. ~**fying** adj satisfactorio

satphone /'sætfəʊn/ n teléfono m satélite

saturat|e /'sætʃəreɪt/ vt saturar. ~**ed** adj saturado; (drenched) empapado

Saturday /'sætədeɪ/ n sábado m

Saturn /'sætən/ n Saturno m

sauce /sɔːs/ n salsa f; (cheek) descaro m. ~**pan** /'sɔːspən/ n cazo m, cacerola f. ~**r** /'sɔːsə(r)/ n platillo m

saucy /'sɔːsɪ/ adj (-ier, -iest) descarado

Saudi /'saʊdɪ/ adj & n saudita (m & f). ~ **Arabia** /-ə'reɪbɪə/ n Arabia f Saudí

sauna /'sɔːnə/ n sauna f

saunter /'sɔːntə(r)/ vi pasearse

sausage /'sɒsɪdʒ/ n salchicha f

savage /'sævɪdʒ/ adj salvaje; (fierce) feroz. ● n salvaje m & f. ● vt atacar. ~**ry** n ferocidad f

sav|e /seɪv/ vt (rescue) salvar; ahorrar (money, time); (prevent) evitar; (Comp) guardar. ● n (football) parada f. ● prep salvo, excepto. □ ~**e up** vi/t ahorrar. ~**er** n ahorrador m. ~**ing** n ahorro m. ~**ings** npl ahorros mpl

saviour /'seɪvɪə(r)/ n salvador m

savour /'seɪvə(r)/ vt saborear. ~**y** adj (appetizing) sabroso; (not sweet) no dulce

saw[1] /sɔː/ see **SEE**[1]

saw[2] /sɔː/ n sierra f. ● vt (pt sawed, pp sawn) serrar. ~**dust** n serrín m. ~**n** /sɔːn/ see **SAW**[2]

saxophone /'sæksəfəʊn/ n saxofón m, saxófono m

say /seɪ/ vt/i (pt said /sed/) decir; rezar (prayer). ● n. **have a** ~ expresar una opinión; (in decision) tener voz en capítulo. **have no** ~ no tener ni voz ni voto. ~**ing** n refrán m

scab /skæb/ n costra f; (fam, blackleg) esquirol m

scaffolding /'skæfəldɪŋ/ n andamios mpl

scald /skɔːld/ vt escaldar

scale /skeɪl/ n (also Mus) escala f; (of fish) escama f. ● vt (climb) escalar. ~ **down** vt reducir (a escala) (drawing); recortar (operation). ~**s** npl (for weighing) balanza f, peso m

scallion /'skælɪən/ n (Amer) cebolleta f

scalp /skælp/ vt quitar el cuero cabelludo a. ● n cuero m cabelludo

scamper /'skæmpə(r)/ vi. ~ **away** irse correteando

scan /skæn/ vt (pt scanned) escudriñar; (quickly) echar un vistazo a; (radar) explorar

scandal /'skændl/ n escándalo m; (gossip) chismorreo m. ~**ize** vt escandalizar. ~**ous** adj escandaloso

Scandinavia /skændɪ'neɪvɪə/ n Escandinavia f. ~**n** adj & n escandinavo (m)

scant /skænt/ adj escaso. ~**y** adj (-ier, -iest) escaso

scapegoat /'skeɪpgəʊt/ n cabeza f de turco

scar /skɑː(r)/ n cicatriz f

scarc|e /skeəs/ adj (-er, -est) escaso. **be** ~**e** escasear. **make o.s.** ~**e** 🅸 mantenerse lejos. ~**ely** adv apenas. ~**ity** n escasez f

scare /'skeə(r)/ vt asustar. **be** ~**d** tener miedo. **be** ~**d of sth** tenerle miedo a algo. ● n susto m. ~**crow** n espantapájaros m

scarf /skɑːf/ n (pl **scarves**) bufanda f; (over head) pañuelo m

scarlet /'skɑːlət/ adj escarlata f. ~ **fever** n escarlatina f

scarves /skɑːvz/ see **SCARF**

scary /'skeərɪ/ adj (-ier, -iest) que da miedo

scathing /'skeɪðɪŋ/ adj mordaz

scatter /'skætə(r)/ vt (throw) esparcir; (disperse) dispersar. ● vi dispersarse. **~ed** /'skætəd/ adj disperso; (occasional) esporádico

scavenge /'skævɪndʒ/ vi escarbar (en la basura)

scenario /sɪ'nɑːrɪəʊ/ n (pl -os) perspectiva f; (of film) guión m

scen|e /siːn/ n escena f; (sight) vista f; (fuss) lío m. **behind the ~es** entre bastidores. **~ery** /'siːnərɪ/ n paisaje m; (in theatre) decorado m. **~ic** /'siːnɪk/ adj pintoresco

scent /sent/ n olor m; (perfume) perfume m; (trail) pista f. ● vt intuir; (make fragrant) perfumar

sceptic /'skeptɪk/ n escéptico m. **~al** adj escéptico. **~ism** /ɪzəm/ n escepticismo m

sceptre /'septə(r)/ n cetro m

schedule /'ʃedjuːl, 'skedjuːl/ n programa f; (timetable) horario m. **behind ~** atrasado. **it's on ~** va de acuerdo a lo previsto. ● vt proyectar. **~d flight** n vuelo m regular

scheme /skiːm/ n proyecto m; (plot) intriga f ● vi (pej) intrigar

schizophrenic /skɪtsə'frenɪk/ adj & n esquizofrénico (m)

scholar /'skɒlə(r)/ n erudito m. **~ly** adj erudito. **~ship** n erudición f; (grant) beca f

school /skuːl/ n escuela f; (Univ) facultad f ● adj (age, holidays, year) escolar. ● vt instruir; (train) capacitar. **~boy** n colegial m. **~girl** n colegiala f. **~ing** n instrucción f. **~master** n (primary) maestro m; (secondary) profesor m. **~mistress** n (primary) maestra f; (secondary) profesora f. **~teacher** n (primary) maestro m; (secondary) profesor m

scien|ce /'saɪəns/ n ciencia f. **study ~ce** estudiar ciencias. **~ce fiction** n ciencia f ficción. **~tific** /'tɪfɪk/ adj científico. **~tist** /'saɪəntɪst/ n científico m

scissors /'sɪsəz/ npl tijeras fpl

scoff /skɒf/ vt 🄴 zamparse. ● vi. **~ at** mofarse de

scold /skəʊld/ vt regañar

scoop /skuːp/ n pala f; (news) primicia f. □ **~ out** vt sacar; excavar (hole)

scooter /'skuːtə(r)/ n escúter m; (for child) patinete m

scope /skəʊp/ n alcance m; (opportunity) oportunidad f

scorch /skɔːtʃ/ vt chamuscar. **~ing** adj 🄴 de mucho calor

score /skɔː(r)/ n tanteo m; (Mus) partitura f; (twenty) veintena f. **on that ~** en cuanto a eso. **know the ~** 🄴 saber cómo son las cosas. ● vt marcar (goal); anotarse (points); (cut, mark) rayar; conseguir (success). ● vi marcar

scorn /skɔːn/ n desdén m. ● vt desdeñar. **~ful** adj desdeñoso

Scorpio /'skɔːpɪəʊ/ n Escorpio m, Escorpión m

scorpion /'skɔːpɪən/ n escorpión m

Scot /skɒt/ n escocés m. **~ch** /skɒtʃ/ n whisky m, güisqui m

---

Scottish Parliament El Parlamento Escocés fue establecido en Edinburgo en 1999. Tiene competencia legislativa y ejecutiva en los asuntos internos de Escocia y poderes tributarios limitados. Los MSPs (Members of the Scottish Parliament) son 129, de los cuales 73 son elegidos directamente y el resto mediante el sistema de representación proporcional.

---

scotch /skɒtʃ/ vt frustrar; acallar (rumours)

Scotch tape n (Amer) celo m, cinta f Scotch

Scot|land /'skɒtlənd/ n Escocia f. **~s** adj escocés. **~tish** adj escocés

scoundrel /'skaʊndrəl/ n canalla f

scour /'skaʊə(r)/ vt fregar; (search) registrar. **~er** n estropajo m

scourge /skɔːdʒ/ n azote m

scout /skaʊt/ n explorador m. **Boy S~** explorador m

scowl /skaʊl/ n ceño m fruncido. ● vi fruncir el ceño

scram /skræm/ vi 🄴 largarse

scramble /'skræmbl/ vi (clamber) gatear. ● n (difficult climb) subida f difícil; (struggle) rebatiña f. **~d egg** n huevos mpl revueltos

scrap /skræp/ n pedacito m; (fam, fight) pelea f. ● vt (pt **scrapped**) dese-

S

char. **~book** n álbum m de recortes.
~s npl sobras fpl

scrape /skreɪp/ n (fig) apuro m. ● vt
raspar; (graze) rasparse; (rub) rascar.
□ **~ through** vi/t aprobar por los
pelos (exam). □ **~ together** vt reunir.
~r n rasqueta f

scrap ~heap n montón m de deshe-
chos. **~ yard** n chatarrería f

scratch /skrætʃ/ vt rayar (furniture, record); (with nail etc) arañar; rascarse
(itch). ● vi arañar. ● n rayón m; (from
nail etc) arañazo m. **start from ~** empezar desde cero. **be up to ~** dar la
talla

scrawl /skrɔːl/ n garabato m. ● vt/i ga-
rabatear

scream /skriːm/ vt/i gritar. ● n grito m

screech /skriːtʃ/ vi chillar; (brakes etc)
chirriar. ● n chillido m; (of brakes etc)
chirrido m

screen /skriːn/ n pantalla f; (folding)
biombo m. ● vt (hide) ocultar; (protect) proteger; proyectar (film)

screw /skruː/ n tornillo m. ● vt atornillar. □ **~ up** vt atornillar; entornar
(eyes); torcer (face); (sl, ruin) fastidiar.
~driver n destornillador m

scribble /ˈskrɪbl/ vt/i garrabatear. ● n
garrabato m

script /skrɪpt/ n escritura f; (of film
etc) guión m

scroll /skrəʊl/ n rollo m (de pergamino). □ **~ down** vi retroceder la
pantalla. □ **~ up** vi avanzar la pantalla

scrounge /skraʊndʒ/ vt/i gorronear.
~r n gorrón m

scrub /skrʌb/ n (land) maleza f. ● vt/i
(pt scrubbed) fregar

scruff /skrʌf/ n. **by the ~ of the
neck** por el pescuezo. **~y** adj (-ier,
-iest) desaliñado

scrup|le /ˈskruːpl/ n escrúpulo m.
~ulous /-jələs/ adj escrupuloso

scrutin|ize /ˈskruːtɪnaɪz/ vt escudri-
ñar; inspeccionar (document). **~y**
/ˈskruːtɪnɪ/ n examen m minucioso

scuffle /ˈskʌfl/ n refriega f

sculpt /skʌlpt/ vt/i esculpir. **~or** n es-
cultor m. **~ure** /-tʃə(r)/ n escultura f.
● vt/i esculpir

scum /skʌm/ n espuma f; (people, pej)
escoria f

scupper /ˈskʌpə(r)/ vt echar por tierra
(plans)

scurry /ˈskʌrɪ/ vi corretear

scuttle /ˈskʌtl/ n cubo m del carbón.
● vt barrenar (ship). ● vi. **~ away** escabullirse rápidamente

scythe /saɪð/ n guadaña f

SE abbr (= **south-east**) SE

sea /siː/ n mar m. **at ~** en el mar; (fig)
confuso. **by ~** por mar. **~food** n
mariscos mpl. **~ front** n paseo m marítimo, malecón m (LAm). **~gull** n gaviota f. **~horse** n caballito m de mar

seal /siːl/ n sello m; (animal) foca f. ● vt
sellar

sea level n nivel m del mar

sea lion n león m marino

seam /siːm/ n costura f; (of coal)
veta f

seaman /ˈsiːmən/ n (pl **-men**) marinero m

seamy /ˈsiːmɪ/ adj sórdido

seance /ˈseɪɑːns/ n sesión f de espiri-
tismo

search /sɜːtʃ/ vt registrar; buscar en
(records). ● vi buscar. ● n (for sth)
búsqueda f; (of sth) registro m; (Comp)
búsqueda f. **in ~ of** en busca de.
□ **~ for** vt buscar. **~ engine** n buscador m. **~ing** adj penetrante. **~light** n
reflector m. **~ party** n partida f de
rescate

sea ~shore n orilla f del mar. **~sick**
adj mareado. **be ~sick** marearse.
~side n playa f

season /ˈsiːzn/ n estación f; (period)
temporada f. **high/low ~** temporada
f alta/baja. ● vt (Culin) sazonar. **~al** adj
estacional; (demand) de estación.
~ed adj (fig) avezado. **~ing** n condimento m. **~ ticket** n abono m (de
temporada)

seat /siːt/ n asiento m; (place) lugar m;
(in cinema, theatre) localidad f; (of
trousers) fondillos mpl. **take a ~** sentarse. ● vt sentar; (have seats for)
(auditorium) tener capacidad para;
(bus) tener asientos para. **~belt** n
cinturón m de seguridad

sea ~ trout n reo m. **~-urchin** n
erizo m de mar. **~weed** n alga f ma-

rina. **~worthy** adj en condiciones de navegar

seclu|ded /sɪ'kluːdɪd/ adj aislado

second /'sekənd/ adj & n segundo (m). **on ~ thoughts** pensándolo bien. ● adv (in race etc) en segundo lugar. ● vt secundar. **~s** npl (goods) artículos mpl de segunda calidad; (fam, more food) **have ~s** repetir. ● /sɪ'kɒnd/ vt (transfer) trasladar temporalmente. **~ary** /'sekəndrɪ/ adj secundario. **~ary school** n instituto m (de enseñanza secundaria)

second ~class adj de segunda (clase). **~hand** adj de segunda mano. **~ly** adv en segundo lugar. **~rate** adj mediocre

secre|cy /'siːkrəsɪ/ n secreto m. **~t** adj & n secreto (m). **in ~t** en secreto

secretar|ial /sekrə'teərɪəl/ adj de secretario; (course) de secretariado. **~y** /'sekrətrɪ/ n secretario m. **S~y of State** (in UK) ministro m; (in US) secretario m de Estado

secretive /'siːkrɪtɪv/ adj reservado

sect /sekt/ n secta f. **~arian** /-'teərɪən/ adj sectario

section /'sekʃn/ n sección f; (part) parte f

sector /'sektə(r)/ n sector m

secular /'sekjʊlə(r)/ adj secular

secur|e /sɪ'kjʊə(r)/ adj seguro; (shelf) firme. ● vt asegurar; (obtain) obtener. **~ely** adv seguramente. **~ity** n seguridad f; (for loan) garantía f

sedat|e /sɪ'deɪt/ adj reposado. ● vt sedar. **~ion** /sɪ'deɪʃn/ n sedación f **~ive** /'sedətɪv/ adj & n sedante (m)

sediment /'sedɪmənt/ n sedimento m

seduc|e /sɪ'djuːs/ vt seducir. **~er** n seductor m. **~tion** /sɪ'dʌkʃn/ n seducción f. **~tive** /sɪ'dʌktɪv/ adj seductor

see /siː/ ● vt (pt saw, pp seen) ver; (understand) comprender; (escort) acompañar. **~ing that** visto que. **~ you later!** ¡hasta luego! ● vi ver. □ **~ off** vt (say goodbye to) despedirse de. □ **~ through** vt llevar a cabo; calar (person). □ **~ to** vt ocuparse de

seed /siːd/ n semilla f; (fig) germen m; (Amer, pip) pepita f. **go to ~** granar; (fig) echarse a perder. **~ling** n planta f

de semillero. **~y** adj (-ier, -iest) sórdido

seek /siːk/ vt (pt sought) buscar; pedir (approval). □ **~ out** vt buscar

seem /siːm/ vi parecer

seen /siːn/ see SEE

seep /siːp/ vi filtrarse

see-saw /'siːsɔː/ n balancín m

seethe /siːð/ vi (fig) estar furioso. **I was seething with anger** me hervía la sangre

see-through /'siːθruː/ adj transparente

segment /'segmənt/ n segmento m; (of orange) gajo m

segregat|e /'segrɪgeɪt/ vt segregar. **~ion** /-'geɪʃn/ n segregación f

seiz|e /siːz/ vt agarrar; (Jurid) incautar. **~e on** vt aprovechar (chance). □ **~e up** vi (Tec) agarrotarse. **~ure** /'siːʒə(r)/ n incautación f; (Med) ataque m

seldom /'seldəm/ adv rara vez

select /sɪ'lekt/ vt escoger; (Sport) seleccionar. ● adj selecto; (exclusive) exclusivo. **~ion** /-ʃn/ n selección f. **~ive** adj selectivo

self /self/ n (pl selves). **he's his old ~ again** vuelve a ser el de antes. **~-addressed** adj con el nombre y la dirección del remitente. **~-catering** adj con facilidades para cocinar. **~-centred** adj egocéntrico. **~-confidence** n confianza f en sí mismo. **~-confident** adj seguro de sí mismo. **~-conscious** adj cohibido. **~-contained** adj independiente. **~-control** n dominio m de sí mismo. **~-defence** n defensa f propia. **~-employed** adj que trabaja por cuenta propia. **~-evident** adj evidente. **~-important** adj presumido. **~-indulgent** adj inmoderado. **~-interest** n interés m (personal). **~-ish** adj egoísta. **~-ishness** n egoísmo m. **~-pity** n autocompasión f. **~-portrait** n autorretrato m. **~-respect** n amor m propio. **~-righteous** adj santurrón. **~-sacrifice** n abnegación f. **~-satisfied** adj satisfecho de sí mismo. **~-serve** (Amer), **~-service**

S

adj & *n* autoservicio (*m*). **~-sufficient** *adj* independiente

sell /sel/ *vt* (*pt* **sold**) vender. ● *vi* venderse. □ **~ off** *vt* liquidar. **~ out** *vi*. **we've sold out of gloves** los guantes están agotados. **~-by date** *n* fecha *f* límite de venta. **~er** *n* vendedor *m*

Sellotape /'seləteɪp/ *n* (®) celo *m*, cinta *f* Scotch

sell-out /'selaʊt/ *n* (*performance*) éxito *m* de taquilla; (*fam*, *betrayal*) capitulación *f*

semblance /'sembləns/ *n* apariencia *f*

semester /sɪ'mestə(r)/ *n* (*Amer*) semestre *m*

semi... /'semɪ/ *pref* semi...

semi|breve /-briːv/ *n* redonda *f*. **~circle** *n* semicírculo *m*. **~colon** /-'kəʊlən/ *n* punto *m* y coma. **~-detached** /-dɪ'tætʃt/ *adj* (house) adosado. **~final** /-'faɪnl/ *n* semifinal *f*

seminar /'semɪnɑː(r)/ *n* seminario *m*

senat|e /'senɪt/ *n* senado *m*. **the S~e** (*Amer*) el Senado. **~or** /-ətə(r)/ *n* senador *m*

send /send/ *vt/i* (*pt* **sent**) mandar, enviar. □ **~ away** *vt* despedir. □ **~ away for** *vt* pedir (por correo). □ **~ for** *vt* enviar a buscar. □ **~ off for** *vt* pedir (por correo). □ **~ up** *vt* 𝔼 parodiar. **~er** *n* remitente *m*. **~-off** *n* despedida *f*

senile /'siːnaɪl/ *adj* senil

senior /'siːnɪə(r)/ *adj* mayor; (*in rank*) superior; (*partner etc*) principal. ● *n* mayor *m* & *f*. **~ citizen** *n* jubilado *m*. **~ high school** *n* (*Amer*) colegio *m* secundario. **~ity** /-'ɒrətɪ/ *n* antigüedad *f*

sensation /sen'seɪʃn/ *n* sensación *f*. **~al** *adj* sensacional

sens|e /sens/ *n* sentido *m*; (*common sense*) juicio *m*; (*feeling*) sensación *f*. **make ~e** *vt* tener sentido. **make ~e of sth** entender algo. **~eless** *adj* sin sentido. **~ible** /'sensəbl/ *adj* sensato; (clothing) práctico. **~itive** /'sensɪtɪv/ *adj* sensible; (*touchy*) susceptible. **~itivity** /-'tɪvətɪ/ *n* sensibilidad *f*. **~ual** /'senʃʊəl/ *adj* sensual. **~uous** /'sensʊəs/ *adj* sensual

sent /sent/ *see* **SEND**

sentence /'sentəns/ *n* frase *f*; (*judgment*) sentencia *f*; (*punishment*) condena *f*. ● *vt*. **~ to** condenar a

sentiment /'sentɪmənt/ *n* sentimiento *m*; (*opinion*) opinión *f*. **~al** /-'mentl/ *adj* sentimental. **~ality** /-'tælətɪ/ *n* sentimentalismo *m*

sentry /'sentrɪ/ *n* centinela *f*

separa|ble /'sepərəbl/ *adj* separable. **~te** /'sepərət/ *adj* separado; (*independent*) independiente. ● *vt* /'sepəreɪt/ separar. ● *vi* separarse. **~tely** /'sepərətlɪ/ *adv* por separado. **~tion** /-'reɪʃn/ *n* separación *f*. **~tist** /'sepərətɪst/ *n* separatista *m* & *f*

September /sep'tembə(r)/ *n* se(p)tiembre *m*

septic /'septɪk/ *adj* séptico

sequel /'siːkwəl/ *n* continuación *f*; (*later events*) secuela *f*

sequence /'siːkwəns/ *n* sucesión *f*; (*of film*) secuencia *f*

Serb /sɜːb/ *adj* & *n* *see* **SERBIAN**. **~ia** /'sɜːbɪə/ *n* Serbia *f* **~ian** *adj* & *n* serbio (*m*)

serenade /serə'neɪd/ *n* serenata *f*. ● *vt* dar serenata a

serene /sɪ'riːn/ *adj* sereno

sergeant /'sɑːdʒənt/ *n* sargento *m*

serial /'sɪərɪəl/ *n* serie *f*. **~ize** *vt* serializar

series /'sɪəriːz/ *n* serie *f*

serious /'sɪərɪəs/ *adj* serio. **~ly** *adv* seriamente; (*ill*) gravemente. **take ~ly** tomar en serio

sermon /'sɜːmən/ *n* sermón *m*

serum /'sɪərəm/ *n* (*pl* **-a**) suero *m*

servant /'sɜːvənt/ *n* criado *m*

serve /sɜːv/ *vt* servir; servir a (country); cumplir (sentence). **~ as** servir de. **it ~s you right** ¡bien te lo mereces! ● *vi* servir; (*in tennis*) sacar. ● *n* (*in tennis*) saque *m*. **~r** *n* (*Comp*) servidor *m*

service /'sɜːvɪs/ *n* servicio *m*; (*of car etc*) revisión *f*. ● *vt* revisar (car etc). **~ charge** *n* (*in restaurant*) servicio *m*. **~s** *npl* (*Mil*) fuerzas *fpl* armadas. **~ station** *n* estación *f* de servicio

serviette /sɜːvɪ'et/ *n* servilleta *f*

servile /'sɜːvaɪl/ *adj* servil

session /'seʃn/ *n* sesión *f*

set /set/ vt (pt **set**, pres p **setting**)
poner; poner en hora (clock etc); fijar
(limit etc); (typeset) componer. ∼ **fire
to** prender fuego a. ∼ **free** vt poner
en libertad. ● vi (sun) ponerse; (jelly)
cuajarse. ● n serie f; (of cutlery etc)
juego m; (tennis) set m; (TV, Radio) aparato m; (in theatre) decorado m; (of
people) círculo m. ● adj fijo. **be** ∼ **on**
estar resuelto a. □ ∼ **back** vt (delay)
retardar; (fam, cost) costar. □ ∼ **off** vi
salir. vt hacer sonar (alarm); hacer explotar (bomb). □ ∼ **out** vt exponer
(argument). vi (leave) salir. □ ∼. **up** vt
establecer. ∼**back** n revés m

settee /se'ti:/ n sofá m

setting /'setɪŋ/ n (of dial, switch) posición f

settle /'setl/ vt (arrange) acordar; arreglar (matter); resolver (dispute);
pagar (bill); saldar (debt). ● vi (live)
establecerse. □ ∼ **down** vi calmarse;
(become more responsible) sentar (la)
cabeza. □ ∼ **for** vt aceptar. □ ∼ **up** vi
arreglar cuentas. ∼**ment** n establecimiento m; (agreement) acuerdo m; (of
debt) liquidación f; (colony) colonia f.
∼**r** n colono m

set ∼**-to** n pelea f. ∼**-up** n Ⓘ sistema
m; (con) tinglado m

seven /'sevn/ adj & n siete (m). ∼**teen**
/sevn'ti:n/ adj & n diecisiete (m).
∼**teenth** adj decimoséptimo. ● n die-
cisieteavo m. ∼**th** adj & n séptimo (m).
∼**tieth** /'sevntɪɪθ/ adj septuagésimo.
● n setentavo m. ∼**ly** /'sevntɪ/ adj & n
setenta (m)

sever /'sevə(r)/ vt cortar; (fig) romper

several /'sevrəl/ adj & pron varios

sever|e /sɪ'vɪə(r)/ adj (-er, -est) severo;
(serious) grave; (weather) riguroso.
∼**ely** adv severamente. ∼**ity** /sɪ
'verətɪ/ n severidad f; (seriousness)
gravedad f

sew /səʊ/ vt/i (pt **sewed**, pp **sewn**, or
sewed) coser. □ ∼ **up** vt coser

sew|age /'su:ɪdʒ/ n aguas fpl residua-
les. ∼**er** /'su:ə(r)/ n cloaca f

sewing /'səʊɪŋ/ n costura f.
∼**-machine** n máquina f de coser

sewn /səʊn/ see **SEW**

sex /seks/ n sexo m. **have** ∼ tener relaciones sexuales. ● adj sexual. ∼**ist**
adj & n sexista (m & f). ∼**ual** /'sekʃʊəl/
adj sexual. ∼**ual intercourse** n relaciones fpl sexuales. ∼**uality** /-'ælətɪ/ n
sexualidad f. ∼**y** adj (-ier, -iest) exci-
tante, sexy, provocativo

shabby /'ʃæbɪ/ adj (-ier, -iest)
(clothes) gastado; (person) pobre-
mente vestido

shack /ʃæk/ n choza f

shade /ʃeɪd/ n sombra f; (of colour)
tono m; (for lamp) pantalla f; (nuance) matiz m; (Amer, over window)
persiana f

shadow /'ʃædəʊ/ n sombra f. ● vt (follow) seguir de cerca a. ∼**y** adj (fig)
vago

shady /'ʃeɪdɪ/ adj (-ier, -iest) som-
breado; (fig) turbio; (character) sospechoso

shaft /ʃɑ:ft/ n (of arrow) astil m; (Mec)
eje m; (of light) rayo m; (of lift, mine)
pozo m

shaggy /'ʃægɪ/ adj (-ier, -iest) peludo

shake /ʃeɪk/ vt (pt **shook**, pp **shaken**)
sacudir; agitar (bottle); (shock) desconcertar. ∼ **hands with** estrechar
la mano a. ∼ **one's head** negar con
la cabeza; (Amer, meaning yes) asentir
con la cabeza. ● vi temblar. □ ∼ **off** vi
deshacerse de. ● n sacudida f

shaky /'ʃeɪkɪ/ adj (-ier, -iest) temblo-
roso; (table etc) inestable

shall /ʃæl/ modal verb. **we** ∼ **see** vere-
mos. ∼ **we go to the cinema?**
¿vamos al cine?

shallow /'ʃæləʊ/ adj (-er, -est) poco
profundo; (fig) superficial

sham /ʃæm/ n farsa f. ● adj fingido

shambles /'ʃæmblz/ npl (fam, mess)
caos m

shame /ʃeɪm/ n (feeling) vergüenza f.
what a ∼**!** ¡qué lástima! ● vt avergonzar. ∼**ful** adj vergonzoso. ∼**less**
adj desvergonzado

shampoo /ʃæm'pu:/ n champú m. ● vt
lavar

shan't /ʃɑ:nt/ = **shall not**

shape /ʃeɪp/ n forma f. ● vt formar; determinar (future). ● vi tomar forma.
∼**less** adj informe

share /ʃeə(r)/ n porción f; (Com) acción f. ● vt compartir; (divide) dividir.
● vi compartir. ∼ **in sth** participar en

S

algo. ☐ ~ **out** vt repartir. ~**holder** n accionista m & f. ~**-out** n reparto m

shark /ʃɑ:k/ n tiburón m

sharp /ʃɑ:p/ adj (-er, -est) (knife etc) afilado; (pin etc) puntiagudo; (pain, sound) agudo; (taste) ácido; (bend) cerrado; (contrast) marcado; (clever) listo; (Mus) sostenido. ● adv en punto. **at seven o'clock ~** a las siete en punto. ● n (Mus) sostenido m. ~**en** vt afilar; sacar punta a (pencil). ~**ener** n (Mec) afilador m; (for pencils) sacapuntas m. ~**ly** adv bruscamente

shatter /'ʃætə(r)/ vt hacer añicos. **he was ~ed by the news** la noticia lo dejó destrozado. ● vi hacerse añicos. ~**ed** /'ʃætəd/adj (exhausted) agotado

shav|e /ʃeɪv/ vt afeitar, rasurar (Mex). ● vi afeitarse, rasurarse (Mex). ● n afeitada f, rasurada f (Mex). **have a ~e** afeitarse. ~**er** n maquinilla f (de afeitar). ~**ing brush** n brocha f de afeitar. ~**ing cream** n crema f de afeitar

shawl /ʃɔ:l/ n chal m

she /ʃi:/ pron ella

sheaf /ʃi:f/ n (pl **sheaves** /ʃi:vz/) gavilla f

shear /ʃɪə(r)/ vt (pp **shorn** or **sheared**) esquilar. ~**s** /ʃɪəz/ npl tijeras fpl grandes

shed /ʃed/ n cobertizo m. ● vt (pt **shed**, pres p **shedding**) perder; derramar (tears); despojarse de (clothes). ~ **light on** arrojar luz sobre

she'd /ʃi:(ə)d/ = **she had**, **she would**

sheep /ʃi:p/ n invar oveja f. ~**dog** n perro m pastor. ~**ish** adj avergonzado

sheer /ʃɪə(r)/ adj (as intensifier) puro; (steep) perpendicular

sheet /ʃi:t/ n sábana f; (of paper) hoja f; (of glass) lámina f; (of ice) capa f

shelf /ʃelf/ n (pl **shelves**) estante m. **a set of shelves** unos estantes

shell /ʃel/ n concha f; (of egg) cáscara f; (of crab, snail, tortoise) caparazón m or f; (explosive) proyectil m, obús m. ● vt pelar (peas etc); (Mil) bombardear

she'll /'ʃi:(ə)l/ = **she had**, **she would**

shellfish /'ʃelfɪʃ/ n invar marisco m; (collectively) mariscos mpl

shelter /'ʃeltə(r)/ n refugio m. **take ~** refugiarse. ● vt darle cobijo a (fugitive); (protect from weather) resguar-

dar. ● vi refugiarse. ~**ed** /'ʃeltəd/ adj (spot) abrigado; (life) protegido

shelv|e /ʃelv/ vt (fig) dar carpetazo a. ~**ing** n estantería f

shepherd /'ʃepəd/ n pastor m. ~**ess** /-'des/ n pastora f

sherbet /'ʃɜ:bət/ n (Amer, water ice) sorbete m

sheriff /'ʃerɪf/ n (in US) sheriff m

sherry /'ʃerɪ/ n (vino m de) jerez m

she's /ʃi:z/ = **she is**, **she has**

shield /ʃi:ld/ n escudo m. ● vt proteger

shift /ʃɪft/ vt cambiar; correr (furniture etc). ● vi (wind) cambiar; (attention, opinion) pasar a; (Amer, change gear) cambiar de velocidad. ● n cambio m; (work) turno m; (workers) tanda f. ~**y** adj (-ier, -iest) furtivo

shilling /'ʃɪlɪŋ/ n chelín m

shimmer /'ʃɪmə(r)/ vi rielar, relucir

shin /ʃɪn/ n espinilla f

shine /ʃaɪn/ vi (pt **shone**) brillar. ● vt sacar brillo a. **~ a light on sth** alumbrar algo con una luz. ● n brillo m

shingle /'ʃɪŋɡl/ n (pebbles) guijarros mpl

shin|ing /'ʃaɪnɪŋ/ adj brillante. ~**y** /'ʃaɪnɪ/ adj (-ier, -iest) brillante

ship /ʃɪp/ n barco m, buque m. ● vt (pt **shipped**) transportar; (send) enviar; (load) embarcar. ~**building** n construcción f naval. ~**ment** n envío m. ~**ping** n transporte m; (ships) barcos mpl. ~**shape** adj limpio y ordenado. ~**wreck** n naufragio m. ~**wrecked** adj naufragado. **be ~wrecked** naufragar. ~**yard** n astillero m

shirk /ʃɜ:k/ vt esquivar

shirt /ʃɜ:t/ n camisa f. **in ~-sleeves** en mangas de camisa

shit /ʃɪt/ n & int (vulgar) mierda f. ● vi (vulgar) (pt **shat**, pres p **shitting**) cagar

shiver /'ʃɪvə(r)/ vi temblar. ● n escalofrío m

shoal /ʃəʊl/ n banco m

shock /ʃɒk/ n (of impact) choque m; (of earthquake) sacudida f; (surprise) shock m; (scare) susto m; (Elec) descarga f; (Med) shock m. **get a ~** llevarse un shock. ● vt escandalizar;

(*apall*) horrorizar. ~**ing** *adj* escandaloso; ⊞ espantoso

shod /ʃɒd/ *see* **SHOE**

shoddy /'ʃɒdɪ/ *adj* (-**ier, -iest**) mal hecho, de pacotilla

shoe /ʃuː/ *n* zapato *m*; (*of horse*) herradura *f*. ●*vt* (*pt* **shod**, *pres p* **shoeing**) herrar (horse). ~**horn** *n* calzador *m*. ~**lace** *n* cordón *m* (de zapato). ~ **polish** *n* betún *m*

shone /ʃɒn/ *see* **SHINE**

shoo /ʃuː/ *vt* ahuyentar

shook /ʃʊk/ *see* **SHAKE**

shoot /ʃuːt/ *vt* (*pt* **shot**) disparar; rodar (film). ●*vi* (hunt) cazar. ●*n* (*of plant*) retoño *m*. □ ~ **down** *vt* derribar. □ ~ **out** *vi* (*rush*) salir disparado. □ ~ **up** *vi* (prices) dispararse; (*grow*) crecer mucho

shop /ʃɒp/ *n* tienda *f*. **go to the** ~**s** ir de compras. **talk** ~ hablar del trabajo. ●*vi* (*pt* **shopping**) hacer compras. **go** ~**ping** ir de compras. □ ~ **around** *vi* buscar el mejor precio. ~ **assistant** *n* dependiente *m*, dependienta *f*, empleado *m*, empleada *f* (*LAm*). ~**keeper** *n* comerciante *m*, tendero *m*. ~**lifter** *n* ladrón *m* (que roba en las tiendas). ~**lifting** *n* hurto *m* (en las tiendas). ~**per** *n* comprador *m*. ~**ping** *n* (*purchases*) compras *fpl*. **do the** ~**ping** hacer la compra, hacer el mandado (Mex). ~**ping bag** *n* bolsa *f* de la compra. ~**ping cart** *n* (*Amer*) carrito *m* (de la compra), ~**ping centre**, ~**ping mall** (*Amer*) *n* centro *m* comercial. ~**ping trolley** *n* carrito *m* de la compra. ~ **steward** *n* enlace *m* sindical. ~ **window** *n* escaparate *m*, vidriera *f* (*LAm*), aparador *m* (Mex)

shore /ʃɔː(r)/ *n* orilla *f*

shorn /ʃɔːn/ *see* **SHEAR**

short /ʃɔːt/ *adj* (-**er, -est**) corto; (*not lasting*) breve; (*person*) bajo; (*curt*) brusco. **a** ~ **time ago** hace poco. **be** ~ **of time/money** andar corto de tiempo/dinero. **Mick is** ~ **for Michael** Mick es el diminutivo de Michael. ●*adv* (stop) en seco. **we never went** ~ **of food** nunca nos faltó comida. ●*n*. **in** ~ en resumen. ~**age** /-ɪdʒ/ *n* escasez *f*, falta *f*. ~**bread** *n*

galleta *f* (de mantequilla). ~ **circuit** *n* cortocircuito *m*. ~**coming** *n* defecto *m*. ~ **cut** *n* atajo *m*. ~**en** *vt* acortar. ~**hand** *n* taquigrafía *f*. ~**ly** *adv* (*soon*) dentro de poco. ~**ly before midnight** poco antes de la medianoche. ~**s** *npl* pantalones *m* cortos, shorts *mpl*; (*Amer, underwear*) calzoncillos *mpl*. ~**sighted** /-'saɪtɪd/ *adj* miope

shot /ʃɒt/ *see* **SHOOT**. ●*n* (*from gun*) disparo *m*; tiro *m*; (*in soccer*) tiro *m*, disparo *m*; (*in other sports*) tiro *m*; (*Photo*) foto *f*. **be a good/poor** ~ ser un buen/mal tirador. **be off like a** ~ salir disparado. ~**gun** *n* escopeta *f*

should /ʃʊd, ʃəd/ *modal verb*. **I** ~ **go** debería ir. **you** ~**n't have said that** no deberías haber dicho eso. **I** ~ **like to see her** me gustaría verla. **if he** ~ **come** si viniese

shoulder /'ʃəʊldə(r)/ *n* hombro *m*. ●*vt* cargar con (responsibility); ponerse al hombro (burden). ~ **blade** *n* omóplato *m*

shout /ʃaʊt/ *n* grito *m*. ●*vt/i* gritar. ~ **at s.o.** gritarle a uno

shove /ʃʌv/ *n* empujón *m*. ●*vt* empujar; (*fam, put*) poner. ●*vi* empujar. □ ~ **off** *vi* ⊞ largarse

shovel /'ʃʌvl/ *n* pala *f*. ●*vt* (*pt* **shovelled**) palear (coal); espalar (snow)

show /ʃəʊ/ *vt* (*pt* **showed**, *pp* **shown**) mostrar; (*put on display*) exponer; poner (film). **I'll** ~ **you to your room** lo acompaño a su cuarto. ●*vi* (*be visible*) verse. ●*n* muestra *f*; (*exhibition*) exposición *f*; (*in theatre*) espectáculo *m*; (*on TV, radio*) programa *m*; (*ostentation*) pompa *f*. **be on** ~ estar expuesto. □ ~ **off** *vt* (*pej*) lucir, presumir de. *vi* presumir, lucirse. □ ~ **up** *vi* (*be visible*) notarse; (*arrive*) aparecer. *vt* (*reveal*) poner de manifiesto; (*embarrass*) hacer quedar mal. ~**case** *n* vitrina *f*. ~**down** *n* confrontación *f*

shower /'ʃaʊə(r)/ *n* (*of rain*) chaparrón *m*; (*for washing*) ducha *f*. **have a** ~, **take a** ~ ducharse. ●*vi* ducharse

showjumping *n* concursos *mpl* hípicos.

shown /ʃəʊn/ *see* **SHOW**

show ~-**off** *n* fanfarrón *m*. ~**room** *n* sala *f* de exposición *f*. ~**y** *adj* (-**ier,**

S

-iest) llamativo; (*attractive*) ostentoso

shrank /ʃræŋk/ *see* **SHRINK**

shred /ʃred/ *n* pedazo *m*; (*fig*) pizca *f*. ● *vt* (*pt* **shredded**) hacer tiras; destruir, triturar (documents). **~der** *n* (*for paper*) trituradora *f*; (*for vegetables*) cortadora *f*

shrewd /ʃruːd/ *adj* (-er, -est) astuto

shriek /ʃriːk/ *n* chillido *m*; (*of pain*) alarido *m*. ● *vt/i* chillar

shrift /ʃrɪft/ *n*. **give s.o. short ~** despachar a uno con brusquedad. **give sth short ~** desestimar algo de plano

shrill /ʃrɪl/ *adj* agudo

shrimp /ʃrɪmp/ *n* gamba *f*, camarón *m* (*LAm*); (*Amer, large*) langostino *m*

shrine /ʃraɪn/ *n* (*place*) santuario *m*; (*tomb*) sepulcro *m*

shrink /ʃrɪŋk/ *vt* (*pt* **shrank**, *pp* **shrunk**) encoger. ● *vi* encogerse; (amount) reducirse; retroceder (*recoil*)

shrivel /ˈʃrɪvl/ *vi* (*pt* **shrivelled**). **~ (up)** (plant) marchitarse; (fruit) resecarse y arrugarse

shroud /ʃraʊd/ *n* mortaja *f*; (*fig*) velo *m*. ● *vt* envolver

Shrove /ʃrəʊv/ *n*. **~ Tuesday** *n* martes *m* de carnaval

shrub /ʃrʌb/ *n* arbusto *m*

shrug /ʃrʌɡ/ *vt* (*pt* **shrugged**) encogerse de hombros

shrunk /ʃrʌŋk/ *see* **SHRINK**. **~en** *adj* encogido

shudder /ˈʃʌdə(r)/ *vi* estremecerse. ● *n* estremecimiento *m*

shuffle /ˈʃʌfl/ *vi* andar arrastrando los pies. ● *vt* barajar (cards). **~ one's feet** arrastrar los pies

shun /ʃʌn/ *vt* (*pt* **shunned**) evitar

shunt /ʃʌnt/ *vt* cambiar de vía

shush /ʃʊʃ/ *int* ¡chitón!

shut /ʃʌt/ *vt* (*pt* **shut**, *pres p* **shutting**) cerrar. ● *vi* cerrarse. ● *adj*. **be ~** estar cerrado. □ **~ down** *vt/i* cerrar. □ **~ up** *vt* cerrar; 🔟 hacer callar. *vi* callarse. **~ter** *n* contraventana *f*; (*Photo*) obturador *m*

shuttle /ˈʃʌtl/ *n* lanzadera *f*; (*by air*) puente *m* aéreo; (*space* **~**) transbordador *m* espacial. ● *vi*. **~** (**back and forth**) ir y venir. **~cock** *n* volante *m*. **~ service** *n* servicio *m* de enlace

shy /ʃaɪ/ *adj* (-er, -est) tímido. ● *vi* (*pt* **shied**) asustarse. **~ness** *n* timidez *f*

sick /sɪk/ *adj* enfermo; (humour) negro; (*fam, fed up*) harto. **be ~** estar enfermo; (*vomit*) vomitar. **be ~ of** (*fig*) estar harto de. **feel ~** sentir náuseas. **get ~** (*Amer*) caer enfermo, enfermarse (*LAm*). **~ leave** *n* permiso *m* por enfermedad, baja *f* por enfermedad. **~ly** /ˈsɪklɪ/ *adj* (-lier, -liest) enfermizo; (taste, smell etc) nauseabundo. **~ness** /ˈsɪknɪs/ *n* enfermedad *f*

side /saɪd/ *n* lado *m*; (*of hill*) ladera *f*; (*of person*) costado *m*; (*team*) equipo *m*; (*fig*) parte *f*. **~ by ~** uno al lado del otro. **take ~s** tomar partido. ● *adj* lateral. □ **~ with** *vt* ponerse de parte de. **~board** *n* aparador *m*. **~ dish** *n* acompañamiento *m*. **~-effect** *n* efecto *m* secundario; (*fig*) consecuencia *f* indirecta. **~line** *n* actividad *f* suplementaria. **~ road** *n* calle *f* secundaria. **~-step** *vt* eludir. **~-track** *vt* desviar del tema. **~walk** *n* (*Amer*) acera *f*, vereda *f* (*LAm*), banqueta *f* (*Mex*). **~ways** *adj* & *adv* de lado

siding /ˈsaɪdɪŋ/ *n* apartadero *m*

sidle /ˈsaɪdl/ *vi*. **~ up to s.o.** acercarse furtivamente a uno

siege /siːdʒ/ *n* sitio *m*

sieve /sɪv/ *n* tamiz *m*. ● *vt* tamizar, cernir

sift /sɪft/ *vt* tamizar, cernir. ● *vi*. **~ through sth** pasar algo por el tamiz

sigh /saɪ/ *n* suspiro. ● *vi* suspirar

sight /saɪt/ *n* vista *f*; (*spectacle*) espectáculo *m*; (*on gun*) mira *f*. **at first ~** a primera vista. **catch ~ of** ver; (*in distance*) avistar. **lose ~ of** perder de vista. **see the ~s** visitar los lugares de interés. **within ~ of** (*near*) cerca de. ● *vt* ver; divisar (land). **~-seeing** *n*. **go ~** ir a visitar los lugares de interés. **~seer** /-siːə(r)/ *n* turista *m* & *f*

sign /saɪn/ *n* (*indication*) señal *f*, indicio *m*; (*gesture*) señal *f*, seña *f*; (*notice*) letrero *m*; (*astrological*) signo *m*. ● *vt* firmar. □ **~ on** *vi* (*for unemployment benefit*) anotarse para recibir el seguro de desempleo

signal /'sɪɡnəl/ *n* señal *f*. ● *vt* (*pt* **signalled**) señalar. ● *vi*. **~ (to s.o.)** hacer señas (a uno); (*Auto*) poner el intermitente, señalizar

signature /'sɪɡnətʃə(r)/ *n* firma *f*. **~tune** *n* sintonía *f*

significan|ce /sɪɡ'nɪfɪkəns/ *n* importancia *f*. **~t** *adj* (*important*) importante; (*fact*) significativo

signify /'sɪɡnɪfaɪ/ *vt* significar

signpost /'saɪmpəʊst/ *n* señal *f*, poste *m* indicador

silen|ce /'saɪləns/ *n* silencio *m*. ● *vt* hacer callar. **~cer** *n* (*on gun and on car*) silenciador *m*. **~t** *adj* silencioso; (*film*) mudo. **remain ~t** quedarse callado. **~tly** *adv* silenciosamente

silhouette /sɪluː'et/ *n* silueta *f*. ● *vt*. **be ~d** perfilarse (**against** contra)

silicon /'sɪlɪkən/ *n* silicio *m*. **~ chip** *n* pastilla *f* de silicio

silk /sɪlk/ *n* seda *f*. **~y** *adj* (*of silk*) de seda; (*like silk*) sedoso

silly /'sɪlɪ/ *adj* (**-ier, iest**) tonto

silt /sɪlt/ *n* cieno *m*

silver /'sɪlvə(r)/ *n* plata *f*. ● *adj* de plata. **~-plated** *adj* bañado en plata, plateado. **~ware** /-weə(r)/ *n* platería *f*

SIM card *n* tarjeta *f* SIM

simil|ar /'sɪmɪlə(r)/ *adj* parecido, similar. **~arity** /-'lærətɪ/ *n* parecido *m*. **~arly** *adv* de igual manera. **~e** /'sɪmɪlɪ/ *n* símil *m*

simmer /'sɪmə(r)/ *vt/i* hervir a fuego lento. □ **~ down** *vi* calmarse

simpl|e /'sɪmpl/ *adj* (**-er, -est**) sencillo, simple; (*person*) (*humble*) simple; (*backward*) simple. **~e-minded** /-'maɪndɪd/ *adj* ingenuo. **~icity** /-'plɪsetɪ/ *n* simplicidad *f*, sencillez *f*. **~ify** /'sɪmplɪfaɪ/ *vt* simplificar. **~y** *adv* sencillamente, simplemente; (*absolutely*) realmente

simulate /'sɪmjʊleɪt/ *vt* simular

simultaneous /sɪml'teɪnɪəs/ *adj* simultáneo. **~ly** *adv* simultáneamente

sin /sɪn/ *n* pecado *m*. ● *vi* (*pt* **sinned**) pecar

since /sɪns/

● *preposition* desde. **he's been living here ~ 1991** vive aquí desde 1991. **~ Christmas** desde Navidad. **~ then** desde entonces. **I haven't been feeling well ~ Sunday** desde el domingo que no me siento bien. **how long is it ~ your interview?** ¿cuánto (tiempo) hace de la entrevista?

● *adverb* desde entonces. **I haven't spoken to her ~** no he hablado con ella desde entonces

● *conjunction*

····➤ desde que. **I haven't seen her ~ she left** no la he visto desde que se fue. **~ coming to Manchester** desde que vine (*or* vino *etc*) a Manchester. **it's ten years ~ he died** hace diez años que se murió

····➤ (*because*) como, ya que. **~ it was quite late, I decided to stay** como *or* ya que era bastante tarde, decidí quedarme

sincer|e /sɪn'sɪə(r)/ *adj* sincero. **~ely** *adv* sinceramente. **yours ~ely, ~ely (yours)** (*in letters*) (saluda) a usted atentamente. **~ity** /-'serətɪ/ *n* sinceridad *f*

sinful /'sɪnfl/ *adj* (*person*) pecador, (*act*) pecaminoso

sing /sɪŋ/ *vt/i* (*pt* **sang**, *pp* **sung**) cantar

singe /sɪndʒ/ *vt* (*pres p* **singeing**) chamuscar

singer /'sɪŋə(r)/ *n* cantante *m & f*

single /'sɪŋɡl/ *adj* solo; (*not double*) sencillo; (*unmarried*) soltero; (*bed, room*) individual, de una plaza (*LAm*); (*ticket*) de ida, sencillo. **not a ~ house** ni una sola casa. **every ~ day** todos los días sin excepción. ● *n* (*ticket*) billete *m* sencillo, boleto *m* de ida (*LAm*). □ **~ out** *vt* escoger; (*distinguish*) distinguir. **~-handed** /-'hændɪd/ *adj & adv* sin ayuda. **~s** *npl* (*Sport*) individuales *mpl*

singular /'sɪŋɡjʊlə(r)/ *n* singular *f*. ● *adj* singular; (*unusual*) raro; (*noun*) en singular

S

sinister /'sɪnɪstə(r)/ adj siniestro

sink /sɪŋk/ vt (pt **sank**, pp **sunk**) hundir. ● vi hundirse. ● n fregadero m (Amer, in bathroom) lavabo m, lavamanos m. □ ~ **in** vi penetrar

sinner /'sɪnə(r)/ n pecador m

sip /sɪp/ n sorbo m. ● vt (pt **sipped**) sorber

siphon /'saɪfən/ n sifón m. ~ **(out)** sacar con sifón. □ ~ **off** vt desviar (money).

sir /sɜː(r)/ n señor m. **S~** n (title) sir m. Dear **S~**, (in letters) De mi mayor consideración:

siren /'saɪərən/ n sirena f

sister /'sɪstə(r)/ n hermana f; (nurse) enfermera f jefe. ~**-in-law** n (pl ~**s-in-law**) cuñada f

sit /sɪt/ vi (pt **sat**, pres p **sitting**) sentarse; (committee etc) reunirse en sesión. **be** ~**ting** estar sentado. ● vt sentar; hacer (exam). □ ~ **back** vi (fig) relajarse. □ ~ **down** vi sentarse. **be** ~**ting down** estar sentado. □ ~ **up** vi (from lying) incorporarse; (straighten back) ponerse derecho. ~**-in** n (strike) encierro m, ocupación f

site /saɪt/ n emplazamiento m; (piece of land) terreno m; (archaeological) yacimiento m. **building** ~ n solar m. ● vt situar

sit ~**ting** n sesión f; (in restaurant) turno m. ~**ting room** n sala f de estar, living m

situat|e /'sɪtjʊeɪt/ vt situar. ~**ion** /-'eɪʃn/ n situación f

six /sɪks/ adj & n seis (m). ~**teen** /sɪk'stiːn/ adj & n dieciséis (m). ~**teenth** adj decimosexto. ● n dieciseisavo m. ~**th** adj & n sexto (m). ~**tieth** /'sɪkstɪɪθ/ adj sexagésimo. ● n sesentavo m. ~**ty** /'sɪkstɪ/ adj & n sesenta (m)

size /saɪz/ n tamaño m; (of clothes) talla f; (of shoes) número m; (of problem, operation) magnitud f. **what** ~ **do you take?** (clothes) ¿qué talla tiene?; (shoes) ¿qué número calza?. □ ~ **up** vt 🔳 evaluar (problem); calar (person)

sizzle /'sɪzl/ vi crepitar

skat|e /skeɪt/ n patín m.● vi patinar. ~**eboard** n monopatín m, patineta f

(Mex). ~**er** n patinador m. ~**ing** n patinaje m. ~**ing-rink** n pista f de patinaje

skeleton /'skelɪtn/ n esqueleto m. ~ **key** n llave f maestra

sketch /sketʃ/ n (drawing) dibujo m; (rougher) esbozo m; (TV, Theatre) sketch m. ● vt esbozar. ● vi dibujar. ~**y** adj (-ier, -iest) incompleto

ski /skiː/ n (pl **skis**) esquí m. ● vi (pt **skied**, pres p **skiing**) esquiar. **go** ~**ing** ir a esquiar

skid /skɪd/ vi (pt **skidded**) patinar. ● n patinazo m

ski ~**er** n esquiador m. ~**ing** n esquí m

skilful /'skɪlfl/ adj diestro

ski-lift /'skiːlɪft/ n telesquí m

skill /skɪl/ n habilidad f; (technical) destreza f. ~**ed** adj hábil; (worker) cualificado

skim /skɪm/ vt (pt **skimmed**) espumar (soup); desnatar, descremar (milk); (glide over) pasar casi rozando. ~ **milk** (Amer), ~**med milk** n leche f desnatada, leche f descremada. ~ **through** vt leer por encima

skimp /skɪmp/ vi. ~ **on sth** escatimar algo. ~**y** adj (-ier, -iest) escaso; (skirt, dress) brevísimo

skin /skɪn/ n piel f. ● vt (pt **skinned**) despellejar. ~**-deep** adj superficial. ~**-diving** n submarinismo m. ~**ny** adj (-ier, -iest) flaco

skip /skɪp/ vi (pt **skipped**) vi saltar; (with rope) saltar a la comba, saltar a la cuerda. ● vt saltarse (chapter); faltar a (class). ● n brinco m; (container) contenedor m (para escombros). ~**per** n capitán m. ~**ping-rope**, ~**rope** (Amer) n comba f, cuerda f de saltar, reata f (Mex)

skirmish /'skɜːmɪʃ/ n escaramuza f

skirt /skɜːt/ n falda f. ● vt bordear; (go round) ladear. ~**ing-board** n rodapié m, zócalo m

skittle /'skɪtl/ n bolo m

skive off /skaɪv/ (vi 🔳, disappear) escurrir el bulto; (stay away from work) no ir a trabajar

skulk /skʌlk/ vi (hide) esconderse. ~ **around** vi merodear

skull /skʌl/ n cráneo m; (*remains*) calavera f

sky /skaɪ/ n cielo m. ∼**lark** n alondra f. ∼**light** n tragaluz m. ∼ **marshal** n guardia m armado a bordo. ∼**scraper** n rascacielos m

slab /slæb/ n (*of concrete*) bloque m; (*of stone*) losa f

slack /slæk/ adj (**-er, -est**) flojo; (person) poco aplicado; (period) de poca actividad. ● vi flojear. ∼**en** vt aflojar. ● vi (person) descansar. □ ∼**en off** vt/i aflojar

slain /sleɪn/ see **SLAY**

slake /sleɪk/ vt apagar

slam /slæm/ vt (*pt* **slammed**). ∼ the door dar un portazo. ∼ the door shut cerrar de un portazo. ∼ on the brakes pegar un frenazo; (*sl, criticize*) atacar violentamente. ● vi cerrarse de un portazo

slander /'slɑːndə(r)/ n calumnia f. ● vt difamar

slang /slæŋ/ n argot m

slant /slɑːnt/ vt inclinar. ● n inclinación f

slap /slæp/ vt (*pt* **slapped**) (*on face*) pegarle una bofetada a; (*put*) tirar. ∼ s.o. on the back darle una palmada a uno en la espalda. ● n bofetada f; (*on back*) palmada f. ● adv de lleno. ∼**dash** adj descuidado; (work) chapucero

slash /slæʃ/ vt acuchillar; (*fig*) rebajar drásticamente. ● n cuchillada f

slat /slæt/ n tablilla f

slate /sleɪt/ n pizarra f. ● vt 🔲 poner por los suelos

slaughter /'slɔːtə(r)/ vt matar salvajemente; matar (animal). ● n carnicería f; (*of animals*) matanza f

slave /sleɪv/ n esclavo m. ● vi ∼ (**away**) trabajar como un negro. ∼**-driver** n 🔲 negrero m. ∼**ry** /-ərɪ/ n esclavitud f

slay /sleɪ/ vt (*pt* **slew**, *pp* **slain**) dar muerte a

sleazy /'sliːzɪ/ adj (**-ier, -iest**) 🔲 sórdido

sled /sled/ (*Amer*), **sledge** /sledʒ/ n trineo m

sledge-hammer n mazo m, almádena f

sleek /sliːk/ adj (**-er, -est**) liso, brillante

sleep /sliːp/ n sueño m. go to ∼ dormirse. ● vi (*pt* **slept**) dormir. ● vt poder alojar. ∼**er** n (*on track*) traviesa f, durmiente m. **be a light/heavy** ∼**er** tener el sueño ligero/pesado. ∼**ing bag** n saco m de dormir. ∼**ing pill** n somnífero m. ∼**less** adj. have a ∼**less night** pasar la noche en blanco. ∼**walk** vi caminar dormido. ∼**y** adj (**-ier, -iest**) soñoliento. **be/feel** ∼**y** tener sueño

sleet /sliːt/ n aguanieve f

sleeve /sliːv/ n manga f; (*for record*) funda f, carátula f. up one's ∼ en reserva. ∼**less** adj sin mangas

sleigh /sleɪ/ n trineo m

slender /'slendə(r)/ adj delgado; (*fig*) escaso

slept /slept/ see **SLEEP**

slew /sluː/ see **SLAY**

slice /slaɪs/ n (*of ham*) lonja f; (*of bread*) rebanada f; (*of meat*) tajada f; (*of cheese*) trozo m; (*of sth round*) rodaja f. ● vt cortar (en rebanadas, tajadas etc)

slick /slɪk/ adj (performance) muy pulido. ● n. (**oil**) ∼ marea f negra

slid|e /slaɪd/ vt (*pt* **slid**) deslizar. ● vi (*intentionally*) deslizarse; (*unintentionally*) resbalarse. ● n resbalón m; (*in playground*) tobogán m, resbaladilla f (*Mex*); (*for hair*) pasador m, broche m (*Mex*); (*Photo*) diapositiva f. ∼**ing scale** n escala f móvil

slight /slaɪt/ adj (**-er, -est**) ligero; (*slender*) delgado. ● vt desairar. ● n desaire m. ∼**est** adj mínimo. **not in the** ∼**est** en absoluto. ∼**ly** adv un poco, ligeramente

slim /slɪm/ adj (**slimmer, slimmest**) delgado. ● vi (*pt* **slimmed**) (*become slimmer*) adelgazar; (*diet*) hacer régimen

slim|e /slaɪm/ n limo m; (*of snail, slug*) baba f. ∼**y** adj viscoso; (*fig*) excesivamente obsequioso

sling /slɪŋ/ n (*Med*) cabestrillo m. ● vt (*pt* **slung**) lanzar

slip /slɪp/ vt (*pt* **slipped**) deslizar. ∼ s.o.'s mind olvidársele a uno. ● vi res-

S

balarse. **it ~ped out of my hands** se me resbaló de las manos. **he ~ped out of the back door** se deslizó por la puerta trasera ● *n* resbalón *m*; (*mistake*) error *m*; (*petticoat*) combinación *f*; (*paper*) trozo *m*. **give s.o. the ~** lograr zafarse de uno. **~ of the tongue** *n* lapsus *m* linguae. □ **~ away** *vi* escabullirse. □ **~ up** *vi* ⊞ equivocarse

slipper /ˈslɪpə(r)/ *n* zapatilla *f*

slippery /ˈslɪpərɪ/ *adj* resbaladizo

slip ~ road *n* rampa *f* de acceso. **~shod** /ˈslɪpʃɒd/ *adj* descuidado. **~-up** *n* ⊞ error *m*

slit /slɪt/ *n* raja *f*; (*cut*) corte *m*. ● *vt* (*pt* slit, *pres p* **slitting**) rajar; (*cut*) cortar

slither /ˈslɪðə(r)/ *vi* deslizarse

slobber /ˈslɒbə(r)/ *vi* babear

slog /slɒɡ/ *vt* (*pt* **slogged**) golpear. ● *vi* caminar trabajosamente. ● *n* golpetazo *m*; (*hard work*) trabajo *m* penoso. □ **~ away** *vi* sudar tinta ⊞

slogan /ˈsləʊɡən/ *n* eslogan *m*

slop /slɒp/ *vt* (*pt* **slopped**) derramar. ● *vi* derramarse

slop|e /sləʊp/ *vi* inclinarse. ● *vt* inclinar. ● *n* declive *m*, pendiente *f*. **~ing** *adj* inclinado

sloppy /ˈslɒpɪ/ *adj* (**-ier, -iest**) (*work*) descuidado; (*person*) desaliñado

slosh /slɒʃ/ *vi* ⊞ chapotear

slot /slɒt/ *n* ranura *f*. ● *vt* (*pt* **slotted**) encajar

slot-machine *n* distribuidor *m* automático; (*for gambling*) máquina *f* tragamonedas

slouch /slaʊtʃ/ *vi* andar cargado de espaldas; (*in chair*) repanchigarse

Slovak /ˈsləʊvæk/ *adj* & *n* eslovaco (*m*). **~ia** *n* Eslovaquia *f*

slovenly /ˈslʌvnlɪ/ *adj* (*work*) descuidado; (*person*) desaliñado

slow /sləʊ/ *adj* (**-er, -est**) lento. **be ~** (*clock*) estar atrasado. **in ~ motion** a cámara lenta. ● *adv* despacio. ● *vt* retardar. ● *vi* ir más despacio. □ **~ down, ~ up** *vt* retardar. *vi* ir más despacio. **~ly** *adv* despacio, lentamente

sludge /slʌdʒ/ *n* fango *m*

slug /slʌɡ/ *n* babosa *f*. **~gish** *adj* lento

slum /slʌm/ *n* barrio *m* bajo

slumber /ˈslʌmbə(r)/ *vi* dormir

slump /slʌmp/ *n* baja *f* repentina; (*in business*) depresión *f*. ● *vi* desplomarse

slung /slʌŋ/ *see* **SLING**

slur /slɜː(r)/ *vt* (*pt* **slurred**). **~ one's words** arrastrar las palabras. ● *n*. **a racist ~** un comentario racista

slush /slʌʃ/ *n* nieve *f* medio derretida. **~ fund** *n* fondo *m* de reptiles

sly /slaɪ/ *adj* (**slyer, slyest**) (*crafty*) astuto. ● *n*. **on the ~** a hurtadillas. **~ly** *adv* astutamente

smack /smæk/ *n* manotazo *m*. ● *adv* ⊞ **~ in the middle** justo en el medio. **he went ~ into a tree** se dio contra un árbol. ● *vt* pegarle a (con la mano)

small /smɔːl/ *adj* (**-er, -est**) pequeño, chico (*LAm*). ● *n*. **the ~ of the back** la región lumbar. **~ ads** *npl* anuncios *mpl* (clasificados), avisos *mpl* (clasificados) (*LAm*). **~ change** *n* suelto *m*. **~pox** /-pɒks/ *n* viruela *f*. **~ talk** *n* charla *f* sobre temas triviales

smart /smɑːt/ *adj* (**-er, -est**) elegante; (*clever*) listo; (*brisk*) rápido. ● *vi* escocer. □ **~en up** *vt* arreglar. *vi* (*person*) mejorar su aspecto, arreglarse. **~ly** *adv* elegantemente; (*quickly*) rápidamente

smash /smæʃ/ *vt* romper; (*into little pieces*) hacer pedazos; batir (*record*). ● *vi* romperse; (*collide*) chocar (**into** con). ● *n* (*noise*) estrépito *m*; (*collision*) choque *m*; (*in sport*) smash *m*. □ **~ up** *vt* destrozar. **~ing** *adj* ⊞ estupendo

smattering /ˈsmætərɪŋ/ *n* nociones *fpl*

smear /smɪə(r)/ *vt* untar (**with** de); (*stain*) manchar (**with** de); (*fig*) difamar. ● *n* mancha *f*

smell /smel/ *n* olor *m*; (*sense*) olfato *m*. ● *vt* (*pt* **smelt**) oler; (*animal*) olfatear. ● *vi* oler. **~ of sth** oler a algo. **~y** *adj* maloliente. **be ~y** oler mal

smelt /smelt/ *see* **SMELL**. ● *vt* fundir

smile /smaɪl/ *n* sonrisa *f*. ● *vi* sonreír. **~ at s.o.** sonreírle a uno

smirk /smɜːk/ *n* sonrisita *f* (de suficiencia etc)

smith /smɪθ/ *n* herrero *m*

smithereens /smɪðəˈriːnz/ *npl*. **smash sth to ~** hacer algo añicos

smock /smɒk/ n blusa f, bata f

smog /smɒg/ n smog m

smok|e /sməʊk/ n humo m. ● vt fumar (tobacco); ahumar (food). ● vi fumar. ∼**eless** adj que arde sin humo. ∼**er** n fumador m. ∼**y** adj (room) lleno de humo

smooth /smuːð/ adj (-er, -est) (texture/stone) liso; (skin) suave; (movement) suave; (sea) tranquilo. ● vt alisar. □ ∼ **out** vt allanar (problems). ∼**ly** adv suavemente; (without problems) sin problemas

smother /ˈsmʌðə(r)/ vt asfixiar (person). ∼ **s.o. with kisses** cubrir a uno de besos

smoulder /ˈsməʊldə(r)/ vi arder sin llama

smudge /smʌdʒ/ n borrón m. ● vi tiznarse

smug /smʌg/ adj (smugger, smuggest) pagado de sí mismo; (expression) de suficiencia

smuggl|e /ˈsmʌgl/ vt pasar de contrabando. ∼**er** n contrabandista m & f. ∼**ing** n contrabando m

snack /snæk/ n tentempié m. ∼ **bar** n cafetería f

snag /snæg/ n problema m

snail /sneɪl/ n caracol m. **at a** ∼'s **pace** a paso de tortuga

snake /sneɪk/ n culebra f, serpiente f

snap /snæp/ vt (pt snapped) (break) romper. ∼ **one's fingers** chasquear los dedos. ● vi romperse; (dog) intentar morder; (say) contestar bruscamente. ∼ **at** (dog) intentar morder; (say) contestar bruscamente. ● n chasquido m; (Photo) foto f. ● adj instantáneo. □ ∼ **up** vt no dejar escapar (offer). ∼**py** adj (-ier, -iest) 🗊 rápido. **make it** ∼**py!** ¡date prisa! ∼**shot** n foto f

snare /sneə(r)/ n trampa f

snarl /snɑːl/ vi gruñir

snatch /snætʃ/ vt. ∼ **sth from s.o.** arrebatarle algo a uno; (steal) robar. ● n (short part) fragmento m

sneak /sniːk/ n soplón m. ● vi (past & pp sneaked or 🗊 snuck) ∼ **in** entrar a hurtadillas. ∼ **off** escabullirse. ∼**ers** /ˈsniːkəz/ npl zapatillas fpl de deporte. ∼**y** adj artero

sneer /snɪə(r)/ n expresión f desdeñosa. ● vi hacer una mueca de desprecio. ∼ **at** hablar con desprecio a

sneeze /sniːz/ n estornudo m. ● vi estornudar

snide /snaɪd/ adj insidioso

sniff /snɪf/ vt oler. ● vi sorberse la nariz

snigger /ˈsnɪgə(r)/ n risilla f. ● vi reírse (por lo bajo)

snip /snɪp/ vt (pt snipped) dar un tijeretazo a. ● n tijeretazo m

sniper /ˈsnaɪpə(r)/ n francotirador m

snippet /ˈsnɪpɪt/ n (of conversation) trozo m. ∼**s of information** datos mpl aislados

snivel /ˈsnɪvl/ vi (pt snivelled) lloriquear

snob /snɒb/ n esnob m & f. ∼**bery** n esnobismo m. ∼**bish** adj esnob

snooker /ˈsnuːkə(r)/ n snooker m

snoop /snuːp/ vi 🗊 husmear

snooze /snuːz/ n sueñecito m. ● vi dormitar

snore /snɔː(r)/ n ronquido m. ● vi roncar

snorkel /ˈsnɔːkl/ n esnórkel m

snort /snɔːt/ n bufido m. ● vi bufar

snout /snaʊt/ n hocico m

snow /snəʊ/ n nieve f. ● vi nevar. **be** ∼**ed in** estar aislado por la nieve. **be** ∼**ed under with work** estar agobiado de trabajo. ∼**ball** n bola f de nieve. ∼**drift** n nieve f amontonada. ∼**fall** n nevada f. ∼**flake** n copo m de nieve. ∼**man** n muñeco m de nieve. ∼**plough** n quitanieves m. ∼**storm** n tormenta f de nieve. ∼**y** adj (day, weather) nevoso; (landscape) nevado

snub /snʌb/ vt (pt snubbed) desairar. ● n desaire m. ∼**-nosed** adj chato

snuck /snʌk/ see SNEAK

snuff out /snʌf/ vt apagar (candle)

snug /snʌg/ adj (snugger, snuggest) cómodo; (tight) ajustado

snuggle (up) /ˈsnʌgl/ vi acurrucarse

so /səʊ/ adv (before a or adv) tan; (thus) así; **and** ∼ **on, and** ∼ **forth** etcétera (etcétera). **I think** ∼ creo que sí. **or** ∼ más o menos. ∼ **long!** ¡hasta luego! ● conj (therefore) así que. ∼ **am I** yo también. ∼ **as to** para. ∼

S

far adv (*time*) hasta ahora. ∼ **far as I know** que yo sepa. ∼ **that** conj para que.

soak /səʊk/ vt remojar. ● vi remojarse. □ ∼ **in** vi penetrar. □ ∼ **up** vt absorber. ∼**ing** adj empapado.

so-and-so /'səʊənsəʊ/ n fulano m

soap /səʊp/ n jabón m. ● vt enjabonar. ∼ **opera** n telenovela f, culebrón m. ∼ **powder** n jabón m en polvo. ∼**y** adj jabonoso

soar /sɔː(r)/ vi (bird/plane) planear; (*rise*) elevarse; (*price*) dispararse. ∼**ing** adj (inflation) galopante

sob /sɒb/ n sollozo m. ● vi (pt sobbed) sollozar

sober /'səʊbə(r)/ adj (not drunk) sobrio

so-called /'səʊkɔːld/ adj denominado; (expert) supuesto

soccer /'sɒkə(r)/ n fútbol m, futbol m (Mex)

sociable /'səʊʃəbl/ adj sociable

social /'səʊʃl/ adj social; (sociable) sociable. ∼**ism** n socialismo m. ∼**ist** adj & n socialista (m & f). ∼**ize** vt socializar. ∼ **security** n seguridad f social. ∼ **worker** n asistente m social

society /sə'saɪətɪ/ n sociedad f

sociolog|ical /səʊsɪə'lɒdʒɪkl/ adj sociológico. ∼**ist** /-'ɒlədʒɪst/ n sociólogo m. ∼**y** /-'ɒlədʒɪ/ n sociología f

sock /sɒk/ n calcetín m

socket /'sɒkɪt/ n (of joint) hueco m; (of eye) cuenca f; (wall plug) enchufe m; (for bulb) portalámparas m

soda /'səʊdə/ n soda f. ∼**-water** n soda f

sodium /'səʊdɪəm/ n sodio m

sofa /'səʊfə/ n sofá m

soft /sɒft/ adj (-er, -est) blando; (light, colour) suave; (gentle) dulce, tierno; (not strict) blando. ∼ **drink** n refresco m. ∼**en** /'sɒfn/ vt ablandar; suavizar (skin). ● vi ablandarse. ∼**ly** adv dulcemente; (speak) bajito. ∼**ware** /-weə(r)/ n software m

soggy /'sɒgɪ/ adj (-ier, -iest) empapado

soil /sɔɪl/ n tierra f; (Amer, dirt) suciedad f. ● vt ensuciar

solar /'səʊlə(r)/ adj solar

sold /səʊld/ see **SELL**

solder /'sɒldə(r)/ vt soldar

soldier /'səʊldʒə(r)/ n soldado m. □ ∼ **on** vi 🄸 seguir al pie del cañon

sole /səʊl/ n (of foot) planta f; (of shoe) suela f. ● adj único, solo. ∼**ly** adv únicamente

solemn /'sɒləm/ adj solemne

solicitor /sə'lɪsɪtə(r)/ n abogado m; (notary) notario m

solid /'sɒlɪd/ adj sólido; (gold etc) macizo; (unanimous) unánime; (meal) sustancioso. ● n sólido m. ∼**s** npl alimentos mpl sólidos. ∼**arity** /sɒlɪ'dærətɪ/ n solidaridad f. ∼**ify** /sə'lɪdɪfaɪ/ vi solidificarse

solitary /'sɒlɪtrɪ/ adj solitario

solitude /'sɒlɪtjuːd/ n soledad f

solo /'səʊləʊ/ n (pl -os) (Mus) solo m. ∼**ist** n solista m & f

solstice /'sɒlstɪs/ n solsticio m

solu|ble /'sɒljʊbl/ adj soluble. ∼**tion** /sə'luːʃn/ n solución f

solve /sɒlv/ vt solucionar (problem); resolver (mystery). ∼**nt** /-vənt/ adj & n solvente (m)

sombre /'sɒmbə(r)/ adj sombrío

---

some /sʌm//səm/

● adjective

····▸ (unspecified number) unos, unas. **he ate** ∼ **olives** comió unas aceitunas

····▸ (unspecified amount) not translated. **I have to buy** ∼ **bread** tengo que comprar pan. **would you like** ∼ **coffee?** ¿quieres café?

····▸ (certain, not all) algunos, -nas. **I like** ∼ **modern writers** algunos escritores modernos me gustan

····▸ (a little) algo de. **I eat** ∼ **meat, but not much** como algo de carne, pero no mucho

····▸ (considerable amount of) **we've known each other for** ∼ **time** ya hace tiempo que nos conocemos

····▸ (expressing admiration) **that's** ∼ **car you've got!** ¡vaya coche que tienes!

● pronoun

····▸ (a number of things or people) algunos, -nas, unos, unas. ∼ **are mine and** ∼ **aren't** algunos or

unos son míos y otros no. **aren't
there any apples? we bought
~ yesterday** ¿no hay manzanas?
compramos algunas ayer

····▸ (*part of an amount*) **he wants
~** quiere un poco. **~ of what
he said** parte *or* algo de lo que
dijo

····▸ (*certain people*) algunos, -nas .
~ say that... algunos dicen
que...

● *adverb*

····▸ (*approximately*) unos, unas, alrededor de. **there were ~ fifty
people there** había unas cincuenta personas, había alrededor
de cincuenta personas

some ~body /-bɑdɪ/ *pron* alguien.
~how *adv* de algún modo. **~how
or other** de una manera u otra.
~one *pron* alguien

somersault /'sʌməsɔːlt/ *n* salto *m*
mortal. ● *vi* dar un salto mortal

some ~thing *pron* algo *m*. **~thing
like** (*approximately*) alrededor de.
~time *adj* ex. ● *adv* algún día.
~time next week un día de la semana que viene. **~times** *adv* a
veces. **~what** *adv* un tanto.
~where *adv* en alguna parte, en
algún lado

son /sʌn/ *n* hijo *m*

sonata /sə'nɑːtə/ *n* sonata *f*

song /sɒŋ/ *n* canción *f*

sonic /'sɒnɪk/ *adj* sónico

son-in-law /'sʌnɪnlɔː/ *n* (*pl* **sons-
in-law**) yerno *m*

sonnet /'sɒnɪt/ *n* soneto *m*

son of a bitch *n* (*pl* **sons of bitches**)
(*esp Amer sl*) hijo *m* de puta

soon /suːn/ *adv* (**-er, -est**) pronto; (*in a
short time*) dentro de poco. **~ after**
poco después. **~er or later** tarde o
temprano. **as ~ as** en cuanto; **as ~
as possible** lo antes posible. **the ~er
the better** cuanto antes mejor

soot /sʊt/ *n* hollín *m*

sooth|e /suːð/ *vt* calmar; aliviar (pain).
~ing *adj* (*medicine*) calmante;
(*words*) tranquilizador

sooty /'sʊtɪ/ *adj* cubierto de hollín

sophisticated /sə'fɪstɪkeɪtɪd/ *adj* so-
fisticado; (*complex*) complejo

sophomore /'sɒfəmɔː(r)/ *n* (*Amer*) estudiante *m & f* de segundo curso (en
la universidad)

sopping /'sɒpɪŋ/ *adj.* **~ (wet)** empapado

soppy /'sɒpɪ/ *adj* (**-ier, -iest**) 🔢 sentimental

soprano /sə'prɑːnəʊ/ *n* (*pl* **-os**) soprano *f*

sordid /'sɔːdɪd/ *adj* sórdido

sore /'sɔː(r)/ *adj* (**-er, -est**) dolorido;
(*Amer fam, angry*) **be ~ at s.o.** estar
picado con uno. **~ throat** *n* dolor *m*
de garganta. **I've got a ~ throat** me
duele la garganta. ● *n* llaga *f*

sorrow /'sɒrəʊ/ *n* pena *f*, pesar *m*

sorry /'sɒrɪ/ *adj* (**-ier, -ier**) arrepentido;
(*wretched*) lamentable. **I'm ~** lo
siento. **be ~ for s.o.** (*pity*) compadecer a uno. **I'm ~ you can't come**
siento que no puedas venir. **say ~**
pedir perdón. **~!** (*apologizing*) ¡lo
siento! ¡perdón!. **~?** (*asking s.o. to repeat*) ¿cómo?

sort /sɔːt/ *n* tipo *m*, clase *f*; (*fam, person*) tipo *m*. **a ~ of** una especie de.
● *vt* clasificar. □ **~ out** *vt* (*organize*)
ordenar; organizar (finances); (*separate out*) separar; solucionar (problem)

so-so /'səʊsəʊ/ *adj* regular

soufflé /'suːfleɪ/ *n* suflé *m*

sought /sɔːt/ *see* **SEEK**

soul /səʊl/ *n* alma *f*

sound /saʊnd/ *n* sonido *m*; (*noise*)
ruido *m*. ● *vt* tocar. ● *vi* sonar; (*seem*)
parecer (*as if que*) **it ~s interesting**
suena interesante.. ● *adj* (**-er, -est**)
sano; (*argument*) lógico; (*secure*) seguro. ● *adv.* **~ asleep** profundamente
dormido. **~ barrier** *n* barrera *f* del
sonido. **~ly** *adv* sólidamente; (*asleep*)
profundamente. **~proof** *adj* insonori-
zado. **~track** *n* banda *f* sonora

soup /suːp/ *n* sopa *f*

sour /'saʊə(r)/ *adj* (**-er, -est**) agrio;
(*milk*) cortado

source /sɔːs/ *n* fuente *f*

south /saʊθ/ *n* sur *m*. ● *adj* sur *a invar*;
(*wind*) del sur. ● *adv* (*go*) hacia el sur.
it's ~ of está al sur de. **S~ Africa** *n*
Sudáfrica *f*. **S~ America** *n* América *f*

S

(del Sur), Sudamérica f. **S~
American** adj & n sudamericano (m).
~-east n sudeste m, sureste m.
~erly /'sʌðəlɪ/ (wind) del sur. **~ern**
/'sʌðən/ adj del sur, meridional.
~erner n sureño m. **~ward** /-wəd/,
~wards adv hacia el sur. **~-west** n
sudoeste m, suroeste m

souvenir /suːvə'nɪə(r)/ n recuerdo m

sovereign /'sɒvrɪn/ n & a soberano
(m)

Soviet /'səʊvɪət/ adj (History) soviético.
the ~ Union n la Unión f Soviética

sow[1] /səʊ/ vt (pt sowed, pp sowed or
sown /səʊn/) sembrar

sow[2] /saʊ/ n cerda f

soy (esp Amer), **soya** /'sɔɪə/ n. **~ bean**
n soja f

spa /spɑː/ n balneario m

space /speɪs/ n espacio m; (room) espacio m, lugar m. ● adj (research etc)
espacial. ● vt espaciar. □ **~ out** vt espaciar. **~craft**, **~ship** n nave f espacial

spade /speɪd/ n pala f. **~s** npl (Cards)
picas fpl

spaghetti /spə'getɪ/ n espaguetis mpl

Spain /speɪn/ n España f

spam /spæm/ n (Comp) correo m basura

span /spæn/ n (of arch) luz f; (of time)
espacio m; (of wings) envergadura f.
● vt (pt spanned) extenderse sobre.
● adj see **SPICK**

Spaniard /'spænjəd/ n español m

spaniel /'spænjəl/ n spaniel m

Spanish /'spænɪʃ/ adj español; (language) castellano, español. ● n (language) castellano m, español m. npl.
the ~ (people) los españoles

spank /spæŋk/ vt pegarle a (en las
nalgas)

spanner /'spænə(r)/ n llave f

spare /speə(r)/ vt. **if you can ~ the
time** si tienes tiempo. **can you ~
me a pound?** ¿tienes una libra que
me des? **~ no effort** no escatimar
esfuerzos. **have money to ~** tener
dinero de sobra. ● adj (not in use) de
más; (replacement) de repuesto; (free)
libre. **~ (part)** n repuesto m. **~
room** n cuarto m de huéspedes. **~**

time n tiempo m libre. **~ tyre** n neumático m de repuesto

sparingly /'speərɪŋlɪ/ adv (use) con
moderación

spark /spɑːk/ n chispa f. ● vt provocar
(criticism); suscitar (interest). **~ing
plug** n (Auto) bujía f

sparkl|e /'spɑːkl/ vi centellear. ● n des-
tello m. **~ing** adj centelleante; (wine)
espumoso

spark plug n (Auto) bujía f

sparrow /'spærəʊ/ n gorrión m

sparse /spɑːs/ adj escaso. **~ly** adv es-
casamente

spasm /'spæzəm/ n espasmo m; (of
cough) acceso m. **~odic** /-'mɒdɪk/ adj
espasmódico; (Med) irregular

spat /spæt/ see **SPIT**

spate /speɪt/ n racha f

spatial /'speɪʃl/ adj espacial

spatter /'spætə(r)/ vt salpicar (**with**
de)

spawn /spɔːn/ n huevas fpl. ● vt generar. ● vi desovar

speak /spiːk/ vt/i (pt spoke, pp
spoken) hablar. **~ for s.o.** hablar en
nombre de uno. □ **~ up** vi hablar
más fuerte. **~er** n (in public) orador
m; (loudspeaker) altavoz m; (of language) hablante m & f

spear /spɪə(r)/ n lanza f. **~head** vt
(lead) encabezar

special /'speʃl/ adj especial. **~ist**
/'speʃəlɪst/ n especialista m & f. **~ity**
/-ɪ'ælətɪ/ n especialidad f. **~ization**
/-əlaɪ'zeɪʃn/ n especialización f. **~ize**
/-əlaɪz/ vi especializarse. **~ized** adj especializado. **~ly** adv especialmente.
~ty n (Amer) especialidad f

species /'spiːʃiːz/ n especie f

specif|ic /spə'sɪfɪk/ adj específico.
~ically adv específicamente; (state)
explícitamente. **~ication** /-ɪ'keɪʃn/ n
especificación f. **~y** /'spesɪfaɪ/ vt especificar

specimen /'spesɪmɪn/ n muestra f

speck /spek/ n (of dust) mota f; (in distance) punto m

specs /speks/ npl Ⓣ see **SPECTACLES**

spectac|le /'spektəkl/ n espectáculo
m. **~les** npl gafas fpl, lentes fpl (LAm),
anteojos mpl (LAm). **~ular**

/·'tækjʊlə(r)/ *adj* espectacular

spectator /spek'teɪtə(r)/ *n* espectador *m*

spectr|e /'spektə(r)/ *n* espectro *m*. **~um** /'spektrəm/ *n* (*pl* **-tra** /-trə/) espectro *m*; (*of views*) gama *f*

speculat|e /'spekjʊleɪt/ *vi* especular. **~ion** /-'leɪʃn/. *n* especulación *f*. **~or** *n* especulador *m*

sped /sped/ *see* SPEED

speech /spiːtʃ/ *n* (*faculty*) habla *f*; (*address*) discurso *m*. **~less** *adj* mudo

speed /spiːd/ *n* velocidad *f*; (*rapidity*) rapidez *f*. ● *vi* (*pt* **speeded**) (*drive too fast*) ir a exceso de velocidad. □ ~ **off**, ~ **away** (*pt* **sped**) *vi* alejarse a toda velocidad. □ ~ **by** (*pt* **sped**) *vi* (*time*) pasar volando. □ ~ **up** (*pt* **speeded**) *vt* acelerar. *vi* acelerarse. **~boat** *n* lancha *f* motora. ~ **camera** *n* cámara *f* de control de velocidad. ~ **dating** *n* cita *f* flash, speed dating *m*. ~ **limit** *n* velocidad *f* máxima. **~ometer** /spiː'dɒmɪtə(r)/ *n* velocímetro *m*. **~way** *n* (*Amer*) autopista *f*. **~y** *adj* (**-ier**, **-iest**) rápido

spell /spel/ *n* (*magic*) hechizo *m*; (*of weather, activity*) período *m*. **go through a bad ~** pasar por una mala racha. ● *vt/i* (*pt* **spelled** or **spelt**) escribir. □ ~ **out** *vt* deletrear; (*fig*) explicar. ~ **checker** *n* corrector *m* ortográfico. **~ing** *n* ortografía *f*

spellbound /'spelbaʊnd/ *adj* embelesado

spelt /spelt/ *see* SPELL

spend /spend/ *vt* (*pt* **spent** /spent/) gastar (*money*); pasar (*time*); dedicar (*care*). ● *vi* gastar dinero

sperm /spɜːm/ *n* (*pl* **sperms** or **sperm**) esperma *f*; (*individual*) espermatozoide *m*

spew /spjuː/ *vt/i* vomitar

spher|e /sfɪə(r)/ *n* esfera *f*. **~ical** /'sferɪkl/ *adj* esférico

spice /spaɪs/ *n* especia *f*

spick /spɪk/ *adj*. ~ **and span** limpio y ordenado

spicy /'spaɪsɪ/ *adj* picante

spider /'spaɪdə(r)/ *n* araña *f*

spik|e /spaɪk/ *n* (*of metal etc*) punta *f*. **~y** *adj* puntiagudo

spill /spɪl/ *vt* (*pt* **spilled** or **spilt**) derramar. ● *vi* derramarse. ~ **over** *vi* (*container*) desbordarse; (*liquid*) rebosar

spin /spɪn/ *vt* (*pt* **spun**, *pres p* **spinning**) hacer girar; hilar (*wool*); centrifugar (*washing*). ● *vi* girar. ● *n*. **give sth a ~** hacer girar algo. **go for a ~** (*Auto*) ir a dar un paseo en coche

spinach /'spɪnɪdʒ/ *n* espinacas *fpl*

spindly /'spɪndlɪ/ *adj* larguirucho

spin-drier /spɪn'draɪə(r)/ *n* centrifugadora *f* (de ropa)

spine /spaɪn/ *n* columna *f* vertebral; (*of book*) lomo *m*; (*on animal*) púa *f*. **~less** *adj* (*fig*) sin carácter

spinning wheel /'spɪnɪŋ/ *n* rueca *f*

spin-off /'spɪnɒf/ *n* resultado *m* indirecto; (*by-product*) producto *m* derivado

spinster /'spɪnstə(r)/ *n* soltera *f*

spiral /'spaɪərəl/ *adj* espiral; (*shape*) de espiral. ● *n* espiral *f*. ● *vi* (*pt* **spiralled**) (*unemployment*) escalar; (*prices*) dispararse. ~ **staircase** *n* escalera *f* de caracol

spire /'spaɪə(r)/ *n* aguja *f*

spirit /'spɪrɪt/ *n* espíritu *m*. **be in good ~s** estar animado. **in low ~s** abatido. **~ed** *adj* animado, fogoso. **~s** *npl* (*drinks*) bebidas *fpl* alcohólicas (de alta graduación). **~ual** /'spɪrɪtjʊəl/ *adj* espiritual

spit /spɪt/ *vt* (*pt* **spat** or (*Amer*) **spit**, *pres p* **spitting**) escupir. ● *vi* escupir. **it's ~ting** caen algunas gotas. ● *n* saliva *f*; (*for roasting*) asador *m*

spite /spaɪt/ *n* rencor *m*. **in ~ of** a pesar de. ● *vt* fastidiar. **~ful** *adj* rencoroso

spittle /'spɪtl/ *n* baba *f*

splash /splæʃ/ *vt* salpicar. ● *vi* (*person*) chapotear. ● *n* salpicadura *f*. **a ~ of paint** un poco de pintura. □ ~ **about** *vi* chapotear. □ ~ **down** *vi* (*spacecraft*) amerizar. □ ~ **out** *vi* gastarse un dineral (**on** en)

splend|id /'splendɪd/ *adj* espléndido. **~our** /-ə(r)/ *n* esplendor *m*

splint /splɪnt/ *n* tablilla *f*

splinter /'splɪntə(r)/ *n* astilla *f*. ● *vi* astillarse

S

split /splɪt/ vt (pt **split**, pres p **splitting**) partir; fisionar (atom); reventar (trousers); (divide) dividir. ● vi partirse; (divide) dividirse. **a ~ting headache** un dolor de cabeza espantoso. ● n (in garment) descosido m; (in wood, glass) rajadura f. □ ~ **up** vi separarse. ~ **second** n fracción f de segundo

splutter /'splʌtə(r)/ vi chisporrotear; (person) farfullar

spoil /spɔɪl/ vt (pt **spoilt** or **spoiled**) estropear, echar a perder; (indulge) consentir, malcriar. ~**s** npl botín m. ~**-sport** n aguafiestas m & f

spoke¹ /spəʊk/ see SPEAK

spoke² /spəʊk/ n (of wheel) rayo m

spoken /'spəʊkən/ see SPEAK

spokesman /'spəʊksmən/ n (pl **-men**) portavoz m

sponge /spʌndʒ/ n esponja f. ● vt limpiar con una esponja. ~ **off**, ~ **on** vt vivir a costillas de. ~ **cake** n bizcocho m

sponsor /'spɒnsə(r)/ n patrocinador m; (of the arts) mecenas m & f; (surety) garante m. ● vt patrocinar. ~**ship** n patrocinio m; (of the arts) mecenazgo m

spontaneous /spɒn'teɪnɪəs/ adj espontáneo. ~**ously** adv espontáneamente

spoof /spuːf/ n 🄸 parodia f

spooky /'spuːkɪ/ adj (**-ier, -iest**) 🄸 espeluznante

spool /spuːl/ n carrete m

spoon /spuːn/ n cuchara f. ~**ful** n cucharada f

sporadic /spə'rædɪk/ adj esporádico

sport /spɔːt/ n deporte m. ~**s car** n coche m deportivo. ~**s centre** n centro m deportivo. ~**sman** /-mən/ n, (pl **-men**), ~**swoman** n deportista m & f

spot /spɒt/ n mancha f; (pimple) grano m; (place) lugar m; (in pattern) lunar m. **be in a ~** 🄸 estar en apuros. **on the ~** allí mismo; (decide) en ese mismo momento. ● vt (pt **spotted**) manchar; (fam, notice) ver, divisar; descubrir (mistake). ~ **check** n control m hecho al azar. ~**less** adj (clothes) impecable; (house) limpísimo. ~**light** n reflector m; (in theatre) foco m. ~**ted** adj moteado; (material) de lunares. ~**ty** adj (**-ier, -iest**) (skin) lleno de granos; (youth) con la cara llena de granos

spouse /spaʊz/ n cónyuge m & f

spout /spaʊt/ n pico m; (jet) chorro m

sprain /spreɪn/ vt hacerse un esguince en. ● n esguince m

sprang /spræŋ/ see SPRING

spray /spreɪ/ n (of flowers) ramillete m; (from sea) espuma f; (liquid in spray form) espray m; (device) rociador m. ● vt rociar

spread /spred/ vt (pt **spread**) (stretch, extend) extender; desplegar (wings); difundir (idea, news). ~ **butter on a piece of toast** untar una tostada con mantequilla. ● vi extenderse; (disease) propagarse; (idea, news) difundirse. ● n (of ideas) difusión f; (of disease, fire) propagación f; (fam, feast) festín m. □ ~ **out** vi (move apart) desplegarse

spree /spriː/ n. **go on a shopping ~** ir de expedición a las tiendas

sprightly /'spraɪtlɪ/ adj (**-ier, -iest**) vivo

spring /sprɪŋ/ n (season) primavera f; (device) resorte m; (in mattress) muelle m, resorte m (LAm); (elasticity) elasticidad f; (water) manantial m. ● adj primaveral. ● vi (pt **sprang**, pp **sprung**) saltar; (issue) brotar. ~ **from sth** (provenir de algo. □ ~ **up** vi surgir. ~**board** n trampolín m. ~**-clean** /-'kliːn/ vi hacer una limpieza general. ~ **onion** n cebolleta f. ~**time** n primavera f. ~**y** adj (**-ier, -iest**) (mattress, grass) mullido

sprinkle /'sprɪŋkl/ vt salpicar; (with liquid) rociar. ● n salpicadura f; (of liquid) rociada f. ~**r** n regadera f

sprint /sprɪnt/ n carrera f corta. ● vi (Sport) esprintar; (run fast) correr. ~**er** n corredor m

sprout /spraʊt/ vi brotar. ● n brote m. (Brussels) ~**s** npl coles fpl de Bruselas

sprung /sprʌŋ/ see SPRING

spud /spʌd/ n 🄸 patata f, papa f (LAm)

spun /spʌn/ see SPIN

spur /spɜː(r)/ n espuela f; (stimulus) acicate m. **on the ~ of the moment** sin pensarlo. ● vt (pt **spurred**). ~

(on) espolear; (*fig*) estimular

spurn /spɜːn/ *vt* desdeñar; (*reject*) rechazar

spurt /spɜːt/ *vi* (liquid) salir a chorros. ● *n* chorro *m*; (*of activity*) racha *f*

spy /spaɪ/ *n* espía *m* & *f*. ● *vt* descubrir, ver. ● *vi* espiar. ~ **on s.o.** espiar a uno

squabble /ˈskwɒbl/ *vi* reñir

squad /skwɒd/ *n* (*Mil*) pelotón *m*; (*of police*) brigada *f*; (*Sport*) equipo *m*. ~ **car** *m* coche *m* patrulla. ~**ron** /ˈskwɒdrən/ *n* (*Mil*, *Aviat*) escuadrón *m*; (*Naut*) escuadra *f*

squalid /ˈskwɒlɪd/ *adj* miserable

squall /skwɔːl/ *n* turbión *m*

squalor /ˈskwɒlə(r)/ *n* miseria *f*

squander /ˈskwɒndə(r)/ *vt* derrochar; desaprovechar (opportunity)

square /skweə(r)/ *n* cuadrado *m*; (*in town*) plaza *f*. ● *adj* cuadrado; (meal) decente; (*fam*, *old-fashioned*) chapado a la antigua. ● *vt* (settle) arreglar; (*Math*) elevar al cuadrado. ● *vi* (agree) cuadrar. □ ~ **up** *vi* arreglar cuentas (with con). ~**ly** *adv* directamente

squash /skwɒʃ/ *vt* aplastar; (suppress) acallar. ● *n*. it was a terrible ~ íbamos (or iban) terriblemente apretujados; (drink) orange ~ naranjada *f*; (*Sport*) squash *m*; (vegetable) calabaza *f*. ~**y** *adj* blando

squat /skwɒt/ *vi* (*pt* **squatted**) ponerse en cuclillas; (occupy illegally) ocupar sin autorización. ● *adj* rechoncho y bajo. ~**ter** *n* ocupante *m* & *f* ilegal, okupa *m* & *f*

squawk /skwɔːk/ *n* graznido *m*. ● *vi* graznar

squeak /skwiːk/ *n* chillido *m*; (*of door*) chirrido *m*. ● *vi* chillar; (door) chirriar; (shoes) crujir. ~**y** *adj* chirriante

squeal /skwiːl/ *n* chillido *m* ● *vi* chillar

squeamish /ˈskwiːmɪʃ/ *adj* impresionable, delicado

squeeze /skwiːz/ *vt* apretar; exprimir (lemon etc). ● *vi*. ~ **in** meterse. ● *n* estrujón *m*; (*of hand*) apretón *m*

squid /skwɪd/ *n* calamar *m*

squiggle /ˈskwɪgl/ *n* garabato *m*

squint /skwɪnt/ *vi* bizquear; (*trying to see*) entrecerrar los ojos. ● *n* estrabismo *m*

squirm /skwɜːm/ *vi* retorcerse

squirrel /ˈskwɪrəl/ *n* ardilla *f*

squirt /skwɜːt/ *vt* (liquid) echar un chorro de. ● *vi* salir a chorros. ● *n* chorrito *m*

St /sənt/ *abbr* (= **saint**) /sənt/ S, San(to); (= **street**) C/, Calle *f*

stab /stæb/ *vt* (*pt* **stabbed**) apuñalar. ● *n* puñalada *f*; (pain) punzada *f*. have a ~ **at sth** intentar algo

stabili|ty /stəˈbɪlətɪ/ *n* estabilidad *f*. ~**ze** /ˈsteɪbɪlaɪz/ *vt/i* estabilizar

stable /ˈsteɪbl/ *adj* (**-er**, **-est**) estable. ● *n* caballeriza *f*, cuadra *f*

stack /stæk/ *n* montón *m*. ● *vt*. ~ **(up)** amontonar

stadium /ˈsteɪdɪəm/ *n* (*pl* **-diums** or **-dia** /-dɪə/) estadio *m*

staff /stɑːf/ *n* (stick) palo *m*; (employees) personal *m*. teaching ~ personal *m* docente. a member of ~ un empleado

stag /stæg/ *n* ciervo *m*. ~**-night**, ~**-party** *n* (before wedding) fiesta *f* de despedida de soltero; (men-only party) fiesta *f* para hombres

stage /steɪdʒ/ *n* (in theatre) escenario *f*; (platform) plataforma *f*; (phase) etapa *f*. the ~ (profession, medium) el teatro. ● *vt* poner en escena (play); (arrange) organizar; (pej) orquestar. ~**coach** *n* diligencia *f*

stagger /ˈstægə(r)/ *vi* tambalearse ● *vt* dejar estupefacto; escalonar (holidays etc). ~**ing** *adj* asombroso

stagna|nt /ˈstægnənt/ *adj* estancado. ~**te** /stægˈneɪt/ *vi* estancarse

staid /steɪd/ *adj* serio, formal

stain /steɪn/ *vt* manchar; (colour) teñir. ● *n* mancha *f*; (dye) tintura *f*. ~**ed glass window** *n* vidriera *f* de colores. ~**less steel** *n* acero *m* inoxidable. ~ **remover** *n* quitamanchas *m*

stair /steə(r)/ *n* escalón *m*. ~**s** *npl* escalera *f*. ~**case**, ~**way** *n* escalera *f*

stake /steɪk/ *n* estaca *f*; (wager) apuesta *f*; (*Com*) intereses *mpl*. be at ~ estar en juego. ● *vt* estacar; jugarse (reputation). ~ **a claim** reclamar

S

stala|ctite /'stæləktaɪt/ n estalactita f. **~gmite** /'stælagmaɪt/ n estalagmita f

stale /steɪl/ adj (-er, -est) no fresco; (bread) duro; (smell) viciado. **~mate** n (Chess) ahogado m; (deadlock) punto m muerto

stalk /stɔːk/ n tallo m. ● vt acechar. ● vi irse indignado

stall /stɔːl/ n (in stable) comparti-miento m; (in market) puesto m. **~s** npl (in theatre) platea f, patio m de bu-tacas. ● vt parar (engine). ● vi (en-gine) pararse; (fig) andar con rodeos

stallion /'stæljən/ n semental m

stalwart /'stɔːlwət/ adj (supporter) leal, incondicional

stamina /'stæmɪnə/ n resistencia f

stammer /'stæmə(r)/ vi tartamudear. ● n tartamudeo m

stamp /stæmp/ vt (with feet) patear; (press) estampar; (with rubber stamp) sellar; (fig) señalar. ● vi dar patadas en el suelo. ● n sello m, estampilla f (LAm), timbre m (Mex); (on passport) sello m; (with foot) patada f; (mark) marca f, señal f. □ **~ out** vt (fig) erra-dicar. **~ed addressed envelope** n sobre m franqueado con su dirección

stampede /stæm'piːd/ n estampida f. ● vi salir en estampida

stance /stɑːns/ n postura f

stand /stænd/ vi (pt stood) estar de pie, estar parado (LAm); (rise) ponerse de pie, pararse; (be) encontrarse; (Pol) presentarse como candidato (**for** en). **the offer ~s** la oferta sigue en pie. **~ to reason** ser lógico. ● vt (endure) soportar; (place) colocar. **~ a chance** tener una posibilidad. ● n posición f, postura f; (for lamp etc) pie m, sostén m; (at market) puesto m; (booth) quiosco m; (Sport) tribuna f. **make a ~ against sth** oponer resistencia a algo. □ **~ back** vi apartarse. □ **~ by** vi estar preparado. vt (support) apoyar. □ **~ down** vi retirarse. □ **~ for** vt sig-nificar. □ **~ in for** vt suplir a. □ **~ out** vi destacarse. □ **~ up** vi ponerse de pie, pararse (LAm). □ **~ up for** vt defender. **~ up for oneself** defen-derse. □ **~ up to** vt resistir a

standard /'stændəd/ n norma f; (level) nivel m; (flag) estandarte m. ● adj es-tándar a invar, normal. **~ize** vt estan-darizar. **~ lamp** n lámpara f de pie. **~s** npl principios mpl

stand ~by n (at airport) stand-by m. **be on ~by** (police) estar en estado de alerta. **~-in** n suplente m & f. **~ing** adj de pie, parado (LAm); (per-manent) permanente f. ● n posición f; (prestige) prestigio m. **~off** n (Amer, draw) empate m; (deadlock) callejón m sin salida. **~point** n punto m de vista. **~still** n. **be at a ~still** estar paralizado. **come to a ~still** (vehicle) parar; (city) quedar paralizado

stank /stæŋk/ see STINK

staple /'steɪpl/ adj principal. ● n grapa f. ● vt sujetar con una grapa. **~r** n grapadora f

star /stɑː(r)/ n (incl Cinema, Theatre) es-trella f; (asterisk) asterisco m. ● vi (pt starred). **~ in a film** protagonizar una película. **~board** n estribor m.

starch /stɑːtʃ/ n almidón m; (in food) fécula f. ● vt almidonar. **~y** (food) adj a base de féculas

stardom /'stɑːdəm/ n estrellato m

stare /steə(r)/ n mirada f fija. ● vi. **~ (at)** mirar fijamente

starfish /'stɑːfɪʃ/ n estrella f de mar

stark /stɑːk/ adj (-er, -est) escueto. ● adv completamente

starling /'stɑːlɪŋ/ n estornino m

starry /'stɑːrɪ/ adj estrellado

start /stɑːt/ vt empezar, comenzar; en-cender (engine); arrancar (car); (cause) provocar; abrir (business). ● vi empezar; (car etc) arrancar; (jump) dar un respingo. **to ~ with** (as linker) para empezar. **~ off by doing sth** empezar por hacer algo. ● n principio m; (Sport) ventaja f; (jump) susto m. **make an early ~** (on journey) salir temprano. **~er** n (Auto) motor m de arranque; (Culin) primer plato m. **~ing-point** n punto m de partida

startle /'stɑːtl/ vt asustar

starv|ation /stɑː'veɪʃn/ n hambre f, inanición f. **~e** /stɑːv/ vt hacer morir de hambre. ● vi morirse de hambre. **I'm ~ing** me muero de hambre

state /steɪt/ n estado m. **be in a ~** estar agitado. **the S~** los Estados mpl

Unidos. ● *vt* declarar; expresar (views); (*fix*) fijar. ● *adj* del Estado; (*Schol*) público; (*with ceremony*) de gala. ~ly *adj* (-ier, -iest) majestuoso. ~ly home *n* casa *f* solariega. ~ment *n* declaración *f*; (*account*) informe *m*. ~sman /-mən/ *n* estadista *m*

state school En Gran Bretaña, colegio estatal de educación gratuita, financiado directa o indirectamente por el gobierno. Abarca la educación primaria y secundaria, colegios especializados, *comprehensives* etc.

static /'stætɪk/ *adj* estacionario. ● *n* (*interference*) estática *f*

station /'steɪʃn/ *n* estación *f*; (*on radio*) emisora *f*; (*TV*) canal *m*. ● *vt* colocar; (*Mil*) estacionar. ~ary *adj* estacionario. ~er's (shop) *n* papelería *f*. ~ery *n* artículos *mpl* de papelería. ~ wagon *n* (*Amer*) ranchera *f*, (coche *m*) familiar *m*, camioneta *f* (*LAm*)

statistic /stə'tɪstɪk/ *n* estadística *f*. ~al *adj* estadístico. ~s *n* (*science*) estadística *f*

statue /'stætʃuː/ *n* estatua *f*

stature /'stætʃə(r)/ *n* talla *f*, estatura *f*

status /'steɪtəs/ *n* posición *f* social; (*prestige*) categoría *f*; (*Jurid*) estado *m*

statut|e /'stætʃuːt/ *n* estatuto *m*. ~ory /-ʊtrɪ/ *adj* estatutario

staunch /stɔːnʃ/ *adj* (-er, -est) leal

stave /steɪv/ *n* (*Mus*) pentagrama *m*. □ ~ off *vt* evitar

stay /steɪ/ *n* (*of time*) estancia *f*, estadía *f* (*LAm*); (*Jurid*) suspensión *f*. ● *vi* quedarse; (*reside*) alojarse. I'm ~ing in a hotel estoy en un hotel. □ ~ in *vi* quedarse en casa. □ ~ up *vi* quedarse levantado

stead /sted/ *n*. in s.o.'s ~ en lugar de uno. stand s.o. in good ~ resultarle muy útil a uno. ~ily *adv* firmemente; (*regularly*) regularmente. ~y *adj* (-ier, -iest) firme; (*regular*) regular; (flow) continuo; (worker) serio

steak /steɪk/ *n*. a ~ un filete. some ~ carne para guisar

steal /stiːl/ *vt* (*pt* stole, *pp* stolen) robar. ~ in *vi* entrar a hurtadillas

stealth /stelθ/ *n*. by ~ sigilosamente. ~y *adj* sigiloso

steam /stiːm/ *n* vapor *m*. let off ~ (*fig*) desahogarse. ● *vt* (*cook*) cocer al vapor. ● *vi* echar vapor. □ ~ up *vi* empañarse. ~ engine *n* máquina *f* de vapor. ~er *n* (*ship*) barco *m* de vapor. ~roller *n* apisonadora *f*. ~y *adj* lleno de vapor

steel /stiːl/ *n* acero *m*. ● *vt*. ~ o.s. armarse de valor. ~ industry *n* industria *f* siderúrgica

steep /stiːp/ ● *adj* (-er, -est) empinado; (increase) considerable; (price) [T] excesivo

steeple /'stiːpl/ *n* aguja *f*, campanario *m*

steeply /'stiːplɪ/ *adv* abruptamente; (increase) considerablemente

steer /stɪə(r)/ *vt* dirigir; gobernar (ship). ● *vi* (*in ship*) estar al timón. ~ clear of evitar. ~ing *n* (*Auto*) dirección *f*. ~ing wheel *n* volante *m*

stem /stem/ *n* (*of plant*) tallo *m*; (*of glass*) pie *m*; (*of word*) raíz *f*. ● *vt* (*pt* stemmed) contener (bleeding). ● *vi*. ~ from provenir de

stench /stentʃ/ *n* hedor *m*

stencil /'stensl/ *n* plantilla *f*

stenographer /ste'nɒgrəfə(r)/ *n* estenógrafo *m*

step /step/ *vi* (*pt* stepped). ~ in sth pisar algo. □ ~ aside *vi* hacerse a un lado. □ ~ down *vi* retirarse. □ ~ in *vi* (*fig*) intervenir. □ ~ up *vt* intensificar; redoblar (security). ● *n* paso *m*; (stair) escalón *m*; (*fig*) medida *f*. take ~s tomar medidas. be in ~ llevar el paso. be out of ~ no llevar el paso. ~brother *n* hermanastro *m*. ~daughter *n* hijastra *f*. ~father *n* padrastro *m*. ~ladder *n* escalera *f* de tijera. ~mother *n* madrastra *f*. ~ping-stone *n* peldaño *m*. ~sister *n* hermanastra *f*. ~son *n* hijastro *m*

stereo /'steriəʊ/ *n* (*pl* -os) estéreo *m*. ● *adj* estéreo *a invar*. ~type *n* estereotipo *m*

steril|e /'steraɪl/ *adj* estéril. ~ize /'sterɪlaɪz/ *vt* esterilizar

sterling /'stɜːlɪŋ/ *n* libras *fpl* esterlinas. ● *adj* (pound) esterlina

S

stern /stɜːn/ n (of boat) popa f. ● adj (-er, -est) severo

stethoscope /'steθəskəʊp/ n estetoscopio m

stew /stjuː/ vt/i guisar. ● n estofado m, guiso m

steward /'stjuːəd/ n administrador m; (on ship) camarero m; (air steward) sobrecargo m, aeromozo m (LAm). ~ess /-'des/ n camarera f; (on aircraft) auxiliar f de vuelo, azafata f

stick /stɪk/ n palo m; (for walking) bastón m; (of celery etc) tallo m. ● vt (pt stuck) (glue) pegar; (fam, put) poner; (thrust) clavar; (fam, endure) soportar. ● vi pegarse; (jam) atascarse. □ ~ out vi sobresalir. □ ~ to vt ceñirse a. □ ~ up for vt 🄸 defender. ~er n pegatina f. ~ing plaster n esparadrapo m; (individual) tirita f, curita f (LAm). ~ler /'stɪklə(r)/ n. be a ~ler for insistir en. ~y /'stɪkɪ/ adj (-ier, -iest) (surface) pegajoso; (label) engomado

stiff /stɪf/ adj (-er, -est) rígido; (joint, fabric) tieso; (muscle) entumecido; (difficult) difícil; (manner) estirado; (drink) fuerte. **have a ~ neck** tener tortícolis. ~en vi (become rigid) agarrotarse; (become firm) endurecerse. ~ly adv rígidamente

stifl|e /'staɪfl/ vt sofocar. ~ing adj sofocante

stiletto (heel) /stɪ'letəʊ/ n (pl -os) tacón m de aguja

still /stɪl/ adj inmóvil; (peaceful) tranquilo; (drink) sin gas. **sit ~, stand ~** quedarse tranquilo. ● adv todavía, aún; (nevertheless) sin embargo. ~born adj nacido muerto. ~ life n (pl -s) bodegón m. ~ness n tranquilidad f

stilted /'stɪltɪd/ adj rebuscado; (conversation) forzado

stilts /stɪlts/ npl zancos mpl

stimul|ant /'stɪmjʊlənt/ n estimulante m. ~ate /-leɪt/ vt estimular. ~ation /-'leɪʃn/ n estímulo m. ~us /-əs/ n (pl -li /-laɪ/) estímulo m

sting /stɪŋ/ n picadura f; (organ) aguijón m. ● vt/i (pt stung) picar

stingy /'stɪndʒɪ/ adj (-ier, -iest) tacaño

stink /stɪŋk/ n hedor m. ● vi (pt stank or stunk, pp stunk) apestar, oler mal

stipulat|e /'stɪpjʊleɪt/ vt/i estipular. ~ion /-'leɪʃn/ n estipulación f

stir /stɜː(r)/ vt (pt stirred) remover, revolver; (move) agitar; estimular (imagination). ● vi moverse. ~ **up trouble** armar lío 🄸. ● n revuelo m, conmoción f

stirrup /'stɪrəp/ n estribo m

stitch /stɪtʃ/ n (in sewing) puntada f; (in knitting) punto m; (pain) dolor m costado. **be in ~es** 🄸 desternillarse de risa. ● vt coser

stock /stɒk/ n (Com, supplies) existencias fpl; (Com, variety) surtido m; (livestock) ganado m; (Culin) caldo m. ~s **and shares, ~s and bonds** (Amer) acciones fpl. **out of ~** agotado. **take ~ of sth** (fig) hacer un balance de algo. ● adj estándar a invar; (fig) trillado. ● vt surtir, abastecer (with de). □ ~ **up** vi abastecerse (with de). ~broker /-brəʊkə(r)/ n corredor m de bolsa. **S~ Exchange** n bolsa f. ~ing n media f. ~pile n reservas fpl. ● vt almacenar. ~-still adj inmóvil. ~-taking n (Com) inventario m. ~y adj (-ier, -iest) bajo y fornido

stodgy /'stɒdʒɪ/ (-dgier, -dgiest) adj pesado

stoke /stəʊk/ vt echarle carbón (or leña) a

stole /stəʊl/ see **STEAL**

stolen /'stəʊlən/ see **STEAL**

stomach /'stʌmək/ n estómago m. ● vt soportar. ~-ache n dolor m de estómago

ston|e /stəʊn/ n piedra f; (in fruit) hueso m; (weight, pl stone) unidad de peso equivalente a 14 libras o 6,35 kg. ● adj de piedra. ● vt apedrear. ~e-deaf adj sordo como una tapia. ~y adj (silence) sepulcral

stood /stʊd/ see **STAND**

stool /stuːl/ n taburete m

stoop /stuːp/ vi agacharse; (fig) rebajarse. ● n. **have a ~** ser cargado de espaldas

stop /stɒp/ vt (pt stopped) (halt, switch off) parar; (cease) terminar; (prevent) impedir; (interrupt) interrumpir. ~ **doing sth** dejar de hacer algo. ~ **it!** ¡basta ya! ● vi (bus) parar, detenerse; (clock) pararse. **it's ~ped raining** ha dejado de llover. ● n (bus etc) parada f; (break on journey) parada f. **put a ~ to sth** poner fin a algo. **come to a ~** detenerse. **~gap** n remedio m provisional. **~over** n escala f. **~page** /'stɒpɪdʒ/ n suspensión f, paradero m (LAm); (of work) huelga f, paro m (LAm); (interruption) interrupción f. **~per** n tapón m. **~watch** n cronómetro m

storage /'stɔːrɪdʒ/ n almacenamiento m

store /stɔː(r)/ n provisión f; (depot) almacén m, (Amer, shop) tienda f; (fig) reserva f. **in ~** en reserva. ● vt (for future) poner en reserva; (in warehouse) almacenar. □ **~ up** vt (fig) ir acumulando. **~keeper** n (Amer) tendero m, comerciante m & f. **~room** n almacén m; (for food) despensa f

storey /'stɔːrɪ/ n (pl **-eys**) piso m, planta f

stork /stɔːk/ n cigüeña f

storm /stɔːm/ n tempestad f. ● vi rabiar. ● vt (Mil) asaltar. **~y** adj tormentoso; (sea, relationship) tempestuoso

story /'stɔːrɪ/ n historia f; (in newspaper) artículo m; (rumour) rumor m; (🗊, lie) mentira f, cuento m. **~-teller** n cuentista m & f

stout /staʊt/ adj (**-er, -est**) robusto, corpulento. ● n cerveza f negra

stove /staʊv/ n estufa f

stow /staʊ/ vt guardar; (hide) esconder. □ **~ away** vi viajar de polizón. **~away** n polizón m & f

straggl|e /'strægl/ vi rezagarse. **~y** adj desordenado

straight /streɪt/ adj (**-er, -est**) recto; (tidy) en orden; (frank) franco; (hair) lacio; (🗊, conventional) convencional. **be ~** estar derecho. ● adv (sit up) derecho; (direct) directamente; (without delay) inmediatamente. **~ away** en seguida, inmediatamente. **~ on** todo recto. **~ out** sin rodeos. ● n recta f. **~en** vt enderezar. □ **~en up** vt ordenar. **~forward** /-'fɔːwəd/ adj franco; (easy) sencillo

strain /streɪn/ n (tension) tensión f; (injury) torcedura f. ● vt forzar (voice, eyesight); someter a demasiada tensión (relations); (sieve) colar. **~ one's**

back hacerse daño en la espalda. **~ a muscle** hacerse un esguince. **~ed** adj forzado; (relations) tirante. **~er** n colador m. **~s** npl (Mus) acordes mpl

strait /streɪt/ n estrecho m. **be in dire ~s** estar en grandes apuros. **~jacket** n camisa f de fuerza

strand /strænd/ n (thread) hebra f. **a ~ of hair** un pelo. ● vt. **be ~ed** (ship) quedar encallado. **I was left ~ed** me abandonaron a mi suerte

strange /streɪndʒ/ adj (**-er, -est**) raro, extraño; (not known) desconocido. **~ly** adv de una manera rara. **~ly enough** aunque parezca mentira. **~r** n desconocido m; (from another place) forastero m

strangle /'strængl/ vt estrangular

strap /stræp/ n correa f; (of garment) tirante m. ● vt (pt **strapped**) atar con una correa

strat|egic /strə'tiːdʒɪk/ adj estratégico. **~egy** /'strætədʒɪ/ n estrategia f

straw /strɔː/ n paja f; (drinking **~**) pajita f, paja f, popote m (Mex). **the last ~** el colmo. **~berry** /-bərɪ/ n fresa f; (large) fresón m

stray /streɪ/ vi (wander away) apartarse; (get lost) extraviarse; (deviate) desviarse (**from** de). ● adj (animal) (without owner) callejero; (lost) perdido. ● n (without owner) perro m/gato m callejero; (lost) perro m/gato m perdido

streak /striːk/ n lista f, raya f; (in hair) reflejo m; (in personality) veta f

stream /striːm/ n arroyo m; (current) corriente f. **a ~ of abuse** una sarta de insultos. ● vi correr. □ **~ out** vi (people) salir en tropel. **~er** n (paper) serpentina f; (banner) banderín m. **~line** vt dar línea aerodinámica a; (simplify) racionalizar. **~lined** adj aerodinámico

street /striːt/ n calle f. **~car** n (Amer) tranvía m. **~ lamp** n farol m. **~ map**, **~ plan** n plano m

strength /streŋθ/ n fuerza f; (of wall etc) solidez f. **~en** vt reforzar (wall); fortalecer (muscle)

strenuous /'strenjʊəs/ adj enérgico; (arduous) arduo; (tiring) fatigoso

stress /stres/ n énfasis f; (*Gram*) acento m; (*Mec, Med, tension*) tensión f. ● vt insistir en

stretch /stretʃ/ vt estirar; (*extend*) extender; forzar (truth); estirar (resources). ● vi estirarse; (*when sleepy*) desperezarse; (*extend*) extenderse; (*be elastic*) estirarse. ● n (*period*) período m; (*of road*) tramo m. **at a ~** sin parar. □ **~ out** vi (person) tenderse. **~er** n camilla f

strict /strɪkt/ adj (**-er, -est**) estricto; (*secrecy*) absoluto. **~ly** adv con severidad; (*rigorously*) terminantemente. **~ly speaking** en rigor

stridden /strɪdn/ see STRIDE

stride /straɪd/ vi (*pt* **strode**, *pp* **stridden**) andar a zancadas. ● n zancada f. **take sth in one's ~** tomarse algo con calma. **~nt** /straɪdnt/ adj estridente

strife /straɪf/ n conflicto m

strike /straɪk/ vt (*pt* **struck**) golpear; encender (match); encontrar (gold, oil); (clock) dar. **it ~s me as odd** me parece raro. ● vi golpear; (*go on strike*) declararse en huelga; (*be on strike*) estar en huelga; (*attack*) atacar; (clock) dar la hora. ● n (*of workers*) huelga f, paro m; (*attack*) ataque m. **come out on ~** ir a la huelga. □ **~ off**, **~ out** vt tachar. **~ up a friendship** trabar amistad. **~r** n huelguista m & f; (*Sport*) artillero m

striking /ˈstraɪkɪŋ/ adj (resemblance) sorprendente; (colour) llamativo

string /strɪŋ/ n cordel m, mecate m (*Mex*); (*Mus*) cuerda f; (*of lies, pearls*) sarta f; (*of people*) sucesión f. □ **~ along** vt 🗉 engañar

stringent /ˈstrɪndʒənt/ adj riguroso

strip /strɪp/ vt (*pt* **stripped**) desnudar (person); deshacer (bed). ● vi desnudarse. ● n tira f; (*of land*) franja f. **~ cartoon** n historieta f

stripe /straɪp/ n raya f. **~d** adj a rayas, rayado

strip lighting n luz f fluorescente

strive /straɪv/ vi (*pt* **strove**, *pp* **striven**). **~ to** esforzarse por

strode /strəʊd/ see STRIDE

stroke /strəʊk/ n golpe m; (*in swimming*) brazada f; (*Med*) ataque m de apoplejía; (*of pen etc*) trazo m; (*of clock*) campanada f; (*caress*) caricia f. **a ~ of luck** un golpe de suerte. ● vt acariciar

stroll /strəʊl/ vi pasearse. ● n paseo m. **~er** n (*Amer*) sillita f de paseo, cochecito m

strong /strɒŋ/ adj (**-er, -est**) fuerte. **~hold** n fortaleza f; (*fig*) baluarte m. **~ly** adv (*greatly*) fuertemente; (*protest*) enérgicamente; (*deeply*) profundamente. **~room** n cámara f acorazada

strove /strəʊv/ see STRIVE

struck /strʌk/ see STRIKE

structur|al /ˈstrʌktʃərəl/ adj estructural. **~e** /ˈstrʌktʃə(r)/ n estructura f

struggle /ˈstrʌɡl/ vi luchar; (*thrash around*) forcejear. ● n lucha f

strum /strʌm/ vt (*pt* **strummed**) rasguear

strung /strʌŋ/ see STRING

strut /strʌt/ n (*in building*) puntal m. ● vi (*pt* **strutted**) pavonearse

stub /stʌb/ n (*of pencil, candle*) cabo m; (*counterfoil*) talón m; (*of cigarette*) colilla. □ **~ out** (*pt* **stubbed**) vt apagar

stubble /ˈstʌbl/ n rastrojo m; (*beard*) barba f de varios días

stubborn /ˈstʌbən/ adj terco

stuck /stʌk/ see STICK. ● adj. **the drawer is ~** el cajón se ha atascado. **the door is ~** la puerta se ha atrancado. **~-up** adj 🗉 estirado

stud /stʌd/ n tachuela f; (*for collar*) gemelo m.

student /ˈstjuːdənt/ n estudiante m & f; (*at school*) alumno m. **~ driver** n (*Amer*) persona que está aprendiendo a conducir

studio /ˈstjuːdɪəʊ/ n (*pl* **-os**) estudio m. **~ apartment**, **~ flat** n estudio m

studious /ˈstjuːdɪəs/ adj estudioso

study /ˈstʌdɪ/ n estudio m. ● vt/i estudiar

stuff /stʌf/ n 🗉 cosas fpl. **what's this ~ called?** ¿cómo se llama esta cosa?. ● vt rellenar; disecar (animal); (*cram*) atiborrar; (*put*) meter de prisa. **~ o.s.** 🗉 darse un atracón. **~ing** n relleno m. **~y** adj (**-ier, -iest**) mal ventilado; (*old-fashioned*) acartonado. **it's**

~y in here está muy cargado el ambiente

stumbl|e /'stʌmbl/ vi tropezar. ~e across, ~e on vt dar con. ~ing-block n tropiezo m, impedimento m

stump /stʌmp/ n (of limb) muñón m; (of tree) tocón m

stun /stʌn/ vt (pt stunned) (daze) aturdir; (bewilder) dejar atónito. ~ning adj sensacional

stung /stʌŋ/ see STING

stunk /stʌŋk/ see STINK

stunt /stʌnt/ n 🔲 ardid m publicitario. ● vt detener, atrofiar. ~ed adj (growth) atrofiado; (body) raquítico. ~man n especialista m. ~woman n especialista f

stupendous /stjuː'pendəs/ adj estupendo

stupid /'stjuːpɪd/ adj (foolish) tonto; (unintelligent) estúpido. ~ity /-'pɪdəti/ n estupidez f. ~ly adv estúpidamente

stupor /'stjuːpə(r)/ n estupor m

sturdy /'stɜːdi/ adj (-ier, -iest) robusto

stutter /'stʌtə(r)/ vi tartamudear. ● n tartamudeo m

sty /staɪ/ n (pl sties) pocilga f; (Med) orzuelo m

styl|e /staɪl/ n estilo m; (fashion) moda f; (design, type) diseño m. in ~ a lo grande. ● vt diseñar. ~ish adj elegante. ~ist n estilista m & f. hair ~ist estilista m & f

stylus /'staɪləs/ n (pl -uses) aguja f (de tocadiscos)

suave /swɑːv/ adj elegante y desenvuelto

subconscious /sʌb'kɒnʃəs/ adj & n subconsciente (m)

subdivide /sʌbdɪ'vaɪd/ vt subdividir

subdued /səb'djuːd/ adj apagado

subject /'sʌbdʒɪkt/ adj sometido. ~ to sujeto a. ● n (theme) tema m; (Schol) asignatura f, materia f (LAm); (Gram) sujeto m; (Pol) súbdito m. ● /səb'dʒekt/ vt someter. ~ive /səb'dʒektɪv/ adj subjetivo

subjunctive /səb'dʒʌŋktɪv/ adj & n subjuntivo (m)

sublime /sə'blaɪm/ adj sublime

submarine /sʌbmə'riːn/ n submarino m

submerge /səb'mɜːdʒ/ vt sumergir. ● vi sumergirse

submi|ssion /səb'mɪʃn/ n sumisión f. ~t /səb'mɪt/ vt (pt submitted) (subject) someter; presentar (application). ● vi rendirse

subordinate /sə'bɔːdɪnət/ adj & n subordinado (m). ● /sə'bɔːdɪneɪt/ vt subordinar

subscri|be /səb'skraɪb/ vi suscribir. ~be to suscribirse a (magazine). ~ber n suscriptor m. ~ption /-rɪpʃn/ n (to magazine) suscripción f

subsequent /'sʌbsɪkwənt/ adj posterior, subsiguiente. ~ly adv posteriormente

subside /səb'saɪd/ vi (land) hundirse; (flood) bajar; (storm, wind) amainar. ~nce /'sʌbsɪdəns/ n hundimiento m

subsidiary /səb'sɪdɪəri/ adj secundario; (subject) complementario. ● n (Com) filial

subsid|ize /'sʌbsɪdaɪz/ vt subvencionar, subsidiar (LAm). ~y /'sʌbsədi/ n subvención f, subsidio m

substance /'sʌbstəns/ n sustancia f

substandard /sʌb'stændəd/ adj de calidad inferior

substantial /səb'stænʃl/ adj (sturdy) sólido; (meal) sustancioso; (considerable) considerable

substitut|e /'sʌbstɪtjuːt/ n (person) substituto m; (thing) sucedáneo m. ● vt/i sustituir. ~ion /-'tjuːʃn/ n sustitución f

subterranean /sʌbtə'reɪnjən/ adj subterráneo

subtitle /'sʌbtaɪtl/ n subtítulo m

subtle /'sʌtl/ adj (-er, -est) sutil; (tactful) discreto. ~ty n sutileza f

subtract /səb'trækt/ vt restar. ~ion /-ʃn/ n resta f

suburb /'sʌbɜːb/ n barrio m residencial de las afueras, colonia f. the ~s las afueras fpl. ~an /sə'bɜːbən/ adj suburbano. ~ia /sə'bɜːbɪə/ n zonas residenciales de las afueras de una ciudad

subversive /səb'vɜːsɪv/ adj subversivo

S

subway /'sʌbweɪ/ n paso m subterráneo; (*Amer*) metro m

succeed /sək'siːd/ vi (plan) dar resultado; (person) tener éxito. **~ in doing** lograr hacer. ● vt suceder

success /sək'ses/ n éxito m. **~ful** adj (person) de éxito, exitoso (*LAm*). **the ~ful applicant** el candidato que obtenga el puesto. **~fully** adj satisfactoriamente. **~ion** /-ʃn/ n sucesión f. **for 3 years in ~ion** durante tres años consecutivos. **in rapid ~ion** uno tras otro. **~ive** adj sucesivo. **~or** n sucesor m

succulent /'sʌkjʊlənt/ adj suculento

succumb /sə'kʌm/ vi sucumbir

such /sʌtʃ/ adj tal (+ noun), tan (+ adj). **~ a big house** una casa tan grande. ● pron tal. **~ and ~** tal o cual. **~ as** como. **~ as it is** tal como es

suck /sʌk/ vt chupar (sweet, thumb); sorber (liquid). □ **~ up** vt (vacuum cleaner) aspirar; (pump) succionar. □ **~ up to** vt Ⅰ dar coba a. **~er** n (plant) chupón m; (fam, person) imbécil m

suckle /'sʌkl/ vt amamantar

suction /'sʌkʃn/ n succión f

sudden /'sʌdn/ adj repentino. **all of a ~** de repente. **~ly** adv de repente

suds /sʌds/ npl espuma f de jabón

sue /suː/ vt (pres p **suing**) demandar (for por)

suede /sweɪd/ n ante m

suet /'suːɪt/ n sebo m

suffer /'sʌfə(r)/ vt sufrir; (tolerate) aguantar. ● vi sufrir; (be affected) resentirse

suffic|e /sə'faɪs/ vi bastar. **~ient** /sə'fɪʃnt/ adj suficiente, bastante. **~iently** adv (lo) suficientemente

suffix /'sʌfɪks/ n (pl **-ixes**) sufijo m

suffocat|e /'sʌfəkeɪt/ vt asfixiar. ● vi asfixiarse. **~ion** /-'keɪʃn/ n asfixia f

sugar /'ʃʊɡə(r)/ n azúcar m & f. **~ bowl** n azucarero m. **~y** adj azucarado.

suggest /sə'dʒest/ vt sugerir. **~ion** /-tʃən/ n sugerencia f

suicid|al /suːɪ'saɪdl/ adj suicida. **~e** /'suːɪsaɪd/ n suicidio m. **commit ~e** suicidarse

suit /suːt/ n traje m; (woman's) traje m de chaqueta; (Cards) palo m; (Jurid) pleito m. ● vt venirle bien a, convenirle a; (clothes) quedarle bien a; (adapt) adaptar. **be ~ed to** (thing) ser apropiado para. **I'm not ~ed to this kind of work** no sirvo para este tipo de trabajo. **~able** adj apropiado, adecuado. **~ably** adv (dressed) apropiadamente; (qualified) adecuadamente. **~case** n maleta f, valija f (*LAm*)

suite /swiːt/ n (of furniture) juego m; (of rooms) suite f

sulk /sʌlk/ vi enfurruñarse

sullen /'sʌlən/ adj hosco

sulphur /'sʌlfə(r)/ n azufre m. **~ic acid** /sʌl'fjʊərɪk/ n ácido m sulfúrico

sultan /'sʌltən/ n sultán m

sultana /sʌl'tɑːnə/ n pasa f de Esmirna

sultry /'sʌltrɪ/ adj (-ier, -iest) (weather) bochornoso; (fig) sensual

sum /sʌm/ n (of money) suma f, cantidad f; (Math) suma f. ● □ **~ up** (pt **summed**) vt resumir. ● vi recapitular

summar|ily /'sʌmərɪlɪ/ adv sumariamente. **~ize** vt resumir. **~y** n resumen m

summer /'sʌmə(r)/ n verano m. **~ camp** n (in US) colonia f de vacaciones. **~time** n verano m. **~y** adj veraniego

---

summer camp En EE.UU., es el campamento de verano, aspecto muy importante en la vida de muchos niños. Las actividades al aire libre se practican en un ambiente natural entre las que se incluyen natación, montañismo, supervivencia al aire libre. En estos campamentos miles de estudiantes trabajan como supervisores.

---

summit /'sʌmɪt/ n (of mountain) cumbre f. **~ conference** n conferencia f cumbre

summon /'sʌmən/ vt llamar; convocar (meeting, s.o. to meeting); (Jurid) citar. □ **~ up** vt armarse de. **~s** n (Jurid) citación f. ● vt citar

sumptuous /'sʌmptjʊəs/ adj suntuoso

sun /sʌn/ n sol m. **~bathe** vi tomar el sol, asolearse (*LAm*). **~beam** n rayo m de sol. ~**burn** n quemadura f de sol. ~**burnt** adj quemado por el sol

Sunday /'sʌndeɪ/ n domingo m

sunflower /'sʌnflaʊə(r)/ n girasol m

sung /sʌŋ/ see **SING**

sunglasses /'sʌnglɑːsɪz/ npl gafas fpl de sol, lentes mpl de sol (LAm)

sunk /sʌŋk/ see **SINK**. ~**en** /'sʌŋkən/ ● adj hundido

sun|**light** n luz f del sol. ~**ny** adj (-ier, -iest) (day) de sol; (place) soleado. **it is** ~**ny** hace sol. ~**rise** n. **at** ~**rise** al amanecer. salida f del sol. ~**roof** n techo m corredizo. ~**set** n puesta f del sol. ~**shine** n sol m. ~**stroke** n insolación f. ~**tan** n bronceado m. **get a** ~**tan** broncearse. ~**tan lotion** n bronceador m

super /'suːpə(r)/ adj Ⓘ genial, super a invar

superb /suː'pɜːb/ adj espléndido

supercilious /suːpə'sɪlɪəs/ adj desdeñoso

superficial /suːpə'fɪʃl/ adj superficial

superfluous /suː'pɜːfluəs/ adj superfluo

superhighway /'suːpəhaɪweɪ/ n (Amer, Auto) autopista f; (Comp) **information** ~ autopista f de la comunicación

superhuman /suːpə'hjuːmən/ adj sobrehumano

superintendent /suːpərɪn'tendənt/ n director m; (Amer, of building) portero m; (of police) comisario m; (in US) superintendente m & f

superior /suː'pɪərɪə(r)/ adj & n superior (m). ~**ity** /-'ɒrətɪ/ n superioridad f

superlative /suː'pɜːlətɪv/ adj inigualable. ● n superlativo m

supermarket /'suːpəmɑːkɪt/ n supermercado m

supernatural /suːpə'nætʃrəl/ adj sobrenatural

superpower /'suːpəpaʊə(r)/ n superpotencia f

supersede /suːpə'siːd/ vt reemplazar, sustituir

supersonic /suːpə'sɒnɪk/ adj supersónico

superstitio|**n** /suːpə'stɪʃn/ n superstición f. ~**us** adj /-əs/ supersticioso

supervis|**e** /'suːpəvaɪz/ vt supervisar. ~**ion** /-'vɪʒn/ n supervisión f. ~**or** n supervisor m

supper /'sʌpə(r)/ n cena f (ligera), comida f (ligera) (LAm)

supple /sʌpl/ adj flexible

supplement /'sʌplɪmənt/ n suplemento m; (to diet, income) complemento m. ● vt complementar (diet, income). ~**ary** /-'mentərɪ/ adj suplementario

suppl|**ier** /sə'plaɪə(r)/ n (Com) proveedor m. ~**y** /sə'plaɪ/ vt suministrar; proporcionar (information). ~**y s.o. with sth** (equipment) proveer a uno de algo; (in business) abastecer a uno de algo. ● n suministro m. ~**y and demand** oferta f y demanda. ~**ies** npl provisiones mpl, víveres mpl; (Mil) pertrechos mpl. **office** ~**ies** artículos mpl de oficina

support /sə'pɔːt/ vt (hold up) sostener; (back) apoyar; mantener (family). ● n apoyo m; (Tec) soporte m. ~**er** n partidario m; (Sport) hincha m & f

suppos|**e** /sə'pəʊz/ vt suponer, imaginarse; (think) creer. **I'm** ~**ed to start work at nine** se supone que tengo que empezar a trabajar a las nueve. ~**edly** adv supuestamente. ~**ition** /sʌpə'zɪʃn/ n suposición f

suppress /sə'pres/ vt reprimir (feelings); sofocar (rebellion). ~**ion** /-ʃn/n represión f

suprem|**acy** /suː'preməsɪ/ n supremacía f. ~**e** /suː'priːm/ adj supremo

sure /ʃʊə(r)/ adj (-er, -est) seguro. **make** ~ **that** asegurarse de que. ● adv ¡claro!. ~**ly** adv (undoubtedly) seguramente; (gladly) desde luego. ~**ly you don't believe that!** ¡no te creerás eso! ~**ty** /-ətɪ/ n garantía f

surf /sɜːf/ n oleaje m; (foam) espuma f. ● vi hacer surf. ● vt (Comp) surfear, navegar

surface /'sɜːfɪs/ n superficie f. ● adj superficial. ● vt recubrir (with de). ● vi salir a la superficie; (problems) aflorar

surfboard /'sɜːfbɔːd/ n tabla f de surf

surfeit /'sɜːfɪt/ n exceso m

S

surf ∼**er** n surfista m & f; (Internet) navegador m. ∼**ing** n surf m

surge /sɜːdʒ/ vi (crowd) moverse en tropel; (sea) hincharse. ● n oleada f; (in demand, sales) aumento m

surg|eon /'sɜːdʒən/ n cirujano m. ∼**ery** n cirugía f; (consulting room) consultorio m; (consulting hours) consulta f. ∼**ical** adj quirúrgico

surly /'sɜːlɪ/ adj (-ier, -iest) hosco

surmise /sə'maɪz/ vt conjeturar

surmount /sə'maʊnt/ vt superar

surname /'sɜːneɪm/ n apellido m

surpass /sə'pɑːs/ vt superar

surplus /'sɜːpləs/ adj & n excedente (m)

surpris|e /sə'praɪz/ n sorpresa f. ● vt sorprender. ∼**ed** adj sorprendido. ∼**ing** adj sorprendente. ∼**ingly** adv sorprendentemente

surrender /sə'rendə(r)/ vt entregar. ● vi rendirse. ● n rendición f

surreptitious /sʌrəp'tɪʃəs/ adj furtivo

surround /sə'raʊnd/ vt rodear; (Mil) rodear, cercar. ∼**ing** adj circundante. ∼**ings** npl alrededores mpl; (environment) ambiente m

surveillance /sɜː'veɪləns/ n vigilancia f

survey /'sɜːveɪ/ n inspección f; (report) informe m; (general view) vista f general. ● /sə'veɪ/ vt inspeccionar; (measure) medir; (look at) contemplar. ∼**or** n topógrafo m, agrimensor m; (of building) perito m

surviv|al /sə'vaɪvl/ n supervivencia f. ∼**e** /sə'vaɪv/ vt/i sobrevivir. ∼**or** n superviviente m & f

susceptible /sə'septəbl/ adj. ∼ **to** propenso a

suspect /sə'spekt/ vt sospechar; sospechar de (person). ● /'sʌspekt/ adj & n sospechoso (m)

suspen|d /sə'spend/ vt suspender. ∼**ders** npl (Amer, braces) tirantes mpl. ∼**se** /-s/ n (in film etc) suspense m, suspenso m (LAm). **keep s.o. in** ∼**se** mantener a uno sobre ascuas. ∼**sion** /-ʃn/ n suspensión f. ∼**sion bridge** n puente m colgante

suspici|on /sə'spɪʃn/ n (belief) sospecha f; (mistrust) desconfianza f. ∼**ous**

/-ʃəs/ adj desconfiado; (causing suspicion) sospechoso

sustain /sə'steɪn/ vt sostener; mantener (conversation, interest); (suffer) sufrir

SW abbr (= south-west) SO

swab /swɒb/ n (specimen) muestra f, frotis m

swagger /'swægə(r)/ vi pavonearse

swallow /'swɒləʊ/ vt/i tragar. ● n trago m; (bird) golondrina f

swam /swæm/ see **SWIM**

swamp /swɒmp/ n pantano m, ciénaga f. ● vt inundar. ∼**y** adj pantanoso

swan /swɒn/ n cisne m

swap /swɒp/ vt/i (pt swapped) intercambiar. ∼ **sth for sth** cambiar algo por algo. ● n cambio m

swarm /swɔːm/ n enjambre m. ● vi (bees) enjambrar; (fig) hormiguear

swarthy /'swɔːðɪ/ adj (-ier, -iest) moreno

swat /swɒt/ vt (pt swatted) matar (con matamoscas etc)

sway /sweɪ/ vi balancearse; (gently) mecerse. ● vt (influence) influir en

swear /sweə(r)/ vt/i (pt swore, pp sworn) jurar. ∼**word** n palabrota f

sweat /swet/ n sudor m, transpiración f. ● vi sudar

sweat|er /'swetə(r)/ n jersey m, suéter m. ∼**shirt** n sudadera f. ∼**suit** n (Amer) chándal m, equipo m de deportes

swede /swiːd/ n nabo m sueco

Swede /swiːd/ n sueco m. ∼**n** /'swiːdn/ n Suecia f. ∼**ish** adj sueco. ● n (language) sueco m. ● npl. **the** ∼ (people) los suecos

sweep /swiːp/ vt (pt swept) barrer; deshollinar (chimney). ● n barrido m. ∼ **away** vt (carry away) arrastrar; (abolish) erradicar. ∼**er** n barrendero m. ∼**ing** adj (gesture) amplio; (changes) radical; (statement) demasiado general

sweet /swiːt/ adj (-er, -est) dulce; (fragrant) fragante; (pleasant) agradable; (kind, gentle) dulce; (cute) rico. **have a** ∼ **tooth** ser dulcero. ● n caramelo m, dulce m (Mex); (dish) postre m. ∼**en** vt endulzar. ∼**heart** n enamorado m; (as *form of address*) amor *m*. ~**ly** *adv* dulcemente. ~ **potato** *n* boniato *m*, batata *f*, camote *m LAm*

swell /swel/ *vt* (*pt* **swelled**, *pp* **swollen** or **swelled**) hinchar; (*increase*) aumentar. ●*vi* hincharse; (*increase*) aumentar. ●*adj* (*Amer fam*) fenomenal. ●*n* (*of sea*) oleaje *m*. ~**ing** *n* hinchazón *m*

sweltering /'sweltərɪŋ/ *vi* sofocante

swept /swept/ *see* SWEEP

swerve /swɜːv/ *vi* virar bruscamente

swift /swɪft/ *adj* (**-er**, **-est**) veloz, rápido; (*reply*) rápido. ●*n* (*bird*) vencejo *m*. ~**ly** *adv* rápidamente

swig /swɪg/ *vt* (*pt* **swigged**) 🔲 beber a grandes tragos. ●*n* 🔲 trago *m*

swim /swɪm/ *vi* (*pt* **swam**, *pp* **swum**) nadar. ●*n* baño *m*. ~**mer** *n* nadador *m*. ~**ming** *n* natación *f*. ~**ming bath(s)** *n*(*pl*) piscina *f* cubierta, alberca *f* techada (*Mex*). ~**ming pool** *n* piscina *f*, alberca *f* (*Mex*). ~**ming trunks** *npl* bañador *m*, traje *m* de baño ~**suit** *n* traje *m* de baño, bañador *m*

swindle /'swɪndl/ *vt* estafar. ●*n* estafa *f*. ~**r** *n* estafador *m*

swine /swaɪn/ *npl* cerdos *mpl*. ●*n* (*pl* **swine**) (*fam, person*) canalla *m & f*. ~ **fever** *n* fiebre *f* porcina

swing /swɪŋ/ *vt* (*pt* **swung**) balancear; (*object on rope*) hacer oscilar. ●*vi* (*dangle*) balancearse; (*swing on a swing*) columpiarse; (*pendulum*) oscilar. ~ **open/shut** abrirse/cerrarse. ●*n* oscilación *f*, vaivén *m*; (*seat*) columpio *m*; (*in opinion*) cambio *m*. **in full** ~ en plena actividad

swipe /swaɪp/ *vt* darle un golpe a; (*fam, snatch*) birlar. ●*n* golpe *m*

Swiss /swɪs/ *adj* suizo (*m*). ●*npl*. **the** ~ los suizos

switch /swɪtʃ/ *n* (*Elec*) interruptor *m*; (*exchange*) intercambio *m*; (*Amer, Rail*) agujas *fpl*.●*vt* cambiar; (*deviate*) desviar. □ ~ **off** *vt* (*Elec*) apagar (light, TV, heating); desconectar (electricity). □ ~ **on** *vt* encender, prender (*LAm*); arrancar (engine). ~**board** *n* centralita *f*

Switzerland /'swɪtsələnd/ *n* Suiza *f*

swivel /'swɪvl/ *vi* (*pt* **swivelled**) girar. ●*vt* hacer girar

swollen /'swəʊlən/ *see* SWELL. ●*adj* hinchado

swoop /swuːp/ *vi* (bird) abatirse; (police) llevar a cabo una redada. ●*n* (*of bird*) descenso *m* en picado or (*LAm*) en picada; (*by police*) redada *f*

sword /sɔːd/ *n* espada *f*

swore /swɔː(r)/ *see* SWEAR

sworn /swɔːn/ *see* SWEAR. ●*adj* (enemy) declarado; (statement) jurado

swot /swɒt/ *vt*/*i* (*pt* **swotted**) (*Schol, fam*) empollar, estudiar como loco. ●*n* (*Schol, fam*) empollón *m*, matado *m* (*Mex*)

swum /swʌm/ *see* SWIM

swung /swʌŋ/ *see* SWING

syllable /'sɪləbl/ *n* sílaba *f*

syllabus /'sɪləbəs/ *n* (*pl* **-buses**) plan *m* de estudios; (*of a particular subject*) programa *m*

symbol /'sɪmbl/ *n* símbolo *m*. ~**ic(al)** /-'bɒlɪk(l)/ *adj* simbólico. ~**ism** *n* simbolismo *m*. ~**ize** *vt* simbolizar

symmetr|ical /sɪ'metrɪkl/ *adj* simétrico. ~**y** /'sɪmətrɪ/ *n* simetría *f*

sympath|etic /sɪmpə'θetɪk/ *adj* comprensivo; (*showing pity*) compasivo. ~**ize** /'sɪmpəθaɪz/ *vi* comprender; (*commiserate*) ~**ize with s.o.** compadecer a uno. ~**y** /'sɪmpəθɪ/ *n* comprensión *f*; (*pity*) compasión *f*; (*condolences*) pésame *m*

symphony /'sɪmfənɪ/ *n* sinfonía *f*

symptom /'sɪmptəm/ *n* síntoma *m*. ~**atic** /-'mætɪk/ *adj* sintomático

synagogue /'sɪnəgɒg/ *n* sinagoga *f*

synchronize /'sɪŋkrənaɪz/ *vt* sincronizar

syndicate /'sɪndɪkət/ *n* agrupación *f*; (*Amer, TV*) agencia *f* de distribución periodística

synonym /'sɪnənɪm/ *n* sinónimo *m*. ~**ous** /-'nɒnɪməs/ *adj* sinónimo

syntax /'sɪntæks/ *n* sintaxis *f*

synthesi|s /'sɪnθəsɪs/ *n* (*pl* **-theses** /-siːz/) síntesis *f*.~**ze** /-aɪz/ *vt* sintetizar

synthetic /sɪn'θetɪk/ *adj* sintético

syringe /'sɪrɪndʒ/ *n* jeringa *f*, jeringuilla *f*

syrup /'sɪrəp/ n (sugar solution) almíbar m; (with other ingredients) jarabe m; (medicine) jarabe m

system /'sɪstəm/ n sistema m, método m; (Tec, Mec, Comp) sistema m. **the digestive** ∼ el aparato digestivo. ∼**atic** /-ə'mætɪk/ adj sistemático. ∼**atically** /-ə'mætɪklɪ/ adv sistemáticamente. ∼**s analyst** n analista m & f de sistemas

Tt

tab /tæb/ n (flap) lengüeta f; (label) etiqueta f

table /'teɪbl/ n mesa f; (list) tabla f. ∼**cloth** n mantel m. ∼ **mat** n salvamanteles m. ∼**spoon** n cuchara f grande; (measure) cucharada f (grande)

tablet /'tæblɪt/ n pastilla f; (pill) comprimido m

table tennis n tenis m de mesa, ping-pong m

tabloid /'tæblɔɪd/ n tabloide m

taboo /tə'buː/ adj & n tabú (m)

tacit /'tæsɪt/ adj tácito

taciturn /'tæsɪtɜːn/ adj taciturno

tack /tæk/ n tachuela f; (stitch) hilván m. ●vt clavar con tachuelas; (sew) hilvanar. ●vi (Naut) virar □ ∼ **on** vt añadir.

tackle /'tækl/ n (equipment) equipo m; (soccer) entrada f fuerte; (US football, Rugby) placaje m. **fishing** ∼ aparejo m de pesca. ●vt abordar (problem); (in soccer) entrarle a; (in US football, Rugby) placar

tacky /'tækɪ/ adj pegajoso

tact /tækt/ n tacto m. ∼**ful** adj diplomático

tactic|al /'tæktɪkl/ adj táctico. ∼**s** npl táctica f

tactless /'tæktləs/ adj indiscreto

tadpole /'tædpəʊl/ n renacuajo m

tag /tæg/ n (label) etiqueta f. □ ∼ **along** (pt **tagged**) vt 🅴 seguir

tail /teɪl/ n (of horse, fish, bird) cola f; (of dog, pig) rabo m. ∼**s** npl (tailcoat) frac m; (of coin) cruz f. ●vt seguir. □ ∼ **off** vi disminuir.

tailor /'teɪlə(r)/ n sastre m. ∼**ed** /'teɪləd/ adj entallado. ∼-**made** n hecho a (la) medida

taint /teɪnt/ vt contaminar

take /teɪk/ vt (pt **took**, pp **taken**) tomar, coger (esp Spain), agarrar (esp LAm); (capture) capturar; (endure) aguantar; (require) requerir; llevar (time); tomar (bath); tomar (medicine); (carry) llevar; aceptar (cheque). **I** ∼ **a size 10** uso la talla 14. □ ∼ **after** vt parecerse a. □ ∼ **away** vt llevarse; (confiscate) quitar. □ ∼ **back** vt retirar (statement etc). □ ∼ **in** vt achicar (garment); (understand) asimilar; (deceive) engañar. □ ∼ **off** vt (remove) quitar, sacar; quitarse (shoes, jacket); (mimic) imitar. vi (aircraft) despegar. □ ∼ **on** vt contratar (employee). □ ∼ **out** vt sacar. □ ∼ **over** vt tomar posesión de; hacerse cargo de (job). vi (assume control) asumir el poder. □ ∼ **up** vt empezar a hacer (hobby); aceptar (challenge); subir (hem); llevar (time); ocupar (space). ●n (Cinema) toma f. ∼-**off** n despegue m. ∼-**over** n (Com) absorción f

takings /'teɪkɪŋz/ npl recaudación f; (at box office) taquilla f

talcum powder /'tælkəm/ n polvos mpl de talco, talco m (LAm)

tale /teɪl/ n cuento m

talent /'tælənt/ n talento m. ∼**ed** adj talentoso

talk /tɔːk/ vt/i hablar. ∼ **to s.o.** hablar con uno. ∼ **about** hablar de. ●n conversación f; (lecture) charla f. □ ∼ **over** vt discutir. ∼**ative** /-ətɪv/ adj hablador

tall /tɔːl/ adj (-**er**, -**est**) alto. ∼ **story** n 🅸 cuento m chino

tally /'tælɪ/ vi coincidir (**with** con)

talon /'tælən/ n garra f

tambourine /tæmbə'riːn/ n pandereta f

tame /teɪm/ adj (-**er**, -**est**) (animal) (by nature) manso; (tamed) domado. ●vt domar (wild animal)

tamper /'tæmpə(r)/ vi. ~ **with** tocar; (alter) alterar, falsificar

tampon /'tæmpɒn/ n tampón m

tan /tæn/ vi (pt tanned) broncearse. ● n bronceado m. **get a** ~ broncearse. ● adj habano

tang /tæŋ/ n sabor m fuerte

tangent /'tændʒənt/ n tangente f

tangerine /tændʒə'riːn/ n mandarina f

tangible /'tændʒəbl/ adj tangible

tangle /'tæŋgl/ vt enredar. **get** ~**d** (**up**) enredarse. ● n enredo m, maraña f

tango /'tæŋgəʊ/ n (pl -os) tango m

tank /tæŋk/ n depósito m; (Auto) tanque m; (Mil) tanque m

tanker /'tæŋkə(r)/ n (ship) buque m cisterna; (truck) camión m cisterna

tantrum /'tæntrəm/ n berrinche m, rabieta f

tap /tæp/ n grifo m, llave f (LAm); (knock) golpecito m. ● vt (pt tapped) (knock) dar un golpecito en; interceptar (phone). ● vi dar golpecitos (**on** en). ~ **dancing** n claqué m

tape /teɪp/ n cinta f; (Med) esparadrapo m. ● vt (record) grabar. ~**-measure** n cinta f métrica

taper /'teɪpə(r)/ vt afilar. ● vi afilarse. □ ~ **off** vi disminuir

tape recorder n magnetofón m, magnetófono m

tapestry /'tæpɪstrɪ/ n tapiz m

tar /tɑː(r)/ n alquitrán m. ● vt (pt tarred) alquitranar

target /'tɑːgɪt/ n blanco m; (fig) objetivo m

tarmac /'tɑːmæk/ n pista f. **T**~ n (Amer, ®) asfalto m

tarnish /'tɑːnɪʃ/ vt deslustrar; empañar (reputation)

tart /tɑːt/ n pastel m; (individual) pastelillo m; (sl, woman) prostituta f, fulana f 🔲. ● vt. ~ **o.s. up** 🔲 engalanarse. ● adj (-er, -est) ácido

tartan /'tɑːtn/ n tartán m, tela f escocesa

task /tɑːsk/ n tarea f. **take to** ~ reprender

tassel /'tæsl/ n borla f

taste /teɪst/ n sabor m, gusto m; (liking) gusto m. ● vt probar. ● vi. ~**e of**

saber a. ~**eful** adj de buen gusto. ~**eless** adj soso; (fig) de mal gusto. ~**y** adj (-ier, -iest) sabroso

tat /tæt/ see **TIT FOR TAT**

tatter|ed /'tætəd/ adj hecho jirones. ~**s** /'tætəz/ npl andrajos mpl

tattoo /tæ'tuː/ n (on body) tatuaje m. ● vt tatuar

tatty /'tætɪ/ adj (-ier, -iest) gastado, estropeado

taught /tɔːt/ see **TEACH**

taunt /tɔːnt/ vt provocar mediante burlas. ● n pulla f

Taurus /'tɔːrəs/ n Tauro m

taut /tɔːt/ adj tenso

tavern /'tævən/ n taberna f

tax /tæks/ n impuesto m. ● vt imponer contribuciones a (person); gravar (thing); (strain) poner a prueba. ~**able** adj imponible. ~**ation** /-'seɪʃn/ n impuestos mpl; (system) sistema m tributario. ~ **collector** n recaudador m de impuestos. ~**-free** adj libre de impuestos

taxi /'tæksɪ/ n (pl -is) taxi m. ● vi (pt taxied, pres p taxiing) (aircraft) rodar por la pista

taxpayer /'tækspeɪə(r)/ n contribuyente m & f

tea /tiː/ n té m; (afternoon tea) merienda f, té m. ~ **bag** n bolsita f de té

teach /tiːtʃ/ vt (pt taught) dar clases de, enseñar (subject); dar clase a (person). ~ **school** (Amer) dar clase(s) en un colegio. ● vi dar clase(s). ~**er** n profesor m; (primary) maestro m. ~**ing** n enseñanza f. ● adj docente

tea ~**cup** n taza f de té. ~ **leaf** n hoja f de té

team /tiːm/ n equipo m. □ ~ **up** vi asociarse (**with** con). ~ **work** n trabajo m de equipo

teapot /'tiːpɒt/ n tetera f

tear¹ /teə(r)/ vt (pt tore, pp torn) romper, rasgar. ● vi romperse, rasgarse. ● n rotura f; (rip) desgarrón m. □ ~ **along** vi ir a toda velocidad. □ ~ **apart** vt desgarrar. □ ~ **off**, ~ **out** vt arrancar. □ ~ **up** vt romper

tear² /tɪə(r)/ n lágrima f. **be in** ~**s** estar llorando. ~**ful** adj lloroso (farewell) triste. ~ **gas** n gas m lacrimógeno

tease /tiːz/ vt tomarle el pelo a

tea ~ **set** n juego m de té. ~**spoon** n cucharita f, cucharilla f; (amount) cucharadita f

teat /tiːt/ n (of animal) tetilla f; (for bottle) tetina f

tea towel /'tiːtaʊəl/ n paño m de cocina

techni|cal /'teknɪkl/ adj técnico. ~**cality** n /-'kælətɪ/ n detalle m técnico. ~**cally** adv técnicamente. ~**cian** /tek'nɪʃn/ n técnico m. ~**que** /tek'niːk/ n técnica f

technolog|ical /teknə'lɒdʒɪkl/ adj tecnológico. ~**y** /tek'nɒlədʒɪ/ n tecnología f

teddy bear /'tedɪ/ n osito m de peluche

tedi|ous /'tiːdɪəs/ adj tedioso. ~**um** /'tiːdɪəm/ n tedio m

teem /tiːm/ vi abundar (with en), estar repleto (with de)

teen|age /'tiːneɪdʒ/ adj adolescente; (for teenagers) para jóvenes. ~**ager** n adolescente m & f. ~**s** /tiːnz/ npl adolescencia f

teeny /'tiːnɪ/ adj (-ier, -iest) ⊞ chiquito

teeter /'tiːtə(r)/ vi balancearse

teeth /tiːθ/ see **TOOTH**. ~**e** /tiːð/ vi. he's ~**ing** le están saliendo los dientes. ~**ing troubles** npl (fig) problemas mpl iniciales

tele|communications /telɪkəmjuːnɪ'keɪʃnz/ npl telecomunicaciones fpl. ~**gram** /'telɪgræm/ n telegrama m. ~**pathic** /telɪ'pæθɪk/ adj telepático. ~**pathy** /tə'lepəθɪ/ n telepatía f

telephon|e /'telɪfəʊn/ n teléfono m. ● vt llamar por teléfono. ~**e booth**, ~**e box** n cabina f telefónica. ~**e call** n llamada f telefónica. ~ **card** n tarjeta f telefónica. ~**e directory** n guía f telefónica. ~**e exchange** n central f telefónica. ~**ist** /tɪ'lefənɪst/ n telefonista m & f

tele|sales /'telɪseɪlz/ npl televentas fpl. ~**scope** n telescopio m. ~**scopic** /-'skɒpɪk/ adj telescópico. ~**text** n teletex(to) m. ~**working** n teletrabajo m

televis|e /'telɪvaɪz/ vt televisar. ~**ion** /'telɪvɪʒn/ n (medium) televisión f. ~**ion (set)** n televisor m

telex /'teleks/ n télex m

tell /tel/ vt (pt told) decir; contar (story, joke); (distinguish) distinguir. ~ **the difference** notar la diferencia. ~ **the time** decir la hora. ● vi (produce an effect) tener efecto; (know) saber. □ ~ **off** vt regañar. ~**ing** adj revelador. ~**-tale** n soplón m. ● adj revelador

telly /'telɪ/ n ⊞ tele f

temp /temp/ n empleado m eventual or temporal

temper /'tempə(r)/ n (mood) humor m; (disposition) carácter m; (fit of anger) cólera f. **be in a** ~ estar furioso. **lose one's** ~ perder los estribos. ~**ament** /'tempramant/ n temperamento m. ~**amental** /-'mentl/ adj temperamental. ~**ate** /'temparat/ adj templado. ~**ature** /'temprɪtʃə(r)/ n temperatura f. **have a** ~**ature** tener fiebre

tempestuous /tem'pestjʊəs/ adj tempestuoso

temple /'templ/ n templo m; (of head) sien f

tempo /'tempəʊ/ n (pl -os or tempi) ritmo m

temporar|ily /'tempərərəlɪ/ adv temporalmente, temporariamente (LAm). ~**y** /'tempərərɪ/ adj temporal, provisional; (job) eventual, temporal

tempt /tempt/ vt tentar. ~**ation** /-'teɪʃn/ n tentación f. ~**ing** adj tentador

ten /ten/ adj & n diez (m)

tenaci|ous /tɪ'neɪʃəs/ adj tenaz. ~**ty** /tɪ'næsətɪ/ n tenacidad f

tenan|cy /'tenənsɪ/ n inquilinato m. ~**t** n inquilino m, arrendatario m

tend /tend/ vi. ~ **to** tender a. ● vt cuidar (de). ~**ency** /'tendənsɪ/ n tendencia f

tender /'tendə(r)/ adj tierno; (painful) sensible. ● n (Com) oferta f. **legal** ~ n moneda f de curso legal. ● vt ofrecer, presentar. ~**ly** adv tiernamente

tendon /'tendən/ n tendón m

tennis /ˈtenɪs/ n tenis m

tenor /ˈtenə(r)/ n tenor m

tens|e /tens/ adj (-er, -est) (taut) tenso, tirante; (person) tenso. ● n (Gram) tiempo m. ~ion /ˈtenʃn/ n tensión f; (between two parties) conflicto m

tent /tent/ n tienda f (de campaña), carpa f (LAm)

tentacle /ˈtentəkl/ n tentáculo m

tentative /ˈtentətɪv/ adj (plan) provisional; (offer) tentativo; (person) indeciso

tenterhooks /ˈtentəhʊks/ npl. **be on ~** estar en ascuas

tenth /tenθ/ adj & n décimo (m)

tenuous /ˈtenjuəs/ adj (claim) poco fundado; (link) indirecto

tenure /ˈtenjʊə(r)/ n tenencia f; (period of office) ejercicio m

tepid /ˈtepɪd/ adj tibio

term /tɜːm/ n (of time) período m; (Schol) trimestre m; (word etc) término m. ~s npl condiciones fpl; (Com) precio m. **on good/bad ~s** en buenas/malas relaciones. ● vt calificar de

termin|al /ˈtɜːmɪnl/ adj terminal. ● n (transport) terminal f; (Comp, Elec) terminal m. ~ate /-eɪt/ vt poner fin a; poner término a (contract); (Amer, fire) despedir. ● vi terminarse. ~ology /-ˈnɒlədʒɪ/ n terminología f

terrace /ˈterəs/ n terraza f; (houses) hilera f de casas

terrain /təˈreɪn/ n terreno m

terrestrial /tɪˈrestrɪəl/ adj terrestre

terribl|e /ˈterəbl/ adj espantoso. ~y adv terriblemente

terrif|ic /təˈrɪfɪk/ adj (fam, excellent) estupendo; (fam, huge) enorme. ~ied /ˈterɪfaɪd/ adj aterrorizado. ~y /ˈterɪfaɪ/ vt aterrorizar. ~ying adj aterrador

territor|ial /terɪˈtɔːrɪəl/ adj territorial. ~y /ˈterɪtrɪ/ n territorio m

terror /ˈterə(r)/ n terror m. ~ism n terrorismo m. ~ist n terrorista m & f. ~ize vt aterrorizar

terse /tɜːs/ adj seco, lacónico

test /test/ n (of machine, drug) prueba f; (exam) prueba f, test m; (of blood) análisis m; (for eyes, hearing) examen m. ● vt probar, poner a prueba (product); hacerle una prueba a (student); evaluar (knowledge); examinar (sight)

testament /ˈtestəmənt/ n (will) testamento m. **Old/New T~** Antiguo/Nuevo Testamento

testicle /ˈtestɪkl/ n testículo m

testify /ˈtestɪfaɪ/ vt atestiguar. ● vi declarar

testimon|ial /testɪˈməʊnɪəl/ n recomendación f. ~y /ˈtestɪmənɪ/ n testimonio m

test ~ match n partido m internacional. ~ **tube** n tubo m de ensayo, probeta f

tether /ˈteðə(r)/ vt atar. ● n. **be at the end of one's ~** no poder más

text /tekst/ n texto m. ● vt mandar un mensaje a. ~book n libro m de texto

textile /ˈtekstaɪl/ adj & n textil (m)

texture /ˈtekstʃə(r)/ n textura f

Thames /temz/ n Támesis m

than /ðæn, ðən/ conj que; (with quantity) de

thank /θæŋk/ vt darle las gracias a, agradecer. ~ **you** gracias. ~ful adj agradecido. ~fully adv (happily) gracias a Dios. ~less adj ingrato. ~s npl agradecimiento m. ~s! 🔡 ¡gracias!. ~s to gracias a

Thanksgiving (Day) /θæŋksˈgɪvɪŋ/ n (in US) el día de Acción de Gracias

that /ðæt, ðət/ adj (pl those) ese, aquel, esa, aquella. ● pron (pl those) ése, aquél, ésa, aquélla. ~ **is** es decir. ~'s **not true** eso no es cierto. ~'s **why** por eso. **is** ~ **you?** ¿eres tú? **like** ~ así. ● adv tan. ~ rel pron que; (with prep) el que, la que, el cual, la cual. ● conj que

thatched /θætʃt/ adj (roof) de paja; (cottage) con techo de paja

thaw /θɔː/ vt descongelar. ● vi descongelarse; (snow) derretirse. ● n deshielo m

the	definite article

····▶ el (m), la (f), los (mpl), las (fpl). ~ **building** el edificio. ~ **windows** las ventanas

! Feminine singular nouns beginning with a stressed or accented *a* or *ha* take the article *el* instead of *la*, e.g. ~ **soul** *el alma*; ~ **axe** *el hacha*; ~ **eagle** *el águila*

Note that when *el* follows the prepositions *de* and *a*, it combines to form *del* and *al*, e.g. **of** ~ **group** *del grupo*. **I went to** ~ **bank** *fui al banco*

••••▶ (*before an ordinal number in names, titles*) *not translated*. **Henry** ~ **Eighth** Enrique Octavo. **Elizabeth** ~ **Second** Isabel Segunda

••••▶ (*in abstractions*) lo. ~ **impossible** lo imposible

theatr|e /ˈθɪətə(r)/ *n* teatro *m*; (*Amer, movie theater*) cine *m*. ~**ical** /-ˈætrɪkl/ *adj* teatral

theft /θeft/ *n* hurto *m*

their /ðeə(r)/ *adj* su, sus *pl*. ~**s** /ðeəz/ *poss pron* (el) suyo *m*, (la) suya *f*, (los) suyos *mpl*, (las) suyas *fpl*

them /ðem, ðəm/ *pron* (*accusative*) los *m*, las *f*; (*dative*) les; (*after prep*) ellos *m*, ellas *f*

theme /θiːm/ *n* tema *m*. ~ **park** *n* parque *m* temático. ~ **song** *n* motivo *m* principal

themselves /ðəmˈselvz/ *pron* ellos mismos *m*, ellas mismas *f*; (*reflexive*) se; (*after prep*) sí mismos *m*, sí mismas *f*

then /ðen/ *adv* entonces; (*next*) luego, después. **by** ~ para entonces. **now and** ~ de vez en cuando. **since** ~ desde entonces. ● *adj* entonces

theology /θɪˈɒlədʒɪ/ *n* teología *f*

theor|etical /θɪəˈretɪkl/ *adj* teórico. ~**y** /ˈθɪərɪ/ *n* teoría *f*

therap|eutic /θerəˈpjuːtɪk/ *adj* terapéutico. ~**ist** /ˈθerəpɪst/ *n* terapeuta *m* & *f*. ~**y** /ˈθerəpɪ/ *n* terapia *f*

there /ðeə(r)/ *adv* ahí; (*further away*) allí, ahí; (*less precise, further*) allá. ~ **is**, ~ **are** hay. ~ **it is** ahí está. **down** ~ ahí abajo. **up** ~ ahí arriba. ● *int*. ~**!** that's the last box ¡listo! ésa es la última caja. ~, ~, **don't cry!** vamos, no llores. ~**abouts** *adv* por

ahí. ~**fore** /-fɔː(r)/ *adv* por lo tanto.

thermometer /θəˈmɒmɪtə(r)/ *n* termómetro *m*

Thermos /ˈθɜːməs/ *n* (®) termo *m*

thermostat /ˈθɜːməstæt/ *n* termostato *m*

thesaurus /θɪˈsɔːrəs/ *n* (*pl* **-ri**/-raɪ/) diccionario *m* de sinónimos

these /ðiːz/ *adj* estos, estas. ● *pron* éstos, éstas

thesis /ˈθiːsɪs/ *n* (*pl* **theses**/-siːz/) tesis *f*

they /ðeɪ/ *pron* ellos *m*, ellas *f*. ~ **say that** dicen *or* se dice que

they'd /ðeɪ(ə)d/ = **they had**, **they would**

they'll /ðeɪl/ = **they will**

they're /ðeɪə(r)/ = **they are**

they've /ðeɪv/ = **they have**

thick /θɪk/ *adj* (**-er, -est**) (layer, sweater) grueso, gordo; (sauce) espeso; (fog, smoke) espeso, denso; (fur) tupido; (*fam, stupid*) burro. ● *adv* espesamente, densamente. ● *n*. **in the** ~ **of** en medio de. ~**en** *vt* espesar. ● *vi* espesarse. ~**et** /-ɪt/ *n* matorral *m*. ~**ness** *n* (*of fabric*) grosor *m*; (*of paper, wood, wall*) espesor *m*

thief /θiːf/ *n* (*pl* **thieves** /θiːvz/) ladrón *m*

thigh /θaɪ/ *n* muslo *m*

thimble /ˈθɪmbl/ *n* dedal *m*

thin /θɪn/ *adj* (**thinner, thinnest**) (person) delgado, flaco; (layer, slice) fino; (hair) ralo

thing /θɪŋ/ *n* cosa *f*. **it's a good** ~ **(that)...** menos mal que.... **just the** ~ exactamente lo que se necesita. **poor** ~**!** ¡pobrecito!

think /θɪŋk/ *vt* (*pt* **thought**) pensar, creer. ● *vi* pensar (**about** en); (*carefully*) reflexionar; (*imagine*) imaginarse. **I** ~ **so** creo que sí. ~ **of** s.o. pensar en uno. **I hadn't thought of that** eso no se me ha ocurrido. ~ **over** *vt* pensar bien. ~ **up** *vt* idear, inventar. ~**er** *n* pensador *m*. ~**-tank** *n* gabinete *m* estratégico

third /θɜːd/ *adj* tercero, (*before masculine singular noun*) tercer. ● *n* tercio *m*, tercera parte *f*. ~ **(gear)** *n* (*Auto*) tercera *f*. ~**-rate** *adj* muy inferior. **T~**

t

World n Tercer Mundo m

thirst /θɜːst/ n sed f. **~y** adj sediento. **be ~y** tener sed

thirt|een /θɜːˈtiːn/ adj & n trece (m). **~teenth** adj decimotercero. ● n treceavo m ● **~ieth** /ˈθɜːtɪəθ/ adj trigésimo. ● n treintavo m. **~y** /ˈθɜːtɪ/ adj & n treinta (m)

this /ðɪs/ adj (pl **these**) este, esta. **~ one** éste, ésta. ● pron (pl **these**) éste, ésta, esto. **like ~** así

thistle /ˈθɪsl/ n cardo m

thong /θɒŋ/ n correa f; (Amer, sandal) chancla f

thorn /θɔːn/ n espina f. **~y** adj espinoso

thorough /ˈθʌrə/ adj (investigation) riguroso; (cleaning etc) a fondo; (person) concienzudo. **~bred** /-bred/ adj de pura sangre. **~fare** n vía f pública; (street) calle f. **no ~fare** prohibido el paso. **~ly** adv (clean) a fondo; (examine) minuciosamente; (completely) perfectamente

those /ðəʊz/ adj esos, esas, aquellos, aquellas. ● pron ésos, ésas, aquéllos, aquéllas

though /ðəʊ/ conj aunque. ● adv sin embargo. **as ~** como si

thought /θɔːt/ see **THINK**. ● n pensamiento m; (idea) idea f. **~ful** adj pensativo; (considerate) atento. **~fully** adv pensativamente; (considerately) atentamente. **~less** adj desconsiderado

thousand /ˈθaʊznd/ adj & n mil (m). **~th** adj & n milésimo (m)

thrash /θræʃ/ vt azotar; (defeat) derrotar

thread /θred/ n hilo m; (of screw) rosca f. ● vt enhebrar (needle); ensartar (beads). **~bare** adj gastado, raído

threat /θret/ n amenaza f. **~en** vt/i amenazar. **~ening** adj amenazador

three /θriː/ adj & n tres (m). **~fold** adj triple. ● adv tres veces

threshold /ˈθreʃhəʊld/ n umbral m

threw /θruː/ see **THROW**

thrift /θrɪft/ n economía f, ahorro m. **~y** adj frugal

thrill /θrɪl/ n emoción f ● vt emocionar. **~ed** adj contentísimo (**with**

con). **~er** n (book) libro m de suspense or (LAm) suspenso; (film) película f de suspense or (LAm) suspenso. **~ing** adj emocionante

thriv|e /θraɪv/ vi prosperar. **~ing** adj próspero

throat /θrəʊt/ n garganta f

throb /θrɒb/ vi (pt **throbbed**) palpitar; (with pain) dar punzadas; (engine) vibrar. **~bing** adj (pain) punzante

throes /θrəʊz/ npl. **be in one's death ~** estar agonizando

throne /θrəʊn/ n trono m

throng /θrɒŋ/ n multitud f

throttle /ˈθrɒtl/ n (Auto) acelerador m (que se acciona con la mano). ● vt estrangular

through /θruː/ prep por, a través de; (during) durante; (by means of) a través de; (Amer, until and including) **Monday ~ Friday** de lunes a viernes. ● adv de parte a parte, de un lado a otro; (entirely) completamente; (to the end) hasta el final. **be ~** (finished) haber terminado. ● adj (train etc) directo. **no ~ road** calle sin salida. **~out** /-ˈaʊt/ prep por todo; (time) durante todo. **~out his career** a lo largo de su carrera

throve /θrəʊv/ see **THRIVE**

throw /θrəʊ/ vt (pt **threw**, pp **thrown**) tirar, aventar (Mex); lanzar (grenade, javelin); (disconcert) desconcertar; 🔲 hacer, dar (party). ● n (of ball) tiro m; (of dice) tirada f. □ **~ away** vt tirar. □ **~ up** vi (vomit) vomitar.

thrush /θrʌʃ/ n tordo m

thrust /θrʌst/ vt (pt **thrust**) empujar; (push in) clavar. ● n empujón m; (of sword) estocada f

thud /θʌd/ n ruido m sordo

thug /θʌg/ n matón m

thumb /θʌm/ n pulgar m. ● vt. **~ a lift** ir a dedo. **~tack** n (Amer) chincheta f, tachuela f, chinche f (Mex)

thump /θʌmp/ vt golpear. ● vi (heart) latir fuertemente. ● n golpazo m

thunder /ˈθʌndə(r)/ n truenos mpl, (of traffic) estruendo m. ● vi tronar. **~bolt** n rayo m. **~storm** n tormenta f eléctrica. **~y** adj con truenos

Thursday /ˈθɜːzdeɪ/ n jueves m

t

thus /ðʌs/ *adv* así

thwart /θwɔːt/ *vt* frustrar

tic /tɪk/ *n* tic *m*

tick /tɪk/ *n* (*sound*) tic *m*; (*insect*) garrapata *f*, (*mark*) marca *f*, visto *m*, palomita *f* (*Mex*); (*fam, instant*) momentito *m*. ● *vi* hacer tictac. ● *vt*. ~ (**off**) marcar

ticket /'tɪkɪt/ *n* (*for bus, train*) billete *m*, boleto *m* (*LAm*); (*for plane*) pasaje *m*, billete *m*; (*for theatre, museum*) entrada *f*; (*for baggage, coat*) ticket *m*; (*fine*) multa *f*. ~ **collector** *n* revisor *m*. ~ **office** *n* (*transport*) mostrador *m* de venta de billetes *or* (*LAm*) boletos; (*in theatre*) taquilla *f*, boletería *f* (*LAm*)

tickl|e /'tɪkl/ *vt* hacerle cosquillas a. ● *n* cosquilleo *m*. ~**ish** /'tɪklɪʃ/ *adj*. **be** ~**ish** tener cosquillas

tidal wave /'taɪdl/ *n* maremoto *m*

tide /taɪd/ *n* marea *f*. **high/low** ~ marea alta/baja. □ ~ **over** *vt* ayudar a salir de un apuro

tid|ily /'taɪdɪlɪ/ *adv* ordenadamente. ~**iness** *n* orden *m*. ~**y** *adj* (**-ier, -iest**) ordenado. ● *vt/i* ~**y** (**up**) ordenar, arreglar

tie /taɪ/ *vt* (*pres p* tying) atar, amarrar (*LAm*); hacer (knot). ● *vi* (*Sport*) empatar. ● *n* (*constraint*) atadura *f*; (*bond*) lazo *m*; (*necktie*) corbata *f*; (*Sport*) empate *m*. ~ **in with** *vt* concordar con. □ ~ **up** *vt* atar. **be** ~**d up** (*busy*) estar ocupado

tier /tɪə(r)/ *n* hilera *f* superpuesta; (*in stadium etc*) grada *f*; (*of cake*) piso *m*

tiger /'taɪɡə(r)/ *n* tigre *m*

tight /taɪt/ *adj* (**-er, -est**) (clothes) ajustado, ceñido; (*taut*) tieso; (control) estricto; (knot, nut) apretado; (*fam, drunk*) borracho. ~**en** *vt* apretar. □ ~**en up** *vt* hacer más estricto. ~**-fisted** /-'fɪstɪd/ *adj* tacaño. ~**ly** *adv* bien, fuerte; (fastened) fuertemente. ~**rope** *n* cuerda *f* floja. ~**s** *npl* (*for ballet etc*) leotardo(s) *m*(*pl*); (*pantyhose*) medias *fpl*

tile /taɪl/ *n* (*decorative*) azulejo *m*; (*on roof*) teja *f*; (*on floor*) baldosa *f*. ● *vt* azulejar; tejar (roof); embaldosar (floor)

till /tɪl/ *prep* hasta. ● *conj* hasta que. ● *n* caja *f*. ● *vt* cultivar

tilt /tɪlt/ *vt* inclinar. ● *vi* inclinarse. ● *n* inclinación *f*

timber /'tɪmbə(r)/ *n* madera *f* (*para construcción*)

time /taɪm/ *n* tiempo *m*; (*moment*) momento *m*; (*occasion*) ocasión *f*; (*by clock*) hora *f*; (*epoch*) época *f*; (*rhythm*) compás *m*. **at** ~**s** a veces. **for the** ~ **being** por el momento. **from** ~ **to** ~ de vez en cuando. **have a good** ~ divertirse, pasarlo bien. **in a year's** ~ dentro de un año. **in no** ~ en un abrir y cerrar de ojos. **in** ~ a tiempo; (*eventually*) con el tiempo. **arrive on** ~ llegar a tiempo. **it's** ~ **we left** es hora de irnos. ● *vt* elegir el momento; cronometrar (race). ~ **bomb** *n* bomba *f* de tiempo. ~**ly** *adj* oportuno. ~**r** *n* cronómetro *m*; (*Culin*) avisador *m*; (*with sand*) reloj *m* de arena; (*Elec*) interruptor *m* de reloj. ~**s** /'taɪmz/ *prep*. **2** ~**s 4 is 8** 2 (multiplicado) por 4 son 8. ~**table** *n* horario *m*

timid /'tɪmɪd/ *adj* tímido; (*fearful*) miedoso

tin /tɪn/ *n* estaño *m*; (*container*) lata *f*. ~ **foil** *n* papel *m* de estaño

tinge /tɪndʒ/ *vt*. **be** ~**d with sth** estar matizado de algo. ● *n* matiz *m*

tingle /'tɪŋɡl/ *vi* sentir un hormigueo

tinker /'tɪŋkə(r)/ *vi*. ~ **with** juguetear con

tinkle /'tɪŋkl/ *vi* tintinear

tinned /tɪnd/ *adj* en lata, enlatado

tin opener *n* abrelatas *m*

tint /tɪnt/ *n* matiz *m*

tiny /'taɪnɪ/ *adj* (**-ier, -iest**) minúsculo, diminuto

tip /tɪp/ *n* punta *f*. ● *vt* (*pt* tipped) (*tilt*) inclinar; (*overturn*) volcar; (*pour*) verter; (*give gratuity to*) darle (una) propina a. □ ~ **off** *vt* avisar. □ ~ **out** *vt* verter. □ ~ **over** *vi* caerse. *n* propina *f*; (*advice*) consejo *m* (práctico); (*for rubbish*) vertedero *m*. ~**ped** *adj* (cigarette) con filtro

tipsy /'tɪpsɪ/ *adj* achispado

tiptoe /'tɪptəʊ/ *n*. **on** ~ de puntillas

tiptop /'tɪptɒp/ *adj* 🅸 de primera. **in** ~ **condition** en excelente estado

tire /'taɪə(r)/ *n* (*Amer*) *see* **TYRE**. ● *vt* cansar. ● *vi* cansarse. ~**d** /'taɪəd/ *adj*

cansado. **get** ~**d** cansarse. ~**d of**
harto de. ~**d out** agotado. ~**less** *adj*
incansable; (efforts) inagotable.
~**some** /-səm/ *adj* (person) pesado;
(task) tedioso

tiring /'taɪərɪŋ/ *adj* cansado, cansador
(*LAm*)

tissue /'tɪʃuː/ *n* (of bones, plants) tejido
m; (paper handkerchief) pañuelo *m* de
papel. ~ **paper** *n* papel *m* de seda

tit /tɪt/ *n* (bird) paro *m*; (🔞, breast)
teta *f*

titbit /'tɪtbɪt/ *n* exquisitez *f*

tit for tat *n*: **it was** ~ fue ojo por
ojo, diente por diente

title /'taɪtl/ *n* título *m*

to /tuː, tə/ *prep* a; (towards) hacia: (in
order to) para; (as far as) hasta; (of)
de. **give it** ~ **me** dámelo. **what did
you say** ~ **him?** ¿qué le dijiste?; **I
don't want** ~ no quiero. **it's twenty**
~ **seven** (by clock) son las siete
menos veinte, son veinte para las
siete (*LAm*). ● *adv.* **pull** ~ cerrar. ~
and fro *adv* de un lado a otro

toad /təʊd/ *n* sapo *m*. ~**stool** *n* hongo
m (no comestible)

toast /təʊst/ *n* pan *m* tostado, tostadas
fpl; (drink) brindis *m*. **a piece of** ~
una tostada, un pan tostado (*Mex*).
drink a ~ **to** brindar por. ● *vt* (Culin)
tostar; (drink to) brindar por. ~**er** *n*
tostadora *f* (eléctrica). tostador *m*

tobacco /tə'bækəʊ/ *n* tabaco *m*. ~**nist**
/-ənɪst/ *n* estanquero *m*

toboggan /tə'bɒgən/ *n* tobogán *m*

today /tə'deɪ/ *n* & *adv* hoy (*m*)

toddler /'tɒdlə(r)/ *n* niño *m* pequeño
(entre un año y dos años y medio de
edad)

toe /təʊ/ *n* dedo *m* (del pie); (of shoe)
punta *f*. **big** ~ dedo *m* gordo (del
pie). **on one's** ~**s** (fig) alerta. ● *vt.* ~
the line acatar la disciplina

**TOEFL - Test of English as a
Foreign Language** Un examen que, a la hora de solicitar el
ingreso a una universidad americana, evalúa el dominio del inglés
de aquellos estudiantes cuya lengua materna no es este idioma.

---

toffee /'tɒfɪ/ *n* toffee *m* (golosina
hecha con azúcar y mantequilla)

together /tə'geðə(r)/ *adv* juntos; (at
same time) a la vez. ~ **with** junto
con

toil /tɔɪl/ *vi* afanarse. ● *n* trabajo *m*
duro

toilet /'tɔɪlɪt/ *n* servicio *m*, baño *m*
(*LAm*). ~ **paper** *n* papel *m* higiénico.
~**ries** /'tɔɪlɪtrɪz/ *npl* artículos *mpl* de
tocador. ~ **roll** *n* rollo *m* de papel higiénico

token /'təʊkən/ *n* muestra *f*; (voucher)
vale *m*; (coin) ficha *f*. ● *adj* simbólico

told /təʊld/ *see* **TELL**

tolera|ble /'tɒlərəbl/ *adj* tolerable;
(not bad) pasable. ~**nce** /'tɒlərəns/ *n*
tolerancia *f*. ~**nt** *adj* tolerante. ~**te**
/-reɪt/ *vt* tolerar. ~**tion** /-'reɪʃən/ *n*
tolerancia *f*

toll /təʊl/ *n* (on road) peaje *m*, cuota *f*
(*Mex*). **death** ~ número *m* de muer-
tos. ~ **call** *n* (Amer) llamada *f* interur-
bana, conferencia *f*. ● *vi* doblar, tocar
a muerto

tomato /tə'mɑːtəʊ/ *n* (pl -oes) tomate
m, jitomate *m* (*Mex*)

tomb /tuːm/ *n* tumba *f*, sepulcro *m*.
~**stone** *n* lápida *f*

tomorrow /tə'mɒrəʊ/ *n* & *adv* mañana
(*f*). **see you** ~! ¡hasta mañana!

ton /tʌn/ *n* tonelada *f* (= 1,016kg). ~**s
of** 🔞 montones de. **metric** ~ tonelada *f* (métrica) (= 1,000kg)

tone /təʊn/ *n* tono *m*. □ ~ **down** *vt*
atenuar; moderar (language). ~**-deaf**
adj que no tiene oído (musical)

tongs /tɒŋz/ *npl* tenacillas *fpl*

tongue /tʌŋ/ *n* lengua *f*. **say sth** ~ **in
cheek** decir algo medio burlándose.
~**-tied** *adj* cohibido. ~**-twister** *n* trabalenguas *m*

tonic /'tɒnɪk/ *adj* tónico. ● *n* (Med, fig)
tónico *m*. ~ **(water)** *n* tónica *f*

tonight /tə'naɪt/ *adv* & *n* esta noche
(*f*); (evening) esta tarde (*f*)

tonne /tʌn/ *n* tonelada *f* (métrica)

tonsil /'tɒnsl/ *n* amígdala *f*. ~**litis**
/-'laɪtɪs/ *n* amigdalitis *f*

too /tuː/ *adv* (excessively) demasiado;
(also) también. **I'm not** ~ **sure** no
estoy muy seguro. ~ **many** demasia-

t

dos. ~ **much** demasiado

took /tʊk/ *see* **TAKE**

tool /tuːl/ *n* herramienta *f*

tooth /tuːθ/ *n* (*pl* **teeth**) diente *m*; (*molar*) muela *f*. ~**ache** *n* dolor *m* de muelas. ~**brush** *n* cepillo *m* de dientes. ~**paste** *n* pasta *f* dentífrica, pasta *f* de dientes. ~**pick** *n* palillo *m* (de dientes)

top /tɒp/ *n* parte *f* superior, parte *f* de arriba; (*of mountain*) cima *f*; (*of tree*) copa *f*; (*of page*) parte *f* superior; (*lid, of bottle*) tapa *f*; (*of pen*) capuchón *m*; (*spinning* ~) trompo *m*, peonza *f*. be ~ **of the class** ser el primero de la clase. **from ~ to bottom** de arriba abajo. **on** ~ **of** encima de; (*besides*) además de. ● *adj* más alto; (*shelf*) superior; (*speed*) máximo; (*in rank*) superior; (*leading*) más destacado. ● *vt* (*pt* **topped**) cubrir; (*exceed*) exceder. ~ **floor** *n* último piso *m*. □ ~ **up** *vt* llenar; (*mobile phone*) recargar el saldo. ~ **hat** *n* chistera *f*. ~**-heavy** /-'hevɪ/ *adj* inestable (por ser más pesado en su parte superior)

topic /'tɒpɪk/ *n* tema *m*. ~**al** *adj* de actualidad

topless /'tɒpləs/ *adj* topless

topple /'tɒpl/ *vi* (*Pol*) derribar; (*overturn*) volcar. ● *vi* caerse

top secret /tɒp'siːkrɪt/ *adj* secreto, reservado

torch /tɔːtʃ/ *n* linterna *f*; (*flaming*) antorcha *f*

tore /tɔː(r)/ *see* **TEAR**[1]

torment /'tɔːment/ *n* tormento *m*. ● /tɔː'ment/ *vt* atormentar

torn /tɔːn/ *see* **TEAR**[1]

tornado /tɔː'neɪdəʊ/ *n* (*pl* **-oes**) tornado *m*

torpedo /tɔː'piːdəʊ/ *n* (*pl* **-oes**) torpedo *m*. ● *vt* torpedear

torrent /'tɒrənt/ *n* torrente *m*. ~**ial** /tə'renʃl/ *adj* torrencial

torrid /'tɒrɪd/ *adj* tórrido; (*affair*) apasionado

tortoise /'tɔːtəs/ *n* tortuga *f*. ~**shell** *n* carey *m*

tortuous /'tɔːtjʊəs/ *adj* tortuoso

torture /'tɔːtʃə(r)/ *n* tortura *f*. ● *vt* torturar

toss /tɒs/ *vt* tirar, lanzar (ball); (*shake*) sacudir. ● *vi*. ~ **and turn** (*in bed*) dar vueltas

tot /tɒt/ *n* pequeño *m*; (*fam, of liquor*) trago *m*. ● *vt* (*pt* **totted**). ~ **up** Ⓣ sumar

total /'təʊtl/ *adj & n* total (*m*). ● *vt* (*pt* **totalled**) ascender a un total de; (*add up*) totalizar. ~**itarian** /təʊtælɪ'teərɪən/ *adj* totalitario. ~**ly** *adv* totalmente

totter /'tɒtə(r)/ *vi* tambalearse

touch /tʌtʃ/ *vt* tocar; (*move*) conmover; (*concern*) afectar. ● *vi* tocar; (*wires*) tocarse. ● *n* toque *m*; (*sense*) tacto *m*; (*contact*) contacto *m*. **be/get/stay in** ~ **with** estar/ponerse/mantenerse en contacto con. □ ~ **down** *vi* (aircraft) aterrizar. □ ~ **up** *vt* retocar. ~**ing** *adj* enternecedor. ~**y** *adj* quisquilloso

tough /tʌf/ *adj* (**-er, -est**) duro; (*strong*) fuerte, resistente; (*difficult*) difícil; (*severe*) severo. ~**en**. ~ (**up**) *vt* endurecer; hacer más fuerte (person)

tour /tʊə(r)/ *n* viaje *m*; (*visit*) visita *f*; (*excursion*) excursión *f*; (*by team etc*) gira *f*. **be on** ~ estar de gira. ● *vt* recorrer; (*visit*) visitar. ~ **guide** *n* guía de turismo

touris|m /'tʊərɪzəm/ *n* turismo *m*. ~**t** /'tʊərɪst/ *n* turista *m & f*. ● *adj* turístico. ~**t office** *n* oficina *f* de turismo

tournament /'tɔːnəmənt/ *n* torneo *m*

tousle /'taʊzl/ *vt* despeinar

tout /taʊt/ *vi*. ~ (**for**) solicitar

tow /təʊ/ *vt* remolcar. ● *n* remolque *m*

toward(s) /tə'wɔːd(z)/ *prep* hacia. **his attitude** ~ **her** su actitud para con ella

towel /'taʊəl/ *n* toalla *f*

tower /'taʊə(r)/ *n* torre *f*. ● *vi*. ~ **above** (building) descollar sobre; (person) destacar sobre. ~ **block** *n* edificio *m* or bloque *m* de apartamentos. ~**ing** *adj* altísimo; (*rage*) violento

town /taʊn/ *n* ciudad *f*; (*smaller*) pueblo *m*. **go to** ~ Ⓣ no escatimar dinero. ~ **hall** *n* ayuntamiento *m*

toxic /'tɒksɪk/ *adj* tóxico

toy /tɔɪ/ *n* juguete *m*. □ ~ **with** *vt* juguetear con (object); darle vueltas a (idea). ~**shop** *n* juguetería *f*

t

trac|e /treɪs/ n señal f, rastro m. ● vt trazar; (draw) dibujar; (with tracing paper) calcar; (track down) localizar. ~**ing paper** n papel m de calcar

track /træk/ n pista f, huellas fpl; (path) sendero m; (Sport) pista f. **the ~(s)** la vía férrea; (Rail) vía f. **keep ~ of** seguirle la pista a (person). ● vt seguirle la pista a. □ ~ **down** vt localizar. ~ **suit** n equipo m (de deportes) chándal m

tract /trækt/ n (land) extensión f; (pamphlet) tratado m breve

traction /'trækʃn/ n tracción f

tractor /'træktə(r)/ n tractor m

trade /treɪd/ n comercio m; (occupation) oficio m; (exchange) cambio m; (industry) industria f. ● vt. ~ **sth for sth** cambiar algo por algo. ● vi comerciar. □ ~ **in** vt (give in partexchange) entregar como parte del pago. ~ **mark** n marca f (de fábrica). ~**r** n comerciante m & f. ~ **union** n sindicato m

tradition /trə'dɪʃn/ n tradición f. ~**al** adj tradicional

traffic /'træfɪk/ n tráfico m. ● vi (pt **trafficked**) comerciar (**in** en). ~ **circle** n (Amer) glorieta f, rotonda f. ~ **island** n isla f peatonal. ~ **jam** n embotellamiento m, atasco m. ~ **lights** npl semáforo m. ~ **warden** n guardia m, controlador m de tráfico

trag|edy /'trædʒɪdɪ/ n tragedia f. ~**ic** /'trædʒɪk/ adj trágico

trail /treɪl/ vi arrastrarse; (lag) rezagarse. ● vt (track) seguir la pista de. ● n (left by animal, person) huellas fpl; (path) sendero m. **be on the ~ of** s.o./sth seguir la pista de uno/algo. ~**er** n remolque m; (Amer, caravan) caravana f, rulot m; (film) avance m

train /treɪn/ n (Rail) tren m; (of events) serie f; (of dress) cola f. ● vt capacitar (employee); adiestrar (soldier); (Sport) entrenar; educar (voice); guiar (plant); amaestrar (animal). ● vi estudiar; (Sport) entrenarse. ~**ed** adj (skilled) cualificado, calificado; (doctor) diplomado. ~**ee** /treɪ'niː/ n aprendiz m; (Amer, Mil) recluta m & f. ~**er** n (Sport) entrenador m; (of animals) amaestrador m. ~**ers** mpl zapa-

tillas fpl de deporte. ~**ing** n capacitación f; (Sport) entrenamiento m

trait /treɪ(t)/ n rasgo m

traitor /'treɪtə(r)/ n traidor m

tram /træm/ n tranvía m

tramp /træmp/ vi. ~ **(along)** caminar pesadamente. ● n vagabundo m

trample /'træmpl/ vt pisotear. ● vi. ~ **on** pisotear

trampoline /'træmpəliːn/ n trampolín m

trance /trɑːns/ n trance m

tranquil /'træŋkwɪl/ adj tranquilo. ~**lity** /-'kwɪlətɪ/ n tranquilidad f; (of person) serenidad f. ~**lize** /'træŋkwɪlaɪz/ vt sedar, dar un sedante a. ~**lizer** n sedante m, tranquilizante m

transaction /træn'zækʃən/ n transacción f, operación f

transatlantic /trænzət'læntɪk/ adj transatlántico

transcend /træn'send/ vt (go beyond) exceder

transcript /'trænskrɪpt/ n transcripción f

transfer /træns'fɜː(r)/ vt (pt **transferred**) trasladar; traspasar (player); transferir (funds, property); pasar (call). ● vi trasladarse. ● /'trænsfɜː(r)/ n traslado m; (of player) traspaso m; (of funds, property) transferencia f; (paper) calcomanía f

transform /træns'fɔːm/ vt transformar. ~**ation** /-ə'meɪʃn/ n transformación f. ~**er** n transformador m

transfusion /træns'fjuːʒn/ n transfusión f

transient /'trænzɪənt/ adj pasajero

transistor /træn'zɪstə(r)/ n transistor m

transit /'trænsɪt/ n tránsito m. ~**ion** /træn'zɪʒn/ n transición f. ~**ive** /'trænsɪtɪv/ adj transitivo

translat|e /trænz'leɪt/ vt traducir. ~**ion** /-ʃn/ n traducción f. ~**or** n traductor m

transmission /trænz'mɪʃn/ n transmisión f

transmit /trænz'mɪt/ vt (pt **transmitted**) transmitir. ~**ter** n transmisor m

t

transparen|cy /træns'pærənsɪ/ n transparencia f; (*Photo*) diapositiva f. **~t** adj transparente

transplant /træns'plɑːnt/ vt trasplantar. ● /'trænsplɑːnt/ n trasplante m

transport /træn'spɔːt/ vt transportar. ● /'trænspɔːt/ n transporte m. **~ation** /-'teɪʃn/ n transporte m

trap /træp/ n trampa f. ● vt (pt **trapped**) atrapar; (*jam*) atascar; (*cut off*) bloquear. **~door** n trampilla f

trapeze /trə'piːz/ n trapecio m

trash /træʃ/ n basura f; (*Amer, worthless people*) escoria f. **~ can** n (*Amer*) cubo m de la basura, bote m de la basura (*Mex*). **~y** adj (souvenir) de porquería; (magazine) malo

travel /'trævl/ vi (pt **travelled**) viajar; (vehicle) desplazarse. ● vt recorrer. ● n viajes mpl. **~ agency** n agencia f de viajes. **~ler** n viajero m. **~ler's cheque** n cheque m de viaje or viajero. **~ling expenses** npl gastos mpl de viaje

trawler /'trɔːlə(r)/ n barca f pesquera

tray /treɪ/ n bandeja f

treacher|ous adj traidor; (*deceptive*) engañoso. **~y** n traición f

treacle /'triːkl/ n melaza f

tread /tred/ vi (pt **trod**, pp **trodden**) pisar. **~ on sth** pisar algo. **~ carefully** andarse con cuidado. ● n (*step*) paso m; (*of tyre*) banda f de rodamiento

treason /'triːzn/ n traición f

treasur|e /'treʒə(r)/ n tesoro m. **~ed** /'treʒəd/ adj (possession) preciado. **~er** /'treʒərə(r)/ n tesorero m. **~y** n erario m, tesoro m. **the T~y** el fisco, la hacienda pública. **Department of the T~y** (*in US*) Departamento m del Tesoro

treat /triːt/ vt tratar; (*Med*) tratar. **~ s.o.** (*to meal etc*) invitar a uno. ● n placer m; (*present*) regalo m

treatise /'triːtɪz/ n tratado m

treatment /'triːtmənt/ n tratamiento m

treaty /'triːtɪ/ n tratado m

treble /'trebl/ adj triple; (clef) de sol; (voice) de tiple. ● vt triplicar. ● vi triplicarse. ● n tiple m & f

tree /triː/ n árbol m

trek /trek/ n caminata f. ● vi (pt **trekked**) caminar

trellis /'trelɪs/ n enrejado m

tremble /'trembl/ vi temblar

tremendous /trɪ'mendəs/ adj formidable; (*fam, huge*) tremendo. **~ly** adv tremendamente

tremor /'tremə(r)/ n temblor m

trench /trentʃ/ n zanja f; (*Mil*) trinchera f

trend /trend/ n tendencia f; (*fashion*) moda f. **~y** adj (-ier, -iest) [i] moderno

trepidation /trepɪ'deɪʃn/ n inquietud f

trespass /'trespəs/ vi. **~ on** entrar sin autorización (en propiedad ajena). **~er** n intruso m

trial /'traɪəl/ n prueba f; (*Jurid*) proceso m, juicio m; (*ordeal*) prueba f dura. **by ~ and error** por ensayo y error. **be on ~** estar a prueba; (*Jurid*) estar siendo procesado

triang|le /'traɪæŋgl/ n triángulo m. **~ular** /-'æŋgjʊlə(r)/ adj triangular

trib|al /'traɪbl/ adj tribal. **~e** /traɪb/ n tribu f

tribulation /trɪbjʊ'leɪʃn/ n tribulación f

tribunal /traɪ'bjuːnl/ n tribunal m

tributary /'trɪbjʊtrɪ/ n (*of river*) afluente m

tribute /'trɪbjuːt/ n tributo m; (*acknowledgement*) homenaje m. **pay ~ to** rendir homenaje a

trick /trɪk/ n trampa f, ardid m; (*joke*) broma f; (*feat*) truco m; (*in card games*) baza f. **play a ~ on** gastar una broma a. ● vt engañar. **~ery** n engaño m

trickle /'trɪkl/ vi gotear. **~ in** (*fig*) entrar poco a poco

trickster /'trɪkstə(r)/ n estafador m

tricky /'trɪkɪ/ adj delicado, difícil

tricycle /'traɪsɪkl/ n triciclo m

tried /traɪd/ see **TRY**

trifl|e /'traɪfl/ n nimiedad f; (*Culin*) postre de bizcocho, jerez, frutas y nata. ● vi. □ **~e with** vt jugar con. **~ing** adj insignificante

trigger /'trɪgə(r)/ n (of gun) gatillo m.
● vt. ～ **(off)** desencadenar

trim /trɪm/ adj (**trimmer, trimmest**)
(slim) esbelto; (neat) elegante. ● vt (pt
trimmed) (cut) recortar; (adorn)
adornar. ● n (cut) recorte m. **in** ～ en
buen estado. **～mings** npl recortes
mpl

trinity /'trɪnɪtɪ/ n. **the (Holy) T～** la
(Santísima) Trinidad

trinket /'trɪŋkɪt/ n chuchería f

trio /'triːəʊ/ n (pl -**os**) trío m

trip /trɪp/ (pt **tripped**) vt ～ **(up)** hacerle una zancadilla a, hacer tropezar
● vi tropezar. ● n (journey) viaje m;
(outing) excursión f; (stumble) traspié m

tripe /traɪp/ n callos mpl, mondongo m
(LAm), pancita f (Mex); (fam, nonsense)
paparruchas fpl

triple /'trɪpl/ adj triple. ● vt triplicar.
● vi triplicarse. **～t** /'trɪplɪt/ n trillizo m

triplicate /'trɪplɪkət/ adj triplicado. **in**
～ por triplicado

tripod /'traɪpɒd/ n trípode m

trite /traɪt/ adj trillado

triumph /'traɪʌmf/ n triunfo m. ● vi
triunfar (**over** sobre). **～al** /-'ʌmfl/ adj
triunfal. **～ant** /-'ʌmfnt/ adj (troops)
triunfador; (moment) triunfal; (smile)
de triunfo

trivial /'trɪvɪəl/ adj insignificante; (con-
cerns) trivial. **～ity** /-'ælətɪ/ n triviali-
dad f

trod, trodden /trɒd, trɒdn/ see
TREAD

trolley /'trɒlɪ/ n (pl -**eys**) carretón m;
(in supermarket, airport) carrito m; (for
food, drink) carrito m, mesa f rodante.
～ **car** n (Amer) tranvía f

trombone /trɒm'bəʊn/ n trombón m

troop /truːp/ n compañía f; (of cavalry)
escuadrón m. ● vi. ～ **in** entrar en tropel. ～ **out** salir en tropel. **～er** n soldado m de caballería; (Amer, state police officer) agente m & f. **～s** npl (Mil)
tropas fpl

trophy /'trəʊfɪ/ n trofeo m

tropic /'trɒpɪk/ n trópico m. **～al** adj
tropical. **～s** npl trópicos mpl

trot /trɒt/ n trote m. ● vi (pt **trotted**)
trotar

trouble /'trʌbl/ n problemas mpl; (awkward situation) apuro m; (inconvenience) molestia f. **be in** ～ estar en
apuros. **get into** ～ meterse en problemas. **look for** ～ buscar camorra.
take the ～ **to do sth** molestarse en
hacer algo. ● vt (bother) molestar;
(worry) preocupar. **～-maker** n alborotador m. **～some** /-səm/ adj problemático. ～ **spot** n punto m conflictivo

trough /trɒf/ n (for drinking) abreva-
dero m; (for feeding) comedero m

troupe /truːp/ n compañía f teatral

trousers /'traʊzəz/ npl pantalón m,
pantalones mpl

trout /traʊt/ n (pl **trout**) trucha f

trowel /'traʊəl/ n (garden) desplanta-
dor m; (for mortar) paleta f

truant /'truːənt/ n. **play** ～ hacer novillos

truce /truːs/ n tregua f

truck /trʌk/ n camión m; (Rail) vagón
m, furgón m; (Amer, vegetables, fruit)
productos mpl de la huerta. ～ **driver**,
～er (Amer) n camionero m. **～ing** n
transporte m por carretera

trudge /trʌdʒ/ vi andar penosamente

true /truː/ adj (-er, -est) verdadero;
(story, account) verídico; (friend) auténtico, de verdad. ～ **to sth/s.o.** fiel
a algo/uno. **be** ～ ser cierto. **come** ～
hacerse realidad

truffle /'trʌfl/ n trufa f; (chocolate)
trufa f de chocolate

truly /'truːlɪ/ adv verdaderamente; (sin-
cerely) sinceramente. **yours** ～ (in letters) cordiales saludos

trump /trʌmp/ n (Cards) triunfo m; (fig)
baza f

trumpet /'trʌmpɪt/ n trompeta f. **～er**
n trompetista m & f, trompeta m & f

truncheon /'trʌntʃən/ n porra f

trunk /trʌŋk/ n (of tree) tronco m;
(box) baúl m; (of elephant) trompa f;
(Amer, Auto) maletero m, cajuela f (Mex).
～s npl bañador m, traje m de baño

truss /trʌs/ vt. **truss (up)** vt atar

trust /trʌst/ n confianza f; (money,
property) fondo m de inversiones; (in-
stitution) fundación f. ～ **on** ～ a ojos cerrados; (Com) al fiado. ● vi. ～ **in s.o./
sth** confiar en uno/algo. ● vt confiar

t

en; (*in negative sentences*) fiarse; (*hope*) esperar. **~ed** *adj* leal. **~ee** /trʌˈstiː/ *n* fideicomisario *m*. **~ful** confiado. **~ing** *adj* confiado. **~worthy**, **~y** *adj* digno de confianza

truth /truːθ/ *n* (*pl* **-s** /truːðz/) verdad *f*; (*of account, story*) veracidad *f*. **~ful** *adj* veraz.

try /traɪ/ *vt* (*pt* **tried**) intentar; probar (food, product); (*be a strain on*) poner a prueba; (*Jurid*) procesar. **~ to do sth** tratar de hacer algo, intentar hacer algo. **~ not to forget** procura no olvidarte. ● *n* tentativa *f*, prueba *f*; (*Rugby*) ensayo *m*. ▫ **~ on** *vt* probarse (garment). ▫ **~ out** *vt* probar. **~ing** *adj* duro; (*annoying*) molesto

tsar /zɑː(r)/ *n* zar *m*

T-shirt /ˈtiːʃɜːt/ *n* camiseta *f*

tub /tʌb/ *n* cuba *f*; (*for washing clothes*) tina *f*; (*bathtub*) bañera *f*; (*for ice cream*) envase *m*, tarrina *f*

tuba /ˈtjuːbə/ *n* tuba *f*

tubby /ˈtʌbɪ/ *adj* (**-ier**, **-iest**) rechoncho

tube /tjuːb/ *n* tubo *m*; (*fam, Rail*) metro *m*; (*Amer fam, television*) tele *f*. **inner ~** *n* cámara *f* de aire

tuberculosis /tjuːbɜːkjʊˈləʊsɪs/ *n* tuberculosis *f*

tub|ing /ˈtjuːbɪŋ/ *n* tubería *f*. **~ular** /-jʊlə(r)/ *adj* tubular

tuck /tʌk/ *n* (*fold*) jareta *f*. ● *vt* plegar; (*put*) meter. ▫ **~ in(to)** *vi* (*fam, eat*) ponerse a comer. ▫ **~ up** *vt* arropar (child)

Tuesday /ˈtjuːzdeɪ/ *n* martes *m*

tuft /tʌft/ *n* (*of hair*) mechón *m*; (*of feathers*) penacho *m*; (*of grass*) mata *f*

tug /tʌg/ *vt* (*pt* **tugged**) tirar de. ● *vi*. **~ at sth** tirar de algo. ● *n* tirón *m*; (*Naut*) remolcador *m*. **~-of-war** *n* juego de tira y afloja

tuition /tjuːˈɪʃn/ *n* clases *fpl*

tulip /ˈtjuːlɪp/ *n* tulipán *m*

tumble /ˈtʌmbl/ *vi* caerse. ● *n* caída *f*. **~down** *adj* en ruinas. **~-drier** *n* secadora *f*. **~r** *n* (*glass*) vaso *m* (*de lados rectos*)

tummy /ˈtʌmɪ/ *n* 🗓 barriga *f*

tumour /ˈtjuːmə(r)/ *n* tumor *m*

tumult /ˈtjuːmʌlt/ *n* tumulto *m*. **~uous** /-ˈmʌltjʊəs/ *adj* (applause) apoteósico

tuna /ˈtjuːnə/ *n* (*pl* **tuna**) atún *m*

tune /tjuːn/ *n* melodía *f*; (*piece*) tonada *f*. **be in ~** estar afinado. **be out of ~** estar desafinado. ● *vt* afinar, sintonizar (radio, TV); (*Mec*) poner a punto. ● *vi*. **~ in (to)** sintonizar (con). ▫ **~ up** *vt/i* afinar. **~ful** *adj* melodioso. **~r** *n* afinador *m*; (*Radio*) sintonizador *m*

tunic /ˈtjuːnɪk/ *n* túnica *f*

tunnel /ˈtʌnl/ *n* túnel *m*. ● *vi* (*pt* **tunnelled**) abrir un túnel

turban /ˈtɜːbən/ *n* turbante *m*

turbine /ˈtɜːbaɪn/ *n* turbina *f*

turbo /ˈtɜːbəʊ/ *n* (*pl* **-os**) turbo(compresor) *m*

turbulen|ce /ˈtɜːbjʊləns/ *n* turbulencia *f*. **~t** *adj* turbulento

turf /tɜːf/ *n* (*pl* **turfs** *or* **turves**) césped *m*; (*segment of grass*) tepe *m*. ▫ **~ out** *vt* 🗓 echar

turgid /ˈtɜːdʒɪd/ *adj* (language) ampuloso

turkey /ˈtɜːkɪ/ *n* (*pl* **-eys**) pavo *m*

Turk|ey /ˈtɜːkɪ/ *f* Turquía *f*. **~ish** *adj* & *n* turco (*m*)

turmoil /ˈtɜːmɔɪl/ *n* confusión *f*

turn /tɜːn/ *vt* hacer girar; volver (head, page); doblar (corner); (*change*) cambiar; (*deflect*) desviar. **~ sth into sth** convertir *or* transformar algo en algo. ● *vi* (handle) girar, dar vueltas; (person) volverse, darse la vuelta. **~ right** girar *or* doblar *or* torcer a la derecha. **~ red** ponerse rojo. **~ into sth** convertirse en algo. ● *n* vuelta *f*; (*in road*) curva *f*; (*change*) giro *m*; (*sequence*) turno *m*; (*fam, of illness*) ataque *m*. **good ~** favor *m*. **in ~** a su vez. ▫ **~ down** *vt* (*fold*) doblar; (*reduce*) bajar; (*reject*) rechazar. ▫ **~ off** *vt* cerrar (tap); apagar (light, TV, etc). *vi* (*from road*) doblar. ▫ **~ on** *vt* abrir (tap); encender, prender (*LAm*) (light etc). ▫ **~ out** *vt* apagar (light etc). *vi* (*result*) resultar. ▫ **~ round** *vi* darse la vuelta. ▫ **~ up** *vi* aparecer. *vt* (*find*) encontrar; levantar (collar); subir (hem); acortar (trousers); poner más fuerte (gas). **~ed-up** *adj* (nose) res-

pingón. ~**ing** n (in town) bocacalle f.
we've missed the ~**ing** nos hemos
pasado la calle (or carretera). ~**ing-
point** n momento m decisivo.

turnip /'tɜːnɪp/ n nabo m

turn ~**over** n (Com) facturación f; (of
staff) movimiento m. ~**pike** n (Amer)
autopista f de peaje. ~**stile** n torniquete m. ~**table** n platina f. ~**-up** n
(of trousers) vuelta f, valenciana f (Mex)

turquoise /'tɜːkwɔɪz/ adj & n turquesa
(f)

turret /'tʌrɪt/ n torrecilla f

turtle /'tɜːtl/ n tortuga f de mar;
(Amer, tortoise) tortuga f

turves /'tɜːvz/ see TURF

tusk /tʌsk/ n colmillo m

tussle /'tʌsl/ n lucha f

tutor /'tjuːtə(r)/ n profesor m particular

tuxedo /tʌk'siːdəʊ/ n (pl -os) (Amer)
esmoquin m, smoking m

TV /tiː'viː/ n televisión f, tele f 🔲

twang /twæŋ/ n tañido m; (in voice)
gangueo m

tweet /twiːt/ n piada f. ● vi piar

tweezers /'twiːzəz/ npl pinzas fpl

twel|fth /twelfθ/ adj duodécimo. ● n
doceavo m. ~**ve** /twelv/ adj & n doce
(m)

twent|ieth /'twentɪəθ/ adj vigésimo.
● n veinteavo m. ~**y** /'twentɪ/ adj & n
veinte (m)

twice /twaɪs/ adv dos veces. ~ **as
many people** el doble de gente

twiddle /'twɪdl/ vt (hacer) girar

twig /twɪg/ n ramita f. ● vi (pt
twigged) 🔲 caer, darse cuenta

twilight /'twaɪlaɪt/ n crepúsculo m

twin /twɪn/ adj & n gemelo (m), mellizo
(m) (LAm)

twine /twaɪn/ n cordel m, bramante m

twinge /twɪndʒ/ n punzada f; (of remorse) punzada f

twinkle /'twɪŋkl/ vi centellear. ● n
centelleo m; (in eye) brillo m

twirl /twɜːl/ vt (hacer) girar. ● vi girar.
● n vuelta f

twist /twɪst/ vt retorcer; (roll) enrollar;
girar (knob); tergiversar (words); (distort) retorcer. ~ **one's ankle** torcerse
el tobillo. ● vi (rope, wire) enrollarse;

(road, river) serpentear. ● n torsión f;
(curve) vuelta f

twit /twɪt/ n 🔲 imbécil m

twitch /twɪtʃ/ vi moverse. ● n tic m

twitter /'twɪtə(r)/ vi gorjear

two /tuː/ adj & n dos (m). ~**-bit** adj
(Amer) de tres al cuarto. ~**-faced** adj
falso, insincero. ~**fold** adj doble.
● adv dos veces. ~**pence** /'tʌpəns/ n
dos peniques mpl. ~**-piece (suit)** n
traje m de dos piezas. ~**-way** adj
(traffic) de doble sentido

tycoon /taɪ'kuːn/ n magnate m

tying /'taɪɪŋ/ see TIE

type /taɪp/ n tipo m. ● vt/i escribir a
máquina. ~**-cast** adj (actor) encasi-
llado, ~**script** n texto m mecanografiado, manuscrito m (de una obra,
novela etc). ~**writer** n máquina f de
escribir. ~**written** adj escrito a máquina, mecanografiado

typhoon /taɪ'fuːn/ n tifón m

typical /'tɪpɪkl/ adj típico. ~**ly** adv típi-
camente

typify /'tɪpɪfaɪ/ vt tipificar

typi|ng /'taɪpɪŋ/ n mecanografía f.
~**st** n mecanógrafo m

tyran|nical /tɪ'rænɪkl/ adj tiránico.
~**ny** /'tɪrənɪ/ n tiranía f. ~**t**
/'taɪərənt/ n tirano m

tyre /'taɪə(r)/ n neumático m, llanta f
(LAm)

Uu

udder /'ʌdə(r)/ n ubre f

UFO /'juːfəʊ/ abbr (= **unidentified flying object**) OVNI m (objeto volante
no identificado)

ugly /'ʌglɪ/ adj (-ier, -iest) feo

UK /juː'keɪ/ abbr (= **United Kingdom**)
Reino m Unido

Ukraine /juː'kreɪn/ n Ucrania f

ulcer /'ʌlsə(r)/ n úlcera f; (external)
llaga f

ultimate /'ʌltɪmət/ adj (eventual) final;
(utmost) máximo. ~**ly** adv en última
instancia; (in the long run) a la larga

ultimatum /ˌʌltɪˈmeɪtəm/ n (pl -ums) ultimátum m

ultra... /ˈʌltrə/ pref ultra... ~**violet** /-ˈvaɪələt/ adj ultravioleta

umbilical cord /ʌmˈbɪlɪkl/ n cordón m umbilical

umbrella /ʌmˈbrelə/ n paraguas m

umpire /ˈʌmpaɪə(r)/ n árbitro m. ● vt arbitrar

umpteen /ˈʌmptiːn/ adj ⊞ tropecientos ⊞. ~**th** adj ⊞ enésimo

un... /ʌn/ pref in..., des..., no, poco, sin

UN /juːˈen/ abbr (= United Nations) ONU f (Organización de las Naciones Unidas)

unable /ʌnˈeɪbl/ adj. be ~ **to** no poder; (be incapable of) ser incapaz de

unacceptable /ʌnəkˈseptəbl/ adj (behaviour) inaceptable; (terms) inadmisible

unaccompanied /ʌnəˈkʌmpənɪd/ adj (luggage) no acompañado; (person, instrument) solo; (singing) sin acompañamiento

unaccustomed /ʌnəˈkʌstəmd/ adj desacostumbrado. be ~ **to** adj no estar acostumbrado a

unaffected /ʌnəˈfektɪd/ adj natural

unaided /ʌnˈeɪdɪd/ adj sin ayuda

unanimous /juːˈnænɪməs/ adj unánime. ~**ly** adv unánimemente; (elect) por unanimidad

unarmed /ʌnˈɑːmd/ adj desarmado

unattended /ʌnəˈtendɪd/ adj sin vigilar

unattractive /ʌnəˈtræktɪv/ adj poco atractivo

unavoidabl|e /ʌnəˈvɔɪdəbl/ adj inevitable. ~**y** adv. I was ~**y** delayed no pude evitar llegar tarde

unaware /ʌnəˈweə(r)/ adj. be ~ **of** ignorar, no ser consciente de. ~**s** /-ˈeəz/ adv desprevenido

unbearabl|e /ʌnˈbeərəbl/ adj insoportable, inaguantable. ~**y** adv inaguantablemente

unbeat|able /ʌnˈbiːtəbl/ adj (quality) insuperable; (team) invencible. ~**en** adj no vencido; (record) insuperado

unbelievabl|e /ʌnbɪˈliːvəbl/ adj increíble. ~**y** adv increíblemente

unbiased /ʌnˈbaɪəst/ adj imparcial

unblock /ʌnˈblɒk/ vt desatascar

unbolt /ʌnˈbəʊlt/ vt descorrer el pestillo de

unborn /ʌnˈbɔːn/ adj que todavía no ha nacido

unbreakable /ʌnˈbreɪkəbl/ adj irrompible

unbroken /ʌnˈbrəʊkən/ adj (intact) intacto; (continuous) ininterrumpido

unbutton /ʌnˈbʌtn/ vt desabotonar, desabrochar

uncalled-for /ʌnˈkɔːldfɔː(r)/ adj fuera de lugar

uncanny /ʌnˈkænɪ/ adj (-ier, -iest) raro, extraño

uncertain /ʌnˈsɜːtn/ adj incierto; (hesitant) vacilante. be ~ **of/about sth** no estar seguro de algo. ~**ty** n incertidumbre f

uncharitable /ʌnˈtʃærɪtəbl/ adj severo

uncivilized /ʌnˈsɪvɪlaɪzd/ adj incivilizado

uncle /ˈʌŋkl/ n tío m

Uncle Sam Es la típica personificación de EE.UU., en que éste es representado por un hombre de barba blanca, vestido con los colores nacionales y con un sombrero de copa adornado con estrellas. Es posible que la imagen se haya extraído del cartel de reclutamiento, en 1917, que llevaba la leyenda: "A Ud. lo necesito".

---

unclean /ʌnˈkliːn/ adj impuro

unclear /ʌnˈklɪə(r)/ adj poco claro

uncomfortable /ʌnˈkʌmfətəbl/ adj incómodo

uncommon /ʌnˈkɒmən/ adj poco común

uncompromising /ʌnˈkɒmprəmaɪzɪŋ/ adj intransigente

unconcerned /ʌnkənˈsɜːnd/ adj indiferente

unconditional /ʌnkənˈdɪʃənl/ adj incondicional

unconnected /ʌnkəˈnektɪd/ adj (unrelated) sin conexión. **the events are**

u

~ estos acontecimientos no guardan ninguna relación (entre sí)

unconscious /ʌn'kɒnʃəs/ adj (Med) inconsciente. **~ly** adv inconscientemente

unconventional /ʌnkən'venʃənl/ adj poco convencional

uncork /ʌn'kɔːk/ vt descorchar

uncouth /ʌn'kuːθ/ adj zafio

uncover /ʌn'kʌvə(r)/ vt destapar; revelar (plot, scandal)

undaunted /ʌn'dɔːntɪd/ adj impertérrito

undecided /ʌndɪ'saɪdɪd/ adj indeciso

undeniab|le /ʌndɪ'naɪəbl/ adj innegable. **~y** adv sin lugar a dudas

under /'ʌndə(r)/ prep debajo de, (less than) menos de; (heading) bajo; (according to) según; (expressing movement) por debajo de. ● adv debajo, abajo

under... pref sub...

under ~carriage n tren m de aterrizaje. **~charge** vt /-'tʃɑːdʒ/ cobrarle de menos a. **~clothes** npl ropa f interior. **~coat, ~coating** (Amer) n (paint) pintura f base; (first coat) primera mano f de pintura. **~cover** adj /-'kʌvə(r)/ secreto. **~current** n corriente f submarina. **~dog** n. the **~dog** el que tiene menos posibilidades. **the ~dogs** npl los de abajo. **~done** adj /-'dʌn/ (meat) poco hecho. **~estimate** /-'estɪmeɪt/ vt (underrate) subestimar. **~fed** /-'fed/ adj subalimentado. **~foot** /-'fʊt/ adv debajo de los pies. **~go** vt (pt -went, pp -gone) sufrir. **~graduate** /-'grædjʊət/ n estudiante m universitario (no licenciado). **~ground** /-'graʊnd/ adv bajo tierra; (in secret) clandestinamente. ● /-'graʊnd/ adj subterráneo; (secret) clandestino. ● n metro m. **~growth** n maleza f. **~hand** /-'hænd/ adj (secret) clandestino; (deceptive) fraudulento. **~lie** /-'laɪ/ vt (pt -lay, pp -lain, pres p -lying) subyacer a. **~line** /-'laɪn/ vt subrayar. **~lying** /-'laɪɪŋ/ adj subyacente. **~mine** /-'maɪn/ vt socavar. **~neath** /-'niːθ/ prep debajo de, abajo de (LAm). ● adv por debajo. **~paid** /-'peɪd/ adj mal pagado. **~pants** npl calzoncillos

mpl. **~pass** n paso m subterráneo; (for traffic) paso m inferior. **~privileged** /-'prɪvəlɪdʒd/ adj desfavorecido. **~rate** /-'reɪt/ vt subestimar. **~rated** /-'reɪtɪd/ adj no debidamente apreciado. **~shirt** n (Amer) camiseta f (interior).

understand /ʌndə'stænd/ vt (pt -stood) entender; (empathize with) comprender, entender. ● vi entender, comprender. **~able** adj comprensible. **~ing** adj comprensivo. ● n (grasp) entendimiento m; (sympathy) comprensión f; (agreement) acuerdo m

under ~statement n subestimación f. **~take** /-'teɪk/ (pt -took, pp -taken) emprender (task); asumir (responsibility). **~take to do sth** comprometerse a hacer algo. **~taker** n director m de pompas fúnebres. **~taking** /-'teɪkɪŋ/ n empresa f; (promise) promesa f. **~tone** n. in an **~tone** en voz baja. **~value** /-'vælju:/ vt subvalorar. **~water** /-'wɔːtə(r)/ adj submarino. ● adv debajo del agua. **~wear** n ropa f interior. **~weight** /-'weɪt/ adj de peso más bajo que el normal. **~went** /-'went/ see **UNDERGO**. **~world** n (criminals) hampa f. **~write** /-'raɪt/ vt (pt -wrote, pp -written) (Com) asegurar; (guarantee financially) financiar

undeserved /ʌndɪ'zɜːvd/ adj inmerecido

undesirable /ʌndɪ'zaɪərəbl/ adj indeseable

undignified /ʌn'dɪgnɪfaɪd/ adj indecoroso

undisputed /ʌndɪs'pju:tɪd/ adj (champion) indiscutido; (facts) innegable

undo /ʌn'du:/ vt (pt -did, pp -done) desabrochar (button, jacket); abrir (zip); desatar (knot, laces)

undoubted /ʌn'daʊtɪd/ adj indudable. **~ly** adv indudablemente, sin duda

undress /ʌn'dres/ vt desvestir, desnudar. ● vi desvestirse, desnudarse

undue /ʌn'dju:/ adj excesivo

undulate /'ʌndjʊleɪt/ vi ondular

unduly /ʌn'dju:lɪ/ adv excesivamente

unearth /ʌn'ɜːθ/ vt desenterrar; descubrir (document)

u

unearthly /ʌn'ɜːθlɪ/ adj sobrenatural. **at an ~ hour** a estas horas intempestivas

uneasy /ʌn'iːzɪ/ adj incómodo

uneconomic /ʌniːkə'nɒmɪk/ adj poco económico

uneducated /ʌn'edjʊkeɪtɪd/ adj sin educación

unemploy|ed /ʌnɪm'plɔɪd/ adj desempleado, parado. **~ment** n desempleo m, paro m

unending /ʌn'endɪŋ/ adj interminable, sin fin

unequal /ʌn'iːkwəl/ adj desigual

unequivocal /ʌnɪ'kwɪvəkl/ adj inequívoco

unethical /ʌn'eθɪkl/ adj poco ético, inmoral

uneven /ʌn'iːvn/ adj desigual

unexpected /ʌnɪk'spektɪd/ adj inesperado; (result) imprevisto. **~ly** adv (arrive) de improviso; (happen) de forma imprevista

unfair /ʌn'feə(r)/ adj injusto; improcedente (dismissal). **~ly** adv injustamente

unfaithful /ʌn'feɪθfl/ adj infiel

unfamiliar /ʌnfə'mɪlɪə(r)/ adj desconocido. **be ~ with** desconocer

unfasten /ʌn'fɑːsn/ vt desabrochar (clothes); (untie) desatar

unfavourable /ʌn'feɪvərəbl/ adj desfavorable

unfeeling /ʌn'fiːlɪŋ/ adj insensible

unfit /ʌn'fɪt/ adj. **I'm ~** no estoy en forma. **~ for human consumption** no apto para el consumo

unfold /ʌn'fəʊld/ vt desdoblar; desplegar (wings); (fig) revelar. ● vi (leaf) abrirse; (events) desarrollarse

unforeseen /ʌnfɔː'siːn/ adj imprevisto

unforgettable /ʌnfə'getəbl/ adj inolvidable

unforgivable /ʌnfə'gɪvəbl/ adj imperdonable

unfortunate /ʌn'fɔːtʃənət/ adj desafortunado; (regrettable) lamentable. **~ly** adv desafortunadamente; (stronger) por desgracia, desgraciadamente

unfounded /ʌn'faʊndɪd/ adj infundado

unfriendly /ʌn'frendlɪ/ adj poco amistoso; (stronger) antipático

unfurl /ʌn'fɜːl/ vt desplegar

ungainly /ʌn'geɪnlɪ/ adj desgarbado

ungrateful /ʌn'greɪtfl/ adj desagradecido, ingrato

unhapp|iness /ʌn'hæpɪnes/ n infelicidad f, tristeza f. **~y** adj (-ier, -iest) infeliz, triste; (unsuitable) inoportuno. **be ~y about sth** no estar contento con algo

unharmed /ʌn'hɑːmd/ adj (person) ileso

unhealthy /ʌn'helθɪ/ adj (-ier, -iest) (person) de mala salud; (complexion) enfermizo; (conditions) poco saludable

unhurt /ʌn'hɜːt/ adj ileso

unification /juːnɪfɪ'keɪʃn/ n unificación f

uniform /'juːnɪfɔːm/ adj & n uniforme (m). **~ity** /-'fɔːmətɪ/ n uniformidad f

unify /'juːnɪfaɪ/ vt unir

unilateral /juːnɪ'lætərəl/ adj unilateral

unimaginable /ʌnɪ'mædʒɪnəbl/ adj inimaginable

unimaginative /ʌnɪ'mædʒɪnətɪv/ adj (person) poco imaginativo

unimportant /ʌnɪm'pɔːtnt/ adj sin importancia

uninhabited /ʌnɪn'hæbɪtɪd/ adj deshabitado; (island) despoblado

unintelligible /ʌnɪn'telɪdʒəbl/ adj ininteligible

unintentional /ʌnɪn'tenʃənl/ adj involuntario

union /'juːnjən/ n unión f; (trade union) sindicato m; (student ~) asociación f de estudiantes. **U~ Jack** n bandera f del Reino Unido

unique /juː'niːk/ adj único

unison /'juːnɪsn/ n. **in ~** al unísono

unit /'juːnɪt/ n unidad f; (of furniture etc) módulo m; (in course) módulo m

unite /juː'naɪt/ vt unir. ● vi unirse. **U~d Kingdom** n Reino m Unido. **U~d Nations** n Organización f de las Naciones Unidas (ONU). **U~d States (of America)** n Estados mpl Unidos (de América)

unity /'juːnɪtɪ/ n unidad f

univers|al /juːnɪˈvɜːsl/ *adj* universal. **~e** /ˈjuːnɪvɜːs/ *n* universo *m*

university /juːnɪˈvɜːsɪtɪ/ *n* universidad *f*. ● *adj* universitario

unjust /ʌnˈdʒʌst/ *adj* injusto. **~ified** /-ɪfaɪd/ *adj* injustificado

unkind /ʌnˈkaɪnd/ *adj* poco amable; (*cruel*) cruel; (remark) hiriente

unknown /ʌnˈnəʊn/ *adj* desconocido

unlawful /ʌnˈlɔːfl/ *adj* ilegal

unleaded /ʌnˈledɪd/ *adj* (fuel) sin plomo

unleash /ʌnˈliːʃ/ *vt* soltar

unless /ʌnˈles, ənˈles/ *conj* a menos que, a no ser que

unlike /ʌnˈlaɪk/ *prep* diferente de. (*in contrast to*) a diferencia de. **~ly** *adj* improbable

unlimited /ʌnˈlɪmɪtɪd/ *adj* ilimitado

unlisted /ʌnˈlɪstɪd/ *adj* (Amer) que no figura en la guía telefónica, privado (Mex)

unload /ʌnˈləʊd/ *vt* descargar

unlock /ʌnˈlɒk/ *vt* abrir (con llave)

unluck|ily /ʌnˈlʌkɪlɪ/ *adv* desgraciadamente. **~y** *adj* (-ier, -iest) (person) sin suerte, desafortunado. **be ~y** tener mala suerte; (bring bad luck) traer mala suerte

unmarried /ʌnˈmærɪd/ *adj* soltero

unmask /ʌnˈmɑːsk/ *vt* desenmascarar

unmentionable /ʌnˈmenʃənəbl/ *adj* inmencionable

unmistakable /ʌnmɪˈsteɪkəbl/ *adj* inconfundible

unnatural /ʌnˈnætʃərəl/ *adj* poco natural; (not normal) anormal

unnecessar|ily /ʌnˈnesəsərɪlɪ/ *adv* innecesariamente. **~y** *adj* innecesario

unnerve /ʌnˈnɜːv/ *vt* desconcertar

unnoticed /ʌnˈnəʊtɪst/ *adj* inadvertido

unobtainable /ʌnəbˈteɪnəbl/ *adj* imposible de conseguir

unobtrusive /ʌnəbˈtruːsɪv/ *adj* discreto

unofficial /ʌnəˈfɪʃl/ *adj* no oficial. **~ly** *adv* extraoficialmente

unpack /ʌnˈpæk/ *vt* sacar las cosas de (bags); deshacer, desempacar (LAm) (suitcase). ● *vi* deshacer las maletas, desempacar (LAm)

unpaid /ʌnˈpeɪd/ *adj* (work) no retribuido, no remunerado; (leave) sin sueldo

unperturbed /ʌnpəˈtɜːbd/ *adj* impasible. **he carried on ~** siguió sin inmutarse

unpleasant /ʌnˈpleznt/ *adj* desagradable

unplug /ʌnˈplʌg/ *vt* desenchufar

unpopular /ʌnˈpɒpjʊlə(r)/ *adj* impopular

unprecedented /ʌnˈpresɪdentɪd/ *adj* sin precedentes

unpredictable /ʌnprɪˈdɪktəbl/ *adj* imprevisible

unprepared /ʌnprɪˈpeəd/ *adj* no preparado; (unready) desprevenido

unprofessional /ʌnprəˈfeʃənəl/ *adj* poco profesional

unprofitable /ʌnˈprɒfɪtəbl/ *adj* no rentable

unprotected /ʌnprəˈtektɪd/ *adj* sin protección; (sex) sin el uso de preservativos

unqualified /ʌnˈkwɒlɪfaɪd/ *adj* sin título; (fig) absoluto

unquestion|able /ʌnˈkwestʃənəbl/ *adj* incuestionable, innegable. **~ing** *adj* (obedience) ciego; (loyalty) incondicional

unravel /ʌnˈrævl/ *vt* (pt unravelled) desenredar; desentrañar (mystery)

unreal /ʌnˈrɪəl/ *adj* irreal. **~istic** /-ˈlɪstɪk/ *adj* poco realista

unreasonable /ʌnˈriːzənəbl/ *adj* irrazonable

unrecognizable /ʌnrekəgˈnaɪzəbl/ *adj* irreconocible

unrelated /ʌnrɪˈleɪtɪd/ *adj* (facts) no relacionados (entre sí); (people) no emparentado

unreliable /ʌnrɪˈlaɪəbl/ *adj* (person) informal; (machine) poco fiable; (information) poco fidedigno

unrepentant /ʌnrɪˈpentənt/ *adj* impenitente

unrest /ʌnˈrest/ *n* (discontent) descontento *m*; (disturbances) disturbios *mpl*

unrivalled /ʌnˈraɪvld/ *adj* incomparable

unroll /ʌnˈrəʊl/ *vt* desenrollar. ● *vi* desenrollarse

u

unruffled /ʌnˈrʌfld/ (person) sereno

unruly /ʌnˈruːlɪ/ adj (class) indisciplinado; (child) revoltoso

unsafe /ʌnˈseɪf/ adj inseguro

unsatisfactory /ʌnsætɪsˈfæktərɪ/ adj insatisfactorio

unsavoury /ʌnˈseɪvərɪ/ adj desagradable

unscathed /ʌnˈskeɪðd/ adj ileso

unscheduled /ʌnˈʃedjuːld/ adj no programado, no previsto

unscrew /ʌnˈskruː/ vt destornillar; desenroscar (lid)

unscrupulous /ʌnˈskruːpjʊləs/ adj inescrupuloso

unseemly /ʌnˈsiːmlɪ/ adj indecoroso

unseen /ʌnˈsiːn/ adj (danger) oculto; (unnoticed) sin ser visto

unselfish /ʌnˈselfɪʃ/ adj (act) desinteresado; (person) nada egoísta

unsettle /ʌnˈsetl/ vt desestabilizar (situation); alterar (plans). ∼**d** adj agitado; (weather) inestable; (undecided) pendiente (de resolución)

unshakeable /ʌnˈʃeɪkəbl/ adj inquebrantable

unshaven /ʌnˈʃeɪvn/ adj sin afeitar, sin rasurar (Mex)

unsightly /ʌnˈsaɪtlɪ/ adj feo

unskilled /ʌnˈskɪld/ adj (work) no especializado; (worker) no cualificado, no calificado

unsociable /ʌnˈsəʊʃəbl/ adj insociable

unsolved /ʌnˈsɒlvd/ adj no resuelto; (murder) sin esclarecerse

unsophisticated /ʌnsəˈfɪstɪkeɪtɪd/ adj sencillo

unsound /ʌnˈsaʊnd/ adj poco sólido

unspecified /ʌnˈspesɪfaɪd/ adj no especificado

unstable /ʌnˈsteɪbl/ adj inestable

unsteady /ʌnˈstedɪ/ adj inestable, poco firme

unstuck /ʌnˈstʌk/ adj despegado. **come** ∼ despegarse; (fail) fracasar

unsuccessful /ʌnsəkˈsesfʊl/ adj (attempt) infructuoso. **be** ∼ no tener éxito, fracasar

unsuitable /ʌnˈsuːtəbl/ adj (clothing) poco apropiado, poco adecuado; (time) inconveniente. **she is** ∼ **for**

the job no es la persona indicada para el trabajo

unsure /ʌnˈʃʊə(r)/ adj inseguro

unthinkable /ʌnˈθɪŋkəbl/ adj inconcebible

untid|iness /ʌnˈtaɪdɪnəs/ n desorden m. ∼**y** adj (**-ier, -iest**) desordenado; (appearance, writing) descuidado

untie /ʌnˈtaɪ/ vt desatar, desamarrar (LAm)

until /ənˈtɪl, ʌnˈtɪl/ prep hasta. ● conj hasta que

untold /ʌnˈtəʊld/ adj incalculable

untouched /ʌnˈtʌtʃt/ adj intacto

untried /ʌnˈtraɪd/ adj no probado

untrue /ʌnˈtruː/ adj falso

unused /ʌnˈjuːzd/ adj nuevo. ● /ʌnˈjuːst/ adj. ∼ **to** no acostumbrado a

unusual /ʌnˈjuːʒʊəl/ adj poco común, poco corriente. **it's** ∼ **to see so many people** es raro ver a tanta gente. ∼**ly** adv excepcionalmente, inusitadamente

unveil /ʌnˈveɪl/ vt descubrir

unwanted /ʌnˈwɒntɪd/ adj superfluo; (child) no deseado

unwelcome /ʌnˈwelkəm/ adj (news) poco grato; (guest) inoportuno

unwell /ʌnˈwel/ adj indispuesto

unwieldy /ʌnˈwiːldɪ/ adj pesado y difícil de manejar

unwilling /ʌnˈwɪlɪŋ/ adj mal dispuesto. **be** ∼ no querer

unwind /ʌnˈwaɪnd/ vt (pt unwound) desenrollar. ● vi (fam, relax) relajarse

unwise /ʌnˈwaɪz/ adj poco sensato

unworthy /ʌnˈwɜːðɪ/ adj indigno

unwrap /ʌnˈræp/ vt (pt unwrapped) desenvolver

unwritten /ʌnˈrɪtn/ adj no escrito; (agreement) verbal

up /ʌp/ adv arriba; (upwards) hacia arriba; (higher) más arriba. ∼ **here** aquí arriba. ∼ **there** allí arriba. ∼ **to** hasta. **he's not** ∼ **yet** todavía no se ha levantado. **be** ∼ **against** enfrentarse con. **come** ∼ subir. **go** ∼ subir. **he's not** ∼ **to the job** no tiene las condiciones necesarias para el trabajo. **it's** ∼ **to you** depende de ti. **what's** ∼? ¿qué pasa? ● prep. **go** ∼ **the stairs** subir la escalera. **it's just**

~ **the road** está un poco más allá. ●*vt* (*pt* **upped**) aumentar. ●*n.* ~**s and downs** *npl* altibajos *mpl*; (*of life*) vicisitudes *fpl*. ~**bringing** /'ʌpbrɪŋɪŋ/ *n* educación *f.* ~**date** /ʌp'deɪt/ *vt* poner al día. ~**grade** /ʌp'greɪd/ *vt* elevar de categoría (person); mejorar (equipment). ~**heaval** /ʌp'hi:vl/ *n* trastorno *m.* ~**hill** /ʌp'hɪl/ *adv* cuesta arriba. ~**hold** /ʌp'həʊld/ *vt* (*pt* **upheld**) mantener (principle); confirmar (decision). ~**holster** /ʌp'həʊlstə(r)/ *vt* tapizar. ~**holstery** *n* tapicería *f.* ~**keep** *n* mantenimiento *m.* ~**-market** /ʌp'mɑ:kɪt/ *adj* de categoría

upon /ə'pɒn/ *prep* sobre. **once** ~ **a time** érase una vez

upper /'ʌpə(r)/ *adj* superior. ~ **class** *n* clase *f* alta

up ~**right** *adj* vertical; (citizen) recto. **place sth** ~**right** poner algo de pie. ~**rising** /'ʌpraɪzɪŋ/ *n* levantamiento *m.* ~**roar** *n* tumulto *m*

upset /ʌp'set/ *vt* (*pt* **upset**, *pres p* **upsetting**) (*hurt*) disgustar; (*offend*) ofender; (*distress*) alterar; desbaratar (plans). ●*adj* (*hurt*) disgustado; (*distressed*) alterado; (*offended*) ofendido; (*disappointed*) desilusionado. ●/'ʌpset/ *n* trastorno *m.* **have a stomach** ~ estar mal del estómago

up ~**shot** *n* resultado *m.* ~**side down** /ʌpsaɪd'daʊn/ *adv* al revés (con la parte de arriba abajo); (*in disorder*) patas arriba. **turn sth** ~**side down** poner algo boca abajo. ~**stairs** /ʌp'steəz/ *adv* arriba. **go** ~**stairs** subir. ●/'ʌpsteəz/ *adj* de arriba. ~**start** *n* advenedizo *m.* ~**state** *adv* (*Amer*). **I live** ~**state** vivo en el norte del estado. ~**stream** /ʌp'stri:m/ *adv* río arriba. ~**take** *n.* **be quick on the** ~**take** agarrar las cosas al vuelo. ~**-to-date** /ʌptə'deɪt/ *adj* al día; (news) de última hora. ~**turn** *n* repunte *m*, mejora *f.* ~**ward** /'ʌpwəd/ *adj* (movement) ascendente; (direction) hacia arriba. ●*adv* hacia arriba. ~**wards** *adv* hacia arriba

uranium /jʊ'reɪnɪəm/ *n* uranio *m*

Uranus /'jʊərənəs/jʊə'reɪnəs/ *n* Urano *m*

urban /'ɜ:bən/ *adj* urbano

urchin /'ɜ:tʃɪn/ *n* pilluelo *m*

urge /ɜ:dʒ/ *vt* instar. ~ **s.o. to do sth** instar a uno a que haga algo. ●*n* impulso *m*; (*wish, whim*) ganas *fpl*. □ ~ **on** *vt* animar

urgen|cy /'ɜ:dʒənsɪ/ *n* urgencia *f.* ~**t** *adj* urgente. ~**tly** *adv* urgentemente, con urgencia

urin|ate /'jʊərɪneɪt/ *vi* orinar. ~**e** /'jʊərɪn/ *n* orina *f*

Uruguay /'jʊərəgwaɪ/ *n* Uruguay *m.* ~**an** *adj* & *n* uruguayo (*m*)

us /ʌs, əs/ *pron* nos; (*after prep*) nosotros *m*, nosotras *f*

US(A) /ju:es'eɪ/ *abbr* (= **United States (of America)**) EE.UU. (*only written*), Estados *mpl* Unidos

usage /'ju:zɪdʒ/ *n* uso *m*

use /ju:z/ *vt* usar; utilizar (service, facilities); consumir (fuel). ●/ju:s/ *n* uso *m*, empleo *m.* **be of** ~ servir. **it is no** ~ es inútil. □ ~ **up** *vt* agotar, consumir. ~**d** /ju:zd/ *adj* usado. ●/ju:st/ *v mod* ~ **to. he** ~**d to say** decía, solía decir. **there** ~**d to be** (antes) había. ●*adj*/ju:st/. **be** ~**d to** estar acostumbrado a. ~**ful** /ju:sfl/ *adj* útil. ~**fully** *adv* útilmente. ~**less** *adj* inútil; (person) incompetente. ~**r** /-zə(r)/ *n* usuario *m.* **drug** ~ *n* consumidor *m* de drogas

usher /'ʌʃə(r)/ *n* (*in theatre etc*) acomodador *m.* □ ~ **in** *vt* hacer pasar; marcar el comienzo de (new era). ~**ette** /-'ret/ *n* acomodadora *f*

USSR *abbr* (History) (= **Union of Soviet Socialist Republics**) URSS

usual /'ju:ʒʊəl/ *adj* usual; (*habitual*) acostumbrado, habitual; (place, route) de siempre. **as** ~ como de costumbre, como siempre. ~**ly** *adv* normalmente. **he** ~**ly wakes up early** suele despertarse temprano

utensil /ju:'tensl/ *n* utensilio *m*

utilize /'ju:tɪlaɪz/ *vt* utilizar

utmost /'ʌtməʊst/ *adj* sumo. ●*n.* **do one's** ~ hacer todo lo posible (**to** para)

utter /'ʌtə(r)/ *adj* completo. ●*vt* pronunciar (word); dar (cry). ~**ly** *adv* totalmente

U-turn /'ju:tɜ:n/ *n* cambio *m* de sentido

u

Vv

vacan|cy /'veɪkənsɪ/ n (job) vacante f; (room) habitación f libre. **~t** adj (building) desocupado; (seat) libre; (post) vacante; (look) ausente

vacate /və'keɪt/ vt dejar

vacation /və'keɪʃn/ n (Amer) vacaciones fpl. **go on ~** ir de vacaciones. **~er** n (Amer) veraneante m & f

vaccin|ate /'væksɪneɪt/ vt vacunar. **~ation** /-'neɪʃn/ n vacunación f. **~e** /'væksiːn/ n vacuna f

vacuum /'vækjʊəm/ n vacío m. **~ cleaner** n aspiradora f

vagina /və'dʒaɪnə/ n vagina f

vague /veɪɡ/ adj (-er, -est) vago; (outline) borroso; (person, expression) despistado. **~ly** adv vagamente

vain /veɪn/ adj (-er, -est) vanidoso; (useless) vano. **in ~** en vano

Valentine's Day /'væləntaɪnz/ n el día de San Valentín

valiant /'vælɪənt/ adj valeroso

valid /'vælɪd/ adj válido. **~ate** /-eɪt/ vt dar validez a; validar (contract). **~ity** /-'ɪdətɪ/ n validez f

valley /'vælɪ/ n (pl -eys) valle m

valour /'vælə(r)/ n valor m

valu|able /'væljʊəbl/ adj valioso. **~ables** npl objetos mpl de valor. **~ation** /-'eɪʃn/ n valoración f. **~e** /'væljuː/ n valor m. ● vt valorar; tasar, valorar, avaluar (LAm) (property). **~e added tax** n impuesto m sobre el valor añadido

valve /vælv/ n válvula f

vampire /'væmpaɪə(r)/ n vampiro m

van /væn/ n furgoneta f, camioneta f; (Rail) furgón m

vandal /'vændl/ n vándalo m. **~ism** n vandalismo m. **~ize** vt destruir

vanilla /və'nɪlə/ n vainilla f

vanish /'vænɪʃ/ vi desaparecer

vanity /'vænɪtɪ/ n vanidad f. **~ case** n neceser m

vapour /'veɪpə(r)/ n vapor m

varia|ble /'veərɪəbl/ adj variable. **~nce** /-əns/ n. **at ~ce** en desacuerdo. **~nt** n variante f. **~tion** /-'eɪʃn/ n variación f

vari|ed /'veərɪd/ adj variado. **~ety** /və'raɪətɪ/ n variedad f. **~ety show** n espectáculo m de variedades. **~ous** /'veərɪəs/ adj (several) varios; (different) diversos

varnish /'vɑːnɪʃ/ n barniz m; (for nails) esmalte m. ● vt barnizar; pintar (nails)

vary /'veərɪ/ vt/i variar

vase /vɑːz/, (Amer) /veɪs/ n (for flowers) florero m; (ornamental) jarrón m

vast /vɑːst/ adj vasto, extenso; (size) inmenso. **~ly** adv infinitamente

vat /væt/ n cuba f

VAT /viːeɪ'tiː/ abbr (= value added tax) IVA m

vault /vɔːlt/ n (roof) bóveda f; (in bank) cámara f acorazada; (tomb) cripta f. ● vt/i saltar

VCR n = **videocassette recorder**

VDU n = **visual display unit**

veal /viːl/ n ternera f

veer /vɪə(r)/ vi dar un viraje, virar

vegeta|ble /'vedʒɪtəbl/ adj vegetal. ● n verdura f. **~rian** /vedʒɪ'teərɪən/ adj & n vegetariano (m). **~tion** /vedʒɪ'teɪʃn/ n vegetación f

vehement /'viːəmənt/ adj vehemente. **~tly** adv con vehemencia

vehicle /'viːɪkl/ n vehículo m

veil /veɪl/ n velo m

vein /veɪn/ n vena f; (in marble) veta f

velocity /vɪ'lɒsɪtɪ/ n velocidad f

velvet /'velvɪt/ n terciopelo m

vendetta /ven'detə/ n vendetta f

vend|ing machine /'vendɪŋ/ n distribuidor m automático. **~or** /'vendə(r)/ n vendedor m

veneer /və'nɪə(r)/ n chapa f, enchapado m; (fig) barniz m, apariencia f

venerate /'venəreɪt/ vt venerar

venereal /və'nɪərɪəl/ adj venéreo

Venetian blind /və'niːʃn/ n persiana f veneciana

Venezuela /venə'zweɪlə/ n Venezuela f. **~n** adj & n venezolano (m)

vengeance /'vendʒəns/ n venganza f. **with a ~** (fig) con ganas

venom /'venəm/ n veneno m. ~ous adj venenoso

vent /vent/ n (conducto m de) ventilación; (air ~) respiradero m. **give** ~ **to** dar rienda suelta a. ● vt descargar

ventilat|e /'ventɪleɪt/ vt ventilar. ~ion /-'leɪʃn/ n ventilación f

ventriloquist /ven'trɪləkwɪst/ n ventrílocuo m

venture /'ventʃə(r)/ n empresa f. ● vt aventurar. ● vi atreverse

venue /'venjuː/ n (for concert) lugar m de actuación

Venus /'viːnəs/ n Venus m

veranda /və'rændə/ n galería f

verb /vɜːb/ n verbo m. ~al adj verbal

verdict /'vɜːdɪkt/ n veredicto m; (opinion) opinión f

verge /vɜːdʒ/ n borde m. □ ~ **on** vt rayar en

verify /'verɪfaɪ/ vt (confirm) confirmar; (check) verificar

vermin /'vɜːmɪn/ n alimañas fpl

versatil|e /'vɜːsətaɪl/ adj versátil. ~ity /-'tɪlətɪ/ n versatilidad f

verse /vɜːs/ n estrofa f; (poetry) poesías fpl. ~d /vɜːst/ adj. **be well-~ed in** ser muy versado en. ~ion /'vɜːʃn/ n versión f

versus /'vɜːsəs/ prep contra

vertebra /'vɜːtɪbrə/ n (pl -brae /-briː/) vértebra f. ~te /-brət/ n vertebrado m

vertical /'vɜːtɪkl/ adj & n vertical (f). ~ly adv verticalmente

vertigo /'vɜːtɪgəʊ/ n vértigo m

verve /vɜːv/ n brío m

very /'verɪ/ adv muy. ~ **much** muchísimo. ~ **well** muy bien. **the** ~ **first** el primero de todos. ● adj mismo. **the** ~ **thing** exactamente lo que hace falta

vessel /'vesl/ n (receptacle) recipiente m; (ship) navío m, nave f

vest /vest/ n camiseta f; (Amer) chaleco m.

vestige /'vestɪdʒ/ n vestigio m

vet /vet/ n veterinario m; (Amer fam, veteran) veterano m. ● vt (pt vetted) someter a investigación (applicant)

veteran /'vetərən/ n veterano m

veterinary /'vetərɪnərɪ/ adj veterinario. ~ **surgeon** n veterinario m

veto /'viːtəʊ/ n (pl -oes) veto m. ● vt vetar

vex /veks/ vt fastidiar

via /'vaɪə/ prep por, por vía de

viable /'vaɪəbl/ adj viable

viaduct /'vaɪədʌkt/ n viaducto m

vibrat|e /vaɪ'breɪt/ vt/i vibrar. ~ion /-ʃn/ n vibración f

vicar /'vɪkə(r)/ n párroco m. ~age /-rɪdʒ/ n casa f del párroco

vice /vaɪs/ n vicio m; (Tec) torno m de banco

vice versa /vaɪsɪ'vɜːsə/ adv viceversa

vicinity /vɪ'sɪnɪtɪ/ n vecindad f. **in the** ~ **of** cerca de

vicious /'vɪʃəs/ adj (attack) feroz; (dog) fiero; (rumour) malicioso. ~ **circle** n círculo m vicioso

victim /'vɪktɪm/ n víctima f. ~ize vt victimizar

victor /'vɪktə(r)/ n vencedor m

Victorian /vɪk'tɔːrɪən/ adj victoriano

victor|ious /vɪk'tɔːrɪəs/ adj (army) victorioso; (team) vencedor. ~y /'vɪktərɪ/ n victoria f

video /'vɪdɪəʊ/ n (pl -os) vídeo m, video m (LAm). ~ **camera** n videocámara f. ~ **(cassette) recorder** n magnetoscopio m. ~ **tape** n videocassette f

vie /vaɪ/ vi (pres p **vying**) rivalizar

Vietnam /vjet'næm/ n Vietnam m. ~ese adj & n vietnamita (m & f)

view /vjuː/ n vista f; (mental survey) visión f de conjunto; (opinion) opinión f. **in my** ~ a mi juicio. **in** ~ **of** en vista de. **on** ~ expuesto. ● vt ver (scene, property); (consider) considerar. ~er n (TV) televidente m & f. ~finder n visor m. ~point n punto m de vista

vigil|ance n vigilancia f. ~ant adj vigilante

vigo|rous /'vɪgərəs/ adj enérgico; (growth) vigoroso. ~ur /'vɪgə(r)/ n vigor m

vile /vaɪl/ adj (base) vil; (food) asqueroso; (weather, temper) horrible

village /'vɪlɪdʒ/ n pueblo m; (small) aldea f. ~r n vecino m del pueblo; (of small village) aldeano m

villain /'vɪlən/ n maleante m & f; (in story etc) villano m

V

vindicate /'vɪndɪkeɪt/ vt justificar

vindictive /vɪn'dɪktɪv/ adj vengativo

vine /vaɪn/ n (on ground) vid f; (climbing) parra f

vinegar /'vɪnɪɡə(r)/ n vinagre m

vineyard /'vɪnjəd/ n viña f

vintage /'vɪntɪdʒ/ n (year) cosecha f. ● adj (wine) añejo; (car) de época

vinyl /'vaɪnɪl/ n vinilo m

viola /vɪ'əʊlə/ n viola f

violat|e /'vaɪəleɪt/ vt violar. ~ion /-'leɪʃn/ n violación f

violen|ce /'vaɪələns/ n violencia f. ~t adj violento. ~tly adv violentamente

violet /'vaɪələt/ adj & n violeta (f); (colour) violeta (m)

violin /'vaɪəlɪn/ n violín m. ~ist n violinista m & f

VIP /viːɑːr'piː/ abbr (= very important person) VIP m

viper /'vaɪpə(r)/ n víbora f

virgin /'vɜːdʒɪn/ adj & n virgen (f)

Virgo /'vɜːɡəʊ/ n Virgo f

virile /'vɪraɪl/ adj viril

virtual /'vɜːtʃʊəl/ adj. traffic is at a ~ standstill el tráfico está prácticamente paralizado. ~ reality n realidad f virtual. ~ly adv prácticamente

virtue /'vɜːtʃuː/ n virtud f. by ~ of en virtud de

virtuous /'vɜːtʃʊəs/ adj virtuoso

virulent /'vɪrʊlənt/ adj virulento

virus /'vaɪərəs/ n (pl -uses) virus m

visa /'viːzə/ n visado m, visa f (LAm)

vise /vaɪs/ n (Amer) torno m de banco

visib|ility /vɪzɪ'bɪlətɪ/ n visibilidad f. ~le /'vɪzɪbl/ adj visible; (sign, improvement) evidente

vision /'vɪʒn/ n visión f; (sight) vista f

visit /'vɪzɪt/ vt visitar; hacer una visita a (person). ● vi hacer visitas. ~ with s.o. (Amer) ir a ver a uno. ● n visita f. pay s.o. a ~ hacerle una visita a uno. ~or n visitante m & f; (guest) visita f

visor /'vaɪzə(r)/ n visera f

visual /'vɪʒjʊəl/ adj visual. ~ize vt imaginar(se); (foresee) prever

vital /'vaɪtl/ adj (essential) esencial; (factor) de vital importancia; (organ) vital. ~ity /vaɪ'tælətɪ/ n vitalidad f

vitamin /'vɪtəmɪn/ n vitamina f.

vivacious /vɪ'veɪʃəs/ adj vivaz

vivid /'vɪvɪd/ adj vivo. ~ly adv intensamente; (describe) gráficamente

vivisection /vɪvɪ'sekʃn/ n vivisección f

vocabulary /və'kæbjʊlərɪ/ n vocabulario m

vocal /'vəʊkl/ adj vocal. ~ist n cantante m & f

vocation /vəʊ'keɪʃn/ n vocación f. ~al adj profesional

vociferous /və'sɪfərəs/ adj vociferador

vogue /vəʊɡ/ n moda f, boga f

voice /vɔɪs/ n voz f. ● vt expresar

void /vɔɪd/ adj (not valid) nulo. ● n vacío m

volatile /'vɒlətaɪl/ adj volátil; (person) imprevisible

volcan|ic /vɒl'kænɪk/ adj volcánico. ~o /vɒl'keɪnəʊ/ n (pl -oes) volcán m

volley /'vɒlɪ/ n (pl -eys) (of gunfire) descarga f cerrada; (sport) volea f. ~ball n vóleibol m

volt /vəʊlt/ n voltio m. ~age /-ɪdʒ/ n voltaje m

volume /'vɒljuːm/ n volumen m; (book) tomo m

voluntar|ily /'vɒləntərəlɪ/ adv voluntariamente. ~y adj voluntario; (organization) de beneficencia

volunteer /vɒlən'tɪə(r)/ n voluntario m. ● vt ofrecer. ● vi. ~ (to) ofrecerse (a)

vomit /'vɒmɪt/ vt/i vomitar. ● n vómito m

voracious /və'reɪʃəs/ adj voraz

vot|e /vəʊt/ n voto m; (right) derecho m al voto; (act) votación f. ● vi votar. ~er n votante m & f. ~ing n votación f

vouch /vaʊtʃ/ vi. ~ for s.o. responder por uno. ~er /-ə(r)/ n vale m

vow /vaʊ/ n voto m. ● vi jurar

vowel /'vaʊəl/ n vocal f

voyage /'vɔɪɪdʒ/ n viaje m; (by sea) travesía f

vulgar /'vʌlɡə(r)/ adj (coarse) grosero, vulgar; (tasteless) de mal gusto. ~ity /-'ɡærətɪ/ n vulgaridad f

vulnerable /'vʌlnərəbl/ adj vulnerable

V

vulture /'vʌltʃə(r)/ n buitre m

vying /'vaɪɪŋ/ see **VIE**

Ww

W abbr (= **West**) O

wad /wɒd/ n (of notes) fajo m; (tied together) lío m; (papers) montón m

waddle /'wɒdl/ vi contonearse

wade /weɪd/ vi caminar (por el agua etc)

wafer /'weɪfə(r)/ n galleta f de barquillo

waffle /'wɒfl/ n 🇬🇧 palabrería f ● vi 🇬🇧 divagar; (in essay, exam) meter paja 🇬🇧. ● n (Culin) gofre m, wafle m (LAm)

waft /wɒft/ vi flotar

wag /wæg/ vt (pt **wagged**) menear. ● vi menearse

wage /weɪdʒ/ n sueldo m. ~s npl salario m, sueldo m. ~r n apuesta f

waggle /'wægl/ vt menear. ● vi menearse

wagon /'wægən/ n carro m; (Rail) vagón m; (Amer, delivery truck) furgoneta f de reparto

wail /weɪl/ vi llorar

waist /weɪst/ n cintura f. ~coat n chaleco m. ~line n cintura f

wait /weɪt/ vi esperar; (at table) servir. ~ **for** esperar. ~ **on s.o.** atender a uno. ● vt (await) esperar (chance, turn). ~ **table** (Amer) servir a la mesa. **I can't ~ to see him** me muero de ganas de verlo. ● n espera f. **lie in** ~ acechar

waiter /'weɪtə(r)/ n camarero m, mesero m (LAm)

wait ~ing-list n lista f de espera. ~**ing-room** n sala f de espera

waitress /'weɪtrɪs/ n camarera f, mesera f (LAm)

waive /weɪv/ vt renunciar a

wake /weɪk/ vt (pt **woke**, pp **woken**) despertar. ● vi despertarse. ● n (Naut) estela f. **in the ~ of** como resultado de. □ ~ **up** vt despertar. vi despertarse

Wales /weɪlz/ n (el país de) Gales

walk /wɔːk/ vi andar, caminar; (not ride) ir a pie; (stroll) pasear. ● vt andar por (streets); llevar de paseo (dog). ● n paseo m; (long) caminata f; (gait) manera f de andar. □ ~ **out** vi salir; (workers) declararse en huelga. □ ~ **out on** vt abandonar. ~**er** n excursionista m & f

walkie-talkie /wɔːkɪ'tɔːkɪ/ n walkie-talkie m

walk ~ing-stick n bastón m. **W~man** /-mən/ n Walkman m (P). ~**-out** n retirada en señal de protesta; (strike) abandono m del trabajo

wall /wɔːl/ n (interior) pared f; (exterior) muro m

> **Wall Street** Una calle en Manhattan, Nueva York, donde se encuentra la Bolsa neoyorquina y las sedes de muchas instituciones financieras. Cuando se habla de Wall Street, a menudo se está refiriendo a esas instituciones.

wallet /'wɒlɪt/ n cartera f, billetera f

wallop /'wɒləp/ vt (pt **walloped**) 🇬🇧 darle un golpazo a.

wallow /'wɒləʊ/ vi revolcarse

wallpaper /'wɔːlpeɪpə(r)/ n papel m pintado

walnut /'wɔːlnʌt/ n nuez f; (tree) nogal m

walrus /'wɔːlrəs/ n morsa f

waltz /wɔːls/ n vals m. ● vi valsar

wand /wɒnd/ n varita f (mágica)

wander /'wɒndə(r)/ vi vagar; (stroll) pasear; (digress) divagar. ● n vuelta f, paseo m. ~**er** n trotamundos m

wane /weɪn/ vi (moon) menguar; (interest) decaer. ● n. **be on the ~** (popularity) estar decayendo

wangle /wæŋgl/ vt 🇬🇧 agenciarse

want /wɒnt/ vt querer; (need) necesitar. ● vi. ~ **for** carecer de. ● n necesidad f; (lack) falta f. ~**ed** adj (criminal) buscado

war /wɔː(r)/ n guerra f. **at** ~ en guerra

warble /'wɔːbl/ vi trinar, gorjear

ward /wɔːd/ n (in hospital) sala f; (child) pupilo m. □ ~ **off** vt conjurar (danger); rechazar (attack)

warden /'wɔːdn/ n guarda m

warder /'wɔːdə(r)/ n celador m (de una cárcel)

wardrobe /'wɔːdrəʊb/ n armario m; (clothes) guardarropa f, vestuario m

warehouse /'weəhaʊs/ n depósito m, almacén m

wares /weəz/ npl mercancía(s) f(pl)

war ~fare n guerra f. **~head** n cabeza f, ojiva f

warm /wɔːm/ adj (-er, -est) (water, day) tibio, templado; (room) caliente; (climate, wind) cálido; (clothes) de abrigo; (welcome) caluroso. **be ~** (person) tener calor. **it's ~ today** hoy hace calor. ● vt. **~ (up)** calentar (room); recalentar (food); (fig) animar. ● vi. **~ (up)** calentarse; (fig) animarse. **~-blooded** /-'blʌdɪd/ adj de sangre caliente. **~ly** adv (heartily) calurosamente. **~th** n calor m; (of colour, atmosphere) calidez f

warn /wɔːn/ vt advertir. **~ing** n advertencia f; (notice) aviso m

warp /wɔːp/ vt alabear. **~ed** /'wɔːpt/ adj (wood) alabeado; (mind) retorcido

warrant /'wɒrənt/ n orden f judicial; (search ~) orden f de registro; (for arrest) orden f de arresto. ● vt justificar. **~y** n garantía f

warrior /'wɒrɪə(r)/ n guerrero m

warship /'wɔːʃɪp/ n buque m de guerra

wart /wɔːt/ n verruga f

wartime /'wɔːtaɪm/ n tiempo m de guerra

wary /'weərɪ/ adj (-ier, -iest) cauteloso. **be ~ of** recelar de

was /wəz, wɒz/ see BE

wash /wɒʃ/ vt lavar; fregar, lavar (LAm) (floor). **~ one's face** lavarse la cara. ● vi lavarse. ● n (in washing machine) lavado m. **have a ~** lavarse. **I gave the car a ~** lavé el coche. □ **~ out** vt (clean) lavar; (rinse) enjuagar. □ **~ up** vi fregar los platos, lavar los trastes (Mex); (Amer, wash face and hands) lavarse. **~able** adj lavable. **~basin**, **~bowl** (Amer) n lavabo m. **~er** n arandela f. **~ing** n lavado m; (dirty clothes) ropa f para lavar; (wet clothes)

ropa f lavada. **do the ~ing** lavar la ropa, hacer la colada. **~ing-machine** n máquina f de lavar, lavadora f. **~ing-powder** n jabón m en polvo. **~ing-up** n. **do the ~ing-up** lavar los platos, fregar (los platos). **~ing-up liquid** n lavavajillas m. **~out** n ⊡ desastre m. **~room** n (Amer) baños mpl, servicios mpl

wasp /wɒsp/ n avispa f

waste /weɪst/ ● adj (matter) de desecho; (land) yermo; (uncultivated) baldío. ● n (of materials) desperdicio m; (of time) pérdida f; (refuse) residuos mpl. ● vt despilfarrar (electricity, money); desperdiciar (talent, effort); perder (time). ● vi. **~-disposal unit** n trituradora f de desperdicios. **~ful** adj poco económico; (person) despilfarrador. **~-paper basket** n papelera f

watch /wɒtʃ/ vt mirar; observar (person, expression); ver (TV); (keep an eye on) vigilar; (take heed) tener cuidado con. ● vi mirar. ● n (observation) vigilancia f; (period of duty) guardia f; (timepiece) reloj m. **~ out** vi (be careful) tener cuidado; (look carefully) estarse atento. **~dog** n perro m guardián. **~man** /-mən/ n (pl -men) vigilante m.

water /'wɔːtə(r)/ n agua f. ● vt regar (plants etc). ● vi (eyes) llorar. **make s.o.'s mouth ~** hacérsele la boca agua, hacérsele agua la boca (LAm). **~ down** vt diluir; aguar (wine). **~-colour** n acuarela f. **~cress** n berro m. **~fall** n cascada f; (large) catarata f. **~ing-can** n regadera f. **~ lily** n nenúfar m. **~logged** /-lɒgd/ adj anegado; (shoes) empapado. **~proof** adj impermeable; (watch) sumergible. **~-skiing** n esquí m acuático. **~tight** adj hermético; (boat) estanco; (argument) irrebatible. **~way** n canal m navegable. **~y** adj acuoso; (eyes) lloroso

watt /wɒt/ n vatio m

wave /weɪv/ n onda f; (of hand) señal f; (fig) oleada f. ● vt agitar; (curl) ondular (hair). ● vi (signal) hacer señales con la mano; ondear (flag). **~band** n banda f de frecuencia. **~length** n longitud f de onda

W

waver /'weɪvə(r)/ vi (be indecisive) vacilar; (falter) flaquear

wavy /'weɪvɪ/ adj (-ier, -iest) ondulado

wax /wæks/ n cera f. ●vi (moon) crecer. **~work** n figura f de cera. **~works** npl museo m de cera

way /weɪ/ n (route) camino m; (manner) manera f, forma f, modo m; (direction) dirección f; (habit) costumbre f. **it's a long ~ from here** queda muy lejos de aquí. **be in the ~** estorbar. **by the ~** a propósito. **either ~** de cualquier manera. **give ~** (collapse) ceder, romperse; (Auto) ceder el paso. **in a ~** en cierta manera. **in some ~s** en ciertos modos. **make ~** dejar paso a. **no ~!** ¡ni hablar! **on my ~ to** de camino a. **out of the ~** remoto; (extraordinary) fuera de lo común. **that ~** por allí. **this ~** por aquí. **~ in** n entrada f. **~lay** /weɪ'leɪ/ vt (pt -laid) abordar. **~ out** n salida f. **~-out** adj ultramoderno, original. **~s** npl costumbres fpl

we /wiː/ pron nosotros m, nosotras f

weak /wiːk/ adj (-er, -est) débil; (structure) poco sólido; (performance, student) flojo; (coffee) poco cargado; (solution) diluido; (beer) suave; (pej) aguado. **~en** vt debilitar. ●vi (resolve) flaquear. **~ling** n alfeñique m. **~ness** n debilidad f

wealth /welθ/ n riqueza f. **~y** adj (-ier, -iest) rico

weapon /'wepən/ n arma f. **~s of mass destruction** armas de destrucción masiva

wear /weə(r)/ vt (pt wore, pp worn) llevar; vestirse de (black, red, etc); (usually) usar. **I've got nothing to ~** no tengo nada que ponerme. ●vi (through use) gastarse; (last) durar. ●n uso m; (damage) desgaste m; **and tear** desgaste m natural. □ **~ out** vt gastar; (tire) agotar. vi gastarse

weary /'wɪərɪ/ adj (-ier, -iest) cansado. ●vt cansar. ●vi cansarse. **~ of** cansarse de

weather /'weðə(r)/ n tiempo m. **what's the ~ like?** ¿qué tiempo hace?. **the ~ was bad** hizo mal tiempo. **be under the ~** 🅸 no andar muy bien 🅸. ●vt (survive) sobrellevar.

~-beaten adj curtido. **~ forecast** n pronóstico m del tiempo. **~-vane** n veleta f

weave /wiːv/ vt (pt wove, pp woven) tejer; entretejer (threads). **~ one's way** abrirse paso. ●vi (person) zigzaguear; (road) serpentear. **~r** n tejedor m

web /web/ n (of spider) telaraña f; (of intrigue) red f. **~ page** n página web. **~ site** n sitio web m

wed /wed/ vt (pt wedded) casarse con. ●vi casarse.

we'd /wiːd//wɪəd/ = **we had**, **we would**

wedding /'wedɪŋ/ n boda f, casamiento m. **~-cake** n pastel m de boda. **~-ring** n anillo m de boda

wedge /wedʒ/ n cuña f

Wednesday /'wenzdeɪ/ n miércoles m

wee /wiː/ adj 🅸 pequeñito. ●n. **have a ~** 🅸 hacer pis 🅸

weed /wiːd/ n mala hierba f. ●vt desherbar. □ **~ out** vt eliminar. **~killer** n herbicida m. **~y** adj (person) enclenque; (Amer, lanky) larguirucho 🅸

week /wiːk/ n semana f. **~day** n día m de semana. **~end** n fin m de semana. **~ly** adj semanal. ●n semanario m. ●adv semanalmente

weep /wiːp/ vi (pt wept) llorar

weigh /weɪ/ vt/i pesar. **~ anchor** levar anclas. □ **~ down** vt (fig) oprimir. □ **~ up** vt pesar; (fig) considerar

weight /weɪt/ n peso m; (sport) pesa f. **put on ~** engordar. **lose ~** adelgazar. **~-lifting** n halterofilia f, levantamiento m de pesos

weir /wɪə(r)/ n presa f

weird /wɪəd/ adj (-er, -est) raro, extraño; (unearthly) misterioso

welcom|e /'welkəm/ adj bienvenido. **you're ~e!** (after thank you) ¡de nada! ●n bienvenida f; (reception) acogida f. ●vt dar la bienvenida a; (appreciate) alegrarse de. **~ing** adj acogedor

weld /weld/ vt soldar. ●n soldadura f. **~er** n soldador m

welfare /'welfeə(r)/ n bienestar m; (aid) asistencia f social. **W~ State** n estado m benefactor

W

well /wel/ *adv* (**better**, **best**) bien. ~ **done!** ¡muy bien!, ¡bravo! **as** ~ también. **as** ~ **as** además de. **we may as** ~ **go tomorrow** más vale que vayamos mañana. **do** ~ (*succeed*) tener éxito. **very** ~ muy bien. ● *adj* bien. **I'm very** ~ estoy muy bien. ● *int* (*introducing, continuing sentence*) bueno; (*surprise*) ¡vaya!; (*indignation, resignation*) bueno. ~ **I never!** ¡no me digas! ● *n* pozo *m*

we'll /wiːl//wɪəl/ = **we will**

well ~**-behaved** /-bɪˈheɪvd/ *adj* que se porta bien, bueno. ~**-educated** /-ˈedjʊkeɪtɪd/ *adj* culto.

wellington (boot) /ˈwelɪŋtən/ *n* bota *f* de goma *or* de agua; (*Amer, short boot*) botín *m*

well ~**-known** /-ˈnəʊn/ *adj* conocido. ~ **off** *adj* adinerado. ~**-stocked** /-ˈstɒkt/ *adj* bien provisto. ~**-to-do** /-təˈduː/ *adj* adinerado

Welsh /welʃ/ *adj* & *n* galés (*m*). **the** ~ *n* los galeses

> **Welsh Assembly** La Asamblea Nacional de Gales empezó a funcionar, en Cardiff, en 1999. Tiene poderes limitados, por lo que no puede imponer impuestos. Consta de 60 miembros o *AMs* (*Assembly Members*); 40 elegidos directamente y el resto, de las listas regionales, mediante el sistema de representación proporcional.

went /went/ *see* **GO**

wept /wept/ *see* **WEEP**

were /wɜː(r), wə(r)/ *see* **BE**

we're /wɪə(r)/ = **we are**

west /west/ *n* oeste *m*. **the W**~ el Occidente *m*. ● *adj* oeste; (*wind*) del oeste. ● *adv* (*go*) hacia el oeste, al oeste. **it's** ~ **of York** está al oeste de York. ~**erly** /-əlɪ/ *adj* (*wind*) del oeste. ~**ern** /-ən/ *adj* occidental. ● *n* (*film*) película *f* del Oeste. ~**erner** /-ən/ *adj* occidental *m* & *f*. **W**~ **Indian** *adj* & *n* antillano (*m*). **W**~ **Indies** *npl* Antillas *fpl*. ~**ward(s)** /-wəd(z)/.

wet /wet/ *adj* (**wetter**, **wettest**) mojado; (*rainy*) lluvioso; (*fam, person*) soso. '~ **paint**' 'pintura fresca'. **get**

~ mojarse. **he got his feet** ~ se mojó los pies. ● *vt* (*pt* **wetted**) mojar; (*dampen*) humedecer. ~ **o.s.** orinarse. ~**back** *n* espalda *f* mojada. ~ **blanket** *n* aguafiestas *m* & *f*. ~ **suit** *n* traje *m* de neopreno

we've /wiːv/ = **we have**

whack /wæk/ *vt* 🛈 golpear. ● *n* 🛈 golpe *m*.

whale /weɪl/ *n* ballena *f*. **we had a** ~ **of a time** 🛈 lo pasamos bomba 🛈

wham /wæm/ *int* ¡zas!

wharf /wɔːf/ *n* (*pl* **wharves** *or* **wharfs**) muelle *m*

what /wɒt/

● *adjective*

····➤ (*in questions*) qué. ~ **perfume are you wearing?** ¿qué perfume llevas?. ~ **colour are the walls?** ¿de qué color son las paredes?

····➤ (*in exclamations*) qué. ~ **a beautiful house!** ¡qué casa más linda!. ~ **a lot of people!** ¡cuánta gente!

····➤ (*in indirect speech*) qué. **I'll ask him** ~ **bus to take** le preguntaré qué autobús hay que tomar. **do you know** ~ **time it leaves?** ¿sabes a qué hora sale?

● *pronoun*

····➤ (*in questions*) qué. ~ **is it?** ¿qué es? ~ **for?** ¿para qué?. ~**'s the problem?** ¿cuál es el problema? ~**'s he like?** ¿cómo es? **what?** (*say that again*) ¿cómo?, ¿qué?

····➤ (*in indirect questions*) qué. **I didn't know** ~ **to do** no sabía qué hacer

····➤ (*relative*) lo que. **I did** ~ **I could** hice lo que pude. ~ **I need is a new car** lo que necesito es un coche nuevo

····➤ (*in phrases*) ~ **about me?** ¿y yo qué? ~ **if she doesn't come?** ¿y si no viene?

whatever /wɒtˈevə(r)/ *adj* cualquiera. ● *pron* (todo) lo que, cualquier cosa que

whatsoever /wɒtsəʊˈevə(r)/ *adj* & *pron* = **whatever**

wheat /wiːt/ n trigo m

wheel /wiːl/ n rueda f. **at the** ~ al volante. ● vt empujar (bicycle etc); llevar (en silla de ruedas etc) (person). ~**barrow** n carretilla f. ~**chair** n silla f de ruedas

wheeze /wiːz/ vi respirar con dificultad

when /wen/ adv cuándo. ● conj cuando. ~**ever** /-'evə(r)/ adv (every time that) cada vez que, siempre que; (at whatever time) **we'll go** ~**ever you're ready** saldremos cuando estés listo

where /weə(r)/ adv & conj donde; (interrogative) dónde. ~ **are you going?** ¿adónde vas? ~ **are you from?** ¿de dónde eres?. ~**abouts** /-əbaʊts/ adv en qué parte. ● n paradero m. ~**as** /-'æz/ conj por cuanto; (in contrast) mientras (que). ~**ver** /weər'evə(r)/ adv (in questions) dónde; (no matter where) en cualquier parte. ● conj donde (+ subjunctive), dondequiera (+ subjunctive)

whet /wet/ vt (pt **whetted**) abrir (appetite)

whether /'weðə(r)/ conj si. **I don't know** ~ **she will like it** no sé si le gustará. ~ **you like it or not** te guste o no te guste

which /wɪtʃ/ adj (in questions) (sing) qué, cuál; (pl) qué, cuáles. ~ **one** cuál. ~ **one of you** cuál de ustedes. ● pron (in questions) (sing) cuál; (pl) cuáles; (relative) que; (object) el cual, la cual, lo cual, los cuales, las cuales. ~**ever** /-'evə(r)/ adj cualquier. ● pron cualquiera que, el que, la que; (in questions) cuál; (pl) cuáles

while /waɪl/ n rato m. **a** ~ **ago** hace un rato. ● conj mientras; (although) aunque. □ ~ **away** vt pasar (time)

whilst /waɪlst/ conj see **WHILE**

whim /wɪm/ n capricho m

whimper /'wɪmpə(r)/ vi gimotear. ● n quejido m

whine /waɪn/ vi (person) gemir; (child) lloriquear; (dog) aullar

whip /wɪp/ n látigo m; (for punishment) azote m. ● vt (pt **whipped** /wɪpt/) fustigar, pegarle a (con la fusta) (horse); azotar (person); (Culin) batir

whirl /wɜːl/ vi girar rápidamente. ~**pool** n remolino m. ~**wind** n torbellino m

whirr /wɜː(r)/ n zumbido m. ● vi zumbar

whisk /wɪsk/ vt (Culin) batir. ● n (Culin) batidor m. ~ **away** llevarse

whisker /'wɪskə(r)/ n pelo m. ~**s** npl (of cat etc) bigotes mpl

whisky /'wɪski/ n whisky m, güisqui m

whisper /'wɪspə(r)/ vt susurrar. ● vi cuchichear. ● n susurro m

whistle /'wɪsl/ n silbido m; (loud) chiflado m; (instrument) silbato m, pito m. ● vi silbar; (loudly) chiflar

white /waɪt/ adj (~r, -est) blanco. **go** ~ ponerse pálido. ● n blanco; (of egg) clara f. ~ **coffee** n café m con leche. ~**-collar worker** n empleado m de oficina. ~ **elephant** n objeto m inútil y costoso. ~**-hot** adj (metal) al rojo blanco. ~ **lie** n mentirijilla f. ~**n** vt/i blanquear. ~**wash** n cal f; (cover-up) tapadera f 🔢. ● vt blanquear, encalar

Whitsun /'wɪtsn/ n Pentecostés m

whiz /wɪz/ vi (pt **whizzed**). ~ **by**, ~ **past** pasar zumbando. ~**-kid** n 🔢 lince m 🔢

who /huː/ pron (in questions) quién; (pl) quiénes; (as relative) que; **the girl** ~ **lives there** la chica que vive allí. **those** ~ **can't come tomorrow** los que no puedan venir mañana. ~**ever** /huː'evə(r)/ pron quienquiera que; (interrogative) quién

whole /həʊl/ adj. **the** ~ **country** todo el país. **there's a** ~ **bottle left** queda una botella entera. ● n todo m, conjunto m; (total) total m. **on the** ~ en general. ~**-hearted** /-'hɑːtɪd/ adj (support) incondicional; (approval) sin reservar. ~**meal** adj integral. ~**sale** n venta f al por mayor. ● adj & adv al por mayor. ~**some** /-səm/ adj sano

wholly /'həʊlɪ/ adv completamente

whom /huːm/ pron que, a quien; (in questions) a quién

whooping cough /'huːpɪŋ/ n tos f convulsa

whore /hɔː(r)/ n puta f

whose /huːz/ pron de quién; (pl) de quiénes. ● adj (in questions) de quién;

W

(*pl*) de quiénes; (*relative*) cuyo; (*pl*) cuyos

why /waɪ/ *adv* por qué. ∼ **not?** ¿por qué no? **that's ∼ I couldn't go** por eso no pude ir. ● *int* ¡vaya!

wick /wɪk/ *n* mecha *f*

wicked /'wɪkɪd/ *adj* malo; (*mischievous*) travieso; (*fam, very bad*) malísimo

wicker /'wɪkə(r)/ *n* mimbre *m & f*. ● *adj* de mimbre. ∼**work** *n* artículos *mpl* de mimbre

wicket /'wɪkɪt/ *n* (*cricket*) rastrillo *m*

wide /waɪd/ *adj* (**-er, -est**) ancho; (*range, experience*) amplio; (*off target*) desviado. **it's four metres ∼** tiene cuatro metros de ancho. ● *adv*. **open ∼!** abra bien la boca. ∼ **awake** *adj* completamente despierto; (*fig*) despabilado. **I left the door ∼ open** dejé la puerta abierta de par en par. ∼**ly** *adv* extensamente; (*believed*) generalmente; (*different*) muy. ∼**n** *vt* ensanchar. ● *vi* ensancharse. ∼**spread** *adj* extendido; (*fig*) difundido

widow /'wɪdəʊ/ *n* viuda *f*. ∼**er** *n* viudo *m*.

width /wɪdθ/ *n* anchura *f*. **in ∼** de ancho

wield /wiːld/ *vt* manejar; ejercer (*power*)

wife /waɪf/ *n* (*pl* **wives**) mujer *f*, esposa *f*

wig /wɪg/ *n* peluca *f*

wiggle /'wɪgl/ *vt* menear. ● *vi* menearse

wild /waɪld/ *adj* (**-er, -est**) (*animal*) salvaje; (*flower*) silvestre; (*country*) agreste; (*enraged*) furioso; (*idea*) extravagante; (*with joy*) loco. **a ∼ guess** una conjetura hecha totalmente al azar. **I'm not ∼ about the idea** la idea no me enloquece. ● *adv* en estado salvaje. **run ∼** (*children*) criarse como salvajes. ∼**s** *npl* regiones *fpl* salvajes. ∼**erness** /'wɪldənɪs/ *n* páramo *m*. ∼**fire** *n*. **spread like ∼fire** correr como un reguero de pólvora. ∼**-goose chase** *n* empresa *f* inútil. ∼**life** *n* fauna *f*. ∼**ly** *adv* violentamente; (*fig*) locamente

will /wɪl/
● *auxiliary verb*

> past **would**; contracted forms
> **I'll, you'll, etc = I will, you**
> **will, etc.; won't = will not**

┈┈➤ (*talking about the future*)

> **!** The Spanish future tense is not always the first option for translating the English future tense. The present tense of *ir + a + verb* is commonly used instead, particularly in Latin American countries. **he'll be here on Tuesday** estará el martes, va a estar el martes; **she won't agree** no va a aceptar, no aceptará

┈┈➤ (*in invitations and requests*) ∼ **you have some wine?** ¿quieres (un poco de) vino? **you'll stay for dinner, won't you?** te quedas a cenar, ¿no?

┈┈➤ (*in tag questions*) **you ∼ be back soon, won't you?** vas a volver pronto, ¿no?

┈┈➤ (*in short answers*) **will it be ready by Monday? - yes, it ∼** ¿estará listo para el lunes? - sí

● *noun*
┈┈➤ (*mental power*) voluntad *f*
┈┈➤ (*document*) testamento *m*

willing /'wɪlɪŋ/ *adj* complaciente. ∼ **to** dispuesto a. ∼**ly** *adv* de buena gana

willow /'wɪləʊ/ *n* sauce *m*

will-power /'wɪlpaʊə(r)/ *n* fuerza *f* de voluntad

wilt /wɪlt/ *vi* marchitarse

win /wɪn/ *vt* (*pt* **won**, *pres p* **winning**) ganar; (*achieve, obtain*) conseguir. ● *vi* ganar. ● *n* victoria *f*. □ ∼ **over** *vt* ganarse a

wince /wɪns/ *vi* hacer una mueca de dolor

winch /wɪntʃ/ *n* cabrestante *m*. ● *vt* levantar con un cabrestante

wind¹ /wɪnd/ *n* viento *m*; (*in stomach*) gases *mpl*. ∼ **instrument** instrumento *m* de viento. ● *vt* dejar sin aliento

wind² /waɪnd/ vt (pt **wound**) (wrap around) enrollar; dar cuerda a (clock etc). ● vi (road etc) serpentear. □ ~ **up** vt dar cuerda a (watch, clock); (fig) terminar, concluir

winding /ˈwaɪndɪŋ/ adj tortuoso

windmill /ˈwɪndmɪl/ n molino m (de viento)

window /ˈwɪndəʊ/ n ventana f; (in shop) escaparate m, vitrina f (LAm), vidriera f (LAm), aparador m (Mex); (of vehicle, booking-office) ventanilla f; (Comp) ventana f, window m. ~ **box** n jardinera f. ~**-shop** vi mirar los escaparates. ~**sill** n alféizar m or repisa f de la ventana

wine /waɪn/ n vino m. ~**-cellar** n bodega f. ~**-glass** n copa f de vino. ~**-growing** n vinicultura f. ● adj vinícola. ~ **list** n lista f de vinos. ~**-tasting** n cata f de vinos

wing /wɪŋ/ n ala f; (Auto) aleta f. **under one's** ~ bajo la protección de uno. ~**er** n (Sport) ala m & f. ~**s** npl (in theatre) bastidores mpl

wink /wɪŋk/ vi guiñar el ojo; (light etc) centellear. ● n guiño m. **not to sleep a** ~ no pegar ojo

win ~**ner** n ganador m. ~**ning-post** n poste m de llegada. ~**nings** npl ganancias fpl

wint|er /ˈwɪntə(r)/ n invierno m. ● vi invernar. ~**ry** adj invernal

wipe /waɪp/ vt limpiar, pasarle un trapo a; (dry) secar. ~ **one's nose** limpiarse la nariz. ● n. **give sth a** ~ limpiar algo, pasarle un trapo a algo. □ ~ **out** vt (cancel) cancelar; (destroy) destruir; (obliterate) borrar. □ ~ **up** vt limpiar

wir|e /ˈwaɪə(r)/ n alambre m; (Elec) cable m. ~**ing** n instalación f eléctrica

wisdom /ˈwɪzdəm/ n sabiduría f. ~ **tooth** n muela f del juicio

wise /waɪz/ adj (-er, -est) sabio; (sensible) prudente; (decision, choice) acertado. ~**ly** adv sabiamente; (sensibly) prudentemente

wish /wɪʃ/ n deseo m; (greeting) saludo m. **make a** ~ pedir un deseo. **best** ~**es, John** (in letters) saludos de John, un abrazo de John. ● vt desear. ~ **s.o. well** desear buena suerte a

uno. **I** ~ **I were rich** ¡ojalá fuera rico! **he** ~**ed he hadn't told her** lamentó habérselo dicho. ~**ful thinking** n ilusiones fpl

wistful /ˈwɪstfl/ adj melancólico

wit /wɪt/ n gracia f; (intelligence) ingenio m. **be at one's** ~**s' end** no saber más qué hacer

witch /wɪtʃ/ n bruja f. ~**craft** n brujería f.

with /wɪð/ prep con; (cause, having) de. **come** ~ **me** ven conmigo. **take it** ~ **you** llévalo contigo. (formal) llévelo consigo. **the man** ~ **the beard** el hombre de la barba. **trembling** ~ **fear** temblando de miedo

withdraw /wɪðˈdrɔː/ vt (pt **withdrew**, pp **withdrawn**) retirar. ● vi apartarse. ~**al** n retirada f. ~**n** adj (person) retraído

wither /ˈwɪðə(r)/ vi marchitarse

withhold /wɪðˈhəʊld/ vt (pt **withheld**) retener; (conceal) ocultar (**from** a)

within /wɪðˈɪn/ prep dentro de. ● adv dentro. ~ **sight** a la vista

without /wɪðˈaʊt/ prep sin. ~ **paying** sin pagar

withstand /wɪðˈstænd/ vt (pt **-stood**) resistir

witness /ˈwɪtnɪs/ n testigo m; (proof) testimonio m. ● vt presenciar; atestiguar (signature). ~**-box** n tribuna f de los testigos

witt|icism /ˈwɪtɪsɪzəm/ n ocurrencia f. ~**y** /ˈwɪtɪ/ adj (-ier, -iest) gracioso

wives /waɪvz/ see **WIFE**

wizard /ˈwɪzəd/ n hechicero m

wizened /ˈwɪznd/ adj arrugado

wobbl|e /ˈwɒbl/ vi (chair) tambalearse; (bicycle) bambolearse; (voice, jelly, hand) temblar. ~**y** adj (chair etc) cojo

woe /wəʊ/ n aflicción f

woke /wəʊk/, **woken** /ˈwəʊkən/ see **WAKE**

wolf /wʊlf/ n (pl **wolves** /wʊlvz/) lobo m

woman /ˈwʊmən/ n (pl **women**) mujer f

womb /wuːm/ n matriz f

women /ˈwɪmɪn/ npl see **WOMAN**

won /wʌn/ see **WIN**

W

wonder /'wʌndə(r)/ n maravilla f; (bewilderment) asombro m. **no ~** no es de extrañarse (**that** que). ● vt (ask oneself) preguntarse. **I ~ whose book this is** me pregunto de quién será este libro; (in polite requests) **I ~ if you could help me?** ¿me podría ayudar? **~ful** adj maravilloso. **~fully** adv maravillosamente

won't /wəʊnt/ = **will not**

wood /wʊd/ n madera f; (for burning) leña f; (area) bosque m. **~ed** adj poblado de árboles, boscoso. **~en** adj de madera. **~land** n bosque m. **~wind** /-wɪnd/ n instrumentos mpl de viento de madera. **~work** n carpintería f; (in room etc) maderaje m. **~worm** n carcoma f. **~y** adj leñoso

wool /wʊl/ n lana f. **pull the ~ over s.o.'s eyes** engañar a uno. **~len** adj de lana. **~ly** adj (-ier, -iest) de lana; (unclear) vago. ● n jersey m

word /wɜːd/ n palabra f; (news) noticia f. **by ~ of mouth** de palabra. **I didn't say a ~** yo no dije nada. **in other ~s** es decir. ● vt expresar. **~ing** n redacción f; (of question) formulación f. **~ processor** n procesador m de textos. **~y** adj prolijo

wore /wɔː(r)/ see **WEAR**

work /wɜːk/ n trabajo m; (arts) obra f. **be out of ~** estar sin trabajo, estar desocupado. ● vt hacer trabajar; manejar (machine). ● vi trabajar; (machine) funcionar; (student) estudiar; (drug etc) surtir efecto. □ **~ off** vt desahogar. □ **~ out** vt resolver (problem); (calculate) calcular; (understand) entender. ● vi (succeed) salir bien; (Sport) entrenarse. □ **~ up** vt. **get ~ed up** exaltarse. **~able** adj (project, solution) factible. **~er** n trabajador m; (manual) obrero m; (in office, bank) empleado m. **~ing** adj (day) laborable; (clothes etc) de trabajo. **in ~ing order** en estado de funcionamiento. **~ing class** n clase f obrera. **~ing-class** adj de la clase obrera. **~man** /-mən/ n (pl -men) obrero m. **~manship** n destreza f. **~s** npl (building) fábrica f; (Mec) mecanismo m. **~shop** n taller m

world /wɜːld/ n mundo m. **out of this ~** maravilloso. ● adj mundial. **W~**

Cup n. **the W~ Cup** la Copa del Mundo. **~ly** adj mundano. **~wide** adj universal. **W~ Wide Web** n World Wide Web m

worm /wɜːm/ n gusano m, lombriz f

worn /wɔːn/ see **WEAR**. ● adj gastado. **~-out** adj gastado; (person) rendido

worr|ied /'wʌrɪd/ adj preocupado. **~y** /'wʌrɪ/ vt preocupar; (annoy) molestar. ● vi preocuparse. ● n preocupación f. **~ying** adj inquietante

worse /wɜːs/ adj peor. **get ~** empeorar. ● adv peor; (more) más. **~n** vt/i empeorar

worship /'wɜːʃɪp/ n culto m; (title) Su Señoría. ● vt (pt worshipped) adorar

worst /wɜːst/ adj peor. **he's the ~ in the class** es el peor de la clase. ● adv peor. ● n. **the ~** lo peor

worth /wɜːθ/ n valor m. ● adj. **be ~** valer. **it's ~ trying** vale la pena probarlo. **it was ~ my while** (me) valió la pena. **~less** adj sin valor. **~while** /-'waɪl/ adj que vale la pena. **~y** /'wɜːðɪ/ adj meritorio; (respectable) respetable; (laudable) loable

would /wʊd/ modal verb. (in conditional sentences) **~ you go?** ¿irías tú? **he ~ come if he could** vendría si pudiera; (in reported speech) **I thought you'd forget** pensé que te olvidarías; (in requests, invitations) **~ you come here, please?** ¿quieres venir aquí? **~ you switch the television off?** ¿podrías apagar la televisión?; (be prepared to) **he ~n't listen to me** no me quería escuchar

wound[1] /wuːnd/ n herida f. ● vt herir

wound[2] /waʊnd/ see **WIND**[2]

wove, woven /wəʊv, 'wəʊvn/ see **WEAVE**

wow /waʊ/ int ¡ah!

wrangle /'ræŋgl/ vi reñir. ● n riña f

wrap /ræp/ vt (pt wrapped) envolver. ● n bata f; (shawl) chal m. **~per** n, **~ping** n envoltura f

wrath /rɒθ/ n ira f

wreak /riːk/ vt sembrar. **~ havoc** causar estragos

wreath /riːθ/ n (pl -ths /-ðz/) corona f

wreck /rek/ n (ship) restos mpl de un naufragio; (vehicle) restos mpl de un avión siniestrado. **be a nervous ~**

tener los nervios destrozados. ● *vt* provocar el naufragio de (ship); destrozar (car); (*Amer, demolish*) demoler; (*fig*) destrozar. **~age** /-ɪdʒ/ *n* restos *mpl*; (*of building*) ruinas *fpl*

wrench /rentʃ/ *vt* arrancar; (*sprain*) desgarrarse; dislocarse (joint). ● *n* tirón *m*; (*emotional*) dolor *m* (causado por una separación); (*tool*) llave *f* inglesa

wrestl|e /'resl/ *vi* luchar. **~er** *n* luchador *m*. **~ing** *n* lucha *f*

wretch /retʃ/ *n* (*despicable person*) desgraciado *m*; (*unfortunate person*) desdichado *m & f*. **~ed** /-ɪd/ *adj* desdichado; (*weather*) horrible

wriggle /'rɪgl/ *vi* retorcerse. **~ out of** escaparse de

wring /rɪŋ/ *vt* (*pt* **wrung**) retorcer (neck). **~ out of** (*obtain from*) arrancar. □ **~ out** *vt* retorcer

wrinkl|e /'rɪŋkl/ *n* arruga *f*. ● *vt* arrugar. ● *vi* arrugarse. **~y** *adj* arrugado

wrist /rɪst/ *n* muñeca *f*. **~watch** *n* reloj *m* de pulsera

writ /rɪt/ *n* orden *m* judicial

write /raɪt/ *vt/i* (*pt* **wrote**, *pp* **written**, *pres p* **writing**) escribir. □ **~ down** *vt* anotar. □ **~ off** *vt* cancelar (debt). **~-off** *n*. the car was a **~-off** el coche fue declarado un siniestro total. **~r** *n* escritor *m*

writhe /raɪð/ *vi* retorcerse

writing /'raɪtɪŋ/ *n* (*script*) escritura *f*; (*handwriting*) letra *f*. **in ~** por escrito. **~s** *npl* obra *f*, escritos *mpl*. **~ desk** *n* escritorio *m*. **~ pad** *n* bloc *m*. **~ paper** *n* papel *m* de escribir

written /'rɪtn/ *see* **WRITE**

wrong /rɒŋ/ *adj* equivocado, incorrecto; (*not just*) injusto; (*mistaken*) equivocado. be **~** no tener razón; (*be mistaken*) equivocarse. what's **~**? ¿qué pasa? it's **~ to steal** robar está mal. what's **~ with that**? ¿qué hay de malo en eso?. ● *adv* mal. go **~** equivocarse; (*plan*) salir mal. ● *n* injusticia *f*; (*evil*) mal *m*. in the **~** equivocado. ● *vt* ser injusto con. **~ful** *adj* injusto. **~ly** *adv* mal; (*unfairly*) injustamente

wrote /rəʊt/ *see* **WRITE**

wrought iron /rɔːt/ *n* hierro *m* forjado

wrung /rʌŋ/ *see* **WRING**

wry /raɪ/ *adj* (**wryer**, **wryest**) irónico. make a **~ face** torcer el gesto

xerox /'zɪərɒks/ *vt* fotocopiar, xerografiar

Xmas /'krɪsməs/ *n abbr* (**Christmas**) Navidad *f*

X-ray /'eksreɪ/ *n* (*ray*) rayo *m* X; (*photograph*) radiografía *f*. **~s** *npl* rayos *mpl*. ● *vt* hacer una radiografía de

xylophone /'zaɪləfəʊn/ *n* xilofón *m*, xilófono *m*

yacht /jɒt/ *n* yate *m*. **~ing** *n* navegación *f* a vela

yank /jæŋk/ *vt* 🆃 tirar de (*violentamente*)

Yankee /'jæŋkɪ/ *n* 🆃 yanqui *m & f*

yap /jæp/ *vi* (*pt* **yapped**) (dog) ladrar (*con ladridos agudos*)

yard /jɑːd/ *n* patio *m*; (*Amer, garden*) jardín *m*; (*measurement*) yarda *f* (= 0.9144 *metre*)

yarn /jɑːn/ *n* hilo *m*; (*fam, tale*) cuento *m*

yawn /jɔːn/ *vi* bostezar. ● *n* bostezo *m*

yeah /jeə/ *adv* 🆃 sí

year /jɪə(r)/ *n* año *m*. be three **~s old** tener tres años. **~ly** *adj* anual. ● *adv* cada año

yearn /'jɜːn/ *vi*. **~ to do sth** anhelar hacer algo. **~ for sth** añorar algo. **~ing** *n* anhelo *m*, ansia *f*

yeast /jiːst/ *n* levadura *f*

yell /jel/ *vi* gritar. ● *n* grito *m*

yellow /'jeləʊ/ *adj & n* amarillo (*m*)

w

x

y

yelp /jelp/ *n* gañido *m*. ● *vi* gañir

yes /jes/ *int* & *n* sí (*m*)

yesterday /'jestədeɪ/ *adv* & *n* ayer (*m*). **the day before ~** anteayer *m*. **~ morning** ayer por la mañana, ayer en la mañana (*LAm*)

yet /jet/ *adv* todavía, aún; (*already*) ya. **as ~** hasta ahora; (*as a linker*) sin embargo. ● *conj* pero

Yiddish /'jɪdɪʃ/ *n* yídish *m*

yield /jiːld/ *vt* (*surrender*) ceder; producir (*crop/mineral*); dar (*results*). ● *vi* ceder. **'yield'** (*Amer, traffic sign*) ceda el paso. ● *n* rendimiento *m*

yoga /'jəʊgə/ *n* yoga *m*

yoghurt /'jɒgət/ *n* yogur *m*

yoke /jəʊk/ *n* (*fig also*) yugo *m*

yokel /'jəʊkl/ *n* palurdo *m*

yolk /jəʊk/ *n* yema *f* (de huevo)

---

you /juː/ *pronoun*

····▶ (*as the subject*) (*familiar form*) (*sing*) tú, vos (*River Plate and parts of Central America*); (*pl*) vosotros, -tras (*Spain*), ustedes (*LAm*); (*formal*) (*sing*) usted; (*pl*) ustedes

> **!** In Spanish the subject pronoun is usually only used to give emphasis or mark contrast.

····▶ (*as the direct object*) (*familiar form*) (*sing*) te; (*pl*) os (*Spain*), los, las (*LAm*); (*formal*) (*sing*) lo *or* (*Spain*) le, la; (*pl*) los *or* (*Spain*) les, las. **I love ~** te quiero

····▶ (*as the indirect object*) (*familiar form*) (*sing*) te; (*pl*) os (*Spain*), les (*LAm*); (*formal*) (*sing*) le; (*pl*) les. **I sent ~ the book yesterday** te mandé el libro ayer

> **!** The pronoun *se* replaces the indirect object pronoun *le* or *les* when the latter is used with the direct object pronoun (*lo*, *la* etc), e.g. **I gave it to ~** se lo di

····▶ (*when used after a preposition*) (*familiar form*) (*sing*) ti, vos (*River Plate and parts of Central America*); (*pl*) vosotros, -tras (*Spain*), ustedes (*LAm*); (*formal*) (*sing*) usted; (*pl*) ustedes

····▶ (*generalizing*) uno, tú (*esp Spain*). **~ feel very proud** uno se siente muy orgulloso, te sientes muy orgulloso (*esp Spain*). **~ have to be patient** hay que tener paciencia

---

you'd /juːd/, /jʊəd/ = **you had**, **you would**

you'll /juːl/, /jʊəl/ = **you will**

young /jʌŋ/ *adj* (-er, -est) joven. **my ~er sister** mi hermana menor. **he's a year ~er than me** tiene un año menos que yo. **~ lady** *n* señorita *f*. **~ man** *n* joven *m*. **~ster** /-stə(r)/ *n* joven *m*

your /jɔː(r)/ *adj* (*belonging to one person*) (*sing, familiar*) tu; (*pl, familiar*) tus; (*sing, formal*) su; (*pl, formal*) sus; (*belonging to more than one person*) (*sing, familiar*) vuestro, -tra, su (*LAm*); (*pl, familiar*) vuestros, -tras, sus (*LAm*); (*sing, formal*) su; (*pl, formal*) sus

you're /jʊə(r)/, /jɔː(r)/ = **you are**

yours /jɔːz/ *poss pron* (*belonging to one person*) (*sing, familiar*) tuyo, -ya; (*pl, familiar*) tuyos, -yas; (*sing, formal*) suyo, -ya; (*pl, formal*) suyos, -yas. (*belonging to more than one person*) (*sing, familiar*) vuestro, -tra; (*pl, familiar*) vuestros, -tras, suyos, -yas (*LAm*); (*sing, formal*) suyo, -ya; (*pl, formal*) suyos, -yas. **an aunt of ~** una tía tuya/suya; **~ is here** el tuyo/la tuya/el suyo/la suya está aquí

yourself /jɔːˈself/ *pron* (*reflexive*). (*emphatic use*) ① tú mismo, tú misma; (*formal*) usted mismo, usted misma. **describe ~f** descríbete; (*Ud form*) descríbase. **stop thinking about ~f** ① deja de pensar en tí mismo; (*formal*) deje de pensar en sí mismo. **by ~f** solo, sola. **~ves** /jɔːˈselvz/ *pron* vosotros mismos, vosotras mismas (*familiar*), ustedes mismos, ustedes mismas (*LAm familiar*), ustedes mismos, ustedes mismas (*formal*); (*reflexive*). **behave ~ves** ¡portaos bien! (*familiar*), ¡pórtense bien! (*formal, LAm familiar*). **by ~ves** solos, solas

youth /juːθ/ *n* (*pl* **youths** /juːðz/) (*early life*) juventud *f*; (*boy*) joven *m*; (*young people*) juventud *f*. **~ful** *adj*

y

joven, juvenil. ~ **hostel** n albergue m juvenil

you've /juːv/ = you have

Yugoslav /ˈjuːɡəslɑːv/ adj & n yugoslavo (m). ~**ia** /-ˈslɑːvɪə/ n Yugoslavia f

Zz

zeal /ziːl/ n fervor m, celo m

zeal|ot /ˈzelət/ n fanático m. ~**ous** /-əs/ adj ferviente; (worker) que pone gran celo en su trabajo

zebra /ˈzebrə/ n cebra f. ~ **crossing** n paso m de cebra

zenith /ˈzenɪθ/ n cenit m

zero /ˈzɪərəʊ/ n (pl -os) cero m

zest /zest/ n entusiasmo m; (peel) cáscara f

zigzag /ˈzɪɡzæɡ/ n zigzag m. ●vi (pt **zigzagged**) zigzaguear

zilch /zɪltʃ/ n ⊠ nada de nada

zinc /zɪŋk/ n cinc m

zip /zɪp/ n cremallera f, cierre m (LAm), zíper m (Mex). ●vt. ~ (up) cerrar (la cremallera). Z~ **code** n (Amer) código m postal. ~ **fastener** n cremallera f. ~**per** n/vt see ZIP

zodiac /ˈzəʊdɪæk/ n zodíaco m, zodiaco m

zombie /ˈzɒmbɪ/ n zombi m & f

zone /zəʊn/ n zona f. **time** ~ n huso m horario

zoo /zuː/ n zoo m, zoológico m. ~**logical** /zuːəˈlɒdʒɪkl/ adj zoológico. ~**logist** /zuːˈɒlədʒɪst/ n zoólogo m, ~**logy** /zuːˈɒlədʒɪ/ n zoología f

zoom /zuːm/. □ ~ **in** vi (Photo) hacer un zoom in (**on** sobre). □ ~ **past** vi/t pasar zumbando. ~ **lens** n teleobjetivo m, zoom m

zucchini /zʊˈkiːnɪ/ n (invar or ~s) (Amer) calabacín m

Numbers/números

zero	0	cero
one (first)	1	uno (primero)
two (second)	2	dos (segundo)
three (third)	3	tres (tercero)
four (fourth)	4	cuatro (cuarto)
five (fifth)	5	cinco (quinto)
six (sixth)	6	seis (sexto)
seven (seventh)	7	siete (séptimo)
eight (eighth)	8	ocho (octavo)
nine (ninth)	9	nueve (noveno)
ten (tenth)	10	diez (décimo)
eleven (eleventh)	11	once (undécimo)
twelve (twelfth)	12	doce (duodécimo)
thirteen (thirteenth)	13	trece (decimotercero)
fourteen (fourteenth)	14	catorce (decimocuarto)
fifteen (fifteenth)	15	quince (decimoquinto)
sixteen (sixteenth)	16	dieciséis (decimosexto)
seventeen (seventeenth)	17	diecisiete (decimoséptimo)
eighteen (eighteenth)	18	dieciocho (decimoctavo)
nineteen (nineteenth)	19	diecinueve (decimonoveno)
twenty (twentieth)	20	veinte (vigésimo)
twenty one (twenty-first)	21	veintiuno (vigésimo primero)
twenty-two (twenty-second)	22	veintidós (vigésimo segundo)
twenty-three (twenty-third)	23	veintitrés (vigésimo tercero)
twenty-four (twenty-fourth)	24	veinticuatro (vigésimo cuarto)
twenty-five (twenty-fifth)	25	veinticinco (vigésimo quinto)
twenty-six (twenty-sixth)	26	veintiséis (vigésimo sexto)
thirty (thirtieth)	30	treinta (trigésimo)

Numbers

thirty-one (thirty-first)	31	treinta y uno (trigésimo primero)
forty (fortieth)	40	cuarenta (cuadragésimo)
fifty (fiftieth)	50	cincuenta (quincuagésimo)
sixty (sixtieth)	60	sesenta (sexagésimo)
seventy (seventieth)	70	setenta (septuagésimo)
eighty (eightieth)	80	ochenta (octogésimo)
ninety (ninetieth)	90	noventa (nonagésimo)
a/one hundred (hundredth)	100	cien (centésimo)
a/one hundred and one (hundred and first)	101	ciento uno (centésimo primero)
two hundred (two hundredth)	200	doscientos (ducentésimo)
three hundred (three hundredth)	300	trescientos (tricentésimo)
four hundred (four hundredth)	400	cuatrocientos (cuadringentésimo)
five hundred (five hundredth)	500	quinientos (quingentésimo)
six hundred (six hundredth)	600	seiscientos (sexcentésimo)
seven hundred (seven hundredth)	700	setecientos (septingentésimo)
eight hundred (eight hundredth)	800	ochocientos (octingentésimo)
nine hundred (nine hundredth)	900	novecientos (noningentésimo)
a/one thousand (thousandth)	1000	mil (milésimo)
two thousand (two thousandth)	2000	dos mil (dos milésimo)
a/one million (millionth)	1,000,000	un millón (millonésimo)

Verbos irregulares ingleses

Infinitivo	Pretérito	Participio pasado	Infinitivo	Pretérito	Participio pasado
be	was	been	**drive**	drove	driven
bear	bore	borne	**eat**	ate	eaten
beat	beat	beaten	**fall**	fell	fallen
become	became	become	**feed**	fed	fed
begin	began	begun	**feel**	felt	felt
bend	bent	bent	**fight**	fought	fought
bet	bet,	bet,	**find**	found	found
	betted	betted	**flee**	fled	fled
bid	bade, bid	bidden, bid	**fly**	flew	flown
bind	bound	bound	**freeze**	froze	frozen
bite	bit	bitten	**get**	got	got, gotten US
bleed	bled	bled	**give**	gave	given
blow	blew	blown	**go**	went	gone
break	broke	broken	**grow**	grew	grown
breed	bred	bred	**hang**	hung,	hung,
bring	brought	brought		hanged	hanged
build	built	built	**have**	had	had
burn	burnt,	burnt,	**hear**	heard	heard
	burned	burned	**hide**	hid	hidden
burst	burst	burst	**hit**	hit	hit
buy	bought	bought	**hold**	held	held
catch	caught	caught	**hurt**	hurt	hurt
choose	chose	chosen	**keep**	kept	kept
cling	clung	clung	**kneel**	knelt	knelt
come	came	come	**know**	knew	known
cost	cost,	cost,	**lay**	laid	laid
	costed (vt)	costed	**lead**	led	led
cut	cut	cut	**lean**	leaned,	leaned,
deal	dealt	dealt		leant	leant
dig	dug	dug	**learn**	learnt,	learnt,
do	did	done		learned	learned
draw	drew	drawn	**leave**	left	left
dream	dreamt,	dreamt,	**lend**	lent	lent
	dreamed	dreamed	**let**	let	let
drink	drank	drunk	**lie**	lay	lain

Infinitivo	Pretérito	Participio pasado	Infinitivo	Pretérito	Participio pasado
lose	lost	lost	**spend**	spent	spent
make	made	made	**spit**	spat	spat
mean	meant	meant	**spoil**	spoilt,	spoilt,
meet	met	met		spoiled	spoiled
pay	paid	paid	**spread**	spread	spread
put	put	put	**spring**	sprang	sprung
read	read	read	**stand**	stood	stood
ride	rode	ridden	**steal**	stole	stolen
ring	rang	rung	**stick**	stuck	stuck
rise	rose	risen	**sting**	stung	stung
run	ran	run	**stride**	strode	stridden
say	said	said	**strike**	struck	struck
see	saw	seen	**swear**	swore	sworn
seek	sought	sought	**sweep**	swept	swept
sell	sold	sold	**swell**	swelled	swollen,
send	sent	sent			swelled
set	set	set	**swim**	swam	swum
sew	sewed	sewn, sewed	**swing**	swung	swung
shake	shook	shaken	**take**	took	taken
shine	shone	shone	**teach**	taught	taught
shoe	shod	shod	**tear**	tore	torn
shoot	shot	shot	**tell**	told	told
show	showed	shown	**think**	thought	thought
shut	shut	shut	**throw**	threw	thrown
sing	sang	sung	**thrust**	thrust	thrust
sink	sank	sunk	**tread**	trod	trodden
sit	sat	sat	**under-**	under-	understood
sleep	slept	slept	**stand**	stood	
sling	slung	slung	**wake**	woke	woken
smell	smelt,	smelt,	**wear**	wore	worn
	smelled	smelled	**win**	won	won
speak	spoke	spoken	**write**	wrote	written
spell	spelled,	spelled,			
	spelt	spelt			

Spanish verbs

Regular verbs:

● in **-ar** (*e.g.* **comprar**)
Present; compr|o, ~as, ~a, ~amos, ~áis, ~an
Future: comprar|é, ~ás, ~á, ~emos, ~éis, ~án
Imperfect: compr|aba, ~abas, ~aba, ~ábamos, ~abais, ~aban
Preterite: compr|é, ~aste, ~ó, ~amos, ~asteis, ~aron
Present subjunctive: compr|e, ~es, ~e, ~emos, ~éis, ~en
Imperfect subjunctive: compr|ara, ~aras, ~ara, ~áramos, ~arais, ~aran
compr|ase, ~ases, ~ase, ~ásemos, ~aseis, ~asen
Conditional: comprar|ía, ~ías, ~ía, ~íamos, ~íais, ~ían
Present participle: comprando
Past participle: comprado
Imperative: compra, comprad

● in **-er** (*e.g.* **beber**)
Present: beb|o, ~es, ~e, ~emos, ~éis, ~en
Future: beber|é, ~ás, ~á, ~emos, ~éis, ~án
Imperfect: beb|ía, ~ías, ~ía, ~íamos, ~íais, ~ían
Preterite: beb|í, ~iste, ~ió, ~imos, ~isteis, ~ieron
Present subjunctive: beb|a, ~as, ~a, ~amos, ~áis, ~an
Imperfect subjunctive: beb|iera, ~ieras, ~iera, ~iéramos, ~ierais, ~ieran

beb|iese, ~ieses, ~iese, ~iésemos, ~ieseis, ~iesen
Conditional: beber|ía, ~ías, ~ía, ~íamos, ~íais, ~ían
Present participle: bebiendo
Past participle: bebido
Imperative: bebe, bebed

● in **-ir** (*e.g.* **vivir**)
Present: viv|o, ~es, ~e, ~imos, ~ís, ~en
Future: vivir|é, ~ás, ~á, ~emos, ~éis, ~án
Imperfect: viv|ía, ~ías, ~ía, ~íamos, ~íais, ~ían
Preterite: viv|í, ~iste, ~ió, ~imos, ~isteis, ~ieron
Present subjunctive: viv|a, ~as, ~a, ~amos, ~áis, ~an
Imperfect subjunctive: viv|iera, ~ieras, ~iera, ~iéramos, ~ierais, ~ieran
viv|iese, ~ieses, ~iese, ~iésemos, ~ieseis, ~iesen
Conditional: vivir|ía, ~ías, ~ía, ~íamos, ~íais, ~ían
Present participle: viviendo
Past participle: vivido
Imperative: vive, vivid

Irregular verbs:

[1] cerrar

Present: cierro, cierras, cierra, cerramos, cerráis, cierran
Present subjunctive: cierre, cierres, cierre, cerremos, cerréis, cierren
Imperative: cierra, cerrad

[2] contar, mover

Present: cuento, cuentas, cuenta, contamos, contáis, cuentan
muevo, mueves, mueve, movemos, movéis, mueven
Present subjunctive: cuente, cuentes, cuente, contemos, contéis, cuenten
mueva, muevas, mueva, movamos, mováis, muevan
Imperative: cuenta, contad
mueve, moved

[3] jugar

Present: juego, juegas, juega, jugamos, jugáis, juegan
Preterite: jugué, jugaste, jugó, jugamos, jugasteis, jugaron
Present subjunctive: juegue, juegues, juegue, juguemos, juguéis, jueguen

[4] sentir

Present: siento, sientes, siente, sentimos, sentís, sienten
Preterite: sentí, sentiste, sintió, sentimos, sentisteis, sintieron
Present subjunctive: sienta, sientas, sienta, sintamos, sintáis, sientan
Imperfect subjunctive: sint|iera, ~ieras, ~iera, ~iéramos, ~ierais, ~ieran
sint|iese, ~ieses, ~iese, ~iésemos, ~ieseis, ~iesen
Present participle: sintiendo
Imperative: siente, sentid

[5] pedir

Present: pido, pides, pide, pedimos, pedís, piden
Preterite: pedí, pediste, pidió, pedimos, pedisteis, pidieron

Present subjunctive: pid|a, ~as, ~a, ~amos, ~áis, ~an
Imperfect subjunctive: pid|iera, ~ieras, ~iera, ~iéramos, ~ierais, ~ieran
pid|iese, ~ieses, ~iese, ~iésemos, ~ieseis, ~iesen
Present participle: pidiendo
Imperative: pide, pedid

[6] dormir

Present: duermo, duermes, duerme, dormimos, dormís, duermen
Preterite: dormí, dormiste, durmió, dormimos, dormisteis, durmieron
Present subjunctive: duerma, duermas, duerma, durmamos, durmáis, duerman
Imperfect subjunctive: durm|iera, ~ieras, ~iera, ~iéramos, ~ierais, ~ieran
durm|iese, ~ieses, ~iese, ~iésemos, ~ieseis, ~iesen
Present participle: durmiendo
Imperative: duerme, dormid

[7] dedicar

Preterite: dediqué, dedicaste, dedicó, dedicamos, dedicasteis, dedicaron
Present subjunctive: dediqu|e, ~es, ~e, ~emos, ~éis, ~en

[8] delinquir

Present: delinco, delinques, delinque, delinquimos, delinquís, delinquen
Present subjunctive: delinc|a, ~as, ~a, ~amos, ~áis, ~an

[9] vencer, esparcir

Present: venzo, vences, vence, vencemos, vencéis, vencen
esparzo, esparces, esparce, esparcimos, esparcís, esparcen

Present subjunctive: venz|a, ∼as, ∼a,
∼amos, ∼áis, ∼an
esparz|a, ∼as, ∼a, ∼amos, ∼áis,
∼an

[10] rechazar

Preterite: rechacé, rechazaste,
rechazó, rechazamos,
rechazasteis, rechazaron
Present subjunctive: rechac|e, ∼es, ∼e,
∼emos, ∼éis, ∼en

[11] conocer, lucir

Present: conozco, conoces, conoce,
conocemos, conocéis, conocen
luzco, luces, luce, lucimos, lucís,
lucen
Present subjunctive: conozc|a, ∼as,
∼a, ∼amos, ∼áis, ∼an
luzc|a, ∼as, ∼a, ∼amos, ∼áis,
∼an

[12] pagar

Preterite: pagué, pagaste, pagó,
pagamos, pagasteis, pagaron
Present subjunctive: pagu|e, ∼es, ∼e,
∼emos, ∼éis, ∼en

[13] distinguir

Present: distingo, distingues,
distingue, distinguimos,
distinguís, distinguen
Present subjunctive: disting|a, ∼as,
∼a, ∼amos, ∼áis, ∼an

[14] acoger, afligir

Present: acojo, acoges, acoge,
acogemos, acogéis, acogen
aflijo, afliges, aflige, afligimos,
afligís, afligen
Present subjunctive: acoj|a, ∼as, ∼a,
∼amos, ∼áis, ∼an

aflij|a, ∼as, ∼a, ∼amos, ∼áis,
∼an

[15] averiguar

Preterite: averigüé, averiguaste,
averiguó, averiguamos,
averiguasteis, averiguaron
Present subjunctive: averigü|e, ∼es,
∼e, ∼emos, ∼éis, ∼en

[16] agorar

Present: agüero, agüeras, agüera,
agoramos, agoráis, agüeran
Present subjunctive: agüere, agüeres,
agüere, agoremos, agoréis,
agüeren
Imperative: agüera, agorad

[17] huir

Present: huyo, huyes, huye, huimos,
huís, huyen
Preterite: huí, huiste, huyó, huimos,
huisteis, huyeron
Present subjunctive: huy|a, ∼as, ∼a,
∼amos, ∼áis, ∼an
Imperfect subjunctive: huy|era, ∼eras,
∼era, ∼éramos, ∼erais, ∼eran
huy|ese, ∼eses, ∼ese, ∼ésemos,
∼eseis, ∼esen
Present participle: huyendo
Imperative: huye, huid

[18] creer

Preterite: creí, creíste, creyó, creímos,
creísteis, creyeron
Imperfect subjunctive: crey|era, ∼eras,
∼era, ∼éramos, ∼erais, ∼eran
crey|ese, ∼eses, ∼ese, ∼ésemos,
∼eseis, ∼esen
Present participle:
creyendo
Past participle: creído

[19] argüir

Present: arguyo, arguyes, arguye, argüimos, argüís, arguyen
Preterite: argüí, argüiste, arguyó, argüimos, argüisteis, arguyeron
Present subjunctive: arguy|a, ~as, ~a, ~amos, ~áis, ~an
Imperfect subjunctive: arguy|era, ~eras, ~era, ~éramos, ~erais, ~eran
arguy|ese, ~eses, ~ese, ~ésemos, ~eseis, ~esen
Present participle: arguyendo
Imperative: arguye, argüid

[20] vaciar

Present: vacío, vacías, vacía, vaciamos, vaciáis, vacían
Present subjunctive: vacíe, vacíes, vacíe, vaciemos, vaciéis, vacíen
Imperative: vacía, vaciad

[21] acentuar

Present: acentúo, acentúas, acentúa, acentuamos, acentuáis, acentúan
Present subjunctive: acentúe, acentúes, acentúe, acentuemos, acentuéis, acentúen
Imperative: acentúa, acentuad

[22] atañer, engullir

Preterite: atañ|i, ~iste, ~ó, ~imos, ~isteis, ~eron
engull|í ~iste, ~ó, ~imos, ~isteis, ~eron
Imperfect subjunctive: atañera, ~eras, ~era, ~éramos, ~erais, ~eran
atañese, ~eses, ~ese, ~ésemos, ~eseis, ~esen
engull|era, ~eras, ~era, ~éramos, ~erais, ~eran

engull|ese, ~eses, ~ese, ~ésemos, ~eseis, ~esen
Present participle: atañendo engullendo

[23] aislar, aullar

Present: aíslo, aíslas, aísla, aislamos, aisláis, aíslan
aúllo, aúllas, aúlla, aullamos aulláis, aúllan
Present subjunctive: aísle, aísles, aísle, aislemos, aisléis, aíslen
aúlle, aúlles, aúlle, aullemos, aulléis, aúllen
Imperative: aísla, aislad aúlla, aullad

[24] abolir

Present: abolimos, abolís
Present subjunctive: not used
Imperative: abolid

[25] andar

Preterite: anduv|e, ~iste, ~o, ~imos, ~isteis, ~ieron
Imperfect subjunctive: anduv|iera, ~ieras, ~iera, ~iéramos, ~ierais, ~ieran
anduv|iese, ~ieses, ~iese, ~iésemos, ~ieseis, ~iesen

[26] dar

Present: doy, das, da, damos, dais, dan
Preterite: di, diste, dio, dimos, disteis, dieron
Present subjunctive: dé, des, dé, demos, deis, den
Imperfect subjunctive: diera, dieras, diera, diéramos, dierais, dieran
diese, dieses, diese, diésemos, dieseis, diesen

[27] estar

Present: estoy, estás, está, estamos, estáis, están
Preterite: estuv|e, ~iste, ~o, ~imos, ~isteis, ~ieron
Present subjunctive: esté, estés, esté, estemos, estéis, estén
Imperfect subjunctive: estuv|iera, ~ieras, ~iera, ~iéramos, ~ierais, ~ieran
estuv|iese, ~ieses, ~iese, ~iésemos, ~ieseis, ~iesen
Imperative: está, estad

[28] caber

Present: quepo, cabes, cabe, cabemos, cabéis, caben
Future: cabr|é, ~ás, ~á, ~emos, ~éis, ~án
Preterite: cup|e, ~iste, ~o, ~imos, ~isteis, ~ieron
Present subjunctive: quep|a, ~as, ~a, ~amos, ~áis, ~an
Imperfect subjunctive: cup|iera, ~ieras, ~iera, ~iéramos, ~ierais, ~ieran
cup|iese, ~ieses, ~iese, ~iésemos, ~ieseis, ~iesen
Conditional: cabr|ía, ~ías, ~ía, ~íamos, ~íais, ~ían

[29] caer

Present: caigo, caes, cae, caemos, caéis, caen
Preterite: caí, caiste, cayó, caímos, caísteis, cayeron
Present subjunctive: caig|a, ~as, ~a, ~amos, ~áis, ~an
Imperfect subjunctive: cay|era, ~eras, ~era, ~éramos, ~erais, ~eran
cay|ese, ~eses, ~ese, ~ésemos, ~eseis, ~esen
Present participle: cayendo

Past participle: caído

[30] haber

Present: he, has, ha, hemos, habéis, han
Future: habr|é, ~ás, ~á, ~emos, ~éis, ~án
Preterite: hub|e, ~iste, ~o, ~imos, ~isteis, ~ieron
Present subjunctive: hay|a, ~as, ~a, ~amos, ~áis, ~an
Imperfect subjunctive: hub|iera, ~ieras, ~iera, ~iéramos, ~ierais, ~ieran
hub|iese, ~ieses, ~iese, ~iésemos, ~ieseis, ~iesen
Conditional: habr|ía, ~ías, ~ía, ~íamos, ~íais, ~ían
Imperative: he, habed

[31] hacer

Present: hago, haces, hace, hacemos, hacéis, hacen
Future: har|é, ~ás, ~á, ~emos, ~éis, ~án
Preterite: hice, hiciste, hizo, hicimos, hicisteis, hicieron
Present subjunctive: hag|a, ~as, ~a, ~amos, ~áis, ~an
Imperfect subjunctive: hic|iera, ~ieras, ~iera, ~iéramos, ~ierais, ~ieran
hic|iese, ~ieses, ~iese, ~iésemos, ~ieseis, ~iesen
Conditional: har|ía, ~ías, ~ía, ~íamos, ~íais, ~ían
Past participle: hecho
Imperative: haz, haced

[32] placer

Present subjunctive: plazca
Imperfect subjunctive: placiera, placiese

[33] poder

Present: puedo, puedes, puede, podemos, podéis, pueden
Future: podr|é, ~ás, ~á, ~emos, ~éis, ~án
Preterite: pud|e, ~iste, ~o, ~imos, ~isteis, ~ieron
Present subjunctive: pueda, puedas, pueda, podamos, podáis, puedan
Imperfect subjunctive: pud|iera, ~ieras, ~iera, ~iéramos, ~ierais, ~ieran
pud|iese, ~ieses, ~iese, ~iésemos, ~ieseis, ~iesen
Conditional: podr|ía, ~ías, ~ía, ~íamos, ~íais, ~ían
Past participle: pudiendo

[34] poner

Present: pongo, pones, pone, ponemos, ponéis, ponen
Future: pondr|é, ~ás, ~á, ~emos, ~éis, ~án
Preterite: pus|e, ~iste, ~o, ~imos, ~isteis, ~ieron
Present subjunctive: pong|a, ~as, ~a, ~amos, ~áis, ~an
Imperfect subjunctive: pus|iera, ~ieras, ~iera, ~iéramos, ~ierais, ~ieran
pus|iese, ~ieses, ~iese, ~iésemos, ~ieseis, ~iesen
Conditional: pondr|ía, ~ías, ~ía, ~íamos, ~íais, ~ían
Past participle: puesto
Imperative: pon, poned

[35] querer

Present: quiero, quieres, quiere, queremos, queréis, quieren
Future: querr|é, ~ás, ~á, ~emos, ~éis, ~án
Preterite: quis|e, ~iste, ~o, ~imos, ~isteis, ~ieron
Present subjunctive: quiera, quieras, quiera, queramos, queráis, quieran
Imperfect subjunctive: quis|iera, ~ieras, ~iera, ~iéramos, ~ierais, ~ieran
quis|iese, ~ieses, ~iese, ~iésemos, ~ieseis, ~iesen
Conditional: querr|ía, ~ías, ~ía, ~íamos, ~íais, ~ían
Imperative: quiere, quered

[36] raer

Present: raigo/rayo, raes, rae, raemos, raéis, raen
Preterite: raí, raíste, rayó, raímos, raísteis, rayeron
Present subjunctive: raig|a, ~as, ~a, ~amos, ~áis, ~an ray|a, ~as, ~a, ~amos, ~áis, ~an
Imperfect subjunctive: ray|era, ~eras, ~era, ~éramos, ~erais, ~eran
ray|ese, ~eses, ~ese, ~ésemos, ~eseis, ~esen
Present participle: rayendo
Past participle: raído

[37] roer

Present: roo, roes, roe, roemos, roéis, roen
Preterite: roí, roíste, royó, roímos, roísteis, royeron
Present subjunctive: ro|a, ~as, ~a, ~amos, ~áis, ~an
Imperfect subjunctive: roy|era, ~eras, ~era, ~éramos, ~erais, ~eran
roy|ese, ~eses, ~ese, ~ésemos, ~eseis, ~esen
Present participle: royendo
Past participle: roído

[38] saber

Present: sé, sabes, sabe, sabemos,
sabéis, saben
Future: sabr|é, ~ás, ~á, ~emos,
~éis, ~án
Preterite: sup|e, ~iste, ~o, ~imos,
~isteis, ~ieron
Present subjunctive: sep|a, ~as, ~a,
~amos, ~áis, ~an
Imperfect subjunctive: sup|iera, ~ieras,
~iera, ~iéramos, ~ierais, ~ieran
sup|iese, ~ieses, ~iese, ~iésemos,
~ieseis, ~iesen
Conditional: sabr|ía, ~ías, ~ía,
~íamos, ~íais, ~ían

[39] ser

Present: soy, eres, es, somos, sois, son
Imperfect: era, eras, era, éramos,
erais, eran
Preterite: fui, fuiste, fue, fuimos,
fuisteis, fueron
Present subjunctive: se|a, ~as, ~a,
~amos, ~áis, ~an
Imperfect subjunctive: fu|era, ~eras,
~era, ~éramos, ~erais, ~eran
fu|ese, ~eses, ~ese, ~ésemos,
~eseis, ~esen
Imperative: sé, sed

[40] tener

Present: tengo, tienes, tiene,
tenemos, tenéis, tienen
Future: tendr|é, ~ás, ~á, ~emos,
~éis, ~án
Preterite: tuv|e, ~iste, ~o, ~imos,
~isteis, ~ieron
Present subjunctive: teng|a, ~as, ~a,
~amos, ~áis, ~an
Imperfect subjunctive: tuv|iera, ~ieras,
~iera, ~iéramos, ~ierais, ~ieran

tuv|iese, ~ieses, ~iese, ~iésemos,
~ieseis, ~iesen
Conditional: tendr|ía, ~ías, ~ía,
~íamos, ~íais, ~ían
Imperative: ten, tened

[41] traer

Present: traigo, traes, trae, traemos,
traéis, traen
Preterite: traj|e, ~iste, ~o, ~imos,
~isteis, ~eron
Present subjunctive: traig|a, ~as, ~a,
~amos, ~áis, ~an
Imperfect subjunctive: traj|era, ~eras,
~era, ~éramos, ~erais, ~eran
traj|ese, ~eses, ~ese, ~ésemos,
~eseis, ~esen
Present participle: trayendo
Past participle: traído

[42] valer

Present: valgo, vales, vale, valemos,
valéis, valen
Future: vald|ré, ~ás, ~á, ~emos,
~éis, ~án
Present subjunctive: valg|a, ~as, ~a,
~amos, ~áis, ~an
Conditional: vald|ría, ~ías, ~ía,
~íamos, ~íais, ~ían
Imperative: vale, valed

[43] ver

Present: veo, ves, ve, vemos, veis, ven
Imperfect: ve|ía, ~ías, ~ía, ~íamos,
~íais, ~ían
Preterite: vi, viste, vio, vimos, visteis,
vieron
Present subjunctive: ve|a, ~as, ~a,
~amos, ~áis, ~an
Past participle: visto

[44] yacer

Present: yazco, yaces, yace, yacemos,
yacéis, yacen
Present subjunctive: yazc|a, ~**as**, ~**a**,
~**amos**, ~**áis**, ~**an**
Imperative: yace, yaced

[45] asir

Present: asgo, ases, ase, asimos, asís,
asen
Present subjunctive: asg|a, ~**as**, ~**a**,
~**amos**, ~**áis**, ~**an**

[46] decir

Present: digo, dices, dice, decimos,
decís, dicen
Future: dir|é, ~**ás**, ~**á**, ~**emos**, ~**éis**,
~**án**
Preterite: dij|e, ~**iste**, ~**o**, ~**imos**,
~**isteis**, ~**eron**
Present subjunctive: dig|a, ~**as**, ~**a**,
~**amos**, ~**áis**, ~**an**
Imperfect subjunctive: dij|era, ~**eras**,
~**era**, ~**éramos**, ~**erais**, ~**eran**
dij|ese, ~**eses**, ~**ese**, ~**ésemos**,
~**eseis**, ~**esen**
Conditional: dir|ía, ~**ías**, ~**ía**,
~**íamos**, ~**íais**, ~**ían**
Present participle: dicho
Imperative: di, decid

[47] reducir

Present: reduzco, reduces, reduce,
reducimos, reducís, reducen
Preterite: reduj|e, ~**iste**, ~**o**, ~**imos**,
~**isteis**, ~**eron**
Present subjunctive: reduzc|a, ~**as**,
~**a**, ~**amos**, ~**áis**, ~**an**
Imperfect subjunctive: reduj|era,
~**eras**, ~**era**, ~**éramos**, ~**erais**,
~**eran**

reduj|ese, ~**eses**, ~**ese**, ~**ésemos**,
~**eseis**, ~**esen**

[48] erguir

Present: yergo, yergues, yergue,
erguimos, erguís, yerguen
Preterite: erguí, erguiste, irguió,
erguimos, erguisteis, irguieron
Present subjunctive: yerg|a, ~**as**, ~**a**,
~**amos**, ~**áis**, ~**an**
Imperfect subjunctive: irgu|iera,
~**ieras**, ~**iera**, ~**iéramos**, ~**ierais**,
~**ieran**
irgu|iese, ~**ieses**, ~**iese**,
~**iésemos**, ~**ieseis**, ~**iesen**
Present participle: irguiendo
Imperative: yergue, erguid

[49] ir

Present: voy, vas, va, vamos, vais, van
Imperfect: iba, ibas, iba, íbamos,
ibais, iban
Preterite: fui, fuiste, fue, fuimos,
fuisteis, fueron
Present subjunctive: vay|a, ~**as**, ~**a**,
~**amos**, ~**áis**, ~**an**
Imperfect subjunctive: fu|era, ~**eras**,
~**era**, ~**éramos**, ~**erais**, ~**eran**
fu|ese, ~**eses**, ~**ese**, ~**ésemos**,
~**eseis**, ~**esen**
Present participle: yendo
Imperative: ve, id

[50] oír

Present: oigo, oyes, oye, oímos, oís,
oyen
Preterite: oí, oíste, oyó, oímos, oísteis,
oyeron
Present subjunctive: oig|a, ~**as**, ~**a**,
~**amos**, ~**áis**, ~**an**
Imperfect subjunctive: oy|era, ~**eras**,
~**era**, ~**éramos**, ~**erais**, ~**eran**

oy|ese, ~eses, ~ese, ~ésemos,
~eseis, ~esen
Present participle: oyendo
Past participle: oído
Imperative: oye, oíd

[51] reír

Present: río, ríes, ríe, reímos, reís,
ríen
Preterite: reí, reíste, rió, reímos,
reísteis, rieron
Present subjunctive: ría, rías, ría,
riamos, riáis, rían
Present participle: riendo
Past participle: reído
Imperative: ríe, reíd

[52] salir

Present: salgo, sales, sale, salimos,
salís, salen
Future: saldr|é, ~ás, ~á, ~emos,
~éis, ~án
Present subjunctive: salg|a, ~as, ~a,
~amos, ~áis, ~an

Conditional: saldr|ía, ~ías, ~ía,
~íamos, ~íais, ~ían
Imperative: sal, salid

[53] venir

Present: vengo, vienes, viene,
venimos, venís, vienen
Future: vendr|é, ~ás, ~á, ~emos,
~éis, ~án
Preterite: vin|e, ~iste, ~o, ~imos,
~isteis, ~ieron
Present subjunctive: veng|a, ~as, ~a,
~amos, ~áis, ~an
Imperfect subjunctive: vin|iera, ~ieras,
~iera, ~iéramos, ~ierais, ~ieran
vin|iese, ~ieses, ~iese, ~iésemos,
~ieseis, ~iesen
Conditional: vendr|ía, ~ías, ~ía,
~íamos, ~íais, ~ían
Present participle: viniendo
Imperative: ven, venid